2016 EDITION | PRIDE & FERRELL

MARKETING

WILLIAM M. PRIDE
Texas A & M University

O. C. FERRELL
University of New Mexico

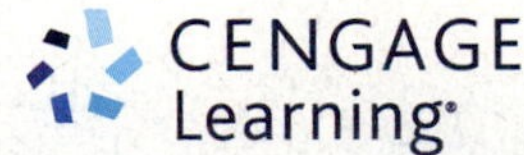

Australia • Brazil • Mexico • Singapore • United Kingdom • United States

Marketing, 18e
William M. Pride, O.C. Ferrell

Vice President, General Manager, Social Science & Qualitative Business: Erin Joyner

Product Director: Mike Schenk

Sr. Product Manager: Jason Fremder

Sr. Content Developer: Julie Fritsch

Product Assistant: Jamie Mack

Marketing Manager: Jeff Tousignant

Sr. Content Project Manager: Colleen A. Farmer

Sr. Media Developer: John Rich

Manufacturing Planner: Ron Montgomery

Marketing Coordinator: Chris Walz

Production Service: Integra Software Services Pvt. Ltd.

Sr. Art Director: Stacy Shirley

Internal Designers: Mike Stratton & Lou Ann Thesing

Cover Designer: Lou Ann Thesing

Cover Image: © zayats-and-zayats/Shutterstock

Intellectual Property Analyst: Jen Nonenmacher

Project Manager: Betsy Hathaway

Library of Congress Control Number: 2014944159

ISBN: 978-1-285-85834-0

Cengage Learning
20 Channel Center Street
Boston, MA 02210
USA

Printed in the United States of America
Print Number: 01 Print Year: 2014

To Nancy, Allen, Carmen, Mike, Ashley, Charlie, and J.R. Pride

To James Collins Ferrell

© zayats-and-zayats/Shutterstock.com

brief contents

© zayats-and-zayats/Shutterstock.com

contents

Part 3: Marketing Research and Target Market Analysis 125

Part 4: Buying Behavior, Global Marketing, and Digital Marketing 189

Part 8: Pricing Decisions 581

Chapter 19: Pricing Concepts 582

Chapter 20: Setting Prices 612

preface

MARKETING IN A CHANGING ENVIRONMENT

The importance of marketing has continued to increase as dynamic changes in the environment evolve. As students prepare for careers in a globally competitive digital world, they will need to gain marketing knowledge that will prepare them to be successful. This new edition of Pride and Ferrell *Marketing* has been revised to engage students and provide the frameworks, concepts, and approaches to decision making that ensure comprehensive understanding of marketing. Our perspective goes beyond learning terminology and concepts to provide decision-making experiences for students through the use of cases, exercises, and debate issues. As students prepare for the new digital world, they also need practice in developing communication skills, especially effective teamwork.

Pride and Ferrell *Marketing* has been developed to make sure that students receive the most comprehensive overview of marketing available. This means that students using this book should develop respect for the importance of marketing and understand that learning marketing requires in-depth knowledge and the mastering of essential concepts. Therefore, key concepts like digital marketing and social networking, product concepts, integrated marketing communications, and social responsibility and ethics in marketing all are presented in stand-alone chapters. To make this edition more efficient, we have combined our coverage of branding and packaging with our discussion of fundamental product concepts in a single chapter titled "Product Concepts, Branding, and Packaging."

We also provide numerous ancillary materials to aid in student comprehension of marketing concepts as well as for increasing instructor resources for teaching this important material. Online materials include quizzes, PowerPoint presentations, videos, and flashcards. Our marketing video case series enables students to learn how real-world companies address marketing challenges. Our Interactive Marketing Plan Worksheets and video program provide students with practical knowledge of the challenges and the planning process of launching a new product. Together these revisions and additional materials will assist students in gaining a full understanding of pertinent marketing practices.

Online social networking has become an increasingly powerful tool for marketers. Most discussions about marketing today bring up issues such as how digital media can lower costs, improve communications, provide better customer support, and achieve improved marketing research. All elements of the marketing mix should be considered when using digital media and social networking. We discuss how digital media and social networking tools can create effective digital marketing strategies that can enhance marketing efforts. In addition, the entire book integrates important digital marketing concepts and examples where appropriate.

We have paid careful attention to enhancing all key concepts in marketing and have built this revision to be current and to reflect important changes in marketing. Our book is a market leader because students find it readable and relevant. Our text reflects the real world of marketing and provides the most comprehensive coverage possible of important marketing topics.

Specific details of this extensive revision are available in the transition guide in the *Instructor's Manual*. We have also made efforts to improve all teaching ancillaries and student learning tools. PowerPoint presentations continue to be a very popular teaching device, and a special effort has been made to upgrade the PowerPoint program to enhance classroom teaching. The *Instructor's Manual* continues to be a valuable tool, updated with engaging in-class activities and projects. The authors and publisher have worked together to provide a comprehensive teaching package and ancillaries that are unsurpassed in the marketplace.

The authors have maintained a hands-on approach to teaching this material and revising the text and its ancillaries. This results in an integrated teaching package and approach that is accurate, sound, and successful in reaching students. The outcome of this involvement fosters trust and confidence in the teaching package and in student learning outcomes. Student feedback regarding this textbook is highly favorable.

WHAT'S NEW TO THIS EDITION?

Our goal is to provide the most up-to-date content, including concepts, examples, cases, exercises, and data, possible. Therefore, in this revision there are significant changes that make learning more engaging and interesting to the students. The following highlight the types of changes that were made in this revision.

- **Foundational content.** Each chapter has been updated with the latest knowledge available related to frameworks, concepts, and academic research. These additions have been seamlessly integrated into the text. Many examples are new and a review of footnotes at the ends of chapters will reveal where new content has been added. Many of the new examples and content changes have been updated to 2014.
- **Opening vignettes: *Marketing Insights*.** All of the chapter-opening vignettes are new or updated. They are written to introduce the theme of each chapter by focusing on actual entrepreneurial companies and how they deal with real-world situations.
- **Boxed features.** Each chapter includes two new or updated boxed features that highlight green marketing, marketing entrepreneurs, emerging trends in marketing, or controversial issues in marketing. The majority of the boxed features are new to this edition; a few have been significantly updated and revised to fit the themes of this edition.

MARKETING INSIGHTS

Publix Provides the Full Service Experience

Publix Super Markets, established in Florida over 83 years ago, is a customer-centered supermarket with stores in five states. The chain has grown to be the seventh-largest private company and the most profitable grocery chain in the United States. How did it achieve such success? It focused on exceptional customer service, high-quality products, and competitive prices. When George Jenkins founded Publix, he wanted to ensure his employees felt valued, so he offered them a stake in the company. Today, Publix is the largest employee-owned company in the United States. It has made *Fortune*'s "100 Best Companies to Work For" every year.

Valued employees translate into satisfied customers. Publix checks out two customers per line to decrease wait

and quickly direct customers to the items they need. This is part of what Publix calls its "full service experience for customers."

When Walmart opened stores in Florida, Publix responded with strong strategic marketing and expansion plans. Walmart operates on the value of low prices, while Publix emphasizes helpful, friendly, and motivated staff who keep the stores clean, organized, and stocked. Publix offers weekly Buy One Get One Free promotions, which some customers argue beat Walmart on value. Publix is always looking for ways to improve the customer experience. This has allowed it to keep the majority of its market share in Florida even as Walmart grows in the state. It achieves this by listening to customer feedback. For example, as a response

- **New Snapshot features.** The Snapshot features are new and engage students by highlighting interesting, up-to-date statistics that link marketing theory to the real world.
- **New research.** Throughout the text we have updated content with the most recent research that supports the frameworks and best practices for marketing.

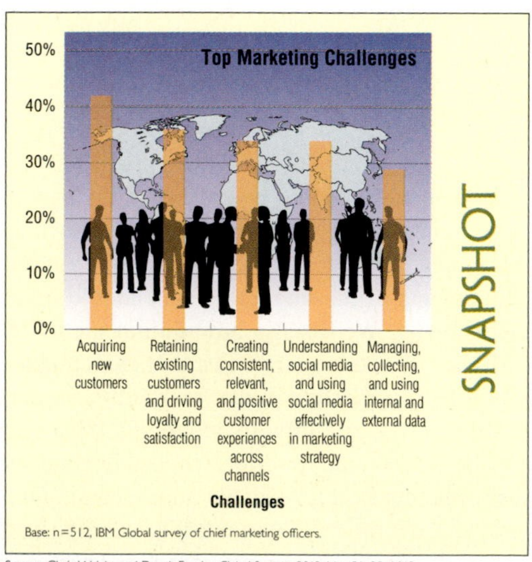

Source: Chris Wright and Derek Franks, *Global Summit 2013*, May 21–23, 2013, http://public.dhe.ibm.com/common/ssi/ecm/en/zzl03043usen/ZZL03043USEN.PDF (accessed October 24, 2013).

- **New illustrations and examples.** New advertisements from well-known firms are employed to illustrate chapter topics. Experiences of real-world companies are used to exemplify marketing concepts and strategies throughout the text. Most examples are new or updated to include digital marketing concepts as well as several new sustainable marketing illustrations.
- **End-of-chapter cases.** Each chapter contains two cases, including a video case, profiling firms to illustrate concrete application of marketing strategies and concepts. Many of our video cases are new to this edition and are supported by current and engaging videos.

© Procter & Gamble

FEATURES OF THE BOOK

As with previous editions, this edition of the text provides a comprehensive and practical introduction to marketing that is both easy to teach and to learn. *Marketing* continues to be one of the most widely adopted introductory textbooks in the world. We appreciate the confidence that adopters have placed in our textbook and continue to work hard to make sure that, as in previous editions, this edition keeps pace with changes. The entire text is structured to excite students about the subject and to help them learn completely and efficiently.

- An *organizational model* at the beginning of each part provides a "road map" of the text and a visual tool for understanding the connections among various components.
- *Objectives* at the start of each chapter present concrete expectations about what students are to learn as they read the chapter.
- Every chapter begins with an *opening vignette*. This feature provides an example of the real world of marketing that relates to the topic covered in the chapter. After reading the vignette, the student should be motivated to want to learn more about concepts and strategies that relate to the varying topics. Students will learn about topics such as international supply chain issues, content marketing, frequent-flier promotions, and price wars. Students will also be introduced to such companies as Shutterfly, H.Bloom, Uniqlo, and Goya Foods.
- Boxed features—*Emerging Trends in Marketing* and *Going Green*—capture dynamic changes in marketing. These changes are influencing marketing strategies and customer behavior. Strong feedback from adopters indicated the need for coverage in these areas.

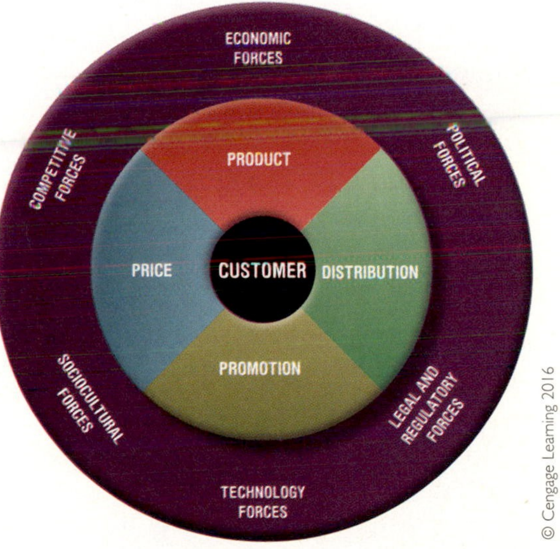

© Cengage Learning 2016

EMERGING TRENDS

Pinterest Provides New Methods for Marketing Research

The pinboard photo-sharing site Pinterest offers a less costly alternative for gathering market research. The social network has appealed to many marketers since its debut, but as its user base grows, businesses are learning how to use Pinterest pages to understand customers. Retailers pin images of their products to their pages and monitor engagement with these images by tracking follower comments, likes, and the number of times their images have been "repined." Pinterest's new feature, called "Rich Pins," encourages consumers themselves to market the product, allowing them to make more specific comments about products such as unique features or pricing. Marketers can also develop different boards of images to target different customer segments.

Nordstrom uses information gleaned from Pinterest to manage its inventory. If a product is getting a lot of attention on Pinterest, Nordstrom makes sure it is in stock. Lowe's also monitors its boards for buyer information. The use of Pinterest in marketing is different from other social networking sites because it is focused primarily around products. One in five Pinterest users buys products after pinning or liking them. Marketers should not overlook this opportunity to use the Pinterest platform as an inexpensive source of collecting primary data on consumer preferences.[a]

© iStockphoto.com/CTR design LLC

- The *Emerging Trends* boxes cover such marketing phenomena as limited-time fast-food products, the revival of barber shops, pet-friendly hotels, and business apps. Featured companies include Ticketmaster, Pinterest, Starbucks, and Salesforce.com.

GOING GREEN

Marketing for the Car-Sharing Business Model: "Share It" Social Media!

Zipcar, the innovative and environmentally friendly solution to car ownership and rental cars, has continued to propel and expand its business model of car sharing. Zipcar is a U.S. membership-based company that allows members to reserve vehicles located across the United States, Spain, Canada, or the United Kingdom. To join, users register online and receive a Zipcard, or electronic key, in the mail. Members are then eligible to reserve a car for an allotted time, by the day or by the hour, and are provided the flexibility and convenience of using any car.

Although the company has experienced growth and an increase in memberships over the years (more than

marketing concept for this type of business has proven a challenge. The car-sharing business model relies heavily on positive word-of-mouth promotion. In order to leverage this, Zipcar has taken to social media and encourages members to share photos and comments about their experiences with car sharing to effectively communicate the value of the business. This type of marketing also lends a sense of authenticity to the brand that the company could not have achieved without the help of its customers.

In 2013, Zipcar was acquired by car rental giant Avis for $500 million. Now a subsidiary of Avis, Zipcar remains a popular alternative for business travelers and

- The *Going Green* boxes introduce students to such topics as plant-based packaging, eco-friendly initiatives at Mall of America, and the use of the word "natural" in advertising. Featured companies include ZipCar, Unilever, Google, SodaStream, and Rodale.
- There are also two types of mini-features found in the text: *Marketing Debate* and *Entrepreneurship in Marketing*.
- The *Marketing Debate* marginal feature discusses controversial issues related to marketing, such as the marketing of free toys in fast food, privacy issues in tracking product returns, child-free seating areas on airliners, marketing on Twitter, marketing of caffeine-enriched foods, the pros and cons of mobile advertising, and the ethics of using MFN clauses.

MARKETING DEBATE

Privacy Issues in Tracking Product Returns

ISSUE: Is it acceptable to collect data on customer product returns?

Retailers have begun compiling return profiles on customers to reduce product return fraud, estimated to cost retailers approximately $8.9 billion annually. Return fraud occurs when customers buy items with the purpose of returning them. It can also involve returning stolen items and switching a lower price tag for a higher one. When a customer brings in an item for a return, the retailer generally asks for the person's identification card. Most think their identity is being confirmed, but some stores use their marketing information system to create a database on the consumer. Although only 1 percent of return profiles are suspicious, honest consumers are also getting their return merchandise history tracked. This could be viewed as a privacy issue. Consumer privacy related to transactions is a major marketing ethics issue, especially when this

ENTREPRENEURSHIP IN MARKETING

Two Moms Go from Zero to $70 Million in 7 Years!

Founders: Kristin Groose Richmond and Kirsten Saenz Tobey
Business: Revolution Foods
Founded: 2006
Success: Company grew from a start-up to $70 million in annual sales in only seven years.

Two entrepreneurial moms started Revolution Foods with the idea of cooking up nutritious meals that students would gobble up. Kristin Groose Richmond and Kirsten Saenz Tobey met at the University of California-Berkeley's Haas School of Business, and their shared interest in healthy foods for children led them to team up at Revolution Foods

Given growing concerns about childhood obesity and the drive to instill healthy eating habits from an early age, they knew parents and school officials would welcome new options for school breakfasts and lunches if the price was right. Revolution Foods proved itself by researching what children like to eat, creating affordable menus featuring foods from local sources, testing the meals in local schools, and continually refining the menus and prices over time.

After winning big customers like the San Francisco Unified School District, the firm now serves more than 1 million meals every week. Building on its success, Revolution Foods is branching out into the consumer market with prepackaged meals sold in supermarkets nationwide.[b]

- The *Entrepreneurship in Marketing* feature focuses on the role of entrepreneurship and the need for creativity in developing successful marketing strategies by featuring successful entrepreneurial companies like Revolution Foods, Xiaomi, Simple, Van Leeuwen Artisan Ice Cream, Lonesome Pine Used Book Store, and B-Reel.
- *Key term definitions* appear in the margins to help students build their marketing vocabulary.
- Figures, tables, photographs, advertisements, and Snapshot features increase comprehension and stimulate interest.
- A complete *chapter summary* reviews the major topics discussed, and the list of important terms provides another end-of-chapter study aid to expand students' marketing vocabulary.
- *Developing Your Marketing Plan* ties the chapter concepts into an overall marketing plan that can be created by completing the Interactive Marketing Plan activity found at **www.cengagebrain.com**. The *Developing Your Marketing Plan* feature allows students to explore each chapter topic in relation to developing and implementing a marketing campaign.
- *Discussion and review questions* at the end of each chapter encourage further study and exploration of chapter content.
- Two *cases* at the end of each chapter help students understand the application of chapter concepts. One of the end-of-chapter cases is related to a video segment. Some examples of companies highlighted in the cases are Axe, Taza, The Food Network, L'Oréal, and Wyndham.

- A *strategic case* at the end of each part helps students integrate the diverse concepts that have been discussed within the related chapters. Examples include Eaton, REI, Apple Inc., and Chevrolet.
- *Appendixes* discuss marketing career opportunities, explore financial analysis in marketing, and present a sample marketing plan.
- A comprehensive *glossary* defines more than 625 important marketing terms.

TEXT ORGANIZATION

We have organized the eight parts of *Marketing* to give students a theoretical and practical understanding of marketing decision making.

Part 1 **Marketing Strategy and Customer Relationships**
In **Chapter 1**, we define marketing and explore several key concepts: customers and target markets, the marketing mix, relationship marketing, the marketing concept, and value-driven marketing. In **Chapter 2**, we look at an overview of strategic marketing topics, such as the strategic planning process; corporate, business-unit, and marketing strategies; the implementation of marketing strategies; performance evaluation of marketing strategies; and the components of the marketing plan.

Part 2 **Environmental Forces and Social and Ethical Responsibilities**
We examine competitive, economic, political, legal and regulatory, technological, and sociocultural forces that can have profound effects on marketing strategies in **Chapter 3**. In **Chapter 4**, we explore social responsibility and ethical issues in marketing decisions.

Part 3 **Marketing Research and Target Market Analysis**
In **Chapter 5**, we provide a foundation for analyzing buyers with a look at marketing information systems and the basic steps in the marketing research process. We look at elements that affect buying decisions to better analyze customers' needs and evaluate how specific marketing strategies can satisfy those needs. In **Chapter 6**, we deal with how to select and analyze target markets—one of the major steps in marketing strategy development.

Part 4 **Buying Behavior, Global Marketing, and Digital Marketing**
We examine consumer buying decision processes and factors that influence buying decisions in **Chapter 7**. In **Chapter 8**, we explore business markets, business customers, the buying center, and the business buying decision process. **Chapter 9** focuses on the actions, involvement, and strategies of marketers that serve international customers. In **Chapter 10**, we discuss digital marketing, social media, and social networking.

Part 5 **Product Decisions**
In **Chapter 11**, we introduce basic concepts and relationships that must be understood to make effective product decisions. Also, we discuss a number of dimensions associated with branding and packaging. We analyze a variety of topics regarding product management in **Chapter 12**, including line extensions and product modification, new-product development, and product deletions. **Chapter 13** discusses services marketing.

Part 6 **Distribution Decisions**
In **Chapter 14**, we look at supply-chain management, marketing channels, and the decisions and activities associated with the physical distribution of products, such as order processing, materials handling, warehousing, inventory management, and transportation. **Chapter 15** explores retailing and wholesaling, including types of retailers and wholesalers, direct marketing and selling, and strategic retailing issues.

Part 7 **Promotion Decisions**

We discuss integrated marketing communications in **Chapter 16**. The communication process and major promotional methods that can be included in promotion mixes are described. In **Chapter 17**, we analyze the major steps in developing an advertising campaign. We also define public relations and how it can be used. **Chapter 18** deals with personal selling and the role it can play in a firm's promotional efforts. We also explore the general characteristics of sales promotion and describe sales promotion techniques.

Part 8 **Pricing Decisions**

In **Chapter 19**, we discuss the importance of price and look at some characteristics of price and nonprice competition. We explore fundamental concepts like demand, elasticity, marginal analysis, and break-even analysis. We then examine the major factors that affect marketers' pricing decisions. In **Chapter 20**, we look at the six major stages of the process marketers use to establish prices.

A COMPREHENSIVE INSTRUCTIONAL RESOURCE PACKAGE

For instructors, this edition of *Marketing* includes an exceptionally comprehensive package of teaching materials.

Instructor's Manual

The *Instructor's Manual* has been revamped to meet the needs of an engaging classroom environment. It has been updated with diverse and dynamic discussion starters, classroom activities, and group exercises. It includes such tools as:

- Quick Reference Guide
- Purpose Statement
- Integrated Lecture Outline
- Discussion Starter recommendations that encourage active exploration of the in-text examples
- Class Exercises and Semester Project Activities
- Suggested Answers to end-of-chapter exercises, cases, and strategic cases
- Guide to teaching Role-Play Team Exercises

Test Bank

The test bank provides more than 4,000 test items, including true/false, multiple-choice, and essay questions. Each objective test item is accompanied by the correct answer, appropriate Learning Objective, level of difficulty, Bloom's level of thinking, Program Interdisciplinary Learning Outcomes, and Marketing Disciplinary Learning Outcomes. Cengage Learning Testing powered by Cognero is a flexible, online system that allows you to:

- Author, edit, and manage test bank content from multiple Cengage Learning solutions
- Create multiple test versions in an instant
- Deliver tests from your LMS, your classroom, or wherever you want

American Marketing Association Professional Certified Marketer®

The American Marketing Association has recently started offering marketing graduates the opportunity of adding the AMA PCM® credentials to their undergraduate or MBA degree, which can serve as a symbol of professional excellence that affirms mastery of marketing knowledge and commitment to quality in the practice of marketing. Certification, which is voluntary, requires passing a rigorous and comprehensive exam and then maintaining your certification through continuing education. Earning your AMA PCM certification demonstrates to employers, peers, and clients that you:

- Have mastered essential marketing knowledge and practices
- Go the extra mile to stay current in the marketing field
- Follow the highest professional standards

The AMA recommends Pride and Ferrell *Marketing* as a suggested resource for AMA PCM students to utilize as they prepare for taking the AMA PCM Certification exam, and the text was used as a source to design the course and as a source for suitable examination questions. Now, more than ever, you need to stand out in the marketplace. AMA's Professional Certified Marketer (PCM®) program is the perfect way to showcase your expertise and set yourself apart.

To learn more about the American Marketing Association and the AMA PCM exam, visit **www.marketingpower.com/Careers/Pages/ProfessionalCertifiedMarketer.aspx**

© Cengage Learning 2014

PowerPoint Slides

PowerPoint continues to be a very popular teaching device, and a special effort has been made to upgrade the PowerPoint program to enhance classroom teaching. Premium lecture slides, containing such content as advertisements, and unique graphs and data, have been created to provide instructors with up-to-date, unique content to increase student application and interest.

Marketing Video Case Series

This series contains videos specifically tied to the video cases found at the end of the book. The videos include information about exciting companies, such as New Belgium Brewing, TOMS Shoes, Starbucks, Dale Carnegie, and The Food Network.

MindTap for *Marketing*, 18e

MindTap is a personalized teaching experience with relevant assignments that guide students to analyze, apply, and improve thinking, allowing you to measure skills and outcomes with ease.

- Personalized Teaching: Becomes yours with a learning path that is built with key student objectives. Control what students see and when they see it. Use it as-is or match to your syllabus exactly—hide, rearrange, add, and create your own content.
- Guide Students: A unique learning path of relevant readings, multimedia, and activities that move students up the learning taxonomy from basic knowledge and comprehension to analysis and application.
- Promote Better Outcomes: Empower instructors and motivate students with analytics and reports that provide a snapshot of class progress, time in course, and engagement and completion rates.

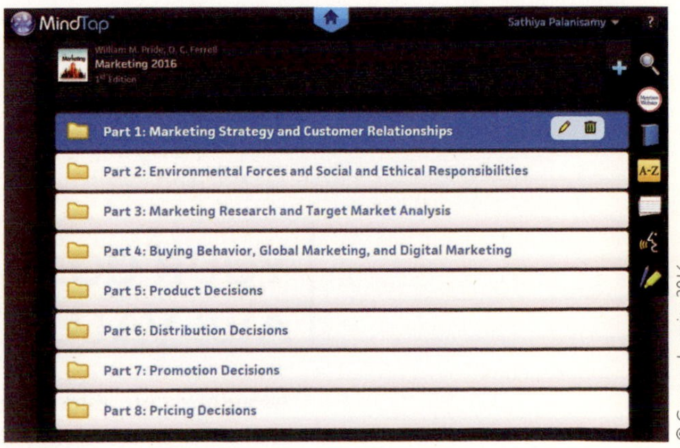

© Cengage Learning 2016

Author's Website

The authors also maintain a website at **http://prideferrell.net** to provide video resources that can be used as supplements and class exercises. The videos have been developed as marketing labs with worksheets for students to use on observing the videos. Some of the videos are accessible through links, and there is also information on where some of the videos can be obtained.

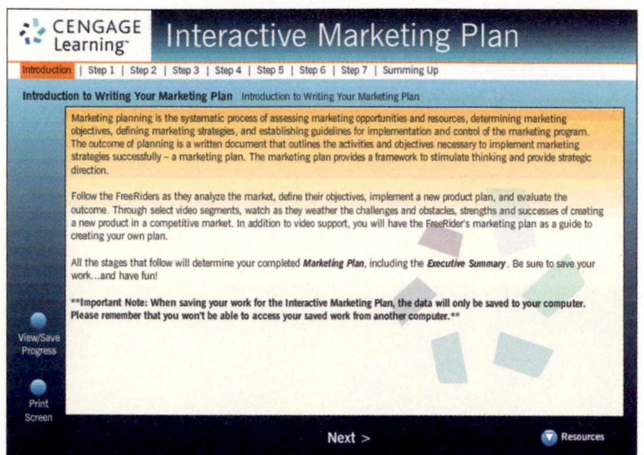

Interactive Marketing Plan

The Marketing Plan Worksheets have been revamped and reproduced within an interactive and multimedia environment. A video program has been developed around the worksheets, allowing students to follow a company through the trials and tribulations of launching a new product. This video helps place the conceptual marketing plan into an applicable light and is supported by a summary of the specific stages of the marketing plan as well as a sample plan based on the events of the video. These elements act as the 1-2-3 punch supporting the student while completing his or her own plan, the last step of the Interactive Marketing Plan. The plan is broken into three functional sections that can either be completed in one simple project or carried over throughout the semester.

SUPPLEMENTS TO MEET STUDENT NEEDS

The complete package available with *Marketing* includes support materials that facilitate student learning. To access additional course materials, please visit **www.cengagebrain.com**. At the CengageBrain.com home page, search for the ISBN of your textbook (from the back cover of your book) using the search box at the top of the page. This will take you to the product page, where the following resources can be found:

- Interactive teaching and learning tools, including:
  - Full-color e-book—Allows you to highlight and search for key terms
  - Quizzes
  - Flashcards
  - Videos
  - An Interactive Marketing Plan
  - And more!

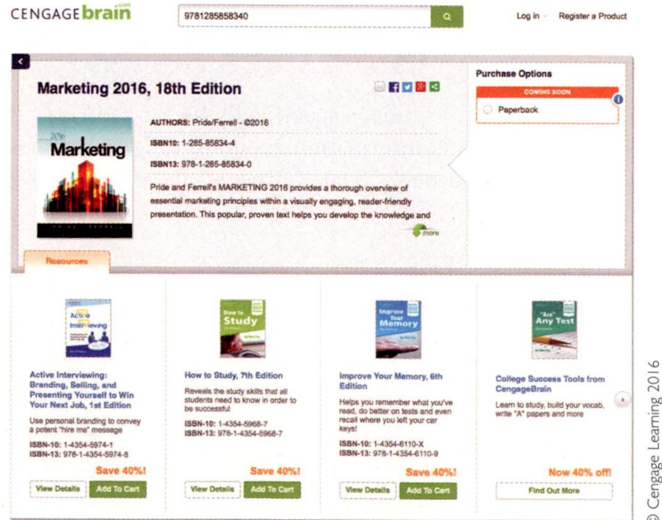

YOUR COMMENTS AND SUGGESTIONS ARE VALUED

As authors, our major focus has been on teaching and preparing learning materials for introductory marketing students. We have traveled extensively to work with students and to understand the needs of professors of introductory marketing courses. We both teach this marketing course on a regular basis and test the materials included in the book, test bank, and other ancillary materials to make sure they are effective in the classroom.

Through the years, professors and students have sent us many helpful suggestions for improving the text and ancillary components. We invite your comments, questions, and criticisms. We want to do our best to provide materials that enhance the teaching and learning of marketing concepts and strategies. Your suggestions will be sincerely appreciated. Please write us, or e-mail us at **w-pride@tamu.edu** or **OFerrell@unm.edu**, or call 979-845-5857 (Bill Pride) or 505-277-3468 (O. C. Ferrell).

ACKNOWLEDGMENTS

Like most textbooks, this one reflects the ideas of many academicians and practitioners who have contributed to the development of the marketing discipline. We appreciate the opportunity to present their ideas in this book.

A number of individuals have made helpful comments and recommendations in their reviews of this or earlier editions. We appreciate the generous help of these reviewers:

Zafar U. Ahmed
Minot State University

Thomas Ainscough
University of Massachusetts–Dartmouth

Sana Akili
Iowa State University

Katrece Albert
Southern University

Joe F. Alexander
University of Northern Colorado

Mark I. Alpert
University of Texas at Austin

David M. Ambrose
University of Nebraska

David Andrus
Kansas State University

Linda K. Anglin
Minnesota State University

George Avellano
Central State University

Emin Babakus
University of Memphis

Julie Baker
Texas Christian University

Siva Balasubramanian
Southern Illinois University

Joseph Ballenger
Stephen F. Austin State University

Guy Banville
Creighton University

Frank Barber
Cuyahoga Community College

Joseph Barr
Framingham State College

Thomas E. Barry
Southern Methodist University

Charles A. Bearchell
California State University–Northridge

Richard C. Becherer
University of Tennessee–Chattanooga

Walter H. Beck, Sr.
Reinhardt College

Russell Belk
University of Utah

John Bennett
University of Missouri–Columbia

W. R. Berdine
California State Polytechnic Institute

Karen Berger
Pace University

Stewart W. Bither
Pennsylvania State University

Roger Blackwell
Ohio State University

Peter Bloch
University of Missouri–Columbia

Wanda Blockhus
San Jose State University

Nancy Bloom
Nassau Community College

Paul N. Bloom
University of North Carolina

James P. Boespflug
Arapahoe Community College

Joseph G. Bonnice
Manhattan College

John Boos
Ohio Wesleyan University

Peter Bortolotti
Johnson & Wales University

Jenell Bramlage
University of Northwestern Ohio

James Brock
Susquehanna College

John R. Brooks, Jr.
Houston Baptist University

William G. Browne
Oregon State University

John Buckley
Orange County Community College

Gul T. Butaney
Bentley College

James Cagley
University of Tulsa

Pat J. Calabros
University of Texas–Arlington

Linda Calderone
State University of New York College of Technology at Farmingdale

Joseph Cangelosi
University of Central Arkansas

William J. Carner
University of Texas–Austin

James C. Carroll
University of Central Arkansas

Terry M. Chambers
Westminster College

Lawrence Chase
Tompkins Cortland Community College

Larry Chonko
Baylor University

Ernest F. Cooke
Loyola College–Baltimore

Robert Copley
University of Louisville

John I. Coppett
University of Houston–Clear Lake

Robert Corey
West Virginia University

Deborah L. Cowles
Virginia Commonwealth University

Sandra Coyne
Springfield College

William L. Cron
Texas Christian University

Gary Cutler
Dyersburg State Community College

Bernice N. Dandridge
Diablo Valley College

Tamara Davis
Davenport University

Lloyd M. DeBoer
George Mason University

Sally Dibb
University of Warwick

Ralph DiPietro
Montclair State University

Paul Dishman
Idaho State University

Suresh Divakar
State University of New York–Buffalo

Casey L. Donoho
Northern Arizona University

Todd Donovan
Colorado State University

Peter T. Doukas
Westchester Community College

Kent Drummond
University of Wyoming

Tinus Van Drunen
University Twente (Netherlands)

Lee R. Duffus
Florida Gulf Coast University

Robert F. Dwyer
University of Cincinnati

Roland Eyears
Central Ohio Technical College

Thomas Falcone
Indiana University of Pennsylvania

James Finch
University of Wisconsin–La Crosse

Letty C. Fisher
SUNY/Westchester Community College

Renée Florsheim
Loyola Marymount University

Charles W. Ford
Arkansas State University

John Fraedrich
Southern Illinois University, Carbondale

David J. Fritzsche
University of Washington

Donald A. Fuller
University of Central Florida

Terry Gable
Truman State University

Robert Garrity
University of Hawaii

Cathy Goodwin
University of Manitoba

Geoffrey L. Gordon
Northern Illinois University

Robert Grafton-Small
University of Strathclyde

Harrison Grathwohl
California State University–Chico

Alan A. Greco
North Carolina A&T State University

Blaine S. Greenfield
Bucks County Community College

Sharon F. Gregg
Middle Tennessee University

Charles Gross
University of New Hampshire

David Hansen
Texas Southern University

Richard C. Hansen
Ferris State University

Nancy Hanson-Rasmussen
University of Wisconsin–Eau Claire

Robert R. Harmon
Portland State University

Mary C. Harrison
Amber University

Lorraine Hartley
Franklin University

Michael Hartline
Florida State University

Salah S. Hassan
George Washington University

Manoj Hastak
American University

Dean Headley
Wichita State University

Esther Headley
Wichita State University

Debbora Heflin-Bullock
California State Polytechnic University–Pomona

Merlin Henry
Rancho Santiago College

Tony Henthorne
University of Southern Mississippi

Lois Herr
Elizabethtown College

Charles L. Hilton
Eastern Kentucky University

Elizabeth C. Hirschman
Rutgers, State University of New Jersey

John R. Huser
Illinois Central College

Joan M. Inzinga
Bay Path College

Deloris James
University of Maryland

Ron Johnson
Colorado Mountain College

Theodore F. Jula
Stonehill College

Peter F. Kaminski
Northern Illinois University

Yvonne Karsten
Minnesota State University

Jerome Katrichis
Temple University

Garland Keesling
Towson University

James Kellaris
University of Cincinnati

Alvin Kelly
Florida A&M University

Philip Kemp
DePaul University

Sylvia Keyes
Bridgewater State College

Roy Klages
State University of New York at Albany

Hal Koenig
Oregon State University

Douglas Kornemann
Milwaukee Area Technical College

Kathleen Krentler
San Diego State University

John Krupa, Jr.
Johnson & Wales University

Barbara Lafferty
University of South Florida

Patricia Laidler
Massasoit Community College

Richard A. Lancioni
Temple University

Irene Lange
California State University–Fullerton

Geoffrey P. Lantos
Stonehill College

Charles L. Lapp
University of Texas–Dallas

Virginia Larson
San Jose State University

John Lavin
Waukesha County Technical Institute

Marilyn Lavin
University of Wisconsin–Whitewater

Monle Lee
Indiana University–South Bend

Ron Lennon
Barry University

Richard C. Leventhal
Metropolitan State College

Marilyn L. Liebrenz-Himes
George Washington University

Jay D. Lindquist
Western Michigan University

Terry Loe
Kennesaw State University

Mary Logan
Southwestern Assemblies of God College

Paul Londrigan
Mott Community College

Anthony Lucas
Community College of Allegheny County

George Lucas
U.S. Learning, Inc.

William Lundstrom
Cleveland State University

Rhonda Mack
College of Charleston

Stan Madden
Baylor University

Patricia M. Manninen
North Shore Community College

Gerald L. Manning
Des Moines Area Community College

Lalita A. Manrai
University of Delaware

Franklyn Manu
Morgan State University

Allen S. Marber
University of Bridgeport

Gayle J. Marco
Robert Morris College

Carolyn A. Massiah
University of Central Florida

James McAlexander
Oregon State University

Donald McCartney
University of Wisconsin–Green Bay

Anthony McGann
University of Wyoming

Jack McNiff
State University of New York College of Technology at Farmington

Carla Meeske
University of Oregon

Jeffrey A. Meier
Fox Valley Technical College

James Meszaros
County College of Morris

Brian Meyer
Minnesota State University

Martin Meyers
University of Wisconsin–Stevens Point

Stephen J. Miller
Oklahoma State University

William Moller
University of Michigan

Carol Morris-Calder
Loyola Marymount University

David Murphy
Madisonville Community College

Keith Murray
Bryant College

Sue Ellen Neeley
University of Houston–Clear Lake

Carolyn Y. Nicholson
Stetson University

Francis L. Notturno, Sr.
Owens Community College

James R. Ogden
Kutztown University of Pennsylvania

Lois Bitner Olson
San Diego State University

Mike O'Neill
California State University–Chico

Robert S. Owen
State University of New York–Oswego

Allan Palmer
University of North Carolina at Charlotte

David P. Paul III
Monmouth University

Terry Paul
Ohio State University

Teresa Pavia
University of Utah

John Perrachione
Truman State University

Michael Peters
Boston College

Linda Pettijohn
Missouri State University

Lana Podolak
Community College of Beaver County

Raymond E. Polchow
Muskingum Area Technical College

Thomas Ponzurick
West Virginia University

William Presutti
Duquesne University

Kathy Pullins
Columbus State Community College

Edna J. Ragins
North Carolina A&T State University

Mohammed Rawwas
University of Northern Iowa

William Rhey
University of Tampa

Glen Riecken
East Tennessee State University

Winston Ring
University of Wisconsin–Milwaukee

Ed Riordan
Wayne State University

Bruce Robertson
San Francisco State University

Robert A. Robicheaux
University of Alabama–Birmingham

Linda Rose
Westwood College Online

Bert Rosenbloom
Drexel University

Robert H. Ross
Wichita State University

Tom Rossi
Broome Community College

Vicki Rostedt
The University of Akron

Catherine Roster
University of New Mexico

Kenneth L. Rowe
Arizona State University

Don Roy
Middle Tennessee State University

Catherine Ruggieri
St. John's University

Elise Sautter
New Mexico State University

Ronald Schill
Brigham Young University

Bodo Schlegelmilch
Vienna University of Economics and Business Administration

Edward Schmitt
Villanova University

Thomas Schori
Illinois State University

Donald Sciglimpaglia
San Diego State University

Stanley Scott
University of Alaska–Anchorage

Harold S. Sekiguchi
University of Nevada–Reno

Gilbert Seligman
Dutchess Community College

Richard J. Semenik
University of Utah

Beheruz N. Sethna
Lamar University

Morris A. Shapero
Schiller International University

Mark Siders
Southern Oregon University

Carolyn F. Siegel
Eastern Kentucky University

Dean C. Siewers
Rochester Institute of Technology

Lyndon Simkin
University of Warwick

Roberta Slater
Cedar Crest College

Paul J. Solomon
University of South Florida

Sheldon Somerstein
City University of New York

Eric R. Spangenberg
University of Mississippi

Rosann L. Spiro
Indiana University

William Staples
University of Houston–Clear Lake

Claire F. Sullivan
Metropolitan State University

Carmen Sunda
University of New Orleans

Robert Swerdlow
Lamar University

Crina Tarasi
Central Michigan University

Ruth Taylor
Texas State University

Steven A. Taylor
Illinois State University

Hal Teer
James Madison University

Ira Teich
Long Island University–C. W. Post

Debbie Thorne
Texas State University

Sharynn Tomlin
Angelo State University

Hale Tongren
George Mason University

James Underwood
University of Southwest Louisiana–Lafayette

Barbara Unger
Western Washington University

Dale Varble
Indiana State University

Bronis Verhage
Georgia State University

R. Vishwanathan "Vish" Iyer
University of Northern Colorado

Charles Vitaska
Metropolitan State College

Kirk Wakefield
Baylor University

Harlan Wallingford
Pace University

Jacquelyn Warwick
Andrews University

James F. Wenthe
Georgia College

Sumner M. White
Massachusetts Bay Community College

Janice Williams
University of Central Oklahoma

Alan R. Wiman
Rider College

John Withey
Indiana University–South Bend

Ken Wright
West Australian College of Advanced Education

We would like to thank Charlie Hofacker and Michael Hartline, both of Florida State University, for many helpful suggestions and insights in developing the chapter on digital marketing and social networking. Michael Hartline also assisted in the development of the marketing plan outline and provided suggestions throughout the text. Catherine Roster, University of New Mexico, and Marty Meyers, University of Wisconsin–Stevens Point, provided important assistance in revising "Marketing Research and Information Systems," "Consumer Buying Behavior," and "Digital Marketing and Social Networking."

We thank Jennifer Sawayda, Jennifer Jackson, Danielle Jolley, and Michelle Urban for their research and editorial assistance in the revision of the chapters. We appreciate the efforts of Marian Wood for developing and revising a number of boxed features and cases. We deeply appreciate the assistance of Laurie Marshall, Clarissa Means, Carolyn Phillips, Elisa Reyna, and Eva Tweedy for providing editorial technical assistance and support.

We express appreciation for the support and encouragement given to us by our colleagues at Texas A&M University and University of New Mexico. We are also grateful for the comments and suggestions we received from our own students, student focus groups, and student correspondents who provided feedback through the website.

A number of talented professionals at Cengage Learning and Integra have contributed to the development of this book. We are especially grateful to Jason Fremder, Colleen Farmer, Julie Fritsch, Sreejith Govindan, Stacy Shirley, John Rich, and Megan Fischer. Their inspiration, patience, support, and friendship are invaluable.

William M. Pride
O. C. Ferrell

ABOUT THE AUTHORS

William M. Pride is Professor of Marketing, Mays Business School, at Texas A&M University. He received his PhD from Louisiana State University. In addition to this text, he is the co-author of Cengage Learning's *Business* text, a market leader. Dr. Pride teaches principles of marketing at both undergraduate and graduate levels and constantly solicits student feedback important to revising a principles of marketing text.

Dr. Pride's research interests are in advertising, promotion, and distribution channels. His research articles have appeared in major journals in the fields of marketing, such as the *Journal of Marketing,* the *Journal of Marketing Research,* the *Journal of the Academy of Marketing Science,* and the *Journal of Advertising.*

Dr. Pride is a member of the American Marketing Association, Academy of Marketing Science, Society for Marketing Advances, and the Marketing Management Association. He has received the Marketing Fellow Award from the Society for Marketing Advances and the Marketing Innovation Award from the Marketing Management Association. Both of these are lifetime achievement awards.

O. C. Ferrell is University Distinguished Professor of Marketing and Bill Daniels Professor of Business Ethics, Anderson School of Management, University of New Mexico. He has also been on the faculties of the University of Wyoming, Colorado State University, University of Memphis, Texas A&M University, Illinois State University, and Southern Illinois University. He received his PhD in marketing from Louisiana State University.

He is past president of the Academic Council of the American Marketing Association and chaired the American Marketing Association Ethics Committee. Under his leadership, the committee developed the AMA Code of Ethics and the AMA Code of Ethics for Marketing on the Internet. He is currently a member of the advisory committee for the AMA marketing certification program. In addition, he is a former member of the Academy of Marketing Science Board of Governors and is a Society of Marketing Advances and Southwestern Marketing Association Fellow and an Academy of Marketing Science Distinguished Fellow. He is the Academy of Marketing Science's vice president of publications. In 2010, he received a Lifetime Achievement Award from the Macromarketing Society and a special award for service to doctoral students from the Southeast Doctoral Consortium. In 2014, Dr. Ferrell received the Cutco Vector Distinguished Marketing Educator Award from the Academy of Marketing Science.

Dr. Ferrell is the co-author of 20 books and more than 100 published articles and papers. His articles have been published in the *Journal of Marketing Research*, the *Journal of Marketing,* the *Journal of Business Ethics*, the *Journal of Business Research,* the *Journal of the Academy of Marketing Science*, and the *Journal of Public Policy & Marketing,* as well as other journals.

part 1

Marketing Strategy and Customer Relationships

PART 1 introduces the field of marketing and offers a broad perspective from which to explore and analyze various components of the marketing discipline. CHAPTER 1 defines *marketing* and explores some key concepts, including customers and target markets, the marketing mix, relationship marketing, the marketing concept, and value. CHAPTER 2 provides an overview of strategic marketing issues, such as the effect of organizational resources and opportunities on the planning process; the role of the mission statement; corporate, business-unit, and marketing strategies; and the creation of the marketing plan.

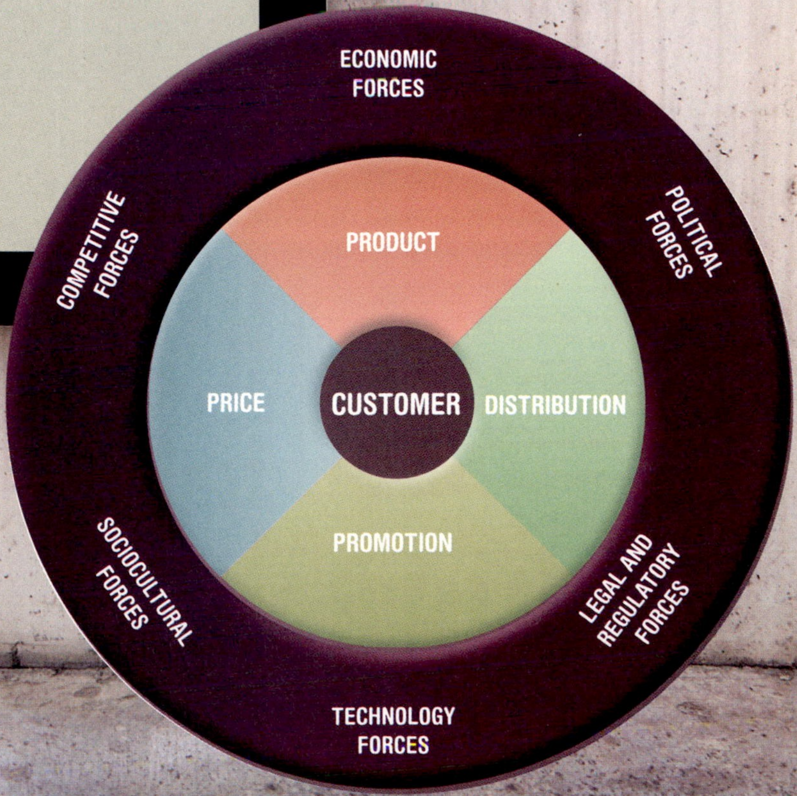

chapter 1

An Overview of Strategic Marketing

OBJECTIVES

1-1 Define *marketing*.

1-2 Explain the different variables of the marketing mix.

1-3 Describe how marketing creates value.

1-4 Briefly describe the marketing environment.

1-5 Summarize the marketing concept.

1-6 Identify the importance of building customer relationships.

1-7 Explain why marketing is important to our global economy.

MARKETING INSIGHTS

Publix Provides the Full Service Experience

Publix Super Markets, established in Florida over 83 years ago, is a customer-centered supermarket with stores in five states. The chain has grown to be the seventh-largest private company and the most profitable grocery chain in the United States. How did it achieve such success? It focused on exceptional customer service, high-quality products, and competitive prices. When George Jenkins founded Publix, he wanted to ensure his employees felt valued, so he offered them a stake in the company. Today, Publix is the largest employee-owned company in the United States. It has made *Fortune*'s "100 Best Companies to Work For" every year.

Valued employees translate into satisfied customers. Publix checks out two customers per line to decrease wait times, and baggers carry the customers' bags to their vehicles. Employees are highly trained to answer questions and quickly direct customers to the items they need. This is part of what Publix calls its "full service experience for customers."

When Walmart opened stores in Florida, Publix responded with strong strategic marketing and expansion plans. Walmart operates on the value of low prices, while Publix emphasizes helpful, friendly, and motivated staff who keep the stores clean, organized, and stocked. Publix offers weekly Buy One Get One Free promotions, which some customers argue beat Walmart on value. Publix is always looking for ways to improve the customer experience. This has allowed it to keep the majority of its market share in Florida even as Walmart grows in the state. It achieves this by listening to customer feedback. For example, as a response to customer feedback, Publix began offering an online deli ordering service to shorten wait times at the counter.[1]

Like all organizations, Publix attempts to provide products that customers want, communicate useful information about them to excite interest, price them appropriately, and make them available when and where customers want to buy them. Even if an organization does all these things well, however, competition from marketers of similar products, economic conditions, and other factors can impact the company's success. Such factors influence the decisions that all organizations must make in strategic marketing.

This chapter introduces the strategic marketing concepts and decisions covered throughout the text. First, we develop a definition of *marketing* and explore each element of the definition in detail. Next, we explore the importance of value-driven marketing. We also introduce the marketing concept and consider several issues associated with its implementation. Additionally, we take a look at the management of customer relationships and relationship marketing. Finally, we examine the importance of marketing in global society.

marketing The process of creating, distributing, promoting, and pricing goods, services, and ideas to facilitate satisfying exchange relationships with customers and to develop and maintain favorable relationships with stakeholders in a dynamic environment

customers The purchasers of organizations' products; the focal point of all marketing activities

1-1 DEFINING MARKETING

If you ask several people what *marketing* is, you are likely to hear a variety of descriptions. Although many people think marketing is advertising or selling, marketing is much more complex than most people realize. In this book we define **marketing** as the process of creating, distributing, promoting, and pricing goods, services, and ideas to facilitate satisfying exchange relationships with customers and to develop and maintain favorable relationships with stakeholders in a dynamic environment. Our definition is consistent with that of the American Marketing Association (AMA), which defines *marketing* as "the activity, set of institutions, and processes for creating, communicating, delivering, and exchanging offerings that have value for customers, clients, partners, and society at large."[2]

© Mars, Inc

Appealing to Target Markets
Snickers are highly desired and hunger-satisfying candy bars.

1-1a Marketing Focuses on Customers

As the purchasers of the products that organizations develop, price, distribute, and promote, **customers** are the focal point of all marketing activities (see Figure 1.1). Organizations have to define their products not as what the companies make or produce but as what they do to satisfy customers. Snickers creates products that satisfy consumer needs. The advertisement shows a zebra chasing a lion to demonstrate that Snickers bars are desirable because of their taste and ability to eliminate hunger.

The essence of marketing is to develop satisfying exchanges from which both customers and marketers benefit. The customer expects to gain a reward or benefit greater than the costs incurred in a marketing transaction. The marketer expects to gain something of value in return, generally the price charged for the product. Through buyer–seller interaction, a customer develops expectations about the seller's future behavior. To fulfill these expectations, the marketer

Figure 1.1 Components of Strategic Marketing

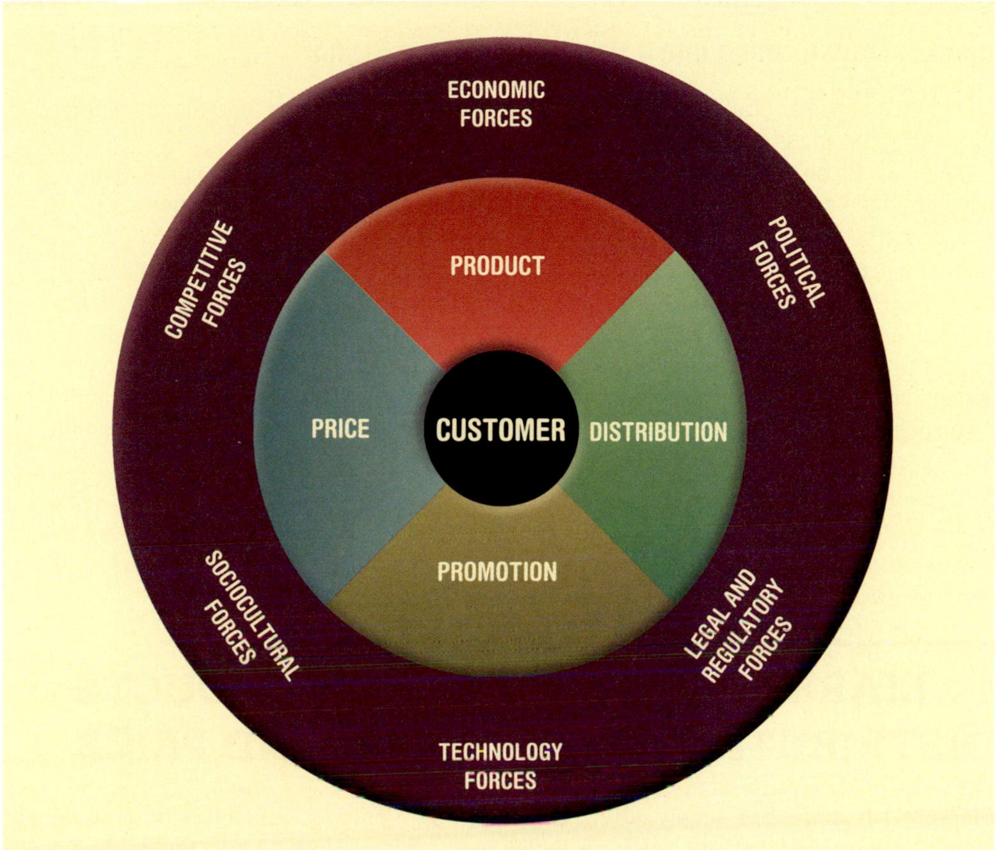

must deliver on promises made. Over time, this interaction results in relationships between the two parties. Fast-food restaurants such as Taco Bell and Subway depend on repeat purchases from satisfied customers—many often live or work a few miles from these restaurants—whereas customer expectations revolve around tasty food, value, and dependable service.

Organizations generally focus their marketing efforts on a specific group of customers, called a **target market**. Marketing managers may define a target market as a vast number of people or a relatively small group. For instance, marketers are increasingly interested in Hispanic consumers. Within the last decade, Hispanics made up more than half of the population gains in the United States. As a result, marketers are developing new ways to reach this demographic. For instance, magazines including *Hearst*, *Conde Nast*, and *Time* have begun increasing inserts and content for Hispanic populations. Although the magazines are still written in English, they contain specific references and themes that appeal to Hispanics.[3] Often companies target multiple markets with different products, promotions, prices, and distribution systems for each one. Vans shoes targets a fairly narrow market segment, especially compared to more diverse athletic shoe companies such as Nike and Reebok. Vans targets skateboarders and snowboarders between the ages of 10 and 24, whereas Nike and Reebok target most sports, age ranges, genders, and price points.[4]

target market A specific group of customers on whom an organization focuses its marketing efforts

Emerging Trends

Starbucks: Transforming into a Health-Conscious Brand

With the acquisition of Evolution Fresh, a juice bar brand, Starbucks is initiating its long-term strategic plan to transform the Starbucks brand into a healthy snack and meal alternative. In offering these juices and smoothies and listing calorie counts on menus, Starbucks is striving to operate in a responsible manner and is encouraging consumers to be responsible when making purchases. Its most recent endeavor is a strategic alliance with Danone, a French yogurt producer, to create a Greek yogurt for its Evolution Fresh brand. The extension of the Evolution Fresh brand is not only a smart business move into the emerging yogurt market but also communicates that Starbucks cares about the quality of food that consumers are eating.

In recent years, Starbucks has become more than just a quick stop for morning coffee. Consumers are spending more time in the afternoons and evenings buying and eating snacks served by the coffee maker. They have also been purchasing Starbucks products in grocery stores, and the Evolution Fresh Greek yogurt will be sold in both locations. CEO Howard Shultz recognizes that consumers find value in these healthy options and continues to find new ways to incorporate this value into the Starbucks brand.[a]

1-2 MARKETING DEALS WITH PRODUCTS, DISTRIBUTION, PROMOTION, AND PRICE

Marketing is more than simply advertising or selling a product; it involves developing and managing a product that will satisfy customer needs. It focuses on making the product available in the right place and at a price acceptable to buyers. It also requires communicating information that helps customers determine whether the product will satisfy their needs. These activities are planned, organized, implemented, and controlled to meet the needs of customers within the target market. Marketers refer to these activities—product, pricing, distribution, and promotion—as the **marketing mix** because they decide what type of each element to use and in what amounts. Marketing creates value through the marketing mix. A primary goal of a marketing manager is to create and maintain the right mix of these elements to satisfy customers' needs for a general product type. Note in Figure 1.1 that the marketing mix is built around the customer.

Marketing managers strive to develop a marketing mix that matches the needs of customers in the target market. Zumiez targets teenage girls and boys with snowboarding and skateboarding clothes. Products are made available in shopping malls (distribution) at competitive prices, supported by promotional activities. Marketing managers must constantly monitor the competition and adapt their product, pricing, promotion, and distribution decisions to create long-term success.

Before marketers can develop a marketing mix, they must collect in-depth, up-to-date information about customer needs. Such information might include data about the age, income, ethnicity, gender, and educational level of people in the target market, their preferences for product features, their attitudes toward competitors' products, and the frequency with which they use the product. Zumiez has to closely monitor trends to adjust its marketing mix to provide constant fashion changes. Armed with market information, marketing managers are better able to develop a marketing mix that satisfies a specific target market.

marketing mix Four marketing activities—product, pricing, distribution, and promotion—that a firm can control to meet the needs of customers within its target market

Let's look more closely at the decisions and activities related to each marketing mix variable.

1-2a The Product Variable

Successful marketing efforts result in products that become part of everyday life. Consider the satisfaction customers have had over the years from Coca-Cola, Levi's jeans, Visa credit cards, Tylenol pain relievers, and 3M Post-it Notes. The product variable of the marketing mix deals with researching customers' needs and wants and designing a product that satisfies them. A **product** can be a good, a service, or an idea. A good is a physical entity you can touch. Oakley sunglasses, Seven for All Mankind jeans, and Axe body spray are all examples of products. A service is the application of human and mechanical efforts to people or objects to provide intangible benefits to customers. Air travel, education, haircutting, banking, medical care, and day care are examples of services. Ideas include concepts, philosophies, images, and issues. For instance, a marriage counselor, for a fee, gives spouses ideas to help improve their relationship. Other marketers of ideas include political parties, churches, and schools.

The product variable also involves creating or modifying brand names and packaging and may include decisions regarding warranty and repair services. For example, the lawn care company TruGreen was originally branded as "Chemlawn." The company adapted its branding and products to provide a healthier and "greener" product offering.

Product variable decisions and related activities are important because they are directly involved with creating products that address customers' needs and wants. To maintain an assortment of products that helps an organization achieve its goals, marketers must develop new products, modify existing ones, and eliminate those that no longer satisfy enough buyers or that yield unacceptable profits.

1-2b The Distribution Variable

To satisfy customers, products must be available at the right time and in convenient locations. Subway, for example, locates not only in strip malls but also inside Walmarts, Home Depots, laundromats, churches, and hospitals, as well as inside Goodwill stores, car dealerships, and appliance stores. There are more than 40,566 Subways in 103 different countries, surpassing McDonald's as the world's largest chain.[5]

In dealing with the distribution variable, a marketing manager makes products available in the quantities desired to as many target market customers as possible, keeping total inventory, transportation, and storage costs as low as possible. A marketing manager also may select and motivate intermediaries (wholesalers and retailers), establish and

product A good, a service, or an idea

Thomas Barwick/Stone/Getty Images

© iStockphoto.com/alvarez

Types of Products
Sports events are intangible goods that provide fans with a fun experience. Bicycles represent a tangible good that consumers can use for recreation.

Distribution
Netflix uses digital distribution that allows consumers to stream movies right off its website.

maintain inventory control procedures, and develop and manage transportation and storage systems. The advent of the Internet and electronic commerce also has dramatically influenced the distribution variable. Companies now can make their products available throughout the world without maintaining facilities in each country. Apple has benefited from the ability to download songs and apps over the Internet. The company has supported growth and global success beyond the presence of physical Apple stores by selling phones, computers, iPads, and accessories online. We examine distribution issues in Chapters 14 and 15.

1-2c The Promotion Variable

The promotion variable relates to activities used to inform individuals or groups about the organization and its products. Promotion can aim to increase public awareness of the organization and of new or existing products. Holiday Inn Express, for example, wants to increase its appeal for younger travelers among Generation X (born between the early 1960s and early 1980s) and Generation Y (born between the early 1980s and early 2000s). The company launched its "Stay Smart" campaign encouraging consumers to offer humorous advice for any topic using social media channels such as Instagram, Twitter, and YouTube. The company adopted comedian Jason Jones as its spokesman. Holiday Inn hopes this interactive experience through digital media will engage younger generations of influential consumers.[6]

Promotional activities also can educate customers about product features. Iams provides wholesome dog food. The company's advertisement seeks to educate dog owners about the potential health benefits of its dog food versus other competitors. In addition, promotional activities can urge people to take a particular stance on a political or social issue, such as smoking or drug abuse. For example, the National Highway Safety Traffic Administration released an ad campaign to deter drunk driving during the holiday season. The campaign carried the message that cops "would see you before you see them." In the advertisement, a transparent cop watches a drunk couple as they leave a party, only to have them arrested as they are driving home.[7]

Promotion can help to sustain interest in established products that have been available for decades, such as Arm & Hammer baking soda or Ivory soap. Many companies are using the

Internet to communicate information about themselves and their products. Campbell's Kitchen provides a diverse array of recipes, coupons, and discussion boards online to support the sales of their soups.[8]

1-2d The Price Variable

The price variable relates to decisions and actions associated with establishing pricing objectives and policies and determining product prices. Price is a critical component of the marketing mix because customers are concerned about the value obtained in an exchange. Price is often used as a competitive tool, and intense price competition sometimes leads to price wars. Higher prices can be used competitively to establish a product's premium image. Waterman and Mont Blanc pens, for example, have an image of high quality and high price that has given them significant status. Other companies are skilled at providing products at prices lower than competitors (consider Walmart's tagline "Save Money, Live Better"). Amazon uses its vast network of partnerships and cost efficiencies to provide products at low prices. Brick-and-mortar retailers have not been able to offer comparable products with prices that low, providing Amazon with a considerable competitive advantage.

The marketing-mix variables are often viewed as controllable because they can be modified. However, there are limits to how much marketing managers can alter them. Economic conditions, competitive structure, and government regulations may prevent a manager from adjusting prices frequently or significantly. Making changes in the size, shape, and design of most tangible goods is expensive; therefore, such product features cannot be altered very often. In addition, promotional campaigns and methods used to distribute products ordinarily cannot be rewritten or revamped overnight.

Promotional Activities
Iams compares the wholesomeness of its dog food with the artificial preservatives found in many other leading dog food brands.

1-3 MARKETING CREATES VALUE

Value is an important element of managing long-term customer relationships and implementing the marketing concept. We view **value** as a customer's subjective assessment of benefits relative to costs in determining the worth of a product (customer value = customer benefits – customer costs). Consumers develop a concept of value through the integration of their perceptions of product quality and financial sacrifice.[9] From a company's perspective, there is a trade-off between increasing the value offered to a customer and maximizing the profits from a transaction.[10]

Customer benefits include anything a buyer receives in an exchange. Hotels and motels, for example, basically provide a room with a bed and bathroom, but each firm provides a different level of service, amenities, and atmosphere to satisfy its guests. Hampton Inn offers the minimum services necessary to maintain a quality, efficient, low-price overnight accommodation. In contrast, the Ritz-Carlton provides every imaginable service a guest might desire. The hotel even allows its staff members to spend up to $2,000 to settle customer complaints.[11] Customers judge which type of accommodation offers the best value according to the benefits they desire and their willingness and ability to pay for the costs associated with the benefits.

value A customer's subjective assessment of benefits relative to costs in determining the worth of a product

Customer costs include anything a buyer must give up to obtain the benefits the product provides. The most obvious cost is the monetary price of the product, but nonmonetary costs

Value-Driven Marketing
Mars, Inc., sells its high-quality Galaxy chocolate bars in the United Kingdom, Ireland, the Middle East, and India. Its chocolate satisfies customer desires at a premium price point.

can be equally important in a customer's determination of value. Two nonmonetary costs are the time and effort customers expend to find and purchase desired products. To reduce time and effort, a company can increase product availability, thereby making it more convenient for buyers to purchase the firm's products. Another nonmonetary cost is risk, which can be reduced by offering good basic warranties or extended warranties for an additional charge.[12] Another risk-reduction strategy is the offer of a 100 percent satisfaction guarantee. This strategy is increasingly popular in today's catalog/telephone/Internet shopping environment. L.L. Bean, for example, uses such a guarantee to reduce the risk involved in ordering merchandise from its catalogs.

The process people use to determine the value of a product is not highly scientific. All of us tend to get a feel for the worth of products based on our own expectations and previous experience. We can, for example, compare the value of tires, batteries, and computers directly with the value of competing products. We evaluate movies, sporting events, and performances by entertainers on the more subjective basis of personal preferences and emotions. For most purchases, we do not consciously try to calculate the associated benefits and costs. It becomes an instinctive feeling that Kellogg's Corn Flakes is a good value or that McDonald's is a good place to take children for a quick lunch. The purchase of an automobile or a mountain bike may have emotional components, but more conscious decision making also may figure in the process of determining value.

When developing marketing activities, it is important to recognize that customers receive benefits based on their experiences. For example, many computer buyers consider services such as fast delivery, ease of installation, technical advice, and training assistance to be important elements of the product. Customers also derive benefits from the act of shopping and selecting products. These benefits can be affected by the atmosphere or environment of a store, such as Red Lobster's nautical/seafood theme. Even the ease of navigating a website can have a tremendous impact on perceived value. For this reason, General Motors has developed a user-friendly way to navigate its website for researching and pricing vehicles. Using the Internet to compare a Chevrolet to a Mercedes could result in different users viewing each automobile as an excellent value. Owners have rated Chevrolet as providing reliable transportation and having dealers who provide acceptable service. A Mercedes may cost twice as much but has been rated as a better-engineered automobile that also has a higher social status than the Chevrolet. Different customers may view each car as being an exceptional value for their own personal satisfaction.

The marketing mix can be used to enhance perceptions of value. A product that demonstrates value usually has a feature or an enhancement that provides benefits. Promotional activities can also help to create image and prestige characteristics that customers consider in their assessment of a product's value. In some cases, value may be perceived simply as the lowest price. Many customers may not care about the quality of the paper towels they buy; they simply want the cheapest ones for use in cleaning up spills because they plan to throw them in the trash anyway. On the other hand, more people are looking for the fastest, most convenient way to achieve a goal and therefore become insensitive to pricing. For example, many busy customers are buying more prepared meals in supermarkets to take home and serve quickly, even though these meals cost considerably more than meals prepared from scratch. In such cases, the products with the greatest convenience may be perceived as having the greatest value. The availability or distribution of products also can enhance their value. Taco Bell wants to have its Mexican fast-food products available at any time and any place people are thinking about consuming food. It therefore has introduced Taco Bell products into supermarkets, vending machines, college campuses, and other convenient locations. Thus, the development of an effective marketing strategy requires understanding the needs and desires of customers and designing a marketing mix to satisfy them and provide the value they want.

1-3a Marketing Builds Relationships with Customers and Other Stakeholders

Marketing also creates value through the building of stakeholder relationships. Individuals and organizations engage in marketing to facilitate **exchanges**, the provision or transfer of goods, services, or ideas in return for something of value. Any product (good, service, or even idea) may be involved in a marketing exchange. We assume only that individuals and organizations expect to gain a reward in excess of the costs incurred.

For an exchange to take place, four conditions must exist. First, two or more individuals, groups, or organizations must participate, and each must possess something of value that the other party desires. Second, the exchange should provide a benefit or satisfaction to both parties involved in the transaction. Third, each party must have confidence in the promise of the "something of value" held by the other. If you go to a Coldplay concert, for example, you go with the expectation of a great performance. Finally, to build trust, the parties to the exchange must meet expectations.

exchanges The provision or transfer of goods, services, or ideas in return for something of value

© testing/Shutterstock.com

Satisfying Stakeholder Needs Apple continues to excel at creating products that satisfy customers, generate jobs, create shareholder wealth, and contribute to greater life enjoyment.

Figure 1.2 **Exchange between Buyer and Seller**

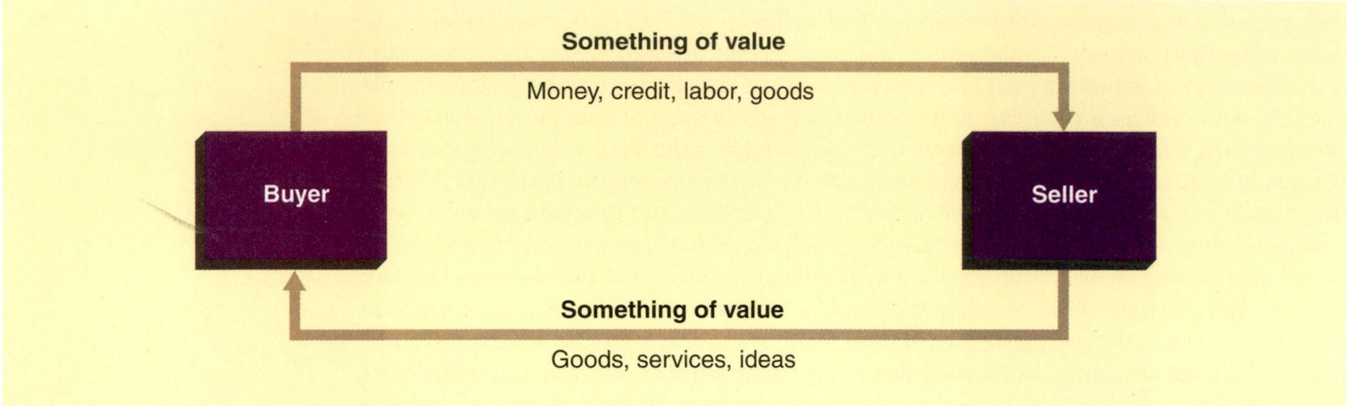

Figure 1.2 depicts the exchange process. The arrows indicate that the parties communicate that each has something of value available to exchange. An exchange will not necessarily take place just because these conditions exist; marketing activities can occur even without an actual transaction or sale. You may see an ad for a Sub-Zero refrigerator, for instance, but you might never buy the luxury appliance. When an exchange occurs, products are traded for other products or for financial resources.

Marketing activities should attempt to create and maintain satisfying exchange relationships. To maintain an exchange relationship, buyers must be satisfied with the good, service, or idea obtained, and sellers must be satisfied with the financial reward or something else of value received. A dissatisfied customer who lacks trust in the relationship often searches for alternative organizations or products. The customer relationship often endures over an extended time period, and repeat purchases are critical for the firm.

Marketers are concerned with building and maintaining relationships not only with customers but also with relevant stakeholders. **Stakeholders** include those constituents who have a "stake," or claim, in some aspect of a company's products, operations, markets, industry, and outcomes; these include customers, employees, investors and shareholders, suppliers, governments, communities, and many others. Developing and maintaining favorable relations with stakeholders is crucial to the long-term growth of an organization and its products. Marketing is an important part of our economic system and society. Therefore, marketing activities contribute to the well-being of society and our standard of living.

1-4 MARKETING OCCURS IN A DYNAMIC ENVIRONMENT

stakeholders Constituents who have a "stake," or claim, in some aspect of a company's products, operations, markets, industry, and outcomes

marketing environment The competitive, economic, political, legal and regulatory, technological, and sociocultural forces that surround the customer and affect the marketing mix

Marketing activities do not take place in a vacuum. The **marketing environment**, which includes competitive, economic, political, legal and regulatory, technological, and sociocultural forces, surrounds the customer and affects the marketing mix (see Figure 1.1). The effects of these forces on buyers and sellers can be dramatic and difficult to predict. Their impact on value can be extensive as market changes can easily impact how stakeholders perceive certain products. They can create threats to marketers but can also generate opportunities for new products and new methods of reaching customers.

The forces of the marketing environment affect a marketer's ability to facilitate value-driven marketing exchanges in three general ways. First, they influence customers by affecting their lifestyles, standards of living, and preferences and needs for products. Because a marketing manager tries to develop and adjust the marketing mix to satisfy customers, effects of environmental forces on customers also have an indirect impact on marketing-mix components. Second, marketing environment forces help to determine whether and how a marketing manager can perform certain marketing activities. Third, environmental forces may affect a marketing manager's decisions and actions by influencing buyers' reactions to the firm's marketing mix.

Marketing environment forces can fluctuate quickly and dramatically, which is one reason why marketing is so interesting and challenging. Because these forces are closely interrelated, changes in one may cause changes in others. For example, evidence linking children's consumption of soft drinks and fast foods to health issues has exposed marketers of such products to negative publicity and generated calls for legislation regulating the sale of soft drinks in public schools. Some companies have responded to these concerns by voluntarily reformulating products to make them healthier or even introducing new products. Coca-Cola reduced the calories in some of its soft drinks by 30 percent and has begun placing calorie counts at the front of its packaging.[13] Changes in the marketing environment produce uncertainty for marketers and at times hurt marketing efforts, but they also create opportunities. For example, when oil prices increase, consumers shift to potential alternative sources of transportation including bikes, buses, light rail, trains, carpooling, more energy-efficient vehicle purchases, or telecommuting when possible. Marketers who are alert to changes in environmental forces not only can adjust to and influence these changes but can also capitalize on the opportunities such changes provide. Marketing-mix variables—product, price, distribution, and promotion—are factors over which an organization has control; the forces of the environment, however, are subject to far less control. Even though marketers know that they cannot predict changes in the marketing environment with certainty, they must nevertheless plan for them. Because these environmental forces have such a profound effect on marketing activities, we explore each of them in considerable depth in Chapter 3.

1-5 UNDERSTANDING THE MARKETING CONCEPT

Some firms have sought success by buying land, building a factory, equipping it with people and machines, and then making a product they believe buyers need. However, these firms frequently fail to attract customers with what they have to offer because they define their business as "making a product" rather than as "helping potential customers satisfy their needs and wants." For example, when digital music became popular, businesses had opportunities to develop new products to satisfy customers' needs. Firms such as Apple developed the iTunes music store as well as new products like the iPod, iPhone, and iPad to satisfy consumers' desires for portable, customized music libraries. Other companies like Pandora and Spotify offered on-demand music streaming to computers and mobile devices. Companies that did not pursue such opportunities struggled to compete as digital music sales rose while physical album sales declined.

According to the **marketing concept**, an organization should try to provide products that satisfy customers' needs through a coordinated set of activities that also allows the organization to achieve its goals. Customer satisfaction is the major focus of the marketing concept. To implement the marketing concept, an organization strives to determine what buyers want and uses this information to develop satisfying products. It focuses on customer analysis, competitor analysis, and integration of the firm's resources to provide customer value and satisfaction, as well as to generate long-term profits.[14] As this advertisement demonstrates, McDonald's provides seasonal and limited-time availability products to satisfy consumer needs and vary their menu. The pumpkin spice latte is an example of a seasonal, limited-time menu addition. The firm also must continue to alter, adapt, and develop products to keep pace with customers' changing desires and preferences. Howard Schultz, founder and CEO of Starbucks, demonstrates the company's grasp on the marketing concept by explaining that Starbucks is

marketing concept
A managerial philosophy that an organization should try to satisfy customers' needs through a coordinated set of activities that also allows the organization to achieve its goals

© McDonalds

The Marketing Concept
McDonald's offers some seasonal and limited-release products to vary their menu and satisfy consumer needs.

not a coffee business that serves people, but rather a "people business serving coffee." Starbucks leadership sees the company as being "in the business of humanity," emphasizing the fact that Starbucks is not only concerned about customers but society as well.[15] Thus, the marketing concept emphasizes that marketing begins and ends with customers. Research has found a positive association between customer satisfaction and shareholder value,[16] and high levels of customer satisfaction also tend to attract and retain high-quality employees and managers.[17]

The marketing concept is not a second definition of marketing. It is a management philosophy guiding an organization's overall activities. This philosophy affects all organizational activities, not just marketing. Production, finance, accounting, human resources, and marketing departments must work together. Marketing is the business function that provides revenue. The implementation of the marketing concept results in sales and profits that are necessary for any organization to exist.

A firm that adopts the marketing concept must satisfy not only its customers' objectives but also its own, or it will not stay in business long. The overall objectives of a business usually relate to profits, market share, sales, or probably a combination of all three. The marketing concept stresses that an organization can best achieve these objectives by being customer oriented. Thus, implementing the marketing concept should benefit the organization as well as its customers.

It is important for marketers to consider not only their current buyers' needs but also the long-term needs of society. Striving to satisfy customers' desires by sacrificing society's long-term welfare is unacceptable. For instance, there is significant demand for large SUVs and trucks. However, environmentalists and federal regulators are challenging automakers to produce more fuel-efficient vehicles with increased mpg standards. The question that remains is whether or not Americans are willing to give up their spacious SUVs for the good of the environment. Automakers are addressing environmental concerns with smaller, more fuel-efficient SUVs. Demand for these SUVs shows that these vehicles are not going away anytime soon.[18] So implementing the marketing concept and meeting the needs of society is a balancing act.

1-5a Evolution of the Marketing Concept

The marketing concept may seem like an obvious approach to running a business. Although satisfying consumers is necessary for business success, historically not all firms were successful in implementing this concept. The development of marketing has been reduced to three time periods, including production, sales, and market orientation. Though this is an oversimplification, these frameworks help to understand marketing over time. There have always been companies that embraced the marketing concept and focused on the interests of consumers.

The Production Orientation

During the second half of the 19th century, the Industrial Revolution was in full swing in the United States. Electricity, rail transportation, division of labor, assembly lines, and mass production made it possible to produce goods more efficiently. With new technology and new ways of using labor, products poured into the marketplace, where demand for manufactured goods was strong. Although mass markets were evolving, firms were developing the ability to produce more products, and competition was becoming more intense.

The Sales Orientation

Though sales have always been needed to make a profit, during the first half of the 20th century competition increased, and businesses realized that they would have to focus more on selling products to many buyers. Businesses viewed sales as the major means of increasing profits, and this period came to have a sales orientation. Businesspeople believed that the most important marketing activities were personal selling, advertising, and distribution. Today, some people incorrectly equate marketing with a sales orientation. On the other hand, some firms still use a sales orientation.

The Market Orientation

Although marketing history reveals that some firms have always produced products that consumers desired, by the 1950s, both businesses and academics developed new philosophies and terminology to explain why this approach is necessary for organizational success. This perspective emphasized that marketers first need to determine what customers want and then produce those products rather than making the products first and then trying to persuade customers that they need them. As more organizations realized the importance of satisfying customers' needs, U.S. businesses entered the marketing era, called *market orientation*.

A **market orientation** requires the "organizationwide generation of market intelligence pertaining to current and future customer needs, dissemination of the intelligence across departments, and organizationwide responsiveness to it."[19] Market orientation is linked to new product innovation by developing a strategic focus to explore and develop new products to serve target markets.[20] For example, with an increasing "green attitude" in this country, consumers like environmentally responsible products offered at fair prices. To meet this demand, Method laundry detergent is eight times more concentrated and can clean 50 loads of laundry from a container the size of a small soft-drink bottle. Top management, marketing managers, non-marketing managers (those in production, finance, human resources, and so on), and customers are all important in developing and carrying out a market orientation. Trust, openness, honoring promises, respect, collaboration, and recognizing the market as the *raison d'etre* are six values required by organizations striving to become more market oriented.[21] Unless marketing managers provide continuous customer-focused leadership with minimal interdepartmental conflict, achieving a market orientation will be difficult. Non-marketing managers must communicate with marketing managers to share information important to understanding the customer. Finally, a market orientation involves being responsive to ever-changing customer needs and wants. Apple Inc. is successful because it understands what consumers want. Trying to assess what customers want, which is difficult to begin with, is further complicated by the speed with which fashions and tastes can change. Today, businesses want to satisfy customers and build meaningful long-term buyer–seller relationships. Doing so helps a firm boost its own financial value.[22]

1-5b Implementing the Marketing Concept

A philosophy may sound reasonable and look good on paper, but this does not mean that it can be put into practice easily. To implement the marketing concept, a market-oriented organization must accept some general conditions and recognize and deal with several problems. Consequently, the marketing concept has yet to be fully accepted by all businesses.

Management must first establish an information system to discover customers' real needs and then use the information to create satisfying products. For example, Rubbermaid is using a social commerce platform (customer/business interaction mechanism) that impacts product development and education as to how to use the product. In reviewing customer interaction,

market orientation An organizationwide commitment to researching and responding to customer needs

Rubbermaid noted that many consumers did not understand how to use its "Produce Saver" food storage container properly. When the company added use and care instructions to its website, the average star rating (a notation of satisfaction) increased significantly. Listening and responding to consumers' frustrations and appreciation is the key in implementing the marketing concept.[23] An information system is usually expensive; management must commit money and time for its development and maintenance. Without an adequate information system, however, an organization cannot be market oriented.

To satisfy customers' objectives as well as its own, a company also must coordinate all of its activities. This may require restructuring its internal operations, including production, marketing, and other business functions. This requires the firm to adapt to a changing external environment, including changing customer expectations. Companies that monitor the external environment can often predict major changes and adapt successfully. For instance, while the majority of Internet companies failed after the dot-com bubble burst in 2000, Amazon.com continued to thrive because it understood its customers and had created a website customized to their wants.[24] The company continues to expand its goods and services and add new features to its website to better serve its customers. On the other hand, Research in Motion (RIM; now called BlackBerry Ltd), the maker of the once-popular Blackberry, failed to adapt its technology for consumer use. After the Apple iPhone was released, RIM's market share significantly decreased.[25]

If marketing is not included in the organization's top-level management, a company could fail to address actual customer needs and desires. Implementing the marketing concept demands the support not only of top management but also of managers and staff at all levels of the organization.

1-6 CUSTOMER RELATIONSHIP MANAGEMENT

Customer relationship management (CRM) focuses on using information about customers to create marketing strategies that develop and sustain desirable customer relationships. Achieving the full profit potential of each customer relationship should be the fundamental goal of every marketing strategy. Marketing relationships with customers are the lifeblood of all businesses. At the most basic level, profits can be obtained through relationships in the following ways: (1) by acquiring new customers, (2) by enhancing the profitability of existing customers, and (3) by extending the duration of customer relationships. In addition to retaining customers, companies also should focus on regaining and managing relationships with customers who have abandoned the firm.[26] Implementing the marketing concept means optimizing the exchange relationship, otherwise known as the relationship between a company's financial investment in customer relationships and the return generated by customers' loyalty and retention.

1-6a Relationship Marketing

Maintaining positive relationships with customers is an important goal for marketers. The term **relationship marketing** refers to "long-term, mutually beneficial arrangements in which both the buyer and seller focus on value enhancement through the creation of more satisfying exchanges."[27] Relationship marketing continually deepens the buyer's trust in the company, and as the customer's confidence grows, this, in turn, increases the firm's understanding of the customer's needs. Buyers and marketers can thus enter into a close relationship in which both participate in the creation of value.[28] Successful marketers respond to customer needs and strive to increase value to buyers over time. Eventually, this interaction becomes a solid relationship that allows for cooperation and mutual dependency. Whole Foods has implemented relationship marketing with the view that customers are its most important stakeholder. One of the company's core values involves "satisfying the customer first."[29]

customer relationship management (CRM)
Using information about customers to create marketing strategies that develop and sustain desirable customer relationships

relationship marketing
Establishing long-term, mutually satisfying buyer–seller relationships

Relationship marketing strives to build satisfying exchange relationships between buyers and sellers by gathering useful data at all customer contact points and analyzing that data to better understand customers' needs, desires, and habits. It focuses on building and using databases and leveraging technologies to identify strategies and methods that will maximize the lifetime value of each desirable customer to the company. It is imperative that marketers educate themselves about their customers' expectations if they are to satisfy their needs; customer dissatisfaction will only lead to defection.[30] In one survey, 36 percent of marketing managers responded that loyalty and maintaining satisfaction were the biggest challenges of their organizations.[31]

To build these long-term customer relationships, marketers are increasingly turning to marketing research and information technology. By increasing customer value over time, organizations try to retain and increase long-term profitability through customer loyalty, which results from increasing customer value. The airline industry is a key player in CRM efforts with its frequent-flyer programs. Frequent-flyer programs enable airlines to track individual information about customers, using databases that can help airlines understand what different customers want and treat customers differently depending on their flying habits. Relationship-building efforts like frequent-flyer programs have been shown to increase customer value.[32]

Source: Chris Wright and Derek Franks, *Global Summit 2013*, May 21–23, 2013, http://public.dhe.ibm.com/common/ssi/ecm/en/zzl03043usen/ZZL03043USEN.PDF (accessed October 24, 2013).

Through the use of Internet-based marketing strategies (e-marketing), companies can personalize customer relationships on a nearly one-on-one basis. A wide range of products, such as computers, jeans, golf clubs, cosmetics, and greeting cards, can be tailored for specific customers. Customer relationship management provides a strategic bridge between information technology and marketing strategies aimed at long-term relationships. This involves finding and retaining customers by using information to improve customer value and satisfaction.

1-6b Customer Lifetime Value

Managing customer relationships requires identifying patterns of buying behavior and using that information to focus on the most promising and profitable customers.[33] Companies must be sensitive to customers' requirements and desires and establish communication to build their trust and loyalty. **Customer lifetime value** predicts the net value (profit or loss) for the future relationship with the customer. Pizza Hut, for example, is estimated to have a customer lifetime value of $8,000, whereas Cadillac estimates its customer lifetime value at $332,000.[34] A customer's value over a lifetime represents an intangible asset to a marketer that can be augmented by addressing the customer's varying needs and preferences at different stages in his or her relationship with the firm.[35] In general, when marketers focus on customers chosen for their lifetime value, they earn higher profits in future periods than when they focus on customers selected for other reasons.[36]

customer lifetime value A key measurement that forecasts a customer's lifetime economic contribution based on continued relationship marketing efforts

The ability to identify individual customers allows marketers to shift their focus from targeting groups of similar customers to increasing their share of an individual customer's purchases. The emphasis changes from *share of market* to *share of customer*. Focusing on share of customer requires recognizing that all customers have different needs and that not all customers weigh the value of a company equally. The most basic application of this idea is the 80/20 rule: 80 percent of business profits come from 20 percent of customers. The goal is to assess the worth of individual customers and thus estimate their lifetime value to the company. The concept of *customer lifetime value* (CLV) may include not only an individual's tendency to engage in purchases but also his or her strong word-of-mouth communication about the company's products. Some customers—those who require considerable hand-holding or who return products frequently—may simply be too expensive to retain due to the low level of profits they generate. Companies can discourage these unprofitable customers by requiring them to pay higher fees for additional services.

CLV is a key measurement that forecasts a customer's lifetime economic contribution based on continued relationship marketing efforts. It can be calculated by taking the sum of the customer's present value contributions to profit margins over a specific time frame. For example, the lifetime value of a Lexus customer could be predicted by how many new automobiles Lexus could sell the customer over a period of years and a summation of the contribution to margins across the time period. Although this is not an exact science, knowing a customer's potential lifetime value can help marketers determine how best to allocate resources to marketing strategies to sustain that customer over a lifetime.

1-7 THE IMPORTANCE OF MARKETING IN OUR GLOBAL ECONOMY

Our definition of marketing and discussion of marketing activities reveal some of the obvious reasons the study of marketing is relevant in today's world. In this section, we look at how marketing affects us as individuals and at its role in our increasingly global society.

1-7a Marketing Costs Consume a Sizable Portion of Buyers' Dollars

Studying marketing will make you aware that many marketing activities are necessary to provide satisfying goods and services. Obviously, these activities cost money. About one-half of a buyer's dollar goes toward marketing costs. If you spend $16 on a new CD, 50 to 60 percent goes toward marketing expenses, including promotion and distribution, as well as profit margins. The production (pressing) of the CD represents about $1, or 6 percent of its price. A family with a monthly income of $3,000 that allocates $600 to taxes and savings spends about $2,400 for goods and services. Of this amount, $1,200 goes toward marketing activities. If marketing expenses consume that much of your dollar, you should know how this money is being used. Marketing costs have an impact on the economy and the standard of living for consumers.

1-7b Marketing Is Used in Nonprofit Organizations

Although the term *marketing* may bring to mind advertising for Burger King, Volkswagen, and Apple, marketing is also important in organizations working to achieve goals other than ordinary business objectives (such as profit). Government agencies at the federal, state, and local levels engage in marketing activities to fulfill their mission and goals. For instance, the Centers for Disease Control promotes its most updated book about international health risks through its website for travelers' health.[37] Universities and colleges engage in marketing activities to recruit new students, as well as to obtain donations from alumni and businesses.

In the private sector, nonprofit organizations also employ marketing activities to create, price, distribute, and promote programs that benefit particular segments of society. The Red Cross provides disaster relief throughout the world and offers promotional messages to encourage donations to support their efforts. Concern USA, an affiliate of the nonprofit

Concern Worldwide, releases advertising to describe its commitment toward reducing suffering and improving the quality of life for individuals across the globe.[38]

1-7c Marketing Is Important to Businesses and the Economy

Businesses must engage in marketing to survive and grow, and marketing activities are needed to reach customers and provide products. Marketing is responsible for generating sales necessary for the operations of a firm and to provide financial returns to investors. Innovation in operations and products drive business success and customer loyalty. Even nonprofit businesses need to understand and utilize marketing to serve their clients or audience.

Marketing activities help to produce the profits that are essential to the survival of individual businesses. Without profits, businesses would find it difficult, if not impossible, to buy more raw materials, hire more employees, attract more capital, and create additional products that, in turn, make more profits. Without profits, marketers cannot continue to provide jobs and contribute to social causes. Companies promote their support of social causes through promotional activities such as the Ralph Lauren advertisement. The Pink Pony generates revenue to fight cancer. Consumers buying Pink Pony products trigger a 25 percent donation to the cause. Therefore, marketing helps create a successful economy and contributes to the well-being of society.

Social Marketing
Marketing is used by companies such as Ralph Lauren to create awareness of its Pink Pony purchases, which generate donations for cancer research.

1-7d Marketing Fuels Our Global Economy

Marketing is necessary to advance a global economy. Advances in technology, along with falling political and economic barriers and the universal desire for a higher standard of living, have made marketing across national borders commonplace while stimulating global economic growth. As a result of worldwide communications and increased international travel, many U.S. brands have achieved widespread acceptance around the world. At the same time, customers in the United States have greater choices among the products they buy because foreign brands such as Toyota (Japan), Bayer (Germany), and Nestlé (Switzerland) sell alongside U.S. brands such as General Motors, Tylenol, and Chevron. People around the world watch CNN and MTV on Samsung and Sony televisions they purchased at Walmart. Electronic commerce via the Internet now enables businesses of all sizes to reach buyers worldwide. We explore the international markets and opportunities for global marketing in Chapter 9.

1-7e Marketing Knowledge Enhances Consumer Awareness

Besides contributing to the well-being of our economy, marketing activities help to improve the quality of our lives. Studying marketing allows us to understand the importance of marketing to customers, organizations, and our economy. Thus, we can analyze marketing efforts that need improvement and how to attain that goal. Today the consumer has more power from information available through websites, social media, and required disclosure. As you become more knowledgeable, it is possible to improve purchasing decisions. In general, you have more accurate information about a product before you purchase it than at any other time in history. Understanding marketing enables us to evaluate corrective measures (such as laws, regulations, and industry guidelines) that could stop unfair, damaging, or unethical marketing practices. Thus, understanding how marketing activities work can help you to be a better consumer and increase your ability to maximize value from purchases.

1-7f Marketing Connects People through Technology

Technology, especially computers and telecommunications, helps marketers to understand and satisfy more customers than ever before. Over the phone and online, customers can provide feedback about their experiences with a company's products. Even products such as Dasani bottled water provide a customer service number and a website for questions or comments. This feedback helps marketers refine and improve their products to better satisfy customer needs. Today marketers must recognize the impact not only of websites but of instant messaging, blogs, online forums, online games, mailing lists, and wikis, as well as text messaging via cell phones and interacting through Facebook. Increasingly, these tools are facilitating marketing exchanges. For example, new apps are being released that allow consumers to pay for their purchases using their smartphones. These apps contain "virtual replicas" of the consumer's credit or debit cards that can be used in lieu of plastic. Recognizing the convenience of this new method, more and more companies are adapting their operations to accept mobile payments.[39]

The Internet allows companies to provide tremendous amounts of information about their products to consumers and to interact with them through e-mail and websites. A consumer shopping for a new car, for example, can access automakers' webpages, configure an ideal vehicle, and get instant feedback on its cost. Consumers can visit Autobytel, Edmund's, and other websites to find professional reviews and obtain comparative pricing information on both new and used cars to help them find the best value. They can also visit a consumer opinion site, such as Yelp, to read other consumers' reviews of the products. They can then purchase a vehicle online or at a dealership. A number of companies employ social media to connect with their customers, utilizing blogs and social networking sites such as Facebook and Twitter. We consider social networking and other digital media in Chapter 10.

Marketers of everything from computers to travel reservations use the Internet for transactions. Southwest Airlines, for example, books most of its passenger revenue via its website.[40] The Internet also has become a vital tool for marketing to other businesses. Successful companies are using technology in their marketing strategies to develop profitable relationships with these customers. As more consumers adopt smartphones, mobile marketing is also becoming a major trend. Table 1.1 shows the most common cell phone activities. Note how many of

Table 1.1 Cell Phone Activities

Activity	Percent of Time Spent on Activity
Text messaging	81
Access Internet	60
E-mail	52
Download apps	50
Get directions, recommendations, or other location-based information	49
Listen to music	48
Participate in video call or video chat	21
"Check in" to share location	8

Source: Pew Research Center's Internet & American Life Project Spring Tracking Survey, April 17–May 19, 2013. *N* = 2,076 cell phone owners. Interviews were conducted in English and Spanish and on land-line and cell phones. The margin of error based on results based on all cell phone owners is +/– 2.4 percentage points.

the activities involve accessing the Internet. Approximately 34 percent of Internet users go online mostly through their phones.[41] We will discuss mobile marketing in more detail in Chapter 10, but it is crucial that marketers recognize these changing technological trends.

1-7g Socially Responsible Marketing: Promoting the Welfare of Customers and Stakeholders

The success of our economic system depends on marketers whose values promote trust and cooperative relationships in which customers and other stakeholders are treated with respect. The public is increasingly insisting that social responsibility and ethical concerns be considered in planning and implementing marketing activities. Although some marketers' irresponsible or unethical activities end up on the front pages of *USA Today* or *The Wall Street Journal,* more firms are working to develop a responsible approach to developing long-term relationships with customers and other stakeholders. In one such instance, OfficeMax partnered with Adopt-A-Classroom, a nonprofit organization, to create an event to end teacher-funded classrooms. Once a year, OfficeMax makes 1,000 teachers' days better all across the United States by surprising them at school with more than $1,000 in school supplies.[42]

Marketing Connects People through Technology
The eBay mobile app on the iPhone allows shoppers to get to the eBay website with just the click of a button.

In the area of the natural environment, companies are increasingly embracing the notion of **green marketing**, which is a strategic process involving stakeholder assessment to create meaningful long-term relationships with customers while maintaining, supporting, and enhancing the natural environment. Safeway, for example, was recognized by Greenpeace as the supermarket chain with the most sustainable seafood buying practices. Understanding that overfishing is a major concern, Safeway discontinued sales of several threatened fish populations and promoted the formation of a marine reserve in the southern Antarctic oceans

green marketing
A strategic process involving stakeholder assessment to create meaningful long-term relationships with customers while maintaining, supporting, and enhancing the natural environment

Going Green

Marketing for the Car-Sharing Business Model: "Share It" Social Media!

Zipcar, the innovative and environmentally friendly solution to car ownership and rental cars, has continued to propel and expand its business model of car sharing. Zipcar is a U.S. membership-based company that allows members to reserve vehicles located across the United States, Spain, Canada, or the United Kingdom. To join, users register online and receive a Zipcard, or electronic key, in the mail. Members are then eligible to reserve a car for an allotted time, by the day or by the hour, and are provided the flexibility and convenience of using any car.

Although the company has experienced growth and an increase in memberships over the years (more than 760,000 since 2000), developing a consistently effective marketing concept for this type of business has proven a challenge. The car-sharing business model relies heavily on positive word-of-mouth promotion. In order to leverage this, Zipcar has taken to social media and encourages members to share photos and comments about their experiences with car sharing to effectively communicate the value of the business. This type of marketing also lends a sense of authenticity to the brand that the company could not have achieved without the help of its customers.

In 2013, Zipcar was acquired by car rental giant Avis for $500 million. Now a subsidiary of Avis, Zipcar remains a popular alternative for business travelers and college students.[b]

to protect Chilean sea bass, a "red-list" fish.[43] Such initiatives not only reduce the negative impact that businesses have on the environment but also serve to enhance their reputations as sustainability concerns continue to grow.

By addressing concerns about the impact of marketing on society, a firm can contribute to society through socially responsible activities as well as increase its financial performance. For example, studies have revealed that market orientation combined with social responsibility improves overall business performance.[44] We examine these issues and many others as we develop a framework for understanding more about marketing in the remainder of this book.

1-7h Marketing Offers Many Exciting Career Prospects

From 25 to 33 percent of all civilian workers in the United States perform marketing activities. The marketing field offers a variety of interesting and challenging career opportunities throughout the world, such as personal selling, advertising, packaging, transportation, storage, marketing research, product development, wholesaling, and retailing. In the most recent recessionary period when unemployment was high, sales positions remained among the most attractive job opportunities. The government reports there are about 1 million new sales positions each year. Marketing positions are among the most secure positions because of the need to manage customer relationships. In addition, many individuals working for nonbusiness organizations engage in marketing activities to promote political, educational, cultural, church, civic, and charitable activities. Whether a person earns a living through marketing activities or performs them voluntarily for a nonprofit group, marketing knowledge and skills are valuable personal and professional assets.

Summary

1-1 Define *marketing*.

Marketing is the process of creating, pricing, distributing, and promoting goods, services, and ideas to facilitate satisfying exchange relationships with customers and to develop and maintain favorable relationships with stakeholders in a dynamic environment. The essence of marketing is to develop satisfying exchanges from which both customers and marketers benefit. Organizations generally focus their marketing efforts on a specific group of customers called a target market. A target market is the group of customers toward which a company directs a set of marketing efforts.

1-2 Explain the different variables of the marketing mix.

Marketing involves developing and managing a product that will satisfy customer needs, making the product available at the right place and at a price acceptable to customers, and communicating information that helps customers determine whether the product will satisfy their needs. These activities—product, price, distribution, and promotion—are known as the marketing mix because marketing managers decide what type of each element to use and in what amounts. Marketing managers strive to develop a marketing mix that matches the needs of customers in the target market. Before marketers can develop a marketing mix, they must collect in-depth, up-to-date information about customer needs. The product variable of the marketing mix deals with researching customers' needs and wants and designing a product that satisfies them. A product can be a good, a service, or an idea. In dealing with the distribution variable, a marketing manager tries to make products available in the quantities desired to as many customers as possible. The promotion variable relates to activities used to inform individuals or groups about the organization and its products. The price variable involves decisions and actions associated with establishing pricing policies and determining product prices. These marketing-mix variables are often viewed as controllable because they can be changed, but there are limits to how much they can be altered.

1-3 Describe how marketing creates value.

Individuals and organizations engage in marketing to facilitate exchanges—the provision or transfer of goods, services, and ideas in return for something of value. Four conditions must exist for an exchange to occur. First, two or more individuals, groups, or organizations must participate, and each must possess something of value that the other party desires. Second, the exchange should provide a benefit or satisfaction to both parties involved in the transaction. Third, each party must have confidence in the promise of the "something of value" held by the other. Finally, to build trust, the parties to the exchange must meet expectations. Marketing activities should attempt to create and maintain satisfying exchange relationships.

1-4 Briefly describe the marketing environment.

The marketing environment, which includes competitive, economic, political, legal and regulatory, technological, and sociocultural forces, surrounds the customer and the marketing mix. These forces can create threats to marketers, but they also generate opportunities for new products and new methods of reaching customers. These forces can fluctuate quickly and dramatically.

1-5 Summarize the marketing concept.

According to the marketing concept, an organization should try to provide products that satisfy customers' needs through a coordinated set of activities that also allows the organization to achieve its goals. Customer satisfaction is the marketing concept's major objective. The philosophy of the marketing concept emerged in the United States during the 1950s after the production and sales eras. Organizations that develop activities consistent with the marketing concept become market-oriented organizations. To implement the marketing concept, a market-oriented organization must establish an information system to discover customers' needs and use the information to create satisfying products. It must also coordinate all its activities and develop marketing mixes that create value for customers in order to satisfy their needs.

1-6 Identify the importance of building customer relationships.

Relationship marketing involves establishing long-term, mutually satisfying buyer–seller relationships. Customer relationship management (CRM) focuses on using information about customers to create marketing strategies that develop and sustain desirable customer relationships. Managing customer relationships requires identifying patterns of buying behavior and using that information to focus on the most promising and profitable customers. A customer's value over a lifetime represents an intangible asset to a marketer that can be augmented by addressing the customer's varying needs and preferences at different stages in his or her relationship with the firm. Customer lifetime value is a key measurement that forecasts a customer's lifetime economic contribution based on continued relationship marketing efforts. Knowing a customer's potential lifetime value can help marketers determine how to best allocate resources to marketing strategies to sustain that customer over a lifetime.

1-7 Explain why marketing is important to our global economy.

Marketing is important to our economy in many ways. Marketing costs absorb about half of each buyer's dollar. Marketing activities are performed in both business and nonprofit organizations. Marketing activities help business organizations to generate profits, and they help fuel the increasingly global economy. Knowledge of marketing enhances consumer awareness. New technology improves marketers' ability to connect with customers. Socially responsible marketing can promote the welfare of customers and society. Green marketing is a strategic process involving stakeholder assessment to create meaningful long-term relationships with customers while maintaining, supporting, and enhancing the natural environment. Finally, marketing offers many exciting career opportunities.

Go to www.cengagebrain.com for resources to help you master the content in this chapter as well as for materials that will expand your marketing knowledge!

Developing Your Marketing Plan

Successful companies develop strategies for marketing their products. The strategic plan guides the marketer in making many of the detailed decisions about the attributes of the product, its distribution, promotional activities, and pricing. A clear understanding of the foundations of marketing is essential in formulating a strategy and in the development of a specific marketing plan. To guide you in relating the information in this chapter to the development of your marketing plan, consider the following:

1. Discuss how the marketing concept contributes to a company's long-term success.
2. Describe the level of market orientation that currently exists in your company. How will a market orientation contribute to the success of your new product?
3. What benefits will your product provide to the customer? How will these benefits play a role in determining the customer value of your product?

The information obtained from these questions should assist you in developing various aspects of your marketing plan found in the "Interactive Marketing Plan" exercise at www.cengagebrain.com.

Important Terms

marketing 4
customers 4
target market 5
marketing mix 6
product 7
value 9
exchanges 11
stakeholders 12
marketing environment 12
marketing concept 13
market orientation 15
customer relationship management (CRM) 16
relationship marketing 16
customer lifetime value 17
green marketing 21

Discussion and Review Questions

1. What is *marketing*? How did you define the term before you read this chapter?
2. What is the focus of all marketing activities? Why?
3. What are the four variables of the marketing mix? Why are these elements known as variables?
4. What is value? How can marketers use the marketing mix to enhance the perception of value?
5. What conditions must exist before a marketing exchange can occur? Describe a recent exchange in which you participated.
6. What are the forces in the marketing environment? How much control does a marketing manager have over these forces?
7. Discuss the basic elements of the marketing concept. Which businesses in your area use this philosophy? Explain why.
8. How can an organization implement the marketing concept?
9. What is customer relationship management? Why is it so important to "manage" this relationship?
10. Why is marketing important in our society? Why should you study marketing?

Video Case 1.1

Cruising to Success: The Tale of New Belgium Brewing

In 1991, electrical engineer Jeff Lebesch and Kim Jordan began making Belgian-style ales in their basement. The impetus for the brewery occurred after Lebesch had spent time in Belgium riding throughout the country on his mountain bike. He believed he could manufacture high-quality Belgian beers in America. After spending time in the Colorado Rockies deciding the values and directions of their new company, the two launched New Belgium Brewing (NBB), with Kim Jordan as marketing director. The company's first beer was named Fat Tire in honor of Lebesch's Belgian mountain biking trek. Fat Tire remains one of NBB's most popular ales.

NBB has come far from its humble basement origins. Today, the Fort Collins–based brewery is the third-largest craft brewer in the country with products available in 37 states. Kim Jordan helms the company as one of the few female CEOs of a large beer firm. "This entrepreneurial thing sneaks up on you," Jordan states. "And even after 20 years, I still have those pinch me moments where I think, wow, this is what we've created here together." While total beer sales are dropping in the United States, sales in the craft beer industry have increased to $8.7 billion. NBB has a sales growth rate of 15 percent.

Creating such success required a corporate culture that stressed creativity and an authentic approach to treating all stakeholders with respect. Though the New Belgium product is a quality craft beer, just as important to the company is how it treats employees, the community, and the environment. Each element of the marketing mix was carefully considered. The company spends a significant amount of time researching and creating its beers, even collaborating with other breweries to create new products. These collaborations have led to products such as its Biere de Garde and Cigar City Collaboration. NBB's culture is focused on making a quality product and satisfying customers. It has even ventured into organic beer with its creation of Mothership Wit Organic Wheat Beer. The company has several product line varieties, including its more popular beers Fat Tire, 1554, Sunshine Wheat, Shift, Blue Paddle, and its new Snapshot Wheat; seasonal beers such as Mighty Arrow and Accumulation; and its

Lips of Faith line, a series of experimental beers including Yuzu and La Folie produced in smaller batches.

The distribution element of the product mix was complex at the outset. In her initial role as marketing director, Jordan needed to convince distributors to carry their products. Often, new companies must work hard to convince distributors to carry their brands because distributors are fearful of alienating more established rivals. However, Jordan tirelessly got NBB beer onto store shelves, even delivering beer in her Toyota station wagon. As a craft brewer, NBB uses a premium pricing strategy. Its products are priced higher than domestic brands such as Coors or Budweiser and have higher profit margins. The popularity of NBB beers has prompted rivals to develop competitive products such as MillerCoors' Blue Moon Belgian White.

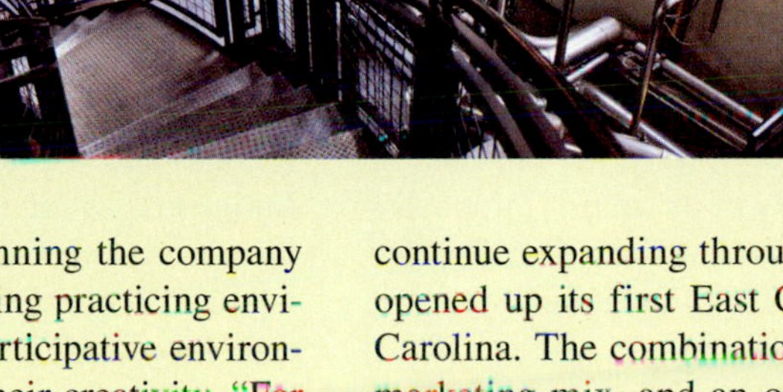
Tim Fleming/Alamy

Perhaps the most notable dimension of NBB's marketing mix is promotion. From the beginning the company based its brand on its core values, including practicing environmental stewardship and forming a participative environment in which all employees can exert their creativity. "For me brand is absolutely everything we are. It's the people here. It's how we interact with one another. And then there's the other piece of that creativity, obviously, which is designing beers," Kim Jordan said. NBB promotion has attempted to portray the company's creativity and its harmony with the natural environment. For instance, one NBB video features a tinkerer repairing a bicycle and riding down the road, while another features NBB "rangers" singing a hip-hop number to promote the company's Ranger IPA ale. The company has also heavily promoted its brand through Facebook and Twitter. This "indie" charm has served to position NBB as a company committed to having fun and being a socially responsible company.

NBB also markets itself as a company committed to sustainability. Sustainability has been a core value at NBB from day one. The company was the first fully wind-powered brewery in the United States. NBB recycles cardboard boxes, keg caps, office materials, and amber glass. The brewery stores spent barley and hop grains in an on-premise silo and invites local farmers to pick up the grains, free of charge, to feed their pigs. The company also provides employees with a cruiser bicycle after one year of employment so they can bike to work instead of drive.

NBB's popularity is allowing it to expand on the East Coast with plans to continue expanding throughout the United States. It has just opened up its first East Coast brewery in Asheville, North Carolina. The combination of a unique brand image, strong marketing mix, and an orientation that considers all stakeholders has turned NBB into a multimillion dollar success.[45]

Questions for Discussion

1. How has New Belgium implemented the marketing concept?
2. What has Kim Jordan done to create success at New Belgium?
3. How does New Belgium's focus on sustainability as a core value contribute to its corporate culture and success?

Case 1.2
Campbell's Wants to Show You the Value of Soup

The Campbell Soup Company is on a mission to create value in the minds of consumers. Value is the customer's subjective assessment of benefits relative to costs in determining the product's worth. Campbell's is very aware of the value equation and is concerned that some consumers may not appreciate the good value of Campbell's soups. To change this perception, Campbell's has intensified its marketing efforts to reposition its soup brands and differentiate them from the competition.

Campbell's Soup was founded in 1869 as a canned-food company. Its iconic red-and-white colors, first adopted in 1898 based upon the colors of the Cornell football team, have since become a core part of the company's brand identity. Although most people associate Campbell's with soup, the company has adopted new product mixes through acquisitions and expansions. Campbell's is divided into three main divisions: Campbell North America, Pepperidge Farm, and International. The company owns such well-known brands as Campbell's, Pace, Pepperidge Farm, and V8.

Campbell's has been largely successful as a company, but in recent years its soup division in North America has diminished. Although product lines such as Pepperidge Farm have performed well globally, simple meal sales within the United States, which includes Campbell's soups, decreased 6 percent. With more than $1 billion in condensed soup sales, such a decrease is a serious threat to Campbell's Soup. In response the company is taking the bold marketing move of increasing its marketing by $100 million in order to reposition how consumers, particularly the younger generation, view condensed soup.

This is not Campbell's first endeavor to alter consumer perceptions of its flagship brand. In the last few years the company has performed extensive marketing research that culminated in changing its iconic labels for its condensed soups and adopting a new advertising slogan. The bowls on the labels got bigger, the soup got steamier, the spoon was abandoned, and the logo was moved toward the bottom. To emphasize the quality and versatility of its soups, Campbell's adopted the tagline "It's Amazing What Soup Can Do" for all of its different soup line-ups within the United States. It is also working on developing marketing initiatives to target Millennials and Hispanics.

However, Campbell's newest marketing initiatives are set to push the limits of how its soups are perceived. For many years Campbell's has been emphasizing the healthy nature of its soups. As consumers have become more health-conscious, Campbell's responded by reducing the sodium in its soup products. Yet because the campaign was not successful in increasing purchases, Campbell's is taking the controversial step of de-emphasizing its health initiatives and pouring marketing dollars into re-portraying its brand as tasty and exciting.

Such a move comes with controversy because Campbell's has raised the amount of sodium in some of its soups. However, when companies try to address nutritional issues but consumers show little interest, the companies are faced with the dilemma of dropping their health campaigns in exchange for adopting attributes, such as taste, that customers value. Campbell's had also introduced discounts on its soups in the hopes of attracting price-conscious consumers. After the move failed to generate increased sales, Campbell's decided to stop discounting its soup products. Without these discounts, Campbell's will have to increase the perceived value of its products to convince consumers to pay more.

Yet Campbell's remains undeterred. The company aims to engage in what Campbell's' CEO calls "disruptive innovation" with the introduction of new product lines, new packaging, and new flavors. For instance, Campbell's released new exotic flavors in pouches to appeal to the younger generation. Campbell's has even tested marketing through new technology channels. The company has released iAds through Apple iPhones and iPads, a tactic that appears to aid brand recall. Initial studies found that consumers who viewed Campbell's iAds were five times more likely to recall them than those who had seen its TV ads. If Campbell's has its way, then a can of soup will become much more valuable to consumers.[46]

Questions for Discussion

1. Evaluate Campbell's success in implementing the marketing concept.
2. How would you define Campbell's target market for soup?
3. How is Campbell's trying to increase the customer's perceived value of its soup?

NOTES

[1] Brian Solomon, "The Wal-Mart Slayer," *Forbes*, August 12, 2013, pp. 96–104; Susan Thurston, "Walmart and Publix Fight for Shoppers' Grocery Dollars," July 14, 2012, www.tampabay.com/news/business/walmart-and-publix-fight-for-shoppers-grocery-dollars/1240266 (accessed August 6, 2013); "100 Best Companies to Work For: Publix Supermarkets," *CNN Money*, http://money.cnn.com/magazines/fortune/bestcompanies/2011/snapshots/67.html (accessed August 6, 2013).

[2] "Definition of Marketing," American Marketing Association, www.marketingpower.com/AboutAMA/Pages/DefinitionofMarketing.aspx (accessed July 7, 2010).

[3] Michael Sebastian, "Magazine's Next Big Goal: Reaching Latinas in English," *Advertising Age*, November 8, 2013, http://adage.com/article/media/publishers-reaching-latina-audiences-english/245036 (accessed November 14, 2013).

[4] "Vans, Inc.," www.jiffynotes.com/a_study_guides/book_notes/cps_03/cps_03_00479.html (accessed December 27, 2010).

[5] Julie Jargon, "Subway Runs Past McDonald's Chain," *The Wall Street Journal*, March 9, 2011, p. B4; Subway, "Store Locator," www.subway.com/storelocator (accessed October 24, 2013).

[6] Nancy Trejos, "Tonight, We Are Young Hangouts," *USA Today*, June 28, 2013, p. 5B.

[7] "Impaired Driving," NHTSA, www.nhtsa.gov/drivesober/video/couple (accessed October 24, 2013).

[8] Campbell's Kitchen, www.campbellskitchen.com/RecipeCategoryHome.aspx?fbid=DKtnA8n1vQ0 (accessed January 4, 2011).

[9] Rajneesh Suri, Chiranjeev Kohli, and Kent B. Monroe, "The Effects of Perceived Scarcity on Consumers' Processing of Price Information," *Journal of the Academy of Marketing Science* 35 (2007): 89–100.

[10] Natalie Mizik and Robert Jacobson, "Trading Off between Value Creation and Value Appropriation: The Financial Implications and Shifts in Strategic Emphasis," *Journal of Marketing* (January 2003): 63–76.

[11] Kasey Wehrum, "How May We Help You?" *Inc.*, March 2011, pp. 63–68.

[12] O. C. Ferrell and Michael Hartline, *Marketing Strategy*. (Mason, OH: Cengage Learning, 2005), p. 108.

[13] Mike Esterl and Paul Ziobro, "Coke's Low-Calorie Push," *The Wall Street Journal*, May 9, 2013, p. B1; Mike Esterl, "With Soda on Defensive, Machines Will List Calories," *The Wall Street Journal*, October 9, 2012, p. B3.

[14] Ajay K. Kohli and Bernard J. Jaworski, "Market Orientation: The Construct, Research Propositions, and Managerial Implications," *Journal of Marketing* (April 1990): 1–18; O. C. Ferrell, "Business Ethics and Customer Stakeholders," *Academy of Management Executive* 18 (May 2004): 126–129.

[15] "Starbucks CEO Howard Schultz Is All Abuzz," *CBS News*, March 27, 2011, www.cbsnews.com/stories/2011/03/27/business/main20047618.shtml (accessed March 30, 2011).

[16] Eugene W. Anderson, Claes Fornell, and Sanal K. Mazvancheryl, "Customer Satisfaction and Shareholder Value," *Journal of Marketing* (October 2004): 172–185.

[17] Xeuming Luo and Christian Homburg, "Neglected Outcomes of Customer Satisfaction," *Journal of Marketing* 70 (April 2007).

[18] Alisa Priddle, Chris Woodyard, and Nathan Bomey, "American Love Affair with SUV Continues," *USA Today*, May 31, 2013, p. 5B.

[19] Kohli and Jaworski, "Market Orientation: The Construct, Research Propositions, and Managerial Implications."

[20] Kwaku Atuahene-Gima, "Resolving the Capability-Rigidity Paradox in New Product Innovation," *Journal of Marketing* 69 (October 2005): 61–83.

[21] Gary F.Gebhardt, Gregory S. Carpenter, and John F. Sherry, Jr., "Creating a Market Orientation: A Longitudinal, Multiform, Grounded Analysis of Cultural Transformation," *Journal of Marketing* 70 (October 2006): 37-55.,

[22] Sunil Gupta, Donald R. Lehmann, and Jennifer Ames Stuart, "Valuing Customers," *Journal of Marketing Research* (February 2004): 7–18.

[23] "Bazaarvoice Enables Rubbermaid to Listen, Learn, and Improve Products Based on Customer Conversations," *Business Wire*, January 21, 2010, www.businesswire.com/portal/site/home/permalink/?ndmViewId=news_view&newsId=20100121005613&newsLang=en (accessed January 12, 2012); "User-Generated R&D: Clay Shirky Explains How to Feed Innovation with Customer Insights," *Bazaarvoice*, May 3, 2011, www.bazaarvoice.com/blog/2011/05/03/user-generated-rd-clay-shirky-explains-how-to-feed-innovation-with-customer-insights (accessed January 12, 2012).

[24] Pradeep Korgaonkar and Bay O'Leary, "Management, Market, and Financial Factors Separating Winners and Losers in e-Business," *Journal of Computer-Mediated Communication* 11, no. 4 (2006): article 12.

[25] Douglas A. McIntrye, "Ten Brands That Will Disappear in 2013," *Fox Business*, June 21, 2012, www.foxbusiness.com/industries/2012/06/21/ten-brands-that-will-disappear-in-2013 (accessed October 24, 2013).

[26] Jacquelyn S. Thomas, Robert C. Blattberg, and Edward J. Fox, "Recapturing Lost Customers," *Journal of Marketing Research* (February 2004): 31–45.

[27] Jagdish N. Sheth and Rajendras Sisodia, "More Than Ever Before, Marketing Is under Fire to Account for What It Spends," *Marketing Management* (Fall 1995): 13–14.

[28] Stephen L. Vargo and Robert F. Lusch, "Service-Dominant Logic: Continuing the Evolution," *Journal of the Academy of Marketing Science* 36 (2008): 1–10.

[29] "Whole Foods Market's Core Values," Whole Foods, www.wholefoodsmarket.com/values/corevalues.php (accessed January 10, 2012).

[30] Chezy Ofir and Itamar Simonson, "The Effect of Stating Expectations on Customer Satisfaction and Shopping Experience," *Journal of Marketing Research* XLIV (February 2007): 164–174.

[31] Chris Wright and Derek Franks, *Global Summit 2013*, May 21–23, 2013, http://public.dhe.ibm.com/common/ssi/ecm/en/zzl03043usen/ZZL03043USEN.PDF (accessed October 24, 2013).

[32] Robert W. Palmatier, Lisa K. Scheer, and Jan-Benedict E. M. Steenkamp, "Customer Loyalty to Whom? Managing the Benefits and Risks of Salesperson-Owned Loyalty," *Journal of Marketing Research* XLIV (May 2007): 185–199.

[33] Werner J. Reinartz and V. Kumar, "On the Profitability of Long-Life Customers in a Noncontractual Setting: An Empirical Investigation and Implications for Marketing," *Journal of Marketing* (October 2000): 17–35.

[34] Customer Insight Group, Inc., "Program Design: Loyalty and Retention," www.customerinsightgroup.com/loyalty_retention.php (accessed January 4, 2011).

[35] V. Kumar and Morris George, "Measuring and Maximizing Customer Equity: A Critical Analysis," *Journal of the Academy of Marketing Science* 35 (2007): 157–171.

[36] Rajkumar Venkatesan and V. Kumar, "A Customer Lifetime Value Framework for Customer Selection and Resource Allocation Strategy," *Journal of Marketing* (October 2004): 106–125.

[37] Centers for Disease Control, "Yellow Book Homepage," wwwnc.cdc.gov/travel/page/yellowbook-home-2014 (accessed October 24, 2013).

[38] Concern USA website, www.concernusa.org (accessed November 25, 2013).

[39] Edward C. Baig, "Mobile Payments Gain Traction," *USA Today*, August 11, 2011, pp. 1A–2A; Jefferson Graham, "Starbucks Expands Mobile Payments to 6,800 Sites," *USA Today*, January 19, 2011, p. 1B.

[40] "Southwest Corporate Fact Sheet," Southwest Airlines, www.swamedia.com/channels/Corporate-Fact-Sheet/pages/corporate-fact-sheet (accessed November 30, 2013).

[41] Joanna Brenner, "Pew Internet: Mobile," *Pew Internet & American Life Project*, September 18, 2013, http://pewinternet.org/Commentary/2012/February/Pew-Internet-Mobile.aspx (accessed October 24, 2013).

[42] "OfficeMax and Store Customers Donate $1.7 Million in Supplies to Benefit Teachers and Schools," *OfficeMax*, October 1, 2013, www.adaymadebetter.com/newsroom (accessed November 20, 2013).

[43] Kim O'Donnel, "Safeway Scales the 'Seafood Scorecard' by Greenpeace," *USA Today*, April 18, 2011, p. 5D.

[44] Anis Ben Brik, Belaid Rettab, and Kemel Mallahi, "Market Orientation, Corporate Social Responsibility, and Business Performance," *Journal of Business Ethics* 99 (2011): 307–324.

[45] New Belgium website, newbelgium.com (accessed November 20, 2013); "New Belgium Brewing: Ethical and Environmental Responsibility," in O. C. Ferrell, John Fraedrich, and Linda Ferrell, *Business Ethics: Ethical Decision Making and Cases*, 9th ed. (Mason, OH: Cengage Learning, 2013), pp. 355–363; "New Belgium Brewery," Amalgamated, http://amalgamatednyc.com/project/tinkerer (accessed March 27, 2012); Norman Miller, "Craft Beer Industry Continues to Grow," *PJ Star*, March 26, 2012, www.pjstar.com/community/blogs/beer-nut/x140148153/Craft-Beer-industry-continues-to-grow (accessed March 27, 2012); "COLLABEERATIONS," Elysian Brewing Company, www.elysianbrewing.com/beer/collabeerations.html (accessed March 27, 2012); Devin Leonard, "New Belgium and the Battle of the Microbrews," *Bloomberg Businessweek*, December 1, 2011, www.businessweek.com/magazine/new-belgium-and-the-battle-of-the-microbrews-12012011.html (accessed March 27, 2012); "Kim's Joy Ride," www.youtube.com/watch?v=L94PE12VaFY (accessed November 20, 2013); Michael Finch II, "The Beer Is Here: New Belgium Brewing Begins Distribution with Events across Alabama," AL.com, January 23, 2014, www.al.com/business/index.ssf/2014/01/the_beer_is_here_new_belgium_b.html (accessed March 25, 2014).

[46] Candice Chol and Michelle Chapman, "Kicking the Can: Campbell's Hit by Fresh Food Shift," *NBC News*, November 19, 2013, www.nbcnews.com/business/campbells-hurting-millennials-turn-noses-canned-soup-2D11624166 (accessed November 20, 2013); E. J. Schultz, "Incoming CEO Sets New Course for Struggling Campbell," *Advertising Age*, July 12, 2011, http://adage.com/article/news/incoming-ceo-sets-struggling-campbell/228673 (accessed November 20, 2013); Campbell Soup Company website, www.campbellsoup.com (accessed November 20, 2013); Carly Weeks, "Campbell's Adding Salt Back to Its Soups," *The Globe and Mail*, July 15, 2011, www.theglobeandmail.com/life/health/new-health/health-news/campbells-adding-salt-back-to-its-soups/article2097659 (accessed November 20, 2013); Ilan Brat, "The Emotional Quotient of Soup Shopping," *The Wall Street Journal*, February 17, 2010, http://online.wsj.com/article/SB10001424052748704804204575069562743700340.html (accessed November 20, 2013); "Campbell Launches *'It's Amazing What Soup Can Do'* Ad Campaign to Promote Campbell's U.S. Soup Brands," *Business Wire*, September 7, 2010, www.businesswire.com/news/home/20100907006087/en/Campbell-Launches-%E2%80%9CIt%E2%80%99s-Amazing-Soup-Do%E2%80%9D-Ad (accessed November 20, 2013); Lisa Terry, "How Campbell Soup Fixed Its Confusing Shelves," *Advertising Age*, July 25, 2011, http://adage.com/article/news/campbell-soup-fixed-confusing-shelves/228858 (accessed November 20, 2013); Kunur Patel, "Apple, Campbell's Say iAds Twice as Effective as TV," *Advertising Age*, February 3, 2011, http://adage.com/article/digital/apple-campbell-s-iads-effective-tv/148630 (accessed November 20, 2013); E. J. Schultz, "Campbell Soups Vows to Hold Line on Marketing," *Advertising Age*, September 2, 2011, http://adage.com/article/news/campbell-soup-vows-hold-line-marketing-economy/229611 (accessed November 20, 2013).

Feature Notes

[a] Bruce Horovitz, "Starbucks to Enter Yogurt Business," *USA Today*, July 25, 2013, www.usatoday.com/story/money/business/2013/07/23/starbucks-yogurt-evolution-fresh-danone-dannon/2578137 (accessed August 12, 2013); Bruce Horovitz, "Starbucks, Taco Bell Make Healthy Eating More Attainable," *USA Today*, June 19, 2013, www.usatoday.com/story/money/business/2013/06/18/starbucks-menu-board-calories-taco-bell-power-protein-menu/2431801 (accessed August 12, 2013); Stephanie Strom, "Want a Yogurt with That Venti Latte? Starbucks and Danone to Join Forces," *The New York Times*, July 23, 2013, www.nytimes.com/2013/07/24/business/starbucks-and-danone-joining-forces-to-sell-yogurt.html?_r=0 (accessed August 12, 2013).

[b] Zipcar, "How It Works," www.zipcar.com/how (accessed August 8, 2013); John Kell, "Avis to Buy Car-Sharing Service Zipcar," *The Wall Street Journal*, January 2, 2013, http://online.wsj.com/article/SB10001424127887324374004578217121433322386.html (accessed August 7, 2013); Joan Voight, "Avis, Zipcar Deal Meets Marketing Challenges," *Ad Week*, January 15, 2013, www.adweek.com/news/advertising-branding/avis-zipcar-deal-meets-marketing-challenges-146421 (accessed August 7, 2013).

chapter 2

Planning, Implementing, and Evaluating Marketing Strategies

OBJECTIVES

2-1 Explain the strategic planning process.

2-2 Identify what is necessary to effectively manage the implementation of marketing strategies.

2-3 Describe the four major elements of strategic performance evaluation.

2-4 Describe the development of a marketing plan.

MARKETING INSIGHTS

Shutterfly's High-Flying Marketing Strategy

How many dot-com companies have faced down competition from Kodak, Walmart, and other corporate giants—and survived to become the industry leader with a healthy 50 percent market share? Since its founding in 1999 as an online site for printing photos and photo books, Shutterfly has provided free, secure, and unlimited storage of uploaded images, promising customers that "we care about your photos as much as you do."

Shutterfly is now flying high in revenue growth thanks to a marketing strategy based on careful research, long-term planning, and a portfolio of complementary business units. The company's main target market is "chief memory officers," women ages 25 to 50 years old who tap Shutterfly's offerings online or via smartphone apps to organize family photos into high-quality printed books or put favorite images on mugs and other products.

To make the most of its strength in technology and profit from market opportunities, Shutterfly has expanded its operations through acquisitions and in-house innovation. Its Tiny Prints unit markets personalized stationery; its Wedding Paper Divas unit markets stylish wedding invitations; and its Treat unit markets personalized greeting cards. In addition, its business division prints brochures for corporate clients such as AT&T.

Because Shutterfly plans and implements so many web-based and social media marketing efforts, often with short-term deadlines, staff experts handle most of the company's marketing internally. The company does rely on an outside advertising agency to plan and produce its television commercials. Looking ahead, can Shutterfly maintain its marketing momentum as new competitors emerge and customers' preferences evolve?[1]

Whether it's Shutterfly or your local print shop, an organization must be able to create customer value and achieve its goals. This occurs through successful strategic marketing management. **Strategic marketing management** is the process of planning, implementing, and evaluating the performance of marketing activities and strategies, both effectively and efficiently. Effectiveness and efficiency are key concepts to understanding strategic marketing management. *Effectiveness* is the degree to which long-term customer relationships help achieve an organization's objectives. *Efficiency* refers to minimizing the resources an organization uses to achieve a specific level of desired customer relationships. Thus, the overall goal of strategic marketing management is to facilitate highly desirable customer relationships and to minimize the costs of doing so.

We begin this chapter with an overview of the strategic planning process and a discussion of the nature of marketing strategy. These elements provide a framework for an analysis of the development, implementation, and evaluation of marketing strategies. We conclude with an examination of how to create a marketing plan.

strategic marketing management The process of planning, implementing, and evaluating the performance of marketing activities and strategies, both effectively and efficiently

strategic planning The process of establishing an organizational mission and formulating goals, corporate strategy, marketing objectives, and marketing strategy

mission statement A long-term view, or vision, of what the organization wants to become

2-1 THE STRATEGIC PLANNING PROCESS

Through the process of **strategic planning**, a company establishes an organizational mission and formulates goals, a corporate strategy, marketing objectives, and a marketing strategy.[2] A market orientation should guide the process of strategic planning to ensure that a concern for customer satisfaction is an integral part of the entire company, leading to the development of successful marketing strategies and planning processes.[3]

Figure 2.1 shows the various components of the strategic planning process, which begins with the establishment or revision of an organization's mission and goals. The corporation and individual business units then develop strategies to achieve these goals. The company performs a detailed analysis of its strengths and weaknesses and identifies opportunities and threats within the external marketing environment. Next, each functional area of the organization (marketing, production, finance, human resources, and so forth) establishes its own objectives and develops strategies to achieve them, which must support the organization's overall goals and mission and should be focused on market orientation. Because this is a marketing book, we are most interested in marketing objectives and strategies. We will examine the strategic planning process by taking a closer look at each component, beginning with organizational mission statements and goals.

© Bluebeam Software, Inc

Corporate Identity
Bluebeam Software has established a corporate identity as a company that can address even the most complicated technological needs of traveling professionals.

2-1a Establishing Organizational Mission Statements and Goals

After an organization has assessed its resources and opportunities, it can begin to establish goals and strategies to leverage them. The goals of any organization should derive from its **mission statement**, a long-term view or vision of what the organization wants to become. For instance, Starbucks' mission, "to inspire and nurture the human spirit—one cup and one neighborhood at a time," speaks to the company's desire to be a gathering place in neighborhoods.[4]

When an organization decides on its mission, it is answering two questions: *Who are our customers*? and *What is our core competency*? Although these questions appear very

Figure 2.1 **Components of the Strategic Planning Process**

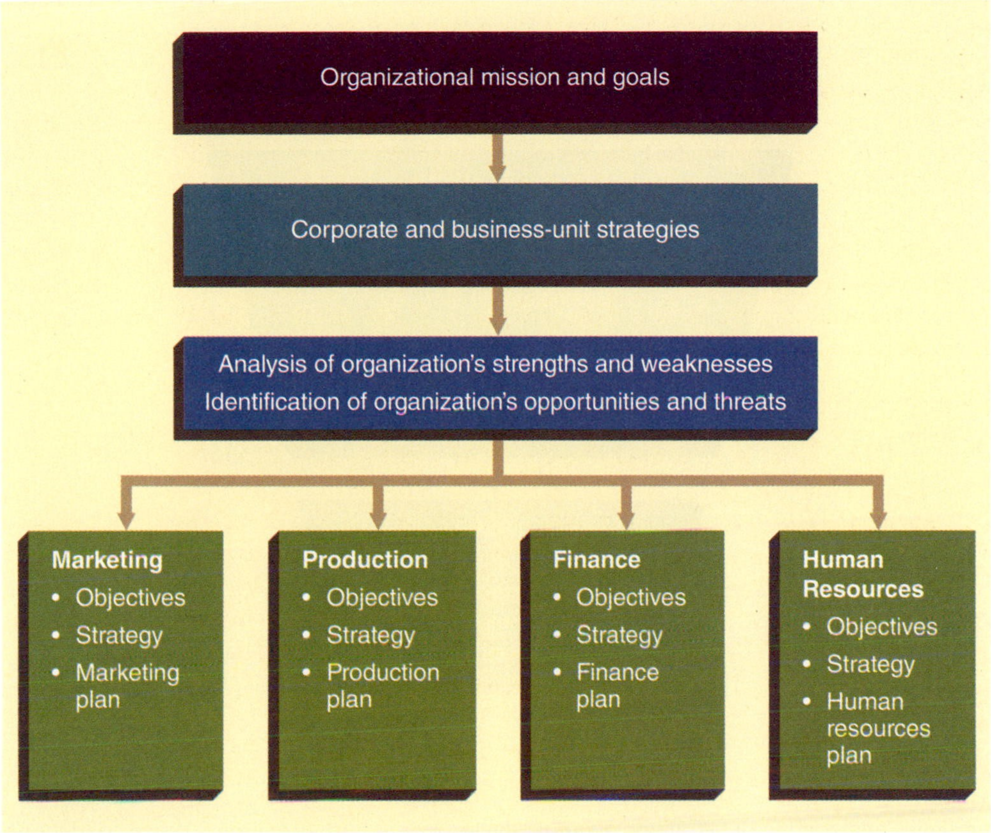

Source: Figure adapted from *Marketing Strategy*, 3rd ed., by O.C. Ferrell and Michael Hartline.

simple, they are two of the most important questions for any company to address. Defining customers' needs and wants gives direction to what the company must do to satisfy them.

Companies try to develop and manage their *corporate identity*—their unique symbols, personalities, and philosophies—to support all corporate activities, including marketing. Managing identity requires broadcasting a company's mission, goals, and values. It also requires implementing a visual identity that sends a consistent image to stakeholders. Mission statements, goals, and objectives must be properly implemented to achieve the desired result. An organization's goals and objectives, derived from its mission statement, guide its planning efforts. Goals focus on the end results the organization seeks. Look at the advertisement for Bluebeam Software. This ad displays the company's desired corporate identity. It shows a man on top of a mountain, who has obviously been hiking, working on his tablet computer. Bluebeam wants its target market to see the company as the go-to choice in cloud computing and software solutions, no matter where you are located in the world. The company's advertisement also indicates that it would like to be associated with young, adventurous professionals, which is underscored by the placement and look of the model in the ad. Bluebeam is making a statement that its corporate identity is in tune with the technologically savvy and adventurous, who travel frequently and have unique technological needs.

2-1b Developing Corporate and Business-Unit Strategies

In most organizations, strategic planning begins at the corporate level and proceeds downward to the business-unit and marketing levels. However, organizations are increasingly developing

Figure 2.2 **Levels of Strategic Planning**

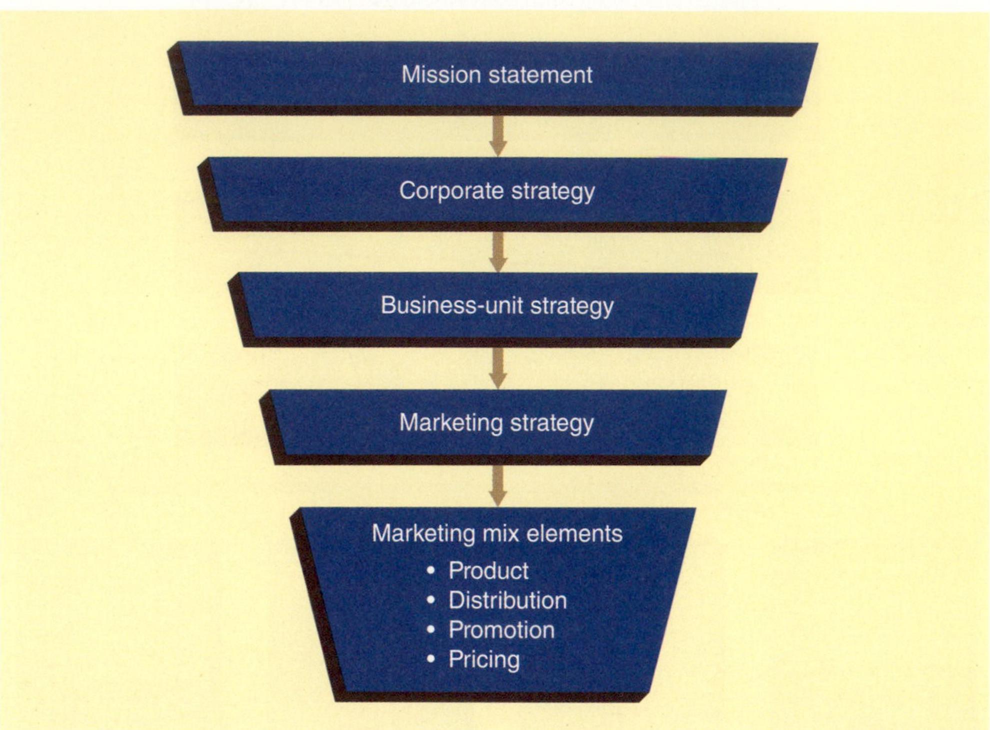

strategies and conducting strategic planning that moves in both directions. When conducting strategic planning, a firm is likely to seek out experts from many levels of the organization to take advantage of in-house expertise and a variety of opinions.

Figure 2.2 shows the relationships among three planning levels: corporate, business unit, and marketing. Corporate strategy is the broadest of the three levels and should be developed with the organization's overall mission in mind. Business-unit strategy should be consistent with the corporate strategy while also serving the unit's needs. Marketing strategy utilizes the marketing mix to develop a message that is consistent with the business-unit and corporate strategies.

Corporate Strategies

Corporate strategy determines the means for utilizing resources in the functional areas of marketing, production, finance, research and development, and human resources to achieve the organization's goals. A corporate strategy outlines the scope of the business and such considerations as resource deployment, competitive advantages, and overall coordination of functional areas. Top management's level of marketing expertise and ability to deploy resources to address the company's markets can affect sales growth and profitability. Corporate strategy addresses the two questions posed in the organization's mission statement: *Who are our customers*? and *What is our core competency*? The term *corporate* in this case does not apply solely to corporations. In this context, it refers to the top-level (i.e., highest) strategy and is used by organizations of all sizes.

corporate strategy A strategy that determines the means for utilizing resources in the various functional areas to reach the organization's goals

Corporate strategy planners are concerned with broad issues such as organizational culture, competition, differentiation, diversification, interrelationships among business units, and environmental and social issues. They attempt to match the resources of the organization with the opportunities and threats in the environment. Take a look at the MasterCard advertisement, for instance. MasterCard identified an opportunity in the marketing environment to target American Express customers who are dissatisfied with the low rate of acceptance of their credit cards abroad. This ad focuses on a hypothetical customer who is visiting London and gets caught in a rainstorm. The person has an immediate need to purchase a pair of rain boots, an act made easier when you have a widely-accepted credit card. The ad is simple in its layout and uses bright colors to catch the viewer's eye. The perspective of the photo is that of the customer standing on a rainy street, and it invites you to imagine what it would be like to have wet feet and need rain boots—a situation that nearly everyone can imagine. MasterCard's strategy is to appeal to nearly everyone who has a credit card, because nearly everyone has been in a situation where they had an unexpected need for a product. The proactive nature of a company's corporate strategy can affect its capacity to innovate.

© Master Card

Business-Unit Strategies
MasterCard targets consumers who want a credit card that is accepted all around the world.

Business-Unit Strategies

After analyzing corporate operations and performance, the next step in strategic planning is to determine future business directions and develop strategies for individual business units. A **strategic business unit (SBU)** is a division, product line, or other profit center within the parent company. Nestlé, for example, has SBUs for Confectionaries and Beverages. Each SBU sells a distinct set of products to an identifiable group of customers and each competes with a well-defined set of competitors. The revenues, costs, investments, and strategic plans of each SBU can be separated from those of the parent company and evaluated. SBUs face different market growth rates, opportunities, competition, and profit-making potential. Business strategy should seek to create value for the company's target markets and attain greater performance, which marketing research suggests requires implementing appropriate strategic actions and targeting appropriate market segments.[5]

Strategic planners should recognize the performance capabilities of each SBU and carefully allocate resources among them. Several tools allow a company's portfolio of SBUs, or even individual products, to be classified and visually displayed according to the attractiveness of markets and the business's relative market share. A **market** is a group of individuals and/or organizations that have needs for products in a product class and have the ability, willingness, and authority to purchase those products. The percentage of a market that actually buys a specific product from a particular company is referred to as that product's (or business unit's) **market share**. Google, for example, has a very dominant share of the search engine market in the United States, at nearly 67 percent.[6] Product quality, order of entry into the market, and market share have been associated with SBU success.[7]

One of the most helpful tools for a marketer is the **market growth/market share matrix**, developed by the Boston Consulting Group (BCG). This approach is based on the philosophy that a product's market growth rate and its market share are important considerations in determining marketing strategy. To develop such a tool, all of the company's SBUs and products are integrated into a single matrix and compared and evaluated to determine appropriate strategies for individual products and overall portfolio strategies. Managers use this model to determine and classify each product's expected future cash contributions and future cash requirements. However, the BCG analytical approach is more of a diagnostic tool than a guide for making strategy prescriptions.

Figure 2.3, which is based on work by the BCG, enables a strategic planner to classify a company's products into four basic types: stars, cash cows, dogs, and question marks. *Stars*

strategic business unit (SBU) A division, product line, or other profit center within the parent company

market A group of individuals and/or organizations that have needs for products in a product class and have the ability, willingness, and authority to purchase those products

market share The percentage of a market that actually buys a specific product from a particular company

market growth/market share matrix A helpful business tool, based on the philosophy that a product's market growth rate and its market share are important considerations in determining its marketing strategy

Figure 2.3 Growth Share Matrix Developed by the Boston Consulting Group

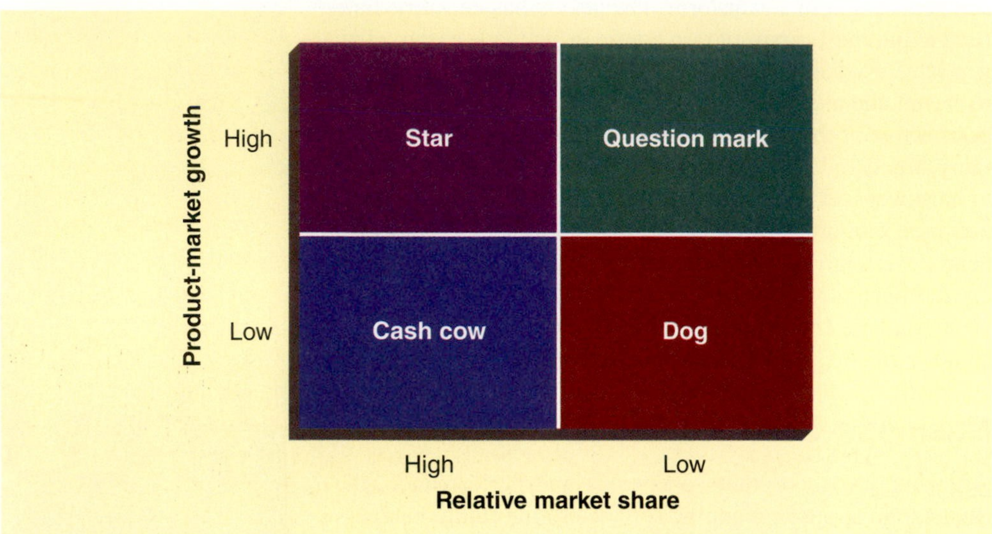

Source: *Perspectives*, No. 66, "The Product Portfolio." Reprinted by permission from The Boston Consulting Group, Inc., Boston, MA, Copyright © 1970.

are products with a dominant share of the market and good prospects for growth. However, they use more cash than they generate to finance growth, add capacity, and increase market share. Samsung's tablet computers might be considered starts because they are gaining market share quickly but remain well behind Apple, the leader. *Cash cows* have a dominant share of the market, but low prospects for growth. They typically generate more cash than is required to maintain market share. Bounty paper towels represent a cash cow for Procter & Gamble because it is a product that consistently sells well. *Dogs* have a subordinate share of the market and low prospects for growth. Dogs are often found in established markets. The cathode ray tube television would probably be considered a dog by a company like Panasonic, as most customers prefer flat screens. *Question marks*, sometimes called "problem children," have a small share of a growing market and generally require a large amount of cash to build market share. The BMW i3 electric car, for example, is a question mark relative to BWM's more established gasoline-powered automobile models.

The long-term health of an organization depends on having a range of products, some that generate cash (and generate acceptable profits) and others that use cash to support growth. The major indicators of a firm's overall health are the size and vulnerability of the cash cows, the prospects for the stars, and the number of question marks and dogs. Particular attention should be paid to products that require large cash flows, as most firms cannot afford to sponsor many such products. If resources are spread too thin, the company will be unable to finance promising new product entries or acquisitions.

2-1c Assessing Organizational Resources and Opportunities

The strategic planning process begins with an analysis of the marketing environment, including the industry in which the company operates or intends to sell its products. As we will see in Chapter 3, the marketing environment (which includes economic, competitive, political, legal and regulatory, sociocultural, and technological forces) can threaten an organization and influence its overall goals affecting the amount and type of resources the company can acquire. However, these forces can also create favorable opportunities that can help an organization achieve its goals and marketing objectives.

Any strategic planning effort must take into account the organization's available financial and human resources and capabilities and how these resources are likely to change over time, as changes may affect the organization's ability to achieve its mission and goals. Adequate resources can help a firm generate customer satisfaction and loyalty, goodwill, and a positive reputation, all of which impact marketing through creating well-known brands and strong financial performance. Coca-Cola, Apple, and Google all benefit from high levels of brand recognition and goodwill. Such strengths also include **core competencies**, things a company does extremely well—sometimes so well that they give the company an advantage over its competition.

Analysis of the marketing environment also includes identifying opportunities in the marketplace, which requires a solid understanding of the company's industry. When the right combination of circumstances and timing permits an organization to take action to reach a particular target market, a **market opportunity** exists. Square®, for instance, began as a small start-up that took advantage of a market opportunity to offer vendors a way to make credit card transactions easier. Square® offers a mobile payment product that latches onto a smartphone and allows small vendors to accept credit card payments anywhere. This has reduced the cost and inconvenience of transactions and allowed for the success of small informal businesses, such as food trucks and farmer's market vendors. Starbucks is even in the process of accepting payments through Square® at some of its stores.[8] Such opportunities are often called **strategic windows**, temporary periods of optimal fit between the key requirements of a market and the particular capabilities of a company competing in that market.[9] When a company matches a core competency to opportunities in the marketplace, it is said to have a **competitive advantage**. Some companies possess manufacturing, technical, or marketing skills that they can tie to market opportunities to create a competitive advantage. Note in the Verizon advertisement that the company focuses on its primary advantage over competing brands—namely, its extensive global 4G network. Verizon has 4G service in more than 200 countries, meaning that its customers are able to use their smartphones in more places than with other carriers. The ad also promotes its low-cost global data package, which makes it less expensive and easier to keep in touch when traveling for business. The photo underscores the wide availability of the Verizon network by showing a woman using her cell phone in what appears to be a remote desert.

A SWOT analysis can be helpful for gauging a firm's capabilities and resources relative to the industry. It can provide a firm with insights into such factors as timing market entry into a new geographic region or product category. We discuss SWOT analysis and first-mover and late-mover advantages in the following sections.

core competencies Things a company does extremely well, which sometimes give it an advantage over its competition

market opportunity A combination of circumstances and timing that permits an organization to take action to reach a particular target market

strategic windows Temporary periods of optimal fit between the key requirements of a market and the particular capabilities of a company competing in that market

competitive advantage The result of a company matching a core competency to opportunities it has discovered in the marketplace

SWOT analysis Assessment of an organization's strengths, weaknesses, opportunities, and threats

© Verizon Wireless

Competitive Advantage
Verizon has a competitive advantage over other mobile carriers because of its extensive global 4G network, allowing customers to have smartphone coverage nearly everywhere in the world.

SWOT Analysis

The **SWOT analysis** assesses an organization's strengths, weaknesses, opportunities, and threats. It is depicted as a four-cell matrix, as in Figure 2.4, and shows how marketers must seek to convert weaknesses into strengths, threats into opportunities, and match internal strengths with external opportunities to develop competitive advantages. Strengths and weaknesses are internal factors that can influence an organization's ability to satisfy target markets. *Strengths* refer to competitive advantages, or core competencies, that give the company an advantage. *Weaknesses* are limitations a company faces in developing or implementing a marketing strategy.

Figure 2.4 The Four-Cell SWOT Matrix

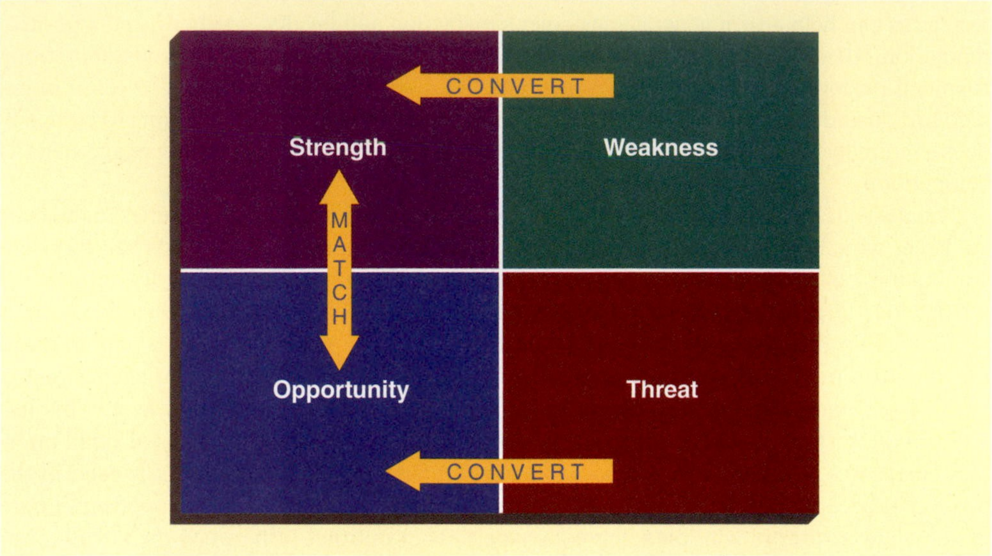

Source: Adapted from Nigel F. Piercy, *Market-Led Strategic*, p. 371.

Consider Walmart, a company that was so dominant for decades that it almost did not need to worry about competitors. However, Amazon has grown into such a threat recently, with its low costs and high customer satisfaction, that Walmart has been forced to acknowledge it has a serious weakness in online sales and technological innovation. To respond to this threat, Walmart developed a presence in Silicon Valley, called WalmartLabs, which acquires start-ups and hires hundreds of young and talented programmers and engineers to help the retailer change with the times and address problems through innovative solutions.[10] Both strengths and weaknesses should be examined from a customer perspective. Only those strengths that relate to satisfying customers should be considered true competitive advantages. Likewise, weaknesses that directly affect customer satisfaction should be considered disadvantages.

Opportunities and threats affect all organizations within an industry, market, or geographic region because they exist outside of and independently of the company. *Opportunities* refer to favorable conditions in the environment that could produce rewards for the organization if acted upon. Opportunities are situations that exist but must be exploited for the company to benefit from them. *Threats,* on the other hand, refer to barriers that could prevent the company from reaching its objectives. Threats must be acted upon to prevent them from limiting the organization's capabilities. Opportunities and threats can stem from many sources within the environment. When a competitor's introduction of a new product threatens a company, a firm may require a defensive strategy. If the company can develop and launch a new product that meets or exceeds the competition's offering, it can transform the threat into an opportunity.

First-Mover and Late-Mover Advantage

first-mover advantage The ability of an innovative company to achieve long-term competitive advantages by being the first to offer a certain product in the marketplace

An important factor that marketers must consider when identifying organizational resources and opportunities is whether the firm has the resources to cultivate a first-mover advantage, or is in a position to choose between developing a first-mover or late-mover advantage. A **first-mover advantage** is the ability of an innovative company to achieve long-term competitive advantages by being the first to offer a certain product in the marketplace. Being the first to enter a market helps a company build a reputation as a pioneer and market leader. Amazon and eBay were both first-mover start-ups that remain leaders as they grow and innovate ahead

Emerging Trends

You Don't Have to Be Old to Cruise

Out with the shuffleboard, in with the heavy metal concerts, circus schools, and water slides. Cruise lines are moving full speed ahead to change perceptions and capture the imagination of first-time cruisers and young families seeking a getaway for adults and children alike.

Cruising has traditionally been associated with older vacationers, and its image has been hurt by recent headlines about accidents and engine problems. To repair the industry's reputation and draw the attention of younger vacationers, cruise marketers are developing new marketing plans with special emphasis on exciting amenities and activities (product) and social media communications (promotion).

Celebrity Cruises recently sold out every cabin for its new "Top Chef" cruise with contestants from the popular television show mingling with passengers and creating exclusive menus for the trip. Royal Caribbean Cruises also sold out its "Full Metal Cruise" featuring heavy metal musicians, a tattoo artist, and specialty beers. Most of these passengers had never cruised before, and the average age was 39. Norwegian Cruise Line is drawing more families than ever before with onboard mini-golf courses, five-story water slides, teen programs, and classes to teach circus skills.

To reach younger vacationers, all the major cruise lines are active on Facebook, YouTube, and other social media. Carnival Cruise Lines even features passengers' social media posts in its television advertising as a way of fueling word of mouth recommendations.[a]

of the competition. For a first mover, the market is, for at least a short period, free of competition as potential competitors work to develop a rival product. Because consumers have no choice initially, being a first mover also helps establish customer brand loyalty in cases when switching to another brand later may be costly or difficult. The first to develop a new product can also protect secrets and technology through patents.

There are risks, however, of being the first to enter a market. There are usually high cost outlays associated with creating a new product, including market research, product development, production, and marketing—or buyer education—costs. Also, early sales growth may not match predictions if the firm overestimates demand or fails to target marketing efforts correctly. The company runs the risk that the product will fail due to market uncertainty, or that the product might not completely meet consumers' expectations or needs.

A **late-mover advantage** is the ability of later market entrants to achieve long-term competitive advantages by not being the first to offer a certain product in a marketplace. Competitors that enter the market later can benefit from the first mover's mistakes and have a chance to improve on the product design and marketing strategy. A late mover is also likely to have lower initial investment costs than the first mover because the first mover has already developed a distribution infrastructure and educated buyers about the product. By the time a late mover enters the market, there is also more data, and therefore more certainty, about product success. Case in point, the competition in the tablet computer market has become fierce. Although Nokia entered the market before Apple, the Apple iPad currently dominates the tablet computer market with a 32 percent share of the global market. Samsung, in second place with 18 percent, has capitalized on its late-mover advantage and is rapidly gaining market share.[11]

There are disadvantages of being a late mover too, though. The company that entered the market first may have patents and other protections on its technology and trade secrets that prevent the late mover from producing a similar product. If customers who have already purchased the first mover's product believe that switching to the late mover's product will be expensive or time-consuming, it may be difficult for the late mover to gain market share.

late-mover advantage The ability of later market entrants to achieve long-term competitive advantages by not being the first to offer a certain product in a marketplace

It is important to note that the timing of entry into the market is crucial. Companies that are relatively quick to enter the market after the first mover have a greater chance of building market share and brand loyalty. Companies that enter the market later on, after many other companies have done so, face stronger competition and have more disadvantages.

2-1d Developing Marketing Objectives and Marketing Strategies

The next phase in strategic planning is the development of marketing objectives and marketing strategies, which are used to achieve marketing objectives. A **marketing objective** states what is to be accomplished through marketing activities. These objectives can be given in terms of product introduction, product improvement or innovation, sales volume, profitability, market share, pricing, distribution, advertising, or employee training activities. A marketing objective of Ritz-Carlton hotels, for example, is to have more than 90 percent of its customers indicate that they had a memorable experience at the hotel. Marketing objectives should be based on a careful study of the SWOT analysis, matching strengths to opportunities, eliminating weaknesses, and minimizing threats.

Marketing objectives should possess certain characteristics. First, a marketing objective should be expressed in clear, simple terms so all marketing and non-marketing personnel in the company understand exactly what they are trying to achieve. Second, an objective should be measurable, which allows the organization to track progress and compare outcomes against beginning benchmarks. For instance, if an objective is to increase market share by 10 percent in the United States, the company should be able to measure market share changes accurately to ensure that it is making gains toward that objective. Third, a marketing objective should specify a time frame for its accomplishment, such as six months or one year. Finally, a marketing objective should be consistent with both business-unit and corporate strategies. This ensures that the company's mission is carried out consistently at all levels of the organization by all personnel. Marketing objectives should be achievable and use company resources effectively, and successful accomplishment should contribute to the overall corporate strategy. A marketing strategy ensures that the firm has a plan in place to achieve its marketing objectives.

marketing objective A statement of what is to be accomplished through marketing activities

marketing strategy A plan of action for identifying and analyzing a target market and developing a marketing mix to meet the needs of that market

A **marketing strategy** is the selection of a target market and the creation of a marketing mix that will satisfy the needs of target market members. A marketing strategy articulates the best use of the company's resources to achieve its marketing objectives.

Going Green

Unilever Aims to Clean the World's Water

Unilever, the Anglo-Dutch company behind such well-known brands as Axe, Lipton, Q-Tips, and Suave, sees sustainability as a long-term key to safeguarding the planet while increasing profits. By 2020, the company aims to grow its revenues by 100 percent and slash its eco-footprint by 50 percent. Becoming greener does more than conserve scarce natural resources: It also lowers costs, inspires employees and retailers, and helps customers lead healthier lives.

In particular, Unilever is focusing on the global challenge of ensuring safe drinking water, because it will not only benefit society but also lead to innovative new products for future growth. Knowing that waterborne disease is a major problem in some emerging nations, the company's research center in India developed an easy-to-operate, affordable home water purifier that works without electricity or any other power source. Under the brand name Pureit, the product was tested in several Indian regions before being marketed throughout the country. Pureit was then marketed in Brazil, Mexico, Indonesia, and Kenya, as well as other countries.

Unilever has sold more than 40 million Pureit filters since 2008, losing a little money on each unit. As sales volume increases, the product will begin to pay for itself. However, it is unlikely to ever be a solid source of profits, which is fine with Unilever as long as it can help clean the world's water.[b]

Selecting the Target Market

Selecting an appropriate target market may be the most important decision a company makes in the strategic planning process and is crucial for strategic success. The target market must be chosen before the organization can adapt its marketing mix to meet the customers' needs and preferences.

If a company selects the wrong target market, all other marketing decisions are likely to be in vain. Toyota, for instance, did not properly identify its target market when introducing the Yaris sedan in China. A success with middle-class consumers ages 18 to 34 elsewhere around the world, the Yaris was a flop in China. Toyota failed to realize that young, middle-class Chinese consumers are highly price sensitive, and the Yaris was priced beyond their reach. Furthermore, those Chinese consumers who could afford the car tended not to like the styling.[12]

Careful and accurate target market selection is crucial to productive marketing efforts. Products, and even whole companies, sometimes fail because marketers misidentify the best target market for their products. Organizations that try to be all things to all people rarely satisfy the needs of any customer group very well. Identification and analysis of a target market provide a foundation on which the company can develop its marketing mix.

When exploring possible target markets, marketing managers try to evaluate how entry could affect the company's sales, costs, and profits. Marketing information should be organized to facilitate a focus on the chosen target customers. Accounting and information systems, for example, can be used to track revenues and costs by customer (or customer group). The firm should offer rewards to managers and employees who focus efforts on profitable customers. Firms should develop teamwork skills that promote a flexible customer orientation that allows the firm to adapt to changes in the marketing environment.

Target Market Selection
Who are the target markets for Head & Shoulders and CoverGirl products? Are they targeting the same customers?

Compare the target markets for the CoverGirl and Head & Shoulders products featured in the accompanying advertisements. Although both of these advertisements show relatively low-cost personal-care products, they are targeted at very different audiences. The ad for Head & Shoulders shampoo features Troy Polamalu, a football safety for the Pittsburgh Steelers who is known for his long hair. Shampoo is a category of product that is more often targeted at women. However, this ad shows Head & Shoulders branching out to male consumers by encouraging them to purchase shampoo endorsed by a famous athlete. The CoverGirl ad, on the other hand, features a woman heavily made up in shades of blue and green. The target market for this ad is women who are not afraid to take fashion and makeup risks and who like to stand out.

Marketers should determine whether a selected target market aligns with the company's overall mission and objectives. If it does, they should assess whether the company has the appropriate resources to develop a marketing mix (product, price, promotion, and distribution) that meets the needs of that target market. The size and number of competitors already marketing products in potential target markets are concerns as well. For example, the market for mobile apps has become so competitive that new entrants must carefully evaluate whether their products represent a new product that would be in demand by the target market or a genuine improvement over what already exists.[13]

Creating Marketing Mixes

Using all relevant information available to conduct in-depth research allows a firm to select the most appropriate target market, which is the basis for creating a marketing mix that satisfies the needs of that market. Thus, the organization should analyze demographic information, customer needs, preferences, and behaviors with respect to product design, pricing, distribution, and promotion. Recognizing that consumers are increasingly interested in reducing waste and helping the environment while also saving money, Glad Products Company launched a global multimedia advertising campaign and marketing strategy focused around increasing consumer awareness of how its bags, wraps, and containers keep food fresh and reduce waste. The campaign was based on research indicating that many households shop for food on Sundays and prepare meals to eat throughout the week, generating a need for reliable food storage. Creating a marketing mix focused around a cause is an increasingly popular strategy among firms.[14]

Marketing-mix decisions should have two additional characteristics: consistency and flexibility. All marketing-mix decisions should be consistent with the business-unit and corporate strategies. Such consistency allows the organization to achieve its objectives on all three levels of planning. Flexibility, on the other hand, permits the organization to alter the marketing mix in response to changes in market conditions, competition, and customer needs. Marketing strategy flexibility has a positive influence on organizational performance.

Utilizing the marketing mix as a tool set, a company can detail how it will achieve a sustainable competitive advantage. A **sustainable competitive advantage** is one that the competition cannot copy in the foreseeable future. Amazon maintains a sustainable competitive advantage in shipping because of its high-tech logistics system and extensive network of distribution centers (40 in the United States, with 5 more under construction), which allows the online giant to offer low prices and fast service. Many retailers struggle to compete with Amazon in terms of low-cost products and fast, reliable, and low-cost shipping.[15] Maintaining a sustainable competitive advantage requires flexibility in the marketing mix when facing uncertain competitive environments.

2-2 MANAGING MARKETING IMPLEMENTATION

Marketing implementation is the process of putting marketing strategies into action. Through planning, marketing managers provide purpose and direction for an organization's marketing efforts and are positioned to implement specific marketing strategies. The effective

sustainable competitive advantage An advantage that the competition cannot copy

marketing implementation The process of putting marketing strategies into action

implementation of any and all marketing activities depends on a well-organized marketing department that is capable of motivating personnel, implementing effective communication, employing good coordination efforts, and setting reasonable and attainable timetables for activity completion.

2-2a Organizing the Marketing Unit

The structure and relationships of a marketing unit, including establishing lines of authority and communication that connect and coordinate individuals, strongly affect marketing activities. Companies that truly adopt the marketing concept develop an organizational culture that is based on a shared set of beliefs that places the customer's needs at the center of decisions about strategy and operations. Technology can help companies adopt the marketing concept. For example, firms increasingly use online Web-tracking to improve information flows and their understanding of customers' needs and wants. Though some feel that this technology is a violation of privacy, tracking companies have helped marketers create very detailed profiles for their target markets, which helps all members of the marketing unit more effectively address the needs of the target market.[16]

Firms must decide whether operations should be centralized or decentralized, a choice that directly impacts marketing decision making and strategy. In a **centralized organization**, top-level managers delegate little authority to lower levels. In a **decentralized organization**, decision-making authority is delegated as far down the chain of command as possible. In centralized organizations, marketing decisions are made at the top levels. However, centralized decision making may prove ineffective in firms that must respond quickly to fluctuations in customer demand. In these organizations, decentralized authority allows the company to adapt more rapidly to customer needs.

How effectively a company's marketing management can implement marketing strategies also depends on how the marketing unit is organized. Organizing marketing activities to align with the overall strategic marketing approach enhances organizational efficiency and performance. A marketing department should clearly outline the hierarchical relationships between personnel and who is responsible for performing certain activities and making decisions.

centralized organization A structure in which top-level managers delegate little authority to lower levels

decentralized organization A structure in which decision-making authority is delegated as far down the chain of command as possible

Recognition
Recognizing outstanding performance is one approach to motivating marketing personnel.

2-2b Motivating Marketing Personnel

People work to satisfy physical, psychological, and social needs. To motivate marketing personnel, managers must address their employees' needs to maintain a high level of workplace satisfaction. It is crucial that the plan to motivate employees be fair, ethical, and well understood to maintain a high level of workplace satisfaction. Employee rewards should also be tied to organizational goals. A firm can motivate its workers through a variety of methods, including by linking pay with performance, informing workers how their performance affects department and corporate results and their own compensation, providing appropriate and competitive compensation, implementing a flexible benefits program, and adopting a participative management approach.

Diversity in the workplace can complicate employee motivational strategies, as different generations and cultures may be motivated by different things. A specific employee might value autonomy or recognition more than a pay increase. Managers can compensate employees, not just with money and fringe benefits, but also with nonfinancial rewards, such as prestige or recognition, job autonomy, skill variety, task significance, increased feedback, or a more relaxed dress code. It is crucial for management to show that it takes pride in its workforce and to motivate employees to take pride in their company.

2-2c Communicating within the Marketing Unit

Marketing managers must be in clear communication with the firm's upper-level management to ensure that they are aware of the firm's goals and achievements and that marketing activities are consistent with the company's overall goals. The marketing unit should also take steps to ensure that its activities are in synch with those of other departments, such as finance or human resources. For instance, marketing personnel should work with the production staff to design products that have the features that marketing research indicates are what customers desire.

It is important that communication flow up, from the front lines of the organization to upper management. Customer-contact employees are in a unique position to understand customers' wants and needs, and pathways should be open for them to communicate this knowledge to marketing managers. In this way, marketing managers can gain access to a rich source of information about what customers require, how products are selling, the effectiveness of marketing activities, and any issues with marketing implementation. Upward communication also allows marketing managers to understand the problems and requirements of lower-level employees, a critical group to keep satisfied, as they are the ones who interface with customers.

Training is an essential element of communicating with marketing employees. An effective training program provides employees with a forum to learn and ask questions, and results in employees who are empowered and can be held accountable for their performance. Many firms utilize a formalized, high-tech information system that tracks data and facilitates communication between marketing managers, sales managers, and sales personnel. Information systems expedite communications within and between departments and support other activities, such as allocating scarce organizational resources, planning, budgeting, sales analyses, performance evaluations, and report preparation.

2-2d Coordinating Marketing Activities

Marketing managers must coordinate diverse employee actions to achieve marketing objectives and must work closely with management in many areas, including research and development, production, finance, accounting, and human resources to ensure that marketing activities align with other functions of the firm. They must also coordinate the activities of internal marketing staff with the marketing efforts of external organizations, including advertising agencies, resellers (wholesalers and retailers), researchers, and shippers. Marketing managers can improve coordination by making each employee aware of how his or her job relates to others and how his or her actions contribute to the achievement of marketing objectives.

2-2e Establishing a Timetable for Implementation

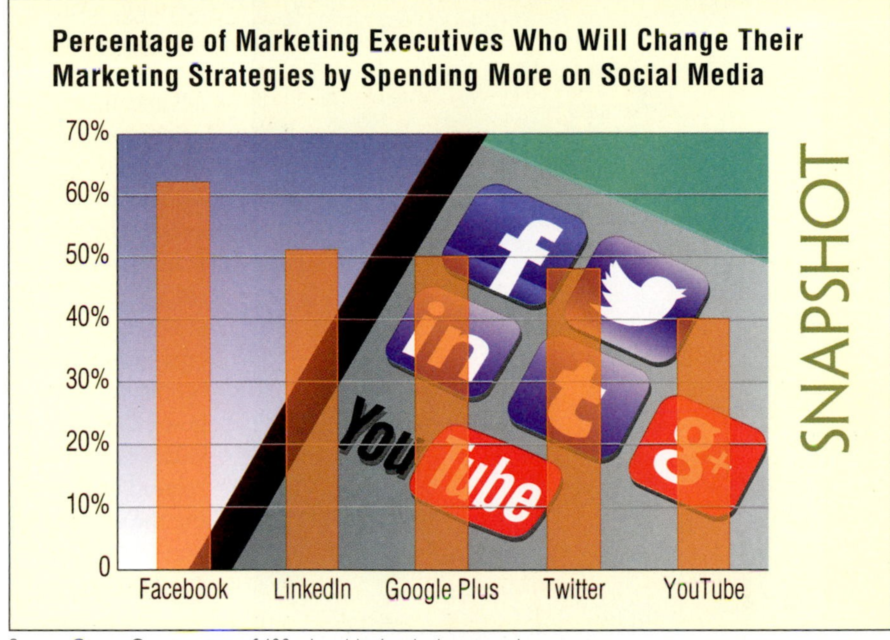

Source: Create Group survey of 400 advertising/marketing executives.

Successful marketing implementation requires that employees know the specific activities for which they are responsible and the timetable for completing them. Establishing an implementation timetable involves several steps: (1) identifying the activities to be performed, (2) determining the time required to complete each activity, (3) separating the activities to be performed in sequence from those to be performed simultaneously, (4) organizing the activities in the proper order, and (5) assigning responsibility for completing each activity to one or more employees, teams, or managers. Completing all implementation activities on schedule requires tight coordination within the marketing unit and among other departments that contribute to marketing activities, such as production. Pinpointing which activities can be performed simultaneously will reduce the total amount of time needed to put a given marketing strategy into practice. Since scheduling can be a complicated task, some organizations use sophisticated computer programs to plan the timing of marketing activities. Microsoft, for instance, has created one of these computer programs, called Microsoft Project. This program allows users to schedule tasks, allocate resources to accomplish these tasks, and monitor a project's progress.[17]

2-3 EVALUATING MARKETING STRATEGIES

To achieve marketing objectives, marketing managers must evaluate marketing strategies effectively. **Strategic performance evaluation** consists of establishing performance standards, measuring actual performance, comparing actual performance with established standards, and modifying the marketing strategy, if needed.

2-3a Establishing Performance Standards

A **performance standard** is an expected level of performance against which actual performance can be compared. A performance standard might be a 20 percent reduction in customer complaints, a monthly sales quota of $150,000, or a 10 percent increase per month in new-customer accounts. Performance standards are derived from marketing objectives that are set while developing the marketing strategy. By establishing marketing objectives, a firm indicates what a marketing strategy is supposed to accomplish. Marketing objectives directly or indirectly set forth performance standards, usually in terms of sales, costs, or communication dimensions, such as brand awareness or product feature recall. Actual performance should be measured in similar terms to facilitate comparisons.

strategic performance evaluation Establishing performance standards, measuring actual performance, comparing actual performance with established standards, and modifying the marketing strategy, if needed

performance standard An expected level of performance against which actual performance can be compared

2-3b Analyzing Actual Performance

The principle means by which a marketer can gauge whether a marketing strategy has been effective in achieving objectives is by analyzing the actual performance of the marketing

© IBM

Analyzing Actual Performance
Products, such as services sold by IBM, can help firms better analyze actual performance to improve their marketing plans.

strategy. Analyzing actual performance associated with communication dimensions is usually achieved by conducting customer research. Generally speaking, technological advancements have made it easier for firms to analyze actual performance. Firms such as IBM, featured in the advertisement, can help companies analyze actual performance using high-tech tools. This ad states that most firms use only 1 percent of the data available to them, and that IBM services can help increase this proportion, improving the quality of decision making. The ad also underscores that having better data can help firms save money and find new customers. The ad emphasizes that IBM can help firms improve analytical capabilities by showing a pie chart with a woman who represents a new customer in one of the slices of the pie—indicating that, with better data, companies can find new customers. In this section, we focus on two bases—sales and cost—for evaluating the actual performance of marketing strategies.

Sales Analysis

Sales analysis uses sales figures to evaluate a firm's current performance. It is a common method of evaluation because sales data are readily available, at least in aggregate form, and can reflect the target market's reactions to a marketing mix. If sales spike after a particular marketing mix is implemented, marketers can be reasonably certain that the marketing mix was effective at reaching the target audience. Information gleaned from sales data alone is not sufficient, however. To be useful, marketers must compare current sales data with forecasted sales, industry sales, specific competitors' sales, and the costs incurred from marketing efforts to achieve the sales volume. For example, knowing that a specialty store attained a $600,000 sales volume this year does not tell management whether its marketing strategy has succeeded. However, if managers know expected sales were $550,000, they are in a better position to determine the effectiveness of the firm's marketing efforts. In addition, if they know the marketing costs needed to achieve the $600,000 volume were 12 percent less than budgeted, they are in an even better position to analyze their marketing strategy precisely.

Although sales may be measured in several ways, the basic unit of measurement is the sales transaction. A sales transaction results in an order for a specified quantity of the organization's product sold under specified terms by a particular salesperson or sales team on a certain date. Organizations should record all information related to a transaction so that they can analyze sales in terms of dollar volume or market share. Firms frequently use dollar volume in their sales analyses because the dollar is a common denominator of sales, costs, and profits. A marketing manager who uses dollar-volume analysis should factor out the effects of price changes, which can skew the numbers by making it seem that more or fewer sales have been made than is the actual case.

A firm's market share is the firm's sales of a product stated as a percentage of industry sales of competing products. Market share analysis lets a company compare its marketing strategy with competitors' strategies. The primary reason for using market share analysis is to estimate whether sales changes have resulted from the firm's marketing strategy or from uncontrollable environmental forces. When a company's sales volume declines but its share of the market stays the same, the marketer can assume that industry sales declined because of outside factors. However, if a company experiences a decline in both sales and market share, it should consider making changes to its marketing strategy to make it more effective.

sales analysis Analysis of sales figures to evaluate a firm's performance

Even though market share analysis can be helpful in evaluating the performance of a marketing strategy, the user must exercise caution when interpreting results. When attributing a sales decline to uncontrollable factors, a marketer must keep in mind that factors in the external marketing environment do not impact all firms equally because firms have varying strategies and objectives. Changes in the strategies of one company can affect the market shares of one or all companies in that industry. Within an industry, the entrance of new firms, the launch of new products by competing firms, or the demise of established products also affects a firm's market share. Market share analysts should attempt to account for these effects. In one case, Apple caused its competitors to reevaluate their marketing strategies when it introduced the iPad and iPhone, spurring competitor innovation and revised marketing strategies.

Marketing Cost Analysis

Although sales analysis is critical for evaluating the performance of a marketing strategy, it provides only a partial picture. A marketing strategy that successfully generates sales may nevertheless be deemed ineffective if it is extremely costly. A firm must take into account the marketing costs associated with a strategy to gain a complete understanding of its effectiveness at achieving a desired sales level. **Marketing cost analysis** breaks down and classifies costs to determine which are associated with specific marketing efforts. Comparing costs of previous marketing activities with results allows a marketer to allocate the firm's marketing resources better in the future. Marketing cost analysis lets a company evaluate the performance of marketing strategy by comparing sales achieved and costs sustained. By pinpointing exactly where a company incurs costs, this form of analysis can help isolate profitable or unprofitable customers, products, and geographic areas.

A company that understands and manages its costs appropriately has a competitive advantage. Evidence shows that a low-cost provider is in a position to engage in aggressive price competition. The Internet offers low-cost marketing options, such as e-mail, social media, and viral videos. It is also the medium where it is easiest for consumers to compare prices, making it a suitable medium to engage in price competition. Bazaarvoice is a company that helps firms create more effective marketing strategies by utilizing social media, targeting key markets, and allowing customers to create and share information about products and brands. Firms like Bazaarvoice help companies efficiently use new technological tools in marketing to maximize impact and keep costs low, while also creating methods for marketers to track customer responses to marketing activities.[18]

One way to analyze costs is by comparing a company's costs with industry averages. Many companies check the amount of money they spend on marketing efforts and other operations against average levels for the industry to identify areas in need of improvement. For example, a business could compare its advertising costs as a percentage of its sales with the industry average. A company might determine it spends 6 percent of its sales on advertising, while the industry average is 2 percent. When looking at industry averages, however, a company should take into account its own unique situation. The company's costs can differ from the industry average for several reasons, including its own marketing objectives, cost structure, geographic location, types of customers, and scale of operations. When comparing its advertising costs with the industry average, for instance, the company just mentioned might be spending a larger proportion on advertising because it is a smaller company competing against industry giants. Or perhaps this firm's advertising objectives are much more aggressive than those of other firms in the industry.

Costs can be categorized in different ways when performing marketing cost analysis. One way is to identify which ones are affected by sales or production volume. Some costs are fixed, meaning they do not change between different units of time, regardless of a company's production or sales volume. Fixed costs are variables such as rent and employees' salaries, which are not affected by fluctuations in production or sales. Fixed costs are generally not very illuminating when determining how to use marketing funds more effectively. For example, it does little good to know that $80,000 is spent for rent annually. The marketing analyst

marketing cost analysis Analysis of costs to determine which are associated with specific marketing efforts

must conduct additional research to determine that, of the $80,000 spent on rent, $32,000 is spent on facilities associated with marketing efforts.

Some costs are directly attributable to production and sales volume. These costs are known as variable costs and are stated as a per quantity (or unit) cost. Variable costs include the cost to produce or sell each unit of a specific product, such as the materials and labor, or the amount of commissions that are paid to salespeople when they sell products.

Another way to categorize costs is based on whether or not they can be linked to a specific business function. Costs that can be linked are allocated, using one or several criteria, to the functions that they support. If the firm spends $80,000 to rent space for production, storage, and sales facilities, the total rental cost can be allocated to each of the three functions using a measurement, such as square footage. Some costs cannot be assigned according to any logical criteria. These are costs such as interest paid on loans, taxes paid to the government, and the salaries of top management.

2-3c Comparing Actual Performance with Performance Standards and Making Changes, If Needed

When comparing actual performance with established performance standards, a firm may find that it exceeded or failed to meet performance standard benchmarks. When actual performance exceeds performance standards, marketers will likely be satisfied and a marketing strategy will be deemed effective. It is important that a firm seek to gain an understanding of why the strategy was effective, because this information may allow marketers to adjust the strategy tactically to be even more effective.

When actual performance does not meet performance standards, marketers should seek to understand why a marketing strategy was less effective than expected. Perhaps a marketing mix variable, such as price, was not ideally suited to the target market, which could result in lower performance. Both environmental changes and aggressive competitive behavior can both cause a marketing strategy to underperform.

When a marketer finds that a strategy is underperforming expectations, a question sometimes arises as to whether the marketing objective, against which performance is measured, is realistic. After studying the problem, the firm may find that the marketing objective is indeed unrealistic. In this case, marketers must alter the marketing objective to bring it in line with more sensible expectations. It is also possible that the marketing strategy is underfunded, which can result in lower performance.

2-4 CREATING THE MARKETING PLAN

The strategic planning process ultimately yields a marketing strategy that is the framework for a **marketing plan**, a written document that specifies the marketing activities to be performed to implement and evaluate the organization's marketing strategies. Developing a clear and well-written marketing plan, though time-consuming, is important. It provides a uniform marketing vision for the firm and is the basis for internal communications. It delineates marketing responsibilities and tasks and outlines schedules for implementation. The plan presents objectives and specifies how resources are to be allocated to achieve them. Finally, the marketing plan helps marketing managers monitor and evaluate the performance of a marketing strategy.

marketing plan A written document that specifies the activities to be performed to implement and control the organization's marketing strategies

A single marketing plan can be developed and applied to the business as a whole, but it is more likely that a company will choose to develop multiple marketing plans, with each relating to a specific brand or product. Multiple marketing plans are part of a larger strategic business plan and are used to implement specific parts of the overall strategy.

Organizations use many different formats when producing a marketing plan. They may be written for strategic business units, product lines, individual products or brands, or specific markets. The key is to make sure that the marketing plan aligns with corporate and business-unit strategies and is accessible to and shared with all key employees. A marketing plan represents a critical element of a company's overall strategy development, and it should reflect the company's culture and be representative of all functional specialists in the firm.

Marketing planning and implementation are closely linked in successful companies. The marketing plan provides a framework to stimulate thinking and provide strategic direction. Implementation is an adaptive response to day-to-day issues, opportunities, and unanticipated situations—such as an economic slowdown that dampens sales—that cannot be incorporated into marketing plans.

Table 2.1 describes the major parts of a typical marketing plan. Each component builds on the last. The first component is the executive summary, which provides an overview of the entire marketing plan so that readers can quickly identify the key issues and their roles in the planning and implementation process. The executive summary includes an introduction, an explanation of the major aspects of the plan, and a statement about the costs.

The next component of the marketing plan is the environmental analysis, which supplies information about the company's current situation with respect to the marketing environment, the target market, and the firm's current objectives and performance. The environmental analysis includes an assessment of all the environmental factors—competitive, economic, political, legal, regulatory, technological, and sociocultural—that can affect marketing activities. It then examines the current needs of the organization's target markets. In the final section of the environmental analysis, the company evaluates its marketing objectives and performance to ensure that objectives are consistent with the changing marketing environment. The next component of the marketing plan is the SWOT analysis (strengths, weaknesses, opportunities, and threats), which use the information gathered in the environmental analysis.

The marketing objectives section of the marketing plan states what the company wants to accomplish through marketing activities, using the SWOT analysis as a guide of where the firm stands in the market. The marketing strategies component outlines how the firm plans to achieve its marketing objectives and discusses the company's target market selection(s) and

Table 2.1 Components of the Marketing Plan

Plan Component	Component Summary	Highlights
Executive Summary	One- to two-page synopsis of the entire marketing plan	1. Stress key points 2. Include one to three key points that make the company unique
Environmental Analysis	Information about the company's current situation with respect to the marketing environment	1. Assessment of marketing environment factors 2. Assessment of target market(s) 3. Assessment of current marketing objectives and performance
SWOT Analysis	Assessment of the organization's strengths, weaknesses, opportunities, and threats	1. Strengths of the company 2. Weaknesses of the company 3. Opportunities in the environment and industry 4. Threats in the environment and industry
Marketing Objectives	Specification of the company's marketing objectives	1. Qualitative measures of what is to be accomplished 2. Quantitative measures of what is to be accomplished
Marketing Strategies	Outline of how the company will achieve its objectives	1. Target market(s) 2. Marketing mix
Marketing Implementation	Outline of how the company will implement its marketing strategies	1. Marketing organization 2. Activities and responsibilities 3. Implementation timetable
Performance Evaluation	Explanation of how the company will evaluate the performance of the implemented plan	1. Performance standards 2. Financial controls 3. Monitoring procedures (audits)

marketing mix. The marketing implementation component of the plan outlines how marketing strategies will be implemented. The success of the marketing strategy depends on the feasibility of marketing implementation. Finally, the performance evaluation section establishes the standards for how results will be measured and evaluated, and what actions the company should take to reduce the differences between planned and actual performance.

It is important to note that most organizations use their own unique formats and terminology to describe the marketing plan. Every marketing plan is, and should be, unique to the organization for which it was created.

Creating and implementing a marketing plan allows the organization to achieve its marketing objectives and its business-unit and corporate goals. However, a marketing plan is only as good as the information it contains and the effort and creativity that went into its development. Therefore, the importance of having a good marketing information system that generates robust and reliable data cannot be overstated. Equally important is the role of managerial judgment throughout the strategic planning process. Although the creation of a marketing plan is an important milestone in strategic planning, it is by no means the final step. To succeed, a company must have a plan that is closely followed, yet flexible enough to allow for adjustments to reflect the changing marketing environment.

Summary

2-1 Explain the strategic planning process.

Through the process of strategic planning, a company identifies or establishes an organizational mission and goals, corporate strategy, marketing objectives, marketing strategy, and a marketing plan. To achieve its marketing objectives, an organization must develop a marketing strategy, which includes identifying a target market and creating a plan of action for developing, distributing, promoting, and pricing products that meet the needs of customers in that target market. The strategic planning process ultimately yields the framework for a marketing plan, a written document that specifies the activities to be performed for implementing and controlling an organization's marketing activities.

An organization's goals should align with its mission statement—a long-term view, or vision, of what the organization wants to become. A well-formulated mission statement gives an organization a clear purpose and direction, distinguishes it from competitors, provides direction for strategic planning, and fosters a focus on customers. An organization's goals, which focus on the end results sought, guide the remainder of its planning efforts.

Corporate strategy determines the means for using resources in the areas of production, finance, research and development, human resources, and marketing to reach the organization's goals. Business-unit strategy focuses on strategic business units (SBUs)—divisions, product lines, or other profit centers within the parent company used to define areas for consideration in a specific strategic marketing plan. The Boston Consulting Group's market growth/market share matrix integrates a company's products or SBUs into a single, overall matrix for evaluation to determine appropriate strategies for individual products and business units.

The marketing environment, including economic, competitive, political, legal and regulatory, sociocultural, and technological forces, can affect the resources available to a company to create favorable opportunities. Resources may help a firm develop core competencies, which are things that a company does extremely well, sometimes so well that it gives the company an advantage over its competition. When the right combination of circumstances and timing permits an organization to take action toward reaching a particular target market, a market opportunity exists. Strategic windows are temporary periods of optimal fit between the key requirements of a market and the particular capabilities of a company competing in that market. When a company matches a core competency to opportunities it has discovered in the marketplace, it is said to have a competitive advantage. A marketer can use SWOT analysis to assess a firm's ability to achieve a competitive advantage.

If marketers want to understand how the timing of entry into a marketplace can create competitive advantage, they can examine the comparative benefits of first-mover and late-mover advantages. The next phase of strategic planning involves the development of marketing objectives and strategies. Marketing objectives state what is to be accomplished through marketing activities, and should be consistent with both business-unit and corporate strategies. Marketing strategies, the most detailed and specific of the three levels of strategy, are composed of two elements: the selection of a target market and the creation of a marketing mix that will satisfy the needs of the target market members. The selection of a target market serves as the basis for the creation of the marketing mix to satisfy the needs of that market. Marketing-mix decisions should also be consistent with business-unit and corporate strategies and be flexible enough to respond to changes in market conditions, competition, and customer needs. Different elements of the marketing mix can be changed to accommodate different marketing strategies.

2-2 Identify what is necessary to effectively manage the implementation of marketing strategies.

Marketing implementation is the process of executing marketing strategies. Through planning, marketing managers provide purpose and direction for an organization's marketing efforts. Marketing managers must understand the problems and elements of marketing implementation before they can effectively implement specific marketing activities. Proper implementation requires creating efficient organizational structures, motivating marketing personnel, properly communicating within the marketing unit, coordinating the marketing activities, and establishing a timetable for implementation.

The marketing unit must have a coherent internal structure in order to organize direct marketing efforts. In a centralized organization, top-level managers delegate very little authority to lower levels, whereas in decentralized organizations, decision-making authority is delegated as far down the chain of command as possible. Motivating marketing employees is crucial to effectively implementing marketing strategies. Marketing managers learn marketing employees' needs and develop different methods to motivate those employees to help the organization meet its goals. Proper communication within the marketing unit is a key element in successful marketing implementation. Communication should move both down (from top management to the lower-level employees) and up (from lower-level employees to top management). Marketing managers must also be able to effectively coordinate marketing activities. This entails both coordinating the activities of the marketing staff within the firms and integrating those activities with the marketing actions of external organizations that are also involved in implementing the marketing strategies. Finally, successful marketing implementation requires that a timetable be established. Establishment of an implementation timetable involves several steps and ensures that employees know the specific activities for which they are responsible and the timeline for completing each activity. Completing all activities on schedule requires tight coordination among departments. Many organizations use sophisticated computer programs to plan the timing of marketing activities.

2-3 Describe the four major elements of strategic performance evaluation.

Strategic performance evaluation consists of establishing performance standards, analyzing actual performance, comparing actual performance with established standards, and modifying the marketing strategy when needed. When actual performance is compared with performance standards, marketers must determine whether a discrepancy exists and, if so, whether it requires corrective action, such as changing the performance standard or improving actual performance. Two possible ways to evaluate the actual performance of marketing strategies are sales analysis and marketing cost analysis.

Sales analysis uses sales figures to evaluate a firm's current performance. It is the most common method of evaluation because sales data are a good indication of the target market's reaction to a marketing mix. Marketers analyze sales by comparing current sales to forecasted sales, industry sales, specific competitors' sales, or the costs incurred to achieve the sales volume. Companies can analyze sales in terms of the dollar volume or market share.

Marketing cost analysis breaks down and classifies costs to determine which are associated with specific marketing efforts. Marketing cost analysis helps marketers decide how to best allocate the firm's marketing resources. Companies can use marketing cost analysis to identify profitable or unprofitable customers, products, and geographic areas. Marketers can compare current costs to previous years' costs, forecasted costs, industry averages, competitors' costs, or to the results generated by those costs. Companies should identify which of its costs are variable and therefore affected by sales or production volumes, and which are fixed and therefore not related to sales volume. Companies should also categorize costs based on whether or not they can be linked to a specific business function, specifically marketing.

2-4 Describe the development of a marketing plan.

A key component of marketing planning is the development of a marketing plan, which outlines all the activities necessary to implement marketing strategies. The plan fosters communication among employees, assigns responsibilities and schedules, specifies how resources are to be allocated to achieve objectives, and helps marketing managers monitor and evaluate the performance of a marketing strategy.

Go to www.cengagebrain.com for resources to help you master the content in this chapter as well as for materials that will expand your marketing knowledge!

Developing Your Marketing Plan

One of the foundations of a successful marketing strategy is a thorough analysis of your company. To make the best decisions about what products to offer, which markets to target, and how to reach those target market members, you must recognize your company's strengths and weaknesses. The information collected in this analysis should be referenced when making many of the decisions in your marketing plan. While writing the beginning of your plan, the information in this chapter can help you with the following issues:

1. Can you identify the core competencies of your company? Do they currently contribute to a competitive advantage? If not, what changes could your company make to establish a competitive advantage?
2. Conduct a SWOT analysis of your company to identify its strengths and weaknesses. Continue your analysis to include the business environment, discovering any opportunities that exist or threats that may impact your company.
3. Using the information from your SWOT analysis, have you identified any opportunities that are a good match with your company's core competencies? Likewise, have you discovered any weaknesses that could be converted to strengths through careful marketing planning?

The information obtained from these questions should assist you in developing various aspects of your marketing plan found in the "Interactive Marketing Plan" exercise at **www.cengagebrain.com**.

Important Terms

strategic marketing management 32
strategic planning 32
mission statement 32
corporate strategy 34
strategic business unit (SBU) 35
market 35
market share 35
market growth/market share matrix 35
core competencies 37
market opportunity 37
strategic windows 37
competitive advantage 37
SWOT analysis 37
first-mover advantage 38
late-mover advantage 39
marketing objective 40
marketing strategy 40
sustainable competitive advantage 42
marketing implementation 42
centralized organization 43
decentralized organization 43
strategic performance evaluation 45
performance standard 45
sales analysis 46
marketing cost analysis 47
marketing plan 48

Discussion and Review Questions

1. Identify the major components of strategic planning, and explain how they are interrelated.
2. Explain how an organization can create a competitive advantage at the corporate strategy level and at the business-unit strategy level.
3. What are some issues to consider in analyzing a company's resources and opportunities? How do these issues affect marketing objectives and marketing strategy?
4. What is SWOT analysis and why is it important?
5. How can an organization make its competitive advantages sustainable over time? How difficult is it to create sustainable competitive advantages?
6. How should organizations set marketing objectives?
7. What are the two major parts of a marketing strategy?
8. When considering the strategic planning process, what factors influence the development of a marketing strategy?
9. Identify and explain the major managerial actions that are a part of managing the implementation of marketing strategies.
10. Which element of the strategic planning process plays a major role in the establishment of performance standards? Explain.
11. When assessing actual performance of a marketing strategy, should a marketer perform marketing cost analysis? Why or why not?
12. Identify and explain the major components of a marketing plan.

Video Case 2.1

BoltBus Offers Affordable Transportation for Tech-Savvy Consumers

Bus service had a stodgy, old-fashioned image when BoltBus began developing a new marketing plan in 2007. Co-owned by Greyhound Lines and Peter Pan Bus Lines, BoltBus noticed that traditional full-fare bus companies were losing market share, and bus travel was on the decline. Time-pressured, price-conscious consumers simply didn't want to sit on a bus for hours or even days as it rattled from stop to stop along a lengthy route. Some of these consumers switched to discount airlines, searching hard for bargain fares to their destination. Others chose to hop on buses operated by a new breed of low-fare, city-to-city bus companies. Instead of operating from existing bus terminals, these bus companies kept costs low by picking up and dropping off passengers at designated street corners in each city.

The marketers at BoltBus recognized a market opportunity in the making. They planned to shake off the outdated image of intercity bus service and create a new premium express bus system for 21st-century travelers on a budget. The brand they chose, BoltBus, conveyed the key benefit of point-to-point speed, contrasted with the old strategy of long routes connecting multiple cities and towns.

© iStockphoto.com/wdstock

Looking at the market, they recognized that college students, young professionals, and young families were interested in comfortable, affordable alternatives to long car trips or pricier air, rail, and bus transportation. These tech-savvy consumers were accustomed to using computers and smartphones for all kinds of daily tasks, including price comparisons. So BoltBus decided to sell tickets through a dedicated website, bypassing the more costly method of selling tickets at bus stations. And, like competitors, BoltBus planned to avoid city bus stations in favor of curbside service, both to keep costs down and to make travel more convenient for customers.

One of the most important decisions BoltBus's marketers made was to keep fares low. During promotions, a limited number of tickets are priced as low as $1 for a one-way trip, an eye-catching figure for travelers on a budget. BoltBus adjusts its prices depending on demand and other factors. In general, the earlier customers buy their tickets, the lower the bus fare. Taking into account low promotional fares, the average BoltBus fare is about $20, quite affordable compared with typical intercity rail and air fares.

The marketers also decided to differentiate BoltBus by upgrading the experience to counter the perception that using intercity bus service means riding dingy, noisy old vehicles. BoltBus's gleaming red deluxe buses feature generous leg room, electric plugs at every seat for powering laptops and phones, and Wi-Fi service to keep passengers connected throughout the trip. BoltBus drivers are professional and friendly, adding to the sociable atmosphere once the bus gets rolling. BoltBus also offers a rewards program to reinforce customer loyalty.

Originally, BoltBus targeted consumers traveling between major East Coast cities, routing buses through a few suburban areas at the suggestion of customers. After establishing a reputation for affordable, comfortable, and speedy bus service, BoltBus expanded to the West Coast, scheduling service to Los Angeles, San Francisco, Portland, Seattle, and other cities. It also began offering limited service to Las Vegas, part of the long-range plan to add routes to interior cities.

Meanwhile, BoltBus's competitors weren't standing still. Megabus, founded a year earlier than BoltBus, operates luxury double-decker express buses equipped with Wi-Fi and power plugs at every seat. Year after year, Megabus has added intercity routes. Today, it serves more than 120 U.S. cities, coast to coast. Other competitors focus on specific city pairs, such as New York and Boston or Philadelphia and New York.

Greyhound, one of BoltBus's owners, has started a premium discount service called Greyhound Express, featuring free Wi-Fi and power plugs on deluxe buses traveling point-to-point between more than a dozen U.S. cities. In addition, Greyhound operates Crucero Direct, a bus service targeting Hispanic American consumers who travel between

Los Angeles, San Ysidro, and San Diego. It also operates special bus service from major cities to casinos in New Jersey, Connecticut, and Las Vegas.

BoltBus and its competitors have attracted so many customers that the bus ridership is no longer in decline. In fact, bus transportation is now the fastest-growing method of travel between U.S. cities. Watch for more growth as BoltBus drives ahead with future marketing plans.[19]

Questions for Discussion

1. How would you describe BoltBus's strengths, weaknesses, opportunities, and threats?
2. Where does BoltBus fit within Greyhound's levels of strategic planning? What challenges does this pose for Greyhound?
3. Why was BoltBus's selection of a target market so vital to the success of its marketing strategy?

Case 2.2

Netflix Uses Technology to Change How We Watch Videos

When Netflix was founded in 1997, the movie rental giant Blockbuster had thousands of stores from coast to coast, filled to the rafters with videocassettes ready for immediate rental to customers. Netflix had a different vision from this well-established, well-financed competitor. Looking at the recent development of DVD technology, Netflix saw an opportunity to change the way consumers rent movies. The entrepreneurial built its marketing strategy around the convenience and low cost of renting DVDs by mail, for one low monthly subscription fee.

Instead of going to a local store to pick out a movie on videocassette, subscribers logged onto the Netflix website to browse the DVD offerings and click to rent. Within a day or two, the DVD would arrive in the customer's mailbox, complete with a self-mailer to return the DVD. And, unlike any other movie rental service, Netflix customers were invited to rate each movie, after which they'd see recommendations tailored to their individual interests.

Fast-forward to the 21st century. Videocassettes are all but obsolete, and Blockbuster, once the dominant brand in movie rentals, is bankrupt. By eliminating the need for brick-and-mortar stores, Netflix has minimized its costs and extended its reach to any place that has postal service and Internet access. The company still rents DVDs by mail, but it has also taken advantage of changes in technology to add video streaming on demand. Now customers can stream movies and television programs to computers, television sets, videogame consoles, DVD players, smartphones, and other web-enabled devices. One plus: Streaming a movie costs Netflix less per customer than paying the postage to deliver and return a DVD to that customer.

Netflix made technology a core competency from the very beginning. Because the business has always been web-based, it can electronically monitor customer activity and analyze everything that customers view or click on. With this data, it can fine-tune the website, determine which movies are most popular among which segments, prepare for peak periods of online activity, and refine the recommendations it makes based on each individual's viewing history and interests. The company also uses its technical know-how to be sure the website looks good on any size screen, from a tiny smartphone to a large-screen television.

A few years ago, planning for a significant rise in demand for streaming entertainment, Netflix decided against investing in expanded systems for this purpose. Instead, it arranged for Amazon Web Services to provide the networking power for streaming. Now, on a typical night, Netflix streaming occupies up to 20,000 servers in Amazon data centers. Demand is so strong, in fact, that Netflix streaming accounts for about one-third of *all* Internet traffic to North American homes during the evening.

Although Blockbuster is no longer a competitive threat, Netflix does face competition from Amazon's own video streaming service, as well as from Hulu, YouTube, and others that stream entertainment content. It also competes with other entertainment providers, including cable, satellite, and broadcast television. To differentiate itself, Netflix has commissioned exclusive programming such as *House of Cards*, *Arrested Development*, and *Orange Is the New Black*. The cost to produce such programs runs to hundreds of millions of dollars. Yet Netflix plans to continue pouring money into exclusive content because of the payoff in positioning, positive publicity, and customer retention.

In addition, the way Netflix releases its exclusive programming reflects its in-depth knowledge of customer behavior. The company found, through data analysis, that customers often indulge in "binge watching" for a series they like, viewing episodes one after another in a short time. Based on this research, Netflix launched all 13 episodes of the inaugural season of *House of Cards* at one time, an industry first. Executives gathered at headquarters to monitor the introduction, cheering as thousands of customers streamed episode after episode. By the end of the first weekend, many customers had watched the entire series and shared their excitement via social media, encouraging others to subscribe and watch. When Netflix won multiple Emmy Awards for *House of Cards* later that year, it was another first—the first time any Internet company had been honored for the quality of its original programming.

One key measure of Netflix's growth is change in the number of monthly subscribers. At the end of 2010, it had 20 million monthly subscribers. These days, it serves more than 40 million subscribers in 41 countries, many of whom only stream movies on demand. Soon it hopes to expand into France, where it must navigate a complex web of rules aimed at protecting French movie producers and theaters from international competition. What's next for Netflix?[20]

Questions for Discussion

1. When Netflix originally entered the movie rental business, was it competing on the basis of a first-mover advantage or a late-mover advantage? Did it rely on the same advantage when it began streaming original content?
2. How does Netflix use its marketing mix to create a sustainable competitive advantage?
3. What performance standards do you think Netflix uses to evaluate the outcome of its marketing strategies?

Strategic Case 1

Consumers Take a Shine to Apple Inc.

Few companies have fans who sleep outside their doors in order to be the first to snag their newest products. However, this is a common occurrence at Apple Inc. The new iPad (Apple's third generation of its iPad product) sold 3 million units four days after the launch. Headquartered in Cupertino, California, Apple went from near bankruptcy, with a 1997 share price of $3.30, to a brand valued at $153 billion and a share price of more than $600.

Apple first entered the public sphere in 1976 with the release of the computer Apple I, created by Apple co-founders Steve Jobs and Steve Wozniak. A few innovations later, the company had more than $1 million in sales. Yet Apple's luck did not last. Its downturn started during the 1980s with a series of product flops and resulted in near bankruptcy for the company. The return of Steve Jobs, who had been ousted in 1985 due to internal conflicts in the company, instituted major changes for Apple. The company successfully adopted a market orientation in which it was able to gather intelligence about customers' current and future needs. For instance, the creation of the iPod and iTunes met customer needs for an efficient way to download a variety of music and listen to it on-the-go. Although it was once unheard of to access the Internet from a cell phone, Apple's iPhone made it commonplace. Apple's investment in the iPad set off a massive surge in demand for tablet computers. Apple has become skilled at recognizing strategic windows of opportunity and acting upon them before the competition.

Apple's Pricing and Promotion Strategies

In addition to its revolutionary products, Apple's success in pricing, promotion, and distribution have also contributed to its popularity. Apple products are traditionally priced high compared to competitors. For example, the new iPad retails for approximately $499 (although models with additional gigabytes are more expensive), while the Amazon Kindle Fire retails for $200. Apple's Mac computers are often more than $1,000. Yet rather than dissuading consumers from adopting the products, the high price point provides Apple with an image of prestige. Apple also stresses the convenience of its products as well as the revolutionary new capabilities they have to offer. Thus, it attempts to create value for customers, prompting them to pay more for Apple products than for those of its competitors.

Even with high-quality products, companies rarely achieve the success of Apple. Apple encourages demand for its products through several types of promotion, including word-of-mouth marketing. Early on, Apple supported "evangelism" of its products, even employing a chief evangelist to spread awareness about Apple and spur demand. Successful evangelists spread enthusiasm about a company among consumers, often through word-of-mouth marketing. These consumers in turn convinced other people about the value of the product. Through product evangelism, Apple created a "Mac cult"—loyal customers eager to share their enthusiasm about the company with others.

Apple's Impact on Marketing

Apple's corporate culture of innovation and loyalty has created a company that massively impacts the marketing strategies of other industries. For some, this impact has been largely negative. Apple's iPhone increased competition in the cellular and smartphone industries, and its iPad competes with electronic readers like Amazon's Kindle. Apple has also taken market share away from competitors such as Research in Motion (RIM). Many RIM BlackBerry users are opting to exchange their BlackBerrys for iPads or Android devices. On the other hand, many companies are seizing upon the opportunity to learn from Apple. One industry in which Apple has made great changes is in retail.

© iStockphoto.com/carterdayne

Apple stores differentiate themselves significantly from other retailers; in fact, Apple took the concept of retail in an entirely new direction. Everything in the Apple store is carefully planned to align with the company's image, from the glass-and-steel design reminiscent of the company's technology to the stations where customers can try out Apple products. Apple stores are a place where customers can both shop and play. Customer service is also important to the Apple store image. Employees are expected to speak with customers within two minutes of them entering the store. Each employee has received extensive training and often receives greater compensation than those at other retail stores to encourage better customer service.

Apple executives constantly look for ways to improve stores, enhance customer service, and increase the time that customers spend in-store. In 2011, the company began to install iPad stations within its stores. The iPads feature a customer service app designed to answer customer questions. If the customer requires additional assistance, he or she can press a help button on the app. The app changes the customer service experience because the representatives comes straight to the customer without the customer actively seeking out the sales representative.

Due to the immense success of Apple stores, other companies are attempting to imitate its retail model. Microsoft and Sony opened some of their own stores, and others use Apple products to enhance their businesses. For instance, some pharmaceutical and car salespeople have adopted the iPad to aid in business transactions, and some restaurants even use the iPad to show menu items.

Apple Going Forward

The death of Steve Jobs concerned some people about the future of Apple. To many customers, Jobs appeared to be a savior who brought the company back from near bankruptcy and who was the driving force behind its innovative products. In the past, whenever rumors of Jobs's health reached the public, Apple's share prices dropped. However, the company remains optimistic. Although Apple must fill its leadership gap and continue innovating to deliver on its promises of quality, the loyalty that fans feel for Apple remains high.[21]

Questions for Discussion

1. How has Apple implemented the marketing concept?
2. Describe the role of Apple stores as an important part of its marketing strategy.
3. What will Apple need to do to maintain product innovation and customer loyalty?

NOTES

[1] Adam Kleinberg, "How Agencies Can Fend Off the Threat of Marketing Services Moving In-House," *Advertising Age*, September 13, 2013, www.adage.com (accessed March 25, 2014); Beth Bulik, "Shutterfly Is Making Digital Photography Look Like a Snap," *Advertising Age*, March 25, 2013, p. 21; Karl Baker, "Shutterfly Soars on Full-Year Sales Forecast," *Bloomberg*, February 6, 2013, www.bloomberg.com (accessed March 25, 2014); Ashlee Vance, "Shutterfly's Improbably Long Lifespan," *Bloomberg Businessweek*, January 7, 2013, pp. 33–34.

[2] O. C. Ferrell and Michael Hartline, *Marketing Strategy*, 6th ed. (Mason, OH: Cengage Learning, 2014), Chapter 2, pp. 14–16.

[3] Christian Homburg, Karley Krohmer, and John P. Workman, Jr., "A Strategy Implementation Perspective of Market Orientation," *Journal of Business Research* 57 (2004): 1331–1340.

[4] "Our Starbucks Mission Statement," Starbucks, www.starbucks.com/about-us/company-information/mission-statement (accessed October 24, 2013).

[5] Stanley F. Slater, G. Tomas, M. Hult, and Eric M. Olson, "On the Importance of Matching Strategic Behavior and Target Market Selection to Business Strategy in High-Tech Markets," *Journal of the Academy of Marketing Science* 35 (2007): 5–17.

[6] Brian Womack, "Google Tops $800 for Record High as Mobile Search Gains," *Bloomberg Businessweek*, February 19, 2013, www.businessweek.com/news/2013-02-19/google-tops-800-for-record-high-as-mobile-search-gains (accessed November 13, 2013).

[7] Robert D. Buzzell, "The PIMS Program of Strategy Research: A Retrospective Appraisal," *Journal of Business Research* 57 (2004): 478–483.

[8] Square, Inc., https://squareup.com/news (accessed October 29, 2013); Milos Dunjic, "Why Starbucks Loves Working with Square," Finextra, October 12, 2013, www.finextra.com/community/FullBlog.aspx?blogid=8335 (accessed October 29, 2013).

[9] Derek F. Abell, "Strategic Windows," *Journal of Marketing* (July 1978): 21.

[10] Matthew Yglesias, "Bentonville Blues," *Slate*, October 21, 2013, www.slate.com/articles/business/moneybox/2013/10/_walmartlabs_why_walmart_won_t_succeed_in_e_commerce_even_if_it_does_everything.html (accessed November 13, 2013).

[11] Brian X. Chen, "Tablet Makers Gear Up for Latest Skirmish," *The New York Times*, October 21,2013, www.nytimes.com/2013/10/21/technology/tablet-makers-gear-up-for-latest-skirmish.html (accessed November 13, 2013).

[12] Norihiko Shirouzu, "Analysis: Oh, What a Sinking Feeling: Toyota Misfires with Chinese Buyers," *Reuters*, October 28, 2012, www.reuters.com/article/2012/10/28/us-toyota-china-idUSBRE89R0KB20121028 (accessed November 13, 2013).

[13] Claire Cain Miller, "Mobile Apps Drive Rapid Changes in Searches," *The New York Times*, January 7, 2013, www.nytimes.com/2013/01/08/business/mobile-apps-drive-rapid-changes-in-search-technology.html (accessed October 24, 2013).

[14] PR Newswire, "Food Network Star Alex Guarnaschelli Joins Glad® to Tackle Food Waste in Homes Across America," *Reuters*, October 16, 2013, www.reuters.com/article/2013/10/16/the-glad-products-idUSnPNCG98433+1e0+PRN20131016 (accessed November 13, 2013).

[15] Jose Pagliery, "Local Shops Fear Amazon's Expansion," *CNN Money*, September 4, 2013, http://money.cnn.com/2013/09/04/smallbusiness/amazon-expansion (accessed November 13, 2013).

[16] Jennifer Valentino-Devries and Jeremy Singer-Vine, "They Know What You're Shopping For," *The Wall Street Journal*, December 7, 2012, http://online.wsj.com/article/SB10001424127887324784404578143144132736214.html(accessed October 24, 2013).

[17] Project Professional 2013, http://office.microsoft.com/en-us/project/professional-project-management-desktop-software-project-professional-FX103797571.aspx (accessed November 12, 2013).

[18] Bazaarvoice, www.bazaarvoice.com (accessed October 24, 2013).

[19] Tim O'Reiley, "BoltBus Beginning LV-L.A. Service with Promotional Fares," *Las Vegas Review-Journal*, December 11, 2013, www.reviewjournal.com (accessed January 23, 2014); Linda Zavoral, "BoltBus to Launch Bay Area–Los Angeles Service," *San Jose Mercury News*, October 18, 2013, www.mercurynews.com (accessed January 23, 2014); Josh Sanburn, "Reinventing the Wheels," *Time*, November 15, 2012, http://business.time.com (accessed January 23, 2014); Jeff Plungis, "Megabus, BoltBus Overcome U.S. Stigma with Cheap Travel," *Bloomberg*, January 7, 2013, www.bloomberg.com (accessed January 23, 2014); "BoltBus" Cengage video.

[20] Julien Ponthus and Leila Abboud, "Netflix Meets with Officials on French Launch," *Reuters*, December 4, 2013, www.reuters.com (accessed March 18, 2014); Brian Stelter, "Netflix Won't Release 'Turbo: Fast' for Binge Viewing," *CNN Money*, December 3, 2013, http://money.cnn.com (accessed March 18, 2014); Ashlee Vance, "The Man Who Ate the Internet," *Bloomberg Businessweek*, May 9, 2013, pp. 56–62; Julia Boorstin, "Exclusive: Netflix CEO Reed Hastings Talks Strategy," *CNBC*, July 23, 2013, www.cnbc.com (accessed March 18, 2014).

[21] Scott Martin, "How Apple Rewrote the Rules of Retailing," *USA Today*, May 19, 2011, p. 1B; Millward Brown Optimor, *BrandZ Top 100 2011*, www.millwardbrown.com/libraries/optimor_brandz_files/2011_brandz_top100_chart.sflb.ash (accessed March 4, 2014); "World's Most Admired Companies: Apple," *CNN Money*, http://money.cnn.com/magazines/fortune/most-admired/2013/list; Martyn Williams, "Timeline: iTunes Store at 10 Billion," *ComputerWorld*, February 24, 2010, www.computerworld.com/s/article/9162018/Timeline_iTunes_Store_at_10_billion (accessed March 4, 2014); Nilofer Merchant, "Apple's Startup Culture," *Bloomberg Businessweek*, June 24, 2010, www.businessweek.com/innovate/content/jun2010/id20100610_525759.htm (accessed March 4, 2014); "The Evangelist's Evangelist," Creating Customer Evangelists, www.creatingcustomerevangelists.com/resources/evangelists/guy_kawasaki.asp (accessed March 4, 2014); "Apple, Inc. (APPL)," *Yahoo! Finance*, http://finance.yahoo.com/q?s=AAPL (accessed March 4, 2014).

Feature Notes

[a] Richard Weiss, "Will Heavy Metal Lure Euro Cruisers Back?" *Bloomberg Businessweek*, May 27, 2013, pp. 24–26; Joe Yonan, "On Celebrity's 'Top Chef' Cruise, Food and Fun Are on the Menu," *The Washington Post*, September 19, 2013, www.washingtonpost.com (accessed February 22, 2014); Carol Christian, "Carnival Cruise's New Ads to Feature 'Real' Photos from Social Media," *Houston Chronicle*, September 19, 2013, www.chron.com; Fran Golden, "Cruise Lines Ramp Up Kid-Friendly Features as Family Market Soars," *Travel Market Report*, January 21, 2013, www.travelmarketreport.com (accessed February 22, 2014).

[b] Marc Gunther, "Unilever's CEO Has a Green Thumb," *Fortune*, June 10, 2013, pp. 124–130; "Unilever Enters Water Business with Purifier," *Business Daily (Kenya)*, April 29, 2013, www.nation.co.ke (accessed January 29, 2014); Ajita Shashidhar, "HUL Pureit Water Filters Are Touching Millions of Lives Worldwide," *Business Today (India)*, June 19, 2013, http://businesstoday.intoday.in (accessed January 29, 2014).

part 2

Environmental Forces and Social and Ethical Responsibilities

PART 2 deals with the marketing environment, social responsibility, and marketing ethics. CHAPTER 3 examines competitive, economic, political, legal and regulatory, technological, and sociocultural forces in the marketing environment, which can have profound effects on marketing strategies. CHAPTER 4 explores the role of social responsibility and ethical issues in marketing decisions.

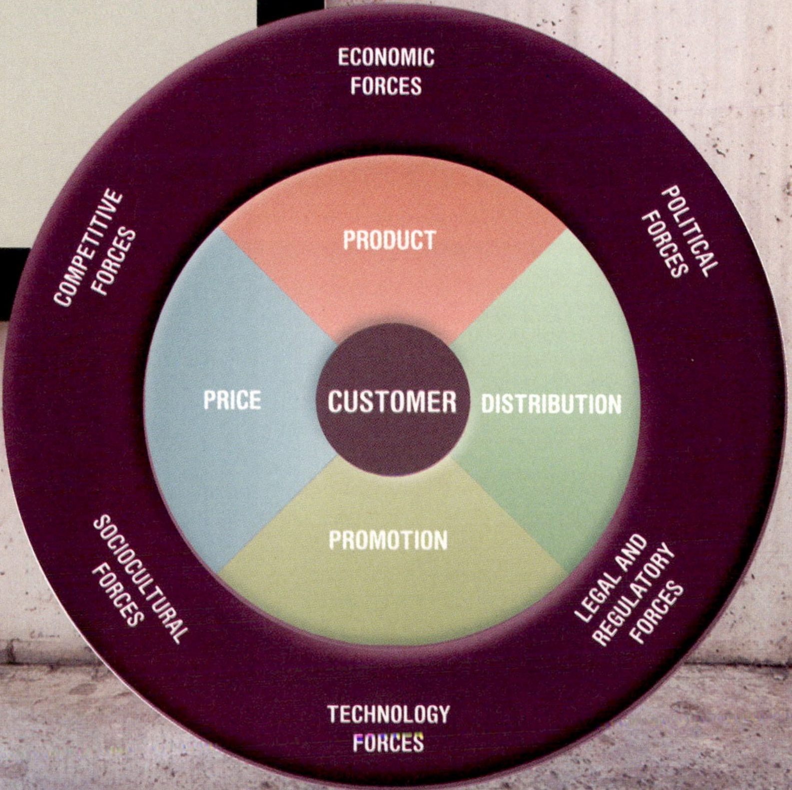

ECONOMIC FORCES
POLITICAL FORCES
LEGAL AND REGULATORY FORCES
TECHNOLOGY FORCES
SOCIOCULTURAL FORCES
COMPETITIVE FORCES
PRODUCT
PRICE
CUSTOMER
DISTRIBUTION
PROMOTION

chapter 3

The Marketing Environment

OBJECTIVES

3-1 Summarize why it is important to examine and respond to the marketing environment.

3-2 Explain how competitive factors affect an organization's ability to compete.

3-3 Articulate how economic factors influence a customer's ability and willingness to buy products.

3-4 Identify the types of political forces in the marketing environment.

3-5 Explain how laws, government regulations, and self-regulatory agencies affect marketing activities.

3-6 Describe how new technology impacts marketing and society.

3-7 Outline the sociocultural issues marketers must deal with as they make decisions.

MARKETING INSIGHTS

The Marketing Success of Goya Foods

In 1936, Spanish immigrant Prudencio Unanue Ortiz identified an opportunity for selling products to the Hispanic market. He created Goya foods after buying the rights to the name *Goya* from a Moroccan sardine company. At first, many stores refused to carry his products. Yet Ortiz recognized that food was a deep-rooted cultural tradition among immigrants. As immigrants from Puerto Rico, the Dominican Republic, Cuba, and other Hispanic cultures began entering New York City, Ortiz developed products that appealed to their native tastes. For instance, the firm sells 40 different bean varieties to appeal to the tastes of those originating from different global regions.

Today the marketing environment for Hispanic food is far different from when Goya Foods began. With more non-Hispanics purchasing Hispanic food items, Goya has begun targeting this demographic by offering tortillas, taco kits, and desired Mexican sides such as jalapeño peppers and ranchero refried pinto beans. Goya also incorporates technology into its marketing campaigns by working with Foodnetwork.com and blogging site Foodbuzz.com to create awareness of the brand. Through these media, the company was able to show non-Latinos how to incorporate Goya foods into their cooking so that consumers could see it was not a special brand but one that could frequently appear on the dinner table.

The company continues to expand its reach, even partnering with Beech-Nut Nutrition to develop Beech-Nut Goya, Hispanic food for babies. As a result of its strong marketing initiatives and ability to recognize new market opportunities, Goya increased its market share to 25 percent and surpassed $1.3 billion in sales to become the largest and fastest growing Hispanic-owned food company in the United States.[1]

Companies like Goya Foods are modifying marketing strategies in response to changes in the marketing environment. Because recognizing and addressing such changes in the marketing environment are crucial to marketing success, we will focus in detail on the forces that contribute to these changes.

This chapter explores the competitive, economic, political, legal and regulatory, technological, and sociocultural forces that constitute the marketing environment. First, we define the marketing environment and consider why it is critical to scan and analyze it. Next, we discuss the effects of competitive forces and explore the influence of general economic conditions: prosperity, recession, depression, and recovery. We also examine buying power and look at the forces that influence consumers' willingness to spend. We then discuss the political forces that generate government actions that affect marketing activities and examine the effects of laws and regulatory agencies on these activities. After analyzing the major dimensions of the technological forces in the environment, we consider the impact of sociocultural forces on marketing efforts.

3-1 EXAMINING AND RESPONDING TO THE MARKETING ENVIRONMENT

The marketing environment consists of external forces that directly or indirectly influence an organization's acquisition of inputs (human, financial, natural resources and raw materials, and information) and creation of outputs (goods, services, or ideas). As we saw in Chapter 1, the marketing environment includes six such forces: competitive, economic, political, legal and regulatory, technological, and sociocultural.

Whether fluctuating rapidly or slowly, environmental forces are always dynamic. Changes in the marketing environment create uncertainty, threats, and opportunities for marketers. Firms providing digital products such as software, music, and movies face many environmental threats as well as opportunities. Advancing technology provides digital delivery of these products, which is an efficient and effective way to reach global markets. On the other hand, technology has made it easier for file-sharing websites to infringe on others' intellectual property. The movie and music industries want more effective legislation in place to crack down on the theft of their products. Most of these developments involve trying to influence controls to stop this threat, including arresting individuals involved in the development of these piracy sites.[2] The marketing environment constantly fluctuates, requiring marketers to monitor it regularly.

Although the future is sometimes hard to predict, marketers try to forecast what may happen. We can say with certainty that marketers continue to modify their marketing strategies and plans in response to dynamic environmental forces. Consider how technological changes have affected the products offered by the mobile phone industry and how the public's growing concern with health and fitness has influenced the products of clothing, food, exercise equipment, and health-care companies. Marketing managers who fail to recognize changes in environmental forces leave their firms unprepared to capitalize on marketing opportunities or to cope with threats created by those changes. Consider Kodak's failure to make the switch from film development to digital photos. Although Kodak helped to develop digital photography, its failure to capitalize on this new innovation led the firm to file for bankruptcy in 2012. It emerged from bankruptcy the next year and has since restructured to focus on packaging, printing, and graphic communications services. Monitoring the environment is crucial to an organization's survival and to the long-term achievement of its goals.

3-1a Environmental Scanning and Analysis

environmental scanning The process of collecting information about forces in the marketing environment

To monitor changes in the marketing environment effectively, marketers engage in environmental scanning and analysis. **Environmental scanning** is the process of collecting information about forces in the marketing environment. Scanning involves observation; secondary sources such as business, trade, government, and general-interest publications; and marketing research. The Internet has become a popular scanning tool because it makes data more accessible and allows companies to gather needed information quickly. Environmental scanning gives companies an edge over competitors in allowing them to take advantage of current trends. However, simply gathering information about competitors and customers is not enough; companies must know *how* to use that information in the strategic planning process. Managers must be careful not to gather so much information that sheer volume makes analysis impossible.

Environmental analysis is the process of assessing and interpreting the information gathered through environmental scanning. A manager evaluates the information for accuracy, tries to resolve inconsistencies in the data, and, if warranted, assigns significance to the findings. Evaluating this information should enable the manager to identify potential threats and opportunities linked to environmental changes. Understanding the current state of the marketing environment and recognizing threats and opportunities that might arise from changes within it help companies in their strategic planning. A threat could be rising interest rates or commodity prices. An opportunity could be increases in consumer income, decreases in the unemployment rate, or adoption of new technology. In particular, environmental analysis can help marketing managers assess the performance of current marketing efforts and develop future marketing strategies.

3-1b Responding to Environmental Forces

Marketing managers take two general approaches to environmental forces: accepting them as uncontrollable or attempting to influence and shape them. An organization that views environmental forces as uncontrollable remains passive and reactive toward the environment. Instead of trying to influence forces in the environment, its marketing managers adjust current marketing strategies to environmental changes. They approach with caution market opportunities discovered through environmental scanning and analysis. On the other hand, marketing managers who believe environmental forces can be shaped adopt a more proactive approach. Consequently, if a market is blocked by traditional environmental constraints, proactive marketing managers may apply economic, psychological, political, and promotional skills to gain access to and operate within it. The meat industry, for instance, tried to lobby against labeling their products with country-of-origin information. Microsoft, Intel, and Google have responded to political, legal, and regulatory concerns about their power in the computer industry by communicating the value of their competitive approaches to various publics. The computer giants contend that their competitive success results in superior products for their customers.

A proactive approach can be constructive and bring desired results. To influence environmental forces, marketing managers seek to identify market opportunities or to extract greater benefits relative to costs from existing market opportunities. The advertisement launched by the National Highway Traffic Safety Commission attempts to bring about desired results by showing the dangers of texting and driving. The advertisement purposefully covers the face of the man texting to demonstrate how texting can distract or "blind" people when they are on the road. Political action is another way to affect environmental forces. The pharmaceutical industry, for example, has lobbied very effectively for fewer restrictions on prescription drug marketing. However, managers must recognize that there are limits to the degree that environmental forces can be shaped. Although an organization may be able to influence legislation through lobbying—as the movie and music industries are doing to try and stop the piracy of their products—it is unlikely that a single organization can significantly change major economic factors such as recessions, interest rates, or commodity prices.

Whether to take a reactive or a proactive approach to environmental forces is a decision for a firm to make based on its strengths or weaknesses. For some organizations, the passive, reactive approach is more appropriate, but for others the aggressive approach leads to better performance. Selection of a particular approach depends on an organization's

environmental analysis The process of assessing and interpreting the information gathered through environmental scanning

AP Images/PRNewsFoto/Outdoor Advertising Association of America

Responding to the Marketing Environment
The sponsors of this ad are trying to educate drivers about the dangers associated with texting and driving.

managerial philosophies, objectives, financial resources, customers, and human resources skills, as well as on the environment within which the organization operates. Both organizational factors and managers' personal characteristics affect the variety of responses to changing environmental conditions. Microsoft, for instance, can take a proactive approach because of its financial resources and the highly visible image of its founder, Bill Gates. However, Microsoft has also been the target of various lawsuits regarding anticompetitive practices, demonstrating that even Microsoft is limited in how far it can influence the business environment.

In the remainder of this chapter, we explore in greater detail the six environmental forces—competitive, economic, political, legal and regulatory, technological, and sociocultural—that interact to create opportunities and threats that must be considered in strategic planning.

3-2 COMPETITIVE FORCES

Few firms, if any, operate free of competition. In fact, for most goods and services, customers have many alternatives from which to choose. Although the five best-selling soft drinks in the United States are Coke, Diet Coke, Pepsi-Cola, Mountain Dew, and Dr Pepper, soft-drink sales in general have flattened as consumers have turned to alternatives such as bottled water, flavored water, fruit juice, and iced tea products.[3] Thus, when marketing managers define the target market(s) their firm will serve, they simultaneously establish a set of competitors.[4] In addition, marketing managers must consider the type of competitive structure in which the firm operates. In this section, we examine types of competition and competitive structures, as well as the importance of monitoring competitors' actions.

competition Other organizations that market products that are similar to or can be substituted for a marketer's products in the same geographic area

brand competitors Firms that market products with similar features and benefits to the same customers at similar prices

product competitors Firms that compete in the same product class but market products with different features, benefits, and prices

3-2a Types of Competitors

Broadly speaking, all firms compete with one another for customers' dollars. More practically, however, a marketer generally defines **competition** as other firms that market products that are similar to or can be substituted for its products in the same geographic area. These competitors can be classified into one of four types. **Brand competitors** market products with similar features and benefits to the same customers at similar prices. For instance, a thirsty, calorie-conscious customer may choose a diet soda such as Diet Coke or Diet Pepsi from the soda machine. However, these sodas face competition from other types of beverages. **Product competitors** compete in the same product class but market products with different features, benefits, and prices. The thirsty dieter might purchase iced tea, juice, a sports beverage, or bottled water instead of a soda.

© iStockPhoto/powerofforever

© iStockPhoto.com/powerofforever

Brand Competition
Diet Coke and Diet Pepsi compete head-to-head in the soft-drink market.

generic competitors Firms that provide very different products that solve the same problem or satisfy the same basic customer need

total budget competitors Firms that compete for the limited financial resources of the same customers

Generic competitors provide very different products that solve the same problem or satisfy the same basic customer need. Our dieter might simply have a glass of water from the kitchen tap to satisfy her thirst. **Total budget competitors** compete for the limited financial resources of the same customers.[5] Total budget competitors for Diet Coke, for example, might include gum, a newspaper, and bananas. Although all four types of competition can affect a firm's marketing performance, brand competitors are the most significant because

Emerging Trends

Ticketmaster's New Strategy to Address Competition

After many years of lobbying regulatory officials to restrict ticket scalpers, Ticketmaster is taking a new approach with its competition-inclusive marketing strategy. Scalpers resell tickets for admission to events at higher prices, without sharing profits with the original seller. Ticketmaster has developed a platform called TM+ that allows scalpers to post their tickets on the Ticketmaster website alongside previously un-purchased tickets. Resellers can determine their own price as long as it is not less than face value. The resellers' tickets are designated on the website so consumers can choose from whom they purchase tickets. This increases competition because customers can see if the resellers are charging significantly more for seats that are the same or similar to others.

To meet the competitive challenge of convincing resellers to post their tickets on their website rather than on other sites such as StubHub, Ticketmaster is offering the use of software without a fee and adding purchase fees to the buyer's price rather than to the seller. Some worry, however, that Ticketmaster may engage in unfair price competition with its new platform and continue to hold tickets for preferred clients. Additionally, other consumers are concerned that tickets will now cost more than they did before. Resellers generally price their tickets higher than face value, and Ticketmaster marks the price up to three times higher to include various fees for processing the tickets.[a]

buyers typically see the different products of these firms as direct substitutes for one another. Consequently, marketers tend to concentrate environmental analyses on brand competitors.

3-2b Types of Competitive Structures

The number of firms that supply a product may affect the strength of competitors. When just one or a few firms control supply, competitive factors exert a different form of influence on marketing activities than when many competitors exist. Table 3.1 presents four general types of competitive structures: monopoly, oligopoly, monopolistic competition, and pure competition.

A **monopoly** exists when an organization offers a product that has no close substitutes, making that organization the sole source of supply. Because the organization has no competitors, it controls the supply of the product completely and, as a single seller, can erect barriers to potential competitors. In reality, most monopolies surviving today are local utilities, which are heavily regulated by local, state, or federal agencies. These monopolies are tolerated because of the tremendous financial resources needed to develop and operate them; few organizations can obtain the financial or political resources to mount any competition against a local water supplier. On the other hand, competition is increasing in the electric and cable television industries.

monopoly A competitive structure in which an organization offers a product that has no close substitutes, making that organization the sole source of supply

oligopoly A competitive structure in which a few sellers control the supply of a large proportion of a product

monopolistic competition A competitive structure in which a firm has many potential competitors and tries to develop a marketing strategy to differentiate its product

pure competition A market structure characterized by an extremely large number of sellers, none strong enough to significantly influence price or supply

An **oligopoly** exists when a few sellers control the supply of a large proportion of a product. In this case, each seller considers the reactions of other sellers to changes in marketing activities. Products facing oligopolistic competition may be homogeneous, such as aluminum, or differentiated, such as packaged delivery services. Usually barriers of some sort make it difficult to enter the market and compete with oligopolies. For example, because of the enormous financial outlay required, few companies or individuals could afford to enter the oil-refining or steel-producing industry. Moreover, some industries demand special technical or marketing skills, a qualification that deters the entry of many potential competitors.

Monopolistic competition exists when a firm with many potential competitors attempts to develop a marketing strategy to differentiate its product. The insurance industry, for instance, is highly competitive, requiring companies to market the benefits of their products. Geico differentiates their products by promoting their value in a tagline from its commercial "15 minutes can save you 15% or more on your car insurance." In monopolistic competition markets, such as insurance, price can effectively differentiate the products.

Pure competition, if it existed at all, would entail an extremely large number of sellers, none of which could significantly influence price or supply. Products would be homogeneous,

Table 3.1 Selected Characteristics of Competitive Structures

Type of Structure	Number of Competitors	Ease of Entry into Market	Product	Examples
Monopoly	One	Many barriers	Almost no substitutes	Water utilities
Oligopoly	Few	Some barriers	Homogeneous or differentiated (with real or perceived differences)	UPS, FedEx, U.S. Postal Service (package delivery)
Monopolistic competition	Many	Few barriers	Product differentiation, with many substitutes	Wrangler, Levi Strauss (jeans)
Pure competition	Unlimited	No barriers	Homogeneous products	Agricultural corn market

and entry into the market would be easy. The closest thing to an example of pure competition is an unregulated farmers' market, where local growers gather to sell their produce. Commodities such as soybeans, corn, and wheat have their markets subsidized or regulated by the government.

Pure competition is an ideal at one end of the continuum, and a monopoly is at the other end. Most marketers function in a competitive environment somewhere between these two extremes.

3-2c Monitoring Competition

Marketers need to monitor the actions of major competitors to determine what specific strategies competitors are using and how those strategies affect their own. Competitive intensity influences a firm's strategic approach to markets.[6] Price is one marketing strategy variable that most competitors monitor. When Delta or Southwest Airlines lowers its fare on a route, most major airlines attempt to match the price. Monitoring guides marketers in developing competitive advantages and in adjusting current marketing strategies and planning new ones. When an airline such as Southwest acquires a competitor such as AirTran, less competition exists in the market.

In monitoring competition, it is not enough to analyze available information; the firm must develop a system for gathering ongoing information about competitors and potential competitors. Information about competitors allows marketing managers to assess the performance of their own marketing efforts and to recognize the strengths and weaknesses in their own marketing strategies. In addition, organizations are rewarded for taking risks and dealing with the uncertainty created by inadequate information.[7] Data about market shares, product movement, sales volume, and expenditure levels can be useful. However, accurate information on these matters is often difficult to obtain.

Monopolistic Competition
Geico uses price promotion to help differentiate its products from others in the monopolistic market for insurance.

3-3 ECONOMIC FORCES

Economic forces in the marketing environment influence both marketers' and customers' decisions and activities. In this section, we examine the effects of general economic conditions as well as buying power and the factors that affect people's willingness to spend.

3-3a Economic Conditions

The overall state of the economy fluctuates in all countries. Changes in general economic conditions affect (and are affected by) supply and demand, buying power, willingness to spend, consumer expenditure levels, and intensity of competitive behavior. Therefore, current economic conditions and changes in the economy have a broad impact on the success of organizations' marketing strategies.

Fluctuations in the economy follow a general pattern, often referred to as the **business cycle**. In the traditional view, the business cycle consists of four stages: prosperity, recession, depression, and recovery. From a global perspective, different regions of the world may be in different stages of the business cycle during the same period. Throughout much of the 1990s, for example, the United States experienced growth (prosperity). The U.S. economy began to slow in 2000, with a brief recession, especially in high-technology industries, in 2001. Many

business cycle A pattern of economic fluctuations that has four stages: prosperity, recession, depression, and recovery

dot-com or Internet companies failed. Japan, however, endured a recession during most of the 1990s and into the early 2000s. Economic variation in the global marketplace creates a planning challenge for firms that sell products in multiple markets around the world. In 2008, the United States experienced an economic downturn due to higher energy prices, falling home values, increasing unemployment, the financial crisis in the banking industry, and fluctuating currency values. That recession was the longest since the Great Depression of the 1930s.

During **prosperity**, unemployment is low and total income is relatively high. Assuming a low inflation rate, this combination ensures high buying power. If the economic outlook remains prosperous, consumers generally are willing to buy. In the prosperity stage, marketers often expand their product offerings to take advantage of increased buying power. They can sometimes capture a larger market share by intensifying distribution and promotion efforts.

Because unemployment rises during a **recession**, total buying power declines. These factors, usually accompanied by consumer pessimism, often stifle both consumer and business spending. As buying power decreases, many customers may become more price and value conscious, and look for basic, functional products. When buying power decreased during the most recent recession, department store sales dropped. Consumers began shopping at off-price retailers such as T.J. Maxx and Ross. Even during the recovery cycle, many consumers opted to continue shopping at off-price retailers to take advantage of the lower prices.[8] The Dollar Store, Dollar Tree, Family Dollar, and Dollar General are among the fastest growing discount and general merchandise chains.[9]

During a recession, some firms make the mistake of drastically reducing their marketing efforts, thus damaging their ability to survive. Obviously, however, marketers should consider some revision of their marketing activities during a recessionary period. Because consumers are more concerned about the functional value of products, a company should focus its marketing research on determining precisely what functions buyers want and make sure those functions become part of its products. Promotional efforts should emphasize value and utility. Marketers must also carefully monitor the needs and expectations of their companies' target markets.

A prolonged recession may become a **depression**, a period in which unemployment is extremely high, wages are very low, total disposable income is at a minimum, and consumers lack confidence in the economy. A depression usually lasts for an extended period, often years, and has been experienced by Russia, Mexico, and Brazil in the 2000s. Although evidence supports maintaining or even increasing spending during economic slowdowns, marketing budgets are more likely to be cut in the face of an economic downturn.

During **recovery**, the economy moves from recession or depression toward prosperity. During this period, high unemployment begins to decline, total disposable income increases, and the economic gloom that reduced consumers' willingness to buy subsides. Both the ability and the willingness to buy rise. Marketers face some problems during recovery; hence, it is difficult to ascertain how quickly and to what level prosperity will return. Large firms such as Procter & Gamble must try to assess how quickly consumers will increase their purchase of higher-priced brands versus economy brands. In this stage, marketers should maintain as much flexibility in their marketing strategies as possible so they can make the needed adjustments.

prosperity A stage of the business cycle characterized by low unemployment and relatively high total income, which together ensure high buying power (provided the inflation rate stays low)

recession A stage of the business cycle during which unemployment rises and total buying power declines, stifling both consumer and business spending

depression A stage of the business cycle when unemployment is extremely high, wages are very low, total disposable income is at a minimum, and consumers lack confidence in the economy

recovery A stage of the business cycle in which the economy moves from recession or depression toward prosperity

buying power Resources, such as money, goods, and services, that can be traded in an exchange

income For an individual, the amount of money received through wages, rents, investments, pensions, and subsidy payments for a given period

3-3b Buying Power

The strength of a person's **buying power** depends on economic conditions and the size of the resources—money, goods, and services that can be traded in an exchange—that enable the individual to make purchases. The major financial sources of buying power are income, credit, and wealth. For an individual, **income** is the amount of money received through wages, rents, investments, pensions, and subsidy payments for a given period, such as a month or a year. Normally this money is allocated among taxes, spending for goods and services, and savings. The median annual household income in the United States is approximately \$51,017.[10] However, because of differences in people's educational levels, abilities, occupations, and wealth, income is not equally distributed in this country.

Marketers are most interested in the amount of money left after payment of taxes because this **disposable income** is used for spending or saving. Because disposable income is a ready source of buying power, the total amount available in a nation is important to marketers. Several factors determine the size of total disposable income. One is the total amount of income, which is affected by wage levels, the rate of unemployment, interest rates, and dividend rates. Because disposable income is income left after taxes are paid, the number and amount of taxes directly affect the size of total disposable income. When taxes rise, disposable income declines; when taxes fall, disposable income increases.

Disposable income that is available for spending and saving after an individual has purchased the basic necessities of food, clothing, and shelter is called **discretionary income**. People use discretionary income to purchase entertainment, vacations, automobiles, education, pets, furniture, appliances, and so on. Changes in total discretionary income affect sales of these products, especially automobiles, furniture, large appliances, and other costly durable goods. Gucci Group sells products that are often purchased with discretionary income. They chose actor James Franco to wear their Gucci Bamboo sunglasses, which sell for more than $600. By using a popular celebrity to model its sunglasses, Gucci hopes to create desirability and an image of exclusivity for the product.

Discretionary Income
Gucci hopes using a popular celebrity to model its Gucci Bamboo Sunglasses will encourage consumers to spend their discretionary income on this luxury product.

Credit enables people to spend future income now or in the near future. However, credit increases current buying power at the expense of future buying power. Several factors determine whether people use, acquire, or forgo credit. First, credit must be available. Interest rates also affect buyers' decisions to use credit, especially for expensive purchases such as homes, appliances, and automobiles. When interest rates are low, the total cost of automobiles and houses becomes more affordable. In the United States, low interest rates in the 2000s induced many buyers to take on the high level of debt necessary to own a home, fueling a tremendous boom in the construction of new homes and the sale of older homes. In contrast, when interest rates are high, consumers are more likely to delay buying such expensive items. Use of credit is also affected by credit terms, such as size of the down payment and amount and number of monthly payments.

Wealth is the accumulation of past income, natural resources, and financial resources. It exists in many forms, including cash, securities, savings accounts, gold, jewelry, and real estate. Global wealth is increasing, with 16 million millionaires worldwide.[11] Like income, wealth is unevenly distributed. A person can have a high income and very little wealth. It is also possible, but not likely, for a person to have great wealth but little income. The significance of wealth to marketers is that as people become wealthier, they gain buying power in three ways: They can use their wealth to make current purchases, to generate income, and to acquire large amounts of credit.

Income, credit, and wealth equip consumers with buying power to purchase goods and services. Marketing managers must be aware of current levels and expected changes in buying power in their own markets because buying power directly affects the types and quantities of goods and services customers purchase. Information about buying power is available from government sources, trade associations, and research agencies. One of the most current and comprehensive sources of buying-power data is the *Sales & Marketing Management Survey of Buying Power,* published annually by *Sales & Marketing Management* magazine. Having buying power, however, does not mean consumers will buy. They must also be willing to use their buying power.

disposable income After-tax income

discretionary income Disposable income available for spending and saving after an individual has purchased the basic necessities of food, clothing, and shelter

wealth The accumulation of past income, natural resources, and financial resources

3-3c Willingness to Spend

People's **willingness to spend**—their inclination to buy because of expected satisfaction from a product—is, to some degree, related to their ability to buy. That is, people are sometimes more willing to buy if they have the buying power. However, a number of other elements also influence willingness to spend. Some elements affect specific products; others influence spending in general. A product's price and value influence almost all of us. Cross pens, for instance, appeal to customers who are willing to spend more for fine writing instruments even when lower-priced pens are readily available. The amount of satisfaction received from a product already owned may also influence customers' desire to buy other products. Satisfaction depends not only on the quality of the currently owned product but also on numerous psychological and social forces. The American Customer Satisfaction Index, computed by the National Quality Research Center at the University of Michigan (see Figure 3.1), offers an indicator of customer satisfaction with a wide variety of businesses. The American Customer Satisfaction Index helps marketers to understand how consumers perceive their industries and businesses and adapt their marketing strategies accordingly.

Factors that affect consumers' general willingness to spend are expectations about future employment, income levels, prices, family size, and general economic conditions. Willingness to spend ordinarily declines if people are unsure whether or how long they will be employed, and it usually increases if people are reasonably certain of higher incomes in the future. Expectations of rising prices in the near future may also increase willingness to spend in the present. For a given level of buying power, the larger the family, the greater the willingness to spend. One reason for this relationship is that as the size of a family increases, more dollars must be spent to provide the basic necessities to sustain family members.

willingness to spend
An inclination to buy because of expected satisfaction from a product, influenced by the ability to buy and numerous psychological and social forces

Figure 3.1 National Customer Satisfaction Index

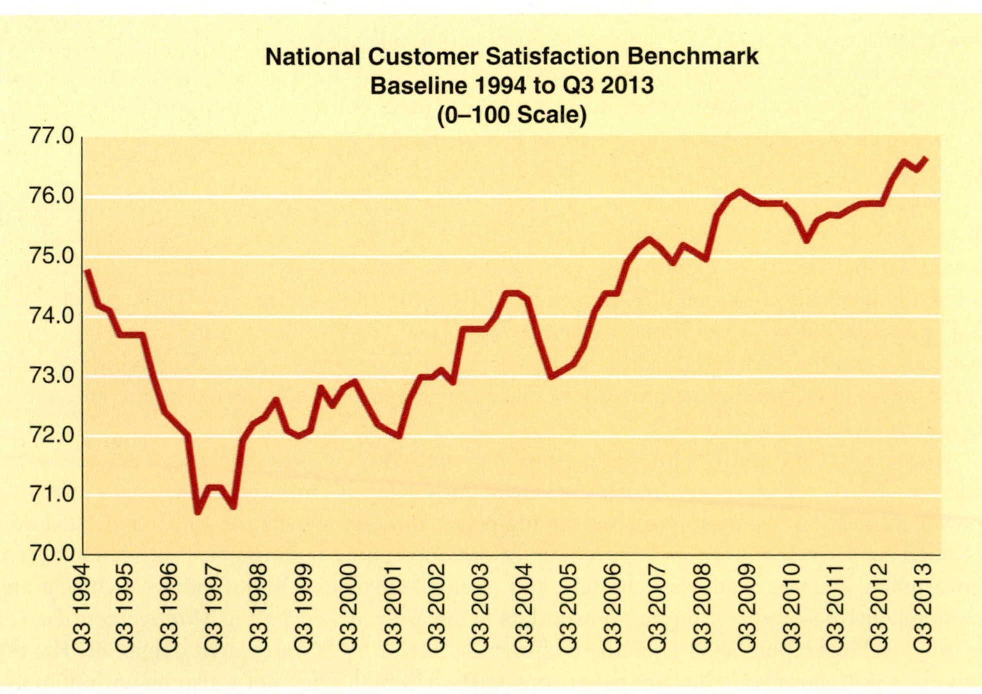

Source: Based on American Customer Satisfaction Index, "Quarterly Benchmarks," http://www.theacsi.org/national-economic-indicator/national-quarterly-benchmarks. (accessed February 3, 2014).

3-4 POLITICAL FORCES

Political, legal, and regulatory forces of the marketing environment are closely interrelated. Legislation is enacted, legal decisions are interpreted by courts, and regulatory agencies are created and operated, for the most part, by elected or appointed officials. Legislation and regulations (or the lack thereof) reflect the current political outlook. After the financial crisis caused a worldwide recession, the government passed the Dodd–Frank Wall Street Reform and Consumer Protection Act of 2010. This agency was created to increase accountability and transparency in the financial industry.[12] The legislation established a new Consumer Financial Protection Bureau to protect consumers from deceptive financial practices.[13] On the other hand, many political leaders blamed this legislation for slowing down the economic recovery and adding extra costs and uncertainty to business decision making. Consequently, the political forces of the marketing environment have the potential to influence marketing decisions and strategies.

Marketing organizations strive to maintain good relations with elected and appointed political officials for several reasons. Political officials well disposed toward particular firms or industries are less likely to create or enforce laws and regulations unfavorable to those companies. Consequently, political officials who believe oil companies are making honest efforts to control pollution are unlikely to create and enforce highly restrictive pollution-control laws. Government contracts can be very profitable, so understanding the competitive bidding process for obtaining contracts is important. Finally, political officials can play key roles in helping organizations secure foreign markets. Government officials will sometimes organize trade missions in which business executives go to foreign countries to meet with potential clients or buyers.[14]

Many marketers view political forces as beyond their control and simply adjust to conditions that arise from those forces. Some firms, however, seek to influence the political process. In some cases, organizations publicly protest the actions of legislative bodies. More often, organizations help elect individuals to political offices who regard them positively. Much of this help is in the form of campaign contributions. AT&T is an example of a company that has attempted to influence legislation and regulation over a long period of time. Since 1990, AT&T has made more than $55 million in corporate donations for use in supporting the campaign funds of political candidates.[15] Some companies choose to donate to the campaign funds of opponents when it is believed to be a close race. Until recently, laws have limited corporate contributions to political campaign funds for specific candidates, and company-sponsored political advertisements could primarily focus only on topics (e.g., health care) and not on candidates. In the 2010 ruling for *Citizens United v. Federal Election Commission*, the Supreme Court ruled that the government is not authorized to ban corporate spending in candidate elections.[16] This means that future elections can be affected by large corporate donations to candidates. Marketers also can influence the political process through political action committees (PACs) that solicit donations from individuals and then contribute those funds to candidates running for political office.

Companies can also participate in the political process through lobbying to persuade public and/or government officials to favor a particular position in decision making. Many organizations concerned about the threat of legislation or regulation that may negatively affect their operations employ lobbyists to communicate their concerns to elected officials. Case in point, as the U.S. government debates whether to pass stricter laws regulating marketing activities over the Internet, social media firms such as Google are sending lobbyists to give their respective viewpoints regarding the proposed legislation.

3-5 LEGAL AND REGULATORY FORCES

A number of federal laws influence marketing decisions and activities. Table 3.2 lists some of the most important laws. In addition to discussing these laws, which deal with competition and consumer protection, this section examines the effects of regulatory agencies and self-regulatory forces on marketing efforts.

Table 3.2 **Major Federal Laws That Affect Marketing Decisions**

Name and Date Enacted	Purpose
Sherman Antitrust Act (1890)	Prohibits contracts, combinations, or conspiracies to restrain trade; establishes as a misdemeanor monopolizing or attempting to monopolize
Clayton Act (1914)	Prohibits specific practices such as price discrimination, exclusive-dealer arrangements, and stock acquisitions whose effect may noticeably lessen competition or tend to create a monopoly
Federal Trade Commission Act (1914)	Created the Federal Trade Commission; also gives the FTC investigatory powers to be used in preventing unfair methods of competition
Robinson–Patman Act (1936)	Prohibits price discrimination that lessens competition among wholesalers or retailers; prohibits producers from giving disproportionate services or facilities to large buyers
Wheeler–Lea Act (1938)	Prohibits unfair and deceptive acts and practices regardless of whether competition is injured; places advertising of foods and drugs under the jurisdiction of the FTC
Lanham Act (1946)	Provides protections for and regulation of brand names, brand marks, trade names, and trademarks
Celler–Kefauver Act (1950)	Prohibits any corporation engaged in commerce from acquiring the whole or any part of the stock or other share of the capital assets of another corporation when the effect would substantially lessen competition or tend to create a monopoly
Fair Packaging and Labeling Act (1966)	Prohibits unfair or deceptive packaging or labeling of consumer products
Magnuson–Moss Warranty (FTC) Act (1975)	Provides for minimum disclosure standards for written consumer product warranties; defines minimum consent standards for written warranties; allows the FTC to prescribe interpretive rules in policy statements regarding unfair or deceptive practices
Consumer Goods Pricing Act (1975)	Prohibits the use of price maintenance agreements among manufacturers and resellers in interstate commerce
Foreign Corrupt Practices Act (1977)	Prohibits American companies from making illicit payments to foreign officials in order to obtain or keep business
Trademark Counterfeiting Act (1980)	Imposes civil and criminal penalties against those who deal in counterfeit consumer goods or any counterfeit goods that can threaten health or safety
Trademark Law Revision Act (1988)	Amends the Lanham Act to allow brands not yet introduced to be protected through registration with the Patent and Trademark Office
Nutrition Labeling and Education Act (1990)	Prohibits exaggerated health claims; requires all processed foods to contain labels with nutritional information
Telephone Consumer Protection Act (1991)	Establishes procedures to avoid unwanted telephone solicitations; prohibits marketers from using an automated telephone dialing system or an artificial or prerecorded voice to certain telephone lines
Federal Trademark Dilution Act (1995)	Grants trademark owners the right to protect trademarks and requires relinquishment of names that match or parallel existing trademarks
Digital Millennium Copyright Act (1996)	Refined copyright laws to protect digital versions of copyrighted materials, including music and movies
Children's Online Privacy Protection Act (2000)	Regulates the collection of personally identifiable information (name, address, e-mail address, hobbies, interests, or information collected through cookies) online from children under age 13
Do Not Call Implementation Act (2003)	Directs the FCC and FTC to coordinate so their rules are consistent regarding telemarketing call practices including the Do Not Call Registry and other lists, as well as call abandonment; in 2008, the FTC amended its rules and banned prerecorded sales pitches for all but a few cases
Credit Card Act (2009)	Implements strict rules on credit card companies regarding topics such as issuing credit to youths, terms disclosure, interest rates, and fees
Dodd–Frank Wall Street Reform and Consumer Protection Act (2010)	Promotes financial reform to increase accountability and transparency in the financial industry, protects consumers from deceptive financial practices, and establishes the Bureau of Consumer Financial Protection

Political Forces
Protestors carry a banner to protest the sale of genetically modified food during a demonstration at a biotechnology industry conference.

3-5a Procompetitive Legislation

Procompetitive laws are designed to preserve competition. Most of these laws were enacted to end various antitrade practices deemed unacceptable by society. The Sherman Antitrust Act, for example, was passed in 1890 to prevent businesses from restraining trade and monopolizing markets. Examples of illegal anticompetitive practices include stealing trade secrets or obtaining other confidential information from a competitor's employees, trademark and copyright infringement, price fixing, false advertising, and deceptive selling methods such as "bait and switch" and false representation of products. The Lanham Act (1946) and the Federal Trademark Dilution Act (1995), for instance, help companies protect their trademarks (brand names, logos, and other registered symbols) against infringement. The latter also requires users of names that match or parallel existing trademarks to relinquish them to prevent confusion among consumers. Antitrust laws also authorize the government to punish companies that engage in such anticompetitive practices. For instance, JP Morgan reached a $13 billion settlement with the Justice Department to resolve allegations that it had sold bad mortgages that harmed homeowners once the financial crisis hit.[17]

Laws have also been created to prevent businesses from gaining an unfair advantage through bribery. The U.S. Foreign Corrupt Practices Act (FCPA) prohibits American companies from making illicit payments to foreign officials in order to obtain or keep business. To illustrate, Diebold Inc., a provider of integrated self-service delivery and security systems, paid $25.2 million to settle allegations that it had bribed government officials in Indonesia and China and falsified records in Russia to secure and retain contracts.[18] The FCPA does allow for small facilitation ("grease") payments to expedite routine government transactions. However, the passage of the U.K. Bribery Act does not allow for facilitation payments.[19] The U.K. Bribery Act is more encompassing than the FCPA and has significant implications for global business. Under this law companies can be found guilty of bribery even if the bribery did not take place within the U.K., and company officials without explicit knowledge about the misconduct can still be held accountable. The law applies to any business with operations in the U.K.[20] However, the U.K. Bribery Law does allow for leniency if the company has an effective compliance program and undergoes periodic ethical assessments.[21] In response to the law, companies have begun to strengthen their compliance programs related to bribery. Kimberly-Clark now requires some of its business partners to consent to audits and keep thorough documentation of their payments.[22]

3-5b Consumer Protection Legislation

Consumer protection legislation is not a recent development. During the mid-1800s, lawmakers in many states passed laws to prohibit adulteration of food and drugs. However, consumer protection laws at the federal level mushroomed in the mid-1960s and early 1970s. A number of them deal with consumer safety, such as the food and drug acts, and are designed to protect people from actual and potential physical harm caused by adulteration or mislabeling. Other laws prohibit the sale of various hazardous products, such as flammable fabrics and toys that may injure children. Others concern automobile safety.

Congress has also passed several laws concerning information disclosure. Some require that information about specific products, such as textiles, furs, cigarettes, and automobiles, be provided on labels. Other laws focus on particular marketing activities: product development and testing, packaging, labeling, advertising, and consumer financing. Concerns about companies' online collection and use of personal information, especially about children, resulted in the passage of the Children's Online Privacy Protection Act (COPPA), which prohibits websites and Internet providers from seeking personal information from children under age 13 without parental consent. Fines for violating COPPA can be severe. The Federal Trade Commission charged the social networking app Path with violating COPPA by collecting personal information from about 3,000 minors without their parents' consent. The company agreed to pay $800,000 to settle the charges.[23]

3-5c Encouraging Compliance with Laws and Regulations

Marketing activities are sometimes at the forefront of organizational misconduct, with fraud and antitrust violations the most frequently sentenced organizational crimes. Legal violations usually begin when marketers develop programs that unwittingly overstep legal bounds. Many marketers lack experience in dealing with complex legal actions and decisions. Some test the limits of certain laws by operating in a legally questionable way to see how far they can get with certain practices before being prosecuted. Other marketers interpret regulations and statutes very strictly to avoid violating a vague law. When marketers

Consumer Credit Card Security
Credit card theft has created the need for consumer vigilance and regulatory agencies' assistance in preventing fraud.

interpret laws in relation to specific marketing practices, they often analyze recent court decisions both to better understand what the law is intended to do and to predict future court interpretations.

The current trend is moving away from legally based organizational compliance programs. Instead, many companies are choosing to provide incentives that foster a culture of ethics and responsibility that encourages compliance with laws and regulations. Developing best practices and voluntary compliance creates rules and principles that guide decision making. Many companies are encouraging their employees to take responsibility for avoiding legal misconduct themselves. The New York Stock Exchange, for example, requires all member companies to have a code of ethics, and some firms try to go beyond what is required by the law. Many firms are trying to develop ethical cultures based on values and proactive assessments of risks to prevent misconduct.

3-5d Regulatory Agencies

Federal regulatory agencies influence many marketing activities, including product development, pricing, packaging, advertising, personal selling, and distribution. Usually these bodies have the power to enforce specific laws, as well as some discretion in establishing operating rules and regulations to guide certain types of industry practices. Because of this discretion and overlapping areas of responsibility, confusion or conflict regarding which agencies have jurisdiction over which marketing activities is common.

Of all the federal regulatory units, the **Federal Trade Commission (FTC)** most heavily influences marketing activities. Although the FTC regulates a variety of business practices, it allocates a large portion of resources to curbing false advertising, misleading pricing, and deceptive packaging and labeling. For instance, the FTC investigated whether Google had engaged in anticompetitive practices by unfairly favoring its own products while making it more difficult for competing products to be displayed prominently in its search results.[24] When it has reason to believe a firm is violating a law, the commission typically issues a complaint stating that the business is in violation and takes appropriate action. If, after it is issued a complaint, a company continues the questionable practice, the FTC can issue a cease-and-desist order demanding that the business stop doing whatever caused the complaint. The firm can appeal to the federal courts to have the order rescinded. However, the FTC can seek civil penalties in court, up to a maximum penalty of $10,000 a day for each infraction if a cease-and-desist order is violated. The commission can require companies to run corrective advertising in response to previous ads deemed misleading (see Figure 3.2).

The FTC also assists businesses in complying with laws and evaluates new marketing methods every year. The agency has held hearings to help firms establish guidelines for

Federal Trade Commission (FTC) An agency that regulates a variety of business practices and curbs false advertising, misleading pricing, and deceptive packaging and labeling

Figure 3.2 Federal Trade Commission Enforcement Tools

Cease-and-desist order
A court order to a business to stop engaging in an illegal practice

Consent decree
An order for a business to stop engaging in questionable activities to avoid prosecution

Redress
Money paid to customer to settle or resolve a complaint

Corrective advertising
A requirement that a business make new advertisement to correct misinformation

Civil penalties
Court-ordered civil fines for up to $10,000 per day for violating a cease-and-desist order

avoiding charges of price fixing, deceptive advertising, and questionable telemarketing practices. It has also held conferences and hearings on electronic (Internet) commerce, identity theft, and childhood obesity. When general sets of guidelines are needed to improve business practices in a particular industry, the FTC sometimes encourages firms within that industry to establish a set of trade practices voluntarily. The FTC may even sponsor a conference that brings together industry leaders and consumers for this purpose.

Unlike the FTC, other regulatory units are limited to dealing with specific goods, services, or business activities. Consider the Food and Drug Administration (FDA), which enforces regulations that prohibit the sale and distribution of adulterated, misbranded, or hazardous food and drug products. For instance, the FDA ordered a generic antidepressant to be pulled from U.S. shelves after determining that it was not the equivalent of the Wellbutrin drug produced by GlaxoSmithKline.[25] Table 3.3 outlines the areas of responsibility of seven federal regulatory agencies.

In addition, all states, as well as many cities and towns, have regulatory agencies that enforce laws and regulations regarding marketing practices within their states or municipalities. State and local regulatory agencies try not to establish regulations that conflict with those of federal regulatory agencies. They generally enforce laws dealing with the production and sale of particular goods and services. The utility, insurance, financial, and liquor industries are commonly regulated by state agencies. Among these agencies' targets are misleading advertising and pricing. Recent legal actions suggest that states are taking a firmer stance against perceived deceptive pricing practices and are using basic consumer research to define deceptive pricing.

State consumer protection laws offer an opportunity for state attorneys general to deal with marketing issues related to fraud and deception. Most states have consumer protection laws that are very general in nature and provide enforcement when new schemes evolve that injure consumers. The New York Consumer Protection Board, for instance, is very proactive in monitoring consumer protection and providing consumer education. New York became the first state to implement an airline passenger rights law. In addition, New York City has banned trans fats and tried to ban large soft drinks.

Table 3.3 Major Federal Regulatory Agencies

Agency	Major Areas of Responsibility
Federal Trade Commission (FTC)	Enforces laws and guidelines regarding business practices; takes action to stop false and deceptive advertising, pricing, packaging, and labelling
Food and Drug Administration (FDA)	Enforces laws and regulations to prevent distribution of adulterated or misbranded foods, drugs, medical devices, cosmetics, veterinary products, and potentially hazardous consumer products
Consumer Product Safety Commission (CPSC)	Ensures compliance with the Consumer Product Safety Act; protects the public from unreasonable risk of injury from any consumer product not covered by other regulatory agencies
Federal Communications Commission (FCC)	Regulates communication by wire, radio, and television in interstate and foreign commerce
Environmental Protection Agency (EPA)	Develops and enforces environmental protection standards and conducts research into the adverse effects of pollution
Federal Power Commission (FPC)	Regulates rates and sales of natural gas producers, thereby affecting the supply and price of gas available to consumers; also regulates wholesale rates for electricity and gas, pipeline construction, and U.S. imports and exports of natural gas and electricity
Consumer Financial Protection Bureau (CFPB)	Regulates the offering and provision of consumer financial products and serves to protect consumers from deceptive financial practices

Source: "Subtitle A—Bureau of Consumer Financial Protection," *One Hundred Eleventh Congress of the United States of America*, 589.

3-5e Self-Regulatory Forces

In an attempt to be good corporate citizens and prevent government intervention, some businesses try to regulate themselves. Similarly, a number of trade associations have developed self-regulatory programs. Though these programs are not a direct outgrowth of laws, many were established to stop or stall the development of laws and governmental regulatory groups that would regulate the associations' marketing practices. Sometimes trade associations establish ethics codes by which their members must abide or risk censure or exclusion from the association. For instance, the Pharmaceutical Research and Manufacturers of America released its "Guiding Principles" to function as a set of voluntary industry rules for drug companies to follow when advertising directly to consumers.[26]

Table 3.4 Self-Regulatory Issues in Marketing

1	Truthful Advertising Messages
2	Health and Childhood Obesity
3	Internet Tracking/User Privacy
4	Concern for Vulnerable Populations
5	Failure to Deliver on Expectations and Promises
6	Sustainable Marketing Practices and Greenwashing
7	Transparent Pricing
8	Understandable Labelling and Packaging
9	Supply-Chain Relationships/Ethical Sourcing
10	Marketing of Dangerous Products
11	Product Quality Failures
12	Nonresponse to Customer Complaints

Perhaps the best-known self-regulatory group is the **Better Business Bureau (BBB)**, which is a system of nongovernmental, independent, local regulatory agencies that are supported by local businesses. More than 150 bureaus help settle problems between consumers and specific business firms. Each bureau also acts to preserve good business practices in a locality, although it usually lacks strong enforcement tools for dealing with firms that employ questionable practices. When a firm continues to violate what the Better Business Bureau believes to be good business practices, the bureau warns consumers through local newspapers or broadcast media. If the offending organization is a BBB member, it may be expelled from the local bureau. In a rare case, the BBB expelled its Los Angeles chapter after the Council of Better Business Bureaus discovered the chapter was operating a pay-for-play scheme and other forms of misconduct.[27] Table 3.4 describes some of the major self-regulatory issues that often occur in the marketing industry.

The Council of Better Business Bureaus is a national organization composed of all local Better Business Bureaus. The National Advertising Division (NAD) of the council operates a self-regulatory program that investigates claims regarding alleged deceptive advertising. For instance, the NAD asked T-Mobile to remove claims from its advertising about competitors after determining that these claims could not be proven true.[28]

Another self-regulatory entity, the **National Advertising Review Board (NARB)**, considers cases in which an advertiser challenges issues raised by the NAD about an advertisement. Cases are reviewed by panels drawn from NARB members that represent advertisers, agencies, and the public. In one case, the NARB determined that companies using the Fair Trade USA seal on its labeling must specify the percentage of fair trade ingredients on the label.[29] The NARB, sponsored by the Council of Better Business Bureaus and three advertising trade organizations, has no official enforcement powers. However, if a firm refuses to comply with its decision, the NARB may publicize the questionable practice and file a complaint with the FTC.

Self-regulatory programs have several advantages over governmental laws and regulatory agencies. Establishment and implementation are usually less expensive, and guidelines are generally more realistic and operational. In addition, effective self-regulatory programs reduce the need to expand government bureaucracy. However, these programs have several limitations. When a trade association creates a set of industry guidelines for its members, nonmember firms do not have to abide by them. Furthermore, many self-regulatory programs lack the tools or authority to enforce guidelines. Finally, guidelines in self-regulatory programs are often less strict than those established by government agencies.

Better Business Bureau (BBB) A system of nongovernmental, independent, local regulatory agencies supported by local businesses that helps settle problems between customers and specific business firms

National Advertising Review Board (NARB) A self-regulatory unit that considers challenges to issues raised by the National Advertising Division (an arm of the Council of Better Business Bureaus) about an advertisement

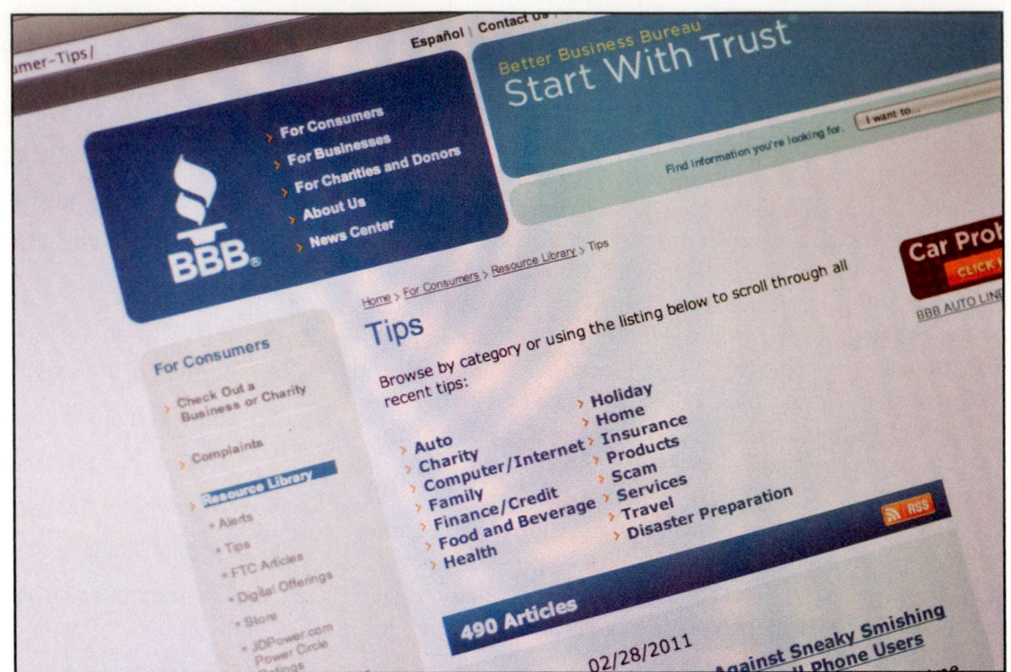

NetPhotos/Alamy

Self-Regulatory Forces The Better Business Bureau is one of the best known self-regulatory organizations.

3-6 TECHNOLOGICAL FORCES

The word *technology* brings to mind scientific advances such as information technology and biotechnology, which have resulted in the Internet, cell phones, cloning, stem-cell research, electric vehicles, iPads, and more. Technology has revolutionized the products created and offered by marketers and the channels by which they communicate about those products. However, even though these innovations are outgrowths of technology, none of them *are* technology. **Technology** is the application of knowledge and tools to solve problems and perform tasks more efficiently. Technology grows out of research performed by businesses, universities, government agencies, and nonprofit organizations. More than half of this research is paid for by the federal government, which supports research in such diverse areas as health, defense, agriculture, energy, and pollution.

The rapid technological growth of the last several decades is expected to accelerate. It has transformed the U.S. economy into the most productive in the world and provided Americans with an ever-higher standard of living and tremendous opportunities for sustained business expansion. Technology and technological advancements clearly influence buyers' and marketers' decisions, so let's take a closer look at the impact of technology and its use in the marketplace.

3-6a Impact of Technology

Technology determines how we, as members of society, satisfy our physiological needs. In various ways and to varying degrees, eating and drinking habits, sleeping patterns, sexual activities, health care, and work performance are all influenced by both existing technology and changes in technology. Because of the technological revolution in communications, for example, marketers can now reach vast numbers of people more efficiently through a variety of media. Social networks, smartphones, and tablet computers help marketers stay in touch with clients, make appointments, and handle last-minute orders or cancellations. A growing number of U.S. households, as well as many businesses, have given up their land-lines in favor

technology The application of knowledge and tools to solve problems and perform tasks more efficiently

Going Green

Google's New Venture: Going Green

Can a multi-billion dollar corporation really become a zero-carbon operation? According to Google's CEO Larry Page, it is certainly going to try. In 2007, Google established the green initiative RE<C, which stands for renewable energy is cheaper than coal, to reduce the company's carbon footprint. The company is taking proactive steps to reduce carbon emissions from its day-to-day operations. It plans to achieve this goal by investing in solar and wind producers, purchasing carbon offsets, and constructing its data centers more efficiently.

The company has marketed its green efforts as something new, innovative, and ambitious that other companies can potentially emulate. For Google, going green has been an initiative that has proven its commitment toward social responsibility. The company realizes that it can give back not only technologically but also proactively by essentially eliminating greenhouse gas emissions. Google began these efforts by marketing the benefits of going green to its employees. It provides its employees with energy efficient modes of transportation and has installed the largest network of electric vehicle charging stations in the United States. Google's green initiatives also enhance its reputation with its target market as many companies and consumers prefer doing business with sustainable firms. If its carbon efficient blueprint becomes a successful endeavor, Google may have found an inadvertent way to market social responsibility by just doing the right thing.[b]

of using cell phones as their primary phones. Currently, about one-third of Americans have exchanged their land-lines for cell phones.[30]

The proliferation of mobile devices has led marketers to employ text and multimedia messaging on cell phones to reach their target markets. Restaurants, for instance, can send their lunch specials to subscribers' cell phones. Because many mobile devices are able to access the Internet, marketers have an increasing number of opportunities for mobile advertising. As consumers become more tech-savvy, marketers must adapt their strategies to take advantage of these new opportunities. Mobile marketing will be discussed in more detail in Chapter 10.

Computers have become a staple in American homes, but the type of computer has been changing drastically in this past decade. Traditional desktop computers appear to be on the decline. Laptops became immensely popular due to their mobility, but analysts estimate that laptops might be entering the maturity stage of the product life cycle. Conversely, tablet computers such as the Apple iPad and Microsoft Surface 2 are experiencing immense growth and may soon supersede laptops in sales.[31] In response many companies are creating apps specifically made for the iPad and similar devices. The rapidly evolving state of technology requires marketers to familiarize themselves with the latest technological changes.

The Internet has become a major tool in most households for communicating, researching, shopping, and entertaining. The percentage of American adults who post or download videos online has grown to 31 percent.[32] Time spent on social networks also makes up a significant portion of a consumer's online activities. One study estimates that users worldwide spend 19 percent of their time online on social networking sites.[33]

Although technology has had many positive impacts on our lives, there are also many negative impacts to consider. We enjoy the benefits of communicating through the Internet; however, we are increasingly concerned about protecting our privacy and intellectual property. Hackers and those who steal digital property are also using advanced technology to harm others. Likewise, technological advances in the areas of health and medicine have led to the creation of new drugs that save lives; however, such advances have also led to cloning and genetically modified foods that have become controversial issues in many segments of

Impact of Technology
Continental Tire provides award-winning products and ground-breaking technology, creating the confidence for their tires to be selected for the Ligenfelter ZL1 Camaro.

society. Consider the impact of cell phones. The ability to call from almost any location has many benefits, but it also has negative side effects, including increases in traffic accidents, increased noise pollution, and fears about potential health risks.[34]

The effects of technology relate to such characteristics as dynamics, reach, and the self-sustaining nature of technological progress. The *dynamics* of technology involve the constant change that often challenges the structures of social institutions, including social relationships, the legal system, religion, education, business, and leisure. *Reach* refers to the broad nature of technology as it moves through society.

The *self-sustaining* nature of technology relates to the fact that technology acts as a catalyst to spur even faster development. As new innovations are introduced, they stimulate the need for more advancement to facilitate further development. Continental Tire has a 140-year history of providing innovative, high-tech tire engineering. The advertisement describes how a special version of the Camaro, Lingenfelter ZL1, selected the continental tire as the "official tire" of Lingenfelter Performance Engineering. Technology initiates a change process that creates new opportunities for new technologies in every industry segment or personal life experience that it touches. At some point, there is a multiplier effect that causes still greater demand for more change to improve performance.[35]

The expanding opportunities for e-commerce, the sharing of business information, the ability to maintain business relationships, and the ability to conduct business transactions via digital networks are changing the relationship between businesses and consumers.[36] Many people use the Internet to purchase consumer electronics, clothing, software, books, furniture, and music. More people now opt to purchase music online or simply listen for free on social networking sites. As a result, CD sales have decreased over the years. In addition, consumers go online to acquire travel-related services, financial services, and information. The forces unleashed by the Internet are particularly important in business-to-business relationships, where uncertainties are being reduced by improving the quantity, reliability, and timeliness of information.

3-6b Adoption and Use of Technology

Many companies lose their status as market leaders because they fail to keep up with technological changes. It is important for firms to determine when a technology is changing the industry and to define the strategic influence of the new technology. The Internet has created the need for ever-faster transmission of signals through 4G, cable broadband, satellite, Wi-Fi, or fiber optic technology. To remain competitive, companies today must keep up with and adapt to technological advances.

The extent to which a firm can protect inventions that stem from research also influences its use of technology. How secure a product is from imitation depends on how easily others can copy it without violating its patent. If groundbreaking products and processes cannot be protected through patents, a company is less likely to market them and make the benefits of its research available to competitors.

Through a procedure known as *technology assessment*, managers try to foresee the effects of new products and processes on their firm's operations, on other business organizations, and on society in general. With information obtained through a technology assessment, management tries to estimate whether benefits of adopting a specific technology outweigh costs to the firm and to society at large. The degree to which a business is technologically based also influences its managers' response to technology.

3-7 SOCIOCULTURAL FORCES

Sociocultural forces are the influences in a society and its culture(s) that bring about changes in people's attitudes, beliefs, norms, customs, and lifestyles. Profoundly affecting how people live, these forces help determine what, where, how, and when people buy products. Like the other environmental forces, sociocultural forces present marketers with both challenges and opportunities. For a closer look at sociocultural forces, we examine three major issues: demographic and diversity characteristics, cultural values, and consumerism.

3-7a Demographic and Diversity Characteristics

Changes in a population's demographic characteristics—age, gender, race, ethnicity, marital and parental status, income, and education—have a significant bearing on relationships and individual behavior. These shifts lead to changes in how people live and ultimately in their consumption of such products as food, clothing, housing, transportation, communication, recreation, education, and health services. We'll look at a few of the changes in demographics and diversity that are affecting marketing activities.

One demographic change that is affecting the marketplace is the increasing proportion of older consumers. According to the U.S. Bureau of the Census, the number of people age 65 and older is expected to more than double by the year 2050, reaching 88.5 million.[37] Consequently, marketers can expect significant increases in the demand for health-care services, recreation, tourism, retirement housing, and selected skin-care products. Even online companies are trying to take advantage of the opportunities Baby Boomers present. Several online dating sites directed toward boomers were recently launched, such as BabyBoomerPeopleMeet.com and SeniorPeopleMeet.com.[38] To reach older customers effectively, of course, marketers must understand the diversity within the mature market with respect to geographic location, income, marital status, and limitations in mobility and self-care.

The number of singles is also on the rise. Singles currently comprise 51 percent of American households.[39] Single people have quite different spending patterns than couples and families with children. They are less likely to own homes and thus buy less furniture and fewer appliances. They spend more heavily on convenience foods, restaurants, travel, entertainment, and recreation. In addition, they tend to prefer smaller packages, whereas families often buy bulk goods and products packaged in multiple servings.

The United States is entering another baby boom, with 27.3 percent of the total population age 18 or younger; the original Baby Boomers, born between 1946 and 1964, account for about 26 percent.[40] The children of the original Baby Boomers differ from one another radically in terms of race, living arrangements, and socioeconomic status. Thus, the newest baby boom is much more diverse than in previous generations.

Despite this trend, the birthrate has begun to decline. The U.S. population experienced the slowest rate of growth in the last decade since the Great Depression. The population grew 9.7 percent to about 317 million. While the birth rate is declining, new immigrants help with population gains.[41]

Another noteworthy population trend is the increasingly multicultural nature of U.S. society. The number of immigrants into the United States has steadily risen during the last 40 years. In the 1960s, 3.3 million people immigrated to the United States; in the 1970s, 4.4 million immigrated; in the 1980s, 7.3 million arrived; in the 1990s, the United States received 9.1 million immigrants; and in the 2000s, more than 8.3 million people have immigrated to the United States.[42]

sociocultural forces
The influences in a society and its culture(s) that change people's attitudes, beliefs, norms, customs, and lifestyles

Table 3.5 The Multicultural Nature of the U.S. Population

Race	% Population 2012	Estimated % 2060
White	78	69
Hispanic	17	31
Black or African American	13	15
Asian	5.1	8.2
American Indian or Alaska Native	1.2	1.5
Native Hawaiian or Pacific Islander	0.2	0.3

Source: U.S. Census Bureau, "U.S. Census Bureau Projections Show a Slower Growing, Older, More Diverse Nation a Half Century from Now," December 12, 2012, www.census.gov/newsroom/releases/archives/population/cb12-243.html (accessed October 26, 2013).

In contrast to earlier immigrants, very few recent ones are of European origin. Another reason for the increasing cultural diversification of the United States is that most recent immigrants are relatively young, whereas U.S. citizens of European origin are growing older. These younger immigrants tend to have more children than their older counterparts, further shifting the population balance. By the turn of the 20th century, the U.S. population had shifted from one dominated by whites to one consisting largely of three racial and ethnic groups: whites, blacks, and Hispanics. The U.S. government projects that by the year 2060, approximately 128.8 million Hispanics, 61.8 million blacks, and 34.4 million Asians will call the United States home.[43] Table 3.5 provides a glimpse into the multicultural nature of the U.S. population. Although the majority of the population still identify themselves as white, Hispanic and Asian ethnicities are expected to grow in the next 50 years, while white non-Hispanics ethnicities are estimated to decrease.

Marketers recognize that these profound changes in the U.S. population bring unique problems and opportunities. But a diverse population means a more diverse customer base, and marketing practices must be modified—and diversified—to meet its changing needs. For instance, since its inception McDonald's has been targeted toward children. Yet this trend is changing as more restaurant-goers consist of Millennials, who spend approximately $247 billion annually at restaurants. McDonald's is responding with more modern-looking restaurants and diverse menus.[44]

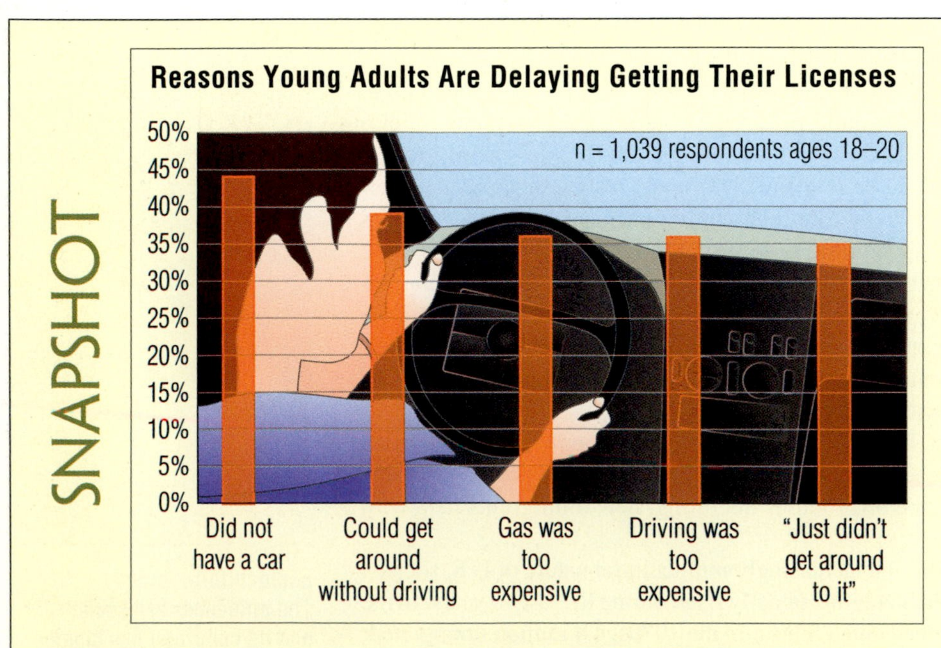

Source: Based on AAA, "Teens Delaying Licensure—A Cause for Concern?" August 1, 2013, http://newsroom.aaa.com/2013/08/teens-delaying-licensure-a-cause-for-concern/ (accessed November 6, 2013).

3-7b Cultural Values

Changes in cultural values have dramatically influenced people's needs and desires for products. Although cultural values do not shift overnight, they do change at varying speeds. Marketers try to monitor these changes, knowing this information can equip them to predict changes in consumers' needs for products, at least in the near future. For instance, automakers are adapting their strategies to appeal to the younger demographic because fewer young adults are choosing to purchase vehicles. Nearly half of young adults remain unlicensed till after their 18th birthday.[45] Many young adults are finding it more preferable to ride their bicycles or carpool than drive their own cars.

Starting in the late 1980s, issues of health, nutrition, and exercise grew in importance. People today are more concerned about the foods they eat and thus are choosing healthier products. Compared to those in the previous two decades, Americans today are more likely to favor smoke-free environments and to consume less alcohol. They have also altered their sexual behavior to reduce the risk of contracting sexually transmitted diseases. Marketers have responded with a proliferation of foods, beverages, and exercise products that fit this new lifestyle, as well as with programs to help people quit smoking and contraceptives that are safer and more effective. Americans are also becoming increasingly open to alternative medicines and nutritionally improved foods. As a result, sales of organic foods, herbs and herbal remedies, vitamins, and dietary supplements have escalated. In addition to the proliferation of new organic brands, such as Earthbound Farm, Horizon Dairy, and Whole Foods' 365, many conventional marketers have introduced organic versions of their products, including Orville Redenbacher, Heinz, and even Walmart.

The major source of cultural values is the family. For years, when asked about the most important aspects of their lives, adults specified family issues and a happy marriage. Today, however, only one out of two marriages is predicted to last. Values regarding the permanence of marriage are changing. Because a happy marriage is prized so highly, more people are willing to give up an unhappy one and seek a different marriage partner or opt to stay single.

Children continue to be very important. Marketers have responded with safer, upscale baby gear and supplies, children's electronics, and family entertainment products. Marketers are also aiming more marketing efforts directly at children because children often play pivotal roles in purchasing decisions. A recent study in Austria reported that children influence twice as many purchase decisions in the supermarket than parents are aware of, and the majority of items children requested are products positioned at their eye level.[46]

Children and family values are also factors in the trend toward more eat-out and take-out meals. Busy families in which both parents work generally want to spend less time in the kitchen and more time together enjoying themselves. Beneficiaries of this trend have primarily been fast-food and casual restaurants like McDonald's, Taco Bell, and Applebee's, but most supermarkets have added more ready-to-cook and ready-to-serve meal components to meet the needs of busy customers. Some also offer dine-in cafés.

Green marketing helps establish long-term consumer relationships by maintaining, supporting, and enhancing the natural environment. One of society's environmental hurdles is proper disposal of waste, especially of nondegradable materials such as disposable diapers and polystyrene packaging. Companies have responded by developing more environmentally sensitive products and packaging. Procter & Gamble, for example, uses recycled materials in some of its packaging and sells environment-friendly refills. Companies like Seventh Generation, which sells products like paper towels and bathroom tissue made from recycled paper as well as eco-friendly cleaning products, have entered the mainstream. Everything the company produces is as environmentally friendly as it can be, in hopes of having as little impact on the

Sociocultural Forces
It is becoming more common for consumers to prefer gluten-free foods for health reasons even if they are not allergic to the ingredient. Food companies are capitalizing on this trend by releasing gluten-free versions of their items.

next seven generations as possible.[47] A number of marketers sponsor recycling programs and encourage their customers to take part in them.

3-7c Consumerism

Consumerism involves organized efforts by individuals, groups, and organizations to protect consumers' rights. The movement's major forces are individual consumer advocates, consumer organizations and other interest groups, consumer education, and consumer laws.

To achieve their objectives, consumers and their advocates write letters or send e-mails to companies, lobby government agencies, broadcast public service announcements, and boycott companies whose activities they deem irresponsible. Consider that a number of consumers would like to eliminate telemarketing and e-mail spam, and some of them have joined organizations and groups attempting to stop these activities. Businesses that engage in questionable practices invite additional regulation. Several organizations, for instance, evaluate children's products for safety, often announcing dangerous products before Christmas so parents can avoid them. Other actions by the consumer movement have resulted in seat belts and air bags in automobiles, dolphin-friendly tuna, the banning of unsafe three-wheel motorized vehicles, and numerous laws regulating product safety and information. We take a closer look at consumerism in the next chapter.

consumerism Organized efforts by individuals, groups, and organizations to protect consumers' rights

Summary

3-1 Summarize why it is important to examine and respond to the marketing environment.

The marketing environment consists of external forces that directly or indirectly influence an organization's acquisition of inputs (personnel, financial resources, raw materials, and information) and generation of outputs (goods, services, and ideas). The marketing environment includes competitive, economic, political, legal and regulatory, technological, and sociocultural forces.

Environmental scanning is the process of collecting information about forces in the marketing environment; environmental analysis is the process of assessing and interpreting information obtained in scanning. This information helps marketing managers predict opportunities and threats associated with environmental fluctuation. Marketing managers may assume either a passive, reactive approach or a proactive, aggressive approach in responding to these environmental fluctuations. The choice depends on the organization's structures and needs and on the composition of environmental forces that affect it.

3-2 Explain how competitive factors affect an organization's ability to compete.

All businesses compete for customers' dollars. A marketer, however, generally defines *competition* as other firms that market products that are similar to or can be substituted for its products in the same geographic area. These competitors can be classified into one of four types: brand competitors, product competitors, generic competitors, and total budget competitors. The number of firms controlling the supply of a product may affect the strength of competitors. The four general types of competitive structures are monopoly, oligopoly, monopolistic competition, and pure competition. Marketers monitor what competitors are currently doing and assess changes occurring in the competitive environment.

3-3 Articulate how economic factors influence a customer's ability and willingness to buy products.

General economic conditions, buying power, and willingness to spend can strongly influence marketing decisions and activities. The overall state of the economy fluctuates in a general pattern known as the business cycle, which consists of four stages: prosperity, recession, depression, and recovery. Consumers' goods, services, and financial holdings make up their buying power, or ability to purchase. Financial sources of buying power are income, credit, and wealth. After-tax income used for spending or saving is disposable income. Disposable income left after an individual has purchased the basic necessities of food, clothes, and shelter is discretionary income. Factors affecting buyers' willingness to spend include product price; level of satisfaction obtained from currently used products; family size; and expectations about future employment, income, prices, and general economic conditions.

3-4 Identify the types of political forces in the marketing environment.

The political, legal, and regulatory forces of the marketing environment are closely interrelated. Political forces may determine what laws and regulations affecting specific marketers are enacted, how much the government purchases, and from which suppliers. They can also be important in helping organizations secure foreign markets. Companies influence political forces in several ways, including maintaining good relationships with political officials, protesting the actions of legislative bodies, helping elect individuals who regard them positively to public office through campaign contributions, and employing lobbyists to communicate their concerns to elected officials.

3-5 Explain how laws, government regulations, and self-regulatory agencies affect marketing activities.

Federal legislation affecting marketing activities can be divided into procompetitive legislation—laws designed to preserve and encourage competition—and consumer protection laws, which generally relate to product safety and information disclosure. Actual effects of legislation are determined by how marketers and courts interpret the laws. Federal guidelines for sentencing concerning violations of these laws represent an attempt to force marketers to comply with the laws.

Federal, state, and local regulatory agencies usually have power to enforce specific laws. They also have some discretion in establishing operating rules and drawing up regulations to guide certain types of industry practices. Industry self-regulation represents another regulatory force; marketers view this type of regulation more favorably than government action because they have more opportunity to take part in creating guidelines. Self-regulation may be less expensive than government regulation, and its guidelines are generally more realistic. However, such regulation generally cannot ensure compliance as effectively as government agencies.

3-6 Describe how new technology impacts marketing and society.

Technology is the application of knowledge and tools to solve problems and perform tasks more efficiently. Consumer demand, buyer behavior, product development, packaging, promotion, prices, and distribution systems are all influenced directly by technology. The rapid technological growth of the last few decades is expected to accelerate. Revolutionary changes in communication technology have allowed marketers to reach vast numbers of people; however, with this expansion of communication has come concern about privacy and intellectual property. And while science and medical research have brought many great advances, cloning and genetically modified foods are controversial issues in many segments of society. Home, health, leisure, and work are all influenced to varying degrees by technology and technological advances. The *dynamics* of technology involves the constant change that challenges every aspect of our society. *Reach* refers to the broad nature of technology as it moves through and affects society.

Many companies lose their status as market leaders because they fail to keep up with technological changes. The ability to protect inventions from competitor imitation is also an important consideration when making marketing decisions.

3-7 Outline the sociocultural issues marketers must deal with as they make decisions.

Sociocultural forces are the influences in a society and its culture that result in changes in attitudes, beliefs, norms, customs, and lifestyles. Major sociocultural issues directly affecting marketers include demographic and diversity characteristics, cultural values, and consumerism.

Changes in a population's demographic characteristics, such as age, income, race, and ethnicity, can lead to changes in that population's consumption of products. Changes in cultural values, such as those relating to health, nutrition, family, and the natural environment, have had striking effects on people's needs for products and therefore are closely monitored by marketers. Consumerism involves the efforts of individuals, groups, and organizations to protect consumers' rights. Consumer rights organizations inform and organize other consumers, raise issues, help businesses develop consumer-oriented programs, and pressure lawmakers to enact consumer protection laws.

Go to www.cengagebrain.com for resources to help you master the content in this chapter as well as materials that will expand your marketing knowledge!

Developing Your Marketing Plan

A marketing strategy is dynamic. Companies must constantly monitor the marketing environment not only to create their marketing strategy but to revise it if necessary. Information about various forces in the marketplace is collected, analyzed, and used as a foundation for several marketing plan decisions. The following questions will help you to understand how the information in this chapter contributes to the development of your marketing plan.

1. Describe the current competitive market for your product. Can you identify the number of brands or market

share they hold? Expand your analysis to include other products that are similar or could be substituted for yours.

2. Using the business cycle pattern, in which of the four stages is the current state of the economy? Can you identify any changes in consumer buying power that would affect the sale and use of your product?
3. Referring to Tables 3.2 and 3.3, do you recognize any laws or regulatory agencies that would have jurisdiction over your type of product?
4. Conduct a brief technology assessment, determining the impact that technology has on your product, its sale, or its use.
5. Discuss how your product could be affected by changes in social attitudes, demographic characteristics, or lifestyles.

The information obtained from these questions should assist you in developing various aspects of your marketing plan found in the "Interactive Marketing Plan" exercise at www.cengagebrain.com.

Important Terms

environmental scanning 62
environmental analysis 63
competition 64
brand competitors 64
product competitors 64
generic competitors 65
total budget competitors 65
monopoly 66
oligopoly 66
monopolistic competition 66
pure competition 66
business cycle 67
prosperity 68
recession 68
depression 68
recovery 68
buying power 68
income 68
disposable income 69
discretionary income 69
wealth 69
willingness to spend 70
Federal Trade Commission (FTC) 75
Better Business Bureau (BBB) 77
National Advertising Review Board (NARB) 77
technology 78
sociocultural forces 81
consumerism 84

Discussion and Review Questions

1. Why are environmental scanning and analysis important to marketers?
2. What are the four types of competition? Which is most important to marketers?
3. In what ways can each of the business cycle stages affect consumers' reactions to marketing strategies?
4. What business cycle stage are we experiencing currently? How is this stage affecting business firms in your area?
5. Define *income*, *disposable income*, and *discretionary income*. How does each type of income affect consumer buying power?
6. How do wealth and consumer credit affect consumer buying power?
7. What factors influence a buyer's willingness to spend?
8. Describe marketers' attempts to influence political forces.
9. What types of problems do marketers experience as they interpret legislation?
10. What are the goals of the Federal Trade Commission? List the ways in which the FTC affects marketing activities. Do you think a single regulatory agency should have such broad jurisdiction over so many marketing practices? Why or why not?
11. Name several nongovernmental regulatory forces. Do you believe self-regulation is more or less effective than governmental regulatory agencies? Why?
12. What does the term *technology* mean to you? Do the benefits of technology outweigh its costs and potential dangers? Defend your answer.
13. Discuss the impact of technology on marketing activities.
14. What factors determine whether a business organization adopts and uses technology?
15. What evidence exists that cultural diversity is increasing in the United States?
16. In what ways are cultural values changing? How are marketers responding to these changes?
17. Describe consumerism. Analyze some active consumer forces in your area.

Video Case 3.1

Preserve Products Challenge Traditional Brands with Green Alternatives

When entrepreneur Eric Hudson started Preserve® Products in 1996, people thought he was crazy. "When we first started the company, a lot of people looked at us like we had three heads, saying, 'Recycled materials are for ashtrays. Recycled materials are for pen holders,'" Hudson said. However, Hudson recognized that cultural values were beginning to shift toward green products. He founded Preserve Products, with the mission "to deliver consumer products that offer great looking design, high performance and are better for the environment than alternative products." The first Preserve product was its recyclable toothbrush. The toothbrush has become one of the organization's more popular products and even had an appearance as Will Ferrell's toothbrush in the movie *Stranger than Fiction.*

More than 15 years later, the green revolution is in full swing and Preserve has become a multi-million dollar company with products available in over a dozen countries. Preserve takes plastics from products at the end of their life cycle and recycles them to create consumer goods such as toothbrushes, razors, kitchenware, mixing bowls, and storage containers. As green products become more mainstream, Preserve has seen an increase in demand from both retailers and consumers. Preserve products can now be found in Wegman's, Whole Foods, Trader Joe's, and Target.

In addition to being recyclable, Preserve products are dishwasher safe and are manufactured in the United States. The company also guarantees that no products have been tested on animals and that it never uses ingredients that could potentially harm consumers. Preserve works to ensure that its products are well-designed and will last for a long time. In 2010 the company won the Spark International Design Silver Award for responsible packaging.

Being a green company is not easy, particularly because many consumers believe that green products are costlier than traditional products. Economic forces like the latest recession have made the cost of goods an even greater concern for consumers. Additionally, greenwashing, or marketing products as being more environmentally-friendly than they really are, is also a problem for Preserve because then consumers become more cautious of trusting green marketing claims. As a result, Preserve works hard to deliver price-competitive, trustworthy products through legitimate retailers.

In order to make its business work, Preserve forms partnerships with both organizations and consumers to get the materials it needs. It has strong relationships with companies like Brita and Seventh Generation, which send their waste to Preserve to be recycled into new products. For instance, Preserve uses the plastic from Stonyfield Farm yogurt cups to create the handles of its recycled toothbrush. Support from these companies is crucial for Preserve to maintain its competitive advantage as a company that offers quality green products.

Additionally, Preserve has been able to use consumers as suppliers. The company encourages their customers to send them used products when they reach the end of their life cycles rather than throwing them into landfills. In 2010 Preserve introduced the Mail-Back package at Whole Foods and Target for its recycled toothbrushes. The package not only protects the toothbrush but also allows consumers to use the package as a mailer to send it back to the company when they are finished with the product. Preserve can therefore reduce costs and widen its distribution range by incorporating consumers into the process. "They can facilitate being part of our supply chain," Hudson said.

Despite its advantages, Preserve must constantly engage in environmental scanning and analysis to effectively respond to changing environmental forces. For instance, Preserve must try to understand consumer perceptions toward green products. One way Preserve achieves this is by remaining in constant dialogue with its customers. "We've sought to have a very innovative approach of really reaching out to our advocates," Hudson said. Preserve uses personal e-mails and electronic newsletters to answer concerns and update consumers on recent events.

Preserve also must constantly analyze the competition. Brand competitors include not only other green consumer product firms but also big brand companies that sell more traditional products. Because the company operates in an environment of monopolistic competition, Preserve strives to differentiate its products and communicate their benefits to relevant stakeholders. Its recent initiative is to work with partners to recycle #5 plastic, which makes up 25 percent of plastic waste but is one of the least-recycled types of plastic.

Preserve has come far in its short history, witnessing a sociocultural shift from little stakeholder concern for green products to strong stakeholder support. As the company continues to research innovative approaches toward reusing products and researching consumers, Preserve appears well poised to compete in the green marketplace.[48]

Questions for Discussion

1. Describe the target market for Preserve products.
2. What environmental forces will be most important to understand for Preserve to be successful?
3. Which elements of the marketing mix are key to Preserve in dealing with competition?

Case 3.2

Whole Foods Capitalizes on Consumer Desires for Organic Food

Whole Foods Market's emphasis on organic food and sustainable fishing practices is not just socially responsible business but also good marketing. Whole Foods has adopted the value of putting the customer first. It keeps this value in mind when conducting environmental scanning to understand the different forces in the marketing environment. By paying careful attention to changing trends, Whole Foods has been able to identify major concerns and tailor its business practices accordingly. For instance, Whole Foods banned the use of the chemical compound Bisphenol-A from its baby bottles and cups even before the Food and Drug Administration recognized that it could be potentially harmful for children.

© iStockphoto.com/ivanastar

Whole Foods was started as a natural foods market in 1980. Through a series of acquisitions the company expanded from a small Austin-based market into a national organic food chain. However, as organic food became more popular, competition increased. Its rival Trader Joe's, for instance, guarantees that products sold under its private-label brand are free from preservatives, genetically-modified ingredients, and trans fats. Whole Foods products are often more expensive than the competition, requiring consumers to spend more disposable income at its stores. These factors require Whole Foods to constantly examine its environment and modify its marketing strategies to increase consumers' willingness to spend in its stores.

One way that Whole Foods has successfully grabbed market share in the organic food industry is by offering a superior product. Whole Foods Market created its own system of quality standards for its food products to assure consumers that it is purchasing superior products, including promoting organically grown foods, selling food that is free from preservatives and sweeteners, and carefully choosing each product in the mix. Whole Foods also tries to create an exciting customer experience in its stores with its free in-store samples, quality customer service, and environmentally-friendly practices.

In 2009, Whole Foods decided to embark upon a healthy living marketing initiative. CEO and co-founder John Mackey believed Whole Foods was deviating from its core principles by selling certain products that were unhealthy. That year Whole Foods adopted a new core value: "Promoting the health of our stakeholders through healthy eating education." Whole Foods partnered with healthy-eating partners to help educate its stakeholders about healthy food choices. Whole Foods stores began to post healthy eating information and recipes throughout its stores and began selling healthy eating cookbooks. For its employee stakeholders, Whole Foods began offering programs to help employees live more healthy lives and provided additional employee discounts to those who achieved health objectives.

Whole Foods also recognizes the importance of the environment, particularly regarding the precarious nature of the world's fisheries. Whole Foods became the first supermarket to offer Marine Stewardship Council (MSC)-certified seafood. Whole Foods has a rating system that color-codes the wild-caught seafood it sells into three ratings: green (sustainable seafood), yellow (medium danger of being overfished), and red (in serious danger of being overfished). Whole Foods phased out all red-rated seafood species by 2013.

Whole Foods' products and sustainability initiatives have factors on its side. The company has been able to benefit from sociocultural perspectives supporting natural and organic food. Whole Foods can also profit, albeit indirectly, from political forces. With the government's fight against childhood obesity and its push for healthier eating, companies like Whole Foods that market healthy food options are likely to prosper. However, Whole Foods does have one major disadvantage: its higher price points, while signaling the fact that it sells premium products, can also harm the company during a recession. When the recession hit, Whole Foods had to make quick changes to its pricing strategies to retain customers. It lowered prices on some of its brands and began to sell "extreme value items" at very low prices. Its adaptions to economic conditions have allowed the company to survive and even prosper. Whole Foods is a good example of a company that offers premium products consumers desire. Whole Foods customers like the company so much that the company has made *Fortune*'s list for "World's Most Admired Companies." [49]

Questions for Discussion

1. How has Whole Foods been successful in the highly competitive supermarket industry?
2. How does the company adjust to changes in economic conditions?
3. How will changes in sociocultural forces provide opportunities for Whole Foods in the future?

NOTES

[1] Erin Carlyle, "How Goya Became One of America's Fastest-Growing Food Companies," *Forbes*, May 8, 2013, www.forbes.com/sites/erincarlyle/2013/05/08/how-goya-became-one-of-americas-fastest-growing-food-companies (accessed July 16, 2013); Grace Flores-Hughes, "Goya Foods Forever! How the Unanue Family Changed American Eating," Vioxxi, June 20, 2013, www.voxxi.com/goya-foods-unanue-family-american-eating (accessed July 16, 2013); Steven Miller, "He Took Hispanic Food to the Masses at Goya Foods," *The Wall Street Journal*, June 14, 2013, http://online.wsj.com/article/SB10001424127887324049504578545663710872842.html (accessed July 16, 2013).

[2] "Dotcom Bust," *The Economist*, January 28, 2012, p. 66; Sven Grundberg, "The Pirate Bay Co-Founder Faces New Allegations," *The Wall Street Journal*, September 11, 2012, online.wsj.com/article/SB100008723963904438841045776451538229833 44.html (accessed December 7, 2012).

[3] Rebecca Orchant, "The Top Sodas in America, in Order from Worst to Best," *The Huffington Post*, October 1, 2013, www.huffingtonpost.com/2013/07/12/best-sodas-in-order-photos_n_3582042.html (accessed November 4, 2013); Natalie Zmuda, "Major Changes at PepsiCo as Marketing Department Reorganizes," *Ad Age*, June 16, 2011, http://adage.com/article/cmo-strategy/pepsico-reorganizes-marketing-department-beverages/228259 (accessed November 4, 2013).

[4] O. C. Ferrell and Michael Hartline, *Marketing Strategy* (Mason, OH: Cengage Learning, 2011).

[5] Ferrell and Hartline, *Marketing Strategy*.

[6] Aron O'Cass and Liem Viet Ngo, "Balancing External Adaptation and Internal Effectiveness: Achieving Better Brand Performance," *Journal of Business Research* 60 (January 2007): 11–20.

[7] Eberhard Stickel, "Uncertainty Reduction in a Competitive Environment," *Journal of Business Research* 51 (2001): 169–177.

[8] John Jannarone, "Discounters Are Still in Fashion," *The Wall Street Journal*, February 25, 2011, p. C8.

[9] Chain Store Guide, *The 50 Fastest Growing Discount Stores & Specialty Retailers* (Tampa, FL: Chain Store Guide, 2010).

[10] Steve Hargreaves, "15% of Americans Living in Poverty," *CNN Money*, September 17, 2013, http://money.cnn.com/2013/09/17/news/economy/poverty-income (accessed November 4, 2013).

[11] Kamila Hinkson, "Where Do Millionaires Live … Toronto Has 118,000," *The Star*, May 9, 2013, www.thestar.com/news/gta/2013/05/09/toronto_has_118000_millionaires.html (accessed November 4, 2013).

[12] Joshua Gallu, "Dodd–Frank May Cost $6.5 Billion and 5,000 Workers," *Bloomberg*, February 14, 2011, www.bloomberg.com/news/2011-02-14/dodd-frank-s-implementation-calls-for-6-5-billion-5-000-staff-in-budget.html (accessed November 4, 2013); Binyamin Appelbaum and Brady Dennis, "Dodd's Overhaul Goes Well Beyond Other Plans," *The Washington Post*, November 11, 2009, www.washingtonpost.com/wp-dyn/content/article/2009/11/09/AR2009110901935.html?hpid=topnews&sid=ST2009111003729 (accessed November 4, 2013).

[13] "Wall Street Reform: Bureau of Consumer Financial Protection (CFPB)," U.S. Treasury, www.treasury.gov/initiatives/Pages/cfpb.aspx (accessed February 22, 2011).

[14] "Trade Mission," BusinessDictionary.com, www.businessdictionary.com/definition/trade-mission.html (accessed February 7, 2012).

[15] "Top All-Time Donors, 1989–2012," OpenSecrets.org, www.opensecrets.org/orgs/list.php (accessed October 28, 2013).

[16] "Campaign Finance," *The New York Times*, October 8, 2010, http://topics.nytimes.com/top/reference/timestopics/subjects/c/campaign_finance/index.html (accessed January 24, 2011).

[17] Doug Stanglin and Kevin McCoy, "JPMorgan, DOJ Near $13B Settlement," *USA Today*, October 19, 2013, www.usatoday.com/story/money/business/2013/10/19/jp-morgan-justice-department-deal-settlement-13b/3052383 (accessed October 28, 2013).

[18] The United States Department of Justice, "Diebold Incorporated Resolves Foreign Corrupt Practices Act Investigation and Agrees to Pay $25.2 Million Criminal Penalty," October 22, 2013, www.justice.gov/opa/pr/2013/October/13-crm-1118.html (accessed November 4, 2013).

[19] Dionne Searcey, "U.K. Law on Bribes Has Firms in a Sweat," *The Wall Street Journal*, December 28, 2010, p. B1; Julius Melnitzer, "U.K. Enacts 'Far-Reaching' Anti-Bribery Act," *Law Times*, February 13, 2011, www.lawtimesnews.com/201102148245/Headline-News/UK-enacts-far-reaching-anti-bribery-act (accessed March 28, 2011).

[20] Julius Melnitzer, "U.K. Enacts 'Far-Reaching' Anti-Bribery Act," *Law Times*, February 13, 2011, www.lawtimesnews.com/201102148245/Headline-News/UK-enacts-far-reaching-anti-bribery-act (accessed March 28, 2011).

[21] Ibid.

[22] Sarah Johnson, "Don't Trust, Verify," *CFO*, February 1, 2012, www.cfo.com/article.cfm/14615752?f=singlepage (accessed February 7, 2012).

[23] Federal Trade Commission, "Path Social Networking App Settles FTC Charges It Deceived Consumers and Improperly Collected Personal Information from Users' Mobile Address Books," February 1, 2013, http://ftc.gov/opa/2013/02/path.shtm (accessed November 4, 2013).

[24] Steve Lohr, "Drafting Antitrust Case, F.T.C. Raises Pressure on Google," *The New York Times*, www.nytimes.com/2012/10/13/technology/ftc-staff-prepares-antitrust-case-against-google-over-search.html?pagewanted=all&_r=0 (accessed November 4, 2013).

[25] Melissa Healy, "Generic Antidepressant Pulled from U.S. Shelves after FDA Finding," *Los Angeles Times*, October 5, 2012, http://articles.latimes.com/2012/oct/05/news/la-heb-generic-antidepressant-equivilency-20121005 (accessed November 4, 2013).

[26] "PhRMA Guiding Principles: Direct to Consumer Advertisements," Pharmaceutical Research and Manufacturers of America, PhRMA, "Direct to Consumer Pharmaceutical Advertising," December 2, 2013, http://www.phrma.org/direct-to-consumer-advertising (accessed May 6, 2014).

[27] Adolfo Flores, "Better Business Bureau Expels Los Angeles Area Chapter," *Los Angeles Times*, March 12, 2013, http://articles.latimes.com/2013/mar/12/business/la-fi-0313-bbb-expelled-20130313 (accessed November 4, 2013).

[28] Jacob Siegal, "T-Mobile's AT&T Attack Ads May Have Gone Too Far [updated]," BGR, September 17, 2013, http://bgr.com/2013/09/17/t-mobile-att-attack-ads (accessed November 4, 2013).

[29] Ryan Zinn, "National Advertising Review Board Determines That Fair Trade USA's 'Fair Trade Certified' Labels Should Reveal Percentage of Fair Trade Content in Body Care Products," Organic Consumers Association, September 18, 2012, www.organicconsumers.org/articles/article_26281.cfm (accessed December 11, 2012).

[30] David Goldman, "Are Landlines Doomed?" *CNN*, April 10, 2012, http://money.cnn.com/2012/04/10/technology/att-verizon-landlines/index.htm (accessed December 11, 2012).

[31] David Sarno, "The Rise of Tablet Computers," *Los Angeles Times*, May 6, 2011, http://articles.latimes.com/2011/may/06/business/la-fi-tablet-era-20110506 (accessed November 4, 2013).

[32] Kristen Purcell, "Online Video 2013," Pew Internet, October 10, 2013, http://articles.latimes.com/2011/may/06/business/la-fi-tablet-era-20110506 (accessed November 4, 2013).

[33] Nick Clayton, "Social Networks Account for 20% of Time Spent Online," *The Wall Street Journal*, December 22, 2011, http://blogs.wsj.com/tech-europe/2011/12/22/social-networks-account-for-20-of-time-spent-online (accessed November 4, 2013).

[34] Debbie McAlister, Linda Ferrell, and O. C. Ferrell, *Business and Society* (Mason, OH: Cengage Learning, 2011), pp. 352–353.

[35] Ibid.

[36] Vladmir Zwass, "Electronic Commerce: Structures and Issues," *International Journal of Electronic Commerce* (Fall 2000): 3–23.

[37] Grayson K. Vincent and Victoria A. Velkoff, "The Next Four Decades: The Older Population in the United States: 2010 to 2050," May 2010, www.census.gov/prod/2010pubs/p25-1138.pdf (accessed November 4, 2013).

[38] www.seniorpeoplemeet.com, babyboomerpeoplemeet.com (accessed March 8, 2010).

[39] Sam Roberts, "New Census Numbers Show Recession's Effect on Families," *International New York Times*, August 27, 2013, www.nytimes.com/2013/08/28/us/new-census-numbers-show-recessions-effect-on-families.html (accessed October 28, 2013).

[40] "State & County Quick Facts," U.S. Census Bureau, http://quickfacts.census.gov/qfd/states/00000.html (accessed December 11, 2012); "10,000 Baby Boomers Retire," Pew Research Center: The Data Bank, December 11, 2012, http://pewresearch.org/databank/dailynumber/?NumberID=1150 (accessed December 11, 2012).

[41] Haya El Nasser, Gregory Korte, and Paul Overberg, "308.7 Million," *USA Today*, December 22, 2010, p. 1A; "U.S. and World Population Clocks," U.S. Census Bureau, www.census.gov/main/www/popclock.html (accessed November 4, 2013).

[42] U.S. Census Bureau, *Statistical Abstract of the United States, 2010*, 58.

[43] U.S. Census Bureau, "U.S. Census Bureau Projections Show a Slower Growing, Older, More Diverse Nation a Half Century from Now," December 12, 2012, www.census.gov/newsroom/releases/archives/population/cb12-243.html (accessed October 26, 2013).

[44] Bruce Horovitz, "At McDonald's, It's All about Millennials Now," *USA Today*, May 23, 2013, p. B1.

[45] AAA, "Teens Delaying Licensure—A Cause for Concern?" August 1, 2013, http://newsroom.aaa.com/2013/08/teens-delaying-licensure-a-cause-for-concern (accessed November 6, 2013).

[46] "Parents Grossly Underestimate the Influence Their Children Wield over In-Store Purchases," *Science News*, March 17, 2009, http://www.sciencedaily.com/releases/2009/03/090316075853.htm (accessed May 6, 2014).

[47] "About Seventh Generation," www.seventhgeneration.com/about (accessed November 4, 2013).

[48] *Recycline* [DVD], Cengage Learning; Preserve Products website, www.preserveproducts.com (accessed November 4, 2013); *Preserve Press Kit*, www.preserveproducts.com/media/presskits/Preserve_MediaKit_2012.pdf (accessed November 4, 2013); Nick Leiber, "America's Most Promising Social Entrepreneurs 2011: Preserve Products," *Bloomberg Businessweek*, http://images.businessweek.com/slideshows/20110621/america-s-most-promising-social-entrepreneurs-2011/slides/19 (accessed November 4, 2013); "Eric Hudson, Recycline," [Interview], YouTube, August 13, 2010, www.youtube.com/watch?v=6hhFPUSMtMg (accessed March 13, 2012); *Recyclables Newsletter: Recycline*, Fall 2006, www.preserveproducts.com/newsletter/newsletter-fall-06.html (accessed November 4, 2013).

[49] "Bisphenol-A," Whole Foods Market, www.wholefoodsmarket.com/products/bisphenol-a.php (accessed November 4, 2013); Joe Dickson, "The FDA Changes Its Tune on Bisphenol-A,"

Whole Foods Market, http://blog.wholefoodsmarket.com/2010/01/the-fda-changes-its-tune-on-bisphenol-a (accessed March 2, 2012); "About Whole Foods Market," Whole Foods Market, www.wholefoodsmarket.com/company (accessed November 4, 2013); "Trader Joe's Product FAQs," Trader Joe's, www.traderjoes.com/about/product-faq.asp (accessed November 4, 2013); "Seafood Sustainability," Whole Foods Market, www.wholefoodsmarket.com/values/seafood.php (accessed November 4, 2013); "Our Quality Standards," Whole Foods Market, www.wholefoodsmarket.com/products/quality-standards.php (accessed March 2, 2012); "Health Starts Here™ Launches at Whole Foods Market®," Whole Foods Market Press Room, January 20, 2010, http://wholefoodsmarket.com/pressroom/blog/2010/01/20/health-starts-here%E2%84%A2-launches-at-whole-foods-market%C2%AE (accessed March 2, 2012); Lisa Baertlein, "Whole Foods Boosts 2011 View, Shares Up," Reuters, July 27, 2011, www.reuters.com/article/2011/07/27/us-wholefoods-idUSTRE76Q6EU20110727 (accessed November 4, 2013); Katy McLaughlin and Timothy W. Martin, "As Sales Slip, Whole Foods Tries Health Push," *The Wall Street Journal*, August 5, 2009, http://online.wsj.com/article/SB124941849645105559.html (accessed March 2, 2012); "World's Most Admired Companies: Whole Foods Market," *CNN Money*, http://money.cnn.com/magazines/fortune/most-admired/2012/snapshots/10572.html (accessed November 4, 2013).

Feature Notes

[a]Hannah Karp, "Ticketmaster Wants In on the Scalping Act," *The Wall Street Journal*, August 11, 2013,http://online.wsj.com/article/SB10001424127887323838204578654220372996886.html (accessed September 3, 2013); Julie Balise, "Ticketmaster Raises White Flag to Scalpers," www.money.msn.com, August 14, 2013, http://money.msn.com/now/post--ticketmaster-raises-white-flag-to-scalpers (accessed May 6, 2014); Live Nation, "TM+ Resell Seller FAQs," Live Support, https://livesupport.custhelp.com/app/answers/detail/a_id/866/~/tm%2B-resale-seller-faqs (accessed September 3, 2013).

[b]Brian Dumaine, "Google's Zero-Carbon Quest," Fortune Tech, http://tech.fortune.cnn.com/2012/07/12/google-zero-carbon (accessed August 17, 2012); Bill Weihl, "Reducing Our Carbon Footprint," Google, May 6, 2009, http://googleblog.blogspot.com/2009/05/reducing-our-carbon-footprint.html#!/2009/05/reducing-our-carbon-footprint.html (accessed August 17, 2012).

chapter 4

Social Responsibility and Ethics in Marketing

OBJECTIVES

4-1 Define the four dimensions of social responsibility.

4-2 State the importance of marketing ethics.

4-3 Describe the three factors of ethical decision making.

4-4 Comment on the requirements for improving ethical decision making.

4-5 Critique the role of social responsibility and ethics in improving marketing performance.

MARKETING INSIGHTS

Supporting Social Causes Can Gain Support for the Brand

For many companies, cause-related marketing is becoming not only a way to build rapport with customers through support of a social cause, but also a way to build upon the company's core competencies and values. In cause-related marketing, firms link their products to a particular social cause. Effective cause-related marketing initiatives can create a positive image of a company among consumers, particularly as consumers are increasingly expecting companies to support social or environmental causes. One study revealed that 85 percent of consumers view companies that engage in cause-related marketing in a more positive light.

Although some firms make one-time donations or decide to temporarily adopt a community project, others have successfully incorporated cause-related marketing into their programs. For instance, IBM established a community service program, Corporate Service Corps, that allows more than 200 teams of 10 to 15 people to volunteer domestically and globally. AT&T has invested more than $100 million in the education system, while its employees have volunteered 270,000 hours of mentoring for students. These programs have bolstered employee satisfaction and job performance and have also demonstrated how corporations can produce positive results within their communities.

Additionally, cause-related marketing has enabled organizations to achieve strong linkages between their support for causes and the products they offer. American Express created a special edition United Way Gift Card in which the company donates the purchase fee for the card to support United Way's work. American Express benefits from both the sale of the gift card as well as the positive perception it generates by aligning its product with a good cause. Aligning cause-related marketing activities with core competencies has proven to be an effective way of creating strong associations between company and cause[1].

© iStockphoto.com/EdStock

Most businesses operate responsibly and within the limits of the law, but organizations often walk a fine line between acting ethically and engaging in questionable behavior. Recent research findings show that ethical companies often have better stock performance, but too often companies are distracted by the short-term costs of implementing ethics programs and the fleeting benefits of cutting ethical corners. Another common mistake companies make is a tendency to believe that because an activity is legal, it is also ethical. In fact, ethics often goes above and beyond the law and should therefore be a critical concern of marketers.

Some of the most common types of unethical practices among companies include deceptive sales practices, bribery, price discrimination, deceptive advertising, misleading packaging, and marketing defective products. Deceptive advertising in particular causes consumers to become defensive toward all promotional messages and distrustful of all advertising, so it hurts not only consumers but marketers as well.[2] Practices of this kind raise questions about marketers' obligations to society. Inherent in these questions are the issues of social responsibility and marketing ethics.

Because social responsibility and ethics often have profound impacts on the success of marketing strategies, we devote this chapter to their role in marketing decision making. We begin by defining social responsibility and exploring its dimensions. We then discuss social responsibility issues, such as sustainability and the marketer's role as a member of the community. Next, we define and examine the role of ethics in marketing decisions. We consider ethical issues in marketing, the ethical decision-making process, and ways to improve ethical conduct in marketing. Finally, we incorporate social responsibility and ethics into strategic market planning.

4-1 THE NATURE OF SOCIAL RESPONSIBILITY

In marketing, **social responsibility** refers to an organization's obligation to maximize its positive impact and minimize its negative impact on society. Social responsibility thus deals with the total effect of all marketing decisions on society. In marketing, social responsibility includes the managerial processes needed to monitor, satisfy, and even exceed stakeholder expectations and needs.[3] Remember from Chapter 1 that stakeholders are groups that have a "stake," or claim, in some aspect of a company's products, operations, markets, industry, and outcomes. CEOs such as Indra Nooyi, chairperson and CEO of PepsiCo, are increasingly recognizing that in the future companies will have to "do better by doing better."[4]

Ample evidence demonstrates that ignoring stakeholders' demands for responsible marketing can destroy customers' trust and even prompt government regulation. Irresponsible actions that anger customers, employees, or competitors may not only jeopardize a marketer's financial standing but have legal repercussions as well. For instance, Johnson and Johnson (J&J) settled with the U.S. Justice Department for $2.2 billion after the Justice Department accused it of marketing the drug Risperdal illegally. One of the accusations levied against J&J was that it failed to warn about negative side effects of the drugs adequately. An investigation was also launched to determine if J&J marketed Risperdal before given approval by the Food and Drug Administration (FDA).[5]

In contrast, socially responsible activities can generate positive publicity and boost sales. IBM, for example, has established a corporate volunteer program that sends employees to developing countries to create opportunities for their citizens. Through this program, IBM has helped Kenya reform its postal system and has aided Tanzania in developing eco-tourism opportunities. Although the program is costly, IBM's efforts have created positive relationships with stakeholders in these countries and have generated approximately $5 million in new business.[6]

social responsibility
An organization's obligation to maximize its positive impact and minimize its negative impact on society

Socially responsible efforts have a positive impact on local communities; at the same time, they indirectly help the sponsoring organization by attracting goodwill, publicity, and potential customers and employees. Thus, although social responsibility is certainly a positive concept in itself, most organizations embrace it in the expectation of indirect long-term benefits. Panera Bread recognizes its key stakeholders, including its customers, employees, and communities. To support its "live consciously" commitment, the company donates all leftover bread each night to people in need in its communities. Panera's philosophy has a positive impact on the communities where it does business. Our own research findings suggest that an organizational culture that supports social responsibility generates greater employee commitment and improved business performance.[7] Table 4.1 provides a sampling of companies that have chosen to make social responsibility a strategic long-term objective.

© Panera Bread

Social Responsibility
Panera's social responsibility in donating bread to the local community impacts key stakeholders, including customers, employees, and communities.

4-1a The Dimensions of Social Responsibility

Socially responsible organizations strive for **marketing citizenship** by adopting a strategic focus for fulfilling the economic, legal, ethical, and philanthropic social responsibilities that their stakeholders expect of them. Companies that consider the diverse perspectives of stakeholders in their daily operations and strategic planning are said to have a *stakeholder orientation*, an important element of social responsibility.[8] A stakeholder orientation in marketing goes beyond customers, competitors, and regulators to include understanding and addressing the needs of all stakeholders, including communities and special-interest groups. As a result, organizations are now under pressure to undertake initiatives that demonstrate a balanced perspective on stakeholder interests.[9] For instance, Pfizer has secured stakeholder input on a number of issues including rising health-care costs and health-care reform.[10] As Figure 4.1 shows, the economic, legal, ethical, and philanthropic dimensions of social responsibility can be viewed as a pyramid.[11]

marketing citizenship The adoption of a strategic focus for fulfilling the economic, legal, ethical, and philanthropic social responsibilities expected by stakeholders

At the most basic level, all companies have an economic responsibility to be profitable so that they can provide a return on investment to their owners and investors, create jobs for the community, and contribute goods and services to the economy. How organizations relate to stakeholders affects the economy. When economic downturns or poor decisions lead companies to lay off employees, communities often suffer as they attempt to absorb the displaced employees. Customers may experience diminished levels of service as a result of fewer experienced employees. Stock prices often decline when layoffs are announced, reducing the value of shareholders' investment portfolios. An organization's sense of economic responsibility is especially significant for employees, raising such issues as equal job opportunities, workplace diversity, job safety, health, and employee privacy. Economic responsibilities require finding a balance in stakeholder interests while recognizing that a firm must make a profit to be sustainable in the long run.

Marketers also have an economic responsibility to engage in fair competition and build ethical customer relationships. Government

Table 4.1 Best Corporate Citizens

1	AT&T, Inc.
2	Mattel, Inc.
3	Bristol Myers Squibb Co.
4	Eaton Corp.
5	Intel Corp.
6	Gap, Inc.
7	Hasbro, Inc.
8	Merck & Co., Inc.
9	Campbell Soup Co.
10	Coca-Cola Enterprises Inc.

Source: "CR's 100 Best Corporate Citizens 2013," *CR*, www.thecro.com/files/100Best2013_web.pdf (accessed November 20, 2013).

Figure 4.1 The Pyramid of Corporate Social Responsibility

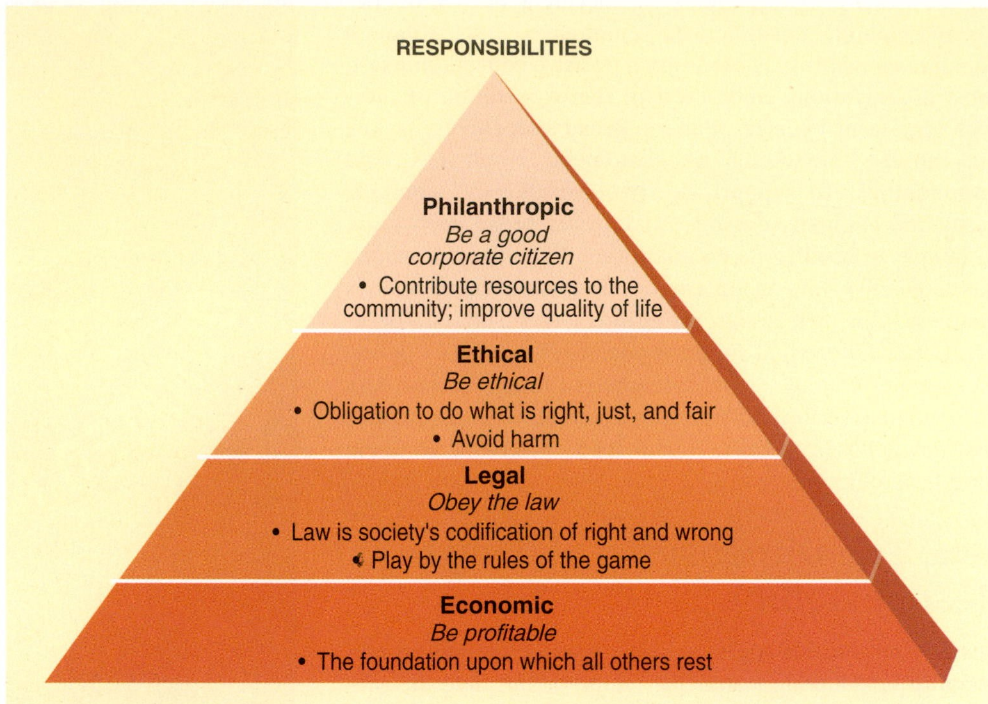

Source: From Archie B. Carroll, "The Pyramid of Corporate Social Responsibility: Toward the Moral Management of Organizational Stakeholders," adaption of Figure 3, p. 42. Reprinted from *Business Horizons*, July/August 1991, by the Foundation for the School of Business at Indiana University. Reprinted with permission.

regulatory agencies often define the activities that constitute fair competition along with unethical issues such as price fixing, deceptive sales practices, false advertising, bribery, and questionable distribution practices. This misconduct can be considered unfair competition that is also damaging to consumers. Companies that engage in questionable conduct damage their reputation and can destroy customer trust. On the other hand, the "World's Most Ethical Companies"—a designation given by the Ethisphere Institute—have a track

John Carey/Photolibrary/Getty Images

The Nature of Social Responsibility
Bananas receive fairtrade certification when their organizations treat farmers humanely and pay them adequate wages. The sticker tells consumers that the bananas are free trade certified.

record of avoiding these types of issues. Starbucks, Cummins, Johnson Controls, Adobe, and Juniper Networks are profitable and have excellent reputations with their customers. Marketers are also expected, of course, to obey laws and regulations. Laws and regulations are designed to keep U.S. companies' actions within the range of acceptable conduct and fair competition. When customers, interest groups, or businesses become outraged over what they perceive as misconduct on the part of a marketing organization, they may urge their legislators to draft new legislation to regulate the behavior or engage in litigation to force the organization to "play by the rules."

Economic and legal responsibilities are the most basic levels of social responsibility for a good reason: Failure to consider them may mean that a marketer is not around long enough to engage in ethical or philanthropic activities. Beyond these dimensions is **marketing ethics**, principles and standards that define acceptable conduct in marketing as determined by various stakeholders, including the public, government regulators, private-interest groups, consumers, industry, and the organization itself. The most basic of these principles have been codified as laws and regulations to encourage marketers to conform to society's expectations for conduct. However, marketing ethics goes beyond legal issues. Ethical marketing decisions foster trust, which helps build long-term marketing relationships. We take a more detailed look at the ethical dimension of social responsibility later in this chapter.

marketing ethics Principles and standards that define acceptable marketing conduct as determined by various stakeholders

cause-related marketing The practice of linking products to a particular social cause on an ongoing or short-term basis

At the top of the pyramid of corporate responsibility (see Figure 4.1) are philanthropic responsibilities. These responsibilities, which go beyond marketing ethics, are not required of a company, but they promote human welfare or goodwill, as do the economic, legal, and ethical dimensions of social responsibility. That many companies have demonstrated philanthropic responsibility is evidenced by the more than $18 billion in annual corporate donations and contributions to environmental and social causes.[12] Even small companies participate in philanthropy through donations and volunteer support of local causes and national charities, such as the Red Cross and the United Way. For example, Charlotte-based printing company Boingo Graphics developed a Boingo Cares program that provides printing services to organizations such as the Humane Society of Charlotte that may otherwise be unable to afford them.[13]

More companies than ever are adopting a strategic approach to corporate philanthropy. Many firms link their products to a particular social cause on an ongoing or short-term basis, a practice known as **cause-related marketing**. Bank of America Merrill Lynch has partnered with the nonprofit organization Water.org in its quest to develop clean water solutions for communities worldwide. In its advertisement, Bank of America Merrill Lynch features a community member getting clean water from an outdoor faucet. The bank calls clean water "liquid assets" in its advertising to explain the value of water in financial terms, linking it to the organization's operations. Such cause-related programs tend to appeal to consumers because they provide an additional reason to "feel good" about a particular purchase. Marketers like the programs because well-designed ones increase sales and create feelings of respect and admiration for the companies involved. Indeed, research findings suggest that 85 percent of American consumers have a more positive opinion of an organization when it supports causes that they care about.[14]

© Bank of America Corporation

Cause-Related Marketing
Bank of America Merrill Lynch demonstrates cause-related marketing through its partnership with nonprofit organization Water.org.

On the other hand, some companies are beginning to extend the concept of corporate philanthropy beyond financial contributions by adopting a **strategic philanthropy** approach, the synergistic use of organizational core competencies and resources to address key stakeholders' interests and achieve both organizational and social benefits. Strategic philanthropy involves employees, organizational resources and expertise, and the ability to link those assets to the concerns of key stakeholders, including employees, customers, suppliers, and social needs. Strategic philanthropy involves both financial and nonfinancial contributions to stakeholders (employee time, goods and services, company technology and equipment, etc.), while also benefiting the company.[15] Salesforce.com, for example, believes in the benefits of strategic philanthropy so strongly that it incorporates community service into its corporate culture. Salesforce.com allows employees 1 percent of their time to volunteer in their communities, sets aside 1 percent of the company's capital for the Salesforce.com Foundation, and donates or discounts licenses of its Customer Relationship Management software to nonprofits worldwide.[16]

4-1b Social Responsibility Issues

Although social responsibility may seem to be an abstract ideal, managers make decisions related to social responsibility every day. To be successful, a business must determine what customers, government regulators, competitors, and society want or expect in terms of social responsibility. Table 4.2 summarizes three major categories of social responsibility issues: sustainability, consumerism, and community relations.

strategic philanthropy The synergistic use of organizational core competencies and resources to address key stakeholders' interests and achieve both organizational and social benefits

sustainability The potential for the long-term well-being of the natural environment, including all biological entities, as well as the interaction among nature and individuals, organizations, and business strategies

Sustainability

One of the more common ways marketers demonstrate social responsibility is through programs designed to protect and preserve the natural environment. **Sustainability** is the potential for the long-term well-being of the natural environment, including all biological entities, as well as the interaction among nature and individuals, organizations, and business strategies. Sustainability includes the assessment and improvement of business strategies, economic sectors, work practices, technologies, and lifestyles—all while maintaining the natural environment. Aubrey Organics uses its advertisement to describe the

Table 4.2 Social Responsibility Issues

Issue	Description	Major Social Concerns
Sustainability	Consumers insisting not only on a good quality of life but also on a healthful environment so they can maintain a high standard of living during their lifetimes	Conservation Water pollution Air pollution Land pollution
Consumerism	Activities undertaken by independent individuals, groups, and organizations to protect their rights as consumers	The right to safety The right to be informed The right to choose The right to be heard
Community relations	Society eager to have marketers contribute to its well-being, wishing to know what marketers do to help solve social problems	Equality issues Disadvantaged members of society Safety and health Education and general welfare

environmental benefits of its products. Not only are the company's products organic, but the company also offsets 100 percent of its electricity to develop more sustainable operations. Many companies are making contributions to sustainability by adopting more eco-friendly business practices and/or supporting environmental initiatives. Method has been largely successful in selling green cleaning supplies. Their success prompted other firms in the industry such as S.C. Johnson to begin their own green product lines.[17] Such efforts generate positive publicity and often increase sales for the companies involved.

Many products have been certified as "green" by environmental organizations such as Green Seal and carry a special logo identifying their organization as green marketers. Lumber products at Home Depot, for instance, may carry a seal from the Forest Stewardship Council to indicate that they were harvested from sustainable forests using environmentally-friendly methods.[18] Likewise, most Chiquita bananas are certified through the Rainforest Alliance's Better Banana Project as having been grown with more environmentally and labor-friendly practices.[19] In Europe, companies can voluntarily apply for the EU Ecolabel to indicate that their products are less harmful to the environment than competing products, based on scientifically determined criteria (see Figure 4.2).

Although demand for economic, legal, and ethical solutions to environmental problems is widespread, the environmental movement in marketing includes many different groups whose values and goals often conflict. Some environmentalists and marketers believe companies should work to protect and preserve the natural environment by implementing the following goals:

Green Marketing
Aubrey Organics make consumers aware of its energy-saving programs and technology through a marketing communications campaign.

1. *Eliminate the concept of waste.* Recognizing that pollution and waste usually stem from inefficiency, the question is not what to do with waste but how to make things without waste.
2. *Reinvent the concept of a product.* Products should be reduced to only three types and eventually just two. The first type is consumables, which are eaten or, when placed in the ground, turn into soil with few harmful side effects. The second type is durable goods—such as cars, televisions, computers, and refrigerators—that should be made, used, and returned to the manufacturer within a closed-loop system. Such products should be designed for disassembly and recycling. The third category is unsalables and includes such products as radioactive materials, heavy metals, and toxins. These products should always belong to the original makers, who should be responsible for the products and their full life-cycle effects. Reclassifying products in this way encourages manufacturers to design products more efficiently.
3. *Make prices reflect the cost.* Every product should reflect or at least approximate its actual cost—not only the direct cost of production but also the cost of air, water, and soil. To illustrate, the cost of a gallon of gasoline is higher when pollution, waste disposal, health effects, and defense expenditures are factored in. Major disasters like the BP oil leak in the Gulf of Mexico also impact the price of gas.
4. *Make environmentalism profitable.* Consumers are beginning to recognize that competition in the marketplace should not occur between companies that are harming the environment and those that are trying to save it.[20]

Figure 4.2 The EU Ecolabel

Consumerism

Another significant issue in socially responsible marketing is consumerism, which we defined in Chapter 3 as the efforts of independent individuals, groups, and organizations to protect the rights of consumers. A number of interest groups and individuals have taken action against companies they consider irresponsible by lobbying government officials and agencies, engaging in letter-writing campaigns and boycotts, and making public-service announcements. Some consumers choose to boycott firms and products out of a desire to support a cause and make a difference.[21] How a firm handles customer complaints affects consumer evaluations and in turn customer satisfaction and loyalty.[22]

The consumer movement has been helped by news-format television programs, such as *Dateline*, *60 Minutes*, and *Prime Time Live*, as well as by 24-hour news coverage from CNN, MSNBC, and Fox News. The Internet too has changed the way consumers obtain information about companies' goods, services, and activities. Consumers can share their opinions about goods and services and about companies they see as irresponsible at consumer-oriented websites, such as epinions.com and ConsumerReview.com, and through blogs and social networking sites.

Ralph Nader, one of the best-known consumer activists, continues to crusade for consumer rights. Consumer activism by Nader and others has resulted in legislation requiring many features that make cars safer: seat belts, air bags, padded dashboards, stronger door latches, head restraints, shatterproof windshields, and collapsible steering columns. Activists' efforts have also facilitated the passage of several consumer protection laws, including the Wholesome Meat Act of 1967, the Radiation Control for Health and Safety Act of 1968, the Clean Water Act of 1972, and the Toxic Substance Act of 1976.

Also of great importance to the consumer movement are four basic rights spelled out in a consumer "bill of rights" that was drafted by President John F. Kennedy. These rights include the right to safety, the right to be informed, the right to choose, and the right to be heard.

Ensuring consumers' *right to safety* means marketers are obligated not to market a product that they know could harm consumers. This right can be extended to imply that

Going Green

SodaStream: Protecting the Environment by Making Soda at Home

The first rendition of SodaStream was introduced in 1903 and became a big hit in Europe. After many years and acquisitions, SodaStream began selling products globally. Today the company is the market leader in the homemade beverage industry. SodaStream is a small appliance that transforms still water into sparkling water. The consumer then adds concentrates to make flavored soda-like beverages.

SodaStream's success is the result of CEO Daniel Birnbaum's promotion of the product as a healthier and greener alternative to prepackaged sodas. As consumers increasingly become more concerned about their health and impact on the environment, SodaStream is becoming a widespread household appliance. The company's promotion efforts focus on the amount of plastic, glass, and aluminum bottles that are thrown away every year. In 2013 SodaStream created an ad to be aired on Super Bowl Sunday. It was estimated that more than 500 million plastic bottles would be discarded on that day alone. The television networks refused to air the ad as many of their sponsors and advertisers were large beverage companies, but SodaStream posted the ad online and received more than two million views on YouTube. In 2014 a censored SodaStream advertisement with endorser Scarlett Johansson aired during the Super Bowl. Again, the commercial was edited to remove a barb at Coke and Pepsi. Since 2009, the company claims it has saved the environment more than three billion bottles through the use of its machines and reusable bottles.[a]

all products must be safe for their intended use, include thorough and explicit instructions for proper and safe use, and have been tested to ensure reliability and quality. The maker of sports supplement Craze suspended production after scientists claimed the product contained a methamphetamine type of compound. This violates consumers' right to safety.[23]

Consumers' *right to be informed* means consumers should have access to and the opportunity to review all relevant information about a product before buying it. Many laws require specific labeling on product packaging to satisfy this right. In addition, labels on alcoholic and tobacco products must inform consumers that these products may cause illness and other problems.

The *right to choose* means consumers should have access to a variety of products and services at competitive prices. They should also be assured of satisfactory quality and service at a fair price. Activities that reduce competition among businesses in an industry might jeopardize this right.

The *right to be heard* ensures that consumers' interests will receive full and sympathetic consideration in the formulation of government policy. The right to be heard also promises consumers fair treatment when they complain to marketers about products. This right benefits marketers, too, because when consumers complain about a product, the manufacturer can use this information to modify the product and make it more satisfying.

The Federal Trade Commission provides a wealth of consumer information at its website (www.ftc.gov/bcp/consumer.shtm) on a variety of topics ranging from automobiles and the Internet to diet, health, fitness, and identity theft.

Community Relations

On the other hand, being a good community citizen also means avoiding harmful actions that could damage the community. Examples include pollution, urban sprawl, and exploitation of the workforce. A firm that participates in the economic viability of the community improves community relations. For example, Cutco Corp. in Olean, New York, gives its employees gift certificates to local stores at Christmas. This supports local businesses and helps build good relationships with the community.

Corporate Contributions
General Mills makes a positive contribution to society through its Yoplait Save Lids to Save Lives Program. During its campaign, customers mail in pink yogurt lids to the organization. For every lid, General Mills donates 10 cents to Susan G. Komen for the Cure® for a maximum donation of $2.5 million.

Although most charitable donations come from individuals, corporate philanthropy is on the rise. Target, for instance, committed $1 billion in its ongoing efforts to improve education. Through the retailer's Take Charge of Education program, customers who use a Target REDcard can designate a specific school to which Target donates 1 percent of their total purchase. The company also provides funds for building new school libraries.[24]

Smaller firms can also make positive contributions to their communities. California-based clothing company Patagonia donates 1 percent of its sales toward preserving and restoring the environment.[25] From a positive perspective, a marketer can significantly improve its community's quality of life through employment opportunities, economic development, and financial contributions to educational, health, cultural, and recreational causes.

4-2 MARKETING ETHICS

As noted earlier, marketing ethics is a dimension of social responsibility that involves principles and standards that define acceptable conduct in marketing. Acceptable standards of conduct in making individual and group decisions in marketing are determined by various stakeholders and by an organization's ethical climate. Marketers must also use their own values and knowledge of ethics to act responsibly and provide ethical leadership for others.

Marketers should be aware of stakeholders, including customers, employees, regulators, suppliers, and the community. When marketing activities deviate from accepted standards, the exchange process can break down, resulting in customer dissatisfaction, lack of trust, and lawsuits. In recent years, a number of ethical scandals have resulted in a massive loss of confidence in the integrity of U.S. businesses. A recent study shows that about 60 percent of U.S. consumers trust businesses today.[26] Trust is an important concern for marketers because it is the foundation for long-term relationships. Consumer lack of trust has increased in recent years due to the financial crisis and deep recession. The questionable conduct of high-profile financial institutions and banks has caused many consumers to critically examine the conduct of all companies. Trust must be built or restored to gain the confidence of customers. Figure 4.3 describes the trust global consumers have for different institutions. Once trust is lost, it can take a lifetime to rebuild. The way to deal with ethical issues is proactively during the strategic planning process, not after major problems materialize.

Our focus here is on the ethical conduct of marketers. It is not our purpose to examine the conduct of consumers, although some do behave unethically (engaging, for instance, in coupon fraud, shoplifting, intellectual property piracy, and other abuses). We discuss consumer misbehavior and ethical issues associated with this misconduct in Chapter 7. Our goal in this chapter is to underscore the importance of resolving ethical issues in marketing and to help you learn about marketing ethics.

ethical issue An identifiable problem, situation, or opportunity requiring a choice among several actions that must be evaluated as right or wrong, ethical or unethical

4-2a Ethical Issues in Marketing

An **ethical issue** is an identifiable problem, situation, or opportunity that requires an individual or organization to choose from among several actions that must be evaluated as right or wrong, ethical or unethical. Any time an activity causes marketing managers or customers

Figure 4.3 Global Trust in Different Industries

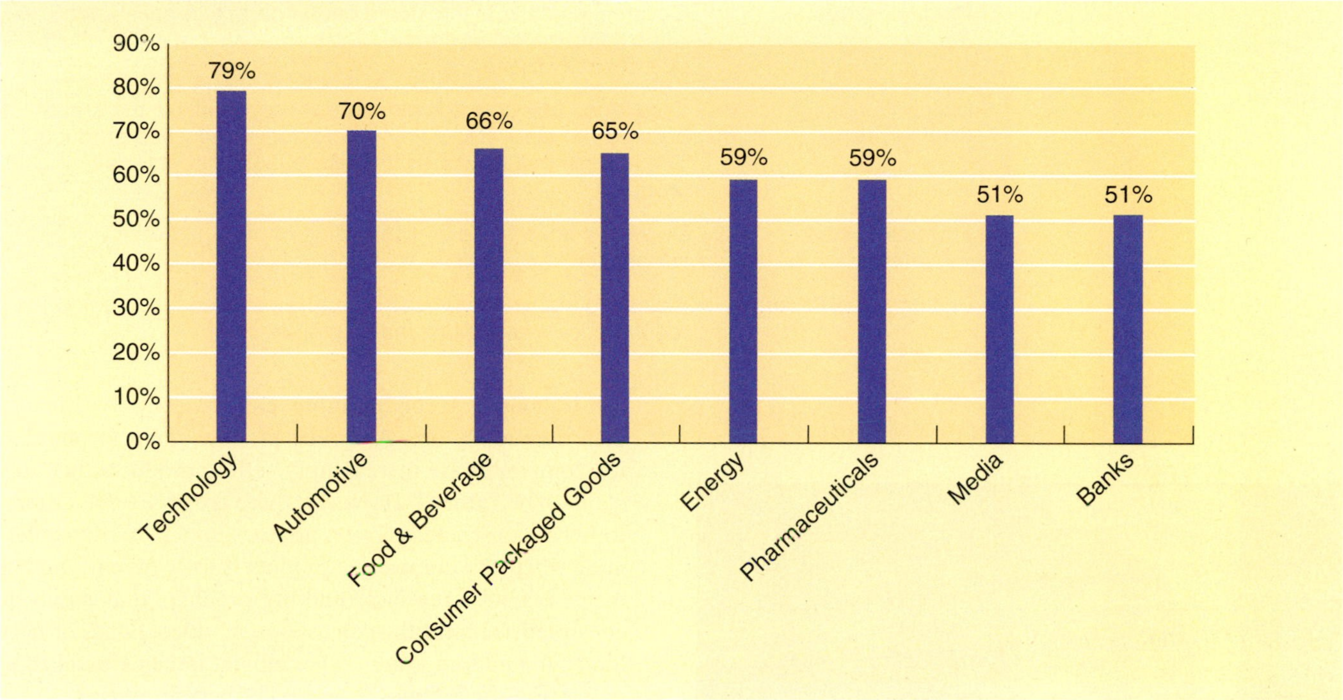

Source: Edelman, *2014 Edelman Trust Barometer Global Insights*, www.edelman.com/insights/intellectual-property/2014-edelman-trust-barometer/about-trust/global-results (accessed March 27, 2014).

in their target market to feel manipulated or cheated, a marketing ethical issue exists, regardless of the legality of that activity. For instance, McDonald's has received criticism from activists who claim that the firm's marketing to children contributes to the obesity epidemic. McDonald's defends its marketing practices and refuses to retire its Ronald McDonald mascot, although it has introduced many healthier food options.[27]

Regardless of the reasons behind specific ethical issues, marketers must be able to identify those issues and decide how to resolve them. Doing so requires familiarity with the many kinds of ethical issues that may arise in marketing. Research findings suggest that the greater the consequences associated with an issue, the more likely it will be recognized as an ethics issue and the more important it will be in making an ethical decision.[28] Some examples of ethical issues related to product, promotion, price, and distribution (the marketing mix) appear in Table 4.3.

Product-related ethical issues generally arise when marketers fail to disclose risks associated with a product or information regarding the function, value, or use of a product. Pressures can build to substitute inferior materials or product components to reduce costs. Ethical issues also arise when marketers fail to inform customers about existing conditions or changes in product quality; such failure is a form of dishonesty about the nature of the product. *Product recalls* occur when companies ask customers to return products found to be defective. Companies that issue product recalls are often criticized for not having adequate quality controls to catch the defective product before it was released. For instance, Chobani recalled some of its Greek yogurt cups after consumers began to get sick from a mold growing in some of the products.[29] The failure to maintain product quality and integrity in production is a significant ethical issue.

Promotion can create ethical issues in a variety of ways, among them false or misleading advertising and manipulative or deceptive sales promotions, tactics, and publicity. One controversial issue in the area of promotion is *greenwashing*, which occurs when products

Table 4.3 Sample Ethical Issues Related to the Marketing Mix

Product Issue *Product information*	Covering up defects that could cause harm to a consumer; withholding critical performance information that could affect a purchase decision.
Distribution Issue *Counterfeiting*	Counterfeit products are widespread, especially in the areas of computer software, clothing, and audio and video products. The Internet has facilitated the distribution of counterfeit products.
Promotion Issue *Advertising*	Deceptive advertising or withholding important product information in a personal-selling situation.
Pricing Issue *Pricing*	Indicating that an advertised sale price is a reduction below the regular price when in fact that is not the case.

are promoted as being more environmentally friendly than they really are. As green products gain in popularity, companies are increasingly selling products that they claim to be "green." However, there are no formal criteria for what constitutes a green product, so it is hard to determine whether a company's product is truly green. Another major ethical issue is promoting products that might be construed as harmful, such as violent video games or fatty foods, to children. Many other ethical issues are linked to promotion, including the use of bribery in personal selling situations. *Bribery* occurs when an incentive (usually money or expensive gifts) is offered in exchange for an illicit advantage. Even a bribe that is offered to benefit the organization is usually considered unethical. Because it jeopardizes trust and fairness, it hurts the organization in the long run. For this reason, sales promotion activities such as games, contests, and other sales attempts must be communicated accurately and transparently.

Ethical Issue
Some concerned parents and advocates have called for the retirement of Ronald McDonald due to his popularity with children. They believe the company is using its mascot to unfairly market unhealthy food to children. McDonald's defends its use of Ronald and has begun offering healthier food options.

In pricing, common ethical issues are price fixing, predatory pricing, and failure to disclose the full price of a purchase. The emotional and subjective nature of price creates many situations in which misunderstandings between the seller and buyer cause ethical problems. Marketers have the right to price their products to earn a reasonable profit, but ethical issues may crop up when a company seeks to earn high profits at the expense of its customers. Some pharmaceutical companies, for example, have been accused of *price gouging,* or pricing products at exorbitant levels, and taking advantage of customers who must purchase the medicine to survive or to maintain their quality of life. Various forms of *bait and switch* pricing schemes attempt to gain consumer interest with a low-priced product, but then switch the buyer to a more expensive product or add-on service. One way companies do this is by telling customers that the lower-priced product they wanted is unavailable. Another issue relates to quantity surcharges that occur when consumers are effectively overcharged for buying a larger package size of the same grocery product.[30]

Ethical issues in distribution involve relationships among producers and marketing intermediaries. Marketing intermediaries, or middlemen (wholesalers and retailers), facilitate the flow of products from the producer to the ultimate customer. Each intermediary performs a different role and agrees to certain rights, responsibilities, and rewards associated with that role. For example, producers expect wholesalers and retailers to honor agreements and keep them informed of inventory needs. Serious ethical issues with regard to distribution include manipulating a product's availability for purposes of exploitation and using coercion to force intermediaries to behave in a specific manner. Several companies have been accused of *channel stuffing*, which involves shipping surplus inventory to wholesalers and retailers at an excessive rate, typically before the end of a quarter. The practice may conceal declining demand for a product or inflate financial statement earnings, which misleads investors.[31] Another ethical issue that has become a worldwide problem is *counterfeiting*. Counterfeit products not only cost the firm, but they can also be dangerous to the consumer. Counterfeit pills of a Novartis anti-malarial drug are becoming more common in Africa. These counterfeits could seriously jeopardize public safety.[32]

As this section has shown, the nature of marketing ethics involves the ethics of all marketing channel members. However, the member managing the product is often held accountable for ethical conduct throughout the total supply chain. Swedish fashion retailer Hennes & Mauritz (H&M) had to act quickly when it found that some of its clothing was being produced in a Cambodian factory where workers had been injured. H&M released a statement that the garments were contracted at the factory without their knowledge. However, this led to criticism regarding H&M's supply-chain controls.[33]

4-2b Ethical Dimensions of Managing Supply-Chain Relationships

Managing supply chains responsibly is one of the greatest difficulties of marketing ethics and therefore needs some additional explanation. Supply chains require constant vigilance on the part of marketers as well as the need to anticipate unforeseen circumstances. Consider Apple Inc., which has a stellar reputation for its high-quality products and technological innovation. Despite Apple's great reputation for quality products, human rights issues have emerged at Chinese suppliers that Apple uses to build and clean its products. Instances of forced overtime, underage workers, explosions, and improper disposal of waste have been recorded at Apple's supplier factories. Although Apple has a Supplier Code of Conduct, problems at its supplier factories have continued. For instance, Chinese-worker rights groups have accused

Marketing Debate

The Marketing of Free Toys in Fast Food

ISSUE: Is the marketing of toys in kid's meals unethical?

Fast food has come under scrutiny for marketing toys with kid's meals. Critics claim it is unethical to entice children to order fast food with toys. Some companies are responding to this discontent. Jack in the Box stopped offering toys and changed the kid's menu to include healthier meal options. Taco Bell is eliminating kid's meals from its menu altogether. San Francisco banned restaurants from offering free toys in kid's meals that do not meet nutritional criteria. However, others argue it is the parents' responsibility to make sure children eat healthy, and pressuring fast-food companies to stop marketing toys infringes on their rights as businesses. As a side note, McDonald's locations in San Francisco now charge 10 cents for the toys and donate the proceeds to charity.[b]

Apple supplier Pegatron of worker safety violations; withholding workers' pay; and poor living conditions.[34]

The issues that Apple has faced highlight the numerous risks that occur in global supply chains. Although companies often create a Supplier Code of Conduct, it requires regular audits to ensure that factories are following compliance standards—which in turn can incur significant costs to companies in both time and finances. Countries with lax labor laws, such as China and Russia, require even more diligent monitoring. Often suppliers hire subcontractors to do some of the work, which increases a company's network of suppliers and the costs of trying to monitor all of them. Finally, company compliance requirements may conflict with the mission of the procurement office. Because it is the procurement division's job to procure resources at the lowest price possible, the division may very well opt to source from less expensive suppliers with questionable ethical practices rather than from more expensive ethical suppliers. Nike faced this problem during the 1990s when it was highly criticized for worker abuses in its supplier factories.[35]

Managing supply-chain ethical decision making is important because many stakeholders hold the firm responsible for all ethical conduct related to product availability. This requires the company to exercise oversight over all of the supplies used in producing a product. Developing good supply-chain ethics is important because it ensures the integrity of the product and the firm's operations in serving customers. For instance, leading healthcare supply company Novation has been recognized for its strong corporate governance and reporting mechanisms in its supply chain. To encourage its suppliers to report misconduct, the company has instituted a vendor grievance and feedback system. This allows vendors to report potential problems before they reach the next level of the supply chain, which reduces the damage such problems will cause if the products continue down the supply chain unchecked.[36]

Fortunately, organizations have been coming up with solutions to promote ethical sourcing practices. First, it is essential for all companies that work with global suppliers to adopt a Global Supplier Code of Conduct and ensure that it is effectively communicated to suppliers. Additionally, companies should encourage compliance and procurement employees to work together to find ethical suppliers at reasonable costs. Marketers must also work to make certain that their company's supply chains are diverse. This can be difficult because sometimes the best product manufacturers are located in a single country. Yet although it is expensive to diversify a company's supply chain, disasters can incapacitate a country.[37] Finally, and perhaps most importantly, companies must perform regular audits on its suppliers and, if necessary, discipline those found to be in violation of company standards.[38] More on supply-chain management will be discussed in Chapter 14.

4-3 THE NATURE OF MARKETING ETHICS

To grasp the significance of ethics in marketing decision making, it is helpful to examine the factors that influence the ethical decision-making process. As Figure 4.4 shows, individual factors, organizational relationships, and opportunity interact to determine ethical decisions in marketing.

4-3a Individual Factors

When people need to resolve ethical conflicts in their daily lives, they often base their decisions on their own values and principles of right or wrong. People learn values and principles through socialization by family members, social groups, religion, and formal education. Because of different levels of personal ethics in any organization, there will be significant ethical diversity among employees. Most firms do not attempt to change an individual's personal ethics but try to hire employees with good character. Therefore, shared ethical values and compliance standards are required to prevent deviation from desired ethical conduct. In

Figure 4.4 **Factors That Influence the Ethical Decision-Making Process**

the workplace, however, recent researchers have established that an organization's culture often has more influence on marketing decisions than an individual's own values.[39]

4-3b Organizational Relationships

Although people can and do make ethical choices pertaining to marketing decisions, no one operates in a vacuum.[40] Ethical choices in marketing are most often made jointly, in work groups and committees, or in conversations and discussions with coworkers. Marketing employees resolve ethical issues based not only on what they learned from their own backgrounds but also on what they learn from others in the organization. The outcome of this learning process depends on the strength of each individual's personal values, opportunity for unethical behavior, and exposure to others who behave ethically or unethically. Superiors, peers, and subordinates in the organization influence the ethical decision-making process. Although people outside the organization, such as family members and friends, also influence decision makers, organizational culture and structure operate through organizational relationships to influence ethical decisions.

organizational, or **corporate, culture** A set of values, beliefs, goals, norms, and rituals that members of an organization share

Organizational, or **corporate, culture** is a set of values, beliefs, goals, norms, and rituals that members of an organization share. These values also help shape employees' satisfaction with their employer, which may affect the quality of the service they provide to customers. A firm's culture may be expressed formally through codes of conduct, memos, manuals, dress codes, and ceremonies, but it is also conveyed informally through work habits, extracurricular activities, and stories. An organization's culture gives its members meaning and suggests rules for how to behave and deal with problems within the organization.

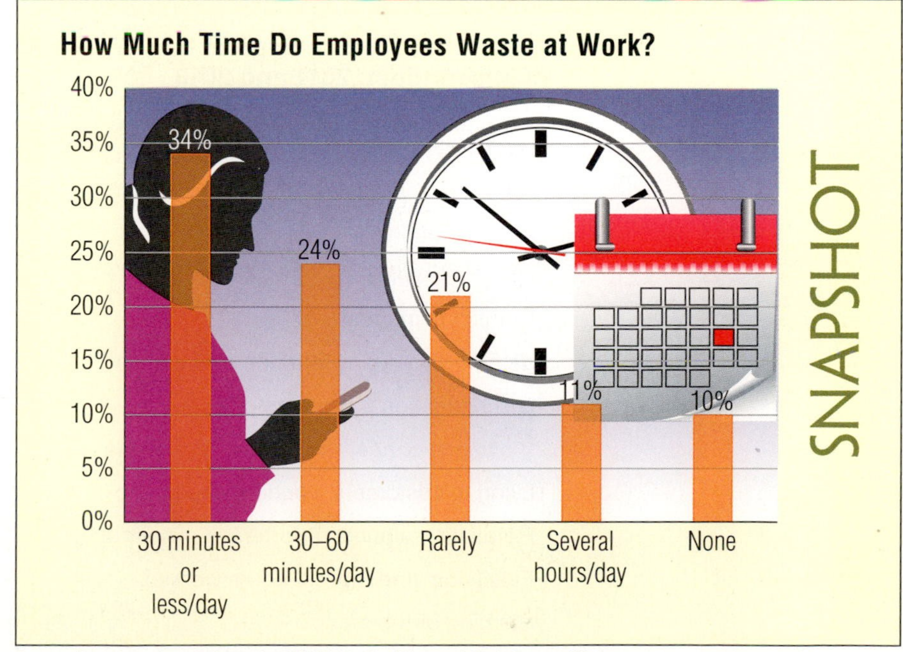

Source: Based on Aaron Gouveia, "2013 Wasting Time at Work Survey," Salary.com, www.salary.com/2013-wasting-time-atwork-survey/slide/2 (accessed November 22, 2013).

With regard to organizational structure, most experts agree that the chief executive officer or vice president of marketing sets the ethical tone for the entire marketing organization. Lower-level managers obtain their cues from top managers, but they too impose some of their personal values on the company. Top-performing sales representatives may influence the conduct of other salespersons as they serve as role models for success. This interaction between corporate culture and executive leadership helps determine the firm's ethical value system.

Coworkers' influence on an individual's ethical choices depends on the person's exposure to unethical behavior. Especially in gray areas, the more a person is exposed to unethical activity by others in the organizational environment, the more likely he or she is to behave unethically. Most marketing employees take their cues from coworkers in learning how to solve problems, including ethical problems.[41] For instance, the most recent National Business Ethics Survey (NBES) found that 41 percent of employees had observed at least one type of misconduct in the past year; about 37 percent of them chose not to report the misconduct to management.[42] Table 4.4 compares the percentage of observed misconduct in the United States between 2011 and 2013. Moreover, researchers suggest that marketing employees who perceive their work environment as ethical experience less role conflict and ambiguity, are more satisfied with their jobs, and are more committed to their employer.[43]

Organizational pressure plays a key role in creating ethical issues. For example, because of pressure to meet a schedule, a superior may ask a salesperson to lie to a customer over the phone about a late product shipment. Similarly, pressure to meet a sales quota may result in overly aggressive sales tactics. Researchers in this area find that superiors and coworkers can generate organizational pressure, which plays a key role in creating ethical issues. Nearly all marketers face difficult issues whose solutions are not obvious or that present conflicts between organizational objectives and personal ethics.

4-3c Opportunity

Another factor that may shape ethical decisions in marketing is opportunity—that is, conditions that limit barriers or provide rewards. A marketing employee who takes advantage of an opportunity to act unethically and is rewarded or suffers no penalty may repeat such acts as

Table 4.4 Percentage of U.S. Workforce Observing Specific Forms of Misconduct, 2011 and 2013

	2011	2013
Overall	45%	41%
Abusive behavior	21%	18%
Lying to employees	20%	17%
Conflict of interest	15%	12%
Violating company Internet use policies	16%	12%
Discrimination against employees	15%	12%
Violations of health or safety regulations	13%	10%
Lying to customers, vendors, the public	12%	10%
Retaliation against reporters of misconduct	n/a	10%
Falsifying time reports/hours worked	12%	10%
Stealing or theft	12%	9%

Source: Based on Ethics Resource Center, *2013 National Business Ethics Survey® of the U.S. Workforce* (Arlington, VA: Ethics Resource Center, 2014), pp. 41–42.

AP Images/Elaine Thompson

Organizational Culture
Bill Gates, founder of Microsoft, reflects the company's organizational culture through his and his wife's personal convictions. Microsoft has been elected as one of the World's Most Ethical Companies.

other opportunities arise. For instance, a salesperson who receives a raise after using a deceptive sales presentation to increase sales is being rewarded and thus will probably continue the behavior. Indeed, opportunity to engage in unethical conduct is often a better predictor of unethical activities than are personal values.[44] Beyond rewards and the absence of punishment, other elements in the business environment may create opportunities. Professional codes of conduct and ethics-related corporate policy also influence opportunity by prescribing what behaviors are acceptable. The larger the rewards and the milder the punishment for unethical conduct, the greater is the likelihood that unethical behavior will occur.

However, just as the majority of people who go into retail stores do not try to shoplift at each opportunity, most marketing managers do not try to take advantage of every opportunity for unethical behavior in their organizations. Although marketing managers often perceive many opportunities to engage in unethical conduct in their companies and industries, researchers have found that most refrain from taking advantage of such opportunities. Moreover, most marketing managers do not believe that unethical conduct in general results in success.[45] Individual factors as well as organizational culture may influence whether an individual becomes opportunistic and tries to take advantage of situations unethically.

4-4 IMPROVING MARKETING ETHICS

It is possible to improve ethical conduct in an organization by hiring ethical employees and eliminating unethical ones, and by improving the organization's ethical standards. One way to approach improvement of an organization's ethical standards is to use a "bad apple–bad barrel" analogy. Some people always do things in their own self-interest, regardless of organizational goals or accepted moral standards; they are sometimes called "bad apples." To eliminate unethical conduct, an organization must rid itself of bad apples through screening techniques and enforcement of the firm's ethical standards. However, organizations sometimes become "bad barrels" themselves, not because the individuals within them are unethical but because the pressures to survive and succeed create conditions (opportunities) that reward unethical behavior. One way to resolve the problem of the bad barrel is to redesign the organization's image and culture so that it conforms to industry and societal norms of ethical conduct.[46]

Without compliance programs and uniform standards and policies regarding conduct, it is hard for employees to determine what conduct is acceptable within the company. In the absence of such programs and standards, employees will generally make decisions based on their observations of how coworkers and superiors behave. To improve ethics, many organizations have developed **codes of conduct** (also called *codes of ethics*) that consist of formalized rules and standards that describe what the company expects of its employees. Most large corporations have formal codes of conduct, but not all codes are effective if implemented improperly. Codes must be periodically revised to identify and eliminate weaknesses in the company's ethical standards and policies. Most codes address specific ethical risk areas in marketing. For instance, IBM's code of conduct has a bribery policy that prohibits accepting gifts of nominal value if the gift in any way influences IBM's business relationship with the giver. However, employees are allowed to accept promotional premiums or gifts of nominal value if based upon bonus programs (such as with hotels and airlines) or if the gift is routinely offered to all other parties with similar relationships to the gift giver.[47] Codes of conduct promote ethical behavior by reducing opportunities for unethical behavior; employees know both what is expected of them and what kind of punishment they face if they violate the rules. Codes help marketers deal with ethical issues or dilemmas that develop in daily operations by prescribing or limiting specific activities.

Codes of conduct do not have to be so detailed that they take every situation into account, but they should provide guidelines that enable employees to achieve organizational objectives in an ethical manner. The American Marketing Association Code of Ethics, reprinted in Table 4.5, does not cover every possible ethical issue, but it provides a useful overview of what marketers believe are sound principles for guiding marketing activities. This code serves as a helpful model for structuring an organization's code of conduct.

If top management develops and enforces ethical and legal compliance programs to encourage ethical decision making, it becomes a force to help individuals make better decisions. According to a National Business Ethics Survey (NBES), a company's ethical culture is the greatest determinant of future misconduct. Thus, a well-implemented ethics program and a strong corporate culture result in the greatest decrease in ethical risks for an organization. Companies that wish to improve their ethics, then, should implement a strong ethics and compliance program and encourage organization wide commitment to an ethical culture.[48] Ethics

codes of conduct Formalized rules and standards that describe what the company expects of its employees

Table 4.5 Code of Ethics of the American Marketing Association

Ethical Norms and Values for Marketers
PREAMBLE
The American Marketing Association commits itself to promoting the highest standard of professional ethical norms and values for its members. Norms are established standards of conduct expected and maintained by society and/or professional organizations. Values represent the collective conception of what people find desirable, important, and morally proper. Values serve as the criteria for evaluating the actions of others. Marketing practitioners must recognize that they serve not only their enterprises but also act as stewards of society in creating, facilitating, and executing the efficient and effective transactions that are part of the greater economy. In this role, marketers should embrace the highest ethical norms of practicing professionals as well as the ethical values implied by their responsibility toward stakeholders (e.g., customers, employees, investors, channel members, regulators, and the host community).
GENERAL NORMS
1. Marketers must first do no harm. This means doing work for which they are appropriately trained or experienced so they can actively add value to their organizations and customers. It also means adhering to all applicable laws and regulations, as well as embodying high ethical standards in the choices they make.
2. Marketers must foster trust in the marketing system. This means that products are appropriate for their intended and promoted uses. It requires that marketing communications about goods and services are not intentionally deceptive or misleading. It suggests building relationships that provide for the equitable adjustment and/or redress of customer grievances. It implies striving for good faith and fair dealing so as to contribute toward the efficacy of the exchange process.
3. Marketers should embrace, communicate, and practice the fundamental ethical values that will improve consumer confidence in the integrity of the marketing exchange system. These basic values are intentionally aspirational and include: Honesty, Responsibility, Fairness, Respect, Openness, and Citizenship.

Ethical Values
Honesty—this means being truthful and forthright in our dealings with customers and stakeholders.
We will tell the truth in all situations and at all times.
We will offer products of value that do what we claim in our communications.
We will stand behind our products if they fail to deliver their claimed benefits.
We will honor our explicit and implicit commitments and promises.
Responsibility—this involves accepting the consequences of our marketing decisions and strategies.
We will make strenuous efforts to serve the needs of our customers.
We will avoid using coercion with all stakeholders.
We will acknowledge the social obligations to stakeholders that come with increased marketing and economic power.
We will recognize our special commitments to economically vulnerable segments of the market such as children, the elderly, and others who may be substantially disadvantaged.
Fairness—this has to do with justly trying to balance the needs of the buyer with the interests of the seller.
We will clearly represent our products in selling, advertising, and other forms of communication; this includes the avoidance of false, misleading, and deceptive promotion.
We will reject manipulations and sales tactics that harm customer trust.
We will not engage in price fixing, predatory pricing, price gouging, or "bait and switch" tactics.
We will not knowingly participate in material conflicts of interest.
Respect—this addresses the basic human dignity of all stakeholders.
We will value individual differences even as we avoid customer stereotyping or depicting demographic groups (e.g., gender, race, sexual) in a negative or dehumanizing way in our promotions.
We will listen to the needs of our customers and make all reasonable efforts to monitor and improve their satisfaction on an ongoing basis.
We will make a special effort to understand suppliers, intermediaries, and distributors from other cultures.
We will appropriately acknowledge the contributions of others, such as consultants, employees, and coworkers, to our marketing endeavors.
Openness—this focuses on creating transparency in our marketing operations.
We will strive to communicate clearly with all our constituencies.
We will accept constructive criticism from our customers and other stakeholders.
We will explain significant product or service risks, component substitutions, or other foreseeable eventualities affecting the customer or their perception of the purchase decision.
We will fully disclose list prices and terms of financing as well as available price deals and adjustments.
Citizenship—this involves a strategic focus on fulfilling the economic, legal, philanthropic, and societal responsibilities that serve stakeholders.
We will strive to protect the natural environment in the execution of marketing campaigns.
We will give back to the community through volunteerism and charitable donations.
We will work to contribute to the overall betterment of marketing and its reputation.
We will encourage supply-chain members to ensure that trade is fair for all participants, including producers in developing countries.
Implementation
Finally, we recognize that every industry sector and marketing subdiscipline (e.g., marketing research, e-commerce, direct selling, direct marketing, advertising) has its own specific ethical issues that require policies and commentary. An array of such codes can be accessed via links on the AMA website. We encourage all such groups to develop and/or refine their industry and discipline-specific codes of ethics in order to supplement these general norms and values.

Source: Copyright © 2010 by the American Marketing Association, www.marketingpower.com/AboutAMA/Pages/Statement%20of%20Ethics.aspx (accessed May 17, 2012).

Figure 4.5 Retaliation against Whistle-Blowers

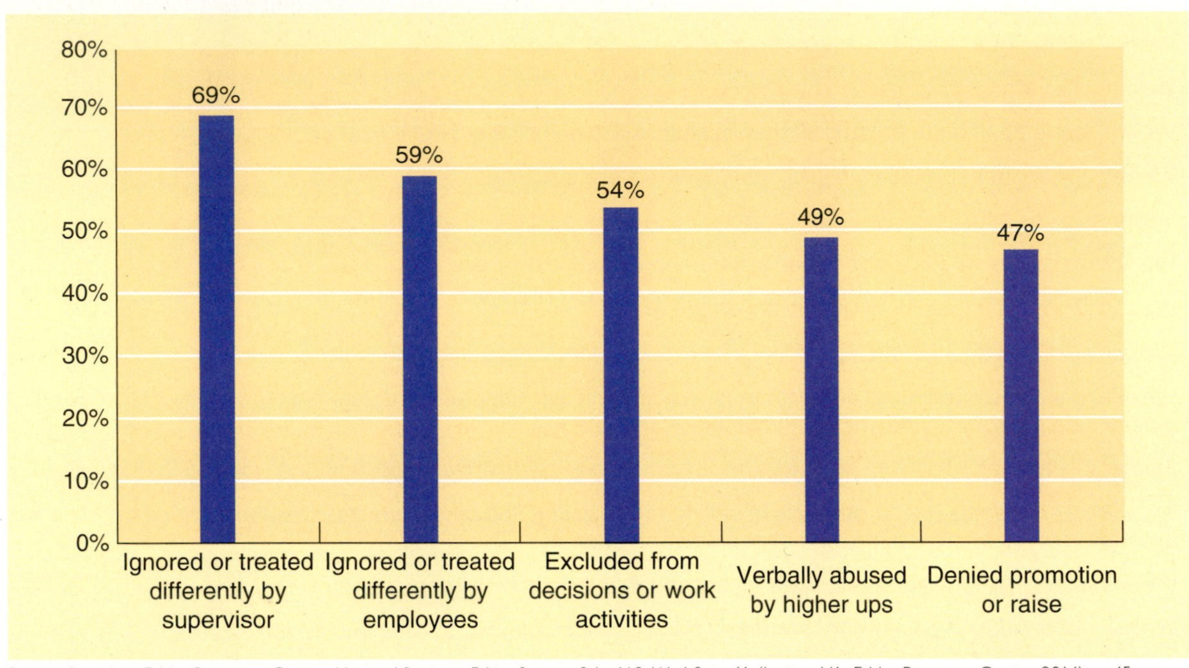

Source: Based on Ethics Resource Center, *National Business Ethics Survey of the U.S. Workforce* (Arlington, VA: Ethics Resource Center, 2014), p. 45.

programs that include written standards of conduct, ethics training, and hotlines increase the likelihood that employees will report misconduct observed in the workplace. When top managers talk about the importance of ethics and model ethical behavior themselves, employees observe significantly fewer instances of unethical conduct. When marketers understand the policies and requirements for ethical conduct, they can more easily resolve ethical conflicts. However, marketers can never fully abdicate their personal ethical responsibility in making decisions. Claiming to be an agent of the business ("the company told me to do it") is unacceptable as a legal excuse and is even less defensible from an ethical perspective.[49] It is also unacceptable for managers to punish those who do report ethical misconduct, although retaliation is still fairly prevalent. The NBES study stated that 21 percent of respondents who reported misconduct said they experienced retaliation, from getting the cold shoulder from other employees to being demoted.[50] Figure 4.5 shows the most common types of retaliation whistle-blowers have said they have experienced.

4-5 INCORPORATING SOCIAL RESPONSIBILITY AND ETHICS INTO STRATEGIC PLANNING

Although the concepts of marketing ethics and social responsibility are often used interchangeably, it is important to distinguish between them. *Ethics* relates to individual and group decisions—judgments about what is right or wrong in a particular decision-making situation—whereas *social responsibility* deals with the total effect of marketing decisions on society. The two concepts are interrelated because a company that supports socially responsible decisions and adheres to a code of conduct is likely to have a positive effect on society. Because ethics and social responsibility programs can be profitable as well, an increasing number of companies are incorporating them into their overall strategic market planning.

As we have emphasized throughout this chapter, ethics is one dimension of social responsibility. Being socially responsible relates to doing what is economically sound, legal, ethical, and socially conscious. One way to evaluate whether a specific activity is ethical and socially responsible is to ask other members of the organization if they approve of it. Contact with concerned consumer groups and industry or government regulatory groups may be helpful. A check to see whether there is a specific company policy about an activity may help resolve ethical questions. If other organizational members approve of the activity and it is legal and customary within the industry, chances are that the activity is acceptable from both an ethical and a social responsibility perspective.

A rule of thumb for resolving ethical and social responsibility issues is that if an issue can withstand open discussion that results in agreement or limited debate, an acceptable solution may exist. Nevertheless, even after a final decision is reached, different viewpoints on the issue may remain. Openness is not the end-all solution to the ethics problem. However, it creates trust and facilitates learning relationships.[51]

Many of society's demands impose costs. For example, society wants a cleaner environment and the preservation of wildlife and their habitats, but it also wants low-priced products. Consider the plight of the gas station owner who asked his customers if they would be willing to spend an additional 1 cent per gallon if he instituted an air filtration system to eliminate harmful fumes. The majority indicated they supported his plan. However, when the system was installed and the price increased, many customers switched to a lower-cost competitor across the street. Thus, companies must carefully balance the costs of providing low-priced products against the costs of manufacturing, packaging, and distributing their products in an environmentally responsible manner.

In trying to satisfy the desires of one group, marketers may dissatisfy others. Regarding the smoking debate, for instance, marketers must balance nonsmokers' desire for a smoke-free environment against smokers' desires, or needs, to continue to smoke. Some anti-tobacco crusaders call for the complete elimination of tobacco products to ensure a smoke-free world. However, this attitude fails to consider the difficulty smokers have in quitting (now that tobacco marketers have admitted their product is addictive) and the impact on U.S. communities and states that depend on tobacco crops for their economic survival. Thus, this issue, like most ethical and social responsibility issues, cannot be viewed in black and white.

Balancing society's demands to satisfy all members of society is difficult, if not impossible. Marketers must evaluate the extent to which members of society are willing to pay for what they want. For instance, customers may want more information about a product but be unwilling to pay the costs the firm incurs in providing the data. Marketers who want to make socially responsible decisions may find the task a challenge because, ultimately, they must ensure their economic survival.

Ethical Treatment of Stakeholders
Although some people believe that electronic cigarettes are a responsible alternative to smoking, e-cigarettes remain controversial due to continued health concerns.

4-5a Social Responsibility and Ethics Improve Marketing Performance

The challenges of ethical conduct are an important part of marketing success. Increasing evidence indicates that being socially responsible and ethical results in increased profits. Recent research findings suggest that a relationship exists between a stakeholder orientation and an organizational climate that supports marketing ethics and social responsibility. Marketing is often the most visible interaction that consumers have with a firm. Also, stakeholders observe marketing activities such as promotion and learn about their activities through the mass media. Anytime there is a product recall or potential unethical act, reputational damage can occur. On the other hand, firms that are highly ethical and build trust with customers are usually not headline stories in the mass media.

The evidence is strong that a broad stakeholder view of the firm can help improve marketing practices that contribute to improved financial, social, and ethical performance.[52] This relationship implies that being ethically and socially concerned is consistent with meeting the demands of customers and other stakeholders. By encouraging employees to understand their markets, companies can help them respond to stakeholders' demands.[53] A stakeholder orientation helps to broaden and redefine marketing beyond a market orientation that focuses on customers and competitors by considering primary stakeholders such as employees, suppliers, regulators, shareholders, customers, and the community. Marketers need to analyze stakeholder relationships to maximize value for specific target markets.

This creates a need to prioritize stakeholders, deal with conflicting demands, and respond with a marketing strategy to provide balance. For instance, car auction company Barrett-Jackson incorporates customer satisfaction into its business model. The company provides its buyers with access to insurance, undergoes extensive background checks to vouch for the authenticity of the classic and custom cars that it auctions, and has hired independent auditors to ensure the fairness and transparency of its business operations.[54] By incorporating ethics into its marketing strategy, Barrett-Jackson has balanced the needs of its stakeholders and developed a solid reputation of trust. All of these actions should be grounded in social responsibility and marketing ethics. The results should be positive relationships with customers and increased financial performance.[55]

AP Images/Tom Uhlman

Social Responsibility Improves Marketing
Walmart deals with consumer environmental concerns through reducing waste in the supply chain and using alternative fuel in some fleet trucks.

A direct association exists between corporate social responsibility and customer satisfaction, profits, and market value.[56] In a survey of consumers, 80 percent indicated that when quality and price are similar among competitors, they would be more likely to buy from the company associated with a particular cause. In addition, young adults aged 18 to 25 are especially likely to take a company's citizenship efforts into account when making not only purchasing but also employment and investment decisions.[57]

Thus, recognition is growing that the long-term value of conducting business in an ethical and socially responsible manner far outweighs short-term costs.[58] Companies that fail to develop strategies and programs to incorporate ethics and social responsibility into their organizational culture may pay the price with poor marketing performance and the potential costs of legal violations, civil litigation, and damaging publicity when questionable activities are made public. Because marketing ethics and social responsibility are not always viewed as organizational performance issues, many managers do not believe they need to consider them in the strategic planning process. Individuals also have different ideas as to what is ethical or unethical, leading them to confuse the need for workplace ethics and the right to maintain their own personal values and ethics. Although the concepts are undoubtedly controversial, it is possible—and desirable—to incorporate ethics and social responsibility into the planning process.

Summary

4-1 Define the four dimensions of social responsibility.

Social responsibility refers to an organization's obligation to maximize its positive impact and minimize its negative impact on society. It deals with the total effect of all marketing decisions on society. Although social responsibility is a positive concept, most organizations embrace it in the expectation of indirect long-term benefits. Marketing citizenship involves adopting a strategic focus for fulfilling the economic, legal, ethical, and philanthropic social responsibilities expected of organizations by their stakeholders, those constituents who have a stake, or claim, in some aspect of the company's products, operations, markets, industry, and outcomes.

At the most basic level, companies have an economic responsibility to be profitable so that they can provide a return on investment to their stockholders, create jobs for the community, and contribute goods and services to the economy. Marketers are also expected to obey laws and regulations. Marketing ethics refers to principles and standards that define acceptable conduct in marketing as determined by various stakeholders, including the public, government regulators, private-interest groups, industry, and the organization itself. Philanthropic responsibilities go beyond marketing ethics; they are not required of a company, but they promote human welfare or goodwill. Many firms use cause-related marketing, the practice of linking products to a social cause on an ongoing or short-term basis. Strategic philanthropy is the synergistic use of organizational core competencies and resources to address key stakeholders' interests and achieve both organizational and social benefits.

Three major categories of issues that fit into the four dimensions of social responsibility are sustainability, consumerism, and community relations. One of the more common ways marketers demonstrate social responsibility is through programs designed to protect and preserve the natural environment. Sustainability is the potential for the long-term well-being of the natural environment, including all biological entities, as well as the interaction among nature and individuals, organizations, and business strategies. Consumerism consists of the efforts of independent individuals, groups, and organizations to protect the rights of consumers. Consumers expect to have the right to safety, the right to be informed, the right to choose, and the right to be heard. Many marketers view social responsibility as including contributions of resources (money, products, and time) to community causes such as the natural environment, arts and recreation, disadvantaged members of the community, and education.

4-2 State the importance of marketing ethics.

Whereas social responsibility is achieved by balancing the interests of all stakeholders in the organization, ethics relates to acceptable standards of conduct in making individual and group decisions. Marketing ethics goes beyond legal issues. Ethical marketing decisions foster mutual trust in marketing relationships.

An ethical issue is an identifiable problem, situation, or opportunity requiring an individual or organization to choose from among several actions that must be evaluated as right or wrong, ethical or unethical. A number of ethical issues relate to the marketing mix (product, promotion, price, and distribution).

4-3 Describe the three factors of ethical decision making.

Individual factors, organizational relationships, and opportunity interact to determine ethical decisions in marketing.

Individuals often base their decisions on their own values and principles of right or wrong. However, ethical choices in marketing are most often made jointly, in work groups and committees, or in conversations and discussions with coworkers. Organizational culture and structure operate through organizational relationships (with superiors, peers, and subordinates) to influence ethical decisions. Organizational, or corporate, culture is a set of values, beliefs, goals, norms, and rituals that members of an organization share. The more a person is exposed to unethical activity by others in the organizational environment, the more likely he or she is to behave unethically. Organizational pressure plays a key role in creating ethical issues, as do opportunity and conditions that limit barriers or provide rewards.

4-4 Comment on the requirements for improving ethical decision making.

It is possible to improve ethical behavior in an organization by hiring ethical employees and eliminating unethical ones, and by improving the organization's ethical standards. If top management develops and enforces ethics and legal compliance programs to encourage ethical decision making, it becomes a force to help individuals make better decisions. To improve company ethics, many organizations have developed codes of conduct—formalized rules and standards that describe what the company expects of its employees. To nurture ethical conduct in marketing, open communication is essential. Firms should also periodically monitor and audit their operations, including their supply chain, to ensure the integrity of the product and the firm's activities. Companies must consistently enforce standards and impose penalties or punishment on those who violate codes of conduct.

4-5 Critique the role of social responsibility and ethics in improving marketing performance.

An increasing number of companies are incorporating ethics and social responsibility programs into their overall strategic marketing planning. To promote socially responsible and ethical behavior while achieving organizational goals, marketers must monitor changes and trends in society's values. They must determine what society wants and attempt to predict the long-term effects of their decisions. Costs are associated with many of society's demands, and balancing those demands to satisfy all of society is difficult. However, increasing evidence indicates that being socially responsible and ethical results in valuable benefits: an enhanced public reputation (which can increase market share), costs savings, and profits.

Go to www.cengagebrain.com for resources to help you master the content in this chapter as well as for materials that will expand your marketing knowledge!

Developing Your Marketing Plan

When developing a marketing strategy, companies must consider that their decisions affect not only their own company but also society in general. Many socially responsible and ethical companies identify their intentions as part of their mission statement, which serves as a guide for making all decisions about the company, including those in the marketing plan. To assist you in relating the information in this chapter to the development of your marketing plan, consider the following:

1. Determine the level of importance that marketing citizenship holds in your company. Identify the various stakeholders who would be affected by your strategic decisions.
2. Referring to Table 4.2 as a guide, discuss how the negative impact of your product's production and use could be minimized.
3. Using Table 4.3, identify additional issues related to your product for each of the 4Ps.

The information obtained from these questions should assist you in developing various aspects of your marketing plan found in the "Interactive Marketing Plan" exercise at www.cengagebrain.com.

Important Terms

social responsibility 94
marketing citizenship 95
marketing ethics 97
cause-related marketing 97
strategic philanthropy 98
sustainability 98
ethical issue 102
organizational (corporate) culture 107
codes of conduct 110

Discussion and Review Questions

1. What is social responsibility? Why is it important?
2. What are stakeholders? What role do they play in strategic marketing decisions?
3. What are four dimensions of social responsibility? What impact do they have on marketing decisions?
4. What is strategic philanthropy? How does it differ from more traditional philanthropic efforts?
5. What are some major social responsibility issues? Give an example of each.
6. What is the difference between ethics and social responsibility?
7. Why is ethics an important consideration in marketing decisions?
8. How do the factors that influence ethical or unethical decisions interact?
9. What ethical conflicts may exist if business employees fly on certain airlines just to receive benefits for their personal frequent-flyer programs?
10. Give an example of how ethical issues can affect each component of the marketing mix.
11. How can the ethical decisions involved in marketing be improved?
12. How can people with different personal values work together to make ethical decisions in organizations?
13. What trade-offs might a company have to make to be socially responsible and responsive to society's demands?
14. What evidence exists that being socially responsible and ethical is worthwhile?

Video Case 4.1

TOMS Shoes Expands One-to-One Model to Eyewear

Although many organizations try to incorporate cause-related marketing into their business operations, TOMS Shoes takes the concept of philanthropy one step further. TOMS blends a for-profit business with a philanthropic component in what it terms the one-to-one model. For every pair of shoes sold, another pair is provided to a child in need. Recently, TOMS has also expanded into eyewear. For every pair of sunglasses sold, a person with vision problems in developing countries receives surgery, prescription glasses, or medical treatment to help restore his or her sight. Unlike many nonprofits, TOMS' for-profit business enables the company to support its philanthropic component, which keeps the company from having to solicit donations.

The idea for TOMS Shoes occurred after founder Blake Mycoskie witnessed the immense poverty in Argentinean villages—poverty so bad that many families could not afford to purchase shoes for their children. Recognizing the importance of shoes to health and education, Mycoskie decided to create a new business that would consist of two parts: TOMS Shoes, a for-profit business that would sell the shoes, and Friends of TOMS, the company's nonprofit subsidiary that would distribute shoes to those in need.

For his original product, Mycoskie decided to adopt the *alpargata* shoe worn in Argentina. The *alpargata* is a slip-on shoe made from canvas or fabric with rubber soles. After a *Los Angeles Times* article featured Mycoskie's new business, demand for the shoes exploded. Unfortunately for Mycoskie, he did not have enough shoes to fill the orders. Mycoskie was able to work out the product shortage, and today TOMS is a thriving business.

After distributing its one-millionth pair of shoes in 2010, TOMS began to consider other products that could be used in the one-to-one model. "When I thought about launching another product with the TOMS model, vision seemed the most obvious choice," Blake Myscoskie explained. Because 80 percent of vision impairment in developing countries is preventable or curable, TOMS decided that for every pair of sunglasses it sold, the company would provide treatment or prescription glasses for those in need. TOMS chose Nepal as the first country to apply its one-to-one model.

TOMS takes its obligations for social responsibility seriously. The company builds the cost of the extra pair of shoes and eye care into the price of the products it sells. TOMS also works closely with local humanitarian organizations. "With TOMS we always work with local nonprofits or NGOs to understand what the need is in a community before we just go in and start giving," said Liza De La Torre, VP of sales and marketing at TOMS.

Customers who do business with TOMS feel committed to the company because they know that their purchases are going toward a good cause, even if they might pay a bit more in the process. TOMS goes to great lengths to educate the public about the importance of its mission. Although it does not have a marketing budget, the company provides internship opportunities and engages brand ambassadors at universities to spread the TOMS message. Every year the company promotes the One Day Without Shoes campaign, in which participants spend one day without shoes to understand what children in developing countries must undergo daily. These events have been supported by celebrities such as Charlize Theron, Kris Ryan, and the Dallas Cowboys Cheerleaders.

Despite TOMS' clear philanthropic component, risks for misconduct still exist. The company uses factories in China, Argentina, and Ethiopia for manufacturing, which creates complex supply-chain relationships that must be carefully managed. TOMS created a set of manufacturing standards based upon International Labor Organization compliance standards for its manufacturers. The company regularly performs audits to check that the factories are complying with company standards. TOMS also seeks to create strong organizational relationships with its employees and volunteers. The company often allows employees to participate in Shoe Drops (distributing the shoes to children) so they can see firsthand how their efforts are helping others.

Despite its success, TOMS' mission is far from complete. As its expansion into eyewear demonstrates, the company is looking for new opportunities for applying its one-to-one model. TOMS demonstrates how an innovative concept and the ability to incorporate philanthropy into business operations can create a successful company that can make a difference.[59]

Questions for Discussion

1. Do you think TOMS is successful because of its unique products, or is it the firm's approach to social responsibility?
2. How does TOMS manage its supply chain in order to ensure ethical and socially responsible conduct?
3. How does TOMS' business model relate to the understanding of stakeholders and strategic philanthropy?

Case 4.2

Ethics Drives Barrett-Jackson Auto Auction Company to Success

Monitoring the ethical behavior of auction companies can be tricky. Consumers might not know the value of the product until after they purchase it, and not all items purchased at auction companies come with sufficient documentation to prove the product's authenticity. It has not been unheard of for sellers to falsify documentation to secure better deals. To avoid these ethical issues, classic and vintage car auction company Barrett-Jackson LLC has created an ethical culture that considers the needs of buyers, sellers, and the community. The company has been recognized as one of the world's most ethical companies by *Ethisphere* magazine.

Barrett-Jackson was founded in 1971 in Scottsdale, Arizona, by classic car lovers Russ Jackson and Tom Barrett. The two men had met a decade earlier when Jackson was considering buying a 1933 Cadillac V16 Town Car from Barrett. The two became lifelong friends and began organizing their own auctions. From the beginning the men recognized the special nature of the products they were auctioning. Buyers place great value on the cars they purchase, with some having searched for years to locate their classic "dream" car. The company would have to exert great delicacy to ensure a fair auction process and authentic products.

After Russ Jackson passed away, his son Craig Jackson began running the company. Like his predecessors, Craig recognized the importance of adopting values to ensure an ethical auction process. "We will separate ourselves and do things in an ethical manner to make sure we set the right standards for our customers. These are the things that have been entrenched in our corporate culture since the beginning," Craig stated.

The company has instituted a number of programs to make certain that the auction process between buyer and seller remains fair. These programs recognize the inherent rights of the stakeholders involved in the transaction. For instance, Barrett-Jackson protects buyers' rights to choose by working to prevent false bids meant to raise the price of the cars. Sometimes car owners will try to bid on their own cars to boost the price. Barrett-Jackson acts to make certain that prices remain fair so that consumers can choose their dream car at a competitive price. Barrett-Jackson also protects the right to safety of both buyers and sellers by using security cameras to monitor stakeholders during the auction and making sure that buyers have the ability to pay. The company also offers access to Barrett-Jackson–endorsed insurance coverage, which reduces the risk of purchase by assuring buyers that their cars can be restored in case of an accident. Barrett-Jackson protects consumers' rights to be informed by making sure to the best of their ability that documentation is truthful and rejects sellers who do not meet their stringent requirements.

Barrett-Jackson also tries to ensure that their stakeholders are provided with a forum to make their voices heard. This includes thoroughly investigating stakeholder concerns even if it might interfere with the sale of a product. For instance, one of the collector vehicles sold by Barrett-Jackson was allegedly the ambulance that carried President John F. Kennedy to the hospital after he was shot. Shortly after the auction of the ambulance was announced, questions concerning the authenticity of these claims arose. Barrett-Jackson responded by undertaking a thorough investigation of the documentation provided on the ambulance. The company responded that it could not offer a 100 percent guarantee that the ambulance was authentic but that the claims were true to the best of its knowledge. By acting to investigate the available documentation and releasing a disclaimer, Barrett-Jackson not only took these claims seriously but told potential buyers about the possible risks involved so they could make an informed decision.

Additionally, Barrett-Jackson practices social responsibility by giving back to the communities in which it does business. Barrett-Jackson has helped raise millions for charities nationwide. The company also engages in strategic philanthropy and created the Barrett-Jackson Cancer Research Fund at the Translational Genomics Research Institute (TGen) in 2010. In honor of Russ Jackson and his son Brian, both victims of cancer, the company raises money to fund research efforts to fight colon and prostate cancer and search for a cure. For example, in 2012 the company raised $125,000 for TGen by auctioning a 1993 Chevrolet Corvette 40th Anniversary coupe.

Barrett-Jackson's emphasis on community relations and customer satisfaction has helped secure its reputation as an ethical company. Buyers and sellers alike can feel confident that they will be treated fairly when doing business with the firm. Barrett-Jackson is a good example of how ethical conduct can increase company success.[60]

Questions for Discussion

1. Why is ethical behavior so important for an auction company such as Barrett-Jackson?
2. In what ways does Barrett-Jackson protect the rights of its buyers and sellers?
3. How do solid community relations help Barrett-Jackson succeed?

Strategic Case 2

REI: An Ethical Consumer Cooperative

Recreational Equipment Incorporated (REI) is a national retail cooperative famous for its outdoor apparel and equipment. A cooperative consists of individuals who have joined together to secure the benefits of a larger organization. In the case of REI, the company is organized as a consumer cooperative. Members of the cooperative receive a portion of the organization's profits annually based on a percentage of their eligible purchases, receive discounts on products and classes, and can vote for board members. REI has 5.1 million active members and generated revenues of $1.93 billion.

Customers are only the beginning of REI's stakeholder orientation. The company also values its communities and the issues that are important to them through philanthropic activities and advocacy efforts. It shows its concern for the environment by promoting and practicing environmentally-friendly behaviors. As a result, REI maintains a strong focus on all stakeholders, an emphasis that has encouraged the organization to offer superior goods and services in areas such as mountain climbing, camping, and other outdoor activities.

REI's values include authenticity, quality, service, respect, integrity, decency, and balance. These values are at the heart of the company's work environment and are reflected in each of their activities. The ethical culture of REI is not just about employees and customers, but includes all stakeholders. Ethical conduct is at the core of its culture.

The concept of REI originated during the 1930s when Lloyd Anderson, a member of the Pacific Northwest Mountaineers, was looking for a high-quality ice axe at a reasonable cost. After searching without success, Anderson found what he needed in an Austrian Alpine Gear catalog for $3.50. His find excited the climbing community around Seattle, prompting Anderson to envision a local business that would carry items for mountain climbers at reasonable prices. In 1938 Lloyd Anderson and his wife Mary, along with 21 fellow climbers, founded an outdoor gear consumer cooperative. At first the cooperative was focused specifically on mountain climbing. Its first full-time employee and eventual CEO was John Whittaker, the first American to successfully climb Mt. Everest. Yet over the years REI grew to include gear for camping and hiking, bicycling, fitness, paddling, and more. Today it is the largest consumer cooperative in the United States.

REI Maintains Customer Satisfaction

REI operates more than 129 retail stores in 32 states. To help customers choose the right product, REI retail locations contain features like bike trails and rock climbing walls that allow customers to test the gear, as well as Internet kiosks to educate consumers about the brands and products it sells. In addition, to make sure that customers purchase products that meet their needs, REI offers a 100% Satisfaction Guarantee. In line with its ethical view of customer satisfaction, REI's return policy used to allow customers to return merchandise at any time and receive a refund. However, some of their customers engaged in misbehavior. They took advantage of REI's policy by either purposefully damaging products and returning them to the store or buying REI merchandise at yard sales and returning them for cash. This misconduct cut into company profits, and REI responded by maintaining its 100% Satisfaction Guarantee but instituting a year-long window for items to be returned.

In changing its policy, REI attempted to maintain fairness to all stakeholders. Its one-year return period gives customers a significant amount of time to decide if they are satisfied. It also helps curb consumer misconduct that could harm other stakeholders. REI learned that although it wants to be ethical to its customers, there are times when it must adopt controls to reduce the potential for unethical conduct.

© iStockphoto.com/RiverNorthPhotography

REI's role in the competitive environment is largely based on quality products. Its competitors, L.L.Bean and Sports Authority, also offer quality products but at lower prices. REI has received some criticism over its higher-priced products, but many of its customers are willing to pay the higher prices because their values align with the company's. REI cooperative members tend to share similar values as well. They receive the added benefit of profiting from their purchases—the more they buy at the store, the more return they will receive in the annual dividends REI provides to members.

REI Uses Marketing to Support Outdoor Initiatives

REI has become an expert in monitoring its environment to ensure that it continues to meet customer needs. For instance, the company uses social media outlets to gauge and address the sociocultural environment. In response to the change in people's desires to reduce their carbon footprint and maintain an active lifestyle, REI produces videos on YouTube and posts on Facebook and Twitter to educate customers about kayaking, road biking, and family camping.

Additionally, REI demonstrates social responsibility by supporting local programs to further conservation and outdoor recreation. A primary focus for REI is youth. REI seeks to inspire and educate the younger generation about the outdoors. The company's Promoting Environmental Awareness in Kids (PEAK) program is one step toward youth engagement. This program teaches kids about outdoor ethics—such as cleaning up waste materials and respecting wildlife—while having fun outdoors. PEAK has two goals: to introduce youth to the wonders of the outdoors, and to practice responsible "No Trace" principles. REI also encourages employees to volunteer in improving and protecting the outdoors. In all of these efforts, REI's philanthropic initiatives contribute to its brand and customer loyalty. Consumers expect businesses to give back to the community, and REI goes beyond what is required.

REI Cares for the Environment

Changing sociocultural trends have made the environment an important stakeholder for businesses. Stakeholders have begun to express an interest in how businesses affect the environment. For this reason, REI develops an annual environmental stewardship report. This not only generates goodwill among stakeholders but also fits well with REI's strategic emphasis on outdoor activities and product offerings. REI has benchmarked four areas of sustainability concern in its stewardship report: (1) greenhouse gas emissions, (2) energy use, (3) waste to landfill, and (4) paper use. The organization also considers its product stewardship responsibilities and has acted as a leader in this area.

REI has been reducing the impact of its greenhouse gas emissions through methods such as the purchase of carbon offsets. During a one-year period, REI reduced its emissions by 7.6 percent, even as the company increased its sales. The company found that transportation contributed the most to greenhouse gas emissions so it began promoting responsible transportation whenever possible, including alternative approaches such as subsidizing vanpools and offering incentives for public transportation. Employee commuting emissions decreased by 27 percent in a one-year period, while product transportation emissions decreased by 9 percent.

Additionally, REI has set the impressive goal of becoming a zero waste-to-landfill company by 2020. The organization is therefore seeking innovative ways to generate less waste and recycle the waste it does generate. These efforts are focused on the entire supply chain by reducing waste before it gets to the retail level. Some of REI's methods include redesigning packaging to reduce waste and increasing recycling. Because REI expanded, its operational waste increased in 2012. However, its total waste decreased by 1.4 percent.

In terms of its paper sourcing, REI wants to ensure that the paper it uses is sourced responsibly. It is impossible for REI to completely eliminate its use of paper, but the company's paper policy encourages the purchase of paper products sourced from post-consumer waste or virgin fiber harvested from forests certified by the Forest Stewardship Council (FSC). Certification implies that the paper-based products have been responsibly sourced. Although REI saw its paper usage increase slightly in 2012, its use of FSC-certified materials also increased.

Finally, REI recognizes that environmental stewardship does not stop after a company sells a product. REI makes product stewardship a key tenet of its sustainability goals. It advocates for a universal standard that can be used to judge a product's sustainability. To that end, REI partnered with Timberland to create the Eco Index. In 2012 the Eco Index was modified to form the HiGG Index, a tool used to measure the sustainability of apparel and footwear products. REI also supports the bluesign® system, a system to responsibly manage chemicals in the supply chain. In 2012, approximately 23 percent of material that REI used was bluesign-certified.

REI also takes its environmental concerns to the political level. Its advocacy efforts center on its desire to protect the environment and promote outdoor recreation. The company has lobbied and continues to lobby for public lands and environmental causes. More specifically, the organization has supported the Land and Water Conservation Fund, the Recreational Trails program, and the Outdoor Industry Association. Additionally, REI is involved with the Washington Wildlife and Recreation Coalition.

Because of REI's customer-based mission, it is able to generate loyalty and enthusiasm among stakeholders. Though some of the company's marketing activities are sales-related, much of it provides stakeholders with information directly related to their outdoor interests and environmental concerns. The marketing citizenship that the company embraces has proven to be a strong force in garnering stakeholder attention, generating profits, and advancing a stakeholder orientation.[61]

Questions for Discussion

1. Describe stakeholder orientation at REI.
2. How does REI implement social responsibility?
3. How do REI's values relate to the development of an ethical culture?

NOTES

[1] Diane Brady, "Volunteerism as a Core Competency," *Bloomberg Businesseek*, November 12–18, 2012, pp. 53–54; David Gould, "Cause Marketing—Where CSR Meets CRM," Special Advertising Section, *Businessweek*, 2012, S8; Arianna Huffington, "Companies and Causes: Social Media Jumpstart a Marketing Revolution," *Huffington Post*, April 6, 2011, www.huffingtonpost.com/arianna-huffington/companies-and-causes-soci_b_845657.html (accessed November 21, 2013); K. Adiwijaya and R. Fauzan, "Cause-Related Marketing: The Influence of Cause-Brand Fit, Firm Motives and Attribute Altruistic to Consumer Inferences and Loyalty and Moderation Effect of Consumer Values," *2012 International Conference on Economics Marketing and Management*, Vol . 28, Singapore; IACSIT Press; IBM, Corporate Service Corps, www.ibm.com/ibm/responsibility/corporateservicecorps (accessed November 21, 2013).

[2] Peter R. Darke and Robin J. B. Ritchie, "The Defensive Consumer: Advertising Deception, Defensive Processing, and Distrust," *Journal of Marketing Research* 4, no. 1 (February 2007): 114–127.

[3] Isabelle Maignan and O. C. Ferrell, "Corporate Social Responsibility and Marketing: An Integrative Framework," *Journal of the Academy of Marketing Science* 32 (January 2004): 3–19.

[4] Indra Nooyi, "The Responsible Company," *The Economist*, March 31, 2008, p. 132.

[5] Jonathon D. Rockoff, "J&J's $2.2 Billion Deal Settling Investigation Is Held Up," *The Wall Street Journal*, May 10, 2013, p. B3.

[6] Anne Tergesen, "Doing Good to Do Well," *The Wall Street Journal*, January 9, 2012, p. B7.

[7] Isabelle Maignan and O. C. Ferrell, "Antecedents and Benefits of Corporate Citizenship: An Investigation of French Businesses," *Journal of Business Research* 51 (2001): 37–51.

[8] Debbie Thorne, Linda Ferrell, and O. C. Ferrell, *Business and Society: A Strategic Approach to Social Responsibility*, 4th ed . (Boston: Houghton Mifflin, 2011), pp. 38–40.

[9] O. C. Ferrell, "Business Ethics and Customer Stakeholders," *Academy of Management Executive* 18 (May 2004): 126–129.

[10] "2007 Corporate Citizenship Report," Pfizer, www.pfizer.com/files/corporate_citizenship/cr_report_2007.pdf (accessed November 21, 2013).

[11] Archie Carroll, "The Pyramid of Corporate Social Responsibility: Toward the Moral Management of Organizational Stakeholders," *Business Horizons* (July/August 1991): 42.

[12] "Giving USA: Charitable Donations Grew in 2012, but Slowly, Like the Economy," Indiana University–Purdue University Indianapolis, June 18, 2013, www.philanthropy.iupui.edu/news/article/giving-usa-2013 (accessed November 21, 2013).

[13] PR Newswire, "Boingo Graphics Recognized as Outstanding Philanthropic Small Business," October 14, 2013, www.prnewswire.com/news-releases/boingo-graphics-recognized-as-outstanding-philanthropic-small-business-227686411.html (accessed November 21, 2013).

[14] "Cone LLC Releases the 2010 Cone Cause Evolution Study," Cone, www.coneinc.com/cause-grows-consumers-want-more (accessed January 17, 2012).

[15] Thorne, Ferrell, and Ferrell, *Business and Society*, p. 335.

[16] "2010 World's Most Ethical Companies—Company Profile: Salesforce.com," *Ethisphere*, pp. Q1, 32.

[17] Dinah Eng [interviewer], "Mopping Up with Green Cleaners," *Fortune*, October 28, 2013, pp. 47–48.

[18] "Welcome to Eco Options," Home Depot, www6.homedepot.com/ecooptions/stage (accessed November 21, 2013).

[19] The Rainforest Alliance, "The Rainforest Alliance's Banana Certification Program," www.rainforest-alliance.org/agriculture/crops/fruits/bananas (accessed November 21, 2013).

[20] Paul Hawken and William McDonough, "Seven Steps to Doing Good Business," *Inc.* (November 1993): 79–90.

[21] Jill Gabrielle Klein, N. Craig Smith, and Andrew John, "Why We Boycott: Consumer Motivations for Boycott Participation," *Journal of Marketing* 68 (July 2004): 92–109.

[22] Christian Homburg and Andreas Fürst, "How Organizational Complaint Handling Drives Customer Loyalty: An Analysis of the Mechanistic and the Organic Approach," *Journal of Marketing* 69 (July 2005): 95–114.

[23] Alison Young, "Maker of Craze Suspends Production," *USA Today*, October 16, 2013, p. 3A.

[24] Target, "Take Charge of Education®," www-secure.target.com/redcard/tcoe/home (accessed November 21, 2013).

[25] "Environmentalism: What We Do," Patagonia, www.patagonia.com/us/patagonia.go?assetid=1960 (accessed November 21, 2013).

[26] Edelman, *Edelman Trust Barometer 2013 Annual Global Study*, www.slideshare.net/EdelmanInsights/global-deck-2013-edelman-trust-barometer-16086761 (accessed November 21, 2013).

[27] Julie Jargon, "'Ronald Is Not a Bad Guy,' CEO Says," *The Wall Street Journal*, May 24, 2013, p. B5.

[28] Tim Barnett and Sean Valentine, "Issue Contingencies and Marketers' Recognition of Ethical Issues, Ethical Judgments and Behavioral Intentions," *Journal of Business Research* 57 (2004): 338–346.

[29] Candice Choi, "Chobani Recalls Some Greek Yogurt Cups," *USA Today*, September 6, 2013, www.usatoday.com/story/money/business/2013/09/05/chobani-recalls-some-greek-yogurt-cups/2769975 (accessed November 20, 2013).

[30] David E. Sprott, Kenneth C. Manning, and Anthony D. Miyazaki, "Grocery Price Setting and Quantity Surcharges," *Journal of Marketing* (July 2003): 34–46.

[31] Stephen Taub, "SEC Probing Harley Statements," *CFO.com*, July 14, 2005, http://ww2.cfo.com/accounting-tax/2005/07/sec-probing-harley-statements (accessed November 21, 2013).

[32] Benoît Faucon, Colum Murphy, and Jeanne Whalen, "Fake-Pill Pipeline Undercuts Africa's Battle with Malaria," *The Wall Street Journal*, May 29, 2013, SA, p. A12.

[33] Kate O'Keefe and Sun Narin, "Supply Chain Trips H&M," *The Wall Street Journal*, May 22, 2013, p. B3.

[34] Charles Duhigg and David Barboza, "Apple's iPad and the Human Costs for Workers in China," *The New York Times*, January 25, 2012, www.nytimes.com/2012/01/26/business/ieconomy-apples-ipad-and-the-human-costs-for-workers-in-china.html?pagewanted=all (accessed November 21, 2013); Paul Mozur, Chao Deng, and Eva Dou, "Worker Group Alleges Abuses at Apple Supplier in China," *The Wall Street Journal*, July 29, 2013, http://online.wsj.com/news/articles/SB10001424127887324170004578633951552047928 (accessed November 21, 2013).

[35] "Monitoring and Auditing Global Supply Chains Is a Must," *Ethisphere*, Q3, (2011): 38–45.

[36] "Health Care Supply Company Novation Earns Ethics Inside Certification," *Ethisphere*, November 8, 2011, http://ethisphere.com/leading-health-care-supply-contracting-company-novation-earns-ethics-inside-certification (accessed February 8, 2012).

[37] Maxwell Murphy, "Reinforcing the Supply Chain," *The Wall Street Journal*, January 11, 2012, p. B6; "Monitoring and Auditing Global Supply Chains Is a Must," pp. 38–45.

[38] "Monitoring and Auditing Global Supply Chains Is a Must," pp. 38–45.

[39] Peggy H. Cunningham and O. C. Ferrell, "The Influence of Role Stress on Unethical Behavior by Personnel Involved in the Marketing Research Process" (working paper, Queens University, Ontario, 2004), p. 35.

[40] Joseph W. Weiss, *Business Ethics: A Managerial, Stakeholder Approach* (Belmont, CA: Wadsworth, 1994), p. 13.

[41] O. C. Ferrell, Larry G. Gresham, and John Fraedrich, "A Synthesis of Ethical Decision Models for Marketing," *Journal of Macromarketing* (Fall 1989): 58–59.

[42] Ethics Resource Center, *2013 National Business Ethics Survey® of the U.S. Workforce* (Arlington, VA: Ethics Resource Center, 2014).

[43] Barry J. Babin, James S. Boles, and Donald P. Robin, "Representing the Perceived Ethical Work Climate Among Marketing Employees," *Journal of the Academy of Marketing Science* 28 (2000): 345–358.

[44] Ferrell, Gresham, and Fraedrich, "A Synthesis of Ethical Decision Models for Marketing."

[45] Lawrence B. Chonko and Shelby D. Hunt, "Ethics and Marketing Management: A Retrospective and Prospective Commentary," *Journal of Business Research* 50 (2000): 235–244.

[46] Linda K. Trevino and Stuart Youngblood, "Bad Apples in Bad Barrels: A Causal Analysis of Ethical Decision Making Behavior," *Journal of Applied Psychology* 75 (1990): 378–385.

[47] IBM, *Business Conduct Guidelines* (Armonk, New York: International Business Machines Corp., 2011).

[48] Ethics Resource Center, "The Ethics Resource Center's 2009 National Business Ethics Survey," p. 41.

[49] Ethics Resource Center, "The Ethics Resource Center's 2007 National Business Ethics Survey," p. ix.

[50] Ethics Resource Center, *2013 National Business Ethics Survey® of the U.S. Workforce* (Arlington, VA: Ethics Resource Center, 2014), p. 27.

[51] Sir Adrian Cadbury, "Ethical Managers Make Their Own Rules," *Harvard Business Review* (September/October 1987): 33.

[52] Isabelle Maignan, Tracy L. Gonzalez-Padron, G. Tomas M. Hult, and O. C. Ferrell, "Stakeholder Orientation: Development and Testing of a Framework for Socially Responsible Marketing," *Journal of Strategic Marketing*, Vol. 19, no. 4, (July 2011): 313–338.

[53] Ferrell, Fraedrich, and Ferrell, *Business Ethics*, pp. 27–30.

[54] "Barrett-Jackson Auction Company: Family, Fairness, and Philanthropy," http://danielsethics.mgt.unm.edu/pdf/Barrett-Jackson%20Case.pdf (accessed November 21, 2013).

[55] G. Thomas Hult, Jeannette Mena, O. C. Ferrell, and Linda Ferrell, "Stakeholder Marketing: A Definition and Conceptual Framework," *AMS Review* 1, no. 1 (2011): 44–65.

[56] Marjorie Kelly, "Holy Grail Found: Absolute, Definitive Proof That Responsible Companies Perform Better Financially," *Business Ethics*, Winter 2005, http://my.opera.com/lounge/forums/topic.dml?id=81271 (accessed November 21, 2013); Xueming Luo and C. B. Bhattacharya, "Corporate Social Responsibility, Customer Satisfaction, and Market Value," *Journal of Marketing* 70 (October 2006), www.marketingpower.com; Isabelle Maignan, O.C. Ferrell, and Linda Ferrell, "A Stakeholder Model for Implementing Social Responsibility in Marketing," *European Journal of Marketing* 39 (September/October 2005): 956–977.

[57] "Cone LLC Releases the 2010 Cone Cause Evolution Study," Cone, www.coneinc.com/cause-grows-consumers-want-more (accessed January 17, 2012).

[58] Maignan, Ferrell, and Ferrell, "A Stakeholder Model for Implementing Social Responsibility in Marketing."

[59] Athima Chansanchai, "Happy Feet: Buy a Pair of TOMS Shoes and a Pair Will Be Donated to a Poor Child Abroad," *Seattle Pi*, June 11, 2007, www.seattlepi.com/default/article/Happy-feet-Buy-a-pair-of-TOMS-shoes-and-a-pair-1240201.php (accessed November 21, 2013); Patrick Cole, "Toms Free Shoe Plan, Boosted by Clinton, Reaches Million Mark," *Bloomberg*, September 15, 2010, www.bloomberg.com/news/2010-09-16/toms-shoe-giveaway-for-kids-boosted-by-bill-clinton-reaches-million-mark.html (accessed November 21, 2013); "Intern at TOMS," TOMS, www.toms.com/our-movement/intern (accessed November 21, 2013); "How We Give," TOMS, www.toms.com/how-we-give (accessed November 21, 2013); "How We Wear Them," TOMS, www.toms.com/how-we-wear-them (accessed November 21, 2013); Booth Moore, "Toms Shoes' Model Is Sell a Pair, Give a Pair Away," *Los Angeles Times*, April 19, 2009, www.latimes.com/features/image/la-ig-greentoms19-2009apr19,0,3694310.story (accessed November 21, 2013); "One Day without Shoes," TOMS, www.onedaywithoutshoes.com (accessed June 3, 2011); "One for One," TOMS, www.toms.com/our-movement/movement-one-for-one (accessed November 21, 2013); Stacy Perman, "Making a Do-Gooder's Business Model Work," *Bloomberg Businessweek*, January 23, 2009, www.businessweek.com/smallbiz/content/jan2009/sb20090123_264702.htm (accessed November 21, 2013); Michelle Prasad, "TOMS Shoes Always Feels Good," *KENTON Magazine*, March 19, 2011, http://kentonmagazine.com/toms-shoes-always-feel-good (accessed November 21, 2013); Craig Sharkton, "Toms Shoes—Philanthropy as a Business Model," sufac.com, August 23, 2008, http://sufac.com/2008/08/toms-shoes-philanthropy-as-a-business-model (accessed June 3, 2011); *TOMS Campus Club Program*, http://images.toms.com/media/content/images/campus-clubs-assets/TOMSCampushandbook_082510_International_final.pdf (accessed November 21, 2013); "TOMS Company Overview," TOMS, www.toms.com/corporate-info (accessed November 21, 2013); "TOMS Manufacturing Practices," TOMS, www.toms.com/manufacturing-practices (accessed November 21, 2013); *TOMS One for One Giving Report*, http://images.toms.com/media/content/images/giving-report/TOMS-Giving-Report-2010.pdf (accessed November 21, 2013); TOMS Shoes, www.toms.com (accessed November 21, 2013); Mike Zimmerman, "The Business of Giving: TOMS Shoes," *Success Magazine*, September 30, 2009, www.successmagazine.com/the-business-of-giving/PARAMS/article/852 (accessed June 3, 2011); "TOMS Eyewear," www.toms.com/eyewear (accessed March 5, 2012); "TOMS Founder Shares Sole-ful Tale," *North Texas Daily*, April 14, 2011, www.ntdaily.com/?p=53882 (accessed March 5, 2012).

[60] "2010 Most Ethical Companies in the World," Barrett-Jackson website, www.barrett-jackson.com/articles/most-ethical-auction-company.asp (accessed June 9, 2011); "2010 World's Most Ethical Companies," *Ethisphere*, http://ethisphere.com/wme2010 (accessed June 8, 2011); "Barrett-Jackson Cancer Research Fund and TGen," TGen website, www.tgenfoundation.org/NetCommunity/Page.aspx?pid=828 (accessed November 21, 2013); "The Barrett-Jackson Legacy," Barrett-Jackson website, www.barrett-jackson.com/about (accessed November 21, 2013); Barrett-Jackson News, "Barrett-Jackson Celebrates Four Decades of Charitable Work at 40th Annual Scottsdale Auction," Barrett-Jackson website, January 18, 2011, http://news.barrett-jackson.com/barrett-jackson-celebrates-four-decades-of-charitable-work-at-40th-annual-scottsdale-auction (accessed November 21, 2013); Paul M. Barrett, "Barrett-Jackson Auction: Dude, There's My Car!" *Bloomberg Businessweek*, January 28, 2011, www.businessweek.com/magazine/content/11_06/b4214071705361.htm (accessed November 21, 2013); Larry Edsall, "Real Buyers. Real Sellers. Real Auctions," Barrett-Jackson website, www.barrett-jackson.com/articles/real-auctions.asp (accessed June 9, 2011). "Reserve Consignments at Barrett-Jackson Palm Beach Auction," *Sports Car Digest*, February 16, 2011, www.sportscardigest.com/reserve-consignments-at-barrett-jackson-palm-beach-auction (accessed November 21, 2013); Beth Schwartz, "Dream Chasers," *Luxury Las Vegas*, November 2009, http://luxurylv.com/2009/11/features/3495 (accessed June 9, 2011); Barrett-Jackson, "Barrett-Jackson Calls Upon Collector Car Specialist Gordon McCall to Run Salon Collection Offering Division," January 22, 2012, http://news.barrett-jackson.com/barrett-jackson-calls-upon-collector-car-specialist-gordon-mccall-to-run-salon-collection-offering-division (accessed November 21, 2013); Bob Golfen, "Dream Cars for Sale at Barrett-Jackson Auction," *Fox News*, January 13, 2012, www.foxnews.com/leisure/2012/ 01/13/dream-cars-for-sale-at-barrett-jackson-auction (accessed March 20, 2012); Hannah Elliot, "Update: Barrett-Jackson Stands Behind JFK Ambulance," *Forbes*, January 21, 2011, www.forbes.com/sites/hannahelliott/2011/01/21/update-barrett-jackson-stands-behind-jfk-ambulance/2 (accessed November 21, 2013); Barrett-Jackson, "Corvette Coupe Raises $125,000 for Cancer Investigations at TGen," January 24, 2012, http://news.barrett-jackson.com/corvette-coupe-raises-125000-for-cancer-investigations-at-tgen (accessed November 21, 2013).

[61] Monte Burke, "A Conversation with REI Chief Executive Sally Jewell," *Forbes*, May 19, 2011, http://blogs.forbes.com/monteburke/2011/05/19/a-conversation-with-rei-chief-executive-sally-jewell (accessed October 17, 2013); *CNN Money*, "100 Best Companies to Work for," http://money.cnn.com/magazines/

fortune/best-companies/2013/snapshots/17.html?iid=bc_fl_list (accessed October 17, 2013); Fair Factories Clearinghouse, "Streamlining Business Practices," www.fairfactories.org/Main/Index.aspx (accessed October 17, 2013); O. C. Ferrell, Geoffrey A. Hirt, and Linda Ferrell, *Business: A Changing World*, 8th ed. (New York: McGraw-Hill Irwin, 2011), p. 138; Christine Frey, "Product-Testing REI Employees Take the Scrapes for Buyers," *Seattle PI*, October 18, 2002, www.seattlepi.com/default/article/Product-testing-REI-employees-take-the-scrapes-1098834.php (accessed October 17, 2013); FSC, "FSC Certification," www.fsc.org/certification.html (accessed October 17, 2013); Global Foresight, "Advisory Board," www.global-foresight.net/about/about-who.html (accessed May 31, 2011); International Labour Organization, "About the ILO," www.ilo.org/global/about-the-ilo/lang--en/index.htm (accessed October 21, 2013); Leave No Trace Website, www.lnt.org/programs/peak/index.html (accessed October 21, 2013); New York Job Source, "Recreation Equipment Inc.," October 6, 2010, http://nyjobsource.com/rei.html (accessed October 21, 2013). REI, *2012 Stewardship Report*, www.rei.com/stewardship/report/2012.html (accessed October 17, 2013); REI, "REI & Youth," www.rei.com/aboutrei/reikids02.html (accessed October 17, 2013); REI, "Being an REI Member Just Got Better: REI Introduces Free Shipping Exclusively for Members," www.rei.com/aboutrei/releases/10free_shipping.html (accessed October 21, 2013); REI, "Board of Directors," www.rei.com/aboutrei/directors.html (accessed October 21, 2013); REI, "Governing Documents of Recreational Equipment, Inc.: Charter of the Nominating and Corporate Governance Committee," www.rei.com/pdf/aboutrei/nomgovcharter09.pdf (accessed October 21, 2013); REI, "Governing Documents of Recreational Equipment, Inc.: Charter of the Audit and Finance Committee," May 20, 2010, www.rei.com/pdf/aboutrei/afcmtecharter.pdf (accessed October 21, 2013); REI, "Overview," www.rei.com/aboutrei/business.html (accessed October 17, 2013); REI, "REI and Youth," www.rei.com/aboutrei/reikids02.html (accessed October 21, 2013); REI, "The REI Member Dividend," https://www.rei.com/membership/dividend (accessed October 21, 2013); REI, "The REI Story," www.rei.com/jobs/story.html (accessed October 21, 2013); REI, "REI Foundation," www.rei.com/aboutrei/csr/2009/rei-foundation.html (accessed June 1, 2011); REI, "REI Outdoor School Classes and Outings," www.rei.com/outdoorschool (accessed June 1, 2011); REI, "REI Outdoor School Facts," www.rei.com/outdoorschool/faqs.html (accessed October 21, 2013); REI, "REI's Culture & Values," www.rei.com/jobs/culture.html (accessed June 1, 2011); REI, "Workforce Diversity," www.rei.com/jobs/diversity.html (accessed June 1, 2011); REI, "Workplace," www.rei.com/stewardship/rei_workplace (accessed October 21, 2013); REI Adventures, www.rei.com/adventures (accessed June 1, 2011); REI Adventures, "Our Trips Include Living Guidebooks," www.rei.com/adventures/resources/guides.html (accessed June 1, 2011); Giselle Tsirulnik, "REI App Ppurpose Is Twofold: Sales and Service," *Mobile Commerce Daily*, March 25, 2011, www.mobilecommercedaily.com/2011/03/25/rei-app-purpose-is-twofold-sales-and-service (accessed June 1, 2011); REI, "Jerry Stritzke Named President and CEO of REI," August 30, 2013, www.rei.com/about-rei/newsroom/2013/jerry-stritzke-named-president-and-ceo-of-rei.html (accessed October 17, 2013); REI, "Factory Fair Labor Compliance: 2011 Stewardship Report," www.rei.com/stewardship/report/2011/workplace/factory-fair-labor.html (accessed October 17, 2013); Amy Martinez, "Retailer REI says a 'Limited Number' of Employees Are Being Laid Off," *Seattle Times*, March 21, 2013, http://seattletimes.com/html/businesstechnology/2020614556_reilayoffsxml.html (accessed October 17, 2013); Daniel Petty, "REI Return Policy Changes: Items Must Be Returned within 1 Year," *The Denver Post*, June 4, 2013, http://blogs.denverpost.com/travel/2013/06/04/rei-return-policy-changes-1-year-purchase/12422 (accessed October 21, 2013); Ariel Webber, "Recreational Equipment Inc. Ads Are Made for Outdoor Enthusiasts," *Trend Hunter Marketing*, February 18, 2013, www.trendhunter.com/trends/recreational-equipment-inc (accessed October 30, 2013); REI, "REI Announces Record Sales for 2012," April 29, 2013, www.rei.com/about-rei/newsroom/2013/rei-announces-record-sales-for-2012.html (accessed October 30, 2013); Elaine Porterfield, "How REI Became the Most Respected Private Company Brand in Washington," *Puget Sound Business Journal*, July 29, 2011, www.bizjournals.com/seattle/print-edition/2011/07/29/how-rei-became-the-most-respected.html?page=all (accessed October 30, 2013).

Feature Notes

[a] Michal Lev-Ram, "SodaStream's Bubbly Rise," *CNN Money*, March 21, 2013, http://money.cnn.com/2013/03/21/news/companies/sodastream-daniel-birnbaum.pr.fortune/index.html (accessed August 7, 2013); Emily Jane Fox, "Super Bowl Showdown: SodaStream vs. Pepsi and Coke," *CNN Money*, February 3, 2013, http://money.cnn.com/2013/02/03/news/companies/sodastream-coke-pepsi-super-bowl/index.html?iid=EL (accessed August 7, 2013); SodaStream website, www.sodastream.com/ (accessed August 7, 2013); "SodaStream Super Bowl Commercial Features Scarlett Johansson and a (Censored) Diss," *The Huffington Post*, February 3, 2014, www.huffingtonpost.com/2014/02/03/sodastream-super-bowl-commercial-scarlett-johansson_n_4713441.html (accessed March 27, 2014).

[b] Bruce Horovitz, "Taco Bell to Drop Kid Meals with Toys," *USA Today*, July 23, 2013, p. 3B; The Huffington Post, "San Francisco Happy Meal Toy Ban Takes Effect, Sidestepped by McDonald's," *Huffington Post*, November 30, 2011, www.huffingtonpost.com/2011/11/30/san-francisco-happy-meal-ban_n_1121186.html (accessed August 5, 2013); Anika Anand, "Jack in the Box to Stop Offering Toys in Kid's Meals," *NBC News*, June 21, 2011, www.nbcnews.com/id/43483446/ns/business-retail/t/jack-box-stop-offering-toys-kids-meals/#.UgAVnhai3ww (accessed August 5, 2013).

part 3

Marketing Research and Target Market Analysis

PART 3 examines how marketers use information and technology to better understand and reach customers. CHAPTER 5 provides a foundation for analyzing buyers through a discussion of marketing information systems and the basic steps in the marketing research process. Understanding elements that affect buying decisions enables marketers to better analyze customers' needs and to evaluate how specific marketing strategies can satisfy those needs. CHAPTER 6 deals with selecting and analyzing target markets, which is one of the major steps in marketing strategy development.

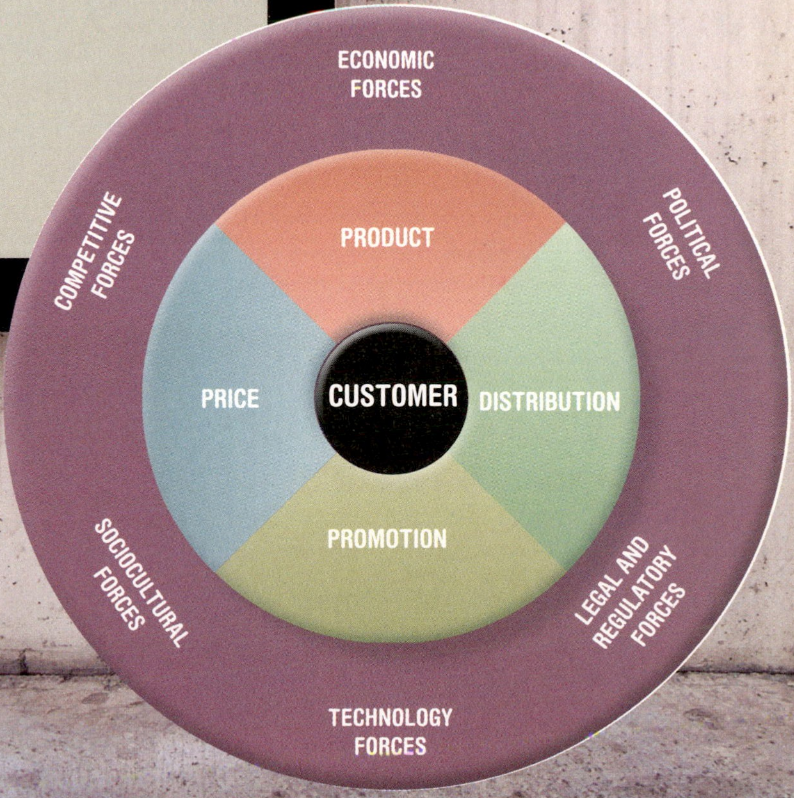

chapter 5

Marketing Research and Information Systems

OBJECTIVES

5-1 Define marketing research and its importance to decision makers.

5-2 Distinguish between exploratory and conclusive research.

5-3 Name the five basic steps in conducting marketing research, including the two types of data and four survey methods.

5-4 Describe the tools, such as databases, big data, decision support systems, and the Internet, useful to marketing decision making.

5-5 Identify ethical and international issues in marketing research.

MARKETING INSIGHTS

The Weather Company Targets Advertising

It is well-known that there is a correlation between the weather and consumer behavior, but this has always been difficult for marketers to accurately measure. With the advent of people's increasing interest in the weather and accessibility to weather and climate information, companies are in a better position to leverage their advertisements against weather forecasts. The Weather Company, with its fine-tuned forecasting and expansion into various media outlets, is helping marketers with this endeavor.

In order for users to get an accurate weather forecast, they have to type in their specific location on a computer or mobile device. A company's advertisement can then be targeted to a specific location in a certain climate. For instance, if there is a high concentration of humidity in the air, the user may see an advertisement for anti-frizz hair products and offer nearby suggestions as to where to purchase the product. Michaels arts and crafts stores use the extended forecast feature to tailor their advertisements because, according to marketing research, people tend to shop for arts and crafts supplies three days before a forecasted rainy day.

Although many consumers are wary of targeted ads, especially when companies use their location to do so, others perceive this kind of advertising more as advice than as a push to purchase products. The advertisement is supplemental to the weather forecast and therefore has value to the user. For instance, in checking the weather and seeing an ad for anti-frizz serum, the user is able to plan how she will wear her hair the following day. She may also remember the advertisement as a solution to a problem she is going to have if the humidity persists.[1]

Marketing research enables marketers to implement the marketing concept by helping them acquire information about whether and how their goods and services satisfy the desires of target market customers. When used effectively, such information facilitates relationship marketing by helping marketers focus their efforts on meeting and even anticipating the needs of their customers. Marketing research and information systems that can provide practical and objective information to help firms develop and implement marketing strategies are therefore essential to effective marketing.

In this chapter, we focus on how marketers gather information needed to make marketing decisions. First, we define marketing research and examine the individual steps of the marketing research process, including various methods of collecting data. Next, we look at how technology aids in collecting, organizing, and interpreting marketing research data. Finally, we consider ethical and international issues in marketing research.

5-1 THE IMPORTANCE OF MARKETING RESEARCH

Marketing research is the systematic design, collection, interpretation, and reporting of information to help marketers solve specific marketing problems or take advantage of marketing opportunities. As the word *research* implies, it is a process for gathering information that is not currently available to decision makers. The purpose of marketing research is to inform an organization about customers' needs and desires, marketing opportunities for products, and changing attitudes and purchase patterns of customers. Market information increases the marketer's ability to respond to customer needs, which leads to improved organizational performance. Detecting shifts in buyers' behaviors and attitudes helps companies stay in touch with the ever-changing marketplace. A fast-food marketer, for example, would be interested to know about the growing popularity of pretzel buns. In a one-year period, companies including 7-Eleven, Wendy's, Sonic, and Dunkin' Donuts released 160 pretzel products into the market.[2] Strategic planning requires marketing research to facilitate the process of assessing such opportunities or threats from competitors.

Marketing research can help a firm better understand market opportunities, ascertain the potential for success for new products, and determine the feasibility of a particular marketing strategy. It can also reveal some surprising trends. A joint survey study was launched by Dunkin' Donuts and CareerBuilder to determine consumers' coffee-drinking habits in the workplace. After surveying 3,684 U.S. workers, the study revealed that more than 60 percent of workers who drink coffee drink at least two cups of coffee a day, and one-third claim they are less productive at work when they do not drink their cup of coffee. This research on consumer coffee consumption provides important information to Dunkin' Donuts as it seeks to compete against other coffee retailers such as Starbucks.[3]

Many types of organizations use marketing research to help them develop marketing mixes to match the needs of customers. Supermarkets have learned from marketing research that roughly half of all Americans prefer to have their dinners ready in 15 to 30 minutes. Such information highlights a tremendous opportunity for supermarkets to offer high-quality "heat-and-eat" meals to satisfy this growing segment of the food market. Political candidates also depend on marketing research to understand the scope of issues their constituents view as important. National political candidates may spend millions surveying voters to better understand issues and craft their images accordingly.

marketing research The systematic design, collection, interpretation, and reporting of information to help marketers solve specific marketing problems or take advantage of marketing opportunities

Changes in the economy have dramatically changed marketers' decision-making strategies. Increasingly, businesses need speed and agility to survive and to react quickly to changing consumer behaviors. Understanding the market is crucial for effective marketing strategies. Evidence shows that automakers use information about consumer vehicle preferences to determine what features are important in the development of new vehicles (see snapshot). Marketing research has shifted its focus toward smaller studies like test marketing,

© iStockphoto.com/IS_ImageSource

Gathering Data
Checkout scanners provide information on what types of products are being purchased. This data can help supermarkets understand their customers' consumption patterns.

small-scale surveys, and short-range forecasting in order to learn about changing dynamics in the marketplace. However, large, high-value research projects remain necessary for long-term success. Though it is acceptable to conduct studies that take six months or more, many companies need real-time information to help them make good decisions. Firms may benefit from historical or secondary data, but due to changes in the economy and buyer behavior, such data are not as useful in today's decision-making environment. As we discuss in this chapter, online research services and the use of big data are helping to supplement and integrate findings in order to help companies make tactical and strategic decisions. In the future, the marketing researcher will need to be able to identify the most efficient and effective ways of gathering information.[4]

The real value of marketing research is measured by improvements in a marketer's ability to make decisions. Starbucks, for instance, has used information about the popularity of tea to launch a new business venture, Teavana tea bar. Market research has shown that although coffee constitutes more sales, tea is the second most consumed beverage after water. Starbucks also knows from research that many tea drinkers do not cross over to coffee, reassuring the chain that its new venture will not cannibalize its coffee business.[5] Marketers should treat information the same way as other resources, and they must weigh the costs and benefits of obtaining information. Information should be considered worthwhile if it results in marketing activities that better

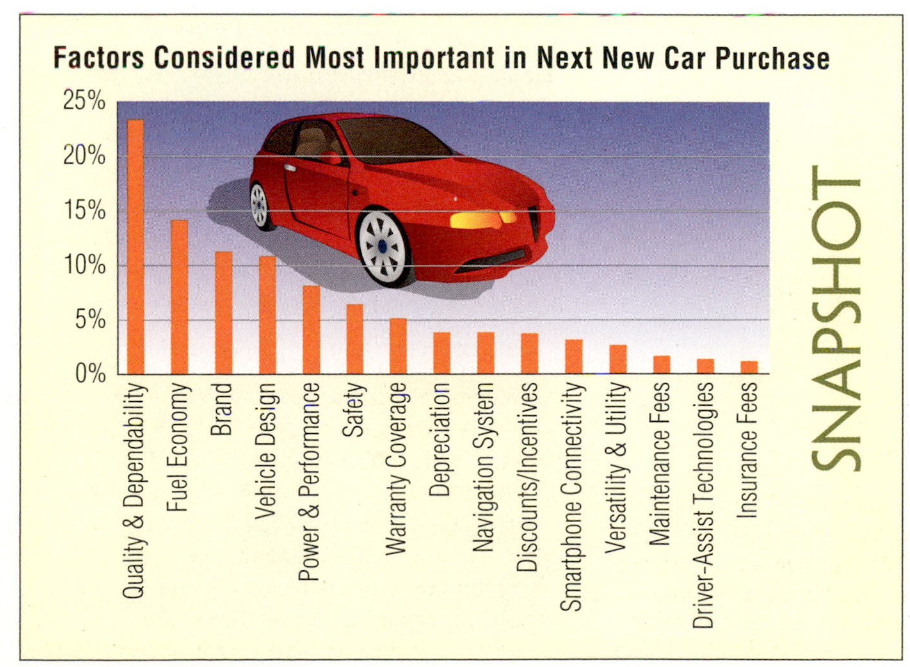

Source: NADAguides.com, May 2013.

satisfy the firm's target customers, lead to increased sales and profits, or help the firm achieve some other goal.

5-2 TYPES OF RESEARCH

The nature and type of research vary based on the research design and the hypotheses under investigation. Marketing research can involve two forms of data. *Qualitative data* yields descriptive non-numerical information. *Quantitative data* yields empirical information that can be communicated through numbers. Marketers may choose to collect either depending upon the research required.

To collect this data, marketers conduct either exploratory research or conclusive research. Although each has a distinct purpose, the major differences between them are formalization and flexibility rather than the specific research methods used. Table 5.1 summarizes the differences.

5-2a Exploratory Research

When marketers need more information about a problem or want to make a tentative hypothesis more specific, they may conduct **exploratory research**. The main purpose of exploratory research is to better understand a problem or situation and/or to help identify additional data needs or decision alternatives.[6] Consider that until recently, there was no research available to help marketers understand how consumers perceive the terms *clearance* versus *sale* in describing a discounted price event. An exploratory study asked one group of 80 consumers to write down their thoughts about a store window sign that said "sale" and another group of 80 consumers to write about a store window sign that read "clearance." The results revealed that consumers expected deeper discounts when the term *clearance* was used, and they expected the quality of the clearance products to be lower than that of products on sale.[7] This exploratory research helped marketers better understand how consumers view these terms and opened up the opportunity for additional research hypotheses about options for retail pricing.

exploratory research
Research conducted to gather more information about a problem or to make a tentative hypothesis more specific

Table 5.1 Differences between Exploratory and Conclusive Research

Research Project Components	Exploratory Research	Conclusive Research
Research purpose	General: to generate insights about a situation	Specific: to verify insights and aid in selecting a course of action
Data needs	Vague	Clear
Data sources	Ill-defined	Well-defined
Data collection form	Open-ended, rough	Usually structured
Sample	Relatively small; subjectively selected to maximize generalization of insights	Relatively large; objectively selected to permit generalization of findings
Data collection	Flexible; no set procedure	Rigid; well-laid-out procedure
Data analysis	Informal; typically nonquantitative	Formal; typically quantitative
Inferences/ recommendations	More tentative than final	More final than tentative

Source: A. Parasuraman, *Marketing Research*, Second Edition. © 2007 Cengage Learning, Inc. Reproduced by permission, www.cengage.com/permissions.

More organizations are starting **customer advisory boards**, which are small groups of actual customers who serve as sounding boards for new product ideas and offer insights into their feelings and attitudes toward a firm's products, promotion, pricing, and other elements of marketing strategy. Though these advisory boards help companies maintain strong relationships with valuable customers, they can also provide great insight into marketing research questions. Oracle maintains customer advisory boards for its subsidiary PeopleSoft to provide insights on how customers view the organization's business application products.[8]

One common method for conducting exploratory research is through a focus group. A **focus group** brings together multiple people to discuss a certain topic in a group setting led by a moderator. Focus groups are often conducted informally, without a structured questionnaire. They allow customer attitudes, behaviors, lifestyles, needs, and desires to be explored in a flexible and creative manner. Questions are open-ended and stimulate respondents to answer in their own words. A traditional focus group session consists of approximately 8 to 12 individuals and is led by a moderator, an independent individual hired by the research firm or the company. The moderator encourages group discussion among all of the participants and can direct the discussion by occasionally asking questions.

Focus groups can provide companies with ideas for new products or be used for initial testing of different marketing strategies for existing products. Illustrative of this, Ford may use focus groups to determine whether to change its advertising to emphasize a vehicle's safety features rather than its style and performance. The less-structured format of focus groups, where participants can interact with one another and build on each other's comments, is beneficial to marketers because it can yield more detailed information to researchers, including information that they might not have necessarily thought to ask participants about beforehand.

A current trend for researchers is online focus groups. In this method, participants sign in to a website and type their comments and responses there. Online focus groups can gather data from large and geographically diverse groups in a less intensive manner than focus-group interviews. Amazon started a digital focus group consisting of some of its "best" customers to preview its entertainment options and provide feedback.[9] Online focus groups are also more convenient for the participants than traditional focus groups. However, this method makes it more difficult to ask participants about a product's smell or taste, if that is relevant to the product being tested. Researchers also cannot observe the participants' nonverbal cues and

customer advisory boards Small groups of actual customers who serve as sounding boards for new-product ideas and offer insights into their feelings and attitudes toward a firm's products and other elements of its marketing strategy

focus group An interview that is often conducted informally, without a structured questionnaire, in small groups of 8 to 12 people, to observe interaction when members are exposed to an idea or a concept

Focus Groups
Focus groups consist of multiple people discussing a certain topic in a group setting. Usually, focus groups are led by a moderator who encourages group discussion.

body language in this setting, which can often reveal "gut" reactions to questions asked or topics discussed.

Focus groups do have a few disadvantages for marketers. Sometimes, the focus group's discussion can be hindered by overly talkative, confrontational, or shy individuals. Some participants may be less than honest in an effort to be sociable or to receive money and/or food in exchange for their participation.[10] For these reasons, focus groups provide only qualitative, not quantitative, data and are thus best used to uncover issues that can then be explored using quantifiable marketing research techniques.

5-2b Conclusive Research

Conclusive research is designed to verify insights through an objective procedure to help marketers make decisions. It is used when the marketer has one or more alternatives in mind and needs assistance in the final stages of decision making. Consider exploratory research that has revealed that the terms *clearance* and *sale* send different signals to consumers. To make a decision about how to use this information, marketers would benefit from a well-defined and structured research project that will help them decide which approach is best for a specific set of products and target consumers. The typically quantitative study should be specific in selecting a course of action and using methods that can be verified. Two such types of conclusive research are descriptive research and experimental research.

If marketers need to understand the characteristics of certain phenomena to solve a particular problem, **descriptive research** can aid them. Descriptive studies may range from general surveys of customers' educations, occupations, or ages to specifics on how often teenagers consume sports drinks or how often customers buy new pairs of athletic shoes. For example, if Nike and Reebok want to target more young women, they might ask 15- to 35-year-old females how often they work out, how frequently they wear athletic shoes for casual use, and how many pairs of athletic shoes they buy in a year. Such descriptive research can be used to develop specific marketing strategies for the athletic-shoe market. Descriptive studies generally demand much prior knowledge and assume that the problem or issue is clearly defined. Some descriptive studies require statistical analysis and predictive tools. The marketer's major task is to choose adequate methods for collecting and measuring data.

Descriptive research is limited in providing evidence necessary to make causal inferences (i.e., that variable X causes a variable Y). **Experimental research** allows marketers to make causal deductions about relationships. Such experimentation requires that an independent variable (one not influenced by or dependent on other variables) be manipulated and the resulting changes in a dependent variable (one contingent on, or restricted to, one value or set of values assumed by the independent variable) be measured. For instance, McDonald's is testing a different version of its dollar menu with items priced at $1, $2, and $5. By manipulating the pricing variable, McDonald's can determine whether consumers are willing to pay higher prices for certain items. Holding variables such as promotion constant, McDonald's can set different prices for items and determine whether the resulting sales are higher than before. If sales increase, then McDonald's managers could make an informed decision about the effect of price on sales.[11] Manipulation of the causal variable and control of other variables are what make experimental research unique. As a result, they can provide much stronger evidence of cause and effect than data collected through descriptive research.

conclusive research
Research designed to verify insights through objective procedures and to help marketers in making decisions

descriptive research
Research conducted to clarify the characteristics of certain phenomena to solve a particular problem

experimental research
Research that allows marketers to make causal inferences about relationships

5-3 THE MARKETING RESEARCH PROCESS

To maintain the control needed to obtain accurate information, marketers approach marketing research as a process with logical steps: (1) locating and defining problems or issues, (2) designing the research project, (3) collecting data, (4) interpreting research findings, and (5) reporting research findings (see Figure 5.1). These steps should be

Figure 5.1 **The Five Steps of the Marketing Research Process**

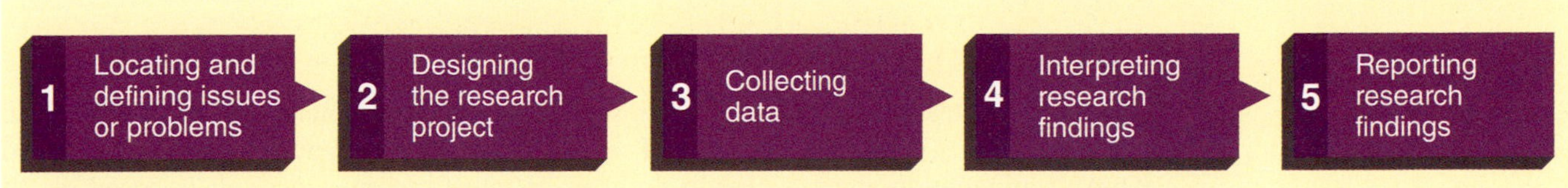

viewed as an overall approach to conducting research rather than as a rigid set of rules to be followed in each project. In planning research projects, marketers must consider each step carefully and determine how they can best adapt the steps to resolve the particular issues at hand.

5-3a Locating and Defining Problems or Research Issues

The first step in launching a research study is problem or issue definition, which focuses on uncovering the nature and boundaries of a situation or question related to marketing strategy or implementation. The first sign of a problem is typically a departure from some normal function, such as the failure to attain objectives. If a corporation's objective is a 12 percent sales increase and the current marketing strategy resulted in a 6 percent increase, this discrepancy should be analyzed to help guide future marketing strategies. Declining sales, increasing expenses, and decreasing profits also signal problems. Customer relationship management (CRM) is frequently based on analysis of existing customers. Armed with this knowledge, a firm could define a problem as finding a way to adjust for biases stemming from existing customers when gathering data or to develop methods for gathering information to help find new customers. Conversely, when an organization experiences a dramatic rise in sales or some other positive event, it may conduct marketing research to discover the reasons and maximize the opportunities stemming from them.

Marketing research often focuses on identifying and defining market opportunities or changes in the environment. When a firm discovers a market opportunity, it may need to conduct research to understand the situation more precisely so it can craft an appropriate marketing strategy. Such market research is quite common in the film industry. Hollywood studios often use pre-screenings or hire market research firms such as Nielsen National Research Group to determine how the audience might respond. These market research firms will also warn studios if their movie release dates are set to "collide" with similar movies with the same target market demographic.[12] Market research has yet to catch on for the Indian film industry Bollywood, however. Indian filmmakers depend less upon market research and more on their individual experiences when creating movies for the public.[13]

To pin down the specific boundaries of a problem or an issue through research, marketers must define the nature and scope of the situation in a way that requires probing beneath the superficial symptoms. The interaction between the marketing manager and the marketing researcher should yield a clear definition of the research needed. Researchers and decision makers should remain in the problem or issue definition stage until they have determined precisely what they want from marketing research and how they will use it. Deciding how to refine a broad, indefinite problem or issue into a precise, researchable statement is a prerequisite for the next step in the research process.

5-3b Designing the Research Project

research design An overall plan for obtaining the information needed to address a research problem or issue

Once the problem or issue has been defined, the next step is to create a **research design**, an overall plan for obtaining the information needed to address it. This step requires formulating a hypothesis and determining what type of research is most appropriate for testing the hypothesis to ensure the results are reliable and valid.

Developing a Hypothesis

The objective statement of a marketing research project should include a hypothesis based on both previous research and expected research findings. A **hypothesis** is an informed guess or assumption about a certain problem or set of circumstances. It is based on all the insight and knowledge available about the problem or circumstances from previous research studies and other sources. So, since data suggest that salsa sales have surpassed ketchup sales in the United States, a food marketer at H.J. Heinz might develop a hypothesis that consumers perceive salsa to be a healthier alternative. As information is gathered, the researcher can test the hypothesis. Movie, theater, sports arena, and concert venue owners who are wondering why sales are down may hypothesize that consumers are staying home more because of rising event prices, widespread availability of home theater systems, broadband Internet access, and families' increasingly busy schedules. Marketers could test this hypothesis by manipulating prices or offering strong incentives for consumers to return. Sometimes, several hypotheses are developed during an actual research project; the hypotheses that are accepted or rejected become the study's chief conclusions.

Research Reliability and Validity

In designing research, marketing researchers must ensure that research techniques are both reliable and valid. A research technique has **reliability** if it produces almost identical results in repeated trials. However, a reliable technique is not necessarily valid. To have **validity**, the research method must measure what it is supposed to measure, not something else. For example, although a group of customers may express the same level of satisfaction based on a rating scale, as individuals they may not exhibit the same repurchase behavior because of different personal characteristics. If the purpose of rating satisfaction was to estimate potential repurchase behavior, this result may cause the researcher to question the validity of the satisfaction scale.[14] A study to measure the effect of advertising on sales would be valid if advertising could be isolated from other factors or from variables that affect sales. The study would be reliable if replications of it produced the same results.

5-3c Collecting Data

The next step in the marketing research process is collecting data to help prove (or disprove) the research hypothesis. The research design must specify what types of data to collect and how they will be collected.

Types of Data

Marketing researchers have two types of data at their disposal. **Primary data** are observed and recorded or collected directly from respondents. This type of data must be gathered by observing phenomena or surveying people of interest. **Secondary data** are compiled both inside and outside the organization for some purpose other than the current investigation. Secondary data include general reports supplied to an enterprise by various data services and internal and online databases. Such reports might concern market share, retail inventory levels, and customers' buying behavior. Commonly, secondary data are already available in private or public reports or have been collected and stored by the organization itself. Due to the opportunity to obtain data via the Internet, more than half of all marketing research now comes from secondary sources.

hypothesis An informed guess or assumption about a certain problem or set of circumstances

reliability A condition that exists when a research technique produces almost identical results in repeated trials

validity A condition that exists when a research method measures what it is supposed to measure

primary data Data observed and recorded or collected directly from respondents

secondary data Data compiled both inside and outside the organization for some purpose other than the current investigation

Sources of Secondary Data
Newspapers such as *The Wall Street Journal* provide important sources for secondary data.

Sources of Secondary Data

Marketers often begin the data-collection phase of the marketing research process by gathering secondary data. They may use available reports and other information from both internal and external sources to study a marketing problem.

Internal sources of secondary data can contribute tremendously to research. An organization's own database may contain information about past marketing activities, such as sales records and research reports, which can be used to test hypotheses and pinpoint problems. From sales reports, a firm may be able to determine not only which product sold best at certain times of the year but also which colors and sizes customers preferred. Such information may have been gathered using customer relationship management tools for marketing, management, or financial purposes.

Accounting records are also an excellent source of data but, surprisingly, are often overlooked. The large volume of data an accounting department collects does not automatically flow to other departments. As a result, detailed information about costs, sales, customer accounts, or profits by product category may not be easily accessible to the marketing area. This condition develops particularly in organizations that do not store marketing information on a systematic basis. A third source of internal secondary data is competitive information gathered by the sales force.

External sources of secondary data include trade associations, periodicals, government publications, unpublished sources, and online databases. Trade associations, such as the American Marketing Association, offer guides and directories that are full of information. Periodicals such as *Bloomberg Businessweek*, *The Wall Street Journal*, *Sales & Marketing Management*, *Advertising Age*, *Marketing Research*, and *Industrial Marketing* publish general information that can help marketers define problems and develop hypotheses. *Survey of Buying Power*, an annual supplement to *Sales & Marketing Management*, contains sales data for major industries on a county-by-county basis. Many marketers also consult federal government publications such as the *Statistical Abstract of the United States*, the *Census of Business*, the *Census of Agriculture*, and the *Census of Population*; most of these government publications are available online. Although the government still conducts its primary census every 10 years, it also conducts the American Community Survey, an ongoing survey sent to population samples on a regular basis.[15] This provides marketers with a more up-to-date demographic picture of the nation's population every year. A company might use survey census data to determine whether to construct a shopping mall in a specific area.[16]

In addition, companies may subscribe to services, such as ACNielsen or Information Resources Inc. (IRI), that track retail sales and other information. For example, IRI tracks consumer purchases using in-store, scanner-based technology. Marketing firms can purchase information from IRI about a product category, such as frozen orange juice, as secondary data.[17] Small businesses may be unable to afford such services, but they can still find a wealth of information through industry publications and trade associations.

Companies such as TiVo are challenging services like ACNielsen by offering year-round second-by-second information about the show and advertising viewing habits of consumers who own the company's DVRs. The data are anonymous and are recorded by the TV viewers' boxes. ACNielsen only measures local program viewing for four months a year. However, TiVo's data gathering is limited. Its privacy-protection policies prevent the company from collecting information that Nielson can provide, such as demographic breakdowns and the number of people watching each TV set. On the other hand, TiVo information can aid local TV news programs in their programming decisions by helping them choose when to air sports and weather and how much time to devote to each segment.[18]

The Internet can be especially useful to marketing researchers. Search engines such as Google can help marketers locate many types of secondary data or to research topics of interest. Of course, companies can mine their own websites for useful information by using CRM tools. Amazon.com, for instance, has built a relationship with its customers by tracking the types of books, music, and other products they purchase. Each time a customer logs on to the website, the company can offer recommendations based on the customer's previous purchases. Such a marketing system helps the company track the changing desires and buying habits of its most valued customers. Furthermore, marketing researchers are increasingly monitoring blogs to discover what consumers are saying about their products—both positive and negative. Some, including yogurt maker Stonyfield Farms, have even established their own blogs as a way to monitor consumer dialogue on issues of their choice. There are many reasons people go online, which can make the job of using the Internet complicated for marketers. Table 5.2 summarizes the external sources of secondary data, excluding syndicated services.

Methods of Collecting Primary Data

population All the elements, units, or individuals of interest to researchers for a specific study

sample A limited number of units chosen to represent the characteristics of a total population

sampling The process of selecting representative units from a total population

probability sampling A type of sampling in which every element in the population being studied has a known chance of being selected for study

random sampling A form of probability sampling in which all units in a population have an equal chance of appearing in the sample, and the various events that can occur have an equal or known chance of taking place

Collecting primary data is a lengthier, more expensive, and more complex process than collecting secondary data. To gather primary data, researchers use sampling procedures, survey methods, and observation. These efforts can be handled in-house by the firm's own research department or contracted to a private research firm such as ACNielsen, Information Resources Inc., or IMS International.

Sampling Because the time and resources available for research are limited, it is almost impossible to investigate all the members of a target market or other population. A **population**, or "universe," includes all the elements, units, or individuals of interest to researchers for a specific study. Consider a Gallup poll designed to predict the results of a presidential election. All registered voters in the United States would constitute the population. By systematically choosing a limited number of units—a **sample**—to represent the characteristics of a total population, researchers can project the reactions of a total market or market segment. (In the case of the presidential poll, a representative national sample of several thousand registered voters would be selected and surveyed to project the probable voting outcome.) **Sampling** in marketing research, therefore, is the process of selecting representative units from a total population. Sampling techniques allow marketers to predict buying behavior fairly accurately on the basis of the responses from a representative portion of the population of interest. Most types of marketing research employ sampling techniques.

There are two basic types of sampling: probability sampling and nonprobability sampling. With **probability sampling**, every element in the population being studied has a known chance of being selected for study. Random sampling is a form of probability sampling. When marketers employ **random sampling**, all the units in a population have an equal chance of appearing in the

Table 5.2 Sources of Secondary Information

Government Sources	
Economic census	www.census.gov/econ/census
Export.gov—country and industry market research	www.export.gov/mrktresearch/index.asp
National Technical Information Services	www.ntis.gov
Industry Canada	www.strategis.ic.gc.ca/engdoc/main.html
Trade Associations and Shows	
American Society of Association Executives	www.asaecenter.org
Directory of Associations	www.marketingsource.com/associations
Trade Show News Network	www.tsnn.com
Magazines, Newspapers, Video, and Audio News Programming	
Resource Library	http://findarticles.com
Google Video Search	www.video.google.com
Google News Directory	www.google.com/news/directory
Yahoo! Video Search	www.video.search.yahoo.com
Corporate Information	
Annual Report Service	www.annualreportservice.com
Bitpipe	www.bitpipe.com
Business Wire—press releases	www.businesswire.com
Hoover's Online	www.hoovers.com
Open Directory Project	www.dmoz.org
PR Newswire—press releases	www.prnewswire.com

Source: Adapted from "Data Collection: Low-Cost Secondary Research," *KnowThis.com*, www.knowthis.com/principles-of-marketing-tutorials/data-collection-low-cost-secondary-research (accessed November 18, 2013).

sample. The various events that can occur have an equal or known chance of taking place. For instance, a specific card in a regulation deck should have a 1 in 52 probability of being drawn at any one time. Sample units are ordinarily chosen by selecting from a table of random numbers statistically generated so that each digit, 0 through 9, will have an equal probability of occurring in each position in the sequence. The sequentially numbered elements of a population are sampled randomly by selecting the units whose numbers appear in the table of random numbers.

Another type of probability sampling is **stratified sampling**, in which the population of interest is divided into groups according to a common attribute, and a random sample is then chosen within each group. The stratified sample may reduce some of the error that could occur in a simple random sample. By ensuring that each major group or segment of the population receives its proportionate share of sample units, investigators avoid including too many or too few sample units from each group. Samples are usually stratified when researchers believe there may be variations among different types of respondents. As an example, many political opinion surveys are stratified by gender, race, age, and/or geographic location.

The second type of sampling, **nonprobability sampling**, is more subjective than probability sampling because there is no way to calculate the likelihood that a specific element of the population being studied will be chosen. Quota sampling, for example, is highly judgmental because the final choice of participants is left to the researchers. In **quota sampling**, researchers divide the population into groups and then arbitrarily choose participants from each group.

stratified sampling A type of probability sampling in which the population is divided into groups with a common attribute and a random sample is chosen within each group

nonprobability sampling A sampling technique in which there is no way to calculate the likelihood that a specific element of the population being studied will be chosen

quota sampling A nonprobability sampling technique in which researchers divide the population into groups and then arbitrarily choose participants from each group

In quota sampling, there are some controls—usually limited to two or three variables, such as age, gender, or race—over the selection of participants. The controls attempt to ensure that representative categories of respondents are interviewed. A study of people who wear eyeglasses, for instance, may be conducted by interviewing equal numbers of men and women who wear eyeglasses. Because quota samples are not probability samples, not everyone has an equal chance of being selected and sampling error therefore cannot be measured statistically. Quota samples are used most often in exploratory studies, when hypotheses are being developed. Often a small quota sample will not be projected to the total population, although the findings may provide valuable insights into a problem. Quota samples are useful when people with some common characteristic are found and questioned about the topic of interest. Consequently, a probability sample used to study people who are allergic to cats would be highly inefficient.

Survey Methods Marketing researchers often employ sampling to collect primary data through mail, telephone, personal interview, online, or social networking surveys. The results of such surveys are used to describe and analyze buying behavior. The survey method chosen depends on the nature of the problem or issue; the data needed to test the hypothesis; and the resources, such as funding and personnel, available to the researcher. Marketers may employ more than one survey method depending on the goals of the research. Surveys can be quite expensive (Procter & Gamble spends about $400 million on consumer research and conducts more than 15,000 research studies annually),[19] but small businesses can turn to sites such as SurveyMonkey.com[20] and zoomerang.com for inexpensive or even free online surveys. Marketing Systems Group describes the various tools it has to meet clients' survey and respondent needs. The advertisement depicts three sails in the company colors. It also emphasizes the quality and strong services that it provides to customers. Table 5.3 summarizes and compares the advantages of the various survey methods.

Table 5.3 Comparison of the Four Basic Survey Methods

	Mail Surveys	Telephone Surveys	Online Surveys	Personal Interview Surveys
Economy	Potentially lower in cost per interview than telephone or personal surveys if there is an adequate response rate.	Avoids interviewers' travel expenses; less expensive than in-home interviews.	The least expensive method if there is an adequate response rate.	The most expensive survey method; shopping mall and focus-group interviews have lower costs than in-home interviews.
Flexibility	Inflexible; questionnaire must be short and easy for respondents to complete.	Flexible because interviewers can ask probing questions, but observations are impossible.	Less flexible; survey must be easy for online users to receive and return; short, dichotomous, or multiple-choice questions work best.	Most flexible method; respondents can react to visual materials; demographic data are more accurate; in-depth probes are possible.
Interviewer bias	Interviewer bias is eliminated; questionnaires can be returned anonymously.	Some anonymity; may be hard to develop trust in respondents.	Interviewer bias is often eliminated with e-mail, but e-mail address on the return eliminates anonymity.	Interviewers' personal characteristics or inability to maintain objectivity may result in bias.
Sampling and respondents' cooperation	Obtaining a complete mailing list is difficult; nonresponse is a major disadvantage.	Sample limited to respondents with telephones; devices that screen calls, busy signals, and refusals are a problem.	The available e-mail address list may not be a representative sample for some purposes. Social media surveys might be skewed as fans may be more likely to take the survey.	Not-at-homes are a problem, which may be overcome by focus-group and shopping mall interviewing.

Gathering information through surveys is becoming increasingly difficult because fewer people are willing to participate. Many people believe responding to surveys requires too much scarce personal time, especially as surveys become longer and more detailed. Others have concerns about how much information marketers are gathering and whether their privacy is being invaded. The unethical use of selling techniques disguised as marketing surveys has also led to decreased cooperation. These factors contribute to nonresponse rates for any type of survey.

In a **mail survey**, questionnaires are sent to respondents, who are encouraged to complete and return them. Mail surveys are used most often when the individuals in the sample are spread over a wide area and funds for the survey are limited. A mail survey is less expensive than a telephone or personal interview survey as long as the response rate is high enough to produce reliable results. The main disadvantages of this method are the possibility of a low response rate and of misleading results if respondents differ significantly from the population being sampled. One method of improving response rates involves attaching a brief personal message on a Post-it® Note to the survey packet. Response rates to these surveys are higher, and the quality and timeliness of the responses are also improved.[21] As a result of these issues, companies are increasingly moving to Internet surveys and automated telephone surveys.

Survey Research
Companies such as Marketing Systems Group provide services to create adequate samples for various types of surveys.

Premiums or incentives that encourage respondents to return questionnaires have been effective in developing panels of respondents who are interviewed regularly by mail. Such mail panels, selected to represent a target market or market segment, are especially useful in evaluating new products and providing general information about customers, as well as records of their purchases (in the form of purchase diaries). Mail panels and purchase diaries are much more widely used than custom mail surveys, but both panels and purchase diaries have shortcomings. People who take the time to fill out a diary may differ from the general population based on income, education, or behavior, such as the time available for shopping activities. Internet and social networking surveys have also greatly gained in popularity, although they are similarly limited as well—given that not all demographics utilize these media equally.

In a **telephone survey**, an interviewer records respondents' answers to a questionnaire over a phone line. A telephone survey has some advantages over a mail survey. The rate of response is higher because it takes less effort to answer the telephone and talk than to fill out and return a questionnaire. If enough interviewers are available, a telephone survey can be conducted very quickly. Thus, political candidates or organizations that want an immediate reaction to an event may choose this method. In addition, a telephone survey permits interviewers to gain rapport with respondents and ask probing questions. Automated telephone surveys, also known as interactive voice response or "robosurveys," rely on a recorded voice to ask the questions while a computer program records respondents' answers. The primary benefit of automated surveys is the elimination of any bias that might be introduced by a live researcher.

Another option is the **telephone depth interview**, which combines the traditional focus group's ability to probe with the confidentiality provided by a telephone survey. This type of interview is most appropriate for qualitative research projects among a small targeted group that is difficult to bring together for a traditional focus group because of members' professions, locations, or lifestyles. Respondents can choose the time and day for the interview. Although

mail survey A research method in which respondents answer a questionnaire sent through the mail

telephone survey A research method in which respondents' answers to a questionnaire are recorded by an interviewer on the phone

telephone depth interview An interview that combines the traditional focus group's ability to probe with the confidentiality provided by telephone surveys

this method is difficult to implement, it can yield revealing information from respondents who otherwise would be unwilling to participate in marketing research.

However, only a small proportion of the population likes to participate in telephone surveys or interviews. This can significantly limit participation and distort representation. Moreover, surveys and interviews conducted over the telephone are limited to oral communication; visual aids or observation cannot be included. Interpreters of results must make adjustments for individuals who are not at home or do not have telephones. Many households are excluded from telephone directories by choice (unlisted numbers) or because the residents moved after the directory was published. Potential respondents often use telephone answering machines, voice mail, or caller ID to screen or block calls; additionally, millions have signed up for "Do Not Call Lists." Moreover, an increasing number of Americans are giving up their fixed telephone lines in favor of cellular or wireless phones. These issues have serious implications for the use of telephone samples in conducting surveys or interviews.

In a **personal interview survey**, participants respond to questions face-to-face. Various audiovisual aids—pictures, products, diagrams, or prerecorded advertising copy—can be incorporated into a personal interview. Rapport gained through direct interaction usually permits more in-depth interviewing, including probes, follow-up questions, or psychological tests. In addition, because personal interviews can be longer, they may yield more information. Respondents can be selected more carefully, and reasons for nonresponse can be explored. One such research technique is the **in-home (door-to-door) interview**. The in-home interview offers a clear advantage when thoroughness of self-disclosure and elimination of group influence are important. In an in-depth interview of 45 to 90 minutes, respondents can be probed to reveal their true motivations, feelings, behaviors, and aspirations. Door-to-door interviewing is increasingly difficult due to respondent and interviewer security and safety issues. This method is particularly limited in gated communities such as condos or apartments.

The nature of personal interviews has changed. In the past, most personal interviews, which were based on random sampling or prearranged appointments, were conducted in the respondent's home. Today, many personal interviews are conducted in shopping malls. **Shopping mall intercept interviews** involve interviewing a percentage of individuals who pass by an "intercept" point in a mall. Like any face-to-face interviewing method, mall intercept interviewing has many advantages. The interviewer is in a position to recognize and react to respondents' nonverbal indications of confusion. Respondents can view product prototypes, videotapes of commercials, and the like, and provide their opinions. The mall environment lets the researcher deal with complex situations. In taste tests, for instance, researchers know that all the respondents are reacting to the same product, which can be prepared and monitored from the mall test kitchen. In addition to the ability to conduct tests requiring bulky equipment, lower cost and greater control make shopping mall intercept interviews popular.

An **on-site computer interview** is a variation of the shopping mall intercept interview in which respondents complete a self-administered questionnaire displayed on a computer monitor. A computer software package can be used to conduct such interviews in shopping malls. After a brief lesson on how to operate the software, respondents proceed through the survey at their own pace. Questionnaires can be adapted so that respondents see only those items (usually a subset of an entire scale) that may provide useful information about their attitudes.

Online and Social Media Surveys We give online surveys and Internet research its own section because as more and more consumers gain Internet access, Internet surveys are likely to become the predominate tool for general population sampling. In an **online survey**, questionnaires can be transmitted to respondents either through e-mail or through a website. Marketing researchers often send these surveys to online panel samples purchased from professional brokers or put together by the company. Marketing research firms that specialize in Internet research can also be used to conduct digital research for their client organizations. Many offer tools that help to complement or enhance online surveys.

Because e-mail is semi-interactive, recipients can ask for clarification of specific questions or pose questions of their own. The potential advantages of online surveys are quick response

personal interview survey A research method in which participants respond to survey questions face-to-face

in-home (door-to-door) interview A personal interview that takes place in the respondent's home

shopping mall intercept interviews A research method that involves interviewing a percentage of individuals passing by "intercept" points in a mall

on-site computer interview A variation of the shopping mall intercept interview in which respondents complete a self-administered questionnaire displayed on a computer monitor

online survey A research method in which respondents answer a questionnaire via e-mail or on a website

Emerging Trends

Pinterest Provides New Methods for Marketing Research

The pinboard photo-sharing site Pinterest offers a less costly alternative for gathering market research. The social network has appealed to many marketers since its debut, but as its user base grows, businesses are learning how to use Pinterest pages to understand customers. Retailers pin images of their products to their pages and monitor engagement with these images by tracking follower comments, likes, and the number of times their images have been "repined." Pinterest's new feature, called "Rich Pins," encourages consumers themselves to market the product, allowing them to make more specific comments about products such as unique features or pricing. Marketers can also develop different boards of images to target different customer segments.

Nordstrom uses information gleaned from Pinterest to manage its inventory. If a product is getting a lot of attention on Pinterest, Nordstrom makes sure it is in stock. Lowe's also monitors its boards for buyer information. The use of Pinterest in marketing is different from other social networking sites because it is focused primarily around products. One in five Pinterest users buys products after pinning or liking them. Marketers should not overlook this opportunity to use the Pinterest platform as an inexpensive source of collecting primary data on consumer preferences.[a]

and lower cost than traditional mail, telephone, and personal interview surveys if the response rate is adequate. In addition, more firms use their websites to conduct surveys.

Social networking sites can also be used to conduct surveys. Marketers can use digital media forums such as chat rooms, blogs, newsgroups, social networks, and research communities to identify trends in interests and consumption patterns. However, using these forums for conducting surveys has some limitations. Often consumers choose to go to a particular social media site or blog and then take the survey; this eliminates randomness and makes it more difficult to obtain a representative sample size. On the other hand, they can provide a very general idea of consumer trends and preferences. Movies, consumer electronics, food, and computers are popular topics in many online communities. Indeed, by "listening in" on these ongoing conversations, marketers may be able to identify new product opportunities and consumer needs. Moreover, this type of online data can be gathered at little incremental cost compared to alternative data sources.

Crowdsourcing combines the words *crowd* and *outsourcing* and calls for taking tasks usually performed by a marketer or researcher and outsourcing them to a crowd, or potential market, through an open call. In the case of digital marketing, crowdsourcing is often used to obtain the opinions or needs of the crowd (or potential markets). Consider Lego's crowdsourcing platform Cuusoo. Cuusoo is a site that invites consumers to submit ideas for Lego sets. Those ideas that get 10,000 votes are reviewed by the firm for possible development. If the Lego set is chosen for development, the creator gets 1 percent of the product's total net sales.[22] Additionally, on threadless.com participants can submit and score T-shirt designs. Designs with the highest votes are printed and then sold. Crowdsourcing is a way for marketers to gather input straight from willing consumers and to actively listen to people's ideas and evaluations on products. It is also important for organizations to harness all of their internal information, and internal social networks can be helpful for that. California-based Blue Shield uses the internal social networking platform Chatter to connect its employees.[23]

crowdsourcing Combines the words *crowd* and *outsourcing* and calls for taking tasks usually performed by a marketer or researcher and outsourcing them to a crowd, or potential market, through an open call

Marketing research will likely rely heavily on online panels and surveys in the future. Furthermore, as negative attitudes toward telephone surveys render that technique less representative and more expensive, the integration of e-mail and voice mail functions into one computer-based system provides a promising alternative for survey research. As the MindField advertisement demonstrates, Internet consumer panels have the strong potential to uncover

Internet Panels
MindField uses consumer Internet panels to help its clients generate important insights about consumer preferences and behavior.

data regarding consumer behavior. MindField gathers quantitative data from a variety of consumers, and its use of the Internet allows the organization to collect information from consumers without worrying about geographic boundaries.

However, there are some ethical issues to consider when using the Internet for marketing research, such as unsolicited e-mail, which could be viewed as "spam," and privacy, as some potential survey respondents fear their personal information will be given or sold to third parties without their knowledge or permission. Additionally, as with direct mail, Internet surveys have a good chance of being discarded, particularly with users who receive dozens of e-mails every day.

Another challenge for researchers is obtaining a sample that is representative of the desired population. Although Internet surveys allow respondents to retain their anonymity and flexibility, they can also enable survey takers to abuse the system. For instance, some survey takers take multiple surveys or pose as other people to make more money. To get around this problem, companies are developing screening mechanisms and instituting limits on how many surveys one person can take.[24] Survey programs such as Qualtrics can also delete surveys that appear suspicious.

Questionnaire Construction A carefully constructed questionnaire is essential to the success of any survey. Questions must be clear, easy to understand, and directed toward a specific objective; that is, they must be designed to elicit information that meets the study's data requirements. Researchers need to define the objective before trying to develop a questionnaire because the objective determines the substance of the questions and the amount of detail. A common mistake in constructing questionnaires is to ask questions that interest the researchers but do not yield information useful in deciding whether to accept or reject a hypothesis. Finally, the most important rule in composing questions is to maintain impartiality. The questions are usually of three kinds: open-ended, dichotomous, and multiple-choice. Problems may develop in the analysis of dichotomous or multiple-choice questions when responses for one outcome outnumber others. For example, a dichotomous question that asks respondents to choose between "buy" or "not buy" might require additional sampling from the disproportionately smaller group if there were not enough responses to analyze.[25] Researchers must also be very careful about questions that a respondent might consider too personal or that might require an admission of activities that other people are likely to condemn. Questions of this type should be worded to make them less offensive.

Observation Methods In using observation methods, researchers record individuals' overt behavior, taking note of physical conditions and events. Direct contact with them is avoided; instead, their actions are examined and noted systematically. For instance, researchers might use observation methods to answer the question, "How long does the average McDonald's restaurant customer have to wait in line before being served?" Observation may include the use of ethnographic techniques, such as watching customers interact with a product in a real-world environment. To increase its ability to observe consumer behavior, Time Warner opened a media lab in New York equipped with eye-tracking stations, in-home simulation, a usability lab, observation rooms, conversation rooms with biometric monitoring, a mock retail store with a checkout, and a theater. The lab tries to simulate a real-world environment to test how consumers would react naturally to different forms of media. Researchers can watch the proceedings from observation rooms in the lab.[26] Observation may also be combined with interviews. For instance, during a personal interview, the condition of a respondent's home or other possessions may be observed and recorded. The interviewer can also directly observe and confirm such demographic information as race, approximate age, and gender.

Data gathered through observation can sometimes be biased if the subject is aware of the observation process. However, an observer can be placed in a natural market environment, such as a grocery store, without influencing shoppers' actions. If the presence of a human observer is likely to bias the outcome or if human sensory abilities are inadequate, mechanical means may be used to record behavior. Mechanical observation devices include cameras, recorders, counting machines, scanners, and equipment that records physiological changes. A special camera can be used to record the eye movements of people as they look at an advertisement; the camera detects the sequence of reading and the parts of the advertisement that receive the greatest attention. The electronic scanners used in supermarkets are very useful in marketing research: They provide accurate data on sales and customers' purchase patterns, and marketing researchers may buy such data from the supermarkets.

Observation is straightforward and avoids a central problem of survey methods: motivating respondents to state their true feelings or opinions. However, observation tends to be descriptive. When it is the only method of data collection, it may not provide insights into causal relationships. Another drawback is that analyses based on observation are subject to the observer's biases or the limitations of the mechanical device.

5-3d Interpreting Research Findings

After collecting data to test their hypotheses, marketers need to interpret the research findings. Interpretation of the data is easier if marketers carefully plan their data analysis methods early in the research process. They should also allow for continual evaluation of the data during the entire collection period. Marketers can then gain valuable insights into areas that should be probed during the formal analysis. Table 5.4 shows that interpreting analytics and implementing insights—as well as research and data collection—is among the top 10 marketing challenges.

The first step in drawing conclusions from most research is to display the data in table format. If marketers intend to apply the results to individual categories of the things or people being studied, cross-tabulation may be useful, especially in tabulating joint occurrences. Using the two variables of gender and purchase rates of automobile tires, for instance, a

Table 5.4 Biggest Marketing Challenges

Rank	Marketing Challenge
1	Acquiring new business
2	Developing/implementing content marketing strategy
3	Measuring ROI
4	Improving customer experience
5	Executing and understanding social media campaigns
6	Establishing thought leadership
7	Developing/implementing brand strategy
8	Interpreting analytics and implementing insights
9	Retaining current customers
10	Conducting research and maintaining data collection

Source: Based on *Marketing News*, December 2013, p. 42.

Interpreting Research Findings
Maritz Research emphasizes that its Capella™ platform helps companies translate data into valuable results.

cross-tabulation could show how men and women differ in purchasing automobile tires. The advertisement promoting the services of marketing research firm Maritz Research states that the bigger marketing research problem is not collecting data but interpreting it adequately. Its photograph of a man getting sprayed with water is meant to convey the problem—and indeed the uselessness—of too much data without the ability to interpret it. Maritz's solution is its platform Capella™, which helps uncover customer service issues and provides companies with a step-by-step plan of addressing them.

After the data are tabulated, they must be analyzed. **Statistical interpretation** focuses on what is typical and what deviates from the average. It indicates how widely responses vary and how they are distributed in relation to the variable being measured. When marketers interpret statistics, they must take into account estimates of expected error or deviation from the true values of the population. The analysis of data may lead researchers to accept or reject the hypothesis being studied. Data require careful interpretation by the marketer. If the results of a study are valid, the decision maker should take action; if a question has been incorrectly or poorly worded, however, the results may produce poor decisions. Consider the research conducted for a food marketer that asked respondents to rate a product on criteria such as "hearty flavor," as well as how important each criterion was to the respondent. Although such results may have had utility for advertising purposes, they are less helpful in product development because it is not possible to discern each respondent's meaning of the phrase "hearty flavor." Managers must understand the research results and relate them to a context that permits effective decision making.

5-3e Reporting Research Findings

The final step in the marketing research process is to report the research findings. Before preparing the report, the marketer must take a clear, objective look at the findings to see how well the gathered facts answer the research question or support or negate the initial hypotheses. In most cases, it is extremely doubtful that the study can provide everything needed to answer the research question. Thus, the researcher must point out the deficiencies in the research and their causes in the report. Research should be meaningful to all participants, especially top managers who develop strategy. Therefore, researchers must try to make certain that their findings are relevant and not just interesting. Research is not useful unless it supports the organization's overall strategy objectives. The more knowledge researchers have about the opportunities and challenges facing an organization, the more meaningful their research report will be. If an outside research agency conducts research, it is even more important to understand the client's business. After conducting research, a research report is the next step. Those responsible for preparing the report must facilitate adjusting the findings to the environment, as elements change over time. Most importantly, the report should be helpful to marketers and managers on an ongoing basis.[27]

The report of research results is usually a formal, written document. Researchers must allow time for the writing task when they plan and schedule the project. Because the report is a means of communicating with the decision makers who will use the research findings, researchers need to determine beforehand how much detail and supporting data to include.

statistical interpretation
Analysis of what is typical and what deviates from the average

They should keep in mind that corporate executives prefer reports that are short, clear, and simply expressed. Researchers often give their summary and recommendations first, especially if decision makers do not have time to study how the results were obtained. A technical report allows its users to analyze data and interpret recommendations because it describes the research methods and procedures and the most important data gathered. Thus, researchers must recognize the needs and expectations of the report user and adapt to them.

Marketing researchers want to know about behavior and opinions, and they want accurate data to help them in making decisions. Careful wording of questions is very important because a biased or emotional word can dramatically change the results. Marketing research and marketing information systems can provide an organization with accurate and reliable customer feedback, which a marketer must have to understand the dynamics of the marketplace. As managers recognize the benefits of marketing research, they assign it a much larger role in decision making.

5-4 USING TECHNOLOGY TO IMPROVE MARKETING INFORMATION GATHERING AND ANALYSIS

Technology makes information for marketing decisions increasingly accessible. The ability of marketers to track customer buying behavior and to better discern what buyers want is changing the nature of marketing. Big data enhances customer relationship management by integrating data from all customer contacts and combining that information to improve customer retention. Information technology permits internal research and quick information gathering to help marketers better understand and satisfy customers. Company responses to e-mail complaints—as well as to communications through mail, telephone, and personal contact—can be used to improve customer satisfaction, retention, and value. Armed with such information, marketers can fine-tune marketing mixes to satisfy their customers' needs.

Consumer feedback is an important aspect of marketing research, and new technology such as digital media is enhancing this process. Ratings and reviews on Internet forums are becoming increasingly popular, with 62 percent of the U.S. online population reading these types of consumer-generated feedback.[28] Online retailers such as Amazon, Netflix, and Priceline are capitalizing on these ratings and reviews by allowing consumers to post comments on their sites concerning books, movies, hotels, and more. Marketers can use these social media forums to closely monitor what their customers are saying. In the case of negative feedback, marketers can communicate with consumers to address problems or complaints more easily than with traditional marketing channels. In one survey, it was noted that a business has the opportunity to turn 18 percent of negative reviewers into loyal customers by responding to their negative feedback. In addition, more than 60 percent of those who receive a reply will replace their negative comments with positive ones.[29] By researching what consumers are saying about their products, companies can understand what features of their product mixes should be promoted or modified.

Finally, the integration of telecommunications and computer technologies allows marketers to access a growing array of valuable information sources related to industry forecasts, business trends, and customer buying behavior. Electronic communication tools can be effectively used to gain accurate information with minimal customer interaction. Most marketing researchers have electronic networking at their disposal. In fact, many firms use marketing information systems and CRM technologies to network all these technologies and organize all the marketing data available to them. In this section, we look at marketing information systems and specific technologies that are helping marketing researchers obtain and manage marketing research data.

5-4a Marketing Information Systems

A **marketing information system (MIS)** is a framework for the day-to-day management and structuring of information gathered regularly from sources both inside and outside the organization. As such, an MIS provides a continuous flow of information about prices, advertising expenditures, sales, competition, and distribution expenses. Marketing information systems can be an important asset for developing effective marketing strategies. Procter & Gamble managers, for instance, search through P&G's proprietary MIS for data to help the company predict which products will work best in different countries.[30] The main focus of the MIS is on data storage and retrieval, as well as on computer capabilities and management's information requirements. Regular reports of sales by product or market categories, data on inventory levels, and records of salespeople's activities are examples of information that is useful in making decisions. In the MIS, the means of gathering data receive less attention than do the procedures for expediting the flow of information.

An effective MIS starts by determining the objective of the information—that is, by identifying decision needs that require certain information. The firm can then specify an information system for continuous monitoring to provide regular, pertinent information on both the external and internal environment. FedEx, for instance, has interactive marketing systems that provide instantaneous communication between the company and customers. Customers can track their packages and receive immediate feedback concerning delivery via the Internet. The company's website provides information about customer usage and allows customers to convey what they think about company services. The evolving telecommunications and computer technologies allow marketers to use information systems to cultivate one-to-one relationships with customers.

marketing information system (MIS) A framework for managing and structuring information gathered regularly from sources inside and outside the organization

database A collection of information arranged for easy access and retrieval

5-4b Databases

Most marketing information systems include internal databases. A **database** is a collection of information arranged for easy access and retrieval. Databases allow marketers to tap into an abundance of information useful in making marketing decisions: internal sales reports, newspaper articles, company news releases, government economic reports, bibliographies, and more, often accessed through a computer system. Information technology has made it

Using Technology for Market Research
Technology can help marketers administer surveys more quickly and efficiently. For instance, surveys on tablet computers make it easy for consumers to answer the questions.

possible to develop databases to guide strategic planning and help improve customer services. Customer relationship management employs database marketing techniques to identify different types of customers and develop specific strategies for interacting with each customer. CRM incorporates these three elements:

1. Identifying and building a database of current and potential consumers, including a wide range of demographic, lifestyle, and purchase information.
2. Delivering differential messages according to each consumer's preferences and characteristics through established and new media channels.
3. Tracking customer relationships to monitor the costs of retaining individual customers and the lifetime value of their purchases.[31]

Many commercial websites require consumers to register and provide personal information to access the site or to make a purchase. Frequent-flyer programs permit airlines to ask loyal customers to participate in surveys about their needs and desires and to track their best customers' flight patterns by time of day, week, month, and year. Also, supermarkets gain a significant amount of data through checkout scanners tied to store discount cards.

Marketing researchers can also use databases, such as LexisNexis, to obtain useful information for marketing decisions. Many commercial databases are accessible online for a fee. Sometimes, they can be obtained in printed form or digitally. With most commercial databases, the user typically conducts a computer search by keyword, topic, or company, and the database service generates abstracts, articles, or reports that can then be printed out.

Information provided by a single firm on household demographics, purchases, television viewing behavior, and responses to promotions such as coupons and free samples is called **single-source data**. BehaviorScan, offered by Information Resources Inc., screens markets with populations between 75,000 and 215,000.[32] This single-source information service monitors consumer household televisions and records the programs and commercials watched. When buyers from these households shop in stores equipped with scanning registers, they present Hotline cards (similar to credit cards) to cashiers. This enables each customer's identification to be electronically coded so the firm can track each product purchased and store the information in a database. The firm also offers new product testing. It is important to gather longitudinal (long-term) information on customers to maximize the usefulness of single-source data.

5-4c Big Data

Big data has the potential to revolutionize the way businesses gather marketing research and develop tailored marketing campaigns. **Big data** involves massive data files that can be obtained from both structured and unstructured databases. Big data often consists of high-volume data that marketers can use to discover unique insights and make more knowledgeable marketing decisions.[33] Big data can include mountains of data collected from social networks, RFID, retailer scanning, purchases, logistics, and production.[34] The amount of data that can be gleaned from consumer activities and purchase patterns yields significant insights for marketers. The complexity of big data requires sophisticated software to store and analyze it.[35] It also requires marketers to identify and understand how to use this data to develop stronger customer relationships.

The positive impact that big data has had upon marketing is undeniable. For instance, Samsung Mobile marketers used data on customers to prioritize key target markets and improve its marketing efforts. The result in the United States was an increase in brand preference from a relative score of –6 to +2.[36] According to research studies, 81 percent of companies that utilize big data effectively in marketing have seen sales increase as a result, as well as an increase of 73 percent in customer satisfaction.[37] Unlike other forms of marketing research, using big data can reveal specific details about consumers that would be hard to discover in other ways. The marketing vice president at DataSift—an organization that analyzes social data—has determined that his company's software can mine 400 pieces of data from a 140-word tweet.[38] The chief marketing officer of Best Buy used big data to focus on the concerns of its highest-value customers. After recognizing these concerns, Best Buy released direct e-mail and direct mail

single-source data Information provided by a single marketing research firm

big data Massive data files that can be obtained from both structured and unstructured databases

promotions specifically tailored toward these customers. The results seem to indicate that the customers became even more loyal to Best Buy after the marketing campaign.[39]

Big data is important because marketers can look at patterns of consumption behavior and discover trends that predict future buying behaviors. Not all of these patterns would be as visible through traditional marketing research methods. It is obvious, for instance, that a woman buying baby supplies is likely pregnant or has a new baby. However, other consumption patterns are less obvious. Target has found that purchases of larger quantities of unscented lotions, cotton balls, scent-free soap, and supplements are also predictors of pregnancy. Target discovered these trends through analyzing its collection of data on consumer purchases. These discoveries have allowed the firm to accurately predict pregnancy. As a result, it has been able to send out marketing materials, such as coupons for diapers, to this demographic in the hopes that they will become future loyal customers.[40] Big data can therefore improve the relationship between company and consumer.

© Burke Inc.

Big Data Generation
Burke is able to take large quantities of data and deliver insights to clients who need to make more informed decisions.

Despite the benefits of big data to marketing research, the challenge for marketers is to figure out how to use pieces of data to develop more targeted marketing strategies. Marketers must know what data to examine, which analytical tools to use, and how to translate this data into customer insights.[41] Big data is useless if an organization's marketers do not know how to use it. Mining big data for customer insights takes much time and energy. In one research study surveying marketers, a little more than half indicated that their organizations had a good understanding of big data. A major reason is that many marketers do not understand the definition of big data or its benefits.[42] Additionally, as with marketing research, big data can still be subject to bias, projection error, and sampling issues.[43]

Although big data yields tremendous insights into consumer preferences, lifestyles, and behaviors, it also creates serious privacy issues. Many consumers do not like to have their purchases or behaviors tracked, and sometimes using big data for marketing purposes creates conflict. Consider Target's detailed data system regarding the consumption behaviors of pregnant women. Using what it learned from big data about the purchase behavior of pregnant women, Target sent out personalized coupon books for baby products. An irate father demanded to see the Target manager and complained that Target had sent his teenage daughter these coupons. A few days later, when the Target manager called to apologize, the father told the manager that he had discovered that his daughter was indeed pregnant. Based on the girl's consumption habits at its stores, Target was able to predict her pregnancy status.[44]

This brings up a major ethical issue. When does big data cross the line into a violation of user privacy? Target customers expressed discomfort at having such personal details tracked. For this reason, the organization became more subtle in its couponing. For instance, instead of sending out coupons simply for baby items, it mixed coupons for baby products with coupons for other items.[45] However, this does not change the fact that companies still know about consumers' personal details and are making use of them.

Although the benefits of big data for marketing are numerous, they may come at the expense of consumer privacy. While some consumers appreciate the added benefits of receiving marketing materials specifically targeted toward their needs, others feel uncomfortable with companies knowing so much about them. At the same time, companies that ignore big data miss out on the opportunity to develop stronger marketing strategies and customer relationships. As the advertisement demonstrates, market researchers need more than surveys and respondents to generate important information. Big data is necessary to uncover valuable insights about customers, and market research firms such as Burke are offering services to help organizations generate this complex information. Avoiding big data could cause a business to sacrifice a competitive advantage. Although there is no easy solution to this issue, consumers can do one thing if they do not want their store purchases tracked: pay in cash.

5-4d Marketing Decision Support Systems

A **marketing decision support system (MDSS)** is customized computer software that aids marketing managers in decision making by helping them anticipate the effects of certain decisions. Some decision support systems have a broader range and offer greater computational and modeling capabilities than spreadsheets; they let managers explore a greater number of alternatives. For instance, an MDSS can determine how sales and profits might be affected by higher or lower interest rates or how sales forecasts, advertising expenditures, production levels, and the like might affect overall profits. For this reason, MDSS software is often a major component of a company's marketing information system. Some decision support systems incorporate artificial intelligence and other advanced computer technologies.

5-5 ISSUES IN MARKETING RESEARCH

Marketers should identify concerns that influence the integrity of research. Ethical issues are a constant risk in gathering and maintaining the quality of information. International issues relate to environmental differences, such as culture, legal requirements, level of technology, and economic development.

5-5a The Importance of Ethical Marketing Research

Marketing managers and other professionals are relying more and more on marketing research, marketing information systems, and new technologies to make better decisions. Therefore, it is essential that professional standards be established by which to judge the reliability of marketing research. Such standards are necessary because of the ethical and legal issues that develop in gathering marketing research data. In the area of online interaction, for example, consumers remain wary of how the personal information collected by marketers will be used, especially whether it will be sold to third parties. In addition, the relationships between research suppliers, such as marketing research agencies, and the marketing managers who make strategy decisions require ethical behavior. Organizations such as the Marketing Research Association have developed codes of conduct and guidelines to promote ethical marketing research. To be effective, such guidelines must instruct marketing researchers on how to avoid misconduct. Table 5.5 recommends explicit steps interviewers should follow when introducing a questionnaire.

Consumer privacy has also become a significant issue. Firms now have the ability to purchase data on customer demographics, interests, and more personal matters such as bankruptcy filings and past marriages. This information has allowed companies to predict customer behavior or current life changes more accurately but may also infringe upon consumer privacy.[46] Videotaping customers in retail stores or tracking shoppers' mobile phones helps retailers understand store traffic, repeat customers, and eye movement. It also raises serious concerns about whether the stores are violating the rights of "honest shoppers."[47] The popularity of the Internet has enabled marketers to collect data on Internet users who visit their websites. Many companies have been able to use this to their advantage. For instance, Amazon,

marketing decision support system (MDSS) Customized computer software that aids marketing managers in decision making

Table 5.5 Guidelines for Questionnaire Introduction

• Allow interviewers to introduce themselves by name.
• State the name of the research company.
• Indicate that this questionnaire is a marketing research project.
• Explain that no sales will be involved.
• Note the general topic of discussion (if this is a problem in a "blind" study, a statement such as "consumer opinion" is acceptable).
• State the likely duration of the interview.
• Assure the anonymity of the respondent and the confidentiality of all answers.
• State the honorarium, if applicable (for many business-to-business and medical studies, this is done up-front for both qualitative and quantitative studies).
• Reassure the respondent with a statement such as, "There are no right or wrong answers, so please give thoughtful and honest answers to each question" (recommended by many clients).

Source: Reprinted with the permission of The Marketing Research Association.

Netflix, and eBay use data to make customized recommendations based on their customers' interests, ratings, or past purchases. Although such data enable companies to offer more personalized services, policy makers fear that it could also allow them to discriminate among consumers who do not appear to make "valuable" customers.[48]

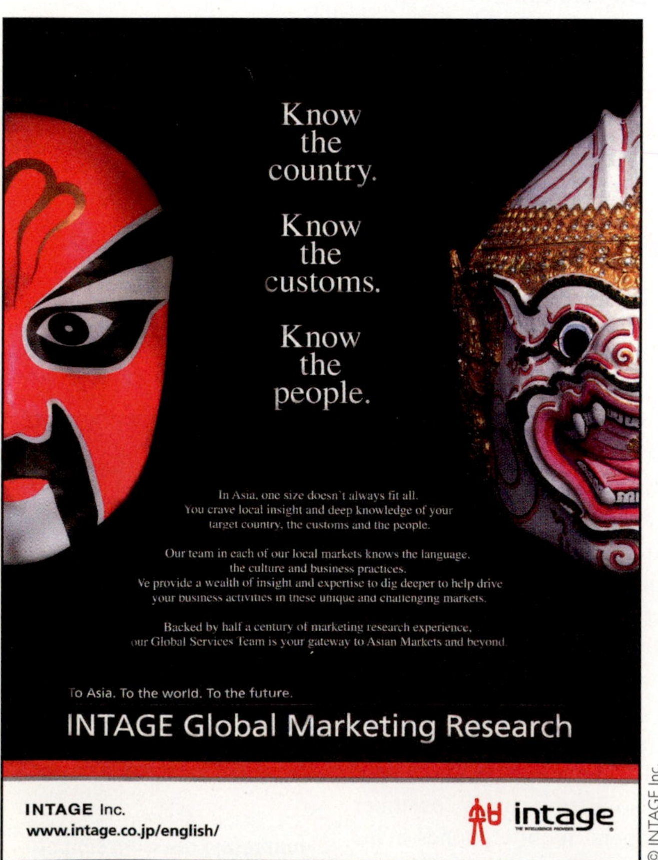

International Marketing Research
Intage provides local insight and deep knowledge of a specific target country, including knowledge of its people and customers.

5-5b International Issues in Marketing Research

As we shall see in Chapter 9, sociocultural, economic, political, legal, and technological forces vary in different regions of the world. These variations create challenges for the organizations that are attempting to understand foreign customers through marketing research. The marketing research process we describe in this chapter is used globally, but to ensure the research is valid and reliable, data-gathering methods may have to be modified to allow for regional differences. To make certain that global and regional differences are satisfactorily addressed, many companies retain a research firm with experience in the country of interest. The advertisement from Intage uses cultural masks to emphasize the differences between countries in Asia. Intage claims that it possesses the necessary knowledge to understand the different cultures and help develop appropriate research studies for clients interested in Asian markets.

Most of the largest marketing research firms derive a significant share of their revenues from research conducted outside the United States. As Table 5.6 indicates, the Nielsen Company, the largest marketing research firm in the world, receives more than half of its revenues from outside the United States.[49]

Table 5.6 **Top U.S. Marketing Research Firms**

Rank	Company	Global Revenues (in Millions of U.S. Dollars)	Percent of Revenues from Outside the United States
1	The Nielsen Co.	$5,429.00	51.2%
2	The Kantar Group	3,338.6	72.2
3	Ipsos	2,301.1	93.2
4	GfK SE	1,947.8	70
5	IMS Health Inc.	775	65

Source: Jack Honomichl, "The 2013 Honomichl Global Top 25 Report," *Marketing News*, August 2013, pp. 29–58.

Experts recommend a two-pronged approach to international marketing research. The first phase involves a detailed search for and analysis of secondary data to gain a greater understanding of a particular marketing environment and to pinpoint issues that must be taken into account in gathering primary research data. Secondary data can be particularly helpful in building a general understanding of the market, including economic, legal, cultural, and demographic issues, as well as in assessing the risks of doing business in that market and in forecasting demand. Marketing researchers often begin by studying country trade reports from the U.S. Department of Commerce, as well as country-specific information from local sources, such as a country's website, and trade and general business publications such as *The Wall Street Journal*. These sources can offer insights into the marketing environment in a particular country and can even indicate untapped market opportunities abroad.

The second phase involves field research using many of the methods described earlier, including focus groups and telephone surveys, to refine a firm's understanding of specific customer needs and preferences. Specific differences among countries can have a profound influence on data gathering. In-home (door-to-door) interviews are illegal in some countries. In developing countries, few people have land-line telephones, as many opt for cell phones, making telephone surveys less practical and less representative of the total population. Primary data gathering may have a greater chance of success if the firm employs local researchers who better understand how to approach potential respondents and can do so in their own languages.[50] Regardless of the specific methods used to gather primary data, whether in the

Marketing Debate

Privacy Issues in Tracking Product Returns

ISSUE: Is it acceptable to collect data on customer product returns?

Retailers have begun compiling return profiles on customers to reduce product return fraud, estimated to cost retailers approximately $8.9 billion annually. Return fraud occurs when customers buy items with the purpose of returning them. It can also involve returning stolen items and switching a lower price tag for a higher one. When a customer brings in an item for a return, the retailer generally asks for the person's identification card. Most think their identity is being confirmed, but some stores use their marketing information system to create a database on the consumer. Although only 1 percent of return profiles are suspicious, honest consumers are also getting their return merchandise history tracked. This could be viewed as a privacy issue. Consumer privacy related to transactions is a major marketing ethics issue, especially when this data could be provided to outside organizations.[b]

United States or abroad, the goal is to recognize the needs of specific target markets to craft the best marketing strategy to satisfy the needs of customers in each market, as we will see in the next chapter.

Summary

5-1 Define marketing research and its importance to decision makers.

Marketing research is the systematic design, collection, interpretation, and reporting of information to help marketers solve specific marketing problems or take advantage of marketing opportunities. It is a process for gathering information not currently available to decision makers. Marketing research can help a firm better understand market opportunities, ascertain the potential for success for new products, and determine the feasibility of a particular marketing strategy. The value of marketing research is measured by improvements in a marketer's ability to make decisions.

5-2 Distinguish between exploratory and conclusive research.

There are two types of marketing research: exploratory research and conclusive research. When marketers need more information about a problem or want to make a tentative hypothesis more specific, they may conduct exploratory research. The main purpose of exploratory research is to better understand a problem or situation and/or to help identify additional data needs or decision alternatives. More organizations are starting customer advisory boards, small groups of actual customers who serve as sounding boards for new product ideas and offer insights into their feelings and attitudes toward a firm's products, promotion, pricing, and other elements of marketing strategy. Another common method for conducting exploratory research is through a focus group. A focus group brings together multiple people to discuss a certain topic in a group setting led by a moderator.

Conclusive research is designed to verify insights through an objective procedure to help marketers make decisions. It is used when the marketer has one or more alternatives in mind and needs assistance in the final stages of decision making. Conclusive research can be descriptive or experimental. If marketers need to understand the characteristics of certain phenomena to solve a particular problem, descriptive research can aid them. Experimental research allows marketers to make causal deductions about relationships. Such experimentation requires that an independent variable (one not influenced by or dependent on other variables) be manipulated and the resulting changes in a dependent variable (one contingent on, or restricted to, one value or set of values assumed by the independent variable) be measured.

5-3 Name the five basic steps in conducting marketing research, including the two types of data and four survey methods.

To maintain the control needed to obtain accurate information, marketers approach marketing research as a process with logical steps: (1) locating and defining problems or issues, (2) designing the research project, (3) collecting data, (4) interpreting research findings, and (5) reporting research findings.

The first step in launching a research study, the problem or issue definition, focuses on uncovering the nature and boundaries of a situation or question related to marketing strategy or implementation. When a firm discovers a market opportunity, it may need to conduct research to understand the situation more precisely so it can craft an appropriate marketing strategy. In the second step, marketing researchers design a research project to obtain the information needed to address it. This step requires formulating a hypothesis and determining what type of research to employ to test the hypothesis so the results are reliable and valid. A hypothesis is an informed guess or assumption about a problem or set of circumstances. Marketers conduct exploratory research when they need more information about a problem or want to make a tentative hypothesis more specific; they use conclusive research to verify insights through an objective procedure. Research is considered reliable if it produces almost identical results in repeated trials; it is valid if it measures what it is supposed to measure.

For the third step of the research process, collecting data, two types of data are available. Primary data are observed and recorded or collected directly from respondents; secondary data are compiled inside or outside the organization for some purpose other than the current investigation. Sources of secondary data include an organization's own database and other internal sources, periodicals, government publications, unpublished sources, and online databases. Methods of collecting primary data include sampling, surveys, observation, and experimentation. Sampling involves selecting representative units from a total population. In probability sampling, every element in the population being studied has a known chance of being selected for study. Nonprobability sampling is more subjective than probability sampling because there is no way to calculate the likelihood that a specific element of the population being studied will be chosen. Marketing researchers employ sampling to collect primary data through mail, telephone, online, or personal interview surveys. A carefully constructed questionnaire is essential to the success of any survey. In using observation methods, researchers record respondents' overt behavior and take note of physical conditions and events. In an experiment, marketing researchers attempt to maintain certain variables while measuring the effects of experimental variables.

To apply research data to decision making, marketers must interpret and report their findings properly—the final two steps in the marketing research process. Statistical interpretation focuses on what is typical or what deviates from the average. After interpreting the research findings, the researchers must prepare a report on the findings that the decision makers can understand and use. Researchers must also take care to avoid bias and distortion.

5-4 Describe the tools, such as databases, big data, decision support systems, and the Internet, useful to marketing decision making.

Many firms use computer technology to create a marketing information system (MIS), a framework for managing and structuring information gathered regularly from sources both inside and outside the organization. A database is a collection of information arranged for easy access and retrieval. Big data involves massive data files that can be obtained from both structured and unstructured databases. A marketing decision support system (MDSS) is customized computer software that aids marketing managers in decision making by helping them anticipate the effects of certain decisions. Online information services and the Internet also enable marketers to communicate with customers and obtain information.

5-5 Identify ethical and international issues in marketing research.

Eliminating unethical marketing research practices and establishing generally acceptable procedures for conducting research are important goals of marketing research. Both domestic and international marketing use the same marketing research process, but international marketing may require modifying data-gathering methods to address regional differences.

Go to www.cengagebrain.com for resources to help you master the content in this chapter as well as materials that will expand your marketing knowledge!

Developing Your Marketing Plan

Decisions about which market opportunities to pursue, what customer needs to satisfy, and how to reach potential customers are not made in a vacuum. The information provided by marketing research activities is essential in developing both the strategic plan and the specific marketing mix. Focus on the following issues as you relate the concepts in this chapter to the development of your marketing plan.

1. Define the nature and scope of the questions you must answer with regard to your market. Identify the types of information you will need about the market to answer those questions. For example, do you need to know about the buying habits, household income levels, or attitudes of potential customers?
2. Determine whether or not this information can be obtained from secondary sources. Visit the websites provided in Table 5.2 as possible resources for the secondary data.
3. Using Table 5.3, choose the appropriate survey method(s) you would use to collect primary data for one of your information needs. What sampling method would you use?

The information obtained from these questions should assist you in developing various aspects of your marketing plan found in the "Interactive Marketing Plan" exercise at www.cengagebrain.com.

Important Terms

marketing research 128
exploratory research 130
customer advisory boards 131
focus group 131
conclusive research 132
descriptive research 132
experimental research 132
research design 133
hypothesis 134
reliability 134
validity 134
primary data 134
secondary data 134
population 136
sample 136
sampling 136
probability sampling 136
random sampling 136
stratified sampling 137

nonprobability sampling 137
quota sampling 137
mail survey 139
telephone survey 139
telephone depth interview 139
personal interview survey 140
in-home (door-to-door) interview 140
shopping mall intercept interviews 140
on-site computer interview 140
online survey 140
crowdsourcing 141
statistical interpretation 144
marketing information system (MIS) 146
database 146
single-source data 147
big data 147
marketing decision support system (MDSS) 149

Discussion and Review Questions

1. What is marketing research? Why is it important?
2. Describe the five steps in the marketing research process.
3. What is the difference between defining a research problem and developing a hypothesis?
4. Describe the different types of approaches to marketing research, and indicate when each should be used.
5. Where are data for marketing research obtained? Give examples of internal and external data.
6. What is the difference between probability sampling and nonprobability sampling? In what situation would random sampling be best? Stratified sampling? Quota sampling?
7. Suggest some ways to encourage respondents to cooperate in mail surveys.
8. If a survey of all homes with listed telephone numbers is to be conducted, what sampling design should be used?
9. Describe some marketing problems that could be solved through information gained from observation.
10. What is a marketing information system, and what should it provide?
11. Define a database. What is its purpose, and what does it include?
12. What is big data? Why is it important to marketing research?
13. How can marketers use online services and the Internet to obtain information for decision making?
14. What role do ethics play in marketing research? Why is it important that marketing researchers be ethical?
15. How does marketing research in other countries differ from marketing research in the United States?

Video Case 5.1

Marketing Research Reveals Marketing Opportunities in the Baby Boomer Generation

For many years, marketers have focused upon consumers between the ages of 18 and 34 to promote products. Marketers feel that wooing consumers early in life will ensure that they become lifetime loyal customers. While this seems logical, research is revealing that Baby Boomers might be a more profitable demographic. Statistics show that although spending for Millennials is actually shrinking, Baby Boomer spending has been increasing. Baby Boomers are estimated to have $3.4 trillion in annual buying power.

The Baby Boomer generation is vastly different from the generations preceding it. Baby Boomers desire to have a variety of products available to them. Many of the products traditionally thought to belong to the younger generation, such as cars and technical products, are actually bought the most by older generations. With approximately 20 percent of the U.S. population estimated to be 65 years or older by 2030, marketers are beginning to research better ways for marketing to Baby Boomers.

In one study researchers attempted to understand how older consumers shop and interact in stores. Because store marketers often target younger generations of consumers, little thought has been given to how accessible these stores are for older generations. The research design involved equipping a person with gloves, neck braces, helmets, blurry goggles, and other equipment to simulate how a person in his or her 70s with arthritis is feeling. Researchers would then observe how the person takes items off of shelves, gets into his or her car, and gets up from chairs.

This research has been shared with many businesses that have interpreted the findings to create a retail environment better suited to this demographic. CVS, for instance, has lowered its shelves, made its store lighting softer, and installed magnifying glasses for hard-to-read labels. Other businesses are using this information to redesign their products. Diamond Foods Inc., for example, has designed the packaging of its Emerald snack nuts to be easier to open, a great help for older consumers whose hands become less mobile as they age. The company also studied consumers with arthritis and decreased the time it takes to rotate the caps to open its products.

Additionally, Baby Boomers have created an opportunity for businesses to market entirely new products. Baby Boomers tend to embrace fitness and exercise regimens as a way to stay fit and prolong their lives. Technology firms are seeing an opportunity to develop products to be installed in the homes of older consumers. These products monitor the movements of the inhabitants and alert family or experts if there are any changes in the inhabitants' movements. A decrease in mobility could signal a change in the person's physical and mental state, which may require medical attention. Although these devices might otherwise seem intrusive, Baby Boomers' desires to stay healthy and prolong life are increasing their demand. Many Baby Boomers are also concerned with preserving their more youthful appearance. Lingerie maker Maidenform has created shapewear, or clothes that help to "tone" the body, targeted toward those ages 35 to 54.

There is one description that marketers must avoid when marketing to Baby Boomers: any words or phrases that make them feel old. Marketing research has revealed that Baby Boomers do not like to be reminded that they are aging. Therefore, many marketing initiatives aimed at older consumers must be subtle. For this reason, Diamond Foods does not market the fact that its packages are easier to open because it does not want to make Baby Boomers feel aged. Even marketers of products that are for older people have overhauled their promotional campaigns to focus less on the concept of aging. Kimberly-Clark's Depend brand for incontinence was widely regarded as "adult diapers." This negative connotation led many to avoid them. To try to counteract this view, Kimberly-Clark released commercials that discussed the benefits of the product but also tried to "de-myth" the brand by discussing its similarity in look and feel to underwear. Many other businesses that sell similar products are following suit.

Although marketers have long focused on Millennials, the demand for products by Baby Boomers is changing the ways that businesses market to consumers. Marketing research is key to understanding the Baby Boomer demographic and creating the goods and services that best meet their needs.[51]

Questions for Discussion

1. Why are Baby Boomers such a lucrative market?
2. How has the marketing research process been used to understand how Baby Boomers shop and interact in stores?
3. How have stores used marketing research findings to tailor their stores and products to appeal to Baby Boomers?

Case 5.2

At Threadless, Customers Design the Product

Loyal customers are also loyal designers at Threadless, a fast-growing T-shirt company based in Chicago. The idea for Threadless grew out of Jake Nickell's hobby of creating digital designs for T-shirts. In 2000, after one of his designs won a contest, 20-year-old Nickell teamed up with his friend Jacob DeHart to start a new business. Their unique marketing twist was that the T-shirts they sold would feature digital designs submitted and selected by customers through online voting. Threadless became a crowdsourcing company, in which tasks usually performed by a marketer or researcher—in this case, product design—are outsourced to the market.

The first contest, which offered a grand prize of two free T-shirts, drew dozens of entries. The designs were placed on the Threadless website, and participants voted on the ones they preferred. Threadless printed and sold 24 copies each of the five top vote-getters. Soon the company began paying $100 for each winning design, an amount it gradually raised above $2,000. By 2002, Threadless had 10,000 customers voting on designs and was selling $100,000 worth of T-shirts.

A decade after its founding, the company's annual sales have skyrocketed beyond $30 million, and customers submit 300 designs per day. Threadless has 2.4 million members registered with its site, creating a large sample size from which to solicit feedback and votes. By marketing only designs that customers approve with their votes, Threadless keeps costs down and profit margins high. Sooner or later, all of its T-shirts sell out, and customers can click to vote for reprinting sold-out designs. Winners receive $2,000 along with a $500 Threadless gift card and $500 for every time the design is printed.

Threadless not only allows aspiring artists and designers to submit and potentially sell their work, but it also acts as a forum for market research. Blogging and critiquing on the Threadless website give designers the ability to interact with one another and receive recommendations on their ideas. This interaction often follows the five-step process of marketing research. For instance, a designer defines a problem she has with her design. She then thinks about what she wants to ask and posts the problem, as well as a picture of the design, on the Threadless blog. Other members post their recommendations, enabling the designer to collect relevant data for solving the problem. She can then interpret the findings to find the best solution and redesign the T-shirt before submitting it. Such interactions are common among the Threadless online community.

After the designers submit their ideas, Threadless creates the equivalent of an online focus group consisting of members from across the world. The T-shirt submissions are posted for members to vote upon, and voters can choose from a score of 0 to 5 on whether this shirt should be printed. They also have the chance to submit their own comments. For those who fall in love with the shirt, Threadless provides a button that the voter can click on to receive an alert. If the shirt gets chosen, the voter will receive a notification that the shirt is available for purchase. Threadless T-shirts and other company apparel can be purchased through the website. By using online customer reviews to create the final product, Threadless is able to eliminate the costs of test marketing.

© iStockphoto.com/AnikaSalsera

Threadless has been so successful that it has opened its own retail store in Chicago to feature and sell its newest collections. Other companies are also getting involved. In 2012 Threadless partnered with Gap to sell T-shirt collections through Gap's website and retail outlets. The company also partnered with the Whole Planet Foundation to create the Whole Planet Foundation T-shirt Design Challenge. Designers submitted their designs for a chance to win a trip abroad, and part of the proceeds for their designs went toward funding entrepreneurs in developing countries.

As co-founder of Threadless, Nickell cannot imagine doing business any other way. "Why wouldn't you want to make the products that people want you to make?" he asks. By paying close attention to its customers' preferences, Threadless now sells 100,000 T-shirts every month. Customers are loyal because they know that their design ideas and votes really count.[52]

Questions for Discussion

1. How has Threadless used crowdsourcing as the foundation of its marketing research?
2. How does Threadless create the equivalent of an online focus group to provide feedback on designs?
3. How has Threadless eliminated the cost of test marketing?

NOTES

[1] Katherine Rosman. "Weather Channel Now Forecasts What You Will Buy," *The Wall Street Journal*, August 14, 2013, http://online.wsj .com/article/SB10001424127887323639704579012674092402660.html (accessed September 3, 2013); Knowledge@Wharton, "Today's Forecast for the Weather Business: Increased Revenues and a Focus on Innovation," Wharton, April 10, 2013, http://knowledge .wharton.upenn.edu/article.cfm?articleid=3229 (accessed September 3, 2013); The Weather Company, "The Weather Company Brands," TWC Media Kit, http://twcmediakit.com/ brands (accessed September 3, 2013).

[2] Bruce Horovitz, "Pretzelmania Spreads from Fast Food to Every Food," *USA Today*, September 26, 2013, p. 2B.

[3] Ali Aceto, "Dunkin' Donuts and CareerBuilder® Survey Reveals Role of Coffee During the WorkDDay," September 27, 2013, www.dunkindonuts.com/DDBlog/2013/09/ dunkin_donuts_andc.html#sthash.ZCpzC6w3 .dpbs (accessed November 22, 2013).

[4] Allison Enright, "Surviving 2010," *Marketing News*, February 28, 2010, pp. 30–33.

[5] Atossa Araxia Abrahamian and Lisa Baertlein, "Manhattan to Get First Teavana Tea Bar since Starbucks Deal," Reuters, October 23, 2013, www.reuters.com/article/2013/10/23/us -starbucks-teavana-idUSBRE99M16B20131023 (accessed November 25, 2013).

[6] Dhruv Grewal Parasuraman and R. Krishnan, *Marketing Research* (Boston: Houghton Mifflin, 2007).

[7] Ken Manning, O. C. Ferrell, and Linda Ferrell, "Consumer Expectations of Clearance vs. Sale Prices," University of New Mexico, working paper, 2013.

[8] John Webb, "Oracle Hosts PeopleSoft Customer Advisory Boards," Oracle, August 21, 2013, https://blogs.oracle.com/peoplesoft/entry/ peoplesoft_customer_advisory_board (accessed November 22, 2013).

[9] Peter Kafka, "Shhh! Amazon Starts a Semi-Secret Digital Focus Group for Its Homegrown TV Shows and Movies," *Fox News*, November 6, 2013, www.foxnews.com/tech/2013/11/06/ shhh-amazon-starts-semi-secret-digital-focus -group-for-its-homegrown-tv-shows (accessed November 25, 2013).

[10] Daniel Gross, "Lies, Damn Lies, and Focus Groups," *Slate*, October 10, 2003, www.slate .com/articles/business/moneybox/2003/10/lies _damn_lies_and_focus_groups.html (accessed July 9, 2012).

[11] Bruce Horovitz, "McDonald's Tests $1 Menu with Higher Price Points," *USA Today*, September 4, 2013, www.usatoday.com/story/ money/business/2013/09/04/mcdonalds-dollar -menu-extra-value-menu/2763981 (accessed December 6, 2013).

[12] Stephen Miller, "Researcher's Data Rewrote Hollywood Endings," *The Wall Street Journal*, December 9, 2011, http://online.wsj.com/article/ SB10001424052970204319004577086782750362996.html?KEYWORDS=market+research +hollywood (accessed February 7, 2012); Edward Jay Epstein, "Hidden Persuaders," *Slate*, July 18, 2005, www.slate.com/articles/arts/the _hollywood_economist/2005/07/hidden _persuaders.html (accessed February 7, 2012).

[13] Diksha Sahni, "Does Bollywood Need Market Research?" *The Wall Street Journal*, March 24, 2011, http://blogs.wsj.com/ indiarealtime/2011/03/24/does-bollywood-need -market-research (accessed February 7, 2012).

[14] Vikas Mittal and Wagner A. Kamakura, "Satisfaction, Repurchase Intent, and Repurchase Behavior: Investigating the Moderating Effects of Customer Characteristics," *Journal of Marketing Research* (February 2001): 131–142.

[15] U.S. Census Bureau, *American Community Survey*, www.census.gov/acs/www (accessed January 20, 2011).

[16] Aaron Gilchrist, "Census Forms Confusion: 'American Community Survey' Is Legit," *nbc12.com*, January 27, 2010, www.nbc12 .com/Global/story.asp?S=11890921 (accessed January 21, 2011).

[17] Symphony IRI Group, "About Us," http:// symphonyiri.com/About/History/tabid/60/ Default.aspy (accessed January 21, 2011).

[18] David Lieberman, "TiVo to Sell Data on What People Watch, Fast-Forward," *USA Today*, April 20, 2010, www.usatoday.com/ tech/news/2009-04-20-tivo-data-new-plan_N .htm (accessed March 19, 2010).

[19] Kelly Tay, "Marketing in a Digital Age," *Business Intelligence*, September 25, 2013, www.businesstimes.com.sg/specials/forward -thinkers/marketing-digital-age-20130925 (accessed November 26, 2013); Brian Terran, "Insights Key to Sustainability Cause, Says P&G Chief Executive," *Research*, September 27, 2012, www.research-live.com/news/news -headlines/insights-key-to-sustainability -cause-says-pg-chief-executive/4008338.article (accessed November 25, 2013).

[20] Procter & Gamble 2009 Annual Report, February 24, 2010, p. 3, http://annualreport .pg.com/annualreport2009/index.shtml (accessed March 20, 2010).

[21] Warren Davies, "How to Increase Survey Response Rates Using Post-it Notes," *GenerallyThinking.com*, August 3, 2009, http:// generallythinking.com/blog/how-to-increase -survey-response-rates-using-post-it-notes (accessed March 9, 2010); Randy Garner, "Post-it Note Persuasion: A Sticky Influence," *Journal of Consumer Psychology* 15 (2005): 230–237.

[22] David Robertson, "Building Success: How Thinking 'Inside the Brick' Saved Lego," *Wired*, October 9, 2013, www.wired.co.uk/ magazine/archive/2013/10/features/building -success (accessed November 25, 2013).

[23] David Rosenbaum, "Who's Out There?" *CFO*, January/February 2012, pp. 44–49.

[24] Sue Shellenbarger, "A Few Bucks for Your Thoughts?" *The Wall Street Journal*, May 18, 2011, http://online.wsj.com/news/articles/SB10001424052748703509104576329110724411724 (accessed March 28, 2014).

[25] Bas Donkers, Philip Hans Franses, and Peter C. Verhoef, "Selective Sampling for Binary Choice Models," *Journal of Marketing Research* (November 2003): 492–497.

[26] Time Warner Media Lab website, www .timewarnermedialab.com (accessed November 26, 2013).

[27] Piet Levy, "10 Minutes with … Gregory A. Reid," *Marketing News*, February 28, 2010, p. 34.

[28] Dr. Paul Marsden, "The Power of Consumer Reviews: It's a Cultural Thing—US vs. UK," *Digital Intelligence Today*, June 13, 2011, http://digitalinnovationtoday.com/the-power-of-consumer-reviews-its-a-cultural-thing-us-vs-uk-data (accessed November 25, 2013).

[29] *Reputation.com*, "How to Make a Negative Review Work in Your Favor," www.reputation.com/reputationwatch/articles/how-make-negative-review-work-your-favor (accessed November 25, 2013).

[30] Lauren Coleman-Lochner, "Why Procter & Gamble Needs to Shave More Indians," *Bloomberg Buinessweek*, June 9, 2011, www.businessweek.com/magazine/content/11_25/b4233021703857.htm (accessed February 7, 2012).

[31] David Aaker, V. Kumar, George Day, and Robert Lane, *Marketing Research*, 10th ed. (New York: Wiley & Sons, 2010).

[32] *BehaviorScan® Testing*, 2011, www.symphonyiri.com/LinkClick.aspx?fileticket=da0Vpb7a728%3D&tabid=348 (accessed December 17, 2013).

[33] Douglas Laney, "The Importance of 'Big Data': A Definition," Gartner, June 2012.

[34] Peter Daboll, "5 Reasons Why Big Data Will Crush Big Research," *Forbes*, December 3, 2013, www.forbes.com/sites/onmarketing/2013/12/03/5-reasons-why-big-data-will-crush-big-research (accessed December 5, 2013).

[35] Danny Bradbury and Tim Anderson, "Big Data and Marketing: An Inevitable Partnership," *The Guardian*, October 16, 2013, www.theguardian.com/technology/2013/oct/16/big-data-and-marketing-an-inevitable-partnership (accessed December 5, 2013).

[36] Amrit Kirpalani, "What Marketing Executives REALLY Think of Big Data," *Direct Marketing News*, November 22, 2013, www.dmnews.com/what-marketing-executives-really-think-of-big-data/article/322236 (accessed December 5, 2013).

[37] Tyler Loechner, "Big Data Generating Big Results for Marketers, But Not All Have Adopted It," *RTM Daily*, October 24, 2013, www.mediapost.com/publications/article/212007/big-data-generating-big-results-for-marketers-but.html (accessed December 5, 2013).

[38] Bradbury and Anderson, "Big Data and Marketing: An Inevitable Partnership."

[39] Amrit Kirpalani, "What Marketing Executives REALLY Think of Big Data."

[40] Kashmir Hill, "How Target Figured Out a Teen Girl Was Pregnant Before Dad Did," *Forbes*, February 16, 2012, www.forbes.com/sites/kashmirhill/2012/02/16/how-target-figured-out-a-teen-girl-was-pregnant-before-her-father-did (accessed December 5, 2013).

[41] SAS, "Big Data, Bigger Marketing," www.sas.com/software/customer-intelligence/big-data-marketing.html (accessed December 5, 2013).

[42] James Rubin, "Survey Demonstrates the Benefits of Big Data," *Forbes*, November 15, 2013, www.forbes.com/sites/forbesinsights/2013/11/15/survey-demonstrates-the-benefits-of-big-data (accessed December 5, 2013).

[43] Peter Daboll, "5 Reasons Why Big Data Will Crush Big Research."

[44] Kashmir Hill, "How Target Figured Out a Girl Was Pregnant Before Dad Did."

[45] Ibid.

[46] Chares Duhigg, "How Companies Learn Your Secrets," *The New York Times*, February 15, 2012, www.nytimes.com/2012/02/19/magazine/shopping-habits.html?_r=1&pagewanted=all (accessed February 28, 2012).

[47] "We Snoop to Conquer," *The Economist*, February 9, 2013, p. 64.

[48] Emily Steel and Julia Angwin, "The Web's Cutting Edge, Anonymity in Name Only," *The Wall Street Journal*, August 4, 2010, http://online.wsj.com/article/SB10001424052748703294904575385532109190198.html (accessed February 7, 2012).

[49] Jack Honomichl, "The 2013 Honomichl Global Top 25 Report," *Marketing News*, August 2013, pp. 29–58.

[50] Reprinted with permission of The Marketing Research Association, P.O. Box 230, Rocky Hill, CT 06067-0230, 860-257-4008.

[51] Ellen Byron, "From Diapers to 'Depends': Marketers Discreetly Retool for Aging Boomers," *The Wall Street Journal*, February 5, 2011, http://online.wsj.com/article/SB10001424052748704013604576104394209062996.html (accessed March 30, 2012); Bruce Horovitz, "Big-Spending Baby Boomers Bend the Rules of Marketing," *USA Today*, November 16, 2010, www.usatoday.com/money/advertising/2010-11-16-1Aboomerbuyers16_CV_N.htm (accessed March 30, 2012).

[52] Threadless website, www.threadless.com (accessed December 5, 2013); KatieSchuppler, "GAP + Threadless," Chicago NOW, March 5, 2012, www.chicagonow.com/fashion-speak/2012/03/gap-threadless (accessed December 5, 2013); Tina Baine, "'Threadless' Hints at Art's Crowdsourced Future," *Santa Cruz (CA) Sentinel*, December 11, 2010, www.santacruzsentinel.com/localnews/ci_16832324 (accessed December 5, 2013); Micha Maidenberg, "Threadless Eyes West Loop," *Chicago Journal*, May 5, 2010, www.chicagojournal.com/news/05-05-2010/Threadless_eyes_West_Loop (accessed December 5, 2013); Julie Shaffer, "Social Climbing," *American Printer*, January 1, 2010, http://americanprinter.com (accessed March 6, 2012); Laurie Burkitt, "Need to Build a Community? Learn from Threadless," *Forbes*, January 7, 2010, www.forbes.com/2010/01/06/threadless-t-shirt-community-crowdsourcing-cmo-network-threadless.html (accessed December 5, 2013); Alicia Wallace, "5 Questions for Jake Nickell, Founder and Chief Strategy Officer of Threadless," *Daily Camera* (Boulder, CO), May 18, 2009, www.dailycamera.com; Max Chafkin, "The Customer Is the Company," *Inc.*, June 1, 2008, www.inc.com/magazine/20080601/the-customer-is-the-company.html (accessed December 5, 2013); International Licensing Industry Merchandisers' Association, "Threadless and Cartoon Network Enterprises Team Up for Regular Show T-shirt Design Challenge!" April 3, 2013, www.licensing.org/news/press-releases/threadless-and-cartoon-network-enterprises-team-up-for-regular-show-t-shirt-design-challenge (accessed December 6, 2013).

Feature Notes

[a] Scott Martin, "Pinterest Ripe for Pinning Down Revenue," *USA Today*, August 22, 2013, p. 4B; Alexandra Samuel, "Data-Driven Pinterest Tactics That Drive Sales," *Harvard Business Review*, July 18, 2013, http://blogs.hbr.org/2013/07/data-driven-pinterest-tactics-sales (accessed October 1, 2013); Andreea Ayers, "How to Use Pinterest for Marketing Research," *Alert* 53, no. 1 (January 2013): 36–37.

[b] Jennifer C. Kerr, "Retailers Tracking What Customers Return," *USA Today*, August 12, 2013, www.usatoday.com/story/money/business/2013/08/12/retailers-tracking-customers-returns/2642607 (accessed September 9, 2013); Josie Rubio, "Point of No Returns? Stores Are Tracking Your Return Merchandise History," *Christian Monitor*, August 17, 2013, www.csmonitor.com/Business/Saving-Money/2013/0817/Point-of-no-returns-Stores-are-tracking-your-return-merchandise-history (accessed September 9, 2013); Michelle Singletary, "Return Fraud Earns Retailers' Wrath," *The Washington Post*, December 10, 2006, www.washingtonpost.com/wp-dyn/content/article/2006/12/09/AR2006120900018.html (accessed September 9, 2013).

chapter 6

Target Markets: Segmentation and Evaluation

OBJECTIVES

6-1 Explain what markets are and how they are generally classified.

6-2 Identify the five steps of the target market selection process.

6-3 Describe the differences among three targeting strategies.

6-4 Identify the major segmentation variables.

6-5 Explain what market segment profiles are and how they are used.

6-6 Explain how to evaluate market segments.

6-7 Identify the factors that influence the selection of specific market segments for use as target markets.

6-8 Discuss sales forecasting methods.

MARKETING INSIGHTS

¡Celebrating Quinceañeras!

Quinceañera celebrations are *de moda*—meaning the tradition of celebrating a young lady's coming-of-age on her 15th birthday—is increasingly trendy in U.S. cities with a large Hispanic-American population. So trendy, in fact, that major companies like Disney and Royal Caribbean have joined local businesses like beauty salons and banquet halls in setting their marketing sights on teenage girls and their families who plan quinceañera parties. Reality television shows, media coverage, and social media buzz have only heightened interest and involvement in this once-in-a-lifetime event.

Disney has targeted the quinceañera market for more than a decade, offering parties at Disneyland California tailored to each girl's personality as well as to her family's budget. The company recently introduced "princess" ball gowns designed with quinceañeras in mind—but also suitable for sweet sixteens—in a range of styles for different tastes and a range of prices for different wallets. As another example, Royal Caribbean offers quinceañeras at sea, complete with private dining areas, special menus, and videographers to capture the memories.

In cities like San Antonio and San Jose, quinceañera expositions bring together dozens of marketers of dresses and tuxedos, floral arrangements, and other goods and services under one roof, often with celebrity hosts. The idea is to attract young ladies to the fashion shows and food fairs while their parents check prices and talk timing. Whether the quinceañera celebration will be large or small, casual or formal, marketers are ready to make it a day to remember from start to finish.[1]

Like most organizations that are trying to compete effectively, Disney and Royal Caribbean Cruises must identify specific customer groups, such as young Latinas and their families, toward which they will direct marketing efforts. This process includes developing and maintaining marketing mixes that satisfy the needs of those customers. In this chapter, we define and explore the concepts of markets and market segmentation. First, we discuss the major requirements of a market. Then, we examine the steps in the target market selection process, including identifying the appropriate targeting strategy, determining which variables to use for segmenting consumer and business markets, developing market segment profiles, evaluating relevant market segments, and selecting target markets. We conclude with a discussion of the various methods for developing sales forecasts.

6-1 WHAT ARE MARKETS?

In Chapter 2, we defined a *market* as a group of individuals and/or organizations that have a desire or need for products in a product class and have the ability, willingness, and authority to purchase those products. You, as a student, are part of the market for textbooks. You are part of other markets as well, such as for computers, clothes, food, and music. To truly be a market, consumers must possess all four characteristics. For instance, teenagers are not part of the market for alcohol. They may have the desire, willingness, and ability to buy liquor, but they do not have the authority to do so because teenagers are prohibited by law from buying alcoholic beverages.

Markets fall into one of two categories: consumer markets and business markets. These categories are based on the characteristics of the individuals and groups that make up a specific market and the purposes for which they buy products. A **consumer market** consists of purchasers and household members who intend to consume or benefit from the purchased products and do not buy products to make a profit. Consumer markets are sometimes referred to as *business-to-consumer (B2C) markets*. Each of us belongs to numerous consumer markets for all the purchases we make in categories such as housing, food, clothing, vehicles, personal services, appliances, furniture, recreational equipment, and other products.

A **business market** consists of individuals or groups that purchase a specific kind of product for one of three purposes: resale, direct use in producing other products, or use in general daily operations. For instance, a producer that buys electrical wire to use in the production of lamps is part of a business market for electrical wire. Some products can be part of either the business or consumer market, depending on their end use. For instance, if you purchase a chair for your home, that chair is part of the consumer market. However, if an office manager purchases the same chair for use in a business office, it is part of the business market. Business markets may be called *business-to-business (B2B)*, *industrial*, or *organizational markets* and can be sub-classified into producer, reseller, government, and institutional markets, as we shall see in Chapter 8.

The advertisements show a product targeted at the consumer market and one targeted at the business market. GoToMeeting by Citrix allows businesspeople to hold meetings and webinars remotely with members of their team. Because its main purpose is to provide a platform for meetings, Citrix aims efforts at the business market. As shown in the advertisement, GoToMeeting allows for team members to see and interact with each other while also displaying other information. Olia hair color, on the other hand, is targeted to a consumer market because hair color has no application in the typical business world. The photo in this advertisement emphasizes the rich color and curl of the woman's hair. You can see from these two advertisements that the one for GoToMeeting focuses on the practical application of the product in the business world, while the advertisement for Olia hair color focuses on how it will make the consumer feel good about herself, emphasizing how marketers will have different objectives depending on which market they target.

consumer market Purchasers and household members who intend to consume or benefit from the purchased products and do not buy products to make profits

business market Individuals, organizations, or groups that purchase a specific kind of product for resale, direct use in producing other products, or use in general daily operations

Citrix

© 2013 Garnier LLC

Types of Markets
GoToMeeting targets business markets by showing how the product can be used to make meetings easier, while Olia is focused on consumer markets by emphasizing how using hair color can help a consumer feel better about her hair.

6-2 TARGET MARKET SELECTION PROCESS

As indicated earlier, the first of two major components of developing a marketing strategy is to select a target market. Although marketers may employ several methods for target market selection, generally they follow a five-step process. This process is shown in Figure 6.1, and we discuss it in the following sections.

Figure 6.1 Target Market Selection Process

1. Identify the appropriate targeting strategy
2. Determine which segmentation variables to use
3. Develop market segment profiles
4. Evaluate relevant market segments
5. Select specific target markets

6-3 STEP 1: IDENTIFY THE APPROPRIATE TARGETING STRATEGY

A target market is a group of people or organizations for which a business creates and maintains a marketing mix specifically designed to satisfy the needs of group members. The strategy used to select a target market is affected by target market characteristics, product attributes, and the organization's objectives and resources. Figure 6.2 illustrates the three basic targeting strategies: undifferentiated, concentrated, and differentiated.

6-3a Undifferentiated Targeting Strategy

An organization sometimes defines an entire market for a product as its target market. When a company designs a single marketing mix and directs it at the entire market for a particular product, it is using an **undifferentiated targeting strategy**. As Figure 6.2 shows, the strategy assumes that all customers in the target market have similar needs, and thus the organization can satisfy most customers with a single marketing mix with little or no variation. Products marketed successfully through the undifferentiated strategy include commodities and staple food items, such as sugar, salt, and conventionally-raised produce.

The undifferentiated targeting strategy is effective under two conditions. First, a large proportion of customers in a total market must have similar needs for the product, a situation termed a **homogeneous market**. A marketer using a single marketing mix for a total market of customers with a variety of needs would find that the marketing mix satisfies very few people. For example, marketers would have little success using an undifferentiated strategy to sell a "universal car" because different customers have varying needs. Second, the organization must have the resources to develop a single marketing mix that satisfies customers' needs in a large portion of a total market and the managerial skills to maintain it.

The reality is that although customers may have similar needs for a few products, for most products their needs are different enough to warrant separate marketing mixes. In such instances, a company should use a concentrated or a differentiated strategy.

undifferentiated targeting strategy A strategy in which an organization designs a single marketing mix and directs it at the entire market for a particular product

homogeneous market A market in which a large proportion of customers have similar needs for a product

heterogeneous market A market made up of individuals or organizations with diverse needs for products in a specific product class

market segmentation The process of dividing a total market into groups with relatively similar product needs to design a marketing mix that matches those needs

market segment Individuals, groups, or organizations sharing one or more similar characteristics that cause them to have similar product needs

6-3b Concentrated Targeting Strategy through Market Segmentation

Although most people will be satisfied with the same white sugar, not everyone wants or needs the same car, furniture, or clothes. A market comprised of individuals or organizations with diverse product needs is called a **heterogeneous market**. Some individuals, for instance, want a Ford truck because they have to haul heavy loads for their work, while others live in the city and enjoy the ease of parking and good gas mileage of a Smart car. The automobile market thus is heterogeneous.

For heterogeneous markets, market segmentation is the best approach. **Market segmentation** is the process of dividing a total market into groups, or segments, that consist of people or organizations with relatively similar product needs. The purpose is to enable a marketer to design a marketing mix that more precisely matches the needs of customers in the selected market segment. A **market segment** consists of individuals, groups, or organizations that share one or more similar characteristics that cause them to have relatively similar product needs. The total market for blue jeans is divided into multiple segments. Price-sensitive customers can buy bargain jeans at Walmart or Ross. Others may need functional jeans, like the Carhartt brand, for work. Still other customers wear jeans as a fashion statement and are willing to spend hundreds of dollars on an exclusive brand such as 7 for All Mankind.

The rationale for segmenting heterogeneous markets is that a company will be most successful in developing a satisfying marketing mix for a portion of a total market whose needs

Figure 6.2 Targeting Strategies

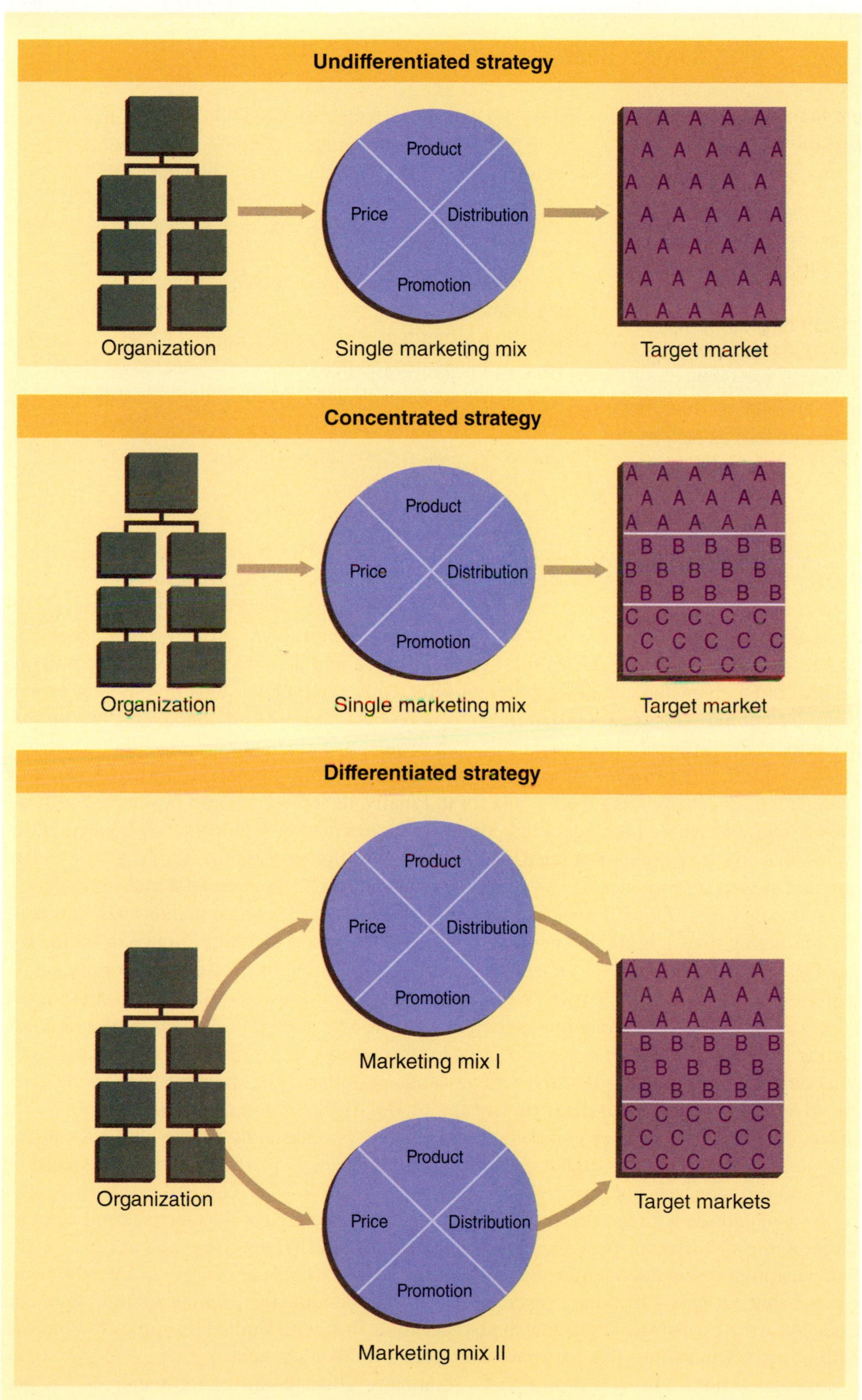

The letters in each target market represent potential customers. Customers with the same letters have similar characteristics and similar product needs.

Marketing Debate

Flying Babies: Separate but Equal?

ISSUE: Should carriers segment the market for air travel based on the benefits of child-free seating areas?

Crying babies can be a nuisance on a short flight but potentially more disturbing to passengers on international flights. With an eye toward allowing business travelers and vacationers to rest or work in peace, several Asian airlines now offer the option of paying for seats in special child-free zones.

The CEO of Malaysia-based AirAsia X says that seating children and their families in a separate section offers benefits for the parents of these youngsters as well as for travelers who choose child-free seating. Parents needn't feel guilty about their babies fussing or crying, and everybody else will enjoy a quieter flight. Passenger feedback has been mostly positive, and consumer research findings suggest many travelers would be willing to pay extra for baby-free seating.

No U.S. airline has banned babies from any seating areas—yet. In fact, most airlines see parents as an attractive target market for family-friendly travel. So should airlines use the benefits of being seated far from noisy children as a variable for segmenting the overall market for air travel?[a]

are relatively similar, since customers' needs tend to vary. The majority of organizations use market segmentation to best satisfy their customers.

For market segmentation to succeed, five conditions must exist. First, customers' needs for the product must be heterogeneous. Otherwise, there is no reason to waste resources segmenting the market. Second, segments must be identifiable and divisible. The company must be able to find a characteristic, or variable, for effectively separating a total market into groups comprised of individuals with relatively uniform product needs. Third, marketers must be able to compare the different market segments with respect to estimated sales potential, costs, and profits. Fourth, at least one segment must have enough profit potential to justify developing and maintaining a special marketing mix for it. Finally, the company must be able to reach the chosen segment with a particular marketing mix. Some market segments may be difficult or impossible to reach because of legal, social, or distribution constraints. Producers of Cuban rum and cigars, for instance, cannot market to U.S. consumers because of a trade embargo.

When an organization directs its marketing efforts toward a single market segment using one marketing mix, it is employing a **concentrated targeting strategy**. Notice in Figure 6.2 that the organization using the concentrated strategy is aiming its marketing mix only at "B" customers. Take a look at the two advertisements for Mont Blanc and Bic pens. Both of these brands are using a concentrated marketing strategy to reach a specific target market, but are aiming their advertisements at very different market segments. Mont Blanc is a very high-end pen company with products that sell for thousands of dollars. The simplicity and elegance of the advertisement speaks to the luxury of the product. Bic, on the other hand, is a brand of cheap, disposable pens. They come in multipacks, are purchased by people who want a reliable and functional pen but do not care about the experience of writing, and are meant to be used and thrown away, not treasured.

As you can see with the two pen brands, the chief advantage of the concentrated strategy is that it allows a firm to specialize. The firm analyzes the characteristics and needs of a distinct customer group and then focuses all its energies on satisfying that group's needs. If the group is big enough, a firm may generate a large sales volume by reaching a single segment. Concentrating on a single segment can also permit a firm with limited resources to compete with larger organizations that may have overlooked smaller segments.

concentrated targeting strategy A market segmentation strategy in which an organization targets a single market segment using one marketing mix

Specialization, however, means that a company allocates all of its resources for one target segment, which can be hazardous. If a company's sales depend on a single segment and the segment's demand for the product declines, the company's financial health also

Advertising Archives

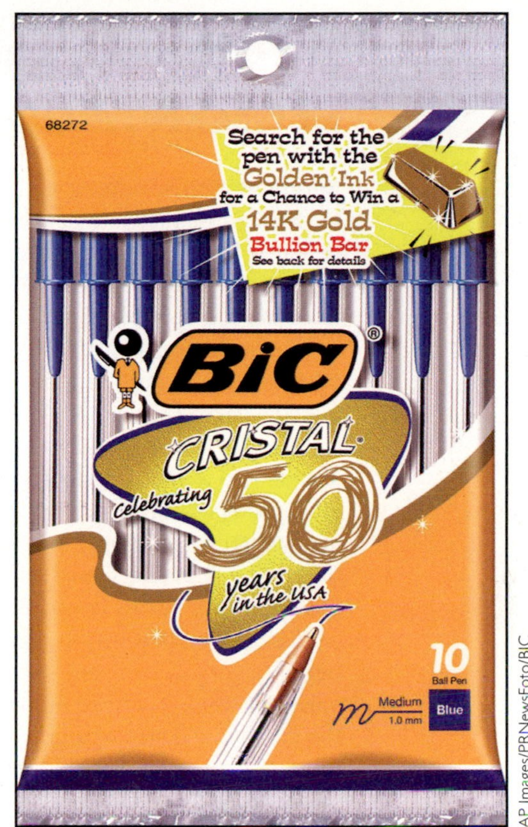

AP Images/PRNewsFoto/BIC

Concentrated Targeting Strategy
Both Mont Blanc and Bic pens use a concentrated targeting strategy to aim at a different, single market segment. They are not competing for the same customers.

deteriorates. The strategy can also prevent a firm from targeting other segments that might be successful, because when a firm penetrates one segment, its popularity may keep it from extending its marketing efforts into other segments.

6-3c Differentiated Targeting Strategy through Market Segmentation

With a **differentiated targeting strategy**, an organization directs its marketing efforts at two or more segments by developing a marketing mix for each segment (See Figure 6.2). After a firm uses a concentrated targeting strategy successfully in one market segment, it may expand its efforts to include additional segments. Enterprise Rent-A-Car is piloting Harley Davidson motorcycle rentals in Las Vegas to satisfy a demand for rental motorcycles among a more thrill-seeking segment of the tourist market. After conducting market research, Enterprise learned that motorcycle riders frequently wish they had more options to ride even when away from home and that they are not satisfied with renting a car. The company anticipates strong demand, especially from foreign tourists who visit the Southwest to experience the Wild West and Route 66 cultures. If successful, the company will expand the availability to additional markets in the region.[2]

A benefit of a differentiated approach is that a firm may increase sales within the total market because its marketing mixes are aimed at more customers. For this reason, a company with excess production capacity may find a differentiated strategy advantageous because the sale of products to additional segments can help to absorb excess capacity. On the other hand, a differentiated strategy often demands more production processes, materials, and people because the different ingredients in each marketing mix will vary. Thus, production costs for a differentiated strategy may be higher than with a concentrated strategy.

differentiated targeting strategy A strategy in which an organization targets two or more segments by developing a marketing mix for each segment

6-4 STEP 2: DETERMINE WHICH SEGMENTATION VARIABLES TO USE

Segmentation variables are the characteristics of individuals, groups, or organizations used to divide a market into segments. Location, age, gender, and rate of product usage can all be bases for segmenting markets. Marketers may use several variables in combination when segmenting a market. For example, Cheerwine is a type of soda pop manufactured in North Carolina and distributed in the southern and mid-Atlantic states. It is targeted at soda drinkers in its distribution area and at young people through heavy use of online and social media for advertising and promotional efforts. Because of its limited availability, the soda has maintained a desirability among fans of cool, regional products.[3]

To select a segmentation variable, markets consider several factors. The segmentation variable should relate to customers' needs for, uses of, or behavior toward the product. It is likely a television marketer will segment television viewers for primetime television by income and age but not by religion, for example, because television viewing does not vary much because of religion. Marketers must select measurable segmentation variables, such as age, location, or gender, if individuals or organizations in a total market are to be classified accurately.

There is no best way to segment markets, and the approach will vary depending on a number of factors. A company's resources and capabilities affect the number and size of segment variables used. The type of product and degree of variation in customers' needs also dictate the number and size of segments targeted. No matter what approach is used, choosing one or more segmentation variables is a critical step in effectively targeting a market. Selecting an inappropriate variable limits the chances of developing a successful marketing strategy. To help you better understand potential segmentation variables, we next examine the differences between the major variables used to segment consumer and business markets.

segmentation variables Characteristics of individuals, groups, or organizations used to divide a market into segments

6-4a Variables for Segmenting Consumer Markets

A marketer that is using segmentation to reach a consumer market can choose one or several variables. As Figure 6.3 shows, segmentation variables can be grouped into four major categories: demographic, geographic, psychographic, and behavioristic.

Figure 6.3 Segmentation Variables for Consumer Markets

Demographic variables
- Age
- Gender
- Race
- Ethnicity
- Income
- Education
- Occupation
- Family size
- Family life cycle
- Religion
- Social class

Geographic variables
- Region
- Urban, suburban, rural
- City size
- County size
- State size
- Market density
- Climate
- Terrain

Psychographic variables
- Personality attributes
- Motives
- Lifestyles

Behavioristic variables
- Volume usage
- End use
- Benefit expectations
- Brand loyalty
- Price sensitivity

Demographic Variables Demographers study aggregate population characteristics such as the distribution of age and gender, fertility rates, migration patterns, and mortality rates. Demographic characteristics that marketers commonly use include age, gender, race, ethnicity, income, education, occupation, family size, family life cycle, religion, and social class. Marketers segment markets by demographic characteristics because they are often closely linked to customers' needs and purchasing behaviors and can be readily measured.

Age is a common variable for segmentation purposes. A trip to the shopping mall highlights the fact that many retailers, including Zara, Aeropostale, and American Eagle Outfitters, target teens and very young adults. If considering segmenting by age, marketers need to be aware of age distribution, how that distribution is changing, and how it will affect the demand for different types of products. The proportion of consumers under age 55 is expected to continue to decrease over time as Baby Boomers (born between 1946 and 1964) age. In 1970, the average age of a U.S. citizen was 27.9. It is currently 37.3.[4] Because of the increasing average age of Americans, many marketers are searching for ways to market their products to older adults. As Figure 6.4 shows, Americans in different age groups have different product needs because of their different lifestyles and health situations. Citizens age 65 and older, for instance, spend the most on health care, while those between ages 35 and 64 spend the most on housing and food.

Figure 6.4 Spending Levels by Age Groups for Selected Product Categories

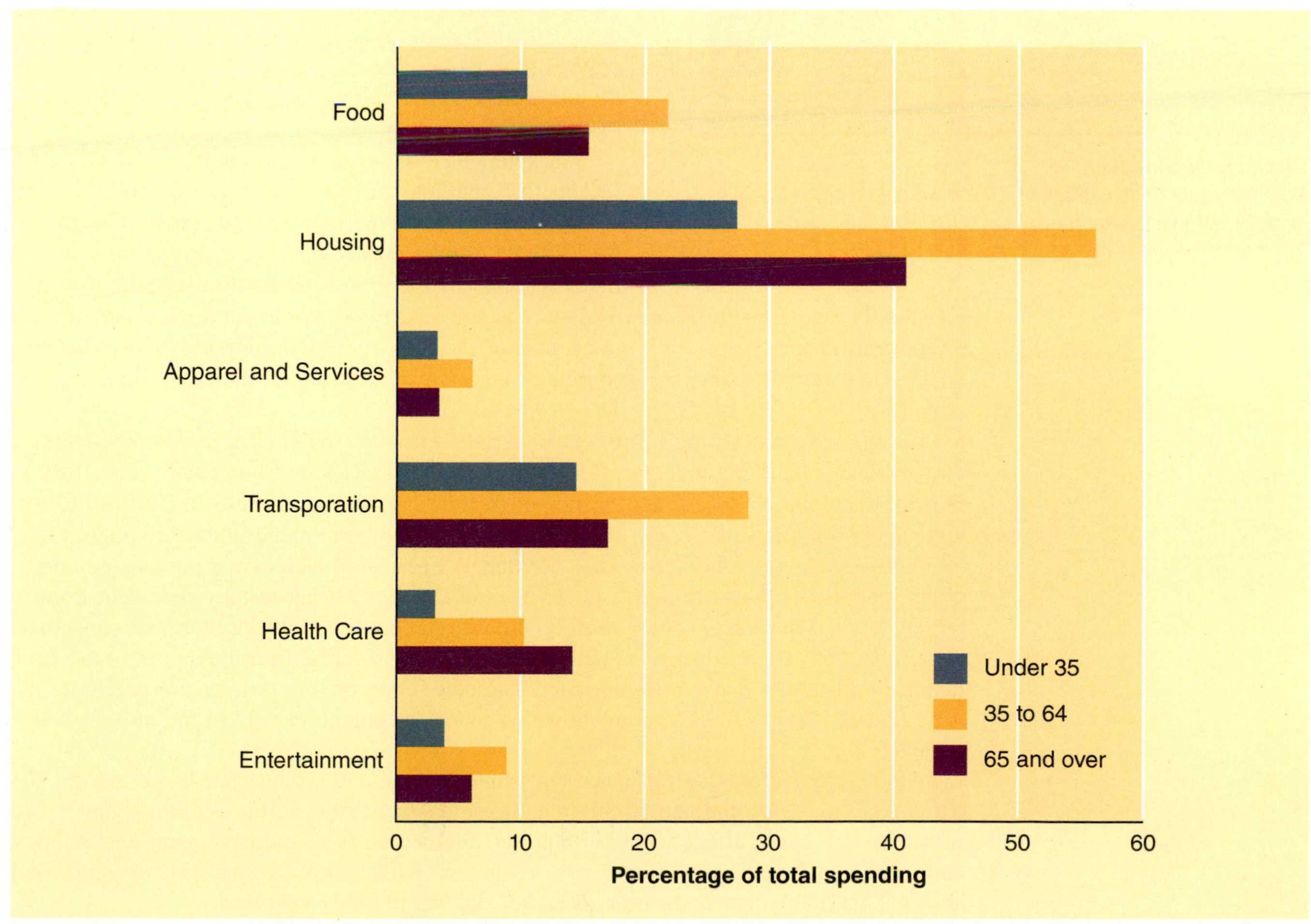

Source: U.S. Department of Labor, Bureau of Labor Statistics, "Age of Reference Person: Average Annual Expenditures and Characteristics," Consumer Expenditure Survey, 2010, Table 3, www.bls.gov/cex/2010/Standard/age.pdf (accessed May 24, 2012).

© 2013 P&G

Gender Segmentation
Downy targets its marketing efforts to women, who do more laundry and make more household purchases than men.

Gender is another demographic variable that is commonly used to segment markets, including clothing, soft drinks, nonprescription medications, magazines, some food items, and personal-care products. After years of being pressured to create marketing strategies that are not targeted by gender, U.S. toymakers have again moved toward segmenting toys by gender. Marketers made this decision based on sales data and customer responses to marketing mixes. They also used cognitive science research findings that indicate how boys and girls do indeed have different toy preferences.[5]

The U.S. Census Bureau reports that females account for 50.8 percent, and males for 49.2 percent, of the total U.S. population.[6] Although they represent only slightly more than half of the population, women disproportionately influence buying decisions. It is estimated that women account for 85 percent of all consumer purchases, causing many marketers to consider female customers when making marketing decisions.[7] Look at the advertisement for Downy Unstoppables laundry scent booster, for instance. Because marketers know that women do the majority of household shopping and do more housework than men, this ad is clearly targeted at females. The model (well-known actress Amy Sedaris, who was on *Sex and the City* and other shows popular among women) is dressed in a tailored 60s-style dress and hairstyle, looking traditionally feminine. The colors of the ad are pastel pink, green, and blue—all very feminine colors. Even the labels on the product depicted in the ad contain floral motifs.

Marketers also use race and ethnicity as variables for segmenting markets for such products as food, music, clothing, cosmetics, banking, and insurance. Cosmetics, for example, is an industry where it is important to match the shade of the products with the skin colors of the target market to maintain customer satisfaction and loyalty. Iman Cosmetics is a line created by the Ethiopian supermodel Iman, with deeper colors designed to flatter the skin tones of women of color, be they Black, Hispanic, or Asian. These products are not made for, nor marketed to, light-skinned women.[8]

Because income strongly influences people's product purchases, it often provides a way to divide markets. Income affects customers' lifestyles and what they can afford to buy. Product markets segmented by income include sporting goods, housing, furniture, cosmetics, clothing, jewelry, home appliances, automobiles, and electronics. Although it may seem obvious to target higher-income consumers because of their larger purchasing power, many marketers choose to target lower-income segments because they represent a much larger population globally. Increasingly, online retailers measure the worth of consumers using a metric called an *e-score.* This metric ranks consumers' lifetime values to the firm, taking into account many variables such as credit score, buying power, and purchase history. E-scores help firms to calculate which market segments represent the most valuable targets.[9]

Among the factors that influence household income and product needs are marital status and the presence and age of children. These characteristics, often combined and called the *family life cycle,* affect needs for housing, appliances, food and beverages, automobiles, and recreational equipment. Family life cycles can be divided in various ways, as Figure 6.5 shows. This figure depicts the process broken down into nine categories.

The composition of the U.S. household in relation to the family life cycle has changed considerably over the last several decades. Single-parent families are on the rise, meaning that the "typical" family no longer necessarily consists of a married couple with children. In fact, husband-and-wife households only account for 48.4 percent of all households in the United States, whereas they used to account for a majority of living arrangements. An estimated 26.7 percent of Americans live alone. Recently, previously small groups have risen in prominence, prompting an interest from marketers. Unmarried households represent 6.6 percent of the total, an increase of 41 percent since 2000. Same-sex partners represent 0.6 percent of households, which is a small proportion of the total population of households, but an increase of more than 81 percent since 2000.[10] People live in many different situations, all of which have different requirements for goods and services. Tracking demographic shifts such as these helps marketers be informed and prepared to satisfy the needs of target markets through new marketing mixes that address their changing lifestyles.

Figure 6.5 Family Life-Cycle Stages as a Percentage of All Households

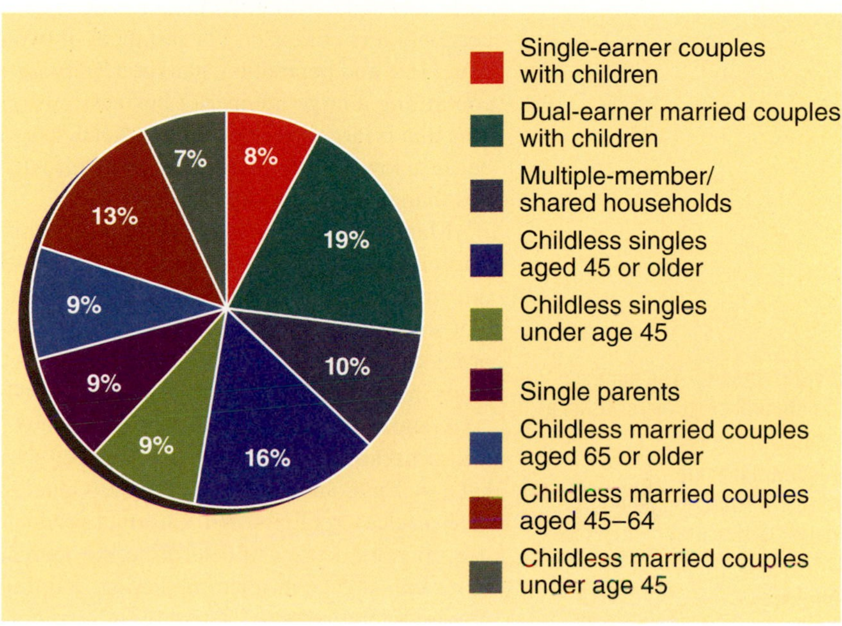

Geographic Variables Geographic variables—climate, terrain, city size, population density, and urban/rural areas—also influence consumer product needs. Markets may be divided using geographic variables because differences in location, climate, and terrain will influence consumers' needs. Consumers in the South, for instance, rarely have a need for snow tires. A company that sells products to a national market might divide the United States into Pacific, Southwest, Central, Midwest, Southeast, Middle Atlantic, and New England regions. A firm that is operating in one or several states might regionalize its market by counties, cities, zip code areas, or other units.

City size can be an important segmentation variable. Many firms choose to limit marketing efforts on cities above a certain size because small populations have been calculated to generate inadequate profits. Other firms actively seek opportunities in smaller towns. A classic example is Walmart, which initially was located only in small towns and even today can be found in towns where other large retailers stay away. If a marketer chooses to divide by a geographic variable, such as by city size, the U.S. Census Bureau provides reporting on population and demographics that can be of considerable assistance to marketers.

Because cities often cut across political boundaries, the U.S. Census Bureau developed a system to classify metropolitan areas (any area with a city or urbanized area with a population of at least 50,000 and a total metropolitan population of at least 100,000). Metropolitan areas are categorized as one of the following: a metropolitan statistical area (MSA), a primary metropolitan statistical area (PMSA), or a consolidated metropolitan statistical area (CMSA). An MSA is an urbanized area encircled by nonmetropolitan counties and is neither socially nor economically dependent on any other metropolitan area. A metropolitan area within a complex of at least 1 million inhabitants can elect to be named a PMSA. A CMSA is a metropolitan area of at least 1 million that has two or more PMSAs. Of the 20 CMSAs, the five largest—New York, Los Angeles, Chicago, San Francisco, and Philadelphia—account for 20 percent of the U.S. population. The federal government provides a considerable amount of socioeconomic information about MSAs, PMSAs, and CMSAs that can aid in market analysis and segmentation.

Market density refers to the number of potential customers within a unit of land area, such as a square mile. Although market density relates generally to population density, the correlation is not exact. For instance, in two different geographic markets of approximately equal size and population, market density for office supplies would be much higher in an area containing a large number of business customers, such as a city downtown, than in another area that is largely residential. Market density may be a useful segmentation variable for firms because low-density markets often require different sales, advertising, and distribution activities than do high-density markets.

Marketers may also use geodemographic segmentation. **Geodemographic segmentation** clusters people by zip codes or neighborhood units based on lifestyle and demographic information. Targeting this way can be effective because people often choose to live in an area that shares their basic lifestyle and political beliefs. Information companies such as Nielsen provide geodemographic data services and products. PRIZM, for example, classifies zip code areas into 66 different cluster types, based on demographic information of residents.[11]

market density The number of potential customers within a unit of land area

geodemographic segmentation A method of market segmentation that clusters people in zip code areas and smaller neighborhood units based on lifestyle and demographic information

micromarketing An approach to market segmentation in which organizations focus precise marketing efforts on very small geographic markets

Geodemographic segmentation allows marketers to engage in micromarketing. **Micromarketing** involves focusing precise marketing efforts on very small geographic markets, such as community and even individual neighborhoods. Providers of financial and healthcare services, retailers, and consumer product companies use micromarketing. Many retailers use micromarketing to determine the merchandise mix for individual stores. Increasingly, firms can engage in micromarketing in online retailing, given the Internet's ability to target precise interest groups. Unlike traditional micromarketing, online micromarketing is not limited by geography. The wealth of consumer information available online allows marketers to appeal efficiently and effectively to very specific consumer niches.

Climate is commonly used as a geographic segmentation variable because of its broad impact on people's behavior and product needs. Product markets affected by climate include air-conditioning and heating equipment, fireplace accessories, clothing, gardening equipment, recreational products, and building materials.

Going Green

Will Guaranteeing Green Guarantee Green for Rodale?

Can Rodale become a successful retailer by targeting people like its readers? The Pennsylvania-based publishing company is best known for health and fitness magazines such as *Prevention*, *Men's Health*, and *Runner's World*. Now, using its knowledge of readers' lifestyles, behavior, and values, Rodale has launched Rodale.com, an online store featuring upscale, eco-friendly products from sustainable sources.

Knowing that the target market cares deeply about the planet's health, Rodale's buyers assess the environmental impact of each supplier, in many cases through on-site visits. They also check for compliance with the voluntary sustainability standards set by independent groups such as the Rainforest Alliance, Green Seal, and Fairtrade International. Because the target market places a high value on aesthetics, Rodale's buyers search out sophisticated, high-quality products that please the senses and protect the planet. Among the eco-luxe products on Rodale's virtual store shelves are stylish handbags made from recycled fabric, specialty herb garden kits, organic cotton towels, all-natural skin cleansers, and designer coats made from recycled merino wool.

To reach its target market, Rodale advertises in its own magazines and places digital ads on selected websites. It also engages and informs customers through posts on social media sites such as Pinterest, Facebook, Twitter, and Tumblr. Looking ahead, will Rodale.com attract loyal shoppers in sufficient numbers to generate sizable profits for its publishing parent?[b]

Psychographic Variables Marketers sometimes use psychographic variables, such as personality characteristics, motives, and lifestyles, to segment markets. A psychographic variable can be used by itself or in combination with other types of segmentation variables.

Personality characteristics can be a useful means of segmentation when a product resembles many competing products and consumers' needs are not significantly related to other segmentation variables. However, segmenting a market according to personality traits can be risky. Although marketing practitioners have long believed consumer choice and product use vary with personality, marketing researchers have generally indicated only a weak relationship. It is difficult to measure personality traits accurately, especially because most personality tests were developed for clinical use, not for segmentation purposes.

When appealing to a personality characteristic, a marketer almost always selects one that many people view positively. Individuals with this characteristic, as well as those who aspire to have it, may be influenced to buy that marketer's brand. Marketers taking this approach do not worry about measuring how many people have the positively-valued characteristic. They assume a sizable proportion of people in the target market either have it or aspire to have it.

Segmentation Based on Motives
Consumers who purchase FEED branded products are dedicated to addressing global hunger.

When motives are used to segment a market, the market is divided according to consumers' reasons for making a purchase. Personal appearance, affiliation, status, safety, and health are examples of motives affecting the types of products purchased and the choice of stores in which they are bought. Marketing efforts based on particular motives can be a point of competitive advantage for a firm. FEED, featured in the advertisement, is a brand of fashion and accessories that donates a portion of each sale to providing meals to the hungry around the world. As you can see on the bottom of the bag featured in the ad, each product is stamped with a number, indicating the meals or vitamin supplements the purchase has provided. The brand is widely available in retailers such as Target and aims its marketing efforts at a market segment that is motivated to purchase products to help make the world a better place. This segment does not mind paying a little bit extra because a portion of all proceeds help those in need.[12]

Lifestyle segmentation groups individuals according to how they spend their time, the importance of things in their surroundings (homes or jobs, for example), beliefs about themselves and broad issues, and some demographic characteristics, such as income and education.[13] Lifestyle analysis provides a broad view of buyers because it encompasses numerous characteristics related to people's activities (e.g., work, hobbies, entertainment, sports), interests (e.g., family, home, fashion, food, technology), and opinions (e.g., politics, social issues, education, the future).

PRIZM, by Nielsen, is commonly used by marketers to segment by demographic variables. It can also be used to segment by lifestyles. PRIZM combines demographics, consumer behavior, and geographic data to help marketers identify, understand, and reach their customers and prospects, resulting in a highly robust tool for marketers.[14] PRIZM divides U.S. households into demographically and behaviorally distinct segments that take into account such factors as likes, dislikes, lifestyles, and purchase behaviors. Used by thousands of marketers, including many within Fortune 500 companies, PRIZM provides marketers with a common tool for understanding and reaching customers in a highly diverse and complex marketplace.

Source: Based on the Data from Entertainment & Media Communication Institute's Center for Skin Cancer Prevention.

Behavioristic Variables Firms can divide a market according to consumer behavior toward a product, which commonly involves an aspect of product use. Therefore, a market may be separated into users—classified as heavy, moderate, or light—and nonusers. To satisfy a specific group, such as heavy users, marketers may create a distinctive product and price or initiate special promotion and distribution activities. Per capita consumption data help determine different levels of usage by product category. To satisfy customers who use a product in a certain way, some feature—packaging, size, texture, or color—may be designed precisely to make the product easier to use, safer, or more convenient.

Benefit segmentation is the division of a market according to benefits that consumers want from the product. Although most types of market segmentation assume a relationship between the variable and customers' needs, benefit segmentation differs in that the benefits customers seek *are* their product needs. Consider that a customer who purchases over-the-counter cold relief medication may be specifically interested in two benefits: stopping a runny nose and relieving chest congestion. Thus, individuals are segmented directly according to their needs. By determining the desired benefits, marketers can divide people into groups by the benefits they seek. The effectiveness of such segmentation depends on three conditions: (1) the benefits sought must be identifiable, (2) using these benefits, marketers must be able to divide people into recognizable segments, and (3) one or more of the resulting segments must be accessible to the firm's marketing efforts.

Marketers can segment consumer markets using many characteristics. They do not, however, use the same variables to segment business characteristics. We will learn about business market segmentation in the next section.

6-4b Variables for Segmenting Business Markets

Like consumer markets, business markets are frequently segmented for marketing purposes. Marketers segment business markets according to geographic location, type of organization, customer size, and product use.

Geographic Location Earlier we noted that the demand for some consumer products can vary considerably among geographic areas because of differences in climate, terrain, or regional customer preferences. Demand for business products also varies according to geographic location. For instance, producers of lumber may divide their markets geographically because customers' needs vary by region. Geographic segmentation may be especially appropriate for producers seeking to reach industries concentrated in certain locations, such as furniture and textile producers concentrated in the Southeast.

benefit segmentation The division of a market according to benefits that consumers want from the product

Type of Organization A company sometimes segments a market by types of organizations within that market because they often require different product features, distribution systems, price structures, and selling strategies. Given these variations, a firm may either concentrate on a single segment with one marketing mix (a concentration targeting strategy) or focus on several groups with multiple mixes (a differentiated targeting strategy). A carpet producer could segment potential customers into several groups, such as automobile makers, commercial carpet contractors (firms that carpet large office buildings), apartment complex developers, carpet wholesalers, and large retail carpet outlets.

Customer Size An organization's size may affect its purchasing procedures and the types and quantities of products it wants. Size can thus be an effective variable for segmenting a business market. To reach a segment of a particular size, marketers may have to adjust one or more marketing mix ingredients. For instance, marketers may want to offer customers who buy in large quantities a discount as a purchase incentive. Personal selling is common and expected in business markets, where a higher level of customer service may be required—larger customers may require a higher level of customer service because of the size and complexity of their orders. Because the needs of large and small buyers tend to be distinct, marketers frequently use different marketing practices to reach target customer groups.

Product Use Certain products, particularly raw materials like steel, petroleum, plastics, and lumber, can be used in numerous ways in the production of goods. These variations will affect the types and amounts of products purchased, as well as the purchasing method. Consider the advertisement for Sappi, a producer of high-quality paper. Paper is a product that can be used for a variety of purposes and targeted at many different markets. In this ad, Sappi is targeting its McCoy line of coated papers at businesses that do design work and that care about crisp colors and paper feel. As part of its marketing strategy, you can see that Sappi produces its own educational publication, *The Standard*, printed on its own paper and features articles on printing and design. The magazine gives the firm added credibility among its target audience, while physically showcasing the product, paper.

Courtesy of Sappi

Segmenting Business Markets
Sappi produces high-quality paper products. It segments based on product use, focusing marketing efforts on companies that produce design work that requires a high grade of paper.

6-5 STEP 3: DEVELOP MARKET SEGMENT PROFILES

A market segment profile describes the similarities among potential customers within a segment and explains the differences among people and organizations in different segments. A profile may cover aspects such as demographic characteristics, geographic factors, product benefits sought, lifestyles, brand preferences, and usage rates. Individuals and organizations within segments should be relatively similar with respect to several characteristics and product needs and differ considerably from those within other market segments. Marketers use market segment profiles to assess the degree to which their products fit potential customers' product needs. Market segment profiles help marketers understand how a business can use its capabilities to serve potential customer groups.

Market segment profiles help a marketer determine which segment or segments are most attractive relative to the firm's strengths, weaknesses, objectives, and resources. Although marketers may initially believe certain segments are attractive, a market segment profile may unveil new information that makes a segment less attractive than thought. Market segment profiles can be useful in helping a firm make marketing decisions relating to a specific market segment or segments.

6-6 STEP 4: EVALUATE RELEVANT MARKET SEGMENTS

After analyzing the market segment profiles, a marketer should be able to narrow his or her focus to several promising segments that warrant further analysis. Marketers should examine sales estimates, competition, and estimated costs associated with each of these segments.

6-6a Sales Estimates

Potential sales for a market segment can be measured along several dimensions, including product level, geographic area, time, and level of competition.[15] With respect to product level, potential sales can be estimated for a specific product item (e.g., Diet Coke) or an entire product line (e.g., Coca-Cola Classic, Diet Coke, and Coke Zero comprise goods in a product line). A manager must also determine the geographic area to include in the estimate. In relation to time, sales estimates can be short range (one year or less), medium range (one to five years), or long range (longer than five years). The competitive level specifies whether sales are being estimated for a single firm or for an entire industry.

Market potential is the total amount of a product that customers will purchase within a specified period at a specific level of industry-wide marketing activity. Market potential can be stated in terms of dollars or units. A segment's market potential is affected by economic, sociocultural, and other environmental forces. The specific level of marketing effort will vary from one firm to another, and each firm's marketing activities together add up to the industry-wide marketing effort total. A marketing manager must also estimate whether and to what extent industry marketing efforts will change over time.

Company sales potential is the maximum percentage share of a market that an individual firm within an industry can expect to capture for a specific product. Several factors influence company sales potential for a market segment. First, the market potential places absolute limits on the size of the company's sales potential—a firm cannot exceed the market potential. Second, the magnitude of industry-wide marketing activities has an indirect but definite impact on the company's sales potential. When Domino's Pizza advertises home-delivered pizza, for instance, it indirectly promotes pizza in general. Maybe you see the ad and it sparks a craving for pizza, but you call the Pizza Hut down the street because it is more familiar to you. Third, the intensity and effectiveness of a company's marketing activities relative to competitors' activities affect the size of the company's sales potential. If a company spends twice as much as any of its competitors on marketing efforts, and if each dollar spent is more effective in generating sales, the firm's sales potential will be high relative to competitors' sales potential.

Two general approaches that measure company sales potential are breakdown and buildup. In the **breakdown approach**, the marketing manager first develops a general economic forecast for a specific time period. Next, the manager estimates market potential based on this forecast. The manager derives the company's sales potential from the forecast and an estimate of market potential. In the **buildup approach**, the marketing manager begins by estimating how much of a product a potential buyer in a specific geographic area, such as a sales territory, will purchase in a given period. The manager then multiplies that amount by the total number of potential buyers in that area. The manager performs the same calculation for each geographic area in which the firm sells products and then adds the totals for each area to calculate market potential. To determine company sales potential, the manager must estimate, based on planned levels of company marketing activities, the proportion of the total market potential the company can reasonably attain.

market potential The total amount of a product that customers will purchase within a specified period at a specific level of industry-wide marketing activity

company sales potential The maximum percentage of market potential that an individual firm within an industry can expect to obtain for a specific product

breakdown approach Measuring company sales potential based on a general economic forecast for a specific period and the market potential derived from it

buildup approach Measuring company sales potential by estimating how much of a product a potential buyer in a specific geographic area will purchase in a given period, multiplying the estimate by the number of potential buyers, and adding the totals of all the geographic areas considered

6-6b Competitive Assessment

Besides obtaining sales estimates, it is crucial to assess competitors that are already operating in the segments being considered. A market segment that initially seems attractive based on sales estimates may turn out to be much less so after a competitive assessment. Such an assessment should ask several questions about competitors: How many exist? What are their strengths and weaknesses? Do several competitors already have major market shares and together dominate the segment? Can our company create a marketing mix to compete effectively against competitors' marketing mixes? Is it likely that new competitors will enter this segment? If so, how will they affect our firm's ability to compete successfully? Answers to such questions are important for proper assessment of the competition in potential market segments.

The market for vacuum cleaners, for instance, has many competitors. Dyson, featured in the advertisement, competes against these other brands by highlighting where its products are superior. Its DC41 model vacuum cleaner has more than twice the suction power of many of its competitors. This fact is underscored in the advertisement by showing the DC41 as much larger in size than popular competitors. This makes the Dyson model more eye-catching in the ad, and the viewer understands that its relative size is an illustration of its power, not of its actual size.

Dyson

Competitive Assessment
Marketers conducted an assessment and determined that Dyson vacuum cleaners can maintain an advantage in a market filled with competing brands by offering vacuum models with more power.

6-6c Cost Estimates

To fulfill the needs of a target segment, an organization must develop and maintain a marketing mix that precisely meets the wants and needs of that segment, which can be expensive. Distinctive product features, attractive package design, generous product warranties, extensive advertising, attractive promotional offers, competitive prices, and high-quality personal service use considerable organizational resources. In some cases, marketers may conclude that the costs to reach some segments are so high that they are essentially inaccessible. Marketers also must consider whether the organization can reach a segment at costs equal to or below competitors' costs. If the firm's costs are likely to be higher, it will be unable to compete in that segment in the long run.

6-7 STEP 5: SELECT SPECIFIC TARGET MARKETS

An important initial consideration in selecting a target market is whether customers' needs differ enough to warrant the use of market segmentation. If segmentation analysis shows customer needs to be homogeneous, the firm's management may decide to use the undifferentiated approach, discussed earlier. However, if customer needs are heterogeneous, which is more likely, marketers must select one or more target markets.

Assuming one or more segments offer significant opportunities to achieve organizational objectives, a marketer must decide which offer the most potential at reasonable costs. Ordinarily, information gathered in the previous step—concerning sales estimates, competitors, and cost estimates—requires careful review in this final step to determining long-term marketing opportunities. At this time, the firm's management must investigate whether the organization has sufficient financial resources, managerial skills, employee expertise, and facilities to compete effectively in selected segments. The firm must also consider the possibility that the requirements of some market segments are at odds with the firm's overall objectives, and that possible legal problems, conflicts with interest groups, and technological advancements will render certain segments unattractive. Finally, marketers must consider long-term versus short-term growth. If long-term prospects look poor, a marketer may ultimately choose not to target a segment because it would be difficult to recoup expenses.

Selecting appropriate target markets is important to an organization's effective adoption and use of the marketing concept philosophy. Identifying the right target market is the key to implementing a successful marketing strategy. Failure to do so can lead to low sales, high costs, and severe financial losses. A careful target market analysis places an organization in a strong position to serve customers' needs and achieve its objectives.

6-8 DEVELOPING SALES FORECASTS

After a company selects a target market or markets, it must develop a **sales forecast**—the amount of a product the company expects to sell during a specific period at a specified level of marketing activity. The sales forecast differs from the company sales potential in that it concentrates on what actual sales will be at a certain level of company marketing effort. The company sales potential assesses what sales are possible at various levels of marketing activities, assuming certain environmental conditions exist. Businesses use the sales forecast for planning, organizing, implementing, and controlling activities. The success of numerous activities depends on this forecast's accuracy. Common problems in failing companies are improper planning and lack of realistic sales forecasts. Overly ambitious sales forecasts can lead to overbuying, overinvestment, and higher costs that weaken a firm's strength and position.

To forecast sales, a marketer can choose from a number of forecasting methods, some arbitrary and quick and others more scientific, complex, and time-consuming. A firm's choice of method or methods depends on the costs involved, type of product, market characteristics, time span and purpose of the forecast, stability of the historical sales data, availability of required information, managerial preferences, and forecasters' expertise and experience.[16] Common forecasting techniques fall into five categories: executive judgment, surveys, time series analysis, regression analysis, and market tests.

sales forecast The amount of a product a company expects to sell during a specific period at a specified level of marketing activities

executive judgment A sales forecasting method based on the intuition of one or more executives

customer forecasting survey A survey of customers regarding the types and quantities of products they intend to buy during a specific period

6-8a Executive Judgment

Executive judgment is the intuition of one or more executives. This is an unscientific but expedient and inexpensive approach to sales forecasting. It is not a very accurate method, but executive judgment may work reasonably well when product demand is relatively stable and the forecaster has years of market-related experience. However, because intuition is heavily influenced by recent experience, the forecast may weight recent sales booms or slumps excessively. Another drawback to executive judgment is that the forecaster has only past experience as a guide for deciding where to go in the future.

6-8b Surveys

Another way to forecast sales is to question customers, sales personnel, or experts regarding their expectations about future purchases. In a **customer forecasting survey**, marketers ask customers what types and quantities of products they intend to buy during a specific period. This approach may be useful to a business with relatively few customers. Consider Lockheed Martin, the U.S. government's largest contractor. Because most of its contracts come from the same customer, the government, Lockheed Martin could conduct customer forecasting surveys effectively. PepsiCo, by contrast, has millions of customers and could not feasibly use a customer survey to forecast future sales.

In a **sales force forecasting survey**, the firm's salespeople estimate anticipated sales in their territories for a specified period. The forecaster combines these territorial estimates to arrive at a tentative forecast. A marketer may survey the sales staff for several reasons, the most important being that the sales staff is the company personnel closest to customers on a daily basis. They, therefore, have first-hand knowledge about customers' product needs. Moreover, when sales representatives assist in developing the forecast, they are invested in the process and are more likely to work toward its achievement. Forecasts can be prepared for single territories, divisions consisting of several territories, regions made up of multiple divisions, and the total geographic market.

When a company wants an **expert forecasting survey**, it hires professionals to help prepare the sales forecast. These experts are usually economists, management consultants, advertising executives, college professors, or other individuals outside the firm with experience in a specific market. Drawing on this experience and their analyses of available information about the company and the market, experts prepare and present forecasts or answer questions. Using experts is a quick way to get information and is relatively inexpensive. However, because they work outside the firm, these forecasters may be less motivated than company personnel to do an effective job.

A more complex form of the expert forecasting survey incorporates the Delphi technique. In the **Delphi technique**, experts create initial forecasts, submit them to the company for averaging, and have the results returned to them so they can make individual refined forecasts. When making calculations using the Delphi technique, experts use the averaged results to eradicate outliers and to refine predictions. The procedure can be repeated several times until the experts, each working separately, reach a consensus. Because this technique gets rid of extreme data, the ultimate goal in using the Delphi technique is to develop a highly reliable sales forecast.

6-8c Time Series Analysis

With **time series analysis**, the forecaster uses the firm's historical sales data to discover a pattern or patterns in sales over time. If a pattern is found, it can be used to forecast sales. This forecasting method assumes that past sales patterns will continue into the future. The accuracy, and thus usefulness, of time series analysis hinges on the validity of this assumption.

In a time series analysis, a forecaster usually performs four types of analyses: trend, cycle, seasonal, and random factor. **Trend analysis** focuses on aggregate sales data, such as the company's annual sales figures, covering a period of many years to determine whether annual sales are generally rising, falling, or staying about the same. Through **cycle analysis**, a forecaster analyzes sales figures (often monthly sales data) for a three- to five-year period to ascertain whether sales fluctuate in a consistent, periodic manner. When performing a **seasonal analysis**, the analyst studies daily, weekly, or monthly sales figures to evaluate the degree to which seasonal factors, such as climate and holiday activities, influence sales. In a **random factor analysis**, the forecaster attempts to attribute erratic sales variations to random, nonrecurring events, such as a regional power failure, a natural disaster, or political unrest in a foreign market. After performing each of these analyses, the forecaster combines the results to develop the sales forecast. Time series analysis is an effective forecasting method for products with reasonably stable demand, but not for products with erratic demand.

sales force forecasting survey A survey of a firm's sales force regarding anticipated sales in their territories for a specified period

expert forecasting survey Sales forecasts prepared by experts outside the firm, such as economists, management consultants, advertising executives, or college professors

Delphi technique A procedure in which experts create initial forecasts, submit them to the company for averaging, and then refine the forecasts

time series analysis A forecasting method that uses historical sales data to discover patterns in the firm's sales over time and generally involves trend, cycle, seasonal, and random factor analyses

trend analysis An analysis that focuses on aggregate sales data over a period of many years to determine general trends in annual sales

cycle analysis An analysis of sales figures for a three- to five-year period to ascertain whether sales fluctuate in a consistent, periodic manner

seasonal analysis An analysis of daily, weekly, or monthly sales figures to evaluate the degree to which seasonal factors influence sales

random factor analysis An analysis attempting to attribute erratic sales variations to random, nonrecurrent events

6-8d Regression Analysis

Like time series analysis, regression analysis requires the use of historical sales data. In **regression analysis**, the forecaster seeks to find a relationship between past sales (the dependent variable) and one or more independent variables, such as population, per capita income, or gross domestic product. Simple regression analysis uses one independent variable, whereas multiple regression analysis includes two or more independent variables. The objective of regression analysis is to develop a mathematical formula that accurately describes a relationship between the firm's sales and one or more variables. However, the formula indicates only an association, not a causal relationship. Once an accurate formula is established, the analyst plugs the necessary information into the formula to derive the sales forecast.

Regression analysis is useful when a precise association can be established. However, a forecaster seldom finds a perfect correlation. Furthermore, this method can be used only when available historical sales data are extensive. Thus, regression analysis is futile for forecasting sales of new products.

6-8e Market Tests

A **market test** involves making a product available to buyers in one or more test areas and measuring purchases and consumer responses to the product, distribution, promotion, and price. Test areas are often midsized cities with populations of 200,000 to 500,000, but they can be towns or small cities with populations of 50,000 to 200,000. Test areas are chosen for their representativeness of a firm's target markets.

A market test provides information about consumers' actual, rather than intended, purchases. In addition, purchase volume can be evaluated in relation to the intensity of other marketing activities such as advertising, in-store promotions, pricing, packaging, and distribution. Forecasters base their sales estimates for larger geographic units on customer response in test areas. McDonald's is partnering with Kraft to test-market packaged McCafé coffee drinks, which are inspired by McDonald's popular McCafé outlets and beverages and compete with Dunkin' Donuts and Starbucks. The products will also compete with Green Mountain Coffee Roasters, Inc.'s Keurig K-cup packaged coffee products. The line of products is marketed as a midrange option, between Kraft's low-end Maxwell House and its high-end Gevalia brands. The decision to test-market packaged coffee products was a result of actively collecting customer feedback and conducting product tests in McDonald's outlets.[17]

Because it does not require historical sales data, a market test is effective for forecasting sales of new products or of existing products in new geographic areas. A market test also gives a marketer an opportunity to test the success of various elements of the marketing mix. However, these tests are often time-consuming and expensive. In addition, a marketer cannot be certain that consumer response during a market test represents the total market response or that such a response will continue in the future.

regression analysis A method of predicting sales based on finding a relationship between past sales and one or more independent variables, such as population or income

market test Making a product available to buyers in one or more test areas and measuring purchases and consumer responses to marketing efforts

6-8f Using Multiple Forecasting Methods

Although some businesses depend on a single sales forecasting method, most firms use several techniques. Sometimes a company is forced to use multiple methods when marketing diverse product lines, but even a single product line may require several forecasts, especially when the product is sold to different market segments. Thus, a producer of automobile tires may rely on one technique to forecast tire sales for new cars and on another to forecast sales of replacement tires. Variation in the length of forecasts may call for several forecasting methods as well. A firm that employs one method for a short-range forecast may find it inappropriate for long-range forecasting. Sometimes a marketer verifies results of one method by using one or more other methods and comparing outcomes.

Summary

6-1 Explain what markets are and how they are generally classified.

A market is a group of people who, as individuals or as organizations, have needs for products in a product class and have the ability, willingness, and authority to purchase such products. Markets can be categorized as consumer markets or business markets, based on the characteristics of the individuals and groups that make up a specific market and the purposes for which they buy products. A consumer market, also known as a *business-to-consumer (B2C) market*, consists of purchasers and household members who intend to consume or benefit from the purchased products and do not buy products for the main purpose of making a profit. A business market, also known as *business-to-business (B2B)*, *industrial*, or *organizational market,* consists of individuals or groups that purchase a specific kind of product for one of three purposes: resale, direct use in producing other products, or use in general daily operations.

6-2 Identify the five steps of the target market selection process.

In general, marketers employ a five-step process when selecting a target market. Step one is to identify the appropriate targeting strategy. Step two is determining which segmentation variables to use. Step three is to develop a market segment profile. Step four is evaluating relevant market segments. Finally, step five is selecting specific target markets. Not all marketers will follow all of these five steps in this order, but this process provides a good general guide.

6-3 Describe the differences among three targeting strategies.

Step one of the target market selection process is to identify the appropriate targeting strategy. When a company designs a single marketing mix and directs it at the entire market for a particular product, it is using an undifferentiated targeting strategy. The undifferentiated strategy is effective in a homogeneous market, whereas a heterogeneous market needs to be segmented through a concentrated targeting strategy or a differentiated targeting strategy. Both of these strategies divide markets into segments consisting of individuals, groups, or organizations that have one or more similar characteristics and can be linked to similar product needs. When using a concentrated strategy, an organization directs marketing efforts toward a single market segment through one marketing mix. With a differentiated targeting strategy, an organization directs customized marketing efforts at two or more segments.

Certain conditions must exist for market segmentation to be effective. First, customers' needs for the product should be heterogeneous. Second, the segments of the market should be identifiable and divisible. Third, the total market should be divided so segments can be compared with respect to estimated sales, costs, and profits. Fourth, at least one segment must have enough profit potential to justify developing and maintaining a special marketing mix for that segment. Fifth, the firm must be able to reach the chosen segment with a particular marketing mix.

6-4 Identify the major segmentation variables.

The second step is determining which segmentation variables to use, which are the characteristics of individuals, groups, or organizations used to divide a total market into segments. The segmentation variable should relate to customers' needs for, uses of, or behavior toward the product. Segmentation variables for consumer markets can be grouped into four categories: demographic (e.g., age, gender, income, ethnicity, family life cycle), geographic (e.g., population, market density, climate), psychographic (e.g., personality traits, motives, lifestyles), and behavioristic (e.g., volume usage, end use, expected benefits, brand loyalty, price sensitivity). Variables for segmenting business markets include geographic location, type of organization, customer size, and product use.

6-5 Explain what market segment profiles are and how they are used.

Step three in the target market selection process is to develop market segment profiles. Such profiles describe the similarities among potential customers within a segment and explain the differences among people and organizations in different market segments. They are used to assess the degree to which the firm's products can match potential customers' product needs. Segments, which may seem attractive at first, may be shown to be quite the opposite after a market segment profile is completed.

6-6 Explain how to evaluate market segments.

Step four is evaluating relevant market segments. Marketers analyze several important factors, such as sales estimates, competition, and estimated costs, associated with each segment. Potential sales for a market segment can be measured along several dimensions, including product level, geographic area, time, and level of competition. Besides obtaining sales estimates, it is crucial to assess competitors that are already operating in the segments being considered. Without competitive information, sales estimates may be misleading. The cost of developing a marketing mix that meets the wants and needs of individuals in that segment must also be considered. If the firm's costs to compete in that market are very high, it may be unable to compete in that segment in the long run.

6-7 Identify the factors that influence the selection of specific market segments for use as target markets.

The final step involves the actual selection of specific target markets. In this step, the company considers whether customers' needs differ enough to warrant segmentation and which segments to target. If customers' needs are heterogeneous, the decision of which segment to target must be made, or whether to enter the market at all. Considerations such as the firm's available resources, managerial skills, employee expertise, facilities, the firm's overall objectives, possible legal problems, conflicts with interest groups, and technological advancements must be considered when deciding which segments to target.

6-8 Discuss sales forecasting methods.

A sales forecast is the amount of a product the company actually expects to sell during a specific period at a specified level of marketing activities. To forecast sales, marketers can choose from a number of methods. The choice depends on various factors, including the costs involved, type of product, market characteristics, and time span and purposes of the forecast. There are five categories of forecasting techniques: executive judgment, surveys, time series analysis, regression analysis, and market tests. Executive judgment is based on the intuition of one or more executives. Surveys include customer, sales force, and expert forecasting. Time series analysis uses the firm's historical sales data to discover patterns in the firm's sales over time and employs four major types of analysis: trend, cycle, seasonal, and random factor. With regression analysis, forecasters attempt to find a relationship between past sales and one or more independent variables. Market testing involves making a product available to buyers in one or more test areas and measuring purchases and consumer responses to distribution, promotion, and price. Many companies employ multiple forecasting methods.

Go to www.cengagebrain.com for resources to help you master the content in this chapter as well as for materials that will expand your marketing knowledge!

Developing Your Marketing Plan

Identifying and analyzing a target market is a major component of formulating a marketing strategy. A clear understanding and explanation of a product's target market is crucial to developing a useful marketing plan. References to various dimensions of a target market are likely to appear in several locations in a marketing plan. To assist you in understanding how information in this chapter relates to the creation of your marketing plan, focus on the following considerations:

1. What type of targeting strategy is being used for your product? Should a different targeting strategy be employed?
2. Select and justify the segmentation variables that are most appropriate for segmenting the market for your product. If your product is a consumer product, use Figure 6.3 for ideas regarding the most appropriate segmentation variables. If your marketing plan focuses on a business product, review the information in the section entitled "Variables for Segmenting Business Markets."
3. Discuss how your product should be positioned in the minds of customers in the target market relative to the product positions of competitors.

The information obtained from these questions should assist you in developing various aspects of your marketing plan found in the "Interactive Marketing Plan" exercise at **www.cengagebrain.com**.

Important Terms

consumer market 162
business market 162
undifferentiated targeting strategy 164
homogeneous market 164
heterogeneous market 164
market segmentation 164
market segment 164
concentrated targeting strategy 166
differentiated targeting strategy 167
segmentation variables 168
market density 172
geodemographic segmentation 172
micromarketing 172
benefit segmentation 174
market potential 176
company sales potential 176
breakdown approach 176
buildup approach 176
sales forecast 178
executive judgment 178
customer forecasting survey 178
sales force forecasting survey 179
expert forecasting survey 179
Delphi technique 179
time series analysis 179
trend analysis 179
cycle analysis 179
seasonal analysis 179
random factor analysis 179
regression analysis 180
market test 180

Discussion and Review Questions

1. What is a market? What are the requirements for a market?
2. In your local area, identify a group of people with unsatisfied product needs who represent a market. Could this market be reached by a business organization? Why or why not?
3. Outline the five major steps in the target market selection process.
4. What is an undifferentiated strategy? Under what conditions is it most useful? Describe a present market situation in which a company is using an undifferentiated strategy. Is the business successful? Why or why not?
5. What is market segmentation? Describe the basic conditions required for effective segmentation. Identify several firms that use market segmentation.
6. List the differences between concentrated and differentiated strategies, and describe the advantages and disadvantages of each.
7. Identify and describe four major categories of variables that can be used to segment consumer markets. Give examples of product markets that are segmented by variables in each category.
8. What dimensions are used to segment business markets?
9. Define *geodemographic segmentation*. Identify several types of firms that might employ this type of market segmentation, and explain why.
10. What is a market segment profile? Why is it an important step in the target market selection process?
11. Describe the important factors that marketers should analyze to evaluate market segments.
12. Why is a marketer concerned about sales potential when trying to select a target market?
13. Why is selecting appropriate target markets important for an organization that wants to adopt the marketing concept philosophy?
14. What is a sales forecast? Why is it important?
15. What are the two primary types of surveys a company might use to forecast sales? Why would a company use an outside expert forecasting survey?
16. Under what conditions are market tests useful for sales forecasting? What are the advantages and disadvantages of market tests?
17. Under what conditions might a firm use multiple forecasting methods?

Video Case 6.1

Family-Owned Ski Butternut Targets Family Skiers

Located in the picturesque Berkshire Mountains of Western Massachusetts, Ski Butternut has been a family-owned, family-oriented ski destination for more than 50 years. The resort includes 22 trails for downhill skiing and snowboarding, two terrain parks for riding, and a dedicated area for snow tubing. Although Ski Butternut hosts some non-ski events during summer and fall, its business goes into high gear when snowy weather arrives, bringing skiers and riders from across Massachusetts, Connecticut, New York, and New Jersey.

Matt Sawyer, Ski Butternut's director of marketing, says the primary target market has always been families with young children who are seeking affordable skiing. Everything from the snack-bar menus to the ski-shop merchandise is presented with families in mind. So that parents can have fun in the snow without worry, the resort has a Children's Center for children who are too young to ski or have no interest. Fifth-graders are invited to ski for free when accompanied by an adult who buys an adult lift ticket. The resort also created two terrain parks for young snowboarders who were clamoring for a more exciting riding experience. Without the terrain parks, Sawyer says, these boarders would have asked their parents to take them to competing mountains in Vermont.

Ski Butternut's research findings show that first-timers are a particularly important segment, because they tend to have a strong allegiance to the resort where they learn to ski. First-timers typically visit the resort seven times before seeking out more challenging mountains. As a result, Ski Butternut has made teaching first-timers to ski or snowboard one of its specialties. For this market, the resort bundles ski or board rentals, lift tickets, and also offers a wide range of individual and group lessons for all ages and abilities at a value price. Because Ski Butternut has trails for different skill levels, beginners can challenge themselves by changing trails within the resort once they feel confident.

Ski Butternut also targets seniors and college students. Knowing that weekends are the busiest period, the resort offers special midweek prices to attract seniors who have free time to ski on weekdays. College students are particularly value-conscious, and they often travel to ski resorts as a group. As a result, Ski Butternut offers weekend and holiday discounts to bring in large numbers of students who would otherwise ski elsewhere. Thanks to Facebook, Twitter, and other social media, students quickly spread the word about special pricing, which enhances Ski Butternut's ability to reach this key segment. In addition, the resort highlights discount pricing for families when targeting specific segments, such as scout troops, military personnel, emergency services personnel, and members of local ski clubs.

Another segment Ski Butternut has selected for marketing attention is ski racers. The resort features professional coaching, lessons, and programs for ski racers in the age group of 8 to 20. Sawyer notes that these ski racers are extremely dedicated to training, which means they're on the slopes as often as possible, a positive for the resort's attendance and revenue. To stay in touch with racers, Ski Butternut has a special website and a dedicated Facebook page.

Sawyer conducts up to 1,200 customer surveys every year to better understand who his customers are and what they need. He also compares the results with skiers who visit mountains of a similar size in other areas. Digging deeper, he analyzes data drawn from the ski shop's rental business to build a detailed picture of customers' demographics, abilities, and preferences. Based on this findings, he knows that the typical family at Ski Butternut consists of two children under age 18 who ski or ride, and at least one parent who skis.

Because they can obtain so much information from and about their customers, Sawyer and his team are able to make better decisions about the marketing mix for each segment. By better matching the media with the audience, they get a better response from advertising, e-mail messages, and other marketing communications. As one example, they found that 15 percent of the visitors to Ski Butternut's website were using a smartphone to access the site. Sawyer has now created a special version of the site specifically for mobile use and created a text-message contest to engage skiers who have smartphones.[18]

Questions for Discussion

1. Of the four categories of variables, which one seems to be the most central to Ski Butternut's segmentation strategy, and why?
2. How is Ski Butternut applying behavioristic variables in its segmentation strategy? Explain your answer.
3. What role do geographic variables play in Ski Butternut's segmentation and targeting?

Case 6.2

Mattel Uses Market Segmentation to Stay on Top

In Mattel's toy chest, Barbie and Draculaura share space with Max Steel, Hot Wheels, American Girl, and Barney. The $6.4 billion company is the global market leader in toys, followed by Lego and Hasbro. Despite intense competition, Mattel wants to retain its market dominance and continue increasing both sales and profits. The toy company aims to stay on top through savvy marketing based on careful targeting and segmentation.

For example, Mattel sees significant revenue potential in targeting boys between the ages of 6 and 11, a customer group that's fascinated with superheroes. Mattel's research findings indicate that boys in this segment like watching videos, reading graphic novels, and playing videogames featuring favorite superheroes. These boys also like discovering new things about their superheroes and figuring out why and how these characters fight their foes.

Mattel targeted this group when it planned a U.S. relaunch of the action figure Max Steel, a superhero toy it has successfully marketed in South America for more than a decade. Max is a high school student who uses his superhero powers to save the world from monsters like Toxcon and Dredd. Months before the new toy appeared in U.S. stores, a Max Steel cartoon premiered on Disney cable channels and a Max Steel website began offering online tournaments, downloadable accessories, and other extras. By the time Max Steel figures and play sets arrived in stores for holiday gift-giving, boys were familiar with the superhero and his background—and were ready to put Max Steel on their wish lists.

The Monster High line of toys and accessories was created for the target market of girls between the ages of 6 and 12 who like vampire romances, zombie stories, and other trendy monster myths. Mattel researchers learned that these girls can be self-conscious about their looks. They're also thinking ahead to high school and to the fun but sometimes stressful school-related social activities.

For this target market, Mattel created a line of unconventional-looking dolls, the children of monsters like Frankenstein. Each has her own personality and personal style, embodying the idea that girls can be attractive even when they don't fit the standard definition of beauty. Instead of Barbie's perfect face and dainty fashions, a Monster High doll has monster features (a werewolf's daughter has wolf ears, a vampire's daughter has prominent canine teeth) and dresses in appealing yet off-beat styles (monster-platform shoes, Goth-style clothing). The target market responded so enthusiastically that Monster High products blossomed into a $1 billion business in less than three years.

© iStockphoto.com/Ivanastar

Barbie's popularity peaked a few years ago, but the brand still has a lot of life left as Mattel refines its targeting to boost worldwide sales beyond $1.3 billion. In China, for example, Mattel originally emphasized Barbie's glamour when communicating with the target market of preteen girls. It opened a glitzy flagship store in Shanghai to showcase Barbie's fashions and accessories—and closed the store when sales fell short of expectations.

As a result of this experience, Mattel decided to take a fresh look at the other target market for dolls, parents and grandparents who buy toys for cherished girls in one-child families. This time, Mattel focused on gift-givers who have high educational aspirations for their daughters and granddaughters. It created new products like Violin Soloist Barbie and Baby Panda Care Barbie, dolls that are good-looking but also have a serious side (musical achievements, saving pandas). Combined with marketing changes to other Mattel brands and products, the company's new targeting strategy helped it to triple sales in China within three years.

Mattel recently decided to target Hispanic American mothers, a fast-growing, increasingly affluent market for all kinds of toys. Its research findings revealed that these mothers either make the buying decisions or are instrumental in the buying decisions for most household purchases. Furthermore, these mothers spend more than non-Hispanic American consumers when they shop for toys—and they tend to be brand-loyal.

Instead of simply translating its English advertisements into Spanish, Mattel dug deeper for cultural insights such as the importance of family and the celebration of Three Kings Day on the twelfth day after Christmas. Based on these findings, Mattel created the marketing theme of "Toy Feliz," meaning "Toy Happy," a twist on the Spanish phrase "Estoy feliz," meaning "I'm happy." Mattel tested the theme in cities with large Hispanic American populations. After the test produced positive results, Mattel began using the theme in television and print ads featuring Barbie, Hot Wheels cars, and other products in its portfolio. It also invited parents to download discount coupons from a special website. Based on the response, Mattel will give this high-potential target market even more marketing attention in the future.[19]

Questions for Discussion

1. Is Mattel using an undifferentiated, concentrated, or differentiated targeting strategy? How do you know?
2. Identify the categories of variables used by Mattel to segment the market for Max Steel action figures. Can you suggest additional variables that Mattel might use in this market?
3. What factors do you think were particularly influential in Mattel's decision to select Hispanic American mothers as a target market?

Strategic Case 3

Home Depot Builds on Research, Segmentation, and Targeting

Nearly 40 years after Home Depot opened its first two stores, the Atlanta-based company is the U.S. market leader in one-stop shopping for home-improvement tools and materials. It rings up $75 billion in annual sales, mainly through more than 2,260 North American stores but also through its online store and mobile-ready website.

Before the rise of Home Depot and its big-box competitors, consumers shopped at small hardware stores where the owners would offer advice and order any obscure tool or odd-sized nail that wasn't in stock. Although do-it-yourselfers might have to wait for out-of-stock or specially-ordered items to be delivered to the store, it was the best option available at the time. Today, however, consumers and contractors all around the country have convenient access to hundreds of thousands of everyday and hard-to-find products stacked on floor-to-ceiling shelves under one giant, warehouse-sized roof.

Over the years, Home Depot has expanded its merchandise selection and service extras to address the needs of specific target markets. One key target market has always been do-it-yourselfers who tackle home projects on their own. Within this market, Home Depot has been giving special marketing attention to women who want to learn how to tackle house repairs or improvements. The retailer is also targeting construction professionals who use Home Depot as a local source of lumber and other building supplies.

© Sergey Yechikov/Shutterstock.com

Getting to Know DIYers

Counting in-store and online purchases, Home Depot completes more than one billion transactions every year. This fills the company's database with all kinds of details concerning who buys what, when, where, and how. Analyzing the data enables Home Depot to keep products in stock where and when they're needed. It also helps the retailer to plan the proper merchandise assortment for each store in each season.

To learn more about its customers, the company regularly conducts shopper surveys and other marketing research studies. Its marketing managers visit stores to hear first-hand from local employees about what their customers like, dislike, return, and request. Reading the reviews of products that customers post on HomeDepot.com also helps the company understand what its customers want and expect.

In addition, its marketers use observation to identify particular customer problems and needs that can be addressed through marketing. For example, the company recently hired a designer to create a new kind of bucket exclusively for the Home Depot. Even though the humble bucket is a mainstay for many household uses, Home Depot wanted to develop something new to showcase its customer-centered innovation. The designer began by observing how people use buckets in and around their homes and gardens. He noticed that women, in particular, have difficulty lifting, carrying, and unloading a conventional bucket full of soil or other contents.

Based on this insight, he redesigned the plastic bucket by forming an indented "grip pocket" on the underside. He also added a large, comfortable handle in addition to a secondary grip opening on one side of the rim. These features make it easier to hold the Big Gripper bucket steady while moving and unloading it, solving a problem experienced by millions of homeowners. The Big Gripper is made in America, adding to the appeal for customers who use their purchases to support U.S. manufacturers.

Watch It, Try It, Do It Yourself

Research findings show that some Home Depot customers are first-timer DIYers and others may have more experience but want to brush up their skills before they undertake a project. To meet these diverse needs, Home Depot offers a variety of free how-to workshops and videos. Consumers can visit the local store for weekly lessons and demonstrations showing everything from how to install closet organizers to how to tile bathroom floors. In "do it herself" workshops, women can test out different power tools, learn how to clean and care for equipment, and get a hands-on feel for common repair techniques. Home Depot even has free children's workshops to teach basic woodworking skills. Participants go home with a handcrafted item such as a racing car, as well as a workshop apron and a special pin. Feedback from these workshops and inquiries about future workshops help Home Depot plan ahead to support customers' informational and instructional needs, which in turn encourages store visits and brand loyalty.

Knowing that many customers can't get to a store workshop or prefer to watch a process several times before trying it themselves at home, Home Depot has also posted dozens of YouTube videos for consumers and professionals. The retailer's free step-by-step demonstrations and product-specific videos have already attracted more than 34 million views. Its thousands of Pinterest pins give customers ideas and inspiration for home improvement, decorating, gardening, and craft projects. By checking the number of views on YouTube and Pinterest, Home Depot can quickly spot the most popular topics and prepare additional videos and posts that fit viewers' interests.

Targeting Online and Mobile Customers

Although online sales are currently a tiny percentage of Home Depot's overall revenues, researchers indicate that time-pressured customers are increasingly interested in browsing online or by cell phone and ordering with a click. Some customers like the ability to buy online and pick up their purchases at the nearest Home Depot store, avoiding any shipping delays. Others are looking for same-day delivery to home or work site, so they can start or finish a project on time.

With speed in mind, retailers like Walmart and Amazon are experimenting with same-day delivery of online purchases. In this competitive environment, Home Depot is investing heavily to improve its back-office technology and expedite shipping so customers receive their orders more quickly. Today, some purchases arrive in just two days but others may not arrive for as long as seven days. In the near future, Home Depot expects to offer two-day delivery by fulfilling online orders from nearby stores. It is also gearing up for same-day delivery of lumber and other materials that contractors and consumers need in a hurry for a project already underway. Customers will have the option of tracking their shipments via updates sent to their cell phones.

For customers on the go, Home Depot's smartphone apps allow convenient access to product specifications, pricing, and customers' reviews. Customers can set up a wish list for products they want from Home Depot. When these customers visit a Home Depot store, sensors detect the app and offer directions to the aisle and shelf where wish-list products are located. The retailer also uses the app to offer coupons on certain products as customers walk through the store. Customers who are not DIYers can find a professional installer or contractor using Home Depot's RedBeacon app.

Targeting the Pros

Purchases and equipment rentals by building professionals account for more than one-third of Home Depot's revenues. The retailer's research findings reveal that these customers are mainly small contractors with no more than five employees and less than $500,000 in annual revenues. For these customers, product availability and price are top concerns. Contractors who buy from Home Depot can schedule delivery at a job site on any day of the week, not just on a weekday. If they run low on lumber or nails, they can use the retailer's Pro app to locate what they need in stock at a nearby Home Depot store, make the purchase, and drive there for immediate pickup. Customers can also consult the app or call Home Depot's experts when they have questions about tools or supplies. If contractors submit an order in advance, the Pro Desk in each store can have all merchandise ready to load when these customers arrive.

The better its contractor customers do, the more they can buy from Home Depot. So to help contractors serve their customers, the retailer offers a number of handy online tools. For example, the retailer has web-based software that contractors can use to prepare estimates and proposals, select specific materials for each job, and calculate costs. Contractors who enroll in the Pro Xtra loyalty program receive special discounts and exclusive offers, among other benefits.

Looking ahead, Home Depot will continue to use marketing research, segmentation, and targeting to increase its customer base, keep customers loyal, and build sales year after year.[20]

Questions for Discussion

1. What hypothesis do you think the product designer formulated before he began researching how consumers use buckets? Do you agree with his decision to use observation rather than another method of collecting primary data? Why?
2. Is Home Depot using differentiated targeting, undifferentiated targeting, or concentrated targeting? How do you know?
3. Which segmentation variables does Home Depot appear to be using to reach consumer markets? Why are these appropriate?
4. Do you think Home Depot is segmenting the contractor market using only business variables or a combination of business and consumer variables? Explain your answer.

NOTES

[1] "The Teenagers of San Antonio Give a Foretaste of America's Hispanic Future," *The Economist*, August 3, 2013, p. 29; Leticia Gutierrez, "Quinceañeras Are Big Business," *Appeal-Democrat (Marysville, CA)*, June 3, 2013, www.appeal-democrat.com (accessed June 3, 2013); Marisa Gerber, "A Fiesta Fit for a Princess," *Los Angeles Times,* August 8, 2013, www.latimes.com/news/local/la-me-quinceanera-dance-20130808-dto,0,315090.htmlstory#axzz2k1Wt10nT (accessed November 7, 2013).

[2] A. Powlowski, "Enterprise Lets 'Easy Rider' Wannabes Rent Motorcycles in Vegas," *NBC News*, October 21, 2013, www.nbcnews.com/business/enterprise-lets-easy-rider-wannabes-rent-motorcycles-vegas-8C11417912 (accessed November 7, 2013).

[3] Cheerwine, www.cheerwine.com (accessed December 17, 2013).

[4] American Community Survey, U.S. Census Bureau, 2011, www.census.gov/compendia/statab/cats/population.html (accessed November 7, 2013).

[5] Elizabeth Sweet, "Guys and Dolls No More?" *The New York Times*, December 21, 2012, www.nytimes.com/2012/12/23/opinion/sunday/gender-based-toy-marketing-returns.html (accessed November 7, 2013).

[6] American Community Survey, U.S. Census Bureau, 2011, www.census.gov/compendia/statab/cats/population.html (accessed November 7, 2013).

[7] "Marketing to Women—Quick Facts," She-Conomy, http://she-conomy.com/report/marketing-to-women-quick-facts (accessed November 7, 2013).

[8] "FAQ," Iman Cosmetics, www.imancosmetics.com/faq (accessed November 2, 2013).

[9] Natasha Singer, "Secret E-Scores Chart Consumers' Buying Power," *The New York Times*, August 19, 2012, www.nytimes.com/2012/08/19/business/electronic-scores-rank-consumers-by-potential-value.html (accessed November 7, 2013).

[10] "Households and Families: 2010," U.S. Census Briefs, www.census.gov/prod/cen2010/briefs/c2010br-14.pdf (accessed November 7, 2013).

[11] "My Best Segments," Nielsen, www.claritas.com/MyBestSegments/Default.jsp?ID=0&menuOption=home&pageName=Home (accessed November 7, 2013).

[12] FEED, www.feedprojects.com (accessed November 1, 2013).

[13] Joseph T. Plummer, "The Concept and Application of Life Style Segmentation," *Journal of Marketing* (January 1974): 33.

[14] Nielsen PRIZM, www.claritas.com/MyBestSegments/Default.jsp?ID=70&pageName=Learn%2BMore&menuOption=learnmore (accessed November 7, 2013).

[15] Philip Kotler and Kevin Keller, *Marketing Management*, 14th ed. (Englewood Cliffs, NJ: Prentice Hall, 2012).

[16] Charles W. Chase, Jr., "Selecting the Appropriate Forecasting Method," *Journal of Business Forecasting* (Fall 1997): 2, 23, 28–29.

[17] Annia Gasparro, "McDonald's Joins with Kraft to Sell Packaged McCafé Coffee in U.S. Stores," *The Wall Street Journal*, October 30, 2013, http://online.wsj.com/news/articles/SB10001424052702304527504579168250062619012?KEYWORDS=mccafe (accessed November 7, 2013).

[18] Jeanette DeForge, "Skiing Areas Spending Millions to Upgrade Snowmaking," *The Republication (Springfield, MA)*, December 4, 2013, www.masslive.com (accessed Jan 20, 2014); Kathleen Mitchell, "Great Barrington Has Become a True Destination," *BusinessWest,* August 26, 2013, www.businesswest.com (accessed Jan 20, 2014); Ski Butternut website, www.skibutternut.com (accessed Jan 20, 2014); "Ski Butternut" Cengage video.

[19] Shareen Pathak, "Competition from Everywhere Has Hasbro, Mattel in Toyland Showdown," *Advertising Age*, December 2, 2013, www.adage.com (accessed Jan 20, 2014); Tanzina Vega, "Spanish Message with One Word That Needs No Translation," *The New York Times,* October 31, 2013, www.nytimes.com (accessed Jan 20, 2014); Mark J. Miller, "Mattel Localizes Barbie for Education-Focused China Market," *Brand Channel,* November 8, 2013, www.brandchannel.com (accessed Jan 20, 2014); Abram Brown, "Life After Barbie," *Forbes,* May 6, 2013, www.forbes.com (accessed Jan 20, 2014).

[20] Joseph Flaherty, "How Home Depot Copied Apple to Build an Ingenious New Bucket," *Wired*, December 31, 2013, www.wired.com/design/2013/12/home-depot-reinvents-buckets (accessed January 15, 2014); Shelly Banjo, "Home Depot Looks to Offer Same-Day Shipping," *The Wall Street Journal,* December 11, 2013, http://online.wsj.com/news/articles/SB10001424052702303932504579251782609141934 (accessed January 15, 2014); Elizabeth Dwoskin and Greg Bensinger, "Tracking Technology Sheds Light on Shopper Habits," *The Wall Street Journal,* December 9, 2013, http://online.wsj.com/news/articles/SB100014240527023033329045792304010308 (accessed January 15, 2014); Shelly Banjo, "Home Depot Beats Wal-Mart, Target Online," *The Wall Street Journal,* November 6, 2013, http://blogs.wsj.com/corporate-intelligence/2013/11/06/home-depot-beats-wal-mart-target-online (accessed January 15, 2014); Geoff Colvin, "Housing Is Back—and So Is Home Depot," *Fortune,* September 26, 2013, http://money.cnn.com/2013/09/19/leadership/home-depot-blake.pr.fortune (accessed January 15, 2014); Chantal Tode, "Home Depot's Redbeacon Escalates App Marketing to Drive Mobile Business," *Mobile Commerce Daily,* August 6, 2013, www.mobilecommercedaily.com/home-depot%E2%80%99s-redbeacon-escalates-app-marketing-to-drive-mobile-business (accessed January 15, 2014).

Feature Notes

[a] David Fickling and Heesu Lee, "Crying Kids on Planes Spawn Child-Free Zones, Flight Nannies," *Bloomberg*, September 13, 2013, www.bloomberg.com (accessed Feb 3, 2014); Ben Mutzabaugh, "Another Airline Rolls Out a 'No-Kids' Zone," *USA Today,* August 26, 2013, www.usatoday.com (accessed Feb 3, 2014); Micheline Maynard, "Should Babies Be Banned from First Class?" *Forbes,* September 15, 2013, www.forbes.com (accessed Feb 3, 2014).

[b] Bill Mickey, "Rodale Launches Standalone E-Commerce Site, Rodale's," *Folio,* May 20, 2013, www.foliomag.com (accessed Feb 11, 2014); Rachel Strugatz, "Rodale Gets into Retail," *WWD*, May 13, 2013, www.wwd.com (accessed Feb 11, 2014); Matthew Flamm, "Rodale Inc.'s Rocky Road," *Crain's New York Business,* December 2, 2012, www.crainsnewyork.com; www.rodales.com.

part 4

Buying Behavior, Global Marketing, and Digital Marketing

PART 4 continues our focus on the customer. Understanding elements that affect buying decisions enables marketers to analyze customers' needs and evaluate how specific marketing strategies can satisfy those needs. CHAPTER 7 examines consumer buying behavior, the decision processes, and factors that influence buying decisions. CHAPTER 8 stresses business markets, organizational buyers, the buying center, and the organizational buying decision process. CHAPTER 9 looks at how marketers can reach global markets and the actions, involvement, and strategies that marketers employ internationally. CHAPTER 10 examines how online social networking and digital media have affected marketing strategies with the creation of new communication channels and the consumer behavior related to these emerging technologies and trends.

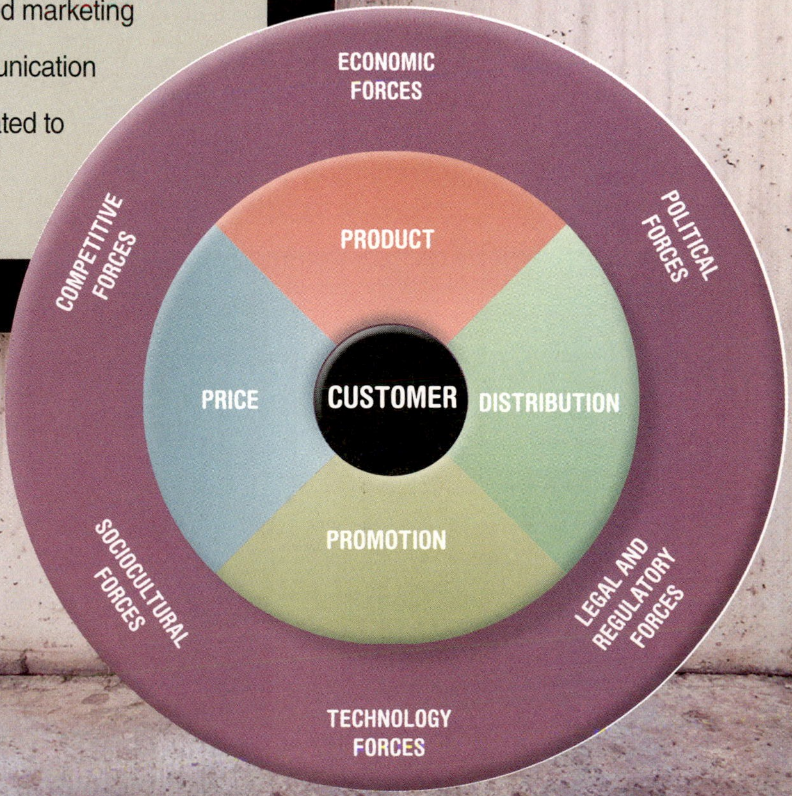

chapter 7

Consumer Buying Behavior

© iStockphoto.com/Yuri

OBJECTIVES

- **7-1** Recognize the stages of the consumer buying decision process.
- **7-2** Describe the types of consumer decision making and the level of involvement.
- **7-3** Explain how situational influences may affect the consumer buying decision process.
- **7-4** Identify the psychological influences that may affect the consumer buying decision process.
- **7-5** Describe the social influences that may affect the consumer buying decision process.
- **7-6** Discuss consumer misbehavior.

MARKETING INSIGHTS

Glasses Are Cool Again, Thanks to Google

One of the pioneers of the Internet Age, Google has also earned a reputation for groundbreaking technology in cell phone systems, mapping, and many other fields. So when the Silicon Valley firm held a contest to select the first people to try Google Glass, an Internet-connected computer device mounted on eyeglass frames, it was inundated with entries. This innovative product wasn't yet available to the public, and Google wanted to get it into the hands of influential people like software developers, educators, sports champions, television stars, podcasters, politicians, and others interested in technology trends—and trendiness.

Through social media, Google asked entrants to describe, in 50 words or less, how they would use Google Glass. The company then selected 10,000 Glass Explorers to receive the futuristic-looking glasses with built-in Wi-Fi and Bluetooth connections, at the pre-release price of $1,500. The company also loaned Google Glass to film schools and other educational institutions so teachers and students could experiment with the product. Within weeks, social and traditional media coverage of the Explorers' experiences showed the world what it was like to use the voice-activated Google Glass to take videos or photos, check the weather, get directions, and much more.

Six months after the contest ended, Google took Google Glass on a national tour to showcase its capabilities. Participants posted photos on Twitter and Instagram, adding to the buzz and helping to shape public attitudes and perceptions ahead of the product's official launch in 2014.[1]

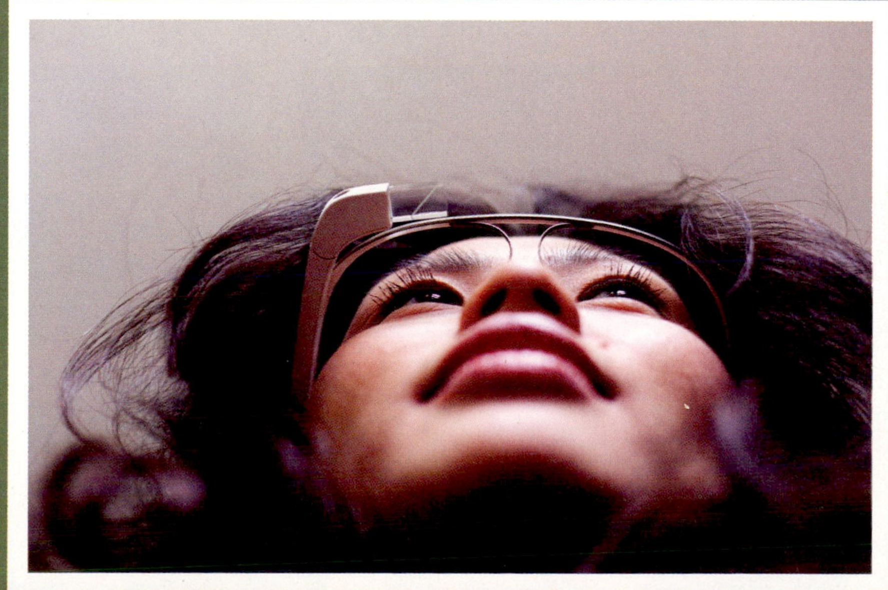

Google and many other online, digital, and traditional marketers go to great lengths to understand their customers' needs and gain a better grasp of customers' **buying behavior**, which is the decision processes and actions of people involved in buying and using products. **Consumer buying behavior** refers to the buying behavior of ultimate consumers—those who purchase products for personal or household use and not for business purposes. Marketers attempt to understand buying behavior for several reasons. First, customers' overall opinions and attitudes toward a firm's products have a great impact on the firm's success. Second, as we saw in Chapter 1, the marketing concept stresses that a firm should create a marketing mix that meets customers' needs. To find out what satisfies consumers, marketers must examine the main influences on what, where, when, and how they buy. Third, by gaining a deeper understanding of the factors that affect buying behavior, marketers are better-positioned to predict how consumers will respond to marketing strategies.

In this chapter, we first examine the major stages of the consumer buying decision process, beginning with problem recognition, information search, and evaluation of alternatives, and proceeding through purchase and postpurchase evaluation. We follow this with an examination of how the customer's level of involvement affects the type of decision making they use and discuss the types of consumer decision-making processes. Next, we examine situational influences—surroundings, time, purchase reason, and buyer's mood and condition—that affect purchasing decisions. We go on to consider psychological influences on purchasing decisions: perception, motives, learning, attitudes, personality and self-concept, and lifestyles. Next, we discuss social influences that affect buying behavior, including roles, family, reference groups and opinion leaders, social classes, and culture and subcultures. We conclude with a discussion of consumer misbehavior.

buying behavior The decision processes and actions of people involved in buying and using products

consumer buying behavior The decision processes and purchasing activities of people who purchase products for personal or household use and not for business purposes

consumer buying decision process A five-stage purchase decision process that includes problem recognition, information search, evaluation of alternatives, purchase, and postpurchase evaluation

7-1 CONSUMER BUYING DECISION PROCESS

The **consumer buying decision process**, shown in Figure 7.1, includes five stages: problem recognition, information search, evaluation of alternatives, purchase, and postpurchase evaluation. Before we examine each stage, consider these important points. First, as shown in Figure 7.1, this process can be affected by numerous influences, which are categorized

Figure 7.1 Consumer Buying Decisions Process and Possible Influences on the Process

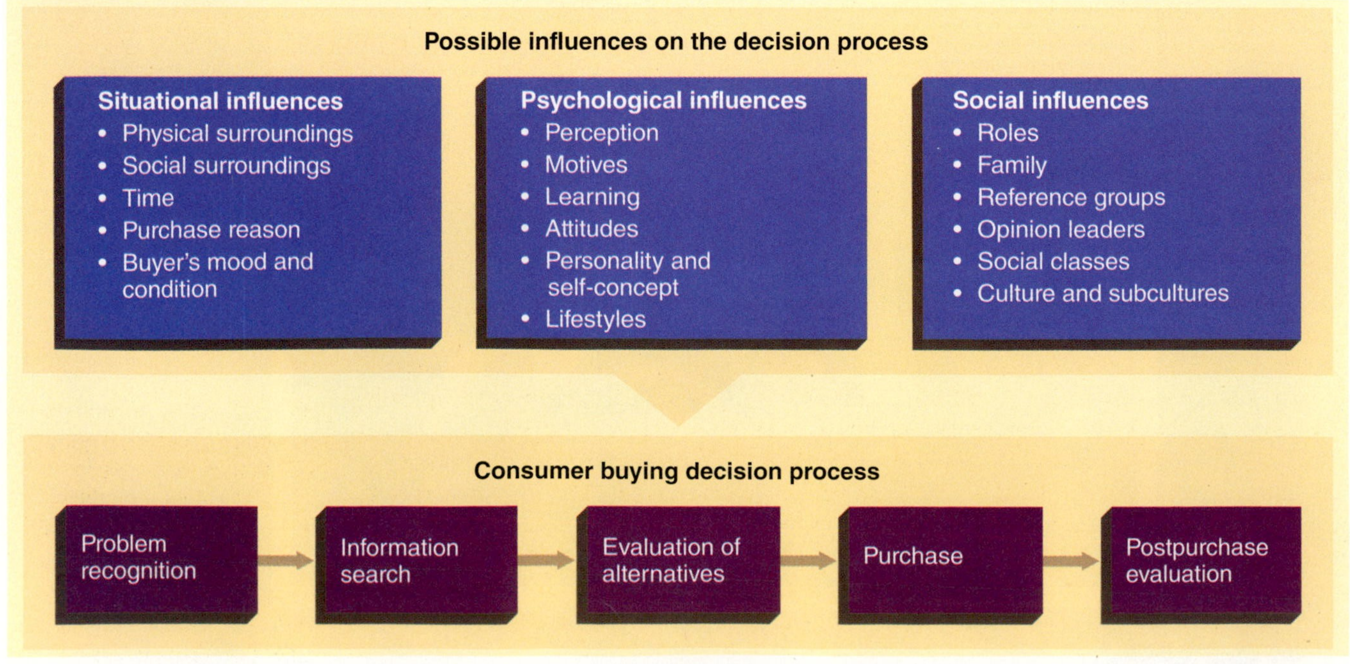

as situational, psychological, and social. Second, the actual act of purchasing is usually not the first stage of the process. Third, not all decision processes lead to a purchase—individuals can end the process at any stage. Finally, not all consumer decisions include all five stages.

7-1a Problem Recognition

Problem recognition occurs when a buyer becomes aware of a difference between a desired state and an actual condition. The speed of consumer problem recognition can be quite rapid or rather slow. Sometimes a person has a problem or need but is unaware of it. Marketers use sales personnel, advertising, and packaging to help trigger recognition of such needs or problems. Consider this advertisement for Amazon's Kindle Fire tablet computer. Such devices can be a great resource for children, allowing them to learn and grow. However, many parents are concerned with children's access to games and non-educational activities. The Kindle Fire solves this problem with its Free Time feature, which allows parents to set a time limit on games and videos, while leaving unlimited reading time.

© Amazon

Problem Recognition
This advertisement is attempting to stimulate problem recognition by calling parents' attention to the time-limiting feature on the Kindle Fire.

7-1b Information Search

After recognizing the problem or need, a buyer will decide whether to pursue satisfying that need. If the consumer chooses to move forward, he or she will next search for product information to help resolve the problem or satisfy the need. If, for example, a consumer realizes that he needs to back up the files on his computer, he will conduct a search on different products that could fulfill this need.

An information search has two aspects. In an **internal search**, buyers search their memories for information about products that might solve their problem. If they cannot retrieve enough information from memory to make a decision, they seek additional information from outside sources in an **external search**. The external search may focus on communication with friends or relatives, comparison of available brands and prices, marketer-dominated sources, and/or public sources. An individual's personal contacts—friends, relatives, and coworkers—often are influential sources of information because the person trusts and respects them. However, consumers should be wary not to overestimate the product knowledge of family and friends. Consumers may also use marketer-dominated sources of information, such as salespeople, advertising, websites, package labeling, and in-store demonstrations and displays because they typically require little effort. The Internet has become a major resource during the consumer buying decision process, with its many sources for product descriptions and reviews and the ease of comparing prices. Buyers can also obtain information from independent sources: government reports, news presentations, publications such as *Consumer Reports*, and reports from product-testing organizations, for instance. Consumers frequently view information from these sources as credible because of their factual and unbiased nature.

Repetition, a technique well-known to advertisers, increases consumers' information retention and recall. When they see or hear an advertising message for the first time, recipients may not grasp all its important details, but they recall more particulars as the message is repeated. However, marketers should be wary not to repeat a message too many times, as consumers can grow tired of it and begin to respond unfavorably. Information can be presented verbally, numerically, or visually. Marketers pay great attention to the visual components of their advertising materials.

internal search An information search in which buyers search their memories for information about products that might solve their problem

external search An information search in which buyers seek information from sources other than their memories

7-1c Evaluation of Alternatives

A successful information search within a product category yields a group of brands that a buyer views as possible alternatives. This group of brands is sometimes called a **consideration set** (or an *evoked set*). Consumers assign a greater value to a brand they have heard of than to one they have not—even when they do not know anything else about the brand other than the name. A consideration set of computers might include laptop, notebook, and tablet computers from Dell, Toshiba, and Apple. A consumer will probably lean initially toward the one with which he or she is most familiar, or that his or her friends prefer, before conducting any additional searches.

To assess the products in a consideration set, the buyer uses **evaluative criteria**: objective characteristics (such as the size) and subjective characteristics (such as style) that are important to him or her. Consider that one buyer may want a large display, whereas another may want a computer with a lot of memory. The buyer assigns a certain level of importance to each criterion. However, some features and characteristics carry more weight than others, depending on consumer preferences. The buyer rates, and eventually ranks, brands in the consideration set using the selected evaluative criteria. It is possible that the evaluation stage may yield no brand the buyer is willing to purchase. In that case, a further information search may be necessary.

Marketers may influence consumers' evaluations by *framing* the alternatives—that is, describing the alternatives and their attributes in a certain manner. Framing can make a characteristic seem more important to a consumer and facilitate its recall from memory. For instance, by stressing a car's superior comfort and safety features over those of a competitor's, a carmaker can direct consumers' attention toward these points. You have experienced the framing effect if you have ever walked into a gourmet grocery or high-end clothing store where the displays make the products seem so appealing that you feel you just have to buy them, only to return home and be less satisfied than you were in the store. Framing has a stronger influence on the decision processes of inexperienced buyers. If the evaluation of alternatives yields one or more brands that the consumer is willing to buy, he or she is ready to move on to the next stage of the decision process: the purchase.

7-1d Purchase

In the purchase stage, the consumer chooses to buy the product or brand yielded by the evaluation of alternatives. However, product availability may influence which brand is ultimately purchased. If the brand that ranked highest in evaluation is unavailable and the buyer is unwilling to wait until it is available again, the buyer may choose to purchase the brand that ranked second. So, if a consumer is at the mall shopping for jeans and the preferred Levis in her size are out of stock but the Lucky brand jeans are not, the consumer may opt to purchase the Lucky brand to save another trip to the mall later.

During this stage, buyers also pick the seller from which they will buy the product—it could be a specific retail shop, chain, or online retailer. The choice of seller may affect final product selection and, therefore, the terms of sale, which, if negotiable, are determined at this stage. Consumers also settle other issues, such as price, delivery, warranties, maintenance agreements, installation, and credit arrangements, at this time. Finally, the actual purchase takes place (although the consumer can still decide to terminate the buying decision process even at this late stage).

7-1e Postpurchase Evaluation

After the purchase, the buyer evaluates the product to ascertain if its actual performance meets expected levels. Many criteria used in evaluating alternatives are applied again during postpurchase evaluation in order to make a comparison. The outcome of this stage is either satisfaction or dissatisfaction, which influences whether the consumer will repurchase the brand or product, complain to the seller, or communicate positively or negatively with other possible buyers.

The postpurchase evaluation stage is especially important for high-priced items. Shortly after the purchase of an expensive product, evaluation may result in **cognitive dissonance**, which involves doubts in the buyer's mind about whether purchasing the product was the right decision.

consideration set A group of brands within a product category that a buyer views as alternatives for possible purchase

evaluative criteria Objective and subjective product characteristics that are important to a buyer

cognitive dissonance A buyer's doubts shortly after a purchase about whether the decision was the right one

Cognitive dissonance is most likely to arise when a person recently bought an expensive, high-involvement product that is found to be lacking some of the desirable features of competing brands. A buyer who is experiencing cognitive dissonance may attempt to return the product or may seek out positive information, such as reviews, to justify choosing it. Marketers sometimes attempt to reduce cognitive dissonance by having salespeople telephone or e-mail recent purchasers to make sure they are satisfied with their new purchases. Salespeople may send recent buyers results of studies showing that other consumers are very satisfied with the brand.

As Figure 7.1 shows, three major categories of influences are believed to affect the consumer buying decision process: situational, psychological, and social. In the remainder of this chapter, we focus on these influences. Although we discuss each major influence separately, their effects on the consumer decision process are interrelated.

7-2 TYPES OF CONSUMER DECISION MAKING AND LEVEL OF INVOLVEMENT

To acquire products that satisfy their current and future needs, consumers engage in different types of decision-making processes that vary depending on the nature of the product. The amount of effort, both mental and physical, that buyers expend in solving problems also varies considerably with the cost and type of product. A major determinant of the type of decision-making process employed depends on the customer's **level of involvement**, which is the degree of interest in a product and the importance the individual places on that product. High-involvement products tend to be those that are visible to others (e.g., real estate, high-end electronics, or automobiles) and are more expensive. High-importance issues, such as health care, are also associated with high levels of involvement. Low-involvement products are much less expensive and have less associated social risk (e.g., grocery or drugstore items).

A person's interest in a product or product category that is ongoing and long-term is referred to as *enduring involvement.* Most consumers have an enduring involvement with very few activities or items—the product categories in which they have the most interest. Many consumers, for instance, have an enduring involvement with Apple products, a brand that inspires loyalty and trust. Consumers will expend a great deal of effort to purchase and learn about Apple products, such as waiting in line for the latest iPhone release and reading articles about the various features of the newest iPad. In contrast, *situational involvement* is temporary and dynamic, and results from a particular set of circumstances, such as the sudden need to buy a new bathroom faucet after the current one starts leaking and will not stop. For a short period of time the consumer will research faucet models, retailers, and prices, but will settle on a choice relatively quickly because the consumer needs a functional bathroom as soon as possible. Once the purchase is made, the consumer's interest and involvement taper off quickly. Consumer involvement may be attached to product categories (e.g., sports), loyalty to a specific brand, interest in a specific advertisement (e.g., a funny commercial) or a medium (e.g., a television show), or to certain decisions and behaviors (e.g., a love of shopping). Interest, such as finding an advertisement entertaining, does not necessarily mean the consumer will become involved with the brand. It may not satisfy a need the customer currently has, or he or she may be loyal to another brand. There are three types of consumer decision making, which vary in involvement level and other factors: routinized response behavior, limited decision making, or extended decision making (Table 7.1).

A consumer uses **routinized response behavior** when buying frequently purchased, low-cost items that require very little search-and-decision effort. A consumer may have a brand preference, but will be satisfied with several brands in the product class. Typically, low-involvement products are bought through routinized response behavior—that is, almost automatically. For example, most buyers spend little time or effort selecting soft drinks or chips.

Buyers engage in **limited decision making** when they buy products occasionally, or from unfamiliar brands in a familiar product category. This type of decision making requires

level of involvement An individual's degree of interest in a product and the importance of the product for that person

routinized response behavior A consumer decision-making process used when buying frequently purchased, low-cost items that require very little search-and-decision effort

limited decision making A consumer decision-making process used when purchasing products occasionally or needing information about an unfamiliar brand in a familiar product category

Table 7.1 Consumer Decision Making

	Routinized Response	Limited	Extended
Product cost	Low	Low to moderate	High
Search effort	Little	Little to moderate	Extensive
Time spent	Short	Short to medium	Lengthy
Brand preference	More than one is acceptable, although one may be preferred	Several	Varies, usually many

slightly more time for information gathering and deliberation. For instance, if Procter & Gamble introduces a new Pantene brand shampoo, interested buyers will seek additional information about the product, perhaps by asking a friend who has used it, watching a commercial about it, or visiting the company's website, before making a trial purchase.

The most complex type of decision making, **extended decision making**, occurs with high-involvement, unfamiliar, expensive, or infrequently purchased items—for instance, a car, home, or college education. The buyer uses many criteria to evaluate alternative brands or choices and spends much time seeking information and deciding before making the purchase.

extended decision making A consumer decision-making process employed when purchasing unfamiliar, expensive, or infrequently bought products

Purchase of a particular product does not elicit the same type of decision-making process every time. We may engage in extended decision making the first time we buy a product, but find that limited decision making suffices when we buy it again. If a routinely purchased brand is discontinued or no longer satisfies us, we may use limited or extended decision making to switch to a new brand. Thus, if we notice that the brand of pain reliever we normally buy is no longer working well, we may seek out a different brand through limited decision making. Most consumers occasionally make purchases solely on impulse and not on the

© iStockphoto.com/DNY59

Low-Involvement Products
Soft drinks, such as Coca-Cola, are low-involvement products because they are inexpensive and purchased frequently. When buying soft drinks, consumers usually employ routinized response behavior.

basis of any of these three decision-making processes. **Impulse buying** involves no conscious planning and stems from a powerful urge to buy something immediately.

7-3 SITUATIONAL INFLUENCES ON THE BUYING DECISION PROCESS

Situational influences result from circumstances, time, and location that affect the consumer buying decision process. Imagine buying an automobile tire after noticing, while washing your car, that the current tire is badly worn. This is a different experience from buying a tire right after a blowout on the highway spoils your road trip because in the prior scenario you can take the time to conduct research and select the best product for your needs. Situational factors can influence the buyer during any stage of the consumer buying decision process and may cause the individual to shorten, lengthen, or terminate the process. Situational factors can be classified into five categories: physical surroundings, social surroundings, time perspective, reason for purchase, and the buyer's momentary mood and condition.[2]

impulse buying An unplanned buying behavior resulting from a powerful urge to buy something immediately

situational influences Influences that result from circumstances, time, and location that affect the consumer buying decision process

Physical surroundings include location, store atmosphere, scents, sounds, lighting, weather, and other factors in the physical environment in which the decision process occurs. Retail chains try to design their store environment and layout in a way that makes shopping as enjoyable and easy as possible, so consumers are more inclined to linger and make purchases. Look at the advertisement for Movado watches, for example. Movado is an exclusive Swiss watch brand, with products selling for hundreds or thousands of dollars. Retail outlets where Movado products are sold are likely to encourage purchases through situational influences, such as appealing displays, highly-attentive salespeople, lighting calculated to enhance the look of the watches, and strategic positioning of products to catch consumers' eyes.

However, dimensions such as weather, traffic sounds, and odors are clearly beyond the marketers' control in some settings. General climatic conditions, for example, may influence a customer's decision to buy a specific type of vehicle (e.g., an SUV) with certain features (e.g., a four-wheel drive). Current weather conditions, or other external factors, may be either encouraging or discouraging to consumers when they seek out specific products.

Social surroundings include characteristics and interactions of others who are present during a purchase decision, such as friends, relatives, salespeople, and other customers. Buyers may feel pressured to behave in a certain way because they are in a public place such as a restaurant, store, or sports arena. Thoughts about who will be around when the product is used or consumed are another dimension of the social setting. Negative elements of physical surroundings, such as an overcrowded store or an argument between a customer and a salesperson, may cause consumers to leave the store before purchasing anything.

The time dimension influences the buying decision process in several ways. It takes varying amounts of time to progress through the steps of the buying decision process, including learning about, searching for, purchasing, and using a product. Time also plays a major role when consumers consider the frequency of product use, the length of time required to use it, and the overall product life. Other time dimensions

Situational Influences
Movado watches are sold at high-end department stores and jewelry stores, where situational influences are likely to affect your purchase decision.

that can influence purchases include time of day, day of the week or month, seasons, and holidays. Thus, a customer under time constraints is likely to either make a quick purchase decision or delay a decision.

The reason for purchase involves what exactly the product purchase should accomplish and for whom. Generally, consumers purchase an item for their own use, for household use, or as a gift. Purchase choices are likely to vary depending on the reason. For example, you will likely choose a nicer product brand for a gift than you would for yourself. If you own a Mont Blanc pen, which is a very expensive brand, it is likely that you received it as a gift from someone very close to you.

The buyer's moods (e.g., anger, anxiety, or contentment) or conditions (e.g., fatigue, illness, or having cash on hand) may also affect the consumer buying decision process. Such moods or conditions are momentary and occur immediately before the situation where a buying decision will be made. They can affect a person's ability and desire to search for or receive information, or seek and evaluate alternatives. Moods can also significantly influence a consumer's postpurchase evaluation. If you are happy immediately after purchase, you may be more likely to attribute the mood to the product and will judge it favorably.

psychological influences Factors that in part determine people's general behavior, thus influencing their behavior as consumers

perception The process of selecting, organizing, and interpreting information inputs to produce meaning

information inputs Sensations received through sight, taste, hearing, smell, and touch

selective exposure The process by which some inputs are selected to reach awareness and others are not

7-4 PSYCHOLOGICAL INFLUENCES ON THE BUYING DECISION PROCESS

Psychological influences partly determine people's general behavior and thus influence their behavior as consumers. Primary psychological influences on consumer behavior are perception, motives, learning, attitudes, personality and self-concept, and lifestyles. Even though these psychological factors operate internally, they are affected strongly by external social forces.

Fish or Fowl?
Do you see fish or birds?

7-4a Perception

People perceive the same event or thing at the same time in different ways. When you first look at the illustration, for instance, do you see fish or birds? Similarly, the same individual may perceive an item in different ways at different times. **Perception** is the process of selecting, organizing, and interpreting information inputs to produce meaning. **Information inputs** are sensations received through sight, taste, hearing, smell, and touch. When we hear an advertisement on the radio, see a friend, smell food cooking at a restaurant, or touch a product, we receive information inputs. Some inputs are more effective in attracting attention than others. For instance, research findings have shown that advertisements for food items that appeal to multiple senses at once are more effective than ones that focus on taste alone.[3] Cinnabon has recognized the power of its cinnamon roll flavor and aroma, and even lends its signature scent and brand to non-food items, such as car fresheners. Most people have positive associations with the warm scent of cinnamon, sugar, and butter, and marketers have found that the brand's scent can successfully sell a wide variety of products.[4]

Selection is the first step in the perceptual process. Perception can be interpreted different ways because, although we constantly receive pieces of information, only some reach our awareness. We would be completely overwhelmed if we paid equal attention to all sensory inputs, so we select some and ignore others. This process is called **selective exposure** because an individual selects (mostly unconsciously) which inputs will reach awareness. If you are concentrating on this paragraph, you probably are not aware that cars outside are making noise, that the room light is on, that a song is playing on your MP3 player, or even that you are touching the page. Even though you receive these inputs, they do not reach your awareness until they are brought to your attention. An individual's current set of needs affects selective exposure. Information inputs that relate to one's strongest needs are more likely to reach conscious awareness. It is not by chance that many fast-food commercials are aired near mealtimes. Customers are more likely to pay attention to these advertisements at times when they are hungry.

The selective nature of perception may also result in two other conditions: selective distortion and selective retention. **Selective distortion** is changing or twisting received information. It occurs when a person receives information inconsistent with personal feelings or beliefs and he or she selectively interprets the information, changing its meaning to align more closely with expectations. Selective distortion explains why people will reject logical information, even when presented with supporting evidence. Selective distortion can both help and hurt marketers. For instance, a consumer may become loyal to a brand and remain loyal, even when confronted with evidence that another brand is superior. However, selective distortion can also lessen the impact of the message on the individual substantially. In **selective retention**, a person remembers information inputs that support personal feelings and beliefs and forgets inputs that do not. After hearing a sales presentation and leaving a store, for example, a customer may quickly forget many selling points if they contradict personal beliefs or preconceived notions about a product.

The second step in the process of perception is perceptual organization. Information inputs that reach awareness are not received in an organized form. To produce meaning, an individual must organize and integrate new information with what is already stored in memory. People use several methods to achieve this. One method is called *figure-ground*. When an individual uses figure-ground, a portion of the information inputs that reach awareness stands out as the figure and others become the background. For example, when looking back at the image of the fish and fowl, when you mentally allow the fish to stand out as the figure, the birds become the background. If you allow the birds to stand out as the figure, the fish become the background. Another method, called *closure*, occurs when a person fills in missing information in a way that conforms to a pattern or statement. In an attempt to draw attention to its brand, a marketer may capitalize on closure by using incomplete images, sounds, or statements in advertisements.

Interpretation, the third step in the perceptual process, is the assignment of meaning to what has been organized. A person interprets information according to what he or she expects or what is familiar. For this reason, a manufacturer who changes a product or its package may face consumer backlash from customers looking for the old, familiar product or package and who do not recognize, or do not like, the new one. In response to research indicating that men are doing more grocery shopping than in the past, many companies are redesigning packaging to appeal more to men—which may be a risky move if loyal consumers do not like the redesigns. Hamburger Helper, for instance, has rebranded to appeal to male shoppers by designing a new box that features large font, dark colors, and emphasizes the meatiness of the food. It also includes the word "ultimate" in the title of the dishes, because researchers revealed it to be a male buzzword with positive associations. Time will tell whether female consumers are turned off by the more male-focused approach.[5] Unless a product or package change is accompanied by a promotional program that makes people aware of the change, an organization may suffer a sales decline.

Although marketers cannot control buyers' perceptions, they often try to influence them. Several problems may arise from such attempts, however. First, a consumer's perceptual process may operate such that a seller's information never reaches the target. For example, a buyer may block out and not notice an advertisement in a magazine. Second, a buyer may receive information but perceive it differently from what was intended, as occurs in selective distortion. For instance, when a toothpaste producer advertises that "35 percent of the people who use this toothpaste have fewer cavities," a customer could potentially infer that 65 percent of users have more cavities. Third, a buyer who perceives information inputs to be inconsistent with prior beliefs is likely to forget the information quickly, as is the case with selective retention.

selective distortion An individual's changing or twisting of information that is inconsistent with personal feelings or beliefs

selective retention Remembering information inputs that support personal feelings and beliefs and forgetting inputs that do not

7-4b Motives

A **motive** is an internal energizing force that directs a person's activities toward satisfying needs or achieving goals. Buyers are affected by a set of motives rather than by just one. At any point in time, certain motives will have a stronger influence on the person than others will. For example, the sensation of being cold is a strong motivator on the decision to purchase a new coat, making the motivation more urgent in the winter than it is in the summer. Motives can be physical feelings, states of mind, or emotions. Some motives may help an individual achieve his or her goals, whereas others create barriers to achievement. Motives also affect the direction and intensity of behavior.

With online shopping increasing annually, marketers have increasingly found a need to understand the motives of online shoppers and how the new shopping medium affects their buying behavior. A research project on this marketing topic divided online shoppers by two basic motivations: utilitarian (or functional) shoppers and hedonic (or nonfunctional) shoppers. Utilitarian consumers shop online because it is a useful and fast way to purchase certain items, whereas hedonic consumers shop online because it is a fun and enjoyable way to find bargains. The researchers found that hedonic consumers spent more time on the Internet for each purchase and shopped online more often than utilitarian consumers. Hedonic consumers were also more likely to make impulse buys online and engage in bidding wars on sites like eBay.[6] Abraham Maslow, an American psychologist, conceived a theory of motivation based on a hierarchy of needs. According to Maslow, humans seek to satisfy five levels of needs, from most to least basic to survival, as shown in Figure 7.2. This pyramid is known as **Maslow's hierarchy of needs**. Maslow proposed that people are constantly striving to move up the hierarchy, fulfilling one level of needs, then aspiring to fulfill the next.

At the most basic level are *physiological needs*, requirements for survival such as food, water, sex, clothing, and shelter, which people try to satisfy first. Food and beverage marketers often appeal to physiological needs, such as sex appeal or hunger. Carl's Jr. is famous for its commercials of lingerie models eating burgers, appealing to two physiological needs at once—hunger and sex. Crest toothpaste, for instance, appeals to the physiological need to have a healthy mouth.

At the next level are *safety needs*, which include security and freedom from physical and emotional pain and suffering. Life insurance, automobile air bags, carbon monoxide detectors, vitamins, and decay-fighting toothpastes are products that consumers purchase to ensure their safety needs are met.

Next are *social needs*—the human requirements for love and affection and a sense of belonging. Advertisements for beauty products, jewelry, and even cars often suggest that purchasing these products will bring love and social acceptance. Certain types of clothing, such

motive An internal energizing force that directs a person's behavior toward satisfying needs or achieving goals

Maslow's hierarchy of needs The five levels of needs that humans seek to satisfy, from most to least important

Figure 7.2 Maslow's Hierarchy of Needs

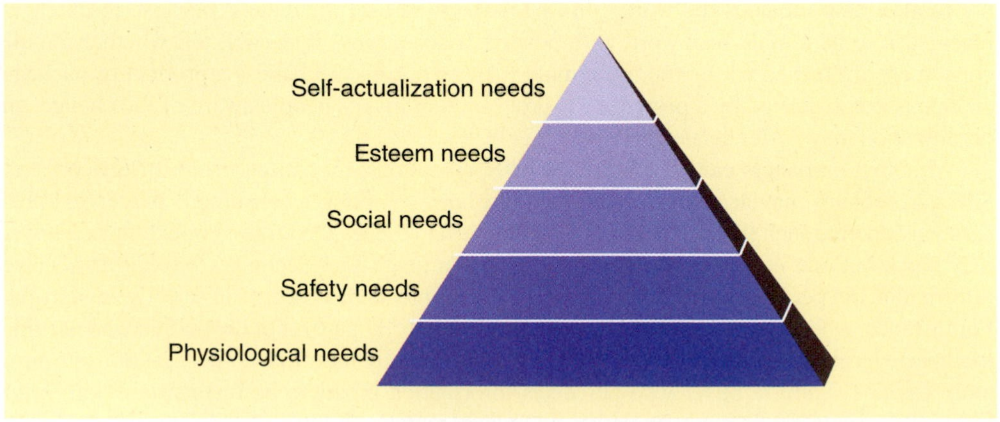

Safety Needs
Crest brand toothpaste appeals to safety needs because it fights tooth decay, resulting in better health for the user.

as items emblazoned with logos or slogans, appeal to the customer's need to belong by displaying his or her affinity for popular brands.

At the level of *esteem needs*, people require respect and recognition from others as well as self-esteem, a sense of one's own worth. Owning a Lexus automobile, purchasing a Chanel handbag, or flying first class can satisfy esteem needs. Many consumers are more willing to purchase products, even if they cost more, from firms that have a reputation for being charitable. Purchasing products from firms that have reputations for being socially responsible can be motivated by a customer's desire to be perceived as a caring individual, thus contributing to satisfying esteem needs.

At the top of the hierarchy are *self-actualization needs*. These refer to people's needs to grow and develop and to become all they are capable of becoming. Many people never reach this level of the hierarchy, but it can be motivating to try. Some products that may send messages that they satisfy these needs include fitness center memberships, education, and self-improvement workshops.

Motives that influence which establishments a customer frequents are called **patronage motives**. A buyer may shop at a specific store because of such patronage motives as price, service, location, product variety, or friendliness of salespeople. To capitalize on patronage motives, marketers try to determine why regular customers frequent a particular store and to emphasize these characteristics in the store's marketing mix.

7-4c Learning

Learning refers to changes in a person's thought processes and behavior caused by information and experience. Consequences of behavior strongly influence the learning process. Behaviors that result in positive consequences tend to be repeated. For instance, a consumer who buys a Snickers candy bar, enjoys the taste, and feels satisfied after eating it is more likely to buy a Snickers bar again. The individual will probably continue to purchase that product until it no longer provides satisfaction. When outcomes of the behavior are no longer satisfying or stand in the way of achieving a desired goal, such as weight loss, the person may switch to a less fattening brand or stop eating candy bars altogether.

Purchasing decisions require customers to process information, an ability that varies by individual. The type of information inexperienced buyers use may differ from the type used

patronage motives Motives that influence where a person purchases products on a regular basis

learning Changes in an individual's thought processes and behavior caused by information and experience

by experienced shoppers who are familiar with the product and purchase situation. Thus, two potential buyers of an antique desk may use different types of information in making their purchase decisions. The inexperienced buyer may judge the desk's value by price and appearance, whereas the more experienced buyer may seek information about the manufacturer, period, and place of origin to assess the desk's quality and value. Consumers who lack experience may seek information from others when making a purchase and even take along an informed "purchase pal." Experienced buyers have greater self-confidence and more knowledge about the product and can recognize which product features are reliable cues to quality.

Marketers help customers learn about their products by helping them gain experience with them, which makes customers feel more comfortable. Free samples, sometimes coupled with coupons, can encourage product trial and reduce purchase risk. For instance, because some consumers may be wary of exotic menu items, restaurants may offer free samples of less common dishes. In-store demonstrations foster knowledge of product uses. A software producer may use point-of-sale product demonstrations to introduce a new product. Test drives give potential new-car purchasers some experience with the automobile's features.

Consumers also learn by experiencing products indirectly through information from salespeople, advertisements, websites, friends, and relatives. Through sales personnel and advertisements, marketers offer information before (and sometimes after) purchases that can create favorable consumer attitudes toward the product. However, marketers may encounter problems in attracting and holding consumers' attention, providing them with information for making purchase decisions and convincing them to try the product.

7-4d Attitudes

An **attitude** is an individual's enduring evaluation of feelings about and behavioral tendencies toward an object or idea. The objects toward which we have attitudes may be tangible or intangible, living or nonliving. For example, we have attitudes toward sex, religion, politics, and music, just as we do toward cars, football, and breakfast cereals. Although attitudes can change over time, they tend to remain stable and do not vary, particularly in the short term. A person's attitudes toward different things do not have equal impact at any one time, and some are stronger than others. Individuals acquire attitudes through experience and interaction with other people.

An attitude consists of three major components: cognitive, affective, and behavioral. The cognitive component is the person's knowledge and information about the object or idea. The affective component comprises the individual's feelings and emotions toward the object or idea. Emotions involve both psychological and biological elements. They relate to feelings and can create visceral responses related to behavior. Love, hate, and anger are emotions that can influence behavior. For some people, certain brands, such as Google, Starbucks, or REI, elicit an emotional response. Firms that successfully create an emotional experience or connection with customers establish a positive brand image that can result in customer loyalty. This means it is important for marketers to generate authentic messages that consumers can relate to on an emotional level. The behavioral component manifests itself in the person's actions regarding the object or idea. Changes in cognitive, affective, or behavioral components may possibly affect other components.

Consumer attitudes toward a company and its products greatly influence success or failure of the firm's marketing strategy. When consumers have strong, negative attitudes toward one or more aspects of a firm's marketing practices, they may not only stop using its products but also urge relatives and friends to do likewise. Because attitudes play an important part in determining consumer behavior, marketers should regularly measure consumer attitudes toward prices, package designs, brand names, advertisements, salespeople, repair services, store locations, features of existing or proposed products, and social responsibility efforts.

Seeking to understand attitudes has resulted in two major academic models: the attitude toward the object model (known as the Fishbein model) and the behavioral intentions model (also known as the Theory of Reasoned Action). These models provide an understanding of the role of attitudes in decision making. The attitude toward the object model can be used to understand, and possibly predict, a consumer's attitude. It consists of three elements: beliefs

attitude An individual's enduring evaluation of feelings about and behavioral tendencies toward an object or idea

about product attributes, the strength of beliefs, and the evaluation of beliefs. These elements combine to form what is called the overall attitude toward the object.[7]

The behavioral intentions model, rather than focusing on attributes, focuses on intentions to act or purchase. This model considers consumer perceptions of what other people, particularly peers, believe is the best choice among a set of alternatives. As its name indicates, this model focuses on attitudes toward the buying behavior, not toward the object. The subjective norm component is important in recognizing that individuals live in an inherently social environment and are influenced by what others think and believe. Consider attitudes toward personal appearance (e.g., what clothes people wear, hairstyles, or body modifications such as piercings or tattoos). Consumers will take into account what others may think of their decisions before committing to products that alter appearance. Many people are motivated to comply with what others hold to be an acceptable norm and stay in close communication through word-of-mouth, traditional, and digital media.

Several methods help marketers gauge consumer attitudes. One of the simplest ways is to question people directly. The Internet and social networking sites are useful tools for marketers seeking to garner information on attitudes directly from consumers. Using sites such as Facebook, companies can ask consumers for feedback and product reviews.

Marketers also evaluate attitudes through attitude scales. An **attitude scale** usually consists of a series of adjectives, phrases, or sentences about an object. Respondents indicate the intensity of their feelings toward the object by reacting to the adjectives, phrases, or sentences. For example, a marketer who is measuring people's attitudes toward shopping might ask respondents to indicate the extent to which they agree or disagree with a number of statements, such as "shopping is more fun than watching television."

attitude scale A means of measuring consumer attitudes by gauging the intensity of individuals' reactions to adjectives, phrases, or sentences about an object

personality A set of internal traits and distinct behavioral tendencies that result in consistent patterns of behavior in certain situations

When marketers determine that a significant number of consumers have negative attitudes toward an aspect of a marketing mix, they may try to change those attitudes. This task is generally lengthy, expensive, and difficult and can require extensive promotional efforts. To alter responses so that more consumers purchase a certain brand, a firm might launch an information-focused campaign to change the cognitive component of a consumer's attitude, or a persuasive (emotional) campaign to influence the affective component. Distributing free samples might help change the behavioral component.

Both business and nonbusiness organizations try to change people's attitudes about many things, from health and safety to prices and product features. Look at the advertisement for Keebler cookies, for instance. As more consumers grow concerned about the ingredients in their food, many parents have cut back on purchasing packaged cookies—for fear of artificial ingredients and preservatives. Keebler seeks to overcome negative attitudes about packaged cookies by prominently featuring natural ingredients, such as butter, sugar, and eggs in this ad. However, Keebler maintains continuity and consumer loyalty to previous products by featuring the familiar Keebler elf.

Communication to Influence Attitudes
Keebler seeks to overcome negative consumer attitudes about packaged cookies with this ad.

7-4e Personality and Self-Concept

Personality is a set of internal traits and distinct behavioral tendencies that result in consistent patterns of behavior in certain situations. An individual's personality is a unique combination of hereditary characteristics and personal experiences. Personalities typically are described as having one or more characteristics, such as compulsiveness, ambition, gregariousness, dogmatism, authoritarianism, introversion, extroversion, and competitiveness. Marketing researchers look for relationships between such characteristics and buying behavior. Even though a few links between several personality traits and buyer behavior have been determined, studies have not proven a definitive link. However, weak association between personality and buying behavior may be the result of unreliable measures, rather than a true lack of a relationship.

A number of marketers are convinced that consumers' personalities do indeed influence types and brands of products purchased. Because of this believed relation, marketers aim advertising at specific personality types. For example, truck commercials often highlight rugged, all-American individualism. Marketers generally focus on positive personality characteristics, such as security consciousness, sociability, independence, or competitiveness, rather than on negatively-valued ones, such as insensitivity or timidity. The PRIZM program, owned by Nielsen, is one consumer framework that takes into account individual personality differences. (See the following "Lifestyles" section.)

A person's self-concept is closely linked to personality. **Self-concept** (sometimes called *self-image*) is one's perception or view of oneself. Individuals develop and alter their self-concepts based on an interaction between psychological and social dimensions. Research findings show that buyers purchase products that reflect and enhance their self-concepts and that purchase decisions are important to the development and maintenance of a stable self-concept.[8] Consumers who feel insecure about their self-concept may purchase products that help them bolster the image of themselves that they would like to project. Consumers' self-concepts may influence whether they buy a product in a specific product category and may affect brand selection as well as the retailers they frequent. Founded by environmentalist Yvon Chouinard, the outfitting company Patagonia appeals to consumers with a self-concept as being outdoor enthusiasts. Many consumers are loyal to the brand because its products and values represent their lifestyle. Patagonia is committed to its mission of sustainability so that people can continue to enjoy nature. It reincorporated under a new organizational structure, a benefit corporation, which further signals that it values doing good as much as making profits.[9]

7-4f Lifestyles

self-concept A perception or view of oneself

lifestyle An individual's pattern of living expressed through activities, interests, and opinions

Many marketers attempt to segment markets by lifestyle. A **lifestyle** is an individual's pattern of living expressed through activities, interests, and opinions. Lifestyle patterns include the ways people spend time, the extent of their interaction with others, and their general outlook on life and living. People partially determine their own lifestyles, but lifestyle is also affected by personality and by demographic factors such as age, education, income, and social class.

Emerging Trends

Who Let the Dogs In?!

Hotels and resorts are rolling out the welcome mat for pet lovers who travel with Fido or Fifi. Just a few years ago, hotels barely tolerated pets. Today, catering to pet owners on the go is not only big business, but it's also smart marketing and an effective way to build customer loyalty.

For example, Kimpton Hotels go all out to accommodate the pet owner's lifestyle. The freebies include "Yappy Hour" get-togethers for dogs and adults, organic snacks, guides to local pet parks, and a "do not disturb" sign to alert staff when a pet is in residence. As a result, more than 100,000 pets—mainly dogs—visit Kimpton's 60 hotels every year, along with their owners. Pet-less guests can even borrow a goldfish for the night through Kimpton's free Guppy Love program.

Some hotels charge a cleaning fee when pets share the room but also provide extras for these special guests. The Revel resort in Atlantic City, New Jersey, promotes "Ruff It at Revel," featuring gourmet dog snacks, a deluxe doggy bed, and a sheltered "Bark Avenue" area for dog-walking in any weather. The Sofitel Miami hotel has a room service menu with pet foods to fit Fido's nutritional needs. The Essex Resort in Vermont now draws 10 percent of its business from pet owners, thanks to events like "Top Dog" getaway weekends.[a]

Lifestyles have a strong impact on many aspects of the consumer buying decision process, from problem recognition to postpurchase evaluation. Lifestyles influence consumers' product needs and brand preferences, types of media they use, and how and where they shop.

One of the most popular frameworks for understanding consumer lifestyles and their influences on purchasing behavior is a product called PRIZM (see also Chapter 6). Originally developed by Claritas, PRIZM was acquired by Nielsen, one of the leading research companies in the world. It divides consumers in the United States into 66 distinct groups based on numerous variables such as education, income, technology use, employment, and social groups.[10] These groups can help marketers understand consumers and how things like lifestyle and education will impact their purchasing habits. Because technology is increasingly important to marketers and plays a huge role in many consumers' lives, Nielsen also released another product, ConneXions, which uses the same lifestyle groups as PRIZM to analyze consumer communications behavior. This information can be valuable to marketers, as it reveals how consumers choose to access information.[11]

7-5 SOCIAL INFLUENCES ON THE BUYING DECISION PROCESS

Forces that other people exert on buying behavior are called **social influences**. As Figure 7.1 shows (located near the beginning of this chapter), they are divided into five major groups: roles, family, reference groups and opinion leaders, social classes, and culture and subcultures.

social influences The forces other people exert on one's buying behavior

roles Actions and activities that a person in a particular position is supposed to perform based on expectations of the individual and surrounding persons

consumer socialization The process through which a person acquires the knowledge and skills to function as a consumer

7-5a Roles

All of us occupy positions within groups, organizations, and institutions. In these positions, we play one or more **roles**, which are sets of actions and activities a person in a particular position is supposed to perform based on the expectations of both the individual and surrounding people. Because every person occupies numerous positions, they have many roles. A man may perform the roles of son, husband, father, employee, employer, church member, civic organization member, and student in an evening college class. Thus, multiple sets of expectations are placed on each person's behavior.

An individual's roles influence both general behavior and buying behavior. The demands of a person's many roles may be diverse, and even at times inconsistent or at odds. Consider the various types of clothes that you buy and wear depending on whether you are going to class, to work, to a party, or to the gym. You and others in these settings have expectations about what is acceptable attire for these activities. Thus, the expectations of those around us affect our purchases of many different types of products.

7-5b Family Influences

Parents teach children how to cope with a variety of problems, including those that help with purchase decisions. Thus, family influences have a direct impact on the consumer buying decision process. **Consumer socialization** is the process through which a person acquires the knowledge and skills to function as a consumer. Often, children

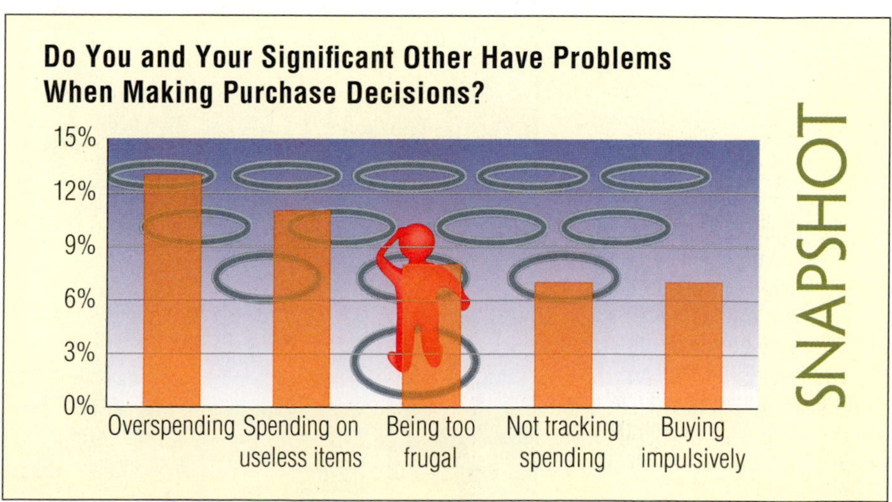

Source: Chase Blueprint survey of 1,212 adults 18 and older.

Table 7.2 Types of Family Decision Making

Decision-Making Type	Decision Maker	Types of Products
Husband dominant	Male head of household	Lawnmowers, hardware and tools, stereos, automobile parts
Wife dominant	Female head of household	Children's clothing, women's clothing, groceries, household furnishings
Autonomic	Equally likely to be made by the husband or wife, but not by both	Men's clothing, luggage, toys and games, sporting equipment, cameras
Syncratic	Made jointly by husband and wife	Vacations, TVs, living room furniture, carpets, financial planning services, family cars

gain this knowledge and set of skills by observing parents and older siblings in purchase situations. Children observe brand preferences and buying practices in their families and, as adults, will retain some of these brand preferences and buying practices as they establish and raise their own families. Buying decisions made by a family are a combination of group and individual decision making.

The extent to which family members take part in family decision making varies among families and product categories. Traditionally, family decision-making processes have been grouped into four categories: autonomic, husband dominant, wife dominant, and syncratic, as shown in Table 7.2. Although female roles have changed over time, women still make the majority of purchase decisions in households. Indeed, research results indicate that women remain the primary decision makers for 85 percent of all consumer buying decisions.[12]

The family lifecycle stage affects individual and joint needs of family members. For example, consider how the car needs of recently married "twenty-somethings" differ from those of the same couple when they are "forty-somethings" with a 13-year-old daughter and a 17-year-old son. Family lifecycle changes can affect which family members are involved in purchase

Family Influences
The consumer decision processes related to the purchase of numerous products are influenced by both parents and children. Children learn about buying many products from their families, which they apply when making similar decisions when they are adults.

decisions and the types of products purchased. Children also have a strong influence on many household purchase decisions.

When two or more family members participate in a purchase, their roles may dictate that each is responsible for performing certain purchase-related tasks, such as initiating the idea, gathering information, determining if the product is affordable, deciding whether to buy the product, or selecting the specific brand. The specific purchase tasks performed depend on the types of products being considered, the kind of family purchase decision process typically employed, and the presence and amount of influence children have in the decision process. Thus, different family members may play different roles in the family buying process.

Within a household, an individual may perform one or more roles related to making buying decisions. The gatekeeper is the household member who collects and controls information, including price and quality comparisons, locations of sellers, and assessment of which brand best suits the family's needs. For example, if a family is planning a summer vacation, the gatekeeper might compare prices for hotels and airfare to determine the best deal. The influencer is a family member who expresses his or her opinions. In the vacation example, an influencer might be a child who wants to go to Disney World or a teenager who wants to go snowboarding. The decider is a member who makes the buying choice. This role switches based on the type and expense of the product being purchased. In the case of a vacation, the decider will more likely be the adults, who possess information, influence, and their own preferences. The buyer is a member who actually makes the purchase. The user is a household member who consumes or uses the product. In this Disney World example, all members of the family are users.

7-5c Reference Groups

A **reference group** is a group, either large or small, with which a person identifies so strongly that he or she adopts the values, attitudes, and behavior of group members. Most people have several reference groups, such as families, work-related groups, fraternities or sororities, civic clubs, professional organizations, or church-related groups.

In general, there are three major types of reference groups: membership, aspirational, and disassociative. A membership reference group is one to which an individual actually belongs. The individual identifies intensely enough with this group to take on the values, attitudes, and behaviors of people in that group. An aspirational reference group is one to which a person aspires to belong. The aspiring member desires to be like group members. A group that a person does not wish to be associated with is a disassociative, or negative, reference group. The individual does not want to take on the values, attitudes, and behavior of group members.

A reference group may serve as an individual's point of comparison and source of information. A customer's behavior may change to be more in line with actions and beliefs of group members. For instance, a person may switch to a different brand of shirt based on reference group members' advice and preferences. An individual may also seek information from the reference group about other factors regarding a prospective purchase, such as where to buy a certain product.

Reference groups can affect whether a person does or does not buy a product at all, buys a type of product within a product category, or buys a specific brand. The extent to which a reference group affects a purchase decision depends on the product's conspicuousness and on the individual's susceptibility to reference group influence. Generally, the more conspicuous a product, the more likely that reference groups will influence a consumer's purchase decision. A product's conspicuousness is determined by whether others can see it and whether it attracts attention. A marketer sometimes tries to use reference group influence in advertisements by suggesting that people in a specific group buy a product and are satisfied with it. Whether this kind of advertising succeeds depends on three factors: how effectively the advertisement communicates the message, the type of product, and the individual's susceptibility to reference group influence. In this type of appeal, the advertiser hopes that many people will accept the suggested group as a reference group and buy (or react more favorably to) the product.

reference group A group that a person identifies with so strongly that he or she adopts the values, attitudes, and behavior of group members

Table 7.3 Examples of Opinion Leaders and Topics

Opinion Leader	Possible Topics
Local religious leader	Charities to support, political ideas, lifestyle choices
Sorority president	Clothing and shoe purchases, hair styles, nail and hair salons
"Movie buff" friend	Movies to see in theaters, rent, or buy; television programs to watch
Family doctor	Prescription drugs, vitamins, health products
"Techie" acquaintance	Computer and other electronics purchases, software purchases, Internet service choices, video game purchases

7-5d Opinion Leaders

An **opinion leader** is a member of an informal group who provides information about a specific topic, such as smartphones, to other group members seeking information. The opinion leader is in a position, or has knowledge or expertise, that makes him or her a credible source of information about a few topics. Opinion leaders are easily accessible and are viewed by other group members as being well informed about one or multiple topics. Opinion leaders are not the foremost authority on all topics, but because such individuals know they are opinion leaders, they feel a responsibility to remain informed about specific topics, and thus seek out advertisements, manufacturers' brochures, salespeople, and other sources of information. Opinion leaders have a strong influence on the behavior of others in their group, particularly relating to product adoption and purchases.

An opinion leader is likely to be most influential when consumers have high product involvement but low product knowledge, when they share the opinion leader's values and attitudes, and when the product details are numerous or complicated. Possible opinion leaders and topics are shown in Table 7.3.

7-5e Social Classes

In all societies, people rank others into higher or lower positions of respect. This ranking process, called social stratification, results in social classes. A **social class** is an open aggregate of people with similar social rank. A class is referred to as *open* because people can move into and out of it. Criteria for grouping people into classes vary from one society to another. In the United States, we take into account many factors, including occupation, education, income, wealth, race, ethnic group, and possessions. A person who is ranking someone into a class does not necessarily apply all of a society's criteria. Sometimes, too, the role of income tends to be overemphasized in social class determination. Although income does help determine social class, the other factors also play a role. Within social classes, both incomes and spending habits differ significantly among members.

Analyses of social class in the United States commonly divide people among three to seven categories. Social scientist Richard P. Coleman suggests that, for purposes of consumer analysis, the population is best divided into the three major status groups (shown in Table 7.4), which are upper, middle, and lower classes. However, he warns marketers that considerable diversity exists in people's life situations within each status group.

To some degree, individuals within social classes develop and assume common behavioral patterns. They may have similar attitudes, values, language patterns, and possessions. Social class influences many aspects of people's lives. Because people most frequently interact with others within their own social class, people are more likely to be influenced by others within their own class than by those in other classes. Social class can influence choice of religion, financial planning decisions, access to education, occupation, and leisure time activities.

opinion leader A member of an informal group who provides information about a specific topic to other group members

social class An open group of individuals with similar social rank

Table 7.4 **Social Class Behavioral Traits and Purchasing Characteristics**

Class (Percent of Population)	Behavioral Traits	Buying Characteristics
Upper Americans		
Upper-upper (0.5)	Social elite Of aristocratic, prominent families Inherited their position in society	Children attend private preparatory schools and best colleges Do not consume ostentatiously Spend money on private clubs, various causes, and the arts
Lower-upper (3.8)	Newer social elite Successful professionals earning very high incomes Earned their position in society	Purchase material symbols of their status, such as large, suburban houses and expensive automobiles Provide a substantial market for luxury product offerings Visit museums and attend live theater Spend money on skiing, golf, swimming, and tennis
Upper-middle (13.8)	Career-oriented, professional degree holders Demand educational attainment of their children	Provide a substantial market for quality product offerings Family lifestyle characterized as gracious yet careful Spend money on movies, gardening, and photography
Middle Americans		
Middle class (32.8)	"Typical" Americans Work conscientiously and adhere to culturally-defined standards Average-pay white-collar workers Attend church and obey the law Often very involved in children's school and sports activities	Greatly value living in a respected neighborhood and keep their homes well furnished Generally price sensitive Adopt conventional consumption tastes and consult category experts Spend on family-oriented, physical activities, such as fishing, camping, boating, and hunting
Working class (32.3)	Average-pay blue-collar workers Live a routine life with unchanging day-to-day activities Hold jobs that entail manual labor and moderate skills Some are union members Socially not involved in civic or church activities; limit social interaction to close neighbors and relatives	Reside in small houses or apartments in depressed areas Impulsive as consumers yet display high loyalty to national brands Seek best bargains Enjoy leisure activities like local travel and recreational parks
Lower Americans		
Upper-lower (9.5)	Low-income individuals who generally fail to rise above this class Reject middle-class morality	Living standard is just above poverty Seek pleasure whenever possible, especially through impulse purchases Frequently purchase on credit
Lower-lower (7.3)	Some are on welfare and may be homeless Poverty stricken Some have strong religious beliefs Some are unemployed In spite of their problems, often good-hearted toward others May be forced to live in less desirable neighborhoods	Spend on products needed for survival Able to convert discarded goods into usable items

Sources: Roger D. Blackwell, Paul W. Miniard, and James F. Engel, *Consumer Behavior*, 10th ed. (Mason, OH: Cengage Learning, 2005); "The Continuing Significance of Social Class Marketing," *Journal of Consumer Research* 10 (December 1983): 265–280; Eugene Sivadas, George Mathew, and David J. Curry, "A Preliminary Examination of the Continued Significance of Social Class in Marketing," *Journal of Consumer Marketing* 14, no. 6 (1997): 463–469.

Social class also influences people's spending, saving, and credit practices. It can determine the type, quality, and quantity of products a person buys and uses. For instance, it affects purchases of clothing, foods, financial and health-care services, travel, recreation, entertainment, and home furnishings. Behaviors within a social class can influence others as well. Most common is the "trickle-down" effect, in which members of lower classes attempt to emulate members of higher social classes, such as purchasing desirable automobiles, large homes, and even selecting certain names for their children. Couture fashions designed for the upper class influence the clothing sold in department stores frequented by the middle class, which eventually is sold to the working class who shop at discount clothing stores. Less often, status float will occur, when a product that is traditionally associated with a lower class gains status and popularity among upper classes. Blue jeans, for example, were originally worn exclusively by the working class. Youth of the 1950s began wearing them as a symbol of rebellion against their parents. By the 1970s and 1980s, jeans had also been adopted by upper-class youth when they began to acquire designer labels. Today, blue jeans are acceptable attire for all social classes and cost anywhere from a few dollars to thousands of dollars, depending on the brand.

Social class also affects an individual's shopping patterns and types of stores patronized. In some instances, marketers attempt to focus on certain social classes through store location and interior design, product design and features, pricing strategies, personal sales efforts, and advertising. Many companies focus on the middle and working classes because they account for such a large portion of the population. Outside the United States, the middle class is growing rapidly in places such as India, China, and Brazil, making these consumers desirable targets for marketing messages. For example, Microsoft acquired phone maker Nokia, largely to give it a competitive advantage in emerging markets. Nokia products are more established than Microsoft in desirable markets, particularly in Latin America. Rather than developing products to compete, Microsoft acquired the company.[13]

Some firms target different classes with a range of products at different price points. Even designers who previously only made clothing for the wealthy have learned about the benefits of offering items at different price points. Numerous fashion houses, such as Isabel Marant and Jason Wu, have produced collaborations with retailers such as Target and H&M, releasing affordable lines for the middle class.[14]

7-5f Culture and Subcultures

Culture is the accumulation of values, knowledge, beliefs, customs, objects, and concepts that a society uses to cope with its environment and passes on to future generations. Culture permeates most things you do and objects you interact with, from the style of buildings in your town, to the type of education you receive, to the laws governing your country. Culture also includes society-specific core values and the degree of acceptability of a wide range of behaviors. For example, in U.S. culture, customers as well as businesspeople are expected to behave ethically.

Culture influences buying behavior because it permeates our daily lives. Our culture determines what we wear and eat and where we reside and travel. Society's interest in the healthfulness of food affects food companies' approaches to developing and promoting their products. Culture also influences how we buy and use products and the satisfaction we get from them.

When U.S. marketers sell products in other countries, they must be aware of the tremendous impact specific cultures have on product purchases and use. Global marketers will find that people in other regions of the world have different attitudes, values, and needs, which call for different methods of doing business and different marketing mixes. Some international marketers fail because they do not or cannot adjust to cultural differences.

A culture consists of various subcultures. A **subculture** is a group of individuals whose characteristics, values, and behavioral patterns are similar within the group and different from those of people in the surrounding culture. Subcultural boundaries are usually based on geographic designations and demographic characteristics, such as age, religion, race, and ethnicity. U.S. culture is marked by many different subcultures. Among them are punk, rocker, gamer, biker, endurance sports enthusiast, cowboy, and business professional. Within

culture The accumulation of values, knowledge, beliefs, customs, objects, and concepts that a society uses to cope with its environment and passes on to future generations

subculture A group of individuals whose characteristics, values, and behavioral patterns are similar within the group and different from those of people in the surrounding culture

subcultures, greater similarities exist in people's attitudes, values, and actions than within the broader culture. Relative to other subcultures, individuals in one subculture may have stronger preferences for specific types of clothing, furniture, food, or consumer electronics. Take a look at the advertisement for Clairol Beautiful Collection line of hair relaxers, for example. Women of African descent who like to wear their hair straight are the subculture targeted by this advertisement. Marketers underscore the long tradition of relaxing hair by showing a women dressed up to look like she is from the 1950s facing the same women wearing contemporary clothing. This ad is clearly appealing to a subculture because most other potential consumers do not have the hair texture to require this product.

Subcultures
Clairol is appealing to the subculture of African American women who like to straighten their hair with its line of Beautiful Collection hair products.

Subcultures can play a significant role in how people respond to advertisements, particularly when pressured to make a snap judgment. It is important for marketers to understand that a person can be a member of more than one subculture and that the behavioral patterns and values attributed to specific subcultures do not necessarily apply to all group members.

The percentage of the U.S. population consisting of ethnic and racial subcultures has grown and is expected to continue to grow. By 2050, about one-half of the U.S. population will be members of racial and ethnic minorities. The U.S. Census Bureau reports that the three largest and fastest-growing ethnic U.S. subcultures are African Americans, Hispanics, and Asians.[15] Nearly 50 percent of children under the age of 5 are now minorities.[16] The population growth of these ethnic and racial subcultures represents a large potential opportunity for marketers because of cultural-specific tastes and desires. Businesses recognize that, to succeed, their marketing strategies have to take into account the values, needs, interests, shopping patterns, and buying habits of these various subcultures.

African American Subculture

In the United States, the African American subculture represents 13.7 percent of the population.[17] The combined buying power of African American consumers is projected to reach $1.1 trillion by 2015.[18] Like all subcultures, African American consumers possess distinct buying patterns. For example, African American consumers spend a larger-than-average proportion of their disposable income on depreciable products such as phone services, children's clothing, and shoes.

Many companies are increasing their focus on the African American community. BET, the television network aimed at African Americans, launched a festival as a means to create a platform for sponsors (including Coca-Cola, Procter & Gamble, and Grey Goose vodka) and the network to speak more directly to African American consumers. This festival is called the BET Experience and includes films, music (featuring big-name artists such as Beyoncé), food, and demonstrations to draw in and interest consumers and to allow them to interact more directly with brands and their products in an entertaining atmosphere.[19]

Hispanic Subculture

Hispanics represent 16.7 percent of the U.S. population.[20] Hispanic buying power is expected to reach $1.5 trillion by 2015.[21] Hispanics represent a large and powerful subculture, and are an attractive consumer group for marketers.

When considering the buying behavior of Hispanics (or any ethnic or racial subculture, for that matter), marketers must keep in mind that this subculture is really composed of many diverse cultures coming from a huge geographic region that encompasses nearly two dozen nationalities, including Cuban, Mexican, Puerto Rican, Caribbean, Spanish, and Dominican. Each has its own history and unique culture that affect consumer preferences and buying behavior. Marketers should also recognize that the terms *Hispanic* and *Latino* refer to an ethnic category rather than a racial distinction. In spite of its complexity, because of the group's growth and purchasing power, understanding the Hispanic subculture is critical to marketers. Like African American consumers, Hispanics spend a larger proportion of their income on groceries, phone services, clothing, and shoes, while they spend less than average on health care, entertainment, and education.[22]

Although most large firms dedicate some marketing resources to the Latino market, spending still does not align with the overall proportion of Latinos in the population. On average, firms only spend around 5 percent to 6 percent of their advertising budgets on marketing directed at Latinos, even though they represent 17 percent of the total population and at least 20 percent of key demographics such as children, teens, and young adults.[23] Some marketers have started to address this gap, including those in commercial real estate, who see potential among the rapidly-growing Latino population as a means of reviving the sagging profits of retailers in shopping spaces such as malls, which have fallen out of favor with other demographic subcultures. Consequently, real estate moguls in Southern California, which boasts a very high Latino population, are drawing in shoppers with Mariachi music, family-oriented promotions centered on Latin American holidays, Spanish language advertisements, and even Spanish-colonial inspired architectural details on storefronts and interiors.[24]

Asian American Subculture

The term *Asian American* includes Filipinos, Chinese, Japanese, Asian Indians, Koreans, and Vietnamese, encompassing people from more than 15 highly diverse ethnic groups. This group represents 5.7 percent of the U.S. population.[25] The individual language, religion, and value system of each group influences its members' purchasing decisions. Some traits of this subculture, however, carry across ethnic divisions, including an emphasis on hard work, strong family ties, and a high value on education. The combined buying power of Asian American consumers is projected to reach $1 trillion by 2017.[26] Though they represent a smaller proportion of the overall population, Asian Americans are the fastest-growing demographic and are projected to increase by 50 percent in a decade. As a group, Asian Americans are also more

Marketing Debate

Customer Tracking Raises Privacy Concerns

ISSUE: Should stores and malls track consumers via their cell phones?

How many shoppers enter a store, which departments do they visit, and how long do they spend in the store or mall? To find out, some stores and malls are tracking consumers by following cell phone Wi-Fi signals. Just as online retailers electronically track the behavior of customers who visit websites, store-based retailers want to better understand buying behavior so they can target shoppers when and where they are planning a purchase. Such tracking would also help stores schedule employees to work in the right department at the right time.

However, tracking raises privacy concerns. Do shoppers know they are being tracked? Can they avoid it? How will the data be used? Public reaction to tracking has been mixed. After media reports of tracking tests, Nordstrom received some shopper complaints and ended a short-lived experiment. On the other hand, thousands of people use apps that offer cash rewards and gifts for allowing themselves to be tracked while they shop.[b]

educated and have household incomes that are 28 percent higher than the median income—making them an appealing target market.

7-6 CONSUMER MISBEHAVIOR

Approaching the topic of inappropriate consumer behavior requires some caution because of varying attitudes and cultural definitions of what comprises misbehavior. However, it is generally agreed that some conduct, such as shoplifting or purchasing illegal drugs, falls under the category of activities that are not accepted by established norms. Therefore, we will define **consumer misbehavior** as behavior that violates generally accepted norms of a particular society. Shoplifting is one of the most obvious misconduct areas, with organized retail crime (where people are paid to shoplift certain goods from retail stores) on the rise. Organized retail crime has become a major threat, not only to retailers, but to all organizations including governments. For instance, an international gang of only five hackers stole 160 million credit card numbers from more than a dozen companies, costing hundreds of millions of dollars in losses. The Internet has facilitated this level of retail crime, which extends across international borders. Because it does not occur in a specific physical location and may be carried out by multiple people, it can be very difficult to track down and stop such activity.[27] Experts estimate that organized retail crime alone costs businesses between $15 billion and $37 billion annually.[28] Aside from selling goods on the black market, consumer motivation for shoplifting includes the low risk of being caught, a desire to be accepted by a group of peers (particularly among young people), and the excitement associated with the activity.

Consumer fraud includes purposeful actions to take advantage of and/or damage others. Fraudulently obtaining credit cards, checks, bank accounts, or false insurance claims fall into this category. Even large companies with sophisticated security systems can be vulnerable to consumer fraud. Major banks, newspapers, governments, and even Twitter have been hacked and mined by criminals for the data their computer systems hold.[29] Some consumers engage in identity theft, which is a serious and growing legal problem—particularly as more shopping is conducted online, where regulations and security are more difficult to enforce. A type of consumer fraud that some consumers might not even consider a crime would be purchasing a dress for a special event, wearing it once, and then returning it.

Piracy is copying computer software, video games, movies, or music. It is a growing legal problem that some estimate costs the electronics and entertainment industries $59 billion annually, although the number is difficult to calculate precisely.[30] The recording industry broadcasts messages explaining why sharing music is not acceptable, but it remains a serious problem. Understanding motivations for piracy can be helpful in developing a plan to combat the issue (see Table 7.5).

Yet another area of concern with consumer misbehavior is abusive consumers. Rude customers engage in verbal or physical abuse, can be uncooperative, and may even break policies. Airlines remove abusive customers if they represent a threat to employees and other passengers. Belligerently drunk customers, especially in environments such as bars and restaurants, have to be removed in order to protect others. Understanding the psychological and social reasons for consumer misconduct can be helpful in preventing or responding to the problem.

consumer misbehavior Behavior that violates generally accepted norms of a particular society

Table 7.5 Motivations for Unethical or Illegal Misbehavior

Justification/rationalization	The thrill of getting away with it
Economic reasons	There is little risk of getting caught
It is accepted by peers	People think they are smarter than others

Source: Kevin J. Shanahan and Michael J. Hyman, "Motivators and Enablers of SCOURing: A Study of Online Piracy in the US and UK," *Journal of Business Research* 63 (September–October 2010): 1095–1102.

Summary

7-1 Recognize the stages of the consumer buying decision process.

The consumer buying decision process includes five stages: problem recognition, information search, evaluation of alternatives, purchase, and postpurchase evaluation. Not all decision processes culminate in a purchase, nor do all consumer decisions include all five stages. Problem recognition occurs when buyers become aware of a difference between a desired state and an actual condition. After recognizing the problem or need, buyers search for information about products to help resolve the problem or satisfy the need. In the internal search, buyers search their memories for information about products that might solve the problem. If they cannot retrieve from memory sufficient information to make a decision, they seek additional information through an external search. A successful search yields a group of brands, called a consideration set, which a buyer views as possible alternatives. To evaluate the products in the consideration set, the buyer establishes certain criteria by which to compare, rate, and rank different products. Marketers can influence consumers' evaluations by framing alternatives. In the purchase stage, consumers select products or brands on the basis of results from the evaluation stage and on other dimensions. Buyers also choose the seller from whom they will buy the product. After the purchase, buyers evaluate the product to determine if its actual performance meets expected levels.

7-2 Describe the types of consumer decision making and the level of involvement.

Buying behavior consists of the decision processes and acts of people involved in buying and using products. Consumer buying behavior is the buying behavior of ultimate consumers. An individual's level of involvement—the importance and intensity of interest in a product in a particular situation—affects the type of decision-making process used. Enduring involvement is an ongoing interest in a product class because of personal relevance, whereas situational involvement is a temporary interest that stems from the particular circumstance or environment in which buyers find themselves. There are three kinds of consumer decision making: routinized response behavior, limited decision making, and extended decision making. Consumers rely on routinized response behavior when buying frequently purchased, low-cost items requiring little search-and-decision effort. Limited decision making is used for products purchased occasionally or when buyers need to acquire information about an unfamiliar brand in a familiar product category. Consumers engage in extended decision making when purchasing an unfamiliar, expensive, or infrequently bought product. Purchase of a certain product does not always elicit the same type of decision making. Impulse buying is not a consciously planned buying behavior but involves a powerful urge to buy something immediately.

7-3 Explain how situational influences may affect the consumer buying decision process.

Three major categories of influences affect the consumer buying decision process: situational, psychological, and social. Situational influences are external circumstances or conditions existing when a consumer makes a purchase decision. Situational influences include surroundings, time, reason for purchase, and the buyer's mood and condition.

7-4 Identify the psychological influences that may affect the consumer buying decision process.

Psychological influences partly determine people's general behavior, thus influencing their behavior as consumers. The primary psychological influences on consumer behavior are perception, motives, learning, attitudes, personality and self-concept, and lifestyles. Perception is the process of selecting, organizing, and interpreting information inputs (sensations received through sight, taste, hearing, smell, and touch) to produce meaning. The three steps in the perceptual process are selection, organization, and interpretation. Individuals have numerous perceptions of packages, products, brands, and organizations that affect their buying decision processes. A motive is an internal energizing force that orients a person's activities toward satisfying needs or achieving goals. Learning refers to changes in a person's thought processes and behavior caused by information and experience. Marketers try to shape what consumers learn to influence what they buy. An attitude is an individual's enduring evaluation, feelings, and behavioral tendencies toward an object or idea and consists of three major components: cognitive, affective, and behavioral. Personality is the set of traits and behaviors that make a person unique. Self-concept, closely linked to personality, is one's perception or view of oneself. Researchers have found that buyers purchase products that reflect and enhance their self-concepts. Lifestyle is an individual's pattern of living expressed through activities, interests, and opinions. Lifestyles influence consumers' needs, brand preferences, and how and where they shop.

7-5 Describe the social influences that may affect the consumer buying decision process.

Social influences are forces that other people exert on buying behavior. They include roles, family, reference groups and opinion leaders, social class, and culture and subcultures. Everyone occupies positions within groups, organizations, and institutions, and each position involves playing a role—a set of actions and activities that a person in a particular position is supposed to perform based on expectations of both the individual and surrounding persons. In a family, children learn from parents and older siblings how to make decisions, such as purchase decisions. Consumer socialization is the process through which a person acquires the knowledge and skills to function as a consumer. The consumer socialization process is partially accomplished through family influences.

A reference group is a group that a person identifies with so strongly that he or she adopts the values, attitudes, and behavior of group members. The three major types of reference groups are membership, aspirational, and disassociative. An opinion leader is a member of an informal group who provides information about a specific topic to other group members.

A social class is an open group of individuals with similar social rank. Social class influences people's spending, saving, and credit practices. Culture is the accumulation of values, knowledge, beliefs, customs, objects, and concepts that a society uses to cope with its environment and passes on to future generations. A culture is made up of subcultures, groups of individuals whose characteristic values and behavior patterns are similar to one another but different from those of the surrounding culture. U.S. marketers focus on three major ethnic subcultures: African American, Hispanic, and Asian American.

7-6 Discuss consumer misbehavior.

Consumer misbehavior is defined as behavior that violates generally accepted norms of a particular society. One form of consumer misbehavior involves shoplifting, or stealing goods from retail stores. Organized retail crime is on the rise and involves people paying others to shoplift certain goods from retail stores, which are then usually sold on the black market. Another form of consumer misbehavior is consumer fraud, which involves purposeful actions to take advantage of and/or damage others. Common examples of consumer fraud are false insurance claims, identity theft, returning an item of clothing after wearing it, and fraudulently obtaining credit cards, checks, and bank accounts. Another form of consumer misbehavior is piracy, the copying or sharing of music, movies, video games, and computer software. One final area of concern with regard to consumer misbehavior is abusive consumers, which include customers who are rude, verbally or physically abusive, and/or uncooperative, which may violate some companies' policies. To respond to or even prevent these growing problems, organizations need to understand the psychological and social reasons for consumer misbehavior.

Go to www.cengagebrain.com for resources to help you master the content in this chapter as well as for materials that will expand your marketing knowledge!

Developing Your Marketing Plan

Understanding the process that an individual consumer goes through when purchasing a product is essential for developing marketing strategy. Knowledge about the potential customer's buying behavior will become the basis for many of the decisions in the specific marketing plan. Using the information from this chapter, you should be able to determine the following:

1. See Table 7.1 What types of decision making are your customers likely to use when purchasing your product?
2. Determine the evaluative criteria that your target market(s) would use when choosing between alternative brands.
3. Using Table 7.2, what types of family decision making, if any, would your target market(s) use?
4. Identify the reference groups or subcultures that may influence your target market's product selection.

The information obtained from these questions should assist you in developing various aspects of your marketing plan found in the "Interactive Marketing Plan" exercise at **www.cengagebrain.com**.

Important Terms

buying behavior 192
consumer buying behavior 192
consumer buying decision process 192
internal search 193
external search 193
consideration set 194
evaluative criteria 194
cognitive dissonance 194
level of involvement 195
routinized response behavior 195
limited decision making 195
extended decision making 196
impulse buying 197
situational influences 197
psychological influences 198
perception 198
information inputs 198
selective exposure 198
selective distortion 199
selective retention 199
motive 200
Maslow's hierarchy of needs 200
patronage motives 201
learning 201
attitude 202
attitude scale 203

personality 204
self-concept 204
lifestyle 204
social influences 205
roles 205
consumer socialization 205
reference group 207
opinion leader 208
social class 208
culture 210
subculture 210
consumer misbehavior 213

Discussion and Review Questions

1. What are the major stages in the consumer buying decision process? Are all these stages used in all consumer purchase decisions? Why or why not?
2. How does a consumer's level of involvement affect his or her choice of decision-making process?
3. Name the types of consumer decision-making processes. List some products you have bought using each type. Have you ever bought a product on impulse? If so, describe the circumstances.
4. What are the categories of situational factors that influence consumer buying behavior? Explain how each of these factors influences buyers' decisions.
5. What is selective exposure? Why do people engage in it?
6. How do marketers attempt to shape consumers' learning?
7. Why are marketers concerned about consumer attitudes?
8. In what ways do lifestyles affect the consumer buying decision process?
9. How do roles affect a person's buying behavior? Provide examples.
10. What are family influences, and how do they affect buying behavior?
11. What are reference groups? How do they influence buying behavior? Name some of your own reference groups.
12. How does an opinion leader influence the buying decision process of reference group members?
13. In what ways does social class affect a person's purchase decisions?
14. What is culture? How does it affect a person's buying behavior?
15. Describe the subcultures to which you belong. Identify buying behavior that is unique to one of your subcultures.
16. What is consumer misbehavior? Describe the various forms of consumer misbehavior.

Video Case 7.1

Starbucks Refines the Customer Experience

Starbucks—the Seattle-based company that popularized the "coffee culture"—is brewing up higher sales through new beverages and new cafés in global markets. A stop at Starbucks has become part of many consumers' daily routines. Some are attracted by the high-quality, brewed-to-order coffees, while others look forward to relaxing and socializing in the "third place" between home and work.

Starbucks has researched and refined every aspect of the customer experience, from the size of its coffees ("tall" is actually "small") to the number of minutes that customers spend waiting in line. To speed up purchases, it offers a pay-by-cell phone option called "mobile pay." Consumers with iPhone or Android cell phones simply download the app and let cashiers scan the Starbucks code on the screen during checkout. The app links to the customer's Starbucks Card, which combines the rewards of a loyalty program with the convenience of a prepaid card for making purchases. Mobile pay is a big hit: in its first 15 months, customers used their cell phones to make more than 42 million payments to Starbucks.

Well established in the intensely competitive U.S. market, Starbucks is growing much more quickly in Asian markets. The company will soon have 1,500 cafés and 30,000 employees in China, where consumers drink, on average, just three cups of coffee every year. By opening in more locations and encouraging consumers to bring their friends for coffee and conversation, Starbucks aims to increase demand and boost sales throughout China. In Japan, where Starbucks now has more than 1,000 cafés, consumers have long enjoyed the tradition of meeting in neighborhood coffee shops.

Through market research, Starbucks stays in touch with what its customers like and what their lifestyles are like. Coffee lovers are still buying their espressos or lattes, but they are also "looking for a healthier lifestyle," says a Starbucks executive. In response to this trend, the company bought Evolution Fresh, which makes premium juices, and opened its first Evolution Fresh store in Bellevue, Washington. On the menu: all-natural, freshly-blended drinks from nutritious fruits and vegetables, plus salads and wraps. Over time, Starbucks is adding Evolution Fresh drinks to the menu in all of its cafés and opening additional Evolution Fresh stores on the East and West Coasts. Although expanding into fresh juices means competing with Jamba Juice and other rivals,

Starbucks is relying on its brand-building expertise to juice up this part of its business.

Taking note of consumer interest in energy drinks, which has blossomed into an $8 billion market, Starbucks has also launched Starbucks Refreshers, a line of carbonated drinks with more than half the caffeine content of an espresso shot. Available in supermarkets and in Starbucks cafés, these all-natural drinks combine green, unroasted coffee with fruit juices for a fruity, non-coffee flavor. To gain significant market share, Starbucks must battle Red Bull, Rockstar, and other well-known marketers of energy drinks.

Starbucks also believes in social responsibility. It offers health-insurance benefits to both part-time and full-time employees and donates generously to community projects. It also protects the environment by recycling in every café and constructing buildings designed to save energy and water. Finally, the company follows ethical purchasing practices to ensure that coffee growers get a fair price for their premium beans.[31]

© iStockphoto.com/shaunl

Questions for Discussion

1. In terms of situational influences and level of involvement, what are the benefits of mobile pay?
2. With Evolution Fresh, which psychological influences on consumer buying decisions does Starbucks seem to be addressing?
3. Why would Starbucks want customers to know that it believes in social responsibility?

Case 7.2

Disney Markets to the Young and the Young at Heart

Walt Disney Company, the corporate home of Mickey and Minnie Mouse, is also home to such well-known characters as the Little Mermaid, Buzz Lightyear, and Iron Man. Disney theme parks and resorts host millions of families every year in Florida, California, Tokyo, Hong Kong, Paris, and beyond. Millions of youngsters log onto the company's Club Penguin website or use its app to play in a unique virtual world. Disney's media empire includes the Disney Channel, ABC, ESPN, and the A&E channels. Its studios turn out hit movies like *Frozen* and *Pirates of the Caribbean.* In short, with $42 billion in annual revenues, Disney knows how to use its understanding of consumer buying behavior to market to the young and the young at heart.

Club Penguin, which Disney acquired in 2007, is a fee-based subscription website marketed to parents on the basis of safety and learning. Disney reassures parents that Club Penguin has safeguards to ensure that children can't use inappropriate language in their online chats, for example, and to set limits on how much time children are allowed to play in Club Penguin. Financial safety is another consideration. Parents know exactly much they'll pay for Club Penguin every month, with no surprise bills for extras. Also, Disney stresses that many Club Penguin activities have an educational element, such as fostering teamwork and creativity. For children, the top reason to join Club Penguin is sociability: They can meet new friends online, compete in team games, and exchange chat messages while they play. Whether children are steered toward Club Penguin by their parents or invited to play online by their peers, Disney reinforces these features and benefits for the purchasers (parents) and the users (children).

Families with young children are a particular target market for Walt Disney World in Orlando and other Disney theme parks. During peak periods, however, families may face long waits for popular rides. To address this inconvenience, Disney introduced the FastPass reservation system, allowing customers to bypass the long lines and "reserve" a spot at a top attraction later in the day. More recently, Disney began testing MagicBand, a wristband intended to streamline the park experience even further. MagicBand serves as an admission ticket and an easy way to make FastPass reservations in advance or on the spot. It can also unlock the user's room in a Disney hotel or resort and, when linked with a credit card, lets the user pay for food or souvenirs with a simple flip of the wrist. And because wristbands are set up individually, Disney can use the data gathered by each band to analyze where users go, and when, and to personalize the park experience by, for example, having employees greet MagicBand users by name.

Disney is expanding into graphic novels for preteen boys. In the past, parents and educators often had negative attitudes toward comic books. These days, however, graphic novels with engaging artwork, complex plots, and interesting characters are perceived as another way to encourage children to read. Libraries and schools have begun to welcome graphic novels, and some book stores now dedicate significant shelf space to graphic novels. For the *Space Mountain* line of graphic novels, Disney built on broad awareness of its Space Mountain theme-park ride to tell the story of space cadets on a time-travel adventure. Knowing that the reading habits of this target market are evolving, Disney released the graphic novels in both printed and electronic form.

Disney has a long line of princess characters designed to appeal to girls from toddler age through teenage. It created Sofia the First, an ordinary preteen girl turned princess, with the attitudes, interests, and aspirations of preschool children and kindergartners in mind. As shown in her popular Disney Junior cable-television program, Sofia's life changes overnight when her mother marries a king. Sofia has to adjust to being part of a step-family, living in a castle, going to a new school, and acting like a princess—challenges that combine the familiar and the magical. Little girls are drawn to Sofia's unique situation and growing self-reliance. Sofia's story also contains elements geared to adults, such as music reminiscent of famous jazz and Motown songs. No wonder parents are buying books, soundtracks, dolls, and other merchandise for their young Sofia fans.[32]

Questions for Discussion

1. Which psychological influences on the buying decision process does Disney address with its marketing efforts?
2. Which social influences on the buying decision process do Disney marketing activities take into account?
3. Which situational influences on the buying decision process are particularly important to Disney's marketing efforts?

NOTES

[1] Olga Kharif, "Will Google Glass Catch On in the Office?" *Bloomberg Businessweek*, September 19, 2013, www.businessweek.com/articles/2013-09-19/google-glass-takes-aim-at-the-workplace (accessed November 15, 2013); Laura Oleniacz, "Google Glass Coming to Durham," *Herald-Sun (Durham, N.C.)*, September 27, 2013, www.heraldsun.com/news/showcase/x1703655280/Google-Glass-coming-to-Durham (accessed November 15, 2013); Jeff Glaze, "For Madison Tech Blogger, Glass Draws Interest," *Wisconsin State Journal*, August 12, 2013, http://host.madison.com/news/local/for-madison-tech-blogger-glass-draws-interest/article_2b8aba81-92da-51d0-bd14-b4e8a11d9734.html (accessed November 15, 2013); Todd R. Weiss, "Google Glass Used by Teacher to Bring Math, Science to Students," *eWeek*, August 2013, p. 2–2.

[2] Russell W. Belk, "Situational Variables and Consumer Behavior," *Journal of Consumer Research* (December 1975): 157–164.

[3] Ryan S. Elder and Ariadna Krishna, "The Effects of Advertising Copy on Sensory Thoughts and Perceived Taste," *Journal of Consumer Research* 36, no. 5 (February 2010): 748–756.

[4] Tom Bara, "The Force behind Cinnabon's 'Almost Pornographic' Global Appeal," *The Wall Street Journal*, September 27, 2013, http://blogs.wsj.com/corporate-intelligence/2013/09/27/the-force-behind-cinnabons-almost-pornographic-global-appeal/?KEYWORDS=sensory+marketing (accessed November 15, 2013).

[5] Bruce St. James, "Marketers Now Targeting Men with Grocery Products," KTAR, October 28, 2013, http://ktar.com/103/1672754/Marketers-now-targeting-men-with-grocery-products (accessed November 15, 2013); Alexander Abad-Santos, "The Rise of the Manly Grocery for the Manly Man," *The Atlantic Wire*, October 17, 2013, www.theatlanticwire.com/entertainment/2013/10/rise-manly-grocery-manly-man/70635 (accessed November 15, 2013).

[6] Sojung Kim and Matthew S. Eastin, "Hedonic Tendencies and the Online Consumer: An Investigation of the Online Shopping Process," *Journal of Internet Commerce* 10, no. 1 (2011): 68–90.

[7] Barry J. Babin and Eric G. Harris, *CB3* (Mason, OH: Cengage Learning, 2012), p. 130.

[8] Aric Rindfleisch, James E. Burroughs, and Nancy Wong, "The Safety of Objects: Materialism, Existential Insecurity, and Brand Connection," *Journal of Consumer Research* 36, no. 1 (June 2009): 1–16.

[9] "Common Threads Initiative," Patagonia, www.patagonia.com/us/common-threads (accessed November 15, 2013); Angus Loten, "With New Law, Profits Take a Back Seat," *The Wall Street Journal*, January 19, 2012, http://online.wsj.com/article/SB10001424052970203735304577168591470161630.html?KEYWORDS=Patagonia (accessed November 15, 2013).

[10] Nielsen PRIZM, www.claritas.com/MyBestSegments/Default.jsp?ID=70&pageName=Learn%2BMore&menuOption=learnmore (accessed November 15, 2013).

[11] Nielsen ConneXions, www.claritas.com/MyBestSegments/Default.jsp?ID=90&pageName=Learn%2BMore&menuOption=learnmore (accessed November 15, 2013).

[12] "Fast Facts," Marketing to Women Conference, www.m2w.biz/fast_facts.php (accessed November 15, 2013).

[13] Timothy B. Lee, "Here's Why Microsoft Is Buying Nokia's Phone Business," *The Washington Post*, September 3, 2013, www.washingtonpost .com/blogs/the-switch/wp/2013/09/03/heres -why-microsoft-is-buying-nokias-phone-business (accessed November 15, 2013).

[14] About H&M, http://about.hm.com/en/About .html (accessed November 15, 2013); "Target Designer Collaborations," *The Huffington Post*, www.huffingtonpost.com/news/target -designer-collaboration (accessed November 15, 2013); Ella Alexander, "Isabel Marant Is H&M's Latest—And Possibly Most Popular Ever," *Vogue* (UK), June 11, 2013, www .vogue.co.uk/news/2013/06/11/hm -design-collaboration-2013—news—updates (accessed November 1, 2013).

[15] "2010 Census Shows Asians Are Fastest-Growing Race Group," U.S. Census, March 21, 2012, www.census.gov/newsroom/releases/ archives/2010_census/cb12-cn22.html (accessed November 15, 2013).

[16] "Most Children Younger Than Age 1 Are Minorities," U.S. Census Newsroom, May 17, 2012, www.census.gov/newsroom/releases/ archives/population/cb12-90.html (accessed November 15, 2013).

[17] "African-American Consumers: Still Vital, Still Growing," Neilsen, 2012, www.nielsen .com/us/en/reports/2012/african-american -consumers--still-vital--still-growing-2012-repo .html (accessed November 15, 2013).

[18] Ibid.

[19] Tanzina Vega, "On the Concert Stage, BET Festival Offers a Broad Brand Experience," *The New York Times*, June 27, 2013, www .nytimes.com/2013/06/28/business/media/ on-the-concert-stage-bet-festival-offers -a-broad-brand-experience.html (accessed November 1, 2013).

[20] American Community Survey, U.S. Census Bureau, 2011.

[21] Hispanic Fast Facts, AHAA, http://ahaa.org/ default.asp?contentID=161 (accessed November 15, 2013).

[22] Jeffrey M. Humphreys, "The Multicultural Economy 2010," Selig Center for Economic Growth, www.terry.uga.edu/selig/buying _power.html (accessed November 15, 2013).

[23] Chiqui Cartagena, "Hispanics Are Creating a New Baby Boom in the United States," CNN, October 14, 2013, www.cnn.com/2013/10/14/ opinion/cartagena-latino-boom (accessed November 1, 2013).

[24] Miriam Jordan, "Mall Owners Woo Hispanic Shoppers," *The Wall Street Journal*, August 13, 2013, http://online.wsj.com/news/articles/SB10 001424127887323446404579010914180363136 (accessed November 1, 2013).

[25] American Community Survey, U.S. Census Bureau, 2011.

[26] Rosa Ramirez, "Asian American Purchasing Power to Rise to $1 Trillion," *National Journal*, November 21, 2012, www.nationaljournal.com/ thenextamerica/economy/asian-american -purchasing-power-to-rise-to-1-trillion -20121121 (accessed November 15, 2013).

[27] Nathaniel Popper and Somini Sengupta, "U.S. Says Ring Stole 160 Million Credit Card Numbers," *The New York Times*, July 25, 2013, http://dealbook.nytimes.com/2013/07/25/ arrests-planned-in-hacking-of-financial -companies (accessed November 1, 2013).

[28] "New Smartphone App Developed to Fight Retail Crime," *PR Web*, January 29, 2013, www.prweb.com/releases/2013/1/ prweb10355345.htm (accessed November 15, 2013).

[29] Michael Chertoff, "How Safe Is Your Data?" *The Wall Street Journal*, January 18, 2013, http://online.wsj.com/article/SB1000142412 7887323968304578246042685303734.html (accessed November 15, 2013).

[30] Don Reisinger, "Software Piracy Hits Record High of $59 Billion," *CNet*, May 12, 2011, http://news.cnet.com/8301-13506_3-20062167 -17.html (accessed November 15, 2013).

[31] Rose Yu, "Starbucks to Brew a Bigger China Pot," *The Wall Street Journal*, April 1, 2012, www.wsj.com (accessed February 12, 2014); Bruce Horovitz, "Starbucks to Jolt Consumers with Refreshers Energy Drink," *USA Today*, March 22, 2012, www.usatoday.com (accessed February 5, 2014); Bruce Horovitz, "Starbucks to Open First Evolution Fresh Juice Store," *USA Today*, March 18, 2012, www.usatoday.com (accessed March 3, 2014); Jennifer Van Grove, "Starbucks Apps Account for 42M Payments," *VentureBeat*, April 9, 2012, www.venturebeat. com (accessed February 17, 2014).

[32] Dean Takahashi, "Disney Takes Its Club Penguin Virtual World to the iPad," *Venture Beat*, December 12, 2013; Steve Smith, "Building the Perfect Princess," *Mediapost*, November 18, 2013, www.mediapost. com (accessed February 26, 2014); Heidi MacDonald, "Disney Expands Its Comics Program," *Publishers Weekly*, November 13, 2013, www.publishersweekly.com (accessed February 5, 2014); Brad Tuttle, "Why Vacationers Will Soon Spend Even More Time and Money at Disney World," *Time*, January 10, 2013, http://business.time.com (accessed March 3, 2014); Katherine Rosman, "Test-Marketing a Modern Princess," *The Wall Street Journal*, April 9, 2013, www.wsj.com (accessed March 2, 2014); www.thewaltdisneycompany.com (accessed March 3, 2014).

Feature Notes

[a] Stephanie Rosenbloom, "Now Checking In: Pampered Pets," *The New York Times*, September 18, 2013, www.nytimes.com; "Best Pet-Friendly Hotels in Miami," *CBS Local News Miami,* September 3, 2013, http://miami .cbslocal.com; Donald Wittkowski, "Dogs Are 'Ruffing It' at Revel," *Press of Atlantic City (Pleasantville, NJ),* May 25, 2013, www .pressofatlanticcity.com.

[b] Paula Ebben, "Stores Spy on Customers by Tracking Cell Phones," *WBZ-TV*, September 26, 2013, http://boston.cbslocal.com; Keli Rabon and Arthur Kane, "Some Stores Track Customers by WiFi on Smart Phones, the Call7 Investigators Found," *Denver Channel,* April 29, 2013, www. thedenverchannel.com; Stephanie Clifford and Quentin Hardy, "Attention, Shoppers: Store Is Tracking Your Cell," *The New York Times,* July 14, 2013, www.nytimes.com.

chapter 8

Business Markets and Buying Behavior

OBJECTIVES

8-1 Distinguish among the four types of business markets.

8-2 Identify the major characteristics of business customers and transactions.

8-3 Identify the attributes of demand for business products.

8-4 Describe the buying center, stages of the business buying decision process, and the factors that affect this process.

8-5 Describe industrial classification systems and how they can be used to identify and analyze business markets.

MARKETING INSIGHTS

iRobot's Avatar Tweaks Teleconferencing

Thanks to iRobot's marketing, tens of thousands of U.S. households own a Roomba vacuum robot. Now iRobot has teamed up with networking giant Cisco to put a fresh face in offices and factories around the world: Ava, an app-controlled robot that can navigate on its own to boardrooms or cubicles and facilitate teleconferences between colleagues who are many miles apart. The robotic technology comes from iRobot and the teleconferencing technology is from Cisco.

Ava (short for "Avatar") sports a large high-definition video screen, an onboard camera, a sensitive microphone, multiple speakers, and Wi-Fi connectivity. It is programmed to automatically map its surroundings and, when activated by app, roll itself into position where needed at a top speed of about one yard per second.

Teleconferencing via Ava can solve a number of problems for business customers. Managers and employees in different facilities can avoid the time and expense of travel by having Ava onsite to conduct video meetings via Wi-Fi. Ava can even check the participants' calendars to determine the best time and date for a video meeting. The robot can also arrange itself so the screen is always at eye level, whether people are seated around a conference table or standing inside a factory. Although the lease price of about $2,000 per month is not cheap, Ava may still be welcomed by corporate decision makers because of the robot's fresh take on calling meetings via the convenience of teleconferencing.[1]

© Daniel Santos Megina / Alamy

Marketers are just as concerned with meeting the needs of business customers as they are of meeting those of consumers. Marketers at iRobot and Cisco, for instance, go to considerable lengths to understand their customers so they can provide better, more satisfying products and develop and maintain long-term customer relationships.

In this chapter, we look at business markets and business buying decision processes. We first discuss various kinds of business markets and the types of buyers that comprise those markets. Next, we explore several dimensions of business buying, such as the characteristics of transactions, attributes and concerns of buyers, methods of buying, and distinctive features of demand for business products. We then examine how business buying decisions are made and who makes the purchases. Finally, we consider how business markets are analyzed.

8-1 BUSINESS MARKETS

As defined in Chapter 6, a business market (also called a *business-to-business market* or *B2B market*) consists of individuals, organizations, or groups that purchase a specific kind of product for one of three purposes: resale, direct use in producing other products, or use in general daily operations. Marketing to businesses employs the same concepts—defining target markets, understanding buying behavior, and developing effective marketing mixes—as marketing to ultimate consumers. However, there are important structural and behavioral differences in business markets. A company that markets to another company must be aware of how its product will affect other firms in the marketing channel, such as resellers and other manufacturers. Business products can also be technically complex, and the market often consists of sophisticated buyers.

Because the business market consists of relatively smaller customer populations, a segment of the market could be as small as a few customers.[2] The market for railway equipment in the United States, for example, is limited to a few major carriers. Some products can be both business and consumer products, especially commodities like corn, bolts, or screws, or supplies like light bulbs or furniture. However, the quantity purchased and the buying methods differ significantly between the consumer and business markets, even for the same products. Business marketing is often based on long-term mutually profitable relationships across members of the marketing channel. Networks of suppliers and customers recognize the importance of building strong alliances based on cooperation, trust, and collaboration.[3] Manufacturers may even co-develop new products, with business customers sharing marketing research findings, production, scheduling, inventory management, and information systems. Business marketing can take a variety of forms, ranging from long-term buyer–seller relationships to quick exchanges of basic products at competitive market prices. For most business marketers, the goal is to understand customer needs and provide a value-added exchange that shifts from attracting customers to keeping customers and developing relationships.

The four categories of business markets are producer, reseller, government, and institutional. In the remainder of this section, we discuss each of these types of markets.

8-1a Producer Markets

producer markets Individuals and business organizations that purchase products to make profits by using them to produce other products or using them in their operations

Individuals and business organizations that purchase products for the purpose of making a profit by using them to produce other products or using them in their operations are classified as **producer markets**. Producer markets include buyers of raw materials, as well as purchasers of semi-finished and finished items, used to make other products. Producer markets include a broad array of industries, including agriculture, forestry, fisheries, mining, construction, transportation, communications, and utilities. As Table 8.1 indicates, the number of business establishments in national producer markets is enormous. For instance, manufacturers buy raw materials and component parts for direct use in product creation. Grocery stores

Table 8.1 **Number of Establishments in Industry Groups**

Industry	Number of Establishments
Agriculture, forestry, fishing, and hunting	21,691
Mining, quarrying, and oil/gas extraction	27,092
Construction	682,684
Manufacturing	299,982
Transportation and warehousing	208,474
Utilities	17,600
Finance and insurance	473,494
Real estate	287,782

Source: Statistics of U.S. Business, all industries, U.S. Bureau of the Census, www.census.gov/econ/susb (accessed November 1, 2013).

and supermarkets are part of producer markets for numerous support products, such as paper and plastic bags, shelves, counters, and scanners. Farmers are part of producer markets for farm machinery, fertilizer, seed, and livestock. Chemical manufacturing plants are also part of producer markets, as they produce materials and ingredients that other firms use in the production of other goods.

Historically, manufacturers have tended to be geographically concentrated. More than half were located in just seven states: New York, California, Pennsylvania, Illinois, Ohio, New Jersey, and Michigan. However, this profile has changed as manufacturing processes are outsourced and factories close in some places and open in others. Manufacturing now also plays a vital role in the economies of states such as Wisconsin, Tennessee, and Kentucky.[4] The United States is also not the manufacturing powerhouse that it once was. In fact, the country has lost nearly a third of its high-tech manufacturing jobs since 2000. Most of this loss is attributable to outsourcing, cutbacks on funding for research and development, and increasingly competitive workforces in other countries, primarily in Asia.[5] The tide has very recently

Producer Markets
Chemical plants are part of the producer market because they produce goods that organizations purchase to use as ingredients in the production of other goods.

begun to turn the other way slowly, with more companies considering locating factories in the United States again as the wage gap between manufacturing jobs in the United States and other places like China has shrunk.[6]

8-1b Reseller Markets

Reseller markets consist of intermediaries, such as wholesalers and retailers, which buy finished goods and resell them for a profit. Aside from making minor alterations, resellers do not change the physical characteristics of the products they handle. Except for items producers sell directly to consumers, all products sold to consumer markets are first sold to reseller markets.

Wholesalers purchase products for resale to retailers, other wholesalers, producers, governments, and institutions. Like manufacturers, wholesalers can also be geographically concentrated. Of the nearly 414,000 wholesalers in the United States, a large number are located in New York, California, Illinois, Texas, Ohio, Pennsylvania, New Jersey, and Florida.[7] Although some products are sold directly to end users, many manufacturers sell their products to wholesalers, which then sell the products to other firms in the distribution system. Thus, wholesalers play a very important role in helping producers get their products to customers.

Retailers purchase products and resell them to final consumers. There are more than 1 million retailers in the United States, employing nearly 14.5 million people and generating approximately $3.9 trillion in annual revenues.[8] The United States continues to be a powerful force in retailing. Half of the top 10 largest retail companies in the world are based in the United States. These retailers are Walmart, The Kroger Co., Costco, Walgreen Co., and The Home Depot Inc.[9] Some retailers—Home Depot, PetSmart, and Staples, for example—carry a large number of items. Supermarkets may handle as many as 50,000 different products. In small, individually-owned retail stores, owners or managers make purchasing decisions. In chain stores, a central office buyer or buying committee frequently decides whether store managers will make a product available for selection. For many products, however, local managers make the actual buying decisions for a particular store.

When making purchase decisions, resellers consider several factors. They evaluate the level of demand for a product to determine the quantity and the price at which the product can be resold. Retailers assess the amount of space required to handle a product relative to its potential profit, sometimes on the basis of sales per square foot of selling area. Because customers often depend on resellers to have products available when needed, resellers typically appraise a supplier's ability to provide adequate quantities when and where they are needed. Resellers also take into account the ease of placing orders and whether producers offer technical assistance or training programs. Before resellers buy a product for the first time, they will try to determine whether the product competes with or complements products they currently handle. These types of concerns distinguish reseller markets from other markets.

reseller markets Intermediaries that buy finished goods and resell them for a profit

government markets Federal, state, county, or local governments that buy goods and services to support their internal operations and provide products to their constituencies

8-1c Government Markets

Federal, state, county, and local governments make up **government markets**. These markets spend billions of dollars annually for a wide range of goods and services—from office supplies and health-care services to vehicles, heavy equipment, and weapons—to support their internal operations and provide citizens with such products as highways, education, water service, energy, and national defense. Government spending accounts for slightly less than 40 percent of the U.S. total gross domestic product (GDP).[10] The amount spent by federal, state, and local units over the decades has gone up on average because the total number of government units and the services they provide have both increased.[11] Costs of providing these services have also risen.

Because government agencies spend public funds to buy the products needed to provide services, they are accountable to the public. This accountability explains their relatively complex buying procedures. Some firms choose not to sell to government buyers because of the additional time and expense the red tape costs them. However, many marketers benefit enough from government contracts that they do not find these procedures to be a stumbling block. For certain products, such as defense-related items, the government may be the only customer.

Governments advertise their purchase needs through releasing bids or negotiated contracts. Although companies may be reluctant to approach government markets because of the complicated bidding process, once they understand the rules of this process, firms can routinely penetrate government markets. To make a sale under the bid system, firms must apply and be approved for placement on a list of qualified bidders. When a government unit wants to buy, it sends out a detailed description of the products to qualified bidders. Businesses whose products fit with the needs described will submit bids. The government unit is usually required to accept the lowest bid.

When buying nonstandard or highly complex products, a government unit often uses a negotiated contract. Under this procedure, the government unit selects only a few firms and then negotiates specifications and terms. It eventually awards the contract to one of the negotiating firms.

Institutional Markets
This pipe organ producer supplies products mainly to churches, which are a part of institutional markets.

8-1d Institutional Markets

Organizations with charitable, educational, community, or other nonbusiness goals constitute **institutional markets**. Members of institutional markets include churches, some hospitals, fraternities and sororities, charitable organizations, and private colleges. Institutions purchase millions of dollars' worth of products annually to support their activities and provide goods, services, and ideas to various audiences. Because institutions often have different goals and fewer resources than other types of organizations, firms may use special marketing efforts to serve them. For example, Aramark provides a variety of services and products to institutional markets, including schools, hospitals, and senior living centers. It frequently ranks as one of the most admired companies in its industry. For areas like university food service, Aramark aims its marketing efforts directly at students.[12] Another example is the pictured pipe organ manufacturer. Because most businesses or individuals have no need for pipe organs, the producer mainly targets its marketing efforts at churches.

8-2 DIMENSIONS OF MARKETING TO BUSINESS CUSTOMERS

Now that we have considered different types of business customers, we look at several dimensions of marketing related to them, including transaction characteristics, attributes of business customers and some of their primary concerns, buying methods, major types of purchases, and the characteristics of demand for business products (see Figure 8.1).

institutional markets Organizations with charitable, educational, community, or other nonbusiness goals

Figure 8.1 **Dimensions of Marketing to Business Customers**

8-2a Characteristics of Transactions with Business Customers

Transactions between businesses differ from consumer sales in several ways. Orders by business customers tend to be much larger than individual consumer sales. Major government contractor Booz Allen Hamilton is sometimes awarded contracts worth up to half a billion dollars to supply medical and IT support assessments and services to various government agencies.[13] Suppliers of large, expensive, or complex goods often must sell products in large quantities to make profits. Consequently, they may prefer not to sell to customers who place small orders.

Some business purchases involve expensive items, such as computer systems. Other products, such as raw materials and component items, are used continuously in production, and their supply may need frequent replenishing. The contract regarding terms of sale of these items is likely to be a long-term agreement.

Discussions and negotiations associated with business purchases can require considerable marketing time and selling effort. Purchasing decisions are often made by committee, orders are frequently large and expensive, and products may be custom built. Several people or departments in the purchasing organization are often involved. For instance, one department expresses a need for a product, a second department develops the specifications, a third stipulates maximum expenditures, and a fourth places the order.

One practice unique to business markets is **reciprocity**, an arrangement in which two organizations agree to buy from each other. Reciprocal agreements that threaten competition are illegal. The Federal Trade Commission and the Justice Department monitor and take actions to stop anticompetitive reciprocal practices, particularly among large firms. Nonetheless, a certain amount of reciprocal activity occurs among small businesses and, to a lesser extent, among larger companies. Because reciprocity influences purchasing agents to deal only with certain suppliers, it can lower morale among agents and lead to less-than-optimal purchases.

reciprocity An arrangement unique to business marketing in which two organizations agree to buy from each other

8-2b Attributes of Business Customers

Business customers also differ from consumers in their purchasing behavior because they are generally better informed about the products they purchase. They typically demand detailed information about a product's functional features and technical specifications to ensure that it meets their needs. Personal goals, however, may also influence business buying behavior. Most purchasing agents seek the psychological satisfaction that comes with organizational advancement and financial rewards. Agents who consistently exhibit rational business buying behavior are likely to attain these personal goals because they help their firms achieve organizational objectives. Today, many suppliers and their customers build and maintain mutually beneficial relationships, sometimes called *partnerships*. Researchers find that even in a partnership between a small vendor and a large corporate buyer, a strong partnership can exist because high levels of interpersonal trust can lead to higher levels of commitment to the partnership by both organizations.[14]

8-2c Primary Concerns of Business Customers

When making purchasing decisions, business customers take into account a variety of factors. Among their chief considerations are price, product quality, service, and supplier relationships. Price is an essential consideration for business customers because it influences operating costs and costs of goods sold, which affects selling price, profit margin, and ultimately the ability to compete. A business customer is likely to compare the price of a product with the benefits the product will yield to the organization, often over a period of years. When purchasing major equipment, a business customer views price as the amount of investment necessary to obtain a certain level of return or savings on business operations.

Most business customers try to maintain a specific level of quality in the products they buy. To achieve this goal, most firms establish standards (usually stated as a percentage of defects allowed) for these products and buy them on the basis of a set of expressed characteristics, commonly called *specifications*. A customer evaluates the quality of the products being considered to determine whether they meet specifications. If a product fails to meet specifications or malfunctions for the ultimate consumer, the customer may drop that product's supplier and switch to a different one. On the other hand, customers are ordinarily cautious about buying products that exceed specifications because such products often cost more, which increases the organization's overall costs. As a result, business customers, therefore, must strike a balance between quality and price when making purchasing decisions.

Emerging Trends

Apps Help Businesses Make Buying Decisions

Business buyers constantly seek out the latest details about product specifications, availability, and price as they weigh decisions about what to buy and from which supplier. In some cases, buyers find they need information at night or on the go. No wonder marketers are coming out with apps to help business customers make more informed decisions, which in turn encourage repeat purchasing and loyalty.

The home improvement retailer Home Depot, for example, understands that builders can run out of lumber or need a special tool right away. With the Home Depot Pro app, the contractor can browse the local store's inventory to see what is in stock, click to buy, and immediately pick up the purchase. The app also connects customers to the Pro Desk if they want to talk with an expert before buying.

General Electric has a Smart Catalog app that accesses electronic catalogs listing thousands of lighting fixtures, motors, and electrical parts, saving buyers the hassle of paging through outdated printed catalogs. Business operations software company SAP sells a purchasing approval app, which streamlines the procurement process for firms and saves time.[a]

Concerns of Business Customers
No matter what the shipping need, Old Dominion promises to deliver a high level of service and customer satisfaction through its shipping service.

Specifications are designed to meet a customer's wants, and anything that does not contribute to meeting those wants may be considered wasteful. Because their purchases tend to be large and sometimes complicated, business buyers value service. Services offered by suppliers directly and indirectly influence customers' costs, sales, and profits. Offering quality customer service can be a means of gaining a competitive advantage over other firms, which leads some businesses to seek out ways to improve their customer service. Long known for its quality customer service and strong customer devotion, The Walt Disney Company offers customer service consulting and training to businesses through its Disney Institute. The service is highly popular, as many firms would like to attract the same level of customer loyalty that Disney does. The Disney Institute has worked with organizations as diverse as Chevrolet and local hospitals.[15]

Typical services business customers desire from suppliers are market information, inventory maintenance, on-time delivery, and repair services. Business buyers may need technical product information, data regarding demand, information about general economic conditions, or supply and delivery information. Purchasers of machinery are especially concerned about obtaining repair services and replacement parts quickly because inoperable equipment is costly, in terms of both repairs and lost productivity.

Maintaining adequate inventory is critical to quality, customer service, customer satisfaction, and managing inventory costs and distribution efficiency. Furthermore, on-time delivery is crucial to ensuring that products are available as needed. Reliable on-time delivery saves business customers money because it enables them to carry only the inventory needed at any given time. Consider the advertisement for Old Dominion Freight Line. The ad shows a hockey player hitting a roll of packaging tape into the back of a truck. At the bottom is the line, "If you're in the skates and sticks business, so are we." This image is meant to show how seriously Old Dominion takes its business and how it is willing to learn about each client's needs. Whatever the business is, be it hockey gear or something else, Old Dominion will transport goods on time and provide other needed services to help a business run efficiently.

Customer expectations about quality of service have increased and broadened over time. Using traditional service quality standards based only on traditional manufacturing and accounting systems is not sufficient. Customers also expect to have access to communication channels that allow them to ask questions, voice complaints, submit orders, and track shipments. Marketers should develop customer service objectives and monitor customer service programs, striving for uniformity of service, simplicity, truthfulness, and accuracy. Firms can observe service by formally surveying customers or informally calling on customers and asking questions about the service they receive. Spending the time and effort to ensure that customers are satisfied can greatly benefit marketers by increasing customer retention.

Finally, business customers are concerned about the costs of developing and maintaining relationships with their suppliers. By building trust with a particular supplier, buyers can reduce their search efforts and uncertainty about prices. Business customers have to keep in mind the overall fit of a supplier and its products with marketing objectives, including distribution and inventory-maintenance costs and efficiency.

8-2d Methods of Business Buying

Although no two business buyers do their jobs the same way, most use one or more of the following purchase methods: *description*, *inspection*, *sampling*, and *negotiation*. The most straightforward is description. When products are standardized and graded according to certain characteristics such as size, shape, weight, and color, a business buyer may be able to purchase simply by describing or specifying quantity, grade, and other attributes. Commodities and raw materials may be purchased this way. Sometimes buyers specify a particular brand or its equivalent when describing the desired product. Purchases based on description are especially common between a buyer and seller with an ongoing relationship built on trust.

Certain products, such as industrial equipment, used vehicles, and buildings, have unique characteristics and may vary with regard to condition. Depending on how they were used and for how long, two products may be in very different conditions, even if they look identical on paper. Consequently, business buyers of such products should base purchase decisions on inspection.

Sampling entails evaluating a portion of the product on the assumption that its characteristics represent the entire lot. This method is appropriate when the product is homogeneous—for instance, grain—and examining the entire lot is not physically or economically feasible.

Some purchases by businesses are based on negotiated contracts. In certain instances, buyers describe exactly what they need and ask sellers to submit bids. They then negotiate with the suppliers that submit the most attractive bids. This approach is generally used for very large or expensive purchases, such as commercial vehicles. This is frequently how government departments conduct business. In other cases, the buyer may be unable to identify specifically what is to be purchased and can provide only a general description, as might be the case for a piece of custom-made equipment. A buyer and seller might negotiate a contract that specifies a base price and provides for the payment of additional costs and fees. These contracts are most commonly used for one-time projects such as buildings, capital equipment, and special projects.

new-task purchase An organization's initial purchase of an item to be used to perform a new job or solve a new problem

straight rebuy purchase A routine purchase of the same products under approximately the same terms of sale by a business buyer

8-2e Types of Business Purchases

Most business purchases are one of three types: new-task, straight rebuy, or modified rebuy. Each type is subject to different influences and require business marketers to modify their selling approaches appropriately. For a **new-task purchase**, an organization makes an initial purchase of an item to be used to perform a new job or solve a new problem. A new-task purchase may require development of product specifications, vendor specifications, and procedures for future product purchases. To make the initial purchase, the business buyer usually needs to acquire a lot of information. New-task purchases are important to suppliers because they can result in a long-term buying relationship if customers are satisfied.

A **straight rebuy purchase** occurs when buyers purchase the same products routinely under approximately the same terms of sale. Buyers require little information for routine purchase decisions and tend to use familiar suppliers that have provided satisfactory service and products in the past. These marketers may set up automatic systems to make reordering easy and convenient for business buyers. A supplier may even monitor the business buyer's inventories and communicate to the buyer what should be ordered and when.

© ASUS Computer International

Types of Business Purchases
When purchasing equipment, such as Asus laptops, business customers are likely to use a modified rebuy strategy as business needs change over time.

For a **modified rebuy purchase**, a new-task purchase is altered after two or three orders, or requirements associated with a straight rebuy purchase are modified. A business buyer might seek faster delivery, lower prices, or a different quality level of product specifications. For example, business customers of Asus computers, featured in the advertisement, probably use modified rebuy purchases as their computing needs change. For instance, a business might choose to upgrade to the ASUS Zenbook™ UX301 because it is highly damage-resistant and combines both a touchscreen and a keyboard. Orders are likely to be similar over time, but demand for specific business products and supplies may fluctuate in cycles that mirror periods of higher and lower customer demand. A modified rebuy situation may cause regular suppliers to compete to keep the account. When a firm changes the terms of a service contract, such as modifying the speed or comprehensiveness of a telecommunication services package, it has made a modified rebuy purchase.

8-3 DEMAND FOR BUSINESS PRODUCTS

Demand for business products (also called *industrial demand*) can be characterized as (1) derived, (2) inelastic, (3) joint, or (4) fluctuating.

8-3a Derived Demand

Because business customers, especially producers, buy products for direct or indirect use in the production of goods and services to satisfy consumers' needs, the demand for business products derives from the demand for consumer products—it is therefore called **derived demand**. In the long run, no demand for business products is totally unrelated to the demand for consumer products. The derived nature of demand is usually multilevel in that business marketers at different levels are affected by a change in consumer demand for a product. The component parts of computers are another example of something that experiences derived demand. Demand for Intel processors, for instance, derives from the demand for computers. The "Intel inside" sticker featured on many computers is meant to stimulate derived demand by encouraging customers to choose a computer with an Intel processor. Change in consumer demand for a product affects demand for all firms involved in the production of that product.

modified rebuy purchase A new-task purchase that is changed on subsequent orders or when the requirements of a straight rebuy purchase are modified

derived demand Demand for business products that stems from demand for consumer products

Derived Demand
The demand for Intel processors derives from the sale of computers that are constructed with Intel processors. The "Intel Inside" message in advertisements and on computer packaging aims at stimulating derived demand.

8-3b Inelastic Demand

With **inelastic demand**, a price increase or decrease does not significantly alter demand for a business product. A product has inelastic demand when the buyer is not sensitive to price or when there are no ready substitutes. Because many business products are more specialized than consumer products, buyers will continue to make purchases even as the price goes up. Because some business products contain many different parts, price increases that affect only one or two parts may yield only a slightly higher per-unit production cost. Because some business products contain a large number of parts that each comprise a small portion of the overall cost, price increases that affect only one or two parts may yield only a slightly higher per-unit production cost. However, when a sizable price increase for a component represents a large proportion of the product's cost, demand may become more elastic because the price increase in the component causes the price at the consumer level to rise sharply. If manufacturers of a key part of solar panels, for instance, substantially increase their prices, forcing the cost of solar photovoltaic panel units to skyrocket, the demand for that source of renewable energy will decrease (or become more elastic) as businesses and consumers reconsider whether there will be a return on investment in installing a solar energy system.

Inelasticity of demand in the business market applies at the industry level, while demand for an individual firm's products may fluctuate. Suppose a spark plug producer increases the price of spark plugs sold to small-engine manufacturers, but its competitors continue to maintain lower prices. The spark plug company that raised its prices will experience reduced unit sales because most small-engine producers will switch to lower-priced brands. A specific firm, therefore, remains vulnerable to elastic demand, while demand across the industry as a whole will not fluctuate drastically.

inelastic demand Demand that is not significantly altered by a price increase or decrease

joint demand Demand involving the use of two or more items in combination to produce a product

8-3c Joint Demand

Certain business products, especially raw materials and components, are subject to joint demand. **Joint demand** occurs when two or more items are used in combination to produce a product. Consider the advertisement for Patron tequila, which emphasizes the quality of the ingredients that go into the products, even the material used in its corks. Demand for the special material Patron uses will increase or decrease jointly with tequila sales, as it is a required component of every bottle of tequila sold. Understanding the effects of joint demand is particularly important for a marketer that sells multiple jointly demanded items. Such a marketer realizes that when a customer begins purchasing one of the jointly demanded items, a good opportunity exists to sell related products.

8-3d Fluctuating Demand

Because the demand for business products is derived from consumer demand, it is subject to dramatic fluctuations. In general, when consumer products are in high demand, producers buy large quantities of raw materials and components to ensure that they meet long-run production requirements. These producers may expand production capacity to meet demands as well, which entails acquiring new equipment and machinery, more workers, and more raw materials and component parts. Conversely, a decline in demand for certain consumer goods reduces demand for business products used to produce those goods.

Joint Demand
The demand for the high-quality cork used in Patron's tequila bottle stoppers increases or decreases jointly as demand for the bottles used for the tequila increases or decreases.

Sometimes, price changes lead to surprising temporary changes in demand. A price increase for a business product initially may cause business customers to buy more of the item in an attempt to stock up because they expect the price to continue to rise. Similarly, demand for a business product may decrease significantly following a price cut because buyers are waiting for further price reductions. Fluctuations in demand can be substantial in industries in which prices change frequently.

8-4 BUSINESS BUYING DECISIONS

Business (organizational) buying behavior refers to the purchase behavior of producers, government units, institutions, and resellers. Although several factors that affect consumer buying behavior (discussed in Chapter 7) also influence business buying behavior, a number of factors are unique to businesses. In this section, we first analyze the buying center to learn who participates in business buying decisions. Then we focus on the stages of the buying decision process and the factors that affect it.

8-4a The Buying Center

Relatively few business purchase decisions are made by just one person. Often purchases are made through a buying center. The **buying center** is the group of people within the organization who make business buying decisions. They include users, influencers, buyers, deciders, and gatekeepers.[16] One person may perform several roles within the buying center, and participants share goals and risks associated with their decisions.

business (organizational) buying behavior The purchase behavior of producers, government units, institutions, and resellers

buying center The people within an organization who make business purchase decisions

Users are the organizational members who will actually use the product. They frequently initiate the purchase process and/or generate purchase specifications. After the purchase, they evaluate product performance relative to the specifications.

Influencers are often technical personnel, such as engineers, who help develop product specifications and evaluate alternatives. Technical personnel are especially important influencers when the products being considered involve new, advanced technology.

Buyers select suppliers and negotiate terms of purchase. They may also be involved in developing specifications. Buyers are sometimes called purchasing agents or purchasing

ENTREPRENEURSHIP IN MARKETING

Two Moms Go from Zero to $70 Million in 7 Years!

Founders: Kristin Groose Richmond and Kirsten Saenz Tobey
Business: Revolution Foods
Founded: 2006
Success: Company grew from a start-up to $70 million in annual sales in only seven years.

Two entrepreneurial moms started Revolution Foods with the idea of cooking up nutritious meals that students would gobble up. Kristin Groose Richmond and Kirsten Saenz Tobey met at the University of California-Berkeley's Haas School of Business, and their shared interest in healthy foods for children led them to team up at Revolution Foods.

Given growing concerns about childhood obesity and the drive to instill healthy eating habits from an early age, they knew parents and school officials would welcome new options for school breakfasts and lunches if the price was right. Revolution Foods proved itself by researching what children like to eat, creating affordable menus featuring foods from local sources, testing the meals in local schools, and continually refining the menus and prices over time.

After winning big customers like the San Francisco Unified School District, the firm now serves more than 1 million meals every week. Building on its success, Revolution Foods is branching out into the consumer market with prepackaged meals sold in supermarkets nationwide.[b]

iStockphoto.com/CRTd

managers. Their choices of vendors and products, especially for new-task purchases, are heavily influenced by others in the buying center. For straight rebuy purchases, the buyer plays a major role in vendor selection and negotiations.

Deciders actually choose the products. Although buyers may be deciders, it is not unusual for different people to occupy these roles. For routinely purchased items, buyers are commonly deciders. However, a buyer may not be authorized to make purchases that exceed a certain dollar limit, in which case higher-level management personnel are deciders.

Finally, *gatekeepers*, such as administrative assistants and technical personnel, control the flow of information to and among the different roles in the buying center. Buyers who deal directly with vendors also may be gatekeepers because they can control information flows. The flow of information from a supplier's sales representatives to users and influencers is often controlled by personnel in the purchasing department.

The number and structure of an organization's buying centers are affected by the organization's size and market position, the volume and types of products being purchased, and the firm's overall managerial philosophy on who should make purchase decisions. The size of a buying center is influenced by the stage of the buying decision process and by the type of purchase (new task, straight rebuy, or modified rebuy). The size of the buying center is generally larger for a new-task purchase than for a straight rebuy. A marketer attempting to sell to a business customer should first determine who the people in the buying center are, the roles they play, and which individuals are most influential in the decision process. Although it may not be feasible to contact all those involved in the buying center, marketers should contact a few of the most influential people.

8-4b Stages of the Business Buying Decision Process

Like consumers, businesses follow a buying decision process. This process is summarized in the lower portion of Figure 8.2. In the first stage, one or more individuals recognize that a problem or need exists. Problem recognition may arise under a variety of circumstances—for instance, when machines malfunction or a firm modifies an existing product or introduces

Figure 8.2 Business (Organizational) Buying Decision Process and Factors That May Influence It

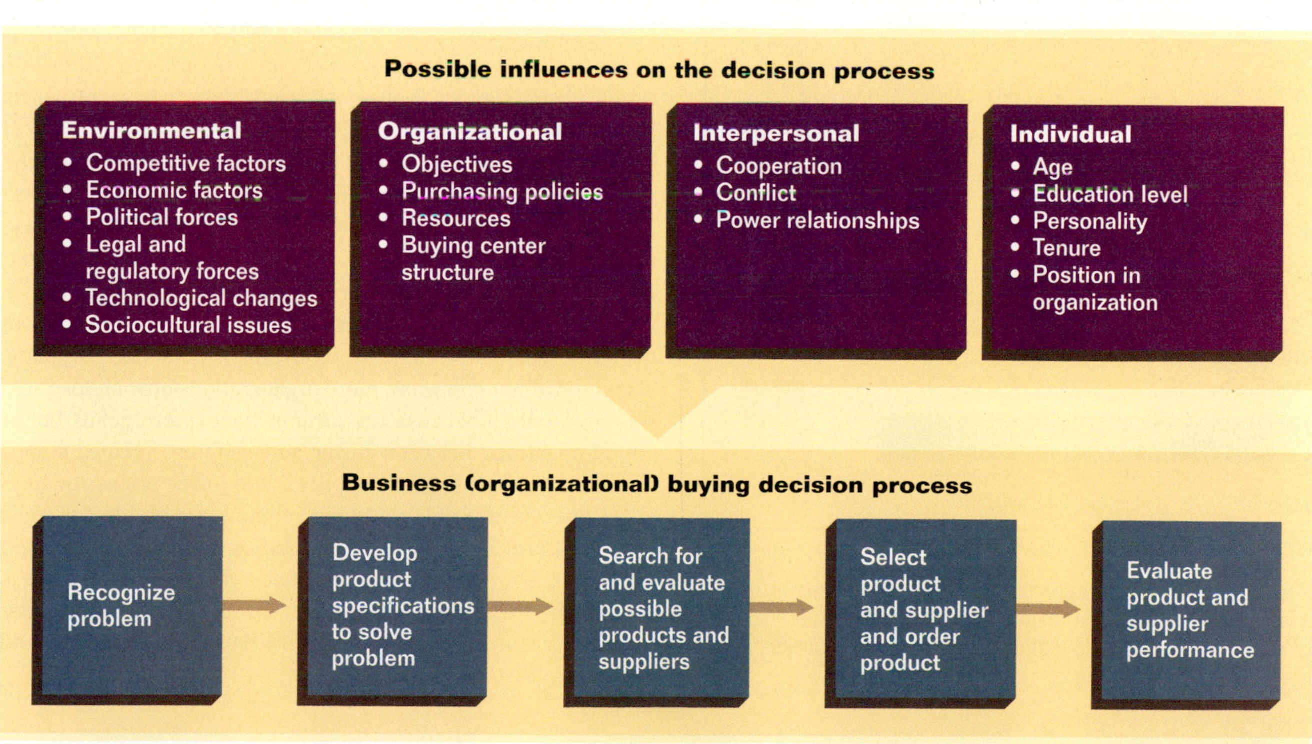

a new one. It may be individuals in the buying center or other individuals in the firm who initially recognize that a problem exists.

The second stage of the process, development of product specifications, requires that buying center participants assess the problem or need and determine what is necessary to resolve or satisfy it. During this stage, users and influencers, such as engineers, provide information and advice for developing product specifications. By assessing and describing needs, the organization should be able to establish product specifications.

Searching for and evaluating potential products and suppliers is the third stage in the decision process. Search activities may involve looking in company files and trade directories, contacting suppliers for information, soliciting proposals from known vendors, and examining various online and print publications. It is common for organizations, particularly those with a reputation for having open hiring policies, to specify a desire to work with diverse vendors, such as those owned by women or by minorities. During this stage, some organizations engage in value analysis, an evaluation of each component of a potential purchase. **Value analysis** examines quality, design, materials, and possibly item reduction or deletion to acquire the product in the most cost-effective way. Some vendors may be deemed unacceptable because they are not large enough to supply needed quantities. Others may be excluded because of poor delivery and service records. Sometimes the product is not available from any vendor and the buyer will work with an innovative supplier to design and produce it. Buyers evaluate products to make sure they meet or exceed product specifications developed in the second stage of the business buying decision process. Usually suppliers are judged according to multiple criteria. A number of firms employ **vendor analysis**, a formal, systematic evaluation of current and potential vendors, focusing on such characteristics as price, product quality, delivery service, product availability, and overall reliability.

value analysis An evaluation of each component of a potential purchase

vendor analysis A formal, systematic evaluation of current and potential vendors

multiple sourcing An organization's decision to use several suppliers

sole sourcing An organization's decision to use only one supplier

The results of deliberations and assessments in the third stage are used during the fourth stage of the process to select the product to be purchased and the supplier. In some cases, the buyer selects and uses several suppliers, a process known as **multiple sourcing**. Firms with federal government contracts are generally required to have several sources for an item to ensure a steady supply. At times, only one supplier is selected, a situation called **sole sourcing**. For organizations that outsource their payroll services, many of these companies will use just one provider. The Intuit advertisement focuses on a problem that many firms have with implementing and maintaining a smooth payroll process. The chewed pencil underscores what a headache payroll can be for many firms. The businesses that recognize that they have this problem are encouraged to purchase Intuit's payroll products to make the process easier and smoother because they cover all business payroll needs.

Sole sourcing has historically been discouraged except in the cases where a product is only available from one company. Though still not common, more organizations now choose sole sourcing, partly because the arrangement often means better communications between buyer and supplier, greater stability and higher profits for suppliers, and lower prices for buyers. However, multiple sourcing remains preferable for most firms because it lessens the possibility of disruption caused by strikes, shortages, or bankruptcies. The actual product is ordered in this fourth stage, and specific details regarding terms, credit arrangements, delivery dates and methods, and technical assistance are finalized.

Sole Sourcing
This advertisement for Intuit points to the problem some firms have with implementing and maintaining a smooth and efficient payroll process. Businesses that outsource payroll processing are likely to use just one vendor.

During the fifth stage, the product's performance is evaluated by comparing it with specifications. Sometimes the product meets the specifications, but its performance fails to adequately solve the problem or satisfy the need recognized in the first stage. In that case, product specifications must be adjusted. The supplier's performance is also evaluated during this stage. If supplier performance is inadequate, the business purchaser seeks corrective action from the supplier or searches for a new one. Results of the evaluation become useful feedback in future business purchase decisions.

This business buying decision process is used in its entirety primarily for new-task purchases. Several stages, but not necessarily all, are used for modified rebuy and straight rebuy situations.

8-4c Influences on the Business Buying Decision Process

Figure 8.2 also lists the four major factors that influence business buying decisions: environmental, organizational, interpersonal, and individual. Environmental factors include competitive and economic factors, political forces, legal and regulatory forces, technological changes, and sociocultural issues. These factors can generate considerable uncertainty for an organization, including in buying decisions. Changes in one or more environmental forces, such as new government regulations or increased competition, can create opportunities and threats that affect purchasing decisions.

Organizational factors that influence the buying decision process include the company's objectives, purchasing policies, resources, and the size and composition of its buying center. An organization may also have certain buying policies to which buying center participants must conform that limit buying decisions. For instance, a firm's policies may mandate contract lengths that are undesirable to many sellers. An organization's financial resources may require special credit arrangements. Any of these conditions could affect purchase decisions.

Interpersonal factors are the relationships among people in the buying center. Trust is crucial in collaborative partnerships. This is especially true when customized products are involved—the buyer may not see the product until it is finished and must trust that the producer is creating it to specifications. Trust and clear communication will ensure that all parties are satisfied with the outcome. Interpersonal dynamics and varying communication abilities within the buying center may complicate processes.

Individual factors are the personal characteristics of participants in the buying center, such as age, education level, personality, and tenure and position in the organization. Consider a 55-year-old manager who has been in the organization for 25 years. This manager is likely to have a greater influence and power over buying center decisions than a 30-year-old employed at the firm only two years. The influence of various factors, such as age and tenure, on the buying decision process depends on the buying situation, the type of product, and the type of purchase (new task, modified rebuy, or straight

Source: American Express OPEN survey of 272 small-business owners ages 48–70.

rebuy). Employees' negotiating styles will vary, as well. To be effective, marketers must know customers well enough to be aware of these individual factors and their potential effects on purchase decisions.

8-5 INDUSTRIAL CLASSIFICATION SYSTEMS

Marketers have access to a considerable amount of information about potential business customers through government and industry publications and websites. Marketers use this information to identify potential business customers and to estimate their purchase potential.

Much information about business customers is based on industrial classification systems. In the United States, marketers historically relied on the *Standard Industrial Classification (SIC) system,* which the federal government developed to classify selected economic characteristics of industrial, commercial, financial, and service organizations. The SIC system was replaced by the **North American Industry Classification System (NAICS)** when the United States joined the North American Free Trade Agreement (NAFTA). NAICS is a single industry classification system used by the United States, Canada, and Mexico to generate comparable statistics among the three NAFTA partners. The NAICS classification is based on production activities. NAICS is also similar to the International Standard Industrial Classification (ISIC) system used in Europe and many other parts of the world.

Whereas the SIC system divided industrial activity into 10 divisions, NAICS divides it into 20 sectors. NAICS contains 1,170 industry classifications, compared with 1,004 in the SIC system. NAICS is comprehensive and up-to-date, and it provides considerably more information about service industries and high-tech products than the SIC system.[17] Table 8.2 shows some NAICS codes for Apple Inc. and AT&T Inc.

North American Industry Classification System (NAICS) An industry classification system that generates comparable statistics among the United States, Canada, and Mexico

Industrial classification systems provide a uniform means of categorizing organizations into groups based on such factors as the types of goods and services provided. Although an industrial classification system is a vehicle for segmentation, it is best used in conjunction

Table 8.2 Examples of NAICS Classification

NAICS Hierarchy for AT&T Inc.		NAICS Hierarchy for Apple Inc.	
Sector 51	Information	Sector 31–33	Manufacturing
Subsector 517	Telecommunications	Subsector 334	Computer and Electronic Manufacturing
Industry Group 5171	Wired Telecommunication Carriers	Industry Group 3341	Computer and Peripheral Equipment Manufacturing
Industry Group 5172	Wireless Telecommunications Carriers		
Industry 51711	Wired Telecommunication Carriers	Industry 33411	Computer and Peripheral Equipment Manufacturing
Industry 51721	Wireless Telecommunications Carriers		
Industry 517110	Wired Telecommunication Carriers	U.S. Industry 334111	Electronic Computer Manufacturing
Industry 517210	Wireless Telecommunications Carriers		

Source: NAICS Association, www.census.gov/eos/www/naics (accessed January 7, 2014).

with other types of data to determine exactly how many and which customers a marketer can reach.

A marketer can take several approaches to determine the identities and locations of organizations in specific groups. One approach is to use state directories or commercial industrial directories, such as *Standard & Poor's Register* and Dun & Bradstreet's *Million Dollar Database*. These sources contain information about a firm, including its name, industrial classification, address, phone number, and annual sales. By referring to one or more of these sources, marketers isolate business customers by industrial classification numbers, determine their locations, and develop lists of potential customers by desired geographic area.

A more expedient, although more expensive, approach is to use a commercial data service. Dun & Bradstreet, for example, can provide a list of organizations that fall into a particular industrial classification group. For each company on the list, Dun & Bradstreet provides the name, location, sales volume, number of employees, type of products handled, names of chief executives, and other pertinent information. Either method can identify and locate effectively a group of potential customers by industry and location. Because some companies on the list will have greater potential than others, marketers must conduct further research to determine which customer or customer group to pursue.

To estimate the purchase potential of business customers or groups of customers, a marketer must find a relationship between the size of potential customers' purchases and a variable available in industrial classification data, such as the number of employees. Thus, a paint manufacturer might attempt to determine the average number of gallons purchased by a type of potential customer relative to the number of employees. Once this relationship is established, it can be applied to customer groups to estimate the size and frequency of potential purchases. After deriving these estimates, the marketer is in a position to select the customer groups with the most sales and profit potential.

Despite their usefulness, industrial classification data pose several problems. First, a few industries do not have specific designations. Second, because transferring products from one establishment to another is counted as a shipment, double counting may occur when products are shipped between two establishments within the same firm. Third, because the Census Bureau is prohibited from providing data that identify specific business organizations, some data (such as value of total shipments) may be understated. Finally, because government agencies provide industrial classification data, a significant lag usually exists between data-collection time and the time when the information is released.

Summary

8-1 Distinguish among the four types of business markets.

Business (B2B) markets consist of individuals, organizations, and groups that purchase a specific kind of product for resale, direct use in producing other products, or use in day-to-day operations. Producer markets include those individuals and business organizations that purchase products for the purpose of making a profit by using them to produce other products or as part of their operations. Intermediaries that buy finished products and resell them to make a profit are classified as reseller markets. Government markets consist of federal, state, county, and local governments, which spend billions of dollars annually for goods and services to support internal operations and to provide citizens with needed services. Organizations with charitable, educational, community, or other nonprofit goals constitute institutional markets.

8-2 Identify the major characteristics of business customers and transactions.

Transactions that involve business customers differ from consumer transactions in several ways. Business transactions tend to be larger and negotiations occur less frequently, though they are often lengthy. They may involve more than one person or department in the purchasing organization. They may also involve reciprocity, an arrangement in which two organizations agree to buy from each other. Business customers are usually better informed than ultimate consumers and are more likely to seek information about a product's features and technical specifications.

Business customers are particularly concerned about quality, service, price, and supplier relationships. Quality is important because it directly affects the quality of products the buyer's firm produces. To achieve an exact level of quality, organizations often buy products on the basis of a set of expressed characteristics, called specifications. Because services have such a direct influence on a firm's costs, sales, and profits, factors such as market information, on-time delivery, and availability of parts are crucial to a business buyer. Although business customers do not depend solely on price to decide which products to buy, price is of primary concern because it directly influences profitability.

Business buyers use several purchasing methods, including description, inspection, sampling, and negotiation. Most organizational purchases are new-task, straight rebuy, or modified rebuy. In a new-task purchase, an organization makes an initial purchase of items to be used to perform new jobs or solve new problems. A straight rebuy purchase occurs when a buyer purchases the same products routinely under approximately the same terms of sale. In a modified rebuy purchase, a new-task purchase is changed the second or third time it is ordered or requirements associated with a straight rebuy purchase are modified.

8-3 Identify the attributes of demand for business products.

Industrial demand differs from consumer demand along several dimensions. Industrial demand derives from demand for consumer products. At the industry level, industrial demand is inelastic. If an industrial item's price changes, product demand will not change as much proportionally. Some industrial products are subject to joint demand, which occurs when two or more items are used in combination to make a product. Finally, because organizational demand derives from consumer demand, the demand for business products can fluctuate significantly.

8-4 Describe the buying center, the stages of the business buying decision process, and the factors that affect this process.

Business (or organizational) buying behavior refers to the purchase behavior of producers, resellers, government units, and institutions. Business purchase decisions are made through a buying center, the group of people involved in making such purchase decisions. Users are those in the organization who actually use the product. Influencers help develop specifications and evaluate alternative products for possible use. Buyers select suppliers and negotiate purchase terms. Deciders choose the products. Gatekeepers control the flow of information to and among individuals occupying other roles in the buying center.

The stages of the business buying decision process are problem recognition, development of product specifications to solve problems, search for and evaluation of products and suppliers, selection and ordering of the most appropriate product, and evaluation of the product's and supplier's performance.

Four categories of factors influence business buying decisions: environmental, organizational, interpersonal, and individual. Environmental factors include competitive forces, economic conditions, political forces, laws and regulations, technological changes, and sociocultural factors. Business factors include the company's objectives, purchasing policies, and resources, as well as the size and composition of its buying center. Interpersonal factors are the relationships among people in the buying center. Individual factors are personal characteristics of members of the buying center, such as age, education level, personality, and tenure and position in the organization.

8-5 Describe industrial classification systems and how they can be used to identify and analyze business markets.

Business marketers have a considerable amount of information available for use in planning marketing strategies. Much of this information is based on an industrial classification system, which categorizes businesses into major industry groups, industry subgroups, and detailed industry categories. The North American Industry Classification System (NAICS) replaced the earlier Standard Industrial Classification (SIC) system and is used by the United States, Canada, and Mexico. It provides marketers with information needed to identify business customer groups. It can best be used for this purpose in conjunction with other information. After identifying target industries, a marketer can obtain the names and locations of potential customers by using government and commercial data sources. Marketers then must estimate potential purchases of business customers by finding a relationship between a potential customer's purchases and a variable available in industrial classification data.

Go to www.cengagebrain.com for resources to help you master the content in this chapter as well as for materials that will expand your marketing knowledge!

Developing Your Marketing Plan

When developing a marketing strategy for business customers, it is essential to understand the process the business goes through when making a buying decision. Knowledge of business buying behavior is important when developing several aspects of the marketing plan. To assist you in relating the information in this chapter to the creation of a marketing plan for business customers, consider the following issues:

1. What are the primary concerns of business customers? Could any of these concerns be addressed with the strengths of your company?
2. Determine the type of business purchase your customer will likely be using when purchasing your product. How would this impact the level of information required by the business when moving through the buying decision process?
3. Discuss the different types of demand that the business customer will experience when purchasing your product.

The information obtained from these questions should assist you in developing various aspects of your marketing plan found in the "Interactive Marketing Plan" exercise at www.cengagebrain.com.

Important Terms

producer markets 222
reseller markets 224
government markets 224
institutional markets 225
reciprocity 226
new-task purchase 229
straight rebuy purchase 229
modified rebuy purchase 230
derived demand 230
inelastic demand 231
joint demand 231
business (organizational) buying behavior 232
buying center 232
value analysis 234
vendor analysis 234
multiple sourcing 234
sole sourcing 234
North American Industry Classification System (NAICS) 236

Discussion and Review Questions

1. Identify, describe, and give examples of the four major types of business markets.
2. Why might business customers generally be considered more rational in their purchasing behavior than ultimate consumers?
3. What are the primary concerns of business customers?
4. List several characteristics that differentiate transactions involving business customers from consumer transactions.
5. What are the commonly used methods of business buying?
6. Why do buyers involved in straight rebuy purchases require less information than those making new-task purchases?
7. How does demand for business products differ from consumer demand?
8. What are the major components of a firm's buying center?
9. Identify the stages of the business buying decision process. How is this decision process used when making straight rebuys?
10. How do environmental, business, interpersonal, and individual factors affect business purchases?
11. What function does an industrial classification system help marketers perform?

Video Case 8.1

Dale Carnegie Focuses on Business Customers

Dale Carnegie was a highly successful entrepreneur and one of the most legendary speakers of the 20th century. His simple but effective two-step formula for connecting with customers and colleagues in business situations was (1) win friends and (2) influence people. He began teaching his methods as part of the Dale Carnegie Course in 1912. In 1936, he published his ground-breaking book, *How to Win Friends and Influence People,* which went on to become an international bestseller and is still available in print, as an audio book, and as an e-book. The original manuscript of this famous book remains on view in the Hauppauge, New York, headquarters of the company that Dale Carnegie founded, inspiring the new leaders who have brought the firm into the 21st century.

Today, Dale Carnegie operates in 85 countries, from China to Cameroon, with 2,700 trainers teaching his methods in 25 languages. In all, more than 8 million people have taken a Dale Carnegie course. The company has trained managers, employees, and teams in multinational corporations, such as Ford, Honda, Adidas, John Deere, 3M, Verizon, American Express, and Apple. It also provides training to people in government agencies, such as the U.S. Department of Veteran Affairs, as well as to small business owners and individuals who want to learn the Carnegie way.

Carnegie's methods can help marketers build a relationship with people at all levels, from the mailroom to the boardroom. Whether the conversation involves a sales call or a factory visit to see a particular piece of equipment, "you can change people's behavior by changing your attitude towards them," says Peter Handal, CEO of Dale Carnegie. Listening carefully, wearing a smile, and being courteous is common sense, yet "it's not common practice," Handal explains, which is where the Dale Carnegie course comes in.

Dale Carnegie's principles still apply in this era of digital communications. For example, choosing positive words in a business e-mail can give recipients a good feeling about the message and the sender. Businesspeople are busy, so many value the efficiency of brief messages sent via text or Twitter. At the same time, adding a personal touch with a quick Skype conversation or recording a relevant video message can be a very effective way to engage business customers. And there's nothing like a face-to-face meeting where the customer can sit with a supplier or technical expert, ask questions, watch a live demonstration or handle a product, and build trust.

As CEO, Peter Handal travels the world to hear what customers and trainers have to say about Dale Carnegie's operations and about their own business situations. He emphasizes the need for managers to listen to what others have to say, even if the news is bad. "That's a very dangerous situation," Handal says. "You can't have everyone on the team in charge, but you have to have everyone be able to speak openly and honestly." In other words, it's important to be nice, but it's also important to speak up so decision makers have all the information they need to proceed.[18]

Questions for Discussion

1. How would you apply Dale Carnegie's methods if you were trying to make a sale to a company with a large buying center?
2. From a marketing perspective, why would people who work for the U.S. Department of Veteran Affairs be as interested in taking a Dale Carnegie course as people who work for American Express?
3. Which concerns of business customers should Dale Carnegie's marketers pay close attention to when selling training services to a company like American Express?

Case 8.2

General Electric Goes Social to Reach Business Buyers

With $147 billion in annual revenue, Connecticut-based General Electric (GE) is a global leader in equipment, software, and services for transportation, health care, energy, and other industries. Both Boeing and Airbus buy GE jet engines for their commercial aircraft. Hospitals and clinics on nearly every continent buy GE's ultrasound imaging equipment and GE's power management systems. Naval officers from many nations order GE's gas turbine engines to power their vessels. Construction companies across North America buy GE kitchen and laundry appliances for the new homes they build. Real estate developers, mining companies, and many other businesses worldwide arrange to obtain loans or lease costly equipment from GE.

Knowing that businesses, institutions, and government agencies need factual data about product features and usage, especially during the early stages of the business buying decision process, GE has put a tremendous amount of information online for quick and easy access. Whether users are thinking about upgrading existing machinery or purchasing agents are researching a product's exact specifications, they can find plenty of details, diagrams, and case studies on GE's websites, available at any hour with just a click or two. In addition, GE's sales and technical personnel are ready to help evaluate a business customer's needs on-site or by phone and suggest solutions tailored to each customer's unique situation.

Another reason for GE's ongoing success in business marketing is that it does not view members of the buying center as mere cogs in the buying process. In the words of GE's chief marketing officer, "customers are people too." GE's marketing experts work hard to make a human connection with both business customers and consumers through marketing communications that polish its image as an innovator in many fields of science and technology.

Philip Scalia / Alamy

The social-media-based "Six Second Science Fair" is a good example. Company marketers posted a few six-second Vine videos of fun experiments to launch a virtual science fair on a special Tumblr page, inviting members of the public to submit their own six-second experiment videos. GE posted these videos on Tumblr and promoted them on Twitter using the hashtag #6SecondScience. The project quickly attracted hundreds of thousands of viewers. Individual videos went viral as viewers retweeted and revined their favorites, giving the GE brand even wider exposure in the business community and the media world.

GE's marketers launched another social-media campaign, "Gravity Day," as a low-key, fun celebration of how Newton got the idea for the principle of gravity by seeing an apple fall from the tree. Once again, GE invited businesses and consumers to submit six-second Vine videos, this time with the theme of dropping an apple in some creative way. Edited together, the segments formed a fun video in which an apple is tossed or juggled or otherwise moved from one video frame to the next. GE promoted "Gravity Day" on its social-media sites and, as before, was rewarded with media coverage and extensive social-media sharing.

Being a big company, GE has jumped into social media in a big way. "Gravity Day" and other Vine video projects are posted on GE's YouTube channel, along with corporate commercials and hundreds of videos demonstrating goods and services. GE's Facebook page has more than 1 million likes, and its Twitter account has more than 175,000 followers. GE also posts behind-the-scenes photos of its facilities, new products, and other images on its Pinterest page, which has more than 20,000 followers. GE's Instagram page, which features photos of the company's innovative products and processes, has more than 155,000 followers. No matter where businesspeople click on social media, GE has a presence, offering numerous opportunities for customers to learn more about the company, its products, its people, and its principles.

GE's marketers demonstrate the company's technical capabilities and social responsibility by providing a wide range of goods and services for the Olympic games. Only a tiny fraction of the Olympics' worldwide viewing audience is in a position to buy energy generation systems, industrial lighting, medical imaging equipment, or jet engines. But seeing GE put its best foot forward during this high-profile event is sure to make a positive impression on those who can sign a purchase order or recommend a supplier.[19]

Questions for Discussion

1. Why is GE's involvement with the Olympics a good way to show that the company understands the primary concerns of business customers?
2. How does derived demand apply to the demand for passenger-jet engines? What are the implications for GE's marketing efforts?
3. In which stage of the business buying decision process is GE's reputation likely to have the most influence on a railroad that is considering the purchase of new locomotives?

NOTES

[1] Christopher Matthews, "Talking Heads," *Time*, June 24, 2013, p. 12; Brad Stone, "Meet the Roomba's Corporate Cousin," *Bloomberg Businessweek*, June 17, 2013, pp. 39–40; Erico Guizzo, "iRobot and Cisco Team Up to Create Ava 500 Telepresence Robot," *Spectrum*, June 10, 2013, http://spectrum.ieee.org/automaton/robotics/industrial-robots/irobot-cisco-ava-500-telepresence-robot (accessed November 26, 2013).

[2] "STP: Segmentation, Targeting, Positioning," American Marketing Association, www.marketingpower.com (accessed November 5, 2013).

[3] Ibid.

[4] Manufacturing Employment Concentrations, http://geocommons.com/maps/1534 (accessed November 5, 2013).

[5] Corilyn Shropshire, "U.S. Lost Quarter of Its High-Tech Jobs in Past Decade," *Chicago Tribune*, January 18, 2012, http://articles.chicagotribune.com/2012-01-18/business/ct-biz-0118-tech-jobs-20120118_1_high-tech-manufacturing-jobs-job-losses-research (accessed November 11, 2013).

[6] Andrew Browne, "The Rebalancing of the World's Manufacturing Sector," *The Wall Street Journal*, September 13, 2013, http://blogs.wsj.com/chinarealtime/2013/09/13/the-rebalancing-of-the-worlds-manufacturing-sector (accessed November 5, 2013).

[7] Statistics of U.S. Business, all industries, U.S. Bureau of the Census, www.census.gov/econ/susb (accessed November 26, 2013).

[8] County Business Patterns, U.S. Census, 2010, http://factfinder2.census.gov/faces/tableservices/jsf/pages/productview.xhtml?pid=BP_2010_00A1&prodType=table (accessed November 26, 2013).

[9] Top 250 Global Retailers, Deloitte, www.stores.org/STORES%20Magazine%20January%202012/global-powers-retailing-top-250 (accessed November 1, 2013).

[10] Total Government Spending, 2012, www.usgovernmentspending.com (accessed November 5, 2013).

[11] U.S. Bureau of the Census, *Statistical Abstract of the United States, 2012*, Table 428, www.census.gov/compendia/statab/2012/tables/12s0428.pdf (accessed November 5, 2013).

[12] "World's Most Admired Companies, 2013," *Fortune*, http://money.cnn.com/magazines/fortune/most-admired/2013/snapshots/2309.html (accessed November 5, 2013).

[13] "Notable Contract Awards," Booz Allen Hamilton, www.boozallen.com/media-center/company-news/notable-contract-awards (accessed November 3, 2013).

[14] Das Narayandas and V. Kasturi Rangan, "Building and Sustaining Buyer–Seller Relationships in Mature Industrial Markets," *Journal of Marketing* (July 2004): 63.

[15] Disney Institute, http://disneyinstitute.com (accessed November 26, 2013); Brooks Barnes, "In Customer Service Consulting, Disney's Small World Is Growing," *The New York Times*, April 21, 2012, www.nytimes.com/2012/04/22/business/media/in-business-consulting-disneys-small-world-is-growing.html (accessed November 5, 2013).

[16] Frederick E. Webster, Jr., and Yoram Wind, "A General Model for Understanding Organizational Buyer Behavior," *Marketing Management* (Winter/Spring 1996): 52–57.

[17] "Development of NAICS," U.S. Census Bureau, www.census.gov/epcd/www/naicsdev.htm (accessed November 3, 2013).

[18] Sunny Thao, "Social Media as a Strategy," *Star Tribune* (Minneapolis), April 7, 2012, www.startribune.com/business/146428825.html (accessed November 26, 2013); "Dale Carnegie Wins Friends in a Digital Age," *CBS News*, April 20, 2012, www.cbsnews.com/news/dale-carnegie-wins-friends-in-a-digital-age (accessed November 26, 2013); Paul Harris, "Digital Makeover for the Self-Help Bible that Helped Millions to Make Friends," *Observer* (London), October 9, 2011, p. 25; Dale Carnegie website, www.dalecarnegie.com (accessed November 26, 2013).

[19] Kate Maddox, "BtoB's Best Marketers: Linda Boff, General Electric," *BtoB*, October 15, 2013, www.btobonline.com (accessed February 20, 2014); Lisa Lacy, "GE Hosts World's First Science Fair on Vine," *ClickZ*, August 13, 2013, www.clickz.com (accessed January 14, 2014); E. J. Schultz, "GE Tells the Secret of Making Geeky Cool," *Advertising Age*, October 5, 2013, www.adage.com (accessed February 6, 2014); Christopher Heine, "GE Gets 30% Better Returns through Smart Content Marketing," *AdWeek*, October 4, 2013, www.adweek.com; www.ge.com (accessed February 26, 2014).

Feature Notes

[a] Home Depot, www.homedepot.com (accessed November 26, 2013); GE Smart Catalog, www.gecatalogs.com (accessed November 26, 2013); SAP Cart Approval Mobile App, www.sap.com/pc/tech/mobile/software/lob-apps/purchasing-approval-app/index.html (accessed January 5, 2014).

[b] Nick Leiber, "Revolution Foods' Quest to Pack More Nutrition into Kids' Lunchboxes," *Bloomberg Businessweek*, September 19, 2013, www.businessweek.com/articles/2013-09-19/revolution-foods-takes-on-kraft-to-get-into-kids-lunchboxes (accessed November 26," 2013); "School Food: Biting Commentary," *The Economist*, May 4, 2013, www.economist.com/news/united-states/21577098-new-company-trying-make-school-meals-healthier-biting-commentary (accessed November 26, 2013); Jill Tucker, "SF School to Get Healthier Lunches," *San Francisco Chronicle*, January 1, 2013, www.sfgate.com/bayarea/article/SF-school-to-get-healthier-lunches-4160062.php (accessed November 26, 2013); "40 Under 40: 35, Kristin Groos Richmond and Kirsten Saenz Tobey," *Fortune*, October 7, 2013, p. 122.

chapter 9

Reaching Global Markets

OBJECTIVES

9-1 Define *international marketing*.

9-2 Differentiate between the six environmental forces that affect international marketing efforts.

9-3 List six important international trade agreements.

9-4 Identify methods of international market entry.

9-5 Summarize the three forms of global organizational structure.

9-6 Describe the use of the marketing mix internationally.

MARKETING INSIGHTS

Accountability and Cultural Challenges with Bangladesh Suppliers

Multinational companies face large production targets that can be costly. Offshore outsourcing is often employed, both to meet these levels and keep costs low. Marketing strategies are impacted as consumers develop concern about worker safety related to the products they buy. Bangladesh, with its 5,000 factories and low minimum wages, has become a popular spot for companies to produce their garments. However, harsh employee treatment, exceedingly long work hours, and decrepit buildings have proven dangerous for factory workers. As a developing nation, the regulation of working conditions and compliance differs significantly from that in the United States.

Over the past few years, there have been reports of preventable building collapses and fires in factories resulting in thousands of deaths. Priority was given to meeting production goals rather than safety. In response, some American and European companies have entered into pacts that set safety standards for suppliers, but some factories have not fully adopted the standards or changed their mentality. One factory was caught keeping two sets of reports: one designed for the companies for which they supply, and another for their own files. The reports sent to the companies showed that employees worked a 48-hour workweek, the maximum set by the safety standards pact, while the factory report showed that employees actually worked more than 100 hours per week. Although companies have taken steps to address safety concerns by participating in the safety pact, without accountability for factory managers the pact will be meaningless. Cultural and legal differences continue to challenge Bangladesh suppliers.[1]

© iStockphoto.com/Günay Mutlu

Technological advances and rapidly changing political and economic conditions are making it easier than ever for companies to market their products overseas as well as at home. With most of the world's population and two-thirds of total purchasing power outside the United States, international markets represent tremendous opportunities for growth. For instance, MasterCard and Visa are expanding into Myanmar in what has been estimated to be one of the last few growth markets for credit card firms.[2] Accessing these markets can promote innovation, while intensifying competition can spur companies to develop global strategies.

In deference to the increasingly global nature of marketing, we devote this chapter to the unique features of global markets and international marketing. We begin by considering the nature of global marketing strategy and the environmental forces that create opportunities and threats for international marketers. Next, we consider several regional trade alliances, markets, and agreements. Then we examine the modes of entry into international marketing and companies' degrees of involvement in it, as well as some of the structures that can be used to organize multinational enterprises. Finally, we examine how firms may alter their marketing mixes when engaging in international marketing efforts. All of these factors must be considered in any marketing plan that includes an international component.

9-1 DEFINE *INTERNATIONAL* MARKETING

9-1a The Nature of Global Marketing Strategy

international marketing Developing and performing marketing activities across national boundaries

International marketing involves developing and performing marketing activities across national boundaries. Global marketing strategies require knowledge about the marketing environment and customers. For the United States, with only 7 percent of the world's population, tremendous opportunities exist globally. Case in point, Walmart has approximately 2.2 million employees and operates 11,000 units in 27 countries outside the United States.[3] General Motors sells more cars in China than in the United States. Consider the advertisement for Berlin, Germany. The advertisement is trying to attract global tourists to the city by portraying Berlin as a place of talent. It encourages consumers to bring their kids with them, implying that Berlin is so special that their children will end up traveling to the city eventually anyway. The advertisement provides a web link that takes users to the Berlin website, which discusses the benefits of and activities in Berlin. Clearly, the advertisement is meant for an international audience.

International Marketing
This advertisement is a part of the marketing used by the city of Berlin to attract tourists.

Firms are finding that international markets provide tremendous opportunities for growth. To encourage international growth, many countries offer significant practical assistance and valuable benchmarking research that will help their domestic firms become more competitive globally. One example is Export.gov, a website managed by the U.S. Department of Commerce's International Trade Administration. Export.gov collects a variety of resources to help businesses who want to export to other countries.[4] A major element of the assistance that governmental organizations can provide for firms (especially small and medium-sized firms) is knowledge of the internationalization process of firms.

Traditionally, most companies—such as McDonald's and KFC—have entered the global marketplace incrementally as they gained knowledge about various markets and opportunities. However, some firms—such as eBay, Google, and Twitter—were founded with the knowledge and resources to expedite their commitment and investment in the global marketplace. These "born globals"—typically small technology-based firms earning as much as 70 percent of their sales outside the domestic home market—export their products almost immediately after being established in market niches in which they compete with larger, more established firms.[5] Whether a firm adopts the traditional approach, the born global approach, or an approach that merges attributes of both approaches to market products, international marketing strategy is a critical element of a firm's global operations. Today, global competition in most industries is intense and becoming increasingly fierce with the addition of newly emerging markets and firms.

9-2 ENVIRONMENTAL FORCES IN GLOBAL MARKETS

Firms that enter international markets often find that they must make significant adjustments in their marketing strategies. The environmental forces that affect foreign markets may differ dramatically from those that affect domestic markets. Walmart, for instance, dissolved its joint venture with Bharti Enterprises in India due to regulatory restrictions placed on foreign firms. Because India requires foreign firms to have local partners, Walmart's pullout will hinder the firm from opening more stores in India in the future.[6] Thus, a successful international marketing strategy requires a careful environmental analysis. Conducting research to understand the needs and desires of international customers is crucial to global marketing success. Many firms have demonstrated that such efforts can generate tremendous financial rewards, increase market share, and heighten customer awareness of their products around the world. In this section, we explore how differences in the sociocultural; economic; political, legal, and regulatory; social and ethical; competitive; and technological forces in other countries can profoundly affect marketing activities.

9-2a Sociocultural Forces

Cultural and social differences among nations can have significant effects on marketing activities. Because marketing activities are primarily social in purpose, they are influenced by beliefs and values regarding family, religion, education, health, and recreation. In terms of families, the world population is over the 7 billion mark, with half residing in countries where fertility is at or below 2.1. Because of these lower fertility rates, the next wave of major population growth will likely take longer and be driven by developing countries.[7] By identifying such major sociocultural deviations among countries, marketers lay groundwork for an effective adaptation of marketing strategy. The sports bar and restaurant Buffalo Wild Wings, for instance, is expanding into the Philippines, the Middle East, and Canada. However, the restaurant will likely have to alter some of its menu items when expanding into the Middle East as Muslims do not drink alcohol.[8]

Local preferences, tastes, and idioms can all prove complicated for international marketers. Although football is a popular sport in the United States and a major opportunity for many television advertisers, soccer is the most popular televised sport in Europe and Latin America. And, of course, marketing communications often must be translated into other languages. Sometimes, the true meaning of translated messages can be misinterpreted or lost. Consider some translations that went awry in foreign markets: KFC's long-running slogan "Finger lickin' good" was translated into Spanish as "Eat your fingers off" and Coors' "Turn it loose" campaign was translated into Spanish as "Drink Coors and get diarrhea."[9]

It can be difficult to transfer marketing symbols, trademarks, logos, and even products to international markets, especially if these are associated with objects that have profound religious or cultural significance in a particular culture. For instance, to honor the 40th National

Day in the United Arab Emirates, PUMA released a shoe designed in the country's national colors. Unfortunately, the company failed to anticipate that shoes are considered unclean in Muslim countries. Many citizens expressed outrage at seeing something that represented their culture placed on what they considered to be dirty. PUMA apologized and removed the product.[10] Cultural differences may also affect marketing negotiations and decision-making behavior. Identifying differences in work-related values of employees across different nationalities helps companies design more effective sales management practices. Cultural differences in the emphasis placed on personal relationships, status, and decision-making styles have been known to complicate dealings between Americans and businesspeople from other countries. In many parts of Asia, a gift may be considered a necessary introduction before negotiation, whereas in the United States or Canada, a gift may be misconstrued as an illegal bribe.

Buyers' perceptions of other countries can influence product adoption and use. Multiple research studies have found that consumer preferences for products depend on both the country of origin and the product category of competing products.[11] When people are unfamiliar with products from another country, their perceptions of the country as a whole may affect their attitude toward the product and influence whether they will buy it. If a country has a reputation for producing quality products and therefore has a positive image in consumers' minds, marketers of products from that country will want to make the country of origin well known. Thus, a generally favorable image of Western computer technology has fueled sales of U.S.-made Dell, Apple, and HP computers and software in Japan. On the other hand, marketers may want to dissociate themselves from a particular country in order to build a brand's reputation as truly global or because a country does not have a good reputation for quality. Because China has had issues with product quality in the past, a Chinese company that purchased Volvo is keeping Volvo positioned as a Swedish brand. The extent to which a product's brand image and country of origin influence purchases is subject to considerable variation based on national culture characteristics.

When products are introduced from one nation into another, acceptance is far more likely if similarities exist between the two cultures. In fact, many similar cultural characteristics exist across countries. For international marketers, cultural differences have implications for product development, advertising, packaging, and pricing. When Walmart expanded into China, for instance, it quickly found that it had to adapt its seafood section because Chinese shoppers like to select their own seafood. This required the stores to build large tanks containing live fish so customers could choose which ones they wanted to purchase.

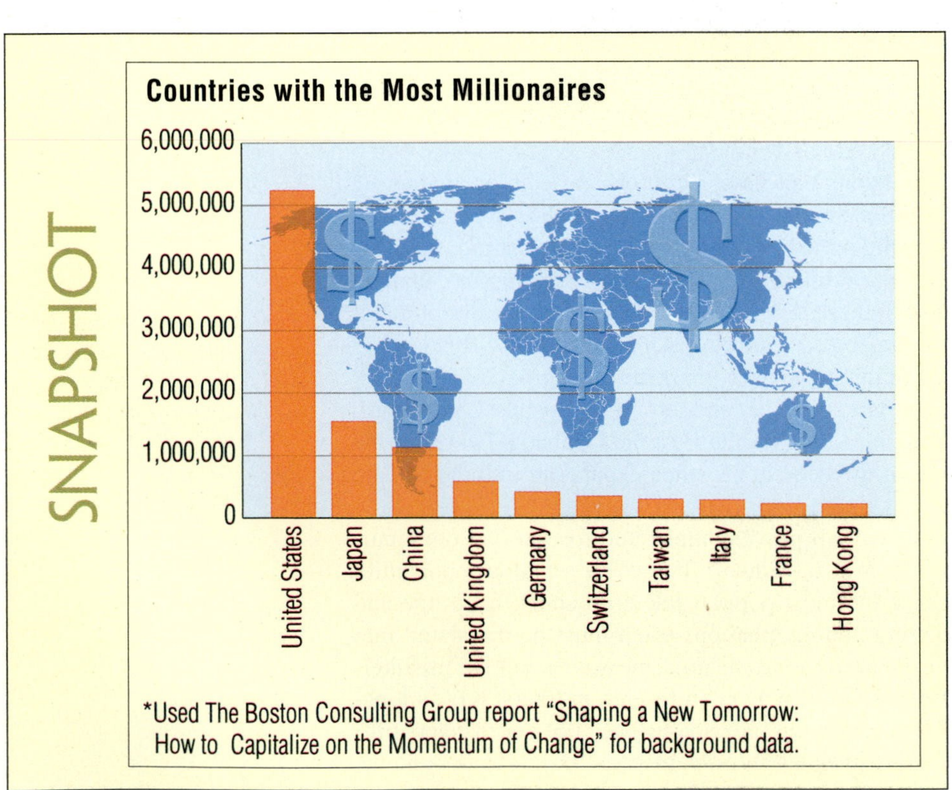

Source: Alexander E. M. Hess, "24/7 Wall St.: Countries with the Most Millionaires," *USA Today*, September 17, 2013, www.usatoday.com/story/money/business/2013/09/15/countries-most-billionaires/2811571/?utm_source=feedburner&utm_medium=feed&utm_campaign=Feed%3A+UsatodaycomMoney-TopStories+%28USATODAY+-+Money+Top+Stories%29 (accessed January 6, 2014).

9-2b Economic Forces

Global marketers need to understand the international trade system, particularly the economic stability of individual nations, as well as trade barriers that may stifle marketing efforts. Economic differences among nations—differences in standards of living, credit, buying power, income distribution, national resources, exchange rates, and the like—dictate many of the adjustments firms must make in marketing internationally.

Instability is one of the guaranteed constants in the global business environment. The United States and the European Union are more stable economically than many other regions of the world. However, even these economies have downturns in regular cycles, and the most recent recession significantly slowed business growth. A number of other countries, including Spain, Russia, Greece, Ireland, and Thailand, have all experienced economic problems, such as depressions, high unemployment, corporate bankruptcies and banking failures, instability in currency markets, trade imbalances, and financial systems that need major reforms. For instance, the rising price of raw materials could increase inflation in developing countries where demand is growing.[12] The constantly fluctuating conditions in different economies require global marketers to carefully monitor the global environment and make changes quickly. Even more stable developing countries, such as Mexico and Brazil, tend to have greater fluctuations in their business cycles than the United States does. Despite this fact, Standard & Poor's downgraded the U.S. debt rating due to continual deficit spending. The credit-rating agency Fitch has also placed the United States on notice for a possible downgrade.[13] Economic instability can also disrupt the markets for U.S. products in places that otherwise might be excellent marketing opportunities. On the other hand, competition from the sustained economic growth of countries like China and India can disrupt markets for U.S. products.

The value of the dollar, euro, and yen has a major impact on the prices of products in many countries. An important economic factor in the global business environment is currency valuation. Many countries have adopted a floating exchange rate, which allows the currencies of those countries to fluctuate, or float, according to the foreign exchange market. Table 9.1 compares the value of the dollar, euro, yen, and yuan. China has been criticized for undervaluing its currency, or valuing its currency below the market value. This gives it an advantage in selling exports, since the Chinese yuan has a lower value than other nations' currencies. It also decreases demand for manufacturers and exporters from other countries.[14] The value of the U.S. dollar is also important. Because many countries float their exchange rates around the dollar, too much or too little U.S. currency in the economy could create inflationary effects or harm exports.[15]

In terms of the value of all products produced by a nation, the United States has the largest gross domestic product in the world at about $16 trillion.[16] **Gross domestic product (GDP)** is an overall measure of a nation's economic standing; it is the market value of a nation's total output of goods and services for a given period. However, it does not take into account the concept of GDP in relation to population (GDP per capita). The United States has a GDP per capita of $50,700. Switzerland is roughly 230 times smaller than the United States—a little larger than the state of Maryland—but its population density is six times greater than that of the United States. Although Switzerland's GDP is about one-forty-fourth the size of U.S. GDP, its GDP per capita is not that much lower. Even Canada, which is comparable in size to the United States, has a lower GDP and GDP per capita.[17] Table 9.2 provides a comparative economic analysis of 15 countries, including the United States. Knowledge about per capita income, credit, and the distribution of income provides general insights into market potential.

gross domestic product (GDP) The market value of a nation's total output of goods and services for a given period; an overall measure of economic standing

Table 9.1 Exchange Rates of Global Currencies*

	1 USD (U.S. dollars)	1 EUR (euro)	1 JPY (Japanese yen)	1 CNY (China yuan renminbi)
1 USD	1.00	0.73	104.19	6.05
1 EUR	1.36	1.00	142.03	8.25
1 JPY	0.0096	0.0070	1.00	0.058
1 CNY	0.17	0.12	17.21	1.00

*As of January 2014

Floating Currency
Although China has increased the value of its currency in recent years, it is still criticized for failing to float its currency according to the foreign exchange market rate.

Table 9.2 **Comparative Analysis of Selected Countries**

Country	Population (in millions)	GDP (U.S.$ in billions)	Exports (U.S.$ in billions)	Imports (U.S.$ in billions)	Internet Users (in millions)	Cell Phones (in millions)
Brazil	201	2,394	242.6	223.2	76.0	248.3
Canada	34.6	1,513	462.9	474.8	27.0	26.3
China	1,349.6	12,610	2,057	1,735	389	1,100
Honduras	8.4	38.42	7.9	11.2	0.7	7.4
India	1,220.8	4,761	298.4	500.4	61.3	893.9
Japan	127.3	4,704	773.9	830.6	99.2	138.4
Jordan	6.5	39.29	7.9	18.4	1.6	9.0
Kenya	44	77.14	6.3	15.1	4.0	30.7
Mexico	116.2	1,788	370.9	370.8	31	100.8
Russia	142.5	2,555	529.6	334.7	40.9	261.9
South Africa	48.6	592	100.7	105	4.4	68.4
Switzerland	8.0	369.4	333.4	287.7	6.2	10.5
Turkey	80.7	1,142	163.4	228.9	27.2	67.7
Thailand	67.4	662.6	226.2	217.8	17.5	84.1
United States	316.7	15,940	1,564	2,299	245	310

Source: Central Intelligence Agency, "Guide to Country Comparisons," *World Factbook*, www.cia.gov/library/publications/the-world-factbook/rankorder/rankorderguide.html (accessed December 11, 2013).

Opportunities for international trade are not limited to countries with the highest incomes. The countries of Brazil, Russia, India, China, and South Africa (BRICS) have attracted attention as their economies appear to be rapidly advancing. The advertisement for the U.S.–India Business Council, for instance, encourages businesses to support the organization in increasing collaboration, innovation, and trade between the two countries. It highlights the major opportunities for businesses investing in India. Other nations are progressing at a much faster rate than they were a few years ago, and these countries—especially in Latin America, Africa, eastern Europe, and the Middle East—have great market potential. Going back to our earlier example, Myanmar offers significant expansion opportunities for credit card companies. In a 1-year period, the number of credit card swiping machines at restaurants and hotels in the country went from zero to 2,500. This benefits both the local population as well as international tourists. However, there is not always a guarantee that terminals will work, and infrastructure problems such as Internet disruptions and unreliable electricity add to the problem.[18] This demonstrates the complex situation that marketers of goods and services in developing countries face when they expand into areas with limited infrastructure. Marketers must also understand the political and legal environments before they can convert buying power of customers in these countries into actual demand for specific products.

Trade with India
India is a lucrative market for many businesses. The U.S.-India Business Council encourages businesses to support collaboration between the two countries so that both can benefit from a strong partnership.

9-2c Political, Legal, and Regulatory Forces

The political, legal, and regulatory forces of the environment are closely intertwined in the United States. To a large degree, the same is true in many countries internationally. Typically, legislation is enacted, legal decisions are interpreted, and regulatory agencies are operated by elected or appointed officials. A country's legal and regulatory infrastructure is a direct reflection of the political climate in the country. In some countries, this political climate is determined by the people via elections, whereas in other countries leaders are appointed or have assumed leadership based on certain powers. Although laws and regulations have direct effects on a firm's operations in a country, political forces are indirect and often not clearly known in all countries. Additionally, businesses from different countries might be similar in nature but operate differently based on legal, political, or regulatory conditions in their home countries. For instance, while airlines operate as private companies in the United States, Emirates airlines is wholly-owned by the Government of Dubai, although it is a commercial enterprise that does not receive government financial support.[19] The advertisement for Emirates airlines stresses the company's large global reach. It is the largest airline in the Middle East with 130 destinations across the world.

On the other hand, some countries have political climates that make it easier for international entrepreneurs to start their own businesses. Table 9.3 lists some of the

Table 9.3 The Best Countries for Entrepreneurs

Rank*	Country
1	Singapore
2	Hong Kong SAR, China
3	New Zealand
4	United States
5	Denmark
6	Norway
7	United Kingdom
8	Republic of Korea
9	Iceland
10	Ireland

*Rankings created by the Small Business Administration on which nations provide the most favorable environment for entrepreneurs.

Source: Alicia Ciccone, "10 Best Countries for Starting a Business," *Huffington Post*, January 10, 2012, www.huffingtonpost.com/2012/01/10/10-easiest-countries-to-s_n_1194511.html (accessed December 12, 2013).

Emirates Airlines
Emirates airlines is quickly growing. This advertisement features the city of Dubai as an unforgettable destination to which Emirates frequently flies.

best countries in which to start a business, according to the Small Business Administration.

The political climate in a country or region, political officials in a country, and political officials in charge of trade agreements directly affect the legislation and regulations (or lack thereof). Within industries, elected or appointed officials of influential industry associations also set the tone for the regulatory environment that guides operations in a particular industry. Consider the American Marketing Association, which has one of the largest professional associations for marketers with 30,000 members worldwide in every area of marketing. It has established a statement of ethics, called "Ethical Norms and Values for Marketers," that guides the marketing profession in the United States.[20]

A nation's political system, laws, regulatory bodies, special-interest groups, and courts all have a great impact on international marketing. A government's policies toward public and private enterprise, consumers, and foreign firms influence marketing across national boundaries. Some countries have established import barriers, such as tariffs. An **import tariff** is any duty levied by a nation on goods bought outside its borders and brought into the country. Because they raise the prices of foreign goods, tariffs impede free trade between nations. Tariffs are usually designed either to raise revenue for a country or to protect domestic products. In the United States, tariff revenues account for a small percentage of total federal revenues, down from about 50 percent of total federal revenues in the early 1900s.

Nontariff trade restrictions include quotas and embargoes. A **quota** is a limit on the amount of goods an importing country will accept for certain product categories in a specific period of time. The United States maintains tariff-rate quotas on imported raw cane sugar, refined and specialty sugar, and sugar-containing products. The goal is to allow countries to export specific products to the United States at a relatively low tariff but acknowledge higher tariffs above predetermined quantities.[21] An **embargo** is a government's suspension of trade in a particular product or with a given country. Embargoes are generally directed at specific goods or countries and are established for political, health, or religious reasons. An embargo may be used to suspend the purchase of a commodity like oil from a country that is involved in questionable conduct, such as human rights violations or terrorism. Products that were created in the United States or by U.S. companies or those containing more than 20 percent of U.S.-manufactured parts cannot be sold to Cuba. Until recently, most Americans were banned from visiting Cuba because of the embargo. However, the administration has begun to allow more Americans to visit Cuba with certain restrictions, suggesting that the tension between the two countries might be diminishing.[22] Laws regarding competition may also serve as trade barriers. Illustrative of this, the European Union has stronger antitrust laws than the United States. Being found guilty of anticompetitive behavior has cost companies like Intel billions of dollars. Because some companies do not have the resources to comply with more stringent laws, this can act as a barrier to trade.

import tariff A duty levied by a nation on goods bought outside its borders and brought into the country

quota A limit on the amount of goods an importing country will accept for certain product categories in a specific period of time

embargo A government's suspension of trade in a particular product or with a given country

exchange controls Government restrictions on the amount of a particular currency that can be bought or sold

Exchange controls, government restrictions on the amount of a particular currency that can be bought or sold, may also limit international trade. They can force businesspeople to buy and sell foreign products through a central agency, such as a central bank. On the other hand, to promote international trade, some countries have joined to form free trade zones, multinational economic communities that eliminate tariffs and other trade barriers. Such regional trade alliances are discussed later in the chapter. As mentioned earlier, foreign currency exchange rates also affect the prices marketers can charge in foreign markets. Fluctuations in the international monetary market can change the prices charged across national boundaries on a daily basis. Thus, these fluctuations must be considered in any international marketing strategy.

Countries may limit imports to maintain a favorable balance of trade. The **balance of trade** is the difference in value between a nation's exports and its imports. When a nation exports more products than it imports, a favorable balance of trade exists because money is flowing into the country. The United States has a negative balance of trade for goods and services of more than $471 billion.[23] A negative balance of trade is considered harmful, because it means U.S. dollars are supporting foreign economies at the expense of U.S. companies and workers. At the same time, U.S. citizens benefit from the assortment of imported products and their typically lower prices.

Many nontariff barriers, such as quotas and minimum price levels set on imports, port-of-entry taxes, and stringent health and safety requirements, still make it difficult for U.S. companies to export their products. For instance, the collectivistic nature of Japanese culture and the high-context nature of Japanese communication make some types of direct marketing messages less effective and may predispose many Japanese to support greater regulation of direct marketing practices.[24] A government's attitude toward importers has a direct impact on the economic feasibility of exporting to that country.

Chris Mellor/Lonely Planet Images/Getty Images

Embargo
Havana Club Rum is an example of a product that cannot be imported into the United States because of the embargo on Cuban products.

9-2d Ethical and Social Responsibility Forces

Differences in national standards are illustrated by what the Mexicans call *la mordida*: "the bite." The use of payoffs and bribes is deeply entrenched in many governments. Because U.S. trade and corporate policy, as well as U.S. law, prohibits direct involvement in payoffs and bribes, U.S. companies may have a hard time competing with foreign firms that engage in these practices. Some U.S. businesses that refuse to make payoffs are forced to hire local consultants, public relations firms, or advertising agencies, which results in indirect payoffs. The ultimate decision about whether to give small tips or gifts where they are customary must be based on a company's code of ethics. However, under the Foreign Corrupt Practices Act of 1977, it is illegal for U.S. firms to attempt to make large payments or bribes to influence policy decisions of foreign governments. Nevertheless, facilitating payments, or small payments to support the performance of standard tasks, are often acceptable. The Foreign Corrupt Practices Act also subjects all publicly held U.S. corporations to rigorous internal controls and record-keeping requirements for their overseas operations.

Many other countries have also outlawed bribery. As we discussed in Chapter 3, the U.K. Bribery Act redefined what many companies consider to be bribery versus gift-giving, causing

balance of trade The difference in value between a nation's exports and its imports multinational firms to update their codes of ethics. Companies with operations in the United Kingdom could still face penalties for bribery, even if the bribery occurred outside the country and managers were not aware of the misconduct.[25] In this case, the U.K. Bribery Act might be considered stricter than the Foreign Corrupt Practices Act. It is thus essential for global marketers to understand the major laws in the countries in which their companies operate.

Differences in ethical standards can also affect marketing efforts. In China and Vietnam, for instance, standards regarding intellectual property differ dramatically from those in the United States, creating potential conflicts for marketers of computer software, music, and books. Pirated and counterfeit goods consume $1 trillion from the world's economy.[26] This explains why British fashion retailer Burberry was concerned when China canceled its retailer trademark for its beige-black-and-red pattern on its leather goods. Without the protection of a trademark, other retailers can make copies of Burberry's leather goods without facing repercussions.[27] The enormous amount of counterfeit products available worldwide, the time it takes to track them down, and legal barriers in certain countries make the pursuit of counterfeiters challenging for many companies.

When marketers do business abroad, they sometimes perceive that other business cultures have different modes of operation. This uneasiness is especially pronounced for marketers who have not traveled extensively or interacted much with foreigners in business or social settings. The perception exists among many in the United States that U.S. firms are different from those in other countries. This inferred perspective of "us" versus "them" is also common in other countries. In business, the idea that "we" differ from "them" is called the self-reference criterion (SRC). The SRC is the unconscious reference to one's own cultural values, experiences, and knowledge. When confronted with a situation, we react on the basis of knowledge we have accumulated over a lifetime, which is usually grounded in our culture of origin. Our reactions are based on meanings, values, and symbols that relate to our culture but may not have the same relevance to people of other cultures.

However, many businesspeople adopt the principle of "When in Rome, do as the Romans do." These businesspeople adapt to the cultural practices of the country they are in and use the host country's cultural practices as the rationalization for sometimes straying from their own ethical values when doing business internationally. By defending the payment of bribes or "greasing the wheels of business" and other questionable practices in this fashion, some businesspeople are resorting to **cultural relativism**—the concept that morality varies from one culture to another and that business practices are therefore differentially defined as right or wrong by particular cultures. Table 9.4 indicates the countries that businesspeople, risk analysts, and the general public perceive as having the most and least corrupt public sectors.

Because of differences in cultural and ethical standards, many companies work both individually and collectively to establish ethics programs and standards for international business conduct. Levi Strauss' code of ethics, for example, bars the firm from manufacturing in countries where workers are known to be abused. Many firms, including Texas Instruments, Coca-Cola, DuPont, Hewlett-Packard, Levi Strauss & Co., Texaco, and Walmart, endorse following international business practices responsibly. These companies support a globally-based resource system called Business for Social Responsibility (BSR). BSR tracks emerging issues and trends, provides information on corporate leadership and best practices, conducts educational workshops and training, and assists organizations in developing practical business ethics tools.[28]

9-2e Competitive Forces

Competition is often viewed as a staple of the global marketplace. Customers thrive on the choices offered by competition, and firms constantly seek opportunities to outmaneuver their competition to gain customers' loyalty. Firms typically identify their competition when they establish target markets worldwide. Customers who are seeking alternative solutions to their product needs find the firms that can solve those needs. However, the increasingly interconnected international marketplace and advances in technology have resulted in competitive forces that are unique to the international marketplace.

cultural relativism The concept that morality varies from one culture to another and that business practices are therefore differentially defined as right or wrong by particular cultures

Table 9.4 Ranking of Countries Based upon Corruption of Public Sector

Country Rank	CPI Score*	Least Corrupt	Country Rank	CPI Score*	Most Corrupt
1	91	Denmark	175	8	Somalia
1	91	New Zealand	175	8	North Korea
3	89	Finland	175	8	Afghanistan
3	89	Sweden	174	11	Sudan
5	86	Norway	173	14	South Sudan
5	86	Singapore	172	15	Libya
7	85	Switzerland	171	16	Iraq
8	83	Netherlands	168	17	Uzbekistan
9	81	Australia	168	17	Turkmenistan
9	81	Canada	168	17	Syria
11	80	Luxembourg	167	18	Yemen
12	78	Germany	163	19	Haiti
12	78	Iceland	163	19	Guinea Bissau

*CPI score relates to perceptions of the degree of public-sector corruption as seen by businesspeople and country analysts and ranges between 10 (highly clear) and 0 (highly corrupt). The United States is perceived as the 19th least-corrupt nation.

Source: Data from Transparency International, *Corruption Perceptions Index 2013* (Berlin, Germany, 2013).

Beyond the types of competition (i.e., brand, product, generic, and total budget competition) and types of competitive structures (i.e., monopoly, oligopoly, monopolistic competition, and pure competition), which are discussed in Chapter 3, firms that operate internationally must do the following:

- Be aware of the competitive forces in the countries they target.
- Identify the interdependence of countries and the global competitors in those markets.
- Be mindful of a new breed of customers: the global customer.

Each country has unique competitive aspects—often founded in the other environmental forces (i.e., sociocultural, technological, political, legal, regulatory, and economic forces)—that are often independent of the competitors in that market. The most globally competitive countries are listed in Table 9.5. Although competitors drive competition, nations establish the infrastructure and the rules for the types of competition that can take place. So, the laws against antitrust in the European Union are often perceived as being stricter than those in the United States. Novartis and Johnson & Johnson were fined more than $22 million after the European Union determined that their Dutch subsidiaries had collaborated to delay the entry of a generic painkiller. This violated EU antitrust laws.[29] Like the United States, other countries allow some monopoly structures to exist. Consider Sweden; their alcohol sales are made through the governmental store Systembolaget, which is legally supported by the Swedish Alcohol Retail Monopoly. According to Systembolaget, the Swedish Alcohol Retail Monopoly exists for one reason: "to minimize alcohol-related problems by selling alcohol in a responsible way."[30]

A new breed of customer—the global customer—has changed the landscape of international competition drastically. In the past, firms simply produced goods or services and provided local markets with information about the features and uses of their goods and services. Customers seldom had opportunities to compare products from competitors, know details about the competing products' features, and compare other options beyond the local (country

Table 9.5 Ranking of the Most Competitive Countries in the World

Rank	Country	Rank	Country
1	Switzerland	11	Norway
2	Singapore	12	Taiwan, China
3	Finland	13	Qatar
4	Germany	14	Canada
5	United States	15	Denmark
6	Sweden	16	Austria
7	Hong Kong SAR	17	Belgium
8	Netherlands	18	New Zealand
9	Japan	19	United Arab Emirates
10	United Kingdom	20	Saudi Arabia

Source: Klaus Schwab (ed.), *The Global Competitiveness Report 2013–2014*, www3.weforum.org/docs/WEF_GlobalCompetitivenessReport_2013-14.pdf (accessed December 10, 2013).

or regional) markets. Now, however, not only do customers who travel the globe expect to be able to buy the same product in most of the world's more than 200 countries, but they also expect that the product they buy in their local store in Miami will have the same features as similar products sold in London or even in Beijing. If either the quality of the product or the product's features are more advanced in an international market, customers will soon demand that their local markets offer the same product at the same or lower prices.

9-2f Technological Forces

Advances in technology have made international marketing much easier. Interactive Web systems, instant messaging, and podcast downloads (along with the traditional vehicles of voice mail, e-mail, and cell phones) make international marketing activities more affordable and convenient. Internet use and social networking activities have accelerated dramatically within the United States and abroad. In Japan, 99 million have Internet access, and 41 million Russians, 61 million Indians, and 389 million Chinese are logging on to the Internet.[31]

In many developing countries that lack the level of technological infrastructure found in the United States and Japan, marketers are beginning to capitalize on opportunities to leapfrog existing technology. Cellular and wireless phone technology is reaching many countries at a more affordable rate than traditional hard-wired telephone systems. Consequently, opportunities for growth in the cell phone market remain strong in Southeast Asia, Africa, and the Middle East. One opportunity created by the rapid growth in mobile devices in Africa is mobile banking. Africa tends to have low infrastructure for physical banks, providing unique opportunities to encourage the growth of electronic banking. Kenya-based mobile phone operator Safaricom runs a money-transfer system called M-PESA that has been adopted by 15 million adult Kenyans.[32]

9-3 REGIONAL TRADE ALLIANCES, MARKETS, AND AGREEMENTS

Although many more firms are beginning to view the world as one huge marketplace, various regional trade alliances and specific markets affect companies engaging in international marketing; some create opportunities, and others impose constraints. In fact, while

Entrepreneurship in Marketing

China's Steve Jobs?

To say the comparisons posed against Lei Jun are daunting is an understatement. The billionaire founder of Xiamoi, China's hottest smartphone company, has continually been compared to the late Steve Jobs. With their passion for innovation, the two seem to possess similar qualities that merit such comparisons. Xiamoi has a current market value of approximately $4 billion.

Although Jun has successfully launched a billion-dollar smartphone company, he has faced challenges of sustaining that growth and finding a way to penetrate global markets. Other challenges Xiamoi faces lie with domination and competition from Apple and Samsung. These two companies alone have created extensive barriers for competitors to enter the global market. Apple products are popular within China and are seen as luxury products. However, the localized appeal of Xiamoi has given it an advantage over Apple. A strength that Xiamoi has over competitors is its ability to create a high-quality, low-priced phone that appeals to the average Chinese consumer. This strategy has proven successful within the Chinese marketplace and Jun hopes it will achieve global success.[a]

trade agreements in various forms have been around for centuries, the last century can be classified as the trade agreement period in the world's international development. Today, there are nearly 200 trade agreements around the world compared with only a select handful in the early 1960s. In this section, we examine several of the more critical regional trade alliances, markets, and changing conditions affecting markets. These include the North American Free Trade Agreement, European Union, Southern Common Market, Asia-Pacific Economic Cooperation, Association of Southeast Asian Nations, and the World Trade Organization.

9-3a The North American Free Trade Agreement (NAFTA)

The **North American Free Trade Agreement (NAFTA)**, implemented in 1994, effectively merged Canada, Mexico, and the United States into one market of nearly 454 million consumers. NAFTA eliminated virtually all tariffs on goods produced and traded among Canada, Mexico, and the United States to create a free trade area. The estimated annual output for this trade alliance is more than $17 trillion.[33]

NAFTA makes it easier for U.S. businesses to invest in Mexico and Canada; provides protection for intellectual property (of special interest to high-technology and entertainment industries); expands trade by requiring equal treatment of U.S. firms in both countries; and simplifies country-of-origin rules, hindering Japan's use of Mexico as a staging ground for further penetration into U.S. markets. Although most tariffs on products coming to the United States were lifted, duties on more sensitive products, such as household glassware, footwear, and some fruits and vegetables, were phased out over a 15-year period.

Canada's more than 34 million consumers are relatively affluent, with a per capita GDP of $43,400.[34] Trade between the United States and Canada totals approximately $680 billion.[35] Canada is the single largest trading partner of the United States, which in turn supports millions of U.S. jobs. NAFTA has also enabled additional trade between Canada and Mexico. Mexico is Canada's fifth-largest export market and third-largest import market.[36]

With a per capita GDP of $15,600, Mexico's more than 116 million consumers are less affluent than Canadian consumers.[37] However, trade between the United States and Mexico totals more than $500 billion.[38] Many U.S. companies, including Hewlett-Packard, IBM, and General Motors, have taken advantage of Mexico's low labor costs and close proximity to the United States to set up production facilities, sometimes called *maquiladoras*. Production at

North American Free Trade Agreement (NAFTA) An alliance that merges Canada, Mexico, and the United States into a single market

the *maquiladoras*, especially in the automotive, electronics, and apparel industries, has grown rapidly as companies as diverse as Ford, John Deere, Motorola, Kimberly-Clark, and VF Corporation set up facilities in north-central Mexican states. Although Mexico experienced financial instability throughout the 1990s—as well as the more recent drug cartel violence—privatization of some government-owned firms and other measures instituted by the Mexican government and businesses have helped Mexico's economy. Needed economic reforms have been initiated, especially in the area of increasing investments and oil production, refining, and distribution. Moreover, increasing trade between the United States and Canada constitutes a strong base of support for the ultimate success of NAFTA.

Mexico is growing faster than Brazil and is estimated to soon become one of the top 10 biggest global economies. Loans to companies in Mexico have been increasing, and as one of the world's largest oil producers, Mexico has the opportunity to increase investment in this profitable commodity. Additionally, while China has taken much outsourcing business from Mexico, a turnaround may be approaching. With an increase in Chinese labor costs and the high transportation costs of transporting goods between China and the United States, many U.S. businesses that outsource are looking toward Mexico as a less costly alternative.[39]

Mexico's membership in NAFTA links the United States and Canada with other Latin American countries, providing additional opportunities to integrate trade among all the nations in the Western Hemisphere. Indeed, efforts to create a free trade agreement among the 34 nations of North and South America are underway. A related trade agreement—the Dominican Republic–Central American Free Trade Agreement (CAFTA-DR)—among Costa Rica, the Dominican Republic, El Salvador, Guatemala, Honduras, Nicaragua, and the United States has also been ratified in all those countries except Costa Rica. The United States exports $20 billion to the CAFTA-DR countries annually.[40]

9-3b The European Union (EU)

The **European Union (EU)**, sometimes also referred to as the *European Community* or *Common Market*, was established in 1958 to promote trade among its members, which initially included Belgium, France, Italy, West Germany, Luxembourg, and the Netherlands. In 1991, East and West Germany united, and by 2013, the EU included the United Kingdom, Spain, Denmark, Greece, Portugal, Ireland, Austria, Finland, Sweden, Cyprus, Poland, Hungary, the Czech Republic, Slovenia, Estonia, Latvia, Lithuania, Slovakia, Malta, Romania, Bulgaria, and Croatia. The Former Yugoslav Republic of Macedonia and Turkey are candidate countries that hope to join the European Union in the near future.[41]

The European Union consists of nearly half a billion consumers and has a combined GDP of nearly $16 trillion.[42] Although it only makes up 7 percent of the population, the EU generates nearly 22 percent of the world's GDP.[43] The EU is a relatively diverse set of democratic European countries. It is not a state that is intended to replace existing country states, nor is it an organization for international cooperation. Instead, its member states have common institutions to which they delegate some of their sovereignty to allow specific matters of joint interest to be decided at the European level. The primary goals of the EU are to establish European citizenship; ensure freedom, security, and justice; promote economic and social progress; and assert Europe's role in world trade.[44] To facilitate free trade among members, the EU is working toward standardizing business regulations and requirements, import duties, and value-added taxes; eliminating customs checks; and creating a standardized currency for use by all members. Many European nations (Austria, Belgium, Finland, France, Germany, Ireland, Italy, Luxembourg, the Netherlands, Portugal, Greece, and Spain) are linked to a common currency, the *euro*, but several EU members have rejected the euro in their countries (e.g., Denmark, Sweden, and the United Kingdom). Although the common currency may necessitate that marketers modify their pricing strategies and subject them to increased competition, it also frees companies that sell products among European countries from the complexities of exchange rates. The long-term goals are to eliminate all trade barriers within the EU, improve the economic efficiency of the EU nations, and stimulate economic growth,

European Union (EU) An alliance that promotes trade among its member countries in Europe

Emerging Trends

Dollar Stores and One Euro Pricing Expand Internationally

Dollar stores have gained popularity in the United States over the last several years, and now the European Union (EU) is catching on to the trend. With severely detrimental economic forces working in the EU, retailers, restaurants, and consumer goods manufacturers are switching to euro pricing to spur customer spending. As euro pricing takes hold, the Dollar Store is seeing an opportunity for international expansion through licensing agreements. With more than 70 countries ready for these agreements, the Dollar Store is poised to make its mark all over the world.

Restaurants have also seen success using the one euro pricing strategy. Implementing weekly specials called "Euromania," where drinks and food items are sold for one euro, Spanish restaurant 1000 Montaditos has been able to triple their sales over the course of 3 years. This unlikely survivor of a severe recession has since increased its Spanish locations by 150 percent and is expecting to add 100 other locations across their borders. This is just one example of how business responsiveness to outside forces can be the difference between success and failure.[b]

thus making the union's economy more competitive in global markets, particularly against Japan and other Pacific Rim nations and North America.

As the EU nations attempt to function as one large market, consumers in the EU may become more homogeneous in their needs and wants. Marketers should be aware, however, that cultural differences among the nations may require modifications in the marketing mix for customers in each nation. Differences in tastes and preferences in these diverse markets are significant for international marketers. But there is evidence that such differences may be diminishing, especially within the younger population that includes teenagers and young professionals. Gathering information about these distinct tastes and preferences is likely to remain a very important factor in developing marketing mixes that satisfy the needs of European customers.

Although the United States and the EU do not always agree, partnerships between the two have been profitable and the two entities generally have a strong positive relationship. Much of this success can be attributed to the shared values of the United States and EU. The EU is mostly democratic and has a strong commitment to human rights, fairness, and the rule of law. As a result, the United States and EU have been able to collaborate on mutually beneficial projects with fewer problems than partnerships with other trade alliances that do not share similar values.[45]

The latest worldwide recession has slowed Europe's economic growth and created a debt crisis. Several members have budget deficits and are struggling to recover. Ireland, Greece, and Portugal required significant bailouts from the European Union, followed by bailout requests from Spain and Cyprus.[46] Standard & Poor's dealt a blow to the EU by downgrading the sovereign debt ratings of several member countries, including France, Portugal, and Italy.[47] Germany, on the other hand, is seeing its impact on the euro-zone increase. Germany is home to many exporting companies, its exports are in high demand in fast-growing economies, and it has a smaller budget deficit and household debt. As a result, Germany is doing better economically than its European counterparts.[48] It continues to maintain its AAA+ rating, signaling to investors that the country is a safe investment.[49]

Due to the massive industry collaboration between the United States and the EU, there have been discussions about the possibility of a trade agreement between the two entities. In many respects, the United States, the EU, and Asia have become largely interdependent in trade and investment. For instance, the United States and the EU have already adopted the "Open Skies" agreement to remove some of the restrictions on transatlantic flights, and the two often collaborate on ways to prevent terrorist attacks, cyber hacking, and crime. The United States and the EU hope that by working together, they can create mutually beneficial relationships that will provide benefits to millions of their citizens.[50]

9-3c The Southern Common Market (MERCOSUR)

The **Southern Common Market (MERCOSUR)** was established in 1991 under the Treaty of Asunción to unite Argentina, Brazil, Paraguay, and Uruguay as a free trade alliance (Paraguay was temporarily suspended from the bloc after the impeachment of a political official).[51] Venezuela joined in 2006. Currently, Bolivia, Chile, Colombia, Ecuador, and Peru are associate members. The alliance represents two-thirds of South America's population and has a combined GDP of more than $2.9 trillion, making it the fourth-largest trading bloc behind NAFTA, the EU, and ASEAN. Like NAFTA, MERCOSUR promotes "the free circulation of goods, services, and production factors among the countries" and establishes a common external tariff and commercial policy.[52]

South America and Latin America are catching the attention of many international businesses. The region is advancing economically with an estimated growth rate of 4 to 5 percent. Another trend is that several of the countries, including some of the MERCOSUR alliance, are starting to experience more stable democracies. Even Cuba, one of the traditionally harshest critics of capitalism in Latin America, is accepting more privatization. After up to 1 million state workers were laid off in 2011, many Cubans had to try to earn their living in the county's private sector. Cuba now has an expanding middle class.[53]

9-3d The Asia-Pacific Economic Cooperation (APEC)

The **Asia-Pacific Economic Cooperation (APEC)**, established in 1989, promotes open trade and economic and technical cooperation among member nations, which initially included Australia, Brunei Darussalam, Canada, Indonesia, Japan, Korea, Malaysia, New Zealand, the Philippines, Singapore, Thailand, and the United States. Since then, the alliance has grown to include China, Hong Kong, Taiwan, Mexico, Papua New Guinea, Chile, Peru, Russia, and Vietnam. The 21-member alliance represents approximately 40 percent of the world's population, 55 percent of world GDP, and nearly 44 percent of global trade. APEC differs from other international trade alliances in its commitment to facilitating business and its practice of allowing the business/private sector to participate in a wide range of APEC activities.[54] Companies of the APEC have become increasingly competitive and sophisticated in global business in the last few decades. Moreover, the markets of the APEC offer tremendous opportunities to marketers who understand them. In fact, the APEC region has consistently been one of the most economically dynamic parts of the world. In the first decade, the APEC countries generated almost 70 percent of the worldwide economic growth, and the APEC region consistently outperformed the rest of the world.[55]

Japanese firms in particular have made tremendous inroads on world markets for automobiles, motorcycles, watches, cameras, and audio and video equipment. Products from Sony, Sanyo, Toyota, Mitsubishi, Canon, Suzuki, and Toshiba are sold all over the world and have set standards of quality by which other products are often judged. Despite the high volume of trade between the United States and Japan, the two economies are less integrated than the U.S. economy is with Canada and the European Union. If Japan imported goods at the same rate as other major nations, the United States would sell billions of dollars more each year to Japan.

The most important emerging economic power is China, which has become one of the most productive manufacturing nations. China, which is now the second-largest trading partner of the United States, has initiated economic reforms to stimulate its economy by privatizing many industries, restructuring its banking system, and increasing public spending on infrastructure. China is a manufacturing powerhouse; however, its high growth rate has decreased in recent years to about 8 percent.[56] Many foreign companies, including Apple and Samsung, have factories in China to take advantage of its low labor costs, and China has become a major global producer in virtually every product category.

For international businesses, the potential of China's consumer market is so vast that it is almost impossible to measure. However, doing business in China entails many risks. China's state capitalism has yielded many economic benefits, including a high average annual growth rate. Yet, at the same time, economists believe that such high growth will not last unless the country focuses less upon exports and more upon the spending power and domestic

Southern Common Market (MERCOSUR) An alliance that promotes the free circulation of goods, services, and production factors, and has a common external tariff and commercial policy among member nations in South America

Asia-Pacific Economic Cooperation (APEC) An alliance that promotes open trade and economic and technical cooperation among member nations throughout the world

consumption of its consumers.[57] Political and economic instability—especially inflation, corruption, and erratic policy shifts—have undercut marketers' efforts to stake a claim in what could become the world's largest market.

Moreover, piracy is a major issue, and protecting a brand name in China is difficult. Because copying is a tradition in China, and laws that protect copyrights and intellectual property are weak and minimally enforced, the country is flooded with counterfeit media, computer software, furniture, and clothing. However, there are signs that piracy laws are beginning to be more enforced in China. Many Chinese Web companies actively search for pirated content to protect their market share. For instance, China's largest Internet video company, Youku Tudou, spends $164 million licensing content and hires Internet sleuths to search the Web for pirated works.[58]

Pacific Rim regions like South Korea, Thailand, Singapore, Taiwan, and Hong Kong are also major manufacturing and financial centers. Even before Korean brand names, such as Samsung, Daewoo, and Hyundai, became household words, these products prospered under U.S. company labels, including GE, GTE, RCA, and J.C.Penney. Singapore boasts huge global markets for rubber goods and pharmaceuticals. Hong Kong is still a strong commercial center after being transferred to Chinese control. Vietnam is one of Asia's fastest-growing markets for U.S. businesses, but Taiwan, given its stability and high educational attainment, has the most promising future of all the Pacific Rim nations as a strong local economy and low import barriers draw increasing imports. The markets of APEC offer tremendous opportunities to marketers who understand them. For instance, YUM! Brands gets 60 percent of its profits from overseas.[59]

Another important trade agreement is the Trans-Pacific Partnership. The Trans-Pacific Strategic Economic Partnership is a proposed trade agreement between Singapore, Brunei, Chile, New Zealand, Vietnam, Malaysia, Japan, Peru, the United States, Canada, Mexico, South Korea, and Australia.[60] Signed in 2005, the partnership seeks to encourage free trade by phasing out import tariffs between member countries.[61] If the partnership succeeds, the trade bloc will become the fifth-largest trading partner for the United States.[62] The agreement would create standards for state-owned enterprises, labor, international property, and the environment.[63] Supporters of the partnership, however, believe it will increase the overall global competitiveness of member countries and could act as a standard for future trade agreements.[64]

Association of Southeast Asian Nations (ASEAN) An alliance that promotes trade and economic integration among member nations in Southeast Asia

9-3e Association of Southeast Asian Nations (ASEAN)

The **Association of Southeast Asian Nations (ASEAN)**, established in 1967, promotes trade and economic integration among member nations in Southeast Asia. The trade pact includes Malaysia, the Philippines, Indonesia, Singapore, Thailand, Brunei Darussalam, Vietnam, Laos, Myanmar, and Cambodia.[65] The region is home to 600 million people with a 5 percent growth rate in GDP. Analysts estimate the ASEAN region will have a combined GDP of $4.7 trillion by 2020.[66] With its motto "One Vision, One Identity, One Community," member nations have expressed the goal of encouraging free trade, peace, and collaboration among member countries.[67] In 1993, the trade bloc passed the Common Effective Preferential Tariff to reduce or phase out tariffs among countries over a 10-year period as well as eliminate non-tariff trade barriers.[68]

Yet, despite these positive growth rates, ASEAN is facing many obstacles in becoming a unified trade bloc.[69] There have also been conflicts among members themselves

Modern Thailand

Encouraging Economic Development in Asia
Thailand provides many opportunities for investment in an environment steeped in hospitality and knowledge.

and concerns over issues such as human rights and disputed territories.[70] Countries such as Thailand struggle with political unrest and regional differences. The advertisement illustrates Thailand's attempt to communicate its scenic beauty and the economic opportunities from doing business in this country. On the other hand, internal political strife poses a threat to companies that invest in Thailand. Therefore, there are great opportunities but also substantial risk.

On the other hand, while many choose to compare ASEAN with the European Union, ASEAN members are careful to point out their differences. Although members hope to increase economic integration by 2015, they expressed that there will be no common currency or fully free labor flows between members. In this way, ASEAN plans to avoid some of the pitfalls that occurred among nations in the EU during the latest worldwide recession.[71]

9-3f The World Trade Organization (WTO)

The **World Trade Organization (WTO)** is a global trade association that promotes free trade among 159 member nations. The WTO is the successor to the **General Agreement on Tariffs and Trade (GATT)**, which was originally signed by 23 nations in 1947 to provide a forum for tariff negotiations and a place where international trade problems could be discussed and resolved. Rounds of GATT negotiations reduced trade barriers for most products and established rules to guide international commerce, such as rules to prevent **dumping**, the selling of products at unfairly low prices.

The WTO came into being in 1995 as a result of the Uruguay Round (1988–1994) of GATT negotiations. Broadly, WTO is the main worldwide organization that deals with the rules of trade between nations; its main function is to ensure that trade flows as smoothly, predictably, and freely as possible between nations. In 2013, 159 nations were members of the WTO.[72]

Fulfilling the purpose of the WTO requires eliminating trade barriers; educating individuals, companies, and governments about trade rules around the world; and assuring global markets that no sudden changes of policy will occur. At the heart of the WTO are agreements that provide legal ground rules for international commerce and trade policy. Based in Geneva, Switzerland, the WTO also serves as a forum for dispute resolution.[73] For example, China filed a complaint with the World Trade Organization alleging that the United States was exaggerating claims that China was dumping 13 types of Chinese products. China went further to accuse the United States of falsely accusing them and imposing anti-dumping duties against their products.[74]

9-4 MODES OF ENTRY INTO INTERNATIONAL MARKETS

Marketers enter international markets and continue to engage in marketing activities at several levels of international involvement. Traditionally, firms have adopted one of four different modes of entering an international market; each successive "stage" represents different degrees of international involvement.

- Stage 1: No regular export activities
- Stage 2: Export via independent representatives (agents)
- Stage 3: Establishment of one or more sales subsidiaries internationally
- Stage 4: Establishment of international production/manufacturing facilities[75]

As Figure 9.1 shows, companies' international involvement today covers a wide spectrum, from purely domestic marketing to global marketing. Domestic marketing involves marketing strategies aimed at markets within the home country; at the other extreme, global marketing entails developing marketing strategies for the entire world (or at least more than one major region of the world). Many firms with an international presence start out as small companies serving local and regional domestic markets and expand to national markets before considering opportunities in foreign markets (the born global firm, described earlier, is one exception

World Trade Organization (WTO) An entity that promotes free trade among member nations by eliminating trade barriers and educating individuals, companies, and governments about trade rules around the world

General Agreement on Tariffs and Trade (GATT) An agreement among nations to reduce worldwide tariffs and increase international trade

dumping Selling products at unfairly low prices

Figure 9.1 Levels of Involvement in Global Marketing

to this internationalization process). Limited exporting may occur even if a firm makes little or no effort to obtain foreign sales. Foreign buyers may seek out the company and/or its products, or a distributor may discover the firm's products and export them. The level of commitment to international marketing is a major variable in global marketing strategies. In this section, we examine importing and exporting, trading companies, licensing and franchising, contract manufacturing, joint ventures, direct ownership, and some of the other approaches to international involvement.

9-4a Importing and Exporting

Importing and exporting require the least amount of effort and commitment of resources. **Importing** is the purchase of products from a foreign source. **Exporting**, the sale of products to foreign markets, enables firms of all sizes to participate in global business. The advertisement for Itaú bank in Latin America highlights the fact that Latin America is the world's largest coffee producer and exporter. This means that trade is a major—and often challenging—activity between Latin American regions and other parts of the world. The bank encourages businesses to invest with it because it knows the Latin American market and can provide valuable insights. A firm may also find an exporting intermediary to take over most marketing functions associated with marketing to other countries. This approach entails minimal effort and cost. Modifications in packaging, labeling, style, or color may be the major expenses in adapting a product for the foreign market.

importing The purchase of products from a foreign source

exporting The sale of products to foreign markets

Latin American Exporting
Itaú uses the example of Latin America's large export coffee market to inform businesses that, as a Latin American company, it knows the market well and can greatly assist its clients.

Export agents bring together buyers and sellers from different countries and collect a commission for arranging sales. Export houses and export merchants purchase products from different companies and then sell them abroad. They are specialists at understanding customers' needs in global markets. Using exporting intermediaries involves limited risk because no foreign direct investment is required.

Buyers from foreign companies and governments provide a direct method of exporting and eliminate the need for an intermediary. These buyers encourage international exchange by contacting overseas firms about their needs and the opportunities available in exporting to them. Indeed, research suggests that many small firms tend to rely heavily on such native contacts, especially in developed markets, and remain production-oriented rather than market-oriented in their approach to international marketing.[76] Domestic firms that want to export with minimal effort and investment should seek out export intermediaries. Once a company becomes involved in exporting, it usually develops more knowledge of the country and becomes more confident in its competitiveness.[77]

9-4b Trading Companies

Marketers sometimes employ a **trading company**, which links buyers and sellers in different countries but is not involved in manufacturing and does not own assets related to manufacturing. Trading companies buy products in one country at the lowest price consistent with quality and sell them to buyers in another country. For instance, WTSC offers a 24-hour-per-day online world trade system that connects 20 million companies in 245 countries, offering more than 60 million products.[78] A trading company acts like a wholesaler, taking on much of the responsibility of finding markets while facilitating all marketing aspects of a transaction. An important function of trading companies is taking title to products and performing all the activities necessary to move the products to the targeted foreign country. For instance, large grain-trading companies that operate out-of-home offices in both the United States and overseas control a major portion of world trade of basic food commodities. These trading companies sell homogeneous agricultural commodities that can be stored and moved rapidly in response to market conditions.

Trading companies reduce risk for firms that want to get involved in international marketing. A trading company provides producers with information about products that meet quality and price expectations in domestic and international markets. Additional services a trading company may provide include consulting, marketing research, advertising, insurance, product research and design, legal assistance, warehousing, and foreign exchange.

9-4c Licensing and Franchising

trading company A company that links buyers and sellers in different countries

licensing An alternative to direct investment that requires a licensee to pay commissions or royalties on sales or supplies used in manufacturing

When potential markets are found across national boundaries, and when production, technical assistance, or marketing know-how is required, **licensing** is an alternative to direct investment. The licensee (the owner of the foreign operation) pays commissions or royalties on sales or supplies used in manufacturing. The licensee may also pay an initial down payment or fee when the licensing agreement is signed. Exchanges of management techniques or technical assistance are primary reasons for licensing agreements. Yoplait, for example, is a French yogurt that is licensed for production in the United States; the Yoplait brand tries to maintain

Franchising
McDonald's has franchises in a number of countries, including this one in Moscow, Russia.

a French image. Similarly, sports organizations like the International Olympic Committee (IOC), which is responsible for the Olympic Games, typically concentrate on organizing their sporting events while licensing the merchandise and other products that are sold.

Licensing is an attractive alternative when resources are unavailable for direct investment or when the core competencies of the firm or organization are not related to the product being sold (such as in the case of Olympics merchandise). Licensing can also be a viable alternative when the political stability of a foreign country is in doubt. In addition, licensing is especially advantageous for small manufacturers wanting to launch a well-known brand internationally. For example, Questor Corporation owns the Spalding name but does not produce a single golf club or tennis ball itself; all Spalding sporting products are licensed worldwide.

Franchising is a form of licensing in which a company (the franchisor) grants a franchisee the right to market its product, using its name, logo, methods of operation, advertising, products, and other elements associated with the franchisor's business, in return for a financial commitment and an agreement to conduct business in accordance with the franchisor's standard of operations. This arrangement allows franchisors to minimize the risks of international marketing in four ways: (1) the franchisor does not have to put up a large capital investment; (2) the franchisor's revenue stream is fairly consistent because franchisees pay a fixed fee and royalties; (3) the franchisor retains control of its name and increases global penetration of its product; and (4) franchise agreements ensure a certain standard of behavior from franchisees, which protects the franchise name.[79]

9-4d Contract Manufacturing

Contract manufacturing occurs when a company hires a foreign firm to produce a designated volume of the firm's product (or a component of a product) to specification and the final product carries the domestic firm's name. The Gap, for example, relies on contract manufacturing for some of its apparel; Nike uses contract manufacturers in Vietnam to produce many of its athletic shoes. Marketing may be handled by the contract manufacturer or by the contracting company.

Three specific forms of contract manufacturing have become popular in the last decade: outsourcing, offshoring, and offshore outsourcing. **Outsourcing** is defined as the contracting of noncore operations or jobs from internal production within a business to an external entity that specializes in that operation. Outsourcing certain elements of a firm's operations to China and Mexico has become popular. The majority of all footwear is now produced in China,

contract manufacturing The practice of hiring a foreign firm to produce a designated volume of the domestic firm's product or a component of it to specification; the final product carries the domestic firm's name

outsourcing The practice of contracting noncore operations with an organization that specializes in that operation

regardless of the brand name of the shoe you wear. Services can also be outsourced. The Food and Drug Administration (FDA) announced it plans to outsource more overseas safety inspections to third parties.[80]

Offshoring is defined as moving a business process that was done domestically at the local factory to a foreign country, regardless of whether the production accomplished in the foreign country is performed by the local company (e.g., in a wholly-owned subsidiary) or a third party (e.g., subcontractor). Typically, the production is moved to reap the advantages of lower cost of operations in the foreign location. **Offshore outsourcing** is the practice of contracting with an organization to perform some or all business functions in a country other than the country in which the product will be sold. Today, some clothing manufacturers that previously engaged in offshore outsourcing are moving production back to the United States to maintain quality and tighter inventory control.[81]

9-4e Joint Ventures

In international marketing, a **joint venture** is a partnership between a domestic firm and a foreign firm or government. Joint ventures are especially popular in industries that require large investments, such as natural resources extraction or automobile manufacturing. Control of the joint venture may be split equally, or one party may control decision making. Joint ventures are often a political necessity because of nationalism and government restrictions on foreign ownership. Samsung has formed a joint venture with Venezuela with the intent to assemble home appliances and other devices within the country.[82] In the past, the Venezuelan government has sometimes been hostile to some direct foreign investment from capitalist countries, particularly that of U.S. companies. Joint ventures may also occur when acquisition or internal development is not feasible or when the risks and constraints leave no other alternative.

Joint ventures also provide legitimacy in the eyes of the host country's citizens. Local partners have firsthand knowledge of the economic and sociopolitical environment and the workings of available distribution networks, and they may have privileged access to local resources (raw materials, labor management, etc.). However, joint venture relationships require trust throughout the relationship to provide a foreign partner with a ready means of implementing its own marketing strategy. Joint ventures are assuming greater global importance because of cost advantages and the number of inexperienced firms that are entering foreign markets. They may be the result of a trade-off between a firm's desire for completely unambiguous control of an enterprise and its quest for additional resources.

Strategic alliances are partnerships formed to create a competitive advantage on a worldwide basis. They are very similar to joint ventures, but while joint ventures are defined in scope, strategic alliances are typically represented by an agreement to work together (which can ultimately mean more involvement than a joint venture). In an international strategic alliance, the firms in the alliance may have been traditional rivals competing for the same market. They may also be competing in certain markets while working together in other markets where it is beneficial for both parties. One such strategic alliance is between Swedish-based AB Volvo and Chinese company Dongfeng Motor Group. The alliance allows Volvo to acquire 45 percent of Dongfeng Motor Group subsidiary Dongfeng Commercial Vehicles. The alliance enables AB Volvo to expand in the Chinese truck market and lends an established brand name to Dongfeng Motor Group.[83] Whereas joint ventures are formed to create a new identity, partners in strategic alliances often retain their distinct identities, with each partner bringing a core competency to the union.

The success rate of international alliances could be higher if a better fit between the companies existed. A strategic alliance should focus on a joint market opportunity from which all partners can benefit. In the automobile, computer, and airline industries, strategic alliances are becoming the predominant means of competing internationally. Competition in these industries is so fierce and the costs of competing on a global basis are so high that few firms have all the resources needed to do it alone. Firms that lack the internal resources essential for international success may seek to collaborate with other companies. A shared mode of leadership among partner corporations combines joint abilities and allows collaboration from a distance. Focusing on customer value and implementing innovative ways to compete create a winning strategy.

offshoring The practice of moving a business process that was done domestically at the local factory to a foreign country, regardless of whether the production accomplished in the foreign country is performed by the local company (e.g., in a wholly-owned subsidiary) or a third party (e.g., subcontractor)

offshore outsourcing The practice of contracting with an organization to perform some or all business functions in a country other than the country in which the product or service will be sold

joint venture A partnership between a domestic firm and a foreign firm or government

strategic alliance A partnership that is formed to create a competitive advantage on a worldwide basis

9-4f Direct Ownership

Once a company makes a long-term commitment to marketing in a foreign country that has a promising market as well as a suitable political and economic environment, **direct ownership** of a foreign subsidiary or division is a possibility. Most foreign investment covers only manufacturing equipment or personnel because the expenses of developing a separate foreign distribution system can be tremendous. The opening of retail stores in Europe, Canada, or Mexico can require a staggering financial investment in facilities, research, and management.

The term **multinational enterprise**, sometimes called *multinational corporation*, refers to a firm that has operations or subsidiaries in many countries. Often, the parent company is based in one country and carries on production, management, and marketing activities in other countries. The firm's subsidiaries may be autonomous so they can respond to the needs of individual international markets, or they may be part of a global network that is led by the headquarters' operations.

At the same time, a wholly-owned foreign subsidiary may be allowed to operate independently of the parent company to give its management more freedom to adjust to the local environment. Cooperative arrangements are developed to assist in marketing efforts, production, and management. A wholly-owned foreign subsidiary may export products to the home country, its market may serve as a test market for the firm's global products, or it may be a component of the firm's globalization efforts. Some U.S. automobile manufacturers, for instance, import cars built by their foreign subsidiaries. A foreign subsidiary offers important tax, tariff, and other operating advantages. Table 9.6 lists some major multinational companies across the world.

One of the greatest advantages of a multinational enterprise is the cross-cultural approach. A subsidiary usually operates under foreign management so it can develop a local identity. In particular, the firm (i.e., seller) is often expected to adapt, if needed, to the buyer's culture. Interestingly, the cultural values of customers in the younger age group (30 years and younger) are becoming increasingly similar around the world. Today, a 20-year-old in Russia is increasingly similar in mindset to a 20-year-old in China and a 20-year-old in the United States, especially with regard to their tastes in music, clothes, and cosmetics. This makes marketing goods and services to the younger population easier today than it was only a generation ago. Nevertheless, there is still great danger involved in having a wholly-owned subsidiary in some parts of the world due to political uncertainty, terrorism threats, and economic instability.

direct ownership A situation in which a company owns subsidiaries or other facilities overseas

multinational enterprise A firm that has operations or subsidiaries in many countries

Table 9.6 Multinational Corporations

Company	Country	Description
Royal Dutch Shell	Netherlands	Oil and gas
Toyota	Japan	Automobiles
Walmart	United States	Retail
Siemens	Germany	Electronics and engineering
Nestlé	Switzerland	Nutritional, snack-food, and health-related consumer goods
Samsung	South Korea	Subsidiaries specializing in electronic components, telecommunications equipment, medical equipment, and more
Unilever	United Kingdom	Consumer goods including cleaning and personal care, foods, beverages
Boeing	United States	Aerospace and defense
Lenovo	China	Computer technology
Subway	United States	Largest fast-food chain

Whereas the most well-known multinational corporations (MNCs) come from developed countries, the world is seeing a rise in MNCs from emerging economies as well. Brazil's Embraer (an aircraft company) and South Africa's MTN (a mobile phone company) are two examples. India's Tata group is even beginning to rival more established MNCs. Tata owns several firms that qualify as MNCs, specializing in such diverse products as cars, hotels, steel, and chemicals. These conglomerates—in which one major entity owns several companies—are becoming an organizational trend among multinationals from developing nations.[84]

9-5 GLOBAL ORGANIZATIONAL STRUCTURES

Firms develop their international marketing strategies and manage their marketing mixes (i.e., product, distribution, promotion, and price) by developing and maintaining an organizational structure that best leverages their resources and core competencies. This organizational structure is defined as the way a firm divides its operations into separate functions and/or value-adding units and coordinates its activities. Most firms undergo a step-by-step development in their internationalization efforts of the firm's people, processes, functions, culture, and structure. The pyramid in Figure 9.2 symbolizes how deeply rooted the international operations and values are in the firm, with the base of the pyramid—structure—being the most difficult to change (especially in the short term). Three basic structures of international organizations exist: export departments, international divisions, and internationally integrated structures (e.g., product division structures, geographic area structures, and matrix structures). The existing structure of the firm, or the structure that the firm chooses to adopt, has implications for international marketing strategy.

Figure 9.2 Organizational Architecture

9-5a Export Departments

For most firms, the early stages of international development are often informal and not fully planned. During this early stage, sales opportunities in the global marketplace motivate a company to engage internationally. For instance, born global firms make exporting a primary objective from their inceptions. For most firms, however, very minimal, if any, organizational adjustments take place to accommodate international sales. Foreign sales are typically so small that many firms cannot justify allocating structural or other resources to the internationalization effort in the infancy of internationalization. Exporting, licensing, and using trading companies are preferred modes of international market entry for firms with an export department structure.

Some firms develop an export department as a subunit of the marketing department, whereas others organize it as a department that structurally coexists at an equal level with the other functional units. Additionally, some companies choose to hire outside export departments to handle their international operations. Lone Star Distribution, a distributor for sports and nutritional supplements, has an export department that helps its clients transport their goods internationally.[85] Another unique case of developing a successful export operation early after its inception is the born global firm of Logitech International. Founded in 1981, Logitech is a Swiss company that designs personal computer peripherals that enable people to effectively work, play, and communicate in the digital world.

As demand for a firm's goods and services grows or its commitments increase due to its internationalization efforts, it develops an international structure. Many firms evolve from using their export department structure to forming an international division.

9-5b International Divisions

A company's international division centralizes all of the responsibility for international operations (and in many cases, all international activities also become centralized in the international division). The typical international division concentrates human resources (i.e., international expertise) into one unit and serves as the central point for all information flow related to international operations (e.g., international market opportunities, international research and development). At the same time, firms with an international division structure take advantage of economies of scale by keeping manufacturing and related functions within the domestic divisions. Firms may develop international divisions at a relatively early stage, as well as a mature stage, of their international development. However, an increasing number of firms are recognizing the importance of going global early on. As such, these firms use exporting, licensing and franchising, trading companies, contract manufacturing, and joint ventures as possible modes of international market entry.

This international division structure illustrates the importance of coordination and cooperation among domestic and international operations. Frequent interaction and strategic planning meetings are required to make this structure work effectively. In particular, firms that use an international division structure are often organized domestically on the basis of functions or product divisions, whereas the international division is organized on the basis of geography. This means that coordination and strategic alignment across domestic divisions and the international division are critical to success. At the same time, lack of coordination between domestic and international operations is commonly the most significant flaw in the international division structure.

An example of a firm that has used the international division structure to achieve worldwide success is Abbott Laboratories, a diversified health-care company that develops products that span prevention and diagnosis to treatment and cures. As international sales grew in the late 1960s, the firm added an international division to its structure. This international division structure has benefits and drawbacks for Abbott, as it does for other firms that use it.[86]

Some argue that to offset the natural "isolation" that may result between domestic and international operations in this structure, the international division structure should be used only when a company (1) intends to market only a small assortment of goods or services internationally and (2) when foreign sales account for only a small portion of total sales.

When the product assortment increases or the percentage of foreign sales becomes significant, an internationally integrated structure may be more appropriate.

9-5c Internationally Integrated Structures

A number of different internationally integrated structures have been developed and implemented by firms in their quest to achieve global success. The three most common structures are the product division structure, the geographic area structure, and the global matrix structure. Firms with these varied structures have multiple choices for international market entry similar to international divisions (e.g., exporting, licensing and franchising, trading companies, contract manufacturing, and joint ventures). However, firms that have internationally integrated structures are the most likely to engage in direct ownership activities internationally.

The product division structure is the form used by the majority of multinational enterprises. This structure lends itself well to firms that are diversified, often driven by their current domestic operations. Each division is a self-contained entity with responsibility for its own operations, whether it is based on a country or regional structure. However, the worldwide headquarters maintain the overall responsibility for the strategic direction of the firm, whereas the product division is in charge of implementation. Procter & Gamble has a long-standing tradition of operating in a product division structure, with leading brands like Pampers, Tide, Pantene, Bounty, Folgers, Pringles, Charmin, Downy, Crest, and Olay.

The geographic area structure lends itself well to firms with a low degree of diversification. Under this domestically influenced functional structure, the world is divided into logical geographical areas based on firms' operations and the customers' characteristics. Accenture, a global management consulting firm, operates worldwide largely based on a geographic area structure. Each area tends to be relatively self-contained, and integration across areas is typically via the worldwide or the regional headquarters. This structure facilitates local responsiveness, but it is not ideal for reducing global costs and transferring core knowledge across the firm's geographic units. A key issue in geographic area structures, as in almost all multinational corporations, is the need to become more regionally and globally integrated.

The global matrix structure was designed to achieve both global integration and local responsiveness. Asea Brown Boveri (ABB), a Swedish-Swiss engineering multinational, is the best-known firm to implement a global matrix structure. ABB is an international leader in power and automation technologies that enable customers to improve their performance while lowering environmental impact. Global matrix structures theoretically facilitate a simultaneous focus on realizing local responsiveness, cost efficiencies, and knowledge transfers. However, few firms can operate a global matrix well, since the structure is based on, for example, product and geographic divisions simultaneously (or a combination of any two traditional structures). This means that employees belong to two divisions and often report to two managers throughout the hierarchies of the firm. An effectively implemented global matrix structure has the benefit of being global in scope while also being nimble and responsive locally. However, a poorly implemented global matrix structure results in added bureaucracy and indecisiveness in leadership and implementation.

9-6 CUSTOMIZATION VERSUS GLOBALIZATION OF INTERNATIONAL MARKETING MIXES

Like domestic marketers, international marketers develop marketing strategies to serve specific target markets. Traditionally, international marketing strategies have customized marketing mixes according to cultural, regional, and national differences. Table 9.7 provides a sample of international issues related to product, distribution, promotion, and price. Many developing countries lack the infrastructure needed for expansive distribution

Table 9.7 Marketing Mix Issues Internationally

	Sample International Issues
Product Element	
Core Product	Is there a commonality of the customer's needs across countries? What will the product be used for and in what context?
Product Adoption	How is awareness created for the product in the various country markets? How and where is the product typically bought?
Managing Products	How are truly new products managed in the country markets vis-à-vis existing products or products that have been modified slightly?
Branding	Is the brand accepted widely around the world? Does the home country help or hurt the brand perception of the consumer?
Distribution Element	
Marketing Channels	What is the role of the channel intermediaries internationally? Where is value created beyond the domestic borders of the firm?
Physical Distribution	Is the movement of products the most efficient from the home country to the foreign market or to a regional warehouse?
Retail Stores	What is the availability of different types of retail stores in the various country markets?
Retailing Strategy	Where do customers typically shop in the targeted countries—downtown, in suburbs, or in malls?
Promotion Element	
Advertising	Some countries' customers prefer firm-specific advertising instead of product-specific advertising. How does this affect advertising?
Public Relations	How is public relations used to manage the stakeholders' interests internationally? Are the stakeholders' interests different worldwide?
Personal Selling	What product types require personal selling internationally? Does it differ from how those products are sold domestically?
Sales Promotion	Is coupon usage a widespread activity in the targeted international markets? What other forms of sales promotion should be used?
Pricing Element	
Core Price	Is price a critical component of the value equation of the product in the targeted country markets?
Analysis of Demand	Is the demand curve similar internationally and domestically? Will a change in price drastically change demand?
Demand, Cost, and Profit Relationships	What are the fixed and variable costs when marketing the product internationally? Are they similar to the domestic setting?
Determination of Price	How do the pricing strategy, environmental forces, business practices, and cultural values affect price?

networks, which can make it harder to get the product to consumers. Pharmaceutical companies are attempting to use Coca-Cola's distribution network to bring important drugs into Africa. Medical kits have been slipped between Coca-Cola bottles stacked in cases and sent to hard-to-reach regions. This allows pharmaceutical firms to get their products to remote regions without having to invest heavily in a distribution network of their own.[87] Realizing that both similarities and differences exist across countries is a critical first step to developing the appropriate marketing strategy effort targeted to particular

Globalization
UPS demonstrates that it is a global firm by depicting flags from various countries waving in the wind. UPS competes in a global market, providing high-quality service and customer relationships.

international markets. Today, many firms strive to build their marketing strategies around similarities that exist instead of customizing around differences.

For many firms, **globalization** of marketing is the goal; it involves developing marketing strategies as though the entire world (or its major regions) were a single entity: A globalized firm markets standardized products in the same way everywhere. Nike and Adidas shoes, for instance, are standardized worldwide. Other examples of globalized products include electronic communications equipment, Western-style clothing, movies, soft drinks, rock and alternative music, cosmetics, and toothpaste. In this advertisement, UPS demonstrates globalization through its depiction of flags from various countries. UPS is using this advertisement to inform consumers that it is a global logistics firm that reaches across the world.

For many years, organizations have attempted to globalize their marketing mixes as much as possible by employing standardized products, promotion campaigns, prices, and distribution channels for all markets. The economic and competitive payoffs for globalized marketing strategies are certainly great. Brand name, product characteristics, packaging, and labeling are among the easiest marketing mix variables to standardize; media allocation, retail outlets, and price may be more difficult. In the end, the degree of similarity among the various environmental and market conditions determines the feasibility and degree of globalization. A successful globalization strategy often depends on the extent to which a firm is able to implement the idea of "think globally, act locally."[88] Even takeout food lends itself to globalization: McDonald's, KFC, and Taco Bell restaurants satisfy hungry customers in both hemispheres, although menus may be altered slightly to satisfy local tastes. When Dunkin' Donuts entered the Chinese market, it served coffee, tea, donuts, and bagels, just as it does in the United States, but in China, the donut case also includes items like green tea and honeydew melon donuts and mochi rings, which are similar to donuts but are made with rice flour. The company has experienced success in China and is planning to open locations in Ho Chi Minh City, Vietnam.[89]

International marketing demands some strategic planning if a firm is to incorporate foreign sales into its overall marketing strategy. International marketing activities often require customized marketing mixes to achieve the firm's goals. Globalization requires a total commitment to the world, regions, or multinational areas as an integral part of the firm's markets; world or regional markets become as important as domestic ones. Regardless of the extent to which a firm chooses to globalize its marketing strategy, extensive environmental analysis and marketing research are necessary to understand the needs and desires of the target market(s) and successfully implement the chosen marketing strategy.

A global presence does not automatically result in a global competitive advantage. However, a global presence generates five opportunities for creating value: (1) to adapt to local market differences, (2) to exploit economies of global scale, (3) to exploit economies of global scope, (4) to mine optimal locations for activities and resources, and (5) to maximize the transfer of knowledge across locations.[90] To exploit these opportunities, marketers need to conduct marketing research and work within the constraints of the international environment and regional trade alliances, markets, and agreements.

globalization The development of marketing strategies that treat the entire world (or its major regions) as a single entity

Summary

9-1 Define *international marketing*.

International marketing involves developing and performing marketing activities across national boundaries. International markets can provide tremendous opportunities for growth and renewed opportunity for the firm.

9-2 Differentiate between the six environmental forces that affect international marketing efforts.

A detailed analysis of the environment is essential before a company enters an international market. Environmental aspects of special importance include sociocultural; economic, political, legal, and regulatory; social and ethical; competitive; and technological forces. Because marketing activities are primarily social in purpose, they are influenced by beliefs and values regarding family, religion, education, health, and recreation. Cultural differences may affect marketing negotiations, decision-making behavior, and product adoption and use. A nation's economic stability and trade barriers can affect marketing efforts. Significant trade barriers include import tariffs, quotas, embargoes, and exchange controls. Gross domestic product (GDP) and GDP per capita are common measures of a nation's economic standing. Political and legal forces include a nation's political system, laws, regulatory bodies, special-interest groups, and courts. In the area of ethics, cultural relativism is the concept that morality varies from one culture to another and that business practices are therefore differentially defined as right or wrong by particular cultures. In addition to considering the types of competition and the types of competitive structures that exist in other countries, marketers also need to consider the competitive forces at work and recognize the importance of the global customer who is well informed about product choices from around the world. Advances in technology have greatly facilitated international marketing.

9-3 List six important international trade agreements.

Various regional trade alliances and specific markets create both opportunities and constraints for companies engaged in international marketing. Important trade agreements include the North American Free Trade Agreement, European Union, Southern Common Market, Asia-Pacific Economic Cooperation, Association of Southeast Asian Nations, and World Trade Organization.

9-4 Identify methods of international market entry.

There are several ways to enter international marketing. Importing (the purchase of products from a foreign source) and exporting (the sale of products to foreign markets) are the easiest and most flexible methods. Marketers may employ a trading company, which links buyers and sellers in different countries but is not involved in manufacturing and does not own assets related to manufacturing. Licensing and franchising are arrangements whereby one firm pays fees to another for the use of its name, expertise, and supplies. Contract manufacturing occurs when a company hires a foreign firm to produce a designated volume of the domestic firm's product to specification, and the final product carries the domestic firm's name. Joint ventures are partnerships between a domestic firm and a foreign firm or government. Strategic alliances are partnerships formed to create competitive advantage on a worldwide basis. Finally, a firm can build its own marketing or production facilities overseas. When companies have direct ownership of facilities in many countries, they may be considered multinational enterprises.

9-5 Summarize the three forms of global organizational structure.

Firms develop their international marketing strategies and manage their marketing mixes by developing and maintaining an organizational structure that best leverages their resources and core competencies. Three basic structures of international organizations include export departments, international divisions, and internationally integrated structures (e.g., product division structures, geographic area structures, and matrix structures).

9-6 Describe the use of the marketing mix internationally.

Although most firms adjust their marketing mixes for differences in target markets, some firms standardize their marketing efforts worldwide. Traditional full-scale international marketing involvement is based on products customized according to cultural, regional, and national differences. Globalization, however, involves developing marketing strategies as if the entire world (or regions of it) were a single entity; a globalized firm markets standardized products in the same way everywhere. International marketing demands some strategic planning if a firm is to incorporate foreign sales into its overall marketing strategy.

Go to www.cengagebrain.com for resources to help you master the content in this chapter as well as for materials that will expand your marketing knowledge!

Developing Your Marketing Plan

When formulating marketing strategy, one of the issues a company must consider is whether to pursue international markets. Although international markets present increased marketing opportunities, they also require more complex decisions when formulating marketing plans. To assist you in relating the information in this chapter to the development of your marketing plan, focus on the following:

1. Review the environmental analysis that was completed in Chapter 3. Extend the analysis for each of the seven factors to include global markets.
2. Using Figure 9.1 as a guide, determine the degree of international involvement that is appropriate for your product and your company.
3. Discuss the concepts of customization and globalization for your product when moving to international markets. Refer to Table 9.7 for guidance in your discussion.

The information obtained from these questions should assist you in developing various aspects of your marketing plan found in the "Interactive Marketing Plan" exercise at www.cengagebrain.com.

Important Terms

international marketing 246
gross domestic product (GDP) 249
import tariff 252
quota 252
embargo 252
exchange controls 252
balance of trade 253
cultural relativism 254
North American Free Trade Agreement (NAFTA) 257
European Union (EU) 258
Southern Common Market (MERCOSUR) 260
Asia-Pacific Economic Cooperation (APEC) 260
Association of Southeast Asian Nations (ASEAN) 261
World Trade Organization (WTO) 262
General Agreement on Tariffs and Trade (GATT) 262
dumping 262
importing 263
exporting 263
trading company 264
licensing 264
contract manufacturing 265
outsourcing 265
offshoring 266
offshore outsourcing 266
joint venture 266
strategic alliance 266
direct ownership 267
multinational enterprise 267
globalization 272

Discussion and Review Questions

1. How does international marketing differ from domestic marketing?
2. What factors must marketers consider as they decide whether to engage in international marketing?
3. Why are the largest industrial corporations in the United States so committed to international marketing?
4. Why do you think this chapter focuses on an analysis of the international marketing environment?
5. If you were asked to provide a small tip (or bribe) to have a document approved in a foreign nation where this practice is customary, what would you do?
6. How will NAFTA affect marketing opportunities for U.S. products in North America (the United States, Mexico, and Canada)?
7. What should marketers consider as they decide whether to license or enter into a joint venture in a foreign nation?
8. Discuss the impact of strategic alliances on international marketing strategies.
9. Contrast globalization with customization of marketing strategies. Is one practice better than the other?
10. What are some of the product issues that you need to consider when marketing luxury automobiles in Australia, Brazil, Singapore, South Africa, and Sweden?

Video Case 9.1

Evo: The Challenge of Going Global

While Bryce Phillips, founder of active sports retailer evo, was skiing in Japan, he was surprised to learn that several skiers at the lodge owned evo products. Although it is evo's intention to become a more global company, the organization does not regularly export to other countries. Yet, even with little export activities, customers from other countries are seeking out evo sports gear.

Evo, short for "evolution," was founded as an online retailer in 2001 and opened its Seattle-based retail store 4 years later. While the retail store provides customers with a physical location to look for products, the online store allows evo to carry a greater selection and extend its global reach. The company caters to active sports enthusiasts with products like ski gear, wakeboards, snowboards, skateboard gear, and street wear. From the beginning, Phillips wanted to use the Web to spread the word about evo worldwide. "When we think about the future, we think about being a global brand in the context that, for the kind of customers that we'd like to attract, we'd like to attract them all over the world," Phillips said. "And being on the Web, the word travels, and your brand can travel very, very quickly."

© Ilja Mašík/Shutterstock.com

Approximately 5 percent of evo's business comes from outside the United States, and the Web's global reach has increased demand for evo's products. Yet, despite these favorable global prospects, evo has been constrained somewhat in its ability to ship internationally. "We are confined in some ways by a lot of our dealer agreements," said Nathan Decker, senior director of e-commerce at evo. He provides two reasons for why vendors create exclusive dealer arrangements with evo: (1) to avoid saturating markets overseas; and (2) to maintain control over their products in order to compete fairly in the global marketplace. By limiting distribution, manufacturers are able to exert some control over other elements of the marketing mix, such as price. The evo website contains a list of brands that the company cannot ship overseas due to contractual agreements. If consumers from foreign countries try to order these brands, they will receive notification that their order has been canceled.

Because retailers often do not own many of the brands they sell, manufacturers can maintain the right to determine where their products are sold and how much to distribute to the company. This represents a major challenge for retailers that want to go global. On the other hand, large retail companies that have a lot of power, such as Walmart, have a better ability to negotiate with manufacturers on global distribution. As evo grows as a brand, the company may gain the power to negotiate more favorable distribution terms with its vendors.

Additionally, dealer contracts cannot prevent consumers themselves from sending the products overseas. As Phillips found out firsthand, the company's popularity has spilled over into other countries. Technology has enabled the company to engage in viral marketing, which aids in increasing the company's global brand exposure. For instance, when mountain gear manufacturer Rossignol decided to launch its skis globally through the evo website, the news was posted on ski websites throughout the world. Evo has also been featured in magazines that have international circulations.

Evo hopes to work with its vendors to make global selling more feasible. "Once we kind of work through that and get the green light from some of our bigger vendors, I think that it'll become more of a strategic focus," Decker said. In the meantime, evo is finding additional ways to increase its global presence. For instance, the company launched evoTrip as a service for adventurous sports enthusiasts who want to travel. EvoTrip arranges the trips with the goal to connect people to local cultures, communities, and sports. In addition to increasing its customer base, evoTrip allows the organization to form relationships with consumers overseas.

Global opportunities are likely to increase as evo continues to grow. In 2011, the company released its first customer catalog, and Phillips has expressed a desire to open more stores across the nation. The organization is also exploring the possibility of expanding its own line of evo-branded products. In doing so, the organization would not be constrained by contractual obligations from its vendors. Creating a global brand remains an important part of evo's endeavors. According to Phillips, "Everything we do, whether it be something we buy or something we sell [or] something we invest in, is connected globally."[91]

Questions for Discussion

1. What are both the positive and negative outcomes from using exclusive dealer agreements that restrict global distribution?
2. What are the unique product features that could make evo a global brand?
3. What should evo's marketing strategy be to go global?

Case 9.2

Starbucks Faces Global Opportunities and Barriers

Although Starbucks has become an important part of America's coffee culture heritage, the idea for the company came from outside its country of origin. While on a business trip in Milan, Italy, in 1983, Starbucks founder and CEO Howard Schultz noticed the popularity of coffee shops as a community gathering place. He realized that, for Italians, coffee was not so much a beverage as it was a social experience. Schultz decided to replicate this coffee culture in the United States, turning Starbucks into the "third place" consumers would frequent after home and work.

Starbucks opened up its first international store in Vancouver, British Columbia, in 1987. Today, the company is a multinational powerhouse with more than 19,000 stores in 62 countries. Globalization offers many advantages to Starbucks. As the coffee industry becomes increasingly saturated in the United States, international expansion allows Starbucks to take advantage of untapped opportunities in other countries.

However, global expansion has not always been so easy. Starbucks has learned that while it must ensure consistency of quality, it must also customize to adapt to local tastes. For example, in the United Kingdom, Starbucks was not initially popular with British consumers. In response, Starbucks began to renovate its stores to create a unique look so that each store fit into the local neighborhood environment. The company rebounded, and today it has nearly 800 stores in the United Kingdom with plans to begin opening franchises in the country.

Starbucks also faces sociocultural barriers in China. The company entered China in 1999 and has since grown to about 550 stores, but what has been particularly challenging for Starbucks is to find a way to get past cultural barriers. In 2007, the company closed its store in the Forbidden City after criticism from the Chinese media.

Due to the backlash from Chinese citizens, Starbucks once again customized its offerings, with more Chinese-inspired food products and coffee-free beverages (Chinese consumers drink an average of three cups of coffee annually). To show support for Chinese business operations, the company opened a coffee farm and processing facilities within the country and reorganized to form a China and Asia Pacific division.

Starbucks must work to ensure that its Western roots and expansion plans do not clash with Chinese values, since the country is a highly lucrative market. Sales in the coffee market grew 20 percent from the year before. However, while the coffee market is booming, Starbucks has also come across economic barriers. Because operating costs are higher in China, and labor costs are increasing, the price of Starbucks drinks in China is 50 to 75 percent higher than in the United States. This makes it harder for Starbucks to attract China's large population of lower-income consumers, and plans to increase prices to keep up with rising costs have angered middle-income customers. Some media outlets in China have accused the firm of ripping off Chinese consumers (an allegation that Starbucks vehemently denies).

Perhaps one of Starbucks' most celebrated successes is its entry into the Indian market. This success is particularly significant due to political barriers for foreign multinationals in India. Until recently, the Indian government mandated that foreign firms could only operate in the country if they created 50-50 joint ventures with domestic firms. The Indian government changed the law to allow companies that only sell one brand of products to develop wholly-owned subsidiaries in the country. However, Starbucks opted to create a 50-50 joint venture with Indian firm Tata Global Beverages. Such a joint venture has many advantages, including an easier transition into the Indian market (Tata Global Beverages is part of the largest business group in the country). On the other hand, Starbucks must still contend with sociocultural and economic barriers. Not only is India more of a tea-driven society, but most domestic coffee companies sell their beverages at a fraction of Starbucks' prices in the United States. Becoming affordable enough to attract the average Indian consumer will require changes in Starbucks' marketing strategies.

Interestingly, there is one notable country in which Starbucks is absent: Italy. While Starbucks modeled itself after Italian-style coffee shops, major differences between the two coffee cultures might hinder Starbucks' acceptance. For instance, the amount of espresso and the proper times to offer certain drinks like cappuccinos (never for breakfast or after heavy meals in Italy) are very different from American coffee-drinking habits. Starbucks announced that it was expanding in Europe with plans to eventually come into Italy. The announcement led to an uproar among some Italian coffee drinkers. To succeed in Italy may require Starbucks to significantly customize its shops and beverages to appeal to Italian tastes.[92]

Questions for Discussion

1. Describe Starbucks' global strategy. Is it engaging in more of a globalization or customization approach?
2. What appear to be some of the most significant barriers Starbucks is facing when expanding into foreign countries?
3. What are some of the most significant obstacles to expansion in Italy, and how can Starbucks overcome them?

NOTES

[1] Shelly Banjo, "In a Bangladesh Factory, Two Sets of Pay Slips," *The Wall Street Journal*, October 4, 2013, pp. B1, B5; Christina Passariello, "Retailers Pick Bangladesh for Future," *The Wall Street Journal*, September 17, 2013, p. B5; Emma Thomasson, "Retailers Divided over Bangladesh Factory Victims Compensation," *Reuters*, September 12, 2013, www.reuters.com/article/2013/09/12/us-bangladesh-retailers-compensation-idUSBRE98B14420130912 (accessed October 22, 2013).

[2] Sanat Vallikappen, "Card Companies Try to Conquer Myanmar," *Bloomberg Businessweek*, October 24, 2013, www.businessweek.com/articles/2013-10-24/visa-mastercard-sign-up-myanmar-banks-to-expand-card-transactions (accessed December 10, 2013).

[3] "Our Locations," Walmart, http://corporate.walmart.com/our-story/our-business/locations (accessed December 10, 2013).

[4] "Export Assistance," Office of the United States Trade Representative, www.ustr.gov/trade-topics/trade-toolbox/export-assistance (accessed February 21, 2012).

[5] Gary A. Knight and S. Tamer Cavusgil, "Innovation, Organizational Capabilities, and the Born-Global Firm," *Journal of International Business Studies* (March 2004): 124–141.

[6] Bruce Einhorn, "India Reforms Suffer with Wal-Mart's Retreat," *Bloomberg Businessweek*, October 10, 2013, www.businessweek.com/articles/2013-10-10/india-reforms-suffer-with-wal-marts-retreat (accessed December 10, 2013).

[7] John Parker, "Another Year, Another Billion," *The Economist: The World in 2011 Special Edition*, p. 28.

[8] Buffalo Wild Wings, "Buffalo Wild Wings to Expand to Philippines," August 28, 2013, http://ir.buffalowildwings.com/releasedetail.cfm?ReleaseID=787647 (accessed December 11, 2013); Meghan Casserly, "Will Buffalo Wild Wings Fly in Dubai?" *Forbes*, December 17, 2012, www.forbes.com/sites/meghancasserly/2012/10/17/will-buffalo-wild-wings-fly-in-dubai/ (accessed December 11, 2013).

[9] Anton Piësch, "Speaking in Tongues," *Inc.* (June 2003): 50.

[10] Adam Wooten, "International Business: Political Passions Quickly Complicate International Marketing Campaigns," *Deseret News*, December 2, 2011, www.deseretnews.com/article/705395176/Political-passions-quickly-complicate-international-marketing-campaigns.html?pg=all (accessed January 6, 2014).

[11] Sadrudin A. Ahmed and Alain D'Astous, "Moderating Effects of Nationality on Country-of-Origin Perceptions: English-Speaking Thailand versus French-Speaking Canada," *Journal of Business Research* 60 (March 2007): 240–248; George Balabanis and Adamantios Diamantopoulos, "Domestic Country Bias, Country-of-Origin Effects, and Consumer Ethnocentrism: A Multidimensional Unfolding Approach," *Journal of the Academy of Marketing Science* (January 2004): 80–95; Harri T. Luomala, "Exploring the Role of Food Origin as a Source of Meanings for Consumers and as a Determinant of Consumers' Actual Food Choices," *Journal of Business Research* 60 (February 2007): 122–129; Durdana Ozretic-Dosen, Vatroslav Skare, and Zoran Krupka, "Assessments of Country of Origin and Brand Cues in Evaluating a Croatian, Western and Eastern European Food Product," *Journal of Business Research* 60 (February 2007): 130–136.

[12] Philip Coggan, "Markets in a Muddle," *The Economist: The World in 2011 Special Edition*, p. 145.

[13] James O'Toole, "Fitch Puts U.S. on Notice for Downgrade," *CNN Money*, October 15, 2013, http://money.cnn.com/2013/10/15/news/economy/fitch-downgrade (accessed December 11, 2013).

[14] Adam Davidson, "How China's Currency Policy Affects You," NPR, April 20, 2006, www.npr.org/templates/story/story.php?storyId=5353313 (accessed January 20, 2012).

[15] Inti Landauro, "Colombia, Mexico Criticize Rich Countries on Monetary, Fiscal Policies," *The Wall Street Journal*, January 24, 2011, http://online.wsj.com/article/BT-CO-20110124-710562.html (accessed January 20, 2012).

[16] Central Intelligence Agency, "Country Comparisons," *The World Factbook*, www.cia.gov/library/publications/the-world-factbook/rankorder/rankorderguide.html (accessed December 11, 2013).

[17] Ibid.

[18] Sanat Vallikappen, "Card Companies Try to Conquer Myanmar."

[19] "Emirates," The Emirates Group, www.theemiratesgroup.com/english/our-brands/air-transportation/emirates-airline.aspx (accessed January 10, 2014).

[20] American Marketing Association, "Statement of Ethics," www.marketingpower.com/AboutAMA/Pages/Statement%20of%20Ethics.aspx (accessed December 11, 2013).

[21] "U.S. Trade Representative Announces Fiscal 2010 Tariff-Rate Quota Allocations for Raw Cane Sugar, Refined Specialty Sugar, Sugar Containing Products," October 1, 2009, www.highbeam.com/doc/1P3-1870093731.html (accessed December 11, 2013).

[22] Marc Frank, "Americans Traveling to Cuba in Record Numbers," *Reuters*, October 18, 2013, www.reuters.com/article/2013/10/18/us-cuba-usa-tourism-idUSBRE99H0J320131018 (accessed December 11, 2013).

[23] U.S. Bureau of the Census, Foreign Trade Division, *U.S. Trade in Goods and Services—Balance of Payments (BOP) Basis*, February 6, 2014, www.census.gov/foreign-trade/statistics/historical/gands.pdf (accessed February 27, 2014).

[24] Charles R. Taylor, George R. Franke, and Michael L. Maynard, "Attitudes toward Direct Marketing and Its Regulation: A Comparison of the United States and Japan," *Journal of Public Policy & Marketing* (Fall 2000): 228–237.

[25] Julius Melnitzer, "U.K. Enacts 'Far-Reaching' Anti-Bribery Act," *Law Times*, February 13, 2011, www.lawtimesnews.com/201102148245/Headline-News/UK-enacts-far-reaching-anti-bribery-act (accessed December 11, 2013).

[26] "Welcome to BASCAP," International Chamber of Commerce, www.iccwbo.org/advocacy-codes-and-rules/bascap (accessed December 11, 2013).

[27] Laurie Burkitt and Kathy Gordon, "Burberry Appeals China Ban on Its Trademark Pattern," *The Wall Street Journal*, November 27, 2013, http://online.wsj.com/news/articles/SB10001424052702303562904579223651626050682 (accessed December 11, 2013).

[28] Business for Social Responsibility, www.bsr.org (accessed December 10, 2013).

[29] Roberta Holland, "European Commission Fines J&J, Novartis €16M for Delaying Generic Painkiller Release," *Compliance Week*, December 11, 2013, www.complianceweek.com/european-commission-fines-jj-novartis-16m-for-delaying-generic-painkiller-release/article/325088 (accessed December 11, 2013).

[30] "This Is Systembolaget," www.systembolaget.se/Applikationer/Knappar/InEnglish/Swedish_alcohol_re.htm (accessed March 23, 2010).

[31] Central Intelligence Agency, "Guide to Country Comparisons," *World Factbook*, www.cia.gov/library/publications/the-world-factbook/rankorder/rankorderguide.html (accessed December 11, 2013).

[32] "Is It a Phone, Is It a Bank?" *The Economist*, March 30, 2013, www.economist.com/news/finance-and-economics/21574520-safaricom-widens-its-banking-services-payments-savings-and-loans-it (accessed December 11, 2013); Olebogeng Mogale, "Mobile Banking Series: An Overview of Why Mobile Banking Remains Important for Financial Inclusion in Africa," *KPMG*, April 22, 2013, www.economist.com/news/finance-and-economics/21574520-safaricom-widens-its-banking-services-payments-savings-and-loans-it (accessed December 11, 2013).

[33] "The North American Free Trade Agreement (NAFTA)," export.gov, http://export.gov/FTA/nafta/index.asp (accessed December 11, 2013).

[34] Central Intelligence Agency, "Guide to Country Comparisons," *World Factbook*, www.cia.gov/library/publications/the-world-factbook/rankorder/rankorderguide.html (accessed December 11, 2013).

[35] Executive Office of the President of the United States, "U.S.-Canada Trade Facts," www.ustr.gov/countries-regions/americas/canada (accessed March 3, 2014).

[36] "Canada's Major Trading Partners—2010," www.dpcdsb.org/NR/rdonlyres/0535EFD9-639D-4D95-B7AA-461E34742340/101643/Canadasmajor_trading_partners_20101.pdf (accessed December 11, 2013).

[37] Central Intelligence Agency, "Guide to Country Comparisons," *World Factbook*, www.cia.gov/library/publications/the-world-factbook/rankorder/rankorderguide.html (accessed December 11, 2013).

[38] Executive Office of the President of the United States, "U.S.-Mexico Trade Facts," www.ustr.gov/countries-regions/americas/mexico (accessed March 3, 2014).

[39] "Special Report: Mexico," *The Economist*, November 24, 2012, pp. 3–16.

[40] "CAFTA-DR (Dominican Republic-Central America FTA)," Office of the United States Trade Representative, www.ustr.gov/trade-agreements/free-trade-agreements/cafta-dr-dominican-republic-central-america-fta (accessed January 23, 2012).

[41] "The History of the European Union," Europa, http://europa.eu/abc/history/index_en.htm (accessed December 11, 2013); "Europe in 12 Lessons," Europa, http://europa.eu/abc/12lessons/lesson_2/index_en.htm (accessed December 11, 2013).

[42] Central Intelligence Agency, "Guide to Country Comparisons," *World Factbook*, www.cia.gov/library/publications/the-world-factbook/rankorder/rankorderguide.html (accessed December 11, 2013).

[43] Herman Van Rompuy, "Europe in the New Global Game," *The Economist: The World in 2011 Special Edition*, p. 97.

[44] "About the European Union," Europa, http://europa.eu/about-eu/index_en.htm (accessed December 11, 2013).

[45] "Special Advertising Section: The European Union and the United States," *Foreign Policy*, January 2013, p. 1.

[46] Bruno Waterfield, "Ireland Forced to Take EU and IMF Bail-Out Package," *The Telegraph*, November 22, 2010, www.telegraph.co.uk/finance/financetopics/financialcrisis/8150137/Ireland-forced-to-take-EU-and-IMF-bail-out-package.html (accessed December 11, 2013); Jonathon House and Alkman Granitsas, "Spain, Cyprus Request Bailout Aid," *The Wall Street Journal*, June 25, 2012, http://online.wsj.com/article/SB10001424052702304458604577488891324210470.html (accessed December 11, 2013).

[47] "Italy's Credit Rating Has Been Downgraded by S&P," *BBC*, July 9, 2013, www.bbc.co.uk/news/business-23250689 (accessed December 11, 2013); David Jolly, "S.&P. Downgrade Deals Blow to French Government," *The New York*

Times, November 8, 2013, www.nytimes.com/2013/11/09/business/international/standard-poors-downgrades-france.html (accessed December 11, 2013); Peter Wise, "S&P Warns of Portugal Rating Cut over Second Bailout Threat," *Financial Times*, September 18, 2013, www.ft.com/intl/cms/s/0/f5109d4c-20a1-11e3-b8c6-00144feab7de.html#axzz2n7MPJRVG (accessed December 11, 2013).

[48] "Powerhouse Deutschland," *Bloomberg Businessweek*, January 3, 2011, p. 93; Alan S. Blinder, "The Euro Zone's German Crisis," *The Wall Street Journal*, http://online.wsj.com/article/SB10001424052970203430404577094313707190708.html (accessed December 11, 2013).

[49] Patrick Donahue, "Germany's AAA Rating Affirmed by Fitch on Budget Consolidation," *Bloomberg*, August 7, 2013, www.bloomberg.com/news/2013-08-07/germany-s-aaa-rating-affirmed-by-fitch-on-budget-consolidation.html (accessed December 11, 2013).

[50] "Special Advertising Section: The European Union and the United States," *Foreign Policy*, January 2013, p. 1.

[51] Daniela DeSantis, "Paraguay's New Leader Wants Back into Mercosur," *Reuters*, September 19, 2013, www.reuters.com/article/2013/09/20/us-paraguay-trade-idUSBRE98J01H20130920 (accessed December 11, 2013); Joanna Klonsky, Stephanie Hanson, and Brianna Lee, "Mercosur: South America's Fractious Trade Bloc," Council on Foreign Relations, July 31, 2012, www.cfr.org/trade/mercosur-south-americas-fractious-trade-bloc/p12762 (accessed December 11, 2013).

[52] Joanna Klonsky, Stephanie Hanson, and Brianna Lee, "Mercosur: South America's Fractious Trade Bloc," Council on Foreign Relations, July 31, 2012, www.cfr.org/trade/mercosur-south-americas-fractious-trade-bloc/p12762 (accessed December 11, 2013); "Agri-Food Regional of the South (Mercosur): Brazil, Argentina, Paraguay," Agriculture and Agrifood Canada, January 2011, www.ats.agr.gc.ca/lat/3947-eng.htm (accessed December 11, 2013).

[53] Johanna Mendelson Forman "Cuba's Emerging Middle Class and Growing Private Sector," *The Huffington Post*, November 12, 2013, www.huffingtonpost.com/2013/11/12/cuba-middle-class_n_4260021.html (accessed December 12, 2013).

[54] "About APEC," Asia-Pacific Economic Cooperation, www.apec.org/home.aspx (accessed December 12, 2013).

[55] Ibid.

[56] Jack Perkowski, "Managing the Dragon's 2013 China Predictions," *Forbes*, January 7, 2013, www.forbes.com/sites/jackperkowski/2013/01/07/managing-the-dragons-2013-china-predictions (accessed December 12, 2013).

[57] "China and the Paradox of Prosperity," *The Economist*, January 28, 2012, p. 9.

[58] Paul Carsten and Jane Lanhee Lee, "Once Piracy Havens, China's Internet Video Websites Turn Police," *Reuters*, December 5, 2013, www.reuters.com/article/2013/12/05/us-china-internet-video-idUSBRE9B414Z20131205 (accessed December 12, 2013).

[59] Karen Cho, "KFC China's Recipe for Success," *INSEAD Knowledge*, July 1, 2009, http://knowledge.insead.edu/KFCinChina090323.cfm? vid=195 (accessed December 12, 2013); Ben Rooney, "China: The New Fast Food Nation," *CNN Money*, July 14, 2010, http://money.cnn.com/2010/07/13/news/companies/Yum_Brands/index.htm (accessed December 12, 2013); Kathy Chu, "For Some U.S. Companies, China Sales Rule," *USA Today*, February 3, 2011, p. 1B.

[60] Lydia DePillis, "Everything You Need to Know about the Trans Pacific Partnership," *The Washington Post*, December 11, 2013, www.washingtonpost.com/blogs/wonkblog/wp/2013/12/11/everything-you-need-to-know-about-the-trans-pacific-partnership (accessed December 12, 2013).

[61] Hiroko Tabuchi, "Premier Says Japan Will Join Pacific Free Trade Talks," *The New York Times*, November 11, 2011, www.nytimes.com/2011/11/12/world/asia/japan-to-join-talks-on-pacific-trade-pact.html (accessed December 12, 2013).

[62] Tom Barkley, "Framework Is Set for New Trade Bloc," *The Wall Street Journal*, November 14, 2011, http://online.wsj.com/article/SB10001424052970203503204577036553639815214.html (accessed December 12, 2013).

[63] David Pilling, "Trans-Pacific Partnership: Far-Reaching Agreement Could Form Powerful New Trade Bloc," *Financial Times*, November 8, 2011, www.ft.com/intl/cms/s/0/47dd4d14-06cc-11e1-90de-00144feabdc0.html#axzz2n7MPJRVG (accessed December 12, 2013).

[64] Tabuchi, "Premier Says Japan Will Join Pacific Free Trade Talks"; Tom Barkley, "Framework Is Set For New Trade Bloc."

[65] Association of Southeast Asian Nations website, www.aseansec.org/ (accessed December 12, 2013).

[66] Parag Khanna, "ASEAN Is Key to 'Asian Century,'" *CNN*, August 15, 2013, www.cnn.com/2013/08/14/opinion/asean-dream-khanna/ (accessed December 12, 2013).

[67] Association of Southeast Asian Nations website, www.aseansec.org (accessed December 12, 2013).

[68] "FAQ—Free Trade Agreement," The Official Portal of Malaysia External Trade Development Association, www.matrade.gov.my/en/malaysian-exporters/going-global/understanding-free-trade-agreements/494-free-trade-agreement-faq (accessed December 12, 2013); www.malaysia.gov.my/EN/Relevant%20Topics/IndustryInMalaysia/Business/BusinessAndEBusiness/BusinessAndAgreement/CEPT/Pages/CEPT.aspx (accessed January 23, 2012).

[69] Nick Mead, "OECD: South-East Asian Economic Outlook to Return to Pre-Crisis Levels," *The Guardian*, http://articles.cnn.com/2011-05-07/world/asia.asean.summit_1_asean-leaders-asean-summit-southeast-asian-nations?_s=PM:WORLD (accessed December 12, 2013).

[70] Kathy Quiano, "ASEAN Summit Starts amid Cloud of Thai-Cambodia Border Row," *CNN*, May 7, 2011, http://articles.cnn.com/2011-05-07/world/asia.asean.summit_1_asean-leaders-asean-summit-southeast-asian-nations?_s=PM:WORLD (accessed December 12, 2013).

[71] Eric Bellman, "Asia Seeks Integration Despite EU's Woes," *The Wall Street Journal*, July 22, 2011, p. A9.

[72] World Trade Organization, "Members and Observers," www.wto.org/english/thewto_e/whatis_e/tif_e/org6_e.htm (accessed December 12, 2013).

[73] "What Is the WTO?" World Trade Organization, www.wto.org/english/thewto_e/whatis_e/whatis_e.htm (accessed December 12, 2013).

[74] "China Files WTO Complaint against U.S. Anti-Dumping Duties," *The Wall Street Journal*, December 3, 2013, http://online.wsj.com/article/BT-CO-20131203-702616.html (accessed December 12, 2013).

[75] Jan Johanson and Finn Wiedersheim-Paul, "The Internationalization of the Firm," *Journal of Management Studies* October(1975): 305–322; Jan Johanson and Jan-Erik Vahlne, "The Internationalization Process of the Firm—A Model of Knowledge Development and Increasing Foreign Commitments," *Journal of International Business Studies* (Spring/Summer 1977): 23–32; S. Tamer Cavusgil and John R. Nevin, "Internal Determinants of Export Marketing Behavior: An Empirical Investigation," *Journal of Marketing Research* (February 1981): 114–119.

[76] Pradeep Tyagi, "Export Behavior of Small Business Firms in Developing Economies: Evidence from the Indian Market," *Marketing Management Journal* (Fall/Winter 2000): 12–20.

[77] Berrin Dosoglu-Guner, "How Do Exporters and Non-Exporters View Their 'Country of Origin' Image Abroad?" *Marketing Management Journal* (Fall/Winter 2000): 21–27.

[78] WTSC Industrial Group website, www.wtsc.eu (accessed December 12, 2013).

[79] Farok J. Contractor and Sumit K. Kundu, "Franchising versus Company-Run Operations: Model Choice in the Global Hotel Sector," *Journal of International Marketing* (November 1997): 28–53.

[80] Catherine Larkin and Anna Edney, "More Outsourcing Planned for FDA Overseas Factory Inspections," *Bloomberg*, February 10, 2011, www.bloomberg.com/news/2011-02-10/fda-to-outsource-international-plant-inspections-as-oversight-criticized.html (accessed December 12, 2013).

[81] "Suddenly, Made in USA Looks Like a Strategy," *Bloomberg Businessweek*, March 28, 2011, pp. 57–58.

[82] Daniel Wallis, "Venezuela Launches Joint Venture with Samsung Electronics," *Reuters*, November 20, 2013, www.reuters.com/article/2013/11/20/us-venezuela-samsung-idUSBRE9AJ14A20131120 (accessed December 12, 2013).

[83] "Volvo in Strategic Alliance with Chinese Motor Company Dongfeng Motor Group," *Global News*, January 26, 2013, http://news.volvogroup.com/2013/01/26/volvo-in-strategic-alliance-with-chinese-company-dongfeng-motor-group (accessed December 12, 2013).

[84] "The 2011 Oil Shock," *The Economist*, March 5, 2011, pp. 14–16.

[85] "Export Department," Lone Star Distribution, www.lonestardistribution.com/index.php/our-companies/export-department (accessed December 12, 2013).

[86] Abbott, www.abbott.com/global/url/content/en_US/10.17:17/general_content/General_Content_00054.htm (accessed December 12, 2013).

[87] Bernhard Warner, "To Get Medicine to Africa, Health Experts Turn to Coca-Cola," *Bloomberg Businessweek*, April 8, 2013, www.businessweek.com/articles/2013-04-08/to-get-medicine-to-africa-health-experts-turn-to-coca-cola (accessed December 12, 2013).

[88] Deborah Owens, Timothy Wilkinson, and Bruce Keillor, "A Comparison of Product Attributes in a Cross-Cultural/Cross-National Context," *Marketing Management Journal* (Fall/Winter 2000): 1–11.

[89] Associated Press, "Starbucks, Dunkin' Donuts to Battle It Out in Vietnam," *The Huffington Post*, January 30, 2013, www.huffingtonpost.com/2013/01/30/starbucks-dunkin-donuts-vietnam_n_2581426.html (accessed December 12, 2013).

[90] Anil K. Gupta and Vijay Govindarajan, "Converting Global Presence into Global Competitive Advantage," *Academy of Management Executive* (May 2001): 45–58.

[91] evo website, www.evo.com (accessed December 12, 2013); Jessica Naziri, "Retailer Grows Up, Along with His Business," *CNBC*, February 15, 2012, www.cnbc.com/id/46386774 (accessed December 12, 2013); "Evo Goes Against the Grain with First Winter Sports," *New Schoolers*, October 15, 2011, www.newschoolers.com/readnews/4209.0/Evo-Goes-Against-The-Grain-With-First-Winter-Sports-Consumer-Catalog?c=2 (accessed December 12, 2013); "Evo Shares Its Retail Secrets," *Skiing Business*, February 7, 2012, http://skiingbusiness.com/11874/profiles/evo-shares-its-retail-secrets (accessed December 12, 2013); "About evoTrip," evo, www.evo.com/about-evotrip.aspx (accessed December 12, 2013).

[92] "Our Heritage," Starbucks, www.starbucks.com/about-us/our-heritage (accessed December 12, 2013); Starbucks, "Starbucks Company Timeline," http://globalassets.starbucks.com/assets/BA6185AA2F9440379CE0857D89DE8412.pdf (accessed December 12, 2013); David Teather, "Starbucks Legend Delivers Recovery by Thinking Smaller," *The Guardian*, January 21, 2010, www.theguardian.com/business/2010/jan/21/starbucks-howard-schultz (accessed December 12, 2013); "How Starbucks Colonised the World," *The Sunday Times*, February 17, 2008, http://business.timesonline.co.uk/tol/business/industry_sectors/leisure/article3381092.ece (accessed July 19, 2011); "Starbucks to Open UK Franchises as Profits Jump," *The Telegraph*, March 14, 2012, www.telegraph.co.uk/finance/newsbysector/retailandconsumer/9043202/Starbucks-to-open-UK-franchises-as-profits-jump.html (accessed December 12, 2013); Lauren Pollock, "Starbucks Adds Division Focused on Asia," *The Wall Street Journal*, July 11, 2011, http://online.wsj.com/article/SB10001424052702303678704576440292712481616.html (accessed December 12, 2013); Matt Hodges, "Schultz Brews Up Major Push in China," *China Daily*, June 10–11, 2011, p. 5; Mariko Sanchanta, "Starbucks Plans Big Expansion in China," *The Wall Street Journal*, April 14, 2010, p. B10; "Asia Pacific," *Starbucks Newsroom*, http://mena.starbucks.com/en/newsroomarticle/sections/about-starbucks/starbucks-coffee-international/asia-pacific.html (accessed December 12, 2013); "Greater China," http://mena.starbucks.com/en/newsroomarticle/sections/about-starbucks/starbucks-coffee-international/greater-china.html (accessed December 12, 2013); Laurie Burkitt, "Starbucks Price Increase Stirs China's Netizens," *The Wall Street Journal*, February 1, 2012, http://blogs.wsj.com/chinarealtime/2012/02/01/starbucks-price-increase-stirs-chinas-netizens (accessed December 12, 2013); Vikas Bajaj, "After a Year of Delays, the First Starbucks Is to Open

in Tea-Loving India This Fall," *The New York Times*, January 30, 2012, www.nytimes.com/2012/01/31/business/global/starbucks-to-open-first-indian-store-this-autumn.html (accessed December 12, 2013); Stephan Faris, "Grounds Zero: A Starbucks-Free Italy," *Bloomberg Businessweek*, February 9, 2012, www.businessweek.com/magazine/grounds-zero-a-starbucksfree-italy-02092012.html (accessed December 12, 2013); Jennifer Askin, "Starbuck's Set to Rock Italy's Café Culture," *ABC News*, April 30, http://abcnews.go.com/Business/story?id=88256 (accessed December 12, 2013); Charles Riley and Sophia Yan, "Starbucks Defends China Prices, Finds Support," *CNN Money*, October 22, 2013, http://money.cnn.com/2013/10/22/news/starbucks-china (accessed December 12, 2013); Seeking Alpha, "Starbucks' CEO Discusses F4Q 2013 Results—Earnings Call Transcript," *Yahoo! Finance*, October 30, 2013, http://finance.yahoo.com/news/starbucks-ceo-discusses-f4q-2013-030232109.html (accessed February 24, 2014).

Feature Notes

[a] Simon Montlake and Ryan Ma, "China's Steve Jobs," *Forbes*, July 18, 2012, www.forbes.com/global/2012/0806/feature-technology-lei-jun-smartphones-china-steve-jobs.html (accessed August 31, 2012); Laura He, "Chinese Billionaire Lei Jun and His iPhone Challenger Jump into Fierce Smartphone Price War," *Forbes*, August 15, 2012, www.forbes.com/sites/laurahe/2012/08/15/lei-jun-and-apples-chinese-challenger-jump-into-fierce-smartphone-price-war (accessed August 31, 2012); Hannah Beech/Chengdu, "The Cult of Apple in China," *Time Magazine*, July 2, 2012, www.time.com/time/magazine/article/0,9171,2117765,00.html (accessed August 31, 2012).

[b] Deborah Ball, "No Need to Ask Price at Euro Stores," *The Wall Street Journal*, August 14, 2013, p. B8; Andrew R, "The World Eats Montadito," *El Pais*, November 11, 2012, http://translate.google.com/translate?hl=en&sl=es&u=http://economia.elpais.com/economia/2012/11/09/actualidad/1352464703_006832.html&prev=/search%3Fq%3Deuromania%2Barticles%2B100%2Bmontaditos%26rlz%3D1C1EODB_enUS550US553%26espv%3D210%26es_sm%3D93%26biw%3D1280%26bih%3D699 (accessed October 21, 2013); Dollar Store, "International," www.dollarstore.com/int/international.html (accessed October 22, 2013).

chapter 10

Digital Marketing and Social Networking

© My Life Graphic/Shutterstock.com

OBJECTIVES

10-1 Define *digital media, digital marketing*, and *electronic marketing*.

10-2 Summarize the growth and importance of digital marketing.

10-3 Describe different types of digital media and how they can be used for marketing.

10-4 Critique the seven different ways consumers use digital media.

10-5 Describe how digital media affect the four variables of the marketing mix.

10-6 Identify legal and ethical considerations in digital marketing.

MARKETING INSIGHTS

Procter & Gamble and Amazon Form a Distribution Network

Digital marketing is necessary for items purchasable online, but it is also important for products that are primarily bought in retail locations. Laundry detergent, for instance, is not an item that consumers have traditionally bought online as it would cost them more when shipping and handling were included. However, the brand of detergent that customers choose will largely depend on the reputation it has online. Powerful brand perceptions are generated online through company messages as well as consumer feedback and comments. The online discussion of brands and products is a hyper version of traditional word-of-mouth communication, making it all the more important for companies to establish themselves online. The better the brand's image online, the more likely consumers will be to put these products on their shopping lists and in their shopping carts.

An important aspect of digital marketing involves distribution. Amazon has developed a program called Vendor Flex, which allows for mutually beneficial partnerships with other companies' warehouses. Procter & Gamble warehouses allot a space for Amazon employees so they can quickly and cost-effectively ship items to customers. With this program, Amazon is changing the landscape of the consumer goods market. Although people are not generally compelled to buy items such as paper towels and toilet paper online, quick and inexpensive delivery is making them think twice. Other companies such as Kimberly Clark and Seventh Generation are partnering with Amazon as well. The Vendor Flex program has increased online sales of consumer products and has exceedingly benefited the partners involved.[1]

Since the 1990s, the Internet and information technology have dramatically changed the marketing environment and the strategies that are necessary for marketing success. Digital media have created exciting opportunities for companies to target specific markets more effectively, develop new marketing strategies, and gather more information about customers. Using digital media channels, marketers are better able to analyze and address consumer needs. Fueled by changing technology, consumer behavior has changed with Internet-enabled consumer empowerment. This has resulted in a shift in the balance of power between consumer and marketer.[2]

One of the defining characteristics of information technology in the 21st century is accelerating change. New systems and applications advance so rapidly that a chapter on this topic has to strain to incorporate the possibilities of the future. When Google first arrived on the scene in 1998, a number of search engines were fighting for dominance. Google, with its fast, easy-to-use format, soon became the number-one search engine. Today, Google provides additional competition to many industries, including advertising, newspaper, mobile phone services, book publishing, and social networking. In the future, wearable computers such as Google Glass and smartwatches have the potential to radically change the computing industry. As you can see, the environment for marketing is changing rapidly based on these factors, as well as unknown future developments within information technology.

In this chapter, we focus on digital marketing strategies—particularly communication channels such as social networks—and discuss how consumers are changing their information searches and consumption behaviors to fit with these emerging technologies and trends. Most importantly, we analyze how marketers can use new media to their advantage to connect with consumers, gather more information about their target markets, and convert this information into successful marketing strategies.

10-1 DEFINING *DIGITAL* MARKETING

Before we move on, we must first provide a definition of digital media. **Digital media** are electronic media that function using digital codes—when we refer to digital media, we are referring to media available via computers, cellular phones, smartphones, and other digital devices that have been released in recent years. A number of terms have been coined to describe marketing activities on the Internet. **Digital marketing** uses all digital media, including the Internet and mobile and interactive channels, to develop communication and exchanges with customers. In this chapter, we focus on how the Internet relates to all aspects of marketing, including strategic planning. Thus, we use the term **electronic marketing**, or **e-marketing**, to refer to the strategic process of distributing, promoting, and pricing products, and discovering the desires of customers using digital media and digital marketing. Our definition of e-marketing goes beyond the Internet and also includes mobile phones, banner ads, digital outdoor marketing, and social networks. With more than 2 billion people accessing the Internet worldwide, marketers are seeing their digital marketing strategies reach consumers from different parts of the world like never before.[3]

digital media Electronic media that function using digital codes; when we refer to digital media, we are referring to media available via computers, cellular phones, smartphones, and other digital devices that have been released in recent years

digital marketing Uses all digital media, including the Internet and mobile and interactive channels, to develop communication and exchanges with customers

electronic marketing (e-marketing) The strategic process of distributing, promoting, and pricing products, and discovering the desires of customers using digital media and digital marketing

10-2 GROWTH AND BENEFITS OF DIGITAL MARKETING

The phenomenal growth of the Internet has provided unprecedented opportunities for marketers to forge interactive relationships with consumers. As the Internet and digital communication technologies have advanced, they have made it possible to target markets more precisely and reach markets that were previously inaccessible. As the world of digital media continues to develop, Internet marketing has been integrated into strategies that include all digital media, including television advertising and other mobile and interactive media that do not use the Internet (advertising media are discussed in detail in Chapter 17). In fact, marketers are using the term *digital marketing* as a catch-all for capturing all digital channels for reaching customers. This area is evolving quickly, and the digital world is still in an early stage of integration into marketing strategy.[4]

One of the most important benefits of e-marketing is the ability of marketers and customers to share information. Through websites, social networks, and other digital media, consumers can learn about everything they consume and use in life. As a result, the Internet is changing the way marketers communicate and develop relationships. Today's marketers can use the Internet to form relationships with a variety of stakeholders, including customers, employees, and suppliers. Many companies use not just e-mail and mobile phones, but also social networking, wikis, media-sharing sites, blogs, mobile applications, and other technologies to coordinate activities and communicate with employees.

For many businesses, engaging in digital and online marketing activities is essential to maintaining competitive advantages. Increasingly, small businesses can use digital media to develop strategies to reach new markets and access inexpensive communication channels. In addition, large companies like Target use online catalogs and company websites to supplement their brick-and-mortar stores. At the other end of the spectrum, companies like Amazon.com, which lack physical stores and sell products solely online, are emerging to challenge traditional brick-and-mortar businesses. Social networking sites are advancing e-marketing by providing features to aid in commerce, such as Facebook developing its own currency to purchase products, send gifts, and engage in the entire shopping experience.[5] Finally, some corporate websites and social media sites provide feedback mechanisms through which customers can ask questions, voice complaints, indicate preferences, and otherwise communicate about their needs and desires.

Benefits of Digital Marketing
Consumers are increasingly using digital devices to pay for purchases rather than using cash.

This increase in digital promotions is providing new business opportunities for Internet services. U.K.-based hibu plc markets its expertise in developing innovative digital solutions for its clients. In its advertising hibu promotes its abilities in website development, digital advertising, and search marketing as a way to make a client's digital investments take off. Due to the diversity of devices in use, hibu claims it can create solutions for phones, laptops, and tablet computers.

One of the biggest mistakes a marketer can make when engaging in digital marketing is to treat it like a traditional marketing channel. Digital media offer a whole new dimension to marketing that marketers must consider when concocting their companies' marketing strategies. Some of the characteristics that distinguish online media from traditional marketing include addressability, interactivity, accessibility, connectivity, and control, as defined in Table 10.1.

New Business Opportunities
Hibu has taken advantage of the new business opportunities of digital marketing by promoting its expertise in website development, display advertising, and search marketing.

10-3 TYPES OF CONSUMER-GENERATED MARKETING AND DIGITAL MEDIA

Although digital and e-marketing have generated exciting opportunities for producers of products to interact with consumers, it is essential to recognize that social media are more consumer-driven than traditional media. Consumer-generated material is having a profound effect on marketing. As the Internet becomes more accessible worldwide, consumers are creating and reading consumer-generated content like never before. Social networks and advances in software technology provide an environment for marketers to utilize consumer-generated content.

Two major trends have caused consumer-generated information to gain importance:

1. The increased tendency of consumers to publish their own thoughts, opinions, reviews, and product discussions through blogs or digital media.
2. Consumers' tendencies to trust other consumers over corporations. Consumers often rely on the recommendations of friends, family, and fellow consumers when making purchasing decisions.

By understanding where online users are likely to express their thoughts and opinions, marketers can use these forums to interact with consumers, address problems, and promote their companies. Types of digital media in which Internet users are likely to participate include social networking

Table 10.1 Characteristics of Online Media

Characteristic	Definition	Example
Addressability	The ability of the marketer to identify customers before they make a purchase	Amazon installs cookies on a user's computer that allow the company to identify the user when he or she returns to the website.
Interactivity	The ability of customers to express their needs and wants directly to the firm in response to its marketing communications	Texas Instruments interacts with its customers on its Facebook page by answering concerns and posting updates.
Accessibility	The ability for marketers to obtain digital information	Google can use Web searches done through its search engine to learn about customer interests.
Connectivity	The ability for consumers to be connected with marketers along with other consumers	Mary Kay offers users the opportunity to sign up for My MK, a system that connects customers with beauty consultants and allows them to develop their own personalized space.
Control	The customer's ability to regulate the information they view as well as the rate and exposure to that information	Consumers use Kayak.com to discover the best travel deals.

sites, blogs, wikis, media-sharing sites, virtual gaming sites, mobile devices, applications and widgets, and more.

10-3a Social Networks

Social networks have evolved quickly in a short period of time. A **social network** is a website where users can create a profile and interact with other users, post information, and engage in other forms of web-based communication. They are widely used by marketers, and marketing strategies are using social networking sites to develop relationships with customers. Each wave of social network has become increasingly sophisticated. Today's social networks offer a multitude of consumer benefits, including music downloads, apps, forums, and games. Marketers are thereby using these sites and their popularity with consumers to promote products, handle questions and complaints, and provide information to assist customers in buying decisions. For instance, in its advertisement *Motor Trend* magazine describes the many ways consumers can "follow" the publication by displaying the app logos of different forms of digital media. Among the apps displayed are those from the digital media sites Facebook, Twitter, Google+, YouTube, Instagram, and Pinterest.

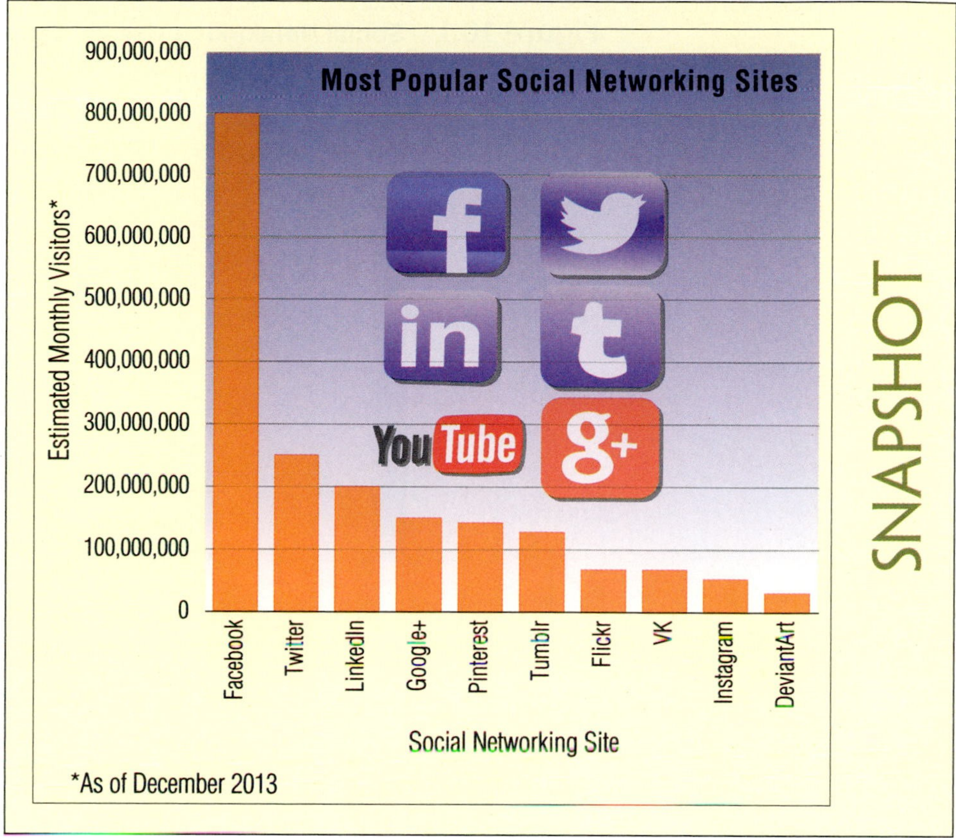

Source: "The 15 Most Popular Social Networking Sites," *eBiz MBA*, December 2013, www.ebizmba.com/articles/social-networking-websites (accessed December 13, 2013).

As the number of social network users increases, interactive marketers are finding opportunities to reach out to consumers in new target markets. CafeMom is a social networking site that offers mothers a forum in which to connect and write about parenting and other topics important to them. At 12 million unique monthly visitors, this particular site is an opportunity to reach out to mothers, a demographic that has a significant influence on family purchasing behavior. Walmart, Playskool, General Mills, and Johnson & Johnson have all advertised through this site.[6] Many countries or regions have their own popular social networking sites as well. For instance, VK is a popular social networking site in Europe. Social networking sites also offer ways for marketers to promote their companies. More information on how marketers use social networks is provided in later sections of this chapter.

Internet users join social networks for many reasons, from chatting with friends to professional networking. Social networks have become very popular among a number of age groups. As Figure 10.1 demonstrates, the majority of social network users are between the ages of 18 and 29, but other age groups are not that far behind. Approximately 72 percent of online adults use social networks.[7] As social networks evolve, both marketers and the owners of social networking sites are realizing the incredible opportunities such networks offer—an influx of advertising dollars for social networking owners and a large reach for the advertiser. As a result, marketers have begun investigating and experimenting with promotion on social networks.

social network A website where users can create a profile and interact with other users, post information, and engage in other forms of web-based communication

Figure 10.1 **Social Networking Use by Age**

Age Groups	18–29	30–49	50–64	65+
Social networking use	89%	78%	60%	43%

Source: Pew Research Center, May 2013.

Courtesy of Motor Trend

Using Social Media to Enhance Promotion
Motor Trend magazine encourages consumers to follow the publication on different social networks, using digital media such as QR codes, Pinterest, Facebook, and YouTube.

Facebook

Facebook is the most popular social networking site in the world. When it was launched in 2004 by Harvard student Mark Zuckerberg and four of his classmates, it was initially limited to Harvard students. In 2006 the site was opened to anyone age 13 or older. Internet users create Facebook profiles and then search the network for people with whom to connect. The social networking giant has surpassed 1 billion users and is still growing.[8]

For this reason, many marketers are turning to Facebook to market products, interact with consumers, and take advantage of free publicity. Consumers can become fans of major companies like Avon by clicking on the "like" icon on their Facebook pages. Organizations also use Facebook and other digital media sites to give special incentives to customers. American Express offers customers special discounts if they link their cards to Facebook, Twitter, and/or Foursquare accounts. This incentive allows the firm to build loyalty and gain more information about customers.[9] Advertising on Facebook has also been increasing. The firm generated $1.8 billion from advertising during a 4-month period, with 49 percent coming from mobile advertising.[10] Promoted posts, one of the features Facebook has to offer businesses, allows companies to develop advertisements that show up in the News Feeds of those who have "liked" the organization and in the News Feeds of their friends.[11]

Additionally, social networking sites are useful for relationship marketing, or the creation of relationships that mutually benefit the marketing business and the customer. Companies are using relationship marketing through Facebook to help consumers feel more connected to their products—and more loyal to the firm. One study discovered that retailers with the highest rate of repeat customers (84 percent or more of their customer base) interact frequently with customers through Facebook and other digital media, resulting in a strong customer following. For instance, Facebook Likes among the top 10 retailers with repeat customers have a median of more than 300,000 Likes. Home shopping network QVC uses Facebook to provide customers with updates, answer questions, and enable customers to interact with shopping experts. Due to this interaction, social networks drove 5.27 percent of QVC's Web traffic.[12] Thanks to Facebook, companies like QVC are able to understand who their customers are and how they can meet their needs.

Twitter

Twitter is a hybrid mix of a social networking site and a micro-blogging site that asks viewers one simple question: "What's happening?" Users can post answers of up to 140 characters, which are then available for their "followers" to read. A limitation of 140 characters may not seem like enough for companies to send an effective message, but some have become experts at using Twitter in their marketing strategies. For instance, JetBlue has had a social media support team since 2010 that monitors Twitter and other postings. The company prides itself on responding quickly to concerns and corresponding with passengers through social media.[13] For sports enthusiasts, the National Football League developed a deal with Twitter to feature football highlights and clips on the site.[14]

Like other social networking sites, Twitter is being used to enhance customer service and create publicity about company products. For example, Zappos posts on Twitter to update followers on company activities and address customer complaints.[15] Progressive Corp. purchases advertisements featuring tweets from its television spokesperson Flo, who provides updates for her more than 20,000 Twitter followers.[16]

Twitter is also expanding into video with its acquisition of the mobile application Vine. In keeping with Twitter's reputation for short, concise postings, Vine allows users to display up to 6 seconds of video and share them with other users. Vine has become highly popular among celebrities and teenagers, with more than 13 million users. Marketers are taking notice. Burberry, for instance, developed a video on Vine that featured its London menswear fashion show.[17]

Marketing Debate

The Odd Challenges of Marketing on Twitter

ISSUE: Should Twitter target users with promoted tweets?

Twitter is facing a backlash. The company is earning advertising revenue with Promoted Tweets. Promoted Tweets are tweet advertisements that companies use to target users. They show up in users' timelines or on Twitter through mobile devices, desktops, laptops, and tablets. However, some users find Promoted Tweets to be invasive. As a form of protest, critics have been re-tweeting advertisements after altering and misspelling words to completely change the message of the original ad. Their aim is to discourage companies from advertising on Twitter by making them look bad and increasing their advertising costs, although Twitter only charges companies for legitimate clicks and re-tweets. Yet while users find Promoted Tweets to be invasive, proponents point out that they help Twitter stay in business so it can keep offering free services to users.[a]

Google+

In 2011 Google launched its Google+ network, a social media site intended to rival Facebook and identify users across Google's various services.[18] The initial launch was invitation-only as a field test. Eventually, Google abandoned the invite-only feature and opened the site to all users over the age of 13.

CEO Larry Page initiated a move to get more people to use Google+ by requiring those that use Google services, such as Gmail and YouTube, to have a Google+ account. This requirement has many implications for Google. For instance, integration between the social network and its other services means that users who post reviews on different Google platforms can no longer do so anonymously—they are now tied to a person's Google+ account.[19] In another controversial move, Google began requiring users who wanted to leave comments on YouTube to do so using Google+.[20] The move has led to a 58 percent jump in users on the site.[21]

Google+ gives digital marketers an opportunity to capitalize on its growing user base. Because Google+ is linked with search results on Google, sharing a firm's information on Google+ could push the firm up through the ranks of Google search results. Google+ postings with links to a company's website encourage more traffic on the corporate website. Google+ also has tools that allow companies to see how often their posts are shared. Additionally, because Google+ is integrated with other Google services, a search for an organization such as Ford will not only bring up information on Ford, but will also display recent posts about Ford that have been placed on Google+.[22] Although Google+ does not yet have the same influence as Facebook, marketers are discovering a number of possibilities to engage users with Google+.

10-3b Blogs and Wikis

blogs Web-based journals (short for "weblogs") in which writers editorialize and interact with other Internet users

Today's marketers must recognize the impact of consumer-generated material like blogs and wikis, as their significance to online consumers has increased a great deal. **Blogs** (short for "weblogs") are web-based journals in which writers can editorialize and interact with other Internet users. More than three-fourths of Internet users read blogs.[23] In fact, the blogging site Tumblr, which allows anyone to post text, hyperlinks, pictures, and other media for free, became one of the top 10 online destinations. The site has approximately 160 million blogs

© iStockphoto.com/fazonl

Blogs
Popular blog-publishing websites provide opportunities for creating original content.

and draws approximately 300 million unique visitors to the site monthly. In 2013 Yahoo! purchased Tumblr for $1.1 billion.[24]

Blogs give consumers control, sometimes more control than companies would like. Whether or not the blog's content is factually accurate, bloggers can post whatever opinions they like about a company or its products. Although companies have filed lawsuits against bloggers for defamation, they usually cannot prevent the blog from going viral. Responding to a negative blog posting is a delicate matter. For instance, although companies sometimes force bloggers to remove blogs, readers often create copies of the blog and spread it across the Internet after the original's removal. In other cases, a positive review of a product posted on a popular blog can result in large increases in sales. Thus, blogs can represent a potent threat to corporations as well as an opportunity.

Blogs have major advantages as well. Rather than trying to eliminate blogs that cast their companies in a negative light, some businesses are using such blogs to answer consumer concerns or defend their corporate reputations. Many major corporations have created their own blogs or encourage employees to blog about the company. Direct selling firm Tastefully Simple operates a blog of easy recipes. Users can look for recipes based on the main ingredient used, type of course, or cooking method.[25] As blogging changes the face of media, companies like Tastefully Simple are using blogs to build enthusiasm for their products and create relationships with consumers.

A **wiki** is a type of software that creates an interface that enables users to add or edit the content of some types of websites. One of the best known is Wikipedia, an online encyclopedia with more than 30 million articles in 287 languages on nearly every subject imaginable (*Encyclopedia Britannica* has 120,000 entries).[26] Wikipedia is consistently one of the top 10 most popular sites on the Web. Because Wikipedia can be edited and read by anyone, it is easy for online consumers to correct inaccuracies in content.[27] This site is expanded, updated, and edited by a large team of volunteer contributors. For the most part, only information that is verifiable through another source is considered appropriate. Because of its open format, Wikipedia has suffered from some high-profile instances of vandalism in which incorrect information was disseminated. Such problems have usually been detected and corrected quickly. Like all social media, wikis have advantages and disadvantages for companies. Wikis on controversial companies like Walmart and Nike often contain negative publicity about the companies, such as worker rights violations. However, some companies have begun to use wikis as internal tools for teams working on a project requiring lots of documentation.[28] Additionally, monitoring wikis provides companies with a better idea of how consumers feel about the company brand.

There is too much at stake financially for marketers to ignore blogs and wikis. Despite this fact, statistics show that less than one-fourth of Fortune 500 companies have a corporate blog.[29] Marketers who want to form better customer relationships and promote their company's products must not underestimate the power of these two tools as new media outlets.

10-3c Media-Sharing Sites

Businesses can also share their corporate messages in more visual ways through media-sharing sites. Media-sharing sites allow marketers to share photos, videos, and podcasts but are more limited in scope in how companies interact with consumers. They tend to be more promotional rather than reactive. This means that while firms can promote their products through videos or photos, they usually do not interact with consumers through personal messages or responses. At the same time, the popularity of these sites provides the potential to reach a global audience of consumers.

Photo-sharing sites allow users to upload and share their photos with the world. Well-known photo-sharing sites include Flickr, Picasa, Shutterfly, Snapfish, and Instagram. Flickr is owned by Yahoo! and is the most popular photo-sharing site on the Internet. A Flickr user can upload images, edit them, classify the images, create photo albums, and share photos or videos with friends without having to e-mail bulky image files or send photos through the mail. However, although Flickr might be a popular photo-sharing site on the Internet,

wiki Type of software that creates an interface that enables users to add or edit the content of some types of websites

Social Photo Sharing
Pinterest, Instagram, Flickr, and Hipstamatic allow users to share photos with a variety of other people on the Internet.

Instagram is the most popular mobile photo-sharing application. Instagram allows users to make their photos look dreamy or retrospective with different tints and share them with their friends.[30] The Eddie Bauer website has an icon on its main website that will take users to its Instagram stream.[31] In 2012 Facebook purchased Instagram for $1 billion with the intention to break into the mobile industry. To compete against Twitter's short-form video service Vine, Facebook has added 13 filters for video to the Instagram app.[32] With more people using mobile apps or accessing the Internet through their smartphones, the use of photo sharing through mobile devices is likely to increase.

Other sites are emerging that take photo sharing to a new level. Pinterest is a photo-sharing bulletin board site that combines photo sharing with elements of bookmarking and social networking. Users can share photos and images with other Internet users, communicating mostly through images that they "pin" to their boards. Other users can "repin" these images to their boards, follow each other, "like" images, and make comments. Marketers have found that an effective way of marketing through Pinterest is to post images conveying a certain emotion that represents their brand.[33] Pinterest has become especially popular among small businesses ever since the site introduced "Rich Pins," a feature that allows retailers to post more information about what is being pinned.[34]

Photo sharing represents an opportunity for companies to market themselves visually by displaying snapshots of company events, company staff, and/or company products. Nike, Audi, and MTV have all used Instagram in digital marketing campaigns.[35] Zales Jewelers has topic boards on Pinterest featuring rings as well as other themes of love, including songs, wedding cake, and wedding dresses.[36] Virgin Mobile has a Flickr photostream that features photos of company events such as product launches.[37] Many businesses with pictures on Flickr have a link connecting their Flickr photostreams to their corporate websites.

Video-sharing sites allow virtually anybody to upload videos, from professional marketers at Fortune 500 corporations to the average Internet user. Some of the most popular video-sharing sites include YouTube, Metacafe.com, and Hulu. Video-sharing sites give companies the opportunity to upload ads and informational videos about their products. A few videos become viral at any given time, and although many of these gain popularity because they embarrass the subject in some way, others reach viral status because people find them entertaining (viral marketing will be discussed in more detail in Chapter 16). Marketers are seizing upon opportunities to use this viral nature to promote awareness of their companies.

For instance, Dove's "Real Beauty Sketches" video became the most viral ad video of all time. Using a forensic artist, the video compared sketches of women as they described themselves to sketches of themselves as others saw them. The video demonstrates that women are more attractive than they generally perceive themselves to be. The video was uploaded onto 33 of Dove's YouTube channels in 25 languages.[38] The resulting publicity helped spread the Dove brand name as well as its association with beauty. YouTube, valued at $15.6 to $21.3 billion, offers the opportunity to spread marketing campaigns at a fraction of the cost of other advertising channels. YouTube has proven so popular that video networks have begun to use the online site as a staging ground for their shows.[39]

A new trend in video marketing is the use of amateur filmmakers. Entrepreneurs have begun to realize that they can use consumer-generated content. Consumer-generated videos save companies money because they do not have to hire advertising firms to develop professional advertising campaigns. Consider the case of Jamal Edwards, an amateur filmmaker who started broadcasting company SBTV. The company creates short videos of rap and pop music stars, places them on YouTube, and generates revenue from advertisements linked to the videos. The videos have resulted in millions of hits, turning the 23-year-old entrepreneur into a multi-millionaire.[40] Marketers believe consumer videos appear more authentic and create enthusiasm for the product among participants.

Podcasting, traditionally used for music and radio broadcasts, is also an important digital marketing tool. **Podcasts** are audio or video files that can be downloaded from the Internet with a subscription that automatically delivers new content to listening devices or personal computers. Podcasts offer the benefit of convenience, giving users the ability to listen to or view content when and where they choose. The fact that the majority of current podcast users are between 18 and 29 years of age makes podcasts a key tool for businesses marketing to this demographic.[41] For instance, the podcast *Mad Money*, hosted by Jim Cramer, gives investment advice and teaches listeners how to analyze stocks and other financial instruments.[42] Companies can use podcasts to demonstrate how to use their products or understand certain features. As podcasting continues to catch on, radio and television networks like CBC Radio, NPR, MSNBC, and PBS are creating podcasts of their shows to profit from this growing trend. Through podcasting, many companies hope to create brand awareness, promote their products, and encourage customer loyalty.

podcast Audio or video file that can be downloaded from the Internet with a subscription that automatically delivers new content to listening devices or personal computers; podcasts offer the benefit of convenience, giving users the ability to listen to or view content when and where they choose

Emerging Trends

Reaching Concentrated Markets through Podcasting

Although podcasting has been around for more than 20 years, it was considered to be a niche form of media. However, the popularity of podcasts is growing as it competes against traditional broadcasting outlets. There is a wide range in the diversity of authors and topics of podcasts, which target specific groups of people with the same interests or social status. The audiences of podcasts are large, ranging in size from several hundred thousand to 2 million subscribers.

Audiences are attracted to podcasts because of quality content and the ease by which they can consume it—in short clips and on mobile devices. This presents opportunities to marketers to advertise or communicate information through their own podcasts. Advertising on a podcast can help marketers address company messages at lower costs than traditional media. For instance, Canadian Internet services and telecommunications company Tucow successfully promoted two of its products through podcast advertising after other forms of advertising failed.

If a company chooses to create its own podcast, it has the freedom to talk about industry trends, brand value, or anything that will pique people's interest in the organization. This has led organizations such as NPR, ESPN, and *Slate* magazine to develop podcasts. Podcasting is also a way to maximize the use of different channels and can serve as a supplement to traditional forms of marketing.[b]

10-3d Virtual Gaming Sites

Virtual gaming sites are offering significant opportunities for marketers to connect with consumers in unique ways. Virtual gaming sites include Second Life, Everquest, FarmVille, and the role-playing game World of Warcraft. Many of these games are role-playing games where the gamer takes on or assumes a particular persona, also known as an *avatar.* These games are social in nature, allowing players to compete against, partner with, or do things for other gamers. In Second Life users connect with other users, communicate with one another, purchase goods with virtual Linden dollars (which are convertible to real dollars on a floating exchange rate of around 250 Linden dollars per $1), and even own virtual businesses.

Real-world marketers and organizations have been eager to capitalize on the popularity of virtual gaming sites. MediaSpike specializes in placing brands into mobile games. Geico Powersports and Mountain Dew are two brands that have worked with MediaSpike to appear in mobile games.[43] Other businesses are looking toward virtual worlds to familiarize consumers with their goods and services. For instance, McDonald's partnered with the virtual gaming site Zynga to bring its virtual store and brand to Zynga's popular virtual gaming site Cityville.[44]

10-3e Mobile Devices

Mobile devices, such as smartphones, mobile computing devices, and tablet computers, allow customers to leave their desktops and access digital networks from anywhere. About 91 percent of American adults have a mobile device.[45] Many of these mobile devices are smartphones, which have the ability to access the Internet, download apps, listen to music, take photographs, and more. Figure 10.2 breaks down smartphone ownership by age and income. Mobile marketing is exploding—marketers spent $15.8 billion on mobile ad spending.[46]

Figure 10.2 Smartphone Ownership by Age and Income

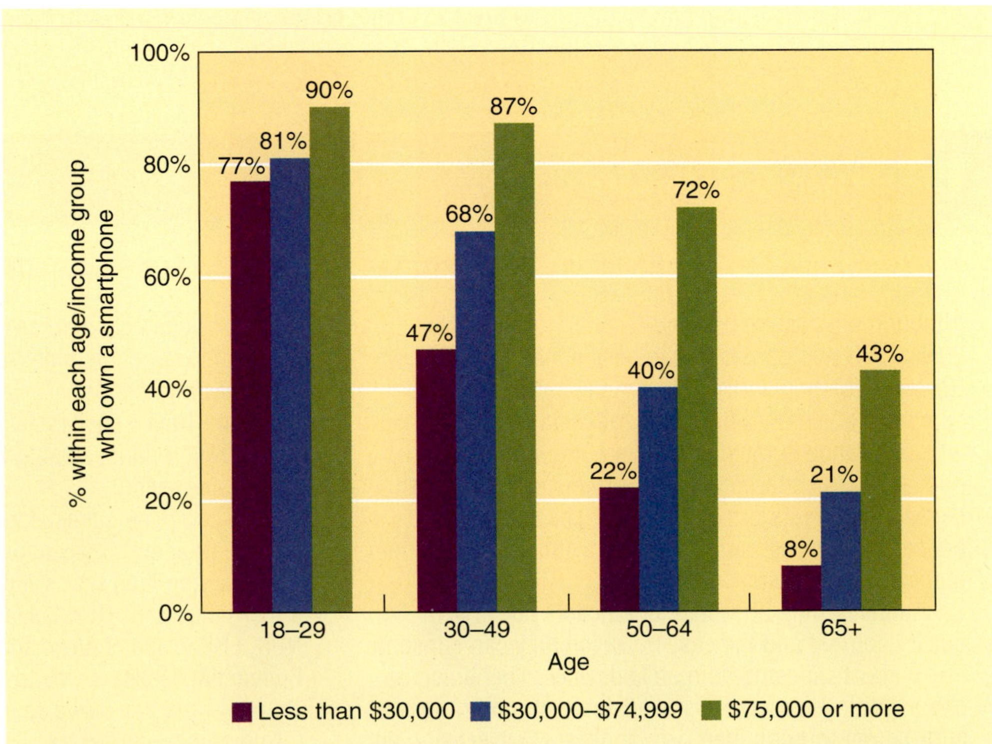

Source: Pew Research Center's Internet & American Life Project, April 17–May 19, 2013, Tracking Survey. Interviews were conducted in English and Spanish and on land-line and cell phones. Margin of error is +/–2.3 percentage points based on adults (*n* = 2,252).

Mobile marketing has proven effective in grabbing consumers' attention. In one study, 88 percent of smartphone users replied that they have noticed mobile advertisements. This rate is unusually high in a world where consumers are often inundated with ads. Despite these promising trends, many brands have yet to take advantage of mobile marketing opportunities. Although most major businesses have websites, not all of these websites are easily viewable on mobile devices.[47]

To avoid being left behind, brands must recognize the importance of mobile marketing. Some of the more common mobile marketing tools include the following:

- *SMS messages:* SMS messages are text messages of 160 words or less. SMS messages have been an effective way to send coupons to prospective customers.[48]
- *Multimedia messages:* Multimedia messaging takes SMS messaging a step further by allowing companies to send video, audio, photos, and other types of media over mobile devices. It is estimated that 98 percent of SMS and MMS messages are viewed, making this an effective way of getting consumers' attention.[49]
- *Mobile advertisements:* Mobile advertisements are visual advertisements that appear on mobile devices. Companies might choose to advertise through search engines, websites, or even games accessed on mobile devices. Marketers spend approximately $3 billion on mobile advertising.[50]
- *Mobile websites:* Mobile websites are websites designed for mobile devices. Approximately 28 percent of Web traffic comes from mobile devices.[51]
- *Location-based networks:* Location-based networks are built for mobile devices. One of the most popular location-based networks is Foursquare, which lets users check in and share their location with others. Foursquare partnered with Visa and MasterCard to offer discounts at participating retailers, including Dunkin' Donuts and Burger King.[52]
- *Mobile applications:* **Mobile applications** are software programs that run on mobile devices and give users access to certain content.[53] Businesses release apps to help consumers access more information about their company or to provide incentives. These are discussed in further detail in the next section.

mobile applications Software programs that run on mobile devices and give users access to certain content

10-3f Applications and Widgets

Applications, or apps, are adding an entirely new layer to the marketing environment, as approximately half of all American adult cell phone users have applications on their mobile devices.[54] The most important feature of apps is the convenience and cost savings they offer to the consumer. Certain apps permit consumers to scan a product's barcode and then compare it with the prices of identical products in other stores or download store discounts. E*Trade has created a mobile app called E*Trade Mobile that allows customers to check on a company's performance. As the advertisement demonstrates, using E*Trade Mobile enables customers to scan a company's barcode and view its performance on iPhone and Android devices.

To remain competitive, companies are beginning to use mobile marketing to offer additional incentives to consumers. Starwood Hotels & Resorts Worldwide developed an app customers can use to research their travel location straight from their smartphones and receive discounts and personalized incentives. Starwood Hotels believes the app will enhance customer relationships, thereby increasing customer

Courtesy of E*Trade

Barcode Scanning
E*Trade's mobile app allows customers to check a company's financial performance by scanning a barcode to assist them with stock purchases.

loyalty.[55] Another application that marketers are finding useful is the QR scanning app. QR codes are black-and-white squares that sometimes appear in magazines, posters, and storefront displays. Smartphone users that have downloaded the QR scanning application can open their smartphones and scan the code, which contains a hidden message accessible with the app. The QR scanning app recognizes the code and opens the link, video, or image on the phone's screen. Marketers are using QR codes to promote their companies and offer consumer discounts.[56]

Mobile technology is also making inroads in transforming the shopping experience. Not only can shoppers use mobile applications to compare prices or download electronic discounts, but they can also use mobile applications to tally up purchases and pay through their smartphones. Mobile payments are gaining traction, and companies like Google are working to capitalize on this opportunity.[57] Google Wallet is a mobile app that stores credit card information on the smartphone. When the shopper is ready to check out, he or she can tap the phone at the point of sale for the transaction to be registered.[58] Square is a company launched by Twitter co-founder Jack Dorsey. The company provides organizations with smartphone swiping devices for credit cards as well as tablets that can be used to tally purchases. A newer service called Square Cash is enabling users to send up to $2,500 digitally through e-mail.[59] Bitcoin is a virtual peer-to-peer currency that can be used to make a payment via smartphone. Smaller organizations have begun to accept Bitcoin at some of their stores. Virtual currency exchanges have run into legal issues, however, due to state money-transmission laws. Bitcoin also fluctuates in value, making it risky for companies to hold onto the virtual currency for long periods.[60] It is not backed by a central bank and its software is run on a network of volunteers' computers. Although the value of Bitcoin has increased, many believe this increase could be because investors are hoarding the money offshore, creating an unsustainable bubble that could burst. However, Bitcoin is being increasingly accepted among officials, and Germany has recognized it as a unit of account.[61] The success of mobile payments in revolutionizing the shopping experience will largely depend upon retailers to adopt this payment system, but companies like Starbucks are already rising to the opportunity.

Widgets are small bits of software on a website, desktop, or mobile device that performs a simple purpose, such as providing stock quotes or blog updates. Marketers might use widgets to display news headlines, clocks, or games on their webpages.[62] Widgets have been used by companies like A&E Television Network as a form of viral marketing—users can download the widget and send it to their friends with a click of a button.[63] Widgets downloaded to a user's desktop can update the user on the latest company or product information, enhancing relationship marketing between companies and their fans. Hotels, restaurants, and other tourist locations can download TripAdvisor widgets to their websites. These widgets display the latest company reviews, rewards, and other TripAdvisor content directly to the company's website.[64] Widgets are an innovative digital marketing tool to personalize webpages, alert users to the latest company information, and spread awareness of the company's products.

10-4 CHANGING DIGITAL MEDIA BEHAVIORS OF CONSUMERS

Consumers now have a greater ability to regulate the information that they view as well as the rate and sequence of their exposure to that information. The Internet is sometimes referred to as a *pull* medium because users determine which websites they are going to view; the marketer has only limited ability to control the content to which users are exposed, and in what sequence. Today, blogs, wikis, podcasts, and ratings are used to publicize, praise, or challenge companies. Digital media require marketers to approach their jobs differently compared to traditional marketing. However, most companies in the United States do not routinely monitor consumers' postings to online social networking sites. In many cases, this represents a missed opportunity to gather information.

widget Small bits of software on a website, desktop, or mobile device that performs a simple purpose, such as providing stock quotes or blog updates

On the other hand, some companies are using the power of the consumer to their advantage. While negative ratings and reviews are damaging to a company, positive customer feedback is free publicity that often helps the company more than corporate messages do. Because consumer-generated content appears more authentic than corporate messages, it can go far in increasing a company's credibility. Additionally, while consumers can use digital media to access more information, marketers can also use the same sites to get information on the consumer—often more information than could be garnered through traditional marketing venues. They can examine how consumers are using the Internet to target marketing messages to their audience. Finally, marketers are also using the Internet to track the success of their online marketing campaigns, creating an entirely new way of gathering marketing research.

10-4a Online Consumer Behavior

As Internet technology evolves, digital media marketers must constantly adapt to new technologies and changing consumer patterns. Unfortunately, with so many new technologies emerging, the attrition rate for digital media channels is very high, with some dying off each year as new ones emerge. As time passes, digital media are becoming more sophisticated so as to reach consumers in more effective ways. Those that are not able to adapt and change eventually fail.

Forrester Research, a technology and market research company, emphasizes the importance of understanding these changing relationships in the online media world. By grouping online consumers into different segments based on how they utilize digital online media, marketers can gain a better understanding of the online market and how best to proceed.[65]

The Social Technographics Profile developed by Forrester Research groups the online community into seven segments according to how they interact with digital media. It is important to note that these segments overlap; many online consumers may belong to multiple segments simultaneously. Table 10.2 provides a description of these seven different groups. *Creators* are those consumers who create their own media outlets, such as blogs, podcasts, consumer-generated videos, and wikis.[66] Creators are becoming increasingly important to online

Table 10.2 Social Technographics

Creators	Publish a blog Publish personal webpages Upload original video Upload original audio/music Write articles or stories and post them
Conversationalists	Update status on social networking sites Post updates on Twitter
Critics	Post ratings/reviews of products or services Comment on someone else's blog Contribute to online forums Contribute to/edit articles in a wiki
Collectors	Use RSS feeds Add tags to webpages or photos "Vote" for websites online
Joiners	Maintain profile on a social networking site Visit social networking sites
Spectators	Read blogs Watch video from other users Listen to podcasts Read online forums Read customer ratings/reviews
Inactives	None of the activities

Source: Charlene Li and Josh Bernoff, *Groundswell* (Boston: Harvard Business Press, 2008), p. 43; "Forrester Unveils New Segment of Social Technographics—The Conversationalists," 360 Digital Connections, January 21, 2010, http://blog.360i.com/social-media/forrester-new-segment-social-technographics-conversationalists (accessed December 19, 2013).

Review Websites
Angie's List has more than 1 million members who access the site to write or receive customer reviews on local businesses.

marketers as a conduit for addressing consumers directly. These types of consumer-generated media are becoming a major part of companies' public relations strategies. For instance, many marketers are pitching new products or stories to professional reporters and bloggers. Bloggers who post this information can reach online consumers as well as reporters in the mainstream media, who often read blogs for story ideas.[67]

The Technographics profile calls its second group of Internet users *conversationalists.* Conversationalists regularly update their Twitter feeds or status updates on social networking sites. Although they are less involved than creators, conversationalists spend time at least once a week (and often more) on digital media sites posting updates.[68] The third category is *critics.* Critics are people who comment on blogs or post ratings and reviews. If you have ever posted a product review or rated a movie, you have engaged in this activity. Critics need to be an important component in a company's digital marketing strategy, because the majority of online shoppers read ratings and reviews to aid in their purchasing decisions. As mentioned before, consumer-generated content like ratings and reviews are viewed as more credible than corporate messages. Consumers often visit review websites like Yelp for recommendations on businesses. Yelp is one of the most comprehensive review sites on businesses, with 42.5 million reviews.[69] A similar review website is Angie's List. As the advertisement demonstrates, Angie's List has detailed reviews on local businesses written by consumers. The advertisement emphasizes that because businesses do not pay to be on Angie's List, the reviews are more reliable because they come from consumers. Hence, marketers should carefully monitor what consumers are saying about their products and address consumer concerns that may affect their corporate reputations.

Collectors are perhaps the least recognized group of the seven. Collectors gather information and organize content generated by critics and creators. The growing popularity of this segment is leading to the creation of social news sites like del.icio.us, reddit, and even Pinterest for photos. Want to know the top news stories according to online consumers? Collectors gather this type of information and post their findings to social networking sites like reddit, where users vote on the sites they like the best. Collectors usually constitute a smaller part of the online population than the other groups; however, they can still have a significant impact on marketing activities.[70] Because collectors are active members in the online community, a company story or site that catches the eye of a collector is likely to be posted and discussed on collector sites and made available to other online users looking for information.

Another Technographics segment, known as *joiners*, is growing dramatically. Anyone who becomes a member of Twitter, Facebook, Google+, or other social networking sites is a joiner.[71] It is not unusual for consumers to be members of several social networking sites at once. Joiners participate in these sites to connect and network with other users, but, as previously discussed, marketers can take significant advantage of these sites to connect with consumers and form customer relationships.

The last two segments are classified as *spectators* and *inactives.* Inactives are online users who do not participate in any digital online media, but as more people begin to use computers as a resource, this number is dwindling. Spectators are the largest group in most countries, and it is not hard to see why. Spectators are those consumers who read what other consumers produce but do not create any content themselves.

Marketers will need to consider what portion of online consumers are creating, conversing, rating, collecting, joining, or simply reading online materials. As with traditional marketing efforts, marketers need to know the best ways to reach their target market. In markets where spectators make up the majority of the online population, companies should post their own corporate messages through blogs and websites promoting their organizations. In a population of joiners, companies could try to connect with their target audience by creating profile pages and inviting consumers to post their thoughts. In areas where a significant portion of the online community consists of creators, marketers should continually monitor what other consumers are saying and incorporate bloggers into their public relations strategies. By knowing how to segment the online population, marketers can better tailor their messages to their target markets.

10-5 E-MARKETING STRATEGY

More than one-fourth of the world's population uses the Internet, and this number is growing at a high rate. These trends display a growing need for businesses to use the Internet to reach an increasingly Web-savvy population. As more shoppers go online for purchases, the power of traditional brick-and-mortar businesses is lessening.

This makes it essential for businesses, small and large alike, to learn how to effectively use new social media. Most businesses are finding it necessary to use digital marketing to gain or maintain market share. When Amazon.com first became popular as an online bookstore in the 1990s, the brick-and-mortar bookseller chain Barnes & Noble quickly made online shopping possible through its website, but did not abandon its physical stores. This "brick-and-clicks" model is now standard for businesses from neighborhood family-owned restaurants to national chain retailers. Some online-only firms, such as eBay, are even experimenting with physical locations. Ebay is testing shoppable windows with giant touchable screens that allow shoppers to shop for and even purchase products.[72] The following sections will examine how businesses are effectively using these social media forums to create effective marketing strategies on the Web.

10-5a Product Considerations

In traditional marketing, marketers must anticipate consumer needs and preferences and then tailor their products to meet these needs. The same is true with marketing products using digital media. Digital media provide an opportunity to add a service dimension to traditional products and create new products that could only be accessible on the Internet. The applications available on the iPad, for instance, provide examples of products that are only available in the digital world. The advertisement from Source Interlink Media directs consumers to its app store. It informs consumers that they can download a variety of different apps depending upon their interests or passions. These represent products that can only be found in the digital realm.

The ability to access product information for any product can have a major impact on buyer decision making. However, with larger companies now launching their own extensive marketing campaigns, and with the constant sophistication of digital technology, many businesses are

Online Products
The mobile applications available for download from the Source Interlink App Store are examples of intangible products only available online.

finding it necessary to continually upgrade their product offerings to meet consumer needs. In managing a product, it is important to pay attention to consumer-generated brand stories that address quality and performance and impact image.[73] As has been discussed throughout this chapter, the Internet represents a large resource to marketers for learning more about consumer wants and needs.

Some companies now use online advertising campaigns and contests to help develop better products. Companies have also begun selling their products through social networking sites. Facebook has partnered with retailers to test a new service to make it easier for consumers to pay for purchases through retailers' mobile apps. This service permits customers to prefill their payment information using information stored on Facebook.[74]

10-5b Distribution Considerations

The role of distribution is to make products available at the right time, at the right place, and in the right quantities. Digital marketing can be viewed as a new distribution channel that helps businesses increase efficiency. The ability to process orders electronically and increase the speed of communications via the Internet reduces inefficiencies, costs, and redundancies while increasing speed throughout the marketing channel. Shipping times and costs have become an important consideration in attracting consumers, prompting many companies to offer consumers low shipping costs or next-day delivery. Amazon.com is now expanding into groceries. The company is testing a grocery delivery service in Los Angeles called Amazon Fresh. In addition to groceries, customers have the added incentive to add in up to 500,000 nonfood items to their grocery orders. It is estimated that Amazon only needs to capture 4 percent share in the markets in which it operates its grocery system within a 10-year period to be profitable.[75]

Distribution involves a push–pull dynamic: The firm that provides a product will push to get that product in front of the consumer, while at the same time connectivity aids those channel members that desire to find each other—the pull side of the dynamic. An iPhone application can help consumers find the closest Starbucks, McDonald's, or KFC. On the other hand, a blog or Twitter feed can help a marketer communicate the availability of products and how and when they can be purchased. This process can help push products through the marketing channel to consumers or enable customers to pull products through the marketing channel.

B2B Promotion
IBM markets its digital solutions to businesses that are having difficulty connecting with customers over multiple mobile devices.

10-5c Promotion Considerations

The majority of this chapter has discussed ways that marketers use digital media and social networking sites to promote products, from creating profiles on social networking sites to connecting with consumers to inserting brands into virtual social games. Social networking sites also allow marketers to approach promotion in entirely new, creative ways. Marketers who choose to capitalize on these opportunities have the chance to boost their firms' brand exposure. For instance, Lubbock-based retailer Polkadot Alley engages frequently with users on Facebook. The owner of the shop often posts discounts and coupons on Facebook to encourage users to become fans and do business with the company.[76]

Digital media has also opened opportunities for business-to-business promotions. As more companies adopt digital marketing strategies, the need for better platforms and digital solutions has grown. Consider IBM's advertisement directed toward business enterprises that struggle with challenges in mobile marketing. IBM claims that approximately 90 percent of people with mobile devices use more than one device per day, which makes it difficult for customers and organizations to interact through mobile. It also makes it more costly for businesses to target customers using mobile devices. IBM promotes its application platform as a cost-effective solution that avoids many of the communication problems between business and customer.

Digital promotions all attempt to increase brand awareness and market to consumers. As a result of online promotion, consumers are more informed, reading consumer-generated content before making purchasing decisions and increasingly shopping at Internet stores. Consumer consumption patterns are changing radically, and marketers must adapt their promotional efforts to meet these new patterns.

10-5d Pricing Considerations

Pricing relates to perceptions of value and is the most flexible element of the marketing mix. Digital media marketing facilitates both price and nonprice competition, because Internet marketing gives consumers access to more information about costs and prices. As consumers become more informed about their options, the demand for low-priced products has grown, leading to the creation of daily deal sites like Groupon, CrowdCut, and LivingSocial. These companies partner with local businesses to offer major discounts to subscribers in order to generate new business. Several marketers are also offering buying incentives like online coupons or free samples to generate consumer demand for their product offerings.

Digital connections can help the customer find the price of the product available from various competitors in an instant. Websites provide price information, and mobile applications can help the customer find the lowest price. Consumers can even bargain with retailers in the store by using a smartphone to show the lowest price available during a transaction. Although this new access to price information benefits the consumer, it also places new pressures on the seller to be competitive and to differentiate products so that customers focus on attributes and benefits other than price.

Until recently, social networks like Facebook and Twitter were mainly used for promotional purposes and customer service. Those who wanted to purchase items were often redirected to the company's website. However, retailers and other organizations are developing e-commerce stores on Facebook so that consumers will not have to leave the site to purchase

Pricing Considerations
Consumers can go online, compare Internet prices with in-store prices, and possibly obtain discounts from companies such as Groupon.

items. Polkadot Alley, for instance, holds auctions on Facebook twice a week. Photos of items to be auctioned are posted, and people interested in shopping during the auction are encouraged to "like" the status. During the auction, a shopper who wants to purchase an item writes a post on Facebook. An application called Soldsie helps process the Facebook transactions. Opening up an e-commerce store on Facebook has caused Polkadot Alley's sales to go from $400,000 to $1.5 million a year.[77] For the business that wants to compete on price, digital marketing provides unlimited opportunities.

10-6 ETHICAL AND LEGAL ISSUES

How marketers use technology to gather information—both online and offline—raises numerous legal and ethical issues. The popularity and widespread use of the Internet grew so quickly in the 1990s that global regulatory systems were unable to keep pace, although today there are a number of laws in place to protect businesses and consumers. Among the issues of concern are personal privacy, fraud, and misappropriation of copyrighted intellectual property.

10-6a Privacy

One of the most significant privacy issues involves the use of personal information that companies collect from website visitors in their efforts to foster long-term relationships with customers. Some people fear that the collection of personal information from website users may violate users' privacy, especially when it is done without their knowledge. Hackers may break into websites and steal users' personal information, enabling them to commit identity theft. Online notebook service Evernote had to reset 50 million passwords after hackers broke into the site.[78] Mobile phone payments are another source of concern. Consumers worry that their information could be hacked, or their phones could be targeted with malware.[79] Malicious mobile apps, used by hackers to steal information, have increased 614 percent in a 1-year period.[80] This requires organizations to implement increased security measures to prevent database theft.

Google, Facebook, and other Internet firms have also come under fire for privacy issues. For instance, when Facebook announced it would give teenagers between the ages of 13 and 17 the ability to make their posts public, privacy advocates quickly protested the move.[81] Google has been a particular target of privacy advocates. Google has the ability to collect a trove of data on consumers who use its various services. Although Google has attempted to develop a "slider" tool that would provide users with a greater ability to control the data collected about them, the tool was abandoned after it was deemed too difficult to implement. However, past privacy snafus have caused Google to make Internet privacy a major priority. For instance, its Google Now product—a new tool that provides information to people before they search for it—underwent many legal and privacy hurdles before its final development. The European Union has been particularly cautious regarding the collection of user data and has instituted more restrictive regulations to control how much data these Internet firms can gather.[82]

Due to consumer concerns over privacy, the FTC is considering developing regulations that would protect consumer privacy by limiting the amount of consumer information that businesses can gather online. Other countries are pursuing similar actions. The European Union passed a law requiring companies to get users' consent before using cookies to track their information. In the United States, some government officials have called for a "do not track" bill, similar to the "do not call" bill for telephones, to allow users to opt out of having their information tracked. Legislators reintroduced a Do Not Track Kids bill that would make it illegal for companies to track children between the ages of 13 and 15 over the Internet or mobile devices without parental permission (currently marketers are prohibited from gathering information about consumers age 13 or younger without parental permission). They also desire a system that would erase information that these teenagers found to be embarrassing.[83]

While consumers may welcome such added protections, Web advertisers, who use consumer information to target advertisements to online consumers, see it as a threat. In response to impending legislation, many Web advertisers are attempting self-regulation in order to stay ahead of the game. For instance, advertising self-regulatory agencies have encouraged members to adopt a do-not-track icon that users can click on to avoid having their online activity monitored. However, it is debatable whether members will choose to participate or honor users' do-not-track requests.[84]

10-6b Online Fraud

Online fraud includes any attempt to conduct dishonest activities online. Online fraud includes, among other things, attempts to deceive consumers into releasing personal information. It is becoming a major source of frustration with social networking sites. Cybercriminals are discovering ways to use sites like Facebook and Twitter to carry out fraudulent activities. Twitter has experienced an influx of fake Twitter accounts to try to boost publicity. A celebrity, for instance, might pay somebody to rebroadcast their tweets on a number of fake Twitter accounts. It is estimated that between 5 and 9 percent of Twitter accounts could be fake. While these accounts might not be used to solicit money or harm users directly, they are used for the express purpose of deceiving users.[85] Mobile payments are another concern. Perhaps the most disturbing is the practice of using social networking sites to pose as charitable institutions or victims of natural disasters. A good method for people to avoid getting scammed through social media sites is to research charities before giving.

In another case, 1.5 million Europeans who had enrolled in customer-loyalty programs found that their personal data had been stolen. Although these consumers dealt with a number of different websites, these websites were all linked by a loyalty program management firm in Ireland.[86] Privacy advocates advise that the best way to stay out of trouble is to avoid giving out personal information, such as social security numbers or credit card information, unless the site is definitely legitimate.

10-6c Intellectual Property

The Internet has also created issues associated with intellectual property, the copyrighted or trademarked ideas and creative materials developed to solve problems, carry out applications, and educate and entertain others. Each year, intellectual property losses in the United States total billions of dollars stemming from the illegal copying of computer programs, movies, compact discs, and books. YouTube has often faced lawsuits on intellectual property

online fraud Any attempt to conduct fraudulent activities online, including deceiving consumers into releasing personal information

Internet Privacy
Companies are attempting to make their websites safe and protect their data from hackers.

infringement. With millions of users uploading content to YouTube, it can be hard for Google to monitor and remove all the videos that may contain copyrighted materials.

The software industry is particularly hard-hit when it comes to the pirating of materials and illegal file sharing. The Business Software Alliance estimates that the global computer software industry loses more than $63 billion a year to illegal theft.[87] Consumers view illegal downloading in different ways, depending on the motivation for the behavior. If the motivation is primarily utilitarian, or for personal gain, then the act is viewed as less ethically acceptable than if it is for a hedonistic reason, or just for fun.[88]

Consumers rationalize pirating software, video games, and music for a number of reasons. First, many consumers feel they just do not have the money to pay for what they want. Second, because their friends engage in piracy and swap digital content, they feel influenced to engage in this activity. Third, for some, the attraction is the thrill of getting away with it and the slim risk of consequences. Fourth, to some extent, there are people who think they are smarter than others; engaging in piracy allows them to show how tech savvy they are.[89]

As digital media continues to evolve, more legal and ethical issues will certainly arise. As a result, marketers and all other users of digital media should make an effort to learn and abide by ethical practices to ensure that they get the most out of the resources available in this growing medium. Doing so will allow marketers to maximize the tremendous opportunities digital media has to offer.

Summary

10-1 Define *digital media, digital marketing,* and *electronic marketing.*

Digital media are electronic media that function using digital codes—when we refer to digital media, we are referring to media available via computers, cellular phones, smartphones, and other digital devices that have been released in recent years. Digital marketing uses all digital media, including the Internet and mobile and interactive channels, to develop communication and exchanges with customers. Electronic marketing refers to the strategic process of distributing, promoting, and pricing products, and discovering the desires of customers using digital media and digital marketing. Our definition of e-marketing goes beyond the Internet and also includes mobile phones, banner ads, digital outdoor marketing, and social networks.

10-2 Summarize the growth and importance of digital marketing.

The phenomenal growth of the Internet has provided unprecedented opportunities for marketers to forge interactive relationships with consumers. As the Internet and digital communication technologies have advanced, they have made it possible to target markets more precisely and reach markets that were previously inaccessible. One of the most important benefits of e-marketing is the ability of marketers and customers to share information. Through websites, social networks, and other digital media, consumers can learn about everything they consume and use in life. As a result, the Internet is changing the way marketers communicate and develop relationships. For many businesses, engaging in digital marketing activities is essential to maintaining competitive advantages.

10-3 Describe different types of digital media and how they can be used for marketing.

Many types of digital media can be used as marketing tools. A social network is a website where users can create a profile and interact with other users, post information, and engage in other forms of web-based communication. Blogs (short for "weblogs") are web-based journals in which writers can editorialize and interact with other Internet users. A wiki is a type of software that creates an interface that enables users to add or edit the content of some types of websites. Media-sharing sites allow marketers to share photos, videos, and podcasts but are more limited in scope in how companies interact with consumers. One type of media sharing is podcasts, which are audio or video files that can be downloaded from the Internet with a subscription that automatically delivers new content to listening devices or personal computers. Virtual gaming sites are three-dimensional game sites that are social in nature and often involve role-playing. Advertising over mobile devices is becoming increasingly common. Mobile applications are software programs that run on mobile devices and give users access to certain content. Widgets are small bits of software on a website, desktop, or mobile device that performs a simple purpose such as displaying stock updates.

As a result of these new marketing channels, digital marketing is moving from a niche strategy to becoming a core consideration in the marketing mix. At the same time, digital technologies are largely changing the dynamic between marketer and consumer. Consumers use social networking sites and mobile applications to do everything from playing games to engaging in commerce. The menu of digital media alternatives continues to grow, requiring marketers to make informed decisions about strategic approaches.

10-4 Critique the seven different ways consumers use digital media.

It is essential that marketers focus on the changing social behaviors of consumers and how they interact with digital media. Consumers now have a greater ability to regulate the information that they view as well as the rate and sequence of their exposure to that information. This is why the Internet is sometimes referred to as a *pull* medium because users determine which websites they are going to view; the marketer has only limited ability to control the content to which users are exposed, and in what sequence. Marketers must modify their marketing strategies to adapt to the changing behaviors of online consumers.

Forrester Research groups online consumers into seven categories depending upon how they use digital media. Creators are those consumers who create their own media outlets. Conversationalists regularly update their Twitter feeds or status updates on social networking sites. Critics are people who comment on blogs or post ratings and reviews. Collectors gather information and organize content generated by critics and creators. Joiners are those who become members of social networking sites. Spectators are those consumers who read what other consumers produce but do not produce any content themselves. Finally, inactives are online users who do not participate in any digital online media, but this number is decreasing as the popularity of digital media grows. Marketers who want to capitalize on social and digital media marketing will need to consider what portion of online consumers are creating, conversing, rating, collecting, joining, or simply reading online materials.

10-5 Describe how digital media affect the four variables of the marketing mix.

The reasons for a digital marketing strategy are many. The low costs of many digital media channels can provide major savings in promotional budgets. Digital marketing is allowing companies to connect with market segments that are harder to reach with traditional media. Despite the challenges involved in such a strategy, digital marketing is opening up new avenues in the relationship between businesses and consumers.

The marketing mix of product, distribution, promotion, and price continues to apply in digital marketing. From a product perspective, digital media provide an opportunity to add a service dimension to traditional products and create new products that could only be accessible on the Internet. Many businesses find it necessary to continually upgrade their product offerings to meet consumer needs. For distribution, the ability to process orders electronically and increase the speed of communications via the Internet reduces inefficiencies, costs, and redundancies while increasing speed throughout the marketing channel. Marketers can promote their products to consumers in new and creative ways using digital media. Finally, from a pricing dimension, digital media facilitate both price and nonprice competition, because Internet marketing gives consumers access to more information about costs and prices.

10-6 Identify legal and ethical considerations in digital marketing.

How marketers use technology to gather information—both online and offline—has raised numerous legal and ethical issues. Privacy is one of the most significant issues, involving the use of personal information that companies collect from website visitors in their efforts to foster long-term relationships with customers. Some people fear that the collection of personal information from website users may violate users' privacy, especially when it is done without their knowledge. Another concern is that hackers may break into websites and steal users' personal information, enabling them to commit identity theft.

Online fraud includes any attempt to conduct dishonest activities online. Online fraud includes, among other things, attempts to deceive consumers into releasing personal information. It is becoming a major source of frustration with social networking sites. Cybercriminals are discovering entirely new ways to use sites like Facebook and Twitter to carry out fraudulent activities. The best way for users to combat fraudulent activity is not to give out personal information except on trustworthy sites.

The Internet has also created issues associated with intellectual property, the copyrighted or trademarked ideas and creative materials developed to solve problems, carry out applications, and educate and entertain others. Each year, intellectual property losses in the United States total billions of dollars stemming from the illegal copying of computer programs, movies, compact discs, and books. The software industry is particularly hard-hit when it comes to pirating material and illegal file sharing.

Go to www.cengagebrain.com for resources to help you master the content in this chapter as well as for materials that will expand your marketing knowledge!

Developing Your Marketing Plan

When developing a marketing strategy using digital media, a marketer must be aware of the strengths and weaknesses of these media. Digital media are relatively new to the field of marketing and have different pros and cons relative to traditional media sources. Different products and target markets may be more or less suited for different digital media outlets.

1. Review the key concepts of addressability, interactivity, accessibility, connectivity, and control in Table 10.1, and explain how they relate to social media. Think about how a marketing strategy focused on social media differs from a marketing campaign reliant on traditional media sources.
2. No matter what marketing media are used, determining the correct marketing mix for your company is always important. Think about how social media might affect the marketing mix.
3. Discuss different digital media and the pros and cons of using each as part of your marketing plan.

The information obtained from these questions should assist you in developing various aspects of your marketing plan found in the "Interactive Marketing Plan" exercise at www.cengagebrain.com.

Important Terms

digital media 284
digital marketing 284
electronic marketing (e-marketing) 284
social network 287
blogs 290
wiki 291
podcast 293
mobile applications 295
widget 296
online fraud 303

Discussion and Review Questions

1. How does digital marketing differ from traditional marketing?
2. Define *interactivity* and explain its significance. How can marketers exploit this characteristic to improve relations with customers?
3. Explain the distinction between push and pull media. What is the significance of control in terms of using websites to market products?
4. Why are social networks becoming an increasingly important marketing tool? Find an example online in which a company has improved the effectiveness of its marketing strategy by using social networks.
5. How has digital media changed consumer behavior? What are the opportunities and challenges that face marketers with this in mind?
6. Describe the different Technographics segments. How can marketers use this segmentation in their strategies?
7. How can marketers exploit the characteristics of the Internet to improve the product element of their marketing mixes?
8. How do the characteristics of digital marketing affect the promotion element of the marketing mix?
9. How have digital media affected the pricing of products? Give examples of the opportunities and challenges presented to marketers in light of these changes.
10. Name and describe the major ethical and legal issues that have developed in response to the Internet. How should policy makers address these issues?

Video Case 10.1

Zappos Drives Sales through Relationship Building on Social Media

Zappos was one of the first companies to incorporate social media into their business, and they have established themselves as a leader in its use. Steven Hill, Vice President of Merchandising, explains, "Social media ... is more about discovering our culture rather than our business." Zappos focuses on building customer relationships through human interaction and emphasizes comments related to service and fun. For example, if a customer experienced a problem with an order or has a question about a product, the Zappos team ensures that these comments are responded to honestly, authentically, and in a timely manner. Sometimes customers will leave fun comments about their experience with the company. Zappos takes these comments just as seriously. Both instances are at the heart of their operations, which is to "deliver happiness."

Zappos does not maintain a specific strategy for marketing on social media, nor do they have a policy for responding to customers. As with any Zappos activity, marketing is guided by the company's core values, including creating "WOW" customer experiences and a culture characterized by fun and a little weirdness. Product Manager Robert Richman explains, "Social media is a communication tool ... and we want to be available to people wherever they're at." If customers are congregating on Facebook, Zappos makes sure to have a presence there so they can engage them in conversation. In fact, Kenshoo, a digital marketing specialist, has recognized Zappos' Facebook activity for its effectiveness. Over a 2-month period, the company initiated 85,000 visits to their webpage through status updates. Forty-two percent of these updates led to purchases, while the other 58 percent left comments or likes on the webpage.

Rob Siefker, Director of the Customer Loyalty Team, emphasizes the importance of using Twitter. He states, "Most people went on Twitter as a way to interact with friends. Some companies went on there and solely focused on the business or service aspect. For us, part of service is being playful ... it makes it much more human to the customer ... it makes it much more personal." Most companies that use social media use it for promotion rather than for truly interacting with customers. This creates a distance between the company and the customer. Mr. Siefker points out that customers "feel when they are being marketed to, and they know there is a reason for it." However, Zappos strives to go beyond using digital media simply for promotion purposes. They want to forge a real connection with customers and describe themselves as a human company, requiring strong interactions between customers and the organization.

The company has been able to achieve rapid growth through their use of values in their marketing activities. They are a large company with a small business feel when it comes to how they treat their customers and how their customers feel about them. This is due in large part to their presence on social media and the way they cross-promote their activities across platforms. For example, if they receive or post a comment on Facebook, they will also share it on Twitter, Google+, YouTube, and Pinterest in order to reach other current or potential customers. While the company focuses mainly on current customers, this activity generates widespread effects such as word-of-mouth marketing that brings in more new customers. The current customers in this sense serve as brand advocates or brand enthusiasts.

Zappos also generates interest by encouraging customers to share promotions and purchases with friends. Another tactic they use on Facebook is to ask people to like their page. It reads, "Let's be in a Like-Like relationship." Then they ask users to sign up for their e-mail list. The order in which they make these requests gives people the impression that Zappos is indeed concerned about building relationships. They also have exclusive content for people who opt to become fans. Once deemed a fan, people are able to see special offers, videos, and promotions and share comments about them. Finally, Zappos uses an engagement strategy called "Fan of the Week Contest," where people are encouraged to take and post photos of themselves with Zappos products. Then users will vote on the best photo, and the one with the most votes wins. Zappos will post the photo on their website for all to see. Overall, Zappos ensures that they are using social media to build relationships by bringing customers closer to the company. Marketing for Zappos is an authentic and human activity that is not about selling products but building relationships.[90]

Questions for Discussion

1. Describe some ways in which Zappos uses digital media tools.
2. How does Zappos encourage word-of-mouth marketing through digital media?
3. How does Zappos use digital media to create an authentic relationship with consumers?

Case 10.2

The Challenges of Intellectual Property in Digital Marketing

Marketing has been forever changed with the advent of social media. Approximately 72 percent of online adults claim to use some form of social media. Marketers are well aware of the strong presence on these sites, as 93 percent of them state they use social media for business purposes. Facebook is most influential, with 47 percent of users claiming that the site impacts their purchase behavior. Platforms such as Instagram, Pinterest, Vine, and YouTube, which reaches the ideal marketing age group of 18–34-year-olds, is a perfect venue for marketers. Starbucks, for example, perpetuates brand awareness by posting images of its products and logo on Instagram, a photo-sharing application. Walmart utilizes YouTube to host its "Associate Stories Video Series," which is a series of interviews with Walmart employees around the globe. These types of activities seem to generate relationships and loyalty.

However, with the growing popularity of digital media also comes the growing tendency to violate the intellectual property of other people. Intellectual property (IP) refers to any creation that is both tangible and intangible and used in commerce. Media such as videos, artwork, music, movies, and writings are often copyrighted, or protected from being used except by the owner's permission. Similarly, trademarks are used to protect brand names and marks from being used by others without permission.

It did not take long for the Internet to impact intellectual property rights. In 1999, the music industry recorded an all-time high in sales with $14.6 billion. A decade later their revenues from music sales totaled $6.3 billion. File-sharing websites such as Pirate Bay provide a platform for people to pirate, or illegally download, music and movies. The music industry has taken a much larger hit from file sharing because of the simplicity of downloading a 5-minute song compared to a video or movie.

It might seem relatively simple for an organization's marketers to ensure that employees do not place content on social media sites that violate another's copyright or trademark. However, the interactive nature of the Internet complicates this issue. For instance, a direct selling firm with thousands of independent distributors remains responsible for what their distributors post concerning their brand or business. If an independent direct seller unknowingly posts content that is copyrighted or trademarked, the company can be held responsible.

Additionally, many digital marketing campaigns make use of user-generated content, such as videos or postings. This provides a significant advantage to marketers as content developed by other users is generally considered more trustworthy than corporate marketing initiatives. However, marketers must also be careful that the users do not post content that infringes on another's intellectual property. For instance, if a user posts something to a popular blog that violates intellectual property law, the blogging company must take down the post immediately or risk being sued.

YouTube has had particular trouble with user-generated content violating copyrights. Millions of consumer-generated videos are uploaded to YouTube, and Google (who owns the site) is hard-pressed to monitor all content to make certain it is original. Viacom, the English Premier League, German performance rights organization GEMA, Kim Kardashian, and Kanye West have all filed lawsuits against YouTube for intellectual property violations (with differing outcomes). Although YouTube is protected somewhat by the Digital Millennium Copyright Act, it must have controls in place to detect potentially copyrighted material and remove any copyrighted material it discovers without permission. A system called Content ID allows rights holders to run against user uploads on YouTube to detect possible copyrighted materials. Still, as long as illegal uploads and downloads continue, YouTube and other digital media sites are likely to face lawsuits from rights holders who feel their intellectual property has been violated. After all, most copyright holders tend to sue web platforms and websites that host copyrighted content rather than against users who download the content because suing individual users would not be feasible.

One way companies can protect themselves is through browse wrap agreements, which is the part of the website that informs users about the conditions of using the site. These agreements should have clear policies regarding intellectual property violations. This demonstrates to outside parties that the organization is committed to warning users against violating intellectual property. However, penalties are not often enforced when users violate the agreement because courts have determined that many of the links for these agreements are not conspicuous enough for users to notice. Recommendations are being made to create a standardized and transparent method for websites to display these browse wrap agreements so that they meet all relevant conditions. These recommendations could have significant implications for global public policy on intellectual property over the Internet.[91]

Questions for Discussion

1. How has Internet piracy impacted organizations?
2. Why is it hard for firms to monitor and protect against intellectual property violations over the Internet?
3. What are some ways organizations can guard against intellectual property violations on their websites?

Strategic Case 4

Eaton Corporation: Experts at Targeting Different Markets

Eaton Corporation is a power management company based in Cleveland, Ohio. Founded by Joseph Eaton in 1911, this $21.8 billion company originally manufactured truck axels. Today, the company produces more than 900,000 different industrial components and employs 103,000 people globally. It sells products in 175 countries. Eaton's goods and services include electrical components and systems for power quality, distribution, and control; hydraulics components, systems, and services for industrial and mobile equipment; aerospace fuel, hydraulics, and pneumatic systems for commercial and military use; and truck and automotive drivetrain and powertrain systems for performance, fuel economy, and safety. Eaton Corporation has also been one of the most profitable companies, with its stock price surpassing the average of the S&P 500 for the past decade. It has been ranked by *Fortune* magazine as number six in industrial and farm equipment.

© iStockphoto.com/FernandoAH

Eaton supplies products that help customers reduce their energy consumption, including monitoring software, power management systems, high-efficiency transformers, hydraulic systems, and truck transmissions. These products help customers to increase the energy efficiency of buildings, vehicles, and machinery; conserve natural resources; shrink their carbon footprints; and reduce their environmental impact. Although the company sells mostly to industrial and government users, it also sells products to consumers for residences and recreation. Eaton's global presence is extensive. The firm is successfully facing political, environmental, and cultural challenges to create a global name for itself. To help in this endeavor, Eaton uses social media sites including Facebook, Twitter, and YouTube to connect with users and spread awareness about its products.

Business Markets

Eaton's businesses consist of two major sectors: electrical and industrial. Its industrial sector is further split up into hydraulic, aerospace, filtration, and vehicle groups. Eaton's vast array of products targets producer, reseller, and government markets. For instance, in the aerospace industry, Eaton offer components such as fuel and inerting systems, hydraulic systems, and motion control for aircraft. It offers electrical systems, hydraulic systems, fueling, and clutches and brakes for military marine vessels. Eaton also uses many intermediaries such as distributors and retailers to sell products to businesses. Because Eaton's business products entail more risk of purchase, the company employs salespeople and has customer support available for its many different product lines. Eaton also has support staff to handle customer emergencies that happen after hours.

Eaton does not limit its industrial products to large businesses only. It also targets smaller businesses that have need of its products. For instance, in one customer transaction, Eaton provided filter bags to help a family-owned mushroom farm improve its filtration system—which was estimated to increase productivity and led to a savings of $22,000 a year. Eaton's Cooper Lighting division also helped a privately-held California firm improve the efficiency of its outdoor lighting system. By installing more energy-efficient lighting, Eaton helped the firm save 50 percent on energy costs.

Eaton markets to its business customers in a variety of ways. It uses digital media such as its website to describe products, and also has a Success Stories page that describes how Eaton technologies improved their customers' operations. It has a sales force to market its products to business customers and resellers. It also develops advertising campaigns to reach its audience. One of its campaigns even won the Eloqua Markie award for Most Creative Marketing Campaign. In its campaign titled "Things Have Changed," Eaton targeted the IT industry by marketing its expertise in the IT and data center solutions. The campaign used the desk toys of an IT manager to get the message across. The campaign also used social media, direct marketing, and event promotions to enhance its advertising campaign. Eaton clearly demonstrates a strong focus on business and government users of its products.

Consumer Markets

While the majority of Eaton's products are sold to business markets, some of its products also target end-use consumers. For instance, Eaton markets its Golf Pride® golf club grip to golfers for both club manufacturers and professional/amateur golfers. These products are found at Dick's Sporting Goods stores and other locations. Eaton also sells residential products including solar devices, circuit breakers, spa panels, and in-ceiling speakers. To help consumers learn about the quality of its products, Eaton offers a virtual tour of a house that demonstrates how its products can be used throughout the home.

Most of Eaton's products represent high-involvement products for consumers due to the expense of the product and the costs of installation. Therefore, Eaton must take steps to emphasize the high quality and significance of its products and, if possible, lower the risks of purchase. Eaton realizes that like its business market, customers are more interested in the functionality of its products. For instance, a home owner is more likely to be concerned with whether a circuit breaker works correctly than how it looks. Eaton puts a major emphasis on service to reassure its customers that the company puts their needs first. It emphasizes on its website that it delivers service 24/7 depending on the customers' needs. Eaton also offers warranties to reassure customers that defects in the product will be addressed. For instance, it offers a 12-month standard warranty on DC products.

Finally, Eaton continually solicits customer feedback in order to assess customer satisfaction. One of the most important ways the company gets customer opinions is through the Customer Relationship Review (CRR). Each year, Eaton conducts more than 1,000 in-person interviews of customers, including at least one person from every major account. Eaton then generates and distributes an Executive Summary that summarizes the company's strengths and weaknesses. In addition, Eaton also creates several smaller and more focused reports for employee use. Eaton considers both business and consumer customers to be important stakeholders.

Global Business and Social Media

Eaton has had a global presence since 1946, when it acquired a minority interest in U.K. firm Hobourn-Eaton Manufacturing Company Limited. Today its global headquarters are located in Dublin, Ireland. Eaton is a truly multinational company with 55 percent of its revenues coming from outside the United States and 24 percent from developing countries. Eaton sees opportunities for massive growth in the Asia-Pacific region and has 18 manufacturing centers in China. However, with these opportunities come challenges that Eaton must face. For instance, China is experiencing increases in safety laws, land prices and taxes, and minimum wage laws. Eaton is choosing to locate more facilities in China to increase its localization so it can handle these challenges more effectively.

Additionally, both the Chinese and Indian governments have set sustainability goals for their countries, meaning that companies will have to increase their sustainability and sale of eco-friendly products. By investing in energy-efficient operations and selling more sustainable products, Eaton has been meeting these environmental challenges head on.

Another major challenge is ethics and compliance. The more Eaton expands into other countries, the harder it will be to ensure that its facilities, suppliers, and partners are adhering to ethical conduct. By creating more of a localized presence in places like China, Eaton has the ability to increase managerial oversight and emphasize ethical expectations. Additionally, the firm has a Global Ethics office that encourages global employees to report questions or concerns. Non-English-speaking employees can write e-mails and letters to the Global Ethics office in their native language, and Eaton will translate them.

Finally, Eaton has found that an effective way of communicating with global customers is through the use of digital media. In addition to its highly informational website, Eaton also offers online catalogs and e-newsletters that can be easily distributed with just a click of a button. Eaton maintains an active presence on Facebook, Twitter, and YouTube, allowing the firm to answer customer questions and provide updates. Eaton maintains different product categories on these social media sites to address different target markets. For instance, it has pages that focus on electrical, vehicle, and filtration products. YouTube videos help to demonstrate how Eaton products work, acting as a sort of sales promotional tool.

Eaton has a company-wide commitment to serving the needs of business, consumer, and global markets. It uses different marketing approaches to target its various markets, including advertising and digital media campaigns. Eaton's strong understanding of its customer markets is the key to its reputation and global success.[92]

Questions for Discussion

1. How does Eaton target business and consumer markets? Are there any differences?
2. Describe ways that Eaton is addressing global challenges.
3. How is Eaton using digital marketing to reach its customers?

NOTES

[1] Serena Ng, "Exploiting Online Media to Sell Soap in Stores," *The Wall Street Journal*, August 21, 2013, p. B5; Brian Clark, "The Perfect Marketing Strategy for Soap, Soda, and Startups," *Forbes*, April 24, 2012, www.forbes.com/sites/brianclark/2012/04/24/entreproducer (accessed October 21, 2013); Serena Ng, "Soap Opera: Amazon Moves In with P&G," *The Wall Street Journal*, October 15, 2013, pp. A1–A2.

[2] Lauren I. Labrecque, Jonas vor dem Esche, Charla Mathwick, Thomas P. Novak, and Charles F. Hofacker, "Consumer Power: Evolution in the Digital Age," *Journal of Interactive Marketing* 27, no. 4 (November 2013): 257–269.

[3] Rachel DiCaro Metscher and Veronica Steele, "10 Questions You Shouldn't Ask about Social Media," *Marketing News*, October 2013, pp. 14–17.

[4] Piet Levy, "The State of Digital Marketing," *Marketing News*, March 15, 2010, pp. 20–21.

[5] Don Fletcher, "Gift Giving on Facebook Gets Real," *Time*, February 15, 2010, www.time.com/time/magazine/article/0,9171,1960260,00.html (accessed December 12, 2013).

[6] "CafeMom," Highland Capital Partners, www.hcp.com/cafemom (accessed December 13, 2013); "Top 15 Most Popular Social Networking Sites," *eBiz*, February 2012, www.ebizmba.com/articles/social-networking-websites (accessed December 13, 2013).

[7] Pew Research Center, "Social Networking Use," 2014, www.pewresearch.org/data-trend/media-and-technology/social-networking-use (accessed January 10, 2014).

[8] Ashlee Vance, "Facebook: The Making of 1 Billion Users," *Bloomberg Businessweek*, October 4, 2012, www.businessweek.com/articles/2012-10-04/facebook-the-making-of-1-billion-users (accessed January 7, 2013).

[9] "Best in Marketing," *Fortune*, September 16, 2013, p. 138.

[10] Scott Martin, "Facebook Posts Profit; Mobile Advertising Up," *USA Today*, October 31, 2013, p. 1B.

[11] Jefferson Graham, "How to Ride Facebook's Giant Wave," *USA Today*, May 30, 2013, p. 5B.

[12] Amy Dusto, "Social Media Interactions Breed Loyal Customers," *Internet Retailer*, November 19, 2013, www.internetretailer.com/2013/11/19/social-media-interactions-breed-loyal-customers (accessed December 19, 2013).

[13] "Best in Customer Service," *Fortune*, September 16, 2013, p. 136.

[14] Amol Sharma, "NFL Throws in with Twitter," *The Wall Street Journal*, September 26, 2013, p. B2.

[15] Zachary Karabell, "To Tweet or Not to Tweet," *Time*, April 11, 2011, p. 24.

[16] Yoree Koh and Suzanne Vranica, "Advertisers Say Twitter Needs More," *The Wall Street Journal*, October 5–6, 2013, pp. B1, B4.

[17] Evelyn M. Rusli and Shira Ovide, "Facebook Plays Catch-Up on Video," *The Wall Street Journal*, June 20, 2013, p. B12.

[18] Alistair Barr, "Google+ Sees a Measurable Plus: 58 Percent More Users,", *USA Today* October 30, 2013, p. 1B.

[19] Amir Efrati, "There's No Avoiding Google+," *The Wall Street Journal*, http://online.wsj.com/news/articles/SB10001424127887324731304578193781852024980 (accessed December 16, 2013).

[20] Paul Tassi, "Google Plus Creates Uproar over Forced YouTube Integration," *Forbes*, November 9, 2013, www.forbes.com/sites/insertcoin/2013/11/09/google-plus-creates-uproar-over-forced-youtube-integration (accessed December 16, 2013).

[21] Alistair Barr, "Google+ Sees a Measurable Plus: 58 Percent More Users."

[22] Allison Rice, "5 Big Reasons Why You Should Consider Google Plus Marketing," *Yahoo! Small Business Advisor*, http://smallbusiness.yahoo.com/advisor/5-big-reasons-why-consider-google-plus-marketing-235637145.html (accessed December 16, 2013).

[23] Paula Berg, "Why Every Brand-Conscious Business Should Blog," *Colorado Biz*, October 2012, p. 8.

[24] Dan Mitchell, "Why Mayer Chose Tumblr," *CNN Money*, May 20, 2013, http://tech.fortune.cnn.com/2013/05/20/why-mayer-chose-tumblr (accessed December 19, 2013); "About Tumblr," *Tumblr*, www.tumblr.com/about (accessed December 19, 2013).

[25] "Easy Recipes for Real Life," Tastefully Simple blog, www.tastefullysimple.com (accessed December 12, 2013); Stacie Schaible, "Dunedin Woman Says 'Mommy' Blogs Hit the Target," *wfla*, December 10, 2013, www.wfla.com/story/24184742/mommy-blogs-hit-the-target (accessed December 13, 2013).

[26] Wikimedia Foundation, "List of Wikipedias," http://meta.wikimedia.org/wiki/List_of_Wikipedias (accessed December 19, 2013); Drake Bennett, "Ten Years of Inaccuracy and Remarkable Detail: Wikipedia," *Bloomberg Businessweek*, January 10, 2011, pp. 57–61.

[27] Charlene Li and Josh Bernoff, *Groundswell* (Boston: Harvard Business Press, 2008), p. 24.

[28] Ibid.

[29] Nora Ganim Barnes and Justina Andonian, "The 2011 Fortune 500 and Social Media Adoption: Have America's Largest Companies Reached a Social Media Plateau?" University of Massachusetts, 2011, www.umassd.edu/cmr/studiesandresearch/2011fortune500 (accessed February 16, 2012).

[30] Steven Bertoni, "How Stanford Made Instagram an Instant Success," *Forbes*, August 20, 2012, pp. 56–63; Jefferson Graham, "Instagram Is a Start-Up Magnet," *USA Today*, August 9, 2012, www.usatoday.com/tech/news/story/2012-08-07/instagram-economy/56883474/1 (accessed August 20, 2012); Karen Rosenberg, "Everyone's Lives, in Pictures," *The New York Times*, April 12, 2012, www.nytimes.com/2012/04/22/sunday-review/everyones-lives-in-pictures-from-instagram.html (accessed August 20, 2012); Kelly Clay, "3 Things You Can Learn about Your Business with Instagram," *Forbes*, August 9, 2012, www.forbes.com/sites/kellyclay/2012/08/09/3-things-you-can-learn-about-your-business-with-instagram (accessed August 20, 2012); Ian Crouch, "Instagram's Instant Nostalgia," *The New Yorker*, April 10, 2012, www.newyorker.com/online/blogs/culture/2012/04/instagrams-instant-nostalgia.html#slide_ss_0=1 (accessed August 20, 2012).

[31] Eddie Bauer website, www.eddiebauer.com/home.jsp (accessed December 12, 2013).

[32] Scott Martin, "Action! Facebook Rolls Out Video Features," *USA Today*, June 21, 2013, p. B1; Victor Luckerson, "A Year Later, Instagram Hasn't Made a Dime. Was It Worth $1 Billion?" *Time*, April 9, 2013, http://business.time.com/2013/04/09/a-year-later-instagram-hasnt-made-a-dime-was-it-worth-1-billion (accessed December 17, 2013).

[33] Laura Schlereth, "Marketers' Interest in Pinterest," *Marketing News*, April 30, 2012, pp. 8–9; The Creative Group, "Pinterest Interest Survey: 17 Percent of Marketers Currently Using or Planning to Join Pinterest," August 22, 2012, www.sacbee.com/2012/08/22/4747399/pinterest-interest-survey-17-percent.html; www.entrepreneur.com/article/222740 (accessed August 24, 2012); Pinterest website, http://pinterest.com (accessed August 24, 2012); http://pinterest.com/wholefoods/whole-planet-foundation (accessed August 27, 2012).

[34] Jefferson Graham, "Small Businesses Are Stuck on Pinterest," *USA Today*, August 22, 2013, p. 4B.

[35] Kelly Clay, "3 Things You Can Learn about Your Business with Instagram," *Forbes*, August 9, 2012, www.forbes.com/sites/kellyclay/2012/08/09/3-things-you-can-learn-about-your-business-with-instagram (accessed August 20, 2012).

[36] Zale Jewelers Pinterest page, www.pinterest.com/zalesjewelers (accessed December 12, 2013).

[37] Virgin Mobile USA, www.flickr.com/photos/37089719@N08 (accessed December 12, 2013).

[38] Laura Stampler, "How Dove's 'Real Beauty Sketches' Became the Most Viral Video Ad of All Time," *Business Insider*, May 22, 2013, www.businessinsider.com/how-doves-real-beauty-sketches-became-the-most-viral-ad-video-of-all-time-2013-5 (accessed December 17, 2013).

[39] Miguel Helft, "How YouTube Changes Everything," *Fortune*, August 12, 2013, pp. 50–60.

[40] Will Smale, "Jamal Edwards: Amateur Film-Maker Turned Multimillionaire," *BBC*, November 10, 2013, www.bbc.co.uk/news/business-24801980 (accessed December 17, 2013).

[41] "2009 Digital Handbook," *Marketing News*, April 30, 2009, p. 14.

[42] "About Made Money," *CNBC*, www.cnbc.com/id/17283246 (accessed December 19, 2013).

[43] Dean Takahashi, "MediaSpike Reaches 20M Monthly Users with Product Placement in Social–Mobile Games," *Venture Beat*, October 24, 2013, http://venturebeat.com/2013/10/24/mediaspike-reaches-20m-monthly-users-with-product-placement-in-socialmobile-games (accessed December 18, 2013).

[44] Brandy Shaul, "CityVille Celebrates the Golden Arches with Branded McDonald's Restaurant," Games.com, October 19, 2011, http://blog.games.com/2011/10/19/cityville-mcdonalds-restaurant (accessed December 18, 2013).

[45] Joanna Brenner, "Pew Internet: Mobile," Pew Internet & American Life Project, September 18, 2013, http://pewinternet.org/Commentary/2012/February/Pew-Internet-Mobile.aspx (accessed December 19, 2013).

[46] Michael Essany, "eMarketer: 2013 Mobile Ad Spending Up 80 Percent," *Mobile Marketing*, September 25, 2013, www.mobilemarketingwatch.com/emarketer-2013-mobile-ad-spending-up-80-36253 (accessed December 18, 2013).

[47] Thomas Claburn, "Google Tells Businesses 'Fall in Love with Mobile,'" *Information Week*, February 28, 2012, www.informationweek.com/news/mobility/business/232601587 (accessed December 19, 2013).

[48] Mark Milian, "Why Text Messages Are Limited to 160 Characters," *Los Angeles Times*, May 3, 2009, latimesblogs.latimes.com/technology/2009/05/invented-text-messaging.html (accessed December 19, 2013); "Eight Reasons Why Your Business Should Use SMS Marketing," Mobile Marketing Ratings, www.mobilemarketingratings.com/eight-reasons-sms-marketing.html (accessed December 19, 2013).

[49] Sara Angeles, "How to Put Text Message Marketing to Work This Holiday Season," *Fox Business*, November 7, 2013, http://smallbusiness.foxbusiness.com/marketing-sales/2013/11/07/how-to-put-text-message-marketing-to-work-this-holiday-season (accessed December 19, 2013).

[50] Suzanne Vranica and Christopher S. Stewart, "Mobile Ads Take Big Leap as Marketers Rev Spending," *The Wall Street Journal*, October 10, 2013, pp. A1–A2.

[51] Jacob Siegal, "Mobile Devices Account for More Than a Quarter of All Internet Traffic," *BGR*, November 8, 2013, http://bgr.com/2013/11/08/mobile-devices-internet-traffic-q3-2013 (accessed December 19, 2013).

[52] Cotton Delo, "Foursquare Partners with Visa and MasterCard to Give Discounts When Users Shop," *Advertising Age*, February 25, 2013, http://adage.com/article/digital/foursquare-partners-visa-mastercard-discounts/240020 (accessed December 18, 2013).

[53] Anita Campbell, "What the Heck Is an App?" *Small Business Trends*, March 7, 2011, http://smallbiztrends.com/2011/03/what-is-an-app.html (accessed December 19, 2013).

[54] "Half of All Adult Cell Phone Owners Have Apps on Their Phones," Pew Internet and American Life Project, November 2, 2011, http://pewinternet.org/~/media/Files/Reports/2011/PIP_Apps-Update-2011.pdf (accessed December 18, 2013).

[55] Catherine Dunn, "Making Room for Technology," *Fortune*, October 7, 2013, p. 49.

[56] Umika Pidaparthy, "Marketers Embracing QR Codes, for Better or Worse," *CNN Tech*, March 28, 2011, http://articles.cnn.com/2011-03-28/tech/qr.codes.marketing_1_qr-smartphone-users-symbian?_s=PM:TECH (accessed December 18, 2013).

[57] Ann Zimmerman, "Check Out the Future of Shopping," *The Wall Street Journal*, May 18, 2011, p. D1.

[58] "Google Wallet," www.google.com/wallet/what-is-google-wallet.html (accessed December 19, 2013).

[59] Walter S. Mossberg, "Square Cash Lets You Say the Money Is in the Email," *The Wall Street Journal*, October 16, 2013, pp. D1, D3.

[60] Sarah E. Needleman, "Banking on Bitcoin's Novelty," *The Wall Street Journal*, June 27, 2013, p. B4; Robin Sidel and Andrew R. Johnson, "States Put Heat on Bitcoin," *The Wall Street Journal*, June 26, 2013, pp. C1–C2.

[61] "The Bitcoin Bubble," *The Economist*, November 30, 2013, p. 13.

[62] Vangie Beal, "All about Widgets," Webopedia™, August 31, 2010, www.webopedia.com/DidYouKnow/Internet/2007/widgets.asp (accessed December 19, 2013).

[63] Rachael King, "Building a Brand with Widgets," *Bloomberg Businessweek*, March 3, 2008, www.businessweek.com/technology/content/feb2008/tc20080303_000743.htm (accessed December 19, 2013).

[64] TripAdvisor, "Welcome to TripAdvisor's Widget Center," www.tripadvisor.com/Widgets (accessed December 16, 2013).

[65] Li and Bernoff, *Groundswell*, p. 41.

[66] Ibid, pp. 41–42.

[67] David Meerman Scott, *The New Rules of Marketing and PR* (Hoboken, NJ: John Wiley & Sons, Inc., 2009), pp. 195–196.

[68] "Forrester Unveils New Segment of Social Technographics—The Conversationalists," 360 *Digital Connections*, January 21, 2010, http://blog.360i.com/social-media/forrester-new-segment-social-technographics-conversationalists (accessed December 19, 2013).

[69] Daniel Roberts, "He'll Do It... His Way," *Fortune*, October 7, 2013, pp. 92–95.

[70] Li and Bernoff, *Groundswell*, p. 44.

[71] Ibid, pp. 44–45.

[72] Alistair Barr, "Shopping? There's a Screen for That," *USA Today*, November 20, 2013, p. 5B.

[73] Sonja Gensler, Franziska Völckner, Yuping Liu-Thompkins, and Caroline Wiertz, "Managing Brands in the Social Environment," *Journal of Interactive Marketing* 27, no. 4 (November 2013): 242–256.

[74] Evelyn M. Rusli, "Facebook Tests Payments Tool," *The Wall Street Journal*, August 16, 2013, p. B4.

[75] Mariam Gottfried, "Amazon Puts Groceries in Its Shopping Cart," *The Wall Street Journal*, October 28, 2013, p. C6.

[76] Melinda F. Emerson, "How to Run a Facebook Commerce Store," *The New York Times*, August 2, 2013, http://boss.blogs.nytimes.com/2013/08/02/how-to-run-a-facebook-commerce-store/?_r=0 (accessed December 19, 2013).

[77] Melinda F. Emerson, "How to Run a Facebook Commerce Store," *The New York Times*, August 2, 2013, http://boss.blogs.nytimes.com/2013/08/02/how-to-run-a-facebook-commerce-store/?_r=0 (accessed December 19, 2013); "How to Shop—Polkadot Alley," *Facebook*, www.facebook.com/ThePolkadotAlley/app_208195102528120 (accessed December 19, 2013).

[78] "Kill or Cure," *The Economist*, September 7, 2013, p. 62.

[79] Brad Stone and Olga Kharif, "Pay as You Go," *Bloomberg Businessweek*, July 18–24, 2011, pp. 66–71.

[80] Paul Davidson, "Is Your Trusty Phone or Tablet Spying on You?" *USA Today*, August 1, 2013, pp. 1B–2B.

[81] Reed Albergotti, "Facebook Draws Fires on Teems," *The Wall Street Journal*, October 18, 2013, p. B5.

[82] Amir Efrati, "Google's Data Trove Dance," *The Wall Street Journal*, July 31, 2013, pp. B1, B4.

[83] Cecilia Kang, "Bill Would Curb Tracking of and Advertising to Children on Internet," *The Washington Post*, November 14, 2013, www.washingtonpost.com/business/technology/bills-would-curb-tracking-of-and-advertising-to-children-on-internet/2013/11/14/dee03382-4d58-11e3-ac54-aa84301ced81_story.html (accessed December 19, 2013); Anne Flaherty, "Senate Chairman Calls for 'Do Not Track' Bill," *Yahoo! News*, April 24, 2013, http://news.yahoo.com/senate-chairman-calls-not-track-bill-201159091–finance.html (accessed December 19, 2013).

[84] Byron Acohido, "Net Do-Not-Track Option Kicks Off to Criticism," *USA Today*, August 30, 2011, p. 2B.

[85] Jeff Elder, "Bogus Accounts Dog Twitter," *The Wall Street Journal*, November 25, 2013, pp. B1, B6.

[86] Carol Matlack, "Now, Your Reward for Being a Loyal Customer: Identity Theft," *Bloomberg Businessweek*, November 13, 2013, www.businessweek.com/articles/2013-11-13/now-your-reward-for-being-a-loyal-customer-identity-theft (accessed December 19, 2013).

[87] Business Software Alliance, "Global Software Piracy, *BSA*, 2011, http://globalstudy.bsa.org/2011 (accessed December 19, 2013).

[88] Aubry R. Fowler III, Barry J. Babin, and May K. Este, "Burning for Fun or Money: Illicit Consumer Behavior in a Contemporary Context," presented at the Academy of Marketing Science Annual Conference, May 27, 2005, Tampa, FL.

[89] Kevin Shanahan and Mike Hyman, "Motivators and Enablers of SCOURing: A Study of Online Piracy in the US and UK," *Journal of Business Research* 63 (2010): 1095–1102.

[90] Todd Wasserman, "Zappos Facebook Activity over 2 Months Drives 85,000 Website Visits," *Mashable*, February 6, 2013, http://mashable.com/2013/02/06/zappos-facebook-results (accessed December 6, 2013); Laura Stampler, "Why Zappos Sees Sponsored Posts on Facebook as 'A Necessary Evil,'" *Business Insider*, February 6, 2013, www.businessinsider.com/zappos-on-facebook-and-social-media-2013-2 (accessed December 6, 2013); Mike Schoultz, "Zappos Marketing Strategy... What Is Their Difference Maker?" *Digital Spark Marketing*, November 12, 2013, www.digitalsparkmarketing.com/creative-marketing/brand/zappos-marketing-strategy (accessed December 6, 2013); Amy Porterfield, "9 Companies Doing Social Media Right and Why," *Social Media Examiner*, April 12, 2011, www.socialmediaexaminer.com/9-companies-doing-social-media-right-and-why (accessed December 6, 2013).

[91] Joanna Brenner, "Pew Internet: Social Networking (Full Detail)," Pew Internet and American Life Project, August 5, 2013, http://pewinternet.org/Commentary/2012/March/Pew-Internet-Social-Networking-full-detail.aspx (accessed December 3, 2013); Tom Pick, "101 Vital Social Media and Digital Marketing Statistics," *Social Media Today*, August 6, 2013, http://socialmediatoday.com/tompick/1647801/101-vital-social-media-and-digital-marketing-statistics-rest-2013 (accessed December 3, 2013); Bas Van Den Beld, "10 Wowing Social Media Statistics," *State of Digital*, October 19, 2012, www.stateofdigital.com/10-wowing-social-media-statistics (accessed December 4, 2013); Belle Beth Cooper, "10 Surprising Social Media Statistics That Will Make You Rethink Your Social Media Strategy," *Fast Company*, November 18, 2013, www.fastcompany.com/3021749/work-smart/10-surprising-social-media-statistics-that-will-make-you-rethink-your-social-stra (accessed December 3, 2013); Venable LLP, "When Marketing through Social Media, Legal Risks Can Go Viral," White Paper, www.venable.com/files/Publication/b4f467b9-0666-4b36-b021-351540962d65/Presentation/PublicationAttachment/019f4e5f-d6f8-4eeb-af43-40a4323b9ff1/Social_Media_white_paper.pdf (accessed December 10, 2013); Christina Warren, "How YouTube Fights Copyright Infringement," *Mashable*, February 17, 2012, http://mashable.com/2012/02/17/youtube-content-id-faq (accessed December 10, 2013); Martin U. Müller interview, "German Court Ruling against YouTube: 'We Don't Want to Sue,

We Want a Contract,' " *Der Spiegel*, April 23, 2012, www.spiegel.de/international/business/german-copyright-group-succeeds-in-case-against-youtube-a-829124.html (accessed December 10, 2013); Sam Gustin, "How Google Beat Viacom in the Landmark YouTube Case," *Time*, April 19, 2013, http://business.time.com/2013/04/19/how-google-beat-viacom-in-the-landmark-youtube-copyright-case-again (accessed December 10, 2013); Jon Brodkin, "YouTube's Defeat of Copyright Owners Is Final in Premier League Case," *ars technica*, http://arstechnica.com/tech-policy/2013/11/youtubes-defeat-of-copyright-owners-is-final-in-premier-league-case (accessed December 10, 2013); The Reliable Source, "Kanye West, Kim Kardashian Sue YouTube Founder for Leaked Proposal Footage," *The Washington Post*, November 4, 2013, www.washingtonpost.com/blogs/reliable-source/wp/2013/11/04/kanye-west-kim-kardashian-sue-youtube-founder-for-leaked-proposal-footage (accessed December 10, 2013); Derek Overbey, "3 Big Brand Social Media Ideas Small Businesses Can Use," *Vertical Response*, November 6, 2013, www.verticalresponse.com/blog/3-big-brand-social-media-ideas-small-businesses-can-use (accessed December 3, 2013); World Intellectual Property Organization, "What Is Intellectual Property?" www.wipo.int/about-ip/en (accessed June 7, 2013); Matt Richtell, "The Napster Decision: The Overview: Appellate Judges Back Limitations on Copying Music," *The New York Times*, February 13, 2001, www.nytimes.com/2001/02/13/business/napster-decision-overview-appellate-judges-back-limitations-copying-music.html?pagewanted=all&src=pm (accessed June 7, 2013); National Paralegal College, "History and Sources of Intellectual Property Law," http://nationalparalegal.edu/public_documents/courseware_asp_files/patents/IntroIP/History.asp (accessed June 7, 2013); International Trademark Association, "Fact Sheets Types of Protection," 2013, www.inta.org/TrademarkBasics/FactSheets/Pages/TrademarksvsGenericTermsFactSheet.aspx (accessed June 7, 2013); David Goldman, "Music's Lost Decade: Sales Cut in Half," *CNN Money*, Feburary 3, 2010, http://money.cnn.com/2010/02/02/news/companies/napster_music_industry (accessed December 10, 2013); Maurizio Borghi, Indranath Gupta, and Eva Hemmungs Wirtén, "Deliverable D26: Reusing Copyrighted Material in User-Generated Content", *Counter© Counterfeiting and Piracy Research* (March 5, 2010); Maurizio Borghi, Maria Lillà Montagnani, and Indranath Gupta, "Deliverable D27: Evaluating Scenarios for Managing Copyright Online," *Counter© Counterfeiting and Piracy Research* (May 30, 2010).

[92] Eaton Corporation, "2012 Annual Report," www.eaton.com/Eaton/OurCompany/InvestorRelations/FinancialReports/AnnualReport/index.htm (accessed October 31, 2013); Eaton Corporation, "Global Ethics & Compliance," www.eaton.com/Eaton/OurCompany/GlobalEthics (accessed October 31, 2013); Ethisphere Institute, 2013 "World's Most Ethical Companies," *Ethisphere*, http://ethisphere.com/worlds-most-ethical/wme-honorees (accessed October 31, 2013); Eaton website, www.eaton.com/Eaton/index.htm (accessed October 31, 2013); Eaton, "Aerospace," www.eaton.com/Eaton/ProductsServices/Aerospace/index.htm?wtredirect=www.eaton.com/aerospace (accessed October 31, 2013); Eaton, "Success Stories: Mushroom Farming Industry," www.eaton.com/Eaton/OurCompany/SuccessStories/ManufacturingIndustrial/Mushroom-Farming-Industry/index.htm (accessed October 31, 2013); *Fortune*, "Most Admired: Industrial and Farm Equipment," *CNN Money*, http://money.cnn.com/magazines/fortune/most-admired/2012/industries/28.html (accessed October 31, 2013); Eaton, "Eaton Receives Eloqua Markie Award for Most Creative Marketing Campaign," November 21, 2012, www.eaton.com/Eaton/OurCompany/NewsEvents/NewsReleases/PCT_403135 (accessed October 31, 2013); Eaton, "Eaton's LED Solutions Allow California Facility to Save More Than 50 Percent on Exterior," September 19, 2013, www.eaton.com/Eaton/OurCompany/NewsEvents/NewsReleases/PCT_508987 (accessed October 31, 2013); Curt Hutchins, *A Transition in Global Markets: Asia-Pacific Is the Future*, 2012, www.amcham-shanghai.org/NR/rdonlyres/73F016E2-0E5F-4BC0-9B99-AC028BD9EA16/17086/CurtHutchins.pdf (accessed October 31, 2013); Anna Clark, "Megatrends: The Power behind Eaton's Global Green Growth," *Green Biz*, June 19, 2013, www.greenbiz.com/blog/2013/06/19/power-behind-eatons-global-green-growth (accessed October 31, 2013).

Feature Notes

[a] Katherine Rosman, "Some Twitter Users Push Back on Ads," *The Wall Street Journal*, August 4, 2013, http://online.wsj.com/article/SB10001424127887324328904578623811676679672.html (accessed August 8, 2013); Nick Douglas, " 'Weird Twitter' Explained," *Daily Dot*, www.dailydot.com/entertainment/weird-twitter-explained-map (accessed August 8, 2013); Mary Beth Quirk, "Twitter Users Rebelling against Promoted Tweets Using Age-Old Tool of Mockery," *Consumerist*, August 5, 2013, http://consumerist.com/2013/08/05/twitter-users-rebelling-against-promoted-tweets-using-age-old-tool-of-mockery (accessed August 8, 2013).

[b] Jefferson Graham, "Remember Podcasting? It's Back—And Booming," *USA Today*, August 16, 2013, pp. B1–B2; Brendan Cournoyer, "3 Reasons Why Podcasts Should Be Part of Your Content Marketing Strategy," *Content Marketing Institute*, January 17, 2012, http://contentmarketinginstitute.com/2012/01/podcasts-content-marketing-strategy (accessed October 1, 2013); Michael Wolf, "Funnymen and iPhones: Why the Podcast Is Finally Coming into Its Own," *Forbes*, April 4, 2013, www.forbes.com/sites/michaelwolf/2013/04/04/funnymen-and-iphones-why-the-podcast-is-finally-coming-into-its-own (accessed October 1, 2013); Christopher Matthews, "Despite Being Oh-So 2005, Podcasting Is Drawing Listeners and Advertisers Alike," *Time*, August 29, 2013, http://business.time.com/2013/08/29/despite-being-oh-so-2005-podcasting-is-drawing-listeners-and-advertisers-alike (accessed October 2, 2013).

part 5

Product Decisions

We are now prepared to analyze the decisions and activities associated with developing and maintaining effective marketing mixes. PART 5 explores the product and price ingredients of the marketing mix. CHAPTER 11 focuses on basic product concepts and on branding and packaging decisions. CHAPTER 12 analyzes various dimensions regarding product management, including line extensions and product modification, new-product development, product deletions, and the management of services as products. In CHAPTER 13, we discuss services marketing, including its importance, key characteristics, marketing strategies for services, and the nature of nonprofit marketing.

chapter 11

Product Concepts, Branding, and Packaging

OBJECTIVES

11-1 Explain the concept of a product.

11-2 Discuss how products are classified.

11-3 Explain the concepts of product line and product mix and how they are related.

11-4 Describe the product life cycle and its impact on marketing strategies.

11-5 Discuss the product adoption process.

11-6 Explain the major components of branding, including brand types, branding strategies, and brand protection.

11-7 Describe the major packaging functions, design considerations, and how packaging is used in marketing strategies.

11-8 Identify the functions of labeling and legal issues related to labeling.

MARKETING INSIGHTS

Nike Races Ahead Using Activity-Tracking Technology

Racing toward a goal of $36 billion in annual revenue by 2017, Nike is pioneering products that help consumers track their activity levels during workouts, sports, and daily lives. First, it developed athletic shoes with built-in sensors to monitor movements such as counting steps or jumps. Through a partnership with Apple, Nike's sensors were set to synch with iPods so users could record their daily performance statistics, upload data to a special website, and compare current activity with their previous records as well as with friends' performance statistics. The digital-monitoring aspect of these products, dubbed Nike Plus, attracted customers who were excited about the ability to record and follow their fitness progress over time—and share their data for a bit of friendly competition.

Nike's next-generation activity-tracking product was the FuelBand, a high-tech wristband with LED lights that change according to the user's movements. Priced at $150, the sleek, black FuelBand offered a number of benefits: It was simple to use, convenient to wear, and discreet enough to disappear under clothing or to be displayed as a fashion statement. The first FuelBands sold out within days, and Nike quickly followed up with an improved version that sported more fitness features and stylish colors for fashion-conscious customers.

Now Nike is facing increased competition from rival wristbands and other wearable gadgets designed to track the user's activity levels. Can Nike maintain its marketing momentum in this fast-growing product category?[1]

Because Nike has long been at the forefront of innovation and style in exercise gear, its products allow it to be a market leader. In this chapter, we first define a product and discuss how products are classified. Next, we examine the concepts of product line and product mix. We then explore the stages of the product life cycle and the effect of each life-cycle stage on marketing strategies. Next, we outline the product adoption process. Then, we discuss branding, its value to customers and marketers, brand loyalty, and brand equity. We examine the various types of brands and consider how companies choose and protect brands, the various branding strategies employed, brand extensions, co-branding, and brand licensing. We also look at the role of packaging, the functions of packaging, issues to consider in packaging design, and how the package can be a major element in marketing strategy. We conclude with a discussion of labeling and some related legal issues.

11-1 WHAT IS A PRODUCT?

good A tangible physical entity

service An intangible result of the application of human and mechanical efforts to people or objects

idea A concept, philosophy, image, or issue

As defined in Chapter 1, a *product* is a good, a service, or an idea received in an exchange. It can be either tangible or intangible and includes functional, social, and psychological utilities or benefits. A **good** is a tangible physical entity, such as an iPad or a Subway sandwich. A **service**, in contrast, is intangible. It is the result of the application of human and mechanical efforts to people or objects. Examples of services include a concert performance by Beyonce, online car insurance, a medical examination, and child day care. BMO Harris Bank, featured in the advertisement, offers a variety of services. It not only offers a place to put money, but also provides research and analysis, business trend reports, and other expertise to help business leaders succeed. The advertisement underscores the value of BMO's services by showing a person using a physical good—a picture frame—to call out the words "Your Vision."

BMO Harris Bank N.A. Member FDIC

Services
BMO Harris Bank offers financial services, such as planning for the future and analysis, to inform decision makers.

An **idea** is a concept, philosophy, image, or issue. Ideas provide the psychological stimulation that aids in solving problems or adjusting to the environment. In the BMO ad, marketers want to establish in consumers' minds that BMO is an expert in helping businesses to develop plans for the future.

It is helpful to think of a total product offering as having three interdependent elements: the core product, its supplemental features, and its symbolic or experiential benefits. The core product consists of a product's fundamental utility or main benefit and usually addresses a fundamental need of the consumer. Most consumers, however, appreciate additional features and services. For instance, a basic cell phone allows consumers to make calls, but increasingly consumers expect supplemental features, such as unlimited texting, widely available high-speed Internet access, and apps. Consumers also may seek out symbolic benefits, such as a trendy brand name, when purchasing a phone.

Supplemental features provide added value or attributes that are in addition to the product's core utility or benefit. Supplemental product features often include perks such as free installation, guarantees, product information, promises of repair or maintenance, delivery, training, or financing. These supplemental attributes are not required to make the core product function effectively, but they help to differentiate one product brand from another and may increase customer loyalty. For instance, *Travel + Leisure* magazine ranks the Wentworth Mansion in Charleston, North Carolina, as one of the best hotels in the world, mostly because of its exceptional service, which includes handmade chocolates on guest pillows each night and personalized attention from the moment guests first arrive and leave their cars with the valet.[2]

Finally, customers also receive benefits based on their experiences with the product, which give symbolic meaning to many products (and brands) for buyers. For some consumers, the simple act of shopping gives them pleasure, which lends to its symbolic value and improves their attitudes about the products they consider buying. Some retailers capitalize on this by striving to create a special, individual experience for customers. The Internet is helping retailers to individualize shopping for consumers before they even enter a store. The department store Selfridges, for example, links the online and in-person shopping experience during the holidays by featuring online "Elves." Customers can click on the "Elf Help" feature of the website gain assistance with gift selection and summon in-person personal shoppers to help them with shopping at Selfridges locations at times of their choosing.[3]

The atmosphere and décor of a retail store, the variety and depth of product choices, the customer support, and even the sounds and smells all contribute to the experiential element. Thus, when buyers purchase a product, they are really buying the benefits and satisfaction they think the product will provide. A Rolex or Patek Philippe watch is purchased to make a statement that the wearer has high status or has achieved financial success, not just for telling time. Services, in particular, are purchased on the basis of expectations. Expectations, suggested by images, promises, and symbols, as well as processes and delivery, help consumers to make judgments about tangible and intangible products. Often symbols and cues are used to make intangible products more tangible, or real, to the consumer. Prudential Insurance, for example, features the Rock of Gibraltar on its logo to symbolize strength and permanency.

11-2 CLASSIFYING PRODUCTS

Products fall into one of two general categories. Products purchased to satisfy personal and family needs are **consumer products**. Those bought to use in a firm's operations, to resell, or to make other products are **business products**. Consumers buy products to satisfy their personal wants, whereas business buyers seek to satisfy the goals of their organizations. Product classifications are important because they may influence pricing, distribution, and promotion decisions. In this section, we examine the characteristics of consumer and business products and explore the marketing activities associated with some of these products.

11-2a Consumer Products

The most widely accepted approach to classifying consumer products is based on characteristics of consumer buying behavior. It divides products into four categories: convenience, shopping, specialty, and unsought products. However, not all buyers behave in the same way when purchasing a specific type of product. Thus, a single product might fit into several categories. To minimize complexity, marketers think in terms of how buyers *generally* behave when purchasing a specific item. Examining the four traditional categories of consumer products can provide further insight.

Convenience Products

Convenience products are relatively inexpensive, frequently purchased items for which buyers exert only minimal purchasing effort. They range from bread, soft drinks, and chewing gum to gasoline and newspapers. The buyer spends little time planning the purchase or comparing available brands or sellers. Even a buyer who prefers a specific brand will generally choose a substitute if the preferred brand is not conveniently available. A convenience product is normally marketed through many retail outlets, such as gas stations, drugstores, and supermarkets. Coca-Cola products, for instance, are available in grocery stores, convenience stores,

consumer products Products purchased to satisfy personal and family needs

business products Products bought to use in a firm's operations, to resell, or to make other products

Convenience products Relatively inexpensive, frequently purchased items for which buyers exert minimal purchasing effort

gas stations, restaurants, and airports—among many other outlets. Because sellers experience high inventory turnover, per-unit gross margins can be relatively low. Producers of convenience products, such as Wrigley's chewing gum, expect little promotional effort at the retail level and thus must provide it themselves with advertising and sales promotion. Packaging and displays are also important because many convenience items are available only on a self-service basis at the retail level, and thus the package plays a major role in selling the product.

Shopping Products

Shopping products are items for which buyers are willing to expend considerable effort in planning and making the purchase. Buyers spend considerable time comparing stores and brands with respect to prices, product features, qualities, services, and perhaps warranties. Shoppers may compare products at a number of outlets such as Best Buy, Amazon.com, Lowe's, or Home Depot. Appliances, bicycles, furniture, stereos, cameras, and shoes exemplify shopping products. These products are expected to last a fairly long time and are more expensive than convenience products. These products, however, are still within the budgets of most consumers and are purchased less frequently than convenience items. Shopping products are distributed via fewer retail outlets than convenience products.

Shopping products Items for which buyers are willing to expend considerable effort in planning and making purchases

Because shopping products are purchased less frequently, inventory turnover is lower, and marketing channel members expect to receive higher gross margins to compensate for the lower turnover. In certain situations, both shopping products and convenience products may be marketed in the same location. For instance, retailers such as Target or Walmart carry shopping products like televisions, furniture, and cameras as well as groceries and other

Convenience versus Shopping Products
Convenience products such as M&M's candies do not require much shopping effort. However, a consumer might expend considerable effort in deciding on, locating, and purchasing a high-end KitchenAid appliance, such as this toaster.

convenience products. Take a look at the two advertisements for convenience versus shopping products. Peanut M&Ms is a convenience product that is inexpensive and widely available. Few consumers will have to exert much effort to locate and purchase Peanut M&Ms. The advertisement does not even mention where M&M's candies are sold because they are so widely available. A KitchenAid toaster, on the other hand, is a shopping product. This ad depicts a high-end toaster model and emphasizes its sleek lines and bright color. Consumers who purchase this product are likely to have conducted research and will seek out this specific KitchenAid model because of its features and reputation for quality.

A marketer must consider several key issues to market a shopping product effectively, including how to allocate resources, whether personal selling is needed, and cooperation within the supply chain. Although advertising for shopping products often requires a large budget, an even larger percentage of the overall budget is needed if marketers determine that personal selling is required. The producer and the marketing channel members usually expect some cooperation from one another with respect to providing parts and repair services and performing promotional activities. Marketers should consider these issues carefully so that they can choose the best course for promoting these products.

specialty products Items with unique characteristics that buyers are willing to expend considerable effort to obtain

unsought products Products purchased to solve a sudden problem, products of which customers are unaware, and products that people do not necessarily think of buying

Specialty Products

Specialty products possess one or more unique characteristics, and generally buyers are willing to expend considerable effort to obtain them. On average, this is the most expensive category of products. Buyers conduct research, plan the purchase of a specialty product, know exactly what they want, and will not accept a substitute. Examples of specialty products include fine jewelry or limited-edition collector's items. When searching for specialty products, buyers do not compare alternatives and are unlikely to base their decision on price. They are concerned primarily with finding an outlet that sells the preselected product. This advertisement for Patek Philippe watches underscores the fact that these are specialty products. The advertisement shows a father, wearing the high-end luxury watch, baking with his son. The caption states, "You never actually own a Patek Philippe. You merely take care of it for the next generation." This is meant to become a family heirloom, hinting that price should be no object. The watch is very expensive and available only at exclusive outlets.

Marketers will approach their efforts for specialty products differently from convenience or shopping products in several ways. Specialty products are often distributed through a very limited number of retail outlets. Similar to shopping products, they are purchased infrequently, causing lower inventory turnover and thus requiring high gross margins to be profitable.

Patek Philippe

Specialty Product
A Swiss-made watch, such as this Patek Philippe model, is a specialty product. It is expensive, exclusive, and is meant to be treasured for a long time.

Unsought Products

Unsought products are those purchased when a sudden problem must be solved, products of which customers are unaware until they see them in a store or online, and products that people do not plan on purchasing. Emergency medical services and automobile repairs are examples of products needed quickly and suddenly to solve a problem. A consumer who is sick or injured has little time to plan to go to an emergency medical center or hospital and will find the closest location to receive service. Likewise, in the event of a broken fan belt in a car, a consumer likely will seek the nearest auto repair facility or call AAA to minimize the length of time before the car is operational again. In such cases, speed of problem resolution is more important than price or other features a buyer might normally consider if there were more time for making a decision.

11-2b Business Products

Business products are usually purchased on the basis of an organization's goals and objectives. Generally, the functional aspects of the product are more important than the psychological rewards sometimes associated with consumer products. Business products can be classified into seven categories according to their characteristics and intended uses: installations, accessory equipment, raw materials, component parts, process materials, MRO supplies (maintenance, repair, and operating), and business services.

Installations

Installations include facilities, such as office buildings, factories, and warehouses, and major nonportable equipment such as production lines and very large machines. Normally, installations are expensive and intended to be used for a considerable length of time. Because installations tend to be costly and involve a long-term investment of capital, these purchase decisions often are made by high-level management. Marketers of installations must frequently provide a variety of services, including training, repairs, maintenance assistance, and even aid in financing.

Accessory Equipment

Accessory equipment does not become part of the final physical product but is used in production or office activities. Examples include file cabinets, fractional-horsepower motors, calculators, and tools. Compared with major equipment, accessory items usually are less expensive, purchased routinely with less negotiation, and are often treated as expense items rather than capital items because they are not expected to last as long. More outlets are required for distributing and selling accessory equipment than for installations, but sellers do not have to provide the multitude of services expected of installations marketers.

Raw Materials

Raw materials are the basic natural materials that actually become part of a physical product. They include minerals, chemicals, agricultural products, and materials from forests and oceans. Corn, for instance, is a raw material that is found in many different products, including food (in many forms), beverages (as corn syrup), and even fuel (as ethanol).

Component Parts

Component parts become part of the physical product and are either finished items ready for assembly or products that need little processing before assembly. Although they become part of a larger product, component parts often can be identified and distinguished easily, even after the product is assembled. Spark plugs, tires, clocks, brakes, and headlights are all component parts of an automobile. Buyers purchase such items according to their own specifications or industry standards, and they expect the parts to be of a specified quality and delivered on time so that production is not slowed or stopped. To cut down on the transportation costs and delivery variability of needed component parts, GM opened a stamping plant in Arlington, Texas, to produce component parts for the automaker's auto assembly facility nearby.[4] Producers that are primarily assemblers, such as auto or computer manufacturers, depend heavily on suppliers of component parts.

installations Facilities and nonportable major equipment

accessory equipment Equipment that does not become part of the final physical product but is used in production or office activities

raw materials Basic natural materials that become part of a physical product

component parts Items that become part of the physical product and are either finished items ready for assembly or items that need little processing before assembly

Process Materials

Process materials are used directly in the production of other products. Unlike component parts, however, process materials are not readily identifiable. Case in point, a salad dressing manufacturer includes vinegar as an ingredient in dressing. The vinegar is a process material because it is not identifiable or extractable from the other ingredients in the dressing. As with component parts, process materials are purchased according to industry standards or the purchaser's specifications.

MRO Supplies

MRO supplies are maintenance, repair, and operating items that facilitate production and operations, but do not become part of the finished product. Many products that were purchased as consumer products could also be considered MRO supplies to businesses. These might include paper, pencils, cleaning supplies, and paints. MRO supplies are sold through numerous outlets and are purchased routinely, much like convenience products in the consumer market. To ensure supplies are available when needed, buyers often deal with more than one seller.

Business Services

Business services are the intangible products that many organizations use in their operations. They include financial, legal, marketing research, information technology, and janitorial services. Firms must decide whether to provide these services internally or obtain them from outside the organization. This decision depends on the costs associated with each alternative and how frequently the services are needed. In this advertisement, Xerox promotes how its products help businesses, such as insurance companies, provide a greater range of business services internally, such as processing claims—creating cost savings and efficiencies and building organizational capacity.

Business Services
Xerox provides products that help businesses conduct more business services in-house to save money and build capacity.

11-3 PRODUCT LINE AND PRODUCT MIX

Marketers must understand the relationships among all the products of their organization to coordinate the marketing of the total group of products. The following concepts help to describe the relationships among an organization's products.

A **product item** is a specific version of a product that can be designated as a distinct offering among an organization's products. A Gap T-shirt represents a product item. A **product line** is a group of closely related product items that are considered to be a unit because of marketing, technical, or end-use considerations.

Specific product items in a product line, such as different dessert flavors or shampoos for oily and dry hair, usually reflect the desires of different target markets or the varying needs of consumers. Thus, to develop the optimal product line, marketers must understand buyers' goals. Firms with high market share are more likely to expand their product lines aggressively, as are marketers with relatively high prices or limited product lines.[5] This pattern can be seen

process materials Materials that are used directly in the production of other products but are not readily identifiable

MRO supplies Maintenance, repair, and operating items that facilitate production and operations but do not become part of the finished product

business services Intangible products that many organizations use in their operations

product item A specific version of a product that can be designated as a distinct offering among a firm's products

product line A group of closely related product items viewed as a unit because of marketing, technical, or end-use considerations

Figure 11.1 The Concepts of Product Mix Width and Depth Applied to U.S. Procter & Gamble Products

Laundry detergents	Toothpastes	Bar soaps	Deodorants	Shampoos	Tissue/Towel
Ivory Snow 1930	Gleem 1952	Ivory 1879	Old Spice 1948	Pantene 1947	Charmin 1928
Dreft 1933	Crest 1955	Camay 1926	Secret 1956	Head & Shoulders 1961	Puffs 1960
Tide 1946		Zest 1952	Sure 1972	Vidal Sassoon 1974	Bounty 1965
Cheer 1950		Safeguard 1963		Pert Plus 1979	
Bold 1965		Oil of Olay 1993		Ivory 1983	
Gain 1966				Infusium 23 1986	
Era 1972				Physique 2000	
Febreze Clean Wash 2000				Herbal Essence 2001	

Depth (vertical) — Width (horizontal)

in many industries, such as the computer industry, where companies are likely to expand their product lines when industry barriers are low or perceived market opportunities exist.

A **product mix** is the composite, or total, group of products that an organization makes available to customers. The **width of product mix** is measured by the number of product lines a company offers. The **depth of product mix** is the average number of different product items offered in each product line. Procter & Gamble offers a broad product mix, comprised of all the health-care, beauty-care, laundry and cleaning, food and beverage, paper, cosmetic, and fragrance products the firm manufactures, some of which are quite deep. Figure 11.1 shows the width and depth of part of Procter & Gamble's product mix. Procter & Gamble is known for using distinctive branding, packaging, segmentation, and consumer advertising to promote individual items in its product lines. Tide, Bold, Gain, Cheer, and Era, for example, are all Procter & Gamble detergents that share the same distribution channels and similar manufacturing facilities, but each is promoted as a distinctive product, adding depth to the product line.

product mix The composite, or total, group of products that an organization makes available to customers

width of product mix The number of product lines a company offers

depth of product mix The average number of different products offered in each product line

product life cycle The progression of a product through four stages: introduction, growth, maturity, and decline

introduction stage The initial stage of a product's life cycle; its first appearance in the marketplace, when sales start at zero and profits are negative

11-4 PRODUCT LIFE CYCLES AND MARKETING STRATEGIES

Product life cycles follow a similar trajectory to biological life cycles, progressing from birth to death. As Figure 11.2 shows, a **product life cycle** has four major stages: introduction, growth, maturity, and decline. As a product moves through each cycle, the strategies relating to competition, pricing, distribution, promotion, and market information must be evaluated and possibly adjusted. Astute marketing managers use the life-cycle concept to make sure that strategies relating to the introduction, alteration, and deletion of products are timed and executed properly. By understanding the typical life-cycle pattern, marketers can maintain profitable product mixes.

11-4a Introduction

The **introduction stage** of the product life cycle begins at a product's first appearance in the marketplace. Sales start at zero and profits are negative because companies must invest in product development and launch prior to selling. Profits may remain low or below zero

Figure 11.2 The Four Stages of the Product Life Cycle

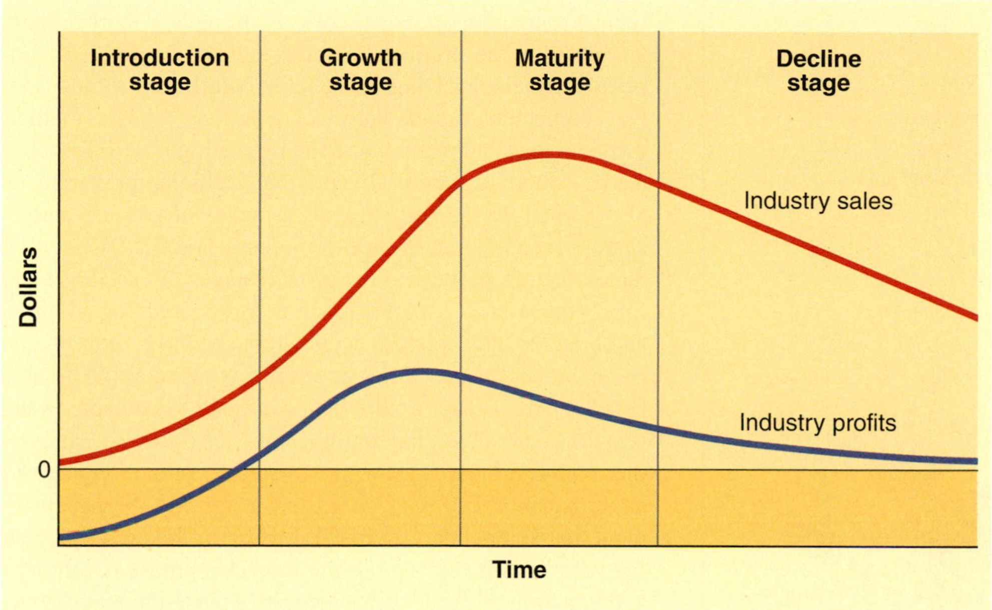

because initial revenues will be low while the company covers large expenses for promotion and distribution. Notice in Figure 11.2 how, as sales move upward from zero over time, profits also increase.

Sales may be slow at first because potential buyers must be made aware of new-product features, uses, and advantages through marketing. Efforts to highlight a new product's value can create a foundation for building brand loyalty and customer relationships.[6] Two difficulties may arise during the introduction stage. First, sellers may lack the resources, technological knowledge, and marketing expertise to launch the product successfully. A large marketing budget is not required to launch a successful product. Marketers can attract attention through such techniques as giving away free samples or through media appearances. Websites, such as Retailmenot.com, help firms with lost-cost promotion by listing coupons and samples for thousands of companies—exposing customers to great deals and new brands.[7] Second, the initial product price may have to be high to recoup expensive marketing research or development costs, which can depress sales. Given these difficulties, it is not surprising that many products never last beyond the introduction stage.

Most new products start off slowly and seldom generate enough sales to bring immediate profits. Although new-product success rates vary a great deal between companies and in different industries, it is estimated that only between 10 and 20 percent of new products succeed in the marketplace.[8] Even among established and successful companies, new-product success rates are rarely above 50 percent.[9] As buyers learn about the new product and express interest, the firm should constantly monitor the product and marketing strategy for weaknesses and make corrections quickly to prevent the product's early demise. Marketing strategy should be designed to attract the segment that is most interested in, most able, and most willing to buy the product. As sales increase, you can see in Figure 11.2 that eventually the firm reaches the breakeven point, which is when profits match expenses.

11-4b Growth

During the **growth stage**, sales rise rapidly and profits reach a peak and then start to decline (see Figure 11.2). The growth stage is critical to a product's survival because competitive reactions to the product's success during this period will affect the product's life expectancy.

growth stage The product life-cycle stage when sales rise rapidly, profits reach a peak, and then they start to decline

Product Variations
Special K Nourish is the first hot cereal that carries the Special K brand, which is more famous for its cold cereals and low-calorie snack foods.

Profits begin to decline late in the growth stage as more competitors enter the market, driving prices down and creating the need for heavy promotional expenses. At this point, a typical marketing strategy seeks to strengthen market share and position the product favorably against aggressive competitors by emphasizing its benefits. Marketers should analyze competing brands' product positions relative to their own and make adjustments to the marketing mix in response to their findings. Aggressive pricing, including price cuts, is also typical during this stage as a means of gaining market share—even if it means short-term loss of profits. The goal of the marketing strategy in the growth stage is to establish and fortify the product's market position by encouraging adoption and brand loyalty. Already well-established as a healthy cold cereal brand, Special K has developed Nourish as the brand's first hot cereal. This product is positioned to compete in the growing market for healthy convenience foods, a category that will continue to grow as consumers remain concerned about nutrition and managing their weight. In the advertisement, marketers underscore the novelty of the item by opening with "this is big" across the top. This phrase is followed at the bottom of the advertisement by a close-up image of the product that clearly shows the healthy fruits and whole grains it contains, all served in a portable cup. Special K Nourish comes in a variety of flavors, all conveniently microwaveable.

Firms should seek to fill gaps in geographic market coverage during the growth period. As a product gains market acceptance, new distribution outlets usually become easier to secure. Marketers sometimes move from an exclusive or a selective exposure to a more intensive network of dealers to achieve greater market penetration. Marketers must also make sure the physical distribution system is running efficiently so that customers' orders are processed accurately and delivered on time.

Promotion expenditures in the growth stage may be slightly lower than during the introductory stage, but are still large. As sales continue to increase, promotion costs should drop as a percentage of total sales, which contributes significantly to increased profits. Advertising messages should stress brand benefits.

11-4c Maturity

During the **maturity stage**, sales peak and start to level off or decline, and profits continue to fall (see Figure 11.2). This stage is characterized by intense competition because many brands are now in the market. Competitors emphasize improvements and differences in their versions of the product. Toothpaste is an example of a product that has many competitors and many variations available on the market. The advertisement for Crest toothpaste, a product in the maturity stage, emphasizes the luxurious nature of this particular product and its superior stain-removing capabilities. The ad also indicates that the toothpaste won a readers' choice award from *Allure* magazine, signaling a level of consumer support and trust in its efficacy. Weaker competitors are squeezed out of the market during this stage.

maturity stage The stage of a product's life cycle when the sales curve peaks and starts to decline, and profits continue to fall

During the maturity phase, the producers who remain in the market are likely to change their promotional and distribution efforts. Advertising and dealer-oriented promotions are typical during this stage of the product life cycle. Marketers also must take into account that as it reaches maturity, buyers' knowledge of the product is likely to be high. Consumers are no longer inexperienced generalists. They have become experienced specialists. Marketers of mature products sometimes expand distribution into global markets, in which case products may have to be adapted to fit differing needs of global customers more precisely. Thus, when automaker Honda wanted to branch into the Indian market it had to create diesel-powered versions of its compact cars because many consumers there preferred to drive cars with diesel engines.[10]

Because many products are in the maturity stage of their life cycles, marketers must know how to deal with them and be prepared to adjust their marketing strategies. There are many approaches to altering marketing strategies during the maturity stage. To increase the sales of mature products, marketers may suggest new uses for them. Maxwell House International Café instant coffee drinks, produced by Kraft Foods, have long been in the maturity stage. In an attempt to extend the product line's life span and to increase market share, Maxwell House marketers developed an advertising campaign that suggests using the sweetened instant flavored coffee drinks as coffee creamer for black coffee. The campaign utilizes print and online digital media to encourage consumers to send vintage-style postcards to their friends to spread the marketing message.[11]

As customers become more experienced and knowledgeable about products during the maturity stage (particularly about business products), the benefits they seek may change as well, necessitating product modifications. Consider Tide laundry detergent, a strong seller for more than 50 years. As consumers' lifestyles have changed and as men continue to contribute to more housework, the brand has released variations on its original products that are suited to modern lifestyles. For instance, the Tide Pod is a pre-proportioned capsule of laundry detergent, making it easier and more convenient to do the laundry and use the correct amount of product.[12]

Product Maturity
Crest 3D White Luxe highlights improved whitening power and variations from other kinds of toothpaste.

During the maturity stage, marketers actively encourage resellers to support the product. Resellers may be offered promotional assistance to lower their inventory costs. In general, marketers go to great lengths to serve resellers and provide incentives for displaying and selling their brand.

Maintaining market share during the maturity stage requires promotion expenditures, which can be large if a firm seeks to increase a product's market share through new uses. Advertising messages in this stage may focus on differentiating a brand from the field of competitors, and sales promotion efforts may be aimed at both consumers and resellers.

11-4d Decline

During the **decline stage**, sales fall rapidly (see Figure 11.2). When this happens, the marketer must consider eliminating items from the product line that no longer earn a profit. The marketer also may cut promotion efforts, eliminate marginal distributors, and finally, plan to phase out the product. This can be seen in the decline in demand for most carbonated beverages such as soda, which has been continuing for decades as consumers turn away from high-calorie soft drinks in favor of bottled teas and flavored waters.[13] This shift in consumer preference has changed the way companies produce and market bottled beverages, with companies expanding their offerings of juices, waters, and healthier drink options.

decline stage The stage of a product's life cycle when sales fall rapidly

Emerging Trends

These Aren't Your Daddy's Records

Vinyl LPs are back, reversing a long-standing decline and extending the life cycle. LPs enjoyed a meteoric rise as the standard technology for recorded music in the middle of the 20th century. As the decades passed, however, LPs were eclipsed by cassette tapes and then by CDs. Today, in the era of digital downloads, music fans and collectors are again buying vinyl, not only for the listening experience but also for the aesthetic appeal of the album artwork.

A growing number of contemporary bands like Daft Punk and the Black Keys are releasing new albums digitally as well as on vinyl. Music labels are also rereleasing older albums on vinyl, bringing past hits by the Beatles, the Talking Heads, and other performers to a new generation of fans who want to get into the groove.

Although digital downloads are by far the most popular music format, LP sales are increasing as CD sales drop year after year. U.S. consumers now buy more than 4 million LPs each year, a tiny percentage of the overall market. Still, this niche is attractive enough that Target, Whole Foods, Urban Outfitters, and other retailers carry a limited selection of LPs in their stores. The Boston-based retailer Newbury Comics never stopped stocking vinyl, even when the format was out of favor. It has profited by ordering albums made exclusively for its stores, such as special-edition LPs pressed on green vinyl, and reselling to buyers who value these as records and as collectors' items.[a]

In the decline stage, marketers must decide whether to reposition the product to extend its life, or whether it is better to eliminate it. Usually a declining product has lost its distinctiveness because similar competing or superior products have been introduced. Competition engenders increased substitution and brand switching among consumers as they become increasingly insensitive to minor product differences. For these reasons, marketers do little to change a product's style, design, or other attributes during its decline. New technology or social trends, product substitutes, or environmental considerations may also indicate that the time has come to delete the product.

During a product's decline, spending on promotion efforts is usually reduced considerably. Advertising of special offers and sales promotions, such as coupons and premiums, may slow the rate of decline temporarily. Firms will maintain outlets with strong sales volumes and eliminate unprofitable outlets. An entire marketing channel may be eliminated if it does not contribute adequately to profits. A channel not used previously, such as a factory outlet or Internet retailer, can help liquidate remaining inventory of a product that is being eliminated. As sales decline, the product becomes harder for consumers to find, but loyal buyers will seek out resellers who still carry it. As the product continues to decline, the sales staff at outlets where it is still sold will shift emphasis to more profitable products.

11-5 PRODUCT ADOPTION PROCESS

Acceptance of new products—especially new-to-the-world products—usually does not happen quickly. It can take a very long time for consumers to become aware of and overcome skepticism about a new product, particularly if it represents a dramatic innovation. Many consumers prefer to wait to adopt a new product until the "second generation," when kinks are more likely to have been worked out. Customers come to accept new products through an adoption process, detailed in Figure 11.3. The stages of the **product adoption process** are as follows:

product adoption process The five-stage process of buyer acceptance of a product: awareness, interest, evaluation, trial, and adoption

Awareness: The buyer becomes aware of the product.
Interest: The buyer seeks information and is receptive to learning about the product.
Evaluation: The buyer considers the product's benefits and decides whether to try it, considering its value versus the competition.

Figure 11.3 **Production Adoption Process**

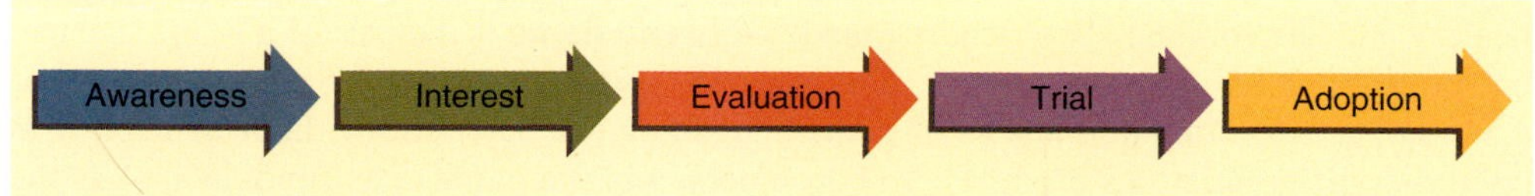

Trial: The buyer examines, tests, or tries the product to determine if it meets his or her needs.

Adoption: The buyer purchases the product and can be expected to use it again whenever the need for this product arises.[14]

In the first stage, when consumers initially become aware that the product exists, they possess little information and are not yet concerned about obtaining more. Consumers enter the interest stage when they become motivated to learn about the product's features, uses, advantages, disadvantages, price, or location. During the evaluation stage, individuals consider whether the product will address the criteria that are crucial to meeting their specific needs. In the trial stage, consumers use or experience the product for the first time, possibly by purchasing a small quantity, taking advantage of free samples, or borrowing the product from someone else. Individuals move into the adoption stage when they need a product of that general type and choose to purchase the new product on a trial basis. However, entering the adoption stage does not mean that the person will eventually adopt the new product. Rejection may occur at any stage. Both product adoption and product rejection can be temporary or permanent.

When an organization introduces a new product, consumers in the target market enter into and move through the adoption process at different rates. For most products, there is also a group of non-adopters who never begin the process. For business marketers, success in managing production innovation, diffusion, and adoption requires great adaptability and significant effort in understanding customers.[15]

Depending on the length of time it takes them to adopt a new product, consumers tend to fall into one of five major adopter categories: innovators, early adopters, early majority, late majority, and laggards.[16] **Innovators** are the first to adopt a new product because they enjoy trying new products and do not mind taking a risk. **Early adopters** choose new products carefully and are viewed as people who are in-the-know by those in the remaining adopter categories. People in the **early majority** adopt just prior to the average person. They are deliberate and cautious in trying new products. Individuals in the **late majority** are skeptical of new products, but eventually adopt them because of economic necessity or social pressure. **Laggards**, the last to adopt a new product, are oriented toward the past. They are suspicious of new products, and when they finally adopt them, it may already have been replaced by an even newer product.

Innovators First adopters of new products

early adopters People who adopt new products early, choose new products carefully, and are viewed as "the people to check with" by later adopters

early majority Individuals who adopt a new product just prior to the average person

late majority Skeptics who adopt new products when they feel it is necessary

laggards The last adopters, who distrust new products

brand A name, term, design, symbol, or other feature that identifies one seller's product as distinct from those of other sellers

11-6 BRANDING

Marketers must make many decisions about products, including choices about brands, brand names, brand marks, trademarks, and trade names. A **brand** is a name, term, design, symbol, or any other feature that identifies one marketer's product as distinct from those of other marketers. A brand may identify a single item, a family of items, or all items of that seller.[17] Some have defined a brand as not just the physical good, name, color, logo, or ad campaign, but everything associated with the product, including its symbolism and experiences.[18] Firms that try to shift the image of a brand risk losing market share. When the Gap brand moved away from its "American Classic" symbolic image in an attempt to change with the times, consumers lost interest and the brand suffered revenue losses. The Body Shop is a bath and body product brand that continues to be strong in spite of fierce competition, largely because of consistent brand messaging that creates an image of a very healthy and environmentally-friendly brand.[19] A **brand name** is the part of a brand that can be spoken—including letters, words, and numbers—such as 7UP or V8. A brand name is essential, as it is often a product's only distinguishing characteristic without which a firm could not differentiate its products. To consumers, a brand name is as fundamental as the product itself. Indeed, many brand names have become synonymous with the product, such as Scotch Tape, Xerox copiers, and Kleenex tissues. Marketers must make efforts, through promotional activities, to ensure that such brand names do not become generic terms, which are not protected under the law.

The element of a brand that is comprised of words—often a symbol or design—is a **brand mark**. Examples of brand marks include the McDonald's Golden Arches, Nike's "swoosh," and Apple's silhouette of an apple with a bite missing. A **trademark** is a legal designation indicating that the owner has exclusive use of a brand or a part of a brand and that others are prohibited by law from its use. To protect a brand name or brand mark in the United States, an organization must register it as a trademark with the U.S. Patent and Trademark Office. Finally, a **trade name** is the full and legal name of an organization, such as Ford Motor Company, rather than the name of a specific product.

11-6a Value of Branding

Both buyers and sellers benefit from branding. Brands help buyers identify specific products that meet their criteria for quality, which reduces the time needed to identify and purchase products by facilitating identification of products that satisfy consumer needs. Without brands, product selection would be more difficult because buyers would have fewer guideposts indicating quality and product features. For many consumers, purchasing certain brands is a form of self-expression. For instance, clothing brand names, such as Nike or Tommy Hilfiger, are important to many consumers because they convey signals about their lifestyle or self-image. Especially when a customer is unable to judge a product's quality, a brand indicates a quality level and image to the customer and reduces a buyer's perceived risk of purchase. Customers want to purchase brands whose quality they trust, such as Coca-Cola, Apple, and Panera. In addition, customers might receive a psychological reward from purchasing and owning a brand that symbolizes high status, such as Aston Martin or Chanel.

Sellers also benefit from branding because brands are identifiers that make repeat purchasing easier for customers, thereby fostering brand loyalty. Furthermore, branding helps a firm introduce a new product by carrying the name and image of one or more existing products—buyers are more likely to experiment with the new product because of familiarity with products carrying firm's existing brand names. It also facilitates promotional efforts because the promotion of each branded product indirectly promotes all other products bearing the same brand. As consumers become loyal to a specific brand, the company's market share will achieve a level of stability, allowing the firm to use its resources more efficiently.

Branding also involves a cultural dimension in that consumers confer their own social meanings onto them. A brand appeals to customers on an emotional level based on its symbolic image and key associations.[20] For some brands, such as Harley-Davidson and Apple, this can result in an almost cult-like following. These brands may develop communities of loyal customers that communicate through get-togethers, online forums, blogs, podcasts, and other means. They may even help consumers to develop their identity and self-concept and serve as a form of self-expression. In fact, the term *cultural branding* has been used to explain how a brand conveys a powerful myth that consumers find useful in cementing their identities.[21] It is also important for marketers to recognize that brands are not completely within their control because a brand exists independently in the consumer's mind.

brand name The part of a brand that can be spoken, including letters, words, and numbers

brand mark The part of a brand that is not made up of words, such as a symbol or design

trademark A legal designation of exclusive use of a brand

trade name The full legal name of an organization

Every aspect of a brand is subject to a consumer's emotional involvement, interpretation, and memory. By understanding how branding influences purchases, marketers can foster customer loyalty.[22]

11-6b Brand Equity

A well-managed brand is an asset to an organization. The value of this asset is often referred to as brand equity. **Brand equity** is the marketing and financial value associated with a brand's strength in a market. In addition to actual proprietary brand assets, such as patents and trademarks, four major elements underlie brand equity: brand name awareness, brand loyalty, perceived brand quality, and brand associations (see Figure 11.4).[23]

Being aware of a brand leads to brand familiarity, which results in a level of comfort with the brand. A consumer is more likely to select a familiar brand than an unfamiliar one because the familiar brand is more likely to be viewed as reliable and of an acceptable level of quality. The familiar brand is also likely to be in a customer's consideration set, whereas the unfamiliar brand is not.

Brand loyalty is a customer's favorable attitude toward a specific brand. If brand loyalty is sufficiently strong, customers will purchase the brand consistently when they need a product in that specific product category. Customer satisfaction with a brand is the most common reason for loyalty to that brand.[24] Brand loyalty has advantages for the customer as well as the manufacturer and seller. It reduces a buyer's risks and shortens the time spent deciding which product to purchase. The degree of brand loyalty is highly variable among product categories. For instance, it is challenging for a firm to foster brand loyalty for products such as fruits or vegetables, because customers can readily judge their quality by looking at them in the grocery store without referring to a brand. The rapid pace of technological change also presents challenges for marketers. With new computers, video games, and other digital devices entering the market at an ever more rapid pace, it can be difficult for marketers to maintain a high level of emotional engagement with consumers, and therefore maintain their loyalty from year to year.[25] Brand loyalty also varies by country, as different cultures may identify with a certain brand to a greater or lesser degree. Globally, international tech brands Apple, Sony, and Panasonic have a higher degree of brand loyalty than brands in other product categories.[26]

There are three degrees of brand loyalty: recognition, preference, and insistence. **Brand recognition** occurs when a customer is aware that the brand exists and views it as an alternative purchase if the preferred brand is unavailable or if the other available brands are unfamiliar. This is the weakest form of brand loyalty. **Brand preference** is a

brand equity The marketing and financial value associated with a brand's strength in a market

brand loyalty A customer's favorable attitude toward a specific brand

brand recognition The degree of brand loyalty in which a customer is aware that a brand exists and views the brand as an alternative purchase if their preferred brand is unavailable

brand preference The degree of brand loyalty in which a customer prefers one brand over competitive offerings

Figure 11.4 **Major Elements of Brand Equity**

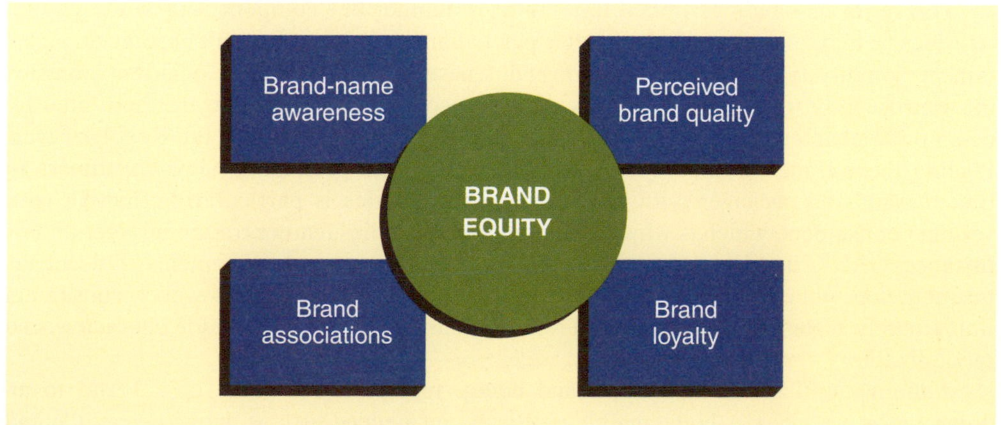

Perceived Quality
Marketers accentuate the quality of the Energizer brand and its long life, which supports the brand's higher price.

stronger degree of brand loyalty. A customer has a definite preference for one brand over competitive offerings, and will purchase this brand if it is available. However, if the brand is not available, the customer will accept a substitute rather than expending the additional effort required to find and purchase the preferred brand. **Brand insistence** is the strongest and least common level of brand loyalty. A customer will accept no substitute and is willing to spend a great deal of time and effort to acquire that brand. If a brand-insistent customer goes to a store and finds the brand unavailable, he or she will seek the brand elsewhere rather than purchase a substitute. Brand insistence also can apply to service products, such as Hilton Hotels, or sports teams, such as the Dallas Cowboys. Although rare, marketers aspire to achieve brand insistence.

Brand loyalty is an important component of brand equity because it reduces a brand's vulnerability to competitors' actions. It allows an organization to retain existing customers and avoid expending significant resources to gain new ones. Loyal customers help to promote a brand by providing visibility and reassuring potential new customers of the brand's quality. Retailers strive to carry the brands known for their strong customer following to satisfy customers because they expect these brands to be available when and where they shop.

Customers associate a particular brand with a certain level of overall quality. As mentioned, customers frequently use a brand name as a proxy for an actual assessment of a product's quality. Although Energizer batteries are not the cheapest on the market, they are considered to be of a higher quality than other battery brands. This advertisement underscores Energizer's reputation for high quality—emphasizing the long life of the batteries. To further underscore that Energizer is a good value, the ad points out that longer-lived batteries mean less battery waste. The image shows the iconic Energizer bunny dwarfed by a huge drum, representing the strong power of the battery brand. Perceived high brand quality helps to support a premium price, allowing a marketer to avoid severe price competition. Also, favorable perceived brand quality can ease the introduction of brand extensions because consumers' high regard for the brand is likely to translate into high regard for the related products.

The set of associations linked to a brand is another key component of brand equity. At times, a marketer works to connect a particular lifestyle or, in some instances, a certain personality type with a specific brand. These types of brand associations contribute significantly to the brand's equity. Brand associations sometimes are facilitated by using trade characters, such as the GEICO Gecko, Cap'n Crunch, and the Keebler Elves. Placing these trade characters in advertisements and on packaging helps consumers to link the ads and packages with the brands. This practice is particularly effective with younger consumers, which is why many cereals and candies feature trade characters.[27] For instance, GEICO usually portrays its gecko trade character in advertisements. This advertisement does not even feature a car in the image or in the large text. However, consumers immediately recognize that it is an ad for car insurance because the trade character is so recognizable.

brand insistence The degree of brand loyalty in which a customer strongly prefers a specific brand and will accept no substitute

Although difficult to measure, brand equity represents the value of a brand to an organization—it includes both tangible assets and intangibles such as public perception and consumer loyalty. Table 11.1 lists the top 10 brands with the highest economic value. Any company that owns a brand listed in Table 11.1 would agree that equity is likely to be the greatest single asset in the organization's possession.

11-6c Types of Brands

There are three categories of brands: manufacturer, private distributor, and generic. **Manufacturer brands** are initiated by producers and ensure that producers are identified with their products at the point of purchase—for example, Green Giant, Dell Computer, and Levi's jeans. A manufacturer brand usually requires a producer to become involved in distribution, promotion, and to some extent, pricing decisions.

Private distributor brands (also called *private brands, store brands,* or *dealer brands*) are initiated and owned by resellers—wholesalers or retailers. The major characteristic of private brands is that the manufacturers are not identified on the products. Retailers and wholesalers use private distributor brands to develop more efficient promotion, generate higher gross margins, and change store image. Private distributor brands give retailers or wholesalers freedom to purchase products of a specified quality at the lowest cost without disclosing the identities of the manufacturers. An example of a wholesaler brand is IGA (Independent Grocers' Alliance). Successful private brands are distributed nationally, and many rival the quality of manufacturer brands. Familiar retailer brand names include Target's Archer Farms and Up and Up, Walmart's Great Value, and Whole Foods' 365 Everyday Value. Sometimes retailers with successful private distributor brands start manufacturing their own products to gain more control over product costs, quality, and design in the

Trade Character
The GEICO gecko is a highly recognizable trade character, even among those who do not use GEICO insurance products.

Table 11.1 **The 10 Most Valuable Brands in the World**

Rank	Brand	Brand Value ($ Millions)
1	Apple	185,071
2	Google	113,669
3	IBM	112,536
4	McDonald's	90,256
5	Coca-Cola	78,415
6	AT&T	75,507
7	Microsoft	69,814
8	Marlboro	69,383
9	Visa	56,060
10	China Mobile	55,368

Source: WWP, *Brandz Top 100 Most Valuable Global Brands 2013*, p. 14.

manufacturer brands A brand initiated by producers to ensure that producers are identified with their products at the point of purchase

private distributor brands A brand initiated and owned by a reseller

hope of increasing profits. Sales of private labels have grown considerably as the quality of store brands has increased. More than 40 percent of shoppers consider themselves frequent buyers of store brands, which accounts for more than $108 billion in revenue at supermarkets, drugstores, and mass merchandisers.[28]

Some products, on the other hand, are not branded at all, which is often called *generic branding*. **Generic brands** indicate only the product category and do not include the company name or other identifying terms. These items are typically staples that would be marketed using an undifferentiated strategy because they lack special features, such as sugar, salt, or aluminum foil. Generic brands usually are sold at lower prices than comparable branded items and compete on the basis of price and value. The prevalence of generic brands has decreased over time, particularly as the quality and value of private brands has increased.

11-6d Selecting a Brand Name

Marketers consider several factors in selecting a brand name. First, the name should be easy for customers (including foreign buyers if the firm intends to market its products in other countries) to say, spell, and recall. Short, one-syllable names, such as Cheer, often satisfy this requirement. Second, the brand name should indicate in some way the product's major benefits and, if possible, should suggest the product's uses and special characteristics. Marketers should always avoid negative or offensive references. Thus, the brand names of household cleaning products such as Ajax dishwashing liquid, Vanish toilet bowl cleaner, Formula 409 multipurpose cleaner, Cascade dishwasher detergent, and Wisk laundry detergent connote strength and effectiveness. There is evidence that consumers are more likely to recall and to evaluate favorably names that convey positive attributes or benefits.[29] Third, to set it apart from competing brands, the brand should be distinctive. Further research findings have shown that creating a brand personality that aligns with the products sold and the target market's self-image is important to brand success—if the target market feels aligned with the brand, they are more likely to develop brand loyalty.[30] If a marketer intends to use a brand for a product line, that brand must be compatible with all products in the line. Finally, a brand should be designed to be used and recognized in all types of media. Finding the right brand has become an increasingly challenging task because many obvious names have already been used.

Marketers can devise brand names from single or multiple words—for example, Dodge Nitro. Letters and numbers, alone or in combination, are used to create such brands as the Honda CR-V or Toshiba's KIRAbook 13 computer. Words, numbers, and letters are combined to yield brand names, such as Apple iPhone 5s or BMW's 528i xDrive sedan. To avoid terms that have negative connotations, marketers sometimes use fabricated words that have absolutely no meaning when created—for example Häagen-Dazs.

Who actually creates brand names? Brand names are generally created by individuals or a team within the organization. Sometimes a name is suggested by individuals who are close to the development of the product. Some organizations have committees that participate in brand-name creation and approval. Large companies that introduce numerous new products annually are likely to have a department that develops brand names. At times, outside consultants and companies that specialize in brand-name development are used.

11-6e Protecting a Brand

A marketer should also design a brand that can be protected easily through registration. A series of court decisions has created a broad hierarchy of protection based on brand type. From most protectable to least protectable, these brand types are fanciful (Exxon), arbitrary (Dr Pepper), suggestive (Spray'n Wash), and descriptive (Minute Rice). Generic brands, such as aluminum foil, are not protectable. Surnames and descriptive, geographic, or functional names are difficult to protect.[31] However, research findings show that consumers prefer these descriptive and suggestive brand names and find them easier to recall compared with fanciful

generic brands A brand indicating only the product category

and arbitrary brand names.[32] A firm should take steps so that its brands are protected and trademarks are renewed as needed.

To guard its exclusive rights to a brand, a company must ensure that the brand is not likely to be considered an infringement on any brand already registered with the U.S. Patent and Trademark Office. Patent infringement cases are at a record high, in part because the Internet allows for easier searching of possible infringement cases. Patent assertion entities buy up vaguely-worded patents and then scour the Internet for businesses that might be perceived of infringing on these patents. They send out letters to unsuspecting companies demanding licensing fees for continued use of the patent. The issue has become such a problem that Congress has started to hear cases that would make it easier for victims of these entities to recoup legal fees.[33] Actually proving that patent infringement has occurred may be complex because infringement is determined by the courts, which base their decisions on whether a brand causes consumers to be confused, mistaken, or deceived about the source of the product. McDonald's is the company probably most famous for aggressively protecting its trademarks against infringement by launching legal charges against a number of companies with *Mc* names. It fears that use of the prefix will give consumers the impression that these companies are associated with or owned by McDonald's.

A marketer should guard against allowing a brand name to become a generic term because these cannot be protected as exclusive brand names. For example, *aspirin*, *escalator*, and *shredded wheat*—all brand names at one time—eventually were declared generic terms that refer to product classes. Thus, they could no longer be protected. To keep a brand name from becoming a generic term, the firm should spell the name with a capital letter and use it as an adjective to modify the name of the general product class and include the word *brand* after the brand name, as in Kool-Aid Brand Soft Drink Mix or Kleenex Brand Tissues.[34] An organization can deal with this problem directly by advertising that its brand is a trademark and should not be used generically. The firm also can indicate that the brand is a registered trademark by using the symbol ®.

A U.S. firm that tries to protect a brand in a foreign country is likely to encounter additional problems. In many countries, brand registration is not possible. In such places, the first firm to use a brand in such a country automatically has the rights to it. In some instances, U.S. companies actually have had to buy their own brand rights from a firm in a foreign country because the foreign firm was the first user in that country.

Marketers trying to protect their brands also must contend with brand counterfeiting. In the United States, for instance, one can purchase counterfeit General Motors parts, Cartier and Rolex watches, Louis Vuitton handbags, Walt Disney character dolls, Microsoft software, Warner Brothers clothing, Mont Blanc pens, and a host of other products illegally marketed by manufacturers that do not own the brands. Annual trade losses caused by counterfeit products are estimated at $360 billion globally.[35] In the wake of financial crises that have spread across Europe, counterfeiting in the food and beverage industry has become common. Investigators have uncovered thousands of cases of fraudulent products entering the market, and even established and trusted brands are not safe. They have found incidences of adulterated wine and spirits, chocolate, olive oil, and beef, among many other products.[36]

11-6f Branding Strategies

Before establishing branding strategies, a firm must decide whether to brand its products at all. If a company's product is homogeneous and is similar to competitors' products, it may be difficult to brand in a way that will result in consumer loyalty. Raw materials and commodities such as coal, carrots, or gravel are hard to brand because of their homogeneity and their physical characteristics.

If a firm chooses to brand its products, it may use individual or family branding, or a combination. **Individual branding** is a policy of naming each product differently. Nestlé S.A., the world's largest food and nutrition company, uses individual branding for many of its 6,000 different brands, such as Nescafé coffee, PowerBar nutritional food, Maggi soups, and

individual branding
A branding strategy in which each product is given a different name

Häagen-Dazs ice cream. A major advantage of individual branding is that, if an organization introduces an inferior product, the negative images associated with it do not influence consumers' decisions to purchase the company's other products. An individual branding strategy may also facilitate market segmentation when a firm wishes to enter many segments of the same market. Separate, unrelated names can be used, and each brand can be aimed at a specific segment. With individual branding, however, a firm cannot capitalize on the positive image associated with successful products.

When using **family branding**, all of a firm's products are branded with the same name, or part of the name, such as the cereals Kellogg's Frosted Flakes, Kellogg's Rice Krispies, and Kellogg's Corn Flakes. In some cases, a company's name is combined with other words, such as with Arm & Hammer Heavy Duty Detergent, Arm & Hammer Pure Baking Soda, and Arm & Hammer Carpet Deodorizer, which uses the "Arm & Hammer" name followed by a description. Unlike individual branding, family branding means that the promotion of one item with the family brand promotes the firm's other products.

Family branding can be a benefit when consumers have positive associations with brands, or a drawback if something happens to make consumers think negatively of the brand. For example, Johnson's Baby, a brand produced by Johnson & Johnson, was criticized for putting potentially harmful chemicals in some of its products, causing some health-conscious consumers to mistrust all the products carrying the brand name. In response to consumer outrage, Johnson & Johnson reformulated the products, restoring trust in the entire family of products.[37]

An organization is not limited to a single branding strategy. A company that uses primarily individual branding for many of its products also may use family branding for a specific product line. Branding strategy is influenced by the number of products and product lines the company produces, the number and types of competing products available, and the size of the firm.

11-6g Brand Extensions

A **brand extension** occurs when an organization uses one of its existing brands to brand a new product in a different product category. For example, HGTV, the home and garden cable channel, extended its brand with the HGTV HOME plant collection, available at garden centers nationwide.[38] A brand extension should not be confused with a line extension, which will be discussed in greater detail in Chapter 12. A line extension refers to using an existing brand on a new product in the same product category, such as new flavors or sizes. For example, when Gatorade introduced Gatorade Frost beverage, featuring different flavors than the Original Gatorade, these products represented a line extension because they were in the same category.[39]

If a brand is extended too many times or extended too far outside its original product category, it can be weakened through dilution of its image and symbolic impact. For example, Zippo, the company known for high-quality lighters, extended its brand into writing implements, camping supplies, and women's fragrances. Research has found that a line extension into premium categories can be an effective strategy to revitalize a brand, but the extension needs to be closely linked to the core brand.[40] Other research supports this by suggesting that diluting a brand by extending it into dissimilar product categories can suppress consumer consideration and choice for the original products carrying the brand.[41] Table 11.2 describes brand extensions that failed because they were too dissimilar to their core product.

family branding Branding all of a firm's products with the same name or part of the name

brand extension An organization uses one of its existing brands to brand a new product in a different product category

co-branding Using two or more brands on one product

11-6h Co-Branding

Co-branding is the use of two or more brands on one product. Marketers employ co-branding to capitalize on the brand equity of multiple brands. Co-branding is popular in several processed-food categories and in the credit card industry. The brands used for co-branding can be owned by the same company. For instance, Benjamin Moore partnered with the retailer, Target, to release a co-branded line of paint colors that coordinate with Target's kids' furniture

Table 11.2 **Worst Brand Extensions**

Brand Name	Core Product	Failed Brand Extension
Smith & Wesson	Firearms	Mountain Bikes
Bic	Pens	Bic Underwear
Cosmopolitan	Magazine	Yogurt
Wrigley	Candy	Life Savers Soda
Coors	Beer	Rocky Mountain Spring Water
Colgate	Consumer products	Colgate Kitchen Entrees
Frito-Lay	Snack foods	Lemonade
Harley-Davidson	Motorcycles	Perfume

Source: "Top 25 Biggest Product Flops of All Time," *DailyFinance*, www.dailyfinance.com/photos/top-25-biggest-product-flops-of-all-time (accessed December 7, 2013).

and accessories collection.[42] Many food items are co-branded initially. Cinnabon has released co-branded items with Kellogg's (cereal) and Pillsbury (Toaster Strudel).

Effective co-branding capitalizes on the trust and confidence customers have in the brands involved. The brands should not lose their identities, and it should be clear to customers which brand is the main brand. Nissan hopes to gain more traction in the truck market with a co-branded model featuring a Cummins diesel engine. Cummins is known for offering high-powered and high-quality engines, and Nissan expects this will make its Titan truck model more appealing to discerning consumers.[43] It is important for marketers to understand before entering a co-branding relationship that when a co-branded product is unsuccessful, both brands are implicated in the failure. To gain customer acceptance, the brands involved must represent a complementary fit in the minds of buyers. Trying to link a brand such as Harley-Davidson with a brand such as Healthy Choice would not achieve co-branding objectives because customers are not likely to perceive these brands as compatible.

11-6i Brand Licensing

A popular branding strategy involves **brand licensing**, an agreement in which a company permits another organization to use its brand on other products for a licensing fee. Royalties may be as low as 2 percent of wholesale revenues or higher than 10 percent. The licensee is responsible for all manufacturing, selling, and advertising functions and bears the costs if the licensed product fails. The top U.S. licensing company is Disney Consumer Products, the products arm of the Walt Disney Company, with $39.3 billion in licensing revenue.[44] Sports is an industry that engages in much licensing, with the NFL, the NCAA, NASCAR, and Major League Baseball all leaders in the retail sales of licensed sports-related products. The advantages of licensing range from extra revenues and the low cost of brand expansion to generating free publicity, developing a new image, or protecting a trademark. The major disadvantages are a lack of manufacturing control and the risks of making consumers feel bombarded with too many unrelated products bearing the same name.

11-7 PACKAGING

Packaging involves the development of a container to hold a product. A package can be a vital part of a product, making it more versatile, safer, and easier to use. It also conveys vital information about the product and is an opportunity to display interesting graphic design elements. Like a brand name, a package can influence customers' attitudes toward a product and

brand licensing An agreement whereby a company permits another organization to use its brand on other products for a licensing fee

their decisions to buy an item. Consequently, packaging convenience can be a major factor in purchase. Producers of jellies, sauces, and ketchups package their products in squeezable plastic containers that can be stored upside down, which make dispensing and storing the product more convenient. Package characteristics help to shape buyers' impressions of a product at the time of purchase and during use. In this section, we examine the main functions of packaging and consider several major packaging decisions. We also analyze the role of the package in a marketing strategy.

11-7a Packaging Functions

Effective packaging involves more than simply putting products in containers and covering them with wrappers. Packaging materials first and foremost serve the basic purpose of protecting the product and maintaining its functional form. Fluids, like milk or orange juice, require packages that are waterproof and durable to preserve and protect their contents. Packaging should prevent damage that could affect the product's usefulness, which leads to higher costs. Packaging techniques have also been developed to prevent product tampering, as this has been a major problem for many firms. Some packages are also designed to deter shoplifting through the inclusion of antitheft devices.

Another function of packaging is to offer convenience to consumers. For instance, single-serving containers for food and drinks that do not require refrigeration appeal to children, parents, and those with active lifestyles because they are easily portable. Packaging can prevent product waste, make storage easier for retailers and for consumers, and even promote greater consumption. Another function of packaging is to promote a product by communicating its features, uses, benefits, and image. Sometimes a reusable package can make the product more desirable. Some Puma shoes, for instance, are packaged in a tote bag. This packaging system reduces shoebox waste, energy expended in packaging production, is lighter and cheaper to ship, and provides consumers with a reusable bag, which is recyclable but can also be used as a small shopping or gym bag.[45] Finally, packaging can be used to communicate symbolically the quality or premium nature of a product. It can also evoke an emotional response.

11-7b Major Packaging Considerations

Marketers must take many factors into account when designing and producing packages. Obviously, a major consideration is cost. Although a number of different packaging materials, processes, and designs are available, costs can vary greatly. In recent years, buyers have shown a willingness to pay more for improved packaging, but there are limits. Marketers should conduct research to determine exactly how much customers are willing to pay for effective and efficient package designs.

Increasingly, firms are finding that they can cut down on the cost of packaging and be more environmentally-friendly through developing minimalist packaging. Redesigned packaging requires fewer materials, is easier and cheaper to ship because it is lighter, and consumers appreciate the lower carbon footprint. Kraft Foods saved more than a million pounds of packaging a year simply by redesigning the zipper on its bags of pre-grated cheese.[46]

As mentioned previously, developing tamper-resistant packaging is very important for certain products. Although no package is completely tamperproof, marketers can develop packages that are difficult to contaminate. At a minimum, all packaging must comply with the Food and Drug Administration's packaging regulations. However, packaging should also make any product tampering evident to resellers and consumers. Although effective tamper-resistant packaging may be expensive to develop, when compared to the potential costs of lost sales, loss of consumer confidence and company reputation, and potentially expensive product liability lawsuits, the costs of ensuring consumer safety through safer packaging are relatively small.

Marketers should consider how much consistency is desirable between the package designs of different products produced by an organization. If a firm's products are unrelated or aimed at very different target markets, no consistency may be the best policy. In many cases, however, packaging uniformity may be best, especially if a firm's products are unrelated or aimed at vastly different target markets. To promote an overall company image, a firm may decide that all packages should be similar or should all feature a major design element. This approach is called **family packaging**. It is generally used for lines of products, as with Campbell's soups, Weight Watchers' foods, or Planters Nuts.

A package's promotional role is an important consideration. Through verbal and nonverbal symbols, the package can inform potential buyers about the product's content, features, uses, advantages, and hazards. Pangea Organics, for instance, shows its commitment to natural ingredients and sustainability by packaging its soaps in containers embedded with seeds. Its boxes are made of recycled ingredients that, when buried in the ground, yield a plant such as a basil or a spruce tree. Packaged in sleek grey boxes with pleasing design features, the label on Pangea's soaps clearly display this creative means of promoting the firm's product and commitment to the cause of sustainability.[47]

A firm can create desirable images and associations by its choice of color, design, shape, and texture. Many cosmetics manufacturers, for example, design their packages to create impressions of luxury and exclusivity. A package performs a promotional function when it is designed to be safer or more convenient to use if such characteristics help stimulate demand.

A package designer must consider size, shape, texture, color, and graphics—as well as functionality—to develop a package that has a definite promotional value. Clever design can make a package appear taller or shorter or larger or smaller, depending on the desire of the marketer and expectations of consumers.

Marketers often carefully consider what colors to use on packages to attract attention and positively influence customers' emotions. People associate specific colors with certain feelings and experiences. Here are some examples:

- White represents sincerity, simplicity, and purity.
- Yellow is associated with cheerfulness, optimism, and friendliness.
- Red connotes excitement and stimulation.
- Pink is considered soft, nurturing, and feminine.
- Blue is soothing; it is also associated with intelligence, trust, and security.
- Black represents power, status, and sophistication.
- Purple is associated with dignity, quality, and luxury.
- Brown is linked to seriousness, ruggedness, and earthiness.
- Green is associated with nature and sustainability.[48]

When opting for color on packaging, marketers must judge whether a particular color will evoke positive or negative feelings when linked to a specific product. Thus, marketers are not likely to package meat or bread in green materials because customers may associate green with mold. Marketers must also determine whether a specific target market will respond favorably or unfavorably to a color.

Packaging also must meet the needs of resellers. Wholesalers and retailers consider whether a package facilitates transportation, storage, and handling. Resellers may refuse to carry certain products if their packages are cumbersome or require too much shelf space. For instance, concentrated versions of laundry detergents and fabric softeners aid retailers and shoppers alike by offering products in smaller containers that are easier to transport, store, and display.

A final consideration is whether to develop packages that are viewed as environmentally responsible. Nearly one-half of all garbage consists of discarded plastic packaging, such as polystyrene containers, plastic soft-drink bottles, and carryout bags. Plastic packaging material does not biodegrade, and paper requires the destruction of valuable forests. Consequently, many companies have changed to environmentally sensitive packaging that is recycled, lighter weight, and uses fewer materials.

family packaging Using similar packaging for all of a firm's products or packaging that has one common design element

Packaging and Marketing Strategy
Offering a range of packaging options that address the different needs of consumers helps Green Mountain Coffee increase sales and customer loyalty.

11-7c Packaging and Marketing Strategy

Packaging can be a major component of a marketing strategy. A new cap or closure, a better box or wrapper, or a more convenient container may give a product a competitive advantage. The right type of package for a new product can help it gain market recognition very quickly. This advertisement for Green Mountain Coffee emphasizes the quality and satisfaction the product can bring, showing someone holding a cup of coffee against a beautiful landscape. The advertisement also emphasizes the different types of packaging in which the coffee is sold, which underscores the range of options available to consumers. If consumers prefer freshly ground coffee, they can purchase the bags. If they like convenience or variety, Keurig K-Cups allow consumers to brew a single serving of coffee in a matter of seconds.

In the case of existing brands, marketers should reevaluate packages periodically. Marketers should view packaging as a strategic tool, especially for consumer convenience products. When considering the strategic uses of packaging, marketers must also analyze the cost of packaging and package changes. In this section, we will examine several ways to use packaging strategically in marketing efforts.

Altering the Package

At times, a marketer changes a package or labeling because the existing design is no longer in style, especially when compared with the packaging of competitive products. Faced with flat sales and criticisms about the poor nutritional profile of many of its food items, McDonald's revamped its menu and its packaging. The new food packaging has a more appealing design. It emphasizes fruits and vegetables and how they can be fun and delicious.[49] A package may be redesigned because new product features need to be highlighted or because new packaging materials have become available. Cleaning supply company Seventh Generation sells its 4× concentrated laundry detergent in a paper bottle, which encloses a plastic shell. The design is innovative, completely recyclable, and requires fewer materials to make.[50]

An organization may also decide to change a product's packaging to make the product safer or more convenient to use. NatureSweet, for example, altered the package for its cherry tomatoes when it introduced a clear plastic container to replace its red mesh bag packaging. The new packaging is more sustainable, makes the product more visible to the consumer, provides greater protection for the tomatoes during transport and handling, and limits ventilation, which increases shelf life.[51]

Secondary-Use Packaging

A secondary-use package can be reused for purposes other than its initial function. For example, a margarine container can be reused to store leftovers, and a jelly container can serve as a drinking glass. Customers often view secondary-use packaging as adding value to products, in which case its use should stimulate unit sales.

Going Green

Goodbye Styrofoam Peanuts, Hello Mushroom Molds!

When the retailer Crate and Barrel ships room dividers, it cushions the corners against damage with foam-like packaging made from the filaments of mushrooms. When the computer manufacturer Dell ships laptops, it encases them in packaging made from pulped bamboo. These are only two examples of how businesses are going green by substituting eco-friendly packaging made from plants for traditional packaging that doesn't biodegrade as quickly or easily.

The mushroom-based packaging used by Crate and Barrel starts as strands that are grown inside custom-made shaped molds. The strands expand to fill the mold's size and shape within a few days, and then the packaging is dried to kill the fungus. Now the "foam" cushions are ready to be fitted over the corners of furniture to protect products in transit. Best of all, the packaging is compostable or can be broken down for mulch, which means less waste clogging landfills for years to come.

Dell, which has manufacturing plants in China, has been testing bamboo packaging for some time. Bamboo is a fast-growing, renewable resource available in abundance in China. The company experimented with pulping the bamboo and drying it inside molds to ensure strength and durability without compromising recyclability. After independent tests confirmed that the bamboo packaging composts properly, Dell began using it to protect laptops shipped from its Chinese factories to warehouses and stores throughout the world.[b]

Category-Consistent Packaging

With category-consistent packaging, the product is packaged in line with the packaging practices associated with a particular product category. Some product categories—for example, mayonnaise, mustard, ketchup, and peanut butter—have traditional package shapes. Other product categories are characterized by recognizable color combinations, such as red and white for soup and red, white, and blue for Ritz-like crackers. When an organization introduces a brand in one of these product categories, marketers will often use traditional package shapes and color combinations to ensure that customers will recognize the new product as being in that specific product category.

Innovative Packaging

Sometimes a marketer employs a unique cap, design, applicator, or other feature to make a product distinctive. Such packaging can be effective when the innovation makes the product safer, easier to use, or provides better protection. Marketers also use innovative or unique packages that are inconsistent with traditional packaging practices to make the brand stand out from its competitors. Basing their packaging on research findings that wine drinkers tend to decide which product to purchase in the store, not in advance, Stack Wine offers its products in unique single-serve cups. The cups are filled with wine, sealed, and come stacked together in four packs. The unique packaging is eye-catching and practical, designed for parties, camping, or other situations where wine glasses are not readily available. It is also a convenient product for the occasional wine drinker, who may not want to open an entire bottle just to have one glass.[52] Unusual packaging sometimes requires expending considerable resources, not only when designing the package but also on making customers aware of the unique package and why it is an improvement. Researchers suggest that uniquely shaped packages that attract attention are likely to be perceived as containing a higher volume of product than comparable products that generate less attention.[53]

Multiple Packaging

Rather than packaging a single unit of a product, marketers sometimes use twin packs, tri-packs, six-packs, or other forms of multiple packaging. For certain types of products, multiple

Innovative Packaging
Using vacuum-sealed packaging is an innovative way to preserve the freshness of apples with minimal waste.

packaging may increase demand because it increases the amount of the product available at the point of consumption (e.g., in one's house). It may also increase consumer acceptance of the product by encouraging the buyer to try the product several times. Multiple packaging can make products easier to handle and store, as in the case of six-packs for soft drinks, and it can facilitate special price offers, such as two-for-one sales. However, multiple packaging does not work well for all types of products. One would not use additional table salt, for example, simply because an extra box is in the pantry.

Handling-Improved Packaging

A product's packaging may be changed to make it easier to handle in the distribution channel—for example, by altering the outer carton or using special bundling, shrink-wrapping, or pallets. In some cases, the shape of the package itself is changed. An ice cream producer, for instance, may adopt a rectangular-shaped package over a cylindrical one to facilitate handling. In addition, at the retail level, the ice cream producer may be able to get more shelf facings with a rectangular package than with a round one. Outer containers for products are sometimes altered so they will proceed more easily through automated warehousing systems.

11-8 LABELING

Labeling is very closely related with packaging and is used for identification, promotional, informational, and legal purposes. Labels can be small or large relative to the size of the product and carry varying amounts of information. The stickers on a banana or apple, for example, are small and display only the brand name of the fruit, the type, and perhaps a stock-keeping unit number. A label can be part of the package itself or a separate feature attached to the package. The label on a can of Coke is actually part of the can, whereas the label on a two-liter bottle of Coke is separate and can be removed. Information presented on a label may include the brand name and mark, the registered trademark symbol, package size and content, product features, nutritional information, presence of allergens, type

labeling Providing identifying, promotional, or other information on package labels

© iStockphoto.com/Oehoeboeroe

Labeling as Marketing Strategy
Labeling can be an important part of the marketing strategy. The label can be attached to the packaging to communicate that the product is eco-friendly. Labeling can include claims about sustainability as well as other information that is potentially valuable to the buyer.

and style of the product, number of servings, care instructions, directions for use and safety precautions, the name and address of the manufacturer, expiration dates, seals of approval, and other facts.

Labels can facilitate the identification of a product by displaying the brand name in combination with a unique graphic design. For instance, Heinz ketchup and Coca-Cola are both easy to identify on a supermarket shelf because of their iconic labels, which feature the name and recognizable brand marks. By drawing attention to products and their benefits, labels can strengthen an organization's promotional efforts. Labels may contain promotional messages, such as "Thirty percent more at no additional cost." Also, a label might be about a new or improved product feature, such as "New, improved scent."

Several federal laws and regulations specify information that must be included on the labels of certain products. Garments must be labeled with the name of the manufacturer, country of manufacture, fabric content, and cleaning instructions. Labels on nonedible items, such as shampoos and detergents, must include both safety precautions and directions for use. The Nutrition Labeling Act of 1990 requires the FDA to review food labeling and packaging for nutrition content, label format, ingredient labeling, food descriptions, and health messages. Any food product making a nutritional claim must follow standardized nutrition labeling. Food product labels must state the number of servings per container, serving size, number of calories per serving, number of calories derived from fat, number of carbohydrates, and amounts of specific nutrients such as vitamins. Many firms that used to feature the word "Natural" on their product labels are retracting that claim in an effort to protect themselves from lawsuits. "Natural" Goldfish crackers have returned to being just Goldfish while Puffins cereal and Naked juice have both removed "All Natural" claims from their labels. Though natural food products are profitable, bringing in more than $40 billion in annual U.S. retail sales, the claim is problematic because there are no regulations for what is natural. Unilever, Ben & Jerry's, and Kashi are just few of many companies that have been taken to court over their "Natural" claims. Until the Food

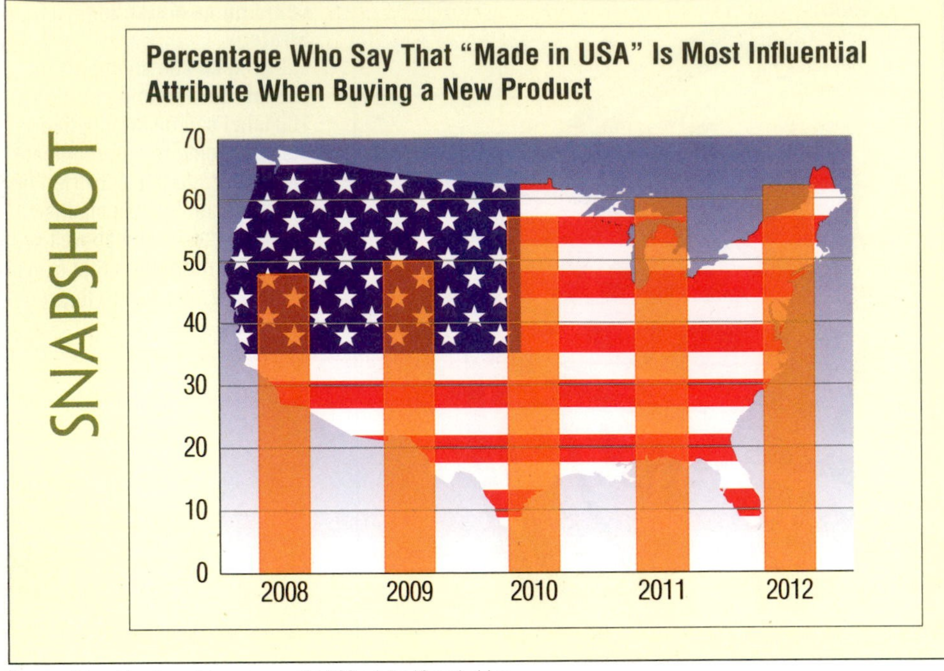

Source: Schneider Associates survey of 1,009 adults 18 and older.

and Drug Administration issues clearer guidelines for what constitutes natural ingredients, it is likely that more companies will change their labels to downplay their "natural" ingredients.[54]

Another concern for many manufacturers are the Federal Trade Commission's (FTC) guidelines regarding "Made in USA" labels, a problem owing to the increasingly global nature of manufacturing. Many countries attach high brand value to American-made brands, including Russia, India, Brazil, and China, giving U.S. firms an even greater incentive to adopt the "Made in USA" label.[55] The FTC requires that "all or virtually all" of a product's components be made in the United States if the label says "Made in USA." The "Made in USA" labeling issue remains complicated, as so many products involve parts sourced, produced, or assembled in places around the globe. Because business shows little sign of becoming less international, the FTC criteria for "Made in USA" are likely to be challenged and may be changed or adapted over time.[56]

Summary

11-1 Explain the concept of a product.

A product is a good, a service, an idea, or any combination of the three received in an exchange. It can be either tangible or intangible and includes functional, social, and psychological utilities or benefits. When consumers purchase a product, they are buying the benefits and satisfaction they think the product will provide.

11-2 Discuss how products are classified.

Products can be classified on the basis of the buyer's intentions. Consumer products are those purchased to satisfy personal and family needs. Business products are purchased for use in a firm's operations, to resell, or to make other products. Consumer products can be subdivided into convenience, shopping, specialty, and unsought products. Business products can be classified as installations, accessory equipment, raw materials, component parts, process materials, MRO supplies, and business services.

11-3 Explain the concepts of product line and product mix and how they are related.

A product item is a specific version of a product that can be designated as a distinct offering among an organization's products. A product line is a group of closely related product items that are considered a unit because of marketing, technical, or end-use considerations. The composite, or total, group of products that an organization makes available to customers is called the product mix. The width of the product mix is measured by the number of product lines the company offers. The depth of the product mix is the average number of different products offered in each product line.

11-4 Describe the product life cycle and its impact on marketing strategies.

The product life cycle describes how product items in an industry move through four stages: introduction, growth, maturity, and decline. The sales curve is at zero at introduction, rises at an increasing rate during growth, peaks during the maturity stage, and then declines. Profits peak toward the end of the growth stage of the product life cycle.

11-5 Discuss the product adoption process.

When customers accept a new product, they usually do so through a five-stage adoption process. The first stage is awareness, when buyers become aware that a product exists. Interest, the second stage, occurs when buyers seek information and are receptive to learning about the product. The third stage is evaluation—buyers consider the product's benefits and decide whether to try it. The fourth stage is trial, during which buyers examine, test, or try the product to determine if it meets their needs. The last stage is adoption, when buyers purchase the product and use it whenever a need for this general type of product arises.

11-6 Explain the major components of branding, including brand types, branding strategies, and brand protection.

A brand is a name, term, design, symbol, or any other feature that identifies one seller's good or service and distinguishes it from those of other sellers. Branding helps buyers to identify and evaluate products, helps sellers to facilitate product introduction and repeat purchasing, and fosters brand loyalty. Brand equity is the marketing and financial value associated with a brand's strength. It represents the value of a brand to an organization. The four major elements underlying brand equity include brand name awareness, brand loyalty, perceived brand quality, and brand associations.

There are three degrees of brand loyalty. Brand recognition occurs when a customer is aware that the brand exists and views it as an alternative purchase if the preferred brand is unavailable or if the other available brands are unfamiliar. Brand preference is a stronger degree of brand loyalty. Brand insistence is the strongest and least common level of brand loyalty

A manufacturer brand is initiated by a producer. A private distributor brand is initiated and owned by a reseller, sometimes taking on the name of the store or distributor. A generic brand indicates only the product category and does not include the company name or other identifying terms. When selecting a brand name, a marketer should choose one that is easy to say, spell, and recall and that alludes to the product's uses, benefits, or special characteristics. Brand names can be devised from words, letters, numbers, nonsense words, or a combination of these. Companies protect ownership of their brands through registration with the U.S. Patent and Trademark Office.

Individual branding designates a unique name for each of a company's products. Family branding identifies all of a firm's products with a single name. A brand extension is the use of an existing name on a new or improved product in a different product category. Co-branding is the use of two or more brands on one product. Through a licensing agreement and for a licensing fee, a firm may permit another organization to use its brand on other products. Brand licensing enables producers to earn extra revenue, receive low-cost or free publicity, and protect their trademarks.

11-7 Describe the major packaging functions, design considerations, and how packaging is used in marketing strategies.

Packaging involves the development of a container and a graphic design for a product. Effective packaging offers protection, economy, safety, and convenience. It can influence a customer's purchase decision by promoting features, uses, benefits, and image. When developing a package, marketers must consider the value to the customer of efficient and effective packaging, offset by the price the customer is willing to pay. Other considerations include how to make the package tamper resistant, whether to use multiple packaging and family packaging, how to design the package as an effective promotional tool, and how best to accommodate resellers. Packaging can be an important part of an overall marketing strategy and can be used to target certain market segments. Modifications in packaging can revive a mature product and extend its product life cycle. Producers alter packages to convey new features or to make them safer or more convenient. If a package has a secondary use, the product's value to the consumer may increase. Innovative packaging enhances a product's distinctiveness.

11-8 Identify the functions of labeling and legal issues related to labeling.

Labeling is closely interrelated with packaging and is used for identification, promotional, and informational and legal purposes. Various federal laws and regulations require that certain products be labeled or marked with warnings, instructions, nutritional information, manufacturer's identification, and perhaps other information.

Go to www.cengagebrain.com for resources to help you master the content in this chapter as well as for materials that will expand your marketing knowledge!

Developing Your Marketing Plan

Identifying the needs of consumer groups and developing products that satisfy those needs are essential when creating a marketing strategy. Successful product development begins with a clear understanding of fundamental product concepts. The product concept is the basis on which many of the marketing plan decisions are made. When relating the information in this chapter to the development of your marketing plan, consider the following:

1. Using Figure 11.1 as a guide, create a matrix of the current product mix for your company.
2. Discuss how the profitability of your product will change as it moves through each of the phases of the product life cycle.
3. Create a brief profile of the type of consumer who is likely to represent each of the product adopter categories for your product.
4. Discuss the factors that could contribute to the failure of your product. How will you define product failure?

The information obtained from these questions should assist you in developing various aspects of your marketing plan found in the "Interactive Marketing Plan" exercise at **www.cengagebrain.com**.

Important Terms

good 318
service 318
idea 318
consumer products 319
business products 319
convenience products 319
shopping products 320
specialty products 321
unsought products 321
installations 322
accessory equipment 322
raw materials 322
component parts 322
process materials 323
MRO supplies 323
business services 323
product item 323
product line 323
product mix 324
width of product mix 324
depth of product mix 324
product life cycle 324
introduction stage 324
growth stage 325
maturity stage 326
decline stage 327
product adoption process 328
innovators 329
early adopters 329
early majority 329
late majority 329
laggards 329
brand 329
brand name 330
brand mark 330
trademark 330
trade name 330
brand equity 331
brand loyalty 331
brand recognition 331
brand preference 331
brand insistence 332
manufacturer brands 333
private distributor brands 333
generic brands 334
individual branding 335
family branding 336
brand extension 336
co-branding 336
brand licensing 337
family packaging 339
labeling 342

Discussion and Review Questions

1. Is a personal computer sold at a retail store a consumer product or a business product? Defend your answer.
2. How do convenience products and shopping products differ? What are the distinguishing characteristics of each type of product?
3. How does an organization's product mix relate to its development of a product line? When should an enterprise add depth to its product line rather than width to its product mix?
4. How do industry profits change as a product moves through the four stages of its life cycle?
5. What are the stages in the product adoption process, and how do they affect the commercialization phase?
6. How does branding benefit consumers and marketers?
7. What is brand equity? Identify and explain the major elements of brand equity.
8. What are the three major degrees of brand loyalty?
9. Compare and contrast manufacturer brands, private distributor brands, and generic brands.
10. Identify the factors a marketer should consider in selecting a brand name.
11. What is co-branding? What major issues should be considered when using co-branding?
12. Describe the functions a package can perform. Which function is most important? Why?
13. What are the main factors a marketer should consider when developing a package?
14. In what ways can packaging be used as a strategic tool?
15. What are the major functions of labeling?

Video Case 11.1

GaGa: Not Just a Lady

Several years before Lady Gaga made her musical debut, Jim King started a company he named GaGa after his beloved grandmother. King, a Rhode Island television news anchor turned entrepreneur, planned to use his grandmother's recipe for frozen dessert as the basis of his first product. Because the lemony dessert contains more butterfat than sherbet and less butterfat than ice cream, he couldn't legally label it as either. So King came up with the idea of calling the product "SherBetter," using the word play to suggest that it's similar to sherbet, but better.

King wasn't intending to compete with major ice cream firms like Hood, Breyers, and Ben & Jerry's. First, as a tiny start-up business, GaGa couldn't begin to match the marketing resources of the national brands. Second, GaGa's focus would be much narrower than the big brands, because sherbets and sorbets make up only a tiny fraction of the overall market for ice cream products. King determined that GaGa would compete on the basis of high quality, all-natural ingredients, and a fresh, creamy taste. He coined the slogan "Smooth as ice cream, fresh like sherbet" to describe SherBetter's appeal.

© iStockphoto.com/loooby

After he cooked up batches of SherBetter in his home kitchen, King drove from grocery store to grocery store until he made a sale to his first retail customer, Munroe Dairy. This initial order for 500 pints of lemon SherBetter was enough to get GaGa off to a solid start. During the first four years of business, the company marketed only one product—the original lemon SherBetter in pint containers. In that time, Stefani Germanotta shot to fame under the stage name of Lady Gaga, giving GaGa's frozen desserts an unexpected but welcome boost in brand awareness and sales.

Four years after founding GaGa, King realized that he could increase sales and increase his brand's visibility in supermarket frozen-food cases by expanding with sufficient products to fill a shelf. Over the next four years, he introduced raspberry, orange, and several other new flavors of SherBetter packed in pint containers. He also launched a line of frozen dessert novelty bars, called "SherBetter on a stick" because they're shaped like ice-cream bars. In addition, he decided to develop a tropical flavor to enhance his product offerings. That led to the introduction of toasted coconut SherBetter, a flavor that tested very well during GaGa's research. As he gained experience, King learned to account for cannibalization of existing products when he launched new products, knowing that overall sales would gain over time.

However, King didn't anticipate that supermarkets would display SherBetter pints and bars in separate freezer sections several doors away from each other. This complicated GaGa's marketing effort, because customers might not know they could buy SherBetter in both bars and pints unless they looked in both frozen-food sections. GaGa simply couldn't afford advertising to promote bars and pints. Instead, King and his wife Michelle, who serves as marketing director, began setting up a table outside the frozen-foods case in different supermarkets and distributing free samples on weekends. They found that when they offered samples, customers responded positively and the store sold a lot of GaGa products that day. This opened the door to repeat purchasing and brand loyalty.

One lesson King learned is that the GaGa brand is more memorable than the SherBetter product name. As a result, he changed the product packaging to emphasize the GaGa brand and its playful implications. After hiring professionals to analyze the company's marketing activities, he also learned that he should focus on what makes GaGa's products unique rather than trying to fit into the broader ice cream product category. The basics of high quality, a unique recipe, and a fun brand have helped King acquire distribution in 1,500 supermarkets and grocery stores throughout the Eastern United States.[57]

Questions for Discussion

1. When GaGa began adding novelty bars in new flavors, what was the effect on the width and depth of its product mix?
2. Why is packaging particularly important for a company like GaGa, which can't afford advertising?
3. Do you think GaGa's SherBetter pints and bars are likely to follow the product life cycle of traditional ice cream products? Explain your answer.

Case 11.2

Wyndham Hotels Portfolio of Brands Satisfies Diverse Customer Needs

Wyndham Worldwide is a global provider of hotels and travel-related services. Its more than 7,200 franchised hotels include Wyndham Grand Collection, Days Inn, Howard Johnson, Wingate at Wyndham, Super 8, Ramada, and Planet Hollywood. While the core product, a place to stay, is virtually the same no matter the hotel, the supplemental and experiential benefits of its hotel chains differ. Wyndham has worked to ensure that each hotel chain maintains its own unique feel to appeal to the appropriate target market.

In many ways, Wyndham's wide range of hotels benefits the company by allowing it to target both budget-conscious consumers and vacationers willing to spend extra money for the resort experience. However, the company must always be careful to market these hotels consistently. For some time, people viewed Wyndham hotels as inconsistent in the quality of services and benefits. The Wyndham CEO believed that past marketing initiatives conflicted with one another to muddle the company's brand identity.

To rectify the problem, Wyndham redesigned some of its hotels and sought to create a solid identity for each hotel chain that would capture the feel of the chain's history and purpose. For instance, the Howard Johnson hotel chain's longer history prompted Wyndham to create an "iconic" atmosphere for these hotels that target leisure travelers and families. The experiential benefits of the Howard Johnson chain therefore include a family-friendly environment and the ability to stay in a classic hotel at a reasonable price.

On the other hand, Wyndham's more upscale hotel chains offer a completely different experience. Its Night Hotel in New York City claims to be "for the traveler who revels in all things after dark." The hotel tries to imbue a "sexy" feel with a chic eatery and bar as well as dark-colored furnishings. Wyndham's TRYP hotels are located in some of the world's biggest cities in Europe, South America, and North America. The hotels are designed to fit in with the local environment and, thus, range from modernistic to historical designs. The hotels are meant to be an extension of the city in which they are located, enabling visitors to experience the excitement of the city even before leaving the hotel's doors.

The hotel product is far from complete without the numerous supplemental benefits that accompany the core product. Travelers have their own expectations of supplemental items that hotels should offer, ranging from intangible items like friendly service to tangible products, such as ample towels and toiletries, pillows, and television. Hotels that do not meet these expectations tend to receive bad reviews and are often shunned by even budget-conscious families. Hotels that go above and beyond these expectations, however, manage to obtain an advantage over their competitors.

Wyndham offers a range of supplemental goods and services to its guests, from discounted hotel packages to large meeting rooms for company conferences. Many Wyndham hotel chains offer their own unique supplemental benefits, as well. Wyndham Gardens offers library lounges for customer comfort, while the more economical Knight's Inn provides a free continental breakfast. Wyndham also provides a reward program for customers who frequently stay at Wyndham hotels. Customers who receive enough points for staying at Wyndham hotels can receive extra days for free. Another program, Wyndham's ByRequest, awards members with free Internet access, expedited check-in, and—after three nights—a snack and drink, extra items like pillows, and the option to have the room personalized to the customer's preferences. Wyndham also rewards female business travelers with its Women on Their Way program. The program's website offers advice and special packages for businesswomen planning their trips.

Wyndham's hotel chains are at different levels of the life cycle. Its Night and TRYP hotel chains, for example, are in the introductory and growth stages, while its Howard Johnson hotel chains are likely in the maturity phase. As a result, Wyndham is more likely to engage in heavy marketing to spread awareness of its newer brands. However, the company is not neglecting its more mature brands. It has worked hard to portray Howard Johnson as an iconic brand and continues to offer benefits packages to encourage families to stay at the chain. The company makes sure to adjust its marketing strategies to suit both the product's benefits and its stage in the product life cycle.

Wyndham has achieved great success in creating a successful product mix to meet the needs of different customers. The company's ability to adapt its marketing strategies to suit its various chains has provided it with unique advantages that make it a formidable competitor to rival hotel companies.[58]

Questions for Discussion

1. How is Wyndham using symbolic and experiential benefits to target its hotels to certain groups of travelers?
2. How is Wyndham using supplemental features at its hotels to create a competitive advantage?
3. How should Wyndham market its hotels according to their stages in the product life cycle?

NOTES

[1] Allan Brettman, "Nike Executives Plot Revenue Course through 2017 for Stock Analysts," *Oregonian*, October 9, 2013, www.oregonlive.com/playbooks-profits/index.ssf/2013/10/nike_executives_plot_revenue_c.html (accessed December 5, 2013); Austin Carr and Whitney Pastorek, "Nike," *Fast Company*, March 2013, pp. 88–156; Leo Kelion, "Nike Shows Off Fuelband SE Activity-Tracking Wristband," *BBC News*, October 15, 2013, www.bbc.co.uk/news/technology-24538852 (accessed December 5, 2013); Kim Gittleson, "Can Nike's Fuelband Really Motivate You to Exercise?" *BBC News*, October 16, 2013, www.bbc.co.uk/news/technology-24543910 (accessed December 5, 2013).

[2] "World's Best Hotel Service, 2013," *Travel and Leisure*, June 2013, www.travelandleisure.com/articles/worlds-best-hotel-service/9 (accessed November 12, 2013).

[3] David Moth, "How Harrods, Macy's and Other Retailers Are Inspiring Christmas Shoppers," *Econsultancy*, November 11, 2013, http://econsultancy.com/us/blog/63769-how-harrods-macy-s-and-other-retailers-are-inspiring-christmas-shoppers (accessed November 12, 2013).

[4] Jeff Bennett, "GM to Open Stamping Plant in Texas", *The Wall Street Journal*, October 13, 2013, http://online.wsj.com/news/articles/SB10001424052702304500404579127860223275366?KEYWORDS=parts+supplier (accessed November 12, 2013).

[5] "Products and Services," General Electric website, www.ge.com/b2b (accessed November 13, 2013).

[6] Michael D. Johnson, Andreas Herrmann, and Frank Huber, "Evolution of Loyalty Intentions," *Journal of Marketing* 70 (April 2006), www.marketingpower.com.

[7] RetailMeNot website, Retailmenot.com (accessed November 23, 2013).

[8] "Top 10 Reasons for New Product Failure," *Green Book*, October 2, 2013, www.greenbook.org/marketing-research/top-10-reasons-for-new-product-failure (accessed November 12, 2013).

[9] Ibid.

[10] Santanu Choudhury, "Honda Lines Up Product Offensive in India," *The Wall Street Journal*, November 25, 2013, http://online.wsj.com/news/articles/SB10001424052702304011304579220932742368894 (accessed November 27, 2013).

[11] Stuart Elliot, "By the Light of the Silvery Spoon, Ads Propose Using Coffee as Creamer," *The New York Times*, September 30, 2013, www.nytimes.com/2013/09/30/business/media/by-the-light-of-the-silvery-spoon-ads-propose-using-coffee-as-creamer.html?_r=1& (accessed November 13, 2013).

[12] Robert Plant, "Incremental Innovation or Breakthroughs? Consider P&G's Tide Pod," *The Wall Street Journal*, September 16, 2013, http://blogs.wsj.com/experts/2013/09/16/incremental-innovation-or-breakthroughs-consider-pgs-tide-pod/?KEYWORDS=improved+product (accessed November 13, 2013).

[13] Candace Choi, "Soda Sales Continue to Decline Despite Flashy Marketing," *The Huffington Post*, July 24, 2013, www.huffingtonpost.com/2013/07/24/soda-sales_n_3645822.html (accessed November 27, 2013).

[14] Adapted from Everett M. Rogers, *Diffusion of Innovations* (New York: Macmillan, 1962), pp. 81–86.

[15] Arch G. Woodside and Wim Biemans, "Managing Relationships, Networks, and Complexity in Innovation, Diffusion, and Adoption Processes," *Business & Industrial Marketing* 20 (July 2005): 247–250.

[16] Ibid, 247–250.

[17] "Dictionary of Marketing Terms," American Marketing Association, www.marketingpower.com (accessed November 28, 2013).

[18] Warren Church, "Investment in Brand Pays Large Dividends," *Marketing News*, November 15, 2006, p. 21.

[19] Antonio Marazza, "A Survivial Guide for Symbolic and Lifestyle Brands," *Forbes*, October 11, 2013, www.forbes.com/sites/onmarketing/2013/10/11/a-survival-guide-for-symbolic-and-lifestyle-brands/2 (accessed November 13, 2013).

[20] C. D. Simms and P. Trott, "The Perception of the BMW Mini Brand: The Importance of Historical Associations and the Development of a Model," *Journal of Product & Brand Management* 15 (2006): 228–238.

[21] Douglas Holt, "Branding as Cultural Activism," *How Brands Become Icons: The Principle of Cultural Branding* (Boston: Harvard Business School Press, 2004), p. 209.

[22] Nigel Hollis, "Branding Unmasked," *Marketing Research* (Fall 2005): 24–29.

[23] David A. Aaker, "*Managing Brand Equity: Capitalizing on the Value of a Brand Name* (New York: Free Press, 1991), pp. 16–17.

[24] Don E. Schulz, "The Loyalty Paradox," *Marketing Management* (September/October 2005): 10–11.

[25] "Customer Loyalty Leaders, 2012," *Brand Keys*, http://brandkeys.com/syndicated-studies/loyalty-leaders-list (accessed November 23, 2013).

[26] "Brand Loyalty Around the Globe: Tech Companies Dominate Top Brands List from Campaign Asia-Pacific—Samsung Claims Top Spot, with Apple, Sony and Panasonic Also Among Highest Ranked: Nestle Is the Only Non-Tech Company in Study's Top Five," *Bull Dog Reporter*, July 6, 0212, www.bulldogreporter.com/dailydog/article/brand-loyalty-around-globe-tech-companies-dominate-top-brands-list-campaign-asia-pa (accessed November 13, 2013).

[27] Simone M. de Droog, Patti M. Valkenburg, and Moniek Buijzen, "Using Brand Characters to Promote Young Children's Liking of and Purchase Requests for Fruit," *Journal of Health Communication: International Perspectives*, 26, no. 1 (2010): 79–89.

[28] "Market Profile," Private Label Manufacturer's Association, http://plma.com/storeBrands/sbt13.html (accessed November 14, 2013).

[29] Chiranjeev S. Kohli, Katrin R. Harich, and Lance Lethesser, "Creating Brand Identity: A Study of Evaluation of New Brand Names," *Journal of Business Research* 58 (2005): 1506–1515.

[30] Richard R. Klink, and Gerard A. Athaide, "Creating Brand Personality with Brand Names," *Marketing Letters* 23, no. 1 (2012): 109–117.

[31] Dorothy Cohen, "Trademark Strategy," *Journal of Marketing* (January 1986): 63.

[32] Chiranjeev Kohli and Rajheesh Suri, "Brand Names That Work: A Study of the Effectiveness of Different Brand Names," *Marketing Management Journal* (Fall/Winter 2000): 112–120.

[33] Dan D'Ambrosio, "Patent Trolls Demand 'Infringement' Fees," *USA Today*, November 12, 2013, www.usatoday.com/story/money/business/2013/11/12/patent-trolls-demand-infringement-fees/3511307 (accessed November 15, 2013).

[34] International Trademark Association, "Fact Sheets: Types of Protection—Trademarks vs. Generic Terms," www.inta.org/TrademarkBasics/FactSheets/Pages/TrademarksvsGenericTermsFactSheet.aspx (accessed July 12, 2013).

[35] "Counterfeit & Pirated Products Account for $360 Billion in Trade Losses," Global Intellectual Property Center, January 8, 2013, www.theglobalipcenter.com/counterfeit-pirated-products-360-billion (accessed November 14, 2013)

[36] Stephen Castle and Doreen Carvajal, "Counterfeit Food More Widespread Than Suspected," *The New York Times*, www.nytimes.com/2013/06/27/business/food-fraud-more-widespread-than-suspected.html (accessed November 14, 2013).

[37] Jane Kay, "Johnson & Johnson Removes Some Chemicals from Baby Shampoo, Other Products," *Scientific American*, May 6, 2013, www.scientificamerican.com/article.cfm?id=johnson-and-johnson-removes-some-chemicals-from-baby-shampoo-other-products (accessed November 22, 2013).

[38] Michael Stone, "Top 10 Licensed Brand Extensions of 2012," *Forbes*, January 22, 2013, www.forbes.com/pictures/femj45gij/hgtv-home-plants (accessed November 14, 2013).

[39] "Gatorade Products," Gatorade website, www.gatorade.com/products/all-products (accessed November 28, 2013).

[40] Shantini Munthree, Geoff Bick, and Russell Abratt, "A Framework for Brand Revitalization," *Journal of Product & Brand Management* 15 (2006): 157–167.

[41] Chris Pullig, Carolyn J. Simmons, and Richard G. Netemeyer, "Brand Dilution: When Do New Brands Hurt Existing Brands?" *Journal of Marketing* 70 (April 2006).

[42] "Target® Colors," Benjamin Moore, http://store.benjaminmoore.com/storefront/shop-by-color/target-paint-colors/target-colors/cndShopByColor-cTarget_Paint_Colors-cTarget_Colors_Fall12-p1.html (accessed November 13, 2013).

[43] Dale Buss, "Nissan Aims at Truck Relevance with Titan-Cummins Diesel Truck," *Forbes*, August 21, 2013, www.forbes.com/sites/dalebuss/2013/08/21/nissan-aims-at-truck-relevance-with-titan-cummins-diesel-deal (accessed November 14, 2013).

[44] "Top 150 Global Licensors, 2013," *License Global*, http://images2.advanstar.com/PixelMags/license-global/digitaledition/05-2013-sp.html#4 (accessed November 14, 2013).

[45] "Puma Clever Little Bag," Fuse Project, www.fuseproject.com/products-47 (accessed November 15, 2013).

[46] Candace Hodder, "What Makes Packaging Sustainable?" *The Dieline*, November 13, 2013, www.thedieline.com/blog/2013/11/13/what-makes-a-package-sustainable.html (accessed November 15, 2013.)

[47] Pangea Organics Facebook Page, www.facebook.com/pangeaskincare (accessed November 15, 2013).

[48] Lauren I. Labrecque and George R. Milne, "Exciting Red and Competent Blue: The Importance of Color in Marketing," *Journal of the Academy of Marketing Science* (January 2011), www.springerlink.com/content/u68v477973076816 (accessed January 24, 2014).

[49] Stephanie Strom, "With Tastes Growing Healthier, McDonald's Aims to Adapt Its Menu," *The New York Times*, September 26, 2013, www.nytimes.com/2013/09/27/business/mcdonalds-moves-toward-a-healthier-menu.html (accessed November 15, 2013).

[50] "Laundry Detergent," Seventh Generation, www.seventhgeneration.com/laundry-detergent (accessed November 15, 2013).

[51] John Kalkowski, "NatureSweet Launches New Tomato Packaging," *Packaging Digest*, October 13, 2011, www.packagingdigest.com/article/519611-NatureSweet_launches_new_tomato_packaging.php (accessed January 23, 2013).

[52] Stack Wine website, http://drinkstack.com (accessed November 15, 2013); Elizabeth Olson, "To Reach Younger Buyers, Vintners Think Outside the Bottle," *The New York Times*, December 26, 2012, www.nytimes.com/2012/12/26/business/media/to-reach-younger-buyers-vintners-rethink-their-packaging.html?_r=1& (accessed November 15, 2013).

[53] Valerie Folkes and Shashi Matta, "The Effect of Package Shape on Consumers' Judgment of Product Volume: Attention as a Mental Contaminant," *Journal of Consumer Research* (September 2004): 390.

[54] Mike Esterl, "Some Food Companies Ditch 'Natural' Label," *The Wall Street Journal*, November 6, 2013, http://online.wsj.com/news/articles/SB10001424052702304470504579163933732367084 (accessed November 15, 2013).

[55] Felix Gillette, "'Made in USA' Still Sells," *Bloomberg Businessweek*, October 11, 2012, www.businessweek.com/articles/2012-10-11/made-in-usa-still-sells (accessed December 7, 2013).

[56] Federal Trade Commission, www.ftc.gov (accessed December 7, 2013).

[57] Curt Nickisch, "GaGa's for Lady Gaga? Coincidental Celebrity Lifts Local Brands," *WBUR radio (Boston)*, February 29, 2012, www.wbur.org (accessed January 21, 2014); GaGa website, www.gonegaga.net (accessed February 3, 2014); "Going Goo Goo for GaGa," *Warwick Online (RI)*, May 12, 2011, www.warwickonline.com (accessed January 2, 2014); "GaGa" Cengage video.

[58] "Wyndham Rewards Loyalty Program with Thanks Again," *The Wall Street Journal*, December 19, 2013, http://online.wsj.com/article/PR-CO-20131219-905488.html (accessed January 14, 2014); Roger Yu, "Travel Q&A: Wyndham CEO Eric Danziger," *USA Today*, January 29, 2009, www.usatoday.com/travel/hotels/2009-01-29-qa-eric-danzinger_N.htm (accessed January 14, 2014); "Wyndham Rewards," Wyndham, https://www.wyndhamrewards.com/trec/consumer/home.action (accessed January 14, 2014); "Women on Their Way by Wyndham Worldwide," www.womenontheirway.com (accessed January 14, 2014); "Wyndham Hotel Group," Wyndham Worldwide, www.wyndhamworldwide.com/about-wyndham-worldwide/wyndham-hotel-group (accessed January 14, 2014).

Feature Notes

[a] Claire Suddath, "Vinyl Records' Renaissance Barely Moves the Sales Needle," *Bloomberg Businessweek*, October 3, 2013, www.businessweek.com/articles/2013-10-03/vinyl-records-renaissance-barely-moves-the-sales-needle (accessed December 5, 2013); Ed Christman, "Vinyl's New Groove," *Billboard*, September 21, 2013, pp. 22–23; Allan Kozinn, "Weaned on CDs, They're Reaching for Vinyl," *The* New York *Times*, June 9, 2013, www.nytimes.com/2013/06/10/arts/music/vinyl-records-are-making-a-comeback.html?pagewanted=all&_r=0 (accessed December 5, 2013).

[b] Pam Allen, "Exclusive: Evocative Design, Sealed Air Corp. and a Warehouse in Iowa," *Albany Business Review*, October 3, 2013, www.bizjournals.com/albany/blog/2013/10/exclusive-ecovative-design-sealed.html (accessed December 5, 2013); Michael Hill, "Firm Uses Mushrooms to Make Eco-Friendly Packaging," *USA Today*, March 11, 2012, http://usatoday30.usatoday.com/money/smallbusiness/story/2012-03-10/mushrooms-as-eco-firendly-packing-materials/53441606/1 (accessed December 5, 2013); Tracey Schelmetic, "Dell Turns to Nature for Packaging Initiative," *Thomas.Net*, January 15, 2013, http://news.thomasnet.com/green_clean/2013/01/15/dell-turns-to-nature-for-packaging-initiative (accessed December 5, 2013).

chapter 12

Developing and Managing Products

OBJECTIVES

12-1 Explain how companies manage existing products through line extensions and product modifications.

12-2 Describe how businesses develop a product idea into a commercial product.

12-3 Discuss the importance of product differentiation and the elements that differentiate one product from another.

12-4 Explain how businesses position their products.

12-5 Discuss how product deletion is used to improve product mixes.

12-6 Describe organizational structures used for managing products.

MARKETING INSIGHTS

Oreo: Constantly Changing to Make the World Happy

Nabisco, which baked its first Oreo sandwich cookies in 1912, has learned how to give an old product new life. More than 100 years after the introduction of the original black-and-white cookie, the brand has grown into a revenue powerhouse, with $2 billion in annual sales worldwide.

Month after month, Nabisco launches new versions of the iconic Oreo to bring loyal customers back to local stores again and again. Sometimes the wafer is different (as in Golden Oreos), and sometimes the filling is different (like Cool Mint Oreos). Sometimes the cookie isn't round (as in Oreo Fun Stix), or it isn't even a cookie (as in Oreo Brownies).

Nabisco also generates buzz by introducing fun variations keyed to the season. For instance, in autumn, the chocolate wafers are embossed with Halloween-themed shapes, such as ghosts, and the filling turns orange. In winter, the chocolate wafers are embossed with cold-weather shapes, like snowmen, while the filling changes to red crème. At times, Nabisco will release a limited-time product without fanfare, as it did with watermelon-filled Oreos and cookies-and-cream–filled Oreos, both produced for a short time one summer. When customers discovered these new products, their social-media comments prompted others to buy and try the new flavors.

Now Nabisco is cultivating a global following with new products created especially for the taste preferences of customers in other cultures—such as Oreos with green tea crème filling (for China), Oreos filled with banana and dulce de leche crème (for Argentina), and Oreos filled with peanut crème (for Indonesia).[1]

Kristoffer Tripplaar/Alamy

To provide products that satisfy target markets and achieve the firm's objectives, a marketer must develop, alter, and maintain an effective product mix—as marketers at Oreo do. An organization's product mix may require adjustment for a variety of reasons. Because customers' attitudes and product preferences change over time, their desire for certain products may wane. For instance, Americans are busier than ever and seek foods that are convenient and easy to eat on the go. McDonald's responded to this demand with its McWrap sandwiches after learning that 65 percent of its customers order through the drive-through. KFC created the Go Cup, which consists of chicken and potato wedges in a bucket-shaped container that fits in most cup holders.[2]

In some cases, a company needs to alter its product mix for competitive reasons. A marketer may have to delete a product from the mix because a competitor dominates the market for that product. IBM sold its personal computer product line to Lenovo because of intense competition in that area. Similarly, a firm may have to introduce a new product or modify an existing one to compete more effectively. A marketer may expand the firm's product mix to take advantage of excess marketing and production capacity.

In this chapter, we examine several ways to improve an organization's product mix. First, we discuss managing existing products through effective line extension and product modification. Next, we examine the stages of new-product development, including idea generation, screening, concept testing, business analysis, product development, test marketing, and commercialization. Then, we go on to discuss the ways companies differentiate their products in the marketplace and follow with a discussion of product positioning and repositioning. Next, we examine the importance of deleting weak products and the methods companies use to eliminate them. Finally, we look at the organizational structures used to manage products.

12-1 MANAGING EXISTING PRODUCTS

An organization can benefit by capitalizing on its existing products. By assessing the composition of the current product mix, a marketer can identify weaknesses and gaps. This analysis can then lead to improvement of the product mix through line extensions and product modifications.

12-1a Line Extensions

A **line extension** is the development of a product that is closely related to one or more products in the existing product line but designed specifically to meet somewhat different customer needs. Researchers have found that men prefer products that are targeted specifically to their gender. Men typically associate diet soda with women and are therefore less likely to consume it. In response, soda manufacturers, such as Dr Pepper, have developed product line extensions, such as Dr Pepper Ten, aimed at getting more men to consume diet or low-calorie beverages with the slogan "It's not for women."[3]

line extension Development of a product that is closely related to existing products in the line but is designed specifically to meet different customer needs

Many of the so-called new products introduced each year are in fact line extensions. Line extensions are more common than new products because they are a less-expensive, lower-risk alternative for increasing sales. A line extension may focus on a different market segment or attempt to increase sales within the same market segment by more precisely satisfying the needs of people in that segment. Firms should be careful of which lines they choose to extend and how. The success of a line extension is enhanced if the parent brand has a high-quality brand image and if there is a good fit between the line extension and its parent.[4] Nestlé launched a Girl Scout Cookie Crunch candy bar as a line extension of its Crunch bars. This extension worked because both Nestlé and the Girl Scouts are known for their sweet treats.[5] On the other hand, Kellogg undermined the strength of its Kashi cereal brand by extending into cereal products that contained genetically modified ingredients. Because Kashi is known for its healthy and organic options, these genetically modified products seemed too mainstream to its health-conscious target market. The brand is returning to its health-conscious roots by releasing cereals featuring the seed quinoa.[6] Line extensions, when successfully applied, can take market share from competitors. For instance, this advertisement for Dyson Hard illustrates a mop similar to a Swiffer Sweepervac. It is an extension of Dyson's line of vacuum cleaners that features the addition of a pre-moistened mopping pad. However, this product is more higher-end compared to the Sweepervac and is positioned to take away market share by appealing to consumers who are willing to pay more for higher quality.

Dyson

Line Extension
The Dyson Hard is an extension of Dyson's line of vacuum cleaners. It is positioned to take away market share from Swiffer, which makes floor-mopping products.

12-1b Product Modifications

Product modification means changing one or more characteristics of a product. A product modification differs from a line extension in that the original product does not remain in the line. Automakers, for instance, use product modifications annually when they create new models of the same brand. Makers of running shoes also follow this practice, releasing new shoe models nearly every year and retiring old ones. Once the new models are introduced, the manufacturers stop producing the previous model. Like line extensions, product modifications entail less risk than developing new products.

Product modification can indeed improve a firm's product mix, but only under certain conditions. First, the product must be modifiable. Second, customers must be able to perceive that a modification has been made. Third, the modification should make the product more consistent with customers' desires so it provides greater satisfaction. One drawback to modifying a successful product is that a consumer who had experience with the original version of the product may view a modified version as a riskier purchase. There are three major types of modifications that can be made to products: quality, functional, and aesthetic.

Quality Modifications

Quality modifications are changes relating to a product's dependability and durability. Usually, the changes are executed by altering the materials or the production process. Reducing a product's quality may allow an organization to lower its price and direct the item at a different target market. In contrast, increasing the quality of a product may give a firm an advantage over competing brands. Higher quality may enable a company to charge a higher price by creating customer loyalty and lowering customer sensitivity to price. Case in point, Nike developed a new, improved process for crafting its shoes. The Flyknit running shoe has an upper that is woven out of revolutionary fibers and fits the foot like a sock. The product debuted at the 2012 Olympics, was featured at the 2014 Olympics, and retails for nearly double that of more basic Nike running shoes.[7] However, higher quality may require the use of more expensive components and processes, which may force the organization to cut costs

product modifications
Changes in one or more characteristics of a product

quality modifications
Changes relating to a product's dependability and durability

Functional Modifications
Functional modifications to the HP ElitePad tablet computer make it compatible with accessories that make it more versatile and durable than competing tablets.

in other areas. Some firms, such as Caterpillar, are finding ways to increase quality while reducing costs.

Functional Modifications

Changes that affect a product's versatility, effectiveness, convenience, or safety are called **functional modifications**, and they usually require that the product be redesigned. Product categories that have undergone considerable functional modification include agricultural equipment, appliances, cleaning products, and telecommunications services. Making programs available in 3D on DirectTV is a functional modification. Functional modifications can increase the number of users of a product and thus enlarge its market. For instance, the iPhone is always adding new features. Powered by Apple's iOS 6 mobile operating system, the iPhone 5 has expanded voice recognition capabilities and is the world's thinnest smartphone made entirely of glass and aluminum.[8] This technology, along with other modifications, makes the iPhone 5 significantly different from previous models. Companies can place a product in a favorable competitive position by providing benefits that competing brands do not offer. Look at the advertisement for the HP ElitePad, a tablet computer that has undergone functional modifications to make it compatible with accessories that expand its versatility and durability. The tablet can be used with a durable case or a keyboard and docking station that make it work like a regular desktop or laptop computer, addressing the problem many consumers experience when typing on tablet touchpads.

Additionally, functional modifications can help an organization achieve and maintain a progressive image. Finally, functional modifications are sometimes made to reduce the possibility of product liability lawsuits, such as adding a kill switch on a machine in case it malfunctions.

Aesthetic Modifications

Aesthetic modifications change the sensory appeal of a product by altering its taste, texture, sound, smell, or appearance. A buyer making a purchase decision is swayed by sensory inputs, and an aesthetic modification may thus strongly affect purchases. The fashion industry relies heavily on aesthetic modifications from season to season. For example, Louis Vuitton clothing, handbags, and leather goods are leaders in the haute couture industry. In order to maintain its reputation for the utmost level of quality and style, the company performs aesthetic modifications on its products regularly. This ensures that Louis Vuitton maintains its reputation for cutting-edge design and high quality. In addition, aesthetic modifications attempt to minimize the amount of illegal product counterfeiting that occurs through constant change in design.

Aesthetic modifications can help a firm differentiate its product from competing brands and thus gain a sizable market share. The major drawback in using aesthetic modifications is that their value is determined subjectively. Although a firm may strive to improve the product's sensory appeal, some customers actually may find the modified product less attractive.

functional modifications Changes affecting a product's versatility, effectiveness, convenience, or safety

aesthetic modifications Changes relating to the sensory appeal of a product

12-2 DEVELOPING NEW PRODUCTS

A firm develops new products as a means of enhancing its product mix and adding depth to a product line. Developing and introducing new products is frequently expensive and risky. However, failure to introduce new products is also risky. For instance, the CD and DVD retailer HMV entered into bankruptcy when the company failed to innovate through introducing new products in the face of changing consumer shopping habits and the increasing preference to purchase music online through such outlets as Amazon.[9]

The term *new product* can have more than one meaning. A genuinely new product offers innovative benefits. For example, Apple is often considered the most innovative company in the country for releasing such products as the iPod, iPhone, and iPad. The firm benefits from this reputation for developing new products that address consumer needs.[10] However, products that are different and distinctly better are often viewed as new, even if they do not represent a truly new product. For instance, the Duracell Powermat 24-Hour Power System is a battery-powered charging pad for mobile devices. Chargers already exist, as do battery-powered devices. However, consumers who use many digital devices are likely to view this mobile and wireless option as an important step forward.[11] This advertisement for a Kohler faucet illustrates a product that represents an innovation over existing faucets. The Karbon model pivots in multiple ways, allowing the user to control the direction of the water stream better and creating a faucet that functions more like a hose, while still having a pleasing modern design.

Product Innovation
Most product innovations build on products already existing in the marketplace. For instance, this Kohler Karbon model faucet represents an innovation over existing faucets by bending in multiple places.

Some popular product innovations of recent decades include cell phones, tablet computers, MP3 players, satellite radio, and smart glasses such as Google Glass. A radically new product involves a complex developmental process, including an extensive business analysis to determine the potential for success. A product such as Google Glass took many years to develop, test, and introduce.[12]

A new product can also be one that a given firm has not marketed previously, although similar products are available from other companies. For instance, this advertisement for the Conair True Glow represents a product that is new to Conair but not totally new to the market. Other companies, such as Clarisonic and Oil of Olay, have introduced similar rotating cleansing brushes. This represents the first cleansing brush released by Conair, however, which is underscored by the phrase "the new clean" written out in the ad.

Finally, a product can be viewed as new when it is brought to one or more markets from another market. Apple, for instance, only recently won a contract to introduce its iPhone in China, the world's largest cell phone market, after being available in most other countries for many years.[13] Before a product is introduced, it goes through the seven phases of the **new-product development process** shown in Figure 12.1: (1) idea generation, (2) screening, (3) concept testing, (4) business analysis, (5) product development, (6) test marketing, and (7) commercialization. A product may be dropped at any stage of development. In this section, we look at the process through which products are developed, from idea inception to fully commercialized product.

new-product development process A seven-phase process for introducing products: idea generation, screening, concept testing, business analysis, product development, test-marketing, and commercialization

Figure 12.1 Phases of New-Product Development

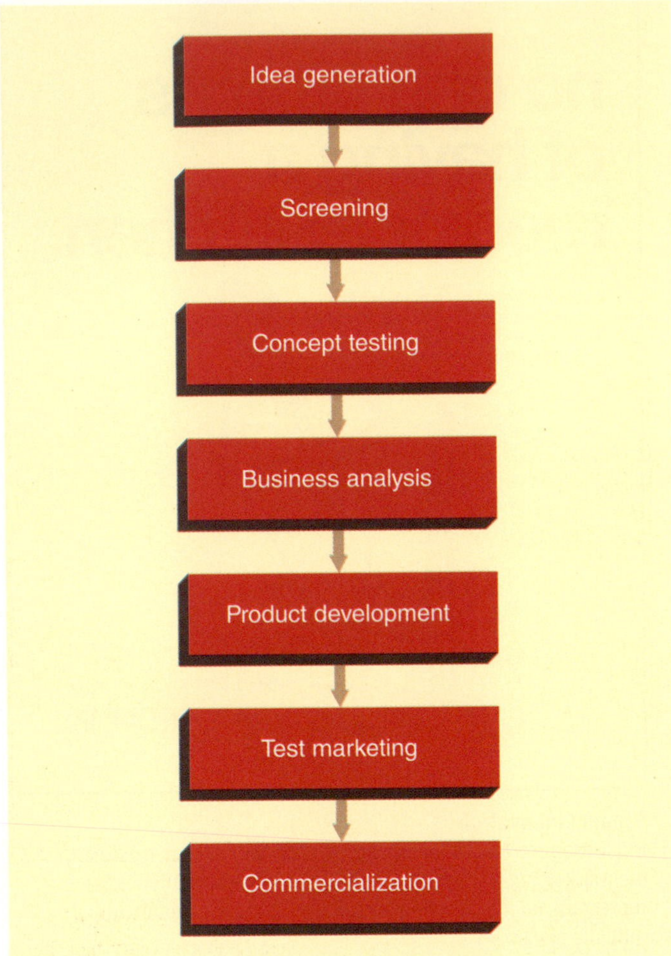

12-2a Idea Generation

Businesses and other organizations seek product ideas that will help them achieve their objectives. This activity is **idea generation**. The fact that only a few ideas are good enough to be commercially successful underscores the challenge of the task.

Although some organizations get their ideas by chance, firms that are most successful at managing their product mixes usually develop systematic approaches for generating new product ideas. At the heart of innovation is a purposeful, focused effort to identify new ways to serve a market.[14] New product ideas can come from several sources. They may stem from internal sources—marketing managers, researchers, sales personnel, engineers, or other organizational personnel. Brainstorming and incentives for good ideas are typical intra-firm devices for stimulating the development of ideas. For instance, the idea for 3M Post-it adhesive-backed notes came from an employee. As a church choir member, he used slips of paper to mark songs in his hymnal. Because the pieces of paper kept falling out, he suggested developing an adhesive-backed note. Over time, employees have become more empowered to express their own product ideas to their supervisors. This collaborative process can be particularly useful to help marketers iron out the details of a new product concept.[15]

New product ideas may also arise from sources outside the firm, such as customers, competitors, advertising agencies, management consultants, and private research organizations. Increasingly, firms are bringing consumers into the product idea development process through online campaigns. The Internet gives marketers the chance to tap into consumer ideas by building online communities and listening to their product needs and wants. These communities provide consumers with a sense of empowerment and allow them to provide insight for new product ideas that can prove invaluable to the firm.[16] The Internet and social media have become very important tools for gathering information from stakeholders, particularly when a firm is targeting younger consumers. The interactivity of the Internet allows other stakeholders to not only suggest and analyze new product ideas but also interact with one another on evaluating and filtering these ideas. After conducting research on popular food and drink flavors, Jack Daniels released a Tennessee Honey-flavored whisky that capitalizes on the boom in artisanal food. Tennessee Honey is marketed via social media.[17] Honey is one of the trendiest flavors of the moment—with cereals, lip balms, cosmetics, and even fragrances all featuring the scent and flavor of honey.[18]

Procter & Gamble is one company that gets nearly half of its ideas from inventors and outside consultants.[19] Many firms offer product development consulting and can be good sources for stimulating new product ideas. For example, Redfusion Studios engages in product design and development for many Fortune 500 companies, such as GE, Georgia-Pacific, Bosch, and Remington.[20] When outsourcing new-product development activities to outside organizations, firms should spell out the specific details of the arrangement and include detailed contractual specifications. Asking customers what they want from products has helped many firms become successful and remain competitive. As more global consumers become interconnected through the Internet, marketers have the chance to tap into consumer ideas by building online communities with them.

idea generation Seeking product ideas to achieve organizational objectives

12-2b Screening

In the process of **screening**, the ideas with the greatest potential are selected for further review. During screening, product ideas are analyzed to determine if they match the organization's objectives and resources. A firm's overall abilities to produce and market the product are also analyzed. Other aspects of an idea to be weighed are the nature and wants of buyers and possible environmental changes. At times, a checklist of new-product requirements is used when making screening decisions. This practice encourages evaluators to be systematic and thus reduces the chances of overlooking some pertinent fact. Most new product ideas are rejected during the screening phase.

12-2c Concept Testing

To evaluate ideas properly, it may be necessary to test product concepts. In **concept testing**, a small sample of potential buyers is presented with a product idea through a written or oral description (and perhaps a few drawings) to determine their attitudes and initial buying intentions regarding the product. For a single product idea, an organization can test one or several concepts of the same product. Concept testing is a low-cost procedure that allows a company to determine customers' initial reactions to a product idea before it invests considerable resources in research and development.

Figure 12.2 shows a concept test for a proposed tick and flea control product. During concept testing, the concept is described briefly, and then a series of questions is presented to a test panel. The questions vary considerably depending on the type of product being tested. Typical questions can include the following: In general, do you find this proposed product attractive? Which benefits are especially attractive to you? Which features are of little or no interest to you? Do you feel that this proposed product would work better for you than the product you currently use? Compared with your current product, what are the primary advantages of the proposed product? If this product were available at an appropriate price, would you buy it? How often would you buy this product? How could the proposed product be improved?

New Product for a Firm
The Conair True Glow is a new product to the Conair family of products, although similar products have been marketed by other firms.

12-2d Business Analysis

During the **business analysis** stage, the product idea is evaluated to determine its potential contribution to the firm's sales, costs, and profits. In the course of a business analysis, evaluators ask a variety of questions: Does the product fit in with the organization's existing product mix? Is demand strong enough to justify entering the market, and will this demand endure? What types of environmental and competitive changes can be expected, and how will these changes affect the product's future sales, costs, and profits?

It is also crucial that a firm determine whether its research, development, engineering, and production capabilities are adequate to develop the product; whether new facilities must be constructed, how quickly they can be built, and how much they will cost; and whether the necessary financing for development and commercialization is on hand or is obtainable based upon terms consistent with a favorable return on investment.

In the business analysis stage, firms seek market information. The results of customer surveys, along with secondary data, supply the specifics needed to estimate potential sales, costs, and profits. For many product ideas in this stage, forecasting sales accurately is difficult. This is

screening Selecting the ideas with the greatest potential for further review

concept testing Seeking a sample of potential buyers' responses to a product idea

business analysis Evaluating the potential impact of a product idea on the firm's sales, costs, and profits

Figure 12.2 Concept Test for a Tick and Flea Control Product

Product description

An insecticide company is considering the development and introduction of a new tick and flea control product for pets. This product would consist of insecticide and a liquid-dispensing brush for applying the insecticide to dogs and cats. The insecticide is in a cartridge that is installed in the handle of the brush. The insecticide is dispensed through the tips of the bristles when they touch the pet's skin (which is where most ticks and fleas are found). The actual dispensing works very much like a felt-tip pen. Only a small amount of insecticide actually is dispensed on the pet because of this unique dispensing feature. Thus, the amount of insecticide that is placed on your pet is minimal compared to conventional methods of applying a tick and flea control product. One application of insecticide will keep your pet free from ticks and fleas for 14 days.

Please answer the following questions:

1. In general, how do you feel about using this type of product on your pet?
2. What are the major advantages of this product compared with the existing product that you are currently using to control ticks and fleas on your pet?
3. What characteristics of this product do you especially like?
4. What suggestions do you have for improving this product?
5. If it is available at an appropriate price, how likely are you to buy this product?

   Very likely Semi-likely Not likely
6. Assuming that a single purchase would provide 30 applications for an average-size dog or 48 applications for an average-size cat, approximately how much would you pay for this product?

especially true for innovative and completely new products. Organizations sometimes employ breakeven analysis to determine how many units they would have to sell to begin making a profit. At times, an organization also uses payback analysis, in which marketers compute the time period required to recover the funds that would be invested in developing the new product. Because breakeven and payback analyses are based on estimates, they are usually viewed as useful but not particularly precise tools.

12-2e Product Development

Product development is the phase in which the organization determines if it is technically feasible to produce the product and if it can be produced at costs low enough to make the final price reasonable. To test its acceptability, the idea or concept is converted into a prototype, or working model. The prototype should reveal tangible and intangible attributes associated with the product in consumers' minds. The product's design, mechanical features, and intangible aspects must be linked to wants in the marketplace. Through marketing research and concept testing, product attributes that are important to buyers are identified. These characteristics must be communicated to customers through the design of the product.

product development Determining if producing a product is technically feasible and cost effective

After a prototype is developed, its overall functioning must be assessed. Its performance, safety, convenience, and other functional qualities are tested both in a laboratory and in the field. Functional testing should be rigorous and lengthy enough to test the product thoroughly. Studies have revealed that the form or design of a product can actually influence how consumers view the product's functional performance.[21] Manufacturing issues that come to light at the prototype stage may require adjustments.

A crucial question that arises during product development is how much quality to build into the product. Thus, a major dimension of quality is durability. Higher quality often calls for better materials and more expensive processing, which increase production costs and, ultimately, the product's price. In determining the specific level of quality that is best for a product, a marketer must ascertain approximately what price the target market views as acceptable. In addition, a marketer usually tries to set a quality level consistent with that of the firm's other products. The quality of competing brands is also a consideration.

The development phase of a new product is often a lengthy and expensive process. As a result, only a relatively small number of product ideas are put into development. If the product appears sufficiently successful during this stage to merit test marketing, then, during the latter part of the development stage, marketers begin to make decisions regarding branding, packaging, labeling, pricing, and promotion for use in the test marketing stage.

12-2f Test Marketing

Test marketing is a limited introduction of a product in geographic areas chosen to represent the intended market. Fast-food chain Chipotle, for example, test marketed a vegan tofu sofritas option at its Baltimore, Philadelphia, Richmond, and Washington, DC, locations before expanding the offering to all East Coast restaurant locations.[22] The aim of test marketing is to determine the extent to which potential customers will buy the product. Test marketing is not an extension of the development stage, but rather a sample launching of the entire marketing mix. It should be conducted only after the product has gone through development and initial plans have been made regarding the other marketing mix variables. Companies use test marketing to lessen the risk of product failure. The dangers of introducing an untested product include undercutting already profitable products and, should the new product fail, loss of credibility with distributors and customers.

Test marketing provides several benefits. It lets marketers expose a product in a natural marketing environment to measure its sales performance. The company can strive to identify weaknesses in the product or in other parts of the marketing mix. A product weakness discovered after

test marketing A limited introduction of a product in geographic areas chosen to represent the intended market

Emerging Trends

The Power of "Limited Time Only" Products

Each time McDonald's puts the McRib back on the menu, bloggers and tweeters spread the word and customers line up to buy a cult-favorite sandwich not available for most of the year. Such limited-time menu items have become a powerful way to differentiate a fast-food brand, build anticipation among loyal customers, boost sales, and compete more effectively.

McDonald's regularly rotates entrées, side dishes, and beverages on and off the menu as the seasons change, holidays come and go, and new food fads emerge. For example, the Shamrock Shake is served only during March, timed to coincide with St. Patrick's Day. McDonald's recently added pumpkin-spice lattes to its October–November McCafé coffee menu, echoing the limited-time offering by Starbucks, which has sold 200 million pumpkin-spice lattes in 9 years of seasonal menu appearances. Riding the wave of pumpkin popularity, Dunkin' Donuts is adding pumpkin mochas to its menu during the fall months.

Burger King has begun introducing wave after wave of limited-time items to entice customers back into its restaurants more often. Battling back against its archrival's McRib, Burger King recently added the BK Rib Sandwich to its summer menu, after months of test-marketing the new sandwich. However, the McRib has a 32-year head start. Will the BK Rib Sandwich be able to develop a strong and loyal following during its limited summer appearances?[a]

a nationwide introduction can be expensive to correct. Moreover, if consumers' early reactions are negative, marketers may be unable to persuade consumers to try the product again. Thus, making adjustments after test marketing can be crucial to the success of a new product. On the other hand, test marketing results may be positive enough to warrant accelerating the product's introduction. Test marketing also allows marketers to experiment with variations in advertising, pricing, and packaging in different test areas and to measure the extent of brand awareness, brand switching, and repeat purchases resulting from these alterations in the marketing mix.

Selection of appropriate test areas is very important because the validity of test marketing results depends heavily on selecting test sites that provide accurate representations of the intended target market. U.S. cities commonly used for test marketing appear in Table 12.1. The criteria used for choosing test cities depend upon the product's attributes, the target market's characteristics, and the firm's objectives and resources.

Test marketing is not without risks. It is expensive, and competitors may try to interfere. A competitor may attempt to "jam" the test program by increasing its own advertising or promotions, lowering prices, and offering special incentives, all to combat consumer recognition and purchase of the new brand. Such tactics can invalidate test results. Sometimes competitors copy the product in the testing stage and rush to introduce a similar product. It is therefore desirable to move to the commercialization phase as soon as possible after successful testing.

Because of these risks, many companies use alternative methods to measure customer preferences. One such method is simulated test marketing. Typically, consumers at shopping centers are asked to view an advertisement for a new product and are given a free sample to take home. These consumers are subsequently interviewed over the phone or through online panels and asked to rate the product. The major advantages of simulated test marketing are greater speed, lower costs, and tighter security, which reduce the flow of information to competitors and reduce jamming. Several marketing research firms, such as ACNielsen Company, offer test marketing services to provide independent assessment of proposed products. Not all products that are test-marketed are launched. At times, problems discovered during test marketing cannot be resolved.

12-2g Commercialization

commercialization Refining and finalizing plans and budgets for full-scale manufacturing and marketing of a product

During the **commercialization** phase, plans for full-scale manufacturing and marketing must be refined and settled and budgets for the project prepared. Early in the commercialization phase, marketing management analyzes the results of test marketing to find out what changes in the marketing mix are needed before introducing the product. The results of test marketing may tell marketers to change one or more of the product's physical attributes,

Table 12.1 Popular Test Markets in the United States

Rank	City
1	Columbus, Ohio
2	Peoria, Illinois
3	Albany, New York
4	Jacksonville, Florida
5	Lexington, Kentucky
6	Des Moines, Iowa
7	Battle Creek, Michigan
8	Greensboro, North Carolina
9	Cleveland, Ohio
10	Phoenix, Arizona

modify the distribution plans to include more retail outlets, alter promotional efforts, or change the product's price. However, as more and more changes are made based on test marketing findings, the test marketing projections may become less valid.

During the early part of this stage, marketers must not only gear up for larger-scale production, but also make decisions about warranties, repairs, and replacement parts. The type of warranty a firm provides can be a critical issue for buyers, especially for expensive, technically complex goods, such as appliances, or frequently used items, such as mattresses. Establishing an effective system for providing repair services and replacement parts is necessary to maintain favorable customer relationships. Although the producer may furnish these services directly to buyers, it is more common for the producer to provide such services through regional service centers. Regardless of how services are provided, it is important to customers that they be performed quickly and correctly.

The product enters the market during the commercialization phase. When introducing a product, a firm may spend enormous sums for advertising, personal selling, and other types of promotion, as well as on manufacturing and equipment costs. Such expenditures may not be recovered for several years. Smaller firms may find this process difficult, but even so they may use press releases, blogs, podcasts, and other tools to capture quick feedback as well as to promote the new product. Another low-cost promotional tool is product reviews in newspapers, magazines, or blogs, which can be especially helpful when they are positive and target the same customers.

Products are not usually launched nationwide overnight, but are introduced in stages through a process called a *rollout*. With a rollout, a product is introduced starting in one geographic area or set of areas and gradually expands into adjacent ones. It may take several years to reach national marketing coverage. Sometimes, the test cities are used as initial marketing areas, and the introduction of the product becomes a natural extension of test marketing. A product test-marketed in Sacramento, California and Fort Collins, Colorado could be introduced first in those cities. After the stage 1 introduction is complete, stage 2 usually includes market coverage of the states where the test cities are located. In stage 3, marketing efforts might be extended to adjacent states. All remaining states would then be covered in stage 4. Figure 12.3 shows these four stages of commercialization.

Figure 12.3 Stages of Expansion into a National Market during Commercialization

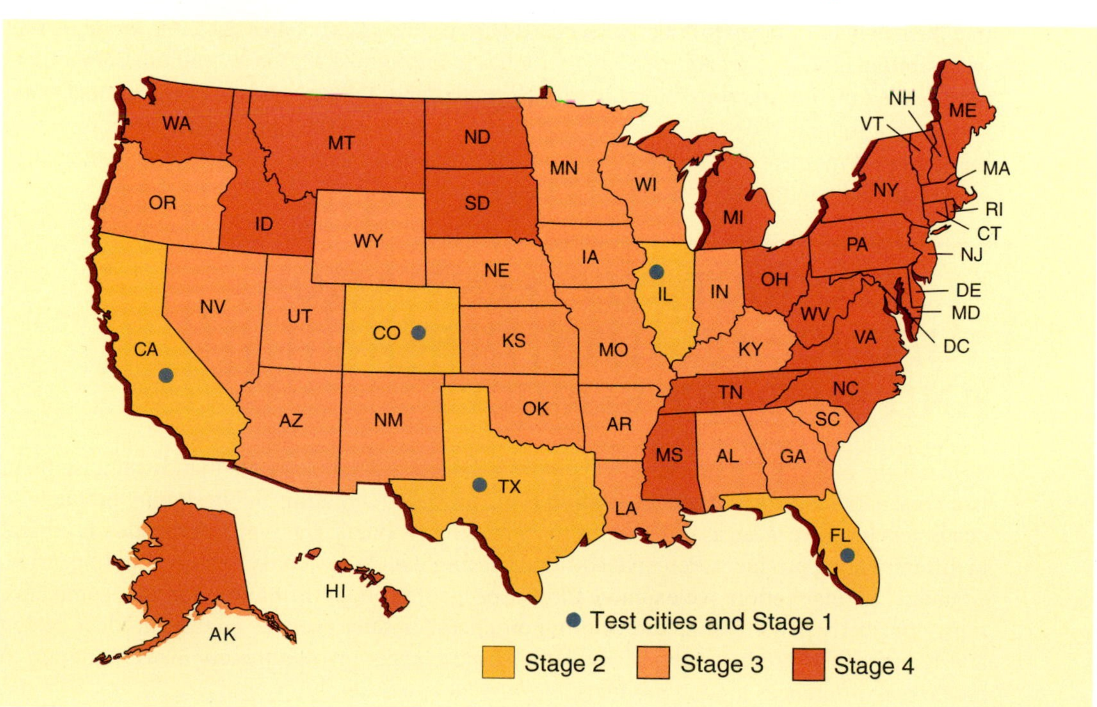

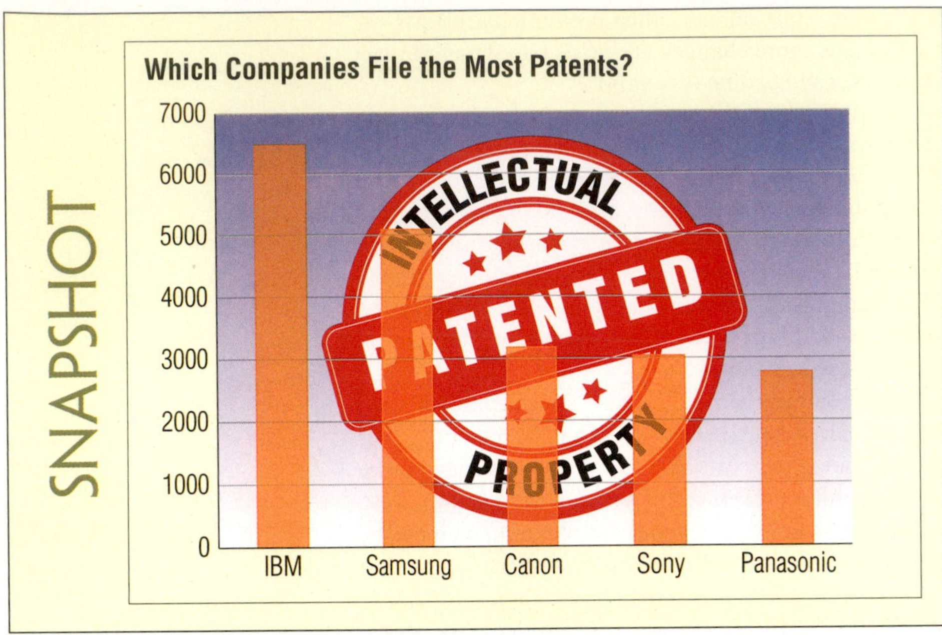

Source: IFI Claims Patent Services.

Product rollouts do not always occur state by state. Other geographic combinations, such as groups of counties that overlap across state borders, are sometimes used. Products destined for multinational markets may also be rolled out one country or region at a time. Gradual product introduction is desirable for several reasons. First, it reduces the risks of introducing a new product. If the product fails, the firm will experience smaller losses if it introduced the item in only a few geographic areas than if it marketed the product nationally. Second, a company cannot introduce a product nationwide overnight, because a system of wholesalers and retailers to distribute the product cannot be established so quickly. Developing a distribution network can take considerable time. Third, if the product is successful from launch, the number of units needed to satisfy nationwide demand for it may be too large for the firm to produce in a short time. Finally, gradual introduction allows for fine-tuning of the marketing mix to satisfy target customers. As electric charging stations become more prevalent around the nation, Tesla Motors has used a rollout strategy to build demand for its innovative electric vehicles. The rollout strategy has also allowed the company to expand production capacity to accommodate growing demand.[23]

Despite the good reasons for introducing a product gradually, marketers realize this approach creates problems. A gradual introduction allows competitors to observe what the firm is doing and monitor results just as the firm's own marketers are doing. If competitors see that the newly introduced product is successful, they may quickly enter the same target market with similar products. In addition, as a product is introduced region by region, competitors may expand their marketing efforts to offset promotion of the new product. Marketers should realize that too much delay in launching a product can cause the firm to miss out on seizing market opportunities, creating competitive offerings, and forming cooperative relationships with channel members.[24]

12-3 PRODUCT DIFFERENTIATION THROUGH QUALITY, DESIGN, AND SUPPORT SERVICES

Some of the most important characteristics of products are the elements that distinguish them from one another. **Product differentiation** is the process of creating and designing products so customers perceive them as different from competing products. Customer perception is critical in differentiating products. Perceived differences might include quality, features, styling, price, or image. In this section, we examine three aspects of product differentiation that companies must consider when creating and offering products for sale: product quality, product design and features, and product support services. These aspects involve the company's attempt to create real differences among products.

product differentiation
Creating and designing products so that customers perceive them as different from competing products

12-3a Product Quality

Quality refers to the overall characteristics of a product that allow it to perform as expected in satisfying customer needs. The words *as expected* are very important to this definition because quality usually means different things to different customers. For some, durability signifies quality. The Craftsman line of tools at Sears is an example of a durable product. Indeed, Sears provides a lifetime guarantee on its tools.

The concept of quality also varies between consumer and business markets. Consumers consider high-quality products to be reliable, durable, and easy to maintain. For business markets, technical suitability, ease of repair, and company reputation are important characteristics. Unlike consumers, most organizations place far less emphasis on price than on product quality.

StriVectin

Level of Quality
StriVectin backs up its quality claims with reports on user satisfaction.

One important dimension of quality is **level of quality**, the amount of quality a product possesses. The concept is a relative one because the quality level of one product is difficult to describe unless it is compared to that of other products. The American Customer Satisfaction Index (ACSI) ranks customer satisfaction among a wide variety of businesses in the United States. For instance, Amazon is the highest-ranked online retailer according to the ACSI index.[25] Dissatisfied customers may curtail their overall spending, which could stifle economic growth. The advertisement for StriVectin NIA-114 anti-aging retinol cream stresses level of quality, comparing the product to prescription skin creams. The advertisement further points out that 97 percent of users reported that it did not irritate their skin (a common problem with retinol-based treatments) and 90 percent saw an improvement in skin texture. These statements back up the claims made in the advertisement of the product's high level of quality.

A second important dimension is consistency. **Consistency of quality** refers to the degree to which a product has the same level of quality over time. Consistency means giving consumers the quality they expect every time they purchase the product. As with level of quality, consistency is a relative concept. It implies a quality comparison within the same brand over time.

The consistency of product quality can also be compared across competing products. It is at this stage that consistency becomes critical to a company's success. Companies that can provide quality on a consistent basis have a major competitive advantage over rivals. FedEx, for example, offers reliable delivery schedules and a variety of options, ranking it at the top of consumer shipping companies.[26] No company has ever succeeded by creating and marketing low-quality products that do not satisfy consumers. Many companies have taken major steps, such as implementing total quality management (TQM), to improve the quality of their products and become more competitive.

Higher product quality means firms will have to charge a higher price for the product. Marketers must therefore consider the balance of quality and price carefully in their planning efforts.

12-3b Product Design and Features

Product design refers to how a product is conceived, planned, and produced. Design is a very complex topic because it involves the total sum of all the product's physical characteristics. Many companies are known for the outstanding designs of their products: Apple for electronics and computers, Cuisinart for kitchen appliances, and Merrell for hiking shoes. Good design is one of the best competitive advantages any brand can possess.

quality The overall characteristics of a product that allow it to perform as expected in satisfying customer needs

level of quality The amount of quality a product possesses

consistency of quality The degree to which a product has the same level of quality over time

product design How a product is conceived, planned, and produced

One component of design is **styling**, or the physical appearance of the product. The style of a product is one design feature that can allow certain products to sell very rapidly. Good design, however, means more than just appearance—design also encompasses a product's functionality and usefulness. For instance, a pair of jeans may look great, but if they fall apart after three washes, the design was poor. Most consumers seek out products that both look good and function well.

Product features are specific design characteristics that allow a product to perform certain tasks. By adding or subtracting features, a company can differentiate its products from those of the competition. Product features can also be used to differentiate products within the same company. For instance, Nike offers a range of shoes designed for purposes from walking, to running, to weightlifting, to cross-training in a gym. In general, the more features a product has, the higher its price and often the higher its perceived quality.

For a brand to have a sustainable competitive advantage, marketers must determine the product designs and features that customers desire. Information from marketing research efforts and databases can help in assessing customers' product design and feature preferences. Being able to meet customers' desires for product design and features at prices they can afford is crucial to a product's long-term success. Marketers must be careful not to misrepresent or overpromise regarding product features or product performance.

12-3c Product Support Services

Many companies differentiate their product offerings by providing support services. Usually referred to as **customer services**, these services include any human or mechanical efforts or activities a company provides that add value to a product. Examples of customer services include delivery and installation, financing arrangements, customer training, warranties and guarantees, repairs, layaway plans, convenient hours of operation, adequate parking, and information through toll-free numbers and websites. Trader Joe's stands out among grocery stores for its stellar customer service. Marketers at Trader Joe's strive to ensure that nothing interrupts the positive experience and to create opportunities for salespeople to connect with customers. The approach ensures that shoppers find and purchase exactly what they want. To create a more personal environment, the store does not even have loudspeakers. As a result, Trader Joe's customers are highly loyal and sales per square foot frequently are triple that of competitors.[27]

styling The physical appearance of a product

product features Specific design characteristics that allow a product to perform certain tasks

customer services Human or mechanical efforts or activities that add value to a product

Whether as a major or minor part of the total product offering, all marketers of goods sell customer services. In the case of markets where all products have essentially the same quality, design, and features, providing good customer service may be the only way a company can

Marketing Debate

Caffeine: Who Needs It?!

ISSUE: Should caffeine-enriched foods and beverages be available to children and teenagers?

Energy drinks, like Red Bull and Monster, are known for their high caffeine content. Caffeine has been added to other foods and beverages to deliver benefits such as a feeling of alertness. Wired Waffles, for example, get their caffeine boost from coffee bean extract. Cracker Jack'D snacks add caffeine through ground-coffee ingredients.

When Wrigley launched Alert Energy Caffeine Gum, however, the Food and Drug Administration expressed concerns about how the caffeine-enriched gum might affect teens and younger children. Although Wrigley was targeting adults, the company quickly halted production, saying a clearer regulatory framework was needed for marketing caffeine-enriched foods.

Frito-Lay, which owns the Cracker Jack brand, continues to market the extra-caffeine version mainly through convenience stores rather than supermarkets because the target market is young men. Java Mallows, which are coffee-flavored marshmallows with caffeine added, were once sold in grocery stores but are now available only online, where children can't click to buy. Should caffeine-added products be available where youngsters and teens can buy them? [b]

differentiate its products. This is especially true in the computer industry. When buying a laptop computer, for example, consumers are likely to shop more for fast delivery, technical support, warranties, and price than for product quality and design, as witnessed by the high volume of "off-the-shelf," non-customized lower-priced laptops sold at retailers such as Best Buy, Costco, Walmart, and Target. Through research, a company can discover the types of services customers want and need. The level of customer service a company provides can profoundly affect customer satisfaction. Additionally, the mere availability of add-on features can enhance the value and quality of a product in the eyes of the consumer.[28]

12-4 PRODUCT POSITIONING AND REPOSITIONING

Once a target market is selected, a firm must consider how to position its product. **Product positioning** refers to the decisions and activities intended to create and maintain a certain concept of the firm's product, relative to competitive brands, in customers' minds. When marketers introduce a product, they try to position it so that it appears to have the characteristics that the target market most desires. This projected image is crucial. For instance, this advertisement for Lindt chocolate positions the confections as a high-end choice for discerning customers. By illustrating a close-up square of chocolate, Lindt underscores the refined characteristics and high-quality ingredients of the product.

product positioning The decisions and activities intended to create and maintain a certain concept of the firm's product, relative to competitive brands, in customers' minds

12-4a Perceptual Mapping

A product's position is the result of customers' perceptions of the product's attributes relative to those of competitive brands. Buyers make numerous purchase decisions on a regular basis. To simplify buying decisions and avoid a continuous reevaluation of numerous products, buyers tend to group, or "position," products in their minds. Rather than allowing customers to position products independently, marketers often try to influence and shape consumers' concepts or perceptions of products through advertising. Marketers sometimes analyze product positions by developing perceptual maps, as shown in Figure 12.4. Perceptual maps are created by questioning a sample of consumers about their perceptions of products, brands, and organizations with respect to two or more dimensions. To develop a perceptual map like the one in Figure 12.4, respondents were asked how they perceive selected pain relievers in regard to price and type of pain for which the products are used. Also, respondents would be asked about their preferences for product features to establish "ideal points" or "ideal clusters," which represent a consensus about what a specific group of customers desire in terms of product features. Then, marketers can compare how their brand is perceived compared with the ideal points.

Product Positioning
Swiss chocolatier Lindt positions its chocolate as a premium product, making it an affordable luxury for those who appreciate fine foods.

12-4b Bases for Positioning

Marketers can use several bases for product positioning. A common basis for positioning products is to use competitors. A firm can position a product to compete head-on with another brand, as PepsiCo has done against Coca-Cola, or to

Figure 12.4 **Hypothetical Perceptual Map for Pain Relievers**

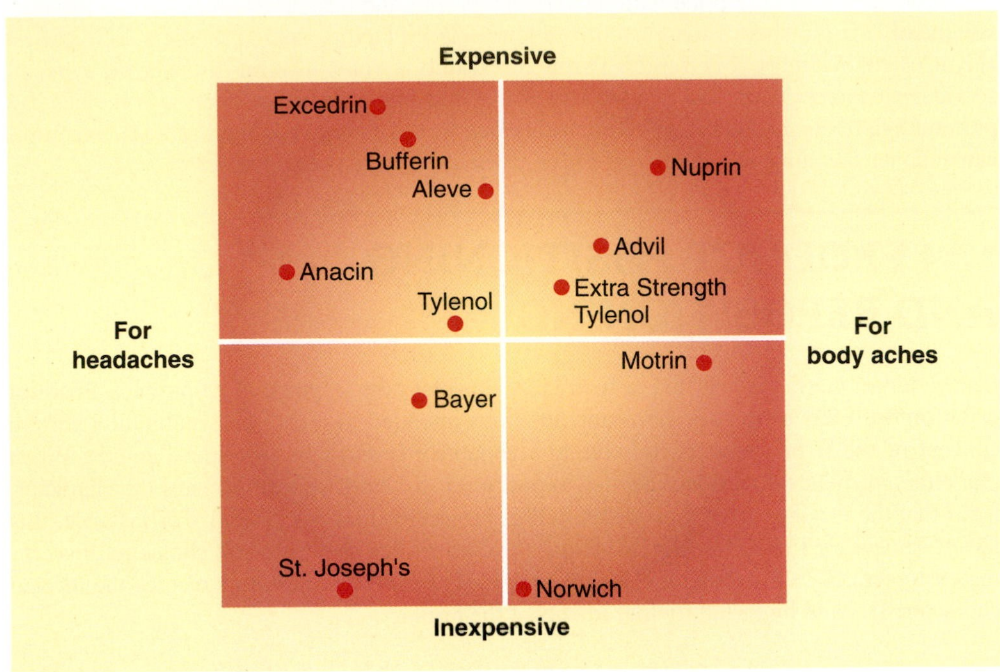

avoid competition, as 7 Up has done relative to Coca-Cola. Head-to-head competition may be a marketer's positioning objective if the product's performance characteristics are at least equal to those of competitive brands and if the product is priced lower. Head-to-head positioning may be appropriate even when the price is higher if the product's performance characteristics are superior. In the Olay body wash advertisement, marketers choose to position Olay Ultra Moisture Body Wash head-to-head with Dove Deep Moisture Body Wash. In the top half of the image, it shows the Dove product washing down the drain, while in the bottom half it shows Olay on a woman's skin. This ad indicates, visually and with words, that Olay moisturizes better than Dove.

Conversely, positioning to avoid competition may be best when the product's performance characteristics do not differ significantly from competing brands. Moreover, positioning a brand to avoid competition may be appropriate when that brand has unique characteristics that are important to some buyers. Prius, for example, does not compete directly with other hybrids. Rather, marketers position it as an eco-friendly hybrid that is also family-friendly. Auto companies are likely to focus on style, fuel efficiency, performance, terms of sale, or safety in their advertisements. Avoiding competition is critical when a firm introduces a brand into a market in which the company already has one or more brands. Marketers usually want to avoid cannibalizing sales of their existing brands, unless the new brand generates substantially larger profits.

A product's position can be based on specific product attributes or features. Apple's iPhone, for instance, is positioned based on product attributes such as its sleek design and compatibility with other Apple products and accessories, such as games and music through the iTunes' store. Style, shape, construction, and color help create the image and generate appeal. If buyers can easily identify the benefits, they are more likely to purchase the product. When the new product does not offer certain preferred attributes, there is room for another new product.

Other bases for product positioning include price, quality level, and benefits provided by the product. The target market can also be a positioning basis for marketers. This type of positioning relies heavily on promoting to the types of people who use the product.

12-4c Repositioning

Positioning decisions are not only for new products. Evaluating the positions of existing products is important because a brand's market share and profitability may be strengthened by product repositioning. Repositioning requires changes in perception and usually changes in product features. For instance, to encourage customers to visit more regularly, Meineke Car Care Centers launched a marketing strategy encouraging consumers to engage in regular car maintenance. The strategy repositions the brand as the go-to company for more proactive car maintenance.[29] When introducing a new product into a product line, one or more existing brands may have to be repositioned to minimize cannibalization of established brands and ensure a favorable position for the new brand.

Repositioning can be accomplished by physically changing the product, its price, or its distribution. Rather than making any of these changes, marketers sometimes reposition a product by changing its image through promotional efforts. Finally, a marketer may reposition a product by aiming it at a different target market.

Head-to-Head Positioning
This advertisement indicates that Olay Ultra Moisture Body Wash moisturizes skin better than Dove Deep Moisture Body Wash.

12-5 PRODUCT DELETION

Generally, a product cannot satisfy target market customers and contribute to the achievement of the organization's overall goals indefinitely. **Product deletion** is the process of eliminating a product from the product mix, usually because it no longer satisfies a sufficient number of customers. Kodak and Fuji, for instance, discontinued sales of most of its varieties of photographic film because of the steep increase in digital photography and decrease in interest in taking photos using film.[30] A declining product reduces an organization's profitability and drains resources that could be used to modify other products or develop new ones. A marginal product may require shorter production runs, which can increase per-unit production costs. Finally, when a dying product completely loses favor with customers, the negative feelings may transfer to some of the company's other products.

Most organizations find it difficult to delete a product. A decision to drop a product may be opposed by managers and other employees who believe that the product is necessary to the product mix. Salespeople who still retain loyal customers may be especially upset when a product is dropped. Companies may spend considerable resources and effort to revive a slipping product with a changed marketing mix and thus avoid having to eliminate it.

Some organizations wait to delete products until after they have become heavy financial burdens. A better approach is some form of systematic review in which each product is evaluated periodically to determine its impact on the overall effectiveness of the firm's product mix. This review should analyze the product's contribution to the firm's sales for a given period, as well as estimate future sales, costs, and profits associated with the product. It should also gauge the value of making changes in the marketing strategy to improve the product's performance. A systematic review allows an organization to improve product performance and ascertain when to delete products. General Motors decided to delete the Hummer, Saturn, Saab, and Pontiac brands in order to lower costs, improve reputation, and become more profitable.

product deletion Eliminating a product from the product mix when it no longer satisfies a sufficient number of customers

Figure 12.5 **Product Deletion Process**

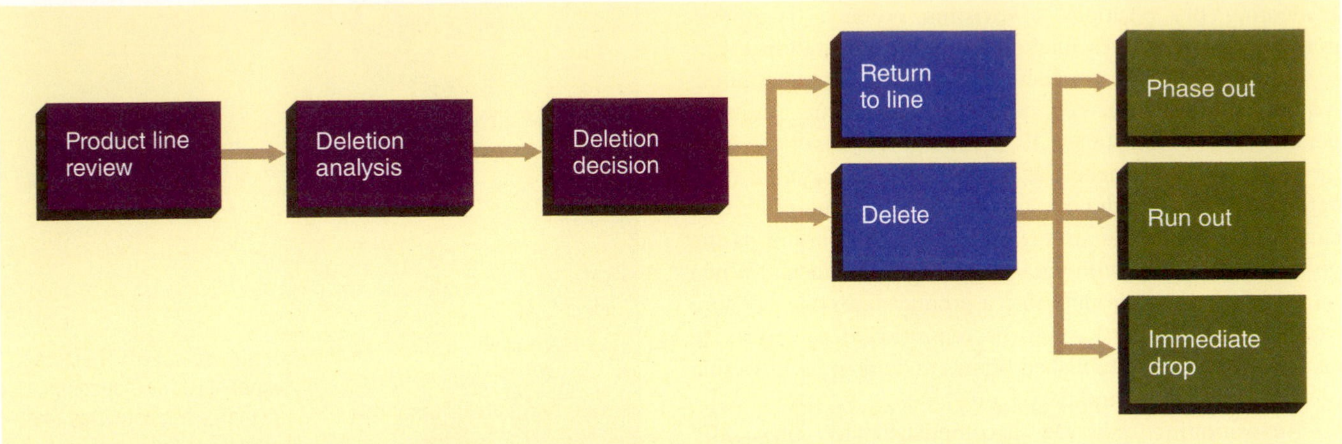

Source: Martin L. Bell, *Marketing: Concepts and Strategy*, 3rd ed., p. 267; Copyright © 1979, Houghton Mifflin Company. Reprinted by permission of Mrs. Martin L. Bell.
© Jim R. Bounds/Bloomberg via Getty Images

There are three basic ways to delete a product: phase it out, run it out, or drop it immediately (see Figure 12.5). A *phase-out* allows the product to decline without a change in the marketing strategy. With this strategy, no attempt is made to give the product new life. A *run-out* exploits any strengths left in the product. Intensifying marketing efforts in core markets or eliminating some marketing expenditures, such as advertising, may cause a sudden temporary jump in profits. This approach is commonly taken for technologically obsolete products, such as older models of computers. Often, the price is reduced to generate a sales spurt. The third alternative, an *immediate drop* of an unprofitable product, is the best strategy when losses are too great to prolong the product's life.

12-6 ORGANIZING TO DEVELOP AND MANAGE PRODUCTS

It should be obvious by now that managing products is a complex task. Often, the traditional functional form of an organization does not fit a company's needs. In this case, management must find an organizational approach that accomplishes the tasks necessary to develop and manage products. Alternatives to functional organization include the product or brand manager approach, the market manager approach, and the venture team approach.

A **product manager** is responsible for a product, a product line, or several distinct products that make up an interrelated group within a multiproduct organization. A **brand manager** is responsible for a single brand. Kraft, for example, has one brand manager for Nabisco Oreos, its number-one-selling cookie, and another for Oscar Mayer Lunchables. Both product and brand managers operate cross-functionally to coordinate the activities, information, and strategies involved in marketing an assigned product. Product managers and brand managers plan marketing activities to achieve objectives by coordinating a mix of distribution, promotion (especially sales promotion and advertising), and price. They must consider packaging and branding decisions and work closely with personnel in research and development, engineering, and production. Marketing researchers help product managers understand consumers and find target markets. Because the brand names of luxury brands like Aston Martin and Porsche can be negatively impacted by association with producers' other mass-market brands, brand managers must balance their brands' independent image with associated brands of the firm. The product or brand manager approach to organization is used by many large, multiple-product companies.

product manager The person within an organization who is responsible for a product, a product line, or several distinct products that make up a group

brand manager The person responsible for a single brand

A **market manager** is responsible for managing the marketing activities that serve a particular group of customers. This organizational approach is effective when a firm engages in different types of marketing activities to provide products to diverse customer groups. A company might have one market manager for business markets and another for consumer markets. Markets can also be divided by geographic region. Thus, the Jack-in-the-Box fast-food chain offers different menu items in New Mexico than it does in Oregon. Because Hindus believe cows are sacred, and India has a large vegetarian population, McDonald's offers lamb and vegetarian options in lieu of beef burgers at its restaurants in India. The chains recognize that different markets have different preferences. These broad market categories might be broken down into more limited market responsibilities.

A **venture team** creates entirely new products that may be aimed at new markets. Unlike a product or market manager, a venture team is responsible for all aspects of developing a product: research and development, production and engineering, finance and accounting, and marketing. Venture team members are brought together from different functional areas of the organization. In working outside established divisions, venture teams have greater flexibility to apply inventive approaches to develop new products that can take advantage of opportunities in highly segmented markets. Companies are increasingly using such cross-functional teams for product development in an effort to boost product quality. Quality may be positively related to information integration within the team, customers' influence on the product development process, and a quality orientation within the firm. When a new product has demonstrated commercial potential, team members may return to their functional areas, or they may join a new or existing division to manage the product.

market manager The person responsible for managing the marketing activities that serve a particular group of customers

venture team A cross-functional group that creates entirely new products that may be aimed at new markets

Summary

12-1 Explain how companies manage existing products through line extensions and product modifications.

Organizations must be able to adjust their product mixes to compete effectively and achieve their goals. Using existing products, a product mix can be improved through line extension and through product modification. A line extension is the development of a product closely related to one or more products in the existing line but designed specifically to meet different customer needs. Product modification is the changing of one or more characteristics of a product. This approach can be achieved through quality modifications, functional modifications, and aesthetic modifications.

12-2 Describe how businesses develop a product idea into a commercial product.

Before a product is introduced, it goes through a 7-phase new-product development process. In the idea generation phase, new product ideas may come from internal or external sources. In the process of screening, ideas are evaluated to determine whether they are consistent with the firm's overall objectives and resources. Concept testing, the third phase, involves having a small sample of potential customers review a brief description of the product idea to determine their initial perceptions of the proposed product and their early buying intentions. During the business analysis stage, the product idea is evaluated to determine its potential contribution to the firm's sales, costs, and profits. In the product development stage, the organization determines if it is technically feasible to produce the product and if it can be produced at a cost low enough to make the final price reasonable. Test marketing is a limited introduction of a product in areas chosen to represent the intended market. Finally, in the commercialization phase, full-scale production of the product begins and a complete marketing strategy is developed.

12-3 Discuss the importance of product differentiation and the elements that differentiate one product from another.

Product differentiation is the process of creating and designing products so that customers perceive them as different from competing products. Product quality, product design and features, and product support services are three aspects of product differentiation that companies consider when creating and marketing products. Product quality includes the overall characteristics of a product that allow it to perform as expected in satisfying customer needs. The level of quality is the amount of quality a product possesses. Consistency of quality is the degree to which a product has the same level of quality over time. Product design refers to how a product is conceived, planned, and produced. Components of product design include styling (the physical appearance of the product) and product features (the specific design characteristics that allow a product to perform certain tasks). Companies often differentiate their products by providing support services, usually called customer services. Customer services are human or mechanical efforts or activities that add value to a product.

12-4 Explain how businesses position their products.

Product positioning relates to the decisions and activities that create and maintain a certain concept of the firm's product in customers' minds. Buyers tend to group, or "position," products in their minds to simplify buying decisions. Marketers try to position a new product so that it appears to have all the characteristics that the target market most desires. Positioning plays a role in market segmentation. Organizations can position a product to compete head-to-head with another brand or to avoid competition. Positioning a product away from competitors by focusing on a specific attribute not emphasized by competitors is one strategy. Other bases for positioning include price, quality level, and benefits provided by the product. Repositioning by making physical changes in the product, changing its price or distribution, or changing its image can boost a brand's market share and profitability.

12-5 Discuss how product deletion is used to improve product mixes.

Product deletion is the process of eliminating a product that no longer satisfies a sufficient number of customers. Although a firm's personnel may oppose product deletion, weak products are unprofitable, consume too much time and effort, may require shorter production runs, and can create an unfavorable impression of the firm's other products. A product mix should be systematically reviewed to determine when to delete products. Products to be deleted can be phased out, run out, or dropped immediately.

12-6 Describe organizational structures used for managing products.

Often, the traditional functional form of organization does not lend itself to the complex task of developing and managing products. Alternative organizational forms include the product or brand manager approach, the market manager approach, and the venture team approach. A product manager is responsible for a product, a product line, or several distinct products that make up an interrelated group within a multiproduct organization. A brand manager is responsible for a single brand. A market manager is responsible for managing the marketing activities that serve a particular group or class of customers. A venture team is sometimes used to create entirely new products that may be aimed at new markets.

Go to www.cengagebrain.com for resources to help you master the content in this chapter as well as materials that will expand your marketing knowledge!

Developing Your Marketing Plan

A company's marketing strategy may be revised to include new products as it considers its SWOT analysis and the impact of environmental factors on its product mix. When developing a marketing plan, the company must decide whether new products are to be added to the product mix or if existing ones should be modified. The information in this chapter will assist you in the creation of your marketing plan as you consider the following:

1. Identify whether your product will be a modification of an existing one in your product mix or a completely new product.
2. If the product is an extension of one in your current product mix, determine the type(s) of modifications that will be performed.
3. Using Figure 12.1 as a guide, discuss how your product idea would move through the stages of new-product development. Examine the idea, using the tests and analyses included in the new-product development process.
4. Discuss how the management of this product will fit into your current organizational structure.

The information obtained from these questions should assist you in developing various aspects of your marketing plan found in the "Interactive Marketing Plan" exercise at www.cengagebrain.com.

Important Terms

line extension 354
product modifications 355
quality modifications 355
functional modifications 356
aesthetic modifications 356
new-product development process 357
idea generation 358
screening 359
concept testing 359
business analysis 359
product development 360
test marketing 361
commercialization 362
product differentiation 364
quality 365
level of quality 365
consistency of quality 365
product design 365
styling 366
product features 366
customer services 366
product positioning 367
product deletion 369
product manager 370
brand manager 370
market manager 371
venture team 371

Discussion and Review Questions

1. What is a line extension, and how does it differ from a product modification?
2. Compare and contrast the three major approaches to modifying a product.
3. Identify and briefly explain the seven major phases of the new-product development process.
4. Do small companies that manufacture just a few products need to be concerned about developing and managing products? Why or why not?
5. Why is product development a cross-functional activity—involving finance, engineering, manufacturing, and other functional areas—within an organization?
6. What is the major purpose of concept testing, and how is it accomplished?
7. What are the benefits and disadvantages of test marketing?
8. Why can the process of commercialization take a considerable amount of time?
9. What is product differentiation, and how can it be achieved?
10. Explain how the term *quality* has been used to differentiate products in the automobile industry in recent years. What are some makes and models of automobiles that come to mind when you hear the terms *high quality* and *poor quality?*
11. What is product positioning? Under what conditions would head-to-head product positioning be appropriate? When should head-to-head positioning be avoided?
12. What types of problems does a weak product cause in a product mix? Describe the most effective approach for avoiding such problems.
13. What type of organization might use a venture team to develop new products? What are the advantages and disadvantages of such a team?

Video Case 12.1

Do AXE Products Make Men More Desirable?

Whether you love them or hate them, the AXE commercials leave an indelible impression. The AXE brand, owned by Unilever, is meant to exude masculinity. First released under the Lynx brand name in France in 1983, AXE products did not hit American shelves until 2002. However, in a short time period, AXE products have revolutionized the male grooming market. AXE is the number-one male grooming brand in both the United States and Canada.

The company features provocative advertisements of women falling over men who wear the AXE body spray. AXE body sprays are its most popular product, but when it first entered the U.S. market, the company was taking a risk. Until that time, body sprays were not marketed to men, as they were considered to be more of a female item. Yet AXE quickly gained popularity by honing in on what many young men care about.

"Our target is really 18 to 24," said AXE brand manager Mike Dwyer. "Our ads are exactly what an 18-to-24-year-old guy is thinking about. It's gears and gadgets, it's sports, or it's girls. We focus very much on girls."

AXE's product features are both tangible and psychological. On the tangible side, the smell of the product needs to be pleasing to both men and women. The psychological features of the product include desirability, masculinity, and seductiveness.

To effectively manage the AXE brand, Unilever has to regularly develop new products and manage existing lines.

Over the years, it has introduced several line extensions, including hairstyling, aftershave, skin care, and shower gel products. The company has also released an AXE fragrance called Anarchy for Her in Canada, so that women can experience the "AXE Effect." Anarchy for Her is meant to complement the Anarchy for Him male fragrance and has more fruity and flowery scents.

Each year, the company introduces a new fragrance. For instance, one of its fragrances includes a chocolate ice cream scent. In order to create scents that resonate with its young male demographic, AXE hires professional perfumers to develop the fragrance and even employs expert "smellers." Such efforts not only made AXE a market leader but also helped the male grooming industry as a whole. It is estimated that, by 2015, male grooming products will be a $33.2 billion industry.

© Robcartorres/Shutterstock.com

AXE's sexualized marketing and its appeal to young men have become what Dwyer has called the "AXE Lifestyle." The styling of the product's package is meant to convey seductiveness (the traditional package is black, but the color changes depending on the product). AXE advertisements try to connect the action of attracting a woman to the product itself. For instance, the chocolate ice cream fragrance featured a commercial where women were licking the man after he used that particular scented body spray. Although AXE promotes itself through Twitter and events, its commercials tend to be its most notable promotion.

Young men have gravitated toward the idea that AXE body spray can make them more desirable. However, what AXE perhaps did not anticipate was its popularity among younger generations: male teenagers and tweens (those between the ages of 10 and 12). Although these younger generations do not have jobs, they have significant influence in the family. Mothers often purchase these products for their children after they request them.

Many of the promotions that appeal to young men seem to appeal to preadolescents—namely, the desire to be accepted and feel "sexy." Because preadolescence is the age when many young men become more conscientiousness of their looks, AXE provides a way for them to feel more confident about their body image. Unfortunately, preadolescents tend to overspray, and some schools have even banned the body spray because it is distracting in class.

Although the AXE brand can profit from its popularity among the tween generation, this trend can also backfire. Young men traditionally have shied away from products that are popular with those young enough to be their "kid brothers." Therefore, AXE makes it clear that its target market is for those between the ages of 18 and 24. To respond to these changing trends, AXE will need to continue developing and adapting products to meet the needs of its target market and take advantage of new market opportunities.[31]

Questions for Discussion

1. How has AXE managed its product mix?
2. How has AXE used line extensions to increase its reach among consumers?
3. Why are younger generations attracted to AXE products?

Case 12.2

Caterpillar Inc. Crawls Over the Competition with Product Development

Caterpillar Inc. is a global manufacturer of construction and mining equipment, machinery, and engines. The company is best known for its more than 300 machines, including tractors, forest machines, off-highway trucks, wheel dozers, and underground mining machines. Many of these machines are sold under the Cat brand, which consists of a Cat logo with the yellow pyramid over part of the "A." Since Caterpillar's machines and equipment are by far their most popular products, the organization must continually develop new products, modify existing ones, and spread awareness of its offerings to maintain its global competitive edge.

The development of new products at Caterpillar involves a series of stages. Overseeing the product development process are product managers. Under their direction, the Caterpillar division will brainstorm ideas for new products or discuss ways to modify existing ones. The company screens relevant product ideas and then undergoes concept testing and business analysis to determine the likely demand and feasibility of the proposed ideas. When it comes to actually developing the product, quality is everything for Caterpillar. Creating high-quality products is embedded in Caterpillar's Code of Conduct as one of its highest values. Therefore, the company has adopted the quality control process of Six Sigma to detect, correct, and reduce problems before the product is released.

After a working product is developed, Caterpillar releases the product on a limited scale and, should these test markets prove favorable, commercializes it on a national or global scale. This allows Caterpillar to gauge not only customer reaction to the product but also work out any manufacturing issues or problems that occur before launching it on a massive scale. When Caterpillar released its Cat CT660 Vocational Truck, it first released the truck into limited markets to make certain that it met quality standards and avoided major glitches. Once it passed these inspection processes, the Cat CT660 Vocational Truck was made available for large-scale shipment.

Not all of Caterpillar's products are new. Many of the company's machines and much of its equipment are modified to meet changing customer needs or adhere to new governmental requirements. For instance, after being criticized for violating the Clean Air Act in 2000, Caterpillar began modifying its engines to be more eco-friendly. Previously, the company's engines were releasing too much pollution into the air, so Caterpillar created Advanced Combustion Emissions Reduction Technology (ACERT) engines to reduce the amount of gases released. Caterpillar's ACERT technology surpassed federal regulation requirements. However, tighter gas emission laws are requiring Caterpillar to modify its products once more. To meet new requirements, Caterpillar partnered with Tenneco Inc. to create the Clean Emissions Module (CEM) to reduce emissions even further. These modules are being placed in Caterpillar's ACERT engines. Caterpillar also refurbishes old machines to increase their life spans, a type of functional modification.

Caterpillar has extended its product line into several different areas, including apparel, watches, toys, and jackets. Line extensions have both benefits and potential downsides. If the line extension has little to do with the core product, then the extension could fail or, even worse, contaminate the brand. On the other hand, line extensions can allow companies to branch out into other areas and increase brand awareness. For instance, Caterpillar-branded toy trucks and tractors allow consumers to become familiar with the Caterpillar name at a young age.

Caterpillar has begun taking its line extensions a step further by licensing the Cat brand name to create Cat-branded lifestyle stores across the world. When first considering Cat-branded stores, Caterpillar was uncertain whether consumers would accept items like apparel and footwear in a retail environment. The company test-marketed the stores over a 2-year period with outlets in the United Arab Emirates and China. Caterpillar has since decided to open stores on a wider global scale. The company has licensed its brand to Wolverine World Wide Inc. for Cat footwear and Summit Resource Imports/SRI Apparel for Cat-branded apparel. Although it is riskier to create a product extension that is vastly different from Caterpillar's core products of machinery and equipment, Caterpillar expects to profit from these licensing arrangements with increased revenue and global brand awareness.

Caterpillar is a company that must continually develop and manage its products to maintain its leadership in the construction industry. Its success at product management will likely lead the company to take advantage of future opportunities in the global market.[32]

Questions for Discussion

1. Why is it so important for Caterpillar to develop new products on a regular basis?
2. Why is Caterpillar so careful to test-market its products prior to commercialization?
3. What are some of the benefits and risks of Caterpillar's line extensions?

NOTES

[1] Olivia B. Waxman, "Cookies n' Crème Oreos: The Most Meta Snack Ever," *Time*, September 20, 2013, http://newsfeed.time.com/2013/09/20/cookies-n-creme-oreos-the-most-meta-snack-ever (accessed December 8, 2013); Andrew Averill, "Watermelon Oreos: The Public Weighs In on Social Media," *Christian Science Monitor*, June 19, 2013, www.csmonitor.com/The-Culture/Family/Modern-Parenthood/2013/0619/Watermelon-Oreos-The-public-weighs-in-on-social-media (accessed December 8, 2013); Stephen Clements, Tanvi Jain, Sherene Jose, and Benjamin Koellmann, "Smart Cookie," *Business Today*, March 31, 2013, pp. 108–112; Bruce Einhorn, "There's More to Oreo than Black and White," *Bloomberg Businessweek*, May 3, 2012, www.businessweek.com/articles/2012-05-03/

theres-more-to-oreo-than-black-and-white (accessed December 8, 2013); Mondelez International website, www.mondelezinternational.com (accessed December 8, 2013).

[2] Tom Gara,"Why Fast Food's Future Needs to Fit in a Cup Holder," *The Wall Street Journal*, October 2, 2013, http://blogs.wsj.com/corporate-intelligence/2013/10/02/why-fast-foods-future-needs-to-fit-in-a-cup-holder/?KEYWORDS=product+size (accessed November 16, 2013).

[3] Carmel Nobel, "Gender Contamination: Why Men Prefer Products Untouched by Women," *Forbes*, November 13, 2013, www.forbes.com/sites/hbsworkingknowledge/2013/11/13/gender-contamination-why-men-prefer-products-untouched-by-women (accessed November 17, 2013).

[4] Robert E. Carter and David J. Curry, "Perceptions versus Performance When Managing Extensions: New Evidence about the Role of Fit between a Parent Brand and an Extension," *Journal of the Academy of Marketing Science*, www.springerlink.com/content/8030v6q35851821t (accessed December 8, 2013).

[5] Brad Tuttle, "Why Some Brand Extensions Are Brilliant and Others Are Just Awkward," *Time*, February 7, 2013, http://business.time.com/2013/02/07/why-some-brand-extensions-are-brilliant-and-others-are-just-awkward (accessed November 17, 2013).

[6] Candace Choi, "Kashi Got Too 'Mainstream,' Says Kellogg CEO," *The Huffington Post*, November 4, 2013, www.huffingtonpost.com/2013/11/04/kashi_n_4213767.html (accessed November 18, 2013).

[7] Christopher Ross, "A Day in the Life of Nike CEO Mark Parker," *The Wall Street Journal*, November 7, 2013, http://online.wsj.com/news/articles/SB10001424052702303376904579135802125126572 (accessed November 17, 2013).

[8] Sam Grobart and Brad Stone, "With iPhone 5, Apple Again Raises the Smartphone Bar," *Bloomberg Businessweek*, September 12, 2012, www.businessweek.com/articles/2012-09-12/with-iphone-5-apple-again-raises-the-smartphone-bar (accessed December 8, 2013).

[9] Mark Scott, "British Retailer HMV Enters Equivalent of Bankruptcy," *The New York Times*, January 15, 2013, http://dealbook.nytimes.com/2013/01/15/british-retailer-hmv-enters-equivalent-of-bankruptcy (accessed January 20, 2014).

[10] Kim Wagner, Eugene Foo, Hadi Zablit, and Andrew Taylor, "Most Innovative Companies, 2013," Boston Consulting Group, September 26, 2013, www.bcgperspectives.com/content/articles/innovation_growth_most_innovative_companies_2013_lessons_from_leaders (accessed December 8, 2013).

[11] Bruce Horovitz, "2013 Product Trends: Quick, Easy and All about Me," *USA Today*, January 4, 2013, www.usatoday.com/story/money/business/2012/12/30/2013-new-product-trends/1767425 (accessed November 17, 2013).

[12] Annie Eisenberg, "Seeking a Staredown with Google Glass," *The New York Times*, October 12, 2013, www.nytimes.com/2013/10/13/business/seeking-a-staredown-with-google-glass.html (accessed December 1, 2013).

[13] Paul Mosur, "Apple Gets iPhone License for China Mobile Network," *The Wall Street Journal*, September 11, 2013, http://online.wsj.com/news/articles/SB10001424127887324549004579068261824600586 (accessed November 17, 2013).

[14] Christoph Fuchs and Martin Schreier, "Customer Empowerment in New Product Development," *Journal of Product Innovation Management* 28, no. 1 (January 2011): 17–31.

[15] Arina Soukhoroukova, Martin Spann, and Bernd Skiera, "Sourcing, Filtering, and Evaluating New Product Ideas: An Empirical Exploration of the Performance of Idea Markets," *Journal of Product Innovation Management* 29, no. 1 (January 2012): 100–112.

[16] Christoph Fuchs and Martin Schreier, "Customer Empowerment in New Product Development," *Journal of Product Innovation Management* 28, no. 1 (January 2011): 17–31.

[17] Christine Birkner, "How Jack Daniel's Generated Buzz for Tennessee Honey," *Marketing News Exclusives*, September 4, 2013, www.marketingpower.com/ResourceLibrary/Pages/newsletters/mne/2013/9/jack-daniels-tennessee-honey.aspx (accessed December 8, 2013).

[18] Stuart Elliot, "Marketers Wax Enthusiastic over Bees and Honey," *The New York Times*, October 16, 2013, www.nytimes.com/2013/10/16/business/media/marketers-wax-enthusiastic-over-bees-and-honey.html?_r=0 (accessed November 16, 2013).

[19] "P&G Open to New Ideas, But Not to Embalming Kits," *Taipei Times*, January 3, 2010, www.taipeitimes.com/News/biz/archives/2010/01/03/2003462552 (accessed November 17, 2013).

[20] Redfusion, www.redfusionstudios.com (accessed November 17, 2013).

[21] JoAndrea Hoegg and Joseph W. Alba, "Seeing Is Believing (Too Much): The Influence of Product Form on Perceptions of Functional Performance," *Journal of Product Innovation Management* 28, no. 3 (May 2011): 346–359.

[22] Maura Judkis, "Chipotle Is Testing Vegan Sofritas on Local Menus," *The Washington Post*, October 10, 2013, www.washingtonpost.com/blogs/going-out-guide/wp/2013/10/10/chipotle-is-testing-vegan-sofritas-on-local-menus (accessed December 1, 2013).

[23] Tim Motovalli, "Plug In, Turn On, Pass Gas Station," *The New York Times*, December 27, 2013, www.nytimes.com/2013/12/29/automobiles/plug-in-turn-on-pass-gas-station.html (accessed January 20, 2014).

[24] Roger J. Calantone and C. Anthony Di Benedetto, "The Role of Lean Launch Execution and Launch Timing on New Product Performance," *Journal of the Academy of Marketing Science*, June 2011, http://rd.springer.com/article/10.1007/s11747-011-0258-1 (accessed January 20, 2014).

[25] ASCI, *ASCI Retail and E-Commerce Report*, 2012, www.theacsi.org/news-and-resources/customer-satisfaction-reports/customer-satisfaction-reports-2012/acsi-retail-and-e-commerce-report-2012 (accessed November 18, 2013).

[26] "Consumer Shipping Benchmarks by Industry," ACSI, www.theacsi.org/index.php?option=com_content&view=article&id=147&catid=&Itemid=212&i=Consumer+Shipping (accessed November 18, 2013).

[27] Jeanne Bliss, "Trader Joe's Customer Experience Obsession," *1 to 1*, May 24, 2012, www.1to1media.com/weblog/2012/05/trader_joes_customer_experienc.html (accessed November 18, 2013).

[28] Marco Bertini, Elie Ofek, and Dan Ariely, "The Impact of Add-On Features on Consumer Product Evaluations," *Journal of Consumer Research* 36, no. 1 (June 2009): 17–28.

[29] Stuart Elliot, "Appealing to a Sense of Value for Car Care," *The New York Times*, September 11, 2013, www.nytimes.com/2013/09/11/business/media/appealing-to-a-sense-of-value-for-car-care.html?_r=0 (accessed November 18, 2013).

[30] David Becker, "Fujifilm Will Soon Discontinue 3×4 Instant B&W Film, Photos Fight Back," *PetaPixel*, November 15, 2013, http://petapixel.com/2013/11/15/fujifilm-ditching-3x4-instant-bw-film-photogs-fight-back (accessed December 1, 2013).

[31] John Berman and Lauren Effron, "The World of AXE Is 'Lick-able, Addictive,'" *ABC News*, March 25, 2011, http://abcnews.go.com/Entertainment/lick-inside-axe-popular-male-grooming-products-brand/story?id=13224549 (accessed December 8, 2013); "AXE Unleashes Anarchy in Canada with First-Ever Female Fragrance," *Canadian Newswire*, February 7, 2012, www.newswire.ca/en/story/917149/axe-unleashes-anarchy-in-canada-with-first-ever-female-fragrance (accessed December 8, 2013); Jan Hoffman, "Masculinity in a Spray Can," *The New York Times*, January 29, 2010, www.nytimes.com/2010/01/31/fashion/31smell.html?pagewanted=1&_r=1 (accessed December 8, 2013); Unilever, "Axe," www.unilever.ca/brands/personalcarebrands/Axe.aspx (accessed December 7, 2013).

[32] Caterpillar, *2010 Sustainability Report*, www.caterpillar.com/cda/files/2646184/7/2010SustainabilityReport.pdf (accessed December 7, 2013); Caterpillar, "Certified Rebuild," *2010 Sustainability Report*, www.caterpillar.com/cda/layout?m=389975&x=7&ids=2646281 (accessed December 7, 2013); "Clean Air Villain of the Month," Clean Air Trust, www.cleanairtrust.org/villain.0800.html (accessed December 7, 2013); Caterpillar, "Vision, Mission, Strategy," www.caterpillar.com/cda/layout?m=692724&x=7 (accessed December 7, 2013); "Caterpillar Inc. (CAT)," *Yahoo! Finance*, http://finance.yahoo.com/q/pr?s=CAT+Profile (accessed December 7, 2013); Caterpillar, "Equipment," www.cat.com/equipment (accessed December 7, 2013); "CATERPILLAR INC (CAT: New York)," *Bloomberg Businessweek*, http://investing.businessweek.com/research/stocks/snapshot/snapshot.asp?ticker=CAT:US (accessed December 7, 2013); "Caterpillar," *Business Insider*, www.businessinsider.com/blackboard/caterpillar (accessed December 7, 2013); Caterpillar, "CAT," www.caterpillar.com/brands/cat (accessed December 7, 2013); Caterpillar, "Products," www.cat.com/products (accessed December 8, 2013); Marc Gunther, "Caterpillar Jumps on the Green Bandwagon," *CNN Money*, May 3, 2007, http://money.cnn.com/2007/05/02/magazines/fortune/pluggedin_Gunther.fortune (accessed December 8, 2013).

Feature Notes

[a] Leslie Patton, "McDonald's Luring Starbucks Crowd with Pumpkin Lattes," *Bloomberg*, September 24, 2013, www.bloomberg.com/news/2013-09-24/mcdonald-s-luring-starbucks-crowd-with-pumpkin-lattes.html (accessed December 7, 2013); Brad Tuttle, "Summer of 2013 Must-Taste Fast Food List: The Top Ten," *Time*, June 5, 2013, http://business.time.com/2013/06/05/summer-of-2013-must-taste-fast-food-list-the-top-ten (accessed December 7, 2013); Sarah Nassauer, "The Calendar of Fast Food," *The Wall Street Journal*, March 6, 2013, http://online.wsj.com/news/articles/SB10001424127887324678604578342240583232674 (accessed December 7, 2013); Bruce Horovitz, "Burger King Rolls Out McRib-Buster," *USA Today*, May 14, 2013, www.usatoday.com/story/money/business/2013/05/14/burger-king-bk-rib-sandwich–mcrib-mcdonalds/2158431 (accessed December 8, 2013).

[b] Michael Hill, "Energy Drinks Go Natural as Market Buzzes Along," *USA Today*, July 1, 2013, www.usatoday.com/story/money/business/2013/07/06/energy-drinks-go-natural/2479993 (accessed December 8, 2013); Kacey Culliney, "Frito-Lay: Cracker Jack'D Caffeinated Snacks Do Not Target Kids," *Bakery and Snacks Magazine*, May 29, 2013, www.bakeryandsnacks.com/Manufacturers/Frito-Lay-Cracker-Jack-D-caffeinated-snacks-do-not-target-kids (accessed December 8, 2013); Saundra Young, "Wrigley Halts Production of Caffeine Gum," *CNN*, May 8, 2013, www.cnn.com/2013/05/08/health/wrigley-caffeine-gum-production/index.html (accessed December 8, 2013); Venessa Wong, "With Caffeinated Snacks, Who Needs Coffee?" *Bloomberg Businessweek*, June 20, 2013, www.businessweek.com/articles/2013-06-20/with-caffeinated-snacks-who-needs-coffee (accessed December 8, 2013).

OBJECTIVES

13-1 Discuss the growth and importance of services.

13-2 Identify the characteristics of services that differentiate them from goods.

13-3 Describe how the characteristics of services influence the development of marketing mixes for services.

13-4 Explain the importance of service quality and explain how to deliver exceptional service quality.

13-5 Discuss the nature of nonprofit marketing.

MARKETING INSIGHTS

Sports Stadiums Score with Super Customer Experiences

From speedy Wi-Fi connections and gourmet snacks to lounges with recliners and high-definition video screens showing other games in progress, sports stadiums are giving more fans more reasons to attend games in person. Although the excitement of live sports is the main attraction, teams also want to give fans a super in-stadium experience when they buy tickets.

For instance, knowing that football fans keep their digital devices close at hand, seats in the new Levi's Stadium where the San Francisco 49ers play have built-in computer tablet holders, and fans can browse the Internet via stadium-wide Wi-Fi. Smartphone apps are available for ordering food, viewing instant replays, and even checking the length of the line for stadium bathrooms. EverBank Field, home of the Jacksonville Jaguars football team, includes a 7,000-square-foot lounge where fans can put their feet up, enjoy a snack, and watch other NFL games on high-definition video screens. The Marlins Park baseball stadium features an aquarium behind home plate and more than a dozen food outlets ranging from traditional burgers and hot dogs to sushi and Cuban specialties.

On the horizon is technology that will help teams determine how many in-stadium fans are looking at the field, how many are watching video screens, how many are checking digital gadgets, and other nuances of behavior. With this information, marketers will be better able to time activities that increase the excitement level, such as giveaways that bring fans to their feet and contests that fans can enter via smartphone text.[1]

© Ken Durden/Shutterstock.com

Sports stadiums offer service products as well as tangible goods. This chapter explores concepts that apply specifically to products that are services. The organizations that market services include for-profit firms (e.g., those offering financial, personal, and professional services) and nonprofit organizations (e.g., educational institutions, churches, charities, and governments).

We begin this chapter with a discussion of the huge importance of service industries in economies, particularly in developed countries like the United States. We then address the unique characteristics of services. Next, we deal with the challenges these characteristics pose in developing and managing marketing mixes for services. We then discuss customers' judgment of service quality and the importance of delivering high-quality services. Finally, we define nonprofit marketing and examine the development of nonprofit marketing strategies.

13-1 THE GROWTH AND IMPORTANCE OF SERVICES

All products—whether goods, services, or ideas—are to some extent intangible. We previously defined a service as an intangible product that involves a deed, a performance, or an effort that cannot be physically possessed.[2] Services are usually provided through the application of human and/or mechanical efforts that are directed at people or objects. For example, a service such as education involves the efforts of service providers (teachers) that are directed at people (students), whereas janitorial and interior decorating services direct their efforts at objects. Services can also involve the use of mechanical efforts directed at people (air or public transportation) or objects (freight transportation). A wide variety of services, such as health care and landscaping, involve both human and mechanical efforts. Although many services entail the use of tangibles such as tools and machinery, the primary difference between a service and a good is that a service is dominated by the intangible portion of the total product.

Services as products should not be confused with the related topic of customer service. Customer service involves any human, mechanical, or electronic activity that adds value to the product. Although customer service is a part of the marketing of goods, service marketers also provide customer services. Many service companies offer service quality guarantees to their customers in an effort to increase value. Hampton Inn, a national chain of mid-price hotels, gives its guests a free night if they are not 100 percent satisfied with their stay (less than one-half of 1 percent of Hampton customers ask for a refund).[3] In some cases, a 100 percent satisfaction guarantee or similar service commitment can motivate employees to provide consistently high-quality service because they are proud to be part of an organization that is so committed to good service.

The importance of services in the U.S. economy led the United States to be known as the world's first service economy. In most developed countries, including Germany, Japan, Australia, and Canada, services account for about 70 percent of the gross domestic product (GDP). More than one-half of new businesses in the United States are service businesses, and service employment is expected to continue to grow. A practice that has gained popularity among U.S. businesses as telecommunications technology has improved is **homesourcing**, in which customer-contact jobs, such as at call centers, are outsourced to the homes of workers. Staffing agencies like Rhema Business Solutions are dedicated to providing homesourcing employees to organizations in a variety of industries, including nursing, marketing and sales, advertising, Web development, and writing.[4] Companies as diverse as 1-800-FLOWERS, J.Crew, and Office Depot all utilize homesourcing for some tasks.

homesourcing A practice whereby customer contact jobs are outsourced into workers' homes

A major catalyst in the growth of consumer services has been long-term economic growth (slowed by a few recessions) in the United States, which has led to increased prosperity and interest in financial services, travel, entertainment, and personal care. The need for child care, domestic services, online dating services, and other time-saving services has increased during the late 20th and early 21st centuries. Many busy consumers want to minimize or avoid such tasks as meal preparation, house cleaning, yard maintenance, and tax preparation to focus on other activities, such as work or family time. Because Americans tend to be health, fitness, and recreation oriented, the demand for services related to exercise and recreation has escalated. Another driver of services is the aging population in the United States, which has spurred expansion of health-care services. Finally, the increasing number and complexity of high-tech goods have spurred demand for support services. Indeed, dramatic changes in information technology have influenced and expanded the services sector in the 21st century. Consider service companies like Google, eBay, and Travelocity, which use technology to provide services that are responsive and well-targeted to customer needs and that have challenged traditional ways of conducting business.

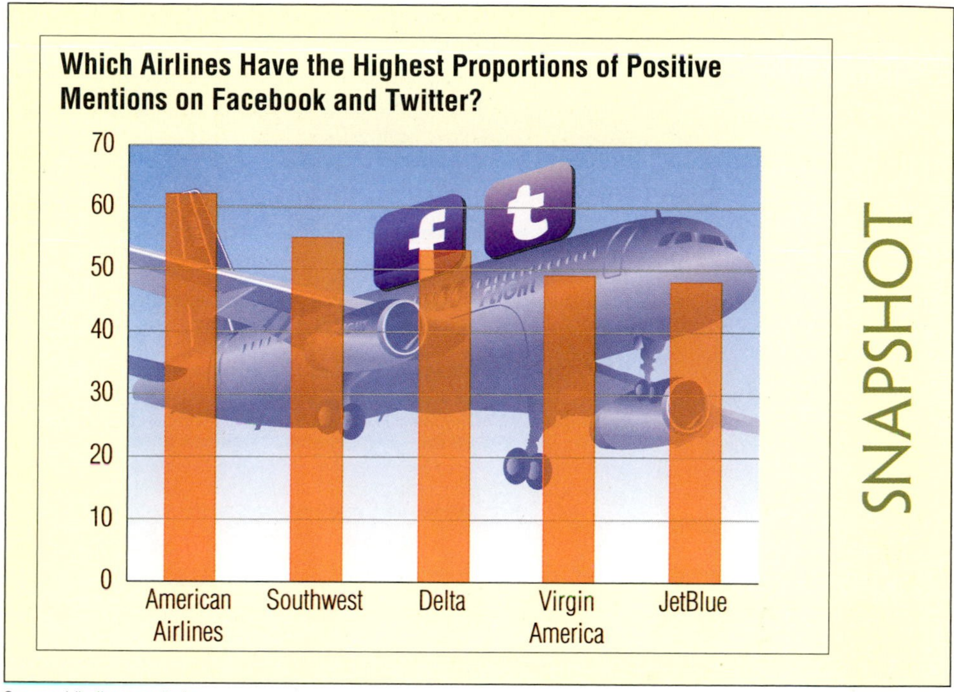

Source: Viralheat analysis.

Business services have grown as well. Business services include support and maintenance, consulting, installation, equipment leasing, marketing research, advertising, temporary office personnel, and janitorial services. The growth in business services can be attributed to the increasingly complex, specialized, and competitive business environment.

A way that might help you view services is using the metaphor of a theater. A play features production elements (such as actors, audience, a setting) and a performance. The actors (service workers) create a performance (service) for the audience (customers) in a setting (service environment) where the performance unfolds. Costumes (uniforms), props (devices, music, machines), and the setting (face-to-face or indirect through telephone or Internet) help complete the metaphor.[5] A service provider such as Disney World illustrates the metaphor: Employees wear costumes, there is an entertainment setting, and most service contact with employees involves playing roles and engaging in planned skits.

13-2 CHARACTERISTICS OF SERVICES

The issues associated with marketing service products are not exactly the same as those associated with marketing goods. To understand these differences, it is first necessary to understand the distinguishing characteristics of services. Services have six basic characteristics: intangibility, inseparability of production and consumption, perishability, heterogeneity, client-based relationships, and customer contact.[6]

13-2a Intangibility

As already noted, the major characteristic that distinguishes a service from a good is intangibility. **Intangibility** means a service is not physical and therefore cannot be touched. It is impossible, for instance, to touch the education that students derive from attending classes—the intangible benefit is becoming more knowledgeable in a chosen field of study. In addition,

intangibility The characteristic that a service is not physical and cannot be perceived by the senses

Figure 13.1 The Tangibility Continuum

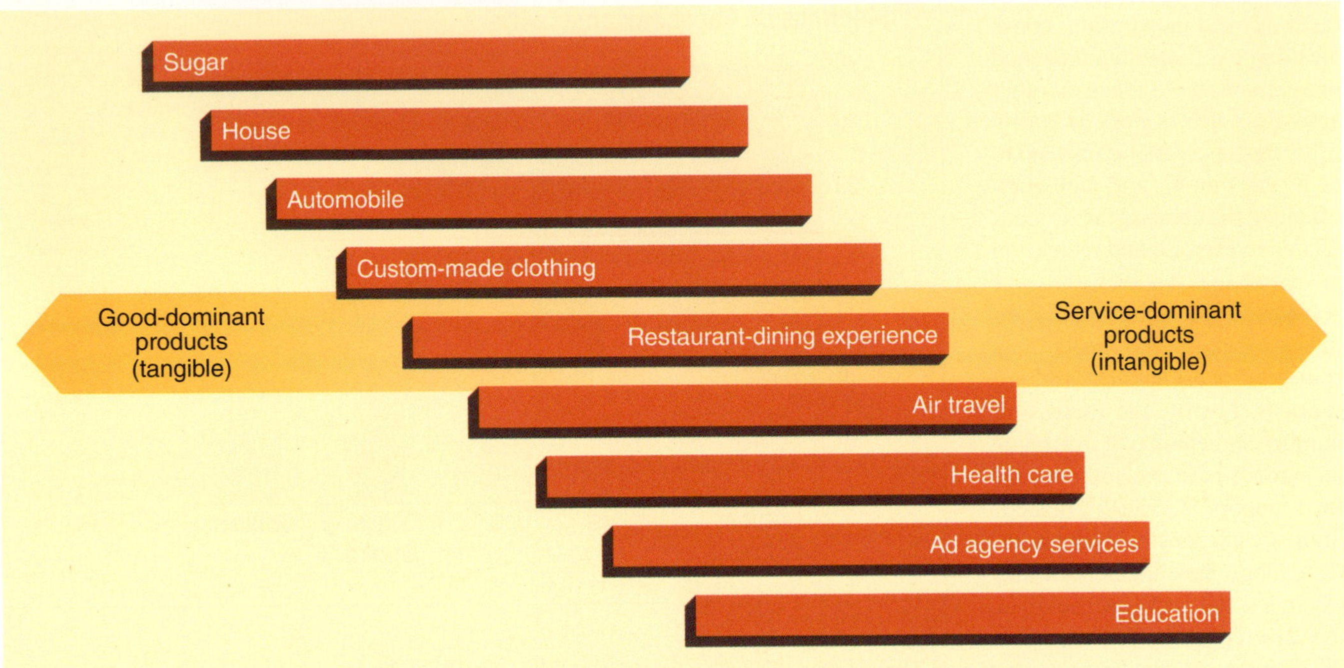

services cannot be physically possessed. Students cannot physically touch knowledge as they can an iPod or a car. The level of intangibility of a service increases the overall importance of the brand image when a customer is deciding which to purchase. A customer trying to select an intangible product usually relies more heavily on the brand to act as a cue to the nature and quality of the service.

Figure 13.1 depicts a tangibility continuum from pure goods (tangible) to pure services (intangible). Pure goods, if they exist at all, are rare because practically all marketers of goods also provide customer services. Even a tangible product like sugar must be delivered to the store, priced, and placed on a shelf before a customer can purchase it. Intangible, service-dominant products such as education or health care are clearly service products. Most products fall somewhere in the middle of this continuum. Products such as a restaurant meal or a hotel stay have both tangible and intangible dimensions. Knowing where the product lies on the continuum is important in creating marketing strategies for service-dominant products.

13-2b Inseparability of Production and Consumption

Another important characteristic of services that creates challenges for marketers is **inseparability**, which refers to the fact that the production of a service cannot be separated from its consumption by customers. For instance, an airline flight is produced and consumed simultaneously—that is, services are produced, sold, and consumed at the same time. In goods marketing, a customer can purchase a good, take it home, and store it until ready for use. The manufacturer of the good may never see an actual customer. Customers, however, often must be present at the production of a service (such as investment consulting or surgery) and cannot take the service home. Indeed, both the service provider and the customer must work together to provide and receive the service's full value. Because of inseparability, customers not only want a specific type of service but expect it to be provided in a specific way by a specific individual. For instance, the production and consumption of a medical exam occur simultaneously, and the patient knows in advance who the physician is and generally

inseparability The quality of being produced and consumed at the same time

© Digital Media Pro/Shutterstock.com

Inseparability of Production and Consumption
An airline flight is characterized by inseparability. That is, production and consumption occur simultaneously and cannot be separated.

understands how the exam will be conducted. Inseparability implies a shared responsibility between the customer and service provider. Training programs for employees in the service sector should stress the importance of the customer in the service experience so that employees understand that the shared responsibility exists.

13-2c Perishability

Services are characterized by **perishability** because the unused service capacity of one time period cannot be stored for future use. For instance, empty seats on an airline flight today cannot be stored and sold to passengers at a later date. Other examples of service perishability include unsold basketball tickets, unscheduled dentists' appointment times, and empty hotel rooms. Although some goods (e.g., meat, milk, or produce) are perishable, goods generally are less perishable than services. If a pair of jeans has been sitting on a department store shelf for a month, the quality is not affected. Goods marketers can handle the supply-demand problem through production scheduling and inventory techniques. Service marketers do not have the same advantage and face several hurdles in trying to balance supply and demand. They can, however, plan for demand that fluctuates according to day of the week, time of day, or season.

13-2d Heterogeneity

Services delivered by people are susceptible to **heterogeneity**, or variation in quality. The quality of manufactured goods is easier to control with standardized procedures, and mistakes are easier to isolate and correct. Because of the nature of human behavior, however, it is very difficult for service providers to maintain a consistent quality of service delivery. This variation in quality can occur from one organization to another, from one service person to another within the same service facility, and from one service facility to another within the same organization. Consequently, the staff people at one bookstore location may be more knowledgeable and therefore more helpful than those at another bookstore owned by the same chain. The quality of the service a single employee provides can vary from customer to customer, day to day, or even hour to hour. Although many service problems are one-time events that cannot be predicted or controlled ahead of time, employee training and the establishment of standard procedures can help increase consistency and reliability. Training

perishability The inability of unused service capacity to be stored for future use

heterogeneity Variation in quality

Heterogeneity
Do you care which chair that you are in? Do you like to go to the same hair care professional most of the time? If so, it is probably because you want the same quality of hair care, such as a haircut that you have received from this individual in the past.

©iStockphoto.com/ranplett

should offer ways that will help employees provide quality service consistently to customers, thus mitigating the issue of heterogeneity. Thus, a business that provides services in a cross-cultural environment may want to train its employees to be more sensitive toward people of different countries and cultures.

Heterogeneity usually increases as the degree of labor intensiveness increases. Many services, such as auto repair, education, and hairstyling, rely heavily on human labor. Other services, such as telecommunications, health clubs, and public transportation, are more equipment intensive. People-based services are often prone to fluctuations in quality from one time period to the next. For instance, the fact that a hairstylist gives a customer a good haircut today does not guarantee that customer a haircut of equal quality from the same hairstylist at a later time. Equipment-based services suffer from this problem to a lesser degree than people-based services. For instance, automated teller machines have low inconsistency in the quality of services compared to receiving the same service in-person at a bank, and barcode scanning has improved the accuracy of service at checkout counters in grocery stores.

13-2e Client-Based Relationships

The success of many services depends on creating and maintaining **client-based relationships**, which are interactions that result in satisfied customers who use a service repeatedly over time.[7] In fact, some service providers such as lawyers, accountants, and financial advisors call their customers *clients* and often develop and maintain close, long-term relationships with them. For such service providers, it is not enough to attract customers. They are successful only to the degree to which they can maintain a group of clients who use their services on an ongoing basis. For example, an accountant may serve a family in his or her area for decades. If the members of this family like the quality of the accountant's services, they are likely to recommend the accountant to other families. If several families repeat this positive word-of-mouth communication, the accountant will likely acquire a long list of satisfied clients.

client-based relationships
Interactions that result in satisfied customers who use a service repeatedly over time

Social media have made it easier for customers to share information about service companies. On Pinterest, users create separate "pinboards" for different categories, such as a planned wedding or party, and other users can use these boards for ideas and inspiration. Marketers are interested in the medium because each "pin" is worth 78 cents in additional revenue and is 100 times more viral than a Twitter tweet—making it a low-cost marketing investment that generates a large return. Pinterest is growing by leaps and bounds and is most popular among young and middle-aged women—the market segment in charge of most household purchasing decisions.[8] Word-of-mouth (or going viral, which is the online equivalent) is a key factor in creating and maintaining client-based relationships. To ensure that it actually occurs, the service provider must take steps to build trust, demonstrate customer commitment, and satisfy customers so well that they become very loyal to the provider and unlikely to switch to competitors.

13-2f Customer Contact

Not all services require a high degree of customer contact, but many do. **customer contact** refers to the level of interaction between the service provider and the customer necessary to deliver the service. High-contact services include health care, real estate, and legal services. Examples of low-contact services are tax preparation, auto repair, travel reservations, and dry cleaning. Technology has enabled many service-oriented businesses to reduce their level of customer contact. Note that high-contact services generally involve actions directed toward people, who must be present during production. A hairstylist's customer, for example, must be physically present at the salon during the styling process. When the customer must be present, the process of production may be just as important as its final outcome. Although it is sometimes possible for the service provider to go to the customer, high-contact services typically require that the customer go to the production facility. Thus, the physical appearance of the facility may be a major component of the customer's overall evaluation of the service. Even in low-contact service situations, the appearance of the facility is important because the customer likely will need to be present to initiate and finalize the service transaction. Consider customers of auto-repair services. They bring in the vehicle and describe its symptoms but often do not remain during the repair process.

Employees of high-contact service providers represent a very important ingredient in creating satisfied customers. A fundamental precept of customer contact is that satisfied employees lead to satisfied customers. Employee satisfaction is one of the most important factors in providing high service quality to customers. Thus, to minimize potential problems, service organizations must take steps to understand and meet the needs of employees by training them adequately, empowering them to make decisions, and rewarding them for customer-oriented behavior.[9] Southwest Airlines encourages customer loyalty and employee retention through training their staff and broadcasting instances of customer satisfaction and standout

customer contact The level of interaction between provider and customer needed to deliver the service

Entrepreneurship in Marketing

A Bank So Simple That's What They Call It!

Entrepreneurs: Joshua Reich and Shamir Karkal
Business: Simple, an online-only bank
Founded: 2009, Portland, Oregon
Success: By the end of its first year, Simple had attracted more than 70,000 customers and processed more than $1 billion in financial transactions.

Joshua Reich and Shamir Karkal launched Simple as an online bank with responsive, personalized customer service for tech-savvy consumers. Simple's customers use their computers and smartphones to deposit checks, pay bills, transfer money into savings, and send money to friends. Instead of paper checks, they get a debit card to pay for purchases and to withdraw money from the ATMs of participating banks. Adding to the appeal, Simple is free, except for fees on a handful of optional, paper-based services.

Service is where Simple really shines, answering customers' questions quickly via e-mail, mobile chat, or a personal phone call. It also provides convenient tools to help customers make informed decisions about managing their money. Customers can set up automatic savings for various goals, see how much is "safe to spend" based on their current situation, and attach personal notes or documents to transaction records as reminders or for tax purposes. In short, the entrepreneurs aim to make banking simple.[a]

customer service through social media channels. Social media can be an inexpensive and effective means of training and engaging employees, as well as spreading awareness of stellar service to customers.[10]

13-3 DEVELOPING AND MANAGING MARKETING MIXES FOR SERVICES

The characteristics of services discussed in the previous section create a number of challenges for service marketers (see Table 13.1). These challenges are especially evident in the development and management of marketing mixes for services. Although such mixes contain the four major marketing-mix variables—product, distribution, promotion, and price—the characteristics of services require that marketers consider additional issues.

13-3a Development of Services

A service offered by an organization is generally a package, or bundle, of services consisting of a core service and one or more supplementary services. A *core service* is the basic service experience or commodity that a customer expects to receive. A *supplementary service* supports the core service and is used to differentiate the service bundle from those of competitors. For example, when a student attends a tutoring session for a class, the core service is the tutoring. Bundled with the core service might be access to outlines with additional information, handouts with practice questions, or online services like a chat room or wiki to address questions that arise outside the designated tutoring time.

Table 13.1 Service Characteristics and Marketing Challenges

Service Characteristics	Resulting Marketing Challenges
Intangibility	Difficult for customer to evaluate. Customer does not take physical possession. Difficult to advertise and display. Difficult to set and justify prices. Service process is usually not protectable by patents.
Inseparability of production and consumption	Service provider cannot mass-produce services. Customer must participate in production. Other consumers affect service outcomes. Services are difficult to distribute.
Perishability	Services cannot be stored. Balancing supply and demand is very difficult. Unused capacity is lost forever. Demand may be very time sensitive.
Heterogeneity	Service quality is difficult to control. Service delivery is difficult to standardize.
Client-based relationships	Success depends on satisfying and keeping customers over the long term. Generating repeat business is challenging. Relationship marketing becomes critical.
Customer contact	Service providers are critical to delivery. Requires high levels of service employee training and motivation. Changing a high-contact service into a low-contact service to achieve lower costs is difficult to achieve without reducing customer satisfaction.

Sources: K. Doublas Hoffman and John E. G. Bateson, *Services Marketing: Concepts, Strategies, and Cases*, 4th ed. (Mason, OH: Cengage Learning, 2011); Valarie A. Zeithaml, A. Parasuraman, and Leonard L. Berry, *Delivering Quality Service: Balancing Customer Perceptions and Expectations* (New York: Free Press, 1990); Leonard L. Berry and A. Parasuraman, *Marketing Services: Competing through Quality* (New York: Free Press, 1991), p. 5.

As discussed earlier, heterogeneity results in variability in service quality and makes it difficult to standardize services. However, heterogeneity provides one advantage to service marketers: It allows them to customize their services to match the specific needs of individual customers. Customization plays a key role in providing competitive advantage for the service provider. Being able to personalize the service to fit the exact needs of the customer accommodates individual needs, wants, or desires.[11] Digital marketing firms must be highly aware of and able to customize their services. Hibu, depicted in the advertisement, is a marketing firm that offers customized digital services that fulfill specific needs for each of its clients. The image of rockets taking off underscores the importance of high-quality and well-targeted marketing to business success.

Customized services can be expensive for both the provider and the customer. Some service marketers therefore face a dilemma: how to provide service at an acceptable level of quality in an efficient and economic manner and still satisfy individual customer needs. To cope with this problem, some service marketers offer standardized packages. Thus, a lawyer may offer a divorce package at a specified price for an uncontested divorce. When service bundles are standardized, the specific actions and activities of the service provider usually are highly specified. Automobile quick-lube providers frequently offer a service bundle for a single price. The specific work to be done on a customer's car is spelled out in detail. Various other equipment-based services are also often standardized into packages. For instance, cable television providers offer several packages, such as "Basic," "Standard," and "Premier."

Hibu

Customized Services
Hibu is a marketing company offering customized digital services, including designing websites, mobile and tablet sites, and e-commerce platforms.

The characteristic of intangibility makes it difficult for customers to evaluate a service prior to purchase. Intangibility requires service marketers, such as stylists or attorneys, to market promises to customers. The customer must place some degree of trust in the service provider to perform the service in a manner that meets or exceeds those promises. Service marketers should take steps to avoid sending messages that consumers might construe as promises that raise customer expectations beyond what the firm can provide.

To cope with the problem of intangibility, marketers employ tangible cues (such as well-groomed, professional-appearing contact personnel and clean, attractive physical facilities) to assure customers about the quality and professionalism of the service. Most service providers require that at least some of their high-contact employees wear uniforms, which help make the service experience more tangible and serve as physical evidence to signal quality, create consistency, and send cues that suggest a desired image.[12] Consider the professionalism, experience, and competence conveyed by an airline pilot's uniform. Life insurance companies sometimes try to make the quality of their policies more tangible by printing them on premium paper and enclosing them in sheaths or high-quality folders. Because customers often rely on brand names as an indicator of product quality, service marketers at organizations whose names are the same as their service brand names should strive to build a strong national image for their companies. For example, USAA insurance, Ritz Carlton hotels, and Starbucks coffee maintain strong, positive national company images because these names are the brand names of the services they provide.

The inseparability of production and consumption and the level of customer contact also influence the development and management of services. The fact that customers are present and may take part in the production of a service means that other customers can impact the outcome of the service. For instance, a restaurant might give a small discount if children are well-behaved. Service marketers can reduce problems by encouraging customers to share the responsibility of maintaining an environment that allows all participants to receive the intended benefits of the service environment.

13-3b Distribution of Services

Marketers deliver services in various ways. In some instances, customers go to a service provider's facility. For instance, most health-care, dry-cleaning, and spa services are delivered at the provider's facilities. Some services are provided at the customer's home or business. Lawn care, air-conditioning and heating repair, and carpet cleaning are examples. Other services are delivered primarily at "arm's length," meaning no face-to-face contact occurs between the customer and the service provider. A number of equipment-based services can be delivered at arm's length, including electric, online, cable television, and telephone services. It can be costly for a firm to install the systems required to deliver high-quality customer service at arm's length, but can be essential in keeping customers satisfied and maintaining market share. To improve the quality of its arm's length service, CenturyLink acquired Tier 3, a cloud computing company. The acquisition allowed the telecommunications provider to offer a more robust package of services that is more accessible than ever.[13]

Marketing channels for services usually are short and direct, meaning the producer delivers the service directly to the end user. Insurance is a service that is frequently offered directly to customers via agents. For example, State Farm underscores the personal touch of its services in this advertisement by highlighting how State Farm agents take the time to meet with customers and truly understand their life insurance needs.

State Farm Life Insurance Company

Direct Marketing Channel
State Farm promotes its direct marketing channel and personal service through agents.

Some services, however, use intermediaries. For example, travel agents facilitate the delivery of airline services, independent insurance agents participate in the marketing of a variety of insurance policies, and financial planners market investment services. The Internet has allowed some service providers to alter marketing and distribution channels. For instance, Stitch Fix is an online personal shopping service, which ships clothing items to subscribers based on a detailed questionnaire. Personal shopping used to be a high-touch service, but the Internet has allowed Stitch Fix to offer a high-quality service at arm's length.[14]

Service marketers are less concerned with warehousing and transportation than are goods marketers. They are very concerned, however, about inventory management, especially balancing supply and demand for services. The service characteristics of inseparability and level of customer contact contribute to the challenges of demand management. In some instances, service marketers use appointments and reservations as approaches for scheduling delivery of services. Health-care providers, attorneys, accountants, and restaurants often use appointments or reservations to plan and pace delivery of their services. To increase the supply of a service, marketers use multiple service sites and also increase the number of contact service providers at each site.

To make delivery more accessible to customers and increase the supply of a service, as well as reduce labor costs, some service providers have replaced some contact personnel with equipment. In other words, they have changed a high-contact service into a low-contact one. By installing ATMs, banks increased production capacity and reduced customer contact. The transition to more automated services is not always seamless, however. Some customers do not like that automated services are less personal and would prefer to talk to a staff person. When designing service delivery, marketers must pay attention to the degree of personalization that customers in their target market desire.

13-3c Promotion of Services

The intangibility of services results in several promotion-related challenges to service marketers. Because it may not be possible to depict the actual performance of a service in an advertisement or display it in a store, explaining a service to customers can be a difficult task. Promotion of services typically includes tangible cues that symbolize the service. Consider Liberty Mutual Insurance, which features the Statue of Liberty on its logo. This image symbolizes strength and reliability to consumers. Although this symbol has nothing to do with the actual service, it makes it much easier for customers to understand the intangible attributes associated with the service.

To make a service more tangible, promotions for services may show pictures of facilities, equipment, and service personnel. Thus, advertisements for fitness centers may depict the equipment available. Marketers may also promote their services as a tangible expression of consumers' lifestyles. The advertisement for Emirates, an airline owned by the United Arab Emirates, specializes in offering customers a luxury service. This advertisement is for a route to Milan, Italy—a destination known for luxury and fashion as well. Through depicting two attractive women biking around sunny Milan, the advertisement emphasizes that the services offered by Emirates are an extension of the lifestyle and types of trips taken by target consumers.

Emirates

Services as an Expression of Lifestyles
Emirates targets wealthy consumers and promotes its services as an expression of the luxury they expect.

Branded marketing can help service firms hone their messages for maximum impact. Contently, for example, is a branded content firm that helps companies align their message to resonate with consumers across multiple media. Contently hires experienced writers and journalists to help companies tell their own stories in ways that are accessible and appealing, helping to improve levels of consumer trust and recognition through posting articles and advertisements on websites, in publications, and in social media.[15] When preparing advertisements, service marketers should be careful to use concrete, specific language to help make services more tangible in customers' minds. Service companies are also careful not to promise too much regarding their services so that customer expectations do not rise to unattainable levels.

Compared with goods marketers, service providers are more likely to promote price, guarantees, performance documentation, availability, and training and certification of contact personnel. It is common, for example, for gyms and yoga or aerobics studios to promote their trainers' degrees and certifications as a way to ensure customers that their trainers are well-qualified to help them reach their fitness goals.

Through their actions, service contact personnel can be directly or indirectly involved in the personal selling of services. Personal selling may be important because personal influence can help the customer visualize the benefits of a given service. Because service contact personnel may engage in personal selling, some companies invest heavily in training. To recapture lost market share and restore customer trust, United Airlines required its staff people to take additional customer service training and instituted a rigorous set of tracking measures to ensure that customers are satisfied. New advertisements emphasize the benefits of flying United, including staff friendliness.[16]

Emerging Trends

Bringing Back the Old-Fashioned Barber Shop

Eclipsed by unisex hair salons for three decades, barber shops are making a big comeback. Coast to coast, men are again seeking out barber shops for an old-fashioned, full-service experience—often with old-fashioned ambiance. Both multi-unit businesses and individual shops are focusing on quality service with the personal touch to attract and retain customers for the long term.

When Jim Valenzuela opened his first V's barber shop in Phoenix, he patterned the interior after barber shops of the past, using nostalgic furnishings such as porcelain chairs and equipment such as hot-towel machines to evoke positive images of old-style, top-quality professionalism. Boosted by loyal customers who appreciate the individualized attention and the traditional services as well as contemporary additions like TVs at each cutting station, the company now has 25 franchised locations.

Many individually-owned barber shops are enjoying new popularity as customers choose to support local small businesses. Personality also plays a pivotal role in differentiating neighborhood barber shops. For example, the Esquire Barber Shop in Uniontown, Pennsylvania, employs only female barbers and sets a family-friendly tone. The University Avenue Barber Shop in Los Gatos, California, fosters a sense of community and continuity, with century-old chairs and a casual atmosphere in which all customers are welcome to join the conversation while they get a trim or a shave.[b]

As noted earlier, intangibility makes experiencing a service prior to purchase difficult, if not impossible in some cases. A car can be test-driven, a snack food can be sampled in a supermarket, and a new brand of bar soap can be distributed as a free sample. Some services can also be offered on a trial basis at little or no risk to the customer, but a number of services cannot be sampled before purchase. Promotional programs that encourage trial use of insurance, health care, or auto repair are difficult to design because, even after purchase of such services, assessing their quality may require a considerable length of time. For instance, an individual may purchase auto insurance from the same provider for 10 years before filing a claim, but the quality of the coverage is based primarily on how the customer is treated and protected when a claim is made.

Because of the heterogeneity and intangibility of services, word-of-mouth communication is particularly important in service promotion. What other people say about a service provider can have a tremendous impact on whether an individual decides to use that provider. Some service marketers attempt to stimulate positive word-of-mouth communication by asking satisfied customers to tell their friends and associates about the service and may even provide incentives to current or new customers. Groupon and Living Social, which offer discounted deals at local businesses in participating cities, offer a free deal to customers who refer friends who then become new customers.

13-3d Pricing of Services

Services should be priced with consumer price sensitivity, the nature of the transaction, and its costs in mind.[17] Prices for services can be established on several different bases. The prices of such services as pest-control, dry cleaning, carpet cleaning, and health consultations are usually based on the performance of specific tasks. Other service prices are based on time spent on the task. For example, attorneys, consultants, counselors, piano teachers, and plumbers usually charge by the hour or day.

Some services use demand-based pricing. When demand for a service is high, the price is also high. Conversely, when demand for a service is low, so is the price. The perishability of services means that, when demand is low, the unused capacity cannot be stored and is lost—resulting in forgone revenues for the firm. Every empty seat on an airline flight or in a movie theater represents lost revenue. Some services are time sensitive, meaning that a significant number of customers desire the service around the same time. This point in time is called *peak demand.* A provider of time-sensitive services brings in most of its revenue during peak demand. For an airline, peak demand is usually early and late in the day. For cruise lines, peak demand occurs in the winter for Caribbean cruises and in the summer for Alaskan or European cruises. Customers can receive better deals on services by purchasing during non-peak times. Marketers may also want to consider that some consumers find demand-based pricing to be a more interesting way to shop for goods and services because it requires them to search for the best deals.[18]

Providers of time-sensitive services can use demand-based pricing to manage the problem of balancing supply and demand. They charge top prices during peak demand and lower prices during off-peak demand to encourage more customers to use the service. This is why the price of a matinee movie is generally lower than the same movie shown at a later time. The Walt Disney World Resort in Orlando, Florida, engages in demand-based pricing. The cost of hotel rooms and other amenities can more than double during holidays or vacation times when the park is at peak capacity.[19]

In cases where customers tend to purchase services in a bundle, marketers must decide whether to offer the services at one price, price them separately, or use a combination of the two methods. Some service providers offer a one-price option for a specific bundle of services and make add-on services available at additional charges. For instance, telecommunication companies like CenturyLink offer services á la cart or as a standard package, and customers can add services according to their needs for additional fees.

Because of the intangible nature of services, customers sometimes rely heavily on price as an indicator of quality. If customers perceive the available services in a service category as being similar in quality, and if the quality of such services is difficult to judge even after these services are purchased, customers may seek out the lowest-priced provider. For example, many customers search for auto insurance providers with the lowest rates because insurance companies tend to offer packages that are easily comparable between firms. If the quality of different service providers is likely to vary, customers may rely heavily on the price–quality association. For instance, if you have to have an appendectomy, will you choose the surgeon who charges $1,500 or the surgeon who only charges $399?

For certain types of services, market conditions may limit how much can be charged for a specific service, especially if the services in this category are perceived as generic in nature. Thus, the prices charged by a self-serve Laundromat are likely to be limited by the competitive rates for laundry services in a given community. Also, state and local government regulations may reduce price flexibility in some industries, such as for auto insurance, utilities, cable television service, and even housing rentals in rent-controlled communities.

13-4 **SERVICE QUALITY**

Delivery of high-quality services is one of the most important and difficult tasks any service organization faces. Because of their characteristics, services are very difficult to evaluate. Hence, customers must look closely at service quality when comparing services. **Service quality** is defined as customers' perceptions of how well a service meets or exceeds their expectations.[20] Research findings by American Express state that 70 percent of American consumers would spend an average of 13 percent more for a product from a company that provides good customer service.[21] Consumers are two times more likely to tell other people about a bad customer service experience than a good one. More than half of the people surveyed admitted to losing their temper with a customer service representative. Finally, 81 percent of participants in the survey believe that small businesses focus more on customer service than larger companies.[22] A survey by RightNow Technologies revealed that 89 percent of consumers surveyed had switched to a competitor at some point because of a bad customer service experience.[23] Customers, not the organization, evaluate

service quality Customers' perceptions of how well a service meets or exceeds their expectations

service quality—a critical distinction because it forces service marketers to examine quality from the customer's viewpoint. Thus, it is important for service organizations to determine what customers expect and then develop service products that meet or exceed those expectations.

13-4a Customer Evaluation of Service Quality

search qualities Tangible attributes that can be judged before the purchase of a product

experience qualities Attributes that can be assessed only during purchase and consumption of a service

credence qualities Attributes that customers may be unable to evaluate even after purchasing and consuming a service

The biggest obstacle for customers in evaluating service quality is the intangible nature of the service. How can customers evaluate something they cannot see, feel, taste, smell, or hear? Evaluation of a good is much easier because all goods possess **search qualities**, tangible attributes like color, style, size, feel, or fit that can be evaluated prior to purchase. Trying on a new coat and taking a car for a test drive are examples of how customers evaluate search qualities. Services, on the other hand, have very few search qualities. Instead, they possess experience and credence qualities. **Experience qualities** are attributes, such as taste, satisfaction, or pleasure, that can be assessed only during the purchase and consumption of a service.[24] Restaurants and vacations are examples of services high in experience qualities. **Credence qualities** are attributes that customers may be unable to evaluate even after the purchase and consumption of the service. Examples of services high in credence qualities are surgical operations, automobile repairs, and legal representation. Most consumers lack the knowledge or skills to evaluate the quality of these types of services. Consequently, they must place a great deal of faith in the integrity and competence of the service provider.

Despite the difficulties in evaluating quality, service quality may be the only way customers can choose one service over another. For this reason, successful service marketers must understand how consumers judge service quality. Table 13.2 defines five dimensions consumers use when evaluating service quality: tangibles, reliability, responsiveness, assurance,

Table 13.2 Dimensions of Service Quality

Dimension	Evaluation Criteria	Examples
Tangibles: Physical evidence of the service	Appearance of physical facilities Appearance of service personnel Tools or equipment used to provide the service	A clean and professional-looking doctor's office A clean and neatly attired repairperson The freshness of food in a restaurant The equipment used in a medical exam
Reliability: Consistency and dependability in performing the service	Accuracy of billing or recordkeeping Performing services when promised	An accurate bank statement A confirmed hotel reservation An airline flight departing and arriving on time
Responsiveness: Willingness or readiness of employees to provide the service	Returning customer phone calls Providing prompt service Handling urgent requests	A server refilling a customer's cup of coffee without being asked An ambulance arriving within 3 minutes
Assurance: Knowledge/competence of employees and ability to convey trust and confidence	Knowledge and skills of employees Company name and reputation Personal characteristics of employees	A highly trained financial adviser A known and respected service provider A doctor's bedside manner
Empathy: Caring and individual attention provided by employees	Listening to customer needs Caring about customers' interests Providing personalized attention	A store employee listening to and trying to understand a customer's complaint A nurse counseling a heart patient

Sources: Adapted from Leonard L. Berry and A. Parasuraman, *Marketing Services: Competing through Quality* (New York: Free Press, 1991); Valarie A. Zeithaml, A. Parasuraman, and Leonard L. Berry, *Delivering Quality Service: Balancing Customer Perceptions and Expectations* (New York: Free Press, 1990); A. Parasuraman, Leonard L. Berry, and Valarie A. Zeithaml, "An Empirical Examination of Relationships in an Extended Service Quality Model," *Marketing Science Institute Working Paper Series*, Report no. 90–112 (Cambridge, MA: Marketing Science Institute, 1990), p. 29.

and empathy. Note that all of these dimensions have links to employee performance. Of the five, reliability is the most important in determining customer evaluations of service quality.[25]

Service marketers pay a great deal of attention to the tangibles of service quality. Tangible elements, such as the appearance of facilities and employees, are often the only aspects of a service that can be viewed before purchase and consumption. Therefore, service marketers must ensure that these tangible elements are consistent with the overall image of the service. When it comes to the appearance of service personnel, something that an organization might want to consider is whether service personnel workers have visible tattoos. Research findings indicate that consumers draw conclusions based on visible tattoos that can affect their overall expectations of the service. In general, visible tattoos on white-collar workers, such as those in the medical and financial services sectors, are still viewed as inappropriate and unprofessional. However, attitudes about tattoos are changing as they become more common. More than 12 percent of workers age 30 and younger have a tattoo, meaning the level of acceptance of body modifications in the service industry, even in traditionally buttoned-up industries like accounting, is bound to increase over time.[26]

Service Quality
NetJets offers a high level of service quality to discerning customers.

Except for the tangibles dimension, the criteria customers use to judge service quality are intangible. For instance, how does a customer judge reliability? Because dimensions like reliability cannot be examined with the senses, customers must rely on other ways of judging service. One of the most important factors in customer judgments of service quality is service expectations. Service expectations are influenced by past experiences with the service, word-of-mouth communication from other customers, and the service company's own advertising. For instance, customers are usually eager to try a new restaurant, especially when friends recommend it. These same customers may have also seen advertisements placed by the restaurant. As a result, they have a preconceived idea of what to expect before they visit the restaurant for the first time. When they finally dine there, the quality they experience will change the expectations they have for their next visit. That is why providing consistently high service quality is important. If the quality of a restaurant, or of any service, begins to deteriorate, customers will alter their own expectations and change their word-of-mouth communication to others accordingly. Another example is air travel. NetJets is a private jet service agency shown in the advertisement. This advertisement underscores the high level of service quality provided to satisfy a discerning audience. Because the target market is high-end business and family travelers who generally will expect the red carpet treatment, the advertisement highlights all of the services NetJets provides.

13-4b Delivering Exceptional Service Quality

Providing high-quality service consistently is very difficult. All consumers have experienced examples of poor service: late flight departures and arrivals, inattentive restaurant servers, rude bank employees, and long lines. Obviously, it is impossible for a service organization to ensure exceptional service quality 100 percent of the time. However, an organization can take many steps to increase the likelihood of providing high-quality service. First, though, the service company must consider the four factors that affect service quality: (1) analysis of customer expectations, (2) service quality specifications, (3) employee performance, and (4) management of service expectations (see Figure 13.2).[27]

Figure 13.2 **Service Quality Model**

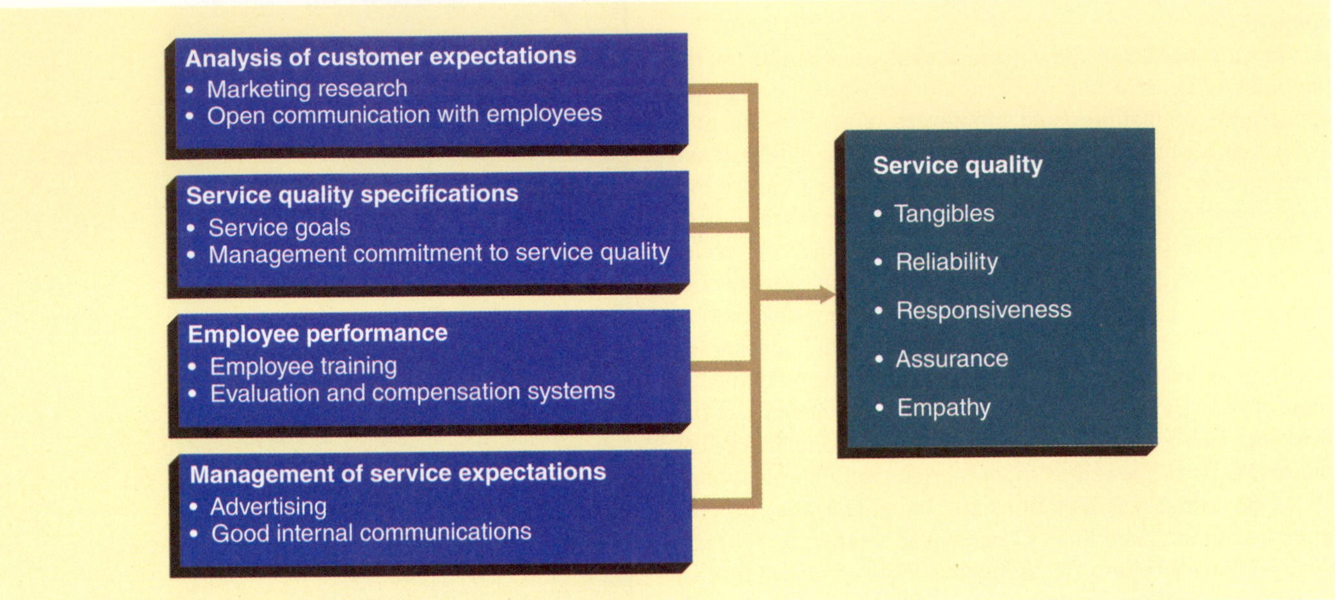

Source: Based on A. Parasuraman, Leonard L. Berry, and Valarie A. Zeithaml, "An Empirical Examination of Relationships in an Extended Service Quality Model," *Marketing Science Institute Working Paper Series*, Report no. 90–112, 1990.

13-4c Analysis of Customer Expectations

Providers need to understand customer expectations when designing a service to meet or exceed those expectations. Only then can they deliver good service. Customers usually have two levels of expectations: desired and acceptable. The desired level of expectations is what the customer really wants. If this level of expectations is provided, the customer will be very satisfied. The acceptable level of expectations is what the customer views as adequate. The difference between these two levels of expectations is called the customer's *zone of tolerance*.[28]

Service companies sometimes use marketing research, such as surveys and focus groups, to discover customer needs and expectations. Social business tools are allowing firms to use resources and data more effectively in developing marketing mixes and strategies. Social business can help firms to respond more quickly to consumer demands, anticipate changes in the marketplace, target internal talent, and improve overall visibility in the marketplace.[29] Other service marketers, especially restaurants, may use comment cards on which customers can complain or provide suggestions. Still another approach is to ask employees. Because customer-contact employees interact daily with customers, they are in good positions to know what customers want from the company. Service managers should interact with their employees regularly by asking their opinions on the best way to serve customers.

Service Quality Specifications

Once an organization understands its customers' needs, it must establish goals to help ensure good service delivery. These goals, or service specifications, are typically set in terms of employee or machine performance. For example, a bank may require its employees to conform to a dress code. Likewise, the bank may require that all incoming phone calls be answered by the third ring. Specifications like these can be very important in providing quality service as long as they are tied to the needs expressed by customers.

Perhaps the most critical aspect of service quality specifications is managers' commitment to service quality. Service managers who are committed to quality become role models for all employees in the organization. Such commitment motivates customer-contact employees to comply with service specifications. It is crucial that all managers within the organization embrace this commitment, especially frontline managers, who are much closer to customers than higher-level managers.

Employee Performance

Once an organization sets service quality standards and managers are committed to them, the firm must find ways to ensure that customer-contact employees perform their jobs well. Contact employees in most service industries (bank tellers, flight attendants, servers, sales clerks, etc.) are often the least-trained and lowest-paid members of the organization. Service organizations that excel realize that contact employees are the most important link to the customer, and thus their performance is critical to customer perceptions of service quality. There is a direct relationship between the satisfaction of a company's contact employees, which is manifested in a positive attitude and a good work ethic, and the satisfaction of its customers. Employee and customer satisfaction levels also have a direct relationship with customer retention and loyalty.[30] The way to ensure that employees perform well is to train them effectively so they understand how to do their jobs. Providing information about customers, service specifications, and the organization itself during the training promotes this understanding.

The evaluation and compensation system the organization uses also plays a part in employee performance. Many service employees are evaluated and rewarded on the basis of output measures, such as sales volume (automobile salespeople) or a low error rate (bank tellers). Systems using output measures may overlook other major aspects of job performance, including friendliness, teamwork, effort, and customer satisfaction. These customer-oriented measures of performance might be a better basis for evaluation and reward. In fact, a number of service marketers use customer satisfaction ratings to determine a portion of service employee compensation.

Management of Service Expectations

Because expectations play such a significant role in customer evaluations of service quality, service companies must set realistic expectations about the service they provide. They can set these expectations through advertising and good internal communication. In their advertisements, service companies make promises about the kind of service they will deliver. As already noted, a service company is forced to make promises because the intangibility of services prevents the organization from showing the benefits in the advertisement. However, the advertiser should not promise more than it can deliver. Doing so will likely mean disappointed customers.

To deliver on promises made, a company needs to have thorough internal communication among its departments, especially management, advertising, and store operations. Assume, for example, that a restaurant's radio advertisements guarantee service within 15 minutes or the meal is free. If top management or the advertising department fails to inform store operations about the 15-minute guarantee, the restaurant will very likely fail to meet its customers' service expectations. Even though customers might appreciate a free meal, the restaurant will lose some credibility as well as revenue. As mentioned earlier, word-of-mouth communication and online viral communication from other customers also shapes customer expectations. However, service companies cannot manage this "advertising" directly. The best way to ensure positive word-of-mouth communication is to provide exceptional service quality. It has been estimated that customers tell four times as many people about bad service as they do about good service.

13-5 NONPROFIT MARKETING

nonprofit marketing
Marketing activities conducted to achieve some goal other than ordinary business goals such as profit, market share, or return on investment

Nonprofit marketing refers to marketing activities that are conducted by individuals and organizations to achieve some goal other than ordinary business goals like profit, market share, or return on investment. Nonprofit marketing is divided into two categories: nonprofit-organization marketing and social marketing. Nonprofit-organization marketing is the use of marketing concepts and techniques by organizations whose goals do not include making profits. Social marketing promotes social causes, such as AIDS research or recycling.

Most of the previously discussed concepts and approaches to service products also apply to nonprofit organizations. Indeed, many nonprofit organizations mainly provide service products. In this section, we examine the concept of nonprofit marketing to determine how it differs from marketing activities in for-profit business organizations. We also explore the marketing objectives of nonprofit organizations and the development of their product strategies.

13-5a How Is Nonprofit Marketing Different?

Many nonprofit organizations strive for effective marketing activities. Charitable organizations and supporters of social causes are major nonprofit marketers in this country. Political parties, unions, religious sects, and fraternal organizations also perform marketing activities, but they are not considered businesses. Where the chief beneficiary of a business enterprise is who owns or holds stock in it, in theory, the only beneficiaries of a nonprofit organization are its clients, its members, or the public at large. The Metropolitan Opera in New York City, for example, is run by the nonprofit Metropolitan Opera Association. Many museums and performing arts institutions are run as nonprofits or have a nonprofit arm. Consider this advertisement for the National Disaster Search Dog Foundation. The advertisement features a cute puppy and informs consumers that it will be saving lives in a year's time. Through the image of the dog, the foundation hopes to create an emotional reaction among those who view the advertisement, convincing them of the importance of its cause.

Search Dog Foundation

Marketing in Nonprofit Organizations
The National Disaster Search Dog Foundation is a nonprofit agency that trains dogs to perform in search and rescue operations. Marketing efforts appeal to consumers on an emotional level, encouraging them to donate to the Foundation.

Nonprofit organizations have greater opportunities for creativity than most for-profit business organizations, but trustees or board members of nonprofit organizations are likely to have difficulty judging the performance of the trained professionals they oversee. It is harder for administrators to evaluate the performance of professors or social workers than it is for sales managers to evaluate the performance of salespeople in a for-profit organization.

Another way nonprofit marketing differs from for-profit marketing is that nonprofit marketing is sometimes quite controversial. Large national nonprofit organizations, such as Greenpeace, the National Rifle Association, and the National Organization for Women, allocate lobbying efforts in their budgets to inform Congress, the White House, and others of their interests and to gain their support. Some nonprofits must devote a large amount to lobbying because their mission is controversial or misunderstood by the general public. However, marketing as a field of study does not attempt to state what an organization's goals should be or debate the issue of nonprofit versus for-profit business goals. Marketing only tries to provide a body of knowledge and concepts to help further an organization's goals. Individuals must decide whether they approve or disapprove of a particular organization's goal orientation. Most marketers would agree that profit and consumer satisfaction are appropriate goals for business enterprises but may disagree about appropriate goals for a nonprofit organization.

13-5b Nonprofit Marketing Objectives

The basic aim of nonprofit organizations is to obtain a desired response from a target market. The response could be a change in values, a financial contribution, the donation of services, or some other type of exchange. Nonprofit marketing objectives are shaped by the nature of the exchange and the goals of the organization. These objectives should state the rationale for the organization's existence. An organization that defines its marketing objective as providing a product can be left without a purpose if the product becomes obsolete. However, servicing and adapting to the perceived needs and wants of a target public, or market, enhance an organization's chance to survive and achieve its goals.

13-5c Developing Nonprofit Marketing Strategies

Nonprofit organizations develop marketing strategies by defining and analyzing a target market then creating and maintaining a total marketing mix that appeals to that market.

Target Markets

We must revise the concept of target markets slightly to apply it to nonprofit organizations. Whereas a business seeks out target groups that are potential purchasers of its product, a nonprofit organization may attempt to serve many diverse groups. For our purposes, a **target public** is a collective of individuals who have an interest in or a concern about an organization, a product, or a social cause. The terms *target market* and *target public* are difficult to distinguish from many non-product or social-cause profit organizations. For instance, the target public for ACCION International is anyone interested in supporting international development and relief work. However, the target market for ACCION's advertisements consists of people in developing nations who want microloans to start businesses and spur economic development.[31]

In nonprofit marketing, direct consumers of the product are called **client publics** and indirect consumers are called **general publics**.[32] For example, the client public for a university is its student body, and its general public includes parents, alumni, and trustees. The client public usually receives most of the attention when an organization develops a marketing strategy.

Developing Marketing Mixes

A marketing strategy limits alternatives and directs marketing activities toward achieving organizational goals. The strategy should include a blueprint for making decisions about product, distribution, promotion, and price. These decision variables should be combined in the best way possible to serve the target market.

In developing the product, nonprofit organizations usually deal with ideas and services. Problems may evolve when an organization fails to define what it provides. What product, for example, does the Peace Corps provide? Its services include vocational training, health services, nutritional assistance, and community development. It also markets the ideas of international cooperation and U.S. foreign policy ideals. The product of the Peace Corps is more difficult to define than the average business product. The marketing of ideas and concepts is more abstract than the marketing of tangibles, and much effort is required to present benefits.

Distribution decisions in nonprofit organizations relate to how ideas and services will be made available to clients. If the product is an idea, selecting the right media to communicate the idea will facilitate distribution. By nature, services consist of assistance, convenience, and availability. Availability is therefore part of the total service. Making a product like health services available requires knowledge of retailing concepts such as site location analysis.

Developing a channel of distribution to coordinate and facilitate the flow of nonprofit products to clients is necessary, but in a nonprofit setting, marketers may need to revise the traditional concept of the marketing channel because the independent wholesalers available to

target public A collective of individuals who have an interest in or concern about an organization, product, or social cause

client publics Direct consumers of a product of a nonprofit organization

general publics Indirect consumers of a product of a nonprofit organization

a business enterprise do not exist in most nonprofit situations. Instead, a very short channel—nonprofit organization to client—is the norm because production and consumption of ideas and services are often simultaneous.

Making promotional decisions may be the first sign that a nonprofit organization is performing marketing activities. Nonprofit organizations use advertising and publicity to communicate with clients and the public. PACER's National Center for Bullying Prevention uses a variety of resources and media to promote its mission. It hosts National Bullying Prevention Month every October, in which thousands of schools participate. It also distributes coloring books to children, sells a CD of anti-bullying songs, and even hosts a fun run. Facebook, CNN, and Yahoo! Kids are multimedia partners of the group.[33] Direct mail continues to be used for fundraising by many social service organizations, such as the Red Cross and Special Olympics. Though direct mail remains important, some organizations have reduced their volume of direct mail in favor of e-mails or other digital communications.

Increasingly, nonprofits are using the Internet to reach fundraising and promotional goals through e-mail, websites, and software that permits online donations. In fact, 73 percent of nonprofits plan to increase their use of e-mail marketing, and 70 percent plan to increase their use of social media. These increases come as many organizations limit the use of print advertisements and direct mail.[34] Online crowdfunding sites, such as Kickstarter, have given nonprofits a new means of reaching many potential donors at once. Similar to telethons, which used to be held live or on television, crowdfunding allows many people to go online and donate small amounts until a goal amount is reached.[35] This model works because it allows people to give to a very targeted cause or project and therefore to feel more connected to where their donations go.[36] Mobile forms of marketing help nonprofits raise more money quickly, particularly among younger target publics. An estimated 96 percent of the global population has some access to cell phones, meaning they can be a powerful tool for doing good, as target publics and client and general publics all have a high level of access.[37]

Many nonprofit organizations also use personal selling, although they may call it by another name. Churches and charities rely on personal selling when they send volunteers to recruit new members or request donations. The U.S. Army uses personal selling when its recruiting officers attempt to persuade men and women to enlist. Special events to obtain funds, communicate ideas, or provide services are also effective promotional activities. Amnesty International, for example, has held worldwide concert tours featuring well-known musical artists to raise funds and increase public awareness of political prisoners around the world.

Although product and promotional techniques may require only slight modification when applied to nonprofit organizations, pricing is generally different and decision making is more complex. The different pricing concepts the nonprofit organization faces include pricing in user and donor markets. Two types of monetary pricing exist: *fixed* and *variable.* There may be a fixed fee for users, or the price may vary depending on the user's ability to pay. When a donation-seeking organization will accept a contribution of any size, it is using variable pricing.

The broadest definition of price (valuation) must be used to develop nonprofit marketing strategies. Financial price, an exact dollar value, may or may not be charged for a nonprofit product. Economists recognize giving up alternatives as a cost. **Opportunity cost** is the value of the benefit given up by selecting one alternative over another. According to this traditional economic view of price, if a nonprofit organization persuades someone to donate time to a cause or to change his or her behavior, the alternatives given up are a cost to (or a price paid by) the individual. Volunteers who answer phones for a university counseling service or a suicide hotline, for example, give up the time they could spend studying or doing other things as well as the income they might earn from working at a for-profit business organization.

For other nonprofit organizations, financial price is an important part of the marketing mix. Nonprofit organizations today raise money by increasing the prices of their services or charging for previously free services. They are using marketing research to determine what kinds of products people will pay for. Pricing strategies of nonprofit organizations often stress public and client welfare over equalization of costs and revenues. If additional funds are needed to cover costs, the organization may solicit donations, contributions, or grants.

opportunity cost The value of the benefit given up by choosing one alternative over another

Summary

13-1 Discuss the growth and importance of services.

Services are intangible products that involve deeds, performances, or efforts that cannot be physically possessed. They are the result of applying human or mechanical efforts to people or objects. Services are a growing part of the U.S. economy. They have six fundamental characteristics: intangibility, inseparability of production and consumption, perishability, heterogeneity, client-based relationships, and customer contact.

13-2 Identify the characteristics of services that differentiate them from goods.

Intangibility means that a service cannot be seen, touched, tasted, or smelled. Inseparability refers to the fact that the production of a service cannot be separated from its consumption by customers. Perishability means unused service capacity of one time period cannot be stored for future use. Heterogeneity is variation in service quality. Client-based relationships are interactions with customers that lead to the repeated use of a service over time. Customer contact is the interaction between providers and customers needed to deliver a service.

13-3 Describe how the characteristics of services influence the development of marketing mixes for services.

Core services are the basic service experiences customers expect. Supplementary services are those that relate to and support core services. Because of the characteristics of services, service marketers face several challenges in developing and managing marketing mixes. To address the problem of intangibility, marketers use cues that help assure customers about the quality of their services. The development and management of service products are also influenced by the service characteristics of inseparability and level of customer contact. Some services require that customers come to the service provider's facility, and others are delivered with no face-to-face contact. Marketing channels for services are usually short and direct, but some services employ intermediaries. Service marketers are less concerned with warehousing and transportation than are goods marketers, but inventory management and balancing supply and demand for services are important issues. The intangibility of services poses several promotion-related challenges. Advertisements with tangible cues that symbolize the service and depict facilities, equipment, and personnel help address these challenges. Service providers are likely to promote price, guarantees, performance documentation, availability, and training and certification of contact personnel. Through their actions, service personnel can be involved directly or indirectly in the personal selling of services.

Intangibility makes it difficult to experience a service before purchasing it. Heterogeneity and intangibility make word-of-mouth communication an important means of promotion. The prices of services are based on task performance, time required, or demand. Perishability creates difficulties in balancing supply and demand because unused capacity cannot be stored. The point in time when a significant number of customers desire a service is called peak demand. Demand-based pricing results in higher prices charged for services during peak demand. When services are offered in a bundle, marketers must decide whether to offer them at one price, price them separately, or use a combination of the two methods. Because services are intangible, customers may rely on price as a sign of quality. For some services, market conditions may dictate the price. For others, state and local government regulations may limit price flexibility.

13-4 Explain the importance of service quality and explain how to deliver exceptional service quality.

Service quality is customers' perception of how well a service meets or exceeds their expectations. Although one of the most important aspects of service marketing, service quality is very difficult for customers to evaluate because the nature of services renders benefits impossible to assess before actual purchase and consumption. These benefits include experience qualities, such as taste, satisfaction, or pleasure, and credence qualities, which customers may be unable to evaluate even after consumption. When competing services are very similar, service quality may be the only way for customers to distinguish among them. Service marketers can increase the quality of their services by following the four-step process of understanding customer expectations, setting service specifications, ensuring good employee performance, and managing customers' service expectations.

13-5 Discuss the nature of nonprofit marketing.

Nonprofit marketing is marketing aimed at nonbusiness goals, including social causes. It uses most of the same concepts and approaches that apply to business situations. Whereas the chief beneficiary of a business enterprise is whoever owns or holds stock in it, the beneficiary of a nonprofit enterprise should be its clients, its members, or its public at large. The goals of a nonprofit organization reflect its unique philosophy or mission. Some nonprofit organizations have very controversial goals, but many organizations exist to further generally accepted social causes.

The marketing objective of nonprofit organizations is to obtain a desired response from a target market. Developing a nonprofit marketing strategy consists of defining and analyzing a target market and creating and maintaining a marketing mix. In nonprofit marketing, the product is usually an idea or a service. Distribution is aimed at the communication of ideas and the delivery of services. The result is a very short marketing channel. Promotion is very important to nonprofit marketing. Nonprofit organizations use advertising, publicity, and personal selling to communicate with clients and the public. Direct mail remains the primary means of fundraising for social services, but some nonprofits use the Internet for fundraising and promotional activities. Price is more difficult to define in nonprofit marketing because of opportunity costs and the difficulty of quantifying the values exchanged.

Go to www.cengagebrain.com for resources to help you master the content in this chapter as well as for materials that will expand your marketing knowledge!

Developing Your Marketing Plan

Products that are services rather than tangible goods present unique challenges to companies when they formulate marketing strategy. A clear comprehension of the concepts that apply specifically to service products is essential when developing the marketing plan. These concepts will form the basis for decisions in several plan areas. To assist you in relating the information in this chapter to the development of your marketing plan for a service product, focus on the following:

1. Using Figure 13.1, determine your product's degree of tangibility. If your product lies close to the tangible end of the continuum, then you may proceed to the questions in the next chapter. If your product is more intangible, then continue with this chapter's issues.
2. Discuss your product with regard to the six service characteristics. To what degree does it possess the qualities that make up each of these characteristics?
3. Using Table 13.1 as a guide, discuss the marketing challenges you are likely to experience.
4. Determine the search, experience, and credence qualities that customers are likely to use when evaluating your service product.
5. Consider how your service product relates to each of the dimensions of service quality. Using Table 13.2 as a guide, develop the evaluation criteria and examples that are appropriate for your product.

The information obtained from these questions should assist you in developing various aspects of your marketing plan found in the "Interactive Marketing Plan" exercise at www.cengagebrain.com.

Important Terms

homesourcing 380
intangibility 381
inseparability 382
perishability 383
heterogeneity 383
client-based relationships 384
customer contact 385
service quality 391
search qualities 392
experience qualities 392
credence qualities 392
nonprofit marketing 395
target public 397
client publics 397
general publics 397
opportunity cost 398

Discussion and Review Questions

1. How important are services in the U.S. economy?
2. Identify and discuss the major characteristics of services.
3. For each marketing-mix element, which service characteristics are most likely to have an impact? Explain.
4. What is service quality? Why do customers find it difficult to judge service quality?
5. Identify and discuss the five components of service quality. How do customers evaluate these components?
6. What is the significance of tangibles in service marketing?
7. How do search, experience, and credence qualities affect the way customers view and evaluate services?
8. What steps should a service company take to provide exceptional service quality?
9. How does nonprofit marketing differ from marketing in for-profit organizations?
10. What are the differences among clients, publics, and customers? What is the difference between a target public and target market?
11. Discuss the development of a marketing strategy for a university. What marketing decisions must be made as the strategy is developed?

Video Case 13.1

UNICEF and the Good Shirts Project

The United Nation's Children's Emergency Fund (UNICEF) was created in 1946 as a nonprofit to protect the welfare and rights of children around the world. Wherever children are threatened by natural disasters, extreme poverty, violence, disease, and other problems, UNICEF works with local and international partners to raise money and deliver services to relieve suffering and meet basic needs.

Now UNICEF has teamed up with New York–based artists Justin and Christine Gignac, plus the online T-shirt retailer Threadless, on the Good Shirts Project. This is a combination fundraiser and educational program, raising awareness of the humanitarian crisis in the Horn of Africa and raising money to provide clean water, food, health supplies, and other desperately needed items for children and adults in Somalia, Kenya, Ethiopia, Eritrea, and Djibouti. "Hundreds of thousands of children are at imminent risk of death," Gignac explains. "Obviously, we need to do something to help and are fortunate to have been included in this effort to raise money for the U.S. Fund for UNICEF to support lifesaving relief efforts."

Good Shirts follows in the footsteps of the Gignacs' previous "Wants for Sale" art series, where they created paintings of items and experiences they wanted—and sold each painting for the amount of money they would have to pay for the item or experience. Similarly, each of the UNICEF shirts is priced at the cost of buying what the shirt shows for people in the Horn of Africa. For example, the white T-shirt featuring a big, colorful mosquito sells for $18.57, which pays for three insecticide-treated nets to protect from malaria. The white T-shirt featuring a green cargo plane sells for $300,000, the cost of chartering a flight from UNICEF's warehouse in Copenhagen to carry aid supplies to Nairobi, Kenya. In all, the artists created a dozen eye-catching T-shirts with light-hearted images "to remind people of the good they're doing by buying one," says Gignac.

Threadless produces the T-shirts and sells them online, with 100 percent of the proceeds going to UNICEF. The artists donate their time and designs, and the BBH New York ad agency provides free marketing assistance. "We're literally letting people wear their donation as a source of pride and as a means to spread the word," says a BBH executive. "If friends get a little competitive over who's being more altruistic, all the better."

To communicate with potential donors and keep the public informed about its services, UNICEF is an active user of social media. It has nearly 1 million followers on Twitter, where it uses the #goodshirts hashtag when tweeting about Good Shirts. UNICEF also has nearly 2 million followers on Facebook and maintains a YouTube channel where videos are posted in multiple languages.

Good Shirts is one of a number of initiatives that UNICEF uses to call attention to world trouble-spots where children are in need of aid. When UNICEF's celebrity ambassadors, including Sarah Jessica Parker, Clay Aiken, and Laurence Fishburne, travel to these areas, they use their fame to spread UNICEF's message and attract media coverage. In a decades-old Halloween tradition, many U.S. children carry orange "Trick or Treat for UNICEF" containers and ask for donations as they go door-to-door in their costumes. No matter where in the world children are threatened, UNICEF is ready to help.[38]

Questions for Discussion

1. Identify UNICEF's target public and client publics. Who is the target market for Good Shirts' social media messages?
2. What ideas and services are involved in UNICEF's product?
3. What kinds of objectives do you think UNICEF set for the Good Shirts Project? How should UNICEF evaluate the results of this project?

Case 13.2

American Express Delivers Service with Calls, Tweets, and Apps

Imagine the customer service challenges involved in satisfying 100 million customers worldwide who use their credit or debit cards to make $888 billion in purchases every year. That's the situation at American Express, the New York–based financial services firm that rings up $31 billion in annual revenues and has 63,000 employees spread across dozens of countries.

Although American Express has been in operation for more than 150 years, it began as a delivery service and did not enter the credit card business until the late 1950s. Since then, the company has expanded to offer a wide range of credit and debit cards for individuals, corporate employees, and small businesses. Its vision is to "make American Express the world's most respected service brand." To do this, it must provide convenient, responsive around-the-clock service to the consumers and executives who carry its cards, as well as to the merchants and small businesses that accept its cards.

© iStockphoto.com/adamdodd

Customers usually prefer to call American Express when they have a question or a problem. At the company's call centers, service representatives can view account details such as demographics, purchasing patterns, and payment patterns while they talk with customers. Thanks to sophisticated software, the reps also have access to special codes that indicate whether a customer is likely to remain loyal or leave. All reps are trained to listen carefully and ask questions that will uncover the source of the problem and lead to an acceptable resolution. Instead of reading from a prepared script, reps are encouraged to take as much time as needed to engage customers in conversation. This allows reps to learn more about each individual's underlying needs, identify a suitable solution to the problem at hand, and—if appropriate—recommend other American Express offerings, all with the goal of satisfying customers and earning their long-term loyalty.

American Express offers customers a number of ways to manage their accounts, check on features and reward benefits, and submit inquiries. Cardholders and merchants can log onto a secure website to access their statements and transaction activity, arrange payments, and request account changes. Online, American Express offers live chat as an option for customers who have a quick question or need immediate assistance while they're at their keyboards. For today's busy lifestyles, the company offers apps for smartphone users to access their account information on the go and to pay for purchases in stores and restaurants. In addition, it maintains a dedicated Twitter account for customer service inquiries, an account that has nearly 45,000 followers.

Because many of American Express's best customers are frequent flyers, the company is opening exclusive VIP lounges in large airports. In addition to lounges in busy U.S. airports such as Las Vegas and Dallas–Fort Worth, the company has customer-only lounges in several overseas airports, including Buenos Aires and Delhi. These luxury lounges offer free food, free Internet access, free concierge service for travel arrangements, and family entertainment areas.

American Express promotes its services and polishes its reputation in traditional advertising media such as television and magazines as well as with posts on its brand-specific social media sites. The company has 5 million Facebook likes, 700,000 Twitter followers, 20,000 people in its Google+ circles, and 31,500 Instagram followers. Drawing on its long history as a service business, American Express recently attracted social media attention and positive response by posting a series of historical brand images, such as a 19th century photo of its New York office and a picture of its earliest credit cards. Social media fans appreciated the nostalgic images and shared them with others, resulting in higher brand awareness and favorable word-of-mouth comments.

The company has also received a lot of publicity from its involvement in Small Business Saturday, an annual event it created to encourage shoppers to buy from local and small businesses on the Saturday after Thanksgiving. Launched in 2010, this high-profile event focuses on the "shop small" message, not the American Express brand. The company urges shoppers to buy locally using any payment method, not just its own cards. In 2013, Small Business Saturday resulted in an estimated $5.7 billion worth of purchases from small, independent businesses. The goodwill this event has generated for American Express over the years adds momentum to the company's marketing as it competes for cardholders and for merchant acceptance, day after day.[39]

Questions for Discussion

1. How is American Express addressing the five dimensions customers use when evaluating service quality? Explain your answer.
2. Why is heterogeneity particularly important to credit card customers?
3. When American Express says its vision is to be "the world's most respected service brand," what are the implications for how it manages service expectations?

Strategic Case 5

100 Years of Product Innovation at Chevrolet

General Motors' Chevrolet brand celebrated its 100th anniversary in 2011. In its 100-year history, Chevrolet embarked on many different vehicle models, some of them widely successful and others deleted from the product mix shortly after introduction. Over the years, it has transitioned from an American icon into a worldwide brand known for its quality and durability. Despite numerous ups and downs in its history, including the recent bankruptcy and bailout of parent company GM, Chevrolet is still going strong after a century of product innovation.

© Scott Olson/Getty Images

History of Product Innovation

Ironically, Chevrolet exists because of its top competitor, Ford Motor. William Durant founded Chevrolet in 1911 to compete head on with Ford's Model T. The brand was named after Louis Chevrolet, a top racer who was hired to design the first Chevrolet. Chevrolet's initial model cost \$2,000. This was a high-priced vehicle at the time, which did not sit well with Durant, who wanted to compete directly against Ford on price. In 1915, Chevrolet released a less expensive model priced at \$490, the same price as a Ford Model T. The company was acquired by General Motors in 1918, and Chevrolet went on to become one of GM's most popular brands.

During much of its history, Chevrolet attempted to position itself as an iconic American brand, using patriotic slogans and courting race car drivers as endorsers to create an image of quality and sportiness. Chevrolet is also credited with being the first automobile maker to come up with the idea of planned product obsolescence. Based on this concept, Chevrolet introduces a new car model each year, a type of product modification. Like all established companies, Chevrolet vehicles underwent several successes and failures. Some vehicles that Chevy thought would succeed failed miserably, often due to safety (the Corvair) or quality (the Vega) issues. On the other hand, its sporty Corvette was immensely popular and still exists today as a sports car icon. Table 13.3 shows the entire portfolio of Chevrolet vehicle models sold in the United States.

After nearly a century in business, Chevrolet faced its greatest threat with GM's bankruptcy in 2009. The company required a massive government bailout, and although GM has begun to rebound, its reputation will take a while to recover. According to GM CEO Dan Akerson, the company "failed because we failed to innovate." However, he sees hope in Chevrolet as an innovation powerhouse and believes the brand will bring GM back from the brink of collapse.

After the Bailout

Today, Chevrolet is a worldwide brand. It achieved record global sales of 4.76 million vehicles in 2011. Although it sold the most vehicles in the United States, China saw a more than 9 percent increase in the number of Chevrolets sold at 595,068 vehicles in 2011. The company positions its vehicles along four values: durability, value, practicality, and friendliness. This lattermost value relies heavily on the customer service that Chevrolet offers among its sales staff and customer support personnel.

Table 13.3 Chevrolet Models Sold within the United States

Cars	SUVs/ Crossovers	Trucks/Vans	Electric Vehicles
Sonic	Equinox	Colorado	Volt
Cruze	Traverse	Avalanche	
Malibu	Tahoe	Silverado	
Corvette	Suburban	Express	
Camaro			
Impala			
Spark			

Source: Based on data gathered from Chevrolet website, www.chevrolet.com/#happygrad (accessed January 26, 2012).

Chevrolet's vehicles are at all stages of the product life cycle. In the decline stage are its SUVs, as SUVs in general have become less popular due to a greater concern for the environment and rising gas prices. Rather than phasing out its SUVs, however, Chevrolet chose to revamp its SUVs to make them more eco-friendly. The company introduced SUV crossover vehicles and the Chevrolet Tahoe Hybrid in the hope of attracting those who like the style of SUVs without the gas inefficiencies. The Corvette is still going strong, although it has likely reached the maturity stage due to new product innovations and changing customer tastes. Additionally, the average Corvette owner is in his or her fifties. The Chevy Cruze is in the growth stage; in 2011, it was the best-selling compact car in the United States. Another car in the growth stage is the Chevrolet Camaro, a product that was initially deleted from the product mix in 2002. After fans demanded to have the Camaro resurrected, Chevrolet reintroduced a redesigned Camaro in 2010. The car went on to win the World Car Design of the Year. Even more popular than its cars are Chevrolet's pickup trucks. Chevrolet introduced its first truck in 1918, and sales of Chevrolet pickup trucks surpassed sales of its cars in 1989. Its Silverado pickup truck is currently in the growth stage as the second best-selling vehicle in 2011. Chevy is also seizing the opportunity to profit from a growing demand for electric vehicles with its introduction of the Chevrolet Volt. The Volt runs on electricity but will use gasoline if all of the electricity is used.

The Chevrolet brand is a model to which marketers aspire. Unlike so many other brands, it has lasted for a century due to its innovative product modifications and ability to rebound from failures. It must continue to seize market opportunities, constantly modify its products, and adapt its brand to changing customer tastes. Successfully meeting these criteria could enable the Chevrolet brand to succeed for another century.[40]

Questions for Discussion

1. Evaluate the product mix brands Cruze, Camaro, and Corvette in terms of their target market.
2. How has GM managed product innovation to sustain the Chevrolet brand for over 100 years?
3. What are the challenges for the Chevrolet brand in the future?

NOTES

[1] "Top Stadium Food in South Florida," *CBS Miami*, October 4, 2013, http://miami.cbslocal.com/top-lists/best-stadium-food-in-miami (accessed December 8, 2013); Ken Belson, "Going to the Game, to Watch Them All on TV," *The New York Times*, September 15, 2013, pp. 1, 4; Mary Dumon, "Levi's Trademarks 49ers Hi-Tech Stadium as 'Field of Jeans,'" *Technorati*, June 7, 2013, http://technorati.com/technology/article/levis-trademarks-49ers-hi-tech-stadium (accessed December 8, 2013); Sean Gregory, "Spy on Sports Fans," *Time*, March 25, 2013, pp. 36–37; Mike Garafolo, "Stadium Innovations a Priority to NFL Owners," *USA Today*, May 20, 2013, www.usatoday.com/story/sports/nfl/2013/05/20/nfl-meeting-stadium-innovations-priority/2344803 (accessed December 8, 2013).

[2] Leonard L. Berry and A. Parasuraman, *Marketing Services: Competing through Quality* (New York: Free Press, 1991), p. 5.

[3] "100% Hampton Guarantee®," Hampton Inn, http://hamptoninn3.hilton.com/en/about/satisfaction.html (accessed December 5, 2013).

[4] Rhema Homesourcing Business Services, www.facebook.com/Homesourcing (accessed November 19, 2013).

[5] Raymond P. Fisk, Stephen J. Grove, and Joby John, *Interactive Services Marketing* (Boston: Houghton Mifflin, 2008), p. 25.

[6] The information in this section is based on Hoffman and Bateson, *Services Marketing: Concepts, Strategies, and Cases*, 57; Valarie A. Zeithaml, A. Parasuraman, and Leonard L. Berry, *Delivering Quality Service: Balancing Customer Perceptions and Expectations* (New York: Free Press, 1990).

[7] J. Paul Peter and James H. Donnelly, *A Preface to Marketing Management* (Burr Ridge, IL: Irwin/McGraw-Hill, 2011).

[8] "About Pinterest," Pinterest, http://about.pinterest.com (accessed November 19, 2013); Addy Dugdale, "How Much Is a Pinterest Pin Worth? More Than a Tweet," *Fast Company*, November 19, 2013, www.fastcompany.com/3021879/fast-feed/how-much-is-a-pinterest-pin-worth-much-more-than-a-tweet (accessed November 19, 2013).

[9] Michael D. Hartline and O. C. Ferrell, "Service Quality Implementation: The Effects of Organizational Socialization and Managerial Actions of Customer Contact Employee Behavior," *Marketing Science Institute Report*, no. 93–122 (Cambridge, MA: Marketing Science Institute, 1993).

[10] Kare Anderson, "The Priceless Power of Socially Empowered Employees," *Forbes*, August 11, 2013, www.forbes.com/sites/kareanderson/2013/08/11/3000 (accessed December 3, 2013).

[11] Hoffman and Bateson, *Services Marketing: Concepts, Strategies, and Cases*, pp. 69–70.

[12] Fisk, Grove, and John, *Interactive Services Marketing*, p. 91.

[13] John Cook, "CenturyLink Buys Tier 3, Creates Cloud Development Center in Seattle Area," *Geek Wire*, November 19, 2013, www.geekwire.com/2013/centurylink-buy-tier-3-establish-cloud-development-center-seattle (accessed November 20, 2013).,

[14] Stitch Fix, www.stitchfix.com/?gclid=CP2jrIDh87oCFUhqfgodF2UAIg (accessed November 20, 2013).

[15] David Carr, "Marrying Companies and Content," *The New York Times*, November 10, 2013, www.nytimes.com/2013/11/11/business/media/marrying-companies-and-content.html (accessed November 20, 2013).

[16] Jane L. Levere, "Old Slogan Returns as United Asserts It Is Customer-Focused," *The New York Times*, September 20, 2013, www.nytimes.com/2013/09/20/business/media/old-slogan-returns-as-united-asserts-it-is-customer-focused.html (accessed December 3. 2013).

[17] Hoffman and Bateson, *Services Marketing: Concepts, Strategies, and Cases*, p. 163.

[18] Stephanie Clifford and Catherine Rampall, "Sometimes, We Want Prices to Fool Us," *The Wall Street Journal*, April 13, 2013, www.nytimes.com/2013/04/14/business/for-penney-a-tough-lesson-in-shopper-psychology.html (accessed November 24, 2013).

[19] Rebecca Dolan, "Ways to Save Money at Walt Disney World," *Kiplinger's*, October 30, 2013, www.kiplinger.com/article/spending/T059-C011-S001-save-money-in-walt-disney-world.html (accessed November 26, 2013).

[20] Zeithaml, Parasuraman, and Berry, *Delivering Quality Service*.

[21] "Good Service Is Good Business: American Consumers Willing to Spend More with Companies That Get Service Right, According to American Express Survey," American Express, May 3, 2011, http://about.americanexpress.com/news/pr/2011/csbar.aspx (accessed December 12, 2013).

[22] Ibid.

[23] Sabina Stoiciu, "The Importance of Excellent Customer Service & Feedback Surveys," *Business 2 Community*, December 2, 2013, www.business2community.com/customer-experience/importance-excellent-customer-service-feedback-surveys-0698146#!oPm8u (accessed December 3, 2013).

[24] Valarie A. Zeithaml, "How Consumer Evaluation Processes Differ between Goods and Services," in *Marketing of Services*, eds., James H. Donnelly and William R. George (Chicago: American Marketing Association, 1981), pp. 186–190.

[25] A. Parasuraman, Leonard L. Berry, and Valarie A. Zeithaml, "An Empirical Examination of Relationships in an Extended Service Quality Model," *Marketing Science Institute Working Paper Services*, no. 90–112 (Cambridge, MA: Marketing Science Institute, 1990), p. 29.

[26] Steve Evans, "Visible Ink: The Mark of the Future Accountant?" *Accounting, Auditing & Accountability Journal* 25, no. 7 (2012), www.emeraldinsight.com/journals.htm?issn=0951-3574&volume=25&issue=7&articleid=17053756&show=html&PHPSESSID=f2t55vncnkm2utjv8l8osp0c26 (accessed December 3, 2013).

[27] Valarie A. Zeithaml, Leonard L. Berry, and A. Parasuraman, "Communication and Control Processes in the Delivery of Service Quality," *Journal of Marketing* (April 1988): 35–48.

[28] Valarie A. Zeithaml, Leonard L. Berry, and A. Parasuraman, "The Nature and Determinants of Customer Expectations of Service," *Journal of the Academy of Marketing Science* (Winter 1993): 1–12.

[29] "Deloitte, Shifting out of First Gear in Social Business: How to Drive Adoption," *The Wall Street Journal, CFO Journal*, December 3, 2013, http://deloitte.wsj.com/cfo/2013/12/03/shifting-out-of-first-gear-in-social-business-how-to-drive-adoption (accessed December 3, 2013).

[30] "I'm Happy, You're Happy: Yet More Evidence That Satisfied Employees Make Satisfied, and Loyal, Customers," *Customer Service Psychology Research*, June 3, 2011, http://customerservicepsychology.wordpress.com/2011/06/03/i%e2%80%99m-happy-you%e2%80%99re-happy-yet-more-evidence-that-satisfied-employees-make-satisfied-and-loyal-customers (accessed December 12, 2013).

[31] "Our Mission and Vision," ACCION International, www.accion.org/page.aspx?pid=501 (accessed December 3, 2013).

[32] Philip Kotler, *Marketing for Nonprofit Organizations*, 2nd ed. (Englewood Cliffs, NJ: Prentice-Hall, 1982), p. 37.

[33] "About Us," Pacer, www.pacer.org/bullying/about (accessed December 3, 2013).

[34] VerticalResponse, "VerticalResponse, Inc. Surveys the State of Non-Profits in America; Reports on Trends in Marketing Channel Use across 2009 and 2010," *Press Release*, February 1, 2010, www.verticalresponse.com/about/press/vr-surveys-non-profits.html (accessed December 12, 2013).

[35] Ben Lamson, "How to Successfully Crowdfund for your Nonprofit," *The Huffington Post*, November 14, 2013, www.huffingtonpost.com/ben-lamson/how-to-successfully-crowd_b_4274202.html (accessed December 3, 2013).

[36] Jennifer Preston, "In Crowdfunding, New Source of Aid after Catastrophe," *The New York Times*, November 7, 2013, www.nytimes.com/2013/11/08/giving/in-crowdfunding-new-source-of-aid-after-catastrophe.html?_r=0 (accessed December 3, 2013).

[37] Esha Chhabra, "Ubiquitous across Globe, Cellphones Have Become Tool for Doing Good," *The New York Times*, November 8, 2013, www.nytimes.com/2013/11/08/giving/ubiquitous-across-globe-cellphones-have-become-tool-for-doing-good.html (accessed December 3, 2013).

[38] Based on information in David Wolinsky, "Threadless Teams with UNICEF for Charitable T-Shirts," NBC Chicago, October 13, 2011, http://www.nbcchicago.com/blogs/inc-well/Threadless-Teams-with-UNICEF-for-Charitable-T-Shirts-131632403.html (accessed December 12, 2013); Piers Fawkes, "Justin Gignac Explains How He'll Raise Millions for UNICEF by Selling T-Shirts," PSFK, October 26, 2011, http://www.psfk.com/2011/10/justin-gignac-explains-how-hell-raise-millions-for-unicef-by-selling-t-shirts.html (accessed December 12, 2013); UNICEF, "Good Shirts Collection Launched to Help UNICEF Aid Children in the Horn of Africa," news release, October 25, 2011, http://www.unicefusa.org/news/releases/unicef-good-shirts.html (accessed December 12, 2013); Unicef website, www.unicef.org (accessed December 12, 2013).

[39] Joe Sharkey, "Airlines' Credit Card Perks Take It on the Chin," *The New York Times*, December 9, 2013, www.nytimes.com/2013/12/10/business/when-airlines-play-hardball-with-favorite-perks.html (accessed January 14, 2014); Patrick Clark, "Small Business Saturday's $5.7 Billion Shopping Spree," *Bloomberg Businessweek*, December 2, 2013, www.businessweek.com/articles/2013-12-02/small-business-saturdays-5-dot-7-billion-shopping-spree (accessed January 14, 2014); Erik Schatzker, "Edward Gilligan, President, American Express, Is Interviewed on Bloomberg TV," *Bloomberg*, November 29, 2013, n.p.; Geoff Colvin, "AmEx Customer Service in Action," *Fortune*, April 19, 2012, http://management.fortune.cnn.com/2012/04/19/amex-customer-service-reps (accessed January 14, 2014); Christopher Heine, "AmEx's Social Data Shows That Nostalgia Is Just Swell," *Adweek*, October 11, 2013, www.adweek.com/news/technology/amexs-social-data-shows-nostalgia-just-swell-153053 (accessed January 14, 2014).

[40] "Chevrolet Turns 100," *Automobile*, November 2011, 53–97; James R. Healy, "100 Years of Chevy," *USA Today*, October 31, 2011, 1B, 2B; Soyoung Kim, "GM Bans Use of 'Chevy' Brand Name Internally," *Reuters*, June 10, 2010, www.reuters.com/article/2010/06/10/gm-chevy-idUSN1024152620100610 (accessed November 14, 2011); "From 0 to 100," *The Economist*, October 29, 2011, 76; "Chevrolet Camaro—World Car Design of the Year 2010," *AUSmotive.com*, April 8, 2010, www.ausmotive.com/2010/04/08/chevrolet-camaro-world-car-design-of-the-year-2010.html (accessed November 14, 2011); "Chevrolet," www.superbrands.com/za/pdfs/CHEV.pdf (accessed November 14, 2011); Joann Muller, "The Best-Selling Vehicles of 2011," *MSNBC*, November 9, 2011, www.msnbc.msn.com/id/45165770/ns/business-forbes_com/t/best-selling-vehicles/ (accessed November 21, 2011); Jason Siu, "Chevrolet Achieves Best Ever Global Sales In 2011," *AutoGuide*, January 20, 2012, www.autoguide.com/auto-news/2012/01/chevrolet-achieves-best-ever-global-sales-in-2011.html (accessed March 21, 2012).

Feature Notes

[a] Melissa Harris, "Making Noise about Finance," *Chicago Tribune*, October 17, 2013, http://articles.chicagotribune.com/2013-10-17/business/ct-biz-1017-confidential-money-20131017_1_chicago-ideas-week-overdraft-fees-money-drop (accessed December 8, 2013); Parimal M. Rohit, "Shamir Karkal's Simple Bank: Making Banking Simple," *IndiaWest*, July 12, 2013, www.indiawest.com/news/12067-shamir-karkal-s-simple-bank-making-banking-simple.html (accessed December 8, 2013); Andre Behrens, "Gamification Done Right," *The New York Times*, June 11, 2013, http://open.blogs.nytimes.com/2013/06/11/gamification-done-right (accessed December 8, 2013); Jenna Wortham, "A Financial Service for People Fed Up with Banks," *The New York Times*, January 8, 2013, www.nytimes.com/2013/01/09/technology/a-financial-service-for-people-fed-up-with-banks.html (accessed December 8, 2013).

[b] Robert Klara, "Barbershops Are Making a Huge Comeback," *Adweek*, October 9, 2013, www.adweek.com/news/advertising-branding/barbershops-are-making-huge-comeback-152932 (accessed December 8, 2013); Judy Peterson, "Old-Fashioned Barber Shops Are Flourishing in Los Gatos," *San Jose Mercury News*, September 16, 2013, www.mercurynews.com/los-gatos/ci_24109390/old-fashioned-barber-shops-are-flourishing-los-gatos (accessed December 8, 2013); Laura Szepesi, "Trio Keep Barber Tradition Alive in Uniontown," *Tribune-Review (Uniontown, PA)*, October 2, 2013, http://triblive.com/news/fayette/4785431-74/esquire-del-grecco#axzz2mv8hvfQL (accessed December 8, 2013).

part 6

Distribution Decisions

Developing products that satisfy customers is important, but it is not enough to guarantee successful marketing strategies. Products must also be available in adequate quantities in accessible locations at the times when customers desire them. PART 6 deals with the distribution of products and the marketing channels and institutions that help to make products available. CHAPTER 14 discusses supply-chain management, marketing channels, and the decisions and activities associated with the physical distribution of products, such as order processing, materials handling, warehousing, inventory management, and transportation. CHAPTER 15 explores retailing and wholesaling, including types of retailers and wholesalers, direct marketing and selling, and strategic retailing issues.

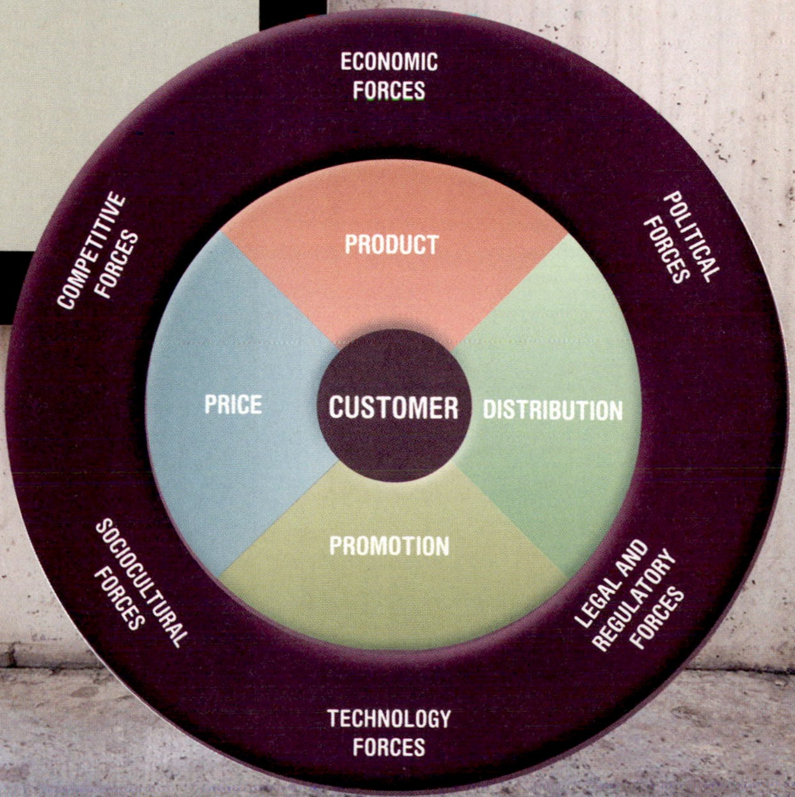

ECONOMIC FORCES
POLITICAL FORCES
LEGAL AND REGULATORY FORCES
TECHNOLOGY FORCES
SOCIOCULTURAL FORCES
COMPETITIVE FORCES
PRODUCT
DISTRIBUTION
PROMOTION
PRICE
CUSTOMER

chapter 14

Marketing Channels and Supply-Chain Management

OBJECTIVES

14-1 Describe the foundations of supply-chain management.

14-2 Explain the role and significance of marketing channels and supply chains.

14-3 Identify the intensity of market coverage.

14-4 Describe strategic issues in marketing channels, including leadership, cooperation, and conflict.

14-5 Explain physical distribution as being a part of supply-chain management.

14-6 Describe legal issues in channel management.

MARKETING INSIGHTS

Making H.Bloom's Business Bloom

Sonu Panda and Bryan Burkhart had never worked with flowers before they launched H.Bloom, a web-based floral business where data are as important as designs. Coming out of the software industry, the co-founders applied their technology know-how to streamlining the process of buying supplies and managing inventory and deliveries to meet customer demand. Their target market was customers (consumers and businesses) that wanted weekly deliveries of fresh floral arrangements.

According to Panda and Burkhart's research findings, 30 to 50 percent of the fresh flowers purchased by local florists spoil before they can be put into arrangements, which affect both pricing and profits. The entrepreneurs realized that they could make their new business bloom by drastically reducing spoilage, passing the savings along in the form of lower prices, and getting arrangements to customers quickly.

By the time H.Bloom opened its virtual storefront in 2010, the co-founders had sophisticated software ready to analyze sales history, project demand, and track minute-to-minute changes in the price, quality, and availability of hundreds of flowers offered by suppliers worldwide. Based on this information, H.Bloom's buyers know instantly when to switch to a different type of rose, for example, if it becomes available in abundance and the price drops by pennies per stem. The company also has software to plan the most efficient delivery routes, saving time and gas—and ensuring that customers can enjoy flowers as fresh as possible for as long as possible. Today, H.Bloom's spoilage is only 2 percent, and its annual revenues have blossomed to $5 million as it serves nine U.S. cities.[1]

The **distribution** component of the marketing mix focuses on the decisions and activities involved in making products available to customers when and where they want to purchase them. H.Bloom uses sophisticated software to make data-driven distribution decisions and address issues. Choosing which channels of distribution to use is a major decision in the development of marketing strategies.

In this chapter, we focus on marketing channels and supply-chain management. First, we explore the concept of the supply chain and its various activities. Second, we elaborate on marketing channels and the need for intermediaries and the primary functions they perform. Next, we outline the types and characteristics of marketing channels, discuss how they are selected, and explore how marketers determine the appropriate intensity of market coverage for a product. We then examine the strategic channel issues of leadership, cooperation, and conflict. We also look at the role of physical distribution within the supply chain, including its objectives and basic functions. Finally, we look at several legal issues that affect channel management.

distribution The decisions and activities that make products available to customers when and where they want to purchase them

supply chain All the activities associated with the flow and transformation of products from raw materials through to the end customer

operations management The total set of managerial activities used by an organization to transform resource inputs into products, services, or both

logistics management Planning, implementing, and controlling the efficient and effective flow and storage of products and information from the point of origin to consumption to meet customers' needs and wants

supply management In its broadest form, refers to the processes that enable the progress of value from raw material to final customer and back to redesign and final disposition

supply-chain management A set of approaches used to integrate the functions of operations management, logistics management, supply management, and marketing channel management so products are produced and distributed in the right quantities, to the right locations, and at the right time

14-1 FOUNDATIONS OF THE SUPPLY CHAIN

An important function of distribution is the joint effort of all involved organizations to create an effective **supply chain**, which refers to all the activities associated with the flow and transformation of products from raw materials through to the end customer. It may help to think of the firms involved in a total distribution system as existing along a conceptual line, the combined impact of which results in an effective supply chain. A distribution system involves firms that are "upstream" in the channel (e.g., suppliers) and "downstream" (e.g., wholesalers and retailers) that work to serve customers and generate competitive advantage. Historically, marketing focused on only certain downstream supply-chain activities, but today marketing professionals are recognizing that they can secure marketplace advantages by effectively integrating activities along the entire length of the supply chain, including operations, logistics, sourcing, and marketing channels. Integrating these activities requires marketing managers to work with other managers in operations, logistics, and supply. **Operations management** is the total set of managerial activities used by an organization to transform resource inputs into goods, services, or both.[2] **Logistics management** involves planning, implementing, and controlling the efficient and effective flow and storage of products and information from the point of origin to consumption to meet customers' needs and wants. The costs of business logistics in the United States are huge, at nearly $1.3 trillion.[3] To put this in perspective, the entire U.S. annual gross domestic product (GDP) is around $15 trillion.[4] **Supply management** (e.g., purchasing, procurement, sourcing) in its broadest form refers to the processes that enable the progress of value from raw material to final customer and back to redesign and final disposition.

Supply-chain management is the set of approaches used to integrate the functions of operations management, logistics management, supply management, and marketing channel management so that products are produced and distributed in the right quantities, to the right locations, and at the right times. It includes activities like manufacturing, research, sales, advertising, and shipping. Supply-chain management involves all entities that facilitate product distribution and benefit from cooperative efforts, including suppliers of raw materials and other components to make goods and services, logistics and transportation firms, communication firms, and other firms that indirectly take part in marketing exchanges. The key tasks involved in supply-chain management are outlined in Table 14.1. Thus, the supply chain includes all entities that facilitate product distribution and benefit from cooperative efforts. Supply-chain managers must encourage cooperation between organizations in the supply chain and understand the trade-offs required to achieve optimal levels of efficiency and service.

Technology has improved supply-chain management capabilities globally. Advances in information technology, in particular, have created an almost seamless distribution process

Table 14.1 Key Tasks in Supply-Chain Management

Marketing Activities	Sample Activities
Operations management	Organizational and system-wide coordination of operations and partnerships to meet customers' product needs
Supply management	Sourcing of necessary resources, goods, and services from suppliers to support all supply-chain members
Logistics management	All activities designed to move the product through the marketing channel to the end user, including warehousing and inventory management
Channel management	All activities related to selling, service, and the development of long-term customer relationships

for matching inventory needs to manufacturer requirements in the upstream portion of the supply chain and to customers' requirements in the downstream portion of the chain. With integrated information sharing among chain members, firms can reduce costs, improve services, and provide increased value to the end customer. Information is a crucial component in operating supply chains efficiently and effectively.

Demand for innovative goods and services has increased and changed over time. Marketers have had to learn to be flexible and responsive to these demands to meet the fluctuating needs of customers by developing and distributing new products and modifying existing ones. Suppliers provide material and service inputs to meet customer needs in the upstream portion of the supply chain. Supply-chain managers can utilize data available through improved information technology to gain knowledge of a firm's customers, which helps to improve products in the downstream portion of the supply chain. Customers are also increasingly a knowledge source in developing the right product in the downstream portion of the supply chain. Firms now understand that managing the entire supply chain is critically important in ensuring that customers get the products when, where, and how they want them. In fact, supply-chain management is one of the industries poised for strong future growth because of the increasing importance of transporting the right products where they need to go safely and on time.[5] Amazon has set the gold standard for supply-chain management—offering customers nearly anything they can imagine at low prices, through a user-friendly website that features product reviews and ratings, perks like offering a variety of shipping options, and an easy return policy. Many companies have struggled to compete with and adapt to such a large and flexible competitor.[6] Amazon has even moved into selling and distributing everyday items, like toilet paper and cleaning supplies, by teaming up with suppliers all over the country to create a seamless distribution system.[7]

In ensuring an efficient supply chain, upstream firms provide direct or indirect input to make the product, and downstream firms are responsible for delivery of the product and after-market services to the ultimate customers. To ensure quality and customer satisfaction, firms must be involved in the management of every aspect of their supply chain, in close partnership with all involved upstream and downstream organizations. Supply-chain management is closely linked to a market orientation. All functional areas of business (marketing, management, production, finance, and information systems) overlap with and are involved in executing a customer orientation and participate in supply-chain management. If a firm has established a marketing strategy based on continuous customer-focused leadership, then supply-chain management will be driven by cooperation and strategic coordination to ensure customer satisfaction. Managers should recognize that supply-chain management is critical to fulfilling customer expectations and that it requires coordination with all areas of the business. Associating a market orientation with supply-chain management should lead to increased firm performance and competitiveness.[8]

14-2 THE ROLE OF MARKETING CHANNELS IN SUPPLY CHAINS

A **marketing channel** (also called a *channel of distribution* or *distribution channel*) is a group of individuals and organizations that direct the flow of products from producers to customers within the supply chain. The major role of marketing channels is to make products available at the right time at the right place in the right quantities. This is achieved by creating synergy among operations management, logistics management, and supply management. Providing customer satisfaction should be the driving force behind marketing channel decisions. Buyers' needs and behavior are, therefore, important concerns of channel members.

Some marketing channels are direct, meaning that the product goes directly from the producer to the customer. For instance, when you order pears online from Harry & David, the product is sent from the manufacturer to the customer. Most channels, however, have one or more **marketing intermediaries** that link producers to other intermediaries or to ultimate consumers through contractual arrangements or through the purchase and reselling of products. Marketing intermediaries perform the activities described in Table 14.2. They also play key roles in customer relationship management, not only through their distribution activities but also by maintaining databases and information systems to help all members of the marketing channel maintain effective customer relationships. For example, MercuryGate provides transportation management software to firms to streamline logistics. The company also works directly with shippers and third-party logistics companies and brokers to ensure that its customers have effective and efficient supply chains by using analytics and a robust information database pulled from its many clients. Its methods work—as its clients, such as Walmart and Siemens, are known for their exemplary supply-chain management.[9]

marketing channel A group of individuals and organizations that direct the flow of products from producers to customers within the supply chain

marketing intermediaries Middlemen that link producers to other intermediaries or ultimate consumers through contractual arrangements or through the purchase and resale of products

Wholesalers and retailers are examples of intermediaries. Wholesalers buy and resell products to other wholesalers, retailers, and industrial customers. Retailers purchase products and resell them to end consumers. Consider your local supermarket, which probably purchased the Advil on its shelves from a wholesaler. The wholesaler purchased that pain medicine, along with other over-the-counter and prescription drugs, from manufacturers like McNeil Consumer Healthcare. Chapter 15 discusses the functions of wholesalers and retailers in marketing channels in detail.

Table 14.2 Marketing Channel Activities Performed by Intermediaries

Marketing Activities	Sample Activities
Marketing information	Analyze sales data and other information in databases and information systems. Perform or commission marketing research.
Marketing management	Establish strategic and tactical plans for developing customer relationships and organizational productivity.
Facilitating exchanges	Choose product assortments that match the needs of customers. Cooperate with channel members to develop partnerships.
Promotion	Set promotional objectives. Coordinate advertising, personal selling, sales promotion, publicity, and packaging.
Price	Establish pricing policies and terms of sales.
Physical distribution	Manage transportation, warehousing, materials handling, inventory control, and communication.

Supply-chain management should begin with a focus on the customer, who is the ultimate consumer and whose satisfaction should be the goal of all the efforts of channel members. Cooperation between channel members should improve customer satisfaction while also increasing coordination, reducing costs, and increasing profits. According to Deloitte Consulting, up to 70 percent of a firm's cost base can be traced back to its supply chain.[10] For this reason, firms are usually interested in taking steps that allow them to reduce waste, such as cutting down on energy requirements. Improving coordination between supply-chain members can help achieve fewer wasted resources and greater speed, and lead to increased environmental sustainability—which can improve a firm's image in the eyes of many consumers.[11] When the buyer, the seller, marketing intermediaries, and facilitating agencies work together, the cooperative relationship results in compromise and adjustments that meet customers' needs regarding delivery, scheduling, packaging, or other requirements.

Each supply-chain member requires information from other channel members. For instance, suppliers need order and forecast information from the manufacturer. They may also need availability information from their own suppliers. Customer relationship management (CRM) systems exploit the information in supply-chain partners' information systems and make it available for easy reference. CRM systems can help all channel members make better marketing strategy decisions that develop and sustain desirable customer relationships. Companies now offer online programs that integrate business data into a social networking site format. Tibbr and Yammer are two such programs. By inputting all data into a single, easy-to-use online system, businesses can achieve greater efficiencies and improve their CRM.[12]

14-2a The Significance of Marketing Channels

Although it is not necessary to make marketing channel decisions before other marketing decisions, they can have a strong influence on the other elements of the marketing mix (i.e., product, promotion, and pricing). Channel decisions are critical because they determine a product's market presence and accessibility. Without marketing channel operations that reach the right customers at the right time, even the best goods and services will not be successful. For example, in spite of spending massive amounts on marketing efforts, Motorola's Moto X smartphone was widely deemed a failure when marketing channel decisions failed to ensure that elements of the marketing mix were reaching the correct target market. Experts attributed the flop to failing to target the best market, positioning it as a high-end phone and making it available exclusively in the United States. If Motorola had chosen global marketing channels, especially in countries where the smartphone market is not yet mature, the Moto X might have been more successful.[13]

Marketing channel decisions have strategic significance because they generally entail long-term commitments among a variety of firms (e.g., suppliers, logistics providers, and operations firms). Furthermore, it is the least flexible component of the marketing mix. Once a firm commits to a distribution channel, it is difficult to change. Marketing channels serve many functions, including creating utility and facilitating exchange efficiencies. Although some of these functions may be performed by a single channel member, most functions are accomplished through both independent and joint efforts of channel members.

Marketing Channels Create Utility

Marketing channels create four types of utility: time, place, possession, and form. *Time utility* is having products available when the customer wants them. Services like Netflix allow customers to watch a movie whenever they want. *Place utility* is making products available in locations where customers wish to purchase them. For example, Zappos allows customers to shop for shoes and accessories anywhere they have access to a mobile device and an Internet connection. *Possession utility* means that the customer has access to the product to use or to store for future use. Possession utility can occur through ownership or through arrangements that give the customer the right to use the product, such as a lease or rental agreement. Channel members sometimes create *form utility* by assembling, preparing, or otherwise refining the product to suit individual customer needs.

Marketing Channels Facilitate Exchange Efficiencies

Even if producers and buyers are located in the same city, there are costs associated with exchanges. Marketing intermediaries can reduce the costs of exchanges by performing certain services or functions efficiently. As Figure 14.1 shows, when four buyers seek products from four producers, 16 separate transactions are possible. If one intermediary serves both producers and buyers, the number of possible transactions is cut in half. Intermediaries are specialists in facilitating exchanges. They provide valuable assistance because of their access to and control over important resources used in the proper functioning of marketing channels. Many firms exist to assist firms with creating supply-chain efficiencies. Take a look at the advertisement for NFI. It shows a man dwarfed by a huge stack of shipping containers, which captures the feeling of being overwhelmed by the task of transporting their goods efficiently and safely—a common feeling among many firms as they grow. Firms like NFI have expert knowledge and have developed distribution networks that can help firms to create supply-chain efficiencies.

Nevertheless, the press, consumers, public officials, and even other marketers freely criticize intermediaries, especially wholesalers. Critics accuse wholesalers of being inefficient and adding to costs. Buyers often think that making the distribution channel as short as possible will decrease the prices for products, but this is not the case.

Critics who suggest that eliminating wholesalers will lower prices for customers fail to recognize that this would not eliminate the need for the services the wholesalers provide. Although wholesalers can be eliminated, their functions cannot. Other channel members would have to perform those functions, perhaps not as efficiently, and customers still would

Figure 14.1 Efficiency in Exchanges Provided by an Intermediary

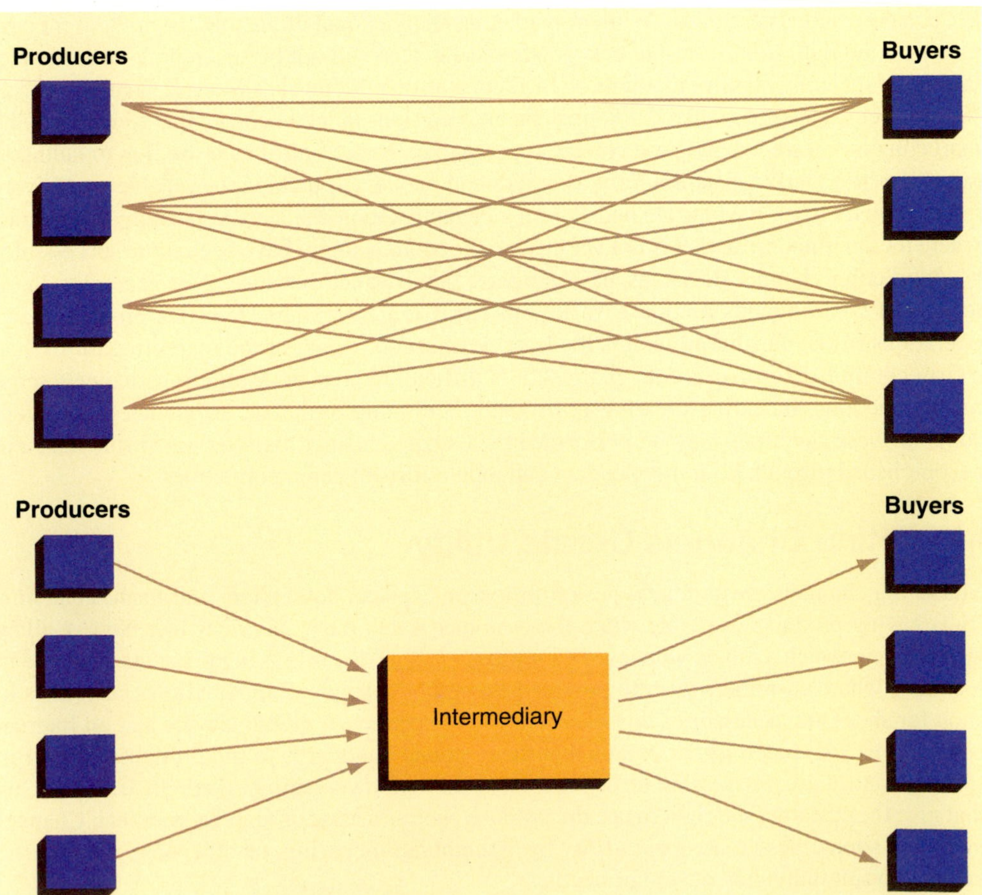

have to pay for them. In addition, all producers would deal directly with retailers or customers, meaning that every producer would have to keep voluminous records and hire sufficient personnel to deal with a multitude of customers. In the end, customers might end up paying a great deal more for products because prices would reflect the costs of an inefficient distribution channel. To mitigate criticisms, wholesalers should only perform the marketing activities that are desired, and they must strive to be as efficient and customer-focused as possible.

14-2b Types of Marketing Channels

Because marketing channels that are appropriate for one product may be less suitable for others, many different distribution paths have been developed. The various marketing channels can be classified generally as channels for consumer products and channels for business products.

Channels for Consumer Products

Figure 14.2 illustrates several channels used in the distribution of consumer products. Channel A depicts the direct movement of products from producer to consumers. For instance, a haircut received at a barber shop moves through channel A because there is no intermediary between the person performing the service and the one receiving it. Direct marketing via the Internet has become a critically important part of some companies' distribution strategies, often as a complement to selling products in traditional

NFI

Supply-Chain Efficiencies
Logistics firms such as NFI can help businesses to create supply-chain efficiencies, distributing their goods quickly and affordably.

Figure 14.2 **Typical Marketing Channels for Consumer Products**

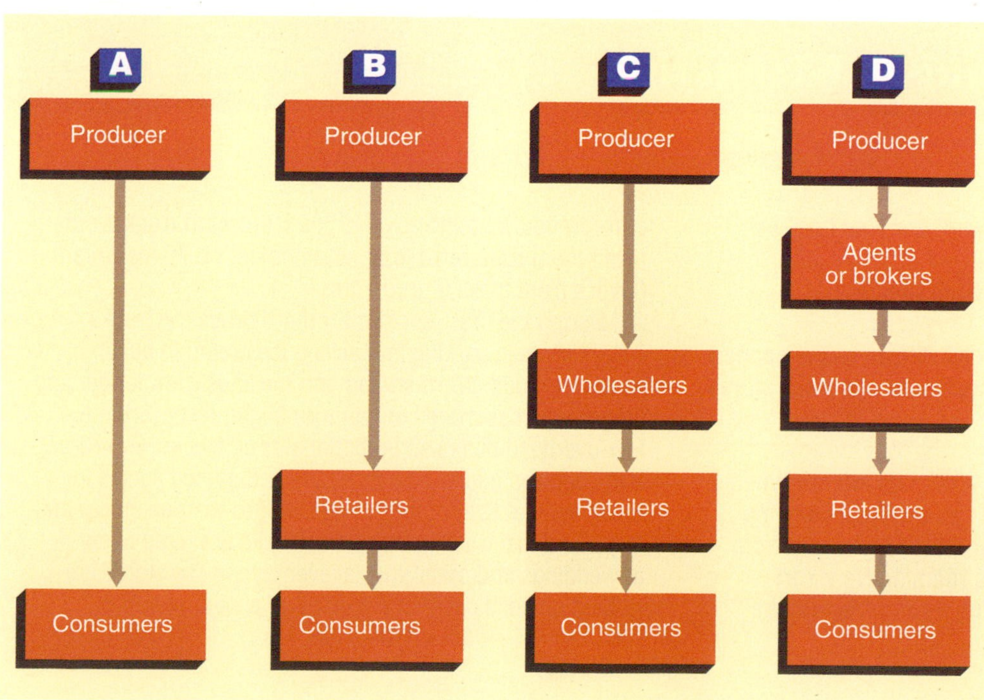

retail stores. A firm must evaluate the benefits of going direct versus the transaction costs involved in using intermediaries.

Channel B, which moves goods from the producer to a retailer and then to customers, is a frequent choice of large retailers because it allows them to buy in quantity from manufacturers. Retailers like Kmart and Walmart sell many items that were purchased directly from producers. New automobiles and new college textbooks are also sold through this type of marketing channel.

Channel C is a common distribution channel for consumer products. It takes goods from the producer to a wholesaler, then to a retailer, and finally to consumers. It is a practical option for producers that sell to hundreds of thousands of customers through thousands of retailers. Some home appliances, hardware, and many convenience goods are marketed through this type of channel. Consider the number of retailers marketing KitchenAid appliances. It would be extremely difficult, if not impossible, for KitchenAid to deal directly with each retailer that sells its brand.

Channel D, wherein goods pass from producer, to agents, to wholesalers, to retailers, and finally to consumers, is used frequently for products intended for mass distribution, such as processed foods. Consequently, to place its Wheat Thins crackers in specific retail outlets, supply-chain managers at Nabisco may hire an agent (or a food broker) to sell the crackers to wholesalers. Wholesalers then sell the Wheat Thins to supermarkets, vending-machine operators, and convenience stores.

Contrary to what you might think, a long channel may actually be the most efficient distribution channel for some goods. When several channel intermediaries perform specialized functions, costs are likely to be lower than when one channel member tries to perform them all. Efficiencies arise when firms that specialize in certain elements of producing a product or moving it through the channel are more effective at performing specialized tasks than the manufacturer. This results in added value to customers and reduced costs throughout the distribution channel.

Channels for Business Products

Figure 14.3 shows four of the most common channels for business products. As with consumer products, manufacturers of business products sometimes work with more than one level of wholesaler.

Entrepreneurship in Marketing

Van Leeuwen Artisan Ice Cream

Entrepreneurs: Pete Van Leeuwen, Ben Van Leeuwen, and Laura O'Neill
Business: Van Leeuwen Artisan Ice Cream
Founded: 2008, New York City
Success: Van Leeuwen Artisan Ice Cream has expanded from two ice-cream trucks to six trucks and three stores within 5 years.

The gourmet food-truck boom was in its infancy when the Van Leeuwen brothers and Laura O'Neill came up with the idea of selling super-premium ice cream from old-fashioned ice-cream trucks roaming New York City. With money invested by family and friends, the entrepreneurs bought two 1950s ice-cream trucks, outfitted them for a retro look, and cooked up 10 ice-cream flavors from fresh ingredients.

During the first year, the brothers drove the trucks 7 days a week, parking and selling ice cream in busy neighborhoods. Word spread and the lines grew longer and longer—just as more competitors began discovering the low-overhead business potential of food trucks. Over time, Van Leeuwen added new products and gained such a loyal following that the company could afford to open stores and buy additional trucks. Today, the trucks are hired to serve at weddings and other special events, and the stores are ringing up solid profits for the trio of entrepreneurs.[a]

Figure 14.3 **Typical Marketing Channels for Business Products**

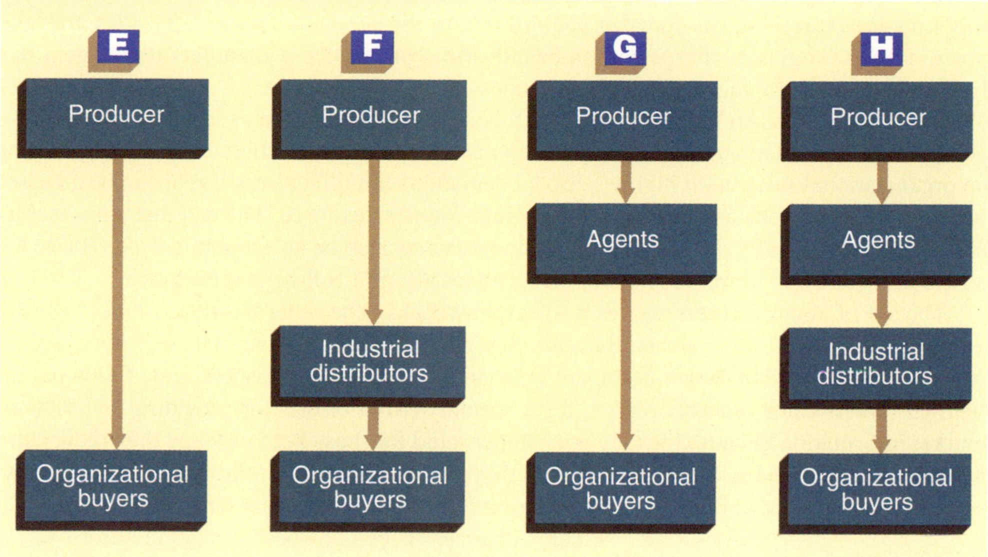

Channel E illustrates the direct channel for business products. In contrast to consumer goods, business products, especially expensive equipment, are most likely to be sold through direct channels. Business customers prefer to communicate directly with producers, especially when expensive or technically complex products are involved. For instance, business buyers of Xerox products not only receive devices and equipment, but ongoing maintenance, technical support, and data analytics. Xerox has moved from being a company known for its copiers to a creative powerhouse that delivers a variety of solutions to its clients. Service through direct channels is a big part of Xerox's success. It digitally collects ongoing information from many of the products it sells to companies and performs preemptive repairs on machines it senses are about to malfunction. This level of service would be impossible through an intermediary.[14]

In channel F, an industrial distributor facilitates exchanges between the producer and the customer. An **industrial distributor** is an independent business that takes title to products and carries inventories. Industrial distributors usually sell standardized items, such as maintenance supplies, production tools, and small operating equipment. Some industrial distributors carry a wide variety of product lines. Applied Industrial Technologies Inc., for instance, carries millions of products from more than 4,000 manufacturers and works with a wide variety of companies from small janitorial services companies to Boeing.[15] Other industrial distributors specialize in one or a small number of lines. Industrial distributors carry an increasing percentage of business products. Overall, these distributors can be most effective when a product has broad market appeal, is easily stocked and serviced, is sold in small quantities, and is needed on demand to avoid high losses.

Industrial distributors offer sellers several advantages. They can perform the needed selling activities in local markets at a relatively low cost to a manufacturer and reduce a producer's financial burden by providing customers with credit services. Also, because industrial distributors usually maintain close relationships with their customers, they are aware of local needs and can pass on market information to producers. By holding adequate inventories in local markets, industrial distributors reduce producers' capital requirements.

Using industrial distributors has several disadvantages. They may be difficult to control because they are independent firms. They often stock competing brands, so a producer cannot depend on them to sell its brand aggressively. Furthermore, industrial distributors incur expenses from maintaining inventories and are less likely to handle bulky or slow-selling items, or items that need specialized facilities or extraordinary selling efforts. In some cases, industrial distributors lack the specialized knowledge necessary to sell and service technical products.

industrial distributor
An independent business organization that takes title to industrial products and carries inventories

The third channel for business products, channel G, employs a *manufacturers' agent,* an independent businessperson who sells complementary products of several producers in assigned territories and is compensated through commissions. Unlike an industrial distributor, a manufacturers' agent does not acquire title to the products and usually does not take possession. Acting as a salesperson on behalf of the producers, a manufacturers' agent has little or no latitude in negotiating prices or sales terms.

Using manufacturers' agents can benefit an organizational marketer. They usually possess considerable technical and market information and have an established set of customers. For an organizational seller with highly seasonal demand, a manufacturers' agent can be an asset because the seller does not have to support a year-round sales force. The fact that manufacturers' agents are typically paid on a commission basis may also be an economical alternative for a firm that has highly limited resources and cannot afford a full-time sales force.

dual distribution The use of two or more marketing channels to distribute the same products to the same target market

The use of manufacturers' agents also has drawbacks. The seller has little control over the actions of manufacturers' agents. Because they work on commission, manufacturers' agents prefer to concentrate on larger accounts. They are often reluctant to spend time following up with customers after the sale, putting forth special selling efforts, or providing sellers with market information because they are not compensated for these activities and they reduce the amount of productive selling time. Because they rarely maintain inventories, manufacturers' agents have a limited ability to provide customers with parts or repair services quickly.

Finally, channel H includes both a manufacturers' agent and an industrial distributor. This channel may be appropriate when the producer wishes to cover a large geographic area, but maintains no sales force due to highly seasonal demand or because it cannot afford one. This channel can also be useful for a business marketer that wants to enter a new geographic market without expanding its sales force.

Dual Distribution
Many firms, including Lancôme, use dual distribution—meaning products are targeted at the same group of consumers via multiple channels. In this case, eyeliner is made available to consumers in department stores and online.

Multiple Marketing Channels and Channel Alliances

To reach diverse target markets, manufacturers may use several marketing channels simultaneously, with each channel involving a different group of intermediaries. A manufacturer often uses multiple channels when the same product is directed to both consumers and business customers. For example, when Heinz markets ketchup for household use, the product is sold to supermarkets through grocery wholesalers or, in some cases, directly to retailers. Ketchup sold to restaurants or institutions, however, follows a different distribution channel.

In some instances, a producer may prefer **dual distribution**, the use of two or more marketing channels to distribute the same products to the same target market. For instance, Kellogg sells its cereals directly to large retail grocery chains (channel B) and food wholesalers that, in turn, sell the cereals to retailers (channel C). Another example of dual distribution is a firm that sells products through retail outlets and its own mail-order catalog or website. Many producers, which previously had sold to wholesalers and retailers, now feature online stores on their company webpages that ship directly from producer to consumer. This is an example of dual distribution because the products are marketed to the same customers through different channels, one involving intermediaries and one direct. Even marketers for makeup, such as the Lancôme eyeliner featured in the advertisement, employ dual distribution. This product is available in department stores, but customers can also purchase it on the producer's website, which is featured prominently on the advertisement. As an extra enticement to shop using the website, the lower left-hand corner of the advertisement tells customers to go to the company website to access makeup tutorials.

A **strategic channel alliance** exists when the products of one organization are distributed through the marketing channels of another. The products of the two firms are often similar with respect to target markets or uses, but they are not direct competitors. A brand of bottled water might be distributed through a marketing channel for soft drinks, or a cereal producer in the United States might form a strategic channel alliance with a European food processor to facilitate international distribution. Such alliances can provide benefits for both the organization that owns the marketing channel and the company whose brand is being distributed through the channel.

14-2c Selecting Marketing Channels

Selecting appropriate marketing channels is important because they are difficult to change once chosen. Although the process varies across organizations, channel selection decisions are usually affected significantly by one or more of the following factors: customer characteristics, product attributes, type of organization, competition, marketing environmental forces, and characteristics of intermediaries (see Figure 14.4).

Customer Characteristics

Marketing managers must consider the characteristics of target market members in channel selection. As we have already seen, the channels that are appropriate for consumers are different from those for business customers. Because of variations in product use, product complexity,

strategic channel alliance An agreement whereby the products of one organization are distributed through the marketing channels of another

Figure 14.4 Selecting Marketing Channels

consumption levels, and need for services, firms develop different marketing strategies for each group. Business customers often prefer to deal directly with producers (or very knowledgeable channel intermediaries such as industrial distributors), especially for highly technical or expensive products, such as mainframe computers, jet airplanes, or heavy machinery that require strict specifications and technical assistance. Businesses also frequently buy in large quantities.

Consumers, on the other hand, generally buy limited quantities of a product, purchase from retailers, and often do not mind limited customer service. When customers are concentrated in a small geographic area, a direct channel may be best, but when many customers are spread across an entire state or nation, distribution through multiple intermediaries is likely to be more efficient.

Product Attributes

The attributes of the product can have a strong influence on the choice of marketing channels. Marketers of complex and expensive products (like automobiles) will likely employ short channels, as will marketers of perishable products (such as dairy and produce). Less-expensive standardized products with long shelf lives, like soft drinks and canned goods, can go through longer channels with many intermediaries. Fragile products that require special handling are likely to be distributed through short channels to minimize the amount of handling and risk of damage. Firms that desire to convey an exclusive image for their products may wish to limit the number of outlets available.

Type of Organization

The characteristics of the organization will have a great impact on the distribution channels chosen. Owing to their size, larger firms are in a better position to deal with vendors or other channel members. They are also likely to have more distribution centers, which reduce delivery times to customers. Large companies can also use an extensive product mix as a competitive tool. A smaller company that uses regional or local channel members, on the other hand, might be in a strong position to cater its marketing mix to serve customers in that particular area, compared with a larger and less-flexible organization. However, smaller firms may not have the resources to develop their own sales force, ship their products long distances, maintain a large inventory, or extend credit. In such cases, they might consider including other channel members that have the resources to provide these services to customers.

Competition

Competition is another important factor for supply-chain managers to consider. The success or failure of a competitor's marketing channel may encourage or dissuade an organization from taking a similar approach. In a highly competitive market, it is important for a company to maintain low costs so it can offer lower prices than its competitors if necessary to maintain a competitive advantage.

Environmental Forces

Environmental forces can play a role in channel selection. Adverse economic conditions might force an organization to use a low-cost channel, even though it reduces customer satisfaction. In contrast, a growing economy may allow a company to choose a channel that previously had been too costly. New technology might allow an organization to add to or modify its channel strategy in beneficial ways, such as adding online retailing or dealing with intermediaries in more direct ways.

The introduction of new technology might cause an organization to add or modify its channel strategy. For instance, many marketers in a variety of industries are finding that it is valuable to maintain online social networking accounts to keep customers up-to-date on new products, offers, and events.

Government regulations can also affect channel selection. As labor and environmental regulations change, an organization may be forced to modify its existing distribution channel structure to comply with new laws. Firms might choose to enact the changes before they are mandated in order to appear proactive. International governmental regulations can complicate the supply chain a great deal, as laws vary from country to country and businesses must make sure they comply with local regulations. Walmart, the largest retailer in the world, decided to suspend retail operations in India, a potentially huge market, because of difficulties in navigating international rules on foreign investment in that country. For smaller companies with fewer resources to devote to negotiating difficult international environments, the challenges can be even greater.[16]

Characteristics of Intermediaries

When an organization believes that an intermediary is not promoting its products adequately or does not offer the correct mix of services, it may reconsider its channel choices. In these instances, the company may choose another channel member to handle its products, it may select a new intermediary, or it might choose to eliminate intermediaries altogether and perform the functions itself.

14-3 INTENSITY OF MARKET COVERAGE

In addition to deciding which marketing channels to use to distribute a product, marketers must determine the appropriate intensity of coverage—that is, the number and kinds of outlets in which a product will be sold. This decision depends on the characteristics of the product and the target market. To achieve the desired intensity of market coverage, distribution must correspond to behavior patterns of buyers. In Chapter 11, we divided consumer products into four categories—convenience, shopping, specialty, and unsought—according to how consumers make purchases. In considering products for purchase, consumers take into account such factors as replacement rate, product adjustment (services), duration of consumption, and time required to find the product.[17] These variables directly affect the intensity of market coverage. As shown in Figure 14.5, the three major levels of market coverage are intensive, selective, and exclusive distribution.

Figure 14.5 Intensity of Market Coverage

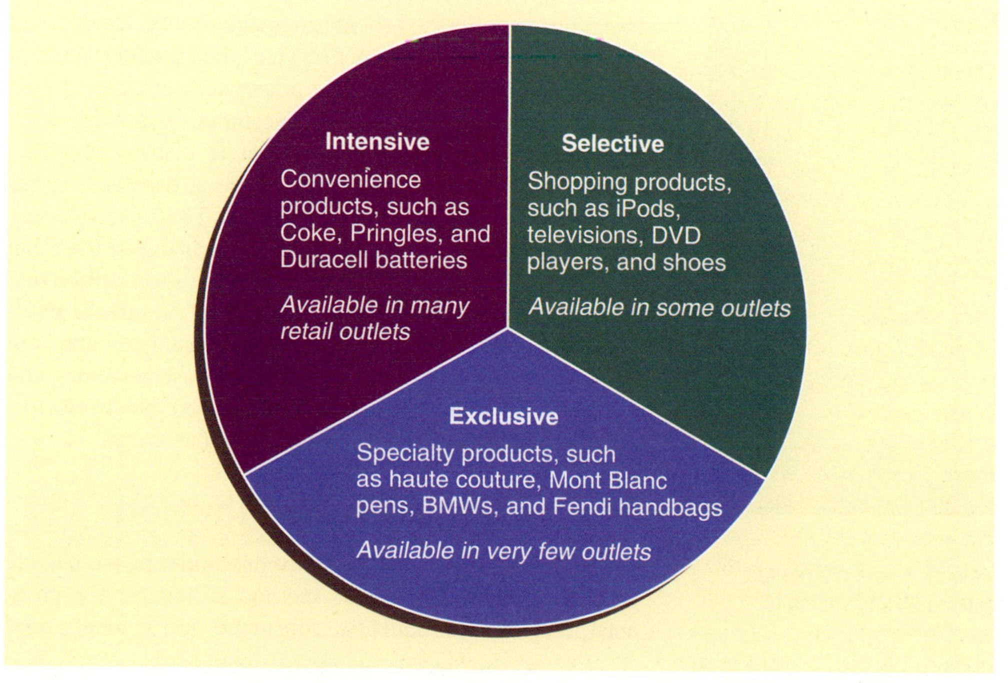

14-3a Intensive Distribution

Intensive distribution uses all available outlets for distributing a product. Intensive distribution is appropriate for products that have a high replacement rate, require almost no service, and are bought based on price cues. Most convenience products like bread, chewing gum, soft drinks, and newspapers are marketed through intensive distribution. Multiple channels may be used to sell through all possible outlets. For example, goods such as soft drinks, snacks, laundry detergent, and pain relievers are available at convenience stores, service stations, supermarkets, discount stores, and other types of retailers. To satisfy consumers seeking to buy these products, they must be available at a store nearby and be obtained with minimal search time. Consumers want to be able to buy these products wherever it is most convenient to them at the lowest price possible while maintaining a reliable level of quality.

intensive distribution Using all available outlets to distribute a product

selective distribution Using only some available outlets in an area to distribute a product

exclusive distribution Using a single outlet in a fairly large geographic area to distribute a product

Sales of low-cost convenience products may be directly related to product availability. Fans of Sriracha brand hot sauce, for instance, were faced with shortages when the California Department of Public Health began to enforce stricter guidelines, halting shipments of the sauce for 30 days.[18] The lack of product availability where consumers demanded it resulted in lost revenues for the company when consumers could not easily find the product in its usual outlets. Companies like Procter & Gamble that produce consumer packaged items rely on intensive distribution for many of their products (e.g., soaps, detergents, food and juice products, and personal-care products) because consumers want ready availability.

Nestle Nespresso

Selective Distribution
Nespresso brand espresso makers and coffees are distributed selectively. Salespeople will be knowledgeable and willing to assist a customer in making a selection.

14-3b Selective Distribution

Selective distribution uses only some available outlets in an area to distribute a product. Selective distribution is appropriate for shopping products, which include durable goods like televisions or computers. Shopping products are more expensive than convenience goods, and consumers are willing to spend more time and possibly visit several retail outlets to compare prices, designs, styles, and other features.

Selective distribution is desirable when a special effort, such as customer service from a channel member, is important to customers. Shopping products require differentiation at the point of purchase. Selective distribution is often used to motivate retailers to provide adequate service. Dealers can offer higher-quality customer service when products are distributed selectively. Consider the advertisement for Nespresso espresso machines and coffees. Nespresso is a moderately high-end brand of coffeemaker that is distributed selectively. Nespresso products are available at dedicated stores and at department stores, such as Macys. This advertisement seeks to cultivate a high-end image by focusing on the clean lines of the machine and the fancy coffee shop drinks that customers can create. When shopping for Nespresso products, salespeople will be able to assist customers and will be knowledgeable about the products. Most perfumes and colognes and some cosmetics are marketed using selective distribution in order to maintain a particular image.

14-3c Exclusive Distribution

Exclusive distribution uses only one outlet in a relatively large geographic area. This method is suitable for products purchased infrequently, consumed over a long period of time, or that require a high level of customer service or information. It is also used for expensive, high-quality products with high profit margins, such as Porsche, BMW, and other luxury automobiles. It is not appropriate for convenience products and many shopping products because an insufficient number of units would be sold to generate an acceptable level of profits on account of those products' lower profit margins.

Exclusive distribution is often used as an incentive to sellers when only a limited market is available for products. Consider Patek Philippe watches that may sell for $10,000 or more. These watches, like luxury automobiles, are available in only a few select locations. Prada, featured in the advertisement, is another brand distributed exclusively. Prada is only available in flagship stores and very exclusive outlets, all located in large cities or resort areas. Items can retail for thousands of dollars, and the brand is frequently worn as a status symbol. This advertisement underscores the exclusive and elite nature of the brand by featuring a famous European actor, Christoph Waltz. A producer using exclusive distribution expects dealers to carry a complete inventory, train personnel to ensure a high level of product knowledge and quality customer service, and participate in promotional programs.

Some products are appropriate for exclusive distribution when first introduced, but as competitors enter the market and the product moves through its life cycle, other types of market coverage and distribution channels become necessary. A problem that can arise with exclusive (and selective) distribution is that unauthorized resellers acquire and sell products or counterfeits, violating the agreement between a manufacturer and its exclusive authorized dealers.

Prada

Exclusive Distribution
Prada uses exclusive distribution, only selling products at flagship stores in large cities or wealthy resort areas.

14-4 STRATEGIC ISSUES IN MARKETING CHANNELS

To maintain customer satisfaction and an effective supply chain, managers must retain a strategic focus on certain competitive priorities, including developing channel leadership, fostering cooperation between channel members, managing channel conflict, and possibly consolidating marketing channels through channel integration.

14-4a Competitive Priorities in Marketing Channels

Increasingly, firms have become aware that supply chains can be a source of competitive advantage and a means of maintaining a strong market orientation because supply-chain decisions cut across all functional areas of business. Building the most effective and efficient supply chain can sustain a business and help it to use resources effectively and be more efficient. Many well-known firms, including Amazon, Dell, FedEx, Toyota, and Walmart, owe much of their success to outmaneuvering rivals with unique supply-chain capabilities. Many countries offer firms opportunities to create an effective and efficient supply chain to support the development of competitive national industries. Although developed nations like Germany, the United States, and Canada remain among the most competitive manufacturing countries, China has ranked number one on Deloitte's annual survey of global manufacturing competitiveness for years, indicating the country's superior capabilities to produce goods at a low price and efficiently distribute them.[19] India, South Korea, and Taiwan have risen to prominence as well.

To unlock the potential of a supply chain, activities must be integrated so that all functions are coordinated into an effective system. Supply chains driven by firm-established goals focus on the "competitive priorities" of speed, quality, cost, or flexibility as the performance objective. Managers must remember, however, to keep a holistic view of the supply chain so that goals such as "speed" or "cost" do not result in dissatisfied or underpaid workers or other such abuses in factories. This should be a particular concern among firms that use international manufacturers because it can be more difficult to monitor working conditions internationally.

14-4b Channel Leadership, Cooperation, and Conflict

Each channel member performs a specific role in the distribution system and agrees (implicitly or explicitly) to accept rights, responsibilities, rewards, and sanctions for nonconformity. Moreover, each channel member holds certain expectations of other channel members. Retailers, for instance, expect wholesalers to maintain adequate inventories and deliver goods on time. Wholesalers expect retailers to honor payment agreements and keep them informed of inventory needs. Channel partnerships can facilitate effective supply-chain management when partners agree on objectives, policies, and procedures for physical distribution efforts associated with the supplier's products. Such partnerships eliminate redundancies and reassign tasks for maximum system-wide efficiency.

Channel cooperation reduces wasted resources, such as time, energy, or materials. A coordinated supply chain can also be more environmentally friendly, a consideration that is increasingly important to many organizations and their stakeholders. In fact, research findings show that companies with environmentally-responsible supply chains tend to be more profitable, particularly when a firm's marketing efforts point out the fact that it has a sustainable supply chain.[20] To reduce the carbon footprint of the U.S. auto industry's production processes, equipment manufacturers and suppliers partnered with the Environmental Protection Agency to form the Suppliers Partnership for the Environment. It is a forum for companies and their supply-chain partners to share environmental best practices and optimize supply-chain productivity. The result is a more efficient and less polluting supply chain.[21] In this section, we discuss channel member behavior—including leadership, cooperation, and conflict—that marketers must understand to make effective channel decisions.

Channel Leadership

Many marketing channel decisions are determined through channel member compromise with a better marketing channel as an end goal. Some marketing channels, however, are organized and controlled by a single leader, or **channel captain** (also called *channel leader*). The channel captain may be a producer, wholesaler, or retailer. Channel captains may establish channel policies and coordinate development of the marketing mix. To attain desired objectives, the captain must possess **channel power**, the ability to influence another channel member's goal achievement. The member that becomes the channel captain will accept the responsibilities and exercise the power associated with this role.

When a manufacturer is a channel captain and it determines that it must increase sales volume to achieve production efficiency, it may encourage growth through offering channel members financing, business advice, ordering assistance, advertising services, sales and service training, and support materials. These benefits usually come with requirements related to sales volume, service quality, training, and customer satisfaction.

Retailers may also be channel captains. Walmart, for example, dominates the supply chain for its retail stores by virtue of the magnitude of its resources (especially information management) and a strong, nationwide customer base. To be part of Walmart's supply chain,

channel captain The dominant leader of a marketing channel or a supply channel

channel power The ability of one channel member to influence another member's goal achievement

other channel members must agree to Walmart's rules. Small retailers may also assume leadership roles when they gain strong customer loyalty in local or regional markets. Retailers that are channel captains control many brands and sometimes replace uncooperative producers. Increasingly, leading retailers are concentrating their buying power among fewer suppliers, which makes it easier to coordinate and maintain a high level of quality and transparency along the entire supply chain. These more selective relationships often involve long-term commitments, which enable retailers to place smaller and more frequent orders as needed, rather than waiting for large-volume discounts, or placing large orders and assuming the risks associated with carrying more inventory than needed.

Wholesalers can assume channel leadership roles as well. Wholesaler leaders may form voluntary chains with several retailers, which they supply with bulk buying or management services. These retailers may also market the wholesalers' own brands. In return, the retailers shift most of their purchasing to the wholesaler leader. The Independent Grocers' Alliance (IGA) is one of the best-known wholesaler leaders in the United States with nearly 5,000 outlets.[22] IGA's power is based on its expertise in advertising, pricing, and purchasing knowledge that it makes available to independent business owners. Wholesaler channel leaders may help retailers with store layouts, accounting, and inventory control.

Channel Cooperation

Channel cooperation is vital if each member is to gain something from the other members. Cooperation enables retailers, wholesalers, suppliers, and logistics providers to speed up inventory replenishment, improve customer service, and cut the costs of bringing products to the consumer.[23] Because the supply chain is an interrelated system, the success of one firm in the channel depends in part on other member firms. Without cooperation, neither overall channel goals nor individual member goals can be realized. Thus, marketing channel members should make a coordinated effort to satisfy market requirements. Channel cooperation leads to greater trust among channel members and improves the overall functioning of the channel. Cooperation also leads to more satisfying relationships among channel members.

There are several ways to improve channel cooperation. If a marketing channel is viewed as a unified supply chain competing with other systems, individual members will be less likely to take actions that create disadvantages for other members. Channel members should agree to direct efforts toward common objectives. To achieve these objectives efficiently, channel members' roles should be defined precisely. Starting from a common basis allows channel members to set benchmarks for reviewing intermediaries' performance and helps to reduce conflicts as each channel member knows what is expected of it.

Channel Conflict

Although all channel members work toward the same general goal—distributing products profitably and efficiently—members sometimes may disagree about the best methods for attaining this goal. Take a look at the advertisement for TAG Heuer watches. This is a very exclusive brand, which is underscored by featuring the famous actor Leonardo DiCaprio as a model. The brand was previously only available via authorized jewelers. Consumers can now purchase the watches directly from the producer via the company's website, creating possible resentment among brick-and-mortar stores if they lose business. If self-interest creates misunderstanding about role expectations, the end result is frustration and conflict for the whole channel. For individual organizations to function together, each channel member must clearly communicate and understand role expectations. Communication difficulties are a potential form of channel conflict because ineffective communication leads to frustration, misunderstandings, and ill-coordinated strategies, jeopardizing further coordination.

Many firms use multiple channels of distribution, especially now that most retail firms have an online presence. The Internet has increased the potential for conflict and resentment between manufacturers and intermediaries. When a manufacturer makes its products

Tag Heuer

Channel Conflict
Exclusive brands like TAG Heuer, which previously were only available at authorized retailers, risk channel conflict now that they are also sold online via the company's website.

available through the Internet, it is employing a direct channel that competes with the retailers that also sell its products.

Channel conflicts also arise when intermediaries overemphasize competing products or diversify into product lines traditionally handled by other intermediaries. When a producer that has traditionally used franchised dealers broadens its retailer base to include other types of retail outlets, for example, conflict can arise with the traditional outlets. Sometimes conflict develops because producers strive to increase efficiency by circumventing intermediaries. Although there is no single method for resolving conflict, partnerships can be reestablished if two conditions are met. First, the role of each channel member must be clearly defined and adhered to. To minimize misunderstanding, all members must be able to expect unambiguous performance levels from one another. Second, members of channel partnerships must agree on means of coordinating channels, which requires strong, but not polarizing, leadership. To prevent channel conflict, producers or other channel members may provide competing resellers with different brands, allocate markets among resellers, define policies for direct sales to avoid potential conflict over large accounts, negotiate territorial issues among regional distributors, and provide recognition to certain resellers for their importance in distributing to others.

14-4c Channel Integration

Channel members can either combine and control activities or pass them to another channel member. Channel functions may be transferred between intermediaries and producers, even to customers. As mentioned earlier in the chapter, supply-chain functions cannot be eliminated. Unless buyers themselves perform the functions, they must pay for the labor and resources needed to perform them.

Various channel stages may be combined, either horizontally or vertically, under the management of a channel captain. Such integration may stabilize supply, reduce costs, and increase channel member coordination.

Vertical Channel Integration

Vertical channel integration combines two or more stages of the channel under one management. This may occur when one member of a marketing channel purchases the operations of another member or simply performs the functions of another member, eliminating the need for that intermediary. The steel industry, because of high costs and the need for reliable distribution channel intermediaries, tends to feature highly vertically integrated firms. For instance, ArcelorMittal and U.S. Steel are both vertically integrated, carrying out many stages of the channel under one roof.[24]

Vertical channel integration represents a more progressive approach to distribution, in which channel members become extensions of one another as they are combined under a single management. Vertically integrated channels can be more effective against competition because of increased bargaining power and the ease of sharing information and responsibilities. At one end of a vertically integrated channel, a manufacturer might provide advertising and training assistance. At the other end, the retailer might buy the manufacturer's products in large quantities and actively promote them.

vertical channel integration
Combining two or more stages of the marketing channel under one management

Integration has been successfully institutionalized in a marketing channel called the **vertical marketing system (VMS)**, in which a single channel member coordinates or manages all activities to maximize efficiencies, resulting in an effective and low-cost distribution system that does not duplicate services. Vertical integration brings most or all stages of the marketing channel under common control or ownership. It can help speed the rate at which goods move through a marketing channel. VMSs account for a large share of retail sales in consumer goods.

Most vertical marketing systems take one of three forms: corporate, administered, or contractual. A *corporate VMS* combines all stages of the marketing channel, from producers to consumers, under a single owner. For example, the Inditex Group, which owns popular clothing retailer Zara, utilizes a corporate VMS to achieve channel efficiencies and maintain a maximum amount of control over the supply chain. Zara's clothing is trendy, requiring the shortest time possible from product development to offering the clothing in stores. Inventory is characterized by very high turnover and frequent changes. Because it has control over all stages of the supply chain, Inditex can maintain an advantage through speed and keeping prices low.[25]

In an *administered VMS,* channel members are independent, but informal coordination achieves a high level of inter-organizational management. Members of an administered VMS may adopt uniform accounting and ordering procedures and cooperate in promotional activities for the benefit of all partners. Although individual channel members maintain autonomy, as in conventional marketing channels, one channel member (such as a producer or large retailer) dominates the administered VMS so that distribution decisions take the whole system into account.

A *contractual VMS* is the most popular type of vertical marketing system. Channel members are linked by legal agreements spelling out each member's rights and obligations. Franchise organizations, such as McDonald's and KFC, are contractual VMSs. Other contractual VMSs include wholesaler-sponsored groups, such as IGA stores, in which independent retailers band together under the contractual leadership of a wholesaler. Retailer-sponsored cooperatives, which own and operate their own wholesalers, are a third type of contractual VMS.

Horizontal Channel Integration

Combining organizations at the same level of operation under one management constitutes **horizontal channel integration**. An organization may integrate horizontally by merging with other organizations at the same level in the marketing channel. The owner of a dry-cleaning firm, for example, might buy and combine several other existing dry-cleaning establishments.

Although horizontal integration permits efficiencies and economies of scale in purchasing, marketing research, advertising, and specialized personnel, it is not always the most effective method of improving distribution. Problems that come with increased size often follow, resulting in decreased flexibility, difficulties coordinating among members, and the need for additional marketing research and large-scale planning. Unless distribution functions for the various units can be performed more efficiently under unified management than under the previously separate managements, horizontal integration will neither reduce costs nor improve the competitive position of the integrating firm.

14-5 PHYSICAL DISTRIBUTION IN SUPPLY-CHAIN MANAGEMENT

Physical distribution, also known as *logistics,* refers to the activities used to move products from producers to consumers and other end users. Physical distribution systems must meet the needs of both the supply chain and customers. Distribution activities are thus an important part of supply-chain planning and can require a high level of cooperation among partners.

vertical marketing system (VMS) A marketing channel managed by a single channel member to achieve efficient, low-cost distribution aimed at satisfying target market customers

horizontal channel integration Combining organizations at the same level of operation under one management

physical distribution Activities used to move products from producers to consumers and other end users

Within the marketing channel, physical distribution activities may be performed by a producer, wholesaler, or retailer, or they may be outsourced. In the context of distribution, *outsourcing* is the contracting of physical distribution tasks to third parties. Most physical distribution activities can be outsourced to outside firms that have special expertise in areas such as warehousing, transportation, inventory management, and information technology. Outsourcing distribution may allow a firm to leverage the expertise of another firm while focusing on its core competencies and freeing up resources to develop value-added capabilities to better serve customers.[26]

Cooperative relationships with third-party organizations, such as trucking companies, warehouses, and data-service providers, can reduce marketing channel costs and boost service and customer satisfaction for all supply-chain partners. When evaluating companies with potential for outsourcing, marketers must be cautious and choose firms that are proven to be efficient and that can help provide excellent customer service. They also need to recognize the importance of logistics functions, like warehousing and information technology, in reducing physical distribution costs associated with outsourcing.

The Internet and technological advancements have revolutionized logistics, allowing many manufacturers to carry out actions and services entirely online, bypassing shipping and warehousing considerations, and transforming physical distribution by facilitating just-in-time delivery, precise inventory visibility, and instant shipment-tracking capabilities. For example, video game and computer software manufacturers have made moves away from physical goods by offering an online download model for their products.[27] Technological advances create new and different problems for manufacturers, such as how to maintain a high level of customer service when customers never enter a store or meet with a salesperson and how to deal with returns of a product that does not exist in a physical form. Because of technology, many companies can now avoid expensive mistakes, reduce costs, and generate increased revenues. Information technology increases the transparency of the supply chain by allowing all marketing channel members to track the movement of goods through the supply chain.[28]

Planning an efficient physical distribution system is crucial to developing an effective marketing strategy because it can decrease costs and increase customer satisfaction. Speed of delivery, flexibility, and quality of service are often as important to customers as costs. Companies that offer the right goods, in the right place, at the right time, in the right quantity, and with the right support services are able to sell more than competitors that do not. Even when the demand for products is unpredictable, suppliers must be able to respond quickly to inventory needs. In such cases, physical distribution costs may be a minor consideration when compared with service, dependability, and timeliness.

Although physical distribution managers try to minimize the costs associated with order processing, inventory management, materials handling, warehousing, and transportation, decreasing the costs in one area often raises them in another. Figure 14.6 shows the percentage of total costs that physical distribution functions represent. A total-cost approach to physical distribution that takes into account all these different functions enables managers to view physical distribution as a system and shifts the emphasis from lowering the costs of individual activities to minimizing overall costs.

Physical distribution managers must be sensitive to the issue of cost trade-offs. Trade-offs are strategic decisions to combine (and recombine) resources for greatest cost-effectiveness. The goal is not always to find the lowest cost, but rather to find the right balance of costs. Higher costs in one functional area of a distribution system may be necessary to achieve lower costs in another. When distribution managers regard the system as a network of integrated functions, trade-offs become useful tools in implementing a unified, cost-effective distribution strategy.

Another important goal of physical distribution involves **cycle time**, the time needed to complete a process. For instance, reducing cycle time while maintaining or reducing costs and/or maintaining or increasing customer service is a winning combination in supply chains and ultimately leads to greater end-customer satisfaction. Firms should aim to find ways to reduce cycle time while maintaining or reducing costs and maintaining or improving customer service.

cycle time The time needed to complete a process

Figure 14.6 Proportional Cost of Each Physical Distribution Function as a Percentage of Total Distribution Costs

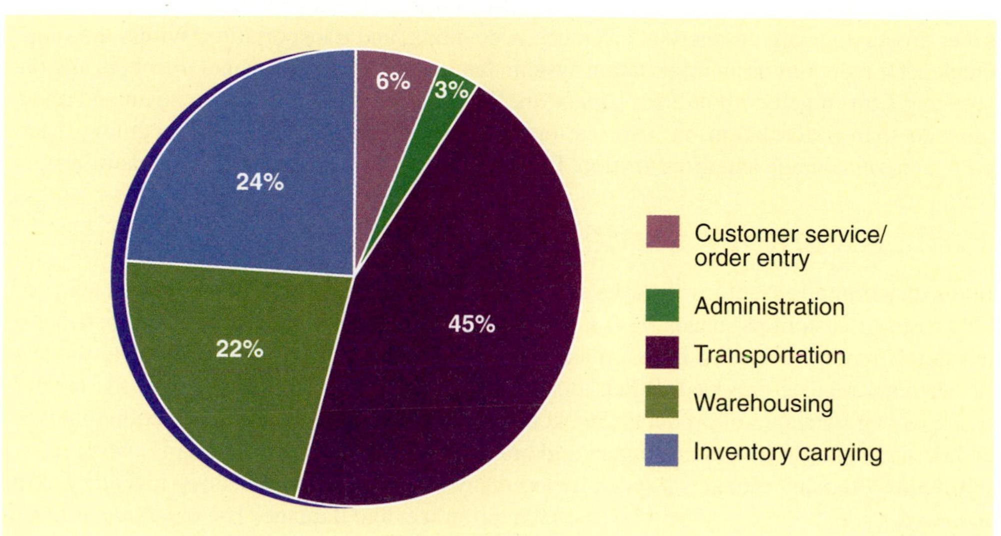

In the process of growing from a tiny business with a highly popular viral video to a large business that ships razor blades to men across the country on a subscription basis, Dollar Shave Club had to find a way to reduce cycle time while maintaining high customer satisfaction and quality. It enlisted the help of a third-party logistics specialist, which allowed it to focus on providing excellent customer service while ensuring on-time deliveries to subscribers.[29] In the rest of this section, we take a closer look at a variety of physical distribution activities, including order processing, inventory management, materials handling, warehousing, and transportation.

14-5a Order Processing

Order processing is the receipt and transmission of sales order information. Although management sometimes overlooks the importance of these activities, efficient order processing facilitates product flow. Computerized order processing provides a platform for information management, allowing all supply-chain members to increase their productivity. When carried out quickly and accurately, order processing contributes to customer satisfaction, decreased costs and cycle time, and increased profits.

Order processing entails three main tasks: order entry, order handling, and order delivery. Order entry begins when customers or salespeople place purchase orders via telephone, regular mail, e-mail, or website. Electronic ordering has become the most common. It is less time-consuming than a paper-based ordering system and reduces costs. In some companies, sales representatives receive and enter orders personally and also handle complaints, prepare progress reports, and forward sales order information.

Order handling involves several tasks. Once an order is entered, it is transmitted to a warehouse to verify product availability and to the credit department to set terms and prices and to check the customer's credit rating. If the credit department approves the purchase, warehouse personnel assemble the order. In many warehouses, automated machines carry out this step. If the requested product is not in stock, a production order is sent to the factory, or the customer is offered a substitute.

When the order has been assembled and packed for shipment, the warehouse schedules delivery with an appropriate carrier. If the customer pays for rush service, overnight delivery by an overnight carrier is used. The customer is sent an invoice, inventory records are adjusted, and the order is delivered.

order processing The receipt and transmission of sales order information

Whether a company uses a manual or an electronic order-processing system depends on which method provides greater speed and accuracy within cost limits. Manual processing suffices for small-volume orders and can be more flexible in certain situations. Most companies, however, use **electronic data interchange (EDI)**, which uses computer technology to integrate order processing with production, inventory, accounting, and transportation. Within the supply chain, EDI functions as an information system that links marketing channel members and outsourcing firms together. It reduces paperwork for all members of the supply chain and allows them to share information on invoices, orders, payments, inquiries, and scheduling. Many companies encourage suppliers to adopt EDI to reduce distribution costs and cycle times.

14-5b Inventory Management

Inventory management involves developing and maintaining adequate assortments of products to meet customers' needs. It is a key component of any effective physical distribution system. Inventory decisions have a major impact on physical distribution costs and the level of customer service provided. When too few products are carried in inventory, the result is *stockouts,* or shortages of products. Stockouts can result in customer dissatisfaction that leads to lower sales, even loss of customers and brand switching. On the other hand, when a firm maintains too many products (especially too many low-turnover products) in inventory, costs increase, as do risks of product obsolescence, pilferage, and damage. The objective of inventory management is to minimize inventory costs while maintaining an adequate supply of goods to satisfy customers. To achieve this objective, marketers focus on two major issues: when to order and how much to order.

To determine when to order, a marketer calculates the *reorder point*: the inventory level that signals the need to place a new order. To calculate the reorder point, the marketer must know the order lead time, the usage rate, and the amount of safety stock required. The *order lead time* refers to the average time lapse between placing the order and receiving it. The *usage rate* is the rate at which a product's inventory is used or sold during a specific time period. *Safety stock* is the amount of extra inventory a firm keeps to guard against stockouts resulting from above-average usage rates and/or longer-than-expected lead times. The reorder point can be calculated using the following formula:

$$\text{Reorder Point} = (\text{Order Lead Time} \times \text{Usage Rate}) + \text{Safety Stock}$$

Thus, if order lead time is 10 days, usage rate is 3 units per day, and safety stock is 20 units, the reorder point is 50 units.

Efficient inventory management with accurate reorder points is crucial for firms that use a **just-in-time (JIT)** approach, in which supplies arrive just as they are needed for use in production or for resale. Companies that use JIT (sometimes referred to as *lean distribution*) can maintain low inventory levels and purchase products and materials in small quantities only when needed. Usually there is no safety stock in a JIT system. Suppliers are expected to provide consistently high-quality products exactly when they are needed. JIT inventory management requires a high level of coordination between producers and suppliers, but it eliminates waste and reduces inventory costs. Toyota was a pioneer of JIT distribution. More recently, Harley Davidson applied JIT distribution methods to reduce costs, increase production flexibility, and improve supply-chain management. The alterations to its supply-chain management system helped Harley successfully turn the business around from near failure.[30] When a JIT approach is used in a supply chain, suppliers may move operations close to their major customers in order to provide goods as quickly as possible.

electronic data interchange (EDI) A computerized means of integrating order processing with production, inventory, accounting, and transportation

inventory management Developing and maintaining adequate assortments of products to meet customers' needs

just-in-time (JIT) An inventory-management approach in which supplies arrive just when needed for production or resale

materials handling Physical handling of tangible goods, supplies, and resources

14-5c Materials Handling

Materials handling, the physical handling of tangible goods, supplies, and resources, is an important factor in warehouse operations, as well as in transportation from points of production to points of consumption. Efficient procedures and techniques for materials handling minimize inventory management costs, reduce the number of times a good is handled, improve customer service, and increase customer satisfaction. Systems for packaging, labeling, loading, and movement must be coordinated to maximize cost reduction and customer satisfaction.

Many firms use radio waves to track materials tagged with radio frequency identification (RFID) through every phase of handling. RFID has greatly improved shipment tracking and reduced cycle times. Hundreds of RFID tags can be read at a time, which represents an advantage over barcodes. Firms are discovering that RFID technology has very broad applications, from tracking inventory to paying for goods and services, asset management, and data collection. For instance, Disney theme parks use RFID in visitor wristbands, called MagicBands. The bands encode visitor wristbands with credit card information, allowing visitors to make purchases with the swipe of a wrist. RFID technology tracks movements within the park to alert them when it is their turn for a nearby ride. Although some are concerned about how much information Disney will be able to collect using the data from wristbands, many of Disney Parks' 30 million annual visitors enjoy the chance not to worry about money and not having to stand in line—which improves the customer experience.[31] Product characteristics often determine handling. For example, the characteristics of bulk liquids and gases determine how they can be moved and stored. Internal packaging is also an important consideration in materials handling. Goods must be packaged correctly to prevent damage or breakage during handling and transportation. Many companies employ packaging consultants during the product design process to help them decide which packaging materials and methods will result in the most efficient handling. Consider the advertisement for Americold, which is a warehousing and logistics company that specializes in the distribution of perishable goods. Firms that produce food items or other goods that must remain cold may want to consider working with such an organization because they feature temperature-controlled warehouses and shipping. Such an operation can help a firm with inventory management by maximizing the shelf life of goods and minimizing loss.

Warehousing and Inventory Management
Americold helps firms that must transport perishable items, such as food, by offering temperature-controlled warehousing and shipping.

Unit loading and containerization are two common methods used in materials handling. With *unit loading,* one or more boxes are placed on a pallet or skid. These units can then be loaded efficiently by mechanical means, such as forklifts, trucks, or conveyer systems. *Containerization* is the consolidation of many items into a single, large container that is sealed at its point of origin and opened at its destination. Containers are usually 8 feet wide, 8 feet high, and 10 to 40 feet long. Their uniform size means they can be stacked and shipped via train, barge, or ship. Once containers reach their destinations, wheel assemblies can be added to make them suitable for ground transportation by truck. Because individual items are not handled in transit, containerization greatly increases efficiency and security in shipping.

14-5d Warehousing

Warehousing, the design and operation of facilities for storing and moving goods, is another important physical distribution function. Warehousing provides time utility by enabling firms to compensate for dissimilar production and consumption rates. When mass production

warehousing The design and operation of facilities for storing and moving goods

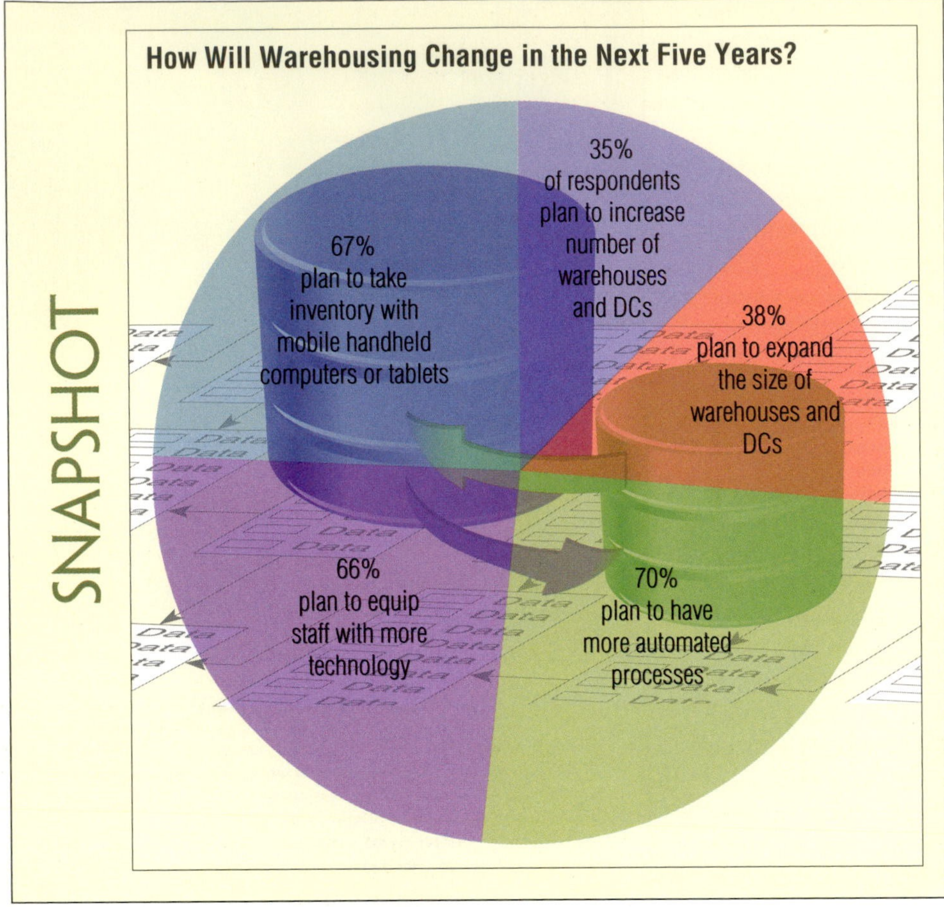

Source: 2013 Warehouse Vision Report, Motorola Solutions.

creates a greater stock of goods than can be sold immediately, companies warehouse the surplus until customers are ready to buy it. Warehousing also helps to stabilize prices and the availability of seasonal items.

Choosing appropriate warehouse facilities is an important strategic consideration because they allow a company to reduce transportation and inventory costs and improve service to customers. The wrong type of warehouse can lead to inefficient physical distribution and added costs. Warehouses fall into two general categories: private and public. In many cases, a combination of private and public facilities provides the most flexible warehousing approach.

Companies operate **private warehouses** for shipping and storing their own products. A firm usually leases or purchases a private warehouse when its warehousing needs in a given geographic market are substantial and stable enough to warrant a long-term commitment to a fixed facility. Private warehouses are also appropriate for firms that require special handling and storage and that want control of warehouse design and operation. Retailers like Sears find it economical to integrate private warehousing with purchasing and distribution for their retail outlets. When sales volumes are fairly stable, ownership and control of a private warehouse may be most convenient and offer cost benefits. Private warehouses, however, face fixed costs, such as insurance, taxes, maintenance, and debt expense. They limit firms' flexibility if they wish to move inventories to different locations. Many private warehouses are being eliminated by direct links between producers and customers, reduced cycle times, and outsourcing to public warehouses.

Public warehouses lease storage space and related physical distribution facilities to other companies. They sometimes provide distribution services, such as receiving, unloading, inspecting, filling orders, financing, displaying products, and coordinating shipments. Distribution Unlimited Inc., for example, offers a wide range of such services through its facilities in New York, which contain more than 8 million square feet of warehouse space.[32]

Public warehouses are especially useful to firms that have seasonal production or demand, low-volume storage needs, and inventories that must be maintained in many locations. They are also useful for firms that are testing or entering new markets or require additional storage space. Additionally, public warehouses serve as collection points during product-recall programs. Whereas private warehouses have fixed costs, public warehouses offer variable (and possibly lower) costs because users rent space and purchase warehousing services only as needed.

private warehouses Company-operated facilities for storing and shipping products

Public warehouses Storage space and related physical distribution facilities that can be leased by companies

Many public warehouses furnish security for products that are used as collateral for loans, a service provided at either the warehouse or the site of the owner's inventory. *Field public warehouses* are established by public warehouses at the owner's inventory location.

The warehouser becomes custodian of the products and issues a receipt that can be used as collateral for a loan. Public warehouses also provide *bonded storage*, a warehousing arrangement in which imported or taxable products are not released until the products' owners pay U.S. customs duties, taxes, or other fees. Bonded warehouses enable firms to defer tax payments on such items until they are delivered to customers.

Distribution centers are large facilities used for receiving, warehousing, and redistributing products to stores or customers. They are specially designed for rapid flow of products and are usually one-story buildings with access to transportation networks, such as major highways and/or railway lines. Many distribution centers are automated, with computer-directed robots, forklifts, and hoists that collect and move products to loading docks. Distribution over large geographic areas can be complicated but having strategically located distribution centers can help a company meet consumer demand. Even Walmart had to build more distribution centers to accommodate a greater number of online sales as it positioned itself to compete directly with Amazon.[33] Although some public warehouses offer such specialized services, most distribution centers are privately owned. They serve customers in regional markets and, in some cases, function as consolidation points for a company's branch warehouses.

14-5e Transportation

Transportation, the movement of products from where they are made to intermediaries and end users, is the most expensive physical distribution function. Freight costs can vary widely among countries, or even regions within the same country, depending on the level of infrastructure and the prevalence of different modes of transportation in an area.[34] Because product availability and timely deliveries depend on transportation functions, transportation decisions directly affect customer service. In some cases, a firm may choose to build its distribution and marketing strategy around a unique transportation system if that system can ensure on-time deliveries and give the firm a competitive edge. Companies may build their own transportation fleets (private carriers) or outsource the transportation function to a common or contract carrier.

distribution centers Large, centralized warehouses that focus on moving rather than storing goods

transportation The movement of products from where they are made to intermediaries and end users

Transportation Modes

The basic transportation modes for moving physical goods are railroads, trucks, waterways, airways, and pipelines. Each has distinct advantages. Many companies adopt physical handling procedures that facilitate the use of two or more modes in combination. Table 14.3 gives more detail on the characteristics of each transportation mode.

Table 14.3 Characteristics and Ratings of Transportation Modes by Selection Criteria

Selection Criteria	Railroads	Trucks	Pipelines	Waterways	Airplanes
Cost	Moderate	High	Low	Very low	Very high
Speed	Average	Fast	Slow	Very slow	Very fast
Dependability	Average	High	High	Average	High
Load flexibility	High	Average	Very low	Very high	Low
Accessibility	High	Very high	Very limited	Limited	Average
Frequency	Low	High	Very high	Very low	Average
Products carried	Coal, grain, lumber, paper and pulp products, chemicals	Clothing, computers, books, groceries and produce, livestock	Oil, processed coal, natural gas	Chemicals, bauxite, grain, motor vehicles, agricultural implements	Flowers, food (highly perishable), technical instruments, emergency parts and equipment, overnight mail

Railroads like Union Pacific and Canadian National carry heavy, bulky freight that must be shipped long distances over land. Railroads commonly haul minerals, sand, lumber, chemicals, and farm products, as well as low-value manufactured goods and automobiles. Railroads are especially efficient for transporting full carloads, which can be shipped at lower rates than smaller quantities, because they require less handling. Many companies locate factories or warehouses near rail lines for convenient loading and unloading.

Trucks provide the most flexible schedules and routes of all major transportation modes in the United States because they can go almost anywhere. Because trucks do not have to conform to a set schedule and can move goods from factory or warehouse to customer, wherever there are roads, they are often used in conjunction with other forms of transport that cannot provide door-to-door deliveries, such as waterways and railroads. Trucks are more expensive and somewhat more vulnerable to bad weather than trains. They are also subject to size and weight restrictions on the loads they carry. Trucks are sometimes criticized for high levels of loss and damage to freight and for delays caused by the re-handling of small shipments.

Waterways are the cheapest method of shipping heavy, low-value, nonperishable goods. Water carriers offer considerable capacity. Powered by tugboats and towboats, barges that travel along intra-coastal canals, inland rivers, and navigation systems can haul at least 10 times the weight of one rail car, and oceangoing vessels can haul thousands of containers. The vast majority of international cargo is transported by water at least part of the way. However, many markets are inaccessible by water transportation and must be supplemented by rail or truck. Droughts and floods also may create difficulties for users of inland waterway transportation. Nevertheless, the growing need to transport goods long distances across the globe will likely increase its use in the future.

Air transportation is the fastest but most expensive form of shipping. It is used most often for perishable goods, for high-value and/or low-bulk items, and for products that require quick delivery over long distances. Some air carriers transport combinations of passengers, freight, and mail. Despite its expense, air transit can reduce warehousing and packaging costs and losses from theft and damage, thus helping the aggregate cost of the mode. Although air transport accounts for a small minority of total cargo carried, it is an important form of transportation in an increasingly time-sensitive business environment.[35] In fact, the success of many businesses is now based on the availability of overnight air delivery service provided by such organizations as

Emerging Trends

Click to Buy and Get Same-Day Delivery

Same-day delivery has become a competitive battleground as online retailers and traditional stores appeal to time-pressured consumers who do not want to wait even one day to receive purchases made online or by smartphone. Walmart has been testing same-day delivery of groceries since 2011, expanding from California to Denver and beyond. Shoppers can click to buy tens of thousands of items and select a 2-hour window for delivery. Branded Walmart To Go trucks bring purchases right to the customer's front door, for a small delivery fee.

This helps Walmart compete more effectively with nonstore retailers like Amazon, which offers same-day delivery of groceries through its AmazonFresh program. Amazon started the delivery service in Seattle and then expanded to California as it prepared warehouses and branded trucks to service customers. The online auction company eBay recently bought a delivery company, Shutl, so it can speed deliveries to customers in major metropolitan areas. Shutl has a high-tech system of routing pickups to different carriers based on location, availability, and other factors.

Even Google is getting into the delivery business with Shopping Express, tested with its own employees and now available in many parts of California. Shopping Express invites customers to click and buy from more than a dozen retailers, including Staples, Whole Foods, and Walgreens, and then select a 3- to 5-hour slot for delivery. Now the companies are waiting to see whether customers will find same-day delivery as convenient and valuable as the instant gratification of buying something in a store and having it right away.[b]

UPS, FedEx, DHL, RPS Air, and the U.S. Postal Service. Many firms offer overnight or same-day shipping to customers.

Pipelines, the most automated transportation mode, usually belong to the shipper and carry the shipper's products. Most pipelines carry petroleum products or chemicals. Slurry pipelines carry pulverized coal, grain, or wood chips suspended in water. Pipelines move products slowly but continuously and at relatively low cost. They are dependable and minimize the problems of product damage and theft. However, contents are subject to as much as 1 percent shrinkage, usually from evaporation—which can result in profit losses. Pipelines also have been a concern to environmentalists, who fear installation and leaks could harm plants and animals.

Choosing Transportation Modes

Logistics managers select a transportation mode based on the combination of cost, speed, dependability, load flexibility, accessibility, and frequency that is most appropriate for their products and generates the desired level of customer service. Table 14.3 shows relative ratings of each transportation mode by these selection criteria.

Marketers compare alternative transportation modes to determine whether the benefits from a more expensive mode are worth the higher costs. A firm wishing to establish international distribution may consider a large logistics firm for its vast network of global partners. Exel Logistics, for instance, offers 500 sites and 40,000 associates in the Americas alone and provides the staffing and expertise to perform many supply-chain management functions at locations around the globe.[36] Look at the Echo advertisement—it is an international logistics company that helps firms to determine which modes of transportation are most important for distributing their products. You can see from the advertisement that Echo will help a firm develop a seamless distribution channel using all available options, including air, rail, and trucks.

intermodal transportation Two or more transportation modes used in combination

freight forwarders Organizations that consolidate shipments from several firms into efficient lot sizes

Coordinating Transportation

To take advantage of the benefits offered by various transportation modes and compensate for shortcomings, marketers often combine and coordinate two or more modes. **Intermodal transportation** is easier than ever because of developments within the transportation industry. It combines the flexibility of trucking with the low cost or speed of other forms of transport. Containerization facilitates intermodal transportation by consolidating shipments into sealed containers for transport by *piggyback* (using truck trailers and railway flatcars), *fishyback* (using truck trailers and water carriers), and *birdyback* (using truck trailers and air carriers). As transportation costs have increased and firms seek to find the most efficient methods possible, intermodal shipping has gained popularity.

Specialized outsourcing agencies provide other forms of transport coordination. Known as **freight forwarders**, these firms combine shipments from several organizations into efficient lot sizes. Small loads (less than 500 pounds) are much more expensive to ship than full carloads or truckloads and may make shipping cost-prohibitive for smaller firms. Freight forwarders help such firms by consolidating small loads from various organizations to allow them to qualify collectively for lower rates. Freight forwarders' profits come from the margin between the higher rates firms would have to pay and the lower carload rates the freight forwarder pays

Echo Global Logistics

Transportation Modes
A logistics company such as Echo can help firms to develop an efficient distribution network using multiple transportation modes.

Intermodal Transportation
Containers facilitate intermodal transportation because they can be transported by ships, trains, and trucks.

© iStockphoto.com/narvikk

for full loads. Because large shipments also require less handling, freight forwarders can reduce delivery time and the likelihood of shipment damage. Freight forwarders also have the insight to determine the most efficient carriers and routes and are useful for shipping goods to foreign markets, including in foreign markets. Shipping firms such as UPS and FedEx offer freight-forwarding services, as do dedicated freight forwarders such as NRA Global Logistics or Worldwide Express. Some companies may prefer to outsource their shipping to freight forwarders because the forwarders provide door-to-door service.

Another transportation innovation is the development of **megacarriers**, freight transportation companies that offer several shipment methods, including rail, truck, and air service. Prior to the development of megacarriers, transportation companies generally only specialized in one mode. To compete with megacarriers, air carriers have increased their ground-transportation services. As the range of transportation alternatives expands, carriers also put greater emphasis on customer service to gain a competitive advantage.

14-6 LEGAL ISSUES IN CHANNEL MANAGEMENT

The numerous federal, state, and local laws governing distribution channel management in the United States are based on the principle that the public is best served by protecting competition and free trade. Under the authority of federal legislation, such as the Sherman Antitrust Act and the Federal Trade Commission Act, courts and regulatory agencies determine under what circumstances channel management practices violate this underlying principle and must be restricted. Although channel managers are not expected to be legal experts, they should be aware that attempts to control distribution functions might have legal repercussions. When shipping internationally, managers must also be aware of international laws and regulations that might affect their distribution activities. The following practices are among those frequently subject to legal restraint.

14-6a Dual Distribution

megacarriers Freight transportation firms that provide several modes of shipment

Earlier, we noted that some companies employ dual distribution by using two or more marketing channels to distribute the same products to the same target market. Courts do not consider this practice illegal when it allows for competition. A manufacturer can also legally open its own retail outlets. However, the courts view a manufacturer that uses company-owned outlets to dominate or drive out of business independent retailers or distributors that handle its products as a threat to competition. In such cases, dual distribution violates the law. To avoid this interpretation, producers should use outlet prices that do not severely undercut independent retailers' prices.

14-6b Restricted Sales Territories

To tighten control over product distribution, a manufacturer may try to prohibit intermediaries from selling outside of designated sales territories. Intermediaries often favor this practice because it provides them with exclusive territories where they can minimize competition. Over the years, the courts have adopted conflicting positions in regard to restricted sales territories. Although the courts have deemed restricted sales territories a restraint of trade among intermediaries handling the same brands (except for small or newly established companies), they have also held that exclusive territories can actually promote competition among dealers handling different brands. At present, the producer's intent in establishing restricted territories and the overall effect of doing so on the market must be evaluated for each individual case.

14-6c Tying Agreements

When a supplier (usually a manufacturer or franchisor) furnishes a product to a channel member with the stipulation that the channel member must purchase other products as well, it has negotiated a **tying agreement**. Suppliers may institute tying agreements as a means of getting rid of slow-moving inventory, or a franchisor may tie the purchase of equipment and supplies to the sale of franchises, justifying the policy as necessary for quality control and protection of the franchisor's reputation.

A related practice is *full-line forcing*, in which a supplier requires that channel members purchase the supplier's entire line to obtain any of the supplier's products. Manufacturers sometimes use full-line forcing to ensure that intermediaries accept new products and that a suitable range of products is available to customers.

The courts accept tying agreements when the supplier is the only firm able to provide products of a certain quality, when the intermediary is free to carry competing products as well, and when a company has just entered the market. Most other tying agreements are considered illegal.

14-6d Exclusive Dealing

When a manufacturer forbids an intermediary to carry products of competing manufacturers, the arrangement is called **exclusive dealing**. Manufacturers receive considerable market protection in an exclusive-dealing arrangement and may cut off shipments to intermediaries that violate the agreement.

The legality of an exclusive-dealing contract is determined by applying three tests. If the exclusive dealing blocks competitors from as much as 15 percent of the market, the sales volume is large, and the producer is considerably larger than the retailer, then the arrangement is considered anticompetitive. If dealers and customers in a given market have access to similar products or if the exclusive-dealing contract strengthens an otherwise weak competitor, the arrangement is allowed.

14-6e Refusal to Deal

For nearly a century, courts have held that producers have the right to choose or reject the channel members with which they will do business. Within existing distribution channels, however, suppliers may not legally refuse to deal with wholesalers or dealers merely because these wholesalers or dealers resist policies that are anticompetitive or in restraint of trade. Suppliers are further prohibited from organizing some channel members in refusal-to-deal actions against other members that choose not to comply with illegal policies.

tying agreement An agreement in which a supplier furnishes a product to a channel member with the stipulation that the channel member must purchase other products as well

exclusive dealing A situation in which a manufacturer forbids an intermediary from carrying products of competing manufacturers

Summary

14-1 Describe the foundations of supply-chain management.

The distribution component of the marketing mix focuses on the decisions and activities involved in making products available to customers when and where they want to purchase them. An important function of distribution is the joint effort of all involved organizations to be part of creating an effective supply chain, which refers to all the activities associated with the flow and transformation of products from raw materials through to the end customer. Operations management is the total set of managerial activities used by an organization to transform resource inputs into goods, services, or both. Logistics management involves planning, implementation, and controlling the efficient and effective flow and storage of goods, services, and information from the point of origin to consumption to meet customers' needs and wants. Supply management in its broadest form refers to the processes that enable the progress of value from raw material to final customer and back to redesign and final disposition. Supply-chain management therefore refers to a set of approaches used to integrate the functions of operations management, logistics management, supply management, and marketing channel management so that goods and services are produced and distributed in the right quantities, to the right locations, and at the right time. The supply chain includes all entities—shippers and other firms that facilitate distribution, as well as producers, wholesalers, and retailers—that distribute products and benefit from cooperative efforts.

14-2 Explain the role and significance of marketing channels and supply chains.

A marketing channel, or channel of distribution, is a group of individuals and organizations that direct the flow of products from producers to customers. The major role of marketing channels is to make products available at the right time, at the right place, and in the right amounts. In most channels of distribution, producers and consumers are linked by marketing intermediaries. The two major types of intermediaries are retailers, which purchase products and resell them to ultimate consumers, and wholesalers, which buy and resell products to other wholesalers, retailers, and business customers.

Marketing channels serve many functions. They create time, place, and possession utilities by making products available when and where customers want them and providing customers with access to product use through sale or rental. Marketing intermediaries facilitate exchange efficiencies, often reducing the costs of exchanges by performing certain services and functions. Although some critics suggest eliminating wholesalers, the functions of the intermediaries in the marketing channel must be performed. As such, eliminating one or more intermediaries results in other organizations in the channel having to do more. Because intermediaries serve both producers and buyers, they reduce the total number of transactions that otherwise would be needed to move products from producer to the end customer.

Channels of distribution are broadly classified as channels for consumer products and channels for business products. Within these two broad categories, different channels are used for different products. Although consumer goods can move directly from producer to consumers, consumer channels that include wholesalers and retailers are usually more economical and knowledge-efficient. Distribution of business products differs from that of consumer products in the types of channels used. A direct distribution channel is common in business marketing. Also used are channels containing industrial distributors, manufacturers' agents, and a combination of agents and distributors. Most producers have multiple or dual channels so the distribution system can be adjusted for various target markets.

Selecting an appropriate marketing channel is a crucial decision for supply-chain managers. To determine which channel is most appropriate, managers must think about customer characteristics, the type of organization, product attributes, competition, environmental forces, and the availability and characteristics of intermediaries. Careful consideration of these factors will assist a supply-chain manager in selecting the correct channel.

14-3 Identify the intensity of market coverage.

A marketing channel is managed such that products receive appropriate market coverage. In choosing intensive distribution, producers strive to make a product available to all possible dealers. In selective distribution, only some outlets in an area are chosen to distribute a product. Exclusive distribution usually gives a single dealer rights to sell a product in a large geographic area.

14-4 Describe strategic issues in marketing channels, including leadership, cooperation, and conflict.

Each channel member performs a different role in the system and agrees to accept certain rights, responsibilities, rewards, and sanctions for nonconformance. Although many marketing channels are determined by consensus, some are organized and controlled by a single leader, or channel captain. A channel captain may be a producer, wholesaler, or retailer. A marketing channel functions most effectively when members cooperate. When they deviate from their roles, channel conflict can arise.

Integration of marketing channels brings various activities under one channel member's management. Vertical integration combines two or more stages of the channel under one management. The vertical marketing system (VMS) is managed centrally for the mutual benefit of all channel members. Vertical marketing systems may be corporate, administered, or contractual. Horizontal integration combines institutions at the same level of channel operation under a single management.

14-5 Explain physical distribution as being a part of supply-chain management.

Physical distribution, or logistics, refers to the activities used to move products from producers to customers and other end users. These activities include order processing, inventory management, materials handling, warehousing, and transportation. An efficient physical distribution system is an important component of an overall marketing strategy because it can decrease costs and increase customer satisfaction. Within the marketing channel, physical distribution activities are often performed by a wholesaler, but they may also be performed by a producer or retailer or outsourced to a third party. Efficient physical distribution systems can decrease costs and transit time while increasing customer service.

Order processing is the receipt and transmission of sales order information. It consists of three main tasks—order entry, order handling, and order delivery—that may be done manually but are more often handled through electronic data interchange systems. Inventory management involves developing and maintaining adequate assortments of products to meet customers' needs. Logistics managers must strive to find the optimal level of inventory to satisfy customer needs while keeping costs down. Materials handling, the physical handling of products, is a crucial element in warehousing and transporting products. Warehousing involves the design and operation of facilities for storing and moving goods. Such facilities may be privately owned or public. Transportation, the movement of products from where they are made to where they are purchased and used, is the most expensive physical distribution function. The basic modes of transporting goods include railroads, trucks, waterways, airways, and pipelines.

14-6 Describe legal issues in channel management.

Federal, state, and local laws regulate channel management to protect competition and free trade. Courts may prohibit or permit a practice depending on whether it violates this underlying principle. Channel management practices frequently subject to legal restraint include dual distribution, restricted sales territories, tying agreements, exclusive dealing, and refusal to deal. When these practices strengthen weak competitors or increase competition among dealers, they may be permitted. In most other cases, when competition may be weakened considerably, they are deemed illegal.

Go to www.cengagebrain.com for resources to help you master the content in this chapter as well as materials that will expand your marketing knowledge!

Developing Your Marketing Plan

One of the key components in a successful marketing strategy is the plan for getting the products to your customer. To make the best decisions about where, when, and how your products will be made available to the customer, you need to know more about how these distribution decisions relate to other marketing-mix elements in your marketing plan. To assist you in relating the information in this chapter to your marketing plan, consider the following issues:

1. Marketing intermediaries perform many activities. Using Table 14.2 as a guide, discuss the types of activities where a channel member could provide needed assistance.
2. Using Figure 14.2 (or Figure 14.3 if your product is a business product), determine which of the channel distribution paths is most appropriate for your product. Given the nature of your product, could it be distributed through more than one of these paths?
3. Determine the level of distribution intensity that is appropriate for your product. Consider the characteristics of your target market(s), the product attributes, and environmental factors in your deliberation.
4. Discuss the physical functions that will be required for distributing your product, focusing on materials handling, warehousing, and transportation.

The information obtained from these questions should assist you in developing various aspects of your marketing plan found in the "Interactive Marketing Plan" exercise at www.cengagebrain.com.

Important Terms

distribution 410
supply chain 410
operations management 410
logistics management 410
supply management 410
supply-chain management 410
marketing channel 412
marketing intermediaries 412
industrial distributor 417

Discussion and Review Questions

1. Define supply-chain management. Why is it important?
2. Describe the major functions of marketing channels. Why are these functions better accomplished through combined efforts of channel members?
3. List several reasons consumers often blame intermediaries for distribution inefficiencies.
4. Compare and contrast the four major types of marketing channels for consumer products. Through which type of channel is each of the following products most likely to be distributed?
   a. New automobiles
   b. Saltine crackers
   c. Cut-your-own Christmas trees
   d. New textbooks
   e. Sofas
   f. Soft drinks
5. Outline the four most common channels for business products. Describe the products or situations that lead marketers to choose each channel.
6. Describe an industrial distributor. What types of products are marketed through an industrial distributor?
7. Under what conditions is a producer most likely to use more than one marketing channel?
8. Identify and describe the factors that may influence marketing channel selection decisions.
9. Explain the differences among intensive, selective, and exclusive methods of distribution.
10. Comment on this statement. "Channel cooperation requires that members support the overall channel goals to achieve individual goals."
11. Explain the major characteristics of each of the three types of vertical marketing systems (VMSs): corporate, administered, and contractual.
12. Discuss the cost and service trade-offs involved in developing a physical distribution system.
13. What are the main tasks involved in order processing?
14. Explain the trade-offs that inventory managers face when they reorder products or supplies. How is the reorder point computed?
15. Explain the major differences between private and public warehouses. How do they differ from a distribution center?
16. Compare and contrast the five major transportation modes in terms of cost, speed, and dependability.
17. Under what conditions are tying agreements, exclusive dealing, and dual distribution judged illegal?

Video Case 14.1

Taza Cultivates Channel Relationships with Chocolate

Taza Chocolate is a small Massachusetts-based manufacturer of stone-ground organic chocolate made in the classic Mexican tradition. Founded in 2006, Taza markets most of its products through U.S. retailers, wholesalers, and distributors. Individual customers around the world can also buy Taza chocolate bars, baking squares, chocolate-covered nuts, and other specialty items directly from the Taza website. If they live in Somerville, Massachusetts, they might even find a Taza employee riding a "chococycle," selling products and distributing samples at an upscale food-truck festival or a weekend market festival.

Taza seeks to make personal connections with all the certified organic growers who supply its ingredients. "Because our process here at the factory is so minimal," says the company's director of sales, "it's really important that we get a very high-quality ingredient. To make sure that we're getting the absolute cream of the [cocoa] crop, we have a direct face-to-face human relationship between us and the actual farmer who's producing those beans."

Dealing directly with suppliers allows Taza to meet its social responsibility goals while ensuring the kind of quality that commands a premium price. "We're a premium brand," explains the director of sales, "and because of the way we do what we do, we have to charge more than your average chocolate bar." A Taza chocolate bar that sells at a retail price of $4.50 carries a wholesale price of about $2.70. The distributor's price, however, is even lower, closer to $2.00.

Distributors buy in the largest quantities, which for Taza means a pallet load rather than a case that a wholesaler would buy. "But wholesale will always be our bread and butter, where we really move the volume and we have good margins," says Taza's director of sales. In the company's experience, distributors are very price-conscious and more interested than wholesalers in promotions and extras.

Taza offers factory tours at its Somerville site, charging a small entrance fee that includes a donation to Sustainable Harvest International. There, visitors can watch the bean-to-bar process from beginning to end, learning about the beans and the stone-ground tradition that differentiates Taza from European chocolates. Visitors enjoy product samples along the way and, at the end of the tour, they can browse through the factory store and buy freshly-made specialties like chipotle chili chocolate and ginger chocolate. On holidays like Halloween and Valentine's Day, Taza hosts special tastings and limited-edition treats to attract customers to its factory store. Its annual beer-and-chocolate pairing event, hosted with the Drink Craft Beer website, is another way to introduce Taza to consumers who appreciate quality foods and drinks.

Taza's marketing communications focus mainly on Facebook, Twitter, blogs, e-mail, and specialty food shows. Also, the company frequently offers samples in upscale and organic food stores in major metropolitan areas. As it does with its growers, Taza seeks to forge personal relationships with its channel partners. "When we send a shipment of chocolate," says the sales director, "sometimes we'll put in a little extra for the people who work there. That always helps because [it's] building that kind of human relationship."

Privately-owned Taza has begun shipping to Canada and a handful of European countries. Its channel arrangements must allow for delivering perishable products that stay fresh and firm, no matter what the weather. As a result, distributors often hold some Taza inventory in refrigerated warehouses to have ready for next-day delivery when retailers place orders.[37]

Questions for Discussion

1. Which distribution channels does Taza use, and why are they appropriate for this company?
2. In what ways does Taza benefit from selling directly to some consumers? What are some potential problems of selling directly to consumers?
3. In what ways are Taza's distribution efforts influenced by the fact that its products are organic?

Case 14.2

Procter & Gamble Tunes Up Channels and Transportation

From Duracell to Dawn, Pampers to Prilosec, Procter & Gamble markets some of the world's best-known brands for household needs, health care, personal care, and baby care. Its portfolio includes 25 brands that bring in more than $1 billion each every year, plus another 15 that bring in at least $500 million every year. In all, Procter & Gamble rings up $84 billion in sales through traditional stores and online retailers in 180 countries.

Because nearly all of Procter & Gamble's products are convenience goods, the company uses intensive distribution market coverage. Among the retailers that carry its products are supermarkets, drug stores, convenience stores, discount stores, and warehouse clubs. Shelf space is valuable, so not all stores carry the entire product line in any given category. In many stores, Procter & Gamble's branded items compete for shelf space not only with other manufacturers' brands, but also with store brands. This isn't always the case, however. For example, Procter & Gamble recently signed an exclusive distribution arrangement with Sam's Club, making Duracell the only national brand of batteries sold in those warehouse stores. And, knowing that warehouse stores have limited back-room storage space, Procter & Gamble makes more frequent deliveries to ensure that its products are always in stock for club members.

Eyeing long-term growth in emerging markets, which already account for 40 percent of its sales, Procter & Gamble is always looking for a distribution edge that will put its products on more shelves. When the company acquired Gillette in 2005, it also obtained access to the marketing channels Gillette had established for its razors, blades, and other accessories. This helped Procter & Gamble gain additional distribution for a wider range of products in India and Brazil, among other nations.

© iStockphoto.com/dem10

Procter & Gamble is testing new Internet and mobile channels for some of its everyday products. In one Toronto experiment, it teamed with the online retailer Well.ca to create posters of frequently-purchased products like Crest toothpaste and Pampers disposable diapers, along with QR (quick response) codes that can be scanned by consumers with QR apps on their smartphones. The posters were positioned in a busy downtown building adjacent to the subway, where time-pressured commuters could take a minute or two to scan the items they wanted to purchase and arrange delivery from Well.ca at a convenient hour. In another Toronto experiment, Procter & Gamble teamed with Walmart Canada to create virtual stores inside 50 bus shelters. As consumers waited for a bus, they used their smartphones to scan QR codes for baby products, beauty products, and other merchandise, and set a time for later delivery. Tests such as these help both the manufacturer and retailers to refine future marketing efforts as technology evolves.

In addition, the Internet retailing pioneer Amazon.com has asked Procter & Gamble to help it speed up delivery of products sold online. At Amazon's request, Procter & Gamble has roped off a small, separate area inside seven of its distribution centers, reserving this space just for the use of Amazon. These centers in the United States, Japan, and Germany hold cartons and cartons of bulky products like Pampers disposable diapers and Bounty paper towels while they await delivery to retailers. Instead of trucking these goods to Amazon's distribution centers when needed, Procter & Gamble simply shifts them to the separate Amazon section of the building. There, Amazon employees select individual items to fulfill customer orders and ship the boxes directly from the distribution center to consumers. Not only does this save time, but it also saves money for both Procter & Gamble and Amazon.

Efficiency is vital when a marketer like Procter & Gamble distributes products in such massive quantities. In North America alone, the company prepares 800,000 shipments annually for delivery to retailers' warehouses and distribution centers. Shaving even a few dollars per shipment adds up to a significant savings over time. Greener transportation is also helping Procter & Gamble save money while it helps protect the planet. Although the company maintains a small fleet of trucks, most of its products are transported by 80 outside trucking companies. Procter & Gamble is working with the truckers to significantly increase the percentage of shipments transported by vehicles that run on compressed natural gas, making physical distribution greener in environmental and financial terms.[38]

Questions for Discussion

1. Do you think Procter & Gamble should use a direct channel to sell to consumers? Identify one or more arguments for and against using a direct channel for disposable diapers and paper towels.
2. What issues in channel conflict might arise from Procter & Gamble's special arrangements with Amazon .com?
3. Would you recommend that Procter & Gamble use any mode of transportation other than trucks to transport cartons to retailers? Explain your answer.

NOTES

[1] Sarah Frier, "Every Rose Has Its Data Points," *Bloomberg Businessweek*, December 24, 2012, pp. 49–50; Jordan Crook, "H.Bloom Floral Service Preps to Launch in 5 New Cities, Starting with Boston on June 11," *TechCrunch*, June 6, 2013,http://techcrunch.com/2013/06/06/h-bloom-floral-service-preps-to-launch-in-5-new-cities-starting-with-boston-on-june-11 (accessed December 21, 2013); Julie DiGiovine, "High-Tech Blooms for Brides," *Boston Magazine*, July 15, 2013, www.bostonmagazine.com/weddings/blog/2013/07/15/high-tech-blooms (accessed December 21, 2013).

[2] Ricky W. Griffin, *Fundamentals of Management* (Mason, OH: South-Western Cengage, 2012), p. 460.

[3] Joseph Bonney, "Logistics Costs Rose 6.6 Percent Last Year," June 13, 2012, www.joc.com/international-logistics/global-sourcing/logistics-costs-rose-66-percent-last-year_20120613.html (accessed December 21, 2013).

[4] GDP, World Bank, http://data.worldbank.org/indicator/NY.GDP.MKTP.CD (accessed December 21, 2013).

[5] Patrick Burnson, "Supply Chain Managers Told to Prepare for Demand Surge in 2014," *Supply Chain Management Review*, November 16, 2013, www.scmr.com/article/supply_chain_managers_told_to_prepare_for_demand_surge_in_2014 (accessed December 12, 2013).

[6] Bob Trebilcock, "Supply Chain: Amazon Is Changing the Rules of the Game," *Modern Materials Handling*, December 14, 2012, www.mmh.com/article/supply_chain_amazon_is_changing_the_rules_of_the_game (accessed December 12, 2013).

[7] Christina Ng, "Soap Opera: Amazon Moves In with P&G," *The Wall Street Journal*, October 14, 2013, http://online.wsj.com/news/articles/SB10001424052702304330904579135840230674458? (accessed December 12, 2013).

[8] Augustine A. Lado, Antony Paulraj, and Injazz J. Chen, "Customer Focus, Supply-Chain Relational Capabilities and Performance: Evidence from U.S. Manufacturing Industries," *The International Journal of Logistics Management* 22, no. 2 (2011): 202–221.

[9] "Solution Highlights," MercuryGate, www.mercurygate.com/solution_highlights (accessed December 12, 2013); April Joyner, "Best Industries 2012: Supply Chain Management," *Inc.*, www.inc.com/ss/best-industries-2012/april-joyner/supply-chain-management-companies-6-that-fill-a-niche (accessed December 12, 2013).

[10] "The Business Case for a Sustainable Supply Chain," *The Wall Street Journal*, September 20, 2012, http://deloitte.wsj.com/cio/2012/09/20/the-business-case-for-a-sustainable-supply-chain (accessed December 15, 2013).

[11] Ibid.

[12] Tibbr, "What's Tibbr," www.tibbr.com/whats-tibbr (accessed December 12, 2013); Yammer, "Overview," https://about.yammer.com (accessed December 12, 2013).

[13] Jonathan Littman, "No More Moto—Google's Not-So-Smart Phones: Why Design Is the New Digital Divide," *The Huffington Post*, November 18, 2013, www.huffingtonpost.com/jonathan-littman/no-more-motogoogles-not-s_b_4293432.html (accessed December 15, 2013).

[14] David Zax, "How Xerox Evolved from Copier Company to Creative Powerhouse," *Fast Company*, December 11, 2013, www.fastcompany.com/3023240/most-creative-people/dreaming-together-how-xerox-keeps-big-ideas-flowing (accessed December 13, 2013).

[15] Applied Industrial Technologies, Inc., www.applied.com (accessed December 13, 2013).

[16] Shelly Banjo, "Walmart Retools International Strategy," *The Wall Street Journal*, October 15, 2013, http://blogs.wsj.com/corporate-intelligence/2013/10/15/wal-mart-retools-international-strategy-closes-some-stores-in-brazil-and-china (accessed December 13, 2013).

[17] Leo Aspinwall, "The Marketing Characteristics of Goods," in *Four Marketing Theories* (Boulder, CO: University of Colorado Press, 1961), pp. 27–32.

[18] AP News, "Sriracha Maker Says Calif. Put Hold on Its Sauces," *Bloomberg Businessweek*, December 11, 2013, www.businessweek.com/ap/2013-12-11/sriracha-maker-california-halting-sauce-shipments (accessed December 13, 2013).

[19] Deloitte, "2013 Global Manufacturing Competitiveness Index," www.deloitte.com/view/en_US/us/Industries/Process-Industrial-Products/manufacturing-competitiveness/mfg-competitiveness-index/index.htm (accessed December 13, 2013).

[20] Adam Vaccaro, "Tell Your Customers about Your Responsible Supply Chain," *Inc.*, November 13, 2013, www.inc.com/adam-vaccaro/supply-chain-corporate-social-responsibility.html (accessed December 13, 2013).

[21] Suppliers Partnership for the Environment website, www.supplierspartnership.org (accessed December 13, 2013).

[22] IGA website, www.iga.com/about.aspx (accessed December 13, 2013).

[23] Wroe Alderson, *Dynamic Marketing Behavior* (Homewood, IL: Irwin, 1965), p. 239.

[24] Ben Levisohn, "Cowen Upgrades U.S. Steel, ArcelorMittal on Rising Steel Prices, Vertical Integration," *Barrons*, December 13, 2013, http://blogs.barrons.com/stockstowatchtoday/2013/12/13/cowen-upgrades-us-steel-arcelormittal-on-rising-steel-prices-verticle-integration (accessed December 13, 2013).

[25] "Inditex Press Dossier," www.inditex.com/en/press/information/press_kit (accessed December 13, 2013), p. 6.

[26] Cliff Holste, "What Shippers Need to Know about Outsourcing," *Supply Chain Digest*, December 11, 2013, www.scdigest.com/experts/Holste_13-12-11.php?cid=7667&ctype=content (accessed December 13, 2013).

[27] Brier Dudley, "Digital Distribution May Prove a Game-Changer for Video Gamers," *Seattle Times*, February 10, 2013, http://seattletimes.com/html/businesstechnology/2020326083_briercolumn11xml.html (accessed December 13, 2013).

[28] Lee Pender, "The Basic Links of SCM," Supply Chain Management Research Center, www.itworld.com/CIO020501_basic_content (accessed December 13, 2013).

[29] Darren Dahl, "Riding the Momentum Created by a Cheeky Video" *The Wall Street Journal*, April 11, 2013, www.nytimes.com/2013/04/11/business/smallbusiness/dollar-shave-club-from-viral-video-to-real-business.html (accessed December 15, 2013).

[30] Jonathan Salem Baskin, "Harley-Davidson Will Be Case History in Social Branding," *Forbes*, July 12, 2013, www.forbes.com/sites/jonathansalembaskin/2013/07/12/harley-davidson-will-be-a-case-history-in-social-branding (accessed December 13, 2013); James R. Hagerty, "Harley Goes Lean to Build Hogs," *The Wall Street Journal*, September 21, 2012, http://online.wsj.com/article/SB10000872396390443720204578004164199848452.html (accessed December 15, 2013).

[31] Matthew Panzarino, "Disney Gets into Wearable Tech with the MagicBand," *The Next Web*, May 29, 2013, http://thenextweb.com/insider/2013/05/29/disney-goes-into-wearable-tech-with-the-magic-band (accessed December 13, 2013).

[32] Distribution Unlimited Inc., http://distributionunlimited.com/operations.php (accessed December 13, 2013).

[33] Shelly Banjo, "Wal-Mart Builds Warehouses for Web Orders," *The Wall Street Journal*, October 1, 2013, http://online.wsj.com/news/articles/SB10001424052702303643304579108070192826030 (accessed December 13, 2013).

[34] Kerri Rantasila and Lauri Ojala, "Measurement of National-Level Logistics Costs and Performance," Discussion Paper 2012, University of Turku (Finland), www.internationaltransportforum.org/jtrc/discussionpapers/dp201204.pdf (accessed December 13, 2013).

[35] David Hummels and Georg Schaur, "Time as a Trade Barrier," *National Bureau of Economic Research*, January 2012, No. 17758, http://papers.nber.org/papers/w17758#fromrss (accessed February 11, 2014).

[36] Excel, www.exel.com/exel/exel_about_exel.jsp (accessed December 13, 2013).

[37] Alex Pearlman, "Taza Chocolate and Drink Craft Beer Prove That Beer and Chocolate Make a Perfect Pair," *Boston Globe*, February 13, 2012, www.boston.com/lifestyle/blogs/thenextgreatgeneration/2012/02/taza_chocolate_and_drink_craft.html (accessed February 11, 2014); Rachel Leah Blumenthal, "A Tour of the Taza Chocolate Factory," *CBS Local News* (Boston), October 26, 2011, http://boston.cbslocal.com/2011/10/26/a-tour-of-the-taza-chocolate-factory (accessed December 21, 2013); Ariel Shearer, "Review: Taza Chocolate," *Boston Phoenix*, October 31, 2011, http://thephoenix.com/boston/food/128984-review-taza-chocolate (accessed December 21, 2013); Courtney Holland, "Sweet Batches of Local Flavor," *Boston Globe*, August 18, 2010, www.boston.com/lifestyle/food/articles/2010/08/18/batch_ice_cream_is_big_on_local_flavor (accessed December 21, 2013); Kerry J. Byrne, "Festival of Food Trucks," *Boston Herald*, August 6, 2010, http://bostonherald.com/entertainment/food_dining/dining_news/2010/08/festival_food_trucks (accessed December 21, 2013).

[38] Steve Banker, "Procter & Gamble, General Mills, and Frito-Lay Move to Natural Gas Fleets," *Forbes*, November 7, 2013, www.forbes.com/sites/stevebanker/2013/11/07/procter-gamble-general-mills-and-frito-lay-transition-to-natural-gas-fleets (accessed February 11, 2014); Serena Ng, "Soap Opera: Amazon Moves In with P&G," *The Wall Street Journal*, October 14, 2013, http://online.wsj.com/news/articles/SB10001424052702304330904579135840230674458 (accessed February 11, 2014); Serena Ng, "Procter & Gamble's Profit Rises on Higher Sales," *Wall Street Journal*, October 25, 2013, http://online.wsj.com/news/articles/SB10001424052702304799404579157181457960644 (accessed February 11, 2014); Barney Jopson, "Procter & Gamble: Time to Freshen Up," *Financial Times*, July 28, 2013, www.ft.com/intl/cms/s/0/e1782cc4-e95a-11e2-9f11-00144feabdc0.html (accessed February 11, 2014); Alicia Androich, "Walmart Canada and P&G Launch Bus Shelter Mobile Store," *Marketing Magazine* (Canada), June 5, 2013, www.marketingmag.ca/news/marketer-news/walmart-canada-and-pg-launch-bus-shelter-mobile-store-80530 (accessed February 11, 2014).

Feature Notes

[a] Sarah Kramer, "Some of His Best Customers Are Canine," *The New York Times*, May 26, 2013, p. CT-2; AnneLise Sorensen, "8 Best Spots in New York City for Ice Cream of Every Stripe," *New York*, July 26, 2013, www.newyork.com/articles/restaurants/8-best-spots-in-new-york-city-for-ice-cream-of-every-stripe-25376 (accessed December 21, 2013); Phyllis Furman, "Food Truck Icon Van Leeuwen Artisan Ice Cream Hits Business Sweet Spot and Cooks Up Growth Plan," *New York Daily News*, August 27, 2012, www.nydailynews.com/new-york/food-truck-icon-van-leeuwen-artisan-ice-cream-hits-business-sweet-spot-cooks-growth-plan-article-1.1143810 (accessed December 21, 2013).

[b] Rachel King, "eBay Expanding Same-Day Delivery Map to 25 Cities with Shutl Buy," *ZDNet*, October 22, 2013, www.zdnet.com/ebay-expanding-same-day-delivery-map-to-25-cities-with-shutl-buy-7000022272 (accessed December 21, 2013); Heather Somerville, "Google Same-Day Delivery Makes Public Debut," *San Jose Mercury News*, September 25, 2013, www.mercurynews.com/business/ci_24171776/exclusive-google-same-day-delivery-makes-public-debut (accessed December 21, 2013); Heather Somerville, "Walmart Expands Grocery Delivery," *San Jose Mercury News*, October 17, 2013, www.mercurynews.com/business/ci_24331014/walmart-expands-grocery-delivery (accessed December 21, 2013); Sarah Perez, "Walmart Expands Same-Day Grocery Delivery to Denver," *TechCrunch*, October 15, 2013, http://techcrunch.com/2013/10/15/walmart-expands-same-day-grocery-delivery-to-denver (accessed December 21, 2013).

chapter 15

Retailing, Direct Marketing, and Wholesaling

OBJECTIVES

15-1 Describe the purpose and function of retailers in the marketing channel.

15-2 Identify the major types of retailers.

15-3 Explain strategic issues in retailing.

15-4 Recognize the various forms of direct marketing, direct selling, and vending.

15-5 Describe franchising and its benefits and weaknesses.

15-6 Explain the nature and functions of wholesalers.

MARKETING INSIGHTS

Uniqlo Enters the U.S. Clothing Market in Style

How can a highly successful Japanese retailer of affordably-priced casual clothing make its name in the U.S. market? Uniqlo is well-known throughout Asia, where it operates 1,200 stores. However, because U.S. shoppers are less familiar with Uniqlo and its private label apparel, the retailer has had to start from scratch to enter this important market.

Uniqlo is using a retail strategy it has used to great effect elsewhere. First, it opens a hip, huge flagship store in a major metro area as a high-profile showcase for the entire product line. This time, Uniqlo opened two flagships, one in New York City and a second in San Francisco. Next, it opens a cluster of smaller stores surrounding each flagship for marketing efficiency. For instance, Uniqlo's Union Square flagship was followed by stores in San Mateo, Santa Clara, and other Bay Area communities. Similarly, the SoHo flagship in New York was followed by stores in Brooklyn, New Jersey, and Connecticut. On both coasts, the cluster of stores benefited from regional advertising and special events. Uniqlo has also used temporary pop-up shops to sell selected products for a limited time. During one winter, it opened a pop-up featuring cold-weather clothing inside a New York City subway station.

Looking ahead, the company has plenty of room to expand on both U.S. coasts and in between. Endorsement deals with athletes like tennis star Novak Djokovic and golf champ Adam Scott are attracting attention and adding cachet. Can Uniqlo achieve its ambitious goal of ringing up $10 billion in U.S. revenues by 2020?[1]

© iStockphoto.com/winhorse

Retailers like Uniqlo are the most visible and accessible marketing channel members to consumers. They represent an important link in the marketing channel because they are both marketers for and customers of producers and wholesalers. They perform many supply-chain functions, such as buying, selling, grading, risk taking, and developing and maintaining information databases about customers. Retailers are in a strategic position to develop relationships with consumers and partnerships with producers and intermediaries in the marketing channel.

In this chapter, we examine the nature of retailing, direct marketing, and wholesaling and their roles in supplying consumers with goods and services. First, we explore the major types of retail stores and consider strategic issues in retailing: location, retail positioning, store image, and category management. Next, we discuss direct marketing, including catalog marketing, response marketing, telemarketing, television home shopping, and online retailing. We also explore direct selling and vending. Then we look at the strengths and weaknesses of franchising, a retailing form that continues to grow in popularity. Finally, we examine the importance of wholesalers in marketing channels, including their functions and classifications.

15-1 RETAILING

Retailing includes all transactions in which the buyer is the ultimate consumer and intends to use the product for personal, family, or household purposes. A **retailer** is an organization that purchases products for the purpose of reselling them to ultimate consumers. Although most retailers' sales are made directly to the consumer, nonretail transactions occur occasionally when retailers sell products to other businesses.

Retailing is important to the national U.S. economy. There are more than 1 million retailers operating in the United States and they employ nearly 15 million people.[2] Retailers contribute a great deal to the U.S. economy, generating more than $4.13 trillion in annual sales.[3]

Retailers add value for customers by providing services and assisting in making product selections. They can also enhance customers' perceptions of the value of products by making buyers' shopping experiences easier or more convenient, such as providing free delivery or offering an online shopping option. Retailers can facilitate comparison shopping, which allows customers to evaluate different options. For instance, car dealerships often cluster in the same general vicinity, as do furniture stores. The Internet also allows consumers to comparison shop easily. Product value is also enhanced when retailers offer services, such as technical advice, delivery, credit, and repair. Finally, retail sales personnel are trained to be able to demonstrate to customers how products can satisfy their needs or solve problems.

Retailers can add significant value to the supply chain, representing a critical link between producers and ultimate consumers by providing the environment in which exchanges occur. Retailers play a major role in creating time, place, and possession and, in some cases, form utility. They perform marketing functions that benefit ultimate consumers by making available broad arrays of products that can satisfy their needs.

Historically, leading retailers like Walmart, Home Depot, Macy's, Staples, and Best Buy have offered consumers a place to browse and compare merchandise to find just what they need. However, such traditional retailing faces challenges from direct marketing channels that provide at-home-shopping options through catalogs, television, and the Internet. Brick-and-mortar retailers have responded to changes in the retail environment in various ways. Many retailers now utilize multiple distribution channels and complement their brick-and-mortar stores with websites where consumers can shop online. To encourage loyalty among shoppers who prefer multiple channels, many offer online-only sales and merchandise that encourage consumers to frequent both their websites and their stores. Partnerships among noncompeting

retailing All transactions in which the buyer intends to consume the product through personal, family, or household use

retailer An organization that purchases products for the purpose of reselling them to ultimate consumers

retailers and other marketing channel members acknowledge the competitive marketing environment and provide additional opportunities for retailers to satisfy the needs of customers and encourage loyalty. For instance, major retailers such as Walmart and Target partner with other retail chains (e.g., McDonald's, KFC, and Starbucks) to feature in-store dining that makes shopping more pleasant. Airports feature many different retailers and service outlets to improve the experience for travelers.

The key to success in retailing is to have a strong customer focus with a retail strategy that provides the level of service, product quality, and innovation that consumers desire. New store formats, service innovations, and advances in information technology have helped retailers to serve customers better. Tech companies, such as AT&T and Verizon, realized the need to provide a quality customer experience in their stores—which often were highly pared-down in their design and level of service.[4] In electronics stores, it is now common to find lounging areas where customers can try out gadgets, highly enthusiastic staff trained in the nuances of every device, and displays designed to be pleasing and eye-catching.

Retailing is also increasingly international. While growth in developed markets has slowed or stopped in many product categories, and the recent global recession slowed economic growth everywhere, many retailers see significant growth potential in international markets. The market for a product category such as cell phones is mature in North America and Europe. However, demand remains strong in places like India, China, and Brazil. These countries all have large, relatively new middle classes with consumers hungry for goods and services. Capitalizing on a market opportunity, supermarket giant Tesco became the first global chain to expand to India since the government passed a newly relaxed international retailing law.[5] It partnered with Tata Group, an Indian conglomerate, to take advantage of India's growing middle class and a market that is projected to be worth nearly $1 trillion. Many major U.S. retailers have international outlets in order to capitalize on international growth. On the other hand, international retailers, such as Aldi, IKEA, and Zara, have also found receptive markets in the United States.

15-2 MAJOR TYPES OF RETAIL STORES

Many types of retail stores exist. One way to classify them is by the breadth of products they offer. Two general categories include general-merchandise retailers and specialty retailers.

15-2a General-Merchandise Retailers

A retail establishment that offers a variety of product lines that are stocked in considerable depth is referred to as a **general-merchandise retailer**. The types of product offerings, mixes of customer services, and operating styles of retailers in this category vary considerably. The primary types of general-merchandise retailers are department stores, discount stores, convenience stores, supermarkets, superstores, hypermarkets, warehouse clubs, and warehouse showrooms (see Table 15.1).

general-merchandise retailer A retail establishment that offers a variety of product lines that are stocked in considerable depth

Department Stores

Department stores are large retail organizations with at least 25 employees that are characterized by wide product mixes. To facilitate marketing efforts and internal management in these stores, related product lines are organized into separate departments such as cosmetics, housewares, apparel, home furnishings, and appliances. This arrangement facilitates marketing and internal management. Often, each department functions as a self-contained business, and buyers for individual departments are fairly autonomous in their decision making.

department stores Large retail organizations characterized by a wide product mix and organized into separate departments to facilitate marketing efforts and internal management

Department stores are distinctly service-oriented. Their total product may include credit, delivery, personal assistance, merchandise returns, and a pleasant atmosphere. Although

Table 15.1 General-Merchandise Retailers

Type of Retailer	Description	Examples
Department store	Large organization offering a wide product mix and organized into separate departments	Macy's, Sears, JCPenney
Discount store	Self-service, general-merchandise store offering brand-name and private-brand products at low prices	Walmart, Target, Kmart
Convenience store	Small, self-service store offering narrow product assortment in convenient locations	7-Eleven
Supermarket	Self-service store offering complete line of food products and some non-food products	Kroger, Safeway, Publix
Superstore	Giant outlet offering all food and non-food products found in supermarkets, as well as most routinely purchased products	Walmart Supercenters, SuperTarget
Hypermarket	Combination supermarket and discount store; larger than a superstore	Carrefour
Warehouse club	Large-scale, members-only establishments combining cash-and-carry wholesaling with discount retailing	Sam's Club, Costco
Warehouse showroom	Facility in a large, low-cost building with large on-premises inventories and minimal service	IKEA

some so-called department stores are actually large, departmentalized specialty stores, most department stores are shopping stores. Consumers can compare price, quality, and service at one store with those at competing stores. Along with large discount stores, department stores are often considered retailing leaders in a community and are found in most places with populations of more than 50,000.

At typical department stores (such as Macy's, Sears, JCPenney, Dillard's, and Neiman Marcus) a large proportion of sales come from apparel, accessories, and cosmetics. These stores carry a broad assortment of other products as well, including luggage, electronics, home

Department Stores
Department stores like Nordstrom offer a wide variety of product lines.

accessories, and sports equipment. Some department stores offer such additional services as automobile insurance, hair care, income tax preparation, and travel and optical services. In some cases, the department store leases space for these specialized services to other businesses, with proprietors managing their own operations and paying rent to the store. Most department stores also sell products through websites, which can service customers who live in smaller markets where no stores are located or who prefer to shop online.

Discount Stores

Department stores have lost sales and market share to discount stores, especially Walmart and Target, in recent decades. **Discount stores** are self-service, general-merchandise outlets that regularly offer brand-name and private-brand products at low prices. Discounters accept lower profit margins than conventional retailers in exchange for high sales volume. To keep inventory turnover high, they carry a wide but carefully selected assortment of products, from appliances to housewares to clothing. Major discount establishments also offer food products, toys, automotive services, garden supplies, and sports equipment.

Walmart and Target have grown to become not only the largest discount stores in the country, but also some of the largest retailers in the world. Walmart is the world's largest retailer, with revenues nearly three times higher than its next competitor Carrefour (a French retailer), and Target is ranked eleventh.[6] Not all discounters are large and international, however. Some, such as Meijer Inc., which has stores in the Midwestern United States, are regional discounters. Most discount stores operate in large (50,000 to 80,000 square feet), no-frills facilities. They usually offer everyday low prices (discussed in Chapter 20), rather than relying on sales events.

Discount retailing developed on a large scale in the early 1950s, when postwar production caught up with strong consumer demand for goods. At first, they were often cash-only operations in warehouse districts, offering goods at savings of 20 to 30 percent over conventional retailers. Facing increased competition from department stores and other discount stores, some discounters improved store services, atmosphere, and location. Some have also raised prices, blurring the distinction between discount store and department store. Target, for example, has grown distinctly more upscale in appearance and offerings over the years. It frequently features low-cost clothing lines by designer labels. It also has become more of a one-stop shop with grocery and pharmacy offerings, as well as clothing, home goods, and electronics. In a further attempt to convince customers to linger, some Target stores even feature in-store Starbucks, Jamba Juice, or Pizza Hut Express outlets.[7]

Convenience Stores

A **convenience store** is a small, self-service store that is open long hours and carries a narrow assortment of products, usually convenience items such as soft drinks and other beverages, snacks, newspapers, tobacco, and gasoline, as well as services such as ATMs. According to the National Association of Convenience Stores, there are more than 149,000 convenience stores in the United States alone, which boast around $700 billion in annual sales.[8] They are typically less than 5,000 square feet, open 24 hours a day and 7 days a week, and stock about 500 items. The convenience store concept was developed in 1927 when Southland Ice in Dallas began stocking basics like milk and eggs along with ice for iceboxes to serve customers who wanted to replenish their supplies. In addition to national chains, there are many family-owned independent convenience stores.

Supermarkets

Supermarkets are large, self-service stores that carry a complete line of food products and some non-food products such as cosmetics and nonprescription drugs. Supermarkets are arranged by department for maximum efficiency in stocking and handling products, but have central checkout facilities. They offer lower prices than smaller neighborhood grocery stores, usually provide free parking, and may also provide services such as check cashing.

discount stores Self-service, general-merchandise stores that offer brand-name and private-brand products at low prices

convenience store A small self-service store that is open long hours and carries a narrow assortment of products, usually convenience items

supermarkets Large, self-service stores that carry a complete line of food products, along with some nonfood products

Consumers make the majority of all their grocery purchases in supermarkets. However, increased availability of grocery items at discount stores, premium markets, other competitors, and online have eroded supermarkets' market share of the grocery segment. Online grocers, especially in larger cities, have done away with the need to go to grocery stores and have put pressure on supermarkets to increase promotions and marketing efforts. Even Amazon offers grocery delivery service. AmazonFresh is a subscription grocery service successfully piloted by Amazon in several West Coast cities. It features more than 500,000 items for same-day or early morning delivery, including groceries and specialty food items, in addition to the broad spectrum of items already available on Amazon. Delivery is free on orders over $35, but the subscription service costs about $300 a year.[9]

Superstores

Superstores, which originated in Europe, are giant retail outlets that carry not only the food and non-food products ordinarily found in supermarkets, but routinely-purchased consumer products such as housewares, hardware, small appliances, clothing, and personal-care products as well. Superstores combine features of discount stores and supermarkets and generally carry about four times as many items as supermarkets. Superstores also offer additional services, including dry cleaning, automotive repair, check cashing, and bill paying. Examples include Walmart Supercenters, some Kroger stores, SuperTarget stores, and Super Kmart Centers.

To cut handling and inventory costs, superstores use sophisticated operating techniques and often have tall shelving that displays entire assortments of products. Superstores can have an area of as much as 200,000 square feet (compared with 20,000 square feet in traditional supermarkets). Sales volume is typically two to three times that of supermarkets, partly because locations near good transportation networks help generate the in-store traffic needed for profitability.

Hypermarkets

Hypermarkets combine supermarket and discount store shopping in one location. Larger than superstores, they range from 225,000 to 325,000 square feet and offer 45,000 to 60,000 different types of low-priced products. They commonly allocate 40 to 50 percent of their space to grocery products and the remainder to general merchandise, including apparel, appliances, housewares, jewelry, hardware, and automotive supplies. Many also lease space to noncompeting businesses, such as banks, optical shops, and fast-food restaurants. All hypermarkets focus on low prices and vast selections.

Retailers have struggled with making the hypermarket concept successful in the United States. Although Kmart, Walmart, and Carrefour have operated hypermarkets in the United States, most of these stores ultimately closed. Such stores may be too large for time-constrained U.S. shoppers. Hypermarkets have been somewhat more popular in Europe, South America, Mexico, the Middle East, and parts of Asia.

Warehouse Clubs

Warehouse clubs, a rapidly growing form of mass merchandising, are large-scale, members-only operations that combine cash-and-carry wholesaling with discount retailing. Sometimes called *buying clubs,* warehouse clubs offer the same types of products as discount stores but in a limited range of sizes and styles. Whereas most discount stores carry around 40,000 items, a warehouse club handles only 3,500 to 5,000 products, usually brand leaders. Sam's Club stores, for example, stock about 4,000 items. Costco currently leads the warehouse club industry with sales of over $105 billion. Sam's Club is second with around $54 billion in store sales.[10] These establishments offer a broad product mix, including food, beverages, books, appliances, housewares, automotive parts, hardware, and furniture.

superstores Giant retail outlets that carry food and nonfood products found in supermarkets, as well as most routinely purchased consumer products

hypermarkets Stores that combine supermarket and discount store shopping in one location

warehouse clubs Large-scale, members-only establishments that combine features of cash-and-carry wholesaling with discount retailing

To keep prices lower than those of supermarkets and discount stores, warehouse clubs offer few services. They also keep advertising to a minimum. Their facilities, frequently located in industrial areas, have concrete floors and aisles wide enough for forklifts. Merchandise is stacked on pallets or displayed on pipe racks. Customers must perform some marketing functions, like transportation of purchases, themselves. Warehouse clubs appeal to price-conscious consumers and small retailers unable to obtain wholesaling services from large distributors.

© iStockphoto.com/slobo

Warehouse Clubs
Sam's Club is a warehouse club that has a wide product mix with limited depth.

Warehouse Showrooms

Warehouse showrooms are retail facilities with five basic characteristics: large, low-cost buildings, warehouse materials-handling technology, vertical merchandise displays, large on-premises inventories, and minimal services. IKEA, a Swedish company that is the world's largest furniture retailer, sells furniture, household goods, and kitchen accessories in warehouse showrooms and through catalogs around the world. These high-volume, low-overhead operations offer few services and retain few personnel. Lower costs are possible at warehouse showrooms because some marketing functions have been shifted to consumers, who must transport, finance, and perhaps store products. Most consumers carry away purchases in the manufacturer's carton, although stores will deliver for a fee.

15-2b Specialty Retailers

In contrast to general-merchandise retailers with their broad product mixes, specialty retailers emphasize narrow and deep assortments. Despite their name, specialty retailers do not sell specialty items (except when specialty goods complement the overall product mix). Instead, they offer substantial assortments in a few product lines. We examine three types of specialty retailers: traditional specialty retailers, category killers, and off-price retailers.

Traditional Specialty Retailers

Traditional specialty retailers are stores that carry a narrow product mix with deep product lines. Sometimes called *limited-line retailers,* they may be referred to as *single-line retailers* if they carry unusual depth in one product category. Specialty retailers commonly sell such shopping products as apparel, jewelry, sporting goods, fabrics, computers, and pet supplies. The Limited, Gap, and Foot Locker are examples of retailers offering limited product lines but great depth within those lines. Sunglass Hut, featured in the advertisement, is a traditional specialty retailer. It only sells sunglasses, but it sells thousands of models from the moderately priced to the extravagant. This advertisement makes it clear what Sunglass Hut sells, featuring two models wearing trendy brands.

Because they are usually small, specialty stores may have high costs in proportion to sales, and satisfying customers may require carrying some products with low turnover rates. Successful specialty stores understand their customers and know what products to carry, which reduces the risk of unsold merchandise. Specialty stores usually offer better selections and more sales expertise than department stores, their main competitors. By capitalizing on

warehouse showrooms Retail facilities in large, low-cost buildings with large on-premises inventories and minimal services

traditional specialty retailers Stores that carry a narrow product mix with deep product lines

Sunglass hut

Traditional Specialty Retailer
Sunglass Hut is a traditional specialty retailer, selling many different brands of sunglasses at a range of prices.

fashion trends, service, personnel, atmosphere, and location, specialty retailers position themselves strategically to attract customers in specific market segments.

Category Killers

A more recent kind of specialty retailer is called the **category killer**, which is a very large specialty store that concentrates on a major product category and competes on the basis of low prices and broad product availability. These stores are referred to as category killers because they expand rapidly and gain sizable market shares, taking business away from smaller, higher-cost retail outlets. Examples of category killers include Home Depot and Lowe's (home improvement), Staples, Office Depot, and OfficeMax (office supply), Barnes & Noble (bookseller), Petco and PetSmart (pet supply), Toys 'R' Us (toys), and Best Buy (consumer electronics). Online retailing has also placed pressure on category killers and taken away market share in recent years. One of the original category killers, Toys 'R' Us now struggles to compete against online retailers, particularly Amazon.[11] To retain a competitive advantage, Toys 'R' Us hired a new CEO, expanded its online presence, and worked with manufacturers to offer exclusive deals and price matching.

Off-Price Retailers

Off-price retailers are stores that buy manufacturers' seconds, overruns, returns, and off-season production runs at below-wholesale prices for resale to consumers at deep discounts. Unlike true discount stores, which pay regular wholesale prices for goods and usually carry second-line brand names, off-price retailers offer limited lines of national-brand and designer merchandise, usually clothing, shoes, or housewares. Consumers appreciate the ability to purchase name-brand goods at discounted prices, and sales at off-price retailers, such as T.J.Maxx, Marshalls, Stein Mart, and Burlington Coat Factory, have grown. Off-price retailers typically perform well in recessionary times, as consumers who want to own name-brand items search for good value.

Off-price stores charge 20 to 50 percent less than department stores for comparable merchandise but offer few customer services. They often feature community dressing rooms and central checkout counters. Some of these stores do not take returns or allow exchanges. Off-price stores may or may not sell goods with the original labels intact. They turn over their inventory up to a dozen times per year, three times as often as traditional specialty stores. They compete with department stores for many of the same price-conscious customers who are knowledgeable about brand names.

To ensure a regular flow of merchandise into their stores, off-price retailers establish long-term relationships with suppliers that can provide large quantities of goods at reduced prices. Manufacturers may approach retailers with samples, discontinued products, or items that have not sold well. Also, off-price retailers may seek out manufacturers, offering to pay cash for goods produced during the manufacturers' off-season. Although manufacturers benefit from such arrangements, they also risk alienating their specialty and department store customers. Department stores tolerate off-price stores as long as they do not advertise brand names, limit merchandise to last season's or lower-quality items,

category killer A very large specialty store that concentrates on a major product category and competes on the basis of low prices and product availability

off-price retailers Stores that buy manufacturers' seconds, overruns, returns, and off-season merchandise for resale to consumers at deep discounts and are located away from the department stores. When off-price retailers obtain large stocks of in-season, top-quality merchandise, tension builds between department stores and manufacturers.

15-3 STRATEGIC ISSUES IN RETAILING

Whereas most business purchases are based on economic planning and necessity, consumer purchases are likely to be influenced by social and psychological factors. Because consumers shop for various reasons—to search for specific items, alleviate boredom, or learn about something new—retailers must do more than simply fill space with merchandise. They must make desired products available, create stimulating shopping environments, and develop marketing strategies that increase store patronage. In this section, we discuss how store location, retail positioning, store image, and category management are used strategically by retailers.

15-3a Location of Retail Stores

You have likely heard the phrase "Location, location, location," commonly used in the real estate business. Location is also critical to business success. Making a good location decision is even more important because, once decided, it is the least flexible variable of the marketing mix. Location is an important strategic decision that dictates the limited geographic trading area from which a store draws its customers. Retailers consider various factors when evaluating potential locations, including position of the firm's target market within the trading area, kinds of products being sold, availability of public transportation, customer characteristics, and placement of competitors' stores.

In choosing a location, a retailer evaluates the relative ease of movement to and from the site, including factors such as pedestrian and vehicular traffic, parking, and transportation. Retailers also evaluate the characteristics of the site itself. They research the types of stores in the area and the size, shape, and visibility of the lot or building under consideration. In addition, they must scrutinize the rental, leasing, or ownership terms. Retailers should look for compatibility with nearby retailers because stores that complement one another draw more customers with similar product needs for everyone. Look at the advertisement for Boucheron Jeweler, a high-end, Paris-based jewelry company. This advertisement prominently announces the fact that Boucheron was the first jewelry store in the very chic square, Place Vendôme, in Paris. The fact that it makes this announcement in French indicates that its target market is worldly and educated. The advertisement also lists its fashionable London locations. By alerting potential customers to the locations of its stores, Boucheron is encouraging its target market to think about the illustrious locales, including their upscale retail neighbors, and to draw an image in their minds about the high quality of the products. The close-up photo of the rings bearing the Boucheron logo underscores the prestige associated with

Location of Retail Stores
Boucheron draws the viewer's attention to its prime locations in London and in the Place Vendôme in Paris.

these products. Having a store in Place Vendôme improves the overall luxury image of Boucheron because it emphasizes in the customers' minds a relationship between the brand and the chic area of Paris.

Some retailers choose to locate in downtown central business districts, whereas others prefer sites within shopping centers. Some retailers, including Toys 'R' Us, Walmart, Home Depot, and many fast-food restaurants, opt for freestanding structures that are not connected to other buildings, but may be located within planned shopping centers. Sometimes, retailers choose to locate in less orthodox settings where competition will be lower and where consumers have limited other options. Pop-up retailers, which are only located in a space for a short time, and retailers that share space are becoming increasingly common as a means of generating consumer buzz while also cutting down on rental costs for all businesses involved. Storefront is a company that helps retailers to find and rent the kind of location that is right for them.[12] Sharing space can let multiple small retailers afford a storefront in a prime location and gives consumers a richer experience by offering stores within a store.[13] For instance, Atlanta's Octane Coffee shares a space with Little Tart Bakeshop, with Little Tart selling its baked goods during the day alongside Octane coffee products, and Octane serving bar snacks and appetizers when the bakeshop closes at 5 p.m.[14]

There are several different types of shopping centers, including neighborhood, community, regional, superregional, lifestyle, power, and outlet centers. **Neighborhood shopping centers** usually consist of several small convenience and specialty stores, such as small grocery stores, gas stations, and fast-food restaurants. These retailers consider their target markets to be consumers who live within two to three miles of their stores, or 10 minutes' driving time. Because most purchases are based on convenience or personal contact, stores within a neighborhood shopping center generally do not coordinate selling efforts. Generally, product mixes consist of essential products, and depth of the product lines is limited. **Community shopping centers** include one or two department stores and some specialty stores, as well as convenience stores. They draw consumers looking for shopping and specialty products not available in neighborhood shopping centers. Because these offer a wider variety of stores, they serve larger geographic areas and consumers are willing to drive longer distances to community shopping centers to shop. Community shopping centers are planned, and retailer efforts are coordinated to attract shoppers. Special events, such as art exhibits, automobile shows, and sidewalk sales, stimulate traffic. Managers of community shopping centers look for tenants that complement the centers' total assortment of products. Such centers have wide product mixes and deep product lines.

Regional shopping centers usually have the largest department stores, widest product mixes, and deepest product lines of all shopping centers. Many shopping malls are regional shopping centers, although some are community shopping centers. With 150,000 or more consumers in their target market, regional shopping centers must have well-coordinated management and marketing activities. Target markets may include consumers traveling from a distance to find products and prices not available in their hometowns. Because of the expense of leasing space in regional shopping centers, tenants are likely to be national chains. Large centers usually advertise, have special events, furnish transportation to some consumer groups (such as seniors), maintain their own security forces, and carefully select the mix of stores. The largest of these centers, sometimes called **superregional shopping centers**, have the widest and deepest product mixes and attract customers from many miles away. Superregional centers often have special attractions beyond stores, such as skating rinks, amusement centers, or upscale restaurants. Mall of America, in the Minneapolis area, is the largest shopping mall in the United States with 520 stores, including Nordstrom and Bloomingdale's, and 50 restaurants. The shopping center also includes a walk-through aquarium, a museum, a seven-acre Nickelodeon theme park, a 14-screen movie theater, hotels, and many special events.[15]

With traditional mall sales declining, some shopping center developers are looking to new formats that differ significantly from traditional shopping centers. A **lifestyle**

neighborhood shopping center A type of shopping center usually consisting of several small convenience and specialty stores

community shopping center A type of shopping center with one or two department stores, some specialty stores, and convenience stores

regional shopping center A type of shopping center with the largest department stores, widest product mixes, and deepest product lines of all shopping centers

superregional shopping center A type of shopping center with the widest and deepest product mixes that attracts customers from many miles away

lifestyle shopping center A type of shopping center that is typically open air and features upscale specialty, dining, and entertainment stores

shopping center is typically an open-air shopping center that features upscale specialty stores, dining, and entertainment, all usually owned by national chains. They are often located near affluent neighborhoods and may have fountains, benches, and other amenities that encourage "casual browsing." Appealing architectural design is an important aspect of these "mini-cities," which may include urban streets or parks, and is intended to encourage consumer loyalty by creating a sense of place. Some lifestyle centers are designed to resemble traditional "Main Street" shopping centers or may have a central theme evidenced by the architecture.[16]

Some shopping center developers are bypassing the traditional department store anchor and combining off-price stores and small stores with category killers in **power shopping center** formats. These centers may be anchored by popular stores, such as the Gap, Toys 'R' Us, PetSmart, and Home Depot. Power shopping centers can take a variety of formats, all vying for the same retail dollar.

Factory outlet malls feature discount and factory outlet stores carrying traditional manufacturer brands, such as Polo Ralph Lauren, Nike, and Guess. The advertisement features the Banana Republic factory store, which sells last season's Banana Republic fashions at discounted prices. This advertisement prominently displays the low starting price of its products, $17.99, and also has a coupon for an additional 20 percent off. Many outlet centers feature upscale products from last season, discounted for quick sale. Manufacturers own these stores and make a special effort to avoid conflict with traditional retailers of their products. Manufacturers place these stores in noncompetitive locations, often outside of metropolitan areas. Factory outlet centers attract value-conscious customers seeking quality and major brand names. They operate in much the same way as regional shopping centers, but usually draw customers, some of whom may be tourists, from a larger shopping radius. Promotional activity is at the heart of these shopping centers. Craft and antique shows, contests, and special events attract a great deal of traffic.

Gap

Factory Outlet Mall
Stores in factory outlet malls feature well-known brands, such as Banana Republic, and offer discounted prices from last season.

15-3b Retail Positioning

The large variety of shopping centers and the expansion of product offerings by traditional stores, along with the increased use of online retailing, have all contributed to intense retailing competition. Retail positioning is therefore an important consideration. **Retail positioning** involves identifying an unserved or underserved market segment and reaching it through a strategy that distinguishes the retailer from others in the minds of customers in the market segment. For instance, H&M is positioned as a low-priced fashion-forward retailer. However, in an effort to be associated with fair business practices, the chain announced that prices would increase to allow the retailer to pay its employees a living wage, repositioning itself as a socially responsible retailer—not just a very low-priced one.[17] This is in contrast to a number of discount and specialty store chains that have positioned themselves to appeal to time- and cash-strapped consumers with convenient locations and layouts as well as low prices. This strategy has helped many retailers gain market share at the expense of large department stores.

power shopping center A type of shopping center that combines off-price stores with category killers

retail positioning Identifying an unserved or underserved market segment and serving it through a strategy that distinguishes the retailer from others in the minds of consumers in that segment

Going Green

Ladybugs Add to Mall of America's Sustainability

Ladybugs for sustainability? That's how the country's largest shopping center, the Mall of America in Bloomington, Minnesota, keeps its 30,000 live plants free of aphids. Instead of spraying chemical pesticide, the mall releases 72,000 ladybugs into its miles of covered corridors, taking care of the aphid problem in an earth-friendly way. The plants, plus 300 trees, act as all-natural air purifiers and bring a touch of the outdoors inside the enclosed mall's 4.2 million square feet of shopping space.

Despite sub-zero outdoor temperatures during the winter, the Mall of America needs no central heating system. Instead, it relies on the heat generated by energy-saving light fixtures dotting the mall's interior, combined with the natural heat generated by sunlight streaming through the many skylights. In addition, shoppers themselves generate enough body heat bustling in and out of the 520 stores to help bring the mall's temperature to a comfortable level.

Every year, the Mall of America and its stores recycle tens of thousands of tons of waste, bypassing local landfills to send paper, glass, and plastic directly to the proper destinations for environmentally-safe recycling. Grease and fat from restaurant fryers are converted into biodiesel to fuel mall vehicles. Finally, waste food from the restaurants is trucked to nearby farms to feed one million hogs every year, adding to the mall's sustainability efforts.[a]

15-3c Store Image

To attract customers, a retail store must project an image—a functional and psychological picture in the consumer's mind—that appeals to its target market. Store environment, merchandise quality, and service quality are key determinants of store image.

Atmospherics, the physical elements in a store's design that appeal to consumers' emotions and encourage buying, help to create an image and position a retailer. Retailers can use different elements—music, color, and complexity of layout and merchandise presentation—to influence customer attention, mood, and shopping behavior.

Exterior atmospheric elements include the appearance of the storefront, display windows, store entrances, and degree of traffic congestion. Exterior atmospherics are particularly important to new customers, who tend to base their judgment of an unfamiliar store on its outside appearance and may not ever enter if they feel intimidated by the appearance of the façade or if the location is inconvenient or unhospitable.

Interior atmospheric elements include aesthetic considerations, such as lighting, wall and floor coverings, dressing facilities, and store fixtures. Interior sensory elements contribute significantly to atmosphere. Bars, for example, consider several factors when it comes to atmospherics, including music tempo and volume, lighting, cleanliness, and physical layout. Most bars tend to sell a similar range of products, so they use atmospherics extensively to differentiate themselves and create a unique environment. In order for a bar to be successful and retain customers, it must monitor atmospheric variables and focus on maintaining customer comfort levels, which may vary depending on target audience. Bar patrons tend to be recreationally and socially motivated, rather than task motivated, so the layout must create a sense of flow and spread the crowd to the right places so customers do not feel claustrophobic.[18]

Color can attract shoppers to a retail display. Many fast-food restaurants use bright colors because these have been shown to make customers feel hungrier and eat faster, which increases turnover.[19] For instance, red is associated with impulsivity and hunger, and yellow is associated with feeling good—both of these colors are common in fast-food restaurants. Green, on the other hand, is calming and associated with wellness, so it is more commonly seen in natural foods stores and restaurants.[20] Sound is another

atmospherics The physical elements in a store's design that appeal to consumers' emotions and encourage buying

© Patrik Dietrich/Shutterstock.com

Atmospherics
Atmospherics in restaurants can greatly influence customers' experiences. Ice bars, like the one pictured here, are bars and restaurants in which the furniture, decorations, and sometimes the building are made completely of ice. They create such a unique ambiance that they attract customers from around the world.

important sensory component of atmosphere. A low-end, family dining restaurant might play fast pop music to encourage customers to eat quickly and leave, increasing turnover and sales. A high-end restaurant, on the other hand, will opt to play soft classical music to enhance the experience and encourage patrons to indulge in multiple courses. Retailers may even employ scent, especially food aromas, to attract customers. Most consumers expect the scent of a store to be congruent with the products that are sold there. Thus, Starbucks should smell like its coffee, Panera like its freshly baked bread, and Yankee Candle like its scented candles. Online retailers are not exempt from concern over atmospherics. Studies have demonstrated that such elements as the layout of a site and the content of digital ads that appear on that site can affect consumer mood and shopping behavior.[21]

15-3d Category Management

Category management is a retail strategy of managing groups of similar, often substitutable products produced by different manufacturers. It first developed in the food industry because supermarkets were concerned about competitive behavior among manufacturers. Supermarkets use category management to allocate space for their many product categories, such as cosmetics, cereals, and soups. The strategy is effective for many different types of retailers. The assortment of merchandise a store chooses through category management is strategic and meant to improve sales and enhance customer satisfaction.

Category management is an important part of developing a collaborative supply chain, which enhances value for customers. Successful category management involves collecting and analyzing data on sales and consumers and sharing the information between the retailer and manufacturer. Walmart, for example, has developed strong supplier relationships with many of its manufacturers, like Procter & Gamble. Collaborative supply chains should designate a single source to develop a system for collecting information on demand, consumer behavior, and optimal product allocations. The key is cooperative interaction between the manufacturers of category products and the retailer to create maximum success for all parties in the supply chain.

category management A retail strategy of managing groups of similar, often substitutable, products produced by different manufacturers

Entrepreneurship in Marketing

Tales of the Lonesome Pine Bookstore

Entrepreneurs: Wendy Welch and Jack Beck
Business: Tales of the Lonesome Pine Bookstore
Founded: 2006, in Big Stone Gap, Virginia
Success: Tales of the Lonesome Pine Bookstore survived the economic downturn in a former coal-mining town and thrived after one founder published a memoir of how the bookstore grew by creating a sense of community among customers.

Wendy Welch and her husband, Jack Beck, have transformed a century-old Edwardian mansion in a tiny mountain town into a bookstore-café-crafts center that now draws customers from hundreds of miles around. Their entrepreneurial adventure began when they bought the house, fixed it up, and installed bookshelves to sell used books in a homey atmosphere.

Making a profit selling books in a town with only 5,000 residents was going to be a challenge, especially in the digital age. However, Welch and Beck forged ahead, offering free tea and coffee and paying close attention to what customers wanted. Business improved when the bookstore began hosting events to bring people together, including needlework nights and jam sessions, and also added a crafts section and a small café. Since Welch's memoir, *The Little Bookstore of Big Stone Gap,* was published, the store has profited from a steady stream of customers visiting from far and wide.[b]

15-4 DIRECT MARKETING, DIRECT SELLING, AND VENDING

Although retailers are the most visible members of the supply chain, many products are sold outside the confines of a retail store. Direct selling and direct marketing account for a huge proportion of the sale of goods globally. Products also may be sold in automatic vending machines, but these account for a very small minority of total retail sales.

15-4a Direct Marketing

Direct marketing is the use of the telephone, Internet, and nonpersonal media to communicate product and organizational information to customers, who can then purchase products via mail, telephone, or the Internet. Direct marketing is one type of nonstore retailing. Sales through direct marketing activities are large, accounting for about 8.7 percent of the entire U.S. GDP.[22]

direct marketing The use of the telephone, Internet, and nonpersonal media to introduce products to customers, who can then purchase them via mail, telephone, or the Internet

nonstore retailing The selling of products outside the confines of a retail facility

catalog marketing A type of marketing in which an organization provides a catalog from which customers make selections and place orders by mail, telephone, or the Internet

Nonstore retailing is the selling of products outside the confines of a retail facility. It is a form of direct marketing that accounts for an increasing percentage of total retail sales, particularly as online retailing becomes more popular. Direct marketing can occur through catalog marketing, direct-response marketing, telemarketing, television home shopping, and online retailing.

Catalog Marketing

In **catalog marketing**, an organization provides a catalog from which customers make selections and place orders by mail, telephone, or the Internet. Catalog marketing began in 1872, when Montgomery Ward issued its first catalog to rural families. There are thousands of catalog marketing companies in the United States, many of which also publish online. Some catalog marketers sell products spread over multiple product lines, while others are more specialized. Take, for example, this catalog cover for the Duluth Trading Company.

Catalog Marketing
The Duluth Trading Company utilizes catalog marketing to sell its work wear for men and women, including its own brand of jeans.

Duluth Trading is a catalog marketer specializing in work wear, as you can see in the humorous illustration of a man wearing jeans, work boots, and a trucker hat. The image is promoting the company's brand of jeans, which are extra durable and flexible to perform well for all kinds of jobs. This cover, while promoting a product, also puts a humorous face on Duluth Trading, perhaps interesting consumers enough to look through the catalog.

Many companies, such as Land's End, Pottery Barn, and Crate & Barrel, sell via catalogs, online, and through retail stores in major metropolitan areas. These retailers generally offer considerable product depth for just a few lines of products. Still other catalog companies specialize in products from a single product line.

The advantages of catalog retailing include efficiency and convenience for customers because they do not have to visit a store. The retailer benefits by being able to locate in remote, low-cost areas, save on expensive store fixtures, and reduce both personal selling and store operating expenses. On the other hand, catalog retailing is inflexible, provides limited service, and is most effective for a selected set of products.

Direct-Response Marketing

Direct-response marketing occurs when a retailer advertises a product and makes it available through mail, telephone, or online orders. Generally, customers use a credit card, but other forms of payment may be permitted. Examples of direct-response marketing include a television commercial offering exercise machines, cosmetics, or household cleaning products available through a toll-free number, and a newspaper or magazine advertisement for a series of children's books available by filling out the form in the ad or calling a toll-free number. Direct-response marketing through television remains a multi-billion dollar industry, although it now competes with the Internet for customers' attention. This marketing method

direct-response marketing
A type of marketing in which a retailer advertises a product and makes it available through mail or telephone orders

has resulted in many products gaining widespread popularity. Some firms, like Russ Reid, specialize in direct-response marketing and assist firms in developing successful promotions. Direct-response marketing is also conducted by sending letters, samples, brochures, or booklets to prospects on a mailing list and asking that they order the advertised products by mail or telephone. In general, products must be priced above $20 to justify the advertising and distribution costs associated with direct-response marketing.

Telemarketing

A number of organizations use the telephone to strengthen the effectiveness of traditional marketing methods. **Telemarketing** is the performance of marketing-related activities by telephone. Some organizations use a prescreened list of prospective clients. Telemarketing can help to generate sales leads, improve customer service, speed up payments on past-due accounts, raise funds for nonprofit organizations, and gather marketing data.

However, increasingly restrictive telemarketing laws have made it a less appealing and less popular marketing method. In 2003, the U.S. Congress implemented a national do-not-call registry, which has more than 200 million numbers on it. The Federal Trade Commission (FTC) enforces violations, and companies are subject to fines of up to $16,000 for each call made to numbers on the list.[23] The Federal Communications Commission (FCC) ruled that companies are no longer allowed to call customers using prerecorded marketing calls simply because they had done business in the past. The law also requires that an "opt-out" mechanism be embedded in the call for consumers who do not wish to receive the calls. Companies that are still allowed to make telemarketing phone calls must pay for access to the do-not-call registry and must obtain updated numbers from the registry at least every three days. Certain exceptions do apply to no-call lists. For example, charitable, political, and telephone survey organizations are not restricted by the national registry.[24] In spite of regulations, many consumers still find robocalls to be a nuisance, and Congress is seeking further measures.[25]

telemarketing The performance of marketing-related activities by telephone

television home shopping A form of selling in which products are presented to television viewers, who can buy them by calling a toll-free number and paying with a credit card

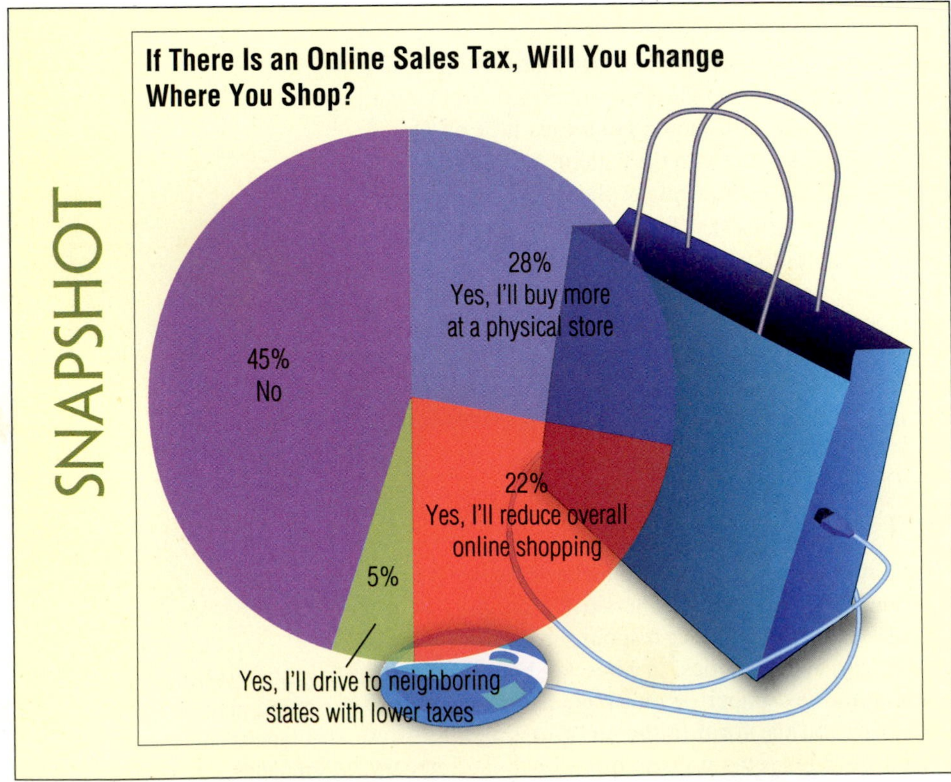

Source: AlixPartners survey of 2,221 online shoppers.

Television Home Shopping

Television home shopping presents products to television viewers, encouraging them to order through toll-free numbers and pay with credit cards. The Home Shopping Network originated and popularized this format. The most popular products sold through television home shopping are jewelry, clothing, housewares, and electronics. Most homes in the United States have access to at least one home shopping channel, with the Home Shopping Network and QVC being the largest.

The television home shopping format offers several benefits. Products can be demonstrated easily, and an adequate amount of time can be spent showing the product so viewers are well-informed. The length of time a product is shown depends not only on the time required for performing demonstrations but also on whether the product is selling. Once the calls peak and begin to decline, hosts switch to a new product. Other benefits are that customers can shop at their convenience and from the comfort of their homes. This method is particularly popular among older consumers, who tend to be less comfortable with online shopping and are less mobile to physically go to a store.

Online Retailing

Online retailing makes products available to buyers through computer connections. The phenomenal growth of Internet use and online information services has created many retailing opportunities. Online retailing is a rapidly-growing segment that most retailers now view as vital to their businesses. Retailers frequently offer exclusive online sales, or may reward customers who visit their websites with special in-store coupons and other promotions and discounts. Online retailing satisfies an increasing expectation among consumers to have multiple channels available to obtain the goods and services they desire at their convenience.

online retailing Retailing that makes products available to buyers through computer connections

direct selling Marketing products to ultimate consumers through face-to-face sales presentations at home or in the workplace

Consumers can perform a wide variety of shopping-related tasks online, including purchasing virtually anything they wish. Consumers can track down rare collectibles, refill their eyeglass prescriptions, and even purchase high-end jewelry or gourmet food. Banks and brokerages offer consumers access to their accounts, where they can perform a wide variety of activities, such as money transfers and stock trading. While online retail sales account for one-tenth of total retail sales, the segment is growing rapidly. Forrester Research projects that online retail sales in the United States will climb to nearly $370 billion by 2017, representing a compound annual growth rate of 10 percent between 2012 and 2017.[26] With ongoing advances in computer technology and consumers ever more pressed for time, online retailing will continue to escalate. Some firms that were primarily catalog retailers are now primarily online retailers, such as Paul Frederick featured in this advertisement. Paul Fredrick sells men's apparel and accessories online and does not sell in stores. The low introductory price offer featured in the advertisement is meant to be an enticement for potential customers to visit the site.

Online security remains a serious concern, even as more people than ever choose to shop online. Some shoppers remain hesitant to use smartphones and other devices for shopping. While major retailers and banks continue to suffer from security breaches, experts do have some tips for keeping shoppers safe. Be wary of suspicious apps, do not click on pop-up ads, shop with a credit (not debit) card, and make sure your antivirus software is consistently up-to-date.[27] Especially during peak shopping seasons such as Black Friday and Cyber Monday, consumers should be wary of online deals that seem too good to be true.

Online Retailers
Companies such as Paul Fredrick sell online only and not in brick-and-mortar stores.

15-4b Direct Selling

Direct selling is the marketing of products to ultimate consumers through face-to-face sales presentations at home or in the workplace. The top five global direct selling companies are Amway, Avon, Herbalife, Vorwerk, and Natura Cosmeticos.[28] Three of these companies, Amway, Avon, and Herbalife, are based in the United States. Direct selling is a highly valuable industry. Amway alone has more than $11.3 billion in annual sales.[29] Direct selling was once associated with door-to-door sales, but it has evolved into a highly professional industry where most contacts with buyers are prearranged through electronic communication or another means

Direct Selling
Mary Kay is a popular makeup brand sold on a person-to-person or party plan basis.

of prior communication. Today, companies identify customers through the mail, telephone, Internet, social networks, or shopping-mall intercepts and then set up appointments with salespeople. Direct selling is most successful in other countries, particularly collective societies like China, where Amway has achieved higher sales than its domestic market, the United States. Collective societies prize the one-on-one attention and feeling like they are connecting with the salesperson.

Although the majority of direct selling takes place on an individual, or person-to-person, basis, it sometimes may be carried out in a group, or "party," plan format. With a party plan, a consumer acts as a host and invites friends and associates to view merchandise, often at someone's home. The informal atmosphere helps to overcome customers' reluctance and encourages them to try out and buy products. Tupperware and Mary Kay were the pioneers of this selling technique and remain global leaders. Mary Kay, featured in the advertisement, remains a popular brand by offering fashion-forward makeup in trendy colors, such as the eye shadows seen here. An advantage to customers who shop with Mary Kay is having an expert come to their home and teach them about application techniques and which colors are most flattering.

Direct selling has benefits and limitations. It gives the marketer an opportunity to demonstrate the product in a comfortable environment where it most likely would be used. The seller can give the customer personal attention, and the product can be presented to the customer at a convenient time and location. Product categories that have been highly successful for direct selling include cosmetics and personal-care products, health products, jewelry, accessories, and household products. Personal attention to the customer is the foundation on which many direct sellers have built their businesses. However, because commissions for salespeople are high, around 30 to 50 percent of the sales price, and great effort is required to isolate promising prospects, overall costs of direct selling make it the most expensive form of retailing. Furthermore, some customers view direct selling negatively, owing to unscrupulous and fraudulent practices used by some direct sellers. Some communities even have local ordinances that control or, in some cases, prohibit direct selling. Despite these negative views held by some individuals, direct selling is still alive and well, bringing in annual revenues of more than $31.6 billion in the United States and nearly $167 billion worldwide.[30]

15-4c Automatic Vending

automatic vending The use of machines to dispense products

Automatic vending is the use of machines to dispense products. It is one of the most impersonal forms of retailing, and it accounts for a very small minority of all retail sales. Small, standardized, routinely purchased products (e.g., snacks and drinks) are best suited for sale in vending machines because consumers buy them out of convenience. Machines in areas of heavy foot traffic provide efficient and continuous service to consumers. High-volume areas, such as in commercial centers of large cities or in airports, may offer a wide range of automatic vending product options. In some markets, vending machines have taken on cult popularity, particularly among urban-dwelling consumers. In larger cities around the world, customers can find a wide variety of products dispensed via vending machine, even high-end and perishable items. For example, the Semi-Automatic machine, located in luxury hotels, dispenses $500 watches and $22 eye cream to travelers who forgot items at home. InstyMeds vending machines dispense prescription medications to customers.[31] Farmers Fridge, a company that services the Chicago area, offers fresh salads via vending machine.[32]

Because vending machines need only a small amount of space and no sales personnel, this retailing method has some advantages over stores. The advantages are partly offset, however, by the high costs of equipment and frequent servicing and repairs.

15-5 FRANCHISING

Franchising is an arrangement in which a supplier, or franchisor, grants a dealer, or franchisee, the right to sell products in exchange for some type of consideration. The franchisor may receive a percentage of total sales in exchange for furnishing equipment, buildings, management know-how, and marketing assistance to the franchisee. The franchisee supplies labor and capital, operates the franchised business, and agrees to abide by the provisions of the franchise agreement. Table 15.2 lists the leading U.S. franchises as well as the types of products they sell, number of franchise outlets, and start-up costs.

Because of changes in the international marketplace, shifting employment options in the United States, the large U.S. service economy, and corporate interest in more joint-venture activity, franchising is a very popular retail option. There are more than 828,100 franchise establishments in the United States, which provide more than 17.4 million jobs across a variety of industries.[33] The gross domestic product of franchised businesses is worth $1.2 trillion.[34]

Franchising offers several advantages to both the franchisee and the franchisor. It enables a franchisee to start a business with limited capital and benefit from the business experience of others. Generally speaking, franchises have lower failure rates than independent retail establishments and are often more successful because they can build on the established reputation

franchising An arrangement in which a supplier (franchisor) grants a dealer (franchisee) the right to sell products in exchange for some type of consideration

Table 15.2 Top U.S. Franchisors and Their Start-Up Costs

Rank	Franchise and Description	Start-Up Costs in U.S. Dollars
1	**Anytime Fitness** Fitness center	$56.29K–353.89K
2	**Hampton Hotels** Midprice hotels	$3.69M–6.57M
3	**Subway** Subs, salads	$85.69K–262.85K
4	**Supercuts** Hair salon	$113.75K–233.6K
5	**Jimmy John's Gourmet Sandwiches** Gourmet sandwiches	$330.5K–519.5K
6	**7-Eleven Inc.** Convenience stores	$50K–1.63M
7	**Servpro** Insurance/disaster restoration and cleaning	$138.55K–187.19K
8	**Denny's Inc.** Family restaurant	$1.12M–2.61M
9	**Pizza Hut Inc.** Pizza, pasta, wings	$297K–2.1M
10	**Dunkin' Donuts** Coffee, doughnuts, baked goods	$294K–1.51M

Source: "2014 Franchise 500," *Entrepreneur*, www.entrepreneur.com/franchises/rankings/franchise500-115608/2014,-1.html (accessed December 22, 2013).

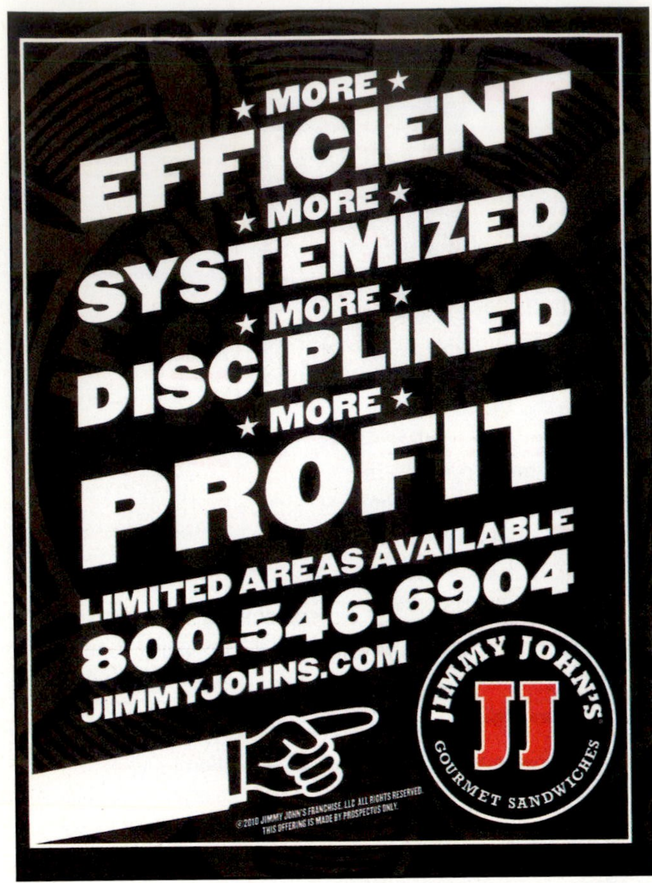

© 2010 Jimmy John's Franchise, LLC.

Franchising
Jimmy John's is a popular sandwich franchise, wherein individual stores are owned and managed by the franchisee.

of a national brand. Nationally, about 57 percent of first-time franchise chains fail, and about 61 percent of independent operators are equally unsuccessful.[35] However, franchise failure rates vary greatly depending on the particular franchise. Nationally-advertised franchises, such as Subway and Burger King, are often assured of sales as soon as they open because customers already know what to expect. If business problems arise, the franchisee can obtain guidance and advice from the franchisor at little or no cost. Also, the franchisee receives materials to use in local advertising and can benefit from national promotional campaigns sponsored by the franchisor.

Through franchise arrangements, the franchisor gains fast and selective product distribution without incurring the high cost of constructing and operating its own outlets. The franchisor, therefore, has more available capital for expanding production and advertising. It can also ensure, through the franchise agreement, that outlets are maintained and operated according to its own standards. Some franchisors do permit their franchisees to modify their menus, hours, or other operating elements to better match their target market's needs. The franchisor benefits from the fact that the franchisee, being a sole proprietor in most cases, is likely to be very highly motivated to succeed. Success of the franchise means more sales, which translates into higher income for the franchisor. This advertisement for Jimmy John's gourmet sandwiches highlights in large bold lettering the advantages of becoming a franchisee, including being "more efficient, more systematized, more disciplined, more profit." Clearly, this advertisement is targeted at potential franchisees, not at potential customers.

Franchise arrangements also have several drawbacks. The franchisor can dictate many aspects of the business: décor, menu, design of employees' uniforms, types of signs, hours of operation, and numerous details of business operations. In addition, franchisees must pay to use the franchisor's name, products, and assistance. Usually, there is a one-time franchise fee and continuing royalty and advertising fees, often collected as a percentage of sales. Franchisees often must work very hard, putting in 10- to 12-hour days six or seven days a week. In some cases, franchise agreements are not uniform, meaning one franchisee may pay more than another for the same services. Finally, the franchisor gives up a certain amount of control when entering into a franchise agreement with an entrepreneur. Consequently, individual establishments may not be operated exactly according to the franchisor's standards.

15-6 WHOLESALING

wholesaling Transactions in which products are bought for resale, for making other products, or for general business operations

wholesaler An individual or organization that sells products that are bought for resale, for making other products, or for general business operations

Wholesaling refers to all transactions in which products are bought for resale, making other products, or general business operations. It does not include exchanges with ultimate consumers. A **wholesaler** is an individual or organization that sells products that are bought for resale, making other products, or general business operations. In other words, wholesalers buy products and resell them to reseller, government, and institutional users. For instance, Sysco, the nation's number-one food-service distributor, supplies restaurants, hotels, schools, industrial caterers, and hospitals with everything from frozen and fresh food and paper products to medical and cleaning supplies. Wholesaling activities are not limited to goods. Service companies, such as financial institutions, also use active wholesale networks. There are more than 414,608 wholesaling establishments in the United States, and more than half of all products sold in this country pass through these firms.[36]

Wholesalers may engage in many supply-chain management activities, which we will discuss. In addition to bearing the primary responsibility for the physical distribution of products from manufacturers to retailers, wholesalers may establish information systems that help producers and retailers manage the supply chain from producer to customer. Many wholesalers use information technology and the Internet to share information among intermediaries, employees, customers, and suppliers and facilitating agencies, such as trucking companies and warehouse firms. Some firms make their databases and marketing information systems available to their supply-chain partners to facilitate order processing, shipping, and product development and to share information about changing market conditions and customer desires. As a result, some wholesalers play a key role in supply chain management decisions.

15-6a Services Provided by Wholesalers

Wholesalers provide essential services to both producers and retailers. By initiating sales contacts with a producer and selling diverse products to retailers, wholesalers serve as an extension of the producer's sales force. Wholesalers also provide financial assistance. They often pay for transporting goods, reduce a producer's warehousing expenses and inventory investment by holding goods in inventory, extend credit and assume losses from buyers who turn out to be poor credit risks, and can be a source of working capital when they buy a producer's output in cash. Wholesalers also serve as conduits for information within the marketing channel, keeping producers up-to-date on market developments and passing along the manufacturers' promotional plans to other intermediaries. Using wholesalers, therefore, gives producers a distinct advantage because the specialized services wholesalers perform allow producers to concentrate on developing and manufacturing products that match customers' needs and wants.

Wholesalers support retailers by assisting with marketing strategy, especially the distribution component. Wholesalers also help retailers select inventory. They are often specialists on market conditions and experts at negotiating final purchases. In industries in which obtaining supplies is important, skilled buying is indispensable. Effective wholesalers make an effort to understand the businesses of their customers. They also must now understand digital marketing and digital communications. Firms such as Williams Commerce specialize in helping wholesalers to adapt to an increasingly digital environment while maintaining the high level of consumer contact that is sometimes required.[37]

Wholesalers can also reduce a retailer's burden of looking for and coordinating supply sources. If the wholesaler purchases for several different buyers, expenses can be shared by all customers. Furthermore, whereas a manufacturer's salesperson offers retailers only a few products at a time, independent wholesalers always have a wide range of products available. Thus, through partnerships, wholesalers and retailers can forge successful relationships for the benefit of customers.

The distinction between services performed by wholesalers and those provided by other businesses has blurred in recent years. Changes in the competitive nature of business, especially the growth of strong retail chains like Walmart, Home Depot, and Best Buy, are changing supply-chain relationships. In many product categories, such as electronics, furniture, and even food products, retailers have discovered that they can deal directly with producers, performing wholesaling activities themselves at a lower cost. However, when a wholesaler is eliminated from a marketing channel, wholesaling activities still have to be performed by a member of the supply chain, whether a producer, retailer, or facilitating agency. Most retailers rely on computer technology to expedite ordering, track deliveries, and monitor handling of goods. Thus, technology has allowed retailers to take over some wholesaling functions.

15-6b Types of Wholesalers

Wholesalers are classified according to several criteria: whether a wholesaler is independently owned or owned by a producer, whether it takes title to (owns) the products it handles, the range of services provided, and the breadth and depth of its product lines. Using these criteria, we discuss three general types of wholesaling establishments including merchant wholesalers, agents and brokers, and manufacturers' sales branches and offices.

Merchant Wholesalers

Merchant wholesalers are independently-owned businesses that take title to goods, assume risks associated with ownership, and generally buy and resell products to other wholesalers, business customers, or retailers. A producer is likely to rely on merchant wholesalers when selling directly to customers would be economically unfeasible. Merchant wholesalers are also useful for providing market coverage, making sales contacts, storing inventory, handling orders, collecting market information, and furnishing customer support. Some merchant wholesalers are even involved in packaging and developing private brands. Merchant wholesalers go by various names, including *wholesaler, jobber, distributor, assembler, exporter,* and *importer.* They fall into two broad categories: full service and limited service (see Figure 15.1).

merchant wholesalers Independently owned businesses that take title to goods, assume ownership risks, and buy and resell products to other wholesalers, business customers, or retailers

full-service wholesalers Merchant wholesalers that perform the widest range of wholesaling

general-merchandise wholesalers Full-service wholesalers with a wide product mix but limited depth within product lines

limited-line wholesalers Full-service wholesalers that carry only a few product lines but many products within those lines

Full-Service Wholesalers **Full-service wholesalers** perform the widest possible range of wholesaling functions. Customers rely on them for product availability, suitable product assortments, breaking large quantities into smaller ones, financial assistance, and technical advice and service. Full-service wholesalers handle either consumer or business products and provide numerous marketing services to their customers. Many large grocery wholesalers, for instance, help retailers with store design, site selection, personnel training, financing, merchandising, advertising, coupon redemption, and scanning. Macdonalds Consolidated is a full-service wholesaler of meat, dairy, and produce goods for grocery retailers in North America. Macdonalds offers many services, including communication management, document management, retailer flyers and merchandising, and rebates for valued customers.[38] Although full-service wholesalers often earn higher gross margins than other wholesalers, their operating expenses are also higher because they perform a wider range of functions.

Full-service wholesalers are categorized as general-merchandise, limited-line, and specialty-line wholesalers. **General-merchandise wholesalers** carry a wide product mix but offer limited depth within product lines. They deal in products such as drugs, nonperishable foods, cosmetics, detergents, and tobacco. **Limited-line wholesalers** carry only a few product lines, such as groceries, lighting fixtures, or oil-well drilling equipment, but offer an extensive assortment of products within those lines. AmerisourceBergen Corporation, for example, is a limited-line wholesaler of pharmaceuticals and health and beauty aids.[39]

Figure 15.1 Types of Merchant Wholesalers

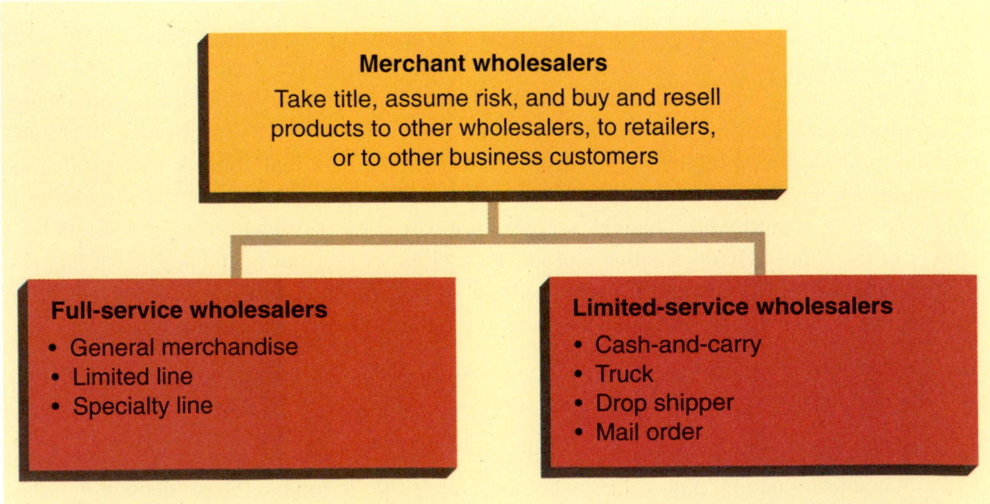

ZUMA Press, Inc./Alamy

Merchant Wholesaler
Grainger is a full-service, limited-line wholesaler of electrical equipment and supplies.

General-line wholesalers provide a range of services similar to those of general-merchandise wholesalers. **Specialty-line wholesalers** offer the narrowest range of products, usually a single product line or a few items within a product line. **Rack jobbers** are full-service, specialty-line wholesalers that own and maintain display racks in supermarkets, drugstores, and discount and variety stores. Retailers provide the space, and they set up displays, mark merchandise, stock shelves, and keep billing and inventory records. Rack jobbers specialize in non-food items with high profit margins, such as health and beauty aids, books, magazines, hosiery, and greeting cards.

specialty-line wholesalers Full-service wholesalers that carry only a single product line or a few items within a product line

rack jobbers Full-service, specialty-line wholesalers that own and maintain display racks in stores

limited-service wholesalers Merchant wholesalers that provide some services and specialize in a few functions

cash-and-carry wholesalers Limited-service wholesalers whose customers pay cash and furnish transportation

truck wholesalers Limited-service wholesalers that transport products directly to customers for inspection and selection

drop shippers Limited-service wholesalers that take title to goods and negotiate sales but never actually take possession of products

Limited-Service Wholesalers

Limited-service wholesalers provide fewer marketing services than do full-service wholesalers and specialize in just a few functions. Producers perform the remaining functions or pass them on to customers or other intermediaries. Limited-service wholesalers take title to merchandise but often do not deliver merchandise, grant credit, provide marketing information, store inventory, or plan ahead for customers' future needs. Because they offer restricted services, limited-service wholesalers charge lower rates and have smaller profit margins than full-service wholesalers. The decision about whether to use a limited-service or a full-service wholesaler depends on the structure of the marketing channel and the need to manage the supply chain to create a competitive advantage. Although limited-service wholesalers are less common than other types, they are important in the distribution of products like specialty foods, perishable items, construction materials, and coal.

Table 15.3 summarizes the services provided by four typical limited-service wholesalers: cash-and-carry wholesalers, truck wholesalers, drop shippers, and mail-order wholesalers. **Cash-and-carry wholesalers** are intermediaries whose customers—often small businesses—pay cash and furnish transportation. Cash-and-carry wholesalers usually handle a limited line of products with a high turnover rate, such as groceries, building materials, and electrical or office supplies. Many small retailers that other types of wholesalers will not take on because of their small size survive because of cash-and-carry wholesalers. **Truck wholesalers**, sometimes called *truck jobbers,* transport a limited line of products directly to customers for on-the-spot inspection and selection. They are often small operators who own and drive their own trucks. They usually have regular routes, calling on retailers and other institutions to determine their needs. **Drop shippers**, also known as *desk jobbers,* take title to products and negotiate sales but never take actual possession of products. They forward orders from retailers,

Table 15.3 Services That Limited-Service Wholesalers Provide

	Cash-and-Carry	Truck	Drop Shipper	Mail Order
Physical possession of merchandise	Yes	Yes	No	Yes
Personal sales calls on customers	No	Yes	No	No
Information about market conditions	No	Some	Yes	Yes
Advice to customers	No	Some	Yes	No
Stocking and maintenance of merchandise in customers' stores	No	No	No	No
Credit to customers	No	No	Yes	Some
Delivery of merchandise to customers	No	Yes	No	No

business buyers, or other wholesalers to manufacturers and arrange for carload shipments of items to be delivered directly from producers to these customers. They assume responsibility for products during the entire transaction, including the costs of any unsold goods. **Mail-order wholesalers** use catalogs instead of a sales force to sell products to retail and business buyers. Wholesale mail-order houses generally feature cosmetics, specialty foods, sporting goods, office supplies, and automotive parts. Mail-order wholesaling enables buyers to choose and order particular catalog items for delivery through various mail carriers. This is a convenient and effective method of selling items to customers in remote areas that other wholesalers might find unprofitable to serve. The Internet has provided an opportunity for mail-order wholesalers to serve a larger number of buyers, selling products over their websites and having the products shipped by the manufacturers.

mail-order wholesalers Limited-service wholesalers that sell products through catalogs

Agents and Brokers

Agents and brokers negotiate purchases and expedite sales but do not take title to products (see Figure 15.2 for types of agents and brokers). Sometimes called *functional middlemen,* they perform a limited number of services in exchange for a commission, which generally is

Figure 15.2 Types of Agents and Brokers

Table 15.4 Services That Agents and Brokers Provide

	Manufacturers' Agents	Selling Agents	Commission Merchants	Brokers
Physical possession of merchandise	Some	Some	Yes	No
Long-term relationship with buyers or sellers	Yes	Yes	Yes	No
Representation of competing product lines	No	No	Yes	Yes
Limited geographic territory	Yes	No	No	No
Credit to customers	No	Yes	Some	No
Delivery of merchandise to customers	Some	Yes	Yes	No

based on the product's selling price. **Agents** represent either buyers or sellers on a permanent basis, whereas **brokers** are intermediaries that buyers or sellers employ temporarily.

Although agents and brokers perform even fewer functions than limited-service wholesalers, they are usually specialists in particular products or types of customers and can provide valuable sales expertise. They know their markets well and often form long-lasting associations with customers. Agents and brokers enable manufacturers to expand sales when resources are limited, benefit from the services of a trained sales force, and hold down personal selling costs. Table 15.4 summarizes the services provided by agents and brokers.

Manufacturers' agents, which account for more than half of all agent wholesalers, are independent intermediaries that represent two or more sellers and usually offer complete product lines to customers. They sell and take orders year-round, much as a manufacturer's sales force does. Restricted to a particular territory, a manufacturer's agent handles noncompeting and complementary products. The relationship between the agent and the manufacturer is governed by written contracts that outline territories, selling price, order handling, and terms of sale relating to delivery, service, and warranties. Manufacturers' agents have little or no control over producers' pricing and marketing policies. They do not extend credit and may be unable to provide technical advice. Manufacturers' agents are commonly used in sales of apparel, machinery and equipment, steel, furniture, automotive products, electrical goods, and some food items.

Selling agents market either all of a specified product line or a manufacturer's entire output. They perform every wholesaling activity except taking title to products. Selling agents usually assume the sales function for several producers simultaneously, and some firms may use them in place of a marketing department. In fact, selling agents are used most often by small producers or by manufacturers that have difficulty maintaining a marketing department because of such factors as seasonal production. In contrast to manufacturers' agents, selling agents generally have no territorial limits and have complete authority over prices, promotion, and distribution. To avoid conflicts of interest, selling agents represent noncompeting product lines. They play a key role in advertising, marketing research, and credit policies of the sellers they represent, at times even advising on product development and packaging.

Commission merchants receive goods on consignment from local sellers and negotiate sales in large, central markets. Sometimes called *factor merchants,* these agents have broad powers regarding prices and terms of sale. They specialize in obtaining the best price possible under market conditions. Most often found in agricultural marketing, commission merchants take possession of truckloads of commodities, arrange for necessary grading or storage, and transport the commodities to auction or markets where they are sold. When sales are completed, the agents deduct commissions and the expense of making the sale and turn over profits to the producer. Commission merchants also offer planning assistance and sometimes extend credit but usually do not provide promotional support.

A broker's primary purpose is to bring buyers and sellers together. Thus, brokers perform fewer functions than other intermediaries. They are not involved in financing or physical

agents Intermediaries that represent either buyers or sellers on a permanent basis

brokers Intermediaries that bring buyers and sellers together temporarily

manufacturers' agents Independent intermediaries that represent two or more sellers and usually offer customers complete product lines

selling agents Intermediaries that market a whole product line or a manufacturer's entire output

commission merchants Agents that receive goods on consignment from local sellers and negotiate sales in large, central markets

possession, have no authority to set prices, and assume almost no risks. Instead, they offer customers specialized knowledge of a particular commodity and a network of established contacts. Brokers are especially useful to sellers of products such as supermarket goods and real estate. Food brokers, for example, connect food and general merchandise to retailer-owned and merchant wholesalers, grocery chains, food processors, and business buyers.

Manufacturers' Sales Branches and Offices

Sometimes called *manufacturers' wholesalers*, manufacturers' sales branches and offices resemble merchant wholesalers' operations. **Sales branches** are manufacturer-owned intermediaries that sell products and provide support services to the manufacturer's sales force. Situated away from the manufacturing plant, they are usually located where large customers are concentrated and demand is high. They offer credit, deliver goods, give promotional assistance, and furnish other services. Customers include retailers, business buyers, and other wholesalers. Manufacturers of electrical supplies, plumbing supplies, lumber, and automotive parts often have branch operations.

Sales offices are manufacturer-owned operations that provide services normally associated with agents. Like sales branches, they are located away from manufacturing plants, but unlike sales branches, they carry no inventory. A manufacturer's sales office (or branch) may sell products that enhance the manufacturer's own product line.

sales branches Manufacturer-owned intermediaries that sell products and provide support services to the manufacturer's sales force

sales offices Manufacturer-owned operations that provide services normally associated with agents

Manufacturers may set up these branches or offices to reach their customers more effectively by performing wholesaling functions themselves. A manufacturer also might set up such a facility when specialized wholesaling services are not available through existing intermediaries. Performing wholesaling and physical distribution activities through a manufacturer's sales branch or office can strengthen supply-chain efficiency. In some situations, though, a manufacturer may bypass its sales office or branches entirely—for example, if the producer decides to serve large retailer customers directly.

Summary

15-1 Describe the purpose and function of retailers in the marketing channel.

Retailing includes all transactions in which buyers intend to consume products through personal, family, or household use. Retailers, organizations that sell products primarily to ultimate consumers, are important links in the marketing channel, because they are both marketers for and customers of wholesalers and producers. Retailers add value, provide services, and assist in making product selections.

15-2 Identify the major types of retailers.

Retail stores can be classified according to the breadth of products offered. Two broad categories are general merchandise retailers and specialty retailers. There are several primary types of general merchandise retailers. Department stores are large retail organizations organized by departments and characterized by wide product mixes in considerable depth. Discount stores are self-service, low-price, general-merchandise outlets. Convenience stores are small self-service stores that are open long hours and carry a narrow assortment of products, usually convenience items. Supermarkets are large self-service food stores that carry some non-food products. Superstores are giant retail outlets that carry all the products found in supermarkets and most consumer products purchased on a routine basis. Hypermarkets offer supermarket and discount store shopping at one location. Warehouse clubs are large-scale, members-only discount operations. Warehouse and catalog showrooms are low-cost operations characterized by warehouse methods of materials handling and display, large inventories, and minimal services.

Specialty retailers offer substantial assortments in a few product lines. They include traditional specialty retailers, which carry narrow product mixes with deep product lines. Category killers are large specialty stores that concentrate on a major product category and compete on the basis of low prices and enormous product availability. Off-price retailers sell brand-name manufacturers' seconds and product overruns at deep discounts.

15-3 Explain strategic issues in retailing.

To increase sales and store patronage, retailers must consider strategic issues. Location determines the trading area from which a store draws its customers and should be evaluated carefully. When evaluating potential sites, retailers take into account a variety of factors, including the location of the firm's target market within the trading area, kinds of products sold, availability of public transportation, customer characteristics, and competitors' locations. Retailers can choose among several types of locations, including freestanding structures, traditional business districts, traditional planned shopping centers (neighborhood, community, regional, and superregional), or nontraditional shopping centers (lifestyle, power, and outlet). Retail positioning involves identifying an unserved or underserved market segment and serving it through a strategy that distinguishes the retailer from others in those customers' minds. Store image, which various customers perceive differently, derives not only from atmospherics but also from location, products offered, customer services, prices, promotion, and the store's overall reputation. Atmospherics refers to the physical elements of a store's design that can be adjusted to appeal to consumers' emotions and thus induce them to buy. Category management is a retail strategy of managing groups of similar, often substitutable products produced by different manufacturers.

15-4 Recognize the various forms of direct marketing, direct selling, and vending.

Direct marketing is the use of the telephone, Internet, and nonpersonal media to communicate product and organizational information to customers, who can then purchase products via mail, telephone, or the Internet. Direct marketing is a type of nonstore retailing, the selling of goods or services outside the confines of a retail facility. Direct marketing may occur through a catalog (catalog marketing), advertising (direct-response marketing), telephone (telemarketing), television (television home shopping), or online (online retailing). Two other types of nonstore retailing are direct selling and automatic vending. Direct selling is the marketing of products to ultimate consumers through face-to-face sales presentations at home or in the workplace. Automatic vending is the use of machines to dispense products.

15-5 Describe franchising and its benefits and weaknesses.

Franchising is an arrangement in which a supplier grants a dealer the right to sell products in exchange for some type of consideration. Franchise arrangements have a number of advantages and disadvantages over traditional business forms, and their use is increasing. There are several advantages for the franchisee. First, franchising enables a franchisee to start a business with limited capital and benefit from the business experience of others. Second, franchises generally have lower failure rates than independent retail establishments and are often more successful because they can build on the franchisor's reputation. Finally, the franchisee receives materials to use in local advertising and can benefit from national promotional campaigns sponsored by the franchisor. In addition, if business problems should arise for the franchise operation, the franchisee can obtain guidance and advice from the franchisor at little or no cost. There are also several advantages for the franchisor. First, the franchisor gains fast and selective product distribution without incurring the high cost of constructing and operating its own outlets. Second, the franchisor has more available capital for expanding production and advertising. Finally, the franchisor benefits from the fact that the franchisee is likely to be highly motivated to succeed—likely resulting in higher income for the franchisor.

There are several disadvantages for the franchisee. The franchisor can dictate many aspects of the business. Franchisees must also pay to use the franchisor's name, products, and assistance; operating a franchise requires hard work and long hours. Another disadvantage is that franchise agreements are not always uniform. Disadvantages for the franchisor include the fact that the franchisor must give up a certain amount of control when entering into an agreement and that individual establishments may not be operated according to standards.

15-6 Explain the nature and functions of wholesalers.

Wholesaling consists of all transactions in which products are bought for resale, making other products, or general business operations. Wholesalers are individuals or organizations that facilitate and expedite exchanges that are primarily wholesale transactions. For producers, wholesalers are a source of financial assistance and information. By performing specialized accumulation and allocation functions, they allow producers to concentrate on manufacturing products. Wholesalers provide retailers with buying expertise, wide product lines, efficient distribution, and warehousing and storage.

Merchant wholesalers are independently-owned businesses that take title to goods and assume ownership risks. They are either full-service wholesalers, offering the widest possible range of wholesaling functions, or limited-service wholesalers, providing only some marketing services and specializing in a few functions. There are several full-service merchant wholesaler types. General-merchandise wholesalers offer a wide but relatively shallow product mix. Limited-line wholesalers offer extensive assortments within a few product lines. Specialty-line wholesalers carry only a single product line or a few items within a line. Rack jobbers own and service display racks in supermarkets and other stores. Limited-service merchant wholesalers include cash-and-carry wholesalers, which sell to small businesses, require payment in cash, and do not deliver. Truck wholesalers sell a limited line of products from their own trucks directly to customers. Drop shippers own goods and negotiate sales, but never take possession of products. Finally, mail-order wholesalers sell to retail and business buyers through direct-mail catalogs.

Agents and brokers negotiate purchases and expedite sales in exchange for a commission, but they do not take title to products. Usually specializing in certain products, they can provide valuable sales expertise. Whereas agents represent buyers or sellers on a permanent basis, brokers are intermediaries that buyers and sellers employ on a temporary basis to negotiate exchanges. Manufacturers' agents offer customers the complete product lines of two or more sellers. Selling agents market a complete product line or a producer's entire output and perform every wholesaling function except taking title to products. Commission merchants are agents that receive goods on consignment from local sellers and negotiate sales in large, central markets.

Manufacturers' sales branches and offices are owned by manufacturers. Sales branches sell products and provide support services for the manufacturer's sales force in a given location. Sales offices carry no inventory and function much as agents do.

Go to www.cengagebrain.com for resources to help you master the content in this chapter as well as for materials that will expand your marketing knowledge!

Developing Your Marketing Plan

Distribution decisions in the marketing plan entail the movement of your product from the producer to the final consumer. An understanding of how and where your customer prefers to purchase products is critical to the development of the marketing plan. As you apply the information in this chapter to your plan, focus on the following issues:

1. Considering your product's attributes and your target market's (or markets') buying behavior, will your product likely be sold to the ultimate customer or to another member of the marketing channel?
2. If your product will be sold to the ultimate customer, what type of retailing establishment is most suitable to your product? Consider the product's characteristics and your target market's buying behavior. Refer to Table 15.1 for retailer types.
3. Discuss how the characteristics of the retail establishment, such as location and store image, have an impact on the consumer's perception of your product.
4. Are direct marketing or direct selling methods appropriate for your product and target market?
5. If your product will be sold to another member in the marketing channel, discuss whether a merchant wholesaler, agent, or broker is most suitable as your channel customer.

The information obtained from these questions should assist you in developing various aspects of your marketing plan found in the "Interactive Marketing Plan" exercise at www.cengagebrain.com.

Important Terms

retailing 448
retailer 448
general-merchandise retailer 449
department stores 449
discount stores 451
convenience store 451
supermarkets 451
superstores 452
hypermarkets 452
warehouse clubs 452
warehouse showrooms 453
traditional specialty retailers 453
category killer 454
off-price retailers 454
neighborhood shopping center 456
community shopping center 456
regional shopping center 456
superregional shopping center 456
lifestyle shopping center 456
power shopping center 457
retail positioning 457
atmospherics 458
category management 459
direct marketing 460
nonstore retailing 460
catalog marketing 460
direct-response marketing 461
telemarketing 462
television home shopping 462
online retailing 463
direct selling 463
automatic vending 464
franchising 465
wholesaling 466
wholesaler 466
merchant wholesalers 468
full-service wholesalers 468
general-merchandise wholesalers 468
limited-line wholesalers 468
specialty-line wholesalers 469
rack jobbers 469
limited-service wholesalers 469
cash-and-carry wholesalers 469
truck wholesalers 469
drop shippers 469
mail-order wholesalers 470
agents 471
brokers 471
manufacturers' agents 471
selling agents 471
commission merchants 471
sales branches 472
sales offices 472

Discussion and Review Questions

1. What value is added to a product by retailers? What value is added by retailers for producers and ultimate consumers?
2. What are the major differences between discount stores and department stores?
3. In what ways are traditional specialty stores and off-price retailers similar? How do they differ?
4. What major issues should be considered when determining a retail site location?
5. Describe the three major types of traditional shopping centers. Give an example of each type in your area.
6. Discuss the major factors that help to determine a retail store's image. How does atmosphere add value to products sold in a store?
7. How is door-to-door selling a form of retailing? Some consumers believe that direct-response orders bypass the retailer. Is this true?
8. If you were opening a retail business, would you prefer to open an independent store or own a store under a franchise arrangement? Explain your preference.
9. What services do wholesalers provide to producers and retailers?
10. What is the difference between a full-service merchant wholesaler and a limited-service merchant wholesaler?
11. Drop shippers take title to products but do not accept physical possession of them, whereas commission merchants take physical possession of products but do not accept title. Defend the logic of classifying drop shippers as merchant wholesalers and commission merchants as agents.
12. Why are manufacturers' sales offices and branches classified as wholesalers? Which independent wholesalers are replaced by manufacturers' sales branches? By sales offices?

Video Case 15.1

L.L.Bean: Open 24/7, Click or Brick

L.L.Bean, based in Freeport, Maine, began life as a one-product firm selling by mail in 1912. Founder Leon Leonwood Bean designed and tested every product he sold, starting with the now-iconic rubber-soled Bean Boot. Today, the catalog business that L.L.Bean began is still going strong, along with 30 U.S. stores and a thriving online retail operation. In addition, L.L.Bean is expanding its retail presence in Japan and China, where customers are particularly drawn to brand names that represent quality and a distinct personality. The company's outdoorsy image and innovative products, combined with a century-old reputation for standing behind every item, have made its stores popular shopping destinations around the world and around the Web.

Although the award-winning L.L.Bean catalog swelled in size during the 1980s and 1990s, it has slimmed down over the years as the online store has grown. Now, using sophisticated marketing database systems, L.L.Bean manages and updates the mailing lists and customer preferences for its catalogs. For targeting purposes, L.L.Bean creates 50 different catalogs that are mailed to selected customers across the United States and in 160 countries worldwide. The company's computer-modeling tools indicate which customers are interested in which products so they receive only the specialized catalogs they desire. Still, says the vice president of stores, "what we find is most customers want some sort of touch point," whether they buy online, in a store, by mail, or by phone.

John Van Decker/Alamy

The company's flagship retail store in Freeport, Maine, like its online counterpart, is open 24 hours a day, 7 days a week, throughout the year. Even on major holidays like Thanksgiving and Christmas, when most other stores are closed, the flagship store is open for business. It stocks extra merchandise and hires additional employees for busy buying periods, as does the online store. Day or night, rain or shine, customers can walk the aisles of the gigantic Freeport store to browse an assortment of clothing and footwear for men, women, and children;

Try out camping gear and other sporting goods; buy home goods like blankets; and check out pet supplies. Every week, the store offers hands-on demonstrations and how-to seminars to educate customers about its products. Customers can pause for a cup of coffee or sit down to a full meal at the in-store café. Thanks to the store's enormous size and entertaining extras, it has become a tourist attraction as well as the centerpiece of L.L.Bean's retail empire.

L.L.Bean's online store continues to grow in popularity. In fact, online orders recently surpassed mail and phone orders, a first in the company's history, and the company also offers a mobile app for anytime, anywhere access via cell phone. The web-based store is busy year-round, but especially during the Christmas shopping season, when it receives a virtual blizzard of orders—as many as 120,000 orders in a day. Unlike the physical stores, which have limited space to hold and display inventory for shoppers to buy in person, the online store can offer every product in every size and color. Customers can order via the Web and have purchases sent to their home or office address or shipped to a local L.L.Bean store for pickup. This latter option is particularly convenient for customers who prefer to pay with cash rather than credit or debit cards.

At the start of L.L.Bean's second century, its dedication to customer satisfaction is as strong as when Leon Leonwood Bean began his mail-order business so many decades ago. "We want to keep ... the customer happy and keep that customer coming back to L.L.Bean over and over," explains the vice president of e-commerce.[40]

Questions for Discussion

1. What forms of direct marketing does L.L.Bean employ? Which additional forms of direct marketing should L.L.Bean consider using?
2. Do you think L.L.Bean's website will ever entirely take the place of its mail-order catalog? Why or why not?
3. What type(s) of location do you think would be most appropriate for future L.L.Bean stores, and why?

Case 15.2

Dick's Sporting Goods Scores with Stores within Stores

Dick's Sporting Goods is scoring big points with customers by setting up stores within stores that each feature an extensive selection of goods from a particular brand. The Pennsylvania-based retailer was founded in 1948 as a bait and tackle shop. Today, the founder's son is CEO, heading up a management team responsible for 558 large-scale Dick's Sporting Goods stores selling sports equipment, clothing, and shoes for team and individual use. Despite competition from other sporting-goods retailers, including Bass Pro Shops and REI, Dick's continues to grow beyond $6 billion in annual sales by putting brand-name merchandise at the core of its strategy for in-store, online, and mobile retailing.

For example, inside some of the larger Dick's stores is a special shop where only Nike-brand products are displayed. Part of the Nike inventory is exclusive to Dick's, which adds to the attraction for customers who prefer that brand. Selected Dick's stores contain a dedicated Under Armour shop or a dedicated North Face shop, again featuring a mix of merchandise available nationwide and some items available only at Dick's. These stores-within-a store not only differentiate Dick's from its rivals, but they also generate higher sales and profits per square foot than other areas of the store.

Not long ago, the retailer teamed up with the National Hockey League to test the sale of league- and team-branded merchandise at Dick's. The NHL operates three flagship specialty stores, and each of the 30 professional hockey teams also sells its own branded merchandise. However, the NHL decided it needed an experienced retail partner with a national presence to expand the NHL shop concept and reach more hockey fans. Now Dick's is working with the NHL to test dedicated shops within three Dick's stores. Averaging 400 square feet, each NHL store-within-a-store offers team merchandise geared to the interests and wallets of a wider range of fans. If the dedicated NHL shops do well, Dick's will open dozens more in the coming years.

Dick's also operates 82 Golf Galaxy specialty stores, catering to golf enthusiasts who appreciate the vast selection of golf-related merchandise, including clothing, shoes, and new or used equipment. Customers can take lessons from golf professionals, test clubs in an indoor driving area and a putting green, and use the interactive golf-course simulator to "play" at some of the world's best-known courses. The full-service retailer offers trade-ins, custom fitting, equipment repair, tee-time reservations, and travel arrangements for golf vacations.

In addition, Dick's is opening a series of smaller specialty stores with narrow but deep assortments for specific target markets. For instance, it operates three True Runner specialty stores stocked with footwear, apparel, and accessories for serious runners. These stores use special technology to analyze each runner's arch and gait so salespeople can make personalized suggestions for appropriate shoes. To encourage runners to drop by, True Runner stores serve as a community hub for running information and provide lockers where customers can leave their belongings while running in the area.

Dick's recently acquired the Field & Stream brand, which has been in existence for more than 140 years. Now the company has begun opening specialty stores under that name to sell equipment and accessories for fishing, camping, and hunting. By 2017, the company expects to have at least 55 Field & Stream specialty stores, coast to coast. Field & Stream stores, like True Runner stores, are smaller than Dick's Sporting Goods and—like all of Dick's stores—are staffed by employees who are knowledgeable and can help customers make informed choices.

Recognizing the potential of e-commerce and growing customer interest in mobile access to retail sites, Dick's has upgraded its website retailing technology and streamlined the process of browsing and buying via smartphone. The idea is to give customer more buying options and achieve the retailer's goal of ringing up $1 billion in online sales by 2017. Nonetheless, store retailing remains the firm's main focus, because most customers like to see sports equipment in person, seek expert advice, and try products before making a purchase. With that in mind, Dick's has invested in a fourth distribution center to be able to receive, sort, and ship merchandise for up to 750 stores. Looking even further ahead, the retailer's research indicates sufficient long-term demand and profit potential for more than 1,000 Dick's Sporting Goods stores nationwide.[41]

Questions for Discussion

1. How would you describe the store image of Dick's Sporting Goods?
2. What effect do you think the opening of NHL stores-within-stores will have on the retail positioning of Dick's Sporting Goods?
3. Would you recommend that Dick's Sporting Goods test direct selling through at-home consultants? Explain your answer.

Strategic Case 6

IKEA Makes the Most of Its Marketing Channels

The furniture and housewares retailer IKEA has a long history of using multiple marketing channels to reach customers near and far. IKEA's founder, Ingvar Kamprad, was a teenage entrepreneur when he started a mail-order business selling postcards and pencils in Sweden more than 70 years ago. Within a few years, he had expanded into reselling locally-made furniture and, in 1951, he printed the first annual IKEA furniture catalog.

© iStockphoto.com/RiverNorthPhotography

Soon, he opened the first IKEA showroom to allow customers to see and try furniture before making a purchase. By 1955, the company was designing and manufacturing many of its own products to meet customers' needs for stylish yet affordable furniture. IKEA came up with innovative designs for bookcases and other furniture items that are packed flat for shipment to stores and then assembled by buyers at home. This kept costs low and allowed the company to charge low prices.

With the opening of its first store outside Sweden in the early 1960s, IKEA was on its way to becoming a global retailing sensation. Today, 770 million people annually pass through the front doors of 345 IKEA stores in 42 countries. The printed IKEA catalog remains a vital marketing tool, with 38 versions now published in 17 languages. More than 10 million people download IKEA's catalog apps to their smartphones every year. In addition, IKEA's websites attract more than 1 billion online visitors yearly. No matter how consumers like to browse and buy, IKEA wants to accommodate their preferences.

What's in Store?

Because in-store transactions account for 95 percent of IKEA's sales, the company puts considerable emphasis on brick-and-mortar retailing. Its warehouse-sized stores carry 10,000 items for the home, from measuring cups, mirrors, and mattresses to towels, toys, and tables. Customers can get ideas and inspiration from dozens of sample rooms filled with furnishings and accessories. They can also use in-store computer kiosks, work with employees, or access software from home to design their own kitchens, see which products fit the project and the budget, and view the results in 3D before ordering anything. Staff experts are on hand to provide design advice for customers who are renovating bathrooms, reorganizing closets, or creating a home office.

IKEA complements the merchandise assortment and on-site customer service with optional, fee-based extras such as delivery and installation. The idea is to extend IKEA's reach beyond the do-it-yourselfers who don't mind lugging bulky boxes and assembling furniture to save money. And, to encourage shoppers to linger, each outlet includes a cafeteria serving traditional dishes like Swedish meatballs, local favorites like chicken wings, and specially-priced children's meals.

One of IKEA's goals is to increase sales of existing stores by enhancing the customer experience. Through extensive in-home research, the company is constantly learning more about customers' aspirations, irritations, lifestyles, and value perceptions, so its local stores can carry the right mix of products at the right prices for each market. For example, based on in-home visits to local customers, the U.K. stores changed their policy of stocking outdoor furniture only during warm months and began selling such merchandise all year long. Supported by a multimedia marketing campaign, IKEA's U.K. sales of outdoor furniture skyrocketed by 58 percent during the year following this change. The U.K. stores are also testing the sale of solar panel kits, in line with the retailer's commitment to earth-friendly renewable energy.

As IKEA blankets the globe with stores, some of its suppliers are opening facilities in nearby areas, to reduce the time and expense of getting products from factory to store. As one example, China-based Liaoyang Ningfeng Woodenware recently created a U.S. subsidiary to manufacture bedroom sets in Virginia for IKEA stores in the United States, Europe, and Asia. The company cited Virginia's abundant raw materials and its well-developed transportation infrastructure as two main reasons for choosing the state for its American division.

At Home in Asia

Although IKEA has slowed the overall pace of new-store openings in recent years, it sees tremendous growth opportunity in emerging markets such as China, where middle-class incomes are rising and consumers are seeking out foreign brands. The company is adding three stores in China every year, competing on the basis of its dual strengths in European styling and vast selection. Initially, IKEA's prices were higher than those of rival retailers, but once it increased the proportion of merchandise sourced from local suppliers, it was able to reduce costs and prices. Now IKEA rings up more than $1 billion in yearly sales through its stores in China and expects double-digit revenue growth in the future.

IKEA has done its homework, stocking products and setting up displays keyed to the specific needs of customers in each area. For instance, apartment-dwellers in the north of China often set aside part of their balconies for food storage, whereas those in the south use part of their balconies for laundry. Therefore, IKEA's in-store exhibits of balcony organizers include storage units reflecting these regional preferences. Because IKEA's China stores are so much larger than local stores and carry a wider array of merchandise, they are extremely popular shopping destinations. In fact, the Beijing store alone draws more customers on a Saturday than an IKEA store in Europe would serve in an entire week. Several couples have even chosen to be married inside one of IKEA's stores in China.

IKEA is also preparing to bring its unique brand of retailing to India, another fast-growing market with great promise. Few large-scale retailers operate in India, and IKEA's fame and novelty have already raised public awareness and anticipation. The most difficult challenge may be navigating all the regulations governing foreign business ownership and the sourcing and shipment of merchandise within India. However, IKEA has the financial strength to wait for profitability as it proceeds with a long-term plan to open 25 stores.

Apps, Social Media, and the Web

Not every customer wants to spend hours in a store, as IKEA well knows. That's why the company has introduced smartphone apps for tech-savvy customers. One app provides access to IKEA's online catalog, enabling customers to check product listings and view photos and videos of merchandise from home or office or anywhere on the go. This app also allows customers to point a smartphone at a space in a room and see how a piece of IKEA furniture such as a sofa or chair would look if placed there. Customers make more informed buying decisions when they can visualize the furniture's position within a real room—and IKEA benefits from fewer merchandise returns. In addition, customers can use an IKEA app to confirm whether an item is in stock at a particular store, to check store hours and directions, and to receive notices of special deals and events.

IKEA uses social media such as Pinterest, Twitter, and Google+ to connect with local customers in many of its markets. By engaging customers with interesting and useful content, the retailer builds brand awareness, polishes its image, and promotes selected products or categories. Its U.S. Facebook page, with more than 3.2 million likes, features product photos, store news, and links to nonprofit groups that IKEA supports, such as UNICEF. Its U.S. Twitter account, named @DesignByIKEA, posts a variety of tweets and Vine videos focusing on seasonal merchandise and solutions to common problems like storage and organization.

Although IKEA has traditionally concentrated on brick-and-mortar retailing, it is upgrading its e-commerce technology and its logistics to accommodate customers who like to browse and buy with a click. The retailer now makes 70 percent of its products available for online purchase and delivery in 13 countries. Within just a few years, all of IKEA's products will be included in its e-commerce offerings.[42]

Questions for Discussion

1. Would you recommend that IKEA continue printing and mailing catalogs or should it switch to an online-only catalog? Explain your answer.
2. If you were in charge of choosing IKEA's next U.S. store location, what factors would you consider in making your decision?
3. How much channel power does IKEA possess? What are the implications for the role it plays in the channel?
4. What are the main logistical issues IKEA must address to be able to make 100 percent of its products available for online purchase and delivery?

NOTES

[1] Renee Frojo, "Uniqlo Piles into Bay Area with Plans for Four New Stores," *San Francisco Business Times*, October 17, 2013, www.bizjournals.com/sanfrancisco/blog/2013/10/uniqlo-commences-bay-area-domination.html?page=all (accessed January 5, 2014); Kyle Stock, "Why Uniqlo Won't Open Stores in the Heartland," *Bloomberg Businessweek*, October 15, 2013, www.businessweek.com/articles/2013-10-15/why-uniqlo-wont-open-stores-in-the-heartland (accessed January 5, 2014); Corinne Lestch, "Uniqlo Kicks Off MTA's Pop-Up Shop Program with Small Shop Showcasing Winter Collection," *New York Daily News*, October 17, 2013, www.nydailynews.com/life-style/fashion/uniqlo-kicks-mta-pop-up-shop-program-article-1.1489357 (accessed January 5, 2014); Eric Wilson, "With Endorsements, Uniqlo Has a Knack for Picking Winners," *The New York Times*, May 22, 2013, www.runway.blogs.nytimes.com/2013/05/22/with-endorsements-uniqlo-has-a-knack-for-picking-winners/?_r=0 (accessed January 5, 2014).

[2] Statistics of U.S. Business, U.S. Bureau of the Census, www.census.gov/econ/susb/index.html (accessed December 15, 2013).

[3] U.S. Bureau of the Census, "Annual Retail Trade Survey," 2010, www.census.gov/retail/index.html#arts (accessed December 15, 2013).

[4] Nick Wingfield, "Tech Companies Press for a Better Retail Experience," *The New York Times*, December 15, 2013, www.nytimes.com/2013/12/16/technology/tech-companies-press-for-a-better-retail-experience.html?_r=0 (accessed December 20, 2013).

[5] Adi Narayan, "Tesco Partners with Tata to Enter Supermarket Business in India," *Bloomberg Businessweek*, December 17, 2013, www.businessweek.com/news/2013-12-17/tesco-partners-with-tata-to-enter-supermarket-business-in-india (accessed December 17, 2013).

[6] Deloitte, "Top 250 Global Retailers," STORES.org, www.stores.org/STORES%20Magazine%20January%202013/global-powers-retailing-top-250 (accessed December 16, 2013).

[7] "Our Stores," Target, http://sites.target.com/site/en/company/page.jsp?contentId=WCMP04-031761 (accessed December 17, 2013).

[8] "About Us," National Association of Convenience Stores Online, www.nacsonline.com/NACS/About_NACS/Pages/default.aspx (accessed December 16, 2013).

[9] Alastair Bair, "Amazon Gives Grocery Business a Tryout," *USA Today*, December 11, 2013, www.usatoday.com/story/tech/2013/12/11/amazon-grocery-san-francisco/3986439 (accessed December 20, 2013).

[10] "Sam's West, Inc. Company Information," Hoover's Online, www.hoovers.com/company-information/cs/company-profile.Sams_West_Inc.22cdd566c68d1f5e.html (accessed January 5, 2014); "Costco Wholesale Corporation Company Information," Hoover's Online, www.hoovers.com/company-information/cs/company-profile.Costco_Wholesale_Corporation.9acf2327527015f2.html (accessed December 16, 2013).

[11] Associated Press, "Toys 'R' Us Reports 3rd Quarter Net Loss; Hurt by Online Retailers, Discounters," *NJ.com*, December 17, 2013, www.nj.com/business/index.ssf/2013/12/toys_r_us_reports_3rd_quarter.html (accessed December 22, 2013).

[12] Storefront website, www.thestorefront.com/about (accessed December 17, 2013).

[13] Jane Hodges, "How Small Shops Economize by Sharing Space," *Entrepreneur*, June 12, 2012, www.entrepreneur.com/article/223702# (accessed December 17, 2013).

[14] Octane Coffee website, http://octanecoffee.com (accessed December 17, 2013).

[15] Mall of America website, www.mallofamerica.com (accessed December 13, 2013).

[16] International Council of Shopping Centers, "ICSC Shopping Center Definitions," http://icsc.org/srch/lib/USDefinitions.pdf (accessed December 17, 2013).

[17] Kathleen Lee Joel, "It's a Good Thing That H&M Might Soon Cost You More," *Daily Life*, December 17, 2013, www.dailylife.com.au/dl-fashion/fashion-coverage/its-a-good-thing-that-hm-might-soon-cost-you-more-20131213-2zc4u.html (accessed December 22, 2013).

[18] Rollo A. S. Grayson and Lisa S. McNeill, "Using Atmospheric Elements in Service Retailing: Understanding the Bar Environment," *Journal of Services Marketing* 23 (October 2009): 517–527.

[19] Tom Buswell, "Restaurant Colors: Triggering Appetite with the Use of Colors," *Send Me the Manager*, January 21, 2013, www.sendmethemanager.com/blog/bid/199532/Restaurant-Colors-Triggering-Appetite-With-the-Use-of-Colors (accessed December 19, 2013).

[20] Ibid.

[21] Charles Dennis, J. Brakus, and Eleftherios Alamanos, "*The Wallpaper Matters: The Influence of the Content of Digital Ads on Customer In-Store Experience,*" *Journal of Marketing Management*, 29 (no. 3/4): 338–355.

[22] Direct Marketing Association, "What Is the Direct Marketing Association?" www.the-dma.org/aboutdma/whatisthedma.shtml (accessed December 16, 2013).

[23] Do Not Call website, www.donotcall.gov (accessed December 21, 2013).

[24] Ibid.

[25] Alejandra Matos, "Washington Trying to Cure Robocall Epidemic," *Star Tribune*, December 14, 2013, www.startribune.com/local/235888131.html (accessed December 21, 2013).

[26] Press Release, "U.S. Online Retail Sales to Reach $370 Billion by 2017," Forrester, March 13, 2013, www.forrester.com/US+Online+Retail+Sales+To+Reach+370+Billion+By+2017/-/E-PRE4764 (accessed January 24, 2014).

[27] Mark Clayton, "Cyber Monday: Nine Tips for Shopping Online Safely," *Christian Science Monitor*, November 29, 2013, www.csmonitor.com/Business/2013/1129/Cyber-Monday-nine-tips-for-shopping-online-safely (accessed December 21, 2013).

[28] "DSN Global 100," *Direct Selling News*, June 1, 2013, http://directsellingnews.com/index.php/view/the_2013_dsn_global_100_list?popup=yes#.UrMoPOLF-dp (accessed December 19, 2013).

[29] Ibid.

[30] Direct Selling Association, "What Is Direct Selling?" www.directselling411.com/about-direct-selling (accessed December 19, 2013).

[31] "Vending Machines of the Past and Present," *The Wall Street Journal*, March 22, 2012, http://online.wsj.com/article/SB10001424052702304724404577295671669812582.html#slide/1 (accessed December 16, 2013); Zafar Aylin, "Prescription Pills, iPods, and Live Bait: There's a Vending Machine for That," *Time*, March 23, 2012, http://newsfeed.time.com/2012/03/23/prescription-pills-ipods-and-live-bait-theres-a-vending-machine-for-that (accessed December 16, 2013).

[32] Ann Abel, "Farmer's Fridge: A Vending Machine You Actually Should Eat From," *Well + Good*, December 16, 2013, www.wellandgoodnyc.com/2013/12/16/farmers-fridge-a-vending-machine-you-actually-should-eat-from (accessed December 21, 2013).

[33] "National Overview," Economic Impact of Franchised Businesses, International Franchise Association Education Foundation, www.buildingopportunity.com/impact/overview.aspx (accessed December 19, 2013).

[34] Ibid.

[35] "Avoiding Atlantis: Building a Franchise Restaurant That Stays Afloat," *PR Newswire*, December 5, 2013, www.prnewswire.com/news-releases/avoiding-atlantis-building-a-franchise-restaurant-that-stays-afloat-234620271.html (accessed December 22, 2013).

[36] Bureau of the Census, "Statistics of U.S. Business," 2010, www.census.gov/econ/susb (accessed December 19, 2013).

[37] "Williams Commerce Report on the Emerging Marketing Tactics Wholesalers Are Pursuing," *PR Web*, www.prweb.com/releases/2013/12/prweb11379890.htm (accessed November 29, 2013).

[38] Macdonalds Consolidated website, www.macdonaldsconsolidated.ca/main.asp (accessed December 18, 2013).

[39] AmerisourceBergen website, www.amerisourcebergen.com/abc (accessed December 19, 2013).

[40] Associated Press, "L.L.Bean Sales Grow Despite Weak Economy," *Chicago Sun-Times*, March 9, 2012, www.suntimes.com/business/11178636-420/ll-bean-sales-grow-despite-weak-economy.html (accessed January 5, 2014); Kelli B. Grant, "Walmart Lets Online Shoppers Pay Cash," *MarketWatch*, March 21, 2012, http://blogs.marketwatch.com/realtimeadvice/2012/03/21/wal-mart-lets-online-shoppers-pay-cash (accessed January 5, 2014); Michael Arndt, "Customer Service Champs: L.L.Bean Follows Its Shoppers to the Web," *Bloomberg Businessweek*, February 18, 2010, www.businessweek.com/magazine/content/10_09/b4168043788083.htm (accessed January 5, 2014); Interviews with L.L.Bean employees and the video, "L.L.Bean Employs a Variety of Promotion Methods to Communicate with Customers"; L.L.Bean website, www.llbean.com (accessed January 5, 2014).

[41] Teresa F. Lindeman, "Dick's Sporting Goods Tests In-Store NHL-Branded Shops," *Pittsburgh Post-Gazette*, December 10, 2013, www.post-gazette.com; Tim Schooley, "Exclusive: NHL Branding 'Super Shops' Within Dick's," *Pittsburgh Business Times*, December 9, 2013, www.bizjournals.com; Shannon Green, "Scoring with Dick's Sporting Goods," *Fortune*, October 28, 2013, p. 79; Mark Brohan, "Dick's Sporting Goods Is Swinging for the E-Commerce Sales Fences," *Internet Retailer*, September 25, 2013, www.internetretailer.com; www.dickssportinggoods.com.

[42] Caroline Baldwin, "IKEA Seeks to Engage Customers with Seamless Shopping Experience," *Computer Weekly*, January 7, 2014, pp. 9–10; "Chinese Furniture Maker to Open VA Plant," *Furniture Today*, December 2, 2013, p. 60; Dominic Basulto, "Big Box Solar and the Clean Energy Revolution," *Washington Post*, October 15, 2013, www.washingtonpost.com/blogs/innovations/wp/2013/10/15/big-box-solar-and-the-clean-energy-revolution (accessed January 17, 2014); "Why IKEA Encourages Chinese to Literally Make Its Stores Their Own," *Advertising Age*, December 9, 2013, p. 19; Anna Ringstrom, "One Size Doesn't Fit All: IKEA Goes Local for India, China," *Reuters*, March 7, 2013, http://in.reuters.com/article/2013/03/07/ikea-expansion-india-china-idINDEE92603L20130307 (accessed January 17, 2014); "All-Year-Round Offer Boosts IKEA Outdoor Furniture 58%," *DIY Week (UK)*, December 13, 2013, p. 5.

Feature Notes

[a] Rebecka Schumann, "72,000 Ladybugs Released Inside Mall of America on Earth Day in Place of Pesticides," *International Business Times*, April 24, 2013, www.ibtimes.com/72000-ladybugs-released-inside-mall-america-earth-day-place-pesticides-photo-1212811 (accessed January 5, 2014); Ken Belson, "Meccas of Shopping Try Hand at Being Misers of Energy," *The New York Times*, April 10, 2012, www.nytimes.com/2012/04/11/business/energy-environment/retailers-seek-to-conserve-energy-to-cut-costs.html (accessed January 5, 2014); "Green Initiatives," *Mall of America*, www.mallofamerica.com/about/future-expansion/green-initiatives (accessed January 5, 2014).

[b] Jeff Minick, "A Rural Bookstore That Beat the Odds," *Smoky Mountain News*, May 8, 2013, www.smokymountainnews.com/component/k2/item/10264-a-rural-bookstore-that-beat-the-odds (accessed January 5, 2014); Chuck Sambuchino, "Debut Author Interview: Wendy Welch, Author of the Memoir, *The Little Bookstore of Big Stone Gap,*" *Writers Digest*, March 30, 2013, www.writersdigest.com/editor-blogs/guide-to-literary-agents/debut-author-interview-wendy-welch-author-of-the-memoir-the-little-bookstore-of-big-stone-gap (accessed January 5, 2014); Wendy Welch, *The Little Bookstore of Big Stone Gap* (New York: St. Martin's Press, 2012).

part 7

Promotion Decisions

PART 7 focuses on communication with target market members and other relevant groups. A specific marketing mix cannot satisfy people in a particular target market unless they are aware of the product and know where to find it. Some promotion decisions relate to a specific marketing mix; others are geared toward promoting the entire organization. CHAPTER 16 discusses integrated marketing communications. It describes the communication process and the major promotional methods that can be included in promotion mixes. CHAPTER 17 analyzes the major steps in developing an advertising campaign. It also explains what public relations is and how it can be used. CHAPTER 18 deals with personal selling and sales promotion efforts, exploring the general characteristics of sales promotion and sales promotion techniques.

chapter 16

Integrated Marketing Communications

OBJECTIVES

16-1 Define integrated marketing communications.

16-2 Describe the steps of the communication process.

16-3 Recognize the definition and objectives of promotion.

16-4 Summarize the four elements of the promotion mix.

16-5 Explain the factors that are used to determine a product's promotion mix.

16-6 Describe how word-of-mouth communication affects promotion.

16-7 Discuss how product placement impacts promotion.

16-8 List major criticisms and defenses of promotion.

MARKETING INSIGHTS

Microsoft Makes Fun of Itself and Generates a Better Image among Consumers

The marketing landscape is changing. Increasingly, people are avoiding traditional promotions that sell to them through television commercials, Internet pop-up ads, or mobile banner ads. This is particularly true for the Millennial generation, who range between the ages of 18 and 34 years old. To reach this lucrative market, many companies are turning to content marketing as part of their integrated marketing strategies. Content marketing uses media to communicate with customers without selling to them.

Microsoft, for example, needed to communicate with the Millennial market about its Internet Explorer 9. Although the firm sent out press releases and received publicity in technological circles, it needed something more to communicate with the Millennial market. The firm partnered with Onion Labs, the satirical newspaper's marketing division, to develop a funny and engaging short video. The video depicted a young person admitting his distaste for Internet Explorer, but after advising his parents to use a different browser, he realizes he likes the new Internet Explorer 9. The video was posted on Microsoft's Tumblr page with an average of 2 views per unique user. It received more than 5,200 tweets, 14,000 Facebook likes, and 675,000 YouTube views. This virtual word-of-mouth communication has created positive buzz marketing for the firm. Although the video did not generate selective demand, it did give the company a better image that will work to its advantage in the future, especially as it enters the mobile phone market where Millennials compose the largest percentage of customers.[1]

© IVY PHOTOS/Shutterstock.com

Organizations like Microsoft employ a variety of promotional methods to communicate with their target markets. Sometimes the messages are planned in advance. Other times, they may be a response to a dramatic change in the marketing environment. Providing information to customers and other stakeholders is vital to initiating and developing long-term relationships with them.

This chapter looks at the general dimensions of promotion. First, we discuss the nature of integrated marketing communications. Next, we analyze the meaning and process of communication. We then define and examine the role of promotion and explore some of the reasons promotion is used. We consider major promotional methods and the factors that influence marketers' decisions to use particular methods. Next, we explain the positive and negative effects of personal and electronic word-of-mouth communication. Finally, we examine criticisms and benefits of promotion.

16-1 THE NATURE OF INTEGRATED MARKETING COMMUNICATIONS

Integrated marketing communications refer to the coordination of promotion and other marketing efforts to ensure maximum informational and persuasive impact on customers. Coordinating multiple marketing tools to produce this synergistic effect requires a marketer to employ a broad perspective. A major goal of integrated marketing communications is to send a consistent message to customers. Toyota embarked upon its "Elevate" integrated marketing campaign to launch the latest Corolla. It released a broadcast featuring the last five decades of the Corolla, print advertisements of the vehicle, digital videos including 6-minute Vine video tutorials to teach dance styles of the past five decades, virtual test drives on smartphones, and physical test drives. In its bid to target both Baby Boomers and Millennials, Toyota combined print, broadcast, digital, social, and experiential media into an effective integrated marketing campaign.[2]

Because various units both inside and outside most companies have traditionally planned and implemented promotional efforts, customers have not always received consistent messages. Integrated marketing communications allow an organization to coordinate and manage its promotional efforts to transmit consistent messages. Integrated marketing communications also enable synchronization of promotion elements and can improve the efficiency and effectiveness of promotion budgets. Thus, this approach fosters not only long-term customer relationships but also the efficient use of promotional resources.

The concept of integrated marketing communications is increasingly effective for several reasons. Mass media advertising, a very popular promotional method in the past, is used less frequently today because of its high cost and lower effectiveness in reaching some target markets. Marketers can now take advantage of more precisely targeted promotional tools, such as TV, direct mail, the Internet, special-interest magazines, DVDs, cell phones, mobile applications, and outdoor boards. Database marketing is also allowing marketers to more precisely target individual customers. Until recently, suppliers of marketing communications were specialists. Advertising agencies provided advertising campaigns, sales promotion companies provided sales promotion activities and materials, and public relations organizations engaged in publicity efforts. Today, a number of promotion-related companies provide one-stop shopping for the client seeking advertising, sales promotion, and public relations, thus reducing coordination problems for the sponsoring company. Because the overall cost of marketing communications has risen significantly, marketers demand systematic evaluations of communication efforts and a reasonable return on investment.

integrated marketing communications Coordination of promotion and other marketing efforts for maximum informational and persuasive impact on customers

The specific communication vehicles employed and the precision with which they are used are changing as both information technology and customer interests become increasingly dynamic. For instance, companies and politicians can hold press conferences where viewers can tweet their questions and have them answered on-screen. Some companies are creating their own branded content to exploit the many vehicles through which consumers obtain information. Thus, HARPER'S Bazaar is allowing companies to place branded content on their website. HARPER'S announced it was introducing a new editorial feature on its website featuring top fashion trends. Advertisers from outside companies can sponsor these features, securing the right to add company products to the list during their sponsorship. On Saturdays HARPER'S offers advertisers the ability to feature their products exclusively.[3]

Today, marketers and customers have almost unlimited access to data about each other. Integrating and customizing marketing communications while protecting customer privacy has become a major challenge. Through digital media, companies can provide product information and services that are coordinated with traditional promotional activities. In fact, gathering information about goods and services is one of the main reasons people go online. This has made online advertising a growing business. Spending on online advertising is expected to surpass spending on newspaper and magazine advertising in 2015.[4] College students in particular say they are influenced by Internet ads when buying online or just researching product purchases. The sharing of information and use of technology to facilitate communication between buyers and sellers are essential for successful customer relationship management.

16-2 PROMOTION AND THE COMMUNICATION PROCESS

Communication is essentially the transmission of information. For communication to take place, both the sender and receiver of information must share some common ground. They must have a common understanding of the symbols, words, and pictures used to transmit information. An individual transmitting the following message may believe he or she is communicating with you:

在工廠吾人製造化粧品,在商店吾人銷售希望。

However, communication has not taken place if you don't understand the language in which the message is written. Thus, we define **communication** as a sharing of meaning. Implicit in this definition is the notion of transmission of information because sharing necessitates transmission.

As Figure 16.1 shows, communication begins with a source. A **source** is a person, group, or organization with a meaning it attempts to share with an audience. A source could be an electronics salesperson wishing to communicate the attributes of 3D television to a buyer in

communication A sharing of meaning through the transmission of information

source A person, group, or organization with a meaning it tries to share with a receiver or an audience

Figure 16.1 **The Communication Process**

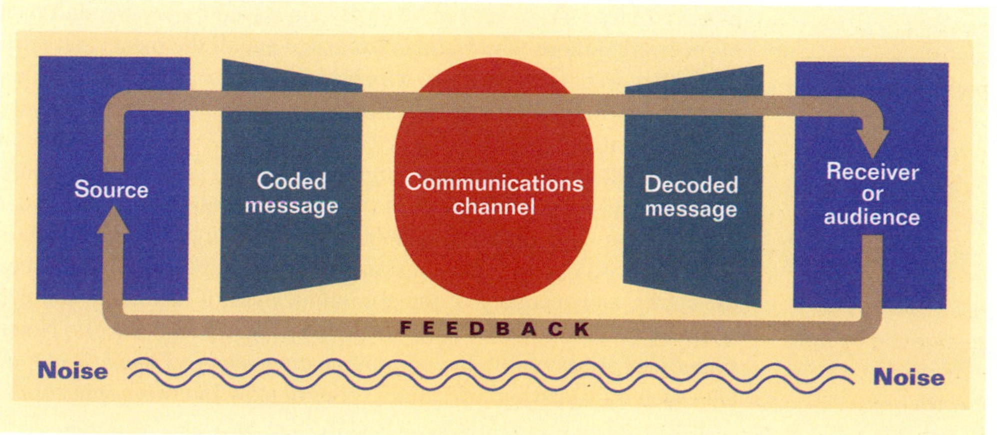

the store or a TV manufacturer using television ads to inform thousands of consumers about its products. Developing a strategy can enhance the effectiveness of the source's communication. For example, a strategy in which a salesperson attempts to influence a customer's decision by eliminating competitive products from consideration has been found to be effective. A **receiver** is the individual, group, or organization that decodes a coded message, and an *audience* is two or more receivers.

To transmit meaning, a source must convert the meaning into a series of signs or symbols representing ideas or concepts. This is called the **coding process**, or *encoding*. When coding meaning into a message, the source must consider certain characteristics of the receiver or audience. This is especially true for advertising. It is important to encode messages to prevent consumers from avoiding a conscious reception. Costs to the consumer in attention, time, and emotional response can diminish the impact of the message.[5] Therefore, signs or symbols must resonate with the receiver.

To share meaning, the source should use signs or symbols familiar to the receiver or audience. Research has shown that persuasive messages from a source are more effective when the appeal matches an individual's personality.[6] Marketers that understand this realize the importance of knowing their target market and ensuring that an advertisement or promotion uses language the target market understands and that depicts behaviors acceptable within the culture. With the Hispanic market growing rapidly, marketers are increasingly using Spanish language media in their advertisements.

When coding a meaning, a source needs to use signs or symbols that the receiver or audience uses to refer to the concepts the source intends to convey. Instead of technical jargon, explanatory language that helps consumers understand the message is more likely to result in positive attitudes and purchase intentions. Marketers try to avoid signs or symbols that may have several meanings for an audience. For instance, *soda* as a general term for soft drinks may not work well in national advertisements. Although in some parts of the United States the word means "soft drink," in other regions it may connote bicarbonate of soda, an ice cream drink, or something one mixes with alcoholic beverages.

receiver The individual, group, or organization that decodes a coded message

coding process Converting meaning into a series of signs or symbols

communications channel The medium of transmission that carries the coded message from the source to the receiver

decoding process Converting signs or symbols into concepts and ideas

noise Anything that reduces a communication's clarity and accuracy

To share a coded meaning with the receiver or audience, a source selects and uses a **communications channel**, the medium of transmission that carries the coded message from the source to the receiver or audience. Transmission media include printed words (newspapers and magazines), broadcast media (television and radio), and digital communication. Table 16.1 summarizes the leading communications channels from which people obtain information and news.

When a source chooses an inappropriate communication channel, several problems may arise. The coded message may reach some receivers, but possibly the wrong receivers. Dieters who adopt the Atkins low-carbohydrate diet, for instance, are more likely to focus on communications that relate to their food concerns, such as "Eat Meat Not Wheat" T-shirts and fast-food chain advertisements that communicate information about the carbohydrate content of menu items. An advertiser that wants to reach this group would need to take this information into account when choosing an appropriate communications channel. At the same time, however, these messages can be easily embraced by the wrong types of receivers—those who want an excuse to eat all the meats and fatty foods they want without guilt, which is not the purpose of the Atkins diet. Thus, finding the right messages that target the right receivers can be a challenging process.

Table 16.1 Sources of News Information for Americans

Television	55%
Internet	21%
Print	9%
Radio	6%
Word-of-mouth	2%

Source: Data from Gallup National Poll of 2,048 Adults, June 24, 2013.

In the **decoding process**, signs or symbols are converted into concepts and ideas. Seldom does a receiver decode exactly the same meaning the source intended. When the result of decoding differs from what was coded, noise exists. **Noise** is anything that reduces the clarity and accuracy of the communication; it has many sources and may affect any or all parts of the communication process. Noise sometimes arises within the communications channel itself. Radio or television transmission difficulties, poor or slow Internet connections, and laryngitis are sources of noise. Noise also occurs when a source uses signs or symbols that are unfamiliar to the receiver or have a meaning different from the one intended. Noise may also originate in the receiver; a receiver may be unaware of a coded message when perceptual processes block it out. Those who do not recycle, for instance, can block messages encouraging "green behaviors" such as recycling.

The receiver's response to a decoded message is **feedback** to the source. The source usually expects and normally receives feedback, although perhaps not immediately. During feedback, the receiver or audience provides the original source with a response to the message. Feedback is coded, sent through a communications channel, and decoded by the receiver, the source of the original communication. Thus, communication is a circular process, as indicated in Figure 16.1.

During face-to-face communication, such as personal selling sales promotions, verbal and nonverbal feedback can be immediate. Instant feedback lets communicators adjust messages quickly to improve the effectiveness of their communications. For example, when a salesperson realizes through feedback that a customer does not understand a sales presentation, the salesperson adapts the presentation to make it more meaningful to the customer. This is why face-to-face communication is the most adaptive and flexible, especially compared to digital, web-based, or telephone communications. In interpersonal communication, feedback occurs through talking, touching, smiling, nodding, eye movements, and other body movements and postures.

When mass communication like advertising is used, feedback is often slow and difficult to recognize. Also, it may be several months or even years before the effects of this promotion will be known. Some relevant and timely feedback can occur in the form of sales increases, inquiries about products, or changes in attitude or brand awareness levels.

Each communication channel has a limit on the volume of information it can handle effectively. This limit, called **channel capacity**, is determined by the least efficient component of the communication process. Consider communications that depend on speech. An individual source can speak only so fast, and there is a limit to how much an individual receiver can take in through listening. Beyond that point, additional messages cannot be decoded; thus, meaning cannot be shared. Although a radio announcer can read several hundred words a minute, a 1-minute advertising message should not exceed 150 words, because most announcers cannot articulate words into understandable messages at a rate beyond 150 words per minute.

feedback The receiver's response to a decoded message

channel capacity The limit on the volume of information a communication channel can handle effectively

Emerging Trends

Chevrolet Incites New Interest with an Old Idea

In an effort to cater to more target markets, Chevrolet introduced the seventh generation of the Corvette Stingray. Chevy found that the Corvette appealed to those in their 50s, making it less attractive to younger customers. Additionally, the popularity of foreign sports cars has also distracted consumers from considering the Corvette as an option. Chevy chose to bring back the Stingray model since it last made its debut in 1976. This is recent enough to incite nostalgia in the older consumer but old enough that it is new to the younger, more affluent consumer.

Due to the specific and unique nature of the new Stingray, the marketing communication for the product also has to be innovative. Chevy has been promoting the vehicle through more exclusive avenues such as auto shows and cover stories in major newspapers as well as auto magazines, which leads to demand via word-of-mouth communication. The company also created a digitalized version of the car for the Sony PlayStation game *Gran Turismo* in order to create buzz among the younger demographic. Publicity, rather than advertising, is key for a product like this because it creates excitement and interest in the market rather than just giving information about the new features of the vehicle. In 2013 Chevy sold 17,000 Corvettes, and the Stingray won Automobile of the Year honors from *Automobile* magazine.[a]

16-3 THE ROLE AND OBJECTIVES OF PROMOTION

Promotion is communication that builds and maintains favorable relationships by informing and persuading one or more audiences to view an organization positively and accept its products. Toward this end, many organizations spend considerable resources on promotion to build and enhance relationships with current and potential customers as well as other stakeholders. Case in point, Procter & Gamble spends about $4.8 billion on advertising yearly, with approximately 35 percent of its marketing budget going toward digital advertising.[7] Marketers also indirectly facilitate favorable relationships by focusing information about company activities and products on interest groups (such as environmental and consumer groups), current and potential investors, regulatory agencies, and society in general. For instance, some organizations promote responsible use of products criticized by society, such as tobacco, alcohol, and violent movies or video games. Companies sometimes promote programs that help selected groups. For example, Safeway's 10% Back to School Program allows customers to contribute toward education during a certain period of the year. Safeway donates 10 percent of the sales price of participating items to the customer's chosen school.[8] Such cause-related marketing links the purchase of products to philanthropic efforts for one or more causes. By contributing to causes that its target markets support, cause-related marketing can help marketers boost sales, increase loyalty, and generate goodwill.

For maximum benefit from promotional efforts, marketers strive for proper planning, implementation, coordination, and control of communications. Effective management of integrated marketing communications is based on information about and feedback from customers and the marketing environment, often obtained from an organization's marketing information system (see Figure 16.2). How successfully marketers use promotion to maintain positive relationships depends to some extent on the quantity and quality of information the organization receives. Because customers derive information and opinions from many different sources, integrated marketing communications planning also takes into account informal methods of communication, such as word of mouth and independent information sources on the Internet. Because promotion is communication that can be managed, we now analyze what this communication is and how it works.

Promotional objectives vary considerably from one organization to another and within organizations over time. Large firms with multiple promotional programs operating simultaneously may have quite varied promotional objectives. For the purpose of analysis, we focus on the eight promotional objectives shown in Table 16.2. Although the list is not exhaustive, one or more of these objectives underlie many promotional programs.

promotion Communication to build and maintain relationships by informing and persuading one or more audiences

Figure 16.2 Information Flows Are Important in Integrated Marketing Communications

Table 16.2 Possible Objectives of Promotion

Create awareness	Retain loyal customers
Stimulate demand	Facilitate reseller support
Encourage product trial	Combat competitive promotional efforts
Identify prospects	Reduce sales fluctuations

16-3a Create Awareness

A considerable amount of promotion efforts focus on creating awareness. For an organization that is introducing a new product or a line extension, making customers aware of the product is crucial to initiating the product adoption process. A marketer that has invested heavily in product development strives to create product awareness quickly to generate revenues to offset the high costs of product development and introduction. Apple often begins to build awareness about new products months before it releases them. It holds an annual developer conference, where CEO Tim Cook often discusses the features of products that will be released later in the year.[9] The M&M'S® Milk Chocolate with peanut butter advertisement creates awareness with its colorful graphic of a giant M&M with peanut butter hair.

primary demand Demand for a product category rather than for a specific brand

pioneer promotion Promotion that informs consumers about a new product

Creating awareness is important for existing products, too. Promotional efforts may aim to increase awareness of brands, product features, image-related issues (such as organizational size or socially responsive behavior), or operational characteristics (such as store hours, locations, and credit availability). Some promotional programs are unsuccessful because marketers fail to generate awareness of critical issues among a significant portion of target market members. Other times, the campaign itself is at fault. A Hyundai commercial that went viral, for instance, was intended to represent the clean emissions of the iX35 Crossover. However, the video was a disaster. The commercial titled "Pipe Job" showed a man failing to kill himself with carbon monoxide poisoning because the car's emissions are so clean. No doubt intending to be edgy, the advertisement was criticized as tasteless and potentially harmful to the serious issue of suicide. Hyundai apologized and stated that its European affiliate advertising agency created the advertisement without Hyundai's request or approval.[10]

Creating Awareness
M&M'S® seeks to create awareness and demand for its peanut butter candy.

16-3b Stimulate Demand

When an organization is the first to introduce an innovative product, it tries to stimulate **primary demand**—demand for a product category rather than for a specific brand of product—through **pioneer promotion**. Pioneer promotion informs potential customers about the product: what it is, what it does, how it can be used, and where it can be purchased. Because pioneer promotion is used in the introductory stage of the product life cycle, meaning there are no competing brands, it neither emphasizes brand names nor compares brands. When Samsung introduced its Galaxy Gear smartwatch, it needed to educate consumers about the benefits of the smartwatch. Initial enthusiasm for the smartwatch was not great, however, because the batteries are not strong enough to perform all the data applications a consumer might wish. Additionally, because the watch is a fashion item, Samsung must work to make the watch fashionable as well as functional. As Samsung improves its products with newer iterations of its Galaxy Gear, it will need to inform consumers about these improvements and what benefits a smartwatch can provide.[11]

© Naked Juice Company

Building Selective Demand
This advertisement builds selective demand by focusing on a specific product—Naked Juice.

To build **selective demand**, demand for a specific brand, a marketer employs promotional efforts that point out the strengths and benefits of a specific brand. Consider the advertisement for Naked Juice. The advertisement shows a bottle of Naked Juice on a scale with kiwi, pineapple, broccoli, and other fruits and vegetables. It emphasizes that consumers can receive one pound of fruit by drinking Naked Juice. Because the advertisement portrays a specific brand, it builds selective demand for the product. Building selective demand also requires singling out attributes important to potential buyers. Selective demand can be stimulated by differentiating the product from competing brands in the minds of potential buyers. Selective demand can also be stimulated by increasing the number of product uses and promoting them through advertising campaigns, as well as through price discounts, free samples, coupons, consumer contests and games, and sweepstakes. For instance, Ace Hardware offers promotions whereby consumers can receive 20 percent off everything that fits into a bag. Such a promotion supports selective demand for Ace Hardware. Promotions for large package sizes or multiple-product packages are directed at increasing consumption, which in turn can stimulate demand. In addition, selective demand can be stimulated by encouraging existing customers to use more of the product.

16-3c Encourage Product Trial

When attempting to move customers through the product adoption process, a marketer may successfully create awareness and interest, but customers may stall during the evaluation stage. In this case, certain types of promotion—such as free samples, coupons, test drives, or limited free-use offers, contests, and games—are employed to encourage product trial. For instance, Starbucks offered free samples of its new Ethiopian coffee among participating Starbucks stores during National Coffee Day and also provided a commemorative Ethiopian tasting cup for each one pound of Ethiopian coffee purchased.[12] Whether a marketer's product is the first in a new product category, a new brand in an existing category, or simply an existing brand seeking customers, trial-inducing promotional efforts aim to make product trial convenient and low risk for potential customers.

16-3d Identify Prospects

Certain types of promotional efforts aim to identify customers who are interested in the firm's product and are likely potential buyers. A marketer may run a television advertisement encouraging the viewer to visit the company's website and share personal information in order to receive something of value from the company. Customers who respond to such a message usually have higher interest in the product, which makes them likely sales

selective demand Demand for a specific brand

prospects. The organization can respond with phone calls, e-mail, or personal contact by salespeople.

16-3e Retain Loyal Customers

Clearly, maintaining long-term customer relationships is a major goal of most marketers. Such relationships are quite valuable. Promotional efforts directed at customer retention can help an organization control its costs, because the costs of retaining customers are usually considerably lower than those of acquiring new ones. Frequent-user programs, such as those sponsored by airlines, car rental agencies, and hotels, aim to reward loyal customers and encourage them to remain loyal. The casual restaurant chain Which Wich® has a customer loyalty program called the Vibe Club that rewards members with discounts and special savings.[13] Some organizations employ special offers that only their existing customers can use. To retain loyal customers, marketers not only advertise loyalty programs but also use reinforcement advertising, which assures current users they have made the right brand choice and tells them how to get the most satisfaction from the product.

16-3f Facilitate Reseller Support

Reseller support is a two-way street: producers generally want to provide support to resellers to assist in selling their products, and in turn they expect resellers to support their products. When a manufacturer advertises a product to consumers, resellers should view this promotion as a form of strong manufacturer support. In some instances, a producer agrees to pay a certain proportion of retailers' advertising expenses for promoting its products. When a manufacturer is introducing a new consumer brand in a highly competitive product category, it may be difficult to persuade supermarket managers to carry this brand. However, if the manufacturer promotes the new brand with free samples and coupon distribution in the retailer's area, a supermarket manager views these actions as strong support and is much more likely to carry the product. To encourage wholesalers and retailers to increase their inventories of its products, a manufacturer may provide them with special offers and buying allowances. In certain industries, a producer's salesperson may provide support to a wholesaler by working with the wholesaler's customers (retailers) in the presentation and promotion of the products. Strong relationships with resellers are important to a firm's ability to maintain a sustainable competitive advantage. The use of various promotional methods can help an organization achieve this goal.

16-3g Combat Competitive Promotional Efforts

At times, a marketer's objective in using promotion is to offset or lessen the effect of a competitor's promotional or marketing programs. This type of promotional activity does not necessarily increase the organization's sales or market share, but it may prevent a sales or market share loss. A combative promotional objective is used most often by firms in extremely competitive consumer markets, such as the fast food, convenience store, and cable/Internet/phone markets. Walmart took a combative promotional approach when it embarked on a campaign stating that it had better prices than rival companies, including Best Buy and Toys "R" Us. Competitors objected to Walmart's claims and stated that the information used was not accurate.[14] It is not unusual for competitors to respond with a counter-pricing strategy or even match a competitor's pricing.

16-3h Reduce Sales Fluctuations

Demand for many products varies from one month to another because of such factors as climate, holidays, and seasons. A business, however, cannot operate at peak efficiency when sales fluctuate rapidly. Changes in sales volume translate into changes in production,

Seasonal Demand
Winter sports gear is subject to seasonal demand, with demand peaking in the winter and bottoming out in the spring and summer. To balance demand, marketers might use promotion such as coupons or advertisements that encourage consumers to purchase these products during off-peak periods.

inventory levels, personnel needs, and financial resources. When promotional techniques reduce fluctuations by generating sales during slow periods, a firm can use its resources more efficiently.

Promotional techniques are often designed to stimulate sales during sales slumps. Hence, Snapper may offer sales prices on lawn mowers into the fall season to extend the selling season. During peak periods, a marketer may refrain from advertising to prevent stimulating sales to the point at which the firm cannot handle all of the demand. On occasion, a company advertises that customers can be better served by coming in on certain days. An Italian restaurant, for example, might distribute coupons that are valid only Monday through Wednesday because on Thursday through Sunday the restaurant is extremely busy.

To achieve the major objectives of promotion discussed here, companies must develop appropriate promotional programs. In the next section, we consider the basic components of such programs: the promotion mix elements.

16-4 THE PROMOTION MIX

Several promotional methods can be used to communicate with individuals, groups, and organizations. When an organization combines specific methods to manage the integrated marketing communications for a particular product, that combination constitutes the promotion mix for that product. The four possible elements of a **promotion mix** are advertising, personal selling, public relations, and sales promotion (see Figure 16.3). For some products, firms use all four elements; for others, they use only two or three. In this section, we provide an overview of each promotion mix element; they are covered in greater detail in the next two chapters.

16-4a Advertising

promotion mix A combination of promotional methods used to promote a specific product

Advertising is a paid nonpersonal communication about an organization and its products transmitted to a target audience through mass media, including television, radio, the Internet, newspapers, magazines, video games, direct mail, outdoor displays, and signs on mass transit vehicles. Advertising is changing as consumers' mass media consumption habits are

Figure 16.3 **The Four Possible Elements of a Promotion Mix**

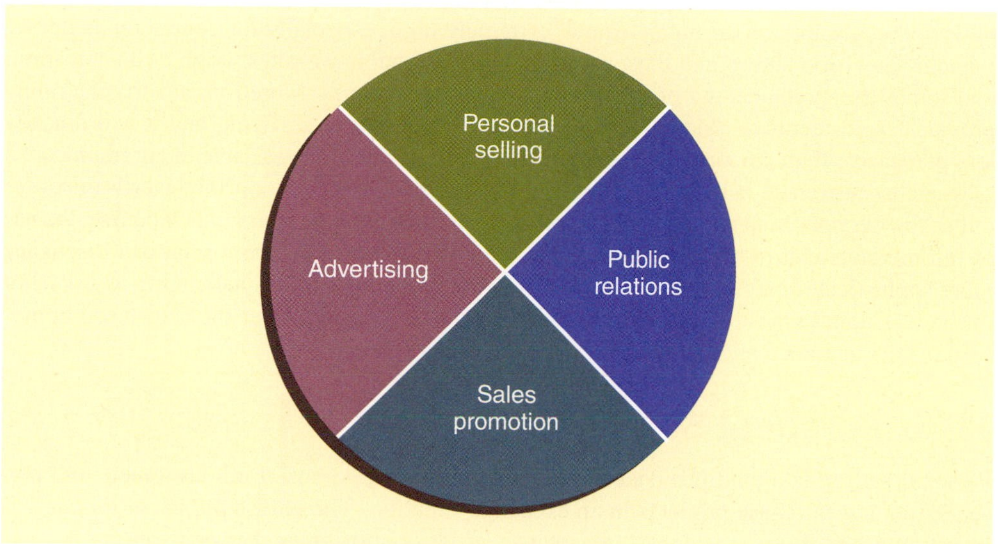

changing. Companies are striving to maximize their presence and impact through digital media; ads are being designed that cater to smaller, more personalized audiences; and traditional media like newspapers are in a decline due to a drop in readership. Individuals and organizations use advertising to promote goods, services, ideas, issues, and people. Being highly flexible, advertising can reach an extremely large target audience or focus on a small, precisely defined segment. For instance, Quizno's advertising focuses on a large audience of potential fast-food customers, ranging from children to adults, whereas advertising for Gulfstream jets aims at a much smaller and more specialized target market.

Advertising offers several benefits. It is extremely cost-efficient when it reaches a vast number of people at a low cost per person. For example, the cost of a 4-color, full-page advertisement in the national edition of Fortune magazine costs $154,400. With a circulation of 830,000, this makes the cost of reaching roughly a thousand subscribers $186.[15] Advertising also lets the source repeat the message several times. Subway credits its promotional and advertising success to a catchy theme and heavy repetition of its "$5.00 footlong" sub sandwich campaign. Furthermore, advertising a product a certain way can add to the product's value, and the visibility an organization gains from advertising can enhance its image. For instance, incorporating touchable elements that generate positive sensory feedback in print advertising can be a positive persuasive tool.[16] At times, a firm tries to enhance its own or its product's image by including celebrity endorsers in advertisements. TAG Heuer and actor Leonardo DiCaprio have teamed together to contribute toward the nonprofit Natural Resources Defense Council. Sales of TAG Heuer Aquaracer 500M Leonardo DiCaprio Limited Edition watches will go toward supporting the environmental advocacy group. By partnering with Leonardo DiCaprio, TAG

© Tag Heuer

Celebrity Endorsers
TAG Heuer and Leonardo DiCaprio have partnered together to support the Natural Resources Defense Council through the sale of limited-edition products.

Heuer not only makes a positive contribution to the environment but also gets the chance to capitalize on DiCaprio's status as a celebrity.

Advertising has disadvantages as well. Even though the cost per person reached may be low, the absolute dollar outlay can be extremely high, especially for commercials during popular television shows and those associated with popular websites. High costs can limit, and sometimes preclude, use of advertising in a promotion mix. Moreover, advertising rarely provides rapid feedback. Measuring its effect on sales is often difficult, and it is ordinarily less persuasive than personal selling. In most instances, the time available to communicate a message to customers is limited to seconds, because people look at a print advertisement for only a few seconds, and most broadcast commercials are 30 seconds or less. Of course, the use of infomercials can increase exposure time for viewers; however, the format can disengage more sophisticated buyers. Finally, using celebrity endorsers can be challenging as well. For instance, Capital One was criticized for retaining Alec Baldwin after the actor used homosexual slurs against a photographer.[17]

16-4b Personal Selling

Personal selling is a paid personal communication that seeks to inform customers and persuade them to purchase products in an exchange situation. The phrase *purchase products* is interpreted broadly to encompass acceptance of ideas and issues. Personal selling is most extensively used in the business-to-business market and also in the business-to-consumer market for high-end products such as homes, cars, electronics, and furniture.

Personal selling has both advantages and limitations when compared with advertising. Advertising is general communication aimed at a relatively large target audience, whereas personal selling involves more specific communication directed at one or several individuals. Reaching one person through personal selling costs considerably more than through advertising, but personal selling efforts often have greater impact on customers. Personal selling also provides immediate feedback, allowing marketers to adjust their messages to improve communication. Such interaction helps them determine and respond to customers' information needs.

When a salesperson and a customer meet face-to-face, they use several types of interpersonal communication. The predominant communication form is language, both

© iStockphoto.com/biffspandex

Personal Selling
Although expensive, personal selling is especially useful in high-risk business-to-business transactions requiring a large amount of investment.

spoken and written. A salesperson and customer frequently use **kinesic communication**, or communication through the movement of head, eyes, arms, hands, legs, or torso. Winking, head nodding, hand gestures, and arm motions are forms of kinesic communication. A good salesperson can often evaluate a prospect's interest in a product or presentation by noting eye contact and head nodding. **Proxemic communication**, a less obvious form of communication used in personal selling situations, occurs when either person varies the physical distance separating them. When a customer backs away from a salesperson, for example, he or she may be displaying a lack of interest in the product or expressing dislike for the salesperson. Touching, or **tactile communication**, is also a form of communication, although less popular in the United States than in many other countries. Handshaking is a common form of tactile communication both in the United States and elsewhere.

16-4c Public Relations

Although many promotional activities focus on a firm's customers, other stakeholders—suppliers, employees, stockholders, the media, educators, potential investors, government officials, and society in general—are important to an organization as well. To communicate with customers and stakeholders, a company employs public relations. Public relations is a broad set of communication efforts used to create and maintain favorable relationships between an organization and its stakeholders. Maintaining a positive relationship with one or more stakeholders can affect a firm's current sales and profits, as well as its long-term survival.

Public relations uses a variety of tools, including annual reports, brochures, event sponsorship, and sponsorship of socially responsible programs aimed at protecting the environment or helping disadvantaged individuals. The goal of public relations is to create and enhance a positive image of the organization. Increasingly, marketers are going directly to consumers with their public relations efforts to bypass the traditional media intermediary (newspapers, magazines, and television). Pampered Chef placed content on YouTube that shows consumers how to make certain recipes. This content familiarizes consumers with Pampered Chef and positions the organization as a helper in the kitchen.[18]

Other tools arise from the use of publicity, which is a component of public relations. Publicity is nonpersonal communication in news-story form about an organization or its products, or both, transmitted through a mass medium at no charge. A few examples of publicity-based public relations tools are news releases, press conferences, and feature articles. To generate publicity, companies sometimes give away products to celebrities in the hope that the celebrities will be seen and photographed with the product, and those photos will stimulate awareness and product trial among their fans. Jaguar Land Rover has provided vehicles for the Royal Family of England for 60 years, and Ford Italia has consistently been providing the Vatican with Ford vehicles. The companies receive publicity when the public sees these important figures driving their vehicles.[19] Ordinarily, public relations efforts are planned and implemented to be consistent with and support other elements of the promotion mix. Public relations efforts may be the responsibility of an individual or of a department within the organization, or the organization may hire an independent public relations agency.

Unpleasant situations and negative events, such as product tampering or an environmental disaster, may generate unfavorable public relations for an organization. For instance, Abercrombie & Fitch faced a public relations nightmare after previous comments from its CEO surfaced indicating that the company did not make clothes for heavier, older, or uncool people. This caused a considerable backlash for consumers offended by the CEO's comments.[20] To minimize the damaging effects of unfavorable coverage, effective marketers have policies and procedures in place to help manage any public relations problems.

Public relations should not be viewed as a set of tools to be used only during crises. To get the most from public relations, an organization should have someone responsible for public relations either internally or externally and should have an ongoing public relations program.

kinesic communication Communicating through the movement of head, eyes, arms, hands, legs, or torso

proxemic communication Communicating by varying the physical distance in face-to-face interactions

tactile communication Communicating through touching

Coupons as Sales Promotion
Johnsonville uses coupons to encourage consumer purchases of its sausage.

16-4d Sales Promotion

Sales promotion is an activity or material that acts as a direct inducement, offering added value or incentive for the product to resellers, salespeople, or consumers. Examples include free samples, games, rebates, sweepstakes, contests, premiums, and coupons. *Sales promotion* should not be confused with *promotion*; sales promotion is just one part of the comprehensive area of promotion. Marketers spend more on sales promotion than on advertising, and sales promotion appears to be a faster-growing area than advertising. Coupons are especially important, particularly for brands such as Johnsonville sausage. Johnsonville encourages consumers to purchase its products by releasing advertisements and dollar-off coupons for its chicken sausage. This is an example of a coupon released by a manufacturer rather than a retail establishment.

Generally, when companies employ advertising or personal selling, they depend on these activities continuously or cyclically. However, a marketer's use of sales promotion tends to be irregular. Many products are seasonal. Toys may be discounted in January after the holiday selling season to move excess inventory. Marketers frequently rely on sales promotion to improve the effectiveness of other promotion mix elements, especially advertising and personal selling. Coupons are still a popular form of sales promotion, although their use seems to be declining. The redemption of digital coupons, however, is growing.[21] Mobile devices are a personal technology, so mobile coupons pose an unusual opportunity to reach consumers wherever they go.

An effective promotion mix requires the right combination of components. To see how such a mix is created, we now examine the factors and conditions affecting the selection of promotional methods that an organization uses for a particular product.

16-5 SELECTING PROMOTION MIX FACTORS

Marketers vary the composition of promotion mixes for many reasons. Although a promotion mix can include all four elements, frequently, a marketer selects fewer than four. Many firms that market multiple product lines use several promotion mixes simultaneously.

16-5a Promotional Resources, Objectives, and Policies

The size of an organization's promotional budget affects the number and relative intensity of promotional methods included in a promotion mix. If a company's promotional budget is extremely limited, the firm is likely to rely on personal selling because it is easier to measure a salesperson's contribution to sales than to measure the sales effectiveness of advertising. Businesses must have sizable promotional budgets to use regional or national advertising. Companies like Procter & Gamble, Unilever, General Motors, and Coca-Cola are among the leaders in worldwide media spending. Organizations with extensive promotional resources generally include more elements in their promotion mixes but having more promotional dollars to spend does not necessarily mean using more promotional methods. Researchers have found that resources spent on promotion activities have a positive influence on shareholder value.

An organization's promotional objectives and policies also influence the types of promotion selected. If a company's objective is to create mass awareness of a new convenience good, such as a breakfast cereal, its promotion mix probably leans heavily toward advertising, sales promotion, and possibly public relations. If a company hopes to educate consumers about the features of a durable good, such as a home appliance, its promotion mix may combine a moderate amount of advertising, possibly some sales promotion designed to attract customers to retail stores, and a great deal of personal selling, because this method is an efficient way to inform customers about such products. If a firm's objective is to produce immediate sales of nondurable services, the promotion mix will probably stress advertising and sales promotion. For instance, dry cleaners and carpet-cleaning firms are more likely to use advertising with a coupon or discount rather than personal selling.

16-5b Characteristics of the Target Market

Size, geographic distribution, and demographic characteristics of an organization's target market help dictate the methods to include in a product's promotion mix. To some degree, market size and diversity determine composition of the mix. If the size is limited, the promotion mix will probably emphasize personal selling, which can be very effective for reaching small numbers of people. Organizations selling to industrial markets and firms marketing products through only a few wholesalers frequently make personal selling the major component of their promotion mixes. When a product's market consists of millions of customers, organizations rely on advertising and sales promotion, because these methods reach masses of people at a low cost per person. When the population density is uneven around the country, marketers may utilize regional advertising and target larger markets.

Geographic distribution of a firm's customers also affects the choice of promotional methods. Personal selling is more feasible if a company's customers are concentrated in a small area than if they are dispersed across a vast region. When the company's customers are numerous and dispersed, regional or national advertising may be more practical.

Distribution of a target market's demographic characteristics, such as age, income, or education, may affect the types of promotional techniques a marketer selects, as well as the messages and images employed. According to the U.S. Census Bureau, so-called traditional families—those composed of married couples with children—account for fewer than one-quarter of all U.S. households.[22] To reach the more than three-quarters of households consisting of single parents, unmarried couples, singles, and "empty nesters" (whose children have left home), more companies are modifying the images used in their promotions.

16-5c Characteristics of the Product

Generally, promotion mixes for business products concentrate on personal selling, whereas advertising plays a major role in promoting consumer goods. This generalization should be treated cautiously, however. Marketers of business products use some advertising to promote products. Advertisements for computers, road-building equipment, and aircraft are fairly common, and some sales promotion is also used occasionally to promote business products. Personal selling is used extensively for consumer durables, such as home appliances, automobiles, and houses, whereas consumer convenience items are promoted mainly through advertising and sales promotion. Public relations appears in promotion mixes for both business and consumer products.

Marketers of highly seasonal products often emphasize advertising—and sometimes sales promotion as well—because off-season sales generally will not support an extensive

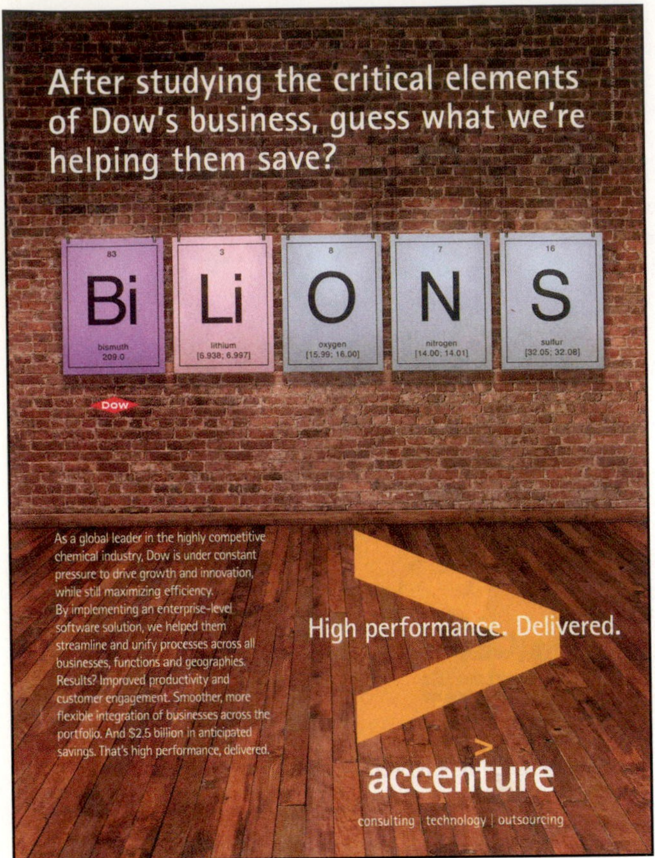

Portraying Characteristics of Service Products
Service products, such as Accenture's consulting, technology, and outsourcing services, are often portrayed using tangible goods that tell a story about the service. In this advertisement, Accenture uses elements of the periodic table to spell out how much money it helped Dow Chemical save.

year-round sales force. Although most toy producers have sales forces to sell to resellers, many of these companies depend chiefly on advertising and strong distribution channels to promote their products.

A product's price also influences the composition of the promotion mix. High-priced products call for personal selling, because consumers associate greater risk with the purchase of such products and usually want information from a salesperson. For low-priced convenience items, marketers use advertising rather than personal selling. Research suggests that consumers visiting a store specifically to purchase a product on sale are more likely to have read flyers and purchased other sale-priced products than consumers visiting the same store for other reasons.[23]

Another consideration in creating an effective promotion mix is the stage of the product life cycle. During the introduction stage, advertising is used to create awareness for both business and consumer products. Sony released commercials for its PlayStation 4 promoting features that appeal to gamers. While Microsoft marketed its Xbox 1 as a mass-market product, Sony's initial advertising focused on gamers who wish to achieve gaming "greatness."[24] For many products, personal selling and sales promotion are also helpful in this stage. In the growth and maturity stages, consumer products require heavy emphasis on advertising, whereas business products often call for a concentration of personal selling and some sales promotion. In the decline stage, marketers usually decrease all promotional activities, especially advertising.

Intensity of market coverage is still another factor affecting the composition of the promotion mix. When products are marketed through intensive distribution, firms depend strongly on advertising and sales promotion. Many convenience products like lotions, cereals, and coffee are promoted through samples, coupons, and refunds. When marketers choose selective distribution, promotion mixes vary considerably. Items handled through exclusive distribution—such as expensive watches, furs, and high-quality furniture—typically require a significant amount of personal selling.

A product's use also affects the combination of promotional methods. Manufacturers of highly personal products, such as laxatives, nonprescription contraceptives, and feminine hygiene products, depend on advertising because many customers do not want to talk with salespeople about these products. Service businesses often use tangible products to promote their intangible services. Accenture is a consulting, technology, and outsourcing firm that helps businesses develop innovative solutions. In this advertisement Accenture describes how it helped Dow Chemical save money through software solutions. Accenture plays on the fact that Dow is a chemical company, using elements from the periodic table to spell out the billions of dollars it has helped Dow save.

16-5d Costs and Availability of Promotional Methods

Costs of promotional methods are major factors to analyze when developing a promotion mix. National advertising and sales promotion require large expenditures. However, if these efforts succeed in reaching extremely large audiences, the cost per individual reached may be quite small, possibly a few pennies. Some forms of advertising are relatively inexpensive. Many small, local businesses advertise products through local newspapers, magazines, radio and television stations, outdoor displays, Internet ads, and signs on mass transit vehicles.

Another consideration that marketers explore when formulating a promotion mix is availability of promotional techniques. Despite the tremendous number of media vehicles in the United States, a firm may find that no available advertising medium effectively reaches a certain target market. The problem of media availability becomes more pronounced when marketers advertise in foreign countries. Some media, such as television, simply may not be available, or advertising on television may be illegal. For instance, the advertising of cigarettes on television is banned in many countries. In addition, regulations or standards for media content may be restrictive in varying global outlets. In some countries, advertisers are forbidden to make brand comparisons on television. Other promotional methods also have limitations. Thus, a firm may wish to increase its sales force but be unable to find qualified personnel.

16-5e Push and Pull Channel Policies

Another element that marketers consider when planning a promotion mix is whether to use a push policy or a pull policy. With a **push policy**, the producer promotes the product only to the next institution down the marketing channel. In a marketing channel with wholesalers and retailers, the producer promotes to the wholesaler because, in this case, the wholesaler is the channel member just below the producer (see Figure 16.4). Each channel member in turn promotes to the next channel member. A push policy normally stresses personal selling. Sometimes sales promotion and advertising are used in conjunction with personal selling to push the products down through the channel.

As Figure 16.4 shows, a firm that uses a **pull policy** promotes directly to consumers to develop strong consumer demand for its products. It does so primarily through advertising and sales promotion. Because consumers are persuaded to seek the products in retail stores, retailers in turn go to wholesalers or the producers to buy the products. This policy is intended to pull the goods down through the channel by creating demand at the consumer level. Consumers are told that if the stores don't have it, then they should request that the stores begin carrying the product. Push and pull policies are not mutually exclusive. At times, an organization uses both simultaneously.

push policy Promoting a product only to the next institution down the marketing channel

pull policy Promoting a product directly to consumers to develop strong consumer demand that pulls products through the marketing channel

Figure 16.4 Comparison of Push and Pull Promotional Strategies

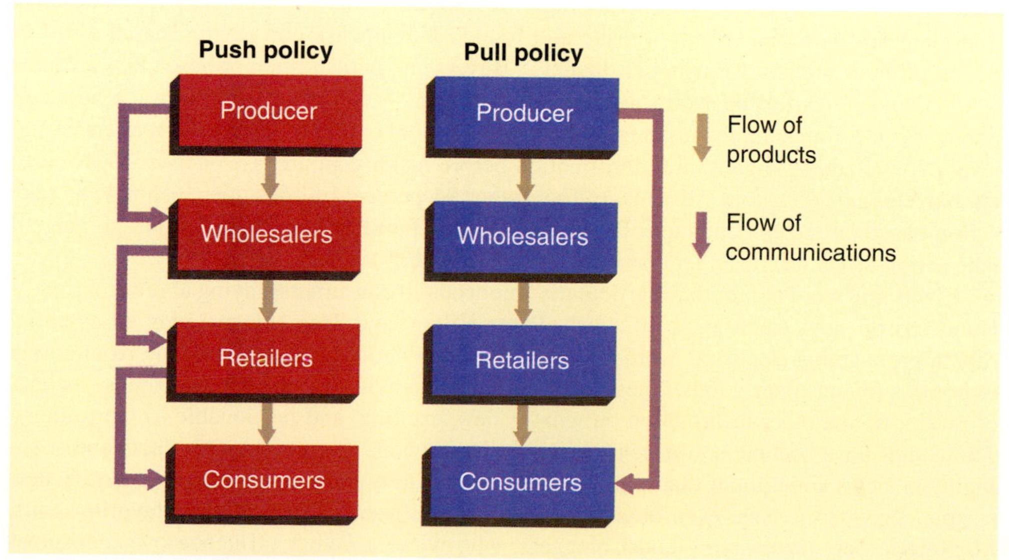

16-6 THE IMPACT OF WORD-OF-MOUTH COMMUNICATIONS ON PROMOTION

When making decisions about the composition of promotion mixes, marketers should recognize that commercial messages, whether from advertising, personal selling, sales promotion, or public relations, are limited in the extent to which they can inform and persuade customers and move them closer to making purchases. Depending on the type of customers and the products involved, buyers to some extent rely on word-of-mouth communication from personal sources, such as family members and friends. **Word-of-mouth communication** is personal, informal exchanges of communication that customers share with one another about products, brands, and companies. Most customers are likely to be influenced by friends and family members when they make purchases. Word-of-mouth communication is very important when people are selecting restaurants and entertainment along with automotive, medical, legal, banking, and personal services like hair care. A study revealed that Kia, Hyundai, and Honda received the best word-of-mouth marketing in the vehicle category in the United States, with the Apple iPhone and Trader Joe's topping the smartphone and grocery categories.[25] Research has identified a link between word-of-mouth communication and new-customer acquisition when there is customer involvement and satisfaction.[26] For this reason, organizations should proactively manage their word-of-mouth communications.[27]

Effective marketers who understand the importance of word-of-mouth communication attempt to identify opinion leaders and encourage them to try their products in the hope that they will spread favorable publicity about them. Apple, for example, has long relied on its nearly cult consumer following to spread by word of mouth their satisfaction with Apple products such as MacBooks, iPods, iPhones, and iPads. The impact of consumer-generated communication—communication not made by companies—is powerful and stands strong compared to commercial messages.[28] Firms need to develop proactive management of word-of-mouth communication that considers both the sender and the receiver.[29]

In addition, customers are increasingly going online for information and opinions about goods and services as well as about the companies. Electronic word of mouth is communicating about products through websites, blogs, e-mail, social networks, or online forums. Users can go to a number of consumer-oriented websites, such as epinions.com and consumerreview.com. At these sites, they can learn about other consumers' feelings toward and experiences with specific products; some sites even encourage consumers to rate products they have tried. Users can also search within product categories and compare consumers' viewpoints on various brands and models. Not surprisingly, research has identified credibility as the most important attribute of a ratings website and found reducing risk and saving search effort to be the primary motives for using such sites.[30] Buyers can peruse Internet-based newsgroups, forums, and blogs to find word-of-mouth information. A consumer looking for a new cell phone service, for example, might inquire in forums about other participants' experiences and level of satisfaction to gain more information before making a purchase decision. A Nielsen Global Survey of Trust in Advertising found that 84 percent of consumer respondents take action based on recommendations they get from their families and friends, while 70 percent take action based on consumer comments posted online.[31]

Electronic word of mouth is particularly important to consumers staying abreast of trends. Hundreds of blogs (such as TechCrunch, Perez Hilton, and Tree Hugger) play an essential role in propagating electronic word-of-mouth communications about everything from gossip to politics to consumer goods. They provide consumers with information on trends, reviews of products, and other information on what is new, exciting, and fashionable for consumers. These sites have become so influential in introducing consumers to new products and shaping their views about them that marketers are increasingly monitoring them to identify new trends; some firms have even attempted to influence users' votes on their favorite items. Marketers must increasingly court bloggers, who wield growing influence over consumer perception of companies, goods, and services.

word-of-mouth communication Personal informal exchanges of communication that customers share with one another about products, brands, and companies

© iStockphoto.com/Arda Guldogan

Electronic Word of Mouth
Consumers tend to trust Internet reviews posted by other consumers, making sites such as Yelp an important tool for investigating new products or businesses.

buzz marketing An attempt to incite publicity and public excitement surrounding a product through a creative event

viral marketing A strategy to get consumers to share a marketer's message, often through e-mail or online videos, in a way that spreads dramatically and quickly

Buzz marketing is an attempt to incite publicity and public excitement surrounding a product through a creative event. Huawai Technologies, for instance, tried to build up buzz for its new smartphone by unveiling its product at the London Roundhouse. The London Roundhouse is a preforming arts center that has hosted past celebrities such as Led Zeppelin. Huawai felt the venue would add to the excitement of the launch. It also developed a YouTube teaser of its new smartphone product to pique consumers' interests.[32]

Buzz marketing works best as a part of an integrated marketing communication program that also uses advertising, personal selling, sales promotion, and publicity. However, marketers should also take care that buzz marketing campaigns do not violate any laws or have the potential to be misconstrued and cause undue alarm. Event marketing is highly influential in gaining the attention of consumers. Consider the buzz created by Red Bull after it sponsored daredevil Felix Baumgartner's jump from 23 miles above the Earth's surface. The jump broke sound barriers and caught the attention of much of the world. In the 6 months following the campaign, sales of Red Bull products rose 7 percent in the United State.[33] Event attendance has a positive effect on brand equity.[34]

Viral marketing is a strategy to get consumers to share a marketer's message, often through e-mail or online video, in a way that spreads dramatically and quickly. At the 2013 Super Bowl, when the lights went out during a temporary power outage, a digital media team took the opportunity to encourage viral marketing for the Oreo brand. The team quickly sent out the tweet "You can still dunk in the dark" to take advantage of the power outage. The tweet was so popular it generated more than 19,000 Facebook likes and was retweeted more than 15,000 times. Oreo's simple tweet to take advantage of the moment earned the brand more publicity

© Delta Faucet Company

Viral Marketing
Delta encourages viral marketing of its newer technology through social media and Pinterest.

than did the advertisement it launched during the Super Bowl.[35] Additionally, Delta uses a mix of print and digital advertising to promote its technology. This print advertisement promotes the company's Delta® Touch2O® faucet. The advertisement also contains a Pinterest tag. Delta encourages consumers who like the technology to scan the tag with the SnapTag® Reader App and post it to Pinterest, a pinboard-style photo-sharing website. Delta hopes that the image will get shared and re-pinned to other Pinterest boards in a type of viral marketing.

Word of mouth, no matter how it is transmitted, is not effective in all product categories. It seems to be most effective for new-to-market and more expensive products. Despite the obvious benefits of positive word of mouth, marketers must also recognize the potential dangers of negative word of mouth. This is particularly important in dealing with online platforms that can reach more people and encourage consumers to "gang up" on a company or product.

16-7 PRODUCT PLACEMENT AS PROMOTION

A growing technique for reaching consumers is the selective placement of products within the context of television programs viewed by the target market. **Product placement** is a form of advertising that strategically locates products or product promotions within entertainment media to reach the product's target markets. Apple is considered to be an expert at product placement. For instance, it partnered with Netflix to have several of its iPads and iPhones in the series *House of Cards*.[36] Such product placement has become more important due to the increasing fragmentation of television viewers who have ever-expanding viewing options and technology that can screen advertisements (e.g., digital video recorders such as TiVo). Researchers have found that 60 to 80 percent of digital video recorder users skip over the commercials when they replay programming.[37]

product placement The strategic location of products or product promotions within entertainment media content to reach the product's target market

In-program product placements have been successful in reaching consumers as they are being entertained. The popular show *Breaking Bad* featured Denny's and the Chrysler 300C model. The companies pursued deals with the show's producers because even though the theme of the show was negative, its popularity meant the brands would get strong exposure.[38] Reality programming in particular has been a natural fit for product placements, because

ENTREPRENEURSHIP IN MARKETING

B-Reel Enhances the Interaction of Products with Consumers

Entrepreneurs: Anders Wahlquist, Petter Westlund, and Pelle Nilsson
The business: B-Reel
Founded: 1999 | Sweden
Success: Advertising/marketing firm B-Reel has been so successful at combining product marketing and entertainment that they now have six offices worldwide.

Product placement has become almost synonymous with advertising, and one company is re-inventing the execution. Founded in 1999, B-Reel has taken advertising and product placement to an advanced level. The advertising production company has defied marketing tradition by creating campaigns that prompt interaction among consumers. Clients including Google, Toshiba, and IKEA have all used B-Reel to create marketing campaigns that engage the viewer.

B-Reel considers a pivotal campaign to be *The Wilderness Downtown*, in which it created an interactive film to promote Google Chrome. The short film allowed users to enter their childhood address, which created a background of a boy running on your street toward your home. Google Maps zoomed and rotated the view for users. The niche of the campaign was that it only worked on Google Chrome, a browser not as popular as others among consumers. About 50 million people watched the campaign, and many downloaded Google Chrome in the process. With many other projects in the works, B-Reel is using a mix of technology and creativity to become masters of buzz marketing.[b]

of the close interchange between the participants and the product (e.g., Sears and *Extreme Makeover Home Edition*; Subway and *The Biggest Loser*; Pepsi and *The X Factor*; Coca-Cola and *American Idol*).

Product placement is not limited to U.S. television shows. The European Parliament approved limited use of product placement, albeit only during certain types of programs and only if consumers were informed at the beginning of the segment that companies had paid to have their products displayed. In general, the notion of product placement has not been favorably viewed in Europe and has been particularly controversial in the United Kingdom. However, new legislation has legalized product placement in U.K. television programs.[39]

16-8 CRITICISMS AND DEFENSES OF PROMOTION

Even though promotional activities can help customers make informed purchasing decisions, social scientists, consumer groups, government agencies, and members of society in general have long criticized promotion. There are two main reasons for such criticism: Promotion does have flaws, and it is a highly visible business activity that pervades our daily lives. Although complaints about too much promotional activity are almost universal, a number of more specific criticisms have been lodged. In this section, we discuss some of the criticisms and defenses of promotion.

16-8a Is Promotion Deceptive?

One common criticism of promotion is that it is deceptive and unethical. During the 19th and early 20th centuries, much promotion was blatantly deceptive. Although no longer widespread, some deceptive promotion still occurs. For instance, the Federal Trade Commission has targeted weight-loss companies. Four companies that sell weight-loss products were fined after determining that they did not have enough evidence to back up their advertising claims. The four companies—including the marketers behind Sensa, L'Occitane Inc., LeanSpa LLC, and HCG Diet—were ordered to pay a combined fine of $34 million to consumers who were misled by their products.[40] Many industries suffer from claims of deception from time to time. One industry that is seemingly constantly bombarded with truthfulness-related claims is the diet products and exercise equipment industry. Some promotions are unintentionally deceiving; for instance, when advertising to children, it is easy to mislead them because they are more naïve than adults and less able to separate fantasy from reality. A promotion may also mislead some receivers, because words can have diverse meanings for different people. However, not all promotion should be condemned because a small portion is flawed. Laws, government regulation, and industry self-regulation have helped decrease deceptive promotion.

16-8b Does Promotion Increase Prices?

Promotion is also criticized for raising prices, but in fact it can lower them. The ultimate purpose of promotion is to stimulate demand. If it does, the business should be able to produce and market products in larger quantities and thus reduce per-unit production research and development, overhead, and marketing costs, which can result in lower prices. As demand for flat-screen TVs and MP3 players, for instance, has increased, their prices have dropped. When promotion fails to stimulate demand, the price of the promoted product increases because promotion costs must be added to other costs. Promotion also helps keep prices lower by facilitating price competition. When firms advertise prices, their prices tend to remain lower than when they are not promoting prices. Gasoline pricing illustrates how promotion fosters price competition. Service stations with the highest prices seldom have highly visible price signs. In addition, results of an analysis for the long-term economic growth for 64 countries indicated that there is a direct relationship between advertising and economic growth. The research findings indicate that advertising is not only related to economic growth but can also bring about economic growth.[41] A Deloitte study found that for every £1 billion ($1.64 billion) spent on advertising in the United Kingdom, a £6 billion ($9.86 billion) increase in annual GDP occurs.[42] This should help clarify debates over the role of promotion in society.

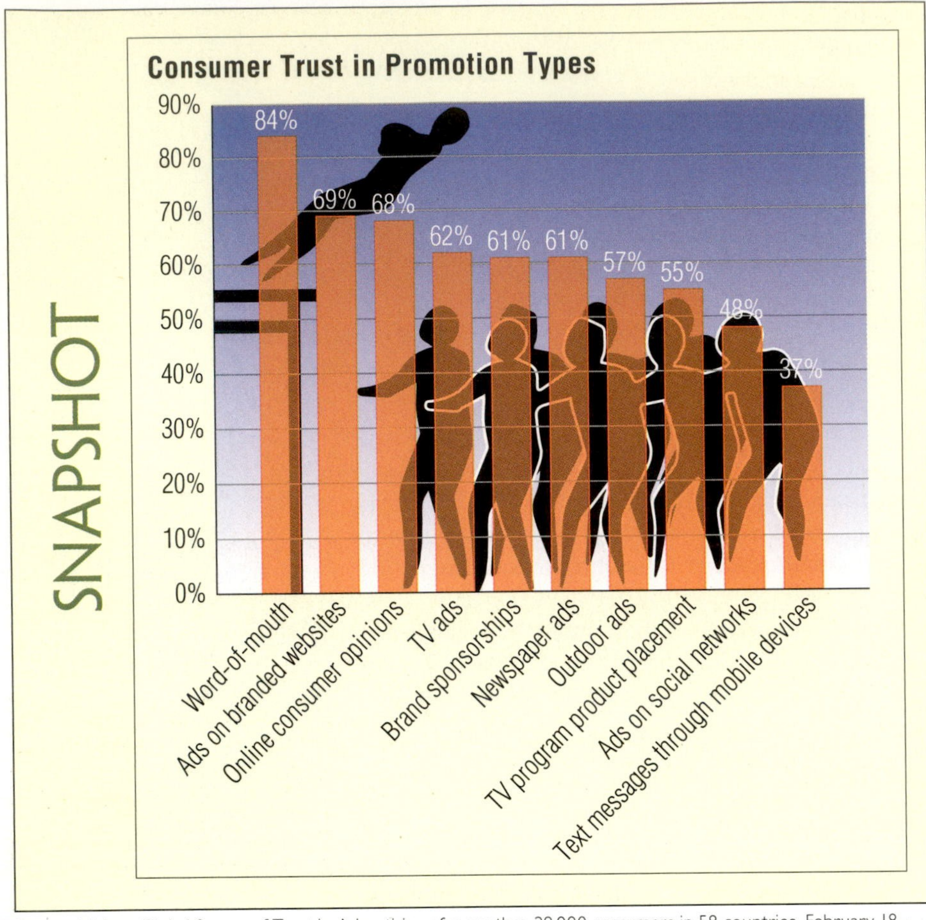

Source: Nielsen Global Survey of Trust in Advertising of more than 29,000 consumers in 58 countries, February 18–March 8, 2013, maximum margin of error ±0.6%.

16-8c Does Promotion Create Needs?

Some critics of promotion claim that it manipulates consumers by persuading them to buy products they do not need, hence creating "artificial" needs. In his theory of motivation, Abraham Maslow (discussed in Chapter 7) indicates that an individual tries to satisfy five levels of needs: physiological needs, such as hunger, thirst, and sex; safety needs; needs for love and affection; needs for self-esteem and respect from others; and self-actualization needs, or the need to realize one's potential. When needs are viewed in this context, it is difficult to demonstrate that promotion creates them. If there were no promotional activities, people would still have needs for food, water, sex, safety, love, affection, self-esteem, respect from others, and self-actualization.

Although promotion may not create needs, it does capitalize on them (which may be why some critics believe promotion creates needs). Many marketers base their appeals on these needs. For instance, several mouthwash, toothpaste, and perfume advertisements associate these products with needs for love, affection, and respect. These advertisers rely on human needs in their messages, but they do not create the needs.

16-8d Does Promotion Encourage Materialism?

Another frequent criticism of promotion is that it leads to materialism. The purpose of promoting goods is to persuade people to buy them; thus, if promotion works, consumers will want to buy more and more things. Marketers assert that values are instilled in the home and that promotion does not change people into materialistic consumers. However, the behavior of today's children and teenagers contradicts this view; many insist on high-priced, brand-name apparel, such as Gucci, Coach, Abercrombie & Fitch, 7 For All Mankind, Jersey Couture, and Ralph Lauren.

16-8e Does Promotion Help Customers without Costing Too Much?

Every year, firms spend billions of dollars for promotion. The question is whether promotion helps customers enough to be worth the cost. Consumers do benefit because promotion informs them about product uses, features, advantages, prices, and locations where they can buy the products. Thus, consumers gain more knowledge about available products and can make more intelligent buying decisions. Promotion also informs consumers about services—for instance, health care, educational programs, and day care—as well as about important social, political, and health-related issues. For example, several organizations, such as the California Department of Health Services, inform people about the health hazards associated with tobacco use.

16-8f Should Potentially Harmful Products Be Promoted?

Finally, some critics of promotion, including consumer groups and government officials, suggest that certain products should not be promoted at all. Primary targets are products associated with violence and other possibly unhealthy activities, such as handguns, alcohol, and tobacco. Cigarette advertisements, for example, promote smoking, a behavior proven to be harmful and even deadly. Tobacco companies, which spend billions on promotion, have countered criticism of their advertising by pointing out that advertisements for red meat and coffee are not censured, even though these products may also cause health problems. Consider the advertisement for Natural American Spirit. The company uses big letters to emphasize its American origins, organic tobacco, and lack of additives. The image of hands depicted as holding dirt reinforces this sustainability image. It also states in large letters that these benefits do not mean that its products are safer than other cigarettes. Despite these disclaimers, critics believe the marketing of these positive claims could deceive people into believing the cigarettes are safer since they are more eco-friendly. On the other hand, those who defend such promotion assert that, as long as it is legal to sell a product, promoting that product should be allowed.

Marketing Harmful Products

Natural American Spirit markets its organic tobacco and lack of additives. Although it has a disclaimer stating that this does not mean it is a healthier cigarette, critics believe it is wrong to market the benefits of products that can cause harm.

Summary

16-1 Define integrated marketing communications.

Integrated marketing communications is the coordination of promotion and other marketing efforts to ensure maximum informational and persuasive impact on customers.

16-2 Describe the steps of the communication process.

Communication is a sharing of meaning. The communication process involves several steps. First, the source translates meaning into code, a process known as coding or encoding. The source should employ signs or symbols familiar to the receiver or audience. The coded message is sent through a communications channel to the receiver or audience. The receiver or audience then decodes the message and usually supplies feedback to the source. When the decoded message differs from the encoded one, a condition called noise exists.

16-3 Recognize the definition and objectives of promotion.

Promotion is communication to build and maintain relationships by informing and persuading one or more audiences. Although promotional objectives vary from one organization to another and within organizations over time, eight primary objectives underlie many promotional programs. Promotion aims to create awareness of a new product, a new brand, or an existing product; to stimulate primary and selective demand; to encourage product trial through the use of free samples, coupons, limited free-use offers, contests, and games; to identify prospects; to retain loyal customers; to facilitate reseller support; to combat competitive promotional efforts; and to reduce sales fluctuations.

16-4 Summarize the four elements of the promotion mix.

The promotion mix for a product may include four major promotional methods: advertising, personal selling, public relations, and sales promotion. Advertising is paid nonpersonal communication about an organization and its products transmitted to a target audience through a mass medium. Personal selling is paid personal communication that attempts to inform customers and persuade them to purchase products in an exchange situation. Public relations is a broad set of communication efforts used to create and maintain favorable relationships between an organization and its stakeholders. Sales promotion is an activity or material that acts as a direct inducement, offering added value or incentive for the product, to resellers, salespeople, or consumers.

16-5 Explain the factors that are used to determine a product's promotion mix.

The promotional methods used in a product's promotion mix are determined by the organization's promotional resources, objectives, and policies; characteristics of the target market; characteristics of the product; and cost and availability of promotional methods. Marketers also consider whether to use a push policy or a pull policy. With a push policy, the producer only promotes the product to the next institution down the marketing channel. Normally, a push policy stresses personal selling. Firms that use a pull policy promote directly to consumers, with the intention of developing strong consumer demand for the products. Once consumers are persuaded to seek the products in retail stores, retailers go to wholesalers or the producer to buy the products.

16-6 Describe how word-of-mouth communication affects promotion.

Most customers are likely to be influenced by friends and family members when making purchases. Word-of-mouth communication is personal, informal exchanges of communication that customers share with one another about products, brands, and companies. Customers may also choose to go online to find electronic word of mouth about products or companies. Buzz marketing is an attempt to incite publicity and public excitement surrounding a product through a creative event. Viral marketing is a strategy to get consumers to share a marketer's message, often through e-mail or online videos, in a way that spreads dramatically and quickly.

16-7 Discuss how product placement impacts promotion.

Product placement is the strategic location of products or product promotions within television program content to reach the product's target market. In-program product placements have been successful in reaching consumers as they are being entertained rather than in the competitive commercial break time periods.

16-8 List major criticisms and defenses of promotion.

Promotional activities can help consumers make informed purchasing decisions, but they have also evoked many criticisms. Promotion has been accused of deception. Although some deceiving or misleading promotions do exist, laws, government regulation, and industry self-regulation minimize deceptive promotion. Promotion has been blamed for increasing prices, but it usually tends to lower them. When demand is high, production and marketing costs decrease, which can result in lower prices. Moreover, promotion helps keep prices lower by facilitating price competition. Other criticisms of promotional activity are that it manipulates consumers into buying products they do not need, that it leads to a more materialistic society, and that consumers do not benefit sufficiently from promotional activity to justify its high cost. Finally, some critics of promotion suggest that potentially harmful products, especially those associated with violence, sex, and unhealthy activities, should not be promoted at all.

Go to www.cengagebrain.com for resources to help you master the content in this chapter as well as for materials that will expand your marketing knowledge!

Developing Your Marketing Plan

A vital component of a successful marketing strategy is the company's plan for communication to its stakeholders. One segment of the communication plan is included in the marketing mix as the promotional element. A clear understanding of the role that promotion plays, as well as the various methods of promotion, is important in developing the promotional plan. The following questions should assist you in relating the information in this chapter to several decisions in your marketing plan.

1. Review the communication process in Figure 16.1. Identify the various players in the communication process for promotion of your product.
2. What are your objectives for promotion? Use Table 16.2 as a guide in answering this question.
3. Which of the four elements of the promotional mix are most appropriate for accomplishing your objectives? Discuss the advantages and disadvantages of each.

4. What role should word-of-mouth communications, buzz marketing, or product placement play in your promotional plan?

The information obtained from these questions should assist you in developing various aspects of your marketing plan found in the "Interactive Marketing Plan" exercise at www.cengagebrain.com.

Important Terms

integrated marketing communications 486
communication 487
source 487
receiver 488
coding process 488
communications channel 488
decoding process 488
noise 488
feedback 489
channel capacity 489
promotion 490
primary demand 491
pioneer promotion 491
selective demand 492
promotion mix 494
kinesic communication 497
proxemic communication 497
tactile communication 497
push policy 501
pull policy 501
word-of-mouth communication 502
buzz marketing 503
viral marketing 503
product placement 504

Discussion and Review Questions

1. What does the term *integrated marketing communications* mean?
2. Define *communication* and describe the communication process. Is it possible to communicate without using all the elements in the communication process? If so, which elements can be omitted?
3. Identify several causes of noise. How can a source reduce noise?
4. What is the major task of promotion? Do firms ever use promotion to accomplish this task and fail? If so, give several examples.
5. Describe the possible objectives of promotion and discuss the circumstances under which each objective might be used.
6. Identify and briefly describe the four promotional methods an organization can use in its promotion mix.
7. What forms of interpersonal communication besides language can be used in personal selling?
8. How do target market characteristics determine which promotional methods to include in a promotion mix? Assume a company is planning to promote a cereal to both adults and children. Along what major dimensions would these two promotional efforts have to differ from each other?
9. How can a product's characteristics affect the composition of its promotion mix?
10. Evaluate the following statement: "Appropriate advertising media are always available if a company can afford them."
11. Explain the difference between a pull policy and a push policy. Under what conditions should each policy be used?
12. In which ways can word-of-mouth communication influence the effectiveness of a promotion mix for a product?
13. Which criticisms of promotion do you believe are the most valid? Why?
14. Should organizations be allowed to promote offensive, violent, sexual, or unhealthy products that can be legally sold and purchased? Support your answer.

Video Case 16.1

Frank Pepe's Pizzeria Napoletana Uses Positive Word of Mouth to Become a Premiere Pizzeria

Frank Pepe's Pizzeria Napoletana has opened one of the most recognizable pizzerias in the United States using word of mouth. After returning from World War I, Frank Pepe initially began with making bread during the week and pizzas on the weekend. After seeing a demand for his product, he utilized his entrepreneurial spirit and focused solely on pizza. Frank Pepe founded Pepe's Pizzeria in 1925, with a heavy influence from his Italian culture, in New Haven, Connecticut.

Frank Pepe developed the New Haven–style thin crust pizza that earned him a reputation as being one of the country's premiere pizzerias. Many people began referring to Frank Pepe as "Old Reliable," which continued to generate positive feedback throughout different communities. Pepe's signature pizza, the White Clam Pizza, was the most notable recipe since the development in the mid-1960s.

Since the beginning, Pepe's has been a family-run business. Frank's wife and children all worked in the original store and, after retiring, they passed the business to their children, who still have a stake in the business today. Through the transition between generations, Pepe's has always aimed to deliver a premium product that is consistent and meets customer standards. As people come into the store, Pepe's employees engage in personal selling by communicating various menu items.

Current CEO Ken Berry places high emphasis upon delivering the promise and guarantee of quality within their product every day. As chief executive operator, he sees the challenge of delivering this promise as a duty that helps protect and build the brand, which the Pepe family initially built. He strives to retain brand equity and rely upon feedback from loyal customers as the company continues to grow.

Including the first and flagship store, there are currently seven pizzerias within Connecticut and New York. With each new store came the difficult task of maintaining the original experience for new, prospective, and loyal customers. When Pepe's began to consistently pursue expansion tactics, some customers appeared dismayed. There were protests and boycotts occurring on opening days, as other happy customers waited in long lines to test the reputation of the premiere pizza.

To ensure customer satisfaction at the new locations, Ken Berry discussed the critical nature of replicating every aspect of the original idea. Everything from the recipes being virtually unchanged to the layout and colors of the stores needed to be congruent to ensure success. He describes Pepe's as an experience that allows customers to step back in time with a handcrafted product.

Another aspect of developing demand for the company in new locations was the advertising tactics used. As Pepe's has always done, they relied upon word of mouth to retain and gain new customers. They place emphasis upon the experience and listen to customer feedback on whether they are delivering a quality product. At times they use direct mail, which can be an effective form of advertising, and try to engage with consumers on Twitter and Facebook to remain connected with them. This is sometimes called electronic word of mouth. A major form of promotion comes in the form of free pizza, which is sales promotion. Generally, the week before a grand opening Pepe's will offer free pizza for a week at that location to allow new ovens to be broken in, workers to understand Pepe's culture, and to showcase the confidence that Pepe's has in their product to the local community.

For the public relations side of the company, Pepe's has a donation request option on their website, where customers are welcome to fill out an application to receive primarily gift cards from the company. They also hold a good neighbor night, which allows an organization to hold a fundraiser at any location. Fifteen percent of proceeds made that night is given to the organization. Although Pepe's loses out on some of proceeds, these events create quality relationships in the community as well as generate a potentially new customer base. They also donate gift cards to nonprofit organizations for fundraising purposes.

Throughout the years Pepe's has strived to deliver a promise to customers by staying true to the original product. They have maintained their brand equity through their dedication and standards set by customers, family members, and all stakeholders associated with the product. For this company, it is clear that through positive word of mouth, advertising does not always need to be a costly expense.[43]

Questions for Discussion

1. What are the various promotional elements that Pepe's uses to communicate with customers?
2. What role does word of mouth play in Pepe's integrated marketing communications?
3. Evaluate free pizza as a form of sales promotion in Pepe's success.

Case 16.2

L'Oréal's Integrated Marketing Communicates a Decades-Old Story

L'Oréal Paris, the French cosmetics division of parent company L'Oréal SA, is an effective architect of integrated marketing communications. They have achieved such status by coordinating a mix of marketing activities through the most appropriate channels and relaying a consistent brand message to customers over several decades. Their success is evidenced by long-term customer relationships, customer loyalty, and influential brand ambassadors over the years. Though L'Oréal Paris has been at times slow to adapt to cultural and demographic changes, they have proven capable of implementing appropriate and synchronized marketing tactics resulting in quick recovery.

L'Oréal's slogan, "Because We're Worth It," is the platform upon which the company's entire marketing strategy is built. Created in 1971, a time when women were seeking to become more empowered, the slogan has remained a powerful force behind the brand. Unlike most company slogans, the L'Oréal slogan has not had significant makeovers due to its simply stated classic message. The slogan has proven resilient in the face of inevitable evolution of brands and consumer tastes. Changes to the company slogan "Because I'm Worth It" have been limited to pronouns. It changed in the 1990s to say "Because You're Worth It," at which point the company launched a global marketing campaign. The slogan has since been translated into 40 languages. In 2010, when nearing its 40th anniversary, the slogan was changed once more to read "Because We're Worth It." The purpose of this change was to refresh their image while remaining loyal to the original message of creating a sense of self-worth and confidence among women.

The company's brand ambassadors have also reinforced the power of the slogan. L'Oréal carefully chooses a wide range of representatives across cultures, ages, and appearances who embody the essence of a strong and empowered woman. Ambassadors such as Aimee Mullins, Beyoncé Knowles, and Jennifer Lopez inspire word-of-mouth communication among customers through advertisements, interviews in which they explain what the brand means to them, and advocacy efforts. Although the slogan's sense of female empowerment may not be as relevant in Europe or America, there is opportunity in Africa and Asia where women's rights are taking hold. L'Oréal's corporate communications team is working to develop more awareness of the brand and greater customer relationships through institutional media relations, corporate social responsibility initiatives, and reputation management. In developing a more global approach, L'Oréal also hires teams of people from multiple countries to research the skin and hair of different people groups.

Although L'Oréal is the largest cosmetics company worldwide, selling an estimated 50 products per second, sales have slipped in recent years. Experts feel that the onset of the digital age and shorter attention spans may be making the slogan less effective and outdated. Despite these concerns, L'Oréal Paris's CEO announced he intends to keep the slogan, and is using it as the basis for digital marketing campaigns. In 2010 the company hired their first chief marketing officer, Marc Speichert, to launch all of the company's brands into the digital realm. Speichert's first contribution was to build a media team to work closely with a consumer insights team to determine what channels and content are appropriate for their different audiences. Based on this information, the company focused on media and Internet displays, social media, TV and print advertising, search optimization, and videos.

As of 2012, L'Oréal became the seventh biggest advertiser in the United States, having spent more than $2 billion dollars on print and television advertising. They have also seen positive results from search optimization and their social media partnership with famous beauty blogger Michelle Phan. The popularity of this marketing component initiated a new cosmetics line to be sold on e-commerce sites as well as in an exclusive location in New York.

L'Oréal's content marketing is based on three pillars: education, empowerment, and aspiration. In line with these three topics, how-to and do-it-yourself videos have been created informing consumers of various beauty tips. Videos focused on empowerment send the message of the brand's strength and confidence rather than just focusing on cosmetics and beauty, leaving customers with a positive outlook. Finally, aspirational videos are reflections of the company's sponsorships with various awards and fashion events, which infuse the brand with elevated perceptions. Overall, these videos and the entirety of the company's content marketing initiatives work together to tell the story of the firm to consumers, creating value and brand awareness among loyal and new users.[44]

Questions for Discussion

1. Describe L'Oréal's integrated marketing strategy. What are the strengths? Weaknesses?
2. Describe the function and effectiveness of brand ambassadors. What are some risks associated with choosing a brand ambassador?
3. Why is it important to have a story to tell when developing content marketing?

NOTES

[1] Content Marketing Institute, "What Is Content Marketing?" *Content Marketing Institute*, http://contentmarketinginstitute.com/what-is-content-marketing (accessed October 23, 2013); Molly Soat, "Success by Self-Depreciation," *Marketing News*, January 2013, pp. 45–50; Jessica Fee, "Why Advertisers Need YouTube," *Mashable*, June 13, 2013, http://mashable.com/2013/06/13/youtube-marketing-advertising (accessed October 23, 2013).

[2] *Toyota–US Newsroom*, "Integrated Marketing Campaign Elevates 2014 Toyota Corolla to New Heights," September 5, 2013, http://pressroom.toyota.com/releases/2014+toyota+corolla+integrated+marketing+campaign.htm (accessed January 7, 2014).

[3] Tanzina Vega, "Harper's Redesigns Its Web Site and Embraces Branded Content," *International*

New York Times, October 14, 2013, www.nytimes.com/2013/10/15/business/media/harpers-redesigns-its-web-site-and-embraces-branded-content.html?_r=0 (accessed January 7, 2014).

[4] Suzanne Vranica, "Ad Spending Expected to Pick Up Pace," *The Wall Street Journal*, December 8, 2013, http://online.wsj.com/news/articles/SB10001424052702303330204579246003193822532 (accessed January 7, 2014).

[5] Pierre Berthon, Karen Robson, and Leyland Pitt, "The Theory and Practice of Advertising: Counting the Cost to the Consumer," *Journal of Advertising Research* 53, no. 3 (2013): 244–246.

[6] Salvador Ruiz and María Sicilia, "The Impact of Cognitive and/or Affective Processing Styles on Consumer Response to Advertising Appeals," *Journal of Business Research* 57 (2004): 657–664.

[7] Jack Neff, "Does P&G Really Drop 35% of Its Marketing Dollars on Advertising?" *Advertising Age*, August 20, 2013, http://adage.com/article/digital/procter-gamble-spends-35-marketing-dollars-digital/243718 (accessed January 6, 2014).

[8] *Safeway*, "10% Back to Schools Program," www.safeway.com/backtoschool (accessed January 7, 2014).

[9] Nick Bilton, "Highlights from Apple's Conference Keynote," *The New York Times*, June 10, 2013, http://bits.blogs.nytimes.com/2013/06/10/live-blog-apple-conference-keynote/?_r=0 (accessed January 9, 2014).

[10] Matthew Herper, "Update: Hyundai Apologizes for Car Ad Depicting Attempted Suicide," *Forbes*, April 25, 2013,www.forbes.com/sites/matthewherper/2013/04/25/a-hyundai-car-ad-depicts-suicide-it-is-so-wrong-i-cant-embed-it-in-this-post (accessed January 9, 2014).

[11] Brad Reed, "Samsung Explains Why Making a Hit Smartwatch Is Insanely Difficult," *BGR*, January 8, 2014, http://bgr.com/2014/01/08/samsung-smartwatch-problems-battery (accessed January 9, 2014).

[12] Starbucks, "A Single-Origin Coffee Unlike Anything in Starbucks 42-Year History, Ethiopia Is Masterfully Roasted for an Exquisite Taste Experience," *Starbucks Newsroom*, September 24, 2013, http://news.starbucks.com/news/starbucks-honors-the-birthplace-of-coffee-with-ethiopia (accessed January 7, 2013).

[13] Which Wich, "Join Our Vibe Club Today. It's Witchin'!" www.whichwich.com/vibe_club (accessed January 8, 2014).

[14] Ann Zimmerman and Shelly Banjo, "Rivals Object to Wal-Mart Ads," *The Wall Street Journal*, January 3, 2013, http://online.wsj.com/news/articles/SB10001424127887323689604578219703156296568 (accessed January 8, 2014).

[15] Time Inc, "Fortune Media Kit," www.fortunemediakit.com/rates.html (accessed January 6, 2014).

[16] "Touch and Its Influence in Persuasion," *Journal of Marketing* 70 (October 2006): 56–69.

[17] Holli McKay, "Capital One Stands by Alec Baldwin; Experts Urge Anger Management Classes," *Fox News*, November 19, 2013, www.foxnews.com/entertainment/2013/11/19/capital-one-stands-by-alec-baldwin-experts-urge-anger-management-classes (accessed January 8, 2014).

[18] Pampered Chef YouTube Channel, www.youtube.com/user/PamperedChefVideo (accessed January 8, 2014).

[19] "George Alexander Louis, Your Chariot—Er, Land Rover—Awaits," *Advertising Age*, July 26, 2013, http://adage.com/article/adages/ford-land-rover-fiat-publicity-pope-royal-baby/243336 (accessed January 6, 2014).

[20] Jena McGregor, "Abercrombie & Fitch's Big, Bad Brand Mistake," *The Washington Post*, May 22, 2013, www.washingtonpost.com/blogs/on-leadership/wp/2013/05/22/abercrombie-fitchs-big-bad-brand-mistake (accessed January 8, 2014).

[21] Inmar, Inc, "Inmar Reports Slight Increase in Coupon Redemption for Q3 2013," *Yahoo! Finance*, October 21, 2013, http://finance.yahoo.com/news/inmar-reports-slight-increase-coupon-185225454.html (accessed January 8, 2014).

[22] United States Census Bureau, "About Three in Four Parents Living with Children Are Married, Census Bureau Reports," November 25, 2013, www.census.gov/newsroom/releases/archives/families_households/cb13-199.html (accessed January 8, 2014).

[23] Rockney G. Walters and Maqbul Jamil, "Exploring the Relationships between Shopping Trip Type, Purchases of Products on Promotion, and Shopping Basket Profit," *Journal of Business Research* 56 (2003): 17–29.

[24] John McDermott, "PlayStation 4 Ads Focus on Hardcore Gamers While Xbox Stresses the Living Room," *Advertising Age*, June 12, 2013, http://adage.com/article/digital/playstation-4-marketing-focuses-gamers-unlike-xbox/242056 (accessed January 8, 2014).

[25] Jeffrey N. Ross, "Honda, Hyundai and Kia Get Best Word-of-Mouth Recommendations in US," *Auto Blog*, December 9, 2013, www.autoblog.com/2013/12/09/honda-hyundai-kia-best-word-of-mouth-recommendations (accessed January 8, 2014).

[26] Tomás Bayón, "The Chain from Customer Satisfaction via Word-of-Mouth Referrals to New Customer Acquisition," *Journal of the Academy of Marketing Science* 35 (June 2007): 233–249.

[27] Rodolfo Vázquez-Casielles, Leticia Suárez-Álvarez, and Ana-Belén Del Río-Lanza, "The Word of Mouth Dynamic: How Positive (and Negative) WOM Drives Purchase Probability: An Analysis of Interpersonal and Non-Interpersonal Factors," *Journal of Advertising Research* 53, no. 1 (2013): 43–60.

[28] Benjamin Lawrence, Susan Fournier, and Frédéric Brunel, "When Companies Don't Make the Ad: A Multimethod Inquiry into the Differential Effectiveness of Consumer-Generated Advertising," *Journal of Advertising* 42, no. 4 (October 2013): 292–307.

[29] Rodolfo Vázquez-Casielles, Leticia Suárez-Álvarez, and Ana Belén del Río-Lanza, "The Word of Mouth Dynamic: How Positive (and Negative) WOM Drives Purchase Probability: An Analysis of Interpersonal and Non-Interpersonal Factors," *Journal of Advertising Research* 53, no. 1 (2013): 43–60.

[30] Pratibha A. Dabholkar, "Factors Influencing Consumer Choice of a 'Rating Web Site': An Experimental Investigation of an Online Interactive Decision Aid," *Journal of Marketing Theory and Practice* 14 (Fall 2006): 259–273.

[31] Nielsen, "Just Do It? Consumer Trust in Advertising and Willingness to Take Action," September 26, 2013, www.nielsen.com/us/en/newswire/2013/just-do-it-consumer-trust-in-advertising-and-willingness-to-ta.html (accessed January 8, 2014).

[32] Juro Osawa, "Huawei Adds Some Spice to Its Consumer Marketing," *The Wall Street Journal*, June 18, 2013, B5.

[33] Natalie Zmuda, "Red Bull's Stratos 'Space Jump' Wowed the World—While Selling a Lot of Product," *Advertising Age*, September 2, 2013, http://adage.com/article/special-report-marketer-alist-2013/red-bull-stratos-space-jump-helped-sell-a-lot-product/243751 (accessed January 8, 2014).

[34] Lia Zarantonello and Bernd H. Schmitt, "The Impact of Event Marketing on Brand Equity: The Mediating Roles of Brand Experience and Brand Attitude," *International Journal of Advertising* 32, no. 2 (2013): 255–280.

[35] E. J. Schultz, "Beyond Super Bowl Stunt, Oreo Finds New Voice in Social Media," *Advertising Age*, February 25, 2013, http://adage.com/article/special-report-digital-alist-2013/ad-age-s-digital-a-list-oreo/239942 (accessed January 6, 2014).

[36] Louis Bedigian, "Apple and Netflix Team Up for Unofficial Product Placement," *Forbes*, February 5, 2013, www.forbes.com/sites/benzingainsights/2013/02/05/apple-and-netflix-team-up-for-unofficial-product-placement (accessed January 8, 2014); Reuters, "Apple Deemed Top of Movie Placement Charts," February 22, 2011, www.reuters.com/article/2011/02/22/us-productplacement-idUSTRE71L69920110222 (accessed January 8, 2014).

[37] Lynna Goch, "The Place to Be," *Best's Review*, February 2005, pp. 64–65.

[38] Jonathan Baskin, "Anathema No More, 'Breaking Bad' Is Redefining Rules for Product Placement," *Forbes*, September 25, 2013, www.forbes.com/sites/jonathansalembaskin/2013/09/25/anathema-no-more-breaking-bad-is-redefining-rules-for-product-placement (accessed January 8, 2014).

[39] Lilly Vitorovich, "Product Placement to Be Allowed in U.K. TV Programs," *The Wall Street Journal*, December 21, 2010, p. B5.

[40] Michelle Castillo, "Sensa, L'Occitane, LeanSpa, HCG Diet Fined by FTC for False Advertising," *CBS News*, January 7, 2014, www.cbsnews.com/news/sensa-loccitane-leanspa-hcg-diet-direct-fined-by-ftc-for-false-advertising (accessed January 8, 2014).

[41] Dennis A. Kopf, Ivonne M. Torres, and Carl Enomoto, "Advertising's Unintended Consequence," *Journal of Advertising* 40, no. 4, (Winter 2011): 5–18.

[42] Charles R. Taylor, "Editorial: On the Economic Effects of Advertising—Evidence That Advertising = Information," *International Journal of Advertising* 32, no. 3 (2013): 339–342.

[43] Pepe's Pizzeria website, www.pepespizzeria.com (accessed January 6, 2014).

[44] Christina Passariello and Max Colchester, "L'Oréal's Slogan Proves Timeless," *The Wall Street Journal*, November 15, 2011, p. B14; Amy Verner, "L'Oréal's 'Because I'm Worth It' Slogan Marks a Milestone," *The Globe and Mail*, December 2, 2011, www.theglobeandmail.com/life/fashion-and-beauty/beauty/beauty-features/lorals-because-im-worth-it-slogan-marks-a-milestone/article2256825 (accessed July 26, 2013); Kate Shapland, "It Was Worth It: L'Oréal Celebrates 40th Anniversary of Landmark Slogan," *Telegraph.co.uk*, November 16, 2011, http://fashion.telegraph.co.uk/beauty/news-features/TMG8894450/It-was-worth-it-LOreal-celebrates-40th-anniversary-of-landmark-slogan.html (accessed July 26, 2013); Rebecca Leffler, "L'Oréal Fetes 40th Anniversary of 'Because You're Worth It' in Paris," *The Hollywood Reporter*, November 14, 2011, www.hollywoodreporter.com/fash-track/l-oreal-jane-fonda-freida-pinto-261216 (accessed July 26, 2013); L'Oréal, "Corporate Communication," www.loreal.com/who-you-can-be/communication/corporate-communication.aspx (accessed July 26, 2013); L'Oréal USA, "Diversity Is a Priority," www.lorealusa.com/_en/_us/html/our-company/our-teams/research-development.aspx (accessed July 26, 2013); Christina Passariello and Max Colchester, "L'Oréal Slogan Must Prove Worth Anew," *The Wall Street Journal*, November 18, 2011, http://online.wsj.com/news/articles/SB10001424052970204323904577037720293895982 (accessed November 20, 2013); Kristen Comings, "Three Keys to L'Oréal's Content Marketing Strategy," *iMedia Connection*, September 30, 2013, www.imediaconnection.com/content/35113.asp#multiview (accessed November 20, 2013); Giselle Abramovich, "L'Oréal: Ads Matter Less," *Digiday*, October 2, 2012, http://digiday.com/brands/adweek-tracking-the-evolution-of-loreal-marketing (accessed November 20, 2013). Kelly Liyakasa, "L'Oréal CMO: Digital Is Changing Our Content, Creative and Conversation," *Ad Exchanger*, September 13, 2013, www.adexchanger.com/digital-marketing-2/loreal-cmo-digital-is-changing-our-content-creative-and-conversation (accessed November 20, 2013). Jack Neff, "L'Oréal Puts U.S. Digital Media Up for Review," *Ad Age*, August 20, 2013, http://adage.com/article/agency-news/l-oreal-puts-u-s-digital-media-review/243732 (accessed November 20, 2013). Daisy Whitney, "Never Say 'Let's Create a Viral Video,'" *Ad Age*, September 13, 2012, http://adage.com/article/media/create-a-viral-video/237181 (accessed November 20, 2013).

Feature Notes

[a] Chris Woodyard, "Corvette Revs Its Image to Attract Younger Buyers," *USA Today*, August 20, 2013, pp. 1B–2B; David Undercuffler, "Car Review: 2014 Corvette Stingray Shifts Away from Tradition," *LA Times*, August 17, 2013, http://articles.latimes.com/2013/aug/17/business/la-fi-autos-chevrolet-corvette-stingray-review-20130817 (accessed August 27, 2013); Paul A Elsenstein, "Chevy Steers 2014 Corvette Stingray into Luxury Market," *NBC News*, August 16, 2013, www.nbcnews.com/business/chevy-steers-2014-corvette-stingray-luxury-market-6C10930051 (accessed August 27, 2013); Chris Isidore and Emily Fox, "Chevrolet Corvette Stingray Wins Car of the Year Honors," *CNN Money*, January 13, 2014, http://money.cnn.com/2014/01/13/autos/car-and-truck-of-the-year (accessed January 27, 2014).

[b] Josh Dean, "The Company That's Changing Advertising," *Inc.*, May 28, 2012, www.inc.com/magazine/201206/josh-dean/b-reel-changing-advertising.html (accessed January 3, 2014); B-Reel website, www.b-reel.com/content (accessed January 3, 2014); Ann-Christine Diaz, "Meet the Creative Shop Using Robots and 'Minority Report' Tech to Sell Your Stuff," *Ad Age*, February 21,2012, http://adage.com/article/digital/meet-creative-shop-robots-wolves-sell-product/232836 (accessed January 3, 2014).

chapter 17

Advertising and Public Relations

OBJECTIVES

17-1 Describe advertising and its different types.

17-2 Summarize the eight major steps in developing an advertising campaign.

17-3 Identify who is responsible for developing advertising campaigns.

17-4 Define *public relations.*

17-5 Describe the different tools of public relations.

17-6 Analyze how public relations is used and evaluated.

MARKETING INSIGHTS

Long Live the Animated Animal Advertiser!

"Yo Quiero Taco Bell!" Despite the fact that the Taco Bell Chihuahua advertising campaign ended in 2000, those from the 1990s still remember this phrase and the small advertiser who uttered these words. Using talking animals and animations as spokescharacters in advertisements has proven to be a powerful tool for many companies. These creatures are able to attract and hold people's attention for longer periods of time and are not subject to the same flaws and scandals as human spokespeople. Often the animals become marketing symbols in themselves, with consumers purchasing clothing with the characters, buying toy versions of the characters for their children, and repeating the slogan of the beloved characters. This aids in brand recall and multiplies the effects of the company's advertising messages.

One example of a successful animal spokescharacter is the Aflac duck. The American Family Life Assurance Company needed to increase awareness in America and Japan, but its long name and the presence of "American" was holding it back. The company shortened its name to the acronym *Aflac*, which sounds like the quacking of a duck. The Aflac duck campaign was born. Despite the incident in which the "voice" of the Aflac duck, Gilbert Gottfried, was fired after making inappropriate comments, the Aflac duck has remained a favorite spokescharacter among consumers. Additionally, the Geico Gecko has also generated positive public relations for the company. The company has turned the Gecko into the primary spokesperson of the firm—he even "wrote" his own book. The popularity of these spokescharacters is effective in developing positive associations between the beloved icon and the brand.[1]

Both large organizations and small companies use conventional and online promotional efforts like advertising to change their corporate images, build brand equity, launch new products, or promote current brands. In this chapter, we explore several dimensions of advertising and public relations. First, we focus on the nature and types of advertising. Next, we examine the major steps in developing an advertising campaign and describe who is responsible for developing such campaigns. We then discuss the nature of public relations and how it is used. We examine various public relations tools and ways to evaluate the effectiveness of public relations. Finally, we focus on how companies deal with unfavorable public relations.

17-1 THE NATURE AND TYPES OF ADVERTISING

advertising Paid nonpersonal communication about an organization and its products transmitted to a target audience through mass media

institutional advertising Advertising that promotes organizational images, ideas, and political issues

Advertising permeates our daily lives. At times, we view it positively; at other times, we feel bombarded and try to avoid it. Some advertising informs, persuades, or entertains us; some bores, annoys, or even offends us. J.C.Penney's back-to-school advertising campaign tried to inform viewers about Arizona jeans parents could buy at its stores with a hip commercial indicating the importance of stylish clothes to children. However, the campaign backfired when the commercial featured a kid sitting alone at a table because he did not have the "cool clothes." Mothers in particular felt that this could promote bullying.[2]

As mentioned in Chapter 16, **advertising** is a paid form of nonpersonal communication that is transmitted to a target audience through mass media, such as television, radio, the Internet, newspapers, magazines, direct mail, outdoor displays, and signs on mass transit vehicles. Advertising can have a profound impact on how consumers view certain products. One example is locally grown and organic produce. Consumers are likely to view locally grown and organic produce as healthier even though there is no evidence to support this view. Organizations use advertising to reach a variety of audiences ranging from small, specific groups, such as stamp collectors in Idaho, to extremely large groups, such as all athletic-shoe purchasers in the United States.

When asked to name major advertisers, most people immediately mention business organizations. However, many nonbusiness organizations—including governments, churches, universities, and charitable organizations—employ advertising to communicate with stakeholders. Each year, the U.S. government spends hundreds of millions of dollars in advertising to advise and influence the behavior of its citizens. Although this chapter analyzes advertising in the context of business organizations, much of the following material applies to all types of organizations. For instance, chambers of commerce promote tourism, such as this advertisement for Arizona, which entices consumers to vacation within the state. The depiction of a hot air balloon floating over a desert landscape lends an air of exoticism and beauty to the advertisement. It is important for cities and states to advertise because tourism generates significant income for their locations.

Arizona Commerce Authority

Nonbusiness Advertising
This Arizona Commerce Authority advertisement is an example of advertising for a nonbusiness organization. Because tourism generates significant income, the Arizona Commerce Authority must advertise to attract tourists who might not be aware of what the state has to offer.

Advertising is used to promote goods, services, ideas, images, issues, people, and anything else advertisers want to publicize or foster. Depending on what is being promoted, advertising can be classified as institutional or product advertising. **Institutional advertising** promotes organizational images, ideas, and political issues. It can be used to create or maintain an organizational image. Institutional advertisements may deal with broad image issues, such as organizational strengths or the friendliness of employees. They may also aim to create a more favorable view of the organization in the eyes of noncustomer groups, such as shareholders, consumer advocacy groups, potential shareholders, or the general public. When a company promotes its position on a public issue—for instance, a tax increase, sustainability, regulations, or international trade coalitions—institutional advertising is referred to as **advocacy advertising**. Such advertising may be used to promote socially approved behavior, such as recycling or moderation in consuming alcoholic beverages. Philip Morris, for example, has run television advertisements encouraging parents to talk to their children about not smoking. Researchers have identified a number of themes that advertisers like Philip Morris can use to increase the effectiveness of antismoking messages for adolescents.[3] This type of advertising not only has social benefits but also helps build an organization's image.

advocacy advertising Advertising that promotes a company's position on a public issue

product advertising Advertising that promotes the uses, features, and benefits of products

pioneer advertising Advertising that tries to stimulate demand for a product category rather than a specific brand by informing potential buyers about the product

competitive advertising Tries to stimulate demand for a specific brand by promoting its features, uses, and advantages relative to competing brands

comparative advertising Compares the sponsored brand with one or more identified brands on the basis of one or more product characteristics

Product advertising promotes the uses, features, and benefits of products. The Hershey's advertisement, for instance, promotes a particular product—Hershey's Semi-Sweet Chocolate Chips. The advertisement includes a photo of a brownie recipe that used Hershey's chocolate chips. It also provides the website for Hershey's Kitchens, which contains hundreds of recipes using Hershey products. There are two types of product advertising: pioneer and competitive. **Pioneer advertising** focuses on stimulating demand for a product category (rather than a specific brand) by informing potential customers about the product's features, uses, and benefits. Sometimes marketers will begin advertising a product before it hits the market. Apple has had great success using this type of advertising for its iPod and iPad. Product advertising that focuses on products before they are available tends to cause people to think about the product more and evaluate it more positively.[4] Pioneer advertising is also employed when the product is in the introductory stage of the product life cycle, exemplified in the launch of the Samsung Galaxy Gear in the smartwatch category. **Competitive advertising** attempts to stimulate demand for a specific brand by promoting the brand's features, uses, and advantages, sometimes through indirect or direct comparisons with competing brands. Cell phone service providers use competitive advertising to position their brands—for example, Verizon against T-Mobile. Advertising effects on sales must reflect competitors' advertising activities. The type of competitive environment will determine the most effective industry approach.

To make direct product comparisons, marketers use a form of competitive advertising called **comparative advertising**, which compares the sponsored brand with one or more identified competing brands on the basis of one or more product characteristics. Surveys show that top creative advertising practitioners view comparative advertising favorably when it clearly identifies the competition.[5] Hindustan Unilever Ltd, for example, used comparative advertising to promote the superiority of its Pepsodent Germicheck toothpaste compared to Colgate's Colgate Strong Teeth in India.[6] Often, the brands that are promoted through comparative advertisements have low market shares and are compared with competitors that have the highest market shares in the product category. Product categories that commonly use comparative advertising include soft drinks, toothpaste, pain relievers, foods, tires, automobiles, and detergents. Under the provisions of the 1988 Trademark Law Revision Act, marketers using comparative

© The Hershey Company

Product Advertising
This Hershey's advertisement promotes a specific product and demonstrates ways it can be used with the depiction of delicious-looking brownies.

advertisements in the United States must not misrepresent the qualities or characteristics of competing products. Other countries may have laws that are stricter or less strict with regard to comparative advertising. For instance, although Colgate asked for an injunction against the Pepsodent advertisement claiming that it misrepresented their product, the Delhi High Court declined their request.[7]

Other forms of competitive advertising include reminder and reinforcement advertising. **Reminder advertising** tells customers that an established brand is still around and still offers certain characteristics, uses, and advantages. Clorox, for example, reminds customers about the many advantages of its bleach products, such as their ability to kill germs, whiten clothes, and remove stains. **Reinforcement advertising** assures current users that they have made the right brand choice and tells them how to get the most satisfaction from that brand. Insurance companies like Geico encourage potential new customers to spend 15 minutes on the phone getting an insurance quote and save 15 percent or more on their policy. Value propositions like Geico's can provide reinforcement to consumers that they are making a good decision as a new or current customer.

reminder advertising Advertising used to remind consumers about an established brand's uses, characteristics, and benefits

reinforcement advertising Advertising that assures users they chose the right brand and tells them how to get the most satisfaction from it

advertising campaign The creation and execution of a series of advertisements to communicate with a particular target audience

17-2 DEVELOPING AN ADVERTISING CAMPAIGN

An **advertising campaign** involves designing a series of advertisements and placing them in various advertising media to reach a particular target audience. As Figure 17.1 shows, the major steps in creating an advertising campaign are (1) identifying and analyzing the target audience, (2) defining the advertising objectives, (3) creating the advertising platform, (4) determining the advertising appropriation, (5) developing the media plan, (6) creating the advertising message, (7) executing the campaign, and (8) evaluating advertising effectiveness. The number of steps and the exact order in which they are carried out may vary according to the organization's resources, the nature of its product, and the type of target audience to be reached. Nevertheless, these general guidelines for developing an advertising campaign are appropriate for all types of organizations.

Figure 17.1 General Steps in Developing and Implementing an Advertising Campaign

17-2a Identifying and Analyzing the Target Audience

The **target audience** is the group of people at whom advertisements are aimed. Advertisements for the Dyson vacuum cleaner target more affluent home owners, whereas the Dirt Devil targets lower- to middle-income households. Identifying and analyzing the target audience are critical processes; the information yielded helps determine other steps in developing the campaign. The target audience may include everyone in the firm's target market. Marketers may, however, direct a campaign at only a portion of the target market. For instance, until recently the upscale yoga apparel organization Lululemon Athletica focused mainly on women. However, the firm is extending its focus to men interested in fitness with new lines of menswear. Menswear now accounts for approximately 13 percent of Lululemon's total revenue.[8]

Advertisers research and analyze advertising targets to establish an information base for a campaign. Information commonly needed includes location and geographic distribution of the target group; the distribution of demographic factors, such as age, income, race, gender, and education; lifestyle information; and consumer attitudes regarding purchase and use of both the advertiser's products and competing products. The exact kinds of information an organization finds useful depend on the type of product being advertised, the characteristics of the target audience, and the type and amount of competition. Additionally, advertisers must be sure to create a campaign that will resonate with the target market. For instance, privacy concerns and irritating ads lead to avoidance, but when online and direct-mail advertising personalizes the information, acceptance of the ad tends to increase.[9] Generally, the more an advertiser knows about the target audience, the more likely the firm is to develop an effective advertising campaign. The advertisement for Outward Bound clearly demonstrates that its target audience is outdoor enthusiasts. Knowing the target market for a company helps in developing an effective marketing mix, including relevant promotions that specifically target this group. The advertisement depicts a mountain climber on the side of a mountain and stresses the fact that Outward Bound offers a different type of education—education for life. When the advertising target is not precisely identified and properly analyzed, the campaign may fail.

Target Audience
Outward Bound displays extreme outdoor activities to appeal to its target audience of outdoor enthusiasts.

17-2b Defining the Advertising Objectives

The advertiser's next step is to determine what the firm hopes to accomplish with the campaign. Because advertising objectives guide campaign development, advertisers should define objectives carefully. Advertising objectives should be stated clearly, precisely, and in measurable terms. Precision and measurability allow advertisers to evaluate advertising success at the end of the campaign in terms of whether objectives have been met. To provide precision and measurability, advertising objectives should contain benchmarks and indicate how far the advertiser wishes to move from these standards. If the goal is to increase sales, the advertiser should state the current sales level (the benchmark) and the amount of sales increase sought through advertising. An advertising objective should also specify a time frame so that advertisers know exactly how long they have to accomplish the objective. An advertiser with average monthly sales of $450,000 (the benchmark) might set the following objective: "Our primary advertising objective is to increase average monthly sales from $450,000 to $540,000 within 12 months."

target audience The group of people at whom advertisements are aimed

Going Green

The Truthfulness of the Word "Natural" in Advertising Claims

Many terms that signify green or environmentally-friendly attributes are vague without clear definitions. The word "natural," displayed in much food advertising, is no exception. PepsiCo.'s Naked Juice brand came under scrutiny for the use of the word "natural." According to a lawsuit, the added vitamins in the juices are synthetic and the drinks contain manmade fibers. The Food and Drug Administration (FDA) admits that the word "natural" is hard to define because so many foods produced and sold on the market have been processed in one way or another. The FDA generally considers non-deceptive use of the word to refer to products that do not contain added colors, artificial flavors, or synthetic substances.

Pepsi Co. agreed to pay a $9 million settlement and refrain from using the word "natural" on its labels and advertisements until the FDA can more specifically define the word. However, it maintains the truthfulness of its "natural" claim. Pepsi also promised that it would hire an independent investigator to ensure that their non-genetically-modified labels are accurate and do not contain genetically modified ingredients. It is important for a company to maintain truthfulness in its advertising, and Pepsi appears willing to make changes.[a]

If an advertiser defines objectives on the basis of sales, the objectives focus on increasing absolute dollar sales or unit sales, increasing sales by a certain percentage, or increasing the firm's market share. Even though an advertiser's long-run goal is to increase sales, not all campaigns are designed to produce immediate sales. Some campaigns aim to increase product or brand awareness, make consumers' attitudes more favorable, heighten consumers' knowledge of product features, or create awareness of positive, healthy consumer behavior, such as nonsmoking. If the goal is to increase product awareness, the objectives are stated in terms of communication. A specific communication objective might be to increase new-product feature awareness, such as increased travel point rewards on a credit card from 0 to 40 percent in the target audience by the end of 6 months.

17-2c Creating the Advertising Platform

Before launching a political campaign, party leaders develop a political platform stating major issues that are the basis of the campaign. Like a political platform, an **advertising platform** consists of the basic issues or selling points that an advertiser wishes to include in the advertising campaign. For instance, Apple advertises its in-store trading program for consumers that want to upgrade to its newest technology.[10] A single advertisement in an advertising campaign may contain one or several issues from the platform. Although the platform sets forth the basic issues, it does not indicate how to present them.

An advertising platform should consist of issues important to customers. One of the best ways to determine those issues is to survey customers about what they consider most important in the selection and use of the product involved. Selling features must not only be important to customers, but they should also be strongly competitive features of the advertised brand. For instance, J.Crew's Ludlow Suit collection capitalizes upon its positioning as "style with substance." The Ludlow collection is marketed as high-quality ("fine Italian fabrics"), high-value products tailored to fit the customer.[11] Although research is the most effective method for determining what issues to include in an advertising platform, customer research can be expensive.

advertising platform Basic issues or selling points to be included in an advertising campaign

Because the advertising platform is a base on which to build the advertising message, marketers should analyze this stage carefully. It has been found that, if the message is viewed as useful, it will create greater brand trust.[12] A campaign can be perfect in terms of selection and analysis of its target audience, statement of its objectives, media strategy, and the form of its message. But the campaign will ultimately fail if the advertisements communicate information that consumers do not deem important when selecting and using the product.

17-2d Determining the Advertising Appropriation

The **advertising appropriation** is the total amount of money a marketer allocates for advertising for a specific time period. Case in point, Panera Bread Co. spends approximately 1.5 percent of its annual sales on advertising.[13] Many factors affect a firm's decision about how much to appropriate for advertising. Geographic size of the market and the distribution of buyers within the market have a great bearing on this decision. Both the type of product advertised and the firm's sales volume relative to competitors' sales volumes also play roles in determining what proportion of revenue to spend on advertising. Advertising appropriations for business products are usually quite small relative to product sales, whereas consumer convenience items, such as the cosmetics sold by L'Oréal, generally have large advertising expenditures relative to sales. For instance, Procter & Gamble spends a relatively high percentage of sales to market its product mix of cosmetics, personal-care products, appliances, detergents, and pet food. Retailers like Walmart usually have a much lower percent of sales spent on advertising.

Of the many techniques used to determine the advertising appropriation, one of the most logical is the **objective-and-task approach**. Using this approach, marketers determine the objectives a campaign is to achieve and then attempt to list the tasks required to accomplish them. The costs of the tasks are calculated and added to arrive at the total appropriation. This approach has one main problem: Marketers sometimes have trouble accurately estimating the level of effort needed to attain certain objectives. A coffee marketer, for example, may find it extremely difficult to determine how much of an increase in national television advertising is needed to raise a brand's market share from 8 to 10 percent.

In the more widely used **percent-of-sales approach**, marketers simply multiply the firm's past sales, plus a factor for planned sales growth or decline, by a standard percentage based on both what the firm traditionally spends on advertising and the industry average. This approach, too, has a major flaw: It is based on the incorrect assumption that sales create advertising rather than the reverse. A marketer using this approach during declining sales will reduce the amount spent on advertising, but such a reduction may further diminish sales. Though illogical, this technique has been favored because it is easy to implement.

Another way to determine advertising appropriation is the **competition-matching approach**. Marketers following this approach try to match their major competitors' appropriations in absolute dollars or to allocate the same percentage of sales for advertising that their competitors do. Although a marketer should be aware of what competitors spend on advertising, this technique should not be used alone because the firm's competitors probably have different advertising objectives and different resources available for advertising. Many companies and advertising agencies review competitive spending on a quarterly basis, comparing competitors' dollar expenditures on print, radio, and television with their own spending levels. Competitive tracking of this nature occurs at both the national and regional levels.

At times, marketers use the **arbitrary approach**, which usually means a high-level executive in the firm states how much to spend on advertising for a certain period. The arbitrary approach often leads to underspending or overspending. Although hardly a scientific budgeting technique, it is expedient.

Deciding how large the advertising appropriation should be is critical. If the appropriation is set too low, the campaign cannot achieve its full potential. When too much money is appropriated, overspending results, and financial resources are wasted.

advertising appropriation The advertising budget for a specific time period

objective-and-task approach Budgeting for an advertising campaign by first determining its objectives and then calculating the cost of all the tasks needed to attain them

percent-of-sales approach Budgeting for an advertising campaign by multiplying the firm's past and expected sales by a standard percentage

competition-matching approach Determining an advertising budget by trying to match competitors' advertising outlays

arbitrary approach Budgeting for an advertising campaign as specified by a high-level executive in the firm

17-2e Developing the Media Plan

Advertisers spend tremendous amounts on advertising media. These amounts have grown rapidly during the past two decades. Figure 17.2 shows the share of advertising revenue allocated to different media categories. Although television and print still comprise a greater share of

Figure 17.2 **Proportion of Total Global Advertising Expenditures Spent on Media**

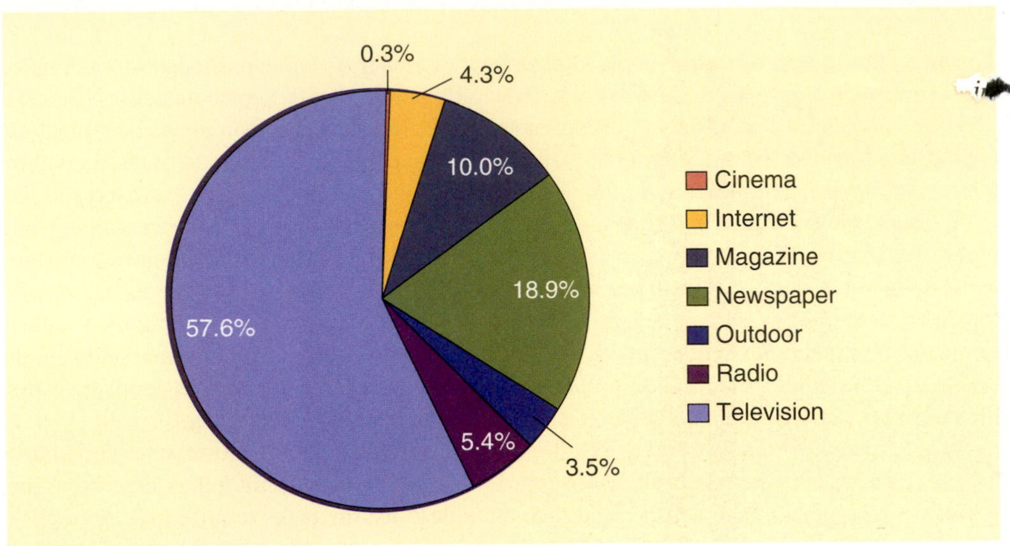

Source: Nielsen, "Global Ad Spend: With Double Digit Gains, Display Ads Drive In-Your-Face Results," October 22, 2013, www.nielsen.com/us/en/newswire/2013/global-ad-spend-with-double-digit-gains-display-ads-drive-in-y.html (accessed January 15, 2014).

media plan A plan that specifies the media vehicles to be used and the schedule for running advertisements

Chrysler Group LLC

Media Plan
In addition to this advertisement found in a magazine, the Dodge Durango was also promoted in newspapers, social media, television, and other promotional outlets. Dodge uses fictional character Ron Burgundy to act as the endorser of its vehicle.

advertising revenue than digital advertising, this last category is expected to grow rapidly during the next few years. To derive maximum results from media expenditures, marketers must develop effective media plans. A **media plan** sets forth the exact media vehicles to be used (specific magazines, television stations, social media, newspapers, and so forth) and the dates and times the advertisements will appear. The media plan for the Dodge Durango consisted of magazines, television, social media, and other promotional outlets. The advertisement shows the fictional Ron Burgundy (portrayed by Will Ferrell) endorsing the Dodge Durango. The plan determines how many people in the target audience will be exposed to the message. The method also determines, to some degree, the effects of the message on those specific target markets. Media planning is a complex task requiring thorough analysis of the target audience. Sophisticated computer models have been developed to attempt to maximize the effectiveness of media plans.

To formulate a media plan, the planners select the media for the campaign and prepare a time schedule for each medium. The media planner's primary goal is to reach the largest number of people in the advertising target that the budget will allow. A secondary goal is to achieve the appropriate message reach and frequency for the target audience while staying within budget. *Reach* refers to the percentage of consumers in the target audience actually exposed to a particular advertisement in a stated period. *Frequency* is the number of times these targeted consumers are exposed to the advertisement.

Media planners begin with broad decisions but eventually make very specific ones. They first decide which kinds of media to use: radio, television, newspapers, digital or online advertising, magazines, direct mail, outdoor displays, or signs on mass transit vehicles. Mobile marketing in particular is growing, with spending on online advertising expected to approximate nearly $20 billion in 2015.[14] Media planners assess different formats and approaches to determine which are most effective. Some media plans are highly focused and use just one medium. Others can be quite complex and dynamic.

Media planners take many factors into account when devising a media plan. They analyze location and demographic characteristics of consumers in the target audience, because people's tastes in media differ according to demographic groups and locations. Media planners also consider the sizes and types of audiences that specific media reach. For instance, *National Geographic* reaches relatively well-educated consumers who are often highly influential decision makers. The magazine has 31 million readers in the United States alone.[15] Many marketers of vehicles, nonprofit organizations, and electronics would consider this an attractive demographic. Declining broadcast television ratings and newspaper and magazine readership have led many companies to explore alternative media, including not only digital advertising but also ads on cell phones, product placements in video games, and advertisements in nontraditional venues. For example, Philadelphia debated whether to allow for advertising in public schools to help generate much-needed cash for the institutions.[16] New media like social networking sites are also attracting advertisers due to their large reach. Research findings have found that, when advertising is a part of a social networking site, consumers need to see the advertising as beneficial, or it may lead them to abandon the site.[17] On the other hand, even in this age of digital media, television remains the most successful medium for advertising.[18]

The rise in digital marketing is creating a dramatic shift for advertising agencies. Whereas competition came mostly from other agencies before, today professional ad agencies face competition from amateur ad makers along with technology companies. For instance, crowdsourcing by organizations like Victor & Spoils is placing the roles of traditional advertising agencies into the hands of creative people worldwide. Digital marketing is not reduced to one medium, but can include platforms such as social networks, e-books, iPads, geotargeting, and mobile apps. Agencies that choose to embrace new advertising media are facing challenges in adapting but are finding increased profits along the way. Big data can open the door to reaching the most desirable customers and have a positive effect on sales.[19] Coca-Cola launched a digital advertising campaign to encourage teen-based participation with its brand. It hired advertising firm Wieden & Kennedy Portland to develop "The Ahh Effect," a campaign involving 61 websites that incorporate games, photos, and videos. Each URL has a different number of "h's" in the word "Ahh" and incorporates different content with which users can interact.[20] Digital marketing enables firms such as Coca-Cola to find more interactive ways to connect with specific target markets at a reasonable price.

The content of the message sometimes affects media choice. Print media can be used more effectively than broadcast media to present complex issues or numerous details in single

Marketing Debate

Pros and Cons of Mobile Advertising

ISSUE: Is mobile advertising an invasion of privacy?

Today, advertising is no longer limited to print and television but has begun reaching consumers on a personal medium—their cell phones. Marketers spend approximately $2.6 billion on mobile advertising, with this number growing each year. This medium has become ideal for advertisers due to social networking, as most consumers access these sites through their mobile phones. Additionally, studies have found that brand recall is higher with certain types of mobile ads. On the other hand, some individuals see mobile advertising as an invasion of privacy. They believe that advertising should be left in the traditional arenas and not displayed over something as personal as their cell phones.[b]

Benefits of Magazine Advertising
Magazine advertisements allow marketers to show their advertisements using bold colors and patterns. This Sherwin Williams advertisement uses a costumed dragon to demonstrate the variety of colors that can be found in its stores.

advertisements. If an advertiser wants to promote beautiful colors, patterns, or textures, media offering high-quality color reproduction, such as magazines or television, should be used instead of newspapers. For instance, food can be effectively promoted in full-color magazine advertisements but far less effectively in black-and-white media. This Sherwin Williams ad shows the benefit of magazine advertising in presenting bold and impactful paint colors.

The cost of media is an important but troublesome consideration. Planners try to obtain the best coverage possible for each dollar spent. However, there is no accurate way to compare the cost and impact of a television commercial with the cost and impact of a newspaper advertisement. A **cost comparison indicator** lets an advertiser compare the costs of several vehicles within a specific medium (such as two magazines) in relation to the number of people each vehicle reaches. The *cost per thousand impressions (CPM)* is the cost comparison indicator for magazines; it shows the cost of exposing 1,000 people to one advertisement.

Figure 17.3 shows the extent to which digital advertising is growing compared to television and newspaper advertising. Emerging media are being used more extensively in light of media fragmentation and decline in traditional media (newspapers and radio). However, although the use of newer forms of media is increasing, many companies continue to spend significant amounts of their marketing dollars advertising in more traditional forums. Because 58 percent of working adults have indicated they still use phone books at work or at home, many marketers continue to pay large sums of money to advertise

Figure 17-3 Digital Advertising Continues Its Rapid Growth

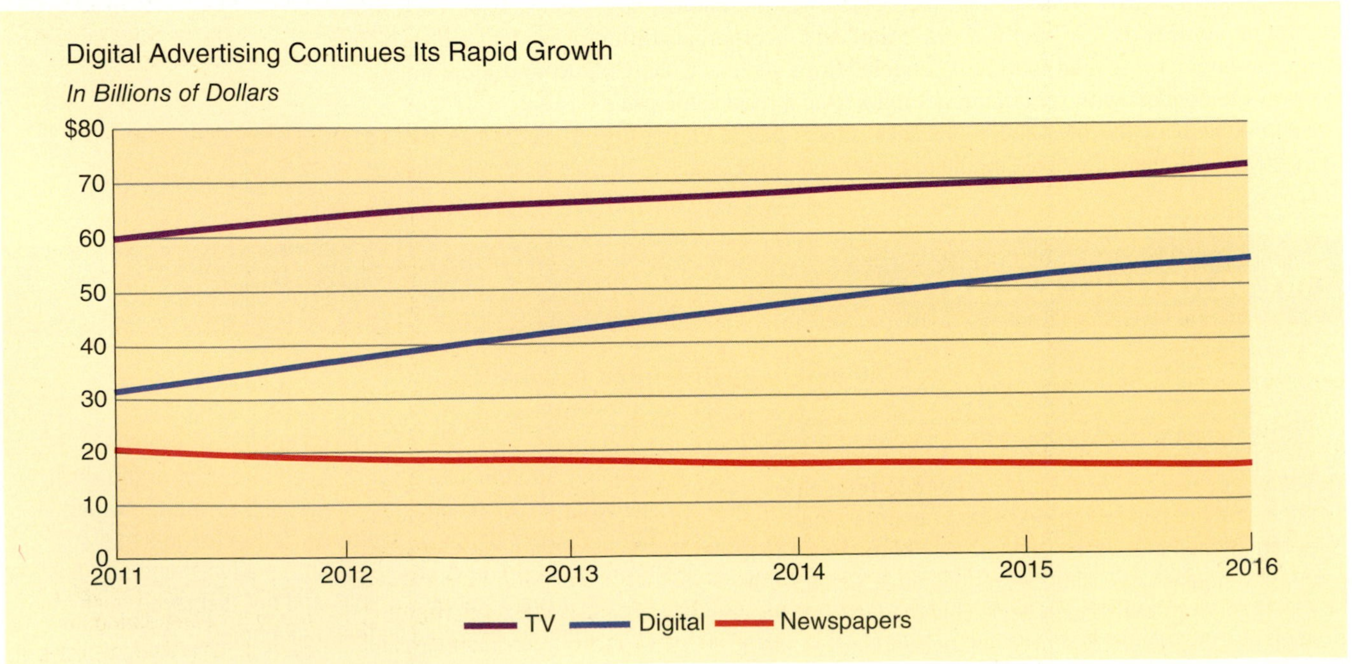

Source: eMarketer, "US Ad Spending Forecast." October 2012.
Note: Mobile is a subset of digital. Figures for 2013–2016 are forecasts.

Table 17.1 Advantages and Disadvantages of Major Media Classes

Medium	Advantages	Disadvantages
Newspapers	Reaches large audience; purchased to be read; geographic flexibility; short lead time; frequent publication; favorable for cooperative advertising; merchandising services	Not selective for socioeconomic groups or target market; short life; limited reproduction capabilities; large advertising volume limits exposure to any one advertisement
Magazines	Demographic selectivity; good reproduction; long life; prestige; geographic selectivity when regional issues are available; read in leisurely manner	High costs; 30- to 90-day average lead time; high level of competition; limited reach; communicates less frequently
Direct mail	Little wasted circulation; highly selective; circulation controlled by advertiser; few distractions; personal; stimulates actions; use of novelty; relatively easy to measure performance; hidden from competitors	Very expensive; lacks editorial content to attract readers; often thrown away unread as junk mail; criticized as invasion of privacy; consumers must choose to read the ad
Radio	Reaches 95 percent of consumers; highly mobile and flexible; very low relative costs; ad can be changed quickly; high level of geographic and demographic selectivity; encourages use of imagination	Lacks visual imagery; short life of message; listeners' attention limited because of other activities; market fragmentation; difficult buying procedures; limited media and audience research
Television	Reaches large audiences; high frequency available; dual impact of audio and video; highly visible; high prestige; geographic and demographic selectivity; difficult to ignore	Very expensive; highly perishable message; size of audience not guaranteed; amount of prime time limited; lack of selectivity in target market
Internet	Immediate response; potential to reach a precisely targeted audience; ability to track customers and build databases; highly interactive medium	Costs of precise targeting are high; inappropriate ad placement; effects difficult to measure; concerns about security and privacy
Yellow Pages	Wide availability; action and product category oriented; low relative costs; ad frequency and longevity; nonintrusive	Market fragmentation; extremely localized; slow updating; lack of creativity; long lead times; requires large space to be noticed
Outdoor	Allows for frequent repetition; low cost; message can be placed close to point of sale; geographic selectivity; operable 24 hours a day; high creativity and effectiveness	Message must be short and simple; no demographic selectivity; seldom attracts readers' full attention; criticized as traffic hazard and blight on countryside; much wasted coverage; limited capabilities

Sources: William F. Arens, *Contemporary Advertising* (Burr Ridge, IL: Irwin/McGraw-Hill, 2011); George E. Belch and Michael Belch, *Advertising and Promotion* (Burr Ridge, IL: Irwin/McGraw-Hill, 2011).

in this medium.[21] Media are selected by weighing the various advantages and disadvantages of each (see Table 17.1).

Like media selection decisions, media scheduling decisions are affected by numerous factors, such as target audience characteristics, product attributes, product seasonality, customer media behavior, and size of the advertising budget. There are three general types of media schedules: continuous, flighting, and pulsing. When a *continuous* schedule is used, advertising runs at a constant level with little variation throughout the campaign period. McDonald's is an example of a company that uses a continuous schedule. With a *flighting* schedule, advertisements run for set periods of time, alternating with periods in which no ads run. For instance, an advertising campaign might have an ad run for 2 weeks, then suspend it for 2 weeks, and then run it again for 2 weeks. Companies like Hallmark, John Deere, and Ray-Ban use a flighting schedule. A *pulsing* schedule combines continuous and flighting schedules: During the entire campaign, a certain portion of advertising runs continuously, and during specific time periods of the campaign, additional advertising is used to intensify the level of communication with the target audience.

cost comparison indicator A means of comparing the costs of advertising vehicles in a specific medium in relation to the number of people reached

17-2f Creating the Advertising Message

The basic content and form of an advertising message are a function of several factors. A product's features, uses, and benefits affect the content of the message. The intensity of the advertising can also have an impact. For instance, push advertising on digital devices refers to advertising that is not requested by the user. Although push advertising might alienate some consumers, younger consumers are more accepting of push advertising if the source is trusted, permission has been given, and the messages are relevant or entertaining.[22] However, research has shown that advertising that pushes too hard to the point that consumers feel uncomfortable may cause consumers to consider the product negatively.[23] With the increase in digital technology, the cost of advertising for marketers is decreasing and advertising is becoming more frequent in venues such as mobile games. Marketers must make sure their advertising is not too intrusive as this could alienate consumers.[24]

Additionally, characteristics of the people in the target audience—gender, age, education, race, income, occupation, lifestyle, life stage, and other attributes—influence both content and form. For instance, gender affects how people respond to advertising claims that use hedging words like *may* and *probably* and pledging words, such as *definitely* and *absolutely*. Researchers have found that women respond negatively to both types of claims, but pledging claims have little effect on men.[25] When Procter & Gamble promotes Crest toothpaste to children, the company emphasizes daily brushing and cavity control, focusing on fun and good flavors like bubblegum. When marketing Crest to adults, P&G focuses on functionality, stressing whitening, enamel protection, breath enhancement, and tartar and plaque control. To communicate effectively, advertisers use words, symbols, and illustrations that are meaningful, familiar, and appealing to people in the target audience.

Another controversy for advertisers is whether to advertise to children. Many countries have restrictions on advertising to this demographic. Sweden and Norway ban advertising directed at children, and Great Britain limits the advertising of foods high in fat, salt, or sugar on television and radio to children under the age of 16. Many firms in the European Union and the United States are attempting self-regulation, developing codes of conduct regarding this type of advertising. Coca-Cola, for instance, promised that it would not target advertising toward children that are under 12 years old.[26]

Spokescharacter
Keebler uses elves to promote the taste and quality of its cookies.

An advertising campaign's objectives and platform also affect the content and form of its messages. If a firm's advertising objectives involve large sales increases, the message may include hard-hitting, high-impact language, symbols, and messages. Slogans such as the Geico gecko's basic message, "15 minutes could save you 15% or more on car insurance," can aid in brand recall. When designing slogans, marketers should make them short, retain them for a long period of time, and provide large marketing budgets to make the slogan memorable.[27] The use of spokescharacters or design elements can also be highly effective. Spokescharacters are visual images that can convey a brand's features, benefits, or brand personality. Flo from Progressive Insurance and the Geico gecko are examples of spokescharacters representing specific brands. The spokescharacter can provide a personality and improve brand equity by directly and indirectly enhancing excitement, sincerity, and trust.[28] Keebler uses the elves as spokescharacters for their cookies. Viewers have come to associate these spokescharacters with the company. In the advertisement, Keebler uses the elves to show the 'elfin magic' that goes into making the cookies so tasty. Thus, the advertising platform is the foundation on which campaign messages are built.

Choice of media obviously influences the content and form of the message. Effective outdoor displays and short broadcast spot announcements require concise, simple messages. Magazine and newspaper advertisements can include considerable detail and long explanations. Because several kinds of media offer geographic selectivity, a precise message can be tailored to a particular geographic section of the target audience. Some magazine publishers produce **regional issues**, in which advertisements and editorial content of copies appearing in one geographic area differ from those appearing in other areas. For instance, the AAA Publishing Network publishes 22 regional magazine titles, including *AAA Horizons* (Connecticut, Rhode Island, and Massachusetts), *AAA Going Places* (Georgia and Tennessee), and *Western Journey* (Idaho and Washington).[29] A company advertising with the AAA Publishing Network might decide to use one message in the New England region and another in the rest of the nation. A company may also choose to advertise in only one region. Such geographic selectivity lets a firm use the same message in different regions at different times.

17-2g Copy

Copy is the verbal portion of an advertisement and may include headlines, subheadlines, body copy, and a signature. Not all advertising contains all of these copy elements. Even handwritten notes on direct-mail advertising that say, "Try this. It works!" seem to increase requests for free samples.[30] The headline is critical because often it is the only part of the copy that people read. It should attract readers' attention and create enough interest to make them want to read the body copy or visit the website. The subheadline, if there is one, links the headline to the body copy and sometimes serves to explain the headline.

Body copy for most advertisements consists of an introductory statement or paragraph, several explanatory paragraphs, and a closing paragraph. Some copywriters have adopted guidelines for developing body copy systematically: (1) identify a specific desire or problem, (2) recommend the product as the best way to satisfy that desire or solve that problem, (3) state product benefits and indicate why the product is best for the buyer's particular situation, (4) substantiate advertising claims, and (5) ask the buyer to take action. When substantiating claims, it is important to present the substantiation in a credible manner. The proof of claims should help strengthen both the image of the product and company integrity. A shortcut explanation of what much advertising is designed to accomplish is the AIDA model. Advertising should create *awareness*, produce *interest*, create *desire*, and ultimately result in a purchase (*action*). Typeface selection can help advertisers create a desired impression using fonts that are engaging, reassuring, or very prominent.[31]

The signature identifies the advertisement's sponsor. It may contain several elements, including the firm's trademark, logo, name, and address. The signature should be attractive, legible, distinctive, and easy to identify in a variety of sizes.

regional issues Versions of a magazine that differ across geographic regions

copy The verbal portion of advertisements

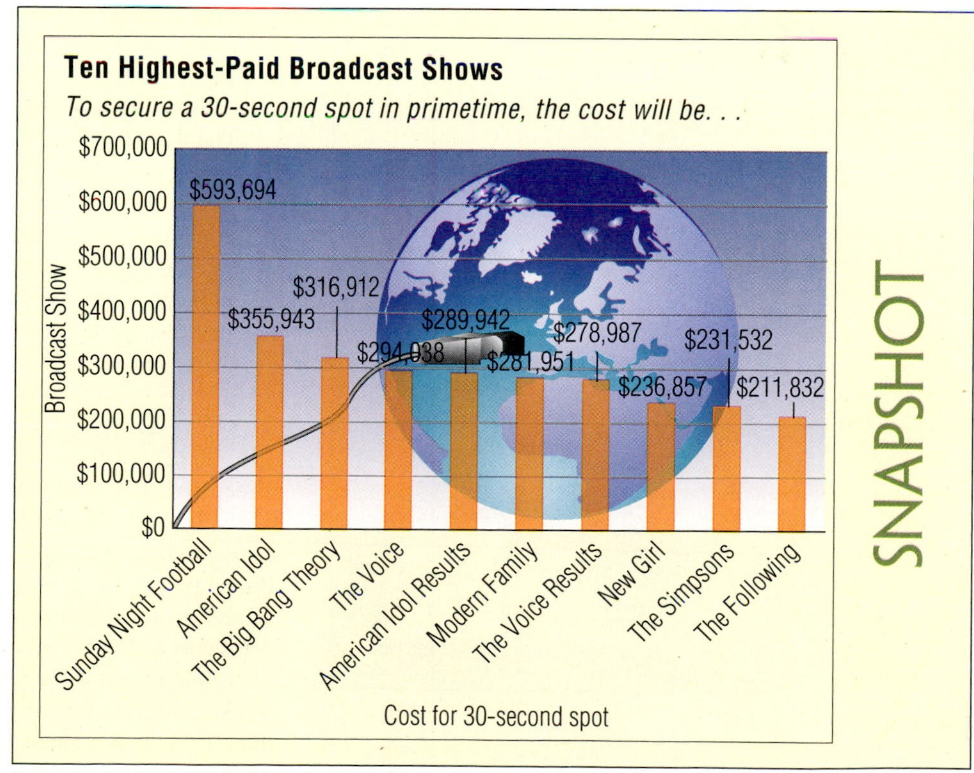

Source: Jeanine Poggi, "TV Ad Prices: Football Is Still King," *Advertising Age*, October 20, 2013, http://adage.com/article/media/tv-ad-prices-football-king/244832 (accessed January 13, 2014).

Often, because radio listeners are not fully "tuned in" mentally to what they're hearing on the radio, radio copy should be informal and conversational to attract listeners' attention. Radio messages are highly perishable and should consist of short, familiar terms, which increase their impact. The length should not require a rate of speech exceeding approximately 2.5 words per second.

In television copy, the audio material must not overpower the visual material, and vice versa. However, a television message should make optimal use of its visual portion, which can be very effective for product use, applications, and demonstrations. Copy for a television commercial is sometimes initially written in parallel script form. Video is described in the left column and audio in the right. When the parallel script is approved, the copywriter and artist combine copy with visual material by using a **storyboard**, which depicts a series of miniature television screens showing the sequence of major scenes in the commercial. Beneath each screen is a description of the audio portion to be used with that video segment. Technical personnel use the storyboard as a blueprint when producing the commercial.

storyboard A blueprint that combines copy and visual material to show the sequence of major scenes in a commercial

artwork An advertisement's illustrations and layout

illustrations Photos, drawings, graphs, charts, and tables used to spark audience interest in an advertisement

layout The physical arrangement of an advertisement's illustration and copy

17-2h Artwork

Artwork consists of an advertisement's illustrations and layout. **Illustrations** are often photographs but can also be drawings, graphs, charts, and tables. Illustrations are used to draw attention, encourage audiences to read or listen to the copy, communicate an idea quickly, or convey ideas that are difficult to express. Illustrations can be more important in capturing attention than text or brand elements, independent of size.[32] They are especially important, because consumers tend to recall the visual portions of advertisements better than the verbal portions. Advertisers use a variety of illustration techniques. They may show the product alone, in a setting, or in use, or show the results of the product's use. For instance, the Petco advertisement shows a close-up of a bulldog to emphasize the importance of protecting your pet's health. The advertisement is meant to market the benefits of Petco instead of a particular Petco product. Illustrations can also take the form of comparisons, contrasts, diagrams, and testimonials.

Components of a Print Ad
This Petco advertisement contains components of a print ad, including a headline, subheadline, body copy, signature, and illustration.

The **layout** of an advertisement is the physical arrangement of the illustration and the copy (headline, subheadline, body copy, and signature). These elements can be arranged in many ways. The final layout is the result of several stages of layout preparation. As it moves through these stages, the layout promotes an exchange of ideas among people developing the advertising campaign and provides instructions for production personnel.

17-2i Executing the Campaign

Execution of an advertising campaign requires extensive planning and coordination, because many tasks must be completed on time and several people and firms are involved. Production companies, research organizations, media firms, printers, and commercial artists are just a few of the people and firms contributing to a campaign.

Implementation requires detailed schedules to ensure that various phases of the work are done on time. Advertising management personnel must evaluate the quality of the work and take corrective action when necessary. After sales of Planters nut products decreased, the company decided to revise its Mr. Peanut mascot. The silent human-sized Mr. Peanut had changed little over the years and had lost his appeal. Planters responded by making the mascot smaller and giving him a voice. Sales began to increase after the new Mr. Peanut began marketing products. Robert Downey, Jr., was originally hired to voice the character and was succeeded by comedian Bill Hader.[33] In some instances, changes are made during the campaign so it meets objectives more effectively. For example, an auto company focusing on gas mileage may need to add more information relative to the competition to achieve its objectives.

17-2j Evaluating Advertising Effectiveness

A variety of ways exist to test the effectiveness of advertising. They include measuring achievement of advertising objectives; assessing effectiveness of copy, illustrations, or layouts; and evaluating certain media.

Advertising can be evaluated before, during, and after the campaign. An evaluation performed before the campaign begins is called a **pretest**. A pretest usually attempts to evaluate the effectiveness of one or more elements of the message. To pretest advertisements, marketers sometimes use a **consumer jury**, a panel of existing or potential buyers of the advertised product. Jurors judge one or several dimensions of two or more advertisements. Such tests are based on the belief that consumers are more likely than advertising experts to know what influences them. Companies can also solicit the assistance of marketing research firms, such as Information Resources Inc. (IRI), to help assess ads.

To measure advertising effectiveness during a campaign, marketers usually rely on "inquiries" or responses. In a campaign's initial stages, an advertiser may use several advertisements simultaneously, each containing a coupon, form, toll-free phone number, QR code, social media, or website through which potential customers can request information. The advertiser records the number of inquiries or responses returned from each type of advertisement. If an advertiser receives 78,528 inquiries from advertisement A, 37,072 from advertisement B, and 47,932 from advertisement C, advertisement A is judged superior to advertisements B and C. Internet advertisers can also assess how many people "clicked" on an ad to obtain more product information.

Evaluation of advertising effectiveness after the campaign is called a **posttest**. Advertising objectives often determine what kind of posttest is appropriate. If the objectives' focus is on communication—to increase awareness of product features or brands or to create more favorable customer attitudes—the posttest should measure changes in these dimensions. Advertisers sometimes use consumer surveys or experiments to evaluate a campaign based on communication objectives. These methods are costly, however. In posttests, generalizations can be made about why advertising is failing or why media vehicles are not delivering the desired results.

For campaign objectives stated in terms of sales, advertisers should determine the change in sales or market share attributable to the campaign. After Will Ferrell began starring in Dodge commercials as fictional anchorman Ron Burgundy, sales of the Dodge Durango soared, climbing 59 percent in a 1-month period.[34] However, changes in sales or market share brought about by advertising cannot be measured precisely; many factors independent of advertisements affect a firm's sales and market share. Competitors' actions, regulatory actions, and changes in economic conditions, consumer preferences, and weather are only a few factors that might enhance or diminish a company's sales or market share. By using data about past and current sales and advertising expenditures, advertisers can make gross estimates of the effects of a campaign on sales or market share. Because it is difficult to determine the direct effects of advertising on sales, many advertisers evaluate print advertisements according to how well consumers can remember them. As more advertisers turn to mobile technology, measuring the recall rate of mobile advertisements is becoming increasingly important. Mobile recall rates appear to be higher than television commercials or Web videos. A mobile video campaign featuring the GMC Terrain vehicle had a 42 percent brand recall rate.[35] Researchers have found that

pretest Evaluation of advertisements performed before a campaign begins

consumer jury A panel of a product's existing or potential buyers who pretest ads

posttest Evaluation of advertising effectiveness after the campaign

ads that play on the theme of social desirability are more memorable when viewed in the presence of other people.

Posttest methods based on memory include recognition and recall tests. Such tests are usually performed by research organizations through surveys. In a **recognition test**, respondents are shown the actual advertisement and asked whether they recognize it. If they do, the interviewer asks additional questions to determine how much of the advertisement each respondent read. When recall is evaluated, respondents are not shown the actual advertisement but instead are asked about what they have seen or heard recently. For Internet advertising, research suggests that the longer a person is exposed to a website containing a banner advertisement, the more likely he or she is to recall the ad.[36]

Recall can be measured through either unaided or aided recall methods. In an **unaided recall test**, respondents identify advertisements they have seen recently but are not shown any clues to help them remember. A similar procedure is used with an **aided recall test**, but respondents are shown a list of products, brands, company names, or trademarks to jog their memories. Research has shown that brand recall is 1.7 times higher among users of a product than non-users.[37] Several research organizations, such as Daniel Starch, provide research services that test recognition and recall of advertisements.

The major justification for using recognition and recall methods is that people are more likely to buy a product if they can remember an advertisement about it than if they cannot. However, recalling an advertisement does not necessarily lead to buying the product or brand advertised. Researchers also use a sophisticated technique called *single-source data* to help evaluate advertisements. With this technique, individuals' behaviors are tracked from television sets to checkout counters. Monitors are placed in preselected homes, and microcomputers record when the television set is on and which station is being viewed. At the supermarket checkout, the individual in the sample household presents an identification card. Checkers then record the purchases by scanner, and data are sent to the research facility. Some single-source data companies provide sample households with scanning equipment for use at home to record purchases after returning from shopping trips. Single-source data supplies information that links exposure to advertisements with purchase behavior.

17-3 WHO DEVELOPS THE ADVERTISING CAMPAIGN?

An advertising campaign may be handled by an individual, a few people within a firm, a firm's own advertising department, or an advertising agency. In very small firms, one or two individuals are responsible for advertising (and for many other activities as well). Usually, these individuals depend heavily on local media (TV, radio, and newspaper) for copywriting, artwork, and advice about scheduling media.

In certain large businesses, especially large retail organizations, advertising departments create and implement advertising campaigns. Depending on the size of the advertising program, an advertising department may consist of a few multiskilled individuals or a sizable number of specialists, including copywriters, artists, social media experts, media buyers, and technical production coordinators. Advertising departments sometimes obtain the services of independent research organizations and hire freelance specialists when a particular project requires it.

Many firms employ an advertising agency to develop advertising campaigns. For example, Perfetti Van Melle, owner of the Mentos brand, hired New York–based McKinney to develop creative television commercials geared toward the Millennial generation.[38] When an organization uses an advertising agency, the firm and the agency usually develop the advertising campaign jointly. How much each participates in the campaign's total development depends on the working relationship between the firm and the agency. Ordinarily,

recognition test A posttest in which respondents are shown the actual ad and are asked if they recognize it

unaided recall test A posttest in which respondents are asked to identify advertisements they have seen recently but are not given any recall clues

aided recall test A posttest that asks respondents to identify recent ads and provides clues to jog their memories

a firm relies on the agency for copywriting, artwork, technical production, and formulation of the media plan. In addition, advertising agencies, because of their size and number of clients, have the ability to reach celebrities for sponsorship or endorsement. The advertising agency for Citizen was able to successfully contract with Eli Manning to promote their line of watches. The advertisement affiliates the Citizen Eco-Drive with the famous champion quarterback. Celebrity endorsements can help create greater awareness and connection with the target audience.

Advertising agencies assist businesses in several ways. An agency, especially a large one, can supply the services of highly skilled specialists—not only copywriters, artists, and production coordinators, but also media experts, researchers, and legal advisors. Agency personnel often have broad advertising experience and are usually more objective than a firm's employees about the organization's products.

Because an agency traditionally receives most of its compensation from a 15 percent commission paid by the media from which it makes purchases, firms can obtain some agency services at low or moderate costs. If an agency contracts for $400,000 of television time for a firm, it receives a commission of $60,000 from the television station. Although the traditional compensation method for agencies is changing and now includes other factors, media commissions still offset some costs of using an agency. Like advertising, public relations can be a vital element in a promotion mix. We turn to this topic next.

The Value of Advertising Agencies
Citizen uses an advertising agency that provides celebrity endorsements and sponsorships.

17-4 PUBLIC RELATIONS

Public relations is a broad set of communication efforts used to create and maintain favorable relationships between an organization and its stakeholders. An organization communicates with various stakeholders, both internal and external, and public relations efforts can be directed toward any and all of them. A firm's stakeholders can include customers, suppliers, employees, shareholders, the media, educators, potential investors, government officials, and society in general. Public relations is also used to respond to negative events. How an organization uses public relations in a crisis often determines how quickly it will recover. Lululemon's chairman was criticized for the way he responded regarding an operations glitch resulting in too-sheer yoga pants. The founder and then-chairman of the company implied that women without a large thigh gap were to blame because the pants were too tight. The chairman ended up leaving after customers expressed outrage.[39] On the other hand, being honest with consumers and responsive to their needs develops a foundation for open communication and trust in the long run.

Public relations can be used to promote people, places, ideas, activities, and even countries. It is often used by nonprofit organizations to achieve their goals. The United Nations started the Free & Equal public relations campaign to promote equality for lesbian, gay, bisexual, transgender, and intersex people across the globe. As part of this campaign, the UN developed fact sheets and creative content such as videos and testimonies to educate and engage consumers.[40] Public relations focuses on enhancing the image of the total organization. Assessing public attitudes and creating a favorable image are no less important

public relations Communication efforts used to create and maintain favorable relations between an organization and its stakeholders

Table 17.2 Top 10 Public Relations Firms

Rank	PR Agency
1	Edelman
2	Weber Shandwick
3	FleishmanHillard
4	MSLGroup
5	Burson Marsteller
6	Ketchum
7	Hill+Knowlton Strategies
8	Ogilvy Public Relations Worldwide
9	Havas PR
10	Brunswick

Source: International Communications Consultancy Organisation, "World PR Report," *The Holmes Report*, http://worldreport.holmesreport.com/sites/all/themes/influence100_theme/Top250table2013_WEB.pdf (accessed January 9, 2014).

than direct promotion of the organization's products. Because the public's attitudes toward a firm are likely to affect the sales of its products, it is very important for firms to maintain positive public perceptions. In addition, employee morale is strengthened if the public perceives the firm positively.[41] Although public relations can make people aware of a company's products, brands, or activities, it can also create specific company images, such as innovativeness or dependability. Companies like Green Mountain Coffee Roasters, Patagonia, Sustainable Harvest, and Honest Tea have reputations for being socially responsible not only because they engage in socially responsible behavior but also because their actions are reported through news stories and other public relations efforts. By getting the media to report on a firm's accomplishments, public relations helps the company maintain positive public visibility. Some firms use public relations for a single purpose; others use it for several purposes. Table 17.2 describes the top 10 public relations firms.

17-5 PUBLIC RELATIONS TOOLS

Companies use a variety of public relations tools to convey messages and create images. Public relations professionals prepare written materials and use digital media to deliver brochures, newsletters, company magazines, news releases, blogs, managed social media sites, and annual reports that reach and influence their various stakeholders. Sometimes, organizations use less conventional tools in their public relations campaigns. Discovery Communications, for example, holds an annual "Discover Your Impact Day," in which employees volunteer in their local communities as a way of giving back. "Discover Your Impact Day" not only enables the firm to make a positive difference but also enhances its own reputation as a socially responsible company. The campaign has been so effective that it has been inducted into the Platinum PR Awards Hall of Fame.[42]

Public relations personnel also create corporate identity materials—such as logos, business cards, stationery, signs, and promotional materials—that make firms immediately recognizable. Speeches are another public relations tool. Because what a company executive says publicly at meetings or to the media can affect the organization's image, the speech must convey the desired message clearly. Event sponsorship, in which a company pays for part or all of a special event, like a benefit concert or a tennis tournament, is another public relations tool. One example is Canon USA's sponsorship of the Special Olympics New York.[43] Sponsoring special events can be an effective means of increasing company or brand recognition with relatively minimal investment. Event sponsorship can gain companies considerable amounts of free media coverage. An organization tries to ensure that its product and the sponsored event target a similar audience and that the two are easily associated in customers' minds. Many companies as well as individuals assist in their charitable giving. Bill Daniels, the founder of Cablevision who passed away in 2000, set up a fund supported with more than a billion dollars to provide financial support for many causes, including business ethics. Bill Daniels believed that ethics is integral to business success, especially in the cable industry. The Daniels Fund is actively supporting business ethics education in Colorado, New Mexico, Utah, and Wyoming. Public relations personnel also organize unique events to "create news" about the company. These may include grand openings with celebrities, prizes, hot-air balloon rides, and other attractions that appeal to a firm's public.

Publicity is a part of public relations. **Publicity** is communication in news-story form about the organization, its products, or both, transmitted through a mass medium at no charge. For instance, when featured on *60 Minutes,* Amazon CEO Jeff Bezos decided to create publicity for the company's plans to use drones (unmanned flying vehicles) to deliver Amazon products in the future. The story was immediately discussed by news outlets such as *USA Today* and *60 Minutes Overtime.*[44] Although public relations has a larger, more comprehensive communication function than publicity, publicity is a very important aspect of public relations. Publicity can be used to provide information about goods or services; to announce expansions or contractions, acquisitions, research, or new-product launches; or to enhance a company's image.

The most common publicity-based public relations tool is the **news release**, sometimes called a *press release,* which is usually a single page of typewritten copy containing fewer than 300 words and describing a company event or product. A news release gives the firm's or agency's name, address, phone number, and contact person. Companies sometimes use news releases when introducing new products or making significant announcements. Dozens of organizations, including Nike, Starbucks, and clean-energy companies, are partnering to create awareness of the economic benefits of national climate and energy legislation through press releases and other media. As Table 17.3 shows, news releases tackle a multitude of specific issues. A **feature article** is a manuscript of up to 3,000 words prepared for a specific publication. A **captioned photograph** is a photograph with a brief description explaining its contents. Captioned photographs are effective for illustrating new or improved products with highly visible features.

There are several other kinds of publicity-based public relations tools. For example, a **press conference** is a meeting called to announce major news events. Media personnel are invited to a press conference and are usually supplied with various written materials and photographs. Letters to the editor and editorials are sometimes prepared and sent to newspapers and magazines. Videos may be made available to broadcasters in the hope that they will be aired.

publicity A news story type of communication about an organization and/or its products transmitted through a mass medium at no charge

news release A short piece of copy publicizing an event or a product

feature article A manuscript of up to 3,000 words prepared for a specific publication

captioned photograph A photograph with a brief description of its contents

press conference A meeting used to announce major news events

Table 17.3 Possible Issues for Publicity Releases

Support of a social cause	New products
Improved warranties	New slogan
Reports on industry conditions	Research developments
New uses for established products	Company's milestones and anniversaries
Product endorsements	Employment, production, and sales changes
Quality awards	Award of contracts
Company name changes	Opening of new markets
Interviews with company officials	Improvements in financial position
Improved distribution policies	Opening of an exhibit
International business efforts	History of a brand
Athletic event sponsorship	Winners of company contests
Visits by celebrities	Logo changes
Reports on new discoveries	Speeches of top management
Innovative business practices	Merit awards
Economic forecasts	Acquisitions and partnerships

Publicity-based public relations tools offer several advantages, including credibility, news value, significant word-of-mouth communications, and a perception of media endorsement. The public may consider news coverage more truthful and credible than an advertisement because news media are not paid to provide the information. In addition, stories regarding a new-product introduction or a new environmentally responsible company policy, for example, are handled as news items and are likely to receive notice. Finally, the cost of publicity is low compared with the cost of advertising.[45]

Publicity-based public relations tools have some limitations. Media personnel must judge company messages to be newsworthy if the messages are to be published or broadcast at all. Consequently, messages must be timely, interesting, accurate, and in the public interest. It may take a great deal of time and effort to convince media personnel of the news value of publicity releases, and many communications fail to qualify. Although public relations personnel usually encourage the media to air publicity releases at certain times, they control neither the content nor the timing of the communication. Media personnel alter length and content of publicity releases to fit publishers' or broadcasters' requirements and may even delete the parts of messages that company personnel view as most important. Furthermore, media personnel use publicity releases in time slots or positions most convenient for them. Other outside public relations messages can be picked up during slow news times. Thus, messages sometimes appear in locations or at times that may not reach the firm's target audiences. Although these limitations can be frustrating, properly managed publicity-based public relations tools offer an organization substantial benefits.

17-6 EVALUATING PUBLIC RELATIONS EFFECTIVENESS

Because of the potential benefits of good public relations, it is essential that organizations evaluate the effectiveness of their public relations campaigns. Research can be conducted to determine how well a firm is communicating its messages or image to its target audiences. *Environmental monitoring* identifies changes in public opinion affecting an organization. A *public relations audit* is used to assess an organization's image among the public or to evaluate the effect of a specific public relations program. A *communications audit* may include a content analysis of messages, a readability study, or a readership survey. If an organization wants to measure the extent to which stakeholders view it as being socially responsible, it can conduct a *social audit.*

One approach to measuring the effectiveness of publicity-based public relations is to count the number of exposures in the media. To determine which releases are published in print media and how often, an organization can hire a clipping service, a firm that clips and sends news releases to client companies. To measure the effectiveness of television coverage, a firm can enclose a card with its publicity releases requesting that the television station record its name and the dates when the news item is broadcast (although station personnel do not always comply). Some multimedia tracking services exist, but they are quite costly.

Counting the number of media exposures does not reveal how many people have actually read or heard the company's message or what they thought about the message afterward. However, measuring changes in product awareness, knowledge, and attitudes resulting from the publicity campaign helps yield this information. To assess these changes, companies must measure these levels before and after public relations campaigns. Although precise measures are difficult to obtain, a firm's marketers should attempt to assess the impact of public relations efforts on the organization's sales. For example, critics' reviews of films can affect the films' box office performance. Interestingly, negative reviews (publicity) harm revenue more than positive reviews help revenue in the early weeks of a film's release.[46]

17-6a Dealing with Unfavorable Public Relations

Thus far, we have discussed public relations as a planned element of the promotion mix. However, companies may have to deal with unexpected and unfavorable publicity resulting from an unsafe product, an accident resulting from product use, controversial actions of employees, or some other negative event or situation. Many companies have experienced unfavorable publicity connected to contamination issues, such as salmonella in peanut butter, lead in toys, and industrial compounds in pet foods. Unfavorable coverage can have quick and dramatic effects. Fines against J.P.Morgan for the "London Whale" trading losses and bad mortgage loans have tarnished its reputation. The company attempted to develop a creative PR campaign that tied into its underwriting of Twitter's IPO with a question-and-answer session on the site. Unfortunately, due to the scandals, many of the tweets that came in were negative and embarrassing to the firm.[47]

Negative events that generate public relations can wipe out a company's favorable image and destroy positive customer attitudes established through years of expensive advertising campaigns and other promotional efforts. Target, for instance, suffered reputational damage after hackers hacked into its system and stole credit card information from millions of its customers. Reputation is often considered a valuable company asset. How an organization deals with unfavorable actions and outcomes can have a significant impact on firm valuation. For example, Penn State University faced a damaged reputation as the result of the negligence and wrongdoing of individuals working in the football program and the complacency of university administrators and leaders. Moreover, today's mass media, including online services and the Internet, disseminate information faster than ever before, and bad news generally receives more media attention than corporate social responsibility.

To protect its image, an organization needs to prevent unfavorable public relations or at least lessen its effect if it occurs. First and foremost, the organization should try to prevent negative incidents and events through safety programs, inspections, training, and effective quality control procedures. Experts insist that sending consistent brand messages and images throughout all communications at all times can help a brand maintain its strength even during a crisis.[48] However, because negative events can strike even the most cautious firms, an organization should have plans in place to handle them when they do occur. Firms need to establish policies and procedures for reducing the adverse impact of news coverage of a crisis or controversy. In most cases, organizations should expedite news coverage of negative events rather than try to discourage or block them. If news coverage is suppressed, rumors and other misinformation may replace facts and create public scrutiny.

An unfavorable event can easily balloon into serious problems or public issues and become very damaging. By being forthright with the press and public and taking prompt action, a firm may be able to convince the public of its honest attempts to deal with the situation, and news personnel may be more willing to help explain complex issues to the public. Dealing effectively with a negative event allows an organization to lessen, if not eliminate, the unfavorable impact on its image. For instance, LIVESTRONG Foundation, founded by cyclist Lance Armstrong to fight against cancer, was caught in the crossfires after Armstrong's drug abuse scandal came out. Because it was associated so closely with its founder, LIVESTRONG risked losing support as public opinion for Armstrong plummeted. The organization immediately created a strong communications plan to emphasize that their goal was to fight cancer, not to be affiliated with an athlete. The CEO of the foundation went on *The Today Show* and National Public Radio to stress their message of serving people. LIVESTRONG's quick thinking in the midst of a crisis earned it the 2013 Platinum PR Award.[49] Experts generally advise companies that are dealing with negative publicity to respond quickly and honestly to the situation and to keep the lines of communication with all stakeholders open. Digital media has enhanced the organizational ability to communicate with key stakeholders and develop dialogues on current issues.

Summary

17-1 Describe advertising and its different types.

Advertising is a paid form of nonpersonal communication transmitted to consumers through mass media, such as television, radio, the Internet, newspapers, magazines, direct mail, outdoor displays, and signs on mass transit vehicles. Both business and nonbusiness organizations use advertising. Institutional advertising promotes organizational images, ideas, and political issues. When a company promotes its position on a public issue such as taxation, institutional advertising is referred to as advocacy advertising. Product advertising promotes uses, features, and benefits of products. The two types of product advertising are pioneer advertising, which focuses on stimulating demand for a product category rather than a specific brand, and competitive advertising, which attempts to stimulate demand for a specific brand by indicating the brand's features, uses, and advantages. To make direct product comparisons, marketers use comparative advertising, which compares two or more brands. Two other forms of competitive advertising are reminder advertising, which reminds customers about an established brand's uses, characteristics, and benefits, and reinforcement advertising, which assures current users they have made the right brand choice.

17-2 Summarize the eight major steps in developing an advertising campaign.

Although marketers may vary in how they develop advertising campaigns, they should follow a general pattern. First, they must identify and analyze the target audience, the group of people at whom advertisements are aimed. Second, they should establish what they want the campaign to accomplish by defining advertising objectives. Objectives should be clear, precise, and presented in measurable terms. Third, marketers must create the advertising platform, which contains basic issues to be presented in the campaign. Advertising platforms should consist of issues important to consumers. Fourth, advertisers must decide how much money to spend on the campaign; they arrive at this decision through the objective-and-task approach, percent-of-sales approach, competition-matching approach, or arbitrary approach.

Advertisers must then develop a media plan by selecting and scheduling media to use in the campaign. Some factors affecting the media plan are location and demographic characteristics of the target audience, content of the message, and cost of the various media. The basic content and form of the advertising message are affected by product features, uses, and benefits; characteristics of the people in the target audience; the campaign's objectives and platform; and the choice of media. Advertisers use copy and artwork to create the message. The execution of an advertising campaign requires extensive planning and coordination.

Finally, advertisers must devise one or more methods for evaluating advertisement effectiveness. Pretests are evaluations performed before the campaign begins; posttests are conducted after the campaign. Two types of posttests are a recognition test, in which respondents are shown the actual advertisement and asked whether they recognize it, and a recall test. In aided recall tests, respondents are shown a list of products, brands, company names, or trademarks to jog their memories. In unaided tests, no clues are given.

17-3 Identify who is responsible for developing advertising campaigns.

Advertising campaigns can be developed by personnel within the firm or in conjunction with advertising agencies. A campaign created by the firm's personnel may be developed by one or more individuals or by an advertising department within the firm. Use of an advertising agency may be advantageous because an agency provides highly skilled, objective specialists with broad experience in advertising at low to moderate costs to the firm.

17-4 Define *public relations*.

Public relations is a broad set of communication efforts used to create and maintain favorable relationships between an organization and its stakeholders. Public relations can be used to promote people, places, ideas, activities, and countries, and to create and maintain a positive company image. Some firms use public relations for a single purpose; others use it for several purposes.

17-5 Describe the different tools of public relations.

Public relations tools include written materials, such as brochures, newsletters, and annual reports; corporate identity materials, such as business cards and signs; speeches; event sponsorships; and special events. Publicity is communication in news-story form about an organization, its products, or both, transmitted through a mass medium at no charge. Publicity-based public relations tools include news releases, feature articles, captioned photographs, and press conferences. Problems that organizations confront in using publicity-based public relations include reluctance of media personnel to print or air releases and lack of control over timing and content of messages.

17-6 Analyze how public relations is used and evaluated.

To evaluate the effectiveness of their public relations programs, companies conduct research to determine how well their messages are reaching their audiences. Environmental monitoring, public relations audits, and counting the number of media exposures are all means of evaluating public relations effectiveness. Organizations should avoid negative public relations by taking steps to prevent negative events that result in unfavorable publicity. To diminish the impact of unfavorable public relations, organizations should institute policies and procedures for dealing with news personnel and the public when negative events occur.

Go to www.cengagebrain.com for resources to help you master the content in this chapter as well as for materials that will expand your marketing knowledge!

Developing Your Marketing Plan

Determining the message that advertising is to communicate to the customer is an important part of developing a marketing strategy. A sound understanding of the various types of advertising and different forms of media is essential in selecting the appropriate methods for communicating the message. These decisions form a critical segment of the marketing plan. To assist you in relating the information in this chapter to the development of your marketing plan, consider the following issues:

1. What class and type of advertising would be most appropriate for your product?
2. Discuss the different methods for determining the advertising appropriation.
3. Using Table 17.1 as a guide, evaluate the different types of media and determine which would be most effective in meeting your promotional objectives (from Chapter 16).
4. What methods would you use to evaluate the effectiveness of your advertising campaign?
5. Review Table 17.3 and discuss possible uses for publicity in your promotional plan.

The information obtained from these questions should assist you in developing various aspects of your marketing plan found in the "Interactive Marketing Plan" exercise at **www.cengagebrain.com**.

Important Terms

advertising 516
institutional advertising 516
advocacy advertising 517
product advertising 517
pioneer advertising 517
competitive advertising 517
comparative advertising 517
reminder advertising 518
reinforcement advertising 518
advertising campaign 518
target audience 519
advertising platform 520
advertising appropriation 521
objective-and-task approach 521
percent-of-sales approach 521
competition-matching approach 521
arbitrary approach 521
media plan 522
cost comparison indicator 525
regional issues 527
copy 527
storyboard 528
artwork 528
illustrations 528
layout 528
pretest 529
consumer jury 529
posttest 529
recognition test 530
unaided recall test 530
aided recall test 530
public relations 531
publicity 533
news release 533
feature article 533
captioned photograph 533
press conference 533

Discussion and Review Questions

1. What is the difference between institutional and product advertising?
2. What is the difference between competitive advertising and comparative advertising?
3. What are the major steps in creating an advertising campaign?
4. What is a target audience? How does a marketer analyze the target audience after identifying it?

5. Why is it necessary to define advertising objectives?
6. What is an advertising platform, and how is it used?
7. What factors affect the size of an advertising budget? What techniques are used to determine an advertising budget?
8. Describe the steps in developing a media plan.
9. What is the function of copy in an advertising message?
10. Discuss several ways to posttest the effectiveness of advertising.
11. What role does an advertising agency play in developing an advertising campaign?
12. What is public relations? Whom can an organization reach through public relations?
13. How do organizations use public relations tools? Give several examples you have observed recently.
14. Explain the problems and limitations associated with publicity-based public relations.
15. In what ways is the effectiveness of public relations evaluated?
16. What are some sources of negative public relations? How should an organization deal with unfavorable public relations?

Video Case 17.1

Scripps Networks Interactive: An Expert at Connecting Advertisers with Programming

Television advertisers have faced challenges in the past several years. People tend to watch fewer television shows at the time of airing or choose to watch them on Internet platforms such as Netflix or Hulu. The use of digital video recorders (DVRs) has also contributed to this challenge as viewers can fast-forward through commercials while watching their favorite shows. Scripps Networks Interactive, parent company to Food Network, HGTV, Travel Channel, DIY Network, Cooking Channel, and Great American Country, has found a way around this issue through product placement and integration, use of social media platforms, and promotion.

Scripps Networks Interactive is unique in that their programming appeals to similar target markets with similar interests. The director of Digital Media and Database Marketing for Scripps Networks Interactive states, "Our programming lends itself so well to speaking to lifestyle and what people are passionate and interested in, and I think our marketing communications strategy is a natural extension of that." This presents a strong opportunity for gaining real results through advertising. At the same time, these promotional initiatives do not always seem like advertising to viewers. One way this is accomplished is through cross-promotional activities across networks. For instance, while watching an episode of *Paula's Home Cooking* on the Food Network, viewers would see a commercial for a *Design Star* episode on HGTV featuring Paula Deen. (In 2013 Paula Deen's contract was not renewed after a racial slur controversy, demonstrating the downside of using celebrity advertisers or spokespeople.) These marketing promotions appear to be natural extensions of the show rather than advertising that is deemed intrusive.

Product placement and integration work well with the lifestyle content of the company's programming because viewers are interested in the content being provided. In most cases, "our audiences ... actually look to our advertisers' products for ideas and as resources," states the senior vice president of Interactive Ad Sales Marketing for Scripps. This creates an opportunity for the company to build strong relationships with advertisers. Advertisers seek out Scripps Networks not only for placement in their shows but also for integration into their social media space. The integration of television product placement and social media advertising has been a benefit for both parties. The senior vice president of Interactive Ad Sales Marketing explains, "If we tie a specific advertiser to *Iron Chef* or to *Chopped*, then there's opportunities for them to be driven from on-air to say 'check out the recipes from this specific episode online at foodnetwork.com.'" Despite the culinary nature of these shows, the advertising platform Scripps has established attracts other vendors, including automobile manufacturers. Lexus, for example, was featured as the car driven by *Restaurant Impossible*'s host Robert Irvine. These clips were then shown on the show's webpage, packaged as a Lexus advertisement.

Scripps has also found a way to integrate product placement into brick and mortar locations as well as on digital space. After Food Network host Guy Fieri won recognition as "The Next Food Network Star," he partnered with TGI Fridays in an endorsement agreement. Fieri hosted a recipe showdown on the Food Network, and TGI Fridays promoted these recipes in their restaurants. Partnerships between chefs and brands have also been developed to create co-branded products. Alex Guarnaschelli, a judge on *Chopped*, was approached by Fisher Nuts to share recipes containing their product. These advertisements were shown on both the Food Network and the Cooking Channel.

Another benefit of this integration is that the company and the advertiser become cooperative marketing partners, where both are working from different directions to promote both the show and the product simultaneously. The general manager of new business for the Food Network explains an example of this kind of relationship with Kohl's and *Worst Cooks in America*: "Kohl's is advertising in it—they are sponsoring it. They are putting things on Pinterest or tweeting. We are doing the same thing in the context of the character, so you get both this top-down and bottom-up thing coming together."

Promotions also work well on this platform. A digital marketer for Scripps Networks describes the effectiveness of promotions. "What makes it more than just a giveaway for money is tying in hooks that engage people to not only sign up to a sweepstakes to win a trip … but making it part of the entertainment experience." For example, the Food Network ran a promotion for its show *The Great Food Truck Race*, where people were asked to go to the Facebook page and nominate or vote for their favorite local food truck. The winners would then be featured on the show's website. This event generated buzz and brought attention to the food trucks around the country that were being nominated. The nominees were featured on commercials aired during the show, where they asked viewers to vote for them online. The fans, businesses, and the show were all involved in generating buzz and promoting one another, creating an effect that is advantageous to all parties.[50]

Questions for Discussion

1. Why is the Food Network such an important venue for many advertisers?
2. Describe some of the ways that Scripps uses product placement on the Food Network.
3. Why do you think even non-food advertisers are attracted to the Food Network?

Case 17.2

Greenwashing in Advertising Hurts Consumers and Companies

The green industry has an estimated value of $40 billion dollars as of 2012. This includes organic food, electric and hybrid vehicles, energy-efficient light bulbs, and green cleaning products. Consumers have been willing to pay a premium for green and sustainable products even during the Great Recession. This trend, however, is changing due to the phenomenon called greenwashing.

Greenwashing occurs when companies deceptively market products as environmentally-friendly. Greenwashing does not have to be completely untrue. For instance, a company might put a label on its product saying that it is "free from chlorofluorocarbons (CFC-free)" as if that is a major accomplishment. CFC-free products are required by law. Greenwashing has decreased consumer trust in the claims that companies are making about their environmentally-friendly products. A survey concluded that consumers' willingness to pay more for green products has dropped between 5 and 12 percentage points from 2008 to 2012.

In the past, the Federal Trade Commission (FTC) has cracked down on companies whose advertisements were inaccurate. For instance, when several companies advertised rayon products as being made from bamboo, the FTC sent warning letters to 78 retailers including Walmart, Kohl's, and The Gap. California sued three companies for labeling plastic bottles as biodegradable, a violation of a California labeling law. Further, one study determined that as many as 95 percent of products marketed as green were guilty of at least one form of greenwashing. In response, the FTC issued a revised set of Green Guides in October of 2012 for businesses to use as they are marketing their products. One of the changes includes advising marketers not to make broad claims about the green attributes of their products. For instance, simply labeling a product as eco-friendly gives the impression that every aspect of the product's production was conducted in an environmentally-friendly manner. The product itself may be green, but the way in which it was produced may have created mass amounts of pollution or large amounts of water waste. Although these guidelines do not carry the force of law, they better enable the FTC to pursue companies that violate standards by engaging in deceptive marketing practices.

The European Union (EU) takes these matters so seriously that it requires advertisers to state their carbon emissions on their advertisements. There are also groups such as the Friends of the Earth Europe who engage consumers in taking a stand against companies who make false green claims. Every year the organization hosts a campaign called the Pinocchio Awards, where people can place votes and expose companies involved in greenwashing or other misleading environmental or socially responsible activities. Each year nine companies are nominated in three different categories. The first is Greener than Green, which includes companies with the most egregious violations; Dirty Hands, Full Wallet encapsulates companies with vague financial, political, and supply-chain policies; and the final category, One for All and All for Me, includes those who hold the most aggressive policies regarding allocation, use, and destruction of natural resources. This tactic puts pressure on companies, not only from the government, but also from consumers to behave in a manner consistent with their claims. It also helps to direct companies away from practices that are harmful to society and the environment.

© iStockphoto.com/bodo23

Greenwashing hurts all businesses in the industry, even those whose claims are accurate and honest. Some companies are taking a unique approach to prove to consumers that they are indeed concerned about their environmental impact. For example, Unilever initiated a sustainable campaign on Facebook and YouTube for its Axe product line called "Showerpooling." The campaign encourages consumers to take showers no longer than 5 minutes and provides them with links on how to install water efficient showerheads. Although this campaign does not contribute directly to profits, it does establish goodwill between the company's brand and the consumer.

Other companies are taking external measures to substantiate their green claims by developing a certification system to help consumers make informed decisions when buying supposedly green products. Partnering with certification organizations such as the Carbon Trust, for example, can validate carbon output claims. However, certification organizations are not always trustworthy either. Some of them charge a fee and do not hold products to rigorous standards. For the time being, the best way for consumers to be informed about eco-friendly products is to do some research before going shopping.[51]

Questions for Discussion

1. Why does greenwashing have such a negative impact?
2. What are some ways that stakeholders have dissuaded greenwashing?
3. What are some actions organizations are taking to demonstrate a genuine commitment toward sustainability?

NOTES

[1] Jason Notte, "16 Greatest Animal Advertisers," *MSN Money*, http://money.msn.com/now/16-greatest-animal-advertisers (accessed August 12, 2013); Carolyn Winter, "Geico's Gecko Has Written a Book," *Bloomberg Businessweek*, February 7, 2013, www.businessweek.com/articles/2013-02-07/geicos-gecko-has-written-a-book (accessed August 13, 2013); Ken Wheaton, "Bell Tolls for Gidget, the Taco Bell Chihuahua," *Ad Age*, July 22, 2009, http://adage.com/article/adages/advertising-icons-taco-bell-chihuahua-dies-15/138062 (accessed August 13, 2013); *Harvard Business Review*, "Growth in Aflac's Two Key Markets 1999–2008," http://hbr.org/web/special-collections/insight/marketing-that-works/aflacs-ceo-explains-how-he-fell-for-the-duck (accessed August 14, 2013).

[2] Mandy Velez, "J.C.Penney Back-to-School Ad 'Promotes Bullying,' Parents Say," *The Huffington Post*, August 14, 2013, www.huffingtonpost.com/2013/08/14/jcpenney-back-to-school-ad_n_3756517.html (accessed January 15, 2014).

[3] Marvin E. Goldberg, Cornelia Pechmann, Guangzhi Zhao, and Ellen Thomas Reibling, "What to Convey in Antismoking Advertisements for Adolescents: The Use of Protection Motivation Theory to Identify Effective Message Themes," *Journal of Marketing* (April 2003): 1–18.

[4] Micael Dahlén, Helge Thorbjørnsen, and Henrik Sjödin, "A Taste of 'Nextopia,'" *Journal of Advertising* 40, no. 1 (Winter 2011): 33–44.

[5] Fred K. Beard, "Practitioner Views of Comparative Advertising: How Practices Have Changed in Two Decades," *Journal of Advertising Research* 53, no. 3 (2013): 313–323.

[6] "Toothpaste War: High Court Rejects Colgate's Plea against Pepsodent," *The Economic Times*, August 21, 2013, http://articles.economictimes.indiatimes.com/2013-08-21/news/41433377_1_colgate-palmolive-germ-attack-power-teeth (accessed January 15, 2014).

[7] Ibid.

[8] Kyle Stock, "Man in Tights: Trying Out Lululemon's Guy Side," *Bloomberg Businessweek*, September 13, 2013, www.businessweek.com/articles/2013-09-13/man-in-tights-trying-out-lululemons-guy-side (accessed January 13, 2014).

[9] Tae Hyun Baek and Mariko Morimoto, "Stay Away from Me," *Journal of Advertising* 41, no. 1 (Spring 2012): 59–76.

[10] "Apple to Offer iPhone Upgrades," *ABC Local*, June 7, 2013, http://abclocal.go.com/wls/story?section=news/consumer&id=9131262 (accessed January 15, 2014).

[11] "The Ludlow Suit by J.Crew," *Fast Company*, March 2012, http://fastcompany.coverleaf.com/fastcompany/201203?pg=6#pg6 (accessed January 13, 2014).

[12] Daniel A. Sheinin, Sajeev Varki, and Christy Ashley, "The Differential Effect of Ad Novelty and Message Usefulness on Brand Judgments," *Journal of Advertising* 40, no. 3 (Fall 2011): 5–17.

[13] Annie Gasparo, "Panera Boosts Ad Budget as 'Fast and Casual' Heats Up," *The Wall Street Journal*, March 8, 2012, p. B7.

[14] John McDermott, "Study: Mobile Marketing Industry to Employ 1.4 Million in 2015," *Advertising Age*, May 9, 2013, http://adage.com/article/digital/study-mobile-marketing-industry-employ-1-4-million-2015/241328 (accessed January 15, 2014).

[15] Crain Communications Inc., "National Geographic," *AdAge 360° Media Guide*, http://brandedcontent.adage.com/360/details.php?brand=23 (accessed January 16, 2014).

[16] Mike Dunn, "Controversial Plan to Allow Advertising on Philadelphia Schools Put on Hold," *CBS Philly*, December 16, 2013, http://philadelphia.cbslocal.com/2013/12/16/controversial-plan-to-allow-advertising-on-philadelphia-schools-put-on-hold (accessed January 16, 2014).

[17] David G. Taylor, Jeffrey E. Lewin, and David Strutton, "Friends, Fans, and Followers: Do Ads Work on Social Networks? How Gender and Age Shape Receptivity," *Journal of Advertising Research* 51, no. 1 (2011): 258–275.

[18] Geoffrey Precourt, "What We Know about TV Today (and Tomorrow)," *Journal of Advertising Research* 53, no. 1 (2013): 3–4.

[19] Gina A. Tran and David Strutton, "What Factors Affect Consumer Acceptance of In-Game Advertisements? Click 'Like' to Manage Digital Content for Players," *Journal of Advertising Research* 53, no. 4 (2013): 455–469.

[20] Shareen Pathak, "Aahhhh! Coke Launches 61 Unique Websites for Teen-Focused Campaign," *Advertising Age*, April 23, 2013, http://adage.com/article/digital/aah-coke-launches-61-web-sites-teen-focused-campaign/241047 (accessed January 16, 2014).

[21] RingCentral Team, "RingCentral in the News: PC Magazine, The Economist and More," RingCentral, http://blog.ringcentral.com/2013/04/ringcentral-in-the-news-pc-magazine-the-economist-and-more (accessed January 16, 2014).

[22] Shintaro Okazaki and Patrick Barwise, "Has the Time Finally Come for the Medium of the Future? Research on Mobile Advertising," 50th Anniversary Supplement, *Journal of Advertising Research* 51, no. 1 (2011): 59–71.

[23] Chingching Chang, "Feeling Ambivalent about Going Green," *Journal of Advertising* 40, no. 4 (Winter 2011): 19–31.

[24] Pierre Berthon, Karen Robson, and Leyland Pitt, "The Theory and Practice of Advertising: Counting the Cost to the Customer," *The Journal of Advertising Research* 53, no. 3 (2013): 244–246.

[25] Ilona A. Berney-Reddish and Charles S. Areni, "Sex Differences in Responses to Probability Markers in Advertising Claims," *Journal of Advertising* 35 (Summer 2006): 7–17.

[26] The Economist Staff, "Cookie Monster Crumbles," *The Economist*, November 23, 2013, pp. 61–62.

[27] Chiranjeev Kohli, Sunil Thomas, and Rajneesh Suri, "Are You in Good Hands? Slogan Recall: What Really Matters," *Journal of Advertising Research* 53, no. 1 (2013): 31–42.

[28] Judith Anne Garretson Folse, Richard G. Netemeyer, and Scot Burton, "Spokescharacters," *Journal of Advertising* 41, no. 1 (Spring 2012): 17–32.

[29] AAA Publishing Network, www.aaapublishingnetwork.com (accessed January 14, 2014).

[30] Daniel J. Howard and Roger A. Kerin, "The Effects of Personalized Product Recommendations on Advertisement Response Rates: The 'Try This. It Works!' Technique," *Journal of Consumer Psychology* 14, no. 3 (2004): 271–279.

[31] Pamela W. Henderson, Joan L. Giese, and Joseph A. Cote, "Impression Management Using Typeface Design," *Journal of Marketing* 68 (October 2004): 60–72.

[32] Rik Pieters and Michel Wedel, "Attention Capture and Transfer in Advertising: Brand, Pictorial, and Text-Size Effects," *Journal of Marketing* 68 (April 2004): 36–50.

[33] David Welch, "Mr. Peanut Gets Smashed," *Bloomberg Businessweek*, March 12–18, 2012, pp. 22–23.

[34] Aaron Taube, "Dodge Has Seen a Huge Surge in Sales from Will Ferrell's Absurd Ron Burgundy Commercials [THE BRIEF]," *Business Insider*, November 5, 2013, www.businessinsider.com/dodge-sales-from-will-ferrells-ron-burgundy-commercials-2013-11 (accessed January 16, 2014).

[35] Lauren Johnson, "GMC Mobile Video Campaign Generates 42pc Brand Recall Rate," *Mobile Marketer*, February 14, 2013, www.mobilemarketer.com/cms/news/video/14783.html (accessed January 16, 2014).

[36] Peter J. Danaher and Guy W. Mullarkey, "Factors Affecting Online Advertising Recall: A Study of Students," *Journal of Advertising Research* 43 (2003): 252–267.

[37] Frank Harrison, "Digging Deeper Down into the Empirical Generalization of Brand Recall: Adding Owned and Earned Media to Paid-Media Touchpoints," *Journal of Advertising Research* 53, no. 2 (June 2013): 181–185.

[38] Stuart Elliot, "An Old Campaign Learns a New Song," *The New York Times*, September 3, 2013, www.nytimes.com/2013/09/04/business/media/an-old-campaign-learns-a-new-song.html (accessed January 16, 2014).

[39] Max Nisen, "The 5 Biggest PR Blunders of 2013," *Business Insider*, December 20, 2013, www.businessinsider.com/biggest-pr-failures-of-2013-2013-12 (accessed January 16, 2014); CTVNews.ca Staff, "Lululemon Founder Chip Wilson Resigns after One Month after Controversial Comments," *CTV News*, December 10, 2013, www.ctvnews.ca/business/lululemon-founder-chip-wilson-resigns-one-month-after-controversial-comments-1.1582415 (accessed January 16, 2014).

[40] Charles Radcliffe, "UN Launches Unprecedented Global Campaign for LGBT Equality," *The Huffington Post*, July 26, 2013, www.huffingtonpost.com/charles-radcliffe/un-launches-unprecedented_b_3650372.html (accessed January 16, 2014).

[41] George E. Belch and Michael A. Belch, *Advertising and Promotion* (Burr Ridge, IL: Irwin/McGraw-Hill, 2008), p. 570.

[42] Steven Goldstein, "2013 Platinum Hall of Fame Inductees," *PR News*, October 15, 2013, www.prnewsonline.com/topics/corporate-responsibility/2013/10/15/2013-platinum-hall-of-fame-inductees (accessed January 16, 2014).

[43] Business Wire, "Canon U.S.A. Sponsors 2013 Special Olympics New York," *Yahoo! Finance*, April 18, 2013, http://finance.yahoo.com/news/canon-u-sponsors-2013-special-130200845.html (accessed January 16, 2014).

[44] Rem Rieder, "Bezos' Drone Plan Delivers a Publicity Coup," *USA Today*, December 3, 2013, p. 5B.

[45] Belch and Belch, *Advertising and Promotion*, pp. 580–581.

[46] Suman Basuroy, Subimal Chatterjee, and S. Abraham Ravid, "How Critical Are Critical Reviews? The Box Office Effects of Film Critics, Star Power, and Budgets," *Journal of Marketing* (October 2003): 103–117.

[47] Emily Greenhouse, "JPMorgan's Twitter Mistake," *The New Yorker*, November 17, 2013, www.newyorker.com/online/blogs/currency/2013/11/jpmorgans-twitter-mistake.html (accessed January 16, 2014).

[48] Deborah L. Vence, "Stand Guard: In Bad Times, an Ongoing Strategy Keeps Image Intact," *Marketing News*, November 16, 2006, p. 15.

[49] Chris Seymour, "2013 Platinum PR Awards: Crisis Management," *PR News*, October 15, 2013, www.prnewsonline.com/topics/crisis-management/2013/10/15/2013-platinum-pr-awards-crisis-management (accessed January 13, 2014).

[50] Brian Steinberg, "Food Net's Endorsements Are Woven Inconspicuously into Its Programming Mix," *Variety*, November 5, 2013, http://variety.com/2013/tv/features/food-net-brand-tie-ins-that-sizzle-but-dont-burn-1200796087 (accessed December 12, 2013); Carey Polis, "'From Scratch' Goes Behind the Scenes at The Food Network," *The Huffington Post*, October 1, 2013, www.huffingtonpost.com/2013/10/01/from-scratch-food-network_n_3984233.html (accessed December 12, 2013); Stuart Elliot, "Two Media Mainstays Expand Their Video Presence," *The New York Times*, October 2, 2013, www.nytimes.com/2013/10/03/business/media/two-media-mainstays-expand-their-video-presence.html (accessed December 12, 2013); John Moulding, "Scripps Network Hails the Impact of Dynamic Advertising Insertion," *Videonet*, October 31, 2013, www.v-net.tv/scripps-networks-hails-the-impact-of-dynamic-advertising-insertion (accessed December 12, 2013).

[51] Part 260O.C. Ferrell and Linda Ferrell, "Are Consumers Being Greenwashed?" http://danielsethics.mgt.unm.edu/pdf/Greenwashing%20DI.pdf (accessed December 10, 2013); Matt Sena, "Green Industry Analysis 2013—Costs and Trends," *Franchise Help*, 2013, www.franchisehelp.com/industry-reports/green-industry-report (accessed December 10, 2013); Jack Neff, "As More Marketers Go Green, Fewer Consumers Willing to Pay for It," *Advertising Age*, September 24, 2012, http://adage.com/article/news/marketers-green-fewer-consumers-pay/237377 (accessed December 10, 2013); Jack Neff, "Consumers Don't Believe Your Green Ad Claims, Survey Finds," *Advertising Age*, September 16, 2013, http://adage.com/article/news/consumers-green-ad-claims-survey-finds/244172 (accessed December 10, 2013); Federal Trade Commission, "FTC Issues Revised 'Green Guides,'" October 1, 2012, www.ftc.gov/news-events/press-releases/2012/10/ftc-issues-revised-green-guides (accessed December 10, 2013); Friends of the Earth Europe, "Pinocchio Awards 2013: Cast Your Vote," October 15, 2013, www.foeeurope.org/pinocchio-awards-2013-cast-vote-151013 (accessed December 10, 2013); Robert Lamb, "Regulating Greenwashing," *How Stuff Works*, http://money.howstuffworks.com/greenwashing.htm (accessed December 10, 2013); Federal Trade Commission, Part 260—Guides for the Use of Environmental Marketing Claims, http://ftc.gov/bcp/grnrule/guides980427.htm (accessed December 12, 2011); Federal Trade Commission, "FTC Warns 78 Retailers,

MARKETING INSIGHTS

Airlines Adapt Frequent-Flyer Incentives

Frequent-flyer programs have bottomed out over the years. These frequent-user incentives were designed as a major form of sales promotion to create loyalty among travelers by allowing them to earn miles for each flight taken. These miles can then be redeemed later for free flights. However, flights are often crowded, making it difficult for passengers to redeem their miles for free seats. This has decreased customer loyalty to any one airline; most customers are enrolled in loyalty programs in at least two airlines. Another contributor to deteriorating loyalty is that travelers cannot tell one airline's frequent-flyer program from another. Furthermore, those with the most miles generally fly all the time and are not interested in spending their free time in an airplane.

As a result, airlines are taking a lesson from credit card rewards programs, where cardholders have the option to redeem their points on a variety of items such as gift cards, vacations, unique experiences, and paying credit card fees. Many airlines have begun adjusting their incentive programs to offer more options. United Airlines, for example, offers online auctions in which consumers can use their miles to bid on experiences such as concerts and a chance to meet the musician backstage. They have also increased the amount of items available for purchase with miles in their catalogs so customers can purchase anything from magazine subscriptions to a MacBook. Delta allows travelers to use their miles to bid for chances to participate in charitable activities such as working with Habitat for Humanity building homes in Mexico. Adapting their sales promotion strategies to appeal to changing consumer tastes may help airlines regain some of the loyalty they have lost.[1]

For many organizations, targeting customers with appropriate personal selling techniques and messages can play a major role in maintaining long-term, satisfying customer relationships, which in turn contribute to company success. Marketing strategy development should involve the sales organization during all stages of development and implementation. Top managers need extensive feedback from the sales force. Managers should strive to make information transparent and jointly analyze sales data. Sales managers should communicate marketing strategy in a language with which salespeople feel comfortable.[2] As we saw in Chapter 16, personal selling and sales promotion are two possible elements in a promotion mix. Personal selling is sometimes a company's sole promotional tool, and it is becoming increasingly professional and sophisticated, with sales personnel acting more as consultants, advisors, and sometimes as partners.

In this chapter, we focus on personal selling and sales promotion. We first consider the purposes of personal selling and then examine its basic steps. Next, we look at types of salespeople and how they are selected. After taking a look at several new types of personal selling, we discuss major sales force management decisions, including setting objectives for the sales force and determining its size; recruiting, selecting, training, compensating, and motivating salespeople; managing sales territories; and controlling and evaluating sales force performance. Then we examine several characteristics of sales promotion, reasons for using sales promotion, and sales promotion methods available for use in a promotion mix.

personal selling Paid personal communication that attempts to inform customers and persuade them to buy products in an exchange situation

18-1 THE NATURE AND GOALS OF PERSONAL SELLING

Personal selling is paid personal communication that attempts to inform customers and persuade them to purchase products in an exchange situation. For instance, a Hewlett-Packard (HP) salesperson describing the benefits of the company's servers, PCs, and printers to a small-business customer is engaging in personal selling. Likewise, a member of the American Marketing Association (AMA) manning a table at an event engages in personal selling to inform interested parties about the benefits of joining the AMA. Personal selling gives marketers the greatest freedom to adjust a message to satisfy customers' information needs. It is the most precise of all promotion methods, enabling marketers to focus on the most promising sales prospects. Personal selling is also the most effective way to form relationships with customers. Edward Jones advertises that it has 11,000 financial sales advisors to provide face-to-face attention to 7 million investors. The advertisement makes it clear that face-to-face personal interaction is superior to a telephone call center. Personal selling is perhaps most important with business-to-business transactions involving the purchase of expensive products. Because of the high-risk factors involved, personal selling is often necessary to assure prospective customers about the quality of the product and answer any questions.[3] Despite these benefits, personal selling is generally the most expensive element in the promotion mix. The average cost of a sales call is more than $400.[4]

Millions of people earn their living through personal selling. Sales careers can offer high income, a great deal of freedom, a high level of training, and a high degree of job satisfaction. Salespeople who delight customers experience an

Courtesy of Edward Jones

The Importance of Personal Selling
Edward Jones engages in personal selling as a superior way to form relationships with customers.

improvement in customer orientation and job skills.[5] Although the public may harbor negative perceptions of personal selling, unfavorable stereotypes of salespeople are changing thanks to the efforts of major corporations, professional sales associations, and academic institutions. Personal selling will continue to gain respect as professional sales associations develop and enforce ethical codes of conduct.[6] Developing ongoing customer relationships today requires sales personnel with high levels of professionalism as well as technical and interpersonal skills.[7]

Personal selling goals vary from one firm to another. However, they usually involve finding prospects, determining their needs, persuading prospects to buy, following up on the sale, and keeping customers satisfied. Identifying potential buyers interested in the organization's products is critical. Because most potential buyers seek information before making purchases, salespeople can ascertain prospects' informational needs and then provide relevant information. To do so, sales personnel must be well trained regarding both their products and the selling process in general.

Salespeople must be aware of their competitors. They must monitor the development of new products and keep abreast of competitors' sales efforts in their sales territories, how often and when the competition calls on their accounts, and what the competition is saying about their product in relation to its own. Salespeople must emphasize the benefits their products provide, especially when competitors' products do not offer those specific benefits. Salespeople often function as knowledge experts for the firm and provide key information for marketing decisions.[8]

Personal selling is changing today based on new technology, how customers gain information about products, and the way customers make purchase decisions. Customer information sharing through social media, mobile and Web applications, and electronic sales presentations are impacting the nature of personal selling. Some firms are adopting social media technology to reach business customers. "Social CRM" (customer relationship management) provides opportunities to manage data in discovering and engaging customers.[9] For instance, the cloud-computing models provided by Salesforce.com to enable firms to manage relationships with their customers can assist in personal selling sales management.

Using websites to manage orders and product information, track inventory, and train salespeople can save companies time and money. Twitter is a relatively new tool that can be

Entrepreneurship in Marketing

Tastefully Simple: From Gift Baskets to Multimillion-Dollar Gourmet Food Firm

Entrepreneurs: Jill Blashack Strahan
Business: Tastefully Simple
Founded: 1995 | Alexandria, Minnesota
Success: Tastefully Simple has grown to become one of the top 100 largest direct selling firms in the world.

Jill Blashack Strahan, founder and CEO of Tastefully Simple, is recognized for her entrepreneurial leadership and vision that created a multimillion-dollar company. Before starting Tastefully Simple, Strahan had a small gift-basket business. However, when the gourmet foods she provided with her baskets proved more profitable than the baskets themselves, she shifted focus. In 1995 Tastefully Simple was conceived with the idea of providing easy-to-prepare foods with a gourmet twist. All of its sales come from the personal sales efforts of consultants. The company's products are offered through independent sales consultants across the United States. Since its founding, the company has come to be one of the top 100 direct selling companies in the world. Tastefully Simple's revenue has grown to more than $95 million.

Tastefully Simple has continually received recognition for being ranked in the top 5 percent of companies nationwide in employee satisfaction. The empowering vision Strahan has provided for potential entrepreneurs, many of them women, has made it a favorite among those with an interest in entrepreneurship.[a]

used to post product information and updates, obtain prospects, recruit new salespeople, and communicate with salespeople. Facebook is another valuable tool that can supplement and support face-to-face contacts. On Facebook, salespeople can carry on conversations very similar to traditional face-to-face social networks. Mobile technology and applications provide salespeople with opportunities to offer service and connect with customers. CRM technology enables improved service, marketing and sales processes, and contact and data management and analysis. CRM can help facilitate the delivery of valuable customer experiences and provide the metrics to measure progress and sales successes.[10]

Few businesses survive solely on profits from one-time customers. For long-run survival, most marketers depend on repeat sales and thus need to keep their customers satisfied. In addition, satisfied customers provide favorable word of mouth and other communications, thereby attracting new customers. Although the whole organization is responsible for achieving customer satisfaction, much of the burden falls on salespeople, because they are almost always closer to customers than anyone else in the company and often provide buyers with information and service after the sale. Indeed, a firm's market orientation has a positive influence on salespeople's attitudes, commitment, and influence on customer purchasing intentions.[11] Additionally, collaboration between sales and other marketing areas is positively related to market orientation that puts customers first, which positively impacts organizational performance.[12] Such contact gives salespeople an opportunity to generate additional sales and offers them a good vantage point for evaluating the strengths and weaknesses of the company's products and other marketing-mix components. Their observations help develop and maintain a marketing mix that better satisfies both the firm and its customers. Sales is no longer an isolated function in a global business world. The sales function is becoming part of a cross-functional strategic solution to customer management. This requires salespersons with both managerial and strategic skills.[13]

18-2 STEPS OF THE PERSONAL SELLING PROCESS

The specific activities involved in the selling process vary among salespeople, selling situations, and cultures. No two salespeople use exactly the same selling methods. Nonetheless, many salespeople move through a general selling process. This process consists of seven steps, outlined in Figure 18.1: prospecting, preapproach, approach, making the presentation, overcoming objections, closing the sale, and following up.

18-2a Prospecting

Developing a database of potential customers is called **prospecting**. Salespeople seek names of prospects from company sales records, trade shows, commercial databases, newspaper announcements (of marriages, births, deaths, and so on), public records, telephone directories, trade association directories, and many other sources. Sales personnel also use responses to traditional and online advertisements that encourage interested persons to send in information request forms. Seminars and meetings targeted at particular types of clients, such as attorneys or accountants, may also produce leads.

Most salespeople prefer to use referrals—recommendations from current customers—to find prospects. For instance, salespeople for Cutco Cutlery, which sells high-quality knives and kitchen cutlery, first make sales calls to their friends and families and then use referrals from them to seek out new prospects. Obtaining referrals requires that the salesperson have a good relationship with the current customer and therefore must have performed well before asking the customer for help. As might be expected, a customer's trust in and satisfaction with a salesperson influence his or her willingness to provide referrals. Research findings show that one referral is as valuable as 12 cold calls.[14] Also, 80 percent of clients are willing to give referrals, but only 20 percent are ever asked. Among the advantages of using referrals are more highly qualified sales leads, greater sales rates, and larger initial transactions. Some companies even award discounts

prospecting Developing a database of potential customers

Figure 18.1 **General Steps in the Personal Selling Process**

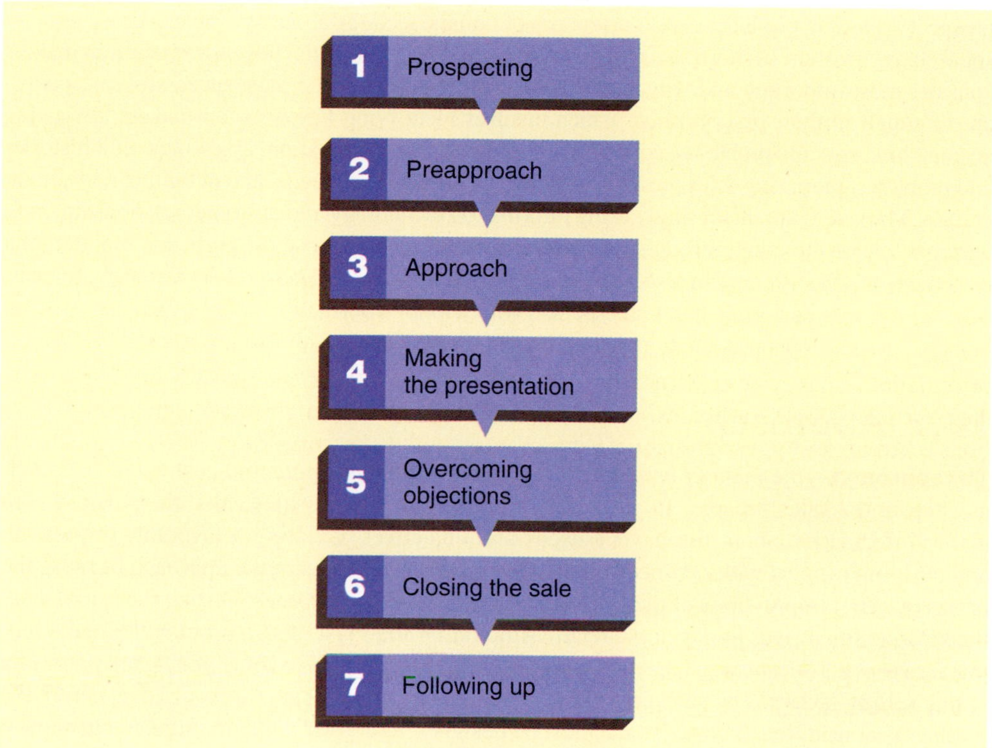

off future purchases to customers who refer new prospects to their salespeople. Consistent activity is critical to successful prospecting. Salespeople must actively search the customer base for qualified prospects that fit the target market profile. After developing the prospect list, a salesperson evaluates whether each prospect is able, willing, and authorized to buy the product. Based on this evaluation, prospects are ranked according to desirability or potential.

Prospecting
Companies often engage in prospecting at trade shows, which allow representatives to demonstrate the latest company products and collect information on consumers who might be interested in the firm's offerings. Company salespeople can later use this information in the preapproach and approach steps of the personal selling process.

18-2b Preapproach

Before contacting acceptable prospects, a salesperson finds and analyzes information about each prospect's specific product needs, current use of brands, feelings about available brands, and personal characteristics. In short, salespeople need to know what potential buyers and decision makers consider most important and why they need a specific product. The most successful salespeople are thorough in their *preapproach,* which involves identifying key decision makers, reviewing account histories and problems, contacting other clients for information, assessing credit histories and problems, preparing sales presentations, identifying product needs, and obtaining relevant literature. Marketers are increasingly using information technology and customer relationship management systems to comb through databases and thus identify their most profitable products and customers. CRM systems can also help sales departments manage leads, track customers, forecast sales, and assess performance. A salesperson with a lot of information about a prospect is better equipped to develop a presentation that precisely communicates with that prospect.

18-2c Approach

The **approach**—the manner in which a salesperson contacts a potential customer—is a critical step in the sales process. In more than 80 percent of initial sales calls, the purpose is to gather information about the buyer's needs and objectives. Creating a favorable impression and building rapport with prospective clients are important tasks in the approach because the prospect's first impressions of the salesperson are usually lasting ones. During the initial visit, the salesperson strives to develop a relationship rather than just push a product. Indeed, coming across as a "salesperson" may not be the best approach because some people are put off by strong selling tactics. The salesperson may have to call on a prospect several times before the product is considered. The approach must be designed to deliver value to targeted customers. If the sales approach is inappropriate, the salesperson's efforts are likely to have poor results.

One type of approach is based on referrals, as discussed in the section on prospecting. The salesperson who uses the "cold canvass" approach calls on potential customers without prior consent. This approach is decreasing. Social media is becoming more typical in gaining the initial contact with a prospect. Repeat contact is another common approach: when making the contact, the salesperson mentions a previous meeting. The exact type of approach depends on the salesperson's preferences, the product being sold, the firm's resources, and the prospect's characteristics.

18-2d Making the Presentation

During the sales presentation, the salesperson must attract and hold the prospect's attention, stimulate interest, and spark a desire for the product. Salespeople who carefully monitor the selling situation and adapt their presentations to meet the needs of prospects generally have more effective sales performance.[15] Salespeople should match their influencing tactics—such as information exchange, recommendations, threats, promises, ingratiation, and inspirational appeals—to their prospects. Different types of buyers respond to different tactics, but most respond well to information exchange and recommendations, and virtually no prospects respond to threats.[16] The salesperson should have the prospect touch, hold, or use the product. If possible, the salesperson should demonstrate the product or invite the prospect to use it. Automobile salespeople, for example, typically invite potential buyers to test-drive the vehicle that interests them. Audiovisual equipment and software may also enhance the presentation.

During the presentation, the salesperson must not only talk, but also listen. Listening is half of the communication process and is often the most important part for a salesperson. Research indicates that salesperson listening and cognitive empathy developed through the sales interaction are linked, suggesting that listening positively affects the relationship between the buyer and seller during a sales presentation.[17] Nonverbal modes of communication are especially beneficial in building trust during the presentation.[18] Nonverbal signals provide a deeper understanding. The sales presentation gives the salesperson the greatest

approach The manner in which a salesperson contacts a potential customer

opportunity to determine the prospect's specific needs by listening to questions and comments and observing responses. Research findings show that complimenting the buyer on his or her questions adds to incremental sales.[19] Even though the salesperson plans the presentation in advance, she or he must be able to adjust the message to meet the prospect's informational needs. Adapting the message in response to the customer's needs generally enhances performance, particularly in new-task or modified rebuy purchase situations.[20]

18-2e Overcoming Objections

An effective salesperson usually seeks out a prospect's objections in order to address them. If they are not apparent, the salesperson cannot deal with them, and the prospect may not buy. One of the best ways to overcome objections is to anticipate and counter them before the prospect raises them. However, this approach can be risky, because the salesperson may mention objections that the prospect would not have raised. If possible, the salesperson should handle objections as they arise. They can also be addressed at the end of the presentation.

18-2f Closing the Sale

Closing is the stage in the personal selling process when the salesperson asks the prospect to buy the product. During the presentation, the salesperson may use a *trial close* by asking questions that assume the prospect will buy. The salesperson might ask the potential customer about financial terms, desired colors or sizes, or delivery arrangements. Reactions to such questions usually indicate how close the prospect is to buying. Properly asked questions may allow prospects to uncover their own problems and identify solutions themselves. One questioning approach uses broad questions (*what, how, why*) to probe or gather information and focused questions (*who, when, where*) to clarify and close the sale. A trial close allows prospects to indicate indirectly that they will buy the product without having to say those sometimes difficult words: "I'll take it."

A salesperson should try to close at several points during the presentation because the prospect may be ready to buy. An attempt to close the sale may result in objections. Thus, closing can uncover hidden objections, which the salesperson can then address. One closing strategy involves asking the potential customer to place a low-risk, trial order.

18-2g Following Up

After a successful closing, the salesperson must follow up the sale. In the follow-up stage, the salesperson determines whether the order was delivered on time and installed properly, if installation was required. He or she should contact the customer to learn if any problems or questions regarding the product have arisen. The follow-up stage is also used to determine customers' future product needs.

Following up also aids the salesperson in creating a solid relationship with the customer. New salespeople might find it difficult to understand the reasons for following up on a sale if the customer seems satisfied with the product. However, a large number of customers who stop buying products do so not out of dissatisfaction but because the company neglected to contact them.[21] Thus, the follow-up stage is vital to establishing a strong relationship and creating loyalty on the part of the buyer.

18-3 TYPES OF SALESPEOPLE

To develop a sales force, a marketing manager decides what kind of salesperson will sell the firm's products most effectively. Most business organizations use several different kinds of sales personnel. Based on the functions performed, salespeople can be classified into three groups: order getters, order takers, and support personnel. One salesperson can, and often does, perform all three functions.

closing The stage in the personal selling process when the salesperson asks the prospect to buy the product

18-3a Order Getters

To obtain orders, salespeople inform prospects and persuade them to buy the product. The responsibility of **order getters** is to increase sales by selling to new customers and increasing sales to present customers. This task is sometimes called *creative selling*. It requires that salespeople recognize potential buyers' needs and give them necessary information. Order getting is frequently divided into two categories: current-customer sales and new-business sales.

Current-Customer Sales

Sales personnel who concentrate on current customers call on people and organizations that have purchased products from the firm before. These salespeople seek more sales from existing customers by following up on previous sales. Current customers can also be sources of leads for new prospects.

order getters Salespeople who sell to new customers and increase sales to current customers

order takers Salespeople who primarily seek repeat sales

New-Business Sales

Business organizations depend to some degree on sales to new customers. New-business sales personnel locate prospects and convert them into buyers. Salespeople help generate new business in many organizations, but even more so in organizations that sell real estate, insurance, appliances, automobiles, and business-to-business supplies and services. These organizations depend in large part on new-customer sales.

© iStockphoto.com/Sportstock

Order Getters
When we think of sales representatives, order getters or order takers probably come to mind. Order getters sell to new customers or increase selling to existing customers. Order takers primarily seek repeat sales. There are also support personnel who facilitate selling but are not involved in solely making sales.

18-3b Order Takers

Taking orders is a repetitive task salespeople perform to perpetuate long-lasting, satisfying customer relationships. **Order takers** primarily seek repeat sales, generating the bulk of many firms' total sales. One of their major objectives is to be certain that customers have sufficient product quantities where and when needed. Most order takers handle orders for standardized products that are purchased routinely and do not require extensive sales efforts. The role of order takers is changing, however, as the position moves more toward one that identifies and solves problems to better meet the needs of customers. There are two groups of order takers: inside order takers and field order takers.

Inside Order Takers

In many businesses, inside order takers, who work in sales offices, receive orders by mail, telephone, and the Internet. Certain producers, wholesalers, and retailers have sales personnel who sell from within the firm rather than in the field. Some inside order takers communicate with customers face to face; retail salespeople, for example, are classified as inside order takers. As more orders are placed electronically, the role of the inside order taker continues to change.

Field Order Takers

Salespeople who travel to customers are outside, or field, order takers. Often, customers and field order takers develop interdependent relationships. The buyer relies on the salesperson to take orders periodically (and sometimes to deliver them), and the salesperson counts on the buyer to purchase a certain quantity of products periodically. Use of small computers has improved the field order taker's inventory and order-tracking capabilities.

18-3c Support Personnel

Support personnel facilitate selling but usually are not involved solely with making sales. They engage primarily in marketing industrial products, locating prospects, educating customers, building goodwill, and providing service after the sale. There are many kinds of sales support personnel; the three most common are missionary, trade, and technical salespeople.

Missionary Salespeople

Missionary salespeople, usually employed by manufacturers, assist the producer's customers in selling to their own customers. Missionary salespeople may call on retailers to inform and persuade them to buy the manufacturer's products. When they succeed, retailers purchase products from wholesalers, which are the producer's customers. Manufacturers of medical supplies and pharmaceuticals often use missionary salespeople, called *detail reps*, to promote their products to physicians, hospitals, and pharmacists.

Trade Salespeople

Trade salespeople are not strictly support personnel, because they usually take orders as well. However, they direct much effort toward helping customers—especially retail stores—promote the product. They are likely to restock shelves, obtain more shelf space, set up displays, provide in-store demonstrations, and distribute samples to store customers. Food producers and processors commonly employ trade salespeople.

Technical Salespeople

Technical salespeople give technical assistance to the organization's current customers, advising them on product characteristics and applications, system designs, and installation procedures. Because this job is often highly technical, the salesperson usually has formal training in one of the physical sciences or in engineering. Technical sales personnel often sell technical industrial products, such as computers, heavy equipment, and steel.

When hiring sales personnel, marketers seldom restrict themselves to a single category, because most firms require different types of salespeople. Several factors dictate how many of each type a particular company should have. Product use, characteristics, complexity, and price influence the kind of sales personnel used, as do the number and characteristics of customers. The types of marketing channels and the intensity and type of advertising also affect the composition of a sales force.

18-4 TEAM SELLING AND RELATIONSHIP SELLING

Personal selling has become an increasingly complex process due in large part to rapid technological innovation. Most importantly, the focus of personal selling is shifting from selling a specific product to building long-term relationships with customers by finding solutions to their needs, problems, and challenges. As a result, the roles of salespeople are changing. Among the newer philosophies for personal selling are team selling and relationship selling.

support personnel Sales staff members who facilitate selling but usually are not involved solely with making sales

missionary salespeople Support salespeople, usually employed by a manufacturer, who assist the producer's customers in selling to their own customers

trade salespeople Salespeople involved mainly in helping a producer's customers promote a product

technical salespeople Support salespeople who give technical assistance to a firm's current customers

18-4a Team Selling

Many products, particularly expensive high-tech business products, have become so complex that a single salesperson can no longer be an expert in every aspect of the product and purchase process. **Team selling**, which involves the salesperson joining with people from the firm's financial, engineering, and other functional areas, is appropriate for such products. The salesperson takes the lead in the personal selling process, but other members of the team bring their unique skills, knowledge, and resources to the process to help customers find solutions to their own business challenges. Selling teams may be created to address a particular short-term situation, or they may be formal, ongoing teams. Team selling is advantageous in situations calling for detailed knowledge of new, complex, and dynamic technologies like jet aircraft and medical equipment. It can be difficult, however, for highly competitive salespersons to adapt to a team selling environment.

18-4b Relationship Selling

Relationship selling, also known as consultative selling, involves building mutually beneficial long-term associations with a customer through regular communications over prolonged periods of time. Like team selling, it is especially used in business-to-business marketing. Relationship selling involves finding solutions to customers' needs by listening to them, gaining a detailed understanding of their organizations, understanding and caring about their needs and challenges, and providing support after the sale. Sales representatives from organizations such as Eli Lilly have begun to change their sales tactics to focus upon building relationships. Rather than spending large amounts of time marketing the benefits of their products, Eli Lilly sales representatives are spending more time listening to the doctors. This sales tactic, known as soft selling, has often led to higher sales from customers who do not feel overly pressured to purchase a product they know little about.[22] Sales relationships are also built on being able to recover when customers are concerned about services. Being proactive in identifying the need for recovery behaviors is a major part of relationship selling.[23] Thus, contacting the customer if delivery time is longer than expected as well as explaining what happened and when the product will be delivered are important.

team selling The use of a team of experts from all functional areas of a firm, led by a salesperson, to conduct the personal selling process

relationship selling The building of mutually beneficial long-term associations with a customer through regular communications over prolonged periods of time

© iStockphoto.com/Jeffrey Smith

Team Selling
Team selling is becoming popular, especially in companies where the selling process is complex and requires a variety of specialized skills.

Relationship selling differs from traditional personal selling due to its adoption of a long-term perspective. Instead of simply focusing on short-term repeat sales, relationship selling involves forming long-term connections that will result in sales throughout the relationship.[24] Relationship selling is well poised to help sellers understand their customers' individual needs. It is particularly important in business-to-business transactions as businesses often require more "individualized solutions" to meet their unique needs than the individual consumer.[25] Relationship selling has significant implications for the seller. Studies show that firms spend six times longer on finding new customers than in keeping current customers.[26] Thus, relationship selling that generates loyal long-term customers is likely to be extremely profitable for the firm both in repeat sales as well as the money saved in trying to find new customers. Finally, as the personal selling industry becomes increasingly competitive, relationship selling is one way that companies can differentiate themselves from rivals to create competitive advantages.[27]

Relationship selling efforts can be improved through sales automation technology tools that enhance interactive communication.[28] McAfee adopted automation software that allowed the firm to score leads and develop more tailored programs to provide prospects with the right information at the right times. This impacted relationships between the firm's buyers and sellers, with the lead to opportunity conversion rate increasing four times what it was before.[29] New applications for customer relationship management are also being provided through companies like Salesforce.com, whose cloud-computing model helps companies keep track of the customer life cycle without having to install any software (applications are downloaded). Social networks are being utilized in sales, adding new layers to the selling process. Sales force CRM, for instance, now allows users to connect with their customers in real time through such networks as Twitter and Facebook. Sales force automation, which involves utilizing information technology to automatically track all stages of the sales process (a part of customer relationship management), has been found to increase salesperson professionalism and responsiveness, customer interaction frequency, and customer relationship quality.[30]

Emerging Trends

Salesforce.com Helps Companies with Relationship Selling

Salesforce.com strives to create mutually beneficial relationships with all of its stakeholders, including customers, employees, and communities. Unlike other companies that struggled through the latest recession, Salesforce.com grew. The company earns approximately $3 billion in annual revenue and has more than 100,000 customers.

Salesforce.com is a customer relationship management (CRM) vendor that provides a cloud-computing model to enable businesses to manage relationships with their customers. Because it can be difficult to manage the sales process, Salesforce.com has also begun offering a number of additional services for businesses such as social media analytics. Users access the company's platform through a subscription and are able to use it from their computers. The massive growth of the company in recent years indicates that customers are happy with Salesforce.com's CRM solutions.

Salesforce.com is also beloved by its employees and communities. The firm provides large bonuses, and some of its employees own stock in the company. Salesforce.com's 1/1/1 Model, which stands for 1 percent time (employees are given 1 percent time to volunteer), 1 percent equity (1 percent of its capital is given to the Salesforce.com Foundation), and 1 percent product (1 percent of its products are donated or discounted to organizations such as nonprofits), has been recognized by top ethics institutions such as the Ethisphere™ Institute. By selling quality CRM products and valuing its own relationships with stakeholders, Salesforce.com has achieved both high growth and a positive reputation.[b]

18-5 SALES FORCE MANAGEMENT

The sales force is directly responsible for generating one of an organization's primary inputs: sales revenue. Without adequate sales revenue, businesses cannot survive. In addition, a firm's reputation is often determined by the ethical conduct of its sales force. Indeed, a positive ethical climate, one component of corporate culture, has been linked with decreased role stress and turnover intention and improved job attitudes and job performance in sales.[31] Research has demonstrated that a negative ethical climate will trigger higher-performing salespeople to leave a company at a higher rate than those in a company perceived to be ethical.[32] The morale and ultimately the success of a firm's sales force depend in large part on adequate compensation, room for advancement, sufficient training, and management support—all key areas of sales management. Salespeople who are not satisfied with these elements may leave. Evaluating the input of salespeople is an important part of sales force management because of its strong bearing on a firm's success. Table 18.1 provides directions on how to attract and retain a top-quality sales force.

We explore eight general areas of sales management: establishing sales force objectives, determining sales force size, recruiting and selecting salespeople, training sales personnel, compensating salespeople, motivating salespeople, managing sales territories, and controlling and evaluating sales force performance.

18-5a Establishing Sales Force Objectives

To manage a sales force effectively, sales managers must develop sales objectives. Sales objectives tell salespeople what they are expected to accomplish during a specified time period. They give the sales force direction and purpose and serve as standards for evaluating and controlling the performance of sales personnel. Sales objectives should be stated in precise, measurable terms; specify the time period and geographic areas involved; and be achievable.

Sales objectives are usually developed for both the total sales force and individual salespeople. Objectives for the entire force are normally stated in terms of sales volume, market share, or profit. Volume objectives refer to dollar or unit sales. The objective for an electric drill producer's sales force, for instance, might be to sell $18 million worth of drills, or

Table 18.1 Directions for Attracting and Retaining a Top Sales Force

Training and development	• On-the-job training • Online individual instruction • Seminars • On-site classroom instruction
Compensation	• Make sure pay mix isn't too risky (high commission, low base) for sales role • Mix base salary with commission, bonus, or both • Base bonuses/commission on reaching sales goals rather than on individual sales dollars • Maintain competitive benefits and expense reimbursement practices
Work/life autonomy	• Offer flexible hours • Consider telecommuting/work-at-home options
Product quality and service	• Ensure goods and services meet customer needs • Provide the appropriate service after the sale

Source: "Attracting & Retaining a Top Sales Force," *Where Great Workplaces Start*, http://greatworkplace.wordpress.com/2010/02/10/attracting-retaining-a-top-sales-force (accessed June 26, 2014).

600,000 drills annually. When sales goals are stated in terms of market share, they usually call for an increase in the proportion of the firm's sales relative to the total number of products sold by all businesses in that industry. When sales objectives are based on profit, they are generally stated in terms of dollar amounts or return on investment.

Sales objectives, or quotas, for individual salespeople are commonly stated in terms of dollar or unit sales volume. Other bases used for individual sales objectives include average order size, average number of calls per time period, and ratio of orders to calls.

18-5b Determining Sales Force Size

Sales force size is important, because it influences the company's ability to generate sales and profits. Moreover, size of the sales force affects the compensation methods used, salespeople's morale, and overall sales force management. Sales force size must be adjusted periodically, because a firm's marketing plans change along with markets and forces in the marketing environment. One danger in cutting back the size of the sales force to increase profits is that the sales organization may lose strength and resiliency, preventing it from rebounding when growth occurs or better market conditions prevail.

Several analytical methods can help determine optimal sales force size. One method involves determining how many sales calls per year are necessary for the organization to serve customers effectively and then dividing this total by the average number of sales calls a salesperson makes annually. A second method is based on marginal analysis, in which additional salespeople are added to the sales force until the cost of an additional salesperson equals the additional sales generated by that person. Although marketing managers may use one or several analytical methods, they normally temper decisions with subjective judgments.

18-5c Recruiting and Selecting Salespeople

To create and maintain an effective sales force, sales managers must recruit the right type of salespeople. In **recruiting**, the sales manager develops a list of qualified applicants for sales positions. Effective recruiting efforts are a vital part of implementing the strategic sales force plan and can help assure successful organizational performance. The costs of hiring and training a salesperson are soaring, reaching more than $60,000 in some industries. Thus, recruiting errors are expensive.

To ensure that the recruiting process results in a pool of qualified applicants, a sales manager establishes a set of qualifications before beginning to recruit. Although marketers have tried for years to identify a set of traits characterizing effective salespeople, no set of generally accepted characteristics exists yet. Experts agree that good salespeople exhibit optimism, flexibility, self-motivation, good time management skills, empathy, and the ability to network and maintain long-term customer relationships. There also seems to be a connection between high sales performance, motivational leadership, and employees who are coachable and highly competitive.[33] Today, companies are increasingly seeking applicants capable of employing relationship-building and consultative approaches as well as the ability to work effectively in team selling efforts. It is desirable to hire salespeople who are disciplined and adaptive with their time.[34]

Sales managers must determine what set of traits best fits their companies' particular sales tasks. Two activities help establish this set of required attributes. First, the sales manager should prepare a job description listing specific tasks salespeople are to perform. Second, the manager should analyze characteristics of the firm's successful salespeople, as well as those of ineffective sales personnel. From the job description and analysis of traits, the sales manager should be able to develop a set of specific requirements and be aware of potential weaknesses that could lead to failure.

A sales manager generally recruits applicants from several sources: departments within the firm, other firms, employment agencies, educational institutions, respondents to advertisements, websites (like Monster.com), and individuals recommended by current employees. The specific sources depend on the type of salesperson required and the manager's experiences and successes with particular recruiting tactics.

recruiting Developing a list of qualified applicants for sales positions

Source: Robert Half Survey of 2,100 chief financial officers, 2013.

The process of recruiting and selecting salespeople varies considerably from one company to another. Companies intent on reducing sales force turnover are likely to have strict recruiting and selection procedures. Sales management should design a selection procedure that satisfies the company's specific needs. Some organizations use the specialized services of other companies to hire sales personnel. The process should include steps that yield the information required to make accurate selection decisions. However, because each step incurs a certain amount of expense, there should be no more steps than necessary. Stages of the selection process should be sequenced so that the more expensive steps, such as a physical examination, occur near the end. Fewer people will then move through higher-cost stages.

Recruitment should not be sporadic; it should be a continuous activity aimed at reaching the best applicants. The selection process should systematically and effectively match applicants' characteristics and needs with the requirements of specific selling tasks. Finally, the selection process should ensure that new sales personnel are available where and when needed.

18-5d Training Sales Personnel

Many organizations have formal training programs; others depend on informal, on-the-job training. Some systematic training programs are quite extensive, whereas others are rather short and rudimentary. Whether the training program is complex or simple, developers must consider what to teach, whom to train, and how to train them.

A sales training program can concentrate on the company, its products, or selling methods. Training programs often cover all three. Such programs can be aimed at newly hired salespeople, experienced salespeople, or both. Training for experienced company salespeople usually emphasizes product information or the use of new technology, although salespeople must also be informed about new selling techniques and changes in company plans, policies, and procedures. Sales managers should use ethics training to institutionalize an ethical climate, improve employee satisfaction, and help prevent misconduct. Ordinarily, new sales personnel require comprehensive training, whereas experienced personnel need both refresher courses on established products and training regarding new-product information and technology changes.

Sales training may be done in the field, at educational institutions, in company facilities, and/or online using web-based technology. For many companies, online training saves time and money and helps salespeople learn about new products quickly. Sales managers might even choose to use online platforms from companies such as GoToMeeting to interact with their sales force face-to-face. GoToMeeting provides an online platform so that sales training and meetings can be conducted face-to-face in high-definition video. Some firms train new employees before assigning them to a specific sales position. Others put them into the field immediately, providing formal training only after they have gained some experience. Training programs for new personnel can be as short as several days or as long as three years; some are even longer. Sales training for experienced personnel is often scheduled when sales activities are not too demanding. Because experienced salespeople usually need periodic retraining, a firm's sales management must determine the frequency, sequencing, and duration of these efforts.

Sales managers, as well as other salespeople, often engage in sales training, whether daily on the job or periodically during sales meetings. In addition, a number of outside companies specialize in providing sales training programs. Materials for sales training programs range from videos, texts, online materials, manuals, and cases to programmed learning devices and digital media. Lectures, demonstrations, simulation exercises, role-plays, and on-the-job training can all be effective training methods. Self-directed learning to supplement traditional sales training has the potential to improve sales performance. The choice of methods and materials for a particular sales training program depends on type and number of trainees, program content and complexity, length and location, size of the training budget, number of trainers, and a trainer's expertise.

Virtual Sales Training
GoToMeeting provides a virtual way to participate in sales training and meetings through face-to-face high-definition video.

18-5e Compensating Salespeople

To develop and maintain a highly productive sales force, an organization must formulate and administer a compensation plan that attracts, motivates, and retains the most effective individuals. The plan should give sales management the desired level of control and provide sales personnel with acceptable levels of income, freedom, and incentive. It should be flexible, equitable, easy to administer, and easy to understand. Good compensation programs facilitate and encourage proper treatment of customers. Obviously, it is quite difficult to incorporate all of these requirements into a single program. Figure 18.2 shows the average salaries for sales representatives.

Figure 18.2 Average Salaries for Sales Representatives

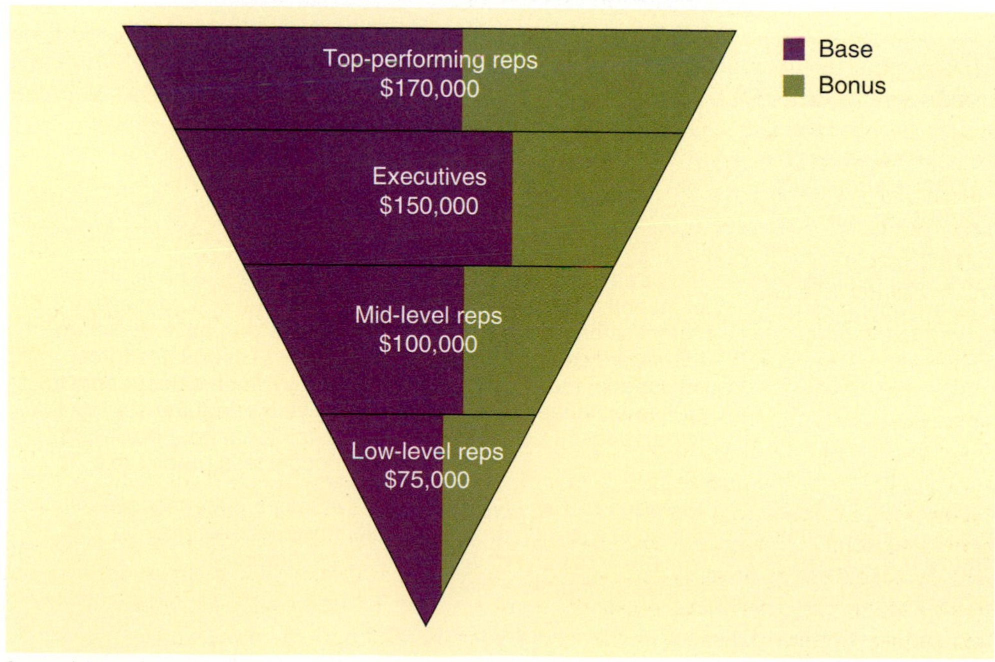

Source: Adapted from Joseph Kornik, "What's It All Worth?" *Sales and Marketing Management*, May 2007, p. 29.

Developers of compensation programs must determine the general level of compensation required and the most desirable method of calculating it. In analyzing the required compensation plan, sales management must ascertain a salesperson's value to the company on the basis of the tasks and responsibilities associated with the sales position. Sales managers may consider a number of factors, including salaries of other types of personnel in the firm, competitors' compensation plans, costs of sales force turnover, and non-salary selling expenses. The average low-level salesperson earns $50,000 to $75,000 annually (including commissions and bonuses), whereas a high-level, high-performing salesperson can make hundreds of thousands a year.

Sales compensation programs usually reimburse salespeople for selling expenses, provide some fringe benefits, and deliver the required compensation level. To achieve this, a firm may use one or more of three basic compensation methods: straight salary, straight commission, or a combination of the two. Table 18.2 lists the major characteristics, advantages, and disadvantages of each method. In a **straight salary compensation plan**, salespeople are paid a specified amount per time period, regardless of selling effort. This sum remains the same until they receive a pay increase or decrease. Although this method is easy to administer and affords salespeople financial security, it provides little incentive for them to boost selling efforts. In a **straight commission compensation plan**, salespeople's compensation is determined solely by sales for a given period. A commission may be based on a single percentage of sales or on a sliding scale involving several sales levels and percentage rates (e.g., sales under $500,000 a quarter would receive a smaller commission than sales over $500,000 each quarter). Although this method motivates sales personnel to escalate their selling efforts, it offers them little financial security, and it can be difficult for sales managers to maintain control over the sales force. Many new salespeople indicate a reluctance to accept the risks associated with straight commission. However, more experienced salespeople know this option can provide the greatest income potential. For these reasons, many firms offer a **combination compensation plan** in which salespeople receive a fixed salary plus a commission based on sales volume. Some combination programs require that a salesperson exceed a certain sales level before earning a commission; others offer commissions for any level of sales.

straight salary compensation plan Paying salespeople a specific amount per time period, regardless of selling effort

straight commission compensation plan Paying salespeople according to the amount of their sales in a given time period

combination compensation plan Paying salespeople a fixed salary plus a commission based on sales volume

When selecting a compensation method, sales management weighs the advantages and disadvantages listed in the table. Researchers have found that higher commissions are the most preferred reward, followed by pay increases, yet preferences on pay tend to vary, depending

Table 18.2 Characteristics of Sales Force Compensation Methods

Compensation Method	When Especially Useful	Advantages	Disadvantages
Straight salary	Compensating new salespeople; firm moves into new sales territories that require developmental work; sales requiring lengthy presale and post-sale services	Gives salespeople security; gives sales managers control over salespeople; easy to administer; yields more predictable selling expenses	Provides no incentive; necessitates closer supervision of salespeople; during sales declines, selling expenses remain constant
Straight commission	Highly aggressive selling is required; non-selling tasks are minimized; company uses contractors and part-timers	Provides maximum amount of incentive; by increasing commission rate, sales managers can encourage salespeople to sell certain items; selling expenses relate directly to sales resources	Salespeople have little financial security; sales managers have minimum control over sales force; may cause salespeople to give inadequate service to smaller accounts; selling costs less predictable
Combination	Sales territories have relatively similar sales potential; firm wishes to provide incentive but still control sales force activities	Provides certain level of financial security; provides some incentive; can move sales force efforts in profitable direction	Selling expenses less predictable; may be difficult to administer

Source: Charles Futrell, *Sales Management*, http://people.tamu.edu/~c-futrell/436/sm_home.html (accessed January 17, 2014).

upon the industry.[35] The Container Store, which markets do-it-yourself organizing and storage products, prefers to pay its sales staff salaries that are 50 to 100 percent higher than those offered by rivals instead of basing pay on commission plans.[36]

18-5f Motivating Salespeople

Although financial compensation is an important incentive, additional programs are necessary for motivating sales personnel. The nature of the jobs, job security, and pay are considered to be the most important factors for the college student going into the sales area today.[37] A sales manager should develop a systematic approach for motivating salespeople to be productive. Sales managers act as models for their sales force. When salespeople perceive their managers as being more customer-oriented and adaptive, they are more likely to imitate these positive behaviors.[38] Salespeople who can identify with their sales managers tend to have higher sales performance and customer satisfaction.[39] Effective sales force motivation is achieved through an organized set of activities performed continuously by the company's sales management.

Sales personnel, like other people, join organizations to satisfy personal needs and achieve personal goals. Sales managers must identify those needs and goals and strive to create an organizational climate that allows each salesperson to fulfill them. Enjoyable working conditions, power and authority, job security, and opportunity to excel are effective motivators, as are company efforts to make sales jobs more productive and efficient. Sales managers who are emotionally intelligent tend to have a positive impact on the creativity of their workers.[40] At the Container Store, for example, first-year sales personnel receive 263 hours of training about the company's products.[41] A strong positive corporate culture leads to higher levels of job satisfaction and organizational commitment and lower levels of job stress.[42]

Motivating Salespeople
Trips or vacation packages are rewards that a high-performing sales person might receive for surpassing his or her sales goals.

Sales contests and other incentive programs can also be effective motivators. These can motivate salespeople to increase sales or add new accounts, promote special items, achieve greater volume per sales call, and cover territories more thoroughly. However, companies need to understand salespersons' preferences when designing contests in order to make them effective in increasing sales. Some companies find such contests powerful tools for motivating sales personnel to achieve company goals. Managers should be careful to craft sales contests that support a strong customer orientation as well as motivate salespeople. In smaller firms lacking the resources for a formal incentive program, a simple but public "thank you" and the recognition from management at a sales meeting, along with a small-denomination gift card, can be very rewarding.

Salesperson turnover is one of the most critical concerns of organizations. Lower organizational commitment has been found to relate directly to job turnover. Identifying with the organization and performance are tied directly to organizational commitment that reduces turnover.[43] Properly designed incentive programs pay for themselves many times over, and sales managers are relying on incentives more than ever. Recognition programs that acknowledge outstanding performance with symbolic awards, such as plaques, can be very effective when carried out in a peer setting. The most common incentive offered by companies is cash, followed by gift cards and travel.[44] Travel reward programs can confer a high-profile honor, provide a unique experience that makes recipients feel special, and build camaraderie among award-winning salespeople. Manufacturing company Hilti rewards the top 10 percent of its sales force by allowing them to attend a President's Club event held in locations such as Hawaii and the Caribbean.[45] However, some recipients of travel awards may feel they already travel too much on the job. Cash rewards are easy to administer, are always appreciated by recipients, and appeal to all demographic groups. However, cash has no visible "trophy" value and provides few "bragging rights." The benefits of awarding merchandise are that the items have visible trophy value. In addition, recipients who are allowed to select the merchandise experience a sense of control, and merchandise awards can help build momentum for the sales force. The disadvantages of using merchandise are that employees may have lower perceived value of the merchandise and the company may experience greater administrative problems. Some companies outsource their incentive programs to companies that specialize in the creation and management of such programs.

18-5g Managing Sales Territories

The effectiveness of a sales force that must travel to customers is somewhat influenced by management's decisions regarding sales territories. When deciding on territories, sales managers must consider size, geographic shape, routing, and scheduling.

Creating Sales Territories

Several factors enter into the design of a sales territory's size and geographic shape. First, sales managers must construct territories that allow sales potential to be measured. Sales territories often consist of several geographic units, such as census tracts, cities, counties, or states, for which market data are obtainable. Sales managers usually try to create territories with similar sales potential, or requiring about the same amount of work. If territories have equal sales potential, they will almost always be unequal in geographic size. Salespeople with larger territories have to work longer and harder to generate a certain sales volume. Conversely, if sales territories requiring equal amounts of work are created, sales potential for those territories will often vary. Think about the effort required to sell in New York and Connecticut versus the sales effort required in a larger, less populated area like Montana or Wyoming. If sales personnel are partially or fully compensated through commissions, they will have unequal income potential. Many sales managers try to balance territorial workloads and earning potential by using differential commission rates. At times, sales managers use commercial programs to help them balance sales territories. Although a sales manager seeks equity when developing and maintaining sales territories, some inequities always prevail. A territory's size and geographical shape should also help the sales force provide the best possible customer coverage and minimize selling costs. Customer density and distribution are important factors.

Routing and Scheduling Salespeople

The geographic size and shape of a sales territory are the most important factors affecting the routing and scheduling of sales calls. Next in importance are the number and distribution of customers within the territory, followed by sales call frequency and duration. Those in charge of routing and scheduling must consider the sequence in which customers are called on, specific roads or transportation schedules to be used, number of calls to be made in a given period, and time of day the calls will occur. In some firms, salespeople plan their own routes and schedules with little or no assistance from the sales manager. In others, the sales manager maintains significant responsibility. No matter who plans the routing and scheduling, the major goals should be to minimize salespeople's non-selling time (time spent traveling and waiting) and maximize their selling time. Sales managers should try to achieve these goals so that a salesperson's travel and lodging costs are held to a minimum.

18-5h Controlling and Evaluating Sales Force Performance

To control and evaluate sales force performance properly, sales management needs information. A sales manager cannot observe the field sales force daily and, thus, relies on salespeople's call reports, customer feedback, contracts, and invoices. Call reports identify the customers called on and present detailed information about interactions with those clients. Sales personnel must often file work schedules indicating where they plan to be during specific time periods. Data about a salesperson's interactions with customers and prospects can be included in the company's customer relationship management system. This information provides insights about the salesperson's performance.

Dimensions used to measure a salesperson's performance are determined largely by sales objectives, normally set by the sales manager. If an individual's sales objective is stated in terms of sales volume, that person should be evaluated on the basis of sales volume generated. Even if a salesperson is assigned a major objective, he or she is ordinarily expected to achieve several related objectives as well. Thus, salespeople are often judged along several dimensions. Sales managers evaluate many performance indicators, including average number of calls per day, average sales per customer, actual sales relative to sales potential, number of new-customer orders, average cost per call, and average gross profit per customer.

To evaluate a salesperson, a sales manager may compare one or more of these dimensions with predetermined performance standards. However, sales managers commonly compare a salesperson's performance with that of other employees operating under similar selling conditions or the salesperson's current performance with past performance. Sometimes, management judges factors that have less direct bearing on sales performance, such as personal appearance, product knowledge, and ethical standards. One concern is the tendency to reprimand top sellers less severely than poor performers for engaging in unethical selling practices.

After evaluating salespeople, sales managers take any needed corrective action to improve sales force performance. They may adjust performance standards, provide additional training, or try other motivational methods. Corrective action may demand comprehensive changes in the sales force.

18-6 SALES PROMOTION

Sales promotion is an activity or material, or both, that acts as a direct inducement, offering added value or incentive for the product, to resellers, salespeople, or consumers. It encompasses all promotional activities and materials other than personal selling, advertising, and public relations. The retailer Payless, for example, often offers buy-one-get-one-free sales on its shoes, a sales promotion tactic known as a bonus or premium. In competitive markets, where products are very similar, sales promotion provides additional inducements that encourage product trial and purchase.

sales promotion An activity and/or material intended to induce resellers or salespeople to sell a product or consumers to buy it

Marketers often use sales promotion to facilitate personal selling, advertising, or both. Companies also employ advertising and personal selling to support sales promotion activities. Marketers frequently use advertising to promote contests, free samples, and premiums. The most effective sales promotion efforts are highly interrelated with other promotional activities. Decisions regarding sales promotion often affect advertising and personal selling decisions, and vice versa.

Sales promotion can increase sales by providing extra purchasing incentives. Many opportunities exist to motivate consumers, resellers, and salespeople to take desired actions. Some kinds of sales promotion are designed specifically to stimulate resellers' demand and effectiveness, some are directed at increasing consumer demand, and some focus on both consumers and resellers. Regardless of the purpose, marketers must ensure that sales promotion objectives are consistent with the organization's overall objectives, as well as with its marketing and promotion objectives.

When deciding which sales promotion methods to use, marketers must consider several factors, particularly product characteristics (price, size, weight, costs, durability, uses, features, and hazards) and target market characteristics (age, gender, income, location, density, usage rate, and shopping patterns). How products are distributed and the number and types of resellers may determine the type of method used. The competitive and legal environment may also influence the choice.

The use of sales promotion has increased dramatically over the past 30 years, primarily at the expense of advertising. This shift in how promotional dollars are used has occurred for several reasons. Heightened concerns about value have made customers more responsive to promotional offers, especially price discounts and point-of-purchase displays. Thanks to their size and access to checkout scanner data, retailers have gained considerable power in the supply chain and are demanding greater promotional efforts from manufacturers to boost retail profits. Declines in brand loyalty have produced an environment in which sales promotions aimed at persuading customers to switch brands are more effective. Finally, the stronger emphasis placed on improving short-term performance results calls for greater use of sales promotion methods that yield quick (although perhaps short-lived) sales increases.[46]

In the remainder of this chapter, we examine several consumer and trade sales promotion methods, including what they entail and what goals they can help marketers achieve.

18-7 CONSUMER SALES PROMOTION METHODS

Consumer sales promotion methods encourage or stimulate consumers to patronize specific retail stores or try particular products. Consumer sales promotion methods initiated by retailers often aim to attract customers to specific locations, whereas those used by manufacturers generally introduce new products or promote established brands. In this section, we discuss coupons, cents-off offers, money refunds and rebates, frequent-user incentives, point-of-purchase displays, demonstrations, free samples, premiums, consumer contests and games, and consumer sweepstakes.

18-7a Coupons

consumer sales promotion methods Sales promotion techniques that encourage consumers to patronize specific stores or try particular products

coupons Written price reductions used to encourage consumers to buy a specific product

Coupons reduce a product's price and aim to prompt customers to try new or established products, increase sales volume quickly, attract repeat purchasers, or introduce new package sizes or features. Savings are deducted from the purchase price. Coupons are the most widely used consumer sales promotion technique. Although coupon usage had been spiraling downward for years, the economic downturn started to reverse this trend. However, coupon redemption has once again started to decrease. Although part of the reason is greater spending power, consumers have indicated that a primary reason for not using coupons is because they cannot find coupons for what they want to buy.[47] Digital coupons via websites and mobile apps are also becoming popular. Social deal sites like Groupon, Living Social, and Crowd

Cut, while not exactly in the coupon area, are encouraging consumers to look for deals or better prices. Starbucks was able to boost sales by offering coupons on daily deal sites such as Living Social as well as giving morning customers discounted drinks if they returned in the afternoon.[48] To take advantage of the new consumer interest in coupons, digital marketing—including mobile, social, and other platforms—is being used for couponing. More than half of Internet users redeemed a digital coupon in 2013.[49]

For best results, coupons should be easily recognized and state the offer clearly. The nature of the product (seasonal demand for it, life-cycle stage, and frequency of purchase) is the prime consideration in setting up a coupon promotion. Paper coupons are distributed on and inside packages, through freestanding inserts, in print advertising, on the back of cash register receipts, and through direct mail. Electronic coupons are distributed online, via in-store kiosks, through shelf dispensers in stores, and at checkout counters.[50] Figure 18.3 indicates that nearly half of the Internet users in the United States have used digital coupons, and this number is likely to grow. When deciding on the distribution method for coupons, marketers should consider strategies and objectives, redemption rates, availability, circulation, and exclusivity. This advertisement for Visine eye drops features a coupon at the bottom offering $2.00 off a Visine purchase. The advertisement depicts the scene of a mother getting up in the middle of the night to feed her baby. However, the faces are replaced by giant eyes to stress the redness and irritation of the mother's eyes. The manufacturer hopes this coupon will increase sales of its product and provides the name of a pharmacy where the product can be found. The coupon distribution and redemption arena has become very competitive. To avoid losing customers, many grocery stores will redeem any coupons offered by competitors. Also, to draw customers to their stores, grocers double and sometimes even triple the value of customers' coupons.

Coupons offer several advantages. Print advertisements with coupons are often more effective at generating brand awareness than print ads without coupons. Generally, the larger the coupon's cash offer, the better the recognition generated. Coupons reward current product

Figure 18.3 U.S. Adult Digital Coupon Users 2012–2015

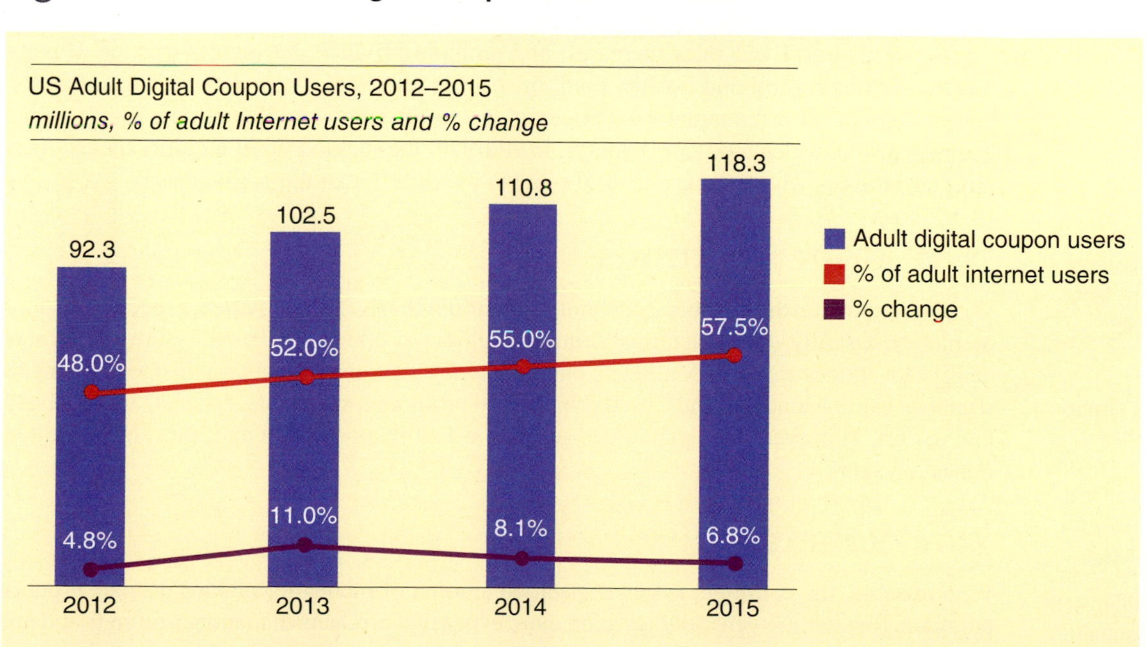

Note: ages 18+; internet users who redeemed a digital coupon/code via any device for online or offline shopping at least once during the calendar year; includes group buying coupons.
Source: eMarketer, Oct 2013

Print Coupons
This advertisement features a coupon from the manufacturer for Visine eye drops.

users, win back former users, and encourage purchases in larger quantities. Because they are returned, coupons also help a manufacturer determine whether it reached the intended target market. The advantages of using electronic coupons over paper coupons include lower cost per redemption, greater targeting ability, improved data-gathering capabilities, and greater experimentation capabilities to determine optimal face values and expiration cycles.[51]

Drawbacks of coupon use include fraud and misredemption, which can be expensive for manufacturers. Coupon fraud—including counterfeit Internet coupons as well as coupons cashed in under false retailer names—costs manufacturers hundreds of millions in losses each year.[52] Another disadvantage, according to some experts, is that coupons are losing their value; because so many manufacturers offer them, consumers have learned not to buy without some incentive, whether that pertains to a coupon, a rebate, or a refund. Furthermore, brand loyalty among heavy coupon users has diminished, and many consumers redeem coupons only for products they normally buy. It is believed that about three-fourths of coupons are redeemed by people already using the brand on the coupon. Thus, coupons have questionable success as an incentive for consumers to try a new brand or product. An additional problem with coupons is that stores often do not have enough of the coupon item in stock. This situation generates ill will toward both the store and the product.

18-7b Cents-Off Offers

With **cents-off offers**, buyers pay a certain amount less than the regular price shown on the label or package. Like coupons, this method can serve as a strong incentive for trying new or unfamiliar products and is commonly used in product introductions. It can stimulate product sales or multiple purchases, yield short-lived sales increases, and promote products during off-seasons. It is an easy method to control and is often used for specific purposes. If used on an ongoing basis, however, cents-off offers reduce the price for customers who would buy at the regular price and may also cheapen a product's image. In addition, the method often requires special handling by retailers who are responsible for giving the discount at the point of sale.

cents-off offers Promotions that allow buyers to pay less than the regular price to encourage purchase

money refunds Sales promotion techniques that offer consumers a specified amount of money when they mail in a proof of purchase, usually for multiple product purchases

rebates Sales promotion techniques in which a consumer receives a specified amount of money for making a single product purchase

18-7c Money Refunds

With **money refunds**, consumers submit proof of purchase and are mailed a specific amount of money. Usually, manufacturers demand multiple product purchases before consumers qualify for money refunds. Marketers employ money refunds as an alternative to coupons to stimulate sales. Money refunds, used primarily to promote trial use of a product, are relatively low in cost. However, they sometimes generate a low response rate and, thus, have limited impact on sales.

18-7d Rebates

With **rebates**, the consumer is sent a specified amount of money for making a single product purchase. Rebates are generally given on more expensive products than money refunds and are used to encourage customers. Marketers also use rebates to reinforce brand loyalty and encourage product purchase. On larger items, such as cars, rebates are often given at the point of sale. Most rebates, however, especially on smaller items, are given after the sale, usually through a mail-in process. This advertisement for Falken Tire shows personnel placing tires on a racecar. Toward the bottom the advertisement informs potential buyers that they can save up to $100 for purchasing four qualifying Falken tires. To qualify, customers must mail in the rebate after purchasing the tires. Researchers find that these mail-in rebates are most effective in situations where consumers require a reason to purchase an item. On the other hand, rebates for products that provide instant gratification are more effective if provided at the point of purchase.[53]

One problem with money refunds and rebates is that many people perceive the redemption process as being too complicated. To eliminate these complications, many marketers allow customers to apply for a rebate online, which eliminates the need for forms that may confuse customers and frustrate retailers. Consumers might also have negative perceptions of manufacturers' reasons for offering rebates. They may believe the products are untested or have not sold well. If these perceptions are not changed, rebate offers may actually degrade product image and desirability.

Rebates
Falken Tire offers customers a mail-in rebate of up to $100 if they purchase Falken tires.

18-7e Frequent-User Incentives

Marriott and United Airlines recently announced a partnership to reward customers for their loyalty to Marriott hotels. Customers who spend 75 nights a year in Marriott hotels will receive Premier Silver status in United's MileagePlus program, providing them with more benefits on their flights.[54] This is an example of a frequent-user incentive program. Many firms develop incentive programs to reward customers who engage in repeat (frequent) purchases. For instance, most major airlines offer frequent-flyer programs that reward customers who have flown a specified number of miles with free tickets for additional travel. JetBlue is now allowing families to pool their frequent-flyer miles.[55] Frequent-user incentives foster customer loyalty to a specific company or group of cooperating companies. They are favored by service businesses, such as airlines, auto rental agencies, hotels, and local coffee shops. Frequent-user programs not only reward loyal customers but also generate data that can contribute significant information about customers that helps marketers foster desirable customer relationships.

18-7f Point-of-Purchase Materials and Demonstrations

Point-of-purchase (POP) materials include outdoor signs, window displays, counter pieces, display racks, and self-service cartons. Innovations in POP displays include sniff-teasers, which give off a product's aroma in the store as consumers walk within a radius of 4 feet, and computerized interactive displays. These items, often supplied by producers, attract attention, inform customers, and encourage retailers to carry particular products. Retailers have also begun experimenting with new forms of POP technology, such as interactive kiosks allowing shoppers to browse through products. A retailer is likely to use point-of-purchase materials if they are attractive, informative, well-constructed, and in harmony with the store's image.

Demonstrations are excellent attention-getters. Manufacturers offer them temporarily to encourage trial use and purchase of a product or to show how a product works. Because labor costs can be extremely high, demonstrations are not used widely. They can be highly effective for promoting certain types of products, such as appliances, cosmetics, and cleaning supplies.

point-of-purchase (POP) materials Signs, window displays, display racks, and similar devices used to attract customers

demonstrations Sales promotion methods a manufacturer uses temporarily to encourage trial use and purchase of a product or to show how a product works

Free Samples
Benjamin Moore & Co. offers a coupon for a free pint color sample to encourage product trial.

Even automobiles can be demonstrated, not only by a salesperson but also by the prospective buyer during a test drive. Cosmetics marketers, such as Estée Lauder and Clinique, sometimes offer potential customers "makeovers" to demonstrate product benefits and proper application.

18-7g Free Samples

Marketers use **free samples** to stimulate trial of a product, increase sales volume in the early stages of a product's life cycle, and obtain desirable distribution. Trader Joe's gives out free samples of its coffee, hoping to entice buyers to make a purchase. Sampling is the most expensive sales promotion method because production and distribution—at local events, by mail or door-to-door delivery, online, in stores, and on packages—entail high costs. However, it can also be one of the most effective sales promotion methods: Arbitron survey results indicate that more than half of consumers who sampled a product plan to purchase it in the future.[56]

Many consumers prefer to get their samples by mail. Other consumers like to sample new food products at supermarkets or try samples of new recipes featuring foods they already like. In designing a free sample, marketers should consider factors like seasonal demand for the product, market characteristics, and prior advertising. Free samples are usually inappropriate for slow-turnover products. Despite high costs, use of sampling is increasing. In a given year, almost three-fourths of consumer products companies may use sampling. Benjamin Moore & Co. provides a free pint color sample for a limited time period through a coupon redeemable at participating retailers. The advertisement underscores the freedom customers should have when painting a wall. The body text claims that each color has a variety of shades and hues, and the coupon gives customers the option of trying out a color they might otherwise not try without the sample.

18-7h Premiums

Premiums are items offered free or at a minimal cost as a bonus for purchasing a product. Like the prize in the Cracker Jack box, premiums are used to attract competitors' customers, introduce different sizes of established products, add variety to other promotional efforts, and stimulate consumer loyalty. Consumers appear to prefer premiums to discounts on products due to the perception that they are receiving something "free."[57] Creativity is essential when using premiums; to stand out and achieve a significant number of redemptions, the premium must match both the target audience and the brand's image. Premiums must also be easily recognizable and desirable. Consumers are more favorable toward a premium when the brand has high equity and there is a good fit between the product and the premium.[58] Premiums are placed on or inside packages and can also be distributed by retailers or through the mail. Examples include a service station giving a free car wash with a fill-up, a free shaving cream with the purchase of a razor, and a free plastic storage box with the purchase of Kraft Cheese Singles.

free samples Samples of a product given out to encourage trial and purchase

premiums Items offered free or at a minimal cost as a bonus for purchasing a product

consumer contests Sales promotion methods in which individuals compete for prizes based on their analytical or creative skills

18-7i Consumer Contests

In **consumer contests**, individuals compete for prizes based on their analytical or creative skills. This method can be used to generate retail traffic and frequency of exposure to promotional messages. Contestants are usually more highly involved in consumer contests than in games or sweepstakes, even though total participation may be lower. Contests may also be used in conjunction with other sales promotional methods, such as coupons. Nikon partnered with *National Geographic* to host the "Full Story" photo contest, a contest in which budding photographers could send in their photo submissions for a chance to win prizes. The winner was given the opportunity to go on assignment to a foreign destination, such as the Galapagos Islands. This contest was beneficial for Nikon because photojournalists were encouraged to submit their stories using the Nikon D600 D-SLR camera. In this way, the company was able to use a consumer contest for product promotion.[59]

18-7j Consumer Games

In **consumer games**, individuals compete for prizes based primarily on chance—often by collecting game pieces like bottle caps or a sticker on a carton of French fries. Because collecting multiple pieces may be necessary to win or increase an individual's chances of winning, the game stimulates repeated business. Development and management of consumer games is often outsourced to an independent public relations firm, which can help marketers navigate federal and state laws that regulate games. Although games may stimulate sales temporarily, there is no evidence to suggest that they affect a company's long-term sales.

Marketers considering games should exercise care. Problems or errors may anger customers and could result in a lawsuit. McDonald's wildly popular Monopoly game promotion, in which customers collect Monopoly real estate pieces on drink and French fry packages, has been tarnished by past fraud after a crime ring, including employees of the promotional firm running the game, was convicted of stealing millions of dollars in winning game pieces. McDonald's later reintroduced the Monopoly game with heightened security. It also introduced an online Monopoly game where consumers can play for prizes by inputting codes.[60]

consumer games Sales promotion methods in which individuals compete for prizes based primarily on chance

18-7k Sweepstakes

Entrants in a **consumer sweepstakes** submit their names for inclusion in a drawing for prizes. To gain an edge over the competition, the games publishing division GameHouse began offering consumers the chance to win a monthly $100,000 sweepstakes through its GameHouse Casino Plus on Facebook.[61] Sweepstakes are employed more often than consumer contests and tend to attract a greater number of participants. However, contestants are

consumer sweepstakes A sales promotion in which entrants submit their names for inclusion in a drawing for prizes

Consumer Games
McDonald's Monopoly is a popular consumer game that gives customers the opportunity to win prizes with the purchase of McDonald's products.

usually more involved in consumer contests and games than in sweepstakes, even though total participation may be lower. Contests, games, and sweepstakes may be used in conjunction with other sales promotion methods like coupons.

18-8 TRADE SALES PROMOTION METHODS

To encourage resellers, especially retailers, to carry their products and promote them effectively, producers use trade sales promotion methods. **Trade sales promotion methods** attempt to persuade wholesalers and retailers to carry a producer's products and market them more aggressively. Marketers use trade sales methods for many reasons, including countering the effect of lower-priced store brands, passing along a discount to a price-sensitive market segment, boosting brand exposure among target consumers, or providing additional incentives to move excess inventory or counteract competitors. These methods include buying allowances, buy-back allowances, scan-back allowances, merchandise allowances, cooperative advertising, dealer listings, free merchandise, dealer loaders, premium or push money, and sales contests.

18-8a Trade Allowances

Many manufacturers offer trade allowances to encourage resellers to carry a product or stock more of it. One such trade allowance is a **buying allowance**, a temporary price reduction offered to resellers for purchasing specified quantities of a product. A soap producer, for example, might give retailers $1 for each case of soap purchased. Such offers provide an incentive for resellers to handle new products, achieve temporary price reductions, or stimulate purchase of items in larger-than-normal quantities. The buying allowance, which takes the form of money, yields profits to resellers and is simple and straightforward. There are no restrictions on how resellers use the money, which increases the method's effectiveness. One drawback of buying allowances is that customers may buy "forward"—that is, buy large amounts that keep them supplied for many months. Another problem is that competitors may match (or beat) the reduced price, which can lower profits for all sellers.

A **buy-back allowance** is a sum of money that a producer gives to a reseller for each unit the reseller buys after an initial promotional deal is over. This method is a secondary incentive in which the total amount of money resellers receive is proportional to their purchases during an initial consumer promotion, such as a coupon offer. Buy-back allowances foster cooperation during an initial sales promotion effort and stimulate repurchase afterward. The main disadvantage of this method is expense.

A **scan-back allowance** is a manufacturer's reward to retailers based on the number of pieces moved through the retailers' scanners during a specific time period. To participate in scan-back programs, retailers are usually expected to pass along savings to consumers through special pricing. Scan-backs are becoming widely used by manufacturers because they link trade spending directly to product movement at the retail level.

A **merchandise allowance** is a manufacturer's agreement to pay resellers certain amounts of money for providing promotional efforts like advertising or point-of-purchase displays. This method is best suited to high-volume, high-profit, easily handled products. A drawback is that some retailers perform activities at a minimally acceptable level simply to obtain allowances. Before paying retailers, manufacturers usually verify their performance. Manufacturers hope that retailers' additional promotional efforts will yield substantial sales increases.

trade sales promotion methods Methods intended to persuade wholesalers and retailers to carry a producer's products and market them aggressively

buying allowance A temporary price reduction to resellers for purchasing specified quantities of a product

buy-back allowance A sum of money given to a reseller for each unit bought after an initial promotion deal is over

scan-back allowance A manufacturer's reward to retailers based on the number of pieces scanned

merchandise allowance A manufacturer's agreement to pay resellers certain amounts of money for providing special promotional efforts, such as setting up and maintaining a display

cooperative advertising An arrangement in which a manufacturer agrees to pay a certain amount of a retailer's media costs for advertising the manufacturer's products

18-8b Cooperative Advertising and Dealer Listings

Cooperative advertising is an arrangement in which a manufacturer agrees to pay a certain amount of a retailer's media costs for advertising the manufacturer's products. The amount allowed is usually based on the quantities purchased. As with merchandise allowances, a retailer must show proof that advertisements did appear before the manufacturer pays the agreed-upon portion of the advertising costs. These payments give retailers additional funds for advertising. Some retailers exploit cooperative-advertising agreements by crowding too many products into one advertisement. Not all available cooperative-advertising dollars are used. Some retailers cannot afford to advertise, while others can afford it but do not want to advertise. A large proportion of all cooperative-advertising dollars is spent on newspaper advertisements.

Dealer listings are advertisements promoting a product and identifying participating retailers that sell the product. Dealer listings can influence retailers to carry the product, build traffic at the retail level, and encourage consumers to buy the product at participating dealers.

18-8c Free Merchandise and Gifts

Manufacturers sometimes offer **free merchandise** to resellers that purchase a stated quantity of products. Occasionally, free merchandise is used as payment for allowances provided through other sales promotion methods. To avoid handling and bookkeeping problems, the "free" merchandise usually takes the form of a reduced invoice.

A **dealer loader** is a gift to a retailer that purchases a specified quantity of merchandise. Dealer loaders are often used to obtain special display efforts from retailers by offering essential display parts as premiums. Thus, a manufacturer might design a display that includes a sterling silver tray as a major component and give the tray to the retailer. Marketers use dealer loaders to obtain new distributors and push larger quantities of goods.

dealer listings Advertisements that promote a product and identify the names of participating retailers that sell the product

free merchandise A manufacturer's reward given to resellers that purchase a stated quantity of products

dealer loader A gift, often part of a display, given to a retailer that purchases a specified quantity of merchandise

premium money (push money) Extra compensation to salespeople for pushing a line of goods

sales contest A sales promotion method used to motivate distributors, retailers, and sales personnel through recognition of outstanding achievements

18-8d Premium Money

Premium money (push money) is additional compensation offered by the manufacturer to salespeople as an incentive to push a line of goods. This method is appropriate when personal selling is an important part of the marketing effort; it is not effective for promoting products sold through self-service. Premium money often helps a manufacturer obtain a commitment from the sales force, but it can be very expensive. The use of this incentive must be in compliance with retailers' policies as well as state and local laws.

18-8e Sales Contest

A **sales contest** is designed to motivate distributors, retailers, and sales personnel by recognizing outstanding achievements. To be effective, this method must be equitable for all individuals involved. One advantage is that it can achieve participation at all distribution levels. Positive effects may be temporary, however, and prizes are usually expensive.

Summary

18-1 Describe the major goals of personal selling.

Personal selling is the process of informing customers and persuading them to purchase products through paid personal communication in an exchange situation. The five general goals of personal selling are finding prospects, determining their needs, persuading prospects to buy, following up on the sale, and keeping customers satisfied.

18-2 Summarize the seven basic steps in the personal selling process.

Many salespeople, either consciously or subconsciously, move through a general selling process as they sell products. In prospecting, the salesperson develops a database of potential customers. Before contacting prospects, the salesperson conducts a preapproach that involves finding and analyzing information about prospects and their needs. The approach is the manner in which the salesperson contacts potential customers. During the sales presentation, the salesperson must attract and hold the prospect's attention to stimulate interest and desire for the product. If possible, the salesperson should handle objections as they arise. During the closing, the salesperson asks the prospect to buy the product or products. After a successful closing, the salesperson must follow up on the sale.

18-3 Identify the types of sales force personnel.

In developing a sales force, marketing managers consider which types of salespeople will sell the firm's products most effectively. The three classifications of salespeople are order getters, order takers, and support personnel. Order getters inform both current customers and new prospects and persuade them to buy. Order takers seek repeat sales and fall into two categories: inside order takers and field order takers. Sales support personnel facilitate selling, but their duties usually extend beyond making sales. The three types of support personnel are missionary, trade, and technical salespeople.

18-4 Describe *team selling* and *relationship selling*.

The roles of salespeople are changing, resulting in an increased focus on team selling and relationship selling. Team selling involves the salesperson joining with people from the firm's financial, engineering, and other functional areas. Relationship selling involves building mutually beneficial long-term associations with a customer through regular communications over prolonged periods of time.

18-5 Discuss eight major decisions in sales force management.

Sales force management is an important determinant of a firm's success because the sales force is directly responsible for generating the organization's sales revenue. Major decision areas and activities are establishing sales force objectives; determining sales force size; recruiting, selecting, training, compensating, and motivating salespeople; managing sales territories; and controlling and evaluating sales force performance.

Sales objectives should be stated in precise, measurable terms and specify the time period and geographic areas involved. The size of the sales force must be adjusted occasionally because a firm's marketing plans change along with markets and forces in the marketing environment.

Recruiting and selecting salespeople involve attracting and choosing the right type of salesperson to maintain an effective sales force. When developing a training program, managers must consider a variety of dimensions, such as who should be trained, what should be taught, and how training should occur. Compensation of salespeople involves formulating and administering a compensation plan that attracts, motivates, and retains the right types of salespeople. Motivated salespeople should translate into high productivity. Managing sales territories focuses on such factors as size, shape, routing, and scheduling. To control and evaluate sales force performance, sales managers use information obtained through salespeople's call reports, customer feedback, and invoices.

18-6 Describe sales promotion.

Sales promotion is an activity or a material (or both) that acts as a direct inducement, offering added value or incentive for the product to resellers, salespeople, or consumers. Marketers use sales promotion to identify and attract new customers, introduce new products, and increase reseller inventories. Sales promotion techniques fall into two general categories: consumer and trade.

18-7 Review consumer sales promotion methods.

Consumer sales promotion methods encourage consumers to patronize specific stores or try a particular product. These sales promotion methods include coupons; cents-off offers; money refunds and rebates; frequent-user incentives; point-of-purchase displays; demonstrations; free samples and premiums; and consumer contests, games, and sweepstakes.

18-8 Review trade sales promotion methods.

Trade sales promotion techniques can motivate resellers to handle a manufacturer's products and market them aggressively. These sales promotion techniques include buying allowances, buy-back allowances, scan-back allowances, merchandise allowances, cooperative advertising, dealer listings, free merchandise, dealer loaders, premium (or push) money, and sales contests.

Go to www.cengagebrain.com for resources to help you master the content in this chapter as well as for materials that will expand your marketing knowledge!

Developing Your Marketing Plan

When developing its marketing strategy, a company must consider the different forms of communication that are necessary to reach a variety of customers. Several types of promotion may be required. Knowledge of the advantages and disadvantages of each promotional element is necessary when developing the marketing plan. Consider the information in this chapter when evaluating your promotional mix.

1. Review the various types of salespeople described in this chapter. Given your promotional objectives (from Chapter 16), do any of these types of salespeople have a place in your promotional plan?
2. Identify the resellers in your distribution channel. Discuss the role that trade sales promotions to these resellers could play in the development of your promotional plan.
3. Evaluate each type of consumer sales promotion as it relates to accomplishing your promotional objectives.

The information obtained from these questions should assist you in developing various aspects of your marketing plan found in the "Interactive Marketing Plan" exercise at **www.cengagebrain.com**.

Important Terms

personal selling 546
prospecting 548
approach 550
closing 551
order getters 552
order takers 552
support personnel 553
missionary salespeople 553
trade salespeople 553
technical salespeople 553
team selling 554
relationship selling 554
recruiting 557
straight salary compensation plan 560
straight commission compensation plan 560
combination compensation plan 560
sales promotion 563
consumer sales promotion methods 564
coupons 564
cents-off offers 566
money refunds 566
rebates 566
point-of-purchase (POP) materials 567
demonstrations 567
free samples 568
premiums 568
consumer contests 568
consumer games 569
consumer sweepstakes 569
trade sales promotion methods 570
buying allowance 570
buy-back allowance 570
scan-back allowance 570
merchandise allowance 570
cooperative advertising 570
dealer listings 571
free merchandise 571
dealer loader 571
premium money (push money) 571
sales contest 571

Discussion and Review Questions

1. What is personal selling? How does personal selling differ from other types of promotional activities?
2. What are the primary purposes of personal selling?
3. Identify the steps of the personal selling process. Must a salesperson include all these steps when selling a product to a customer? Why or why not?
4. How does a salesperson find and evaluate prospects? Do you consider any of these methods to be ethically questionable? Explain.
5. Are order getters more aggressive or creative than order takers? Why or why not?
6. Why are team selling and relationship selling becoming more prevalent?
7. Identify several characteristics of effective sales objectives.
8. How should a sales manager establish criteria for selecting sales personnel? What do you think are the general characteristics of a good salesperson?
9. What major issues or questions should management consider when developing a training program for the sales force?
10. Explain the major advantages and disadvantages of the three basic methods of compensating salespeople. In general, which method would you prefer? Why?
11. What major factors should be taken into account when designing the size and shape of a sales territory?
12. How does a sales manager, who cannot be with each salesperson in the field on a daily basis, control the performance of sales personnel?
13. What is sales promotion? Why is it used?
14. For each of the following, identify and describe three techniques and give several examples: (a) consumer sales promotion methods and (b) trade sales promotion methods.
15. What types of sales promotion methods have you observed recently? Comment on their effectiveness.

Video Case 18.1

Nederlander Organization Rewards the Audience

The Nederlander Organization is in its 100th year of managing Broadway-type theaters in several states and the United Kingdom. It is a theatrical organization that owns concert venues and Broadway theaters. Nederlander describes itself as a lifestyle company, which puts them in a specific niche with a specific type of customer. Josh Lesnick, president and CEO of Audience Rewards, explains, "I think with something like the arts, customers obviously want a good deal. They want a value-add, but it's really about the experience."

The organization engages in promotional activities for various concerts as well as production of Broadway shows. The success of such activities relies on building and maintaining strong relationships with the many theater owners and ticketing organizations. Nederlander Organization has leveraged these relationships with their Audience Rewards program, a type of sales promotion that has allowed them to build strong relationships with customers by enhancing their experience.

The unique nature of the industry and smaller size of their target market allow Nederlander to create a valuable experience for customers through personal selling and sales promotion activities. Josh Lesnick describes Audience Rewards as being similar to a frequent-flyer program. Customers can become members for free and are entered into the ticketing system. When they buy tickets and go to shows, they collect points and are able to redeem them for free or discounted tickets and other rewards. The program was developed as an alternative to traditional discounting. "[It is] another way to incentivize customers to go to the theater more, to spend more money, to try out new art."

Nederlander's sales promotion program strongly benefits smaller venues. The theater industry is composed of many small privately-owned theaters, and each show is marketed individually. This can make it difficult and expensive for companies to advertise and promote their shows. Nederlander's Audience Rewards program helps ease this complexity because they work with many theater owners who support and take part in the program. Lesnick explains that it provides "a central platform to market across all the vendors and art."

The Audience Rewards program also depends on outside relationships with major companies that sponsor the rewards for the program. Acquiring such partnerships can be a challenge for most small companies; however, Nederlander's target market is an attractive opportunity for large companies. A market dominated by 30- to 59-year-old females with an annual income of approximately $200,000 "appeals to our corporate partners because they want to get access to our customers," Lesnick explains. The program has also provided Nederlander with the opportunity to develop new products such as co-branded credit cards and Broadway-wide gift cards. With these new additions, customers and corporate partners are receiving valuable benefits. Customers are not only able to receive free and discounted tickets, but they are also able to redeem their points to participate in special red-carpet events and backstage passes to meet performers. Corporate partners receive the benefit of access to a more specific and profitable target market.

Before the institution of the Audience Rewards program, Nederlander was bringing in hundreds of thousands of dollars in ticket sales without the use of technology or innovative customer relationship management techniques. Sean Free, vice president of Sales and Ticketing, comments on the types of technologies used by businesses for marketing and business strategies. He states that "e-mail blasts, and the retargeting efforts that people are now doing, and following people on the Internet through IP addresses … is all very new … and Broadway is usually one of the last industries to follow through with the latest technology." Despite the tendency for the industry's slow reaction, Nederlander's implementation of the Audience Rewards program has served as a catalytic innovation for the company. For instance, 6 months before the premier of the Broadway show *Evita*, Nederlander, in conjunction with some of its partners, sent out 5 million promotional e-mails to more than 1 million members over a 10-day period. Lesnick explains that the e-mails "created a sense of urgency and an incentive to buy early." This "generated in the pre-sale [revenue] of over $1 million … which allowed the company to strategically realign their money to make other decisions."

In addition to the many benefits of this program, sales promotion has provided Nederlander Organization with a competitive advantage over other companies. Because this program relies on the relationships and support of the theater owners and outside companies with whom Nederlander has already solidified relationships, they have created a barrier to entry for other theater organizations due to their strong relationship marketing. This loyalty program has proven to be profitable and good for all partners and members involved with the company.[62]

Questions for Discussion

1. Why do you think more targeted promotional efforts such as personal selling and sales promotion are necessary for Nederlander's specific target market?
2. How does Nederlander's Audience Rewards program result in a competitive advantage?
3. Describe how Nederlander's strong customer relationship management results in increased loyalty to the organization.

Case 18.2

Mistine Develops Successful Integrated Marketing Strategy

Mistine understands the power of promotion in building brand awareness. Owned by Thai firm Better Way, Mistine was launched in 1991 as a direct selling cosmetics firm. The company's adoption of a direct selling model enabled it to become a first mover in the Thai direct selling market. Yet unlike similar firms, Mistine decided to do things differently by becoming the first direct selling company in the world to engage in mass media advertising. Its integrated marketing campaigns have propelled Mistine into one of Thailand's most accepted brands.

Mistine owes its early promotional success to Dr. Amornthep Deerojanawong, co-founder of Better Way. Dr. Deerojanawong began to advertise the company's low-cost but quality cosmetic products through media interviews and seminars. His credibility as a doctor developed trust in Mistine products. To reach a mass audience, however, Mistine had to invest in television advertising. Its first television campaign was meant to spread awareness about the company. With the tagline "Mistine is here!" Mistine's television campaign was widely successful and increased brand awareness from 10 percent to roughly 70 percent. The company markets itself as "The Asian brand for Asian women" as a way to promote the fact that its products are made to complement Asian skin tones.

Mistine continues to engage in heavy advertising, launching campaigns featuring popular actresses, actors, and bands as Mistine brand ambassadors. Many of these celebrities have been featured on Channel 7 or RS Entertainment, Thai television channels with soap operas popular among Mistine's core market. Mistine has become an expert at choosing celebrities that resonate with these target markets. To take advantage of the favorable impression of Korean cosmetics (especially among teenagers), Mistine used a famous Korean band to promote its BB Powder. The company has also created its own Facebook page to extend its worldwide reach.

In addition to its well-known advertisements, Mistine has also garnered publicity for its cause-related marketing campaigns. The firm is adept at linking causes that people care about with its products. For instance, the company featured famous Thai movie actress Petchara Chaowarat to present the company's "Diamond" lipstick collection. By utilizing Chaowarat—considered the "biggest-name actress in Thailand"—to promote the brand, Mistine not only made its brand appear prestigious but also engaged in cause-related marketing by agreeing to donate part of the lipstick's revenue to the Thailand Association for the Blind (Petchara Chaowarat was struck by blindness during her acting career). This form of public relations allowed Mistine to leave a favorable impression among its target market.

Although customers can find Mistine products in retail stores or order them through the firm's catalog or website, personal selling remains a crucial component to Mistine's integrated marketing strategy. Each day, Mistine salespeople make their rounds to meet customers and prospective customers. This face-to-face interaction enables salespeople to interact with potential customers by presenting product benefits, answering questions, and handling objections. Additionally, it provides Mistine with the opportunity to develop relationships between its sales force and its customers. An advanced computer system tracks sales, and Mistine's fleet of trucks can deliver the products within 1 week of ordering. Mistine's strong distribution system, efficient sales force, and quick delivery services have gained the company many loyal fans—particularly among Thai housewives, factory workers, and teenagers. Additionally, by expanding into different distribution channels Mistine has been able to reach new target markets.

Mistine's effective use of advertising, public relations, and personal selling has provided it with a competitive edge over its rivals. In fact, the company has been so successful that it is expanding into countries such as Myanmar, Indonesia, Ghana, South Africa, and the Democratic Republic of the Congo. As it continues to expand, Mistine will have to change its promotional strategies to account for different cultural values and infrastructures. However, if it can achieve the marketing success that it has in Thailand, then the cosmetics company will be well on its way to becoming a popular global brand.[63]

Questions for Discussion

1. How has Mistine used different promotional strategies to increase brand awareness?
2. Why is personal selling useful for marketing Mistine products?
3. What has given Mistine its competitive advantage in the Thai direct selling market?

Strategic Case 7

Indy Racing League (IRL) Focuses on Integrated Marketing Communications

For the first 17 years of its existence, the Championship Auto Racing Teams (known as CART, and later as Champ Car) dominated auto racing in the United States. Open-wheel racing, involving cars whose wheels are located outside the body of the car rather than underneath the body or fenders as found on street cars, enjoyed greater notoriety than any other forms of racing—including stock-car racing like NASCAR. However, not everyone associated with open-wheel racing in the United States welcomed the success enjoyed by CART. One person with major concerns about the direction of CART was Tony George, president of the Indianapolis Motor Speedway and founder of the Indianapolis 500.

In 1994, George announced that he was creating a new open-wheel league that would compete with CART, beginning in 1996. The Indy Racing League (IRL) was divisive to open-wheel racing in the United States, as team owners were forced to decide whether to remain with CART or move to the new IRL. Only IRL members would be allowed to race in the Indianapolis 500—the world's largest spectator sport and the premiere open-wheeled racing competition. CART teams responded by planning their own event on the same day as the Indianapolis 500. The real challenge for the new IRL was developing an integrated marketing communications program to ensure maximum informational and persuasive impact on potential fans (customers). The rift between CART and the IRL resulted in both parties being unable to use the terms "IndyCar" and "Indy car." Eventually, the IRL was able to reassume the IndyCar brand name, but the temporary loss of the brand name created a challenge for promoting the new league.

A 2001 ESPN Sports Poll survey found that 56 percent of American auto racing fans said stock-car racing was their favorite type of racing, with open-wheel racing third at 9 percent. The diminished appeal of open-wheel racing contributed to additional problems with sponsor relationships. Three major partners left CART, including two partners (Honda and Toyota) that provided engines and technical support to CART and its teams. During the same time, the IRL struggled to find corporate partners as a weakened economy and a fragmented market for open-wheel racing made both the IRL and CART less attractive to sponsors.

The IRL experienced ups and downs in the years following the split. Interest in IRL as measured by television ratings took a noticeable dip between 2002 and 2004, with 25 percent fewer viewers tuning in during 2004 than just 2 years earlier. Some sponsors pulled out, including talk-show host David Letterman. Furthermore, Tony George resigned his top positions with the IRL and the Indianapolis Motor Speedway (IMS) in July 2009. He was a proponent of using profits from IMS to support operations of the IRL, funneling an estimated hundreds of millions of dollars over the years to sustain the IRL.

In response to declining interest in IRL, marketing initiatives were taken to reverse the trend by recognizing the various promotional tools available. For instance, the league dedicated a marketing staff in 2001 to their operations. In 2005, the IRL launched a new ad campaign that targeted 18- to 34-year-old males. The campaign was part of a broader strategy to expand the association of IRL beyond a sport for middle-aged Midwestern males to a younger market. IRL has created profiles on social networking sites like Facebook and Twitter to further target this market.

In support of this effort, two developments can be noted. First, IRL has followed a trend observed in NASCAR and has involved several celebrities in the sport through team ownership. Among the celebrities involved with IRL teams are NBA star Carmelo Anthony, former NFL quarterback Jim Harbaugh, and actor Patrick Dempsey. Another celebrity involved with the IRL was rock star Gene Simmons. He is a partner in Simmons Abramson Marketing, which was hired to help the IRL devise new marketing strategies. The firm's entertainment marketing savvy was tapped to help the IRL connect with fans on an emotional level through its drivers, whom Simmons referred to as "rock stars in rocket ships."

Second, driver personalities began to give the IRL some visibility. The emergence of Danica Patrick as a star in the IRL broadened the appeal of the league and assisted in efforts to reach young males. Patrick was a 23-year-old IRL rookie in 2005 who finished fourth in the Indianapolis 500. The combination of the novelty of a female driver, her captivating looks, provocative advertising (particularly her Go Daddy ads), and personality made her the darling of American sports in 2005. Before moving on to NASCAR in 2012, Patrick's effect on the IRL was very noticeable; the IRL reported gains in event attendance, merchandise sales, website traffic, and television ratings during Patrick's rookie season. Patrick drew the interest of many companies that hired her as a product endorser, including Motorola, Boost Mobile, and XM Radio. In addition, she has appeared in photo shoots in *FHM* and the 2008 and 2009 *Sports Illustrated* swimsuit issues. Another Indy racer, Scott Dixon, received notoriety for his 33 wins and three championships (the most wins of any racer in the league so far), including the 2013 Izod IndyCar Series championship. Other drivers such as Helio Castroneves, Ryan Hunter-Reay, and Marco Andretti have also increased awareness of the IRL.

Driver personalities are critical to the promotion and communication process. Most of the drivers endorse their respective sponsors and end up in television advertising promoting the product. This is often done while showing the driver in an Indy racing car, also promoting the league. Drivers to some extent engage in personal selling by interacting with fans, signing autographs, and making personal appearances. Public relations for the drivers is important in television talk-show appearances and various other word-of-mouth communication that is created when spectators start discussing the drivers. It is even possible for drivers to appear in television programs as a type of product placement, promoting themselves, the Indy League, and the IRL.

Mark Scheuern / Alamy

The Future

In 2008 the IRL and Champ Car decided to reunify. Although reunification was a major step toward competing against its rival NASCAR, the organization knew it needed to engage in strong integrated marketing communications if it wanted to grow its market share.

One major development for the IndyCar Series was a new television broadcast partner. ABC had televised the Indianapolis 500 for more than four decades. The IRL will continue that relationship, but most of the other races on the IndyCar Series schedule (at least 13 per season) are televised by VERSUS, a cable channel that replaced ESPN as IRL's broadcast partner. Although VERSUS has a smaller audience than ESPN, it covers fewer sports and plans to give the IndyCar Series more coverage than ESPN did when it owned the broadcast rights. In addition, VERSUS signed a 10-year contract with the IRL. VERSUS was later changed to the NBC Sports Network.

Perhaps the biggest development for IRL in recent years is its acquisition of a title sponsorship. A title sponsorship is the use of a corporate brand name to be associated with all communication about the league. Due to the decline in its popularity, the IRL lacked a title sponsor for many years. In 2009, the clothing provider Izod decided to become the official title sponsor of the IRL for six years. This sponsorship is beneficial for the IRL, particularly as it came at a time when many sponsors for NASCAR and the IRL were pulling out due to the recession.

Auto racing is the fastest-growing spectator sport in the United States. Unfortunately, the disagreement among top leadership in open-wheel racing divided the sport, leading to a period of decline in open-wheel racing, while other forms of auto racing have grown. Therefore, the new IRL must strengthen its standing in the American motorsports market. The support of major celebrities like Patrick Dempsey and the popularity of drivers like Scott Dixon have boosted the ratings of the IRL, but not enough to overtake NASCAR. The loss of Danica Patrick as a full-time driver to NASCAR also created a challenge for the IRL. With the two major open-wheel leagues unified once more, the IRL must begin the task of reconnecting with former fans and building connections with a new audience.[64]

Questions for Discussion

1. How does the Indy Racing League utilize the various components of integrated marketing communication?
2. How do driver appearances on television and at public events contribute to promoting the Indy Racing League?
3. What is the link between sponsorships of cars and drivers by corporations and promotion of the IRL?

NOTES

[1] Charisse Jones, "Frequent-Flyer Rewards Go Beyond Free Flights," *USA Today*, June 24, 2013, pp. 1B–2B; Charisse Jones, "Frequent -Flyer Plans Inspire Middling Loyalty," *USA Today*, August 20, 2013, p. 5B; Lisa Gerstner, "Best of the Rewards Cards," *Kiplinger's Personal Finance*, July 2013, pp. 54–56.

[2] Avinash Malshe and Avipreet Sohi, "What Makes Strategy Making z\across the Sales -Marketing Interface More Successful?" *Journal of the Academy of Marketing Science* 37, no. 4 (Winter 2009): 400–421.

[3] "Advantages of Personal Selling," *KnowThis .com*, www.knowthis.com/principles-of -marketing-tutorials/personal-selling/ advantages-of-personal-selling (accessed April 2, 2012).

[4] "Research and Markets: The Cost of the Average Sales Call Today Is More Than 400 Dollars," *M2 Presswire*, February 28, 2006.

[5] Donald C. Barnes, Joel E. Collier, Nicole Ponder, and Zachary Williams, "Investigating the Employee's Perspective of Customer Delight," *Journal of Personal Selling & Sales Management* 33, no. 1 (Winter 2013): 91–104.

[6] Jon M. Hawes, Anne K. Rich, and Scott M. Widmier, "Assessing the Development of the Sales Profession," *Journal of Personal Selling & Sales Management* 24 (Winter 2004): 27–37.

[7] Dawn R. Deeter-Schmelz and Karen Norman Kennedy, "A Global Perspective on the Current State of Sales Education in the College Curriculum, *Journal of Personal Selling & Sales Management* 31, no. 1 (Winter 2011): 55–76.

[8] Willem Verbeke, Bart Dietz, and Ernst Verwaal, "Drivers of Sales Performance: A Contemporary Meta-Analysis. Have Salespeople Become Knowledge Brokers?" *Journal of the Academy of Marketing Science* 39 (2011): 407–428.

[9] Michael Rodriguez and Robert M. Peterson, "Generating Leads via Social CRM: Early Best Practices for B2B Sales," abstract in Concha Allen (ed.), "Special Abstract Section: 2011 National Conference in Sales Management," *Journal of Personal Selling* 31, no. 4 (Fall 2011): 457–458.

[10] Ed Peelena, Kees van Montfort, Rob Beltman, and Arnoud Klerkx, "An Empirical Study into the Foundation of CRM Success," *Journal of Strategic Marketing* 17, no. 6 (December 2009): 453–471.

[11] Eli Jones, Paul Busch, and Peter Dacin, "Firm Market Orientation and Salesperson Customer Orientation: Interpersonal and Intrapersonal Influence on Customer Service and Retention in Business-to-Business Buyer–Seller Relationships," *Journal of Business Research* 56 (2003): 323–340.

[12] Kenneth Le Meunier-FitzHugh and Nigel F. Piercy, "Exploring the Relationship between Market Orientation and Sales and Marketing Collaboration," *Journal of Personal Selling & Sales Management* 31, no. 3 (Summer 2011): 287–296.

[13] Kaj Storbacka, Pia Polsa, and Maria Sääksjärvi, "Management Practices in Solution Sales—Multilevel and Cross-Functional Framework," *Journal of Personal Selling & Sales Management* 31, no. 1 (Winter 2011): 35–54.

[14] Julie T. Johnson, Hiram C. Barksdale Jr., and James S. Boles, "Factors Associated with Customer Willingness to Refer Leads to Salespeople," *Journal of Business Research* 56 (2003): 257–263.

[15] Ralph W. Giacobbe, Donald W. Jackson, Jr., Lawrence A. Crosby, and Claudia M. Bridges, "A Contingency Approach to Adaptive Selling Behavior and Sales Performance: Selling Situations and Salesperson Characteristics," *Journal of Personal Selling & Sales Management* 26 (Spring 2006): 115–142.

[16] Richard G. McFarland, Goutam N. Challagalla, and Tasadduq A. Shervani, "Influence Tactics for Effective Adaptive Selling," *Journal of Marketing* 70 (October 2006).

[17] Susie Pryor, Avinash Malshe, and Kyle Paradise, "Salesperson Listening in the Extended Sales Relationship: An Exploration of Cognitive, Affective, and Temporal Dimensions," *Journal of Personal Selling & Sales Management* 33, no. 2 (Spring 2013): 185–196.

[18] John Andy Wood, "NLP Revisted: Nonverbal Communications and Signals of Trustworthiness," *Journal of Personal Selling & Sales Management* 26 (Spring 2006): 198–204.

[19] John Dunyon, Valerie Gossling, Sarah Willden, and John S. Seiter, "Compliments and Purchasing Behavior in Telephone Sales Interactions," abstract in Dawn R. Deeter -Schmelz (ed.), "Personal Selling & Sales Management Abstracts," *Journal of Personal Selling & Sales Management* 31, no. 2 (Spring 2011): 186.

[20] Stephen S. Porter, Joshua L. Wiener, and Gary L. Frankwick, "The Moderating Effect of Selling Situation on the Adaptive Selling Strategy—Selling Effectiveness Relationship," *Journal of Business Research* 56 (2003): 275–281.

[21] Tammy Stanley, "Follow-Up: The Success Recipe Salespeople Don't See," *Direct Selling News*, May 2010, www.directsellingnews.com/ index.php/entries_archive_display/follow_up _the_success_recipe_salespeople_dont_see (accessed February 5, 2011).

[22] Jonathon D. Rockoff, "Drug Sales Reps Try a Softer Pitch," *The Wall Street Journal*, January 10, 2012, B1–B2.

[23] Gabriel R. Gonzalez, K. Douglas Hoffman, Thomas N. Ingram, and Raymond W. LaForge, "Sales Organization Recovery Management and Relationship Selling: A Conceptual Model and Empirical Test," *Journal of Personal Selling & Sales Management* 30, no. 3 (Summer 2010): 223–238.

[24] Barton A. Weitz and Kevin D. Bradford, "Personal Selling and Sales Management: A Relationship Marketing Perspective," *Journal of the Academy of Marketing Science* 27, no. 2 (1999): 241–254.

[25] Eli Jones, Steven P. Brown, Andris A. Zoltners, and Barton A. Weitz, "The Changing Environment of Selling and Sales Management," *Journal of Personal Selling & Sales Management* 25, no. 2 (Spring 2005): 105–111.

[26] "The Right Questions and Attitudes Can Beef Up Your Sales, Improve Customer Retention," *Selling* (June 2001): 3.

[27] Jones et al., 105–111.

[28] Gary K. Hunter and William D. Perreault Jr., "Making Sales Technology Effective," *Journal of Marketing* 71 (January 2007): 16–34.

[29] David Moth, "Marketing Automation: Six Case Studies and an Infographic on How It

Improves Sales and Revenue," *Econsultancy*, November 7, 2013, http://econsultancy.com/blog/63748-marketing-automation-six-case-studies-and-an-infographic-on-how-it-improves-sales-and-revenue (accessed January 17, 2014).

[30] Othman Boujena, Johnston J. Wesley, and Dwight R. Merunka, "The Benefits of Sales Force Automation: A Customer's Perspective," *Journal of Personal Selling & Sales Management* 29, no. 2 (2009): 137–150.

[31] Fernando Jaramillo, Jay Prakash Mulki, and Paul Solomon, "The Role of Ethical Climate on Salesperson's Role Stress, Job Attitudes, Turnover Intention, and Job Performance," *Journal of Personal Selling & Sales Management* 26 (Summer 2006): 272–282.

[32] Christophe Fournier, John F. Tanner, Jr., Lawrence B. Chonko, and Chris Manolis, "The Moderating Role of Ethical Climate on Salesperson Propensity to Leave," *Journal of Personal Selling & Sales Management* 3, no. 1 (Winter 2009–2010): 7–22.

[33] Kirby L. J. Shannahan, Alan J. Bush, and Rachelle J. Shannahan, "Are Your Salespeople Coachable? How Salesperson Coachability, Trait Competitiveness, and Transformational Leadership Enhance Sales Performance," *Journal of the Academy of Marketing Science* 41 (2013): 40–54.

[34] Christophe Fournier, William A. Weeks, Christopher P. Blocker, and Lawrence B. Chonko, "Polychronicity and Scheduling's Role in Reducing Role Stress and Enhancing Sales Performance," *Journal of Personal Selling & Sales Management* 33, no. 2 (Spring 2013): 197–210.

[35] Tara Burnthorne Lopez, Christopher D. Hopkins, and Mary Anne Raymond, "Reward Preferences of Salespeople: How Do Commissions Rate?" *Journal of Personal Selling & Sales Management* 26 (Fall 2006): 381–390.

[36] "Container Store CEO Pitches 'Conscious Capitalism,'" The University of Texas at Dallas News Center, December 15, 2011, www.utd.edu/news/2011/12/15-14731_Container-Store-CEO-Pitches-Conscious-Capitalism_article.html (accessed January 17, 2014).

[37] Denny Bristow, Douglas Amyx, Stephen B. Castleberry, and James J. Cochran, "A Cross-Generational Comparison of Motivational Factors in a Sales Career among Gen-X and Gen-Y College Students," *Journal of Personal Selling & Sales Management* 31, no. 1 (Winter 2011): 35–54.

[38] Subhra Chakrabarty, Gene Brown, and Robert E. Widing, "Distinguishing between the Roles of Customer-Oriented Selling and Adaptive Selling in Managing Dysfunctional Conflict in Buyer–Seller Relationships," *Journal of Personal Selling & Sales Management* 33, no. 3 (Summer 2013): 245–260.

[39] Michael Ahearne, Till Haumann, Forian Kraus, and Jan Wieseke, "It's a Matter of Congruence: How Interpersonal Identification between Sales Managers and Salespersons Shapes Sales Success," *Journal of the Academy of Marketing Science* 41 (2013): 625–648.

[40] Felicia G. Lassk and C. David Shephard, "Exploring the Relationship between Emotional Intelligence and Salesperson Creativity," *Journal of Personal Selling & Sales Management* 33, no. 1 (Winter 2013): 25–38.

[41] The Container Store, "Putting Our Employees First," What We Stand for Blog, http://standfor.containerstore.com/putting-our-employees-first (accessed January 17, 2014).

[42] John W. Barnes, Donald W. Jackson, Jr., Michael D. Hutt, and Ajith Kumar, "The Role of Culture Strength in Shaping Salesforce Outcomes," *Journal of Personal Selling & Sales Management* 26 (Summer 2006): 255–270.

[43] James B. DeConinck, "The Effects of Leader–Member Exchange and Organizational Identification on Performance and Turnover among Salespeople," *Journal of Personal Selling & Sales Management* 31, no. 1 (Winter 2011): 21–34.

[44] Patricia Odell, "Motivating the Masses," *Promo*, September 1, 2005, http://promomagazine.com/research/pitrends/marketing_motivating_masses (accessed April 20, 2011).

[45] "50 Best Companies to Sell For—2013," *Selling Power*, www.sellingpower.com/2013/50-best-companies-to-sell-for (accessed January 17, 2014).

[46] George E. Belch and Michael A. Belch, *Advertising and Promotion* (Burr Ridge, IL: Irwin/McGraw-Hill, 2004), pp. 514–522.

[47] Brad Tuttle, "Why Americans Are Cutting Coupons out of Their Lives," *Time*, February 28, 2013, http://business.time.com/2013/02/28/why-americans-are-cutting-coupons-out-of-their-lives (accessed January 17, 2014).

[48] Julie Jargon, "Coupons Boost Starbucks," *The Wall Street Journal*, November, 2, 2012, p. B6.

[49] "Majority of US Internet Users Will Redeem Digital Coupons in 2013," *eMarketer*, October 21, 2013, www.emarketer.com/Article/Majority-of-US-Internet-Users-Will-Redeem-Digital-Coupons-2013/1010313 (accessed January 17, 2014).

[50] Arthur L. Porter, "Direct Mail's Lessons for Electronic Couponers," *Marketing Management Journal* (Spring/Summer 2000): 107–115.

[51] Ibid.

[52] Coupon Information Corporation, www.cents-off.com/faq.php?st=1fe91 (accessed February 5, 2011).

[53] John T. Gourville and Dilip Soman, "The Consumer Psychology of Mail-in Rebates," *Journal of Product & Brand Management* 20, no. 2 (2011): 147–157.

[54] Nancy Trejos, "Marriott, United Deal Perks Up Rewards," *USA Today*, July 15, 2013, p. 1B.

[55] Charisse Jones, "JetBlue Will Allow Families to Pool Frequent-Flier Miles," *USA Today*, October 11, 2013, p. 4B.

[56] Arbitron Inc., *Arbitron Product Sampling Study*, 2008, www.arbitron.com/downloads/product_sampling_study.pdf (accessed January 24, 2013).

[57] Katherine Hobson, "A Sales Promotion That Works for Shoes May Not for Chocolate," *The Wall Street Journal*, February 8, 2011, http://blogs.wsj.com/health/2011/02/08/a-sales-promotion-that-works-for-shoes-may-not-for-chocolate (accessed April 3, 2012).

[58] Teresa Montaner, Leslie de Chernatony, and Isabel Buil, "Consumer Response to Gift Promotions," *Journal of Product & Brand Management* 20, no. 2 (2011): 101–110.

[59] "Nikon Announces Winner of 'The Full Story' Photo Contest," *National Geographic*, January 25, 2013, http://press.nationalgeographic.com/2013/01/25/nikon-announces-winner-of-the-full-story-photo-contest (accessed January 21, 2014).

[60] Kim Bhasin, "How McDonald's Monopoly Game Became So Ridiculously Successful," *Business Insider*, October 24, 2011, www.businessinsider.com/mcdonalds-monopoly-facts-2011-10 (accessed January 21, 2014); Sandra Grauschopf, "Cheapest Ways to Get McDonald's Monopoly Game Pieces," *About.com*, http://contests.about.com/od/

mcdonaldsmonopolygame/a/Cheapest-Ways-To-Get-Mcdonalds-Monopoly-Game-Pieces.htm (accessed January 21, 2014); Associated Press, "Twenty-One Indicted in McDonald's Scam," *St. Petersburg Times*, September 11, 2001, www.sptimes.com/News/091101/Worldandnation/Twenty_one_indicted_i.shtml (accessed April 3, 2012).

[61] Mike Snider, "Online Game Offers $100,000," *USA Today,* August 1, 2013, p. 3B.

[62] Kenneth Jones, "Broadway's Major Producers Join with Regional Presenters for Audience Rewards Program," *Playbill*, June 28, 2007, www.playbill.com/news/article/109186-Broadways-Major-Producers-Join-With-Regional-Presenters-for-Audience-Rewards-Program (accessed December 11, 2013); Nederlander Organization—Announcements, "Audience Rewards Hits 1 Million Members," August 25, 2012, www.nederlander.com/press_03.html (accessed December 11, 2013); Audience Rewards, "Our History," www.audiencerewards.com/redeemcenter/infopage.cfm?id=25 (accessed December 11, 2013).

[63] Adapted from "Mistine: Direct Selling in the Thai Cosmetics Market," in O.C. Ferrell and Michael D. Hartline, *Marketing Strategy*, 6th ed. (Mason, OH: Cengage Learning, 2014); "Petchara Making an Appearance," *Wise Kwai's Thai Film Journal*, September 29, 2009, http://thaifilmjournal.blogspot.com/2009/09/petchara-making-appearance.html (accessed November 27, 2012).

[64] Some of this material is adapted from "The Indy Racing League (IRL): Driving for First Place" by Don Roy, originally published in O. C. Ferrell and Michael D. Hartline, *Marketing Strategy*, 5th ed. (Mason, OH: Cengage Learning, 2011), pp. 428–435. These facts are from "A Brief History of CART and Champ Car Racing," www.fsdb.net/champcar/history/index.htm; "Celebrities Who Are Revved Up over Racing," *Street & Smith's Sports Business Journal*, May 22, 2006, p. 27; "Hot Wheels Announces Partnership with the IndyCar Series, Indianapolis 500," *Entertainment Newsweekly*, April 24, 2009, p. 140; Marty O'Brien, "Helio Castroneves Is Happier Making Headlines on the Race Tack," *Daily Press*, June 27, 2009; John Ourand, "IRL to Get at Least 7 Hours Weekly on Versus," *Street & Smith's Sports Business Journal*, February 23, 2009, p. 7; Jennifer Pendleton, "Danica Patrick," *Advertising Age*, November 7, 2005, p. S4; Anthony Schoettle, "IRL Ratings Continue Their Skid," *Indianapolis Business Journal*, November 1, 2004, p. 3; "Kiss Rocker Lends Voice to Indy Races," *Knight Ridder Tribune Business News*, April 1, 2006, p. 1; "Turnkey Sports Poll," *Street & Smith's Sports Business Journal*, May 22, 2006, p. 24; J. K. Wall, "Indy Racing League Sets Sights on Marketing Dollars," *Knight Ridder Tribune Business News*, May 27, 2004, p. 1; Scott Warfield, "IRL in Line to Court Young Males," *Street & Smith's Sports Business Journal*, November 29, 2004, p. 4; Jeff Wolf, "George's Ouster Clouds IRL's Future," *Las Vegas Review-Journal*, July 3, 2009; Nate Ryan, "Circuits One Again, But Gains from Split Came at Dear Cost," *USA Today*, April 17, 2008, pp. 1C–2C; Associated Press, "Rahal-Letterman Team Out of IRL, Lacks Sponsor," *ESPN Racing*, January 29, 2009, http://sports.espn.go.com/espn/wire?section=auto&id=3868795&campaign=rsssrch=irl (accessed January 16, 2014); "Team History," *Penske Racing*, 2008, www.penskeracing.com/about/index.cfm?cid=14189 (accessed January 16, 2014); Andretti Autosport website, http://andrettiautosport.com/home.php (accessed January 16, 2014); Larry Hawley, "IRL: Izod, Racing Make for Unique Match," *Los Angeles Times*, November 4, 2009, www.latimes.com/news/isn-110409-indycar-izod-sponsor,0,2329604.story#axzz2qaFswZ7H (accessed January 16, 2014); David Newton, "Danica Adds Coke to Her Portfolio," *ESPN*, May 10, 2012, http://espn.go.com/racing/blog/_/name/newton_david/id/7916132/nascar-danica-patrick-joins-coca-cola-racing-family (accessed January 16, 2014); Jeff Olson and Heather Tucker, "Scott Dixon Wins Third IndyCar Championship," *USA Today*, October 20, 2013, www.usatoday.com/story/sports/motor/indycar/2013/10/20/indycar-championship-scott-dixon-helio-castroneves-mavtv-500/3089857 (accessed January 16, 2014).

Feature Notes

[a] "Tastefully Simple Founder and Founding Partner Recognized," *Echo Press*, October 19, 2012, http://dev1.echopress.com/event/article/id/98803 (accessed January 16, 2014); Beth Douglass Silcox and Barbara Seale, "The Most Influential Women in Direct Selling," *Direct Selling News*, October 2012, pp. 58–59; "About Us," Tastefully Simple Website, www.tastefullysimple.com/WhoWeAre.aspx (accessed January 16, 2014); "DSN Global 100: The Top Direct Selling Companies in the World," *Direct Selling News*, June 1, 2012, http://directsellingnews.com/index.php/view/dsn_global_100_the_top_direct_selling_companies_in_the_world/P7#.UIGzEPUmx8F (accessed January 16, 2014); "DSN Global 100," *Direct Selling News*, June 1, 2014, http://directsellingnews.com/index.php/view/the_2013_dsn_global_100_list?popup=yes#.UthLx_XLQ4k (accessed January 16, 2014).

[b] "2010 World's Most Ethical Companies—Company Profile: Salesforce.com," *Ethisphere*, Q1, pp. 32–33; Milton Moskowitz and Charles Kapelke, "25 Top-Paying Companies," CNNMoney, January 26, 2011, http://money.cnn.com/galleries/2011/pf/jobs/1101/gallery.best_companies_top_paying.fortune/index.html (accessed January 31, 2011); "Salesforce.com Named One of the 'World's Most Ethical Companies' in 2010 for the Fourth Consecutive Year," *Salesforce.com*, March 29, 2010, www.salesforce.com/company/news-press/press-releases/2010/03/100329.jsp (accessed October 28, 2013); Salesforce Foundation Home Page, http://foundation.force.com/home (accessed October 28, 2013); Salesforce.com, www.salesforce.com/company (accessed October 28, 2013); Chris Kanaracus, "Salesforce.Com's Benioff Talks Growth, Microsoft," *CIO*, June 6, 2011, www.cio.com/article/683621/Salesforce.Com_s_Benioff_Talks_Growth_Microsoft (accessed October 28, 2013); Salesforce, "2013 Annual Report," *Salesforce.com*, 2013, www2.sfdcstatic.com/assets/pdf/investors/fy13_annual_report.pdf, (accessed October 28, 2013).

part 8

Pricing Decisions

To provide a satisfying marketing mix, an organization must set a price that is acceptable to target market members. PART 8 centers on pricing decisions that can have numerous effects on other parts of the marketing mix. For instance, price can influence how customers perceive the product, what types of marketing institutions are used to distribute the product, and how the product is promoted. CHAPTER 19 discusses the importance of price and looks at some characteristics of price and nonprice competition. It explores fundamental concepts, such as demand, elasticity, marginal analysis, and break-even analysis. The chapter then examines the major factors that affect marketers' pricing decisions. CHAPTER 20 discusses six major stages that marketers use to establish prices.

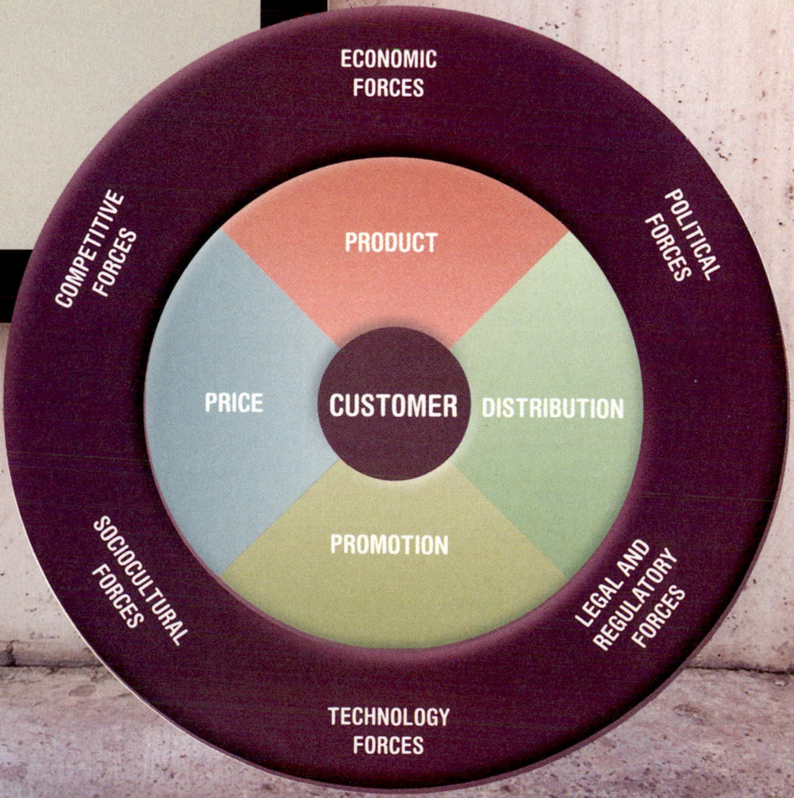

ECONOMIC FORCES
POLITICAL FORCES
LEGAL AND REGULATORY FORCES
TECHNOLOGY FORCES
SOCIOCULTURAL FORCES
COMPETITIVE FORCES
PRODUCT
DISTRIBUTION
PROMOTION
PRICE
CUSTOMER

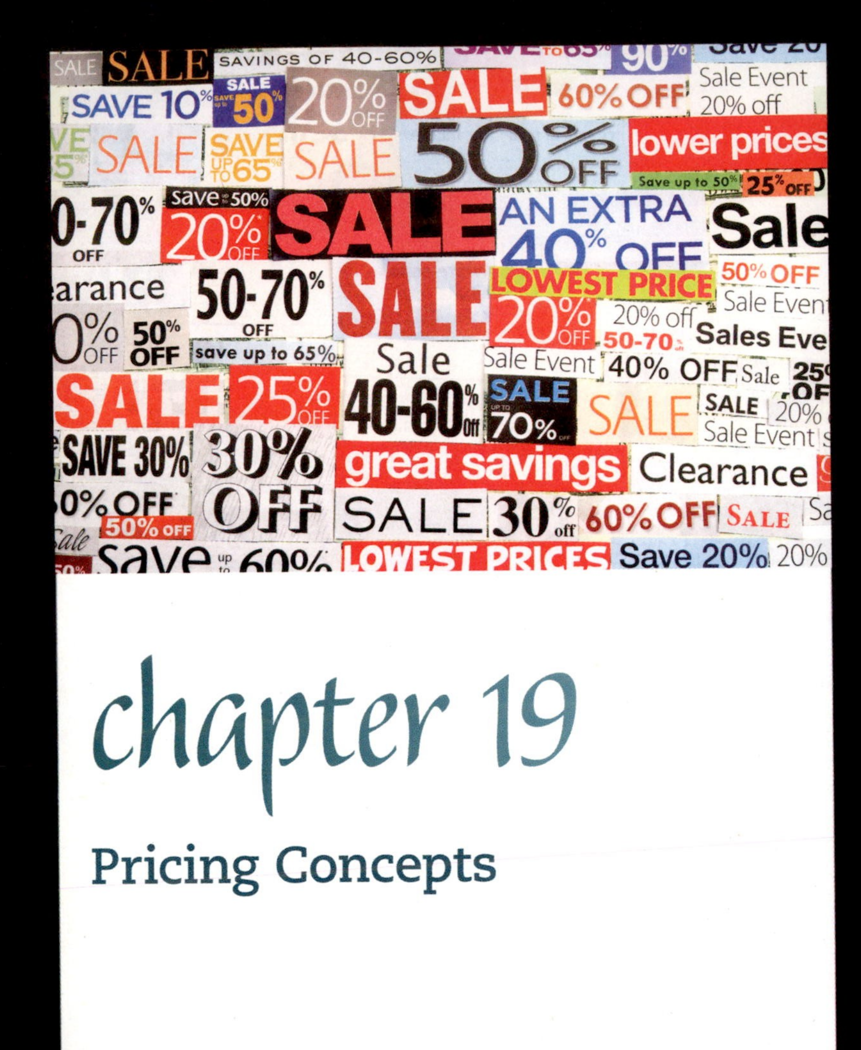

chapter 19

Pricing Concepts

OBJECTIVES

19-1 Summarize why price is important to the marketing mix.

19-2 Compare price competition with nonprice competition.

19-3 Explain the importance of demand curves and the price elasticity of demand.

19-4 Describe the relationships among demand, costs, and profits.

19-5 Describe eight key factors that may influence marketers' pricing decisions.

19-6 Identify seven methods companies can use to price products for business markets.

MARKETING INSIGHTS

Electric Vehicle Price Wars Attempt to Spur Demand

Electric vehicle makers are under pressure by the government to get 1 million of these environmentally-friendly rides as soon as possible. Unfortunately, demand for the vehicles has been low due to high prices, the lack of widespread charging infrastructures, and the inability to travel long distances on a single charge. When supply eclipses demand, companies must lower their prices. For electric vehicle makers, this has resulted in a price war. General Motors (GM), for example, reduced the price of its newest Volt models by $5,000, with the intention of creating models in the future that result in savings between $7,000 and $10,000 per vehicle. Ford's electric Focus model was offered at a $4,000 discount, and the Nissan Leaf sticker price was cut by $6,400. This steep discount benefited Nissan more than the other automakers, accounting for a more than 300 percent increase from the year before. Honda is also competing by adding collision and vehicle theft coverage, maintenance, roadside assistance, and a home charging station in addition to reduced prices. Pricing of electric cars remains very dynamic, with frequent discounts and adjustments to market conditions.

Leasing options are also being reduced. Customers are more comfortable making a short-term commitment to these vehicles because the perceived risk of purchasing one is high. The Chevy Volt monthly lease price is $299, the Honda Fit EV is $259, and the Daimler AG electric model is $139. All of these discounts are in addition to the federal and municipal government subsidies customers receive on these purchases and leases. It remains to be seen whether demand for these vehicles will rise or whether firms must continually discount their vehicles to make sales.[1]

Many firms, including automobile manufacturers, use pricing as a tool to compete against major competitors. However, their rivals also may employ pricing as a major competitive tool. In some industries, firms are very successful even if they don't have the lowest prices. The best price is not always the lowest price.

In this chapter, we focus first on the nature of price and its importance to marketers. We then consider some characteristics of price and nonprice competition. Next, we discuss several pricing-related concepts, such as demand, elasticity, and break-even analysis. Then we examine in some detail the numerous factors that can influence pricing decisions. Finally, we discuss selected issues related to pricing products for business markets.

19-1 THE IMPORTANCE OF PRICE IN MARKETING

The purpose of marketing is to facilitate satisfying exchange relationships between buyer and seller. **Price** is the value paid for a product in a marketing exchange. Many factors may influence the assessment of value, including time constraints, price levels, perceived quality, and motivations to use available information about prices.[2] In most marketing situations, the price is apparent to both buyer and seller. However, price does not always take the form of money paid. In fact, **barter**, the trading of products, is the oldest form of exchange. Money may or may not be involved. Barter among businesses, because of the relatively large values of the exchanges, usually involves trade credit. Corporate barter amounts to an estimated \$12 billion.[3] Certain websites help facilitate B2B bartering.

Buyers' interest in price stems from their expectations about the usefulness of a product or the satisfaction they may derive from it. Because consumers have limited resources, they must allocate those resources to obtain the products they most desire. They must decide whether the utility gained in an exchange is worth the buying power sacrificed. Almost anything of value—ideas, services, rights, and goods—can be assessed by a price. In our society, financial price is the measurement of value commonly used in exchanges.

As pointed out in Chapter 11, developing a product may be a lengthy process. It takes time to plan promotion and to communicate benefits. Distribution usually requires a long-term commitment to dealers that will handle the product. Often, price is the only thing a marketer can change quickly to respond to changes in demand or to actions of competitors. Under certain circumstances, however, the price variable may be relatively inflexible.

Price is a key element in the marketing mix because it relates directly to the generation of total revenue. The following equation is an important one for the entire organization:

$$\text{profit} = \text{total revenue} - \text{total costs}$$

$$\text{profit} = (\text{price} \times \text{quantity sold}) - \text{total costs}$$

Price affects an organization's profits in several ways because it is a key component of the profit equation and can be a major determinant of quantities sold. For instance, price is a top priority for airlines, particularly the price of tickets for front-of-the-plane service for business and other premium-class passengers. Tickets for first class can top \$6,500. Although the majority of passengers who fly on airlines choose to fly coach, it is estimated that these types of passengers comprise 75 percent of the revenue on cross-country flights.[4] Furthermore, total costs are influenced by quantities sold. Consequently, to reach your sales objectives, you would have to sell many more of the Italian Officina Del Tempo watches than Rolex watches because of the dramatic difference in price. The advertisement for the Officina Del Tempo is big and bold, while the advertisement for the Rolex watch uses more white space and lighter colors to underscore its more luxurious nature.

price The value paid for a product in a marketing exchange

barter The trading of products

Because price has a psychological impact on customers, marketers can use it symbolically. By pricing high, they can emphasize the quality of a product and try to increase the prestige associated with its ownership. By lowering a price, marketers can emphasize a bargain and

© Rolex.

Divino Inc.

Differences in Price
Because Rolex watches are much higher-priced than Officina Del Tempo watches, Rolex needs to sell fewer units to achieve its sales objectives.

attract customers who go out of their way to save a small amount of money. Thus, as this chapter details, price can have strong effects on a firm's sales and profitability.

19-2 PRICE AND NONPRICE COMPETITION

The competitive environment strongly influences the marketing-mix decisions associated with a product. Pricing decisions are often made according to the price or nonprice competitive situation in a particular market. Price competition exists when consumers have difficulty distinguishing competitive offerings and marketers emphasize low prices. Nonprice competition involves a focus on marketing-mix elements other than price.

19-2a Price Competition

When engaging in **price competition**, a marketer emphasizes price as an issue and matches or beats competitors' prices. To compete effectively on a price basis, a firm should be the low-cost seller of the product. If all firms producing the same product charge the same price for it, the firm with the lowest costs is the most profitable. Firms that stress low price as a key marketing-mix element tend to market standardized products. A seller competing on price may change prices frequently, or at least must be willing and able to do so. Best Buy, for instance, had to be willing to adopt price-matching policies in order to compete with online competitors. The retailer was having trouble with showrooming, a practice where consumers come into their stores, find what they want to purchase, and then purchase it online at a lower price. Best Buy instituted a permanent price-matching plan that would match the lower prices of its online competitors. Only 10 percent of customers take advantage of Best Buy's

price competition Emphasizing price as an issue and matching or beating competitors' prices

Nonprice Competition
Sheba avoids price competition in its promotion of its high-quality, natural pet patés for cats.

price-matching policy.[5] Whenever competitors change their prices, the company usually responds quickly and aggressively.

Price competition gives marketers flexibility. They can alter prices to account for changes in their costs or respond to changes in demand for the product. If competitors try to gain market share by cutting prices, a company competing on a price basis can react quickly to such efforts. However, a major drawback of price competition is that competitors have the flexibility to adjust prices too. If they quickly match or beat a company's price cuts, a price war may ensue. For instance, electronics retailers are facing a price war in electronics. As we have already mentioned, Best Buy's adoption of a price-matching policy has benefited the firm, but it has also led the firm to announce it would slash prices drastically if needed to keep up with competitors. Similarly, Walmart claimed it would also slash prices for some electronics. The biggest electronics retailers, including Best Buy, Walmart, Target, and Staples, all claim that they will match their competitors' pricing, which is inciting a massive price war. Chronic price wars like this one can substantially weaken organizations.[6]

19-2b Nonprice Competition

Nonprice competition occurs when a seller decides not to focus on price and instead emphasizes distinctive product features, service, product quality, promotion, packaging, or other factors to distinguish its product from competing brands. Thus, nonprice competition allows a company to increase its brand's unit sales through means other than changing the brand's price. Mars, for example, markets not only Snickers and M&M's but also has an upscale candy line called Ethel's Chocolate. With the tagline "eat chocolate, not preservatives," Ethel's Chocolate competes on the basis of taste, attractive appearance, and hip packaging, and, thus, has little need to engage in price competition.[7] A major advantage of nonprice competition is that a firm can build customer loyalty toward its brand. The Sheba cat food advertisement provides a message about its premium pet food with natural ingredients. This product competes through nonprice competition.

If customers prefer a brand because of nonprice factors, they may not be easily lured away by competing firms and brands. In contrast, when price is the primary reason customers buy a particular brand, a competitor is often able to attract those customers through price cuts.

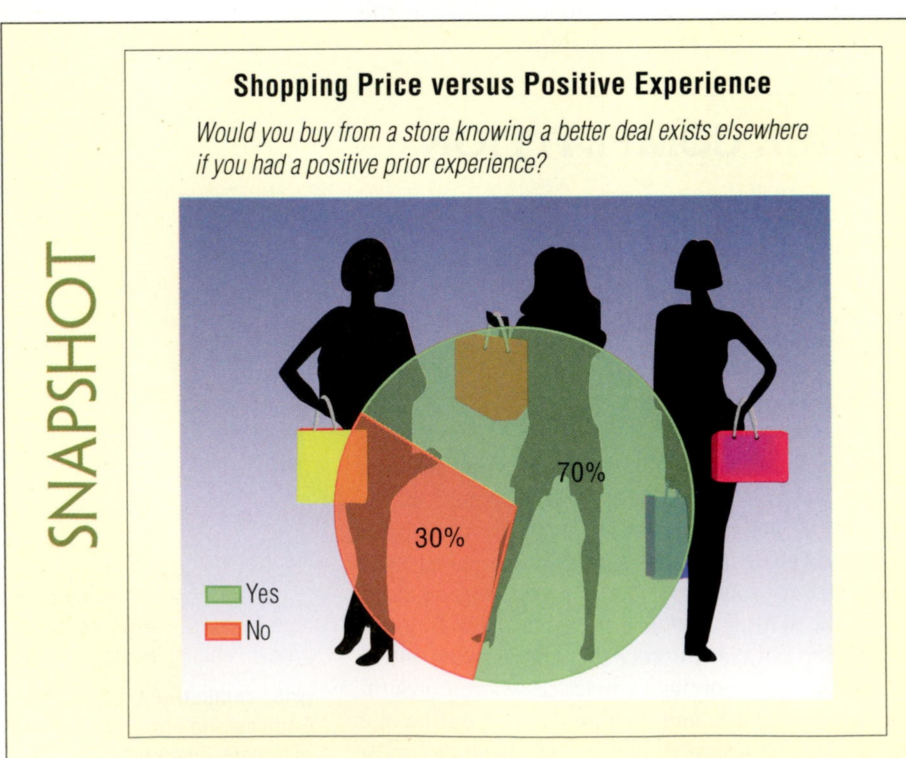

Source: Riverbed survey of 2,074 adults, 2013.

Nonprice competition is effective only under certain conditions. A company must be able to distinguish its brand through unique product features, higher product quality, effective promotion, distinctive packaging, or excellent customer service. Cartier is known for producing jewelry that demands a premium price due to its status as a luxury brand. The jeweler has received a reputation as the "jeweler of kings," with Elizabeth Taylor, Queen Elizabeth II, Kate Middleton, the Duchess of Windsor, and Princess Grace of Monaco bearers of Cartier jewelry.[8] Notice the advertisement showing a Cartier ring and a leopard featured at its left. The leopard has nothing directly to do with the ring. Rather, its beauty and exotic qualities emphasize the exclusivity of the Cartier product. The price of the ring is not mentioned anywhere on the advertisement. Instead, Cartier is using concepts such as quality, fashion, and exclusivity to describe its jewelry. Buyers must not only be able to perceive these distinguishing characteristics but must also view them as important. The distinguishing features that set a particular brand apart from competitors should be difficult, if not impossible, for competitors to imitate. Finally, the firm must extensively promote the brand's distinguishing characteristics to establish its superiority and set it apart from competitors in the minds of buyers.

Even a marketer that is competing on a nonprice basis cannot ignore competitors' prices. This organization must be aware of them and sometimes be prepared to price its brand near or slightly above competing brands. Therefore, price remains a crucial marketing-mix component even in environments that call for nonprice competition.

Nonprice Competition
Cartier does not mention price anywhere in this advertisement. Rather, it uses nonprice characteristics such as quality, status, and exclusivity to market its jewelry.

19-3 DEMAND CURVES AND PRICE ELASTICITY

Determining the demand for a product is the responsibility of marketing managers, who are aided in this task by marketing researchers and forecasters. Marketing research and forecasting techniques yield estimates of sales potential, or the quantity of a product that could be sold during a specific period. These estimates are helpful in establishing the relationship between a product's price and the quantity demanded.

19-3a The Demand Curve

For most products, the quantity demanded goes up as the price goes down, and the quantity demanded goes down as the price goes up. Case in point, prices have fallen precipitously for LCD television sets in recent years. This change in price is largely due to high levels of competition and newer technologies. In order to compensate, most makers of LCD TVs responded by continuing to lower prices. Thus, an inverse relationship exists between price and quantity demanded. As long as the marketing environment and buyers' needs, ability (purchasing power), willingness, and authority to buy remain stable, this fundamental inverse relationship holds.

Figure 19.1 illustrates the effect of one variable, price, on the quantity demanded. The classic **demand curve** (*D*1) is a graph of the quantity of products expected to be sold at

nonprice competition Emphasizing factors other than price to distinguish a product from competing brands

demand curve A graph of the quantity of products expected to be sold at various prices if other factors remain constant

Figure 19.1 Demand Curve Illustrating the Price/Quantity Relationship and Increase in Demand

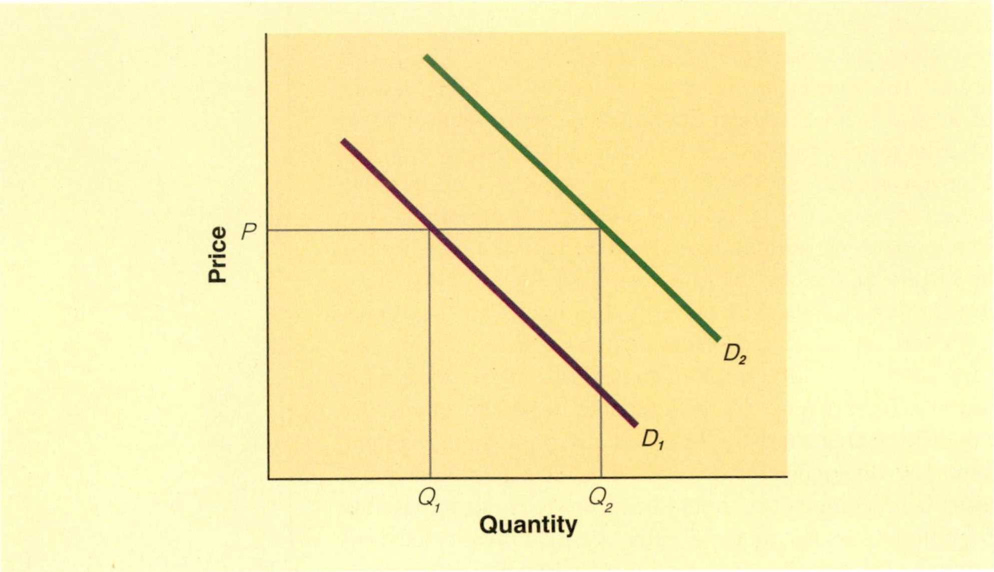

various prices if other factors remain constant. It illustrates that, as price falls, quantity demanded usually rises. Demand depends on other factors in the marketing mix, including product quality, promotion, and distribution. An improvement in any of these factors may cause a shift to demand curve *D*2. In such a case, an increased quantity (*Q*2) will be sold at the same price (*P*).

Many types of demand exist, and not all conform to the classic demand curve shown in Figure 19.1. Prestige products, such as selected perfumes and jewelry, tend to sell better at higher prices than at lower ones. This advertisement for Tod's Shoes provides a close-up of the high-priced shoe to demonstrate its quality and craftsmanship. These products are desirable partly because their expense makes buyers feel elite. If the price fell drastically and many people owned these products, they would lose some of their appeal. The demand curve in Figure 19.2 shows the relationship between price and quantity demanded for prestige products. Quantity demanded is greater, not less, at higher prices. For a certain price range—from *P*1 to *P*2—the quantity demanded (*Q*1) goes up to *Q*2. After a certain point, however, raising the price backfires: If the price goes too high, the quantity demanded goes down. The figure shows that if price is raised from *P*2 to *P*3, quantity demanded goes back down from *Q*2 to *Q*1.

Tod's Group

Prestige Pricing
Luxury products such as Tod's shoes sell better at higher prices than lower prices because they are considered to be a more exclusive product unaffordable for the average consumer.

19-3b Demand Fluctuations

Changes in buyers' needs, variations in the effectiveness of other marketing-mix variables, the presence of substitutes, and dynamic environmental factors can influence demand. Restaurants and utility companies experience large fluctuations in demand daily. Toy manufacturers, fireworks suppliers,

Figure 19.2 Demand Curve Illustrating the Relationship between Price and Quantity for Prestige Products

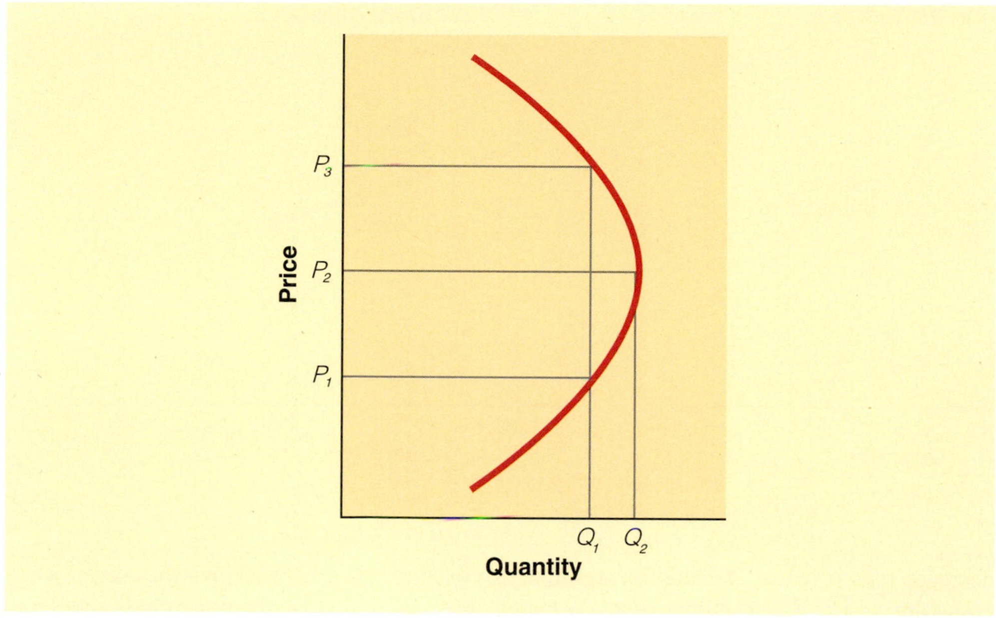

and air-conditioning and heating contractors also face demand fluctuations because of the seasonal nature of their products. Flowers, for instance, are in higher demand in the United States around Valentine's Day and Mother's Day. As consumer habits and needs have changed in recent years, the demand for movie rental stores has declined as consumers increasingly use services like Netflix or stream movies on the Internet. In some cases, demand fluctuations are predictable. It is no surprise to restaurants and utility company managers that demand fluctuates. However, changes in demand for other products may be less predictable, leading to problems for some companies. Other organizations anticipate demand fluctuations and develop new products and prices to meet consumers' changing needs.

19-3c Assessing Price Elasticity of Demand

Up to this point, we have seen how marketers identify the target market's evaluation of price and its ability to purchase and how they examine demand to learn whether price is related inversely or directly to quantity. The next step is to assess price elasticity of demand. **Price elasticity of demand** provides a measure of the sensitivity of demand to changes in price. It is formally defined as the percentage change in quantity demanded relative to a given percentage change in price (see Figure 19.3).[9] The percentage change in quantity demanded caused by a percentage change in price is much greater for elastic demand than for inelastic demand. For a product like electricity, demand is relatively inelastic: When its price increases from *P*1 to *P*2, quantity demanded goes down only a little, from *Q*1 to *Q*2. For products like recreational vehicles, demand is relatively elastic: When price rises sharply, from *P*1 to *P*2, quantity demanded goes down a great deal, from *Q*1 to *Q*2.

If marketers can determine the price elasticity of demand, setting a price is much easier. By analyzing total revenues as prices change, marketers can determine whether a product is price elastic. Total revenue is price times quantity. Thus, 10,000 cans of paint sold in one year at a price of $10 per can equals $100,000 of total revenue. If demand is *elastic*, a change in price causes an opposite change in total revenue: An increase in price will decrease total revenue, and a decrease in price will increase total revenue. *Inelastic* demand results in a change in the same direction as total revenue: An increase in price will increase total revenue, and a decrease in price will

price elasticity of demand A measure of the sensitivity of demand to changes in price

Figure 19.3 Elasticity of Demand

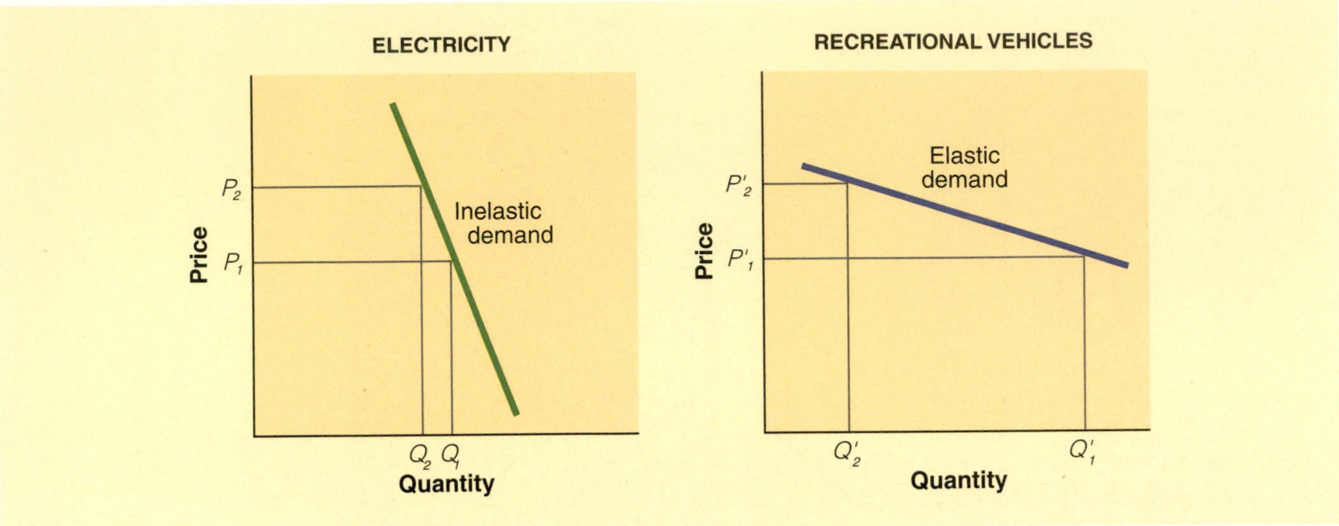

decrease total revenue. Demand for gasoline, for example, is relatively inelastic—even when prices are close to $4 per gallon—because people must still drive to work, run errands, and shop, all of which require fuel for their vehicles. Although higher gasoline prices force more consumers to change some behaviors in an effort to reduce the amount of gasoline they use, most cut spending in other areas instead because they require a certain level of fuel for weekly activities like commuting. The following formula determines the price elasticity of demand:

$$\text{price elasticity of demand} = \frac{\%\ \text{change in quantity demanded}}{\%\ \text{change in price}}$$

Price Elasticity of Demand Oil and gas are examples of products that have inelastic demand. When the price goes up, consumers do not significantly reduce consumption, and when the price goes down, they do not significantly increase their consumption.

For instance, if demand falls by 8 percent when a seller raises the price by 2 percent, the price elasticity of demand is –4 (the negative sign indicating the inverse relationship between price and demand). If demand falls by 2 percent when price is increased by 4 percent, elasticity is –1/2. The less elastic the demand, the more beneficial it is for the seller to raise the price. Products without readily available substitutes and for which consumers have strong needs (e.g., electricity or appendectomies) usually have inelastic demand. Marketers cannot base prices solely on elasticity considerations. They must also examine the costs associated with different sales volumes and evaluate what happens to profits.

19-4 DEMAND, COST, AND PROFIT RELATIONSHIPS

The analysis of demand, cost, and profit is important, because customers are becoming less tolerant of price increases, forcing manufacturers to find new ways to control costs. In the past, many customers desired premium brands and were willing to pay extra for those products. Today, customers pass up certain brand names if they can pay less without sacrificing quality. To stay in business, a company must set prices that not only cover its costs but also meet customers' expectations. In this section, we explore two approaches to understanding demand, cost, and profit relationships: marginal analysis and break-even analysis.

19-4a Marginal Analysis

Marginal analysis examines what happens to a firm's costs and revenues when production (or sales volume) changes by one unit. Both production costs and revenues must be evaluated. To determine the costs of production, it is necessary to distinguish among several types of costs. **Fixed costs** do not vary with changes in the number of units produced or sold. Consequently, a paint manufacturer's cost of renting a factory does not change because production increases from one to two shifts a day or because twice as much paint is sold. Rent may go up, but not because the factory has doubled production or revenue. **Average fixed cost** is the fixed cost per unit produced and is calculated by dividing fixed costs by the number of units produced.

Variable costs vary directly with changes in the number of units produced or sold. The wages for a second shift and the cost of twice as much paint are extra costs incurred when production is doubled. Variable costs are usually constant per unit; that is, twice as many workers and twice as much material produce twice as many cans of paint. **Average variable cost**, the variable cost per unit produced, is calculated by dividing the variable costs by the number of units produced.

Total cost is the sum of average fixed costs and average variable costs times the quantity produced. The **average total cost** is the sum of the average fixed cost and the average variable cost. **Marginal cost (MC)** is the extra cost a firm incurs when it produces one more unit of a product.

Table 19.1 illustrates various costs and their relationships. Notice that average fixed cost declines as output increases. Average variable cost follows a U shape, as does average total cost. Because average total cost continues to fall after average variable cost begins to rise, its lowest point is at a higher level of output than that of average variable cost. Average total cost is lowest at five units at a cost of $22.00, whereas average variable cost is lowest at three units at a cost of $10.67. As Figure 19.4 shows, marginal cost equals average total cost at the latter's lowest level. In Table 19.1, this occurs between five and six units of production. Average total cost decreases as long as marginal cost is less than average total cost and increases when marginal cost rises above average total cost.

Marginal revenue (MR) is the change in total revenue that occurs when a firm sells an additional unit of a product. Figure 19.5 depicts marginal revenue and a demand curve. Most

fixed costs Costs that do not vary with changes in the number of units produced or sold

average fixed cost The fixed cost per unit produced

variable costs Costs that vary directly with changes in the number of units produced or sold

average variable cost The variable cost per unit produced

total cost The sum of average fixed and average variable costs times the quantity produced

average total cost The sum of the average fixed cost and the average variable cost

marginal cost (MC) The extra cost incurred by producing one more unit of a product

marginal revenue (MR) The change in total revenue resulting from the sale of an additional unit of a product

Table 19.1 Costs and Their Relationships

1 Quantity	2 Fixed Cost	3 Average Fixed Cost (2) ÷ (1)	4 Average Variable Cost	5 Average Total Cost (3) + (4)	6 Total Cost (5) × (1)	7 Marginal Cost
1	$40	$40.00	$20.00	$60.00	$60	
						$10
2	40	20.00	15.00	35.00	70	
						2
3	40	13.33	10.67	24.00	72	
						18
4	40	10.00	12.50	22.50	90	
						20
5	40	8.00	14.00	22.00	110	
						30
6	40	6.67	16.67	23.33	140	
						40
7	40	5.71	20.00	25.71	180	

Figure 19.4 Typical Marginal Cost and Average Total Cost Relationship

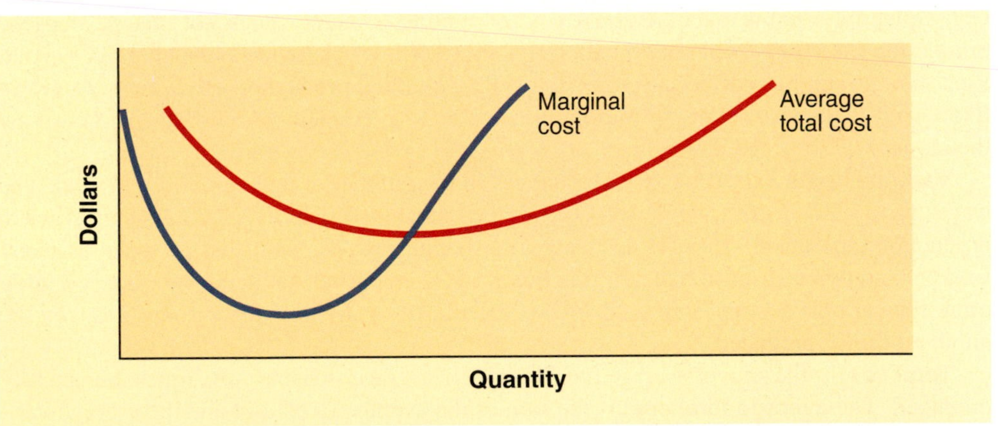

firms in the United States face downward-sloping demand curves for their products; in other words, they must lower their prices to sell additional units. This situation means that each additional unit of product sold provides the firm with less revenue than the previous unit sold. MR then becomes less-than-average revenue, as Figure 19.5 shows. Eventually, MR reaches zero, and the sale of additional units actually hurts the firm.

However, before the firm can determine whether a unit makes a profit, it must know its cost, as well as its revenue, because profit equals revenue minus cost. If MR is a unit's addition to revenue and MC is a unit's addition to cost, MR minus MC tells us whether the unit is profitable. Table 19.2 illustrates the relationships among price, quantity sold, total revenue, marginal revenue, marginal cost, and total cost. It indicates where maximum profits are possible at various combinations of price and cost. Notice that the total cost and the marginal cost figures in Table 19.2 are calculated and appear in Table 19.1.

Figure 19.5 **Typical Marginal Revenue and Average Revenue Relationship**

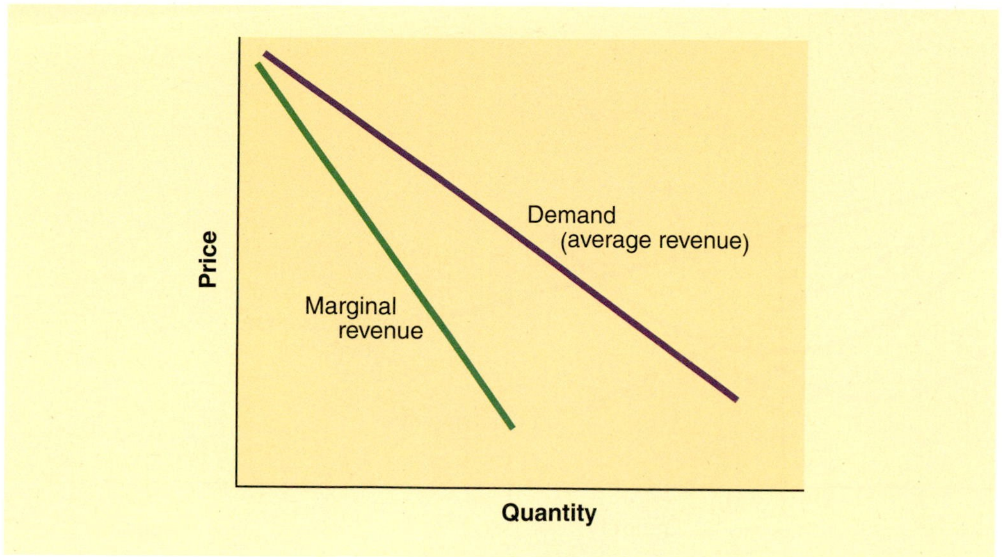

Profit is the highest where MC = MR. In Table 19.2, note that at a quantity of four units, profit is the highest and MR – MC = 0. The best price is $33, and the profit is $42. Up to this point, the additional revenue generated from an extra unit sold exceeds the additional cost of producing it. Beyond this point, the additional cost of producing another unit exceeds the additional revenue generated, and profits decrease. If the price were based on minimum average total cost—$22 (Table 19.1)—it would result in a lower profit of $40 (Table 19.2) for five units priced at $30 versus a profit of $42 for four units priced at $33.

Graphically combining Figures 19.4 and 19.5 into Figure 19.6 shows that any unit for which MR exceeds MC adds to a firm's profits, and any unit for which MC exceeds MR subtracts from profits. The firm should produce at the point where MR equals MC, because this is the most profitable level of production.

This discussion of marginal analysis may give the false impression that pricing can be highly precise. If revenue (demand) and cost (supply) remained constant, prices could be set for maximum profits. In practice, however, cost and revenue change frequently. The competitive tactics of other firms or government action can quickly undermine a company's expectations

Table 19.2 **Marginal Analysis Method for Determining the Most Profitable Price***

1 Price	2 Quantity Sold	3 Total Revenue (1) × (2)	4 Marginal Revenue	5 Marginal Cost	6 Total Cost	7 Profit (3) – (6)
$57	1	$57	$57	$60	$60	$-3
50	2	100	43	10	70	30
38	3	114	14	2	72	42
33*	**4**	**132**	**18**	**18**	**90**	**42**
30	5	150	18	20	110	40
27	6	162	12	30	140	22
25	7	175	13	40	180	-5

*Boldface indicates the best price–profit combination.

Figure 19.6 **Combining the Marginal Cost and Marginal Revenue Concepts for Optimal Profit**

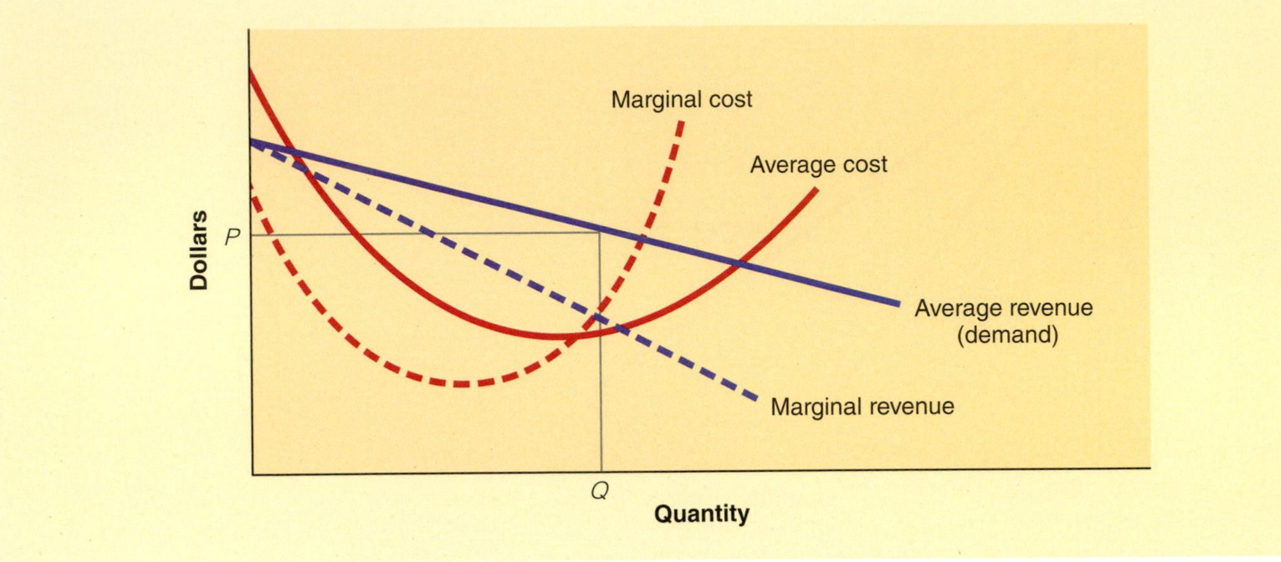

of revenue. Thus, marginal analysis is only a model from which to work. It offers little help in pricing new products before costs and revenues are established. On the other hand, in setting prices of existing products, especially in competitive situations, most marketers can benefit by understanding the relationship between marginal cost and marginal revenue.

19-4b Break-Even Analysis

break even point The point at which the costs of producing a product equal the revenue made from selling the product

The point at which the costs of producing a product equal the revenue made from selling the product is the **break even point**. If a paint manufacturer has total annual costs of $100,000 and sells $100,000 worth of paint in the same year, the company has broken even.

Figure 19.7 illustrates the relationships among costs, revenue, profits, and losses involved in determining the break even point. Knowing the number of units necessary to break even

Figure 19.7 **Determining the Break Even Point**

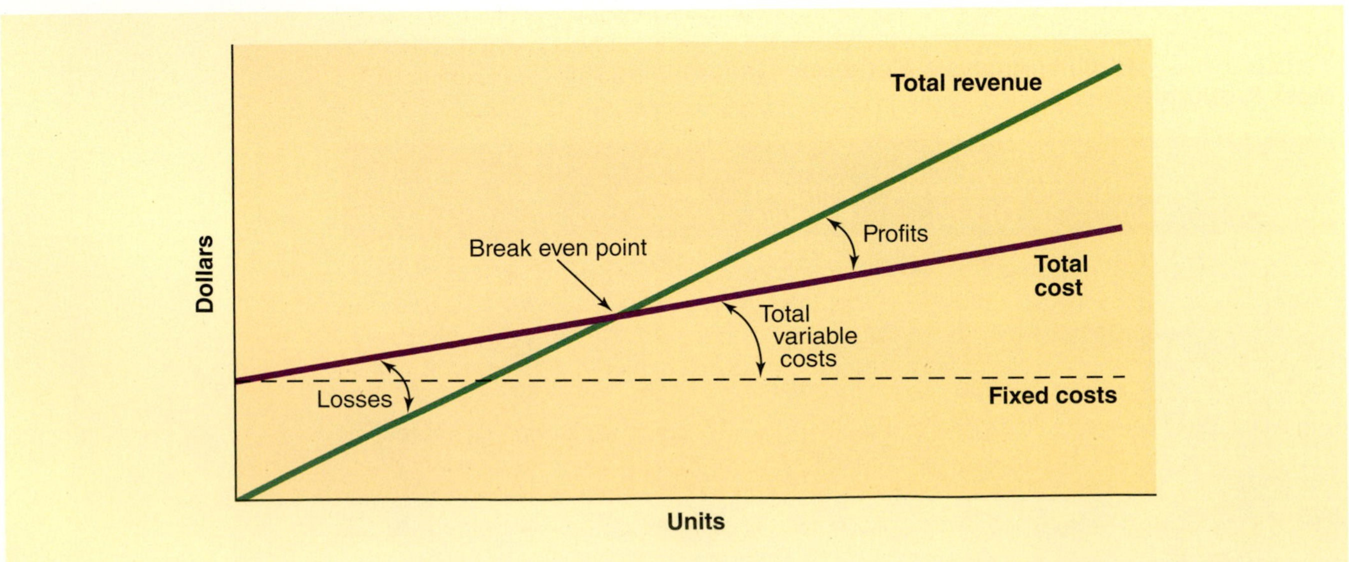

is important in setting the price. If a product priced at $100 per unit has an average variable cost of $60 per unit, the contribution to fixed costs is $40. If total fixed costs are $120,000, the break even point in units is determined as follows:

$$\begin{aligned}\text{break evenpoint} &= \frac{\text{fixed costs}}{\text{per-unit contribution to fixed costs}}\\ &= \frac{\text{fixed costs}}{\text{price} - \text{variable costs}}\\ &= \frac{\$120{,}000}{\$40}\\ &= 3{,}000 \text{ units}\end{aligned}$$

To calculate the break even point in terms of dollar sales volume, the seller multiplies the break even point in units by the price per unit. In the preceding example, the break even point in terms of dollar sales volume is 3,000 (units) times $100, or $300,000.

To use break even analysis effectively, a marketer should determine the break even point for each of several alternative prices. This determination allows the marketer to compare the effects on total revenue, total costs, and the break even point for each price under consideration. Although this comparative analysis may not tell the marketer exactly what price to charge, it will identify highly undesirable price alternatives that should definitely be avoided.

Break-even analysis is simple and straightforward. It does assume, however, that the quantity demanded is basically fixed (inelastic) and that the major task in setting prices is to recover costs. It focuses more on how to break even than on how to achieve a pricing objective, such as percentage of market share or return on investment. Nonetheless, marketing managers can use this concept to determine whether a product will achieve at least a break-even volume.

19-5 FACTORS THAT AFFECT PRICING DECISIONS

Pricing decisions can be complex because of the number of factors to consider. Frequently, there is considerable uncertainty about the reactions to price among buyers, channel members, and competitors. Price is also an important consideration in marketing planning, market analysis, and sales forecasting. It is a major issue when assessing a brand's position relative to competing brands. Most factors that affect pricing decisions can be grouped into one of the eight categories shown in Figure 19.8. In this section, we explore how each of these groups of factors enters into price decision making.

19-5a Organizational and Marketing Objectives

Marketers should set prices that are consistent with the organization's goals and mission. For example, a retailer trying to position itself as being value-oriented may wish to set prices that are quite reasonable relative to product quality. In this case, a marketer would not want to set premium prices on products but would strive to price products in line with this overall organizational goal.

Pricing decisions should also be compatible with the firm's marketing objectives. For instance, suppose one of a producer's marketing objectives is a 12 percent increase in unit sales by the end of the following year. Assuming buyers are price sensitive, increasing the price or setting a price above the average market price would not be in line with this objective.

Figure 19.8 Factors That Affect Pricing Decisions

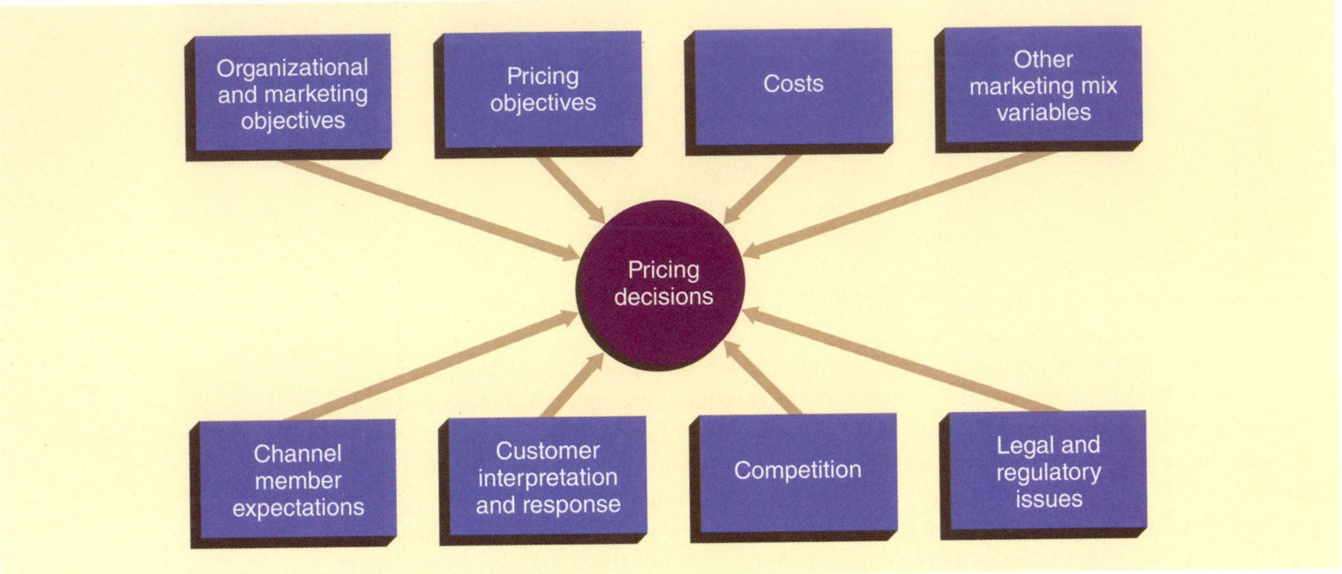

19-5b Types of Pricing Objectives

The types of pricing objectives a marketer uses obviously have considerable bearing on the determination of prices. For instance, an organization that uses pricing to increase its market share would likely set the brand's price below those of competing brands of similar quality to attract competitors' customers. A marketer sometimes uses temporary price reductions in the hope of gaining market share. If a business needs to raise cash quickly, it will likely use temporary price reductions, such as sales, rebates, and special discounts. We examine pricing objectives in more detail in the next chapter.

19-5c Costs

Clearly, costs must be an issue when establishing price. A firm may temporarily sell products below cost to match competition, generate cash flow, or even increase market share, but in the long run, it cannot survive by selling its products below cost. Even a firm that has a high-volume business cannot survive if each item is sold slightly below its cost. A marketer should be careful to analyze all costs so they can be included in the total cost associated with a product.

To maintain market share and revenue in an increasingly price-sensitive market, many marketers have concentrated on reducing costs. For instance, hotels are cutting costs of food delivery by offering no-frills room service. In the past, hotels have attempted to make room service special, with stainless steel plates and rolling tables. However, revenue generated from room service has decreased in recent years, leading hotels to conclude that guests do not really care about having a fancy dining experience in their rooms. As a result, hotels including Hilton Worldwide and the Hudson Hotel are using no-frills tactics such as brown-bag delivery to reduce the costs of food service.[10]

Labor-saving technologies, a focus on quality, and efficient manufacturing processes have brought productivity gains that translate into reduced costs and lower prices for customers. Boeing has increased its learning curve in the production of 787 Dreamliners as it learns more about quality and manufacturing processes. This has decreased cash costs by a 25 percent compound annual growth rate in a 3-year period of production. Boeing will need to double its learning rate in order to break even for its target year of 2015.[11]

Besides considering the costs associated with a particular product, marketers must take into account the costs the product shares with others in the product line. Products often share some costs, particularly the costs of research and development, production, and distribution. Most marketers view a product's cost as a minimum, or floor, below which the product cannot be priced.

19-5d Other Marketing-Mix Variables

All marketing-mix variables are highly interrelated. Pricing decisions can influence evaluations and activities associated with product, distribution, and promotion variables. A product's price frequently affects the demand for that item. A high price, for instance, may result in low unit sales, which in turn may lead to higher production costs per unit. Conversely, lower per-unit production costs may result from a low price. For many products, buyers associate better product quality with a high price and poorer product quality with a low price. This perceived price–quality relationship influences customers' overall image of products or brands. Case in point, some individuals view Mercedes Benz vehicles as higher quality than other brands and are willing to pay a higher price. Individuals who associate quality with a high price are likely to purchase products with well-established and recognizable brand names.

The price of a product is linked to several dimensions of its distribution. Premium-priced products are often marketed through selective or exclusive distribution. Lower-priced products in the same product category may be sold through intensive distribution. Pepsi, for instance, has a multitude of distribution outlets to get their products to the consumer. The advertisement shows an attractive woman enjoying a Diet Pepsi. Unlike advertisements for more exclusive products that are clearly not meant for the average consumer, this advertisement is meant to portray that anyone can enjoy the good taste of Diet Pepsi at their convenience.

As another example, high-end Cross pens are distributed through selective distribution and disposable Bic pens through intensive distribution. Moreover, an increase in physical distribution costs, such as shipping, may have to be passed on to customers. When fuel prices increase significantly, some distribution companies pass on these additional costs through surcharges or higher prices. When setting a price, the profit margins of marketing channel members, such as wholesalers and retailers, must also be considered. Channel members must be adequately compensated for the functions they perform.

Price may determine how a product is promoted. Bargain prices are often included in advertisements. Premium prices are less likely to be advertised, though they are sometimes included in advertisements for upscale items like luxury cars or fine jewelry. Higher-priced products are more likely than lower-priced ones to require personal selling. Furthermore, the price structure can affect a salesperson's relationship with customers. A complex pricing structure takes longer to explain to customers, is more likely to confuse potential buyers, and may cause misunderstandings that result in long-term customer dissatisfaction. Anyone who has tried to decipher his or her cell phone bill will empathize with the frustration that complex pricing structures can bring about. Trying to decipher charges for anytime, weekend, daytime, and roaming minutes, not to mention charges for smartphone data usage, can be confusing.

Intensive Distribution
Pepsi products are sold through intensive distribution at grocery stores, convenience stores, discount stores, and vending machines because like other soft drinks, the brand is a low-priced product.

19-5e Channel Member Expectations

When making price decisions, a producer must consider what members of the distribution channel expect. A channel member certainly expects to receive a profit for the functions it performs. The amount of profit expected depends on what the intermediary could make if it were handling a competing product instead. Also, the amount of time and the resources required to carry the product influence intermediaries' expectations.

Channel members often expect producers to give discounts for large orders and prompt payment. At times, resellers expect producers to provide several support activities, such as sales training, service training, repair advisory service, cooperative advertising, sales promotions, and perhaps a program for returning unsold merchandise to the producer. These support activities clearly have associated costs that a producer must consider when determining prices.

19-5f Customers' Interpretation and Response

When making pricing decisions, marketers should address a vital question: How will our customers interpret our prices and respond to them? *Interpretation* in this context refers to what the price means or what it communicates to customers. Does the price mean "high quality" or "low quality," or "great deal," "fair price," or "rip-off"? Customer *response* refers to whether the price will move customers closer to purchase of the product and the degree to which the price enhances their satisfaction with the purchase experience and with the product after purchase.

Customers' interpretation of and response to a price are to some degree determined by their assessment of value, or what they receive compared with what they give up to make the purchase. In evaluating what they receive, customers consider product attributes, benefits, advantages, disadvantages, the probability of using the product, and possibly the status associated with the product. In assessing the cost of the product, customers will likely consider its price, the amount of time and effort required to obtain it, and perhaps the resources required to maintain it after purchase.

At times, customers interpret a higher price as higher product quality. They are especially likely to make this price–quality association when they cannot judge the quality of the product themselves. This is not always the case, however. Whether price is equated with quality depends on the types of customers and products involved. Obviously marketers that rely on customers making a price–quality association and that provide moderate- or low-quality products at high prices will be unable to build long-term customer relationships.

When interpreting and responding to prices, how do customers determine if the price is too high, too low, or about right? In general, they compare prices with internal or external reference prices. An **internal reference price** is a price developed in the buyer's mind through experience with the product. It reflects a belief that a product should cost approximately a certain amount. To arrive at an internal reference price, consumers may consider one or more values, including what they think the product "ought" to cost, the price usually charged for it, the last price they paid, the highest and lowest amounts they would be willing to pay, the price of the brand they usually buy, the average price of similar products, the expected future price, and the typical discounted price.[12] Researchers have found that less-confident consumers tend to have higher internal reference prices than consumers with greater confidence, and frequent buyers—perhaps because of their experience and confidence—are more likely to judge high prices unfairly.[13] As consumers, our experiences have given each of us internal reference prices for a number of products. For instance, most of us have a reasonable idea of how much to pay for a 6-pack of soft drinks, a loaf of bread, or a cup of coffee.

internal reference price A price developed in the buyer's mind through experience with the product

external reference price A comparison price provided by others

For the product categories with which we have less experience, we rely more heavily on external reference prices. An **external reference price** is a comparison price provided by others, such as retailers or manufacturers. Some grocery and electronics stores, for example, will show other stores' prices next to their price of a particular good if their price is lower than the competitor's price. This provides a reference point for consumers unfamiliar with the product category. Customers' perceptions of prices are also influenced by their expectations about future price increases, what they paid for the product recently, and what they would like to pay for the product. Other factors affecting customers' perceptions of whether the price is right include time or financial constraints, the costs associated with searching for lower-priced products, and expectations that products will go on sale.

Buyers' perceptions of a product relative to competing products may allow the firm to set a price that differs significantly from rivals' prices. If the product is deemed superior to most of the competition, a premium price may be feasible. However, even products with superior quality can be overpriced. Strong brand loyalty sometimes provides the opportunity to charge a premium price. On the other hand, if buyers view a product less than favorably (though not extremely negatively), a lower price may generate sales.

In the context of price, buyers can be characterized according to their degree of value consciousness, price consciousness, and prestige sensitivity. Marketers who understand these characteristics are better able to set pricing objectives and policies. **Value-conscious** consumers are concerned about both price and quality of a product.[14] During uncertain economic periods, customers become more value and price conscious and tend to limit discretionary spending. Whole Foods has introduced discounts for its products to take market share away from traditional grocery stores and shed its reputation as an overpriced retailer. Although this appeals to more value-conscious consumers, it has impacted Whole Foods' profit margins.[15] These value-conscious consumers may perceive value as quality per unit of price or as not only economic savings but also the additional gains expected from one product over a competitor's brand. The first view is appropriate for commodities like bottled water, bananas, and gasoline. If a value-conscious consumer perceives the quality of gasoline to be the same for Exxon and Shell, he or she will go to the station with the lower price. For consumers looking not just for economic value but additional gains they expect from one brand over another, a product differentiation value could be associated with benefits and features that are believed to be unique.[16] For instance, a BMW may be considered to be better than a Cadillac.

value-conscious Concerned about price and quality of a product

price-conscious Striving to pay low prices

prestige-sensitive Drawn to products that signify prominence and status

Price-conscious individuals strive to pay low prices. They want the lowest prices, even if the products are not of the highest quality. Amazon.com has long been known for a willingness to sacrifice profit margins in favor of offering the lowest prices. Price-conscious consumers might also shop at Walmart due to its "Everyday Low Price" guarantee. McDonald's highlights its low prices for its dollar menu and more options in its advertising. McDonald's competes heavily on price because the fast-food market is so competitive. The advertisement suggests to consumers that they can receive good food at lower prices. This type of advertisement appeals to the price-conscious consumer.

Prestige-sensitive buyers focus on purchasing products that signify prominence and status. For instance, Patek Philippe & Co. is known for its high-quality watches and has been a premier watchmaker worldwide for more than 160 years. It retailed its limited-edition World Time watch sold only in Beijing and Shanghai for about $72,000.[17]

Some consumers vary in their degree of value, price, and prestige consciousness. In some market segments, consumers "trade up" to higher-status products in categories such as automobiles, home appliances, restaurants, and even pet food, yet remain price conscious regarding cleaning and grocery products. This trend has benefited marketers like Starbucks, BMW, Whole Foods, and PETCO, which can charge premium prices for high-quality, prestige products.

Price-Conscious Consumers
McDonald's appeals to the price-conscious consumer in marketing the low prices of its food items.

Emerging Trends

Monitoring Driving Behaviors as a Means to Lower Insurance Prices

Car insurance firms are using Usage Based Insurance (UBI) to offer discounts to good drivers. UBI is a digital device that plugs into a vehicle and monitors when, how fast, and for how long a person drives. Periodically, the insurance company reviews this information, and if the driver receives a good grade, he or she is offered a discount. The best drivers can see discounts up to 40 percent off their insurance bill. Some are skeptical of this technology because of the information collected, how it will be used, and with whom it will be shared. Others, however, are not bothered by the privacy concerns if they can save hundreds of dollars per year. A survey revealed that one in three insured drivers would consider switching to UBI.

Insurance policies have previously been based on demographics that do not always reflect a person's driving habits. UBI is a way to catalogue a driver's actual behaviors and habits while driving. It also has the added benefit of reducing insurance fraud because the insurance company can actually see whether a vehicle was involved in an accident. There is also an environmental aspect to this device. Those with a UBI who debate whether to drive to a specific location will consider the mileage registered in the UBI. If the extra mileage will bump them into the next mileage category, they may be deterred from driving.[a]

19-5g Competition

A marketer needs to know competitors' prices so it can adjust its own prices accordingly. This does not mean a company will necessarily match competitors' prices; it may set its price above or below theirs. However, for some organizations, matching competitors' prices is an important strategy for survival. Wendy's and McDonald's, for instance, both aggressively promote their lower-priced items and try to convince consumers that their restaurants offer better deals.[18]

When adjusting prices, a marketer must assess how competitors will respond. Will competitors change their prices and, if so, will they raise or lower them? In Chapter 3, we described several types of competitive market structures. The structure that characterizes the industry to which a firm belongs affects the flexibility of price setting. Because of reduced pricing regulation, for instance, firms in the telecommunications industry have moved from a monopolistic market structure to an oligopolistic one, which has resulted in significant price competition.

When an organization operates as a monopoly and is unregulated, it can set whatever prices the market will bear. However, the company may not price the product at the highest-possible level to avoid government regulation or penetrate a market by using a lower price. If the monopoly is regulated, it normally has less pricing flexibility; the regulatory body lets it set prices that generate a reasonable but not excessive return. A government-owned monopoly may price products below cost to make them accessible to people who otherwise could not afford them. Transit systems, for example, sometimes operate this way. However, government-owned monopolies sometimes charge higher prices to control demand. In some states with state-owned liquor stores, the price of liquor is higher than in states where liquor stores are not owned by a government body.

The automotive and airline industries exemplify oligopolies, in which only a few sellers operate and barriers to competitive entry are high. Companies in such industries can raise their prices in the hope that competitors will do the same. When an organization cuts its price to gain a competitive edge, other companies are likely to follow suit. This happens frequently in the credit card industry. Discover Financial Services is one company that has been successful at adopting cash incentives as a competitive tool. The advertisement leads consumers to believe that they are getting a good deal by using the Discover credit card. Discover uses the advertisement to market itself as the number-one cash rewards program. This is Discover's way of attempting to differentiate itself from other major competitors in the industry. However, generally there is very little advantage gained through price cuts in an oligopolistic market structure because competitors will often follow suit.

A market structure characterized by monopolistic competition has numerous sellers with product offerings that are differentiated by physical characteristics, features, quality, and brand images. The distinguishing characteristics of its product may allow a company to set a different price from its competitors. However, firms in a monopolistic competitive market structure are likely to practice nonprice competition, discussed earlier in this chapter.

Under conditions of perfect competition, many sellers exist. Buyers view all sellers' products as the same. All firms sell their products at the going market price, and buyers will not pay more than that. This type of market structure, then, gives a marketer no flexibility in setting prices. Farming, as an industry, has some characteristics of perfect competition. Farmers sell their products at the going market price. At times, for example, corn, soybean, and wheat growers have had bumper crops and been forced to sell them at depressed market prices. In countries in which farm subsidies are provided, the effects of perfect competition are reduced.

Oligopolistic Competition
Discover uses a cash reward program to encourage adoption of its credit card over those of its competitors.

19-5h Legal and Regulatory Issues

Legal and regulatory issues influence pricing decisions. To curb inflation, the federal government can invoke price controls, freeze prices at certain levels, or determine the rates at which firms may increase prices. In some states and many other countries, regulatory agencies set prices on such products as insurance, dairy products, and liquor.

Many regulations and laws affect pricing decisions and activities in the United States. The Sherman Antitrust Act prohibits conspiracies to control prices, and in interpreting the act, courts have ruled that price-fixing among firms in an industry is illegal. Marketers must refrain from fixing prices by developing independent pricing policies and setting prices in ways that do not even hint at collusion. Two Japanese executives of car-parts maker Denso Corp. were sentenced to more than a year in a U.S. prison after a price-fixing probe indicated that several car-parts manufacturers had colluded on price. The men pled guilty to conspiracy to fix prices. Denso provided parts for Toyota Motor Corp., among other clients, and is one of at least nine parts makers to plead guilty to price-fixing.[19] Both the Federal Trade Commission Act and the Wheeler-Lea Act prohibit deceptive pricing. Some other nations and trade agreements have similar prohibitions. Determining what is anticompetitive in different countries can be complicated. Consequently, China fined Mead Nutrition, Danone, New Zealand company Fonterra, and other companies $110 million for allegedly fixing the prices of foreign baby formula.[20] In establishing prices, marketers must guard against deceiving customers.

The Robinson-Patman Act has had a particularly strong impact on pricing decisions. For various reasons, marketers may wish to sell the same type of product at different prices. Provisions in the Robinson-Patman Act, as well as those in the Clayton Act, limit the use of such price differentials. **Price discrimination**, the practice of employing price differentials that tend to injure competition by giving one or more buyers a competitive advantage over other buyers, is prohibited by law. Many people are surprised to learn that they may be charged a different price for the same product as somebody else. Companies selling over the Web have used user information on geographic location, frequency of purchase, or other characteristics

price discrimination
Employing price differentials that injure competition by giving one or more buyers a competitive advantage

Marketing Debate

MFN Clause: Scandal or Money Saver?

ISSUE: Was Apple using MFN clauses to fix prices on e-books?

Most-Favored-Nation (MFN) clauses occur when a seller promises the lowest price to a buyer. They have been widely used for years across many industries as a form of risk control to protect investments. However, a federal court case involving Apple and its electronic book (e-book) pricing has brought these clauses under scrutiny. Apple was accused of price-fixing by having e-book publishers set their own prices, a measure known as the "Agency Pricing Model." According to this agreement, the publishers could not allow other retailers to sell the same titles for less. This led to other online retailers having to sell their e-books at \$3–\$5 more. Although Apple claims that they were only trying to get the lowest price for their customers, others claim Apple was engaging in price-fixing to secure the best prices.[b]

to determine which price a consumer would be most willing to pay. Although this is currently not considered to be illegal, many Internet shoppers have expressed discontent because they view the practice as unfair.[21] However, not all price differentials are considered to be illegal or unfair. A marketer can use price differentials if they do not hinder competition, result from differences in the costs of selling or transportation to various customers, or arise because the firm has had to cut its price to a particular buyer to meet competitors' prices. Airlines, for example, may charge different customers different prices for the same flights based on the availability of seats at the time of purchase. As a result, flyers sitting in adjacent seats may have paid vastly different fares because one passenger booked weeks ahead, whereas the other booked on the spur of the moment a few days before when only a few seats were still available. A global problem impacting business pricing strategies is the growing market for counterfeit goods. Counterfeit goods are regulated on a country-by-country basis. More sales that are lost to the "gray market" means lower profits and potentially higher prices for the legitimate goods. For instance, Brahmin Leather Works uses colorful advertising to sell its higher-priced handbags. Because Brahmin accessories sell for premium prices, the company must be on the lookout for counterfeiters who want to capitalize on their success.

Counterfeit Products
Efforts to copy luxury goods result in declining profits for manufacturers such as Brahmin.

19-6 PRICING FOR BUSINESS MARKETS

Business markets consist of individuals and organizations that purchase products for resale, use those products in their own operations, or produce other products. Establishing prices for this category of buyers sometimes differs from setting prices for consumers. Differences in the size of purchases, geographic factors, and transportation considerations require sellers to adjust prices. In this section, we discuss several issues unique to the pricing of business products, including discounts, geographic pricing, and transfer pricing.

19-6a Price Discounting

Producers commonly provide intermediaries with discounts, or reductions, from list prices. Although many types of discounts exist, they usually fall into one of five categories: trade, quantity, cash, seasonal, and allowance. Table 19.3 summarizes some reasons to use each type of discount and provides examples. Such discounts can be a significant factor in a marketing strategy.

Trade Discounts

A reduction off the list price given by a producer to an intermediary for performing certain functions is called a **trade (functional) discount**. A trade discount is usually stated in terms of a percentage or series of percentages off the list price. Intermediaries are given trade discounts as compensation for performing various functions, such as selling, transporting, storing, final processing, and perhaps providing credit services. Although certain trade discounts are often a standard practice within an industry, discounts vary considerably among industries. It is important that a manufacturer provide a trade discount large enough to offset the intermediary's costs, plus a reasonable profit, to entice the reseller to carry the product.

trade (functional) discount A reduction off the list price a producer gives to an intermediary for performing certain functions

quantity discounts Deductions from the list price for purchasing in large quantities

cumulative discounts Quantity discounts aggregated over a stated time period

Quantity Discounts

Deductions from list price that reflect the economies of purchasing in large quantities are called **quantity discounts**. Quantity discounts are used in many industries and pass on to the buyer cost savings gained through economies of scale.

Quantity discounts can be either cumulative or noncumulative. **Cumulative discounts** are quantity discounts aggregated over a stated time period. Purchases totaling $10,000 in

Table 19.3 Discounts Used for Business Markets

Type	Reasons for Use	Examples
Trade	To attract and keep effective resellers by compensating them for performing certain functions, such as transportation, warehousing, selling, and providing credit	A college bookstore pays about (functional) one-third less for a new textbook than the retail price a student pays.
Quantity	To encourage customers to buy large quantities when making purchases and, in the case of cumulative discounts, to encourage customer loyalty	Large department store chains purchase some women's apparel at lower prices than do individually owned specialty stores.
Cash	To reduce expenses associated with accounts receivable and collection by encouraging prompt payment of accounts	Numerous companies serving business markets allow a 2 percent discount if an account is paid within 10 days.
Seasonal	To allow a marketer to use resources more efficiently by stimulating sales during off-peak periods	Florida hotels provide companies holding national and regional sales meetings with deeply discounted accommodations during the summer months.
Allowance	In the case of a trade-in allowance, to assist the buyer in making the purchase and potentially earning a profit on the resale of used equipment; in the case of a promotional allowance, to ensure that dealers participate in advertising and sales support programs	A farm equipment dealer takes a farmer's used tractor as a trade-in on a new one. Nabisco pays a promotional allowance to a supermarket for setting up and maintaining a large, end-of-aisle display for a 2-week period.

a 3-month period, for example, might entitle the buyer to a 5 percent, or $500, rebate. Such discounts are intended to reflect economies in selling and encourage the buyer to purchase from one seller. **Noncumulative discounts** are one-time reductions in prices based on the number of units purchased, the dollar value of the order, or the product mix purchased. Like cumulative discounts, these discounts should reflect some economies in selling or trade functions.

Cash Discounts

A **cash discount**, or price reduction, is given to a buyer for prompt payment or cash payment. Accounts receivable are an expense and a collection problem for many organizations. A policy to encourage prompt payment is a popular practice and sometimes a major concern in setting prices.

Discounts are based on cash payments or cash paid within a stated time. For instance, "2/10 net 30" means that a 2 percent discount will be allowed if the account is paid within 10 days. If the buyer does not make payment within the 10-day period, the entire balance is due within 30 days without a discount. If the account is not paid within 30 days, interest may be charged.

Seasonal Discounts

A price reduction to buyers who purchase goods or services out of season is a **seasonal discount**. These discounts let the seller maintain steadier production during the year. Thus, it is usually much cheaper to purchase and install an air-conditioning unit in the winter than it is in the summer. This is because demand for air conditioners is very low during the winter in most parts of the country, and price, therefore, is also lower than in peak-demand season.

Allowances

Another type of reduction from the list price is an **allowance** , a concession in price to achieve a desired goal. Trade-in allowances, for example, are price reductions granted for turning in a used item when purchasing a new one. Allowances help make the buyer better able to make the new purchase. Another example is a promotional allowance, a price reduction granted to dealers for participating in advertising and sales support programs intended to increase sales of a particular item.

19-6b Geographic Pricing

Geographic pricing involves reductions for transportation costs or other costs associated with the physical distance between buyer and seller. Prices may be quoted as F.O.B. (free-on-board) factory or destination. An **F.O.B. factory** price indicates the price of the merchandise at the factory, before it is loaded onto the carrier, and thus excludes transportation costs. The buyer must pay for shipping. An **F.O.B. destination** price means the producer absorbs the costs of shipping the merchandise to the customer. This policy may be used to attract distant customers. Although F.O.B. pricing is an easy way to price products, it is sometimes difficult to administer, especially when a firm has a wide product mix or when customers are widely dispersed. Because customers will want to know about the most economical method of shipping, the seller must be informed about shipping rates.

To avoid the problems involved in charging different prices to each customer, **uniform geographic pricing**, sometimes called *postage-stamp pricing*, may be used. The same price is charged to all customers regardless of geographic location, and the price is based on average shipping costs for all customers. Paper products and office equipment are often priced on a uniform basis.

noncumulative discounts One-time price reductions based on the number of units purchased, the dollar value of the order, or the product mix purchased

cash discount A price reduction given to buyers for prompt payment or cash payment

seasonal discount A price reduction given to buyers for purchasing goods or services out of season

allowance A concession in price to achieve a desired goal

geographic pricing Reductions for transportation and other costs related to the physical distance between buyer and seller

F.O.B. factory The price of merchandise at the factory before shipment

F.O.B. destination A price indicating the producer is absorbing shipping costs

uniform geographic pricing Charging all customers the same price, regardless of geographic location

Zone pricing sets uniform prices for each of several major geographic zones; as the transportation costs across zones increase, so do the prices. For instance, a Florida manufacturer's prices may be higher for buyers on the Pacific coast and in Canada than for buyers in Georgia.

Base-point pricing is a geographic pricing policy that includes the price at the factory, plus freight charges from the base point nearest the buyer. This approach to pricing has virtually been abandoned because of its questionable legal status. The policy resulted in all buyers paying freight charges from one location, such as Detroit or Pittsburgh, regardless of where the product was manufactured.

When the seller absorbs all or part of the actual freight costs, **freight absorption pricing** is being used. The seller might choose this method because it wishes to do business with a particular customer or to get more business; more business will cause the average cost to fall and counterbalance the extra freight cost. This strategy is used to improve market penetration and retain a hold in an increasingly competitive market.

19-6c Transfer Pricing

Transfer pricing occurs when one unit in an organization sells a product to another unit. The price is determined by one of the following methods:

- *Actual full cost:* calculated by dividing all fixed and variable expenses for a period into the number of units produced.
- *Standard full cost:* calculated based on what it would cost to produce the goods at full plant capacity.
- *Cost plus investment:* calculated as full cost plus, the cost of a portion of the selling unit's assets used for internal needs.
- *Market-based cost:* calculated at the market price less a small discount to reflect the lack of sales effort and other expenses.

The choice of transfer pricing method depends on the company's management strategy and the nature of the units' interaction. An organization must also ensure that transfer pricing is fair to all units involved in the transactions.

zone pricing Pricing based on transportation costs within major geographic zones

base-point pricing Geographic pricing that combines factory price and freight charges from the base point nearest the buyer

freight absorption pricing Absorption of all or part of actual freight costs by the seller

transfer pricing Prices charged in sales between an organization's units

Summary

19-1 Summarize why price is important to the marketing mix.

Price is the value paid for a product in a marketing exchange. Barter, the trading of products, is the oldest form of exchange. Price is a key element in the marketing mix, because it relates directly to generation of total revenue. The profit factor can be determined mathematically by multiplying price by quantity sold to get total revenue and then subtracting total costs. Price is the only variable in the marketing mix that can be adjusted quickly and easily to respond to changes in the external environment.

19-2 Compare price competition with nonprice competition.

A product offering can compete on either a price or a nonprice basis. Price competition emphasizes price as the product differential. Prices fluctuate frequently, and price competition among sellers is aggressive. Nonprice competition emphasizes product differentiation through distinctive features, service, product quality, or other factors. Establishing brand loyalty by using nonprice competition works best when the product can be physically differentiated and the customer can recognize these differences.

19-3 Explain the importance of demand curves and the price elasticity of demand.

An organization must determine the demand for its product. The classic demand curve is a graph of the quantity of products expected to be sold at various prices if other factors hold constant. It illustrates that, as price falls, the quantity demanded usually increases. However, for prestige products, there is a direct positive relationship between price and quantity demanded: Demand increases as price increases. Next, price elasticity of demand, the percentage change in quantity demanded relative to a given percentage change in price, must be determined. If demand is elastic, a change in price causes an opposite change in total revenue. Inelastic demand results in a parallel change in total revenue when a product's price is changed.

19-4 Describe the relationships among demand, costs, and profits.

Analysis of demand, cost, and profit relationships can be accomplished through marginal analysis or break-even analysis. Marginal analysis examines what happens to a firm's costs and revenues when production (or sales volume) is changed by one unit. Marginal analysis combines the demand curve with the firm's costs to develop a price that yields maximum profit. Fixed costs do not vary with changes in the number of units produced or sold; average fixed cost is the fixed cost per unit produced. Variable costs vary directly with changes in the number of units produced or sold. Average variable cost is the variable cost per unit produced. Total cost is the sum of average fixed cost and average variable cost times the quantity produced. The optimal price is the point at which marginal cost (the cost associated with producing one more unit of the product) equals marginal revenue (the change in total revenue that occurs when one additional unit of the product is sold). Marginal analysis is only a model; it offers little help in pricing new products before costs and revenues are established.

Break-even analysis, determining the number of units that must be sold to break even, is important in setting price. The point at which the costs of production equal the revenue from selling the product is the break even point. To use break-even analysis effectively, a marketer should determine the break even point for each of several alternative prices. This makes it possible to compare the effects on total revenue, total costs, and the break even point for each price under consideration. However, this approach assumes the quantity demanded is basically fixed and the major task is to set prices to recover costs.

19-5 Describe eight key factors that may influence marketers' pricing decisions.

Eight factors enter into price decision making: organizational and marketing objectives, pricing objectives, costs, other marketing mix variables, channel member expectations, customer interpretation and response, competition, and legal and regulatory issues. When setting prices, marketers should make decisions consistent with the organization's goals and mission. Pricing objectives heavily influence price-setting decisions. Most marketers view a product's cost as the floor below which a product cannot be priced. Because of the interrelationship among the marketing mix variables, price can affect product, promotion, and distribution decisions. The revenue channel members expect for their functions must also be considered when making price decisions.

Buyers' perceptions of price vary. Some consumer segments are sensitive to price, but others may not be. Thus, before determining price, a marketer needs to be aware of its importance to the target market. Knowledge of the prices charged for competing brands is essential to allow the firm to adjust its prices relative to competitors' prices. Government regulations and legislation also influence pricing decisions.

19-6 Identify seven methods companies can use to price products for business markets.

The categories of discounts include trade, quantity, cash, seasonal, and allowance. A trade discount is a price reduction for performing such functions as storing, transporting, final processing, or providing credit services. If an intermediary purchases in large enough quantities, the producer gives a quantity discount, which can be either cumulative or noncumulative. A cash discount is a price reduction for prompt payment or payment in cash. Buyers who purchase goods or services out of season may be granted a seasonal discount. An allowance, such as a trade-in allowance, is a concession in price to achieve a desired goal.

Geographic pricing involves reductions for transportation costs or other costs associated with the physical distance between buyer and seller. With an F.O.B. factory price, the buyer pays for shipping from the factory. An F.O.B. destination price means the producer pays for shipping; this is the easiest way to price products, but it is difficult to administer. When the seller charges a fixed average cost for transportation, it is using uniform geographic pricing. Zone prices are uniform within major geographic zones; they increase by zone as transportation costs increase. With base-point pricing, prices are adjusted for shipping expenses incurred by the seller from the base point nearest the buyer. Freight absorption pricing occurs when a seller absorbs all or part of the freight costs.

Transfer pricing occurs when a unit in an organization sells products to another unit in the organization. Methods used for transfer pricing include actual full cost, standard full cost, cost plus investment, and market-based cost.

Go to www.cengagebrain.com for resources to help you master the content in this chapter as well as for materials that will expand your marketing knowledge!

Developing Your Marketing Plan

The appropriate pricing of a product is an important factor in developing a successful marketing strategy. The price contributes to the profitability of the product and can deter competition from entering the market. A clear understanding of pricing concepts is essential in developing a strategy and marketing plan. Consider the information in this chapter when focusing on the following issues:

1. Does your company currently compete based on price or nonprice factors? Should your new product continue with this approach?
2. Discuss the level of elasticity of demand for your product. Is additional information needed for you to determine its elasticity?
3. At various price points, calculate the break even point for sales of your product.
4. Using Figure 19.8 as a guide, discuss the various factors that affect the pricing of your product.

The information obtained from these questions should assist you in developing various aspects of your marketing plan found in the "Interactive Marketing Plan" exercise at **www.cengagebrain.com**.

Important Terms

price 584
barter 584
price competition 585
nonprice competition 587
demand curve 587
price elasticity of demand 589
fixed costs 591
average fixed cost 591
variable costs 591
average variable cost 591
total cost 591
average total cost 591
marginal cost (MC) 591
marginal revenue (MR) 591
break even point 594
internal reference price 598
external reference price 598
value-conscious 599
price-conscious 599
prestige-sensitive 599
price discrimination 601
trade (functional) discount 603
quantity discounts 603
cumulative discounts 603
noncumulative discounts 604
cash discount 604
seasonal discount 604
allowance 604
geographic pricing 604
F.O.B. factory 604
F.O.B. destination 604
uniform geographic pricing 604
zone pricing 605
base-point pricing 605
freight absorption pricing 605
transfer pricing 605

Discussion and Review Questions

1. Why are pricing decisions important to an organization?
2. Compare and contrast price and nonprice competition. Describe the conditions under which each form works best.
3. Why do most demand curves demonstrate an inverse relationship between price and quantity?
4. List the characteristics of products that have inelastic demand, and give several examples of such products.
5. Explain why optimal profits should occur when marginal cost equals marginal revenue.
6. Chambers Company has just gathered estimates for conducting a break-even analysis for a new product. Variable costs are $7 a unit. The additional plant will cost $48,000. The new product will be charged $18,000 a year for its share of general overhead. Advertising expenditures will be $80,000, and $55,000 will be spent on distribution. If the product sells for $12, what is the break even point in units? What is the break even point in dollar sales volume?
7. In what ways do other marketing-mix variables affect pricing decisions?
8. What types of expectations may channel members have about producers' prices? How might these expectations affect pricing decisions?
9. How do legal and regulatory forces influence pricing decisions?
10. Compare and contrast a trade discount and a quantity discount.
11. What is the reason for using the term *F.O.B.*?
12. What are the major methods used for transfer pricing?

Video Case 19.1

Pricing Renewable Energy Projects: Think Long-Term

John Miggins, a former sales representative for Standard Renewable Energy in Oklahoma, would tell customers to think long-term when thinking about buying renewable energy equipment for residential or commercial use. Although solar panels or a wind turbine will allow customers to generate enough power to replace much or all of the electricity they currently buy from a utility company, the out-of-pocket cost is hardly a quick fix for kilowatt sticker shock. Installing a wind turbine can cost $17,500, and a solar power setup for an average home can cost up to $40,000.

Still, demand for renewable energy equipment has been steadily rising for more than a decade as consumers and businesses have become interested in environmentally friendly power sources. Manufacturers around the world are constantly introducing new, high-efficiency offerings for homes, factories, and other buildings. At the same time, the combination of technological advances, higher supply, and increased global competition has put downward pressure on prices. At one point, so many manufacturers were making so many silicon solar panels that the surplus and the competition pushed panel prices down by 50 percent in 1 year.

These dramatic price drops, and a variety of governmental tax incentives for buying energy-efficient products for homes and businesses, are bringing the cost of renewable energy much closer to the cost of energy from conventional sources, such as coal and nuclear power. As prices move ever lower, the market expands, because more consumers and business buyers see solar and wind generation as viable alternatives to their current power sources. These days, small and midsize solar panel installations and wind turbines are popping up in many places, like homes and individual businesses. In addition, power companies are installing renewable energy equipment to generate electricity on a large scale.

John Miggins warned his customers against expecting a quick return on their investment in renewable energy equipment. He stated that businesses that install solar panels usually get 60 percent of their investment back within 6 years and 100 percent back within 10 years. Consumer installations do not earn back their cost as quickly as commercial installations, simply because homes do not use as much electricity as businesses. Miggins also recognized that customers care about things other than price—they also want a feeling of security and a sense of confidence in the seller who provides their new energy equipment.

When Miggins worked for Standard Renewable Energy, his prices took into account the company's buying power and sales volume. The pieces of equipment he ordered for customers were bundled with larger deliveries to the company's facilities, which reduced the shipping costs paid by individual buyers. And toward the end of a month, when Miggins wanted to close deals and make his sales quota, customers were likely to get an even better price when they placed an order.[22]

Questions for Discussion

1. When pricing its products, what external factors should Standard Renewable Energy pay particular attention to, and why?
2. How are value-conscious, price-conscious, and prestige-conscious customers likely to react to the price of a wind turbine?
3. Does geographic pricing affect what business customers pay for a wind turbine they buy from Standard Renewable Energy compared to prices paid by nonbusiness customers? Explain your answer.

Case 19.2

Take You Out to the Ball Game? Let Me Check the Price First

When the Chicago White Sox play the Chicago Cubs, the Sox raise single-game ticket prices, because the cross-town rivalry attracts so many local fans. The Atlanta Braves raise ticket prices when the Yankees come to town, knowing that fans will flock to the stadium for this matchup. The San Francisco Giants, Minnesota Twins, Oakland Athletics, Chicago Cubs, and other baseball teams also change single-game ticket prices depending on demand. This trend toward dynamic pricing is now spreading to other sports. The Washington Capitals hockey team and the Washington

Wizards basketball team are two of a growing list of teams that use this pricing approach for single-game tickets (not for season tickets).

Before baseball's Giants instituted dynamic pricing, team marketers wondered how fans would react. "They are familiar with this type of pricing in the airline and hotel industry," says the head of ticket sales, "but this was a big leap for a sports team to implement the idea into the box office." Although the Giants had been varying prices depending on which team was visiting, its marketers knew that demand was higher at certain points in the season and on different days of the week. Switching to dynamic pricing enables the Giants to stimulate demand during slower periods and increase revenue during periods of peak demand.

© iStockphoto.com/Franckreporter

The Chicago White Sox team uses dynamic pricing to get as many people into the seats as possible. The team has a committee that meets weekly to review sales data for individual games and for the season, and decide on price changes for the coming week. Except for seats that have been sold to season ticket holders, single-game tickets may be priced up or down at any time. Buyers who get their tickets well in advance usually get the best prices, especially for games scheduled early in the season and games against teams that are not high in the standings. Filling seats also means higher revenues from team merchandise, parking fees, and food sales.

Marketers for the Minnesota Twins like the flexibility of dynamic pricing. In the past, they had to set prices months before the season started, to have time to print brochures and tickets. Now they can make last-minute price adjustments after checking weather forecasts, team rankings, player trades, pitching line-ups, and other factors. If they've priced tickets for a particular game too low—meaning sales are much better than expected—or too high, they can boost ticket sales by making price changes as game day approaches. The Twins also use dynamic pricing to get fans excited about specially priced "Steal of the Week," single-game tickets that are offered online only.

Will all major league sports teams eventually adopt dynamic pricing? The answer depends on whether fans raise a fuss over price changes, and whether the teams currently using it are successful in filling seats and raising revenue. Some teams are testing such pricing on a small scale, applying it only to designated seating sections or specific games to determine public reaction. But if a baseball team hits a home run in pricing, chances are good that it will expand this dynamic approach to the rest of its stadium and the rest of its schedule.[23]

Questions for Discussion

1. How does dynamic pricing allow a team to judge the price elasticity of demand for a particular game and then use this information in future pricing decisions?
2. What other marketing-mix variables must teams consider when using dynamic pricing to set ticket prices? Why?
3. Do you think price competition plays a role in the way baseball teams price their single-game tickets? Explain your answer.

NOTES

[1] Jeff Bennett, "Volt Falls to Electric-Car Price War," *The Wall Street Journal*, August 6, 2013, http://online.wsj.com/article/SB10001424127887324653004578649951845301298.html (accessed August 12, 2013); Ben Klayman and Paul Lienert, "GM, Daimler Amp Up U.S. Electric Car Price War," *Reuters*, August 6, 2013, www.reuters.com/article/2013/08/06/us-autos-gm-volt-idUSBRE97511S20130806 (accessed August 12, 2013); Brooke Crothers, "Electric Car Price War? Chevy Chimes in with Volt Incentives," *Cnet*, June 12, 2013, http://news.cnet.com/8301-11386_3-57589046-76/electric-car-price-war-chevy-chimes-in-with-volt-incentives (accessed August 12, 2013); Brian Thevenot, "Electric Cars Are Getting as Cheap as Gasoline Rivals," *Los Angeles Times*, June 1, 2013, http://articles.latimes.com/2013/jun/01/autos/la-fi-0601-hy-autos-electric-cars-20130531 (accessedAugust 12, 2013).

[2] Rajneesh Suri and Kent B. Monroe, "The Effects of Time Constraints on Consumers' Judgments of Prices and Products," *Journal of Consumer Research* (June 2003): 92.

[3] "Modern Trade & Barter," International Reciprocal Trade Association, 2013, www.irta.com/index.php/about/modern-trade-barter (accessed January 3, 2014).

[4] Mary Jane Credeur and Mary Schlangenstein, "The Battle Royal for the Forward Cabin," *Bloomberg Businessweek*, June 3–9, 2013, p. 26.

[5] Drew Fitzgerald, "Fear of 'Showrooming' Fades," *The Wall Street Journal*, November 14, 2013, p. B1.

[6] Drew Fitzgerald and Paul Ziobro, "Price War Looms for Electronics," *The Wall Street Journal*, November 20, 2013, pp. B1, B6.

[7] "About Ethel M.® Chocolates," www.ethelm.com/about_us/default.aspx (accessed January 22, 2014).

[8] Kim Willsher, "The Jeweller of Kings: Cartier Exhibition Opens at the Grand Palais, Paris," *The Guardian*, December 3, 2013, www.theguardian.com/world/2013/dec/03/cartier-exhibition-opens-paris-jeweller-kings (accessed February 10, 2014).

[9] *Dictionary of Marketing Terms*, American Marketing Association, www.marketingpower.com/_layouts/Dictionary.aspx (accessed January 3, 2014).

[10] Nancy Trejos, "Hotel Room Service Finds Its Way into a Paper Bag," *USA Today*, May 16, 2013, p. 5B.

[11] Agustino Fontevecchia, "Boeing Bleeding Cash as 787 Dreamliners Cost $200M but Sell for $116M, but Productivity Is Improving," *Forbes*, May 21, 2013, www.forbes.com/sites/afontevecchia/2013/05/21/boeing-bleeding-cash-as-787-dreamliners-cost-200m-but-sell-for-116m-but-productivity-is-improving (accessed January 22, 2014).

[12] Russell S. Winer, *Pricing* (Cambridge, MA: Marketing Science Institute, 2005), p. 20.

[13] Manoj Thomas and Geeta Menon, "When Internal Reference Prices and Price Expectations Diverge: The Role of Confidence," *Journal of Marketing Research* XLIV (August 2007): 401–409.

[14] Lichtenstein, Ridgway, and Netemeyer, "Price Perceptions and Consumer Shopping Behavior."

[15] Tess Stynes, "Whole Foods Reduces Its Guidance," *The Wall Street Journal*, November 7, 2013, p. B8.

[16] Gerald E. Smith and Thomas T. Nagle, "A Question of Value," *Marketing Management* (July/August 2005): 39–40.

[17] Mina Choi, "Is This Watch Worth $72,000?" *The Wall Street Journal*, March 15, 2013, http://blogs.wsj.com/scene/2013/03/15/is-this-watch-worth-72000 (accessed January 22, 2014).

[18] Annie Gasparro, "McDonald's, Wendy's in Price Fight," *The Wall Street Journal*, May 9, 2013, p. B3.

[19] Brent Kendall, "Japan Car-Parts Executives Face Prison Terms in U.S.," *The Wall Street Journal*, May 22, 2013, p. B3.

[20] Kazunori Takada and Michael Martina, "China Fines Milk Powder Makers $110 Million for Price Fixing," *Reuters*, August 7, 2013, www.reuters.com/article/2013/08/07/us-meadjohnson-china-idUSBRE97512S20130807 (accessed January 3, 2014).

[21] Jennifer Valentino-Devries, Jeremy Singer-Vine, and Ashkan Soltani, "Websites Vary Prices, Based on Users' Information," *The Wall Street Journal*, December 24, 2012, http://online.wsj.com/news/articles/SB10001424127887323777204578189391813881534 (accessed January 21, 2014).

[22] Based on information in Diane Cardwell, "Renewable Sources of Power Survive, but in a Patchwork," *The New York Times*, April 10, 2012, www.nytimes.com/2012/04/11/business/energy-environment/renewable-energy-advances-in-the-us-despite-obstacles.html?_r=0 (accessed January 22, 2014); James Murray, "McKinsey: Solar Will Be Cost Competitive within a Decade," *Business Green*, April 18, 2012, www.businessgreen.com/bg/news/2168375/mckinsey-solar-cost-competitive-decade (accessed January 22, 2014); Ucilia Wang, "First Solar Struggles Amid Decline of Thin-Film Solar Market," *Forbes*, April 18, 2012, www.forbes.com/sites/uciliawang/2012/04/18/how-first-solar-struggles-amid-decline-of-thin-film-solar-market (accessed January 22, 2014).

[23] Based on information in Doug Williams, "Dynamic Pricing Is New Trend in Ticket Sales," ESPN, April 23, 2012, http://espn.go.com/blog/playbook/dollars/post/_/id/597/dynamic-pricing-is-new-trend-in-ticket-sales (accessed January 22, 2014); Patrick Rishe, "Dynamic Pricing: The Future of Ticket Pricing in Sports," *Forbes*, January 6, 2012, www.forbes.com/sites/prishe/2012/01/06/dynamic-pricing-the-future-of-ticket-pricing-in-sports/2 (accessed January 22, 2014); Tim Tucker, "Braves Join New Trend in Ticketing: Dynamic Pricing," *Atlanta Journal-Constitution*, February 15, 2012, www.ajc.com/news/sports/baseball/braves-join-new-trend-in-ticketing-dynamic-pricing/nQRMH (accessed January 22, 2014); Ed Sherman, "White Sox Get Dynamic about Ticket Pricing," *Crain's Chicago Business*, February 2, 2012, www.chicagobusiness.com/article/20120202/BLOGS04/120209957/white-sox-get-dynamic-about-ticket-pricing (accessed January 22, 2014); Ameet Sachdev, "Baseball Teams Get Dynamic with Ticket Pricing," *The Chicago Tribune*, May 12, 2013, http://articles.chicagotribune.com/2013-05-12/business/ct-biz-0512-stub-hub–20130512_1_stubhub-bleacher-ticket-ticket-reselling (accessed January 22, 2014).

Feature Notes

[a] Leslie Scism, "State Farm Is There: As You Drive," *The Wall Street Journal*, August 4, 2013, http://online.wsj.com/article/SB10001424127887323420604578647950497541958.html (accessed August 13, 2013); Marcus Amick, "Like It or Not, Insurance Rates Are Being Driven by Tech That Tracks How and Where You Drive," *Digital Trends*, August 2, 2013, www.digitaltrends.com/cars/like-it-or-not-insurance-rates-driven-by-technology-that-tracks-how-and-where-you-drive-is-gaining-momentum (accessed August 13, 2013); Karl Henkel, "Pay-as-You-Drive Insurance Catching On," *Detroit News*, August 21, 2013, www.detroitnews.com/article/20130821/AUTO01/308210113/Pay-you-drive-insurance-catching-on?odyssey=mod%7Cnewswell%7Ctext%7CFRONTPAGE%7Cs (accessed August 22, 2013).

[b] Joe Polazzolo, "Apple Ruling Heaps Doubt on 'MFN' Clauses," *The Wall Street Journal*, July 14, 2013, http://online.wsj.com/article/SB10001424127887323664204578605880157245830.html (accessed August 8, 2013); WSJ Staff, "Apple E-Books Suit: What Is 'Agency Pricing'?" *The Wall Street Journal*, April 11, 2012, http://blogs.wsj.com/digits/2012/04/11/what-is-agency-pricing (accessed August 8, 2013); Connie Guglielmo, "Publishers Object to Government's Remedies against Apple in E-Book Case," *Forbes*, August 8, 2013, www.forbes.com/sites/connieguglielmo/2013/08/08/publishers-object-to-governments-remedies-against-apple-in-e-book-case (accessed August 8, 2013).

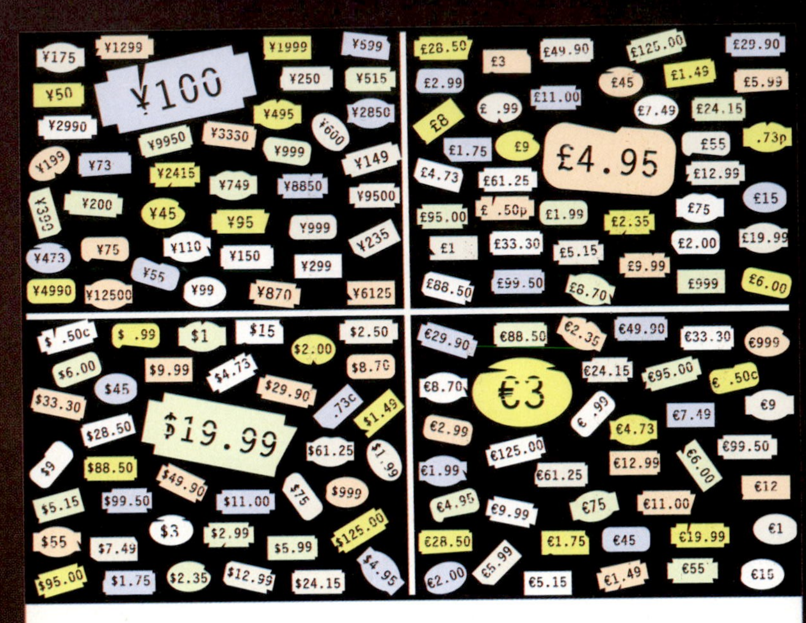

chapter 20

Setting Prices

OBJECTIVES

20-1 Identify issues related to developing pricing objectives.

20-2 Discuss the importance of identifying the target market's evaluation of price.

20-3 Explain how marketers analyze competitors' prices.

20-4 Describe the bases used for setting prices.

20-5 Explain the different types of pricing strategies.

20-6 Describe the selection of a specific price.

MARKETING INSIGHTS

Getting a Present Every Month through Subscription Pricing

Subscription pricing is a fast-growing trend in many product categories, with customers signing up to receive monthly deliveries of items selected for the season, for a theme, or for personal taste. From deluxe snacks and designer accessories to beauty creams and bow ties, subscription pricing can bring almost anything to the customer's mailbox, month after month.

Birchbox was an early pioneer in subscription pricing of boxed shipments of sample-size beauty products. In 2010, Birchbox's founders invited subscribers to sign up online, specify personal-care preferences, and receive a box of samples every month for one low fee, including shipping costs. Three years later, Birchbox had 400,000 subscribers and was ringing up $40 million in annual revenue from subscriptions and from the sale of full-size products.

For customers, one big benefit of subscription pricing is value. The products in each box are generally valued at two or three times the price of a month's subscription. Another appeal is the element of surprise. Subscribers don't know exactly what they'll receive in any given month. Finally, subscriptions allow customers to try different products without making a major investment. For marketers, subscriptions can lead to a steady revenue stream, long-term customer loyalty, and opportunities for testing new products.

Even the world's largest retailer has tried subscription pricing. In a year-long test, Walmart's Goodies unit offered a monthly box of snacks worth much more than the subscription price of $7. When Goodies was discontinued, Walmart said it had learned many lessons it would apply to its future marketing efforts.[1]

Because price has such a profound impact on a firm's success, finding the right pricing strategy is crucial. Marketers at some firms have discovered that customers are willing to pay a fee every month to receive products in the mail that save them time and money or introduce them to new problem-solving goods. However, marketers must carefully select a pricing strategy that is both profitable for the company and reasonable to the customers. Selecting a pricing strategy is one of the fundamental components of the process of setting prices.

In this chapter, we examine six stages of a process that marketers can use when setting prices. Figure 20.1 illustrates these stages. Stage 1 is the development of a pricing objective that is compatible with the organization's overall marketing objectives. Stage 2 entails assessing the target market's evaluation of price. Stage 3 involves evaluating competitors' prices, which helps determine the role of price in the marketing strategy. Stage 4 requires choosing a basis for setting prices. Stage 5 is the selection of a pricing strategy, or the guidelines for using price in the marketing mix. Stage 6, determining the final price, depends on environmental forces and marketers' understanding and use of a systematic approach to establishing prices. These stages are guidelines that provide a logical sequence for establishing prices, not rigid steps that must be followed in a particular order.

20-1 DEVELOPMENT OF PRICING OBJECTIVES

The first step in setting prices is developing **pricing objectives**—goals that describe what a firm wants to achieve through pricing. Developing pricing objectives is an important task because they form the basis for decisions for other stages of the pricing process. Thus, pricing objectives must be stated explicitly and in measurable terms. Objectives should also include a time frame for accomplishing them.

Marketers must ensure that pricing objectives are consistent with the firm's marketing and overall objectives because pricing objectives influence decisions in many functional areas, including finance, accounting, and production. A marketer can use both short- and long-term pricing objectives and can employ one or multiple pricing objectives. For instance, a firm may wish to increase market share by 18 percent over the next three years, achieve a 15 percent return on investment, and promote an image of quality in the marketplace. In this section,

pricing objectives Goals that describe what a firm wants to achieve through pricing

Figure 20.1 Stages for Establishing Prices

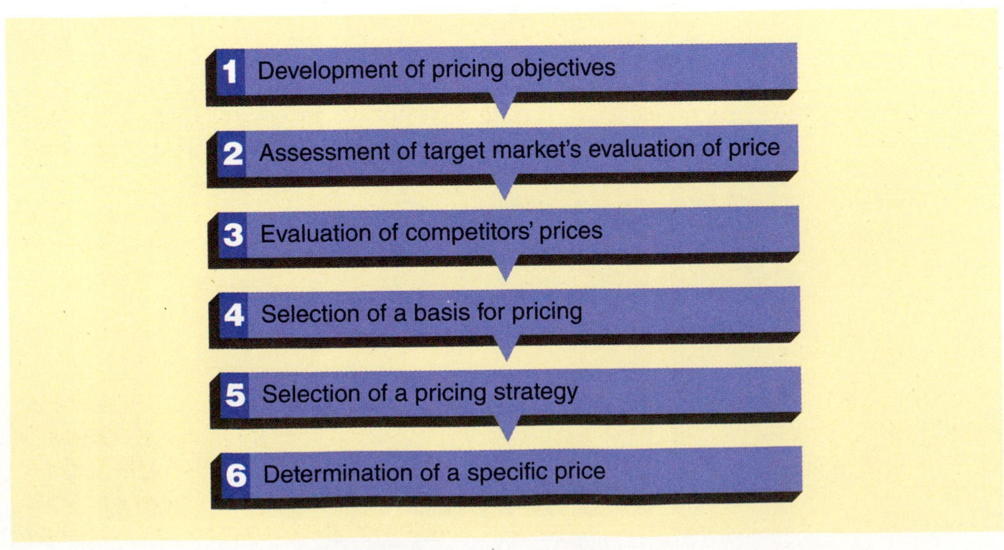

Table 20.1 Pricing Objectives and Typical Actions Taken to Achieve Them

Objective	Possible Action
Survival	Adjust price levels so the firm can increase sales volume to match organizational expenses.
Profit	Identify price and cost levels that allow the firm to maximize profit.
Return on investment	Identify price levels that enable the firm to yield targeted ROI.
Market share	Adjust price levels so the firm can maintain or increase sales relative to competitors' sales.
Cash flow	Set price levels to encourage rapid sales.
Status quo	Identify price levels that help stabilize demand and sales.
Product quality	Set prices to recover research and development expenditures and establish a high-quality image.

we examine some of the pricing objectives companies might set. Table 20.1 shows the major pricing objectives and typical actions associated with them.

20-1a Survival

Survival is one of the most fundamental pricing objectives. This generally involves temporarily setting prices low, at times below costs, in order to attract more sales. Because price is a flexible ingredient in the marketing mix, survival strategy can be useful in keeping a company afloat by increasing sales volume. Most organizations will tolerate setbacks, such as short-run losses and internal upheaval, if necessary for survival.

20-1b Profit

Although a business may claim that its objective is to maximize profits for its owners, the objective of profit maximization is rarely operational because its achievement is difficult to measure. Therefore, profit objectives tend to be set at levels that the owners and top-level decision makers view as satisfactory and attainable. Specific profit objectives may be stated in terms of either actual dollar amounts or a percentage of sales revenues.

20-1c Return on Investment

Pricing to attain a specified rate of return on the company's investment is a profit-related pricing objective. A return on investment (ROI) pricing objective generally requires some trial and error, as it is unusual for all data and inputs required to determine the necessary ROI to be available when first setting prices. Many pharmaceutical companies use ROI pricing objectives because of the high level of investment in research and development required.

20-1d Market Share

Many firms establish pricing objectives to maintain or increase market share, which is a product's sales in relation to total industry sales. For instance, Google priced its Nexus 7 tablet at less than half of an iPad Mini Retina, but offers similar features to its higher-priced competitor. Developing a product with high-end specifications that retails at a low-end price has helped Google to gain traction in the fiercely competitive tablet computer market.[2] High relative market shares often translate into high profits for firms. The Profit Impact of Market Strategies (PIMS) studies, conducted annually since the 1960s, have shown that both market share and product quality influence profitability.[3] Thus, marketers often use an increase in market share as a primary pricing objective.

Maintaining or increasing market share need not depend on growth in industry sales. An organization can increase its market share even if sales for the total industry are flat or decreasing. On the other hand, a firm's sales volume can increase while its market share decreases if the overall market grows.

20-1e Cash Flow

Some companies set prices so they can recover cash as quickly as possible. Financial managers understandably want to recover quickly the capital spent to develop products. Choosing this pricing objective may have the support of a marketing manager if he or she anticipates a short product life cycle. Although it may be acceptable in some situations, the use of cash flow and recovery as an objective oversimplifies the contribution of price to profits. If this pricing objective results in high prices, competitors with lower prices may gain a large share of the market.

20-1f Status Quo

In some cases, an organization is in a favorable position and desires nothing more than to maintain the status quo. Status quo objectives can focus on several dimensions, such as maintaining a certain market share, meeting (but not beating) competitors' prices, achieving price stability, and maintaining a favorable public image. A status quo pricing objective can reduce a firm's risks by helping to stabilize demand for its products. A firm that chooses status quo pricing objectives risks minimizing pricing as a competitive tool, which could lead to a climate of nonprice competition. Professionals such as accountants and attorneys often operate in such an environment.

Emerging Trends

Paying for the Fast Lane

More states and cities are adding special toll lanes that allow drivers to pay extra for the privilege of avoiding traffic congestion during rush hours and other periods of peak demand. The objective of such price-managed highways is to keep traffic moving, not necessarily to bring in incremental revenue. In some cases, the tolls vary depending on current traffic conditions. In Virginia, for example, sensors track the speed and volume of traffic along I-495 leading toward Washington, DC, and tolls are increased or decreased every few minutes as conditions change. Similar projects in Minnesota and California monitor traffic and adjust tolls every few minutes during the morning and afternoon commute.

Although price-managed lanes are relatively new, early results suggest that they are accomplishing their objective of unsnarling traffic. When Florida added two toll lanes between Fort Lauderdale and Miami on I-95, drivers who paid the toll arrived much sooner than they would have in the regular lanes or even in the high-occupancy carpool lane. And because many drivers opted for the toll lanes, speeds on the non-toll lanes increased as well.

Price-managed lanes in Houston have not only reduced congestion in the non-toll lanes, but they've also encouraged commuters to use mass transit. One month after authorities increased the one-way toll from $5 to $7, the transit authority reported a 15 percent increase in the number of passengers boarding commuter buses at rush hour. Despite commuter gripes about paying more for the fast lane, price-managed lanes may be coming to a highway near you very soon.[a]

20-1g Product Quality

A company may have the objective of leading its industry in product quality. A high price may signal to customers that the product is of a high quality. Attaining a high level of product quality is generally more expensive for the firm, as the costs of materials, research, and development may be greater. With a basic pair of boots retailing for hundreds of dollars, Timberland is not a low-priced brand. However, it is a brand associated with quality and timeless style, as shown in this advertisement. An image of one of the brand's boots is placed against a backdrop that shows a close-up of the fine quality leather and precise stitching featured in all Timberland products. The line at the bottom, "Best then. Better now . . ." indicates that the company has always cared about quality and continues to offer a great product. The products and brands that customers perceive to be of high quality are more likely to survive in a competitive marketplace because they trust these products more, even if the prices are higher.

Product Quality Pricing Objective
This advertisement emphasizes the high quality of Timberland boots, which is something that the company has taken pride in for more than 40 years.

20-2 ASSESSMENT OF THE TARGET MARKET'S EVALUATION OF PRICE

After developing pricing objectives, marketers must assess the target market's evaluation of price. Despite the general assumption that price is a major issue for buyers, the importance of price varies depending on the type of product, target market, and the purchase situation. For instance, buyers are probably more sensitive to gasoline prices than luggage prices. We purchase gasoline regularly and notice fluctuations in price, but since luggage is more likely to be perceived as a long-term investment, we expect to pay more for it. With respect to the type of target market, adults frequently must pay more than children for goods and services, including clothing, meals, and movie tickets, because they consume a larger quantity.

The purchase situation also affects the buyer's view of price. Most moviegoers would never pay, in other situations, the prices charged for soft drinks, popcorn, and candy at concession stands. The markup for popcorn in movie theaters can be up to 1,275 percent.[4] Nevertheless, consumers are willing to pay the markup to enhance their movie experience by enjoying buttery popcorn at the theater. By assessing the target market's evaluation of price, a marketer is in a better position to know how much emphasis to put on price in the overall marketing strategy. Information about the target market's price evaluation may also help a marketer determine how far above the competition the firm can set its prices.

Today, because some consumers seek less-expensive products and the Internet allows consumers to shop more selectively than ever before, some manufacturers and retailers focus on the value of products in their communications with customers. Value is more than just a product's price. It combines price with quality attributes, which customers use to differentiate among competing brands. Generally, consumers want to maximize the value they receive for their money. Consumers may even perceive relatively expensive products, such as organic produce, to have great value if the products have desirable features or characteristics. Consumers are also generally willing to pay a higher price for products that offer convenience and save time. Table 20.2 illustrates this point by showing the unit price difference between

Table 20.2 Examples of Perceptions of Product Value

Basic, Cost-Effective Product	Expensive, Time-Saving Product
Whole loose bagels, \$0.59 each	Sliced packaged bagels, \$0.65 each
Whole broccoli, \$1.49/lb	Florets broccoli, \$3.99/lb
Whole carrots, \$1.49/lb	Baby carrots, \$3.99/lb
Whole chicken, \$1.49/lb	Cut-up chicken, \$1.99/lb
Whole feta cheese, \$3.23/8 oz	Crumbled feta cheese, \$8.65/8 oz
Whole Granny Smith apples, \$1.99/lb	Sliced Granny Smith apples, \$3.97/lb
Lean ground chuck (ground), \$3.99/lb	Lean ground chuck (patties), \$5.99/lb

Source: "Supermarket Smarts," *Consumer Reports ShopSmart*, www.shopsmartmag.org/files/Supermarket_smarts.pdf (accessed December 28, 2013).

basic food products and time-saving food products. Companies that offer both affordable prices and high quality, like Target, have altered consumers' expectations about how much quality they must sacrifice for low prices. Understanding the importance of a product to customers, as well as their expectations about quality and value, helps marketers assess correctly the target market's evaluation of price.

20-3 EVALUATION OF COMPETITORS' PRICES

In most cases, marketers are in a better position to establish prices when they know the prices charged for competing brands, which is the next step in establishing prices. Learning competitors' prices should be a regular part of marketing research. Some grocery and department stores even employ comparative shoppers who systematically collect data on prices at competitors' stores. Companies may also purchase price lists from syndicated marketing research services.

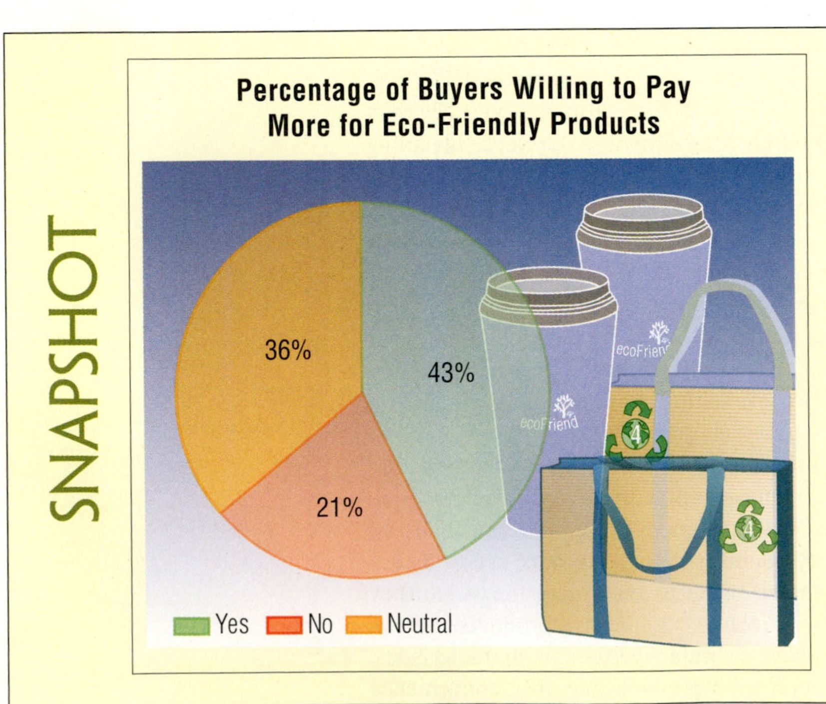

Source: Better Homes and Gardens/ BrandSpark survey of 2,735 consumers.

Uncovering competitors' prices is not always an easy task, especially in producer and reseller markets, where prices are often closely guarded. Even if a marketer has access to competitors' price lists, they may not reflect the actual prices at which competitive products sell because negotiation is involved.

Knowing the prices of competing brands is essential for a marketer. Regardless of its actual costs, a firm does not want to sell its product at a price that is significantly above competitors' prices because the products may not sell as well, or at a price that is significantly below because customers may believe the product is of low quality. Particularly in an industry in which price competition prevails, a marketer needs competitive price information to ensure that a firm's prices are the same as, or slightly lower than, competitors' prices.

Dior

e.l.f.

Competitor's Prices
Both Christian Dior and e.l.f. Cosmetics emphasize the quality of their makeup. However, these products sell for very different prices. Which would you prefer to buy?

In some instances, an organization's prices are designed to be slightly above competitors' prices, such as with Apple brand products, to lend an exclusive image and to signal product quality to consumers. Compare the two advertisements below. One is for Christian Dior brand lipstick, a high-end brand. Marketers underscore the exclusive image by featuring the actress, Natalie Portman, in the advertisement. The other is for eyes lips face (e.l.f.) brand makeup, whose lipsticks are priced starting at only $1, according to the advertisement. This advertisement does not feature a celebrity, but instead focuses on the products themselves and their low prices. Both of these brands emphasize the high quality of their makeup.

20-4 SELECTION OF A BASIS FOR PRICING

The fourth step in establishing prices involves selecting a basis for pricing: cost, demand, and/or competition. Marketers determine the appropriate pricing basis by analyzing the type of product, the market structure of the industry, the brand's market share position relative to competing brands, and customer characteristics. Although we discuss each basis separately in this section, an organization generally considers at least two, or perhaps all three, dimensions. Thus, if a company uses cost as a primary basis for setting prices, its marketers are still aware of and concerned about competitors' prices. If a company uses demand as a basis for pricing, marketers still must consider costs and competitors' prices. Indeed, cost is a factor in every pricing decision because it establishes a price minimum below which the firm will not be able to recoup its production and other costs. Demand, likewise, sets an effective price maximum above which customers are unlikely to buy the product. Setting appropriate prices can be a difficult balance for firms. A high price may reduce demand for the product, but a low price will hurt profit margins and may instill in customers a perception that the product is of low quality. Firms must weigh many different factors when setting prices, including costs, competition, customer buying behavior and price sensitivity, manufacturing capacity, and product life cycles.

20-4a Cost-Based Pricing

With **cost-based pricing**, a flat dollar amount or percentage is added to the cost of the product, which means marketers calculate and apply a desired level of profit to the cost of the product and apply it uniformly. Cost-based pricing does not necessarily take into account the economic aspects of supply and demand, nor must it relate to just one pricing strategy or pricing objective. It is a straightforward and easy-to-implement method. Two common forms of cost-based pricing are cost-plus and markup pricing.

Cost-Plus Pricing

With **cost-plus pricing**, the seller's costs are determined (usually during a project or after a project is completed), and then a specified dollar amount or percentage of the cost is added to the seller's cost to establish the price. When production costs are difficult to predict, cost-plus pricing is appropriate. Projects involving custom-made equipment and commercial construction are often priced using this technique. The government also frequently expects cost-plus pricing from defense contractors. One pitfall for the buyer is that the seller may increase stated costs to gain a larger profit base. Furthermore, some costs, such as overhead, may be difficult to determine. In periods of rapid inflation, cost-plus pricing is popular, especially when the producer must use raw materials that frequently fluctuate in price. In industries in which cost-plus pricing is common and sellers have similar costs, price competition will not be especially intense.

Markup Pricing

With **markup pricing**, commonly used by retailers, a product's price is derived by adding a predetermined percentage of the cost, called *markup*, to the cost of the product. For instance, most supermarkets mark up prices by at least 25 percent, whereas warehouse clubs, like Costco and Sam's Club, have a lower average markup of around 14 percent.[5] Markups can vary a great deal depending on the product and the situation. Although the percentage markup in a retail store varies from one category of goods to another—35 percent of cost for hardware items and 100 percent of cost for greeting cards, for example—the same percentage is often used to determine the prices on items within a single product category, and the percentage markup may be largely standardized across an industry at the retail level. Using a rigid percentage markup for a specific product category reduces pricing to a routine task that can be performed quickly.

The following example illustrates how percentage markups are determined and distinguishes between two methods of stating a markup. Assume a retailer purchases a can of tuna at 45 cents and adds 15 cents to the cost, making the price 60 cents. There are two ways to look at the markup, as a percentage of cost or as a percentage of selling price:

$$\text{markup as percentage of cost} = \frac{\text{markup}}{\text{cost}}$$

$$= \frac{15}{45}$$

$$= 33.3\%$$

cost-based pricing Adding a dollar amount or percentage to the cost of the product

cost-plus pricing Adding a specified dollar amount or percentage to the seller's cost

markup pricing Adding to the cost of the product a predetermined percentage of that cost

$$\text{markup as percentage of selling price} = \frac{\text{markup}}{\text{selling price}}$$
$$= \frac{15}{60}$$
$$= 25.0\%$$

The markup as a percentage of cost is 33.3 percent, while the markup as a percentage of price is only 25 percent. Obviously, when discussing a percentage markup, it is important to know whether the markup is based on cost or selling price.

Markups normally reflect expectations about operating costs, risks, and stock turnovers. Wholesalers and manufacturers often suggest standard retail markups that are considered profitable. To the extent that retailers use similar markups for the same product category, price competition is reduced. In addition, using rigid markups is convenient and is the major reason retailers favor this method.

20-4b Demand-Based Pricing

Marketers sometimes base prices on the level of demand for the product. When **demand-based pricing** is used, customers pay a higher price at times when demand for the product is strong and a lower price when demand is weak. For instance, hotels often offer reduced rates during periods of low demand when they have excess capacity in the form of empty rooms. The belief behind this pricing basis is that it is better to take a lower profit margin on a sale than no revenue at all. Some telephone companies, such as Sprint and AT&T, also use demand-based pricing by charging peak and off-peak rates or offering free cell phone minutes during off-peak times. Some concert and sporting venues also have implemented demand-based pricing for ticket sales. For instance, all tickets for Minnesota Twins baseball games are sold using demand-based pricing. Ticket prices are adjusted daily based on real-time market conditions using Digonex's Sports and Entertainment Analytical Ticketing System (SEATS™), a pricing system that optimizes prices based upon many factors.[6]

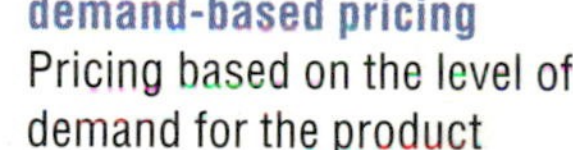

demand-based pricing Pricing based on the level of demand for the product

To use this pricing basis, a marketer must be able to estimate the quantity of a product consumers will demand at different times and how demand will be affected by changes in

Demand-Based Pricing
Airline companies engage in demand-based pricing. When demand for a specific flight is higher, the fares will be higher, and when demand is lower, the fares will be lower.

the price. The marketer then chooses the price that generates the highest total revenue. The effectiveness of demand-based pricing depends on the marketer's ability to estimate demand accurately. Compared with cost-based pricing, demand-based pricing places a firm in a better position to reach high profit levels, as long as demand is strong at times and buyers value the product at levels sufficiently above the product's cost.

20-4c Competition-Based Pricing

With **competition-based pricing**, an organization considers costs to be secondary to competitors' prices. This is a common method among producers of relatively homogeneous products, particularly when the target market considers price to be an important purchase consideration. A firm that uses competition-based pricing may choose to set their prices below competitors' or at the same level. Competitors believe that Amazon's competition-based pricing model has been an attempt to gain monopoly control of many retail markets. Amazon uses highly sophisticated analytics to gauge consumer demand and compare its prices to competitors. To stay ahead of the competition, Amazon adjusts its prices more than 2.5 million times each day. To compare, Walmart and Best Buy change their prices about 50,000 times each month.[7]

20-5 SELECTION OF A PRICING STRATEGY

A *pricing strategy* is a course of action designed to achieve pricing objectives, which are set to help marketers solve the practical problems of setting prices. The extent to which a business uses any of the following strategies depends on its pricing and marketing objectives, the markets for its products, the degree of product differentiation, the product's life-cycle stage, and other factors. Generally, pricing strategies help marketers solve the practical problems of establishing prices. Table 20.3 lists the most common pricing strategies, which we discuss in this section.

competition-based pricing Pricing influenced primarily by competitors' prices

Table 20.3 Common Pricing Strategies

Differential Pricing	**Psychological Pricing**
Negotiated pricing	Reference pricing
Secondary-market pricing	Bundle pricing
Periodic discounting	Multiple-unit pricing
Random discounting	Everyday low prices
	Odd-even pricing
New-Product Pricing	Customary pricing
Price skimming	Prestige pricing
Penetration pricing	
	Professional Pricing
Product-Line Pricing	
Captive pricing	**Promotional Pricing**
Premium pricing	Price leaders
Bait pricing	Special-event pricing
Price lining	Comparison discounting

20-5a Differential Pricing

An important issue in pricing decisions is whether to use a single price or different prices for the same product. Using a single price has several benefits. A primary advantage is simplicity. A single price is easily understood by both employees and customers. Since many salespeople and customers dislike negotiating prices, having a single price reduces the risk of a marketer developing an adversarial relationship with customers. The use of a single price does create some challenges, however. If the single price is too high, some potential customers may be unable to afford the product. If it is too low, the organization loses revenue from those customers who would have paid more had the price been higher.

Differential pricing means charging different prices to different buyers for the same quality and quantity of product. A recent ruling has cleared the way for vendors to use differential pricing by depending on the form of payment. It would allow them to charge more to customers who pay with a credit card, versus those who pay with a debit card or cash.[8] For differential pricing to be effective, the market must consist of multiple segments with different price sensitivities. When this method is employed, caution should be used to avoid confusing or antagonizing customers. Differential pricing can occur in several ways, including negotiated pricing, secondary-market pricing, periodic discounting, and random discounting.

Negotiated Pricing

Negotiated pricing occurs when the final price is established through bargaining between the seller and the customer. Negotiated pricing occurs in a number of industries and at all levels of distribution. Even when there is a predetermined stated price or a price list, manufacturers, wholesalers, and retailers still may negotiate to establish the final sales price. Consumers commonly negotiate prices for houses, cars, and used equipment. Customers rarely pay the list price on a car, for instance, because they go to a car dealership expecting to negotiate with the seller until they arrive at a price that is satisfactory to both the customer and the seller. Negotiation can be very important in setting a good price, and all negotiators should enter into a discussion with a strategy in mind. This involves preparing negotiation tactics and understanding all the variables and risks at play.[9] Managing personal chemistry between the negotiators is just as important as settling on prices. The negotiation process can help build relationships and increase understanding between different parties in a supply-chain relationship.

Secondary-Market Pricing

Secondary-market pricing means setting one price for the primary target market and a different price for another market. Often the price charged in the secondary market is lower. However, when the costs of serving a secondary market are higher than normal, secondary-market customers may have to pay a higher price. Examples of secondary markets include a geographically-isolated domestic market, a market in a foreign country, and a segment willing to purchase a product during off-peak times (such as "early-bird" diners at restaurants and off-peak hour cell phone users). Secondary markets give an organization an opportunity to use excess capacity and stabilize the allocation of resources.

Periodic Discounting

Periodic discounting is the temporary reduction of prices on a patterned or systematic basis. As a result, many retailers have annual holiday sales, and some apparel stores have regular seasonal sales. From the marketer's point of view, a major problem with periodic discounting is customers can predict when the reductions will occur and may delay their purchases until they can take advantage of the lower prices. Periodic discounting is less effective in an environment where many consumers shop online because they can more easily comparison shop for a better deal even during non-sale times.

differential pricing Charging different prices to different buyers for the same quality and quantity of product

negotiated pricing Establishing a final price through bargaining between seller and customer

secondary-market pricing Setting one price for the primary target market and a different price for another market

periodic discounting Temporary reduction of prices on a patterned or systematic basis

Random Discounting

To alleviate the problem of customers knowing when discounting will occur, some organizations employ **random discounting**—that is, they reduce their prices temporarily on a nonsystematic basis. When price reductions of a product occur randomly, current users of that brand are not able to predict when the reductions will occur. Therefore, they are less likely to delay their purchases in anticipation of buying the product at a lower price. Marketers also use random discounting to attract new customers. Random discounting can also be useful to draw attention to a relatively new product. Many grocery store items, such as a new kind of yogurt or cereal, will use random discounting. Marketers must be careful not to use random discounting too often, however, because customers will learn to wait for the discounts.

Whether they use periodic discounting or random discounting, retailers often employ tensile pricing when putting products on sale. *Tensile pricing* involves making a broad statement about price reductions, as opposed to detailing specific price discounts. Examples of tensile pricing would be statements like "20 to 50 percent off," "up to 75 percent off," and "save 10 percent or more." Generally, the tensile price that mentions only the maximum reduction (such as "up to 50 percent off") generates the highest customer response.[10]

20-5b New-Product Pricing

Setting the base price for a new product is a necessary part of formulating a marketing strategy. Marketers can easily adjust the base price in industries that are not subject to government price controls, and its establishment is one of the most fundamental decisions in the marketing mix. The base price can be set high to recover development costs quickly or provide a reference point for developing discount prices for different market segments. When a marketer sets base prices, he or she considers how quickly competitors are expected to enter the market, whether they will mount a strong campaign on entry, and what effect their entry will have on the development of primary demand. Two strategies used in new-product pricing are price skimming and penetration pricing.

Price Skimming

Some consumers are willing to pay a high price for an innovative product, either because of its novelty or because of the prestige or status that ownership confers. **Price skimming** is the strategy of charging the highest possible price for a product during the introduction stage of its life cycle. The seller essentially "skims the cream" off the market, which helps a firm to recover the high costs of R&D more quickly. This approach provides the most flexible introductory base price. Demand tends to be inelastic in the introductory stage of the product life cycle.

Price skimming can provide several benefits. A skimming policy can generate much-needed initial cash flows to help offset development costs. Price skimming protects the marketer from problems that arise when the price is set too low to cover costs. When a firm introduces a product, its production capacity may be limited. A skimming price can help keep demand consistent with the firm's production capabilities. However, price skimming strategies can be dangerous because they may make the product appear more lucrative than it actually is to potential competitors. A firm also risks misjudging demand and facing insufficient sales at the higher price. New-product prices should be based on both the value to the customer and competitive products.

Penetration Pricing

At the opposite extreme, **penetration pricing** is the strategy of setting a low price for a new product. The main purpose of setting a low price is to build market share quickly to encourage product trial by the target market and discourage competitors from entering the market. This approach is less flexible for a marketer than price skimming, because it is more difficult to raise the price of a product from a penetration price than to lower or discount a skimming

random discounting Temporary reduction of prices on an unsystematic basis

price skimming Charging the highest possible price that buyers who most desire the product will pay

penetration pricing Setting prices below those of competing brands to penetrate a market and gain a significant market share quickly

price. It is not unusual for a firm to use a penetration price after having skimmed the market with a higher price.

Penetration pricing can be especially beneficial when a marketer suspects that competitors could enter the market easily. If the low price stimulates sales, the firm may be able to order longer production runs, increasing economies of scale and resulting in decreased production costs per unit. If penetration pricing allows the marketer to gain a large market share quickly, competitors may be discouraged from entering the market. In addition, because the lower per-unit penetration price results in lower per-unit profit, the market may not appear to be especially lucrative to potential new entrants. A disadvantage of penetration pricing is that it places a firm in a less-flexible pricing position. Again, it is more difficult to raise prices significantly than it is to lower them.

20-5c Product-Line Pricing

product-line pricing Establishing and adjusting prices of multiple products within a product line

captive pricing Pricing the basic product in a product line low, while pricing related items higher

Rather than considering products on an item-by-item basis when determining pricing strategies, some marketers employ product-line pricing. **Product-line pricing** means establishing and adjusting the prices of multiple products within a product line. When marketers use product-line pricing, their goal is to maximize profits for an entire product line rather than to focus on the profitability of an individual product item. Product-line pricing can provide marketers with pricing flexibility. Thus, marketers can set prices so that one product is profitable, whereas another is less profitable but increases market share by virtue of having a low price and, therefore, selling more units.

Before setting prices for a product line, marketers evaluate the relationship among the products in the line. When products in a line are complementary, sales increases in one item raise demand for other items. For instance, desktop printers and toner cartridges are complementary products. However, when products in a line function as substitutes for one another, buyers of one product in the line are unlikely to purchase one of the other products in the same line. In this case, marketers must be sensitive to how a price change for one of the brands may affect the demand not only for that brand but also for the substitute brands. For instance, if decision makers at Procter & Gamble were considering a price change for Tide detergent, they would likely also be concerned about how the price change might influence sales of other detergents, such as Cheer, Bold, and Gain.

When marketers employ product-line pricing, they have several strategies from which to choose. These include captive pricing, premium pricing, bait pricing, and price lining.

Captive Pricing

When marketers use **captive pricing**, the basic product in a product line is priced low, but the price on the items required to operate or enhance it are higher. A common example of captive pricing is printer ink. The printer is priced quite low to attract sales, but the printer ink replacement cartridges are very expensive. Look at the advertisement for the Gillette Fusion ProGlide Styler for another example. The Styler is a multi-use facial hair grooming tool for men who have moustaches, beards, or sideburns—something that the advertisement makes clear from the image of a man's moustache. The tool itself is not very expensive, but the replacement blades

Captive Pricing
The Gillette Fusion ProGlide Styler is an example of a captive pricing strategy because the original razor is sold at a low price, but replacement blades are more expensive. Consumers cannot substitute another brand of blades.

are highly specialized and retail for nearly twice the cost of the original kit. Because the tool requires specific replacement blades, consumers cannot purchase generic or off-brand replacements to save money.

Premium Pricing

Premium pricing occurs when the highest-quality product, or the most-versatile and most desirable version of a product in a product line, is assigned the highest price. Other products in the line are priced to appeal to price-sensitive shoppers or to those who seek product-specific features. Marketers that use premium pricing often realize a significant portion of their profits from the premium-priced products. Examples of product categories in which premium pricing is common are small kitchen appliances, beer, ice cream, and television cable service. For example, Talenti brand frozen treats sells its gelato products for around 50 percent more than other non-premium frozen desserts. Talenti gelato comes in grown-up flavors such as Alphonso Mango and Argentine Caramel and features clear plastic packaging, underscoring that it is of a premium quality.[11]

Bait Pricing

To attract customers, marketers may put a low price on one item in the product line with the intention of selling a higher-priced item in the line. This strategy is known as **bait pricing**. Producers of smartphones and tablets may engage in bait pricing, selling ultra-low-priced models that lure in customers but charging extra for the most desirable features. Additional apps and subscription services can cost owners of these gadgets even more, and customers rarely factor in these costs when calculating the overall expense of the purchase.[12]

As long as a retailer has sufficient quantities of the advertised low-priced model available for sale, this strategy is acceptable. However, it may generate customer resentment if customers go to the store looking for the low-priced model and only find the high-priced model in stock. If this is done intentionally, it is called *bait and switch.* Bait and switch occurs when retailers have no intention of selling the bait product. They use the low price merely to entice customers into the store to sell them higher-priced products. Bait and switch is unethical, and in some states it is even illegal.

Price Lining

Price lining is the strategy of selling goods only at certain predetermined prices that reflect explicit price breaks. For instance, a shop may sell men's ties only at $22 and $37. This strategy is common in clothing and accessory stores. It eliminates minor price differences from the buying decision—both for customers and for managers who buy merchandise to sell in these stores.

The basic assumption in price lining is that the demand for various groups or sets of products is inelastic. If the prices are attractive, customers will concentrate their purchases without responding to slight changes in price. Thus, a women's dress shop that carries dresses priced at $85, $55, and $35 may not attract many more sales with a drop to $83, $53, and $33. The "space" between the price of $85 and $55, however, can stir changes in consumer response, with consumers viewing the higher-priced item as of higher quality. With price lining, the demand curve looks like a series of steps, as shown in Figure 20.2.

premium pricing Pricing the highest-quality or most versatile products higher than other models in the product line

bait pricing Pricing an item in a product line low with the intention of selling a higher-priced item in the line

price lining Setting a limited number of prices for selected groups or lines of merchandise

psychological pricing Pricing that attempts to influence a customer's perception of price to make a product's price more attractive

20-5d Psychological Pricing

Psychological pricing attempts to influence a customer's perception of price to make a product's price more attractive. Psychological pricing strategies encourage purchases based on consumers' emotional responses, rather than on economically rational ones. These strategies are used primarily for consumer products, rather than business products, because most business purchases follow a systematic and rational approach. In this section, we consider several

Figure 20.2 **Price Lining**

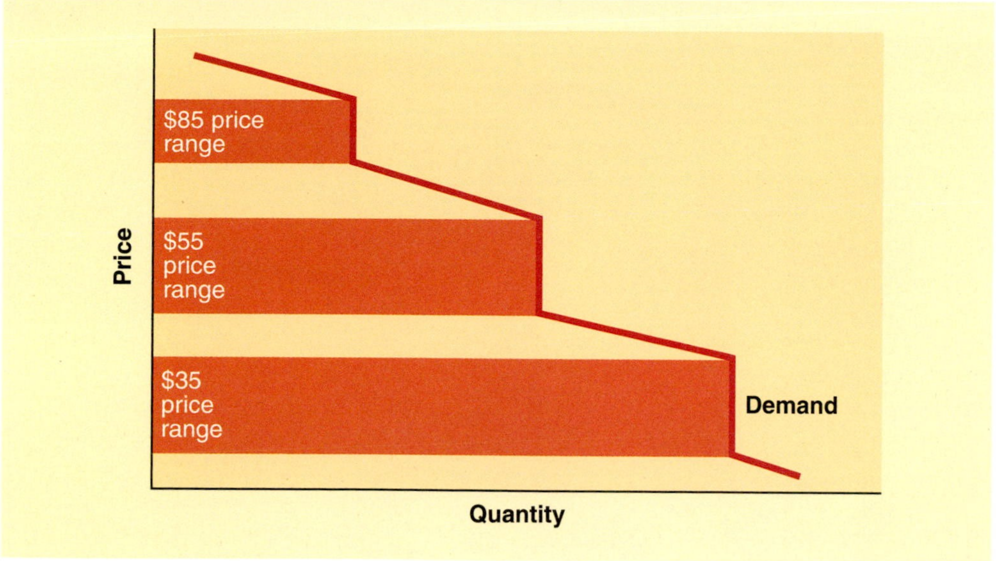

forms of psychological pricing: reference pricing, bundle pricing, multiple-unit pricing, everyday low prices (EDLP), odd-even pricing, customary pricing, and prestige pricing.

Reference Pricing

Reference pricing means pricing a product at a moderate level and physically positioning it next to a more expensive model or brand in the hope that the customer will use the higher price as a reference price (i.e., a comparison price). Because of the comparison, the customer is expected to view the moderate price more favorably than he or she would if the product were considered alone. Reference pricing is based on the "isolation effect," meaning an alternative is less attractive when viewed by itself than when compared with other alternatives.

Bundle Pricing

Bundle pricing is the packaging together of two or more products, usually of a complementary nature, to be sold for a single price. To be attractive to customers, the single price generally is markedly less than the sum of the prices of the individual products. Being able to buy the bundled combination may be of value to the customer, increasing convenience and reducing the time required to shop. Bundle pricing is common for banking and travel services, computers, and automobiles with option packages. Bundle pricing is also common among products that are used in tandem. Comcast Xfinity, for instance, offers a special rate when consumers bundle television, Internet, and phone service. Bundle pricing can help to increase customer satisfaction. It can also help firms sell slow-moving inventory and increase revenues by bundling it with products with a higher turnover.

Multiple-Unit Pricing

Many retailers (and especially supermarkets) practice **multiple-unit pricing**, which is setting a single price for two or more units of a product, such as two cans for 99 cents, rather than 50 cents per can. Especially for frequently-purchased products, this strategy can increase sales by encouraging consumers to purchase multiple units when they might otherwise have only purchased one at a time. Customers benefit from the cost savings and convenience this pricing

reference pricing Pricing a product at a moderate level and displaying it next to a more expensive model or brand

bundle pricing Packaging together two or more complementary products and selling them at a single price

multiple-unit pricing Packaging together two or more identical products and selling them at a single price

Bundle Pricing
Telecommunications companies, such as Comcast, offer bundle pricing on services such as Internet, phone, and television packages.

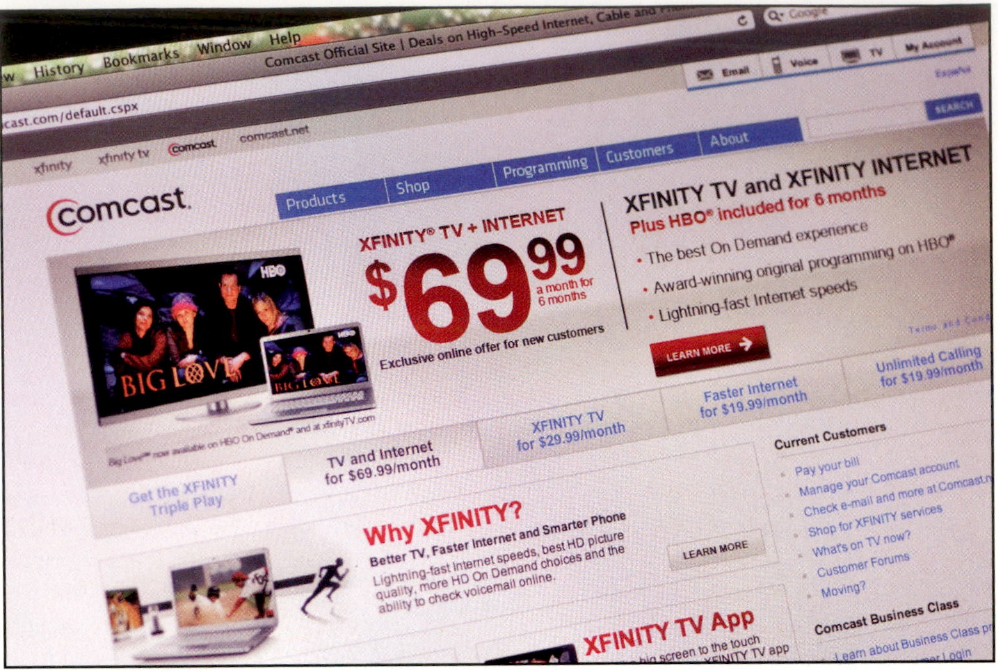

NetPhotos/Alamy

everyday low prices (EDLP) Pricing products low on a consistent basis

© 2013 Target Brands

Everyday Low Prices
This advertisement for Merona brand clothing features Target's EDLPs for apparel and shoes, emphasizing the value of these fashion-forward items.

strategy affords. A company may use multiple-unit pricing to attract new customers to its brands and, in some instances, to increase consumption. When customers buy in larger quantities, their consumption of the product may increase as it is more available. Customers who see the single price and who expect eventually to use more than one unit of the product will likely be inclined to purchase multiple units.

Discount stores and especially warehouse clubs, like Sam's Club and Costco, are major users of multiple-unit pricing. For certain products in these stores, customers receive significant per-unit price reductions when they buy packages containing multiple units of the same product.

Everyday Low Prices (EDLP)

To reduce or eliminate the use of frequent short-term price reductions, some organizations use an approach referred to as **everyday low prices (EDLP)**. When EDLPs are used, a marketer sets a low price for its products on a consistent basis, rather than setting higher prices and frequently discounting them. EDLPs, though not deeply discounted, are set low enough to make customers feel confident they are receiving a good deal. EDLPs are employed by retailers, such as Walmart, and by manufacturers, such as Procter & Gamble. A company that uses EDLP benefits from reduced promotional costs, reduced losses from frequent markdowns, and more stable sales. Look at the advertisement for Merona brand clothing, a Target store brand, which features the EDLPs of a variety of fashionable clothing and shoe choices. The advertisement shows the style and the value of this brand of clothing and reminds consumers that they must shop at Target to purchase it.

A major problem with this approach is that customers can have mixed responses. In some instances, customers believe that EDLPs are a marketing gimmick and not truly the good deal that they proclaim. Some retailers have encountered a backlash against EDLP from consumers who enjoy the thrill of hunting down the best sales. For instance, when JCPenney opted to stop promotions and coupons in favor of EDLP, some customers stopped shopping there. JCPenney marketers discovered the hard way that many consumers want to see the 20 percent off markdown and use coupons because it helps to reinforce the feeling that they are getting a good deal. The company ultimately backtracked on the EDLP policy after seeing sharp declines in sales.[13]

Odd-Even Pricing

odd-even pricing Ending the price with certain numbers to influence buyers' perceptions of the price or product

customary pricing Pricing on the basis of tradition

prestige pricing Setting prices at an artificially high level to convey prestige or a quality image

Odd-even pricing involves ending a price with certain numbers. Through this strategy, marketers try to influence buyers' perceptions of the product. It aligns with the belief among many retailers that consumers respond more positively to odd-number prices, such as $4.99, than to whole-dollar prices, such as $5, for items where customers are looking for value. Odd pricing is the strategy of setting prices using odd numbers that are slightly below whole-dollar amounts. Nine and five are the most popular ending figures for odd-number prices. This strategy assumes more of a product will be sold at $99.95 than at $100. Sellers who use this odd pricing believe that odd numbers increase sales because consumers register the dollar amount, not the cents. Odd-number pricing has been the subject of various psychological studies, but the results have been inconclusive.

Even prices, on the other hand, are often used to give a product an exclusive or upscale image. An even price is believed to influence a customer to view the product as being a high-quality, premium brand. A shirt maker, for example, may print on a premium shirt package a suggested retail price of $42.00 instead of $41.95.

Customary Pricing

With **customary pricing**, certain goods are priced on the basis of tradition. This is a less common pricing strategy now than it was in the past. An example would be the 25-cent gumballs sold in gumball machines—the price has remained at that level for probably as long as you can remember. In cases of customary pricing, it is common for the amount of product sold at the customary price to go down over time, to compensate for inflation and increases in the cost of raw materials.[14]

Prestige Pricing

With **prestige pricing**, prices are set at an artificially high level to convey a quality image. Prestige pricing is used especially when buyers associate a higher price with higher quality. Hermès is a brand that has successfully used prestige pricing to set prices extremely high to convey an aura of ultra-luxury. Even in an economic climate where other luxury brands struggled to maintain sales, Hermès has grown rapidly in the 21st century—bolstered by its elite image.[15] A simple scarf, such as the one depicted in the advertisement, retails for nearly $600. Although the advertisement depicts nothing more than a man bundled up in the snow with the phrase "A sporting life!" it manages to convey a sense of a

Hermes of Paris

Prestige Pricing
Hermès is a premium brand that engages in prestige pricing to convey an image of wealth and luxury.

desirable, luxurious lifestyle—which consumers can seek to emulate through purchasing Hermès brand products.

Typical product categories that are subject to prestige pricing include perfumes, liquor, jewelry, cars, and some food items. Upscale appliances or furniture capitalizes on the desire of some consumer segments to "trade up" for high-quality products. These consumers are willing to pay extra for a Sub-Zero refrigerator or a Viking commercial range because these products are high quality and project an image that the customers can afford the best.

20-5e Professional Pricing

Professional pricing is used by people who have great skill or experience in a particular field. Although costs are considered when setting prices, professionals often believe their fees should not relate directly to the time and/or effort spent in specific cases. Rather, professionals may charge a standard fee regardless of the problems involved in performing the job. Some doctors' and lawyers' fees are prime examples, such as $75 for an office visit, $2,000 for an appendectomy, and $995 for a divorce. Other professionals set prices using different methods. Like other marketers, professionals have costs associated with facilities, labor, insurance, equipment, and supplies. Professionals have an ethical responsibility not to overcharge customers.

20-5f Promotional Pricing

Price—as an ingredient in the marketing mix—often is coordinated with promotion. The two variables are sometimes so interrelated that the pricing policy is promotion-oriented. Examples of promotional pricing include price leaders, special-event pricing, and comparison discounting.

Price Leaders

Sometimes a firm prices a few products below the usual markup, near cost, or below cost, which results in what are known as **price leaders**. This type of pricing is used most often in supermarkets and restaurants to attract customers by offering them especially low prices on a few items, with the expectation that they will purchase other items as well. Management expects that sales of regularly-priced products will more than offset the reduced revenues from the price leaders.

Special-Event Pricing

To increase sales volume, many organizations coordinate price with advertising or sales promotions for seasonal or special situations. **Special-event pricing** involves advertised sales or price cutting linked to a holiday, season, or event. If the pricing objective is survival, then special sales events may be designed to generate the necessary operating capital. Special-event pricing entails coordination of production, scheduling, storage, and physical distribution. Special-event pricing can be an effective strategy to combat sales lags.

Comparison Discounting

Comparison discounting sets the price of a product at a specific level and simultaneously compares it with a higher price. The higher price may be the product's previous price, the price of a competing brand, the product's price at another retail outlet, or a manufacturer's suggested retail price. Customers may find comparative discounting informative, and it can have a significant impact on their purchases.

professional pricing Fees set by people with great skill or experience in a particular field

price leaders Products priced near or even below cost

special-event pricing Advertised sales or price cutting linked to a holiday, a season, or an event

comparison discounting Setting a price at a specific level and comparing it with a higher price

Entrepreneurship in Marketing

Nick D'Aloisio, Teen Millionaire App-Genius

Entrepreneur: Nick D'Aloisio
Business: Summly app
Founded: 2011, in London, England
Success: D'Aloisio created a free iPhone app to summarize news stories and achieved nearly one million downloads in six months.

When Nick D'Aloisio was 12, he programmed an iPhone app that acts like a tiny treadmill for fingers, priced it low to attract users, and earned $126 on the first day of downloads. This experience encouraged him to keep developing apps. A few years later, he became frustrated while sifting through the results of an Internet search. He needed an app to summarize stories as a way of determining which to read and which to skip.

D'Aloisio created and released Trimit, his text-summary app, in July 2011, priced at 99 cents per download. Trimit quickly drew the attention of a deep-pocketed investor, who provided D'Aloisio with the resources he needed to refine the app's capabilities. When D'Aloisio renamed the app Summly and reintroduced it in 2012, he also changed the price to free. His goal in giving the app away was to build a large user base and eventually offer a paid, premium version of the app or profit from deals with publishers who wanted their content optimized for Summly's audience. Instead, Yahoo! bought the app for $30 million in 2013, hired the teen entrepreneur, and relaunched the app as Yahoo! News Digest in 2014.[b]

However, because this pricing strategy on occasion has led to deceptive pricing practices, the Federal Trade Commission has established guidelines for comparison discounting. If the higher price against which the comparison is made is the price formerly charged for the product, the seller must have made the previous price available to customers for a reasonable time period. If sellers present the higher price as the one charged by other retailers in the same trade area, they must be able to demonstrate that this claim is true. When they present the higher price as the manufacturer's suggested retail price, the higher price must be close to the price at which a reasonable proportion of the product was sold. Some manufacturers' suggested retail prices are so high that very few products are actually sold at those prices. In such cases, it is deceptive to use comparison discounting. The Internet has allowed consumers to be more wary of comparison discounting and less susceptible to being fooled, as they can easily compare the listed price for a product with comparable products online.

20-6 DETERMINATION OF A SPECIFIC PRICE

A pricing strategy will yield a certain price or range of prices, which is the final step in the pricing process. However, marketers may need to refine this price in order to make it consistent with circumstances (such as a sluggish economy) and with pricing practices in a particular market or industry. Pricing strategies should help in setting a final price. If they are to do so, marketers must establish pricing objectives, have considerable knowledge about target market customers, and determine demand, price elasticity, costs, and competitive factors. Additionally, the way marketers use pricing in the marketing mix will affect the final price.

In the absence of government price controls, pricing remains a flexible and convenient way to adjust the marketing mix. In many situations, marketers can adjust prices quickly—over a few days or even in minutes. Such flexibility is unique to this component of the marketing mix.

Summary

20-1 Identify issues related to developing pricing objectives.

Setting pricing objectives is critical because pricing objectives form a foundation on which the decisions of subsequent stages are based. Organizations may use numerous pricing objectives, including short-term and long-term ones, and different objectives for different products and market segments. Pricing objectives are overall goals that describe the role of price in a firm's long-range plans. There are several major types of pricing objectives. The most fundamental pricing objective is the organization's survival. Price can usually be easily adjusted to increase sales volume or combat competition to help the organization stay alive. Profit objectives, which are usually stated in terms of sales dollar volume or percentage change, are normally set at a satisfactory level rather than at a level designed to maximize profits. A sales growth objective focuses on increasing the profit base by raising sales volume. Pricing for return on investment (ROI) has a specified profit as its objective. A pricing objective to maintain or increase market share links market position to success. Other types of pricing objectives include cash flow, status quo, and product quality.

20-2 Discuss the importance of identifying the target market's evaluation of price.

Assessing the target market's evaluation of price tells the marketer how much emphasis to place on price and may help determine how far above the competition the firm can set its prices. Understanding how important a product is to customers relative to other products, as well as customers' expectations of quality, helps marketers correctly assess the target market's evaluation of price.

20-3 Explain how marketers analyze competitors' prices.

A marketer needs to be aware of the prices charged for competing brands. This allows the firm to keep its prices in line with competitors' prices when nonprice competition is used. If a company uses price as a competitive tool, it can price its brand below competing brands.

20-4 Describe the bases used for setting prices.

The three major dimensions on which prices can be based are cost, demand, and competition. When using cost-based pricing, the firm determines price by adding a dollar amount or percentage to the cost of the product. Two common cost-based pricing methods are cost-plus and markup pricing. Demand-based pricing is based on the level of demand for the product. To use this method, a marketer must be able to estimate the amounts of a product that buyers will demand at different prices. Demand-based pricing results in a high price when demand for a product is strong and a low price when demand is weak. In the case of competition-based pricing, costs and revenues are secondary to competitors' prices.

20-5 Explain the different types of pricing strategies.

A pricing strategy is an approach or a course of action designed to achieve pricing and marketing objectives. Pricing strategies help marketers solve the practical problems of establishing prices. The most common pricing strategies are differential pricing, new-product pricing, product-line pricing, psychological pricing, professional pricing, and promotional pricing.

When marketers employ differential pricing, they charge different buyers different prices for the same quality and quantity of products. For example, with negotiated pricing, the final price is established through bargaining between seller and customer. Secondary-market pricing involves setting one price for the primary target market and a different price for another market. Oftentimes the price charged in the secondary market is lower. Marketers employ periodic discounting when they temporarily lower their prices on a patterned or systematic basis because of such reasons as a seasonal change, a model-year change, or a holiday. Random discounting occurs on an unsystematic basis.

Two strategies used in new-product pricing are price skimming and penetration pricing. With price skimming, the organization charges the highest price that buyers who most desire the product will pay. A penetration price is a low price designed to penetrate a market and gain a significant market share quickly.

Product-line pricing establishes and adjusts the prices of multiple products within a product line. This strategy includes captive pricing, in which the marketer prices the basic product in a product line low and prices related items higher. Premium pricing is setting prices on higher-quality or more versatile products higher than those on other models in the product line. Bait pricing is when the marketer tries to attract customers by pricing an item in the product line low with the intention of selling a higher-priced item in the line. Price lining is when the organization sets a limited number of prices for selected groups or lines of merchandise.

Psychological pricing attempts to influence customers' perceptions of price to make a product's price more attractive. With reference pricing, marketers price a product at a moderate level and position it next to a more expensive model or brand. Bundle pricing is packaging together two or more complementary products and selling them at a single price. With multiple-unit pricing, two or more identical products are packaged together and sold at a single price. To reduce or eliminate use of frequent short-term price reductions, some organizations employ everyday low pricing (EDLP), setting a low price for products on a consistent basis. When employing odd-even pricing, marketers try to influence buyers' perceptions of the price or the product by ending the price with certain numbers. Customary pricing is based on traditional prices. With prestige pricing, prices are set at an artificially high level to convey prestige or a quality image.

Professional pricing is used by people who have great skill or experience in a particular field, therefore allowing them to set the price. This concept carries the idea that professionals have an ethical responsibility not to overcharge customers. As an ingredient in the marketing mix, price is often coordinated with promotion. The two variables are sometimes so closely interrelated that the pricing policy is promotion-oriented. Promotional pricing includes price leaders, special-event pricing, and comparison discounting.

Price leaders are products priced below the usual markup, near cost, or below cost. Special-event pricing involves advertised sales or price cutting linked to a holiday, season, or event. Marketers that use a comparison discounting strategy price a product at a specific level and compare it with a higher price.

20-6 Describe the selection of a specific price.

A pricing strategy will yield a certain price or range of prices. Pricing strategies should help in setting a final price. If they are to do so, marketers must establish pricing objectives, have considerable knowledge about target market customers, and determine demand, price elasticity, costs, and competitive factors. Additionally, the way marketers use pricing in the marketing mix will affect the final price. Pricing remains a flexible and convenient way to adjust the marketing mix.

Go to www.cengagebrain.com for resources to help you master the content in this chapter as well as materials that will expand your marketing knowledge!

Developing Your Marketing Plan

Setting the right price for a product is a crucial part of a marketing strategy. Price helps to establish a product's position in the mind of the consumer and can differentiate a product from its competition. Several decisions in the marketing plan will be affected by the pricing strategy that is selected. To assist you in relating the information in this chapter to the development of your marketing plan, focus on the following:

1. Using Table 20.1 as a guide, discuss each of the seven pricing objectives. Which pricing objectives will you use for your product? Consider the product life cycle, competition, and product positioning for your target market during your discussion.
2. Review the various types of pricing strategies in Table 20.3. Which of these is the most appropriate for your product?
3. Select a basis for pricing your product (cost, demand, and/or competition). How will you know when it is time to revise your pricing strategy?

The information obtained from these questions should assist you in developing various aspects of your marketing plan found in the "Interactive Marketing Plan" exercise at www.cengagebrain.com.

Important Terms

pricing objectives 614
cost-based pricing 620
cost-plus pricing 620
markup pricing 620
demand-based pricing 621
competition-based pricing 622
differential pricing 623
negotiated pricing 623
secondary-market pricing 623
periodic discounting 623
random discounting 624
price skimming 624
penetration pricing 624
product-line pricing 625
captive pricing 625
premium pricing 626
bait pricing 626
price lining 626
psychological pricing 626
reference pricing 627
bundle pricing 627
multiple-unit pricing 627
everyday low prices (EDLP) 628
odd-even pricing 629
customary pricing 629
prestige pricing 629
professional pricing 630
price leaders 630
special-event pricing 630
comparison discounting 630

Discussion and Review Questions

1. Identify the six stages in the process of establishing prices.
2. How does a return on an investment pricing objective differ from an objective of increasing market share?
3. Why must marketing objectives and pricing objectives be considered when making pricing decisions?
4. Why should a marketer be aware of competitors' prices?
5. What are the benefits of cost-based pricing?
6. Under what conditions is cost-plus pricing most appropriate?
7. A retailer purchases a can of soup for 24 cents and sells it for 36 cents. Calculate the markup as a percentage of cost and as a percentage of selling price.
8. What is differential pricing? In what ways can it be achieved?
9. For what types of products would price skimming be most appropriate? For what types of products would penetration pricing be more effective?
10. Describe bundle pricing, and give three examples using different industries.
11. What are the advantages and disadvantages of using everyday low prices?
12. Why do customers associate price with quality? When should prestige pricing be used?
13. Are price leaders a realistic approach to pricing? Explain your answer.

Video Case 20.1

Pricing at the Farmers' Market

Whether they're outside the barn or inside the city limits, farmers' markets are becoming more popular as consumers increasingly seek out fresh and local foods. Today, more than 7,000 farmers' markets are open in the United States, selling farm products year-round or only in season. Although some are located within a short drive of the farms where the fruits and vegetables are grown, many operate only on weekends, setting up stands in town squares and city parks to offer a combination of shopping and entertainment. "These markets are establishing themselves as part of our culture in ways that they didn't used to be, and that bodes well for their continued growth," says the director of LocalHarvest.org, which produces a national directory of farmers' markets.

© Jeffrey M. Frank/Shutterstock.com

Selling directly to the public enables farmers to build relationships with local shoppers and encourage repeat buying week after week as different items are harvested. It also allows farmers to realize a larger profit margin than if they sold to wholesalers and retailers. This is because the price at which intermediaries buy must have enough room for them to earn a profit when they resell to a store or to consumers. Farmers who market to consumers without intermediaries can charge almost as much—or sometimes even more than—consumers would pay in a supermarket. In many cases, consumers are willing to pay a higher price for top-quality local products, and even more for products that have been certified organic by a recognized authority. Competition is a factor, however. Consumers who browse the farmer's market will quickly see the range of prices that farmers are charging that day for peppers, peaches, or pumpkins. Competition between farmers' markets is another issue, as a new crop of markets appears every season.

Urban Farmz, like other vendors, is adding unique and complementary merchandise to its traditional line-up of agricultural items. Diversifying by selling certified organic soap at its stand, online, and to wholesale accounts will "juice up the brand," as Caleb, a spokesperson for Urban Farmz, says. The producers of the organic soap sell it for $14 per bar on their own website, and they ask Urban Farmz to avoid any conflict by selling at a higher price. Thinking fast, Caleb suggests a retail price of $15.95 per bar, saying that this will give Urban Farmz a reasonable profit margin.

Will buyers accept this price? It's time for some competitive homework. The lavender–lemon verbena scent is very popular, and certified-organic products have cachet. Caleb thinks that visitors to the Urban Farmz website will probably not click away to save a dollar or two by buying elsewhere since they would have to pay the other site's shipping fee, as well as the Urban Farmz site's shipping fee. Urban Farmz will also have to set a separate wholesale price when it sells the soap to local restaurants. Will this new soap be the product that boosts Urban Farmz's profits and turn the name into a lifestyle brand?[16]

Questions for Discussion

1. In the pursuit of profits, how might Urban Farmz use a combination of cost-based, demand-based, and competition-based pricing for the products it sells? Explain your answer.
2. Urban Farmz wants to price the organic soap at $15.95 per bar, while the soap maker prices the same soap at $14 per bar. What perceptions do you think consumers will have of each price? What recommendations do you have regarding this price difference?
3. Would you recommend that Urban Farmz use promotional pricing at the farmers' markets where it regularly sells its products? If so, which techniques would you suggest, and why?

Case 20.2

Under Armour Uses Pricing in the Race for Market Share

Baltimore-based Under Armour is on a mission "to make all athletes better through passion, design, and the relentless pursuit of innovation." Founded by Kevin Plank in 1995, the company made its name with a unique moisture-wicking shirt to keep athletes dry and comfortable during games and workouts. Over the years, it has introduced a wide variety of innovative clothing, accessories, and footwear for specific sports and to support athletic performance in challenging situations, such as in hot, cold, or wet weather conditions. It has raised its public profile through marketing efforts such as outfitting college football teams and U.S. Olympic teams, sponsoring the Under Armour All-American football game, and endorsement deals with outstanding athletes like Olympic medalists Michael Phelps and Lindsey Vonn.

With more than $2.2 billion in annual sales, Under Armour is growing quickly and setting its long-term sights on catching up with industry giants such as Nike and Adidas. Despite high brand awareness, Under Armour has limited financial resources that must be stretched across every product line, whereas Nike, Adidas, and other major competitors possess the financial strength to introduce and promote a multitude of products in multiple categories at one time. Therefore, Kevin Plank, who founded the firm and also serves as CEO, is focusing Under Armour's resources on the specific, high-opportunity markets.

For instance, Plank wants to increase Under Armour's share of the extremely competitive but highly lucrative market for athletic shoes. Since introducing its first athletic shoes in 2006, the company has increased shoe sales at double-digit rates year after year, taking market share from rivals in certain specialized segments. In the market for cleats, Under Armour rocketed to second place only months after launching its first line of football cleats and baseball cleats.

Plank recently set the ambitious goal of making Under Armour the third-largest brand in running shoes, trailing only market-leading Nike and the runner-up brand, Asics. Running shoes are a $7 billion market—and Plank sees product-line pricing as the key to becoming a major player here. The company initially set premium prices starting at $100 per pair, based on each athletic shoe's innovative features and benefits. But it can't significantly increase market share in running shoes without offering a range of products at a range of prices for buyers with different needs and motivations.

So although Under Armour will continue to offer higher-priced running shoes, it is also introducing new running shoes priced between $70 and $100 per pair. This will attract new customers and lay the foundation for repeat purchasing, because customers who are satisfied with their experience will be more likely to buy from Under Armour again. Just as important, these customers may decide to trade up to more expensive footwear the next time they buy from Under Armour. Thanks to this pricing strategy, Under Armour's share is already inching up, and it has become the number-three brand at some of its retailers. However, the race is far from over. The company still holds less than 5 percent of the market for running shoes, whereas market-leader Nike holds a commanding 57 percent market share.

In combination with pricing, Under Armour is relying on innovative product development for growth. Although the company's initial moisture-wicking clothing products were designed for men, it also sees considerable sales and profit opportunity in the market for women's athletic apparel. Looking ahead, it plans to build the women's line into a $1 billion business and, ultimately, generate enough momentum for sales of the company's women's clothing to surpass sales of men's clothing in the future.

To keep the innovations coming, Under Armour holds an annual "Future Show" competition offering cash prizes and contracts to encourage inventors to submit new product ideas. Two years after an inventor won the competition with a unique zipper that athletes can operate with one hand, his invention was incorporated into thousands of Under Armour jackets and outerwear. Under Armour is currently testing another winner's invention, LED lights embedded in shirts, jackets, and backpacks so athletes can see and be seen in the dark as they jog, compete, or practice. Although the technology might result in prices as high as $250 per product, Under Armour believes sports-minded customers will see the value in these cutting-edge products.[17]

Questions for Discussion

1. Of the various pricing objectives, which one does Under Armour appear to be pursuing in its marketing of running shoes, and why?
2. When Under Armour prepares to set the price for a new shirt equipped with LED lights, how much emphasis should it place on its evaluation of competitors' prices?
3. Would you recommend that Under Armour use cost-based pricing, demand-based pricing, or competition-based pricing for a new shirt equipped with LED lights? Explain your answer.

Strategic Case 8

Newspapers Test Pricing for Digital Editions

Pricing is one of the most difficult challenges facing U.S. newspapers in the 21st century. The entire industry is feeling a tremendous financial squeeze. Revenues from display advertising have plummeted as many marketers engage customers via social media, Internet ads, special events, daily deal sites, and other promotional methods that sidestep newspapers. Just as important, revenues from paid classified ads have also slumped. Instead of buying classified ads to fill job openings, sell new or used cars, and sell or trade household items, large numbers of consumers and businesses are turning to auction websites, online employment sites, and social media sites.

© iStockphoto.com/fazon1

Looking at trends in paid newspaper subscriptions, the news isn't much better. During the first decade of this century, weekday newspaper circulation fell by 17 percent, and the outlook for a turnaround in print subscriptions is not positive. One reason is that some people—younger consumers, in particular—prefer to get their news online or from television. With the rise of mobile devices like smartphones, tablet computers, and e-book readers, on-the-go consumers have a quick and easy way to click for news, at any time and from any place. The printed newspaper doesn't have the very latest news—but online sources do. Another reason is that many cash-strapped subscribers have cut back on buying newspapers, either because they're worried about their jobs or because they're saving money for other purchases.

In short, newspapers simply can't continue to do business as they did in the last century and expect to prosper in this century. Once-strong newspapers like the *Rocky Mountain News* have been forced to shut down, while others (like the *Christian Science Monitor*) have abandoned print in favor of online-only editions. Now, with fewer paying customers and fewer advertisers, newspapers are taking a long, hard look at their pricing strategies to find new ways of improving circulation revenues and profits in the digital age. Some newspapers continue to offer news for free, on the basis that this builds their brands online and offers extra value to readers who want to see updated news whenever it breaks. Other newspapers are trying a *paywall,* allowing only paid subscribers to see online content that's "walled off" to prevent free access.

Pricing the Digital *Wall Street Journal*

How do you price the online version of a print newspaper for readers? Should the Internet or mobile edition be entirely free because there are no print costs? Should it be free to customers who subscribe to the print edition? Should some content be free and some fee-only? Or should you set a price for reading almost anything other than today's headlines?

The Wall Street Journal was one of the first newspapers to confront these questions and try to find pricing approaches that made sense for its situation. A national newspaper that's heavy on U.S. and international business news, the *Journal* also covers general news and politics, economics, investment issues, the arts, and lifestyle trends. Many of its subscribers are professionals, investors, or businesspeople who need to follow the latest happenings in their field and stay updated on world events.

During the mid-1990s, the *Journal* recognized that it had an unusual opportunity to pioneer a new pricing strategy for online news content. It started with a free website, quickly attracted 600,000 registered users, and within a few months, it announced a change to subscriber pricing. Once the site set its prices at $49 per year for online-only access and $29 for print subscribers who wanted to view online material, only 5 percent of the registered users chose to pay for access.

The *Journal* was prepared for this kind of response. Whereas other newspapers were testing prices for individual articles or for weekly access, the *Journal* believed it offered subscribers long-term value that they wouldn't appreciate if they could pay for content by the article or by the week. "It's easier for people to see the total value of a package if you have to pay for it all," said the online editor. Giving business readers a comprehensive overview of global markets day after day means "we're not a news site, we're a competitive advantage tool," said another *Journal* executive.

Despite the steep drop in visitors after the *Journal* began selling subscriptions, the site had 100,000 paid subscribers within a year. Within two years, it had 200,000 paid subscribers and was nearly at the breakeven point. Since then, the *Journal* has increased its online subscription prices and instituted subscription pricing for access via apps on mobile devices. Today, the newspaper has more than 500,000 digital subscribers, including 80,000 who access the online edition by phone, tablet, or e-book reader. Non-subscribers have access to a limited amount of the *Journal*'s online content, and new-subscriber deals encourage people to sign up rather than be casual visitors. Thanks to the *Journal* site's loyal and lucrative subscriber base, a growing number of major advertisers are willing to pay to reach this audience online, which contributes millions more to the newspaper's bottom line.

Pricing Digital Versions of Gannett Newspapers

Unlike *The Wall Street Journal*, which attracts many business readers, Gannett newspapers are for the general public. In addition to *USA Today*, its national newspaper, Gannett also owns 80 other papers in 30 states. No two of these local papers are exactly alike. Some papers (like the *Indianapolis Star* in Indianapolis, Indiana) serve big cities, while others (like the *Times Recorder* in Zanesville, Ohio) serve smaller communities. In recent years, Gannett's circulation revenue has been dropping, and the company has decided to increase revenue by instituting monthly subscription pricing for the digital versions of its local newspapers. *USA Today* was not included in this new pricing strategy because of its national distribution.

To start, Gannett tested pricing for online access to three of its local newspaper sites to learn about "consumer engagement and willingness to pay for unique local content," says a spokesperson. Based on the results of those tests, which included full access via computer and mobile devices, Gannett then announced that 80 of its local papers would limit non-subscriber access to digital content. Each local paper was responsible for setting the price, following the general principle that non-subscribers could view no more than 15 articles per month (or as few as five if the paper wants to be more restrictive). To view more content, consumers could choose a monthly subscription for digital-only access using a wide range of devices or a monthly subscription combining print and digital access. Even subscribing to Sunday-only editions will be sufficient to qualify for digital access, if a local paper chooses to price content in that way.

Will consumers pay for digital versions of local newspapers? Some experts believe that local residents will pay for in-depth local coverage and the very latest news, which they can't easily get for free from other sources. If consumers like to read a particular columnist or a regular feature that only appears in the local paper, they will have to pay to see that content online or in print. With the rapid penetration of tablet computers and smartphones, the ability to access local content digitally is increasingly more appealing than reading a once-a-day newspaper in print. Other experts say that consumers have grown accustomed to unlimited online access over the years, and they won't be receptive to paying for what was previously free. However, if consumers find themselves reaching the pre-set limit of how many articles they can read online, they may find that it's easier to pay than to have to click around and find the content elsewhere for free.

Gannett expects its new digital pricing strategy to increase revenues by as much as $100 million per year, once the pricing is implemented by all 80 papers. "This is a turning point for us," says an executive. Meanwhile, other local newspapers are testing different ways to price online content, also hoping that subscribers will sign up and then remain loyal. Will paywalls pay off?[18]

Questions for Discussion

1. When *The Wall Street Journal* began charging for online access, the number of visitors to its site dropped dramatically and slowly began rising again. What does this suggest about the price elasticity of demand for its products?
2. Would consumers have an internal reference price for digital newspaper content? Explain your answer.
3. What type of psychological pricing are Gannett and *The Wall Street Journal* using when they offer print and digital subscriptions together for one price? What do you think of this approach to pricing?
4. Should Gannett and *The Wall Street Journal* be looking at competitors' prices when setting their own prices? Why or why not?

NOTES

[1] Katie Evans, "No More Online Goodies for Wal-Mart Shoppers," *InternetRetailer*, October 28, 2013, www.internetretailer.com/2013/10/28/no-more-online-goodies-wal-mart-shoppers (accessed January 8, 2014); Alice Short, "Cool Stuff in a Box," *Los Angeles Times*, October 5, 2013, www.latimes.com/fashion/alltherage/la-atr-cool-stuff-in-a-box-20131004,0,2220202.story (accessed January 8, 2014); Colleen Leahey, "Thinking Outside the Box," *Fortune*, October 7, 2013, p. 118.

[2] Adrian Campos, "How Google Plans to Win the Tablet Market with the Nexus 7," *Daily Finance*, December 23, 2013, www.dailyfinance.com/2013/12/23/how-google-plans-to-win-tablets-market-with-nexus (accessed December 30, 2013).

[3] "The Profit Impact of Market Strategies (PIMS) Overview," The Strategic Planning Institute, http://pimsonline.com/about_pims_db.htm (accessed December 29, 2013).

[4] "10 Outrageous Markups You'd Never Guess You Were Paying," *Reader's Digest*, www.rd.com/slideshows/10-outrageous-markups-youd-never-guess-you-were-paying/#slideshow=slide2 (accessed January 1, 2014).

[5] John Miley, "Warehouse Stores: Deal or No Deal?" *Kiplinger*, June 9, 2011, www.kiplinger.com/quiz/warehouse-store-deals (accessed January 1, 2014).

[6] "Demand Based Pricing," *This Is Twins Territory*, http://mlb.mlb.com/min/ticketing/demandbased_pricing.jsp (accessed December 27, 2013).

[7] Roberto A. Ferdman, "Amazon Changes its Prices More Than 2.5 Million Times a Day," *Quartz*, December 14, 2013, http://qz.com/157828/amazon-changes-its-prices-more-than-2-5-million-times-a-day (accessed December 27, 2013).

[8] Hilary Stout, "An Easing of Rules on Charges by Amex," *The New York Times*, December 19, 2013, www.nytimes.com/2013/12/20/business/an-easing-of-rules-on-charges-by-amex.html (accessed December 27, 2013).

[9] Kristi Hedges, "Six Surprising Negotiation Tactics That Get You the Best Deal," *Forbes*, December 5, 2013, www.forbes.com/sites/work-in-progress/2013/12/05/six-surprising-negotiation-tactics-that-get-you-the-best-deal (accessed December 27, 2013).

[10] Joan Lindsay Mulliken and Ross D. Petty, "Marketing Tactics Discouraging Price Search: Deception and Competition," *Journal of Business Research* 64, no. 1 (January 2011): 67–73, www.sciencedirect.com/science/article/pii/S0148296309002641 (accessed December 29, 2013).

[11] Lindsay Gellman, "Gelato Makers Hope Foodie Flavors Will Lift Frozen Treat Industry," *The Wall Street Journal*, November 12, 2013, http://online.wsj.com/news/articles/SB10001424052702303309504579186070387414180 (accessed February 2, 2014).

[12] Hilary Osborne, "Parents Buying Tablets for Children Urged to Look Out for Hidden Costs," *The Guardian*, December 25, 2013, www.theguardian.com/technology/2013/dec/25/parents-tablets-children-hidden-costs (accessed December 30, 2013).

[13] Stephanie Clifford and Catherine Rampell, "Sometimes, We Want Prices to Fool Us," *The New York Times*, April 14, 2013, www.nytimes.com/2013/04/14/business/for-penney-a-tough-lesson-in-shopper-psychology.html (accessed December 30, 2013).

[14] Timothy Sexton, "Customary Pricing: Why Paying the Same Low Price May Not Be the Great Deal It Seems," *Yahoo!*, August 30, 3013, http://voices.yahoo.com/customary-pricing-why-paying-same-low-price-may-12293434.html?cat=46 (accessed December 30, 2013).

[15] Manuela Mesco and Nadya Masidlover, "Some Lux Brands Struggle to Move Further Upscale," *The Wall Street Journal*, November 14, 2013, http://online.wsj.com/news/articles/SB10001424052702304243904579198060042193986 (accessed December 30, 2013).

[16] Based on information in "Urban Farmz" video, Cengage, 2011; Jennifer Shutt, "Market Benefits Farmers, Residents," *Delmarva Now* (Salisbury, Maryland), April 18, 2012, www.delmarvanow.com; Jenna Telesca, "Farmers' Markets Grow 17%, Continuing Trend," *Supermarket News*, August 22, 2011, http://supermarketnews.com/produce/farmers-markets-grow-17-continuing-trend (accessed January 11, 2014); Katie Zezima, "As Farmers' Markets Go Mainstream, Some Fear a Glut," *The New York Times*, August 20, 2011, http://www.nytimes.com/2011/08/21/us/21farmers.html?_r=0 (accessed February 10, 2014);

Elizabeth Weise, "Fresh Crop of Farmers Markets Is Spring Up," *USA Today*, August 8, 2011, 5B.

[17] Sarah Meehan, "Year in Review: Under Armour Stock Price Balloons on New Products, Growth Potential," *Baltimore Business Journal*, March 4, 2014, http://www.bizjournals.com/baltimore/news/2013/12/19/under-armour-stock-price-growth-2013.html?page=2 (accessed July 17, 2014); Sarah Meehan, "For Under Armour, Lower Price Points Lead to Stronger Shoe Sales," *Baltimore Business Journal*, October 29, 2013, http://www.bizjournals.com/baltimore/news/2013/10/29/under-armour-grows-shoe-sales-by.html (accessed March 17, 2014); Lorraine Mirabella, "Under Armour Profit Up 27 Percent in Third Quarter," *Baltimore Sun*, October 24, 2013, http://articles.baltimoresun.com/2013-10-24/business/bs-bz-under-armour-earnings-20131024_1_kevin-plank-charged-cotton-brad-dickerson (accessed March 17, 2014).

[18] Based on information in Ryan Nakashima, "Newspapers Erect Pay Walls in Hunt for New Revenue," *Yahoo! News*, April 3, 2012, http://news.yahoo.com/newspapers-erect-pay-walls-hunt-revenue-174925369.html (accessed January 11, 2014); Tom Rosenstiel, Mark Jurkowitz, and Hong Ji, "The Search for a New Business Model," *Pew Research Center's Journalism.org*, March 5, 2012, www.journalism.org/2012/03/05/search-new-business-model (accessed January 11, 2014); Russell Adams, "Papers Put Faith in Paywalls," *The Wall Street Journal*, March 4, 2012, http://online.wsj.com/news/articles/SB10001424052970203833004577251822631536422 (accessed January 11, 2014); Jeff Bercovici, "Gannett Building Paywalls Around All Its Papers Except *USA Today*," *Forbes*, February 22, 2012, www.forbes.com/sites/jeffbercovici/2012/02/22/gannett-building-paywalls-around-all-its-papers-except-usa-today (accessed January 11, 2014); Justin Ellis, "From Salinas to Burlington: Can an Army of Paywalls Big and Small Buoy Gannett?" *Nieman Journalism Lab*, February 28, 2012, www.niemanlab.org/2012/02/from-salinas-to-burlington-can-an-army-of-paywalls-big-and-small-bouy-gannett (accessed January 11, 2014); Elizabeth Gardner, "200,000 Paying for Wall St. Journal Interactive," *InternetWorld*, April 20, 1998, p. 10.

Feature Notes

[a] Dug Begley, "Price Hike Has Desired Effect, So Far, on Katy Toll Lanes," *Houston Chronicle*, October 15, 2013, www.houstonchronicle.com/news/columnists/begley/article/Price-hike-has-desired-effect-so-far-on-Katy-4895563.php (accessed January 8, 2014); Tess Kalinowski, "Do High Occupancy Toll Lanes Really Help Congestion?" *Toronto Star*, May 21, 2013, www.thestar.com/news/gta/2013/05/21/do_high_occupancy_toll_lanes_really_help_congestion.html (accessed January 8, 2013); Hank Silverberg, "Express Toll Lanes Show to Catch on Nationwide," *WTOP (Washington, D.C.)*, April 22, 2013, www.wtop.com/654/3295089/Express-toll-lanes-slow-to-catch-on-nationwide (accessed January 8, 2014).

[b] James Vincent, "CES 2014: Yahoo! Rebrands Nick D'Aloisio's Summly App for Mobile-News Focus," *Independent*, January 17, 2014, www.independent.co.uk/life-style/gadgets-and-tech/ces-2014-yahoo-rebrands-nick-daloisios-summly-app-for-mobilenews-focus-9045993.html (accessed February 2, 2014); Darrell Etherington, "Summly's Nick D'Aloisio on Yahoo!'s Approach to Ephemerality, and Its Startup Mentality," *TechCrunch*, October 17, 2013, http://techcrunch.com/2013/10/17/summlys-nick-daloisio-on-yahoos-approach-to-ephemerality-and-its-startup-mentality (accessed January 8, 2014); Victor Luckerson, "Q&A with the 17-Year-Old Who Sold an App to Yahoo! for $30 Million," *Time*, March 29, 2013, http://business.time.com/2013/03/27/why-is-that-17-year-olds-25-million-news-app-even-legal (accessed January 8, 2013); "Summly, iPhone App Disrupting the News," *The Guardian*, November 1, 2012, www.theguardian.com/technology/appsblog/2012/nov/01/summly-iphone-app-news (accessed January 8, 2014); Olivia Solon, "Nick D'Aloisio: Young People Need to Learn Entrepreneurship, Not Just Coding," *Wired*, October 17, 2013, www.wired.co.uk/news/archive/2013-10/17/nick-summly (accessed January 8, 2014).

© zayats-and-zayats/Shutterstock.com

glossary

accessory equipment Equipment that does not become part of the final physical product but is used in production or office activities

advertising Paid nonpersonal communication about an organization and its products transmitted to a target audience through mass media

advertising appropriation The advertising budget for a specific time period

advertising campaign The creation and execution of a series of advertisements to communicate with a particular target audience

advertising platform Basic issues or selling points to be included in an advertising campaign

advocacy advertising Advertising that promotes a company's position on a public issue

aesthetic modifications Changes relating to the sensory appeal of a product

agents Intermediaries that represent either buyers or sellers on a permanent basis

aided recall test A posttest that asks respondents to identify recent ads and provides clues to jog their memories

allowance A concession in price to achieve a desired goal

approach The manner in which a salesperson contacts a potential customer

arbitrary approach Budgeting for an advertising campaign as specified by a high-level executive in the firm

artwork An advertisement's illustrations and layout

Asia-Pacific Economic Cooperation (APEC) An alliance that promotes open trade and economic and technical cooperation among member nations throughout the world

Association of Southeast Asian Nations (ASEAN) An alliance that promotes trade and economic integration among member nations in Southeast Asia

atmospherics The physical elements in a store's design that appeal to consumers' emotions and encourage buying

attitude An individual's enduring evaluation of feelings about and behavioral tendencies toward an object or idea

attitude scale A means of measuring consumer attitudes by gauging the intensity of individuals' reactions to adjectives, phrases, or sentences about an object

automatic vending The use of machines to dispense products

average fixed cost The fixed cost per unit produced

average total cost The sum of the average fixed cost and the average variable cost

average variable cost The variable cost per unit produced

bait pricing Pricing an item in a product line low with the intention of selling a higher-priced item in the line

balance of trade The difference in value between a nation's exports and its imports

barter The trading of products

base-point pricing Geographic pricing that combines factory price and freight charges from the base point nearest the buyer

benefit segmentation The division of a market according to benefits that consumers want from the product

Better Business Bureau (BBB) A system of nongovernmental, independent, local regulatory agencies supported by local businesses that helps settle problems between customers and specific business firms

big data Massive data files that can be obtained from both structured and unstructured databases

blogs Web-based journals (short for "weblogs") in which writers editorialize and interact with other Internet users

brand A name, term, design, symbol, or other feature that identifies one seller's product as distinct from those of other sellers

brand competitors Firms that market products with similar features and benefits to the same customers at similar prices

brand equity The marketing and financial value associated with a brand's strength in a market

brand extension An organization uses one of its existing brands to brand a new product in a different product category

brand insistence The degree of brand loyalty in which a customer strongly prefers a specific brand and will accept no substitute

brand licensing An agreement whereby a company permits another organization to use its brand on other products for a licensing fee

brand loyalty A customer's favorable attitude toward a specific brand

brand manager The person responsible for a single brand

brand mark The part of a brand that is not made up of words, such as a symbol or design

brand name The part of a brand that can be spoken, including letters, words, and numbers

brand preference The degree of brand loyalty in which a customer prefers one brand over competitive offerings

brand recognition The degree of brand loyalty in which a customer is aware that a brand exists and views the brand as an alternative purchase if their preferred brand is unavailable

breakdown approach Measuring company sales potential based on a general economic forecast for a specific period and the market potential derived from it

break even point The point at which the costs of producing a product equal the revenue made from selling the product

brokers Intermediaries that bring buyers and sellers together temporarily

buildup approach Measuring company sales potential by estimating how much of a product a potential buyer in a specific geographic area will purchase in a given period, multiplying the estimate by the number of potential buyers, and adding the totals of all the geographic areas considered

bundle pricing Packaging together two or more complementary products and selling them at a single price

business analysis Evaluating the potential impact of a product idea on the firm's sales, costs, and profits

business (organizational) buying behavior The purchase behavior of producers, government units, institutions, and resellers

business cycle A pattern of economic fluctuations that has four stages: prosperity, recession, depression, and recovery

business market Individuals, organizations, or groups that purchase a specific kind of product for resale, direct use in producing other products, or use in general daily operations

business products Products bought to use in a firm's operations, to resell, or to make other products

business services Intangible products that many organizations use in their operations

buy-back allowance A sum of money given to a reseller for each unit bought after an initial promotion deal is over

buying allowance A temporary price reduction to resellers for purchasing specified quantities of a product

buying behavior The decision processes and actions of people involved in buying and using products

buying center The people within an organization who make business purchase decisions

buying power Resources, such as money, goods, and services, that can be traded in an exchange

buzz marketing An attempt to incite publicity and public excitement surrounding a product through a creative event

captioned photograph A photograph with a brief description of its contents

captive pricing Pricing the basic product in a product line low, while pricing related items higher

cash-and-carry wholesalers Limited-service wholesalers whose customers pay cash and furnish transportation

cash discount A price reduction given to buyers for prompt payment or cash payment

catalog marketing A type of marketing in which an organization provides a catalog from which customers make selections and place orders by mail, telephone, or the Internet

category killer A very large specialty store that concentrates on a major product category and competes on the basis of low prices and product availability

category management A retail strategy of managing groups of similar, often substitutable, products produced by different manufacturers

cause-related marketing The practice of linking products to a particular social cause on an ongoing or short-term basis

centralized organization A structure in which top-level managers delegate little authority to lower levels

cents-off offers Promotions that allow buyers to pay less than the regular price to encourage purchase

channel capacity The limit on the volume of information a communication channel can handle effectively

channel captain The dominant leader of a marketing channel or a supply channel

channel power The ability of one channel member to influence another member's goal achievement

client-based relationships Interactions that result in satisfied customers who use a service repeatedly over time

client publics Direct consumers of a product of a nonprofit organization

closing The stage in the personal selling process when the salesperson asks the prospect to buy the product

co-branding Using two or more brands on one product

codes of conduct Formalized rules and standards that describe what the company expects of its employees

coding process Converting meaning into a series of signs or symbols

cognitive dissonance A buyer's doubts shortly after a purchase about whether the decision was the right one

combination compensation plan Paying salespeople a fixed salary plus a commission based on sales volume

commercialization Refining and finalizing plans and budgets for full-scale manufacturing and marketing of a product

commission merchants Agents that receive goods on consignment from local sellers and negotiate sales in large, central markets

communication A sharing of meaning through the transmission of information

communications channel The medium of transmission that carries the coded message from the source to the receiver

community shopping center A type of shopping center with one or two department stores, some specialty stores, and convenience stores

company sales potential The maximum percentage of market potential that an individual firm within an industry can expect to obtain for a specific product

comparative advertising Compares the sponsored brand with one or more identified brands on the basis of one or more product characteristics

comparison discounting Setting a price at a specific level and comparing it with a higher price

competition Other organizations that market products that are similar to or can be substituted for a marketer's products in the same geographic area

competition-based pricing Pricing influenced primarily by competitors' prices

competition-matching approach Determining an advertising budget by trying to match competitors' advertising outlays

competitive advantage The result of a company matching a core competency to opportunities it has discovered in the marketplace

competitive advertising Tries to stimulate demand for a specific brand by promoting its features, uses, and advantages relative to competing brands

component parts Items that become part of the physical product and are either finished items ready for assembly or items that need little processing before assembly

concentrated targeting strategy A market segmentation strategy in which an organization targets a single market segment using one marketing mix

concept testing Seeking a sample of potential buyers' responses to a product idea

conclusive research Research designed to verify insights through objective procedures and to help marketers in making decisions

consideration set A group of brands within a product category that a buyer views as alternatives for possible purchase

consistency of quality The degree to which a product has the same level of quality over time

consumer buying behavior The decision processes and purchasing activities of people who purchase products for personal or household use and not for business purposes

consumer buying decision process A five-stage purchase decision process that includes problem recognition, information search, evaluation of alternatives, purchase, and postpurchase evaluation

consumer contests Sales promotion methods in which individuals compete for prizes based on their analytical or creative skills

consumer games Sales promotion methods in which individuals compete for prizes based primarily on chance

consumer jury A panel of a product's existing or potential buyers who pretest ads

consumer market Purchasers and household members who intend to consume or benefit from the purchased products and do not buy products to make profits

consumer misbehavior Behavior that violates generally accepted norms of a particular society

consumer products Products purchased to satisfy personal and family needs

consumer sales promotion methods Sales promotion techniques that encourage consumers to patronize specific stores or try particular products

consumer socialization The process through which a person acquires the knowledge and skills to function as a consumer

consumer sweepstakes A sales promotion in which entrants submit their names for inclusion in a drawing for prizes

consumerism Organized efforts by individuals, groups, and organizations to protect consumers' rights

contract manufacturing The practice of hiring a foreign firm to produce a designated volume of the domestic firm's product or a component of it to specification; the final product carries the domestic firm's name

convenience products Relatively inexpensive, frequently purchased items for which buyers exert minimal purchasing effort

convenience store A small self-service store that is open long hours and carries a narrow assortment of products, usually convenience items

cooperative advertising An arrangement in which a manufacturer agrees to pay a certain amount of a retailer's media costs for advertising the manufacturer's products

copy The verbal portion of advertisements

core competencies Things a company does extremely well, which sometimes give it an advantage over its competition

corporate strategy A strategy that determines the means for utilizing resources in the various functional areas to reach the organization's goals

cost-based pricing Adding a dollar amount or percentage to the cost of the product

cost comparison indicator A means of comparing the costs of advertising vehicles in a specific medium in relation to the number of people reached

cost-plus pricing Adding a specified dollar amount or percentage to the seller's cost

coupons Written price reductions used to encourage consumers to buy a specific product

credence qualities Attributes that customers may be unable to evaluate even after purchasing and consuming a service

crowdsourcing Combines the words *crowd* and *outsourcing* and calls for taking tasks usually performed by a marketer or researcher and outsourcing them to a crowd, or potential market, through an open call

cultural relativism The concept that morality varies from one culture to another and that business practices are therefore differentially defined as right or wrong by particular cultures

culture The accumulation of values, knowledge, beliefs, customs, objects, and concepts that a society uses to cope with its environment and passes on to future generations

cumulative discounts Quantity discounts aggregated over a stated time period

customary pricing Pricing on the basis of tradition

customer advisory boards Small groups of actual customers who serve as sounding boards for new-product ideas and offer insights into their feelings and attitudes toward a firm's products and other elements of its marketing strategy

customer contact The level of interaction between provider and customer needed to deliver the service

customer forecasting survey A survey of customers regarding the types and quantities of products they intend to buy during a specific period

customer lifetime value A key measurement that forecasts a customer's lifetime economic contribution based on continued relationship marketing efforts

customer relationship management (CRM) Using information about customers to create marketing strategies that develop and sustain desirable customer relationships

customer services Human or mechanical efforts or activities that add value to a product

customers The purchasers of organizations' products; the focal point of all marketing activities

cycle analysis An analysis of sales figures for a 3- to 5-year period to ascertain whether sales fluctuate in a consistent, periodic manner

cycle time The time needed to complete a process

database A collection of information arranged for easy access and retrieval

dealer listings Advertisements that promote a product and identify the names of participating retailers that sell the product

dealer loader A gift, often part of a display, given to a retailer that purchases a specified quantity of merchandise

decentralized organization A structure in which decision-making authority is delegated as far down the chain of command as possible

decline stage The stage of a product's life cycle when sales fall rapidly

decoding process Converting signs or symbols into concepts and ideas

Delphi technique A procedure in which experts create initial forecasts, submit them to the company for averaging, and then refine the forecasts

demand-based pricing Pricing based on the level of demand for the product

demand curve A graph of the quantity of products expected to be sold at various prices if other factors remain constant

demonstrations Sales promotion methods a manufacturer uses temporarily to encourage trial use and purchase of a product or to show how a product works

department stores Large retail organizations characterized by a wide product mix and organized into separate departments to facilitate marketing efforts and internal management

depression A stage of the business cycle when unemployment is extremely high, wages are very low, total disposable income is at a minimum, and consumers lack confidence in the economy

depth of product mix The average number of different products offered in each product line

derived demand Demand for business products that stems from demand for consumer products

descriptive research Research conducted to clarify the characteristics of certain phenomena to solve a particular problem

differential pricing Charging different prices to different buyers for the same quality and quantity of product

differentiated targeting strategy A strategy in which an organization targets two or more segments by developing a marketing mix for each segment

digital marketing Uses all digital media, including the Internet and mobile and interactive channels, to develop communication and exchanges with customers

digital media Electronic media that function using digital codes; when we refer to digital media, we are referring to media available via computers, cellular phones, smartphones, and other digital devices that have been released in recent years

direct marketing The use of the telephone, Internet, and nonpersonal media to introduce products to customers, who can then purchase them via mail, telephone, or the Internet

direct ownership A situation in which a company owns subsidiaries or other facilities overseas

direct-response marketing A type of marketing in which a retailer advertises a product and makes it available through mail or telephone orders

direct selling Marketing products to ultimate consumers through face-to-face sales presentations at home or in the workplace

discount stores Self-service, general-merchandise stores that offer brand-name and private-brand products at low prices

discretionary income Disposable income available for spending and saving after an individual has purchased the basic necessities of food, clothing, and shelter

disposable income After-tax income

distribution The decisions and activities that make products available to customers when and where they want to purchase them

distribution centers Large, centralized warehouses that focus on moving rather than storing goods

drop shippers Limited-service wholesalers that take title to goods and negotiate sales but never actually take possession of products

dual distribution The use of two or more marketing channels to distribute the same products to the same target market

dumping Selling products at unfairly low prices

early adopters People who adopt new products early, choose new products carefully, and are viewed as "the people to check with" by later adopters

early majority Individuals who adopt a new product just prior to the average person

electronic data interchange (EDI) A computerized means of integrating order processing with production, inventory, accounting, and transportation

electronic marketing (e-marketing) The strategic process of distributing, promoting, and pricing products, and discovering the desires of customers using digital media and digital marketing

embargo A government's suspension of trade in a particular product or with a given country

environmental analysis The process of assessing and interpreting the information gathered through environmental scanning

environmental scanning The process of collecting information about forces in the marketing environment

ethical issue An identifiable problem, situation, or opportunity requiring a choice among several actions that must be evaluated as right or wrong, ethical or unethical

European Union (EU) An alliance that promotes trade among its member countries in Europe

evaluative criteria Objective and subjective product characteristics that are important to a buyer

everyday low prices (EDLP) Pricing products low on a consistent basis

exchange controls Government restrictions on the amount of a particular currency that can be bought or sold

exchanges The provision or transfer of goods, services, or ideas in return for something of value

exclusive dealing A situation in which a manufacturer forbids an intermediary from carrying products of competing manufacturers

exclusive distribution Using a single outlet in a fairly large geographic area to distribute a product

executive judgment A sales forecasting method based on the intuition of one or more executives

experience qualities Attributes that can be assessed only during purchase and consumption of a service

experimental research Research that allows marketers to make causal inferences about relationships

expert forecasting survey Sales forecasts prepared by experts outside the firm, such as economists, management consultants, advertising executives, or college professors

exploratory research Research conducted to gather more information about a problem or to make a tentative hypothesis more specific

exporting The sale of products to foreign markets

extended decision making A consumer decision-making process employed when purchasing unfamiliar, expensive, or infrequently bought products

external reference price A comparison price provided by others

external search An information search in which buyers seek information from sources other than their memories

family branding Branding all of a firm's products with the same name or part of the name

family packaging Using similar packaging for all of a firm's products or packaging that has one common design element

feature article A manuscript of up to 3,000 words prepared for a specific publication

Federal Trade Commission (FTC) An agency that regulates a variety of business practices and curbs false advertising, misleading pricing, and deceptive packaging and labeling

feedback The receiver's response to a decoded message
first-mover advantage The ability of an innovative company to achieve long-term competitive advantages by being the first to offer a certain product in the marketplace
fixed costs Costs that do not vary with changes in the number of units produced or sold
F.O.B. destination A price indicating the producer is absorbing shipping costs
F.O.B. factory The price of merchandise at the factory before shipment
focus group An interview that is often conducted informally, without a structured questionnaire, in small groups of 8 to 12 people, to observe interaction when members are exposed to an idea or a concept
franchising An arrangement in which a supplier (franchiser) grants a dealer (franchisee) the right to sell products in exchange for some type of consideration
free merchandise A manufacturer's reward given to resellers that purchase a stated quantity of products
free samples Samples of a product given out to encourage trial and purchase
freight absorption pricing Absorption of all or part of actual freight costs by the seller
freight forwarders Organizations that consolidate shipments from several firms into efficient lot sizes
full-service wholesalers Merchant wholesalers that perform the widest range of wholesaling functions
functional modifications Changes affecting a product's versatility, effectiveness, convenience, or safety
General Agreement on Tariffs and Trade (GATT) An agreement among nations to reduce worldwide tariffs and increase international trade
general-merchandise retailer A retail establishment that offers a variety of product lines that are stocked in considerable depth
general-merchandise wholesalers Full-service wholesalers with a wide product mix but limited depth within product lines
general publics Indirect consumers of a product of a nonprofit organization
generic brand A brand indicating only the product category
generic competitors Firms that provide very different products that solve the same problem or satisfy the same basic customer need
geodemographic segmentation A method of market segmentation that clusters people in zip code areas and smaller neighborhood units based on lifestyle and demographic information
geographic pricing Reductions for transportation and other costs related to the physical distance between buyer and seller
globalization The development of marketing strategies that treat the entire world (or its major regions) as a single entity
good A tangible physical entity
government markets Federal, state, county, or local governments that buy goods and services to support their internal operations and provide products to their constituencies
green marketing A strategic process involving stakeholder assessment to create meaningful long-term relationships with customers while maintaining, supporting, and enhancing the natural environment
gross domestic product (GDP) The market value of a nation's total output of goods and services for a given period; an overall measure of economic standing
growth stage The product life-cycle stage when sales rise rapidly, profits reach a peak, and then they start to decline
heterogeneity Variation in quality
heterogeneous market A market made up of individuals or organizations with diverse needs for products in a specific product class
homesourcing A practice whereby customer contact jobs are outsourced into workers' homes
homogeneous market A market in which a large proportion of customers have similar needs for a product
horizontal channel integration Combining organizations at the same level of operation under one management
hypermarkets Stores that combine supermarket and discount store shopping in one location
hypothesis An informed guess or assumption about a certain problem or set of circumstances
idea A concept, philosophy, image, or issue
idea generation Seeking product ideas to achieve organizational objectives
illustrations Photos, drawings, graphs, charts, and tables used to spark audience interest in an advertisement
import tariff A duty levied by a nation on goods bought outside its borders and brought into the country
importing The purchase of products from a foreign source
impulse buying An unplanned buying behavior resulting from a powerful urge to buy something immediately
income For an individual, the amount of money received through wages, rents, investments, pensions, and subsidy payments for a given period
individual branding A branding strategy in which each product is given a different name
industrial distributor An independent business organization that takes title to industrial products and carries inventories
inelastic demand Demand that is not significantly altered by a price increase or decrease
information inputs Sensations received through sight, taste, hearing, smell, and touch
in-home (door-to-door) interview A personal interview that takes place in the respondent's home
innovators First adopters of new products
inseparability The quality of being produced and consumed at the same time
installations Facilities and nonportable major equipment
institutional advertising Advertising that promotes organizational images, ideas, and political issues
institutional markets Organizations with charitable, educational, community, or other nonbusiness goals
intangibility The characteristic that a service is not physical and cannot be perceived by the senses
integrated marketing communications Coordination of promotion and other marketing efforts for maximum informational and persuasive impact on customers
intensive distribution Using all available outlets to distribute a product
intermodal transportation Two or more transportation modes used in combination
internal reference price A price developed in the buyer's mind through experience with the product

internal search An information search in which buyers search their memories for information about products that might solve their problem

international marketing Developing and performing marketing activities across national boundaries

introduction stage The initial stage of a product's life cycle; its first appearance in the marketplace, when sales start at zero and profits are negative

inventory management Developing and maintaining adequate assortments of products to meet customers' needs

joint demand Demand involving the use of two or more items in combination to produce a product

joint venture A partnership between a domestic firm and a foreign firm or government

just-in-time (JIT) An inventory-management approach in which supplies arrive just when needed for production or resale

kinesic communication Communicating through the movement of head, eyes, arms, hands, legs, or torso

labeling Providing identifying, promotional, or other information on package labels

laggards The last adopters, who distrust new products

late majority Skeptics who adopt new products when they feel it is necessary

late-mover advantage The ability of later market entrants to achieve long-term competitive advantages by not being the first to offer a certain product in a marketplace

layout The physical arrangement of an advertisement's illustration and copy

learning Changes in an individual's thought processes and behavior caused by information and experience

level of involvement An individual's degree of interest in a product and the importance of the product for that person

level of quality The amount of quality a product possesses

licensing An alternative to direct investment that requires a licensee to pay commissions or royalties on sales or supplies used in manufacturing

lifestyle An individual's pattern of living expressed through activities, interests, and opinions

lifestyle shopping center A type of shopping center that is typically open air and features upscale specialty, dining, and entertainment stores

limited decision making A consumer decision-making process used when purchasing products occasionally or needing information about an unfamiliar brand in a familiar product category

limited-line wholesalers Full-service wholesalers that carry only a few product lines but many products within those lines

limited-service wholesalers Merchant wholesalers that provide some services and specialize in a few functions

line extension Development of a product that is closely related to existing products in the line but is designed specifically to meet different customer needs

logistics management Planning, implementing, and controlling the efficient and effective flow and storage of products and information from the point of origin to consumption to meet customers' needs and wants

mail-order wholesalers Limited-service wholesalers that sell products through catalogs

mail survey A research method in which respondents answer a questionnaire sent through the mail

manufacturer brand A brand initiated by producers to ensure that producers are identified with their products at the point of purchase

manufacturers' agents Independent intermediaries that represent two or more sellers and usually offer customers complete product lines

marginal cost (MC) The extra cost incurred by producing one more unit of a product

marginal revenue (MR) The change in total revenue resulting from the sale of an additional unit of a product

market A group of individuals and/or organizations that have needs for products in a product class and have the ability, willingness, and authority to purchase those products

market density The number of potential customers within a unit of land area

market growth/market share matrix A helpful business tool, based on the philosophy that a product's market growth rate and its market share are important considerations in determining its marketing strategy

market manager The person responsible for managing the marketing activities that serve a particular group of customers

market opportunity A combination of circumstances and timing that permits an organization to take action to reach a particular target market

market orientation An organizationwide commitment to researching and responding to customer needs

market potential The total amount of a product that customers will purchase within a specified period at a specific level of industry-wide marketing activity

market segment Individuals, groups, or organizations sharing one or more similar characteristics that cause them to have similar product needs

market segmentation The process of dividing a total market into groups with relatively similar product needs to design a marketing mix that matches those needs

market share The percentage of a market that actually buys a specific product from a particular company

market test Making a product available to buyers in one or more test areas and measuring purchases and consumer responses to marketing efforts

marketing The process of creating, distributing, promoting, and pricing goods, services, and ideas to facilitate satisfying exchange relationships with customers and to develop and maintain favorable relationships with stakeholders in a dynamic environment

marketing channel A group of individuals and organizations that direct the flow of products from producers to customers within the supply chain

marketing citizenship The adoption of a strategic focus for fulfilling the economic, legal, ethical, and philanthropic social responsibilities expected by stakeholders

marketing concept A managerial philosophy that an organization should try to satisfy customers' needs through a coordinated set of activities that also allows the organization to achieve its goals

marketing cost analysis Analysis of costs to determine which are associated with specific marketing efforts

marketing decision support system (MDSS) Customized computer software that aids marketing managers in decision making

marketing environment The competitive, economic, political, legal and regulatory, technological, and sociocultural forces that surround the customer and affect the marketing mix

marketing ethics Principles and standards that define acceptable marketing conduct as determined by various stakeholders

marketing implementation The process of putting marketing strategies into action

marketing information system (MIS) A framework for managing and structuring information gathered regularly from sources inside and outside the organization

marketing intermediaries Middlemen that link producers to other intermediaries or ultimate consumers through contractual arrangements or through the purchase and resale of products

marketing mix Four marketing activities—product, pricing, distribution, and promotion—that a firm can control to meet the needs of customers within its target market

marketing objective A statement of what is to be accomplished through marketing activities

marketing plan A written document that specifies the activities to be performed to implement and control the organization's marketing strategies

marketing research The systematic design, collection, interpretation, and reporting of information to help marketers solve specific marketing problems or take advantage of marketing opportunities

marketing strategy A plan of action for identifying and analyzing a target market and developing a marketing mix to meet the needs of that market

markup pricing Adding to the cost of the product a predetermined percentage of that cost

Maslow's hierarchy of needs The five levels of needs that humans seek to satisfy, from most to least important

materials handling Physical handling of tangible goods, supplies, and resources

maturity stage The stage of a product's life cycle when the sales curve peaks and starts to decline, and profits continue to fall

media plan A plan that specifies the media vehicles to be used and the schedule for running advertisements

megacarriers Freight transportation firms that provide several modes of shipment

merchandise allowance A manufacturer's agreement to pay resellers certain amounts of money for providing special promotional efforts, such as setting up and maintaining a display

merchant wholesalers Independently owned businesses that take title to goods, assume ownership risks, and buy and resell products to other wholesalers, business customers, or retailers

micromarketing An approach to market segmentation in which organizations focus precise marketing efforts on very small geographic markets

mission statement A long-term view, or vision, of what the organization wants to become

missionary salespeople Support salespeople, usually employed by a manufacturer, who assist the producer's customers in selling to their own customers

mobile applications software programs that run on mobile devices and give users access to certain content

modified rebuy purchase A new-task purchase that is changed on subsequent orders or when the requirements of a straight rebuy purchase are modified

money refunds Sales promotion techniques that offer consumers a specified amount of money when they mail in a proof of purchase, usually for multiple product purchases

monopolistic competition A competitive structure in which a firm has many potential competitors and tries to develop a marketing strategy to differentiate its product

monopoly A competitive structure in which an organization offers a product that has no close substitutes, making that organization the sole source of supply

motive An internal energizing force that directs a person's behavior toward satisfying needs or achieving goals

MRO supplies Maintenance, repair, and operating items that facilitate production and operations but do not become part of the finished product

multinational enterprise A firm that has operations or subsidiaries in many countries

multiple sourcing An organization's decision to use several suppliers

multiple-unit pricing Packaging together two or more identical products and selling them at a single price

National Advertising Review Board (NARB) A self-regulatory unit that considers challenges to issues raised by the National Advertising Division (an arm of the Council of Better Business Bureaus) about an advertisement

negotiated pricing Establishing a final price through bargaining between seller and customer

neighborhood shopping center A type of shopping center usually consisting of several small convenience and specialty stores

new-product development process A seven-phase process for introducing products: idea generation, screening, concept testing, business analysis, product development, test-marketing, and commercialization

new-task purchase An organization's initial purchase of an item to be used to perform a new job or solve a new problem

news release A short piece of copy publicizing an event or a product

noise Anything that reduces a communication's clarity and accuracy

noncumulative discounts One-time price reductions based on the number of units purchased, the dollar value of the order, or the product mix purchased

nonprice competition Emphasizing factors other than price to distinguish a product from competing brands

nonprobability sampling A sampling technique in which there is no way to calculate the likelihood that a specific element of the population being studied will be chosen

nonprofit marketing Marketing activities conducted to achieve some goal other than ordinary business goals such as profit, market share, or return on investment

nonstore retailing The selling of products outside the confines of a retail facility

North American Free Trade Agreement (NAFTA) An alliance that merges Canada, Mexico, and the United States into a single market

North American Industry Classification System (NAICS) An industry classification system that generates comparable statistics among the United States, Canada, and Mexico

objective-and-task approach Budgeting for an advertising campaign by first determining its objectives and then calculating the cost of all the tasks needed to attain them

odd-even pricing Ending the price with certain numbers to influence buyers' perceptions of the price or product

off-price retailers Stores that buy manufacturers' seconds, overruns, returns, and off-season merchandise for resale to consumers at deep discounts

offshore outsourcing The practice of contracting with an organization to perform some or all business functions in a country other than the country in which the product or service will be sold

offshoring The practice of moving a business process that was done domestically at the local factory to a foreign country, regardless of whether the production accomplished in the foreign country is performed by the local company (e.g., in a wholly owned subsidiary) or a third party (e.g., subcontractor)

oligopoly A competitive structure in which a few sellers control the supply of a large proportion of a product

online fraud Any attempt to conduct fraudulent activities online, including deceiving consumers into releasing personal information

online retailing Retailing that makes products available to buyers through computer connections

online survey A research method in which respondents answer a questionnaire via e-mail or on a website

on-site computer interview A variation of the shopping mall intercept interview in which respondents complete a self-administered questionnaire displayed on a computer monitor

operations management The total set of managerial activities used by an organization to transform resource inputs into products, services, or both

opinion leader A member of an informal group who provides information about a specific topic to other group members

opportunity cost The value of the benefit given up by choosing one alternative over another

order getters Salespeople who sell to new customers and increase sales to current customers

order processing The receipt and transmission of sales order information

order takers Salespeople who primarily seek repeat sales

organizational (corporate) culture A set of values, beliefs, goals, norms, and rituals that members of an organization share

outsourcing The practice of contracting noncore operations with an organization that specializes in that operation

patronage motives Motives that influence where a person purchases products on a regular basis

penetration pricing Setting prices below those of competing brands to penetrate a market and gain a significant market share quickly

percent-of-sales approach Budgeting for an advertising campaign by multiplying the firm's past and expected sales by a standard percentage

perception The process of selecting, organizing, and interpreting information inputs to produce meaning

performance standard An expected level of performance against which actual performance can be compared

periodic discounting Temporary reduction of prices on a patterned or systematic basis

perishability The inability of unused service capacity to be stored for future use

personal interview survey A research method in which participants respond to survey questions face-to-face

personal selling Paid personal communication that attempts to inform customers and persuade them to buy products in an exchange situation

personality A set of internal traits and distinct behavioral tendencies that result in consistent patterns of behavior in certain situations

physical distribution Activities used to move products from producers to consumers and other end users

pioneer advertising Advertising that tries to stimulate demand for a product category rather than a specific brand by informing potential buyers about the product

pioneer promotion Promotion that informs consumers about a new product

podcast Audio or video file that can be downloaded from the Internet with a subscription that automatically delivers new content to listening devices or personal computers; podcasts offer the benefit of convenience, giving users the ability to listen to or view content when and where they choose

point-of-purchase (POP) materials Signs, window displays, display racks, and similar devices used to attract customers

population All the elements, units, or individuals of interest to researchers for a specific study

posttest Evaluation of advertising effectiveness after the campaign

power shopping center A type of shopping center that combines off-price stores with category killers

premium money (push money) Extra compensation to salespeople for pushing a line of goods

premium pricing Pricing the highest-quality or most versatile products higher than other models in the product line

premiums Items offered free or at a minimal cost as a bonus for purchasing a product

press conference A meeting used to announce major news events

prestige pricing Setting prices at an artificially high level to convey prestige or a quality image

prestige sensitive Drawn to products that signify prominence and status

pretest Evaluation of advertisements performed before a campaign begins

price The value paid for a product in a marketing exchange

price competition Emphasizing price as an issue and matching or beating competitors' prices

price conscious Striving to pay low prices

price discrimination Employing price differentials that injure competition by giving one or more buyers a competitive advantage

price elasticity of demand A measure of the sensitivity of demand to changes in price

price leaders Products priced near or even below cost

price lining Setting a limited number of prices for selected groups or lines of merchandise

price skimming Charging the highest possible price that buyers who most desire the product will pay

pricing objectives Goals that describe what a firm wants to achieve through pricing

primary data Data observed and recorded or collected directly from respondents

primary demand Demand for a product category rather than for a specific brand

private distributor brand A brand initiated and owned by a reseller

private warehouses Company-operated facilities for storing and shipping products

probability sampling A type of sampling in which every element in the population being studied has a known chance of being selected for study

process materials Materials that are used directly in the production of other products but are not readily identifiable

producer markets Individuals and business organizations that purchase products to make profits by using them to produce other products or using them in their operations

product A good, a service, or an idea

product adoption process The five-stage process of buyer acceptance of a product: awareness, interest, evaluation, trial, and adoption

product advertising Advertising that promotes the uses, features, and benefits of products

product competitors Firms that compete in the same product class but market products with different features, benefits, and prices

product deletion Eliminating a product from the product mix when it no longer satisfies a sufficient number of customers

product design How a product is conceived, planned, and produced

product development Determining if producing a product is technically feasible and cost effective

product differentiation Creating and designing products so that customers perceive them as different from competing products

product features Specific design characteristics that allow a product to perform certain tasks

product item A specific version of a product that can be designated as a distinct offering among a firm's products

product life cycle The progression of a product through four stages: introduction, growth, maturity, and decline

product line A group of closely related product items viewed as a unit because of marketing, technical, or end-use considerations

product-line pricing Establishing and adjusting prices of multiple products within a product line

product manager The person within an organization who is responsible for a product, a product line, or several distinct products that make up a group

product mix The composite, or total, group of products that an organization makes available to customers

product modifications Changes in one or more characteristics of a product

product placement The strategic location of products or product promotions within entertainment media content to reach the product's target market

product positioning The decisions and activities intended to create and maintain a certain concept of the firm's product, relative to competitive brands, in customers' minds

professional pricing Fees set by people with great skill or experience in a particular field

promotion Communication to build and maintain relationships by informing and persuading one or more audiences

promotion mix A combination of promotional methods used to promote a specific product

prospecting Developing a database of potential customers

prosperity A stage of the business cycle characterized by low unemployment and relatively high total income, which together ensure high buying power (provided the inflation rate stays low)

proxemic communication Communicating by varying the physical distance in face-to-face interactions

psychological influences Factors that in part determine people's general behavior, thus influencing their behavior as consumers

psychological pricing Pricing that attempts to influence a customer's perception of price to make a product's price more attractive

public relations Communication efforts used to create and maintain favorable relations between an organization and its stakeholders

public warehouses Storage space and related physical distribution facilities that can be leased by companies

publicity A news story type of communication about an organization and/or its products transmitted through a mass medium at no charge

pull policy Promoting a product directly to consumers to develop strong consumer demand that pulls products through the marketing channel

pure competition A market structure characterized by an extremely large number of sellers, none strong enough to significantly influence price or supply

push policy Promoting a product only to the next institution down the marketing channel

quality The overall characteristics of a product that allow it to perform as expected in satisfying customer needs

quality modifications Changes relating to a product's dependability and durability

quantity discounts Deductions from the list price for purchasing in large quantities

quota A limit on the amount of goods an importing country will accept for certain product categories in a specific period of time

quota sampling A nonprobability sampling technique in which researchers divide the population into groups and then arbitrarily choose participants from each group

rack jobbers Full-service, specialty-line wholesalers that own and maintain display racks in stores

random discounting Temporary reduction of prices on an unsystematic basis

random factor analysis An analysis attempting to attribute erratic sales variations to random, nonrecurrent events

random sampling A form of probability sampling in which all units in a population have an equal chance of appearing in the sample, and the various events that can occur have an equal or known chance of taking place

raw materials Basic natural materials that become part of a physical product

rebates Sales promotion techniques in which a consumer receives a specified amount of money for making a single product purchase

receiver The individual, group, or organization that decodes a coded message

recession A stage of the business cycle during which unemployment rises and total buying power declines, stifling both consumer and business spending

reciprocity An arrangement unique to business marketing in which two organizations agree to buy from each other

recognition test A posttest in which respondents are shown the actual ad and are asked if they recognize it

recovery A stage of the business cycle in which the economy moves from recession or depression toward prosperity

recruiting Developing a list of qualified applicants for sales positions

reference group A group that a person identifies with so strongly that he or she adopts the values, attitudes, and behavior of group members

reference pricing Pricing a product at a moderate level and displaying it next to a more expensive model or brand

regional issues Versions of a magazine that differ across geographic regions

regional shopping center A type of shopping center with the largest department stores, widest product mixes, and deepest product lines of all shopping centers

regression analysis A method of predicting sales based on finding a relationship between past sales and one or more independent variables, such as population or income

reinforcement advertising Advertising that assures users they chose the right brand and tells them how to get the most satisfaction from it

relationship marketing Establishing long-term, mutually satisfying buyer–seller relationships

relationship selling The building of mutually beneficial long-term associations with a customer through regular communications over prolonged periods of time

reliability A condition that exists when a research technique produces almost identical results in repeated trials

reminder advertising Advertising used to remind consumers about an established brand's uses, characteristics, and benefits

research design An overall plan for obtaining the information needed to address a research problem or issue

reseller markets Intermediaries that buy finished goods and resell them for a profit

retail positioning Identifying an unserved or underserved market segment and serving it through a strategy that distinguishes the retailer from others in the minds of consumers in that segment

retailer An organization that purchases products for the purpose of reselling them to ultimate consumers

retailing All transactions in which the buyer intends to consume the product through personal, family, or household use

roles Actions and activities that a person in a particular position is supposed to perform based on expectations of the individual and surrounding persons

routinized response behavior A consumer decision-making process used when buying frequently purchased, low-cost items that require very little search-and-decision effort

sales analysis Analysis of sales figures to evaluate a firm's performance

sales branches Manufacturer-owned intermediaries that sell products and provide support services to the manufacturer's sales force

sales contest A sales promotion method used to motivate distributors, retailers, and sales personnel through recognition of outstanding achievements

sales force forecasting survey A survey of a firm's sales force regarding anticipated sales in their territories for a specified period

sales forecast The amount of a product a company expects to sell during a specific period at a specified level of marketing activities

sales offices Manufacturer-owned operations that provide services normally associated with agents

sales promotion An activity and/or material intended to induce resellers or salespeople to sell a product or consumers to buy it

sample A limited number of units chosen to represent the characteristics of a total population

sampling The process of selecting representative units from a total population

scan-back allowance A manufacturer's reward to retailers based on the number of pieces scanned

screening Selecting the ideas with the greatest potential for further review

search qualities Tangible attributes that can be judged before the purchase of a product

seasonal analysis An analysis of daily, weekly, or monthly sales figures to evaluate the degree to which seasonal factors influence sales

seasonal discount A price reduction given to buyers for purchasing goods or services out of season

secondary data Data compiled both inside and outside the organization for some purpose other than the current investigation

secondary-market pricing Setting one price for the primary target market and a different price for another market

segmentation variables Characteristics of individuals, groups, or organizations used to divide a market into segments

selective demand Demand for a specific brand

selective distortion An individual's changing or twisting of information that is inconsistent with personal feelings or beliefs

selective distribution Using only some available outlets in an area to distribute a product

selective exposure The process by which some inputs are selected to reach awareness and others are not

selective retention Remembering information inputs that support personal feelings and beliefs and forgetting inputs that do not

self-concept A perception or view of oneself

selling agents Intermediaries that market a whole product line or a manufacturer's entire output

service An intangible result of the application of human and mechanical efforts to people or objects

service quality Customers' perceptions of how well a service meets or exceeds their expectations

shopping mall intercept interview A research method that involves interviewing a percentage of individuals passing by "intercept" points in a mall

shopping products Items for which buyers are willing to expend considerable effort in planning and making purchases

single-source data Information provided by a single marketing research firm

situational influences Influences that result from circumstances, time, and location that affect the consumer buying decision process

social class An open group of individuals with similar social rank

social influences The forces other people exert on one's buying behavior

social network A website where users can create a profile and interact with other users, post information, and engage in other forms of Web-based communication

social responsibility An organization's obligation to maximize its positive impact and minimize its negative impact on society

sociocultural forces The influences in a society and its culture(s) that change people's attitudes, beliefs, norms, customs, and lifestyles

sole sourcing An organization's decision to use only one supplier

source A person, group, or organization with a meaning it tries to share with a receiver or an audience

Southern Common Market (Mercosur) An alliance that promotes the free circulation of goods, services, and production factors, and has a common external tariff and commercial policy among member nations in South America

special-event pricing Advertised sales or price cutting linked to a holiday, a season, or an event

specialty products Items with unique characteristics that buyers are willing to expend considerable effort to obtain

specialty-line wholesalers Full-service wholesalers that carry only a single product line or a few items within a product line

stakeholders Constituents who have a "stake," or claim, in some aspect of a company's products, operations, markets, industry, and outcomes

statistical interpretation Analysis of what is typical and what deviates from the average

storyboard A blueprint that combines copy and visual material to show the sequence of major scenes in a commercial

straight commission compensation plan Paying salespeople according to the amount of their sales in a given time period

straight rebuy purchase A routine purchase of the same products under approximately the same terms of sale by a business buyer

straight salary compensation plan Paying salespeople a specific amount per time period, regardless of selling effort

strategic alliance A partnership that is formed to create a competitive advantage on a worldwide basis

strategic business unit (SBU) A division, product line, or other profit center within the parent company

strategic channel alliance An agreement whereby the products of one organization are distributed through the marketing channels of another

strategic marketing management The process of planning, implementing, and evaluating the performance of marketing activities and strategies, both effectively and efficiently

strategic performance evaluation Establishing performance standards, measuring actual performance, comparing actual performance with established standards, and modifying the marketing strategy, if needed

strategic philanthropy The synergistic use of organizational core competencies and resources to address key stakeholders' interests and achieve both organizational and social benefits

strategic planning The process of establishing an organizational mission and formulating goals, corporate strategy, marketing objectives, and marketing strategy

strategic windows Temporary periods of optimal fit between the key requirements of a market and the particular capabilities of a company competing in that market

stratified sampling A type of probability sampling in which the population is divided into groups with a common attribute and a random sample is chosen within each group

styling The physical appearance of a product

subculture A group of individuals whose characteristics, values, and behavioral patterns are similar within the group and different from those of people in the surrounding culture

supermarkets Large, self-service stores that carry a complete line of food products, along with some nonfood products

superregional shopping center A type of shopping center with the widest and deepest product mixes that attracts customers from many miles away

superstores Giant retail outlets that carry food and nonfood products found in supermarkets, as well as most routinely purchased consumer products

supply chain All the activities associated with the flow and transformation of products from raw materials through to the end customer

supply-chain management A set of approaches used to integrate the functions of operations management, logistics management, supply management, and marketing channel management so products are produced and distributed in the right quantities, to the right locations, and at the right time

supply management In its broadest form, refers to the processes that enable the progress of value from raw material to final customer and back to redesign and final disposition

support personnel Sales staff members who facilitate selling but usually are not involved solely with making sales

sustainability The potential for the long-term well-being of the natural environment, including all biological entities, as well as the interaction among nature and individuals, organizations, and business strategies

sustainable competitive advantage An advantage that the competition cannot copy

SWOT analysis Assessment of an organization's strengths, weaknesses, opportunities, and threats

tactile communication Communicating through touching

target audience The group of people at whom advertisements are aimed

target market A specific group of customers on whom an organization focuses its marketing efforts

target public A collective of individuals who have an interest in or concern about an organization, product, or social cause

team selling The use of a team of experts from all functional areas of a firm, led by a salesperson, to conduct the personal selling process

technical salespeople Support salespeople who give technical assistance to a firm's current customers

technology The application of knowledge and tools to solve problems and perform tasks more efficiently

telemarketing The performance of marketing-related activities by telephone

telephone depth interview An interview that combines the traditional focus group's ability to probe with the confidentiality provided by telephone surveys

telephone survey A research method in which respondents' answers to a questionnaire are recorded by an interviewer on the phone

television home shopping A form of selling in which products are presented to television viewers, who can buy them by calling a toll-free number and paying with a credit card

test marketing A limited introduction of a product in geographic areas chosen to represent the intended market

time series analysis A forecasting method that uses historical sales data to discover patterns in the firm's sales over time and generally involves trend, cycle, seasonal, and random factor analyses

total budget competitors Firms that compete for the limited financial resources of the same customers

total cost The sum of average fixed and average variable costs times the quantity produced

trade (functional) discount A reduction off the list price a producer gives to an intermediary for performing certain functions

trade name The full legal name of an organization

trade sales promotion methods Methods intended to persuade wholesalers and retailers to carry a producer's products and market them aggressively

trade salespeople Salespeople involved mainly in helping a producer's customers promote a product

trademark A legal designation of exclusive use of a brand

trading company A company that links buyers and sellers in different countries

traditional specialty retailers Stores that carry a narrow product mix with deep product lines

transfer pricing Prices charged in sales between an organization's units

transportation The movement of products from where they are made to intermediaries and end users

trend analysis An analysis that focuses on aggregate sales data over a period of many years to determine general trends in annual sales

truck wholesalers Limited-service wholesalers that transport products directly to customers for inspection and selection

tying agreement An agreement in which a supplier furnishes a product to a channel member with the stipulation that the channel member must purchase other products as well

unaided recall test A posttest in which respondents are asked to identify advertisements they have seen recently but are not given any recall clues

undifferentiated targeting strategy A strategy in which an organization designs a single marketing mix and directs it at the entire market for a particular product

uniform geographic pricing Charging all customers the same price, regardless of geographic location

unsought products Products purchased to solve a sudden problem, products of which customers are unaware, and products that people do not necessarily think of buying

validity A condition that exists when a research method measures what it is supposed to measure

value A customer's subjective assessment of benefits relative to costs in determining the worth of a product

value analysis An evaluation of each component of a potential purchase

value conscious Concerned about price and quality of a product

variable costs Costs that vary directly with changes in the number of units produced or sold

vendor analysis A formal, systematic evaluation of current and potential vendors

venture team A cross-functional group that creates entirely new products that may be aimed at new markets

vertical channel integration Combining two or more stages of the marketing channel under one management

vertical marketing system (VMS) A marketing channel managed by a single channel member to achieve efficient, low-cost distribution aimed at satisfying target market customers

viral marketing A strategy to get consumers to share a marketer's message, often through e-mail or online videos, in a way that spreads dramatically and quickly

warehouse clubs Large-scale, members-only establishments that combine features of cash-and-carry wholesaling with discount retailing

warehouse showrooms Retail facilities in large, low-cost buildings with large on-premises inventories and minimal services

warehousing The design and operation of facilities for storing and moving goods

wealth The accumulation of past income, natural resources, and financial resources

wholesaler An individual or organization that sells products that are bought for resale, for making other products, or for general business operations

wholesaling Transactions in which products are bought for resale, for making other products, or for general business operations

widget Small bits of software on a website, desktop, or mobile device that performs a simple purpose, such as providing stock quotes or blog updates

width of product mix The number of product lines a company offers

wiki Type of software that creates an interface that enables users to add or edit the content of some types of websites

willingness to spend An inclination to buy because of expected satisfaction from a product, influenced by the ability to buy and numerous psychological and social forces

word-of-mouth communication Personal informal exchanges of communication that customers share with one another about products, brands, and companies

World Trade Organization (WTO) An entity that promotes free trade among member nations by eliminating trade barriers and educating individuals, companies, and governments about trade rules around the world

zone pricing Pricing based on transportation costs within major geographic zones

name index

© zayats-and-zayats/Shutterstock.com

organization index

C

D

E

F

G

T

subject index

A

C

D

E

F

G

H

I

J

K

L

M

N

O

P

Q

R

S

T

U

X

Y

Z